1, 2, 3 → 301

4, → 483

ADVANCED FINANCIAL ACCOUNTING

Second Edition

Richard E. Baker

Department of Accountancy
Northern Illinois University

Valdean C. Lembke

Department of Accounting
University of Iowa

Thomas E. King

Department of Accounting
Southern Illinois University at Edwardsville

McGraw-Hill, Inc.

New York St. Louis San Francisco Auckland Bogotá
Caracas Lisbon London Madrid Mexico City Milan
Montreal New Delhi San Juan Singapore
Sydney Tokyo Toronto

This book was set in Times Roman by Better Graphics, Inc.
The editors were Johanna Schmid and Bernadette Boylan;
the production supervisor was Annette Mayeski.
The cover was designed by Circa '86.
Arcata Graphics/Martinsburg was printer and binder.

ADVANCED FINANCIAL ACCOUNTING

3 4 5 6 7 8 9 0 AGMAGM 9 0 9 8 7 6 5 4 3

ISBN 0-07-003447-8

Library of Congress Cataloging-in-Publication Data

Baker, Richard E.
    Advanced financial accounting / Richard E. Baker, Valdean C. Lembke, Thomas E. King.—2nd ed.
        p.   cm.
    Includes index.
    ISBN 0-07-003447-8
    1. Accounting.   I. Lembke, Valdean C.   II. King, Thomas E.
    III Title.
HF5635.B165   1993
657′ .046—dc20   92-9163

When ordering this title, use ISBN 0-07-112974-X

This book is printed on acid-free paper.

ABOUT THE AUTHORS

RICHARD E. BAKER is the Ernst & Young Distinguished Professor of Accountancy at Northern Illinois University. In 1991 he was recognized as an inaugural University Presidential Teaching Professor, the highest teaching recognition of his university. He received his B.S. degree from the University of Wisconsin—River Falls and his MBA and Ph.D. from the University of Wisconsin—Madison. His activities in the American Accounting Association include being president of the midwest region. His service activities include participation on several main committees of the American Accounting Association and the Federation of Schools of Accountancy (FSA), including serving as national co-chair of the 1990 FSA committee on Recognizing, Measuring, and Rewarding Teaching Effectiveness. Many of his service efforts have involved the promotion of the integration of the microcomputer into the accounting classroom. Professor Baker has served as an Associate Editor of *The Journal of Accounting Education* and as a reviewer for *Issues in Accounting Education*. He has received numerous teaching awards at both the undergraduate and graduate levels. His most recent published research studies have concentrated on ways to make the learning/teaching experience as effective as possible. Other published research includes studies in financial reporting and mergers and acquisitions. Professor Baker's major teaching areas are advanced financial accounting and financial statement analysis. He is a CPA and also teaches advanced financial accounting topics in CPA exam review courses.

VALDEAN C. LEMBKE is Professor of Accounting in the College of Business Administration at The University of Iowa. He received his B.S. degree from Iowa State University and his MBA and Ph.D. from the University of Michigan. He has internal audit and public accounting experience. He has been active in the American Accounting Association, including service as vice president of the midwest region and book review editor for *Issues in Accounting Education*. Professor Lembke has been a faculty member at The University of Iowa for twenty years, where he was named the first recipient of the Gilbert P. Maynard Excellence in Accounting Instruction award. He has served two terms as department head and is currently head of the Professional Program in Accounting. Professor Lembke has authored or coauthored articles in journals such as *The Accounting Review*, the *Journal of Accounting, Auditing and Finance*, the *Journal of Accountancy*, and the *Internal Auditor*. He also coauthored with Thomas King the chapter on business combinations and consolidated financial statements in the *Accountant's Encyclopedia*. His teaching has been primarily in undergraduate and graduate coursework in financial accounting.

THOMAS E. KING is Professor of Accounting in the School of Business at Southern Illinois University at Edwardsville. He received his B.S. degree from California State University, Northridge, and his MBA and Ph.D. from the University of California, Los Angeles. He is a CPA and received an Elijah Watt Sells Award and the Illinois gold medal for his scores on the Uniform CPA Examination. He has a number of years of business and consulting experience and has been teaching for over twenty years. Professor King coauthored with Valdean Lembke the chapter on business combinations and consolidated financial statements in the *Accountant's Encyclopedia* and has authored or coauthored over a dozen articles appearing in journals such as the *Journal of Accountancy*, *The Accounting Review*, *Accounting Horizons*, the *Journal of Accounting, Auditing and Finance*, *the Journal of Accounting Education*, and *Financial Executive*. He currently serves on the Editorial Board of *Advances in Accounting* and is on the Board of Governors of the St. Louis Chapter of the Institute of Internal Auditors. Professor King teaches undergraduate and graduate courses in financial accounting.

CONTENTS

iv

PREFACE

The second edition of *Advanced Financial Accounting* is a comprehensive and highly illustrated presentation of the accounting and reporting principles used in a variety of business entities. The daily business press carries many stories about the merger and acquisition mania of multicorporate entities, the foreign activities of multinational firms, the operations of governmental and nonprofit entities, and other topics typically included in advanced accounting. Accountants must know how to deal with the accounting and reporting ramifications of these events.

KEY FEATURES

Important features of this book are the clear and readable discussions of concepts and the detailed demonstrations of these concepts through illustrations and explanations. The many favorable responses to the first edition confirm our belief that clear presentation and comprehensive illustrations are key to learning the sophisticated topics in an advanced accounting course. Other key features of the Second Edition include the following:

• *A building-block approach based on a strong conceptual foundation.* Students are provided with a thorough conceptual foundation before advancing to the procedures. The basics of the topics are discussed first, and the complexities are added gradually in successive steps.

• *The use of a continuous case for each major subject matter area.* The comprehensive case of Peerless Products Corporation and its subsidiary, Special Foods, Inc., has been continued. An important advantage of using a continuous, comprehensive case is that students must become familiar with only one set of data and can then move more quickly through the discussion and illustrations. The case adds realism to the study of advanced accounting and permits students to see the effects of each successive step on the financial reports of a company. After students become familiar with the basic example, they can focus on the point of each new illustration without having to absorb a new set of data. Comparisons of different outcomes from alternative accounting methods can be quickly and readily evaluated because the same base illustration is used to discuss each alternative. The accounting and reporting procedures for each alternative are presented and then compared and contrasted with one another. Students can clearly see each step of the process and can more easily assess the important differences between alternatives. The positive feedback about the use of the comprehensive case methodology in the first edition confirms our beliefs about the efficiency and effectiveness of this approach for learning advanced accounting.

• *Extensive illustrations of key concepts.* The book is heavily illustrated with complete workpapers, financial statements, and other computations and comparisons used in developing an understanding of each topic. The illustrations are clearly cross-referenced to the relevant text discussion. Workpaper entries presented in the consolidation material are separately identified with an (E) and are shaded to clearly differentiate them from book entries. The extensive use of illustrations makes the learning process more efficient by allowing students to quickly and readily see the applications of the concepts. In addition, the illustrations reinforce understanding of the concepts by demonstrating the effects of the accounting concepts on the financial statements. In this manner, students understand that the many workpaper procedures typically covered in advanced accounting are the means to a desired end, not the end in themselves.

• *Comprehensive coverage with significant flexibility.* The subject matter of advanced accounting is expanding at an unprecedented rate. New topics are being added, and traditional topics require more extensive coverage. Flexibility is therefore essential in an advanced accounting text. Most one-term courses are unable to cover all the topics included in this text. In recognition of time constraints, this text is structured to provide the most efficient use of the time available. The self-contained units of subject matter allow for substantial flexibility in sequencing the course materials. In addition, individual chapters are organized to allow for opportunities to go into greater depth on some topics through the use of the "Additional Considerations" sections. Several chapters include appendixes containing discussions of alternative accounting procedures or illustrations of procedures or concepts that are of a supplemental nature.

ORGANIZATION

The first part of the text covers business combinations and intercorporate ownership. The preparation of consolidated financial statements is discussed, beginning with the basic consolidation process and continuing through a variety of intercompany transactions. The continuous case of Peerless Products Corporation and its subsidiary, Special Foods, Inc., is used to demonstrate the concepts of consolidation. Accounting procedures for branches and agencies also are considered in this section of the text.

The next part of the text deals with multinational operations, including the treatment of transactions denominated in foreign currencies and the translation of the financial statements of foreign entities. These concepts are presented in the context of Peerless Products Corporation and its German subsidiary.

Special reporting issues in preparing segment and interim reports are discussed and illustrated. In addition, the role of the Securities and Exchange Commission in the regulation of accounting for publicly traded companies is examined.

The next section of the text focuses on partnership accounting and financial reporting in the context of the continuous example of the ABC Partnership. Partnership formation and operation are presented in one chapter, and a separate chapter covers partnership dissolution and alternative forms of liquidation.

As a reflection of its increasing importance, thorough coverage is given to the accounting and financial reporting requirements for governmental and not-for-profit organizations. Two extensive chapters dealing with state and local governmental entities are followed by two chapters providing comprehensive coverage of accounting for colleges and universities, health care providers, voluntary health and welfare organizations, and other not-for-profit organizations. Each chapter is constructed around a comprehensive, integrated case example and presents the essential linkages between the accounting principles used to measure transactions and the financial reporting required for these entities.

The last part of the text presents the accounting and financial reporting procedures for entities in financial difficulty. The chapter focuses again on the example of Peerless Products Corporation. Troubled debt restructurings are presented first, followed by an extensive discussion and illustration of the accounting and financial reporting requirements for companies in legal reorganization or bankruptcy.

FEATURES OF THE REVISION

Every effort was made to make this edition the most comprehensive and current advanced accounting text. The following are the major features of the revision:

• *Updating to reflect recent changes in accounting and financial reporting requirements.* Significant revisions were made in the chapters on health care providers, voluntary health and welfare organizations, and other not-for-profit organizations. Changes as a result of GASB pronouncements on requiring cash flow statements for enterprise funds, the measurement focus and basis of accounting for governmental entities, and reporting component units have been fully integrated into the two chapters on governmental accounting. The recent change in financial reporting for business entities in legal reorganization is fully integrated into the chapter on accounting for companies in financial difficulty. Recent FASB "Discussion Memorandums" on consolidation procedures and bases of measurement are considered in the chapters on consolidation.

• *Additional student learning tools.* Revised text and new illustrations have been developed to clarify complex topics. For example, adopters of the first edition indicated that students had difficulty differentiating budgetary from real accounts for governmental entities. For the second edition, the convention of capitalizing budgetary accounts, as used in the 1988 *Governmental Accounting, Auditing and Financial Reporting,* is used in the two chapters on governmental accounting. New illustrations in the two international accounting chapters help students understand the timeline aspects of multinational operations. New illustrations presenting overviews and comparisons of alternative accounting methods are integrated throughout the text. These new illustrations will enhance students' study and understanding of the topics.

• *Significantly enhanced end-of-chapter materials.* The end-of-chapter materials have been revised and a much broader selection of materials has been provided. Based on comments from users of the text, many of the problems and exercises from the first edition have been retained. A wide range of questions, cases, exercises, and problems are presented at the end of each chapter to permit the instructor to make selections consistent with teaching objectives. Advanced accounting provides important preparation for the Uniform CPA Examination, and CPA Examination questions from recent exams have been included to ensure up-to-date coverage of the exam. Additional integrated, comprehensive problems have been provided as alternative assignment materials. A number of the exercises have been revised to cover more effectively the range of topics presented in each chapter. Items related to the "Additional Considerations" sections of the chapters are noted with an asterisk (*) next to the item number. Those items related to appendixes are denoted by "A" or "B" to designate the specific appendix. Finally, additional cases in many of the chapters provide opportunities for students to use discovery learning skills and to enhance their written communication skills.

ANCILLARY PROGRAM

This text is accompanied by a full ancillary program with items designed to complement your teaching efforts and your students' learning process. If you would like information and costs on the supplemental materials, please contact your local McGraw-Hill representative. We value both your interest and our supplements.

Student Supplements

In addition to the learning aids contained in the text, the following supplements are available to help students learn advanced accounting:

Study guide Closely coordinated with the text, this study guide contains summaries of the key concepts presented in each chapter and provides self-diagnostic and review materials in the form of multiple-choice, true/false, and fill-in-the-blank questions, as well as both short and comprehensive exercises, and problems. The solutions are given in the study guide so that students can readily assess their achievement level and identify topics that need further review.

Accounting workpapers The workpapers are the forms needed to solve most end-of-chapter problems in the text. To increase efficiency for the students, the forms already contain trial balances, other opening data, and column headings.

Checklist of key answers Key answers are provided for many of the end-of-chapter materials in the text.

Instructor Supplements

These teaching aids have been prepared by the authors of the textbook, each of whom has taught advanced accounting for many years. The following supplements are available:

Solutions manual Solutions are provided for all questions, cases, exercises, and problems in the text. Solutions are carefully explained and logically presented. Answers to many of the multiple-choice questions include computations and explanations. Instructors can prepare transparencies directly from the solutions manual or can choose from the overhead transparencies available for selected exercises and problems.

Overhead transparencies Large-type transparencies have been prepared for approximately 100 exercises and problems in the text.

Instructor's resource manual This manual consists of a summary and overview of each chapter and a key point outline that may be used to guide class discussion of each chapter. Teaching ideas are offered for the effective use of discovery learning activities, the use of electronic spreadsheeting in advanced accounting, and ways to increase student interest in the material. Descriptions are provided for each case, exercise, and problem to help instructors assign end-of-chapter materials that meet the specific learning objectives of the course. A large number of key exhibits from the text are presented in large type to make the production of lecture-enhancing transparencies easy. Additional problems are also presented for selected chapters which can be used to demonstrate chapter topics.

Test bank This comprehensive collection of both conceptual and procedural test items has been completely revised. The material is organized by chapter and includes a large variety of multiple-choice questions and exercises and problems that can be used to measure student achievement in the topics in each chapter. The test items are closely coordinated with the text to ensure consistency.

Computerized testing program Questions in the Test Bank are available through RHTest, the computerized testing program. With RHTest, instructors can create and print tests quickly and easily. The computerized testing program allows instructors to edit, add, and delete questions, and to print scrambled versions of the same test.

Computer templates for workpaper problems Spreadsheet templates are provided for problems from the text that require extensive workpaper format solutions. This software is available for both DOS-based and Macintosh computers. Students can work with the electronic spreadsheet to solve consolidation and other workpaper problems.

ACKNOWLEDGMENTS

This text includes the thoughts and contributions of many individuals, and we wish to express our sincere appreciation to them. First, and foremost, we thank all the students in our advanced accounting classes, from whom we have learned so much. In many respects, this text is an outcome of the learning experiences we have shared with our students.

We are indebted to our colleagues in advanced accounting for helping us reach our goal of writing the best possible advanced financial accounting text. We appreciate the many valuable comments and suggestions from the instructors who used the first edition of the text. Their comments and suggestions have contributed to making this text a more effective learning tool. We especially wish to thank: Mark Bettner, Bucknell University; Dennis Bline, University of Texas, San Antonio; David Doran, Pennsylvania State University, Erie; John Engstrom, Northern Illinois University; David Gotlob, Indiana University—Purdue University at Fort Wayne; Sharron Hoffmans, University of Texas, El Paso; James Lahey, Northern Illinois University; Philip Meyer, Boston University; Jon Nance, Southwest Missouri State University; Terence Reilly, Albright College; Max Rexroad, Illinois State University; Andrew Rosman, University of Connecticut; Norlin Rueschhoff, University of Notre Dame; John Simon, Northern Illinois University; Ted Skekel, University of Texas, San Antonio; and James Stice, Brigham Young University.

We also wish to thank Wayne Higley, Buena Vista College, and Wayne W. McManus, Defiance College; for their assistance in revising end-of-chapter materials for several chapters in the text. Typing and problem-checking assistance were provided by Carol Denton, Northern Illinois University, and Maria Blase, Susan Brune, Juliet Bussing, Fran Schnaare, and Tricia Verhoff, Southern Illinois University, Edwardsville. Virginia Bidgood, University of Nevada, Las Vegas, served as the comprehensive problem-checker and reviewed all solutions to the end-of-chapter materials for both accuracy and completeness. We are grateful for the assistance and direction of the McGraw-Hill team, including Bernadette Boylan, Judy Motto, and Annette Mayeski, and, especially, our senior editor, Johanna Schmid, who provided tremendous support and guidance for the revision project.

We appreciate the cooperation of the American Institute of Certified Public Accountants and the Institute of Management Accountants for providing permission to adapt and use materials from the Uniform CPA Examinations and the CMA Examinations, respectively.

Above all, we extend our deepest appreciation to our wives and children, who continue to provide the encouragement and support necessary to complete this project.

Richard E. Baker

Valdean C. Lembke

Thomas E. King

CHAPTER 1

CORPORATE EXPANSION AND ACCOUNTING FOR BUSINESS COMBINATIONS

The business environment in the United States is perhaps the most dynamic and vibrant in the world. Each day, new companies and new products enter the marketplace, and others are forced to leave or to change substantially in order to survive. In this setting, existing companies often find it necessary to combine their operations with those of other companies or to establish new operating units in emerging areas of business activity.

In recent years, the business world has witnessed many corporate acquisitions and combinations, often involving some of the nation's largest and best-known companies. Some of these combinations have captured the attention of the public because of the personalities involved, the daring strategies employed, and the huge sums of money at stake.

A *business combination* occurs when two or more companies join under common control. The concept of *control* relates to the ability to dictate operating and financial policies. Traditionally, control over a company has been gained by acquiring a majority of the company's outstanding voting stock. However, the diversity of financial and operating arrangements employed in recent years also raises the possibility of gaining control with less than majority ownership.

A number of accounting and reporting issues arise when two or more companies join under common ownership. One set of issues involves how to account for the business combination. The procedures used can have a substantial effect on financial statements prepared subsequent to the combination. Other issues involve how to account for intercorporate ownership interests in periods following an acquisition and how to report the results of operations and the financial positions of related companies.

The first 10 chapters of this text focus on accounting and financial reporting when two or more companies are involved. Chapter 1 deals explicitly with accounting and reporting issues related to business combinations. The second chapter focuses on accounting and reporting for stock ownership in other companies. The next eight chapters systematically develop the reporting procedures used by related companies to prepare financial statements as if the companies actually were a single company. Financial statements prepared for two or more legally separate corporations as if they actually were a single company are referred to as *consolidated financial statements*. Chapter 11 covers divisional reporting and the reporting process for companies operating through branches.

THE DEVELOPMENT OF MULTICORPORATE ENTITIES

The simple business setting in which one company has two or three manufacturing plants and produces products for a local or regional market is much less common now than it was several decades ago. As companies have grown in size, they often have developed complex organizational and ownership structures.

Reasons for Corporate Expansion

Both corporate shareholders and management tend to have an interest in seeing a company grow in size. Economies of scale often exist with regard to production and distribution costs. By expanding into new markets or acquiring other companies already in those markets, companies can develop new earning potential, and those in cyclical industries can add greater stability to earnings through diversification. In some cases, companies expand the scope of their operations in response to governmental incentives, such as those encouraging trade with certain countries or the development of low-cost housing.

Corporate management often is rewarded with higher salaries as company size increases. In addition, prestige frequently increases with the size of a company and with a reputation for the successful acquisition of other companies. As a result, corporate management often finds it personally advantageous to increase company size.

Forms of Corporate Expansion

Companies historically have attempted to grow through a combination of new product development and expansion of existing product lines into new markets. In many cases, however, entry into new product areas or geographic regions is more easily accomplished through acquisition of other companies. As a result, many companies have entered into business combinations over the past several decades as a means of attaining growth and diversification.

Business combinations may take one of several legal forms, as illustrated in Figure 1-1. A *statutory merger* is a type of business combination in which only one

FIGURE 1-1 Types of business combinations.

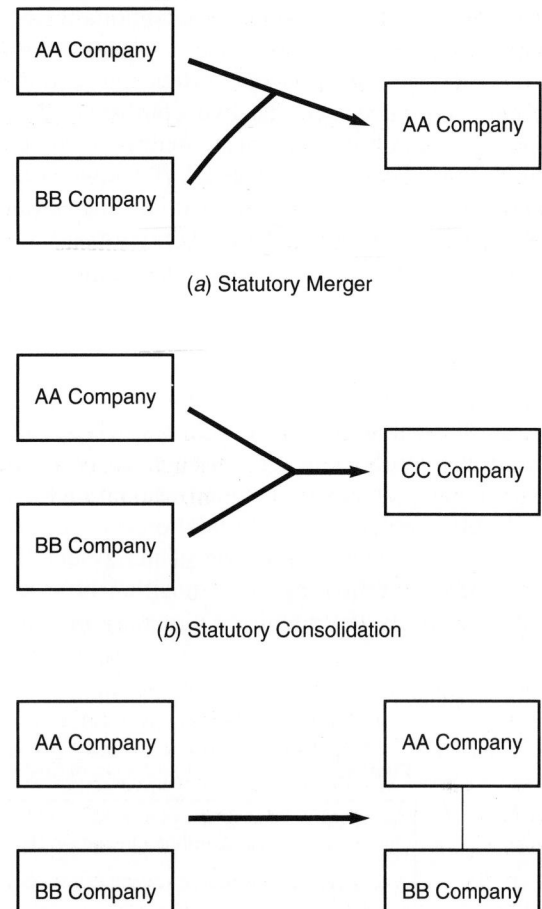

(a) Statutory Merger

(b) Statutory Consolidation

(c) Stock Acquisition

of the combining companies survives and the other loses its separate identity. The assets and liabilities of the acquired company are transferred to the acquiring company, and the acquired company is dissolved, or *liquidated*. The operations of the previously separate companies are carried on in a single legal entity following the merger.

A *statutory consolidation* is a business combination in which both the combining companies are dissolved and the assets and liabilities of both companies are transferred to a newly created corporation. The operations of the previously separate companies are carried on in a single legal entity, and neither of the combining companies remains in existence after a statutory consolidation. In many situations, however, the resulting corporation is new in form only, while in substance it actually is one of the combining companies reincorporated with a new name.

A *stock acquisition* occurs when one company acquires the voting shares of another company and the two companies continue to operate as separate, but related, legal entities. Because neither of the combining companies is liquidated, the acquiring company must report its ownership interest in the other company as an investment. In a stock acquisition, the acquiring company need not acquire all the other company's stock to gain control.

The relationship that is created in a stock acquisition is referred to as a *parent-subsidiary relationship*. A *parent company* is one that owns a majority of the voting stock of another company, referred to as a *subsidiary*. The parent-subsidiary relationship is important because the parent has the ability to control the subsidiary.

As illustrated in Figure 1-2, a stock acquisition occurs when one company acquires a majority of the voting stock of another company and both companies remain in existence as separate legal entities following the business combination. Statutory mergers and consolidations may be effected through acquisition of stock as well as through acquisition of net assets. To complete a statutory merger or consolidation following an acquisition of stock, the acquired company is liquidated and only the acquiring company or a newly created company remains in existence.

FIGURE 1-2 Determining the type of business combination.

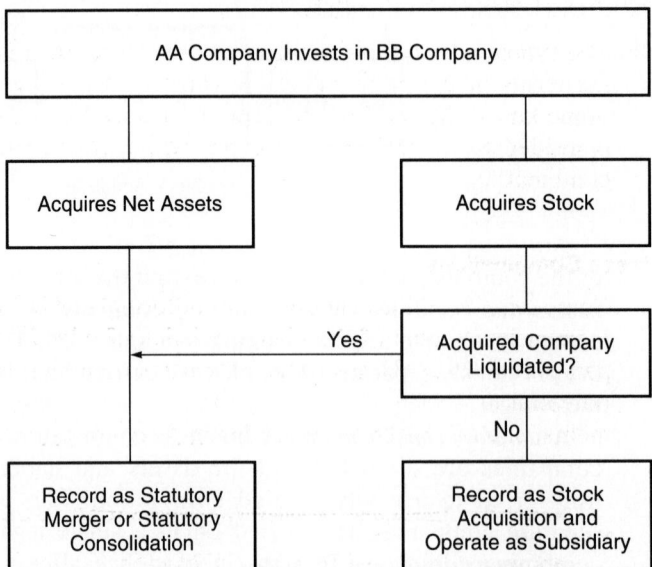

The legal form of a business combination, the substance of the combination agreement, and the circumstances surrounding the combination all affect how the combination is recorded initially and the accounting and reporting procedures used subsequent to the combination.

Frequency of Business Combinations and Multicorporate Entities

Very few major companies function as single legal entities in our modern business environment. Virtually all the 600 companies included in a recent edition of *Accounting Trends and Techniques* had at least one subsidiary, with more than a few broadly diversified companies having several hundred subsidiaries.[1]

Some subsidiary companies are established by incorporating a part of the operations of an existing company, while others are acquired in business combinations. Business combinations are a continuing and frequent part of the business environment. The number of companies involved in business combinations has decreased from the more active periods in the 1960s and 1970s; nevertheless, in each of the years since 1980, approximately one-third of the 600 companies included in *Accounting Trends and Techniques* have participated in business combinations.[2] Notable examples of recent business combinations include both domestic and international acquisitions, such as the merger of American Telephone & Telegraph Co. with NCR Corp., Chemical Banking Corp. with Manufacturers Hanover Corp., Federated Department Stores (U.S.) with Campeau Corp. (Canadian), British Steel PLC (U.K.) with Investor Group (U.S.), and CBS, Inc. (U.S.) with Sony Corp. (Japan).

EXPANSION THROUGH BUSINESS COMBINATIONS

The types of business combinations found in today's business environment and the terms of the combination agreements are as diverse as the firms involved. Some knowledge of the form and the substance of various types of combinations is needed to appreciate the accounting issues that arise in dealing with business combinations.

Types of Business Combinations

Companies enter into various types of formal and informal arrangements that may have at least some of the characteristics of a business combination. Most companies tend to avoid recording informal agreements on their books because of the potential difficulty of enforcing them. In fact, some types of informal arrangements, such as those aimed at fixing prices or apportioning potential customers,

---

[1] *Accounting Trends and Techniques*, American Institute of Certified Public Accountants (New York), 1989, p. 41.
[2] *Accounting Trends and Techniques*, 1990, p. 49.

are illegal. Formal agreements generally are enforceable and are more likely to be recognized on the books of the participants.

Informal Arrangements   Informal arrangements take many different forms. A simple *gentlemen's agreement* may be all that is needed to establish an amiable long-term relationship in a joint business venture. In other cases, companies with complementary products or services develop implicit working relationships. For example, a building contractor always may use a particular electrical or plumbing subcontractor. Companies that are partially dependent on each other may use *interlocking directorates*, in which one or more members serve on the boards of directors of both companies, as a means of providing a degree of mutual direction without taking formal steps to join together.

The informality and freedom that make informal arrangements workable also are strong factors against combining financial statements and treating the companies as if they were a single entity. Another key factor in most informal arrangements is the continuing separation of ownership and the ease with which the informal arrangements can be terminated. Without some type of combined ownership, the essentials of a business combination generally are absent.

Formal Agreements   Formal business combinations usually are accompanied by written agreements. These agreements specify the terms of the combination, including the form of the combined company, the consideration to be exchanged, the disposition of outstanding securities, and the rights and responsibilities of the participants. Consummation of such an agreement requires recognition on the books of one or more of the companies that are a party to the combination.

In some cases, a formal agreement may be equivalent in substance to a business combination, yet different in form. For example, a company entering into an agreement to lease all the assets of another company for a period of several decades is, in effect, acquiring the other company. Similarly, an operating agreement giving to one company full management authority over the operations of another company for an extended period of time may be viewed as a means of effecting a business combination. In spite of the substance of these types of agreements, they usually are not treated as business combinations from an accounting perspective.

Methods of Effecting Business Combinations

A business combination involves joining under common ownership two or more previously separate companies. Business combinations can be characterized as either *friendly combinations* or *unfriendly combinations*. In a friendly combination, the managements of the companies involved come to agreement on the terms of the combination and recommend approval by the stockholders. Such combinations usually are effected in a single transaction involving an exchange of assets or voting shares. In an unfriendly combination, the managements of the companies involved are unable to agree on the terms of a combination, and the management of one of the companies makes a ***tender offer*** directly to the shareholders of the other company. A tender offer invites the shareholders of the other company to "tender," or exchange, their shares for securities or assets of the acquiring company. If sufficient shares are tendered, the acquiring company gains voting control of the other company and can install its own management by exercising its voting rights. Threats of unfriendly takeovers used by outside parties to force high-priced repurchases of stock by the company or other concessions by management have been termed "greenmail" and have been used quite successfully by some members of the financial community. Examples include Revlon's threatened takeover of Gillette Co., James Goldsmith's acquisition of Goodyear Tire & Rubber shares, Minorco's threatened takeover of Salomon, Inc., and various activities by T. Boone Pickens and Carl Icahn.

Threats of hostile takeovers have caused a number of companies to establish a variety of antitakeover measures, including "golden parachutes," which give existing corporate officers various types of salary and pension guarantees or other protection in the event their company is taken over. The State of New York recently extended its "poison pen" law for 2 more years. Under this legislation, additional shares can be issued to existing shareholders at reduced prices, making the cost of acquiring sufficient shares under a hostile takeover prohibitively expensive.

A business combination can be effected by one company's acquiring either the assets or the voting stock of another company.

Acquisition of Assets   Sometimes one company acquires another company's assets through direct negotiations with its management. The agreement also may involve the acquiring company's assuming the other company's liabilities. Combinations of this sort take forms (*a*) or (*b*) in Figure 1-1. The selling company generally distributes to its stockholders the assets or securities received in the combination from the acquiring company and liquidates, leaving only the acquiring company as the surviving legal entity.

The acquiring company accounts for the combination by recording each asset acquired, each liability assumed, and the consideration given in exchange.

Acquisition of Stock   A business combination effected through a stock acquisition does not necessarily have to involve the acquisition of all of a company's outstanding voting shares. For one company to gain control over another through stock ownership, a majority (that is, greater than 50 percent) of the outstanding voting shares normally is required. An acquisition of less than a majority of the outstanding voting shares is not regarded as a business combination. When a majority of the voting stock is held by a single stockholder, the remaining shares are referred to as the ***minority*** or ***noncontrolling interest***.

In those cases where voting control of another company is acquired and both companies remain in existence as separate legal entities following the business combination, the cost of the stock of the acquired company is recorded on the books of the acquiring company as an investment and subsequently is accounted for as a parent-subsidiary relationship. Alternatively, the acquired company may be liquidated and the assets and liabilities transferred to the acquiring company or a newly created company. To do so, all or substantially all of the voting stock of the acquired company must be obtained. An acquisition of stock and subsequent liquidation of the acquired company is equivalent to an acquisition of assets.

Valuation of Business Entities

All parties involved in a business combination must feel there is an opportunity to benefit before they will agree to participate. Determining whether a particular combination proposal is advantageous can be difficult. Both the value of a company's assets and its future earning potential are important in assessing the value of the company.

Value of Individual Assets and Liabilities   The value of a company's individual assets and liabilities usually is determined by appraisal. For some items, the value may be determined with relative ease, such as investments that are traded actively in the securities markets, or short-term payables. For other items the appraisal may be much more subjective, such as the value of land located in an area where there have been few recent sales. In addition, certain intangibles typically are not reported on the balance sheet. For example, the costs of developing new ideas, new products, and new production methods normally are expensed as research and development costs in the period incurred.

Current liabilities often are viewed as having fair values equal to their book values because they will be paid at face amount within a short time. Long-term liabilities, however, must be valued based on current interest rates if different from the effective rates at the issue dates of the liabilities. For example, if $100,000 of 10-year, 6 percent bonds, paying interest annually, had been issued at par 3 years ago, and the current market rate of interest for the same type of security is 10 percent, the value of the liability currently is computed as follows:

Present value for 7 years at 10% of principal payment of $100,000	
($100,000 × .51316)	$51,316
Present value at 10% of 7 interest payments of $6,000	
($6,000 × 4.86842)	29,211
Present value of bond	$80,527

Although accurate assessments of the value of assets and liabilities may be difficult, they form an important part of the overall determination of the value of an enterprise.

Value of Potential Earnings   In many cases, assets operated together as a group have a value that exceeds the sum of their individual values. This "going-concern value" makes it desirable to operate the assets as an ongoing entity rather than sell them individually. A company's earning power as an ongoing enterprise is of obvious importance in valuing that company.

There are different approaches to measuring the value of a company's future earnings. Sometimes companies are valued based on a multiple of their current earnings. For example, if Bargain Company reports earnings of $35,000 for the current year, the value of the company based on a multiple of 10 times current earnings is $350,000. The appropriate multiple to use is a matter of judgment and is based on factors such as the riskiness and variability of the earnings and the anticipated degree of growth.

Another method of valuing a company is to compute the present value of the anticipated future net cash flows generated by the company. This requires assessing the amount and timing of future cash flows and discounting them back to the present value at the discount rate determined to be appropriate for the type of enterprise. For example, if Bargain Company is expected to generate cash flows of $35,000 for each of the next 25 years, the present value of the firm at a discount rate of 10 percent is $317,696, computed as follows:

Annual cash flow generated	$ 35,000
Present value factor for an annuity of 25 annual payments at 10%	×9.07704
Present value of future earnings	$ 317,696

Estimating the potential for future earnings requires numerous assumptions and estimates. Not surprisingly, the buyer and seller often have difficulty agreeing on the value of a company's expected earnings.

Valuation of Consideration Exchanged   When one company acquires another, a value must be placed on the consideration given in the exchange. Little difficulty is encountered when cash is used in an acquisition, but valuation may be more difficult when securities are exchanged, particularly new untraded securities or securities with unusual features. For example, General Motors completed an acquisition in 1985 using a new Series B common stock that pays dividends based on subsequent earnings of the acquired company rather than on the earnings of General Motors as a whole. Some companies have used non-interest-bearing bonds (zero coupon bonds), which have a fair value sufficiently below par value to compensate the holder for interest. Other companies have used various types of convertible securities. Unless these securities, or others that are considered equivalent, are being traded in the market, estimates must be made of their value. The approach generally followed is to use the value of some similar security with a determinable market value and adjust for the estimated value of the differences in the features of the two securities.

ACCOUNTING AND REPORTING ALTERNATIVES

There are two methods of accounting for formal business combinations: *purchase* and *pooling of interests*. Pooling of interests accounting is appropriate for business combinations only when there is a continuity of ownership; that is, the owners of the combining companies continue as the owners of the combined company. For example, if one company acquires another by issuing shares of common stock in exchange for the common stock of the other company, the stockholders of both combining companies continue as owners of the combined company. A pooling of interests can occur only when one company uses its own common stock to acquire the assets or stock of another company.

On the other hand, purchase accounting is appropriate if an important ownership interest is eliminated in the business combination. For example, if one company acquires for cash the stock or assets of another company, the owners of the acquired company do not continue as owners of the combined company, having taken cash rather than an ownership interest.

Under pooling of interests accounting, the book values of the assets, liabilities, and owners' equities of the combining companies are carried forward to the combined company as if the companies had always been combined; that is, the balance sheet items are not adjusted to fair values. Under purchase accounting, assets acquired and liabilities assumed are reported by the acquiring company at their fair values at the date of combination. Accounting for business combinations is summarized in Figure 1-3.

Note from Figure 1-3 that the acquiring company can acquire either the net assets or the common stock of the other company without affecting whether the business combination is accounted for as a purchase or pooling of interests. In general, an acquisition of net assets is associated with a statutory merger or consolidation, and an acquisition of stock is associated with the companies' remaining as separate legal entities in a parent-subsidiary relationship. However, the choice of legal form does not determine whether purchase or pooling of

FIGURE 1-3 Business combination alternatives.

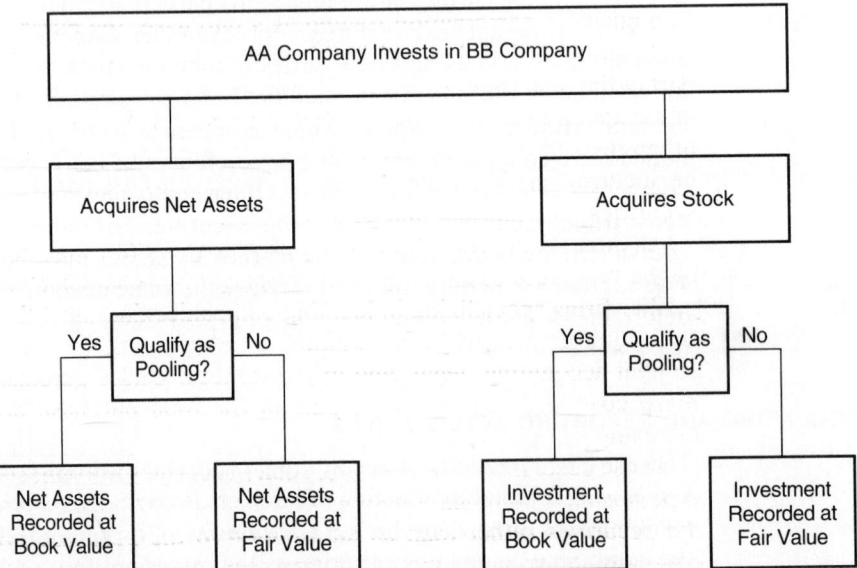

interests treatment is used in recording the business combination. The consideration given by the acquiring company in the exchange tends to be one of the key factors in determining the appropriate accounting method.

PURCHASE ACCOUNTING

All business combinations were treated as purchases before pooling of interests accounting was adopted as an acceptable alternative several decades ago. Although pooling of interests accounting was very widespread through the 1960s, the issuance in 1970 of **APB Opinion No. 16**, "Business Combinations" (APB 16), significantly restricted the use of pooling. Today only about 10 percent of business combinations are treated as poolings of interests.

Nature of Purchase Treatment

When an asset is purchased, consideration is given in exchange for the ownership rights to the item acquired. Thus, purchase treatment is appropriate for business combinations in which owners of one or more of the companies give up their ownership rights.

When an asset is purchased, the buyer records the asset at the total cost incurred in acquiring that asset. If a collection of assets is purchased for a single lump-sum purchase price, the total cost must be allocated to the individual assets acquired based on their fair values. The same principles apply to the purchase of an ongoing business as to the purchase of individual assets or groups of assets.

Determining the Purchase Price

In a business combination treated as a purchase, the purchaser considers all the costs associated with acquiring the net assets or stock of the other company as part of the total purchase price. The value of the consideration given to the owners of the acquired company normally constitutes the largest part of the total cost, but other costs also may be significant. There are three types of other costs that may be incurred in effecting a business combination: direct costs, costs of issuing securities, and indirect and general costs.

All direct costs associated with purchasing another company are treated as part of the total cost of the acquired company. For example, finders' fees often are paid to firms specializing in locating companies that meet the particular needs of the acquiring company. In addition, business combinations often result in substantial accounting, legal, and appraisal fees. Under purchase accounting, all of these costs are capitalized as part of the total purchase price of the acquired company.

Those costs incurred in issuing equity securities in connection with a purchase-type business combination should be treated as a reduction in the issue price of the securities rather than as an addition to the purchase price of the acquired company. Such costs include listing fees, audit and legal fees related to stock registration, and brokers' commissions. Costs incurred in issuing bonds payable as part of a purchase-type business combination should be accounted for as bond issue costs and amortized over the term of the bonds.

All indirect and general costs related to a business combination or to the issuance of securities in a combination should be expensed as incurred. For example, the salary costs of accountants on the staff of the acquiring company in a business combination would be expensed, even though some of their time was spent on matters related to the combination.

To illustrate the treatment of the costs incurred in a purchase-type business combination, assume that on January 1, 19X1, Point Corporation purchases all the assets and liabilities of Sharp Company in a statutory merger by issuing to Sharp 10,000 shares of $10 par common stock. The shares issued have a total market value of $600,000. Point incurs legal and appraisal fees of $40,000 in connection with the combination and stock issue costs of $25,000. The total purchase price is equal to the value of the shares issued by Point plus the additional costs incurred related to the acquisition of assets:

Fair value of stock issued	$600,000
Other acquisition costs	40,000
Total purchase price	$640,000

The stock issued by Point to effect the combination is valued at its fair value minus the issue costs:

Fair value of stock issued	$600,000
Stock issue costs	(25,000)
Recorded amount of stock	$575,000

Combination Effected through Purchase of Net Assets

When one company acquires the net assets of another in a purchase-type business combination, the acquiring company records on its books the individual assets and liabilities acquired in the combination and the consideration given in exchange. Once the total purchase price of an acquisition has been determined, it must be assigned to the individual assets and liabilities acquired. Each identifiable asset and liability acquired is valued at its fair value at the date of combination. Any amount of the purchase price in excess of the fair value of the identifiable assets and liabilities acquired is viewed as the price paid for *goodwill*. In theory, goodwill is the excess earning power of the acquired company; in practice, goodwill represents the premium paid to acquire control.

In the Sharp Company acquisition, the total purchase price was computed to be $640,000. Assume the book values and fair values of Sharp's individual assets and liabilities given in Figure 1-4. When transferred to Point, these individual assets and liabilities must be recorded on Point's books at their fair values at the date of the business combination.

FIGURE 1-4 Sharp Company balance sheet information, December 31, 19X0.

Assets, Liabilities, and Equities	Book Value	Fair Value
Cash and Receivables	$ 40,000	$ 40,000
Inventory	60,000	80,000
Land	50,000	70,000
Buildings and Equipment	400,000	350,000
Accumulated Depreciation	(150,000)	
Patent		80,000
Total Assets	$400,000	$620,000
Current Liabilities	$100,000	$110,000
Common Stock ($5 par)	100,000	
Additional Paid-In Capital	50,000	
Retained Earnings	150,000	
Total Liabilities and Equities	$400,000	
Fair Value of Net Assets		$510,000

The relationship between the total purchase price paid for the net assets of Sharp, the fair value of Sharp's net assets, and the book value of Sharp's net assets is illustrated in the following diagram:

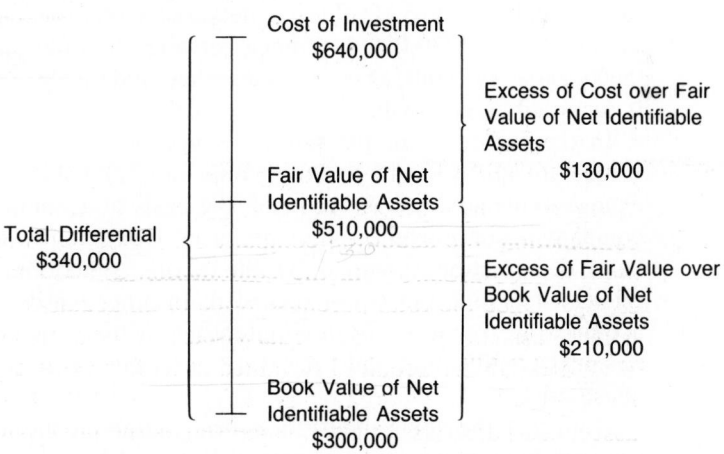

The $40,000 of other acquisition costs associated with the combination and the $25,000 of stock issue costs usually are incurred before the time that the assets of Sharp are received by Point. To facilitate accumulating these amounts before recording the combination, they may be recorded by Point in separate temporary "suspense" accounts as incurred:

(1)	Deferred Merger Costs	40,000	
	Cash		40,000
	Record costs related to purchase of Sharp Company.		
(2)	Deferred Stock Issue Costs	25,000	
	Cash		25,000
	Record costs related to issuance of common stock.		

(*Note*: Journal entries used in the text to illustrate the various accounting procedures are numbered sequentially within individual chapters for easy reference. Each journal entry number appears only once in a chapter.)

On the date of combination, Point records the combination with the following entry:

(3)	Cash and Receivables	40,000	
	Inventory	80,000	
	Land	70,000	
	Buildings and Equipment	350,000	
	Patent	80,000	
	Goodwill	130,000	
	Current Liabilities		110,000
	Common Stock		100,000
	Additional Paid-In Capital		475,000
	Deferred Merger Costs		40,000
	Deferred Stock Issue Costs		25,000
	Record purchase of Sharp Company.		

Entry (3) records all the individual assets and liabilities of Sharp, both tangible and intangible, on Point's books at their fair values on the date of combination. The total fair value of Sharp's net assets recorded is $510,000 ($620,000 − $110,000). The $130,000 difference between the total purchase price of $640,000 ($600,000 + $40,000), as computed earlier, and the fair value of Sharp's net assets is recorded as goodwill.

In the recording of the purchase-type business combination, Sharp's book values are not relevant to Point; only the fair values are recorded. Because a change in ownership has occurred, the basis of accounting used by the acquired company is not relevant to the purchaser. Consistent with this view, the accumulated depreciation recorded by Sharp on its buildings and equipment is not relevant to Point and is not recorded. In other words, the assets and liabilities acquired are recorded by the purchaser in the same way as if there were no business combination and they were purchased as a group for a lump-sum purchase price.

Note that the costs incurred in bringing about the merger are recorded in a separate temporary account entitled Deferred Merger Costs until the transfer of assets to Point is recorded. Because the merger costs are considered part of the total purchase price, the temporary account must be closed with entry (3) and these costs assigned, along with the remainder of the purchase price, to the net assets recorded. Similarly, the stock issue costs are recorded in a temporary account and then treated as a reduction in the proceeds received from the issuance of the stock by reducing the amount of additional paid-in capital recorded. Thus, the stock issued is recorded at its $600,000 fair value less the $25,000 of issue costs, with the $100,000 par value recorded in the common stock account and the remaining $475,000 recorded as additional paid-in capital.

Temporary accounts normally are used to accumulate the merger and stock issue costs because numerous individual costs often are incurred at different times before a business combination. Merger costs incurred after a combination is recorded may be debited directly to goodwill, while stock issue costs incurred subsequently are charged to additional paid-in capital.

Entries Recorded by Acquired Company On the date of the combination, Sharp records the following entry to recognize receipt of the Point shares and the transfer of all individual assets and liabilities to Point:

(4)	Investment in Point Stock	600,000	
	Current Liabilities	100,000	
	Accumulated Depreciation	150,000	
	Cash and Receivables		40,000
	Inventory		60,000
	Land		50,000
	Buildings and Equipment		400,000
	Gain on Sale of Net Assets		300,000
	Record transfer of assets to Point Corporation.		

The fair value of Point Corporation shares is recognized by Sharp at the time of the exchange and a gain of $300,000 is recorded. It is assumed that the motivation for Sharp's shareholders in entering into the business combination was to become shareholders of Point. The distribution of Point shares and the liquidation of Sharp are recorded on Sharp's books with the following entry:

(5)	Common Stock	100,000	
	Additional Paid-In Capital	50,000	
	Retained Earnings	150,000	
	Gain on Sale of Net Assets	300,000	
	Investment in Point Stock		600,000
	Record distribution of Point Corporation stock.		

Recording Goodwill Goodwill is viewed in accounting as the combination of all those factors that permit a company to earn above-average profits. As with any asset, goodwill is valued based on its original cost to the purchaser, where objectively determinable. Many of the expenditures made by companies may or may not lead to an increase in earning power. Because expenditures for "self-developed" goodwill often are not distinguishable from current operating costs, **APB Opinion No. 17**, "Intangible Assets" (APB 17), requires that such expenditures be expensed as incurred. When goodwill is purchased in connection with a business combination, however, the amount of the expenditure is viewed as objectively determinable and is capitalized. In a purchase-type business combination, the cost of goodwill purchased is measured as the excess of the total purchase price over the fair value of the net identifiable assets acquired.

The goodwill recorded when Point purchases Sharp Company is valued at $130,000, the difference between the total purchase price of $640,000 and the $510,000 fair value of Sharp's net identifiable assets. In accordance with the requirements of **APB 17**, the goodwill recorded in entry (3) at the time of the combination must be amortized over its economic life, not to exceed a period of 40 years.

Negative Goodwill   Sometimes the purchase price of an acquired company is less than the fair value of the net identifiable assets acquired. This difference often is referred to as *negative goodwill*.

The existence of negative goodwill might be viewed as implying that the acquired company should be liquidated because the assets and liabilities are worth more individually than together as an ongoing enterprise. On the other hand, the view usually adopted in practice is that the acquisition represents a *bargain purchase*.

APB 16 requires negative goodwill to be allocated against the noncurrent assets acquired, excluding marketable securities, in proportion to their fair values. In other words, all the assets and liabilities acquired by the purchaser are to be valued initially at their fair values; then, the noncurrent assets acquired, excluding marketable securities, are to be written down by a proportionate share of the negative goodwill. The current assets and liabilities are not affected by the write-down. In the unlikely event that the balances of the noncurrent assets are reduced to zero and some negative goodwill remains unallocated, the excess should be reported on the balance sheet as a deferred credit. Subsequently, this amount is amortized over the period benefited by the bargain purchase, not to exceed 40 years.

To illustrate the treatment of negative goodwill, assume that Point Corporation purchases all the assets and liabilities of Sharp Company at a total cost of $460,000 rather than the $640,000 assumed previously. In this case, the relationship between the total purchase price paid for the stock of Sharp, the fair value of Sharp's net assets, and the book value of Sharp's net assets is illustrated in the following diagram:

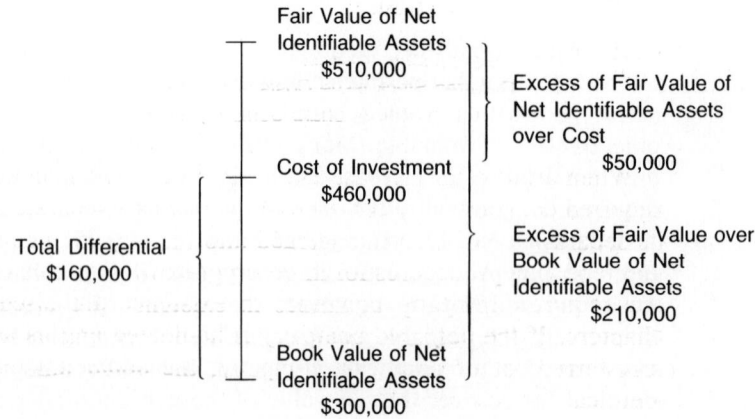

The fair values of Sharp's assets and liabilities total $510,000. The $510,000 total fair value of the net identifiable assets acquired exceeds the $460,000 purchase price by $50,000. This $50,000 of total negative goodwill is apportioned as follows:

Item	Book Value	Fair Value	Reduction	Amount Recorded
Cash and Receivables	$ 40,000	$ 40,000		$ 40,000
Inventory	60,000	80,000		80,000
Land	50,000	70,000	70/500 × $50,000 = $ 7,000	63,000
Buildings and Equipment (net)	250,000	350,000	350/500 × 50,000 = 35,000	315,000
Patent		80,000	80/500 × 50,000 = 8,000	72,000
Total Identifiable Assets	$400,000	$620,000	$50,000	$570,000
Current Liabilities	100,000	110,000		110,000
Net Identifiable Assets	$300,000	$510,000		$460,000

Combination Effected through Purchase of Stock

Many business combinations are effected by purchasing the voting stock of another company rather than by acquiring its net assets. In such a situation, the acquired company continues to exist, and the purchasing company records an investment in the common stock of the acquired company rather than the individual assets and liabilities. As with the purchase of the assets and liabilities, the cost of the investment is based on the total value of the consideration given in purchasing the shares, together with any additional costs incurred in bringing about the combination. For example, if Point Corporation (1) exchanges 10,000 shares of its stock with a total market value of $600,000 for all the shares of Sharp Company in a purchase transaction and (2) incurs and records merger costs of $40,000 and stock issue costs of $25,000 comparable to the prior example, the following entry is recorded by Point upon receipt of the Sharp stock:

(6)	Investment in Sharp Stock	640,000	
	Common Stock		100,000
	Additional Paid-In Capital		475,000
	Deferred Merger Costs		40,000
	Deferred Stock Issue Costs		25,000
	Record purchase of Sharp Company stock.		

When a business combination is effected through an acquisition of stock, the acquired company may continue to operate as a separate company or it may lose its separate identity and be merged into the acquiring company. The accounting and reporting procedures for intercorporate investments in common stock where the acquired company continues in existence are discussed in the next nine chapters. If the acquired company is liquidated and its assets and liabilities are transferred to the acquiring company, the dollar amounts recorded would be identical to those in entry (3).

Financial Reporting Subsequent to a Purchase

Financial statements prepared subsequent to a purchase-type business combination reflect the combined entity only from the date of combination. When a combination occurs during a fiscal period, income earned by the acquired company before the combination is not reported in the income statement of the combined enterprise. If the combined company presents comparative financial statements that include statements for periods before the combination, those statements include only the activities and financial position of the acquiring company and not those of the acquired company.

To illustrate financial reporting subsequent to a purchase-type business combination, assume the following information for Point Corporation and Sharp Company:

	19X0	19X1
Point Corporation:		
Separate Income (excluding any income from Sharp)	$300,000	$300,000
Shares Outstanding, December 31	30,000	40,000
Sharp Company:		
Net Income	$ 60,000	$ 60,000

Point Corporation acquires all the stock of Sharp Company at book value on January 1, 19X1, in a purchase-type business combination by issuing 10,000 shares of common stock. Subsequently, Point Corporation presents comparative financial statements for the years 19X0 and 19X1. The net income and earnings per share that Point presents in its comparative financial statements for the 2 years are as follows:

19X0:	
Net Income	$300,000
Earnings per Share ($300,000/30,000 shares)	$ 10.00
19X1:	
Net Income ($300,000 + $60,000)	$360,000
Earnings per Share ($360,000/40,000 shares)	$ 9.00

If Point Corporation had purchased Sharp Company in the middle of 19X1 instead of at the beginning, Point would include only Sharp's earnings subsequent to acquisition in its 19X1 income statement. If Sharp earned $25,000 in 19X1 before acquisition by Point and $35,000 after the combination, Point would report total net income for 19X1 of $335,000 ($300,000 + $35,000).

Disclosure Requirements

A number of disclosures are required following a business combination to provide financial statement readers with information about the combination and the expected effects of the combination on operating results. **APB 16** requires the following disclosures in the notes to the financial statements when purchase treatment is used:[3]

1. The name and a brief description of the acquired company.

2. A statement that purchase treatment has been used.

3. Information on the total cost incurred in making the purchase. When an exchange of stock occurs, the number of shares issued and remaining to be issued should be disclosed, along with the dollar amount assigned to the shares.

4. The portion of the year for which operating results of the acquired company have been included.

5. A description of the plan for amortization of goodwill and the amortization method.

6. Information on any contingent payments or commitments and their accounting treatment.

Pro forma financial statement data also should be presented to provide statement readers with a better understanding of the potential operating impact of the business combination. At a minimum, supplemental information should be provided to show:

1. Operating results as if the acquisition had been made at the start of the period.

2. When comparative financial statements are presented, operating results for the preceding period as if the acquisition had occurred at the start of that period.

POOLING OF INTERESTS ACCOUNTING

Pooling of interests accounting is the other primary method used to account for business combinations. Against the wishes of the companies involved, pooling of interests accounting was first applied to public utilities by regulatory bodies about half a century ago. Owners of companies subject to rate regulation typically are permitted to earn a fair return on their asset base. If assets are written up, the owners are allowed to earn a higher dollar return because of the higher asset base. The term *pooling* first was used in 1943 in describing the required carryforward of book values for rate-making purposes when two companies had merged, even though the managements of the companies wanted to restate the assets of the acquired company. Not long thereafter, the first nonregulated companies voluntarily opted to use pooling treatment. Before that time, all business combinations were considered to be purchases.

Excluding rate-making situations, the managements of companies involved in business combinations often prefer accounting for the combinations as poolings because of the impact on the financial statements subsequent to the combination. Purchase accounting requires the purchased assets and liabilities to be valued at

---

[3] *Accounting Principles Board Opinion No. 16*, "Business Combinations," August 1970, par. 95.

their fair values. In many cases, the fair values of an acquired company's assets are higher than the previous book values, and if the assets are tangible with limited lives or are intangible, these higher fair values must be amortized. Under pooling of interests accounting, the book values of both the acquiring company and the acquired company are carried forward. Therefore, income often is higher subsequent to the combination under pooling accounting than under purchase accounting because of lower depreciation and amortization charges. Further, the higher asset values recorded under purchase accounting negatively impact ratios such as return on investment because of the lower income amount in the numerator and the higher asset amount in the denominator.

Pooling procedures may lead to "instant earnings" when combinations are consummated late in the fiscal year, because the earnings of the pooled companies are combined for the entire year. Additional earnings also could be created if assets acquired in the pooling are sold at amounts considerably greater than their book values. For example, a piece of land with a book value of $40,000 and a fair value of $60,000 might be acquired in a business combination and immediately sold for $60,000. If the combination is treated as a pooling, the combined company recognizes a $20,000 gain ($60,000 − $40,000) on the sale; if the combination is treated as a purchase, no gain ($60,000 − $60,000) is recognized at the time of sale.

Attempts to restrict the use of pooling of interests accounting were notably unsuccessful before the issuance of **APB 16** in 1970. In particular, **Accounting Research Bulletin No. 48**, "Business Combinations" (ARB 48), issued by the AICPA's Committee on Accounting Procedure in 1957, established criteria for determining whether a business combination should be treated as a purchase or pooling. However, because some of the provisions of **ARB 48** were subject to judgment, and because of a lack of general acceptance, the pronouncement had little impact during much of the period from 1957 to 1970.

Thus, before **APB 16** became effective, companies had rather broad latitude in recording business combinations and there were many abuses of pooling of interests accounting. For example, some combinations were recorded as "part purchase, part pooling" combinations because they seemed to involve elements of both. Others were treated originally as purchases and later changed to "retroactive poolings" as the standards eroded.

APB 16 sets very stringent requirements for the use of pooling of interests accounting. Many of the rules established in **APB 16** are quite complex and exist primarily to eliminate the previous abuses of pooling accounting.

Nature of Pooling Treatment

The notion of continuity of ownership is central to the pooling of interests concept. Therefore, an exchange of voting common stock is essential for a combination to be viewed as a pooling of interests. Through the exchange of stock, the shareholder groups of two previously separate companies are joined together, in effect, pooling their interests to share jointly the rewards and risks of ownership from that point forward. Pooling is viewed as different from purchase accounting in that no new assets are invested, nor do any of the original owners withdraw assets or give up their ownership rights by participating in the exchange. A pooling is simply a coming together of previously separate owners. Following this line of thought, there is no purchase or sale of ownership, and there are no grounds for establishing a new basis of accountability.

The requirements of **APB 16** for use of pooling accounting attempt to assure a continuity of ownership. In particular, pooling of interests accounting may be used only in combinations where one company exchanges its voting common stock for at least 90 percent of the other company's common stock or for all its net assets. Numerous other conditions, discussed later in the chapter, must be met as well.

Distinguishing Characteristics of Pooling

Pooling of interests accounting treats a business combination as a "nonevent" in that the combining companies are viewed as if they always had been together. The unique attributes of pooling of interests accounting are the carryforward of assets and liabilities at book value and the carryforward of retained earnings. This contrasts with purchase accounting, in which the acquired assets and liabilities are recorded at their fair values and retained earnings of the acquired company is not recorded. Further, under pooling of interests accounting, no goodwill is recorded as arising from the combination, while under purchase accounting goodwill often is recorded.

Consistent with the view that the combining companies always have been together, comparative financial statements for periods before a combination that are included in financial reports issued subsequent to the combination are retroactively restated as if the companies always had been combined. All costs associated with the combination or with issuing the stock used in the combination are expensed as incurred; none of the costs of bringing about the combination are capitalized, nor are the stock issue costs deducted from the recorded amount of the stock. The stock issued is recorded at the book value of the net assets received in exchange.

The carryforward of book values and retained earnings in pooling accounting generally is viewed favorably by the managements of the combining companies. As indicated previously, the use of the book values rather than fair values often results in lower amortization charges and higher income subsequent to a pooling-type combination as compared with a purchase-type combination. Further, the absence of recorded goodwill, and subsequent amortization, in a pooling results in higher income in later years than under purchase accounting. In addition to the income effect, the carryforward of the acquired company's retained earnings under pooling may give management more flexibility with respect to dividends subsequent to the combination.

Combination Effected through Acquisition of Net Assets

When one company is merged into another in a pooling of interests, the assets and liabilities of that company are recorded on the books of the continuing company at their book values. The stock issued is recorded at the book value of the net assets received in exchange. Thus, the stockholders' equity accounts of the continuing company are increased so that the total stockholders' equity of the combined company after the combination is equal to the sum of the stockholders' equity accounts of the combining companies before the combination.

Pooling of interests accounting can be illustrated with the merger of Point Corporation and Sharp Company. Balance sheet data as of December 31, 19X0, are presented for the two companies in Figure 1-5. Note that, while fair values may be relevant for determining the amount of stock to be exchanged in the combination, only book values are needed for recording the combination.

Assume that on January 1, 19X1, in a statutory merger accounted for as a pooling of interests, Point Corporation issues 10,000 shares of its $10 par common stock in exchange for all the assets and liabilities of Sharp Company. Sharp distributes the shares to its shareholders and retires its own stock. The entry to record the combination on Point's books is as follows:

(7)	Cash and Receivables	40,000	
	Inventory	60,000	
	Land	50,000	
	Buildings and Equipment	400,000	
	Accumulated Depreciation		150,000
	Current Liabilities		100,000
	Common Stock (Point Corporation)		100,000
	Additional Paid-In Capital		50,000
	Retained Earnings		150,000
	Record pooling-type merger with Sharp.		

Point simply records the assets and liabilities of Sharp on its books using the book values and contra accounts carried by Sharp. Similarly, the stockholders' equity amounts of Sharp are carried over to Point's books. In this example, the total par value of Point's stock issued for Sharp's assets and liabilities is $100,000 and is the same as the total par value of Sharp's stock. Point's common stock issued in the combination replaces that of Sharp, and the other stockholders' equity accounts of Sharp are brought on to Point's books.

The total stockholders' equity of the combined company is always equal to the sum of the stockholders' equity accounts of the combining companies in a pooling of interests. In this example, the individual stockholders' equity accounts of the combined company also are equal to the sums of the individual stockholders' equity accounts of the combining companies. This occurs only because the total par value of the stock issued in the combination by Point is equal to the total par value of Sharp's stock that is retired. If the total par values were different, total stockholders' equity would not change but the totals of individual stockholders' equity items would.

FIGURE 1-5 Point Corporation and Sharp Company balance sheets, December 31, 19X0.

	Book Values	
Assets, Liabilities, and Equities	Point	Sharp
Cash and Receivables	$ 75,000	$ 40,000
Inventory	125,000	60,000
Land	100,000	50,000
Buildings and Equipment	600,000	400,000
Accumulated Depreciation	(200,000)	(150,000)
Total Assets	$700,000	$400,000
Current Liabilities	$150,000	$100,000
Common Stock		
Point Corporation ($10 par)	300,000	
Sharp Company ($5 par)		100,000
Additional Paid-In Capital	30,000	50,000
Retained Earnings	220,000	150,000
Total Liabilities and Equities	$700,000	$400,000

Note that any merger costs or stock issue costs incurred in effecting the combination would have been expensed as incurred.

Entries Recorded by Acquired Company   On the date of combination, Sharp records the following entry to recognize receipt of the Point shares and the transfer of all individual assets and liabilities to Point:

(8)	Investment in Point Stock	300,000	
	Current Liabilities	100,000	
	Accumulated Depreciation	150,000	
	Cash and Receivables		40,000
	Inventory		60,000
	Land		50,000
	Buildings and Equipment		400,000
	Record transfer of assets to Point Corporation.		

The amount recorded by Sharp as its investment in Point Corporation shares is based on the book value of Sharp's net assets in the pooling case. The distribution of Point shares and the liquidation of Sharp are recorded on Sharp's books with the following entry:

(9)	Common Stock	100,000	
	Additional Paid-In Capital	50,000	
	Retained Earnings	150,000	
	Investment in Point Stock		300,000
	Record distribution of Point Corporation stock.		

Differences in Total Par Value

In most poolings, the total par value of the shares issued in the combination is different from the total par value of the stock acquired. This occurs because the number of shares issued usually is different from the number of shares acquired and the per-share par values often are different.

If the total par value of the stock issued in the combination is different from the total par value of the stock acquired, the combined stockholders' equity amounts cannot be determined by a simple summing of the individual stockholders' equity accounts of the combining companies. To illustrate, the following bar graph can be constructed by summing the individual stockholders' equity accounts of the combining companies:

Total Stockholders' Equity

```
┌─────────────────────────┐
│                         │
│      Capital Stock      │
│ ─ ─ ─ ─ ─ ─ ─ ─ ─ ─ ─ ─ │
│       Additional        │
│      Paid-In Capital    │
│ ─ ─ ─ ─ ─ ─ ─ ─ ─ ─ ─ ─ │
│                         │
│    Retained Earnings    │
│                         │
└─────────────────────────┘
```

If the total par value of the common stock of the combined company is less than the sum of the total par values of the stock of the combining companies, the dashed boundary between capital stock and additional paid-in capital shifts upward. Thus, the total amount assigned to capital stock is less, and the amount assigned to additional paid-in capital increases. On the other hand, if the total par value of the stock of the combined company exceeds the total par values of the stock of the combining companies, the dashed boundary between capital stock and additional paid-in capital shifts downward. The total amount assigned to capital stock is more, and the amount assigned to additional paid-in capital decreases. If the total par value of the stock issued in the combination is large enough, the dashed boundary shifts downward past additional paid-in capital; the total additional paid-in capital of the combined company is eliminated, and combined retained earnings is reduced.

The effect of differences in the total par value of stock issued in a business combination is illustrated in Figure 1-6. The figure, based on the Point and Sharp merger, shows the composition of the stockholders' equity accounts of the combined entity in four different cases. Each case reflects a different number of shares issued in the combination, resulting in a different total par value. In each case, the $850,000 total stockholders' equity of the combined entity is equal to the sum of the totals reported by the individual companies at the time of combination ($550,000 + $300,000). To focus attention on the stockholders' equity accounts,

FIGURE 1-6 Stockholders' equity accounts after pooling of interests, January 1, 19X1.

Item	Original Stockholders' Equity Accounts		Changes in Stockholders' Equity Account Balances Recorded by Point			
	Point	Sharp	Case 1	Case 2	Case 3	Case 4
Shares Issued by Point:						
Number of Shares			10,000	8,000	14,000	21,000
Total Par Value			$100,000	$ 80,000	$140,000	$210,000
Common Stock	$300,000	$100,000	$100,000	$ 80,000	$140,000	$210,000
Additional Paid-In Capital	30,000	50,000	50,000	70,000	10,000	(30,000)
Retained Earnings	220,000	150,000	150,000	150,000	150,000	120,000
Total Stockholders' Equity	$550,000	$300,000	$300,000	$300,000	$300,000	$300,000

Stockholders' Equity Accounts of Combined Company

Sum of Original Stockholders' Equity Accounts	Case 1	Case 2	Case 3	Case 4
Capital Stock $400,000	Capital Stock $400,000	Capital Stock $380,000	Capital Stock $440,000	Capital Stock $510,000
Additional Paid-In Capital $80,000	Additional Paid-In Capital $80,000	Additional Paid-In Capital $100,000	Additional Paid-In Capital $40,000	
Retained Earnings $370,000	Retained Earnings $370,000	Retained Earnings $370,000	Retained Earnings $370,000	Retained Earnings $340,000

the illustrative journal entries given below combine all the assets acquired and liabilities assumed into a single account called "Net Assets of Sharp Company."

Case 1 The like stockholders' equity accounts of the combining companies are summed without adjustment when the total par values of the shares exchanged are equal. As illustrated previously with the expanded entry (7), the entry on Point's books to record the combination reflects the issuance of Point's stock and the carryover of Sharp's additional paid-in capital and retained earnings:

(10) Net Assets of Sharp Company	300,000	
Common Stock		100,000
Additional Paid-In Capital		50,000
Retained Earnings		150,000

Case 2 When the total par value of the shares issued is less than the par value of the shares replaced, the difference is reflected as an increase in additional paid-in capital. The entry to record the combination on Point's books when Point issues 8,000 shares having a total par value of $80,000 in exchange for Sharp's stock having a total par value of $100,000 is:

(11) Net Assets of Sharp Company	300,000	
Common Stock		80,000
Additional Paid-In Capital		70,000
Retained Earnings		150,000

Point records additional paid-in capital equal to Sharp's additional paid-in capital ($50,000) plus the difference in the total par value of the shares exchanged ($100,000 − $80,000).

Case 3 When the total par value of the shares issued is greater than the total par value of the shares acquired, the difference is treated as a reduction in the combined additional paid-in capital. The entry to record the combination on Point's books when Point issues 14,000 shares having a total par value of $140,000 in exchange for Sharp's stock having a total par value of $100,000 is:

(12) Net Assets of Sharp Company	300,000	
Common Stock		140,000
Additional Paid-In Capital		10,000
Retained Earnings		150,000

Point records additional paid-in capital equal to Sharp's additional paid-in capital ($50,000) minus the difference in the total par value of the shares exchanged ($140,000 − $100,000).

Case 4 When Point issues 21,000 shares, the $210,000 par value of the shares issued exceeds the $100,000 par value of Sharp's shares retired by enough to eliminate the combined additional paid-in capital and part of the combined retained earnings, as follows:

Par value of Point's shares issued	$210,000
Par value of Sharp's shares replaced	(100,000)
Increase in total par value	$110,000
Additional paid-in capital of Sharp	(50,000)
Additional paid-in capital of Point	(30,000)
Reduction in combined retained earnings	$ 30,000

The entry to record the combination on the books of Point in this last case is:

(13)	Net Assets of Sharp Company	300,000	
	Additional Paid-In Capital	30,000	
	Common Stock		210,000
	Retained Earnings		120,000

Because of the large increase in the total par value of the stock outstanding, this entry does not record any additional paid-in capital and instead eliminates the additional paid-in capital already carried on Point's books. Only $120,000 of retained earnings is carried over from Sharp to Point, reflecting the $30,000 reduction in combined retained earnings. Note that although one of the distinguishing features of a pooling of interests is that the retained earnings of all combining companies is carried forward, this can occur only where there is sufficient additional paid-in capital to absorb any increase in the total par value of the common stock outstanding.

Combination Effected through Acquisition of Stock

In substance, there may be no difference between acquiring all of a company's assets and liabilities and acquiring all its common stock. The net effect is the same, although the form of the combination is not. When common shares are exchanged in a pooling-type business combination, the stock received by the acquiring company is recorded as an investment at the book value of those shares. The stockholders' equity accounts of the acquiring company are affected in the same way as if the net assets of the other company had been acquired. For example, if Point Corporation issues 10,000 shares of its $10 par common stock in exchange for all the common stock of Sharp Company, Point records the stock acquisition with the following entry:

(14)	Investment in Sharp Stock	300,000	
	Common Stock		100,000
	Additional Paid-In Capital		50,000
	Retained Earnings		150,000
	Record pooling-type combination with Sharp.		

The stock investment is recorded by Point at the book value of the shares indicated in Sharp's balance sheet shown in Figure 1-5. The stock issued is recorded at its total par value ($10 × 10,000 shares). Because the total par value of the shares issued is the same as the total par value of the shares received in the exchange, no adjustments are needed for differences in total par values and the other stockholders' equity balances of Sharp are carried over to the books of Point.

Following an exchange of stock, the acquiring (parent) company may choose to maintain the separate existence of the acquired (subsidiary) company and continue to operate it as a separate company. On the other hand, the parent may decide to liquidate the subsidiary and merge all the assets and liabilities into the parent. In this latter case, the ultimate effect is the same as if the original combination had been a merger.

Because **APB 16** requires that only 90 percent of a company's common stock be acquired in an exchange of shares in order for the combination to be treated as a pooling, not all poolings involve a 100 percent acquisition. For poolings in which less than 100 percent of the other company's stock is acquired, the acquiring company records the shares acquired at their book value and records its proportionate share of the acquired company's stockholders' equity accounts. For example, if Point Corporation issues 9,000 of its shares in exchange for 90 percent of the common stock of Sharp Company, Point records the investment in Sharp stock at the book value of the 90 percent ownership interest acquired and 90 percent of the amounts of Sharp's stockholders' equity accounts, as follows:

(15)	Investment in Sharp Stock	270,000	
	Common Stock		90,000
	Additional Paid-In Capital		45,000
	Retained Earnings		135,000
	Record pooling-type combination with Sharp.		

Financial Reporting Subsequent to a Pooling

When a company prepares financial statements subsequent to a pooling-type business combination, the financial statements give effect to the combination as if the combination had occurred before the periods covered by the statements. Even if the combination takes place at a time other than at the beginning of a fiscal period, the income statement for that period reports the income for the combining companies as if they had been combined for the entire period. If the combined company presents comparative financial statements that include statements for periods before the combination, those statements include the operating activities and financial position of the combining companies as if the companies always had been combined.

To illustrate financial reporting subsequent to a pooling-type business combination, assume the following information for Point Corporation and Sharp Company:

	19X0	19X1
Point Corporation:		
Separate Income (excluding any income from Sharp)	$300,000	$300,000
Shares Outstanding, December 31	30,000	40,000
Sharp Company:		
Net Income	$ 60,000	$ 60,000

Point Corporation acquires all the stock of Sharp Company on January 1, 19X1, in a pooling-type business combination by issuing 10,000 shares of common stock. Subsequently, Point Corporation presents comparative financial statements for the years 19X0 and 19X1. The net income and earnings per share that Point presents in its comparative financial statements for the 2 years are as follows:

19X0:
Net Income ($300,000 + $60,000) $360,000
Earnings per Share ($360,000/40,000 shares) $ 9.00
19X1:
Net Income ($300,000 + $60,000) $360,000
Earnings per Share ($360,000/40,000 shares) $ 9.00

If Point Corporation had acquired Sharp Company in the middle of 19X1 instead of at the beginning, Point still would include the entire amount of Sharp's earnings in its 19X1 income statement.

Disclosure Requirements

APB 16 requires the following disclosures in the notes to the financial statements when pooling treatment is used:[4]

1. The name and a brief description of the acquired company.
2. A statement that pooling treatment has been used.
3. Description and number of shares issued in the exchange.
4. For the separate companies, revenue, extraordinary items, net income, changes in stockholders' equity, and the amount and handling of intercompany transactions for the portion of the current period before the date of combination.
5. A description of any adjustments of net assets or income related to changes in accounting procedures.
6. A description of the impact of a change in the fiscal period of a combining company.
7. A reconciliation of revenue and income previously reported by the stock-issuing company with the restated amounts reported for those periods for the combined company.

[4] Ibid., par. 64.

In addition, a material profit or loss from disposing of a significant part of the assets of the combining companies must be reported separately in the income statement as an extraordinary item.

SUMMARY ILLUSTRATION OF PURCHASE AND POOLING ACCOUNTING

To summarize the previous discussion and to highlight the differences between purchase and pooling of interests accounting, assume that Premium Corporation enters into a business combination with Standard Company on January 1, 19X2. The balance sheets for the two companies immediately before the combination are shown in Figure 1-7. Information about the fair values of the assets and liabilities also is included.

On January 1, 19X2, Premium Corporation exchanges 4,000 of its $10 par common shares for all the outstanding shares of Standard Company. Immediately thereafter, Standard Company is liquidated by transferring all its assets and liabilities to Premium and retiring all the stock of Standard held by Premium.

Purchase Accounting

On the date of combination, Premium's shares have a market value of $60 each. Therefore, the total consideration given in the exchange by Premium is $240,000 ($60 × 4,000 shares). The relationship between the total purchase price paid for

FIGURE 1-7 Premium Corporation and Standard Company balance sheet information, December 31, 19X1.

Assets, Liabilities, and Equities	Premium Corporation		Standard Company	
	Book Value	Fair Value	Book Value	Fair Value
Accounts Receivable	$100,000	$100,000	$ 10,000	$ 10,000
Inventory	200,000	220,000	30,000	55,000
Land	50,000	70,000	50,000	30,000
Buildings and Equipment	450,000	400,000	120,000	125,000
Accumulated Depreciation	(150,000)		(20,000)	
Total Assets	$650,000	$790,000	$190,000	$220,000
Accounts Payable	$ 50,000	$ 50,000	$ 40,000	$ 40,000
Common Stock ($10 par)	200,000		50,000	
Additional Paid-In Capital	30,000		10,000	
Retained Earnings	370,000		90,000	
Total Liabilities and Equities	$650,000		$190,000	
Fair Value of Net Assets		$740,000		$180,000

the stock of Standard Company, the fair value of Standard's net assets, and the book value of Standard's net assets is illustrated in the following diagram:

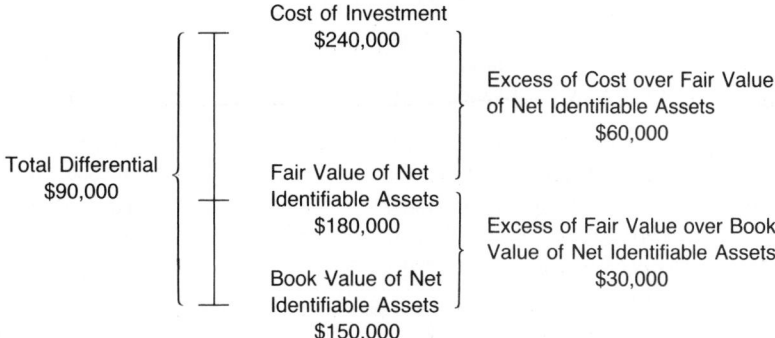

Premium records the combination with the following journal entry:

(16)	Investment in Standard Stock	240,000	
	Common Stock		40,000
	Additional Paid-In Capital		200,000
	Record purchase of Standard stock.		

The transfer of the assets and liabilities of Standard to Premium and the retirement of Standard's stock are recorded by Premium with the following entry:

(17)	Accounts Receivable	10,000	
	Inventory	55,000	
	Land	30,000	
	Buildings and Equipment	125,000	
	Goodwill	60,000	
	Accounts Payable		40,000
	Investment in Standard Stock		240,000
	Record assets acquired and liabilities assumed in purchase of Standard Company.		

The $60,000 difference between the $240,000 purchase price and the $180,000 fair value of the net identifiable assets received is recorded as goodwill. The resulting balance sheet for the combined entity is presented in Figure 1-8. As is always true in a purchase-type business combination, the retained earnings of the combined company is the retained earnings of the acquiring company; the retained earnings of the acquired company is not carried over to the acquiring company.

Pooling of Interests Accounting

When pooling of interests accounting is used to record the combination, the book values of the assets and liabilities and the retained earnings of the combining

(handwritten margin notes: BV Acqing, FV Acqed, BV≠BV, BV+BV, BV+FV, BV+BV, BV+BV)

FIGURE 1-8 Balance sheets for Premium Corporation and Standard Company combined, January 1, 19X2.

Assets, Liabilities, and Equities	Purchase	Pooling
Accounts Receivable	$110,000	$110,000
Inventory	255,000	230,000
Land	80,000	100,000
Buildings and Equipment	575,000	570,000
Accumulated Depreciation	(150,000)	(170,000)
Goodwill	60,000	
Total Assets	$930,000	$840,000
Accounts Payable	$ 90,000	$ 90,000
Common Stock ($10 par)	240,000	240,000
Additional Paid-In Capital	230,000	50,000
Retained Earnings	370,000	460,000
Total Liabilities and Equities	$930,000	$840,000

companies are carried over to the combined company. Premium records the pooling-type business combination with the following entry:

(18)	Investment in Standard Stock	150,000	
	Common Stock		40,000
	Additional Paid-In Capital		20,000
	Retained Earnings		90,000
	Record pooling-type combination with Standard.		

The resulting $10,000 reduction in total par value of the shares outstanding is added to additional paid-in capital, and the full balance of Standard's retained earnings is carried over to Premium's books.

Premium records the transfer of the individual assets and liabilities from Standard with the following entry:

(19)	Accounts Receivable	10,000	
	Inventory	30,000	
	Land	50,000	
	Buildings and Equipment	120,000	
	Accumulated Depreciation		20,000
	Accounts Payable		40,000
	Investment in Standard Stock		150,000
	Record assets acquired and liabilities assumed in pooling-type combination.		

The resulting balance sheet, shown in Figure 1-8, reflects the carryforward of accumulated depreciation and retained earnings from Standard, along with the other book values of Standard.

The stockholders' equity section of the combined balance sheet in Figure 1-8 is based on Premium Corporation's issuing 4,000 shares of its $10 par stock to acquire 100 percent of Standard's stock. If 7,500 shares are issued by Premium instead, the $25,000 increase ($75,000 − $50,000) in the par value of shares outstanding precludes the carryforward of Standard's $10,000 of additional paid-in capital and causes a reduction of $15,000 in the additional paid-in capital already carried on the books of Premium. The entry recorded by Premium in this case is:

(20)	Investment in Standard Stock	150,000	
	Additional Paid-In Capital	15,000	
	Common Stock		75,000
	Retained Earnings		90,000
	Record pooling-type combination with Standard.		

If Premium issues 10,000 shares in the combination, the increase in the total par value of the shares outstanding is $50,000 ($100,000 − $50,000). In this case, no additional paid-in capital is carried over from Standard, all Premium's additional paid-in capital is eliminated, and combined retained earnings must be reduced by $10,000. Therefore, only $80,000 ($90,000 − $10,000) of Standard's retained earnings is carried over to Premium's books. The combination is recorded by the following entry on Premium's books:

(21)	Investment in Standard Stock	150,000	
	Additional Paid-In Capital	30,000	
	Common Stock		100,000
	Retained Earnings		80,000
	Record pooling-type combination with Standard.		

Earnings Subsequent to Combination

Income of the combined company subsequent to the combination generally is affected by the method used to account for the combination. To illustrate, assume that the combined company reports net income of $200,000 for 19X2 after accounting for the January 1 combination of Premium and Standard as a pooling of interests. If the combination had been treated as a purchase, goodwill of $60,000 recorded in entry (17) would have to be amortized subsequent to the combination. Also, the $5,000 cost to Premium over the book value of Standard's buildings and equipment would have to be amortized. The additional cost to Premium of Standard's inventory would have to be recognized as well. Assuming a 10-year expected life of the goodwill and a remaining life of 5 years for the buildings and equipment and assuming that all Standard's inventory at the date of combination is sold in 19X2, the combined company's income for 19X2 would be $32,000 less under purchase treatment than under pooling:

Income following pooling of interests	$200,000
Amortization of goodwill ($60,000/10)	(6,000)
Additional depreciation ($5,000/5)	(1,000)
Excess over book value of inventory	(25,000)
Income following purchase	$168,000

ADDITIONAL CONSIDERATIONS—CRITERIA FOR POOLING OF INTERESTS

APB 16 allows both purchase and pooling of interests as methods of accounting for business combinations, but these methods may not be viewed as alternatives to one another. A series of 12 related conditions is set forth in **APB 16** as prerequisite to pooling treatment. If all the criteria are met, the transaction must be recorded as a pooling of interests. If any are not met, the combination must be treated as a purchase. The companies involved in a combination are not permitted a choice of methods except through the structuring of the combination.

The criteria or conditions established in **APB 16** are meant to assure that combinations treated as poolings contain the essential elements of a pooling. In particular, the conditions aim at assuring a continuity of ownership. The basic idea of a pooling is that previously independent ownership groups join together in a combination, pool their resources, and operate together from that point forward by sharing the rewards and risks of ownership. This contrasts with the nature of a purchase, which involves one ownership group acquiring rights of ownership from others and the others no longer sharing in the rewards and risks of ownership.

The criteria established by **APB 16** for determining whether purchase or pooling accounting is appropriate are divided into three categories:

1. Attributes of the combining companies
2. Manner of combining interests
3. Absence of planned transactions

Each of the categories, in turn, contains several criteria that must be met in order to use pooling treatment.

Attributes of the Combining Companies

Two conditions relating to independence must be satisfied for the combining companies to be eligible for pooling treatment.

1. Each of the combining companies is autonomous and has not been a subsidiary or division of another corporation within 2 years before the plan of combination is initiated.

Two or more previously independent companies must come together through an exchange of ownership if pooling treatment is to be used. Combining only selected subsets of operations is not consistent with bringing together two independent companies to operate as a single entity. An exception to the 2-year requirement is made for entities divested because of judicial or regulatory actions. A new company meets the condition unless it is a successor to another company that would not meet the condition.

2. Each of the combining companies is independent of the other combining companies.

On the date the plan of combination is initiated and consummated, the combining companies can hold no more than 10 percent in total of the outstanding voting common stock of any combining company (excluding shares acquired pursuant to the plan of combination). Because of this requirement of independence before the combination, a company cannot already hold a significant number of shares of another company and qualify for pooling treatment when it acquires the remaining ownership.

Manner of Combining Interests

A total of seven conditions are specified in this category.

1. The combination is effected in a single transaction or is completed in accordance with a specific plan within 1 year after the plan is initiated.

The acquisition of a company's stock over some long period of time is indicative of purchasing that stock, particularly if the terms of acquisition change from transaction to transaction. The 1-year time limit is extended if the delay is beyond the control of the companies involved because of litigation or regulatory action.

2. A corporation offers and issues only common stock with rights identical to those of the majority of its outstanding voting common stock in exchange for substantially all the voting common stock interest of another company at the date the plan of combination is consummated.

The term "substantially all" is defined by the APB as meaning at least 90 percent of the voting common stock of the other company outstanding on the date the combination is consummated. Therefore, to use pooling treatment, one company must issue its voting common stock in exchange for at least 90 percent of the outstanding voting common stock of the other company in consummating the business combination. The shares issued in the exchange must have rights identical with those of the majority of the issuing company's outstanding voting stock.

Intercorporate shareholdings of the companies before the exchange must be considered in determining whether the 90 percent rule has been satisfied. Shares of any combining company held by another combining company are, for purposes of applying the 90 percent rule, considered outstanding but are not counted in the shares exchanged. Further, shares of the issuing company held by a combining company must be restated into an equivalent number of the combining company's shares and deducted from the number actually exchanged. To illustrate, assume that A Company, B Company, and C Company enter into a combination agreement whereby A issues one of its shares for every two shares of B and C. Further assume:

a. Before the combination, A Company holds 20 shares of C, and C holds 30 shares of A.

b. Before the combination, B holds 40 shares of C, which it exchanges under the terms of the combination agreement.

c. C Company has 1,000 shares outstanding.

d. At the completion of the exchange, A Company holds all the shares of B and a total of 980 shares of C.

e. All the shares of C acquired by A are acquired in exchange for A's common stock except for those shares of C already held by A and 10 shares acquired for cash.

For applying the 90 percent rule, the imputed number of C's shares exchanged is computed as follows:

Number of shares of C held by A after exchange		980
Deduct: Shares of C exchanged by B	40	
Shares of C acquired for cash	10	
Shares of C held by A before the exchange	20	
Shares of A held by C before the exchange, restated into an equivalent number of C's shares (30 shares × 2)	60	
		(130)
Imputed number of C's shares acquired in the exchange		850

This combination cannot be treated as a pooling of interests, because only 85 percent (850/1,000) of C's shares are viewed as being acquired in the exchange.

By including under this condition cases in which companies each have holdings in one another, the pronouncement precludes attempts to circumvent the 90 percent rule by selectively choosing which company is to acquire the other.

APB 16 also permits pooling treatment in recording an exchange of common shares for all the other company's net assets. When the issuing company acquires the other company's net assets rather than its stock, all the net assets (not 90 percent) must be acquired in exchange for the issuing company's common stock to qualify for pooling treatment. The combining company may retain temporarily some monetary assets to satisfy any remaining obligations so long as the assets not so used are transferred to the issuing company.

 3. None of the combining companies changes the equity interest of the voting common stock in contemplation of effecting the combination either within 2 years before the plan of combination is initiated or between the dates the combination is initiated and consummated; changes in contemplation of effecting the combination may include distributions to stockholders and additional issuances, exchanges, and retirements of securities.

Retiring the shares of certain stockholders or making abnormal distributions to stockholders results in a lack of continuity of ownership and is indicative of a purchase. For example, an unusually large dividend paid to the shareholders of a combining company would preclude pooling treatment.

4. Each of the combining companies reacquires shares of voting common stock only for purposes other than business combinations, and no company reacquires more than a normal number of shares between the dates the plan of combination is initiated and consummated.

Reacquisitions of stock for cash or other assets result in a discontinuity of ownership. However, normal reacquisitions having a legitimate business purpose unrelated to business combinations are acceptable. For example, shares might be needed in case outstanding stock options were exercised.

5. The ratio of the interest of an individual common stockholder to those of other common stockholders in a combining company remains the same as a result of the exchange of stock to effect the combination.

The relative ownership interests of individual shareholders in a combining company must not be changed by the exchange of shares. Note that this condition relates only to the common shareholders in a particular combining company and does not deal with preferred shareholders. For example, it does not preclude the issuance of common stock in exchange for the preferred stock of a combining company.

6. The voting rights to which the common stock ownership interests in the resulting combined corporation are entitled are exercisable by the stockholders; the stockholders are neither deprived of nor restricted in exercising those rights for a period.

Voting rights are an important element of ownership. Changing or withholding those rights is not consistent with the notion of pooling.

7. The combination is resolved at the date the plan is consummated, and no provisions of the plan relating to the issue of securities or other consideration are pending.

Companies that believe themselves to be merger candidates sometimes posture their activities and reports in the most favorable light. As a safeguard, an exchange offer may provide for a certain number of shares at the time of the business combination and additional shares at some future time if certain performance measures are met. This criterion effectively blocks use of pooling in cases where contingent payments are involved.

Absence of Planned Transactions

Three conditions deal with actions after the combination is completed that are considered inconsistent with the idea of a pooling of interests.

1. The combined corporation does not agree directly or indirectly to retire or reacquire all or part of the common stock issued to effect the combination.

This criterion precludes the use of pooling in situations where the effects of an exchange of shares are negated by an accompanying agreement to buy back the shares exchanged. This criterion is aimed at the substance of an exchange rather than the form.

+/ no equity chong-

2. The combined corporation does not enter into other financial arrangements for the benefit of the former stockholders of a combining company, such as a guarantee of loans secured by stock issued in the combination, which in effect negates the exchange of equity securities.

This condition precludes pooling treatment in situations where the form of the transaction involves an exchange of shares but the substance of the exchange is the same as if the shares acquired were purchased for cash.

3. The combined corporation does not intend or plan to dispose of a significant part of the assets of the combining companies within 2 years after the combination other than disposals in the ordinary course of business of the formerly separate companies and elimination of duplicate facilities or excess capacity.

The concept of a pooling implies the continuity of the activities of the formerly separate companies. While the sale or disposition of duplicate facilities and excess capacity does not violate the spirit of pooling, disposing of a major segment of any combining company following the combination does.

SUMMARY OF KEY CONCEPTS AND TERMS

Business combinations are an important part of the American business scene. There are three types of formal business combinations: (1) statutory mergers, where one of the combining companies loses its separate legal identity and the other company continues with the assets and liabilities of both companies; (2) statutory consolidations, where both combining companies join to form a new company; and (3) stock acquisitions, where both combining companies maintain their separate existence, with one company owning the common stock of the other.

The two methods of accounting for business combinations are the purchase and pooling of interests methods. **APB 16** sets forth the conditions for the use of the two methods. In general, pooling of interests accounting is appropriate for combinations where there is a continuity of ownership; the owners of the separate combining companies must become the owners of the combined company. Purchase accounting is required for all combinations not meeting the specific pooling requirements of **APB 16**. In most purchase-type business combinations, a significant ownership interest is eliminated.

Under purchase accounting, the acquiring company records the assets and liabilities acquired at their fair values. Any excess of the purchase price over the fair value of the net identifiable assets acquired is recorded as goodwill. The retained earnings of the acquired company is not carried forward because past earnings cannot be purchased; only assets and liabilities can be purchased. For financial reporting, the combination is given effect as of the date of combination.

Under pooling accounting, the combining companies are treated as if they always had been combined. All assets and liabilities of the combining companies are carried forward at book values, and the retained earnings amounts of both companies normally are carried forward. Goodwill does not arise in a pooling-type combination. For financial reporting, the combination is treated as if it occurred before the earliest period for which statements are presented.

Bargain purchase	Noncontrolling interest
Business combination	Parent company
Consolidated financial statements	Parent-subsidiary relationship
Control	Pooling of interests
Friendly combinations	Purchase
Gentlemen's agreement	Statutory consolidation
Goodwill	Statutory merger
Interlocking directorates	Stock acquisition
Liquidated	Subsidiary
Minority interest	Tender offer
Negative goodwill	Unfriendly combinations

QUESTIONS

Q1-1 Describe each of the three legal forms that a business combination might take.

Q1-2 What does continuity of ownership mean, and how is it important in business combinations?

Q1-3 What are the major differences between purchase and pooling of interests treatment in recording a business combination?

Q1-4 Why is it considered appropriate to carry forward retained earnings of all the combining companies in a pooling of interests?

Q1-5 How does goodwill arise in a business combination? Under what conditions is it recorded?

Q1-6 When a purchase-type business combination occurs after the start of the year, the income earned by the acquired company between the beginning of the year and the date of combination is excluded from the net income reported by the combined company for the year. Why? How would the treatment differ if the combination were accounted for as a pooling? Why?

Q1-7 What is the maximum balance in retained earnings that can be reported by the combined entity following a business combination under (a) purchase treatment and (b) pooling of interests treatment?

Q1-8 What factors may make it attractive for a company to complete a business combination by acquiring the stock of another company and operating it as a subsidiary?

Q1-9 How does negative goodwill arise in a business combination? How is it normally treated for financial reporting purposes?

Q1-10 How is a business combination likely to be recorded if convertible preferred stock is used to acquire the voting common shares of another company? Why?

Q1-11 How does the treatment of prior-period financial statement data differ between purchase and pooling of interests accounting?

Q1-12 Which of the costs incurred in completing a business combination can be capitalized under (a) purchase treatment and (b) pooling of interests treatment?

Q1-13 Which of the costs incurred in completing a business combination should be treated as a reduction of additional paid-in capital under **(a)** purchase treatment and **(b)** pooling of interests treatment?

Q1-14* What effect do treasury stock transactions have on a company's ability to use pooling of interests treatment in recording a business combination?

Q1-15* Give two examples of planned transactions that would prevent a business combination from being recorded as a pooling of interests.

Q1-16* According to the 90 percent rule from **APB Opinion No. 16**, how are intercorporate shareholdings before a business combination that is to be effected through an exchange of shares taken into consideration when determining how to account for the combination?

CASES

C1-1 Determination of Additional Paid-In Capital Balances

The controller of Green Products Corporation is concerned about the amount of additional paid-in capital her company will report in its balance sheet following a business combination with Blackstone Company. The controller has asked you to assist in answering the following questions:

Required

    a. How is the amount of additional paid-in capital determined when purchase treatment is used in recording a business combination?

    b. How is the amount of additional paid-in capital determined when pooling of interests treatment is used in recording a business combination?

    c. Is the amount of additional paid-in capital likely to be greater following a purchase or a pooling of interests? Why?

C1-2 Goodwill and the Effects of Purchase versus Pooling of Interests Treatment

Midvale Corporation plans to acquire ownership of Bostwick Corporation in an exchange of common shares to take place in the middle of the current year. The president of Midvale Corporation is attempting to anticipate the financial statement impact of acquiring Bostwick Corporation and is particularly interested in the goodwill that might arise in the business combination.

    a. From an accounting perspective, explain the nature of goodwill. Is goodwill an asset? Explain. Under what conditions is goodwill recorded and at what amount?

    b. After it is recorded, how is goodwill treated?

    c. Other than goodwill, what dollar amounts will be reported differently in the financial statements of the combined company prepared subsequent to the combination if the combination is recorded as a pooling of interests rather than a purchase?

    d. Which method of accounting for the business combination is likely to result in higher reported net income for the combined company in the year of the combination? Why?

* Indicates item relates to ''Additional Considerations.''

C1-3   Differences between Purchase and Pooling of Interests [AICPA Adapted]

Flavin Company entered into a business combination with Stevens Company in the middle of the year. The combination was accounted for as a pooling of interests. Both companies use the same methods of accounting.

Flavin Company acquired all the assets and liabilities of Rubin Company in the middle of the year. This combination was accounted for as a purchase and resulted in goodwill. Both companies use the same methods of accounting.

Flavin Company effected both combinations through the issuance of equity securities, and registration fees for the equity securities involved in the combinations were incurred. There were no intercompany transactions before or after the combinations.

Required

a. **(1)** In the business combination accounted for as a pooling of interests, how should the recorded assets and liabilities of the separate companies be accounted for? What is the rationale for accounting for a business combination as a pooling of interests?

(2) In the business combination accounted for as a pooling of interests, how should the registration fees and direct costs related to effecting the business combination be accounted for?

(3) In the business combination accounted for as a pooling of interests, how should the results of operations for the year in which the business combination occurred be reported?

b. **(1)** In the business combination accounted for as a purchase, how should the assets acquired and liabilities assumed be recorded? What is the rationale for accounting for a business combination as a purchase?

(2) In the business combination accounted for as a purchase, how should the registration fees and direct costs related to effecting the business combination be accounted for?

(3) In the business combination accounted for as a purchase, how should the results of operations of the acquired company for the year in which the business combination occurred be reported?

C1-4*   Pooling of Interests Criteria [AICPA Adapted]

Crown Company and Jewel Company, both of which have only voting common stock, are considering a merger whereby Crown would be the surviving company. The terms of the combination provide that the transaction would be carried out by Crown exchanging one share of its stock for two shares of Jewel's stock. Before the date of the contemplated exchange, Crown had purchased 5 percent of Jewel's stock, which it holds as an investment. Jewel at the same date owned 2 percent of Crown's stock. All the remaining outstanding stock of Jewel will be acquired by Crown in the contemplated exchange. Neither of the two companies has ever had any affiliation as a subsidiary or division of any other company.

Required

a. Without enumerating specific criteria, how is a determination made as to whether a business combination is accounted for as a pooling of interests or as a purchase?

b. On the basis of the facts above, discuss the specific criteria that would qualify or disqualify this business combination for pooling of interests treatment.

c. What additional requirements must be met in order to account for this business combination as a pooling of interests?

C1-5* Use of Pooling of Interests Method

Appleton Corporation expanded its distribution network into the Southeast by joining together with an established company headquartered in Atlanta. Under its combination plan, Appleton Corporation acquired a majority of the common stock of Berger Company by issuing three shares of its own voting common stock for each common share of Berger tendered. In addition, Appleton acquired 2 percent of Berger's common stock by issuing preferred shares. Within 6 months of initiating its plan of acquisition, Appleton had acquired all of Berger's common stock with the exception of 5 percent held by stockholders who refused to sell or exchange their shares.

On the date of initiation of the combination, Appleton held 4 percent of Berger's stock, which it had acquired many years ago. Also at the initiation of the combination, Berger held shares of Appleton's common stock that it had acquired several years before.

As part of the combination plan, Appleton issued shares of its common stock to acquire all of Berger's preferred stock. Appleton planned to dispose of several of Berger's factories upon completion of the combination to eliminate duplication of facilities.

Required

a. Without regard to the specific facts of this case, should pooling be allowed as a method of accounting for business combinations? What is the rationale underlying the use of pooling of interests accounting?

b. List all of the factors in this case that might preclude Appleton Corporation from accounting for its combination with Berger Company as a pooling of interests.

EXERCISES

E1-1 Multiple-Choice Questions on Recording Business Combinations
[AICPA Adapted]

Select the correct answer for each of the following questions.

1. Which of the following is a potential abuse that can arise when a business combination is accounted for as a pooling of interests?
   a. Assets of the investee may be overvalued when the price paid by the investor is allocated among specific assets.
   b. Earnings of the pooled entity may be increased because of the combination only and *not* as a result of efficient operations.
   c. Liabilities may be undervalued when the price paid by the investor is allocated to the specific liabilities.
   d. An undue amount of cost may be assigned to goodwill, thus potentially allowing for an overstatement of pooled earnings.

2. In a business combination accounted for as a pooling of interests, the combined corporation's retained earnings usually equals the sum of the retained earnings of the individual combining corporations. Assuming there is *no* contributed capital other than capital stock at par value, which of the following describes a situation where the combined retained earnings must be increased or decreased?
    a. Increased if the par value dollar amount of the outstanding shares of the combined corporation exceeds the total capital stock of the separate combining companies.
    b. Increased if the par value dollar amount of the outstanding shares of the combined corporation is less than the total capital stock of the combining companies.
    c. Decreased if the par value dollar amount of the outstanding shares of the combined corporation exceeds the total capital stock of the separate combining companies.
    d. Decreased if the par value dollar amount of the outstanding shares of the combined corporation is less than the total capital stock of the separate combining companies.

3. Two calendar-year corporations combine on July 1, 19X5. The combination is properly accounted for as a pooling of interests. How should the results of operations have been reported for the year ended December 31, 19X5?
    a. Combined from July 1 to December 31 and disclosed for the separate companies from January 1 to June 30.
    b. Combined from July 1 to December 31 and disclosed for the separate companies for the entire year.
    c. Combined for the entire year and disclosed for the separate companies from January 1 to June 30.
    d. Combined for the entire year and disclosed for the separate companies for the entire year.

4. In a business combination accounted for as a purchase, how should the excess of fair value of net assets acquired over cost be treated?
    a. Amortized as a credit to income over a period *not* to exceed 40 years.
    b. Amortized as a charge to expense over a period *not* to exceed 40 years.
    c. Amortized directly to retained earnings over a period *not* to exceed 40 years.
    d. Allocated as a reduction of noncurrent assets other than long-term investments in marketable securities.

5. Goodwill represents the excess of the cost of an acquired company over the:
    a. Sum of the fair values assigned to identifiable assets acquired less liabilities assumed.
    b. Sum of the fair values assigned to tangible assets acquired less liabilities assumed.
    c. Sum of the fair value assigned to intangible assets acquired less liabilities assumed.
    d. Book value of an acquired company.

6. In a business combination accounted for as a purchase, costs of registering equity securities to be issued by the acquiring company are a (an):
    a. Expense of the combined company for the period in which the costs were incurred.
    b. Direct addition to stockholders' equity of the combined company.
    c. Reduction of the otherwise determinable fair value of the securities.
    d. Addition to goodwill.

7. Costs incurred in effecting a business combination accounted for as a pooling of interests should be:
    a. Added to the cost of the investment account of the parent corporation.

b. Deducted from additional paid-in capital of the combined corporation.
c. Deducted in determining net income of the combined corporation for the period in which the costs were incurred.
d. Capitalized and subsequently amortized over a period not exceeding 40 years.

8. The Action Corporation issued nonvoting preferred stock with a fair market value of $4,000,000 in exchange for all the outstanding common stock of Master Corporation. On the date of the exchange, Master had tangible net assets with a book value of $2,000,000 and a fair value of $2,500,000. In addition, Action issued preferred stock valued at $400,000 to an individual as a finder's fee in arranging the transaction. As a result of this transaction, Action should record an increase in net assets of:
a. $2,000,000.
b. $2,500,000.
c. $2,900,000.
d. $4,400,000.

9. Which of the following is the appropriate basis for valuing fixed assets acquired in a business combination accounted for as a purchase carried out by exchanging cash for common stock?
a. Historical cost.
b. Book value.
c. Cost plus any excess of purchase price over book value of asset acquired.
d. Fair value.

E1-2 Multiple-Choice Questions Contrasting Purchase and Pooling Treatments
[AICPA Adapted]

Select the correct answer for each of the following questions.

1. On April 1, 19X6, The Ash Company paid $400,000 for all the issued and outstanding common stock of Tray Corporation in a transaction properly accounted for as a purchase. The assets and liabilities of Tray Corporation on April 1, 19X6, follow:

Cash	$ 40,000
Inventory	120,000
Property and Equipment (net of accumulated depreciation of $160,000)	240,000
Liabilities	(90,000)

On April 1, 19X6, it was determined that the inventory of Tray had a fair value of $95,000 and the property and equipment (net) had a fair value of $280,000. What should be the amount computed as goodwill by Ash as a result of the business combination?
a. $0.
b. $25,000.
c. $75,000.
d. $90,000.

2. Ethel Corporation issued voting common stock with a stated value of $90,000 in exchange for *all* the outstanding common stock of Lum Company. The combination was properly accounted for as a pooling of interests. The stockholders' equity section of Lum Company at the date of the combination was as follows:

Common Stock	$ 70,000
Capital Contributed in Excess of Stated Value	7,000
Retained Earnings	50,000
	$127,000

What should the increase in stockholders' equity of Ethel Corporation be at the date of acquisition as a result of the business combination?

a. $0.
b. $37,000.
c. $90,000.
d. $127,000.

Items 3 and 4 are based on the following information:

On June 30, 19X5, Axel, Inc., acquired Belle, Inc., in a business combination properly accounted for as a pooling of interests. Axel exchanged six of its shares of common stock for each share of Belle's outstanding common stock. June 30 was the fiscal year-end for both companies. There were *no* intercompany transactions during the year. The balance sheets immediately before the combination follow.

	Axel	Belle	
	Book Value	**Book Value**	**Fair Value**
Current Assets	$ 40,000	$ 30,000	$ 45,000
Equipment (net)	150,000	120,000	140,000
Land	30,000		
Total Assets	$220,000	$150,000	$185,000
Current Liabilities	$ 35,000	$ 15,000	$ 15,000
Notes Payable	40,000		
Bonds Payable		100,000	100,000
Common Stock ($1 par)	75,000		
Common Stock ($5 par)		50,000	
Retained Earnings	70,000	(15,000)	
Total Liabilities and Equities	$220,000	$150,000	

3. What was the retained earnings balance on the combined balance sheet on June 30, 19X5?
   a. $45,000.
   b. $55,000.
   c. $70,000.
   d. $80,000.

4. How should the combined net income for the year be computed?
   a. Use only Axel's income, because the combination occurred on the last day of the fiscal year.
   b. Use only Belle's income, because the combination occurred on the last day of the fiscal year.
   c. Add both companies' incomes even though the combination occurred on the last day of the fiscal year.
   d. Add both companies' incomes and subtract the annual amortization of goodwill.

5. In a business combination how should plant and equipment of the acquired corporation generally be reported under each of the following methods?

	Pooling of Interests	Purchase
a.	Fair value	Recorded value
b.	Fair value	Fair value
c.	Recorded value	Recorded value
d.	Recorded value	Fair value

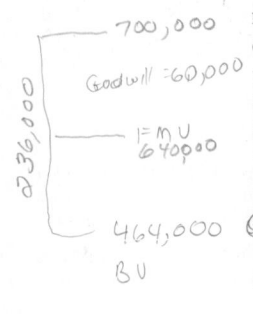

6. A and B Companies have been operating separately for 5 years. Each company has a minimal amount of liabilities and a simple capital structure consisting solely of voting common stock. A Company, in exchange for 40 percent of its voting stock, acquires 80 percent of the common stock of B Company. This was a "tax-free" stock-for-stock (type B) exchange for tax purposes. B Company assets have a total net fair market value of $800,000 and a total net book value of $580,000. The fair market value of the A stock used in the exchange was $700,000. The goodwill on this acquisition would be:
   a. Zero; this would be a pooling of interest.
   b. $60,000.
   c. $120,000.
   d. $236,000.

7. A supportive argument for the pooling of interests method of accounting for a business combination is that:
   a. It was developed within the boundaries of the historical cost system and is compatible with it.
   b. One company is clearly the dominant and continuing entity.
   c. Goodwill is generally a part of any acquisition.
   d. A portion of the total cost is assigned to individual assets acquired on the basis of their fair values.

E1-3 Multiple-Choice Questions on Reported Balances [AICPA Adapted]

Select the correct answer for each of the following questions.

Items 1 and 2 are based on the following data:

On January 1, 19X1, Rolan Corporation issued 10,000 shares of common stock in exchange for all Sandin Corporation's outstanding stock. Condensed balance sheets of Rolan and Sandin immediately before the combination are as follows:

	Rolan	Sandin
Total Assets	$1,000,000	$500,000
Liabilities	$ 300,000	$150,000
Common Stock ($10 par)	200,000	100,000
Retained Earnings	500,000	250,000
Total Liabilities and Equities	$1,000,000	$500,000

Rolan's common stock had a market price of $60 per share on January 1, 19X1. The market price of Sandin's stock was not readily ascertainable.

1. Assuming that the combination of Rolan and Sandin qualifies as a purchase, Rolan's investment in Sandin's stock will be stated in Rolan's balance sheet immediately after the combination in the amount of:
   a. $100,000.
   b. $350,000.
   c. $500,000.
   d. $600,000.

2. Assuming that the combination of Rolan and Sandin qualifies as a pooling of interests, rather than as a purchase, what should be reported as retained earnings in the consolidated balance sheet immediately after the combination?
   a. $500,000.
   b. $600,000.
   c. $750,000.
   d. $850,000.

3. On February 15, 19X5, Reed Corporation paid $1,500,000 for all the issued and outstanding common stock of Cord, Inc., in a transaction properly accounted for as a purchase. The book values and fair values of Cord's assets and liabilities on February 15, 19X5, were as follows:

	Book Value	Fair Value
Cash	$ 160,000	$ 160,000
Receivables	180,000	180,000
Inventory	290,000	270,000
Property, Plant, and Equipment	870,000	960,000
Liabilities	(350,000)	(350,000)
Net Worth	$1,150,000	$1,220,000

What is the amount of goodwill resulting from the business combination?
   a. $0.
   b. $70,000.
   c. $280,000.
   d. $350,000.

4. On April 1, 19X9, the Jack Company paid $800,000 for all the issued and outstanding common stock of Ann Corporation in a transaction properly accounted for as a purchase. The recorded assets and liabilities of Ann Corporation on April 1, 19X9, were as follows:

Cash	$ 80,000
Inventory	240,000
Property and Equipment (net of accumulated depreciation of $320,000)	480,000
Liabilities	(180,000)

On April 1, 19X9, it was determined that the inventory of Ann had a fair value of $190,000 and that the property and equipment had a fair value of $560,000. What is the amount of goodwill resulting from the business combination?
   a. $0.
   b. $50,000.
   c. $150,000.
   d. $180,000.

E1-4   Stock Acquisition

McDermott Corporation has been in the midst of a major expansion program. Much of its growth had been internal, but in 19X3 McDermott decided to continue its expansion through the acquisition of other companies. The first company acquired was Tippy, Inc., a small manufacturer of inertial guidance systems for aircraft and missiles. On June 10, 19X3, McDermott issued 17,000 shares of its $25 par common stock for all 40,000 of Tippy's $10 par common shares. At the date of combination, Tippy reported additional paid-in capital of $100,000 and retained earnings of $350,000. McDermott's stock was selling for $58 per share immediately prior to the combination. Subsequent to the combination, Tippy operated as a subsidiary of McDermott.

Required

Present the journal entry or entries that McDermott would make to record the business combination with Tippy as a: **(a)** purchase; **(b)** pooling of interests.

E1-5   Stockholders' Equity Totals under Pooling Treatment

Center Company and North Corporation agreed to merge on January 1, 19X6, in a business combination recorded as a pooling of interests. Abbreviated balance sheet data for the two companies included the following:

Balance Sheet Item	Center Company	North Corporation
Net Assets	$550,000	$250,000
Common Stock	$200,000	$100,000
Additional Paid-In Capital	20,000	10,000
Retained Earnings	330,000	140,000
Total Liabilities and Equities	$550,000	$250,000

The acquisition is completed by exchanging shares of Center Company's $10 par value common stock for the net assets of North Corporation.

Required

Prepare the stockholders' equity section of the balance sheet for the combined company if Center Company issues the following number of shares:

a. 8,000 shares
b. 12,000 shares
c. 16,000 shares

E1-6   Balances Reported under Purchase and Pooling Treatments

Elm Corporation and Maple Company have announced terms of an exchange agreement under which Elm will issue 8,000 shares of its $10 par value common stock to acquire all the assets of Maple Company. Elm shares currently are trading at $50, and Maple $5 par value shares are trading at $18 each. Historical cost and fair value balance sheet data on January 1, 19X8, are as follows:

Balance Sheet Item	Elm Corporation		Maple Company	
	Book Value	Fair Value	Book Value	Fair Value
Cash and Receivables	$150,000	$150,000	$ 40,000	$ 40,000
Land	100,000	170,000	50,000	85,000
Buildings and Equip-ment (net)	300,000	400,000	160,000	230,000
Total Assets	$550,000	$720,000	$250,000	$355,000
Common Stock	$200,000		$100,000	
Additional Paid-In Capital	20,000		10,000	
Retained Earnings	330,000		140,000	
Total Equities	$550,000		$250,000	

Required

What will be the amount reported immediately following the business combination for each of the following items in the combined company's balance sheet under **(a)** purchase treatment and **(b)** pooling of interests treatment?

1. Common Stock
2. Cash and Receivables
3. Land
4. Buildings and Equipment (net)
5. Goodwill
6. Additional Paid-In Capital
7. Retained Earnings

E1-7 Combining Balance Sheets under Pooling Treatment

The balance sheets of Regal Company and Sour Corporation contained the following balances on January 1, 19X3:

Regal Company
Balance Sheet
January 1, 19X3

Cash and Receivables	$100,000	Accounts Payable	$ 50,000
Inventory	200,000	Common Stock	
Land	50,000	($10 par value)	300,000
Buildings and Equipment	400,000	Additional Paid-In Capital	100,000
Less: Accumulated		Retained Earnings	150,000
Depreciation	(150,000)		
		Total Liabilities	
Total Assets	$600,000	and Equities	$600,000

Sour Corporation
Balance Sheet
January 1, 19X3

Cash and Receivables	$ 40,000	Accounts Payable	$ 10,000
Inventory	100,000	Common Stock	
Land	60,000	($5 par value)	100,000
Buildings and Equipment	700,000	Additional Paid-In Capital	50,000
Less: Accumulated		Retained Earnings	490,000
Depreciation	(250,000)		
		Total Liabilities	
Total Assets	$650,000	and Equities	$650,000

Required

Prepare a balance sheet for the combined entity immediately after Regal Company acquires the net assets of Sour Corporation on January 1, 19X3, by issuing 8,000 shares of its voting common stock in a pooling of interests.

E1-8   Goodwill Recognition

Spur Corporation reported the following balance sheet amounts on December 31, 19X6:

Balance Sheet Item	Historical Cost	Fair Value
Cash and Receivables	$ 50,000	$ 40,000
Inventory	100,000	150,000
Land	40,000	30,000
Plant and Equipment	400,000	350,000
Less: Accumulated Depreciation	(150,000)	
Patent		130,000
Total Assets	$440,000	$700,000
Accounts Payable	$ 80,000	$ 85,000
Common Stock	200,000	
Additional Paid-In Capital	20,000	
Retained Earnings	140,000	
Total Liabilities and Equities	$440,000	

Required

Blanket Company purchases the assets and liabilities of Spur Corporation for $670,000 cash on December 31, 19X6. Give the entry made by Blanket Company to record the purchase.

E1-9   Negative Goodwill

Musial Corporation used debentures with a par value of $600,000 to acquire 100 percent of the net assets of Sorden Company on January 1, 19X7. On that date, the fair value of the bonds issued by Musial Corporation was $564,000, and the following balance sheet data were reported by Sorden Company:

Balance Sheet Item	Historical Cost	Fair Value
Cash and Receivables	$ 55,000	$ 50,000
Inventory	105,000	200,000
Land	60,000	100,000
Plant and Equipment	400,000	300,000
Less: Accumulated Depreciation	(150,000)	
Goodwill	10,000	
Total Assets	$480,000	$650,000
Accounts Payable	$ 50,000	$ 50,000
Common Stock	100,000	
Additional Paid-In Capital	60,000	
Retained Earnings	270,000	
Total Liabilities and Equities	$480,000	

Required

Give the journal entry recorded by Musial Corporation at the time of exchange.

E1-10 Combined Balance Sheet under Purchase and Pooling Treatments

The following balance sheets were prepared for Timber and Bell Corporations on January 1, 19X6, just before they entered into a business combination:

Item	Timber Corporation Book Value	Fair Value	Bell Corporation Book Value	Fair Value
Cash and Receivables	$ 300,000	$ 300,000	$ 50,000	$ 50,000
Inventory	400,000	600,000	100,000	245,000
Buildings and Equipment	800,000	870,000	300,000	250,000
Less: Accumulated Depreciation	(200,000)		(150,000)	
Total Assets	$1,300,000	$1,770,000	$300,000	$545,000
Accounts Payable	$ 100,000	$ 100,000	$ 40,000	$ 40,000
Bonds Payable	400,000	440,000	60,000	85,000
Common Stock:				
$10 par value	300,000			
$5 par value			100,000	
Additional Paid-In Capital	100,000		20,000	
Retained Earnings	400,000		80,000	
Total Liabilities and Equities	$1,300,000		$300,000	

Required

a. Assume Timber acquires the net assets of Bell in a business combination considered to be a pooling of interests. Prepare a balance sheet for the combined company immediately following the acquisition if Timber issues 15,000 shares of stock to complete the transfer. Timber shares are selling for $40 at the time.

b. Assume that Timber acquires the net assets of Bell by issuing 15,000 shares of stock in a business combination treated as a purchase. Prepare a balance sheet for the combined company immediately after the acquisition if the market price of Timber shares is **(1)** $40 and **(2)** $20 at the time the acquisition occurs.

PROBLEMS

P1-11 Recording Procedures under Pooling of Interests Treatment

Obscure Advertising and Brown Company are considering joining forces in a business combination to be recorded as a pooling of interests. The balance sheet data of the two companies at the time of merger are as follows:

Balance Sheet Item	Obscure Advertising	Brown Company
Cash	$ 75,000	$ 10,000
Accounts Receivable	5,000	7,000
Inventory	70,000	60,000
Land	5,000	8,000
Buildings and Equipment	100,000	150,000
Less: Accumulated Depreciation	(40,000)	(120,000)
Total Assets	$215,000	$115,000
Accounts Payable	$ 75,000	$ 70,000
Common Stock	50,000	30,000
Additional Paid-In Capital	8,000	4,000
Retained Earnings	82,000	11,000
Total Liabilities and Equities	$215,000	$115,000

The shareholders of Brown Company agree to accept 4,000 shares of Obscure Advertising's $10 par value shares in exchange for the net assets of Brown Company in a business combination considered to be a pooling of interests.

Required

a. Give the journal entry to be recorded by Obscure Advertising when it issues its shares in exchange for the net assets of Brown Company.

b. Prepare the balance sheet for Obscure Advertising immediately following the merger.

c. Give the journal entry to be recorded by Obscure Advertising if it issues its 4,000 shares in exchange for all of the common stock of Brown Company, instead of for Brown's net assets, and if both companies remain as separate corporations.

P1-12 Journal Entries—Purchase versus Pooling Treatment

On January 1, 19X3, Broom Corporation issued 6,000 shares of its $10 par value common stock to acquire the assets and liabilities of Barrel Stave Corporation. Broom Corporation shares were selling at $90 on that date. Historical cost and fair value balance sheet data for Barrel Stave Corporation at the time of acquisition were as follows:

Balance Sheet Item	Historical Cost	Fair Value
Cash and Receivables	$ 50,000	$ 50,000
Inventory	120,000	200,000
Buildings and Equipment	400,000	300,000
Less: Accumulated Depreciation	(150,000)	
Total Assets	$420,000	$550,000
Accounts Payable	$ 50,000	$ 50,000
Common Stock ($20 par value)	200,000	
Retained Earnings	170,000	
Total Liabilities and Equities	$420,000	

Broom Corporation incurred listing fees of $10,000 and audit fees of $5,000 in issuing its new shares and paid a finder's fee of $25,000 in locating the merger candidate.

Required

Record the journal entries for the exchange assuming (a) purchase treatment was used and (b) pooling of interests treatment was used in recording the acquisition.

P1-13   Purchase Treatment with Goodwill

Obscure Advertising agreed to purchase the net assets of Brown Company for $65,000 cash on January 1, 19X4. The balance sheet data for the two companies and fair value information for Brown Company immediately before the business combination were:

		Brown Company	
Balance Sheet Item	Obscure Advertising	Book Value	Fair Value
Cash	$ 75,000	$ 10,000	$ 10,000
Accounts Receivable	5,000	7,000	3,000
Inventory	70,000	60,000	65,000
Land	5,000	8,000	12,000
Buildings and Equipment	100,000	150,000	40,000
Less: Accumulated Depreciation	(40,000)	(120,000)	
Total Assets	$215,000	$115,000	$130,000
Accounts Payable	$ 75,000	$ 70,000	$ 70,000
Common Stock	50,000	30,000	
Additional Paid-In Capital	8,000	4,000	
Retained Earnings	82,000	11,000	
Total Liabilities and Equities	$215,000	$115,000	

Brown Company had 1,500 shares of $20 par value stock outstanding before the merger, and Obscure Advertising had 5,000 shares of $10 par value stock outstanding.

Required

   a. Give the journal entry to be recorded by Obscure Advertising at the time it purchases the net assets of Brown Company.

   b. Prepare the balance sheet for Obscure Advertising immediately following the acquisition.

c. Give the journal entry to be recorded by Obscure Advertising if it purchases all of Brown Company's common stock for $65,000 cash instead of acquiring the net assets; both companies remain as separate corporations.

P1-14 Negative Goodwill

Eagle Company purchased the net assets of Lark Corporation on January 3, 19X8, for $565,000 cash. In addition, $5,000 of direct costs were incurred in consummating the combination. At the time of acquisition Lark Corporation reported the following historical cost and current market data:

Balance Sheet Item	Book Value	Fair Value
Cash and Receivables	$ 50,000	$ 50,000
Inventory	100,000	150,000
Buildings and Equipment (net)	200,000	300,000
Patent		200,000
Total Assets	$350,000	$700,000
Accounts Payable	$ 30,000	$ 30,000
Common Stock	100,000	
Additional Paid-In Capital	80,000	
Retained Earnings	140,000	
Total Liabilities and Equities	$350,000	

Required

Give the journal entry or entries recorded by Eagle Company to record its purchase of the net assets of Lark Corporation.

P1-15 Journal Entries—Purchase versus Pooling Treatment

On January 1, 19X3, More Products Corporation issues 12,000 shares of its $10 par value stock to acquire the net assets of Light Steel Company. Underlying book value and fair value information for the balance sheet items of Light Steel Company at the time of acquisition are as follows:

Balance Sheet Item	Book Value	Fair Value
Cash	$ 60,000	$ 60,000
Accounts Receivable	100,000	100,000
Inventory (lifo basis)	60,000	115,000
Land	50,000	70,000
Buildings and Equipment	400,000	350,000
Less: Accumulated Depreciation	(150,000)	
Total Assets	$520,000	$695,000
Accounts Payable	$ 10,000	$ 10,000
Bonds Payable	200,000	180,000
Common Stock ($5 par value)	150,000	
Additional Paid-In Capital	70,000	
Retained Earnings	90,000	
Total Liabilities and Equities	$520,000	

Light Steel shares were selling at $18 and More Products shares were selling at $50 just before the merger announcement. Additional cash payments made by More Corporation in completing the acquisition were:

Finder's fee paid to firm that located Light Steel	$10,000
Audit fee for stock issued by More Products	3,000
Stock registration fee for new shares of More Products	5,000
Legal fees paid to assist in transfer of net assets	9,000
Cost of SEC registration of More Products shares	1,000

Required

   a. Prepare all journal entries to be recorded on More Products' books assuming the business combination is recorded as a pooling of interests.
   b. Prepare all journal entries to be recorded on More Products' books assuming the business combination is recorded as a purchase.

P1-16   Pooling Treatment

Ramrod Manufacturing acquired all the assets and liabilities of Stafford Industries on January 1, 19X7, in exchange for 4,000 shares of its $20 par value common stock. Balance sheet data for both companies just before the merger are given as follows:

	Ramrod Manufacturing		Stafford Industries	
Balance Sheet Items	**Book Value**	**Fair Value**	**Book Value**	**Fair Value**
Cash	$ 70,000	$ 70,000	$ 30,000	$ 30,000
Accounts Receivable	100,000	100,000	60,000	60,000
Inventory	200,000	375,000	100,000	160,000
Land	50,000	80,000	40,000	30,000
Buildings and Equipment	600,000	540,000	400,000	350,000
Less: Accumulated Depreciation	(250,000)		(150,000)	
Total Assets	$770,000	$1,165,000	$480,000	$630,000
Accounts Payable	$ 50,000	$ 50,000	$ 10,000	$ 10,000
Bonds Payable	300,000	310,000	150,000	145,000
Common Stock:				
$20 par value	200,000			
$5 par value			100,000	
Additional Paid-In Capital	40,000		20,000	
Retained Earnings	180,000		200,000	
Total Liabilities and Equities	$770,000		$480,000	

Ramrod shares were selling for $150 on the date of acquisition.

Required

Assuming pooling of interests accounting is appropriate for the business combination, prepare the following:

a. Journal entries to record the acquisition on Ramrod's books

b. A balance sheet for the combined enterprise immediately following the business combination

P1-17   Purchase Treatment

Required

Using the data presented in Problem 1-16, prepare (1) journal entries to record the acquisition on Ramrod's books and (2) a balance sheet immediately following the business combination when purchase accounting is used in recording the acquisition.

P1-18   Purchase and Pooling of Interests Workpapers [AICPA Adapted]

Shadow Corporation was merged into Star Corporation on August 31, 19X4, with Shadow Corporation going out of existence. Both corporations had fiscal years ending on August 31, and Star Corporation will retain this fiscal year. The worksheet on page 57 contains a balance sheet for each corporation as of August 31, 19X4, immediately before the merger. You have obtained the following additional information as of the date of the merger:

1. The fair values of the assets and liabilities on August 31, 19X4, of Star Corporation and Shadow Corporation were as follows:

	Star	Shadow
Current Assets	$ 4,950,000	$ 3,400,000
Plant and Equipment (net)	22,000,000	14,000,000
Patents	570,000	360,000
Deferred Market Research Costs	150,000	40,000
Total Assets	$27,670,000	$17,800,000
Liabilities	(2,650,000)	(2,100,000)
Net Assets	$25,020,000	$15,700,000

2. Star Corporation capitalized its fiscal year 19X4 market research costs and has always amortized them over 5 years beginning with the year of expenditure. All market research costs of Star have been appropriately capitalized and amortized for the current and preceding years. Shadow Corporation incurred $50,000 of market research costs that were expensed during the fiscal year ending August 31, 19X4. Shadow did not have any market research costs in any year before 19X4. Shadow will adopt Star's method of accounting for market research costs.

3. Internally generated general expenses incurred because of the merger were $25,000 and are included in the current assets of Star as a prepaid expense.

4. There were no intercompany transactions during the year.

5. Before the merger, Star had 3,000,000 shares of common stock authorized, 1,200,000 shares issued, and 1,100,000 shares outstanding. Shadow had 750,000 shares of common stock authorized, issued, and outstanding.

Required

For each of the following situations, prepare a balance sheet workpaper similar in form to the one below. Enter the balances recorded on Star Corporation's books when Shadow Corporation is liquidated and the resulting balance sheet totals for the combined entity.

a. Star Corporation exchanged 400,000 shares of previously unissued common stock and 100,000 shares of treasury stock for all the outstanding common stock of Shadow Corporation. All the conditions for pooling of interests accounting were met.

b. Star Corporation purchased the assets and assumed the liabilities of Shadow Corporation by paying $3,100,000 cash and issuing debentures of $16,900,000 at face value.

Star Corporation and Shadow Corporation
Worksheet for Pooling of Interests and Purchase Accounting
August 31, 19X4

	Star Corporation	Shadow Corporation	Debit	Credit	Balance Sheet Totals for Combined Entity
Current Assets	4,350,000	3,000,000			
Plant and Equipment (net)	18,500,000	11,300,000			
Patents	450,000	200,000			
Deferred Market Research	150,000				
	23,450,000	14,500,000			
Liabilities	2,650,000	2,100,000			
Common Stock ($10 par value)	12,000,000				
Common Stock ($5 par value)		3,750,000			
Paid-In Capital in Excess of Par	4,200,000	3,200,000			
Retained Earnings	5,850,000	5,450,000			
	24,700,000	14,500,000			
Less: Treasury Stock, at Cost, 100,000 Shares	(1,250,000)				
	23,450,000	14,500,000			

(Amounts Recorded by Star span Debit/Credit columns)

P1-19 Business Combinations

Below are the balance sheets of the Boogie Musical Corporation and the Toot-Toot Tuba Company as of December 31, 19X5.

Boogie Musical Corporation
Balance Sheet
December 31, 19X5

Assets		Liabilities and Equities	
Cash	$ 23,000	Accounts Payable	$ 48,000
Accounts Receivable	85,000	Notes Payable	65,000
Allowance for Uncollectible Accounts	(1,200)	Mortgage Payable	200,000
Inventory	192,000	Bonds Payable	200,000
Plant and Equipment	980,000	Capital Stock ($10 par)	500,000
Accumulated Depreciation	(160,000)	Premium on Capital Stock	1,000
Other Assets	14,000	Retained Earnings	118,800
	$1,132,800		$1,132,800

Toot-Toot Tuba Company
Balance Sheet
December 31, 19X5

Assets		Liabilities and Equities	
Cash	$ 3	Accounts Payable	$ 8,200
Accounts Receivable	17,000	Notes Payable	10,000
Allowance for Uncollectible Accounts	(600)	Mortgage Payable	50,000
Inventory	78,500	Bonds Payable	100,000
Plant and Equipment	451,000	Capital Stock ($50 par)	100,000
Accumulated Depreciation	(225,000)	Premium on Capital Stock	150,000
Other Assets	26,100	Retained Earnings	(71,197)
	$347,003		$347,003

In preparation for a possible business combination, a team of experts from Boogie Musical made a thorough examination and audit of Toot-Toot Tuba. They found that Toot-Toot's assets and equities were correctly stated except that they estimated uncollectible accounts at $1,400. They also estimated the market value of the inventory at $35,000 and the market value of the plant and equipment at $500,000. The business combination took place on January 1, 19X6, and on that date Boogie Musical acquired all the assets and liabilities of Toot-Toot Tuba. On that date, Boogie's common stock was selling for $55 per share.

Required

  a. Record the combination on Boogie's books assuming that the combination is treated as a purchase and Boogie issues 9,000 of its $10 par common shares in exchange for Toot-Toot's assets and liabilities.

  b. Record the combination on Boogie's books assuming that the combination is treated as a pooling of interests and Boogie issues 9,000 of its $10 par common shares in exchange for Toot-Toot's assets and liabilities.

  c. Present the capital section of Boogie's balance sheet immediately after the combination, assuming that the combination is treated as a pooling of interests and Boogie issues 26,000 shares of its common stock in exchange for all the assets and liabilities of Toot-Toot.

  d. Record the combination on Boogie's books assuming that the combination is treated as a pooling of interests and Boogie issues 9,000 of its $10 par common shares to acquire all Toot-Toot's common stock. Both companies retain their separate identities subsequent to the combination.

P1-20   Combined Balance Sheets under Purchase and Pooling Treatments

Bilge Pumpworks and Seaworthy Rope Company agreed to merge on January 1, 19X3. On the date of the merger agreement, the companies report the following data:

Balance Sheet Items	Bilge Pumpworks		Seaworthy Rope Company	
	Book Value	Fair Value	Book Value	Fair Value
Cash and Receivables	$ 90,000	$ 90,000	$ 20,000	$ 20,000
Inventory	100,000	150,000	30,000	42,000
Land	100,000	140,000	10,000	15,000
Plant and Equipment	400,000 ⎫	300,000	200,000 ⎫	140,000
Less: Accumulated Depreciation	(150,000) ⎭		(80,000) ⎭	
Total Assets	$540,000	$680,000	$180,000	$217,000
Current Liabilities	$ 80,000	$ 80,000	$ 20,000	$ 20,000
Capital Stock	200,000		20,000	
Capital in Excess of Par Value	20,000		5,000	
Retained Earnings	240,000		135,000	
Total Liabilities and Equities	$540,000		$180,000	

Bilge Pumpworks has 10,000 shares of its $20 par value shares outstanding on January 1, 19X3, and Seaworthy has 4,000 shares of $5 par value stock outstanding. The market values of the shares are $300 and $50, respectively.

Required

a. Bilge issues 700 shares of stock in exchange for all the net assets of Seaworthy. Prepare a balance sheet for the combined entity immediately following the merger assuming (1) the acquisition is recorded as a purchase and (2) the acquisition is recorded as a pooling of interests.

b. Prepare the stockholders' equity section of the combined company under both purchase and pooling of interests treatments assuming Bilge acquires all the net assets of Seaworthy by issuing the following shares:

(1) 1,100 shares of common
(2) 1,800 shares of common
(3) 3,000 shares of common

P1-21   Comprehensive Problem with Incomplete Data

On January 1, 19X7, Speedy Plumbers issued shares of its $5 par value stock to acquire all the shares of Flash Heating Company, which was liquidated immediately thereafter. The balance sheet for Speedy Plumbers and balance sheets for the combined company under both purchase and pooling of interests treatment are presented.

		Combined Company	
Balance Sheet Item	**Speedy Plumbers**	**Pooling**	**Purchase**
Cash	$ 70,000	$100,000	$ 100,000
Accounts Receivable	130,000	180,000	180,000
Inventory	100,000	170,000	220,000
Land	100,000	160,000	175,000
Buildings and Equipment	400,000	600,000	550,000
Less: Accumulated Depreciation	(150,000)	(230,000)	(150,000)
Goodwill			55,000
Total Assets	$650,000	$980,000	$1,130,000
Accounts Payable	$ 40,000	$ 60,000	$ 60,000
Bonds Payable	100,000	160,000	160,000
Common Stock	200,000	240,000	240,000
Additional Paid-In Capital	60,000	130,000	420,000
Retained Earnings	250,000	390,000	250,000
Total Liabilities and Equities	$650,000	$980,000	$1,130,000

Required

Shortly after the above information was compiled, a fire destroyed the accounting records. You have been employed to determine the answers to a number of questions raised by the owners of the newly combined company.

  a. What was the value of the shares issued by Speedy Plumbers to acquire Flash Heating Company?
  b. What was the fair value of the net assets held by Flash Heating immediately before the combination?
  c. How many shares of Speedy Plumbers were issued in completing the combination?
  d. What was the market price per share of Speedy Plumbers stock at the date of combination?
  e. Was the full retained earnings balance of Flash Heating carried forward in the pooling case? How do you know?
  f. What was the book value of the net assets of Flash Heating at combination?
  g. Flash Heating uses a lifo inventory basis. How much did its inventory increase in value between the date purchased and the time of the business combination?
  h. What was the balance in working capital reported by Flash Heating before the business combination?

P1-22 Reporting Results of Operations

On July 1, 19X2, Amalgamated Transport acquired all of the assets and liabilities of the Swamp Island Railroad by issuing 25,000 common shares. At the date of acquisition, Amalgamated's stock was selling for $96 per share; the net book value of the Swamp Island Railroad on that date was $2,200,000. All the excess of the purchase price over Swamp

Island's net book value was attributable to goodwill with a life of 5 years from the date of combination. The following annual results of operations were reported by Amalgamated and Swamp Island prior to the combination and by the combined company subsequent to the combination:

	19X1	19X2	19X3
Revenue:			
Amalgamated	$1,400,000	$2,000,000	$2,100,000
Swamp Island	350,000		
Net Income:			
Amalgamated	500,000	620,000	700,000
Swamp Island	100,000		

These results of operations reflect the amounts actually reported for each year; the amounts reported for periods subsequent to the combination are based on the combination's having been treated as a pooling of interests.

The revenues and income for both companies have been earned evenly throughout individual years. For the first half of 19X2, Amalgamated earned net income of $255,000 on revenue of $800,000; Swamp Island earned $55,000 on revenue of $200,000. There were no intercompany transactions between the two companies at any time. Amalgamated had 100,000 shares of common stock outstanding prior to the combination.

Required

Present the amounts that would appear for 19X1, 19X2, and 19X3 in Amalgamated Transport's comparative income statement prepared at the end of its fiscal year on December 31, 19X3, for (1) revenues, (2) net income, and (3) earnings per share assuming the business combination was treated as a:

a. Pooling of interests
b. Purchase

P1-23 Comprehensive Problem: Purchase and Pooling of Interests

Integrated Industries, Inc., entered into a business combination agreement with Hydrolized Chemical Corporation (HCC) to assure an uninterrupted supply of key raw materials and to realize certain economies from combining the operating processes and the marketing efforts of the two companies. Under the terms of the agreement, Integrated Industries issued 180,000 shares of its $1 par common stock in exchange for all the assets and liabilities of HCC. The Integrated Industries shares then were distributed to the shareholders of HCC, and HCC was liquidated.

Immediately prior to the combination, HCC's balance sheet appeared as follows, with fair values also indicated:

	Book Values	Fair Values
Assets:		
Cash	$ 28,000	$ 28,000
Accounts Receivable	258,000	251,500
Less: Allowance for Bad Debts	(6,500)	
Inventory	381,000	395,000
Long-Term Investments	150,000	175,000
Land	55,000	100,000
Rolling Stock	130,000	63,000
Plant and Equipment	2,425,000	2,500,000
Less: Accumulated Depreciation	(614,000)	
Patents	125,000	500,000
Special Licenses	95,800	100,000
Total Assets	$3,027,300	$4,112,500
Liabilities:		
Current Payables	$ 137,200	$ 137,200
Mortgages Payable	500,000	520,000
Equipment Trust Notes	100,000	95,000
Debentures Payable	1,000,000	950,000
Less: Discount on Debentures	(40,000)	
Total Liabilities	$1,697,200	$1,702,200
Stockholders' Equity:		
Common Stock ($5 par)	600,000	
Additional Paid-In Capital from Common Stock	500,000	
Additional Paid-In Capital from Retirement of Preferred Stock	22,000	
Retained Earnings	220,100	
Less: Treasury Stock (1,500 shares)	(12,000)	
Total Liabilities and Equity	$3,027,300	

Immediately prior to the combination, Integrated Industries common stock was selling for $14 per share. Integrated Industries incurred direct costs of $135,000 in arranging the business combination and $42,000 of costs associated with registering and issuing the common stock used in the combination.

Required

a. Prepare all journal entries that Integrated Industries should have entered on its books to record the combination as a (1) purchase; (2) pooling of interests.

b. Present all journal entries that should have been entered on the books of HCC to record the combination and the distribution of the stock received, assuming the combination was treated as a (1) purchase; (2) pooling of interests.

CHAPTER 2

REPORTING INTERCORPORATE INVESTMENTS IN COMMON STOCK

Many companies invest in the common stock of other corporations. Some companies invest in common stock to earn a good return by taking advantage of potentially profitable situations. Others acquire common stock to (1) gain control over other companies, (2) enter new market or product areas through companies established in those areas, (3) assure a supply of raw materials or other production inputs, (4) assure a customer for production output, (5) gain economies associated with greater size, (6) diversify, (7) gain new technology, or (8) lessen competition. Examples of intercorporate investments include IBM's acquisition of a sizable portion of Intel's stock to assure a supply of computer components, Polaroid's acquisition of a majority of the common stock of Advanced Color Technology, Inc., to move into the computer products field, and Texaco's much-litigated acquisition of Getty Oil's stock to acquire oil and gas reserves.

There are a number of aspects of accounting for intercorporate investments in common stock that differ from accounting for other types of investments. This chapter presents the accounting and reporting procedures for investments in common stock.

METHODS OF REPORTING INVESTMENTS IN COMMON STOCK

Three methods of reporting intercorporate investments in common stock are found in practice: (1) consolidation, (2) the equity method, and (3) the cost method. The method used depends on the level of influence or control that the investor is able to exercise over the investee.

Consolidation involves combining for financial reporting the individual assets, liabilities, revenues, and expenses of two or more related companies as if they were part of a single company. This process includes the elimination of all intercompany ownership and activities. Consolidation normally is appropriate where one company, referred to as the *parent*, controls another company, referred to as a *subsidiary,* through ownership of more than 50 percent of the subsidiary's outstanding common stock. In some instances, control may be gained by other means. The specific requirements for consolidation are discussed in Chapter 3. A subsidary that is not consolidated with the parent is referred to as an *unconsolidated subsidiary* and is shown as an investment in the parent's balance sheet. Under current accounting standards, most subsidiaries are consolidated.

The *equity method* is used for external reporting when the investor, because of its stock ownership, exercises *significant influence* over the operating and financial policies of the investee and consolidation is not appropriate. The equity method may not be used in place of consolidation when consolidation is appropriate, and therefore its primary use is in reporting nonsubsidiary investments. This method is used most often when one company holds between 20 and 50 percent of another company's common stock. Under the equity method, the investor recognizes income from the investment as the income is earned by the investee. Instead of combining the individual assets, liabilities, revenues, and expenses of the investee with those of the investor, as in consolidation, the investment is reported as one line in the investor's balance sheet, and income recognized from the investee is reported as one line in the investor's income statement. The investment represents the investor's share of the investee's net assets, and the income recognized is the investor's share of the investee's net income.

The *cost method* is used for reporting investments when both consolidation and equity-method reporting are inappropriate. Under the cost method, the investor recognizes income from the investment when the income is distributed by the investee as dividends.

Figure 2-1 summarizes the relationship between methods used to report intercorporate investments in common stock and levels of ownership. This chapter focuses on the cost and equity methods of accounting for investments in common

FIGURE 2-1 Financial-reporting basis by level of common stock ownership.

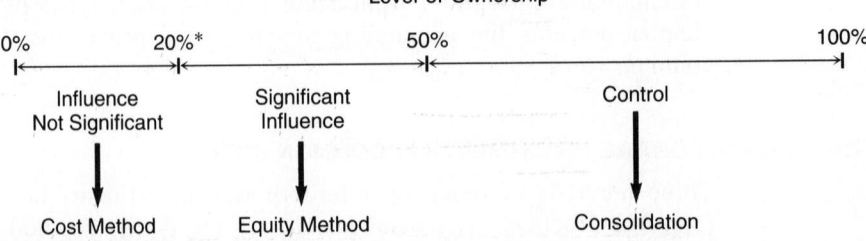

* May vary, depending on circumstances.

stock. The preparation of consolidated financial statements is discussed in Chapters 3 through 10.

THE COST METHOD

Intercorporate investments accounted for by the cost method are carried by the investor at historical cost. Income is recorded by the investor as dividends are declared by the investee. The cost method is used when the investor lacks the ability either to control or to exercise significant influence over the investee, or when the ability to control or significantly influence the investee is temporary. The inability of an investor to exercise either control or significant influence over an investee may result from the size of the investment, usually at common stock ownership levels of less than 20 percent. In some situations, other factors, such as the bankruptcy of the investee, prevent the investor from exercising control or significant influence regardless of the size of the investment.

Accounting Procedures under the Cost Method

The cost method is consistent with the treatment normally accorded noncurrent assets. At the time of purchase, the investor records its investment in common stock at the total cost incurred in making the purchase. Subsequently, the carrying amount of the investment remains unchanged under the cost method; the investment continues to be carried at its original cost until the time of sale. Income from the investment is recognized by the investor as dividends are declared by the investee. Once the investee declares a dividend, the investor has a legal claim against the investee for a proportionate share of the dividend and realization of the income is considered certain enough to be recognized. Recognition of investment income before a dividend declaration is considered inappropriate because the investee's income is not available to the owners until a dividend is declared.

To illustrate the cost method, assume that ABC Company purchases 20 percent of XYZ Company's common stock for $100,000 at the beginning of the year. During the year, XYZ has net income of $50,000 and pays dividends of $20,000. ABC Company should record the following entries relating to its investment in XYZ:

(1)	Investment in XYZ Company Stock	100,000	
	Cash		100,000
	Record purchase of XYZ Company stock.		
(2)	Cash	4,000	
	Dividend Income		4,000
	Record dividend income from XYZ Company:		
	$20,000 × .20		

Note that ABC records only its share of the distributed earnings of XYZ and makes no entry regarding the undistributed portion. The carrying amount of the investment remains at its original cost of $100,000.

Declaration of Dividends in Excess of Earnings since Acquisition

A special treatment is required under the cost method in situations in which an investor holds common stock in a company that declares dividends in excess of the income it has earned since its stock was acquired by the investor. The dividends received are viewed first as representing earnings of the investee from the purchase date of the investment to the declaration date of the dividend. All dividends declared by the investee in excess of its earnings since acquisition by the investor are viewed by the investor as *liquidating dividends*. The investor's share of these liquidating dividends is treated as a return of capital, and the investment account balance is reduced by that amount. Blocks of an investee's stock acquired at different times should be treated separately for purposes of computing liquidating dividends.

Liquidating Dividends Illustrated   To illustrate the computation of liquidating dividends received by the investor, assume that Investor Company purchases 10 percent of the common stock of Investee Company on January 2, 19X1. The annual income and dividends of Investee Company, the amount of dividend income recognized by Investor each year under the cost method, and the reduction of the carrying amount of Investor's investment in Investee Company where appropriate are as follows:

	Investee Company			Investor Company		
Year	Net Income	Dividends	Cumulative Undistributed Income	Cash Received	Dividend Income	Reduction of Investment
19X1	$100,000	$ 70,000	$ 30,000	$ 7,000	$ 7,000	
19X2	100,000	120,000	10,000	12,000	12,000	
19X3	100,000	120,000	-0-	12,000	11,000	$1,000
19X4	100,000	120,000	-0-	12,000	10,000	2,000
19X5	100,000	70,000	30,000	7,000	7,000	

Investor Company records its 10 percent share of Investee's dividend as income in 19X1 because the income of Investee exceeds its dividend. In 19X2, Investee's dividend exceeds earnings for the year, but the cumulative dividends declared since January 2, 19X1, the date Investor acquired Investee's stock, do not exceed Investee's earnings since that date. Hence, Investor again records its 10 percent share of the dividend as income. By the end of 19X3, dividends declared by Investee Company since January 2, 19X1, total $310,000, while Investee's income since that date totals only $300,000. Thus, from Investor's point of view, $10,000 of the 19X3 dividend represents a return of capital while the remaining $110,000 represents a distribution of earnings. Investor's share of each amount is 10 percent. The entry to record the 19X3 dividend on Investor's books is:

(3) Cash	12,000	
Investment in Investee Company Stock		1,000
Dividend Income		11,000

Record receipt of 19X3 dividend from Investee Company:
$12,000 = $120,000 × .10
$1,000 = ($310,000 − $300,000) × .10
$11,000 = ($120,000 − $10,000) × .10

Once a liquidating dividend has been recorded by the investor, the comparison in future periods between cumulative earnings and dividends of the investee should be based on the date of the last liquidating dividend rather than the date the investor acquired the investee's stock. For example, liquidating dividends are recorded by Investor Company in 19X3 and 19X4. In years after 19X4, Investor Company compares earnings and dividends of Investee from the date of the most recent liquidating dividend in 19X4 rather than comparing from January 2, 19X1. All the dividend paid in 19X5 is considered by Investor to be a distribution of earnings.

Liquidating Dividends following Switch from Equity Method   If the investor previously carried the investment using the equity method and, because of the sale of a portion of the investment, switches to the cost method, the date of the switch in methods replaces the date of acquisition as the reference date for distinguishing liquidating dividends. From that point forward, the investor should compare earnings and dividends of the investee starting at the date of the switch to the cost method.

Investee's View of Liquidating Dividends   Dividends received by an investor in excess of earnings since acquisition, while viewed as liquidating dividends by the investor, usually are not liquidating dividends from the investee's point of view. This type of dividend might occur, for example, when an investee's stock is acquired shortly before a dividend is declared. The investee does not consider a dividend to be a liquidating dividend unless the investee's retained earnings is insufficient or the investee specifically declares a liquidating dividend for all common shareholders.

Acquisition at Interim Date

The acquisition of an investment at other than the beginning or end of a fiscal period generally does not create any major problems when the cost method is used in accounting for the investment. The only potential difficulty involves determining whether some part of the payment received by the investor is a liquidating dividend when the investee declares a dividend soon after the investor purchases stock in the investee. In this situation, the investor must estimate the amount of the investee's earnings for the portion of the period during which the investor held the investee's stock and may record dividend income only on that portion.

Changes in the Number of Shares Held

Changes in the number of shares of an investment resulting from stock dividends, stock splits, or reverse splits receive no formal recognition in the accounts of the investor. The carrying value of the investment before the stock dividend or split becomes the carrying amount of the new, greater or lesser number of shares. Purchases and sales of shares, of course, do require journal entries but do not result in any unusual difficulties under the cost method.

Purchases of Additional Shares   A purchase of additional shares of a stock already held is recorded at cost in the same way as an initial purchase of shares. The investor's new percentage ownership of the investee then is calculated, and other evidence, if available, is evaluated to determine if the total investment still should be carried at cost or if the investor should switch to the equity method. When the additional shares give the investor the ability to exercise significant influence over the investee, the equity method should be applied retroactively from the date of the original investment, as illustrated later in this chapter.

Sales of Shares   If all or part of an intercorporate investment in stock is sold, the transaction is accounted for in the same manner as the sale of any other noncurrent asset. A gain or loss on the sale is recognized for the difference between the proceeds received and the carrying amount of the investment sold.

If shares of the stock have been purchased at more than one price, a determination must be made at the time of sale as to which of the shares are sold. The specific shares sold may be identified through segregation, numbered stock certificates, or other means. Where specific identification is impractical, either a fifo or weighted-average cost flow assumption may be used. However, the weighted-average method is not acceptable for tax purposes and, thus, is used infrequently for financial reporting purposes in practice.

THE EQUITY METHOD

The equity method of accounting for intercorporate investments in common stock is intended to reflect the investor's changing equity or interest in the investee. This method is a rather curious one in that the balance in the investment account generally is not carried at either cost or market value, nor does the balance necessarily represent a pro rata share of the investee's book value. Instead, the investment is recorded at the initial purchase price and adjusted each period for the investor's share of the investee's profits or losses and the dividends declared by the investee.

Use of the Equity Method

APB Opinion No. 18 (as amended) "The Equity Method of Accounting for Investments in Common Stock" (APB 18), requires that the equity method be used for reporting investments, other than temporary investments, in common stock of the following:[1]

1. Corporate joint ventures. A *corporate joint venture* is a corporation owned and operated by a small group of businesses, none of which own a majority of the joint venture's common stock.

2. Companies in which the investor's voting stock interest gives the investor the "ability to exercise significant influence over operating and financial policies" of that company.

The second condition is the broader of the two and establishes the "significant influence" criterion. Because there may be difficulty in assessing the degree of influence in some cases, **APB 18** states the following rule:[2]

> . . . an investment (direct or indirect) of 20% or more of the voting stock of an investee should lead to a presumption that in the absence of evidence to the contrary an investor has the ability to exercise significant influence over an investee. Conversely, an investment of less than 20% of the voting stock of an investee should lead to a presumption that an investor does not have the ability to exercise significant influence unless such ability can be demonstrated.

In most cases, an investment of 20 to 50 percent in another company's voting stock is reported under the equity method. Notice, however, that the 20 percent rule does not apply if other evidence is available that provides a better indication of the ability or inability of the investor to significantly influence the investee. Examples of such evidence are discussed later in the chapter.

Regardless of the level of ownership, the equity method is not appropriate if (1) the investment is temporary or (2) the investor's influence is limited by circumstances other than stock ownership, such as bankruptcy of the investee or severe restrictions placed on the availability of a foreign investee's earnings or assets by a foreign government.

Until a recent amendment of **APB 18** by the Financial Accounting Standards Board, companies often chose to exclude some subsidiaries from consolidation. The unconsolidated subsidiaries were required to be reported using the equity method. Under current reporting standards, however, virtually all majority-owned subsidiaries must be consolidated and may not be reported using the equity method. The only exceptions to consolidation are for subsidiaries for which the parent's control is temporary or the parent lacks the ability to control because of other factors; under the continuing provisions of **APB 18,** these subsidiaries normally are reported using the cost method.

Investor's Equity in the Investee

Under the equity method, the investor records its investment at the original cost. This amount is adjusted periodically for changes in the investee's stockholders'

[1] *Accounting Principles Board Opinion No. 18,* "The Equity Method of Accounting for Investments in Common Stock," March 1971, pars. 14–17.
[2] Ibid., par. 17.

equity occasioned by the investee's profits, losses, and dividend declarations. The relationship between the changes in the investment account as carried on the investor's books and the investee's stockholders' equity can be characterized in the following way:

Investee's Retained Earnings	Investor's Investment Account
Increased by income	Increased by equity income accrual
Decreased by losses	Decreased by equity loss accrual
Decreased by dividends	Decreased by dividend recognition

Recognition of Income

Under the equity method, the investor's income statement includes the investor's proportionate share of the investee's income or loss each period. The carrying amount of the investment is adjusted by the same amount to reflect the change in the net assets of the investee resulting from the investee's income.

To illustrate, assume ABC Company acquires significant influence over XYZ Company by purchasing 20 percent of the common stock of the XYZ Company at the beginning of the year. XYZ Company reports income for the year of $60,000. ABC Company records its $12,000 share of XYZ's income with the following entry:

(4)	Investment in XYZ Company Stock	12,000	
	Income from Investee		12,000
	Record income from investment in XYZ Company:		
	$60,000 × .20		

This entry may be referred to as the *equity accrual* and normally is made as an adjusting entry at the end of the period. If the investee reports a loss for the period, the investor recognizes its share of the loss and reduces the carrying amount of the investment by that amount.

Because of the ability to exercise significant influence over the policies of the investee, realization of income from the investment is considered to be sufficiently assured to warrant recognition by the investor as the income is earned by the investee. This differs from the case in which the investor does not have the ability to significantly influence the investee and the investment must be reported using the cost method; in that case, income from the investment is recognized only upon declaration of a dividend by the investee.

Recognition of Dividends

Dividends from an investment are not recognized as income under the equity method because the investor's share of the investee's income is recognized as it is earned by the investee. Instead, such dividends are viewed as distributions of previously recognized income that already has been capitalized in the carrying amount of the investment. The investor must consider investee dividends declared as a reduction in its equity in the investee and, accordingly, reduce the carrying amount of its investment. In effect, all dividends from the investee are treated as liquidating dividends under the equity method. Thus, if ABC Company owns 20 percent of XYZ's common stock and XYZ declares and pays a $20,000 dividend, the following entry is recorded on the books of ABC to record its share of the dividend:

(5) Cash	4,000	
Investment in XYZ Company Stock		4,000
Record receipt of dividend from XYZ: $20,000 × .20		

Carrying Amount of the Investment

Because the investment account carried on the investor's books is adjusted for the investor's share of the investee's income or losses and dividends, the carrying amount of the investment usually is not the same as the original cost to the investor. Only if the investee pays dividends in the exact amount of its earnings will the carrying amount of the investment subsequent to acquisition be equal to its original cost. If the earnings of the investee subsequent to investment by the investor exceed the investee's dividends during that time, the carrying amount of the investment will be greater than its original cost. On the other hand, if the investee's dividends exceed its income, the carrying amount of the investment will be less than its original cost.

To illustrate the change in the carrying amount of the investment, assume that after ABC acquires 20 percent of XYZ's common stock for $100,000, XYZ earns income of $60,000 and pays dividends of $20,000. The carrying amount of the investment starts with the original cost of $100,000 and is increased by ABC's share of XYZ's income, which is $12,000. The carrying amount is reduced by ABC's share of XYZ's dividends, which is $4,000. Thus, the carrying amount of the investment at the end of the period is $108,000 ($100,000 + $12,000 − $4,000). The investment account on ABC's books appears as follows:

Investment in XYZ Common Stock

Original cost	100,000		
Equity accrual		Dividends	
($60,000 × .20)	12,000	($20,000 × .20)	4,000
Ending balance	108,000		

The $8,000 increase in the investment account represents ABC's 20 percent share of XYZ's undistributed earnings ($60,000 − $20,000) for the period.

Acquisition at Interim Date

When an investment is purchased, the investor begins accruing income from the investee under the equity method at the date of acquisition. No income earned by the investee before the date of acquisition of the investment may be accrued by the investor. When the purchase occurs between balance sheet dates, the amount of income earned by the investee from the date of acquisition to the end of the fiscal period may need to be estimated by the investor in recording the equity accrual.

To illustrate, assume that ABC acquires 20 percent of XYZ's common stock on October 1, 19X1, for $109,000. XYZ earns income of $60,000 uniformly throughout 19X1 and pays dividends of $20,000 on December 20, 19X1. The carrying amount of the investment is increased by $3,000, which represents ABC's share of XYZ's net income earned between October 1, 19X1, and December 31, 19X1, and is decreased by $4,000 as a result of dividends received at year-end.

Investment in XYZ Common Stock

Original cost	109,000		
Equity accrual		Dividends	
($60,000 × 1/4 × .20)	3,000	($20,000 × .20)	4,000
Ending balance	108,000		

Difference between Cost of Investment and Underlying Book Value

When one corporation buys the common stock of another, the purchase price normally is based on the market price of the shares acquired rather than the book values of the investee's assets and liabilities. As a result, there often is a difference between the cost of the investment to the investor and the book value of the investor's proportionate share of the underlying net assets of the investee. This difference is referred to as a *differential*.

There are several reasons why the cost of an investment might exceed the book value of the underlying net assets and give rise to a positive differential. One reason is that the investee's recorded assets may be worth more than their book values. Another reason could be the existence of unrecorded goodwill associated with the excess earning power of the investee. In either case, the portion of the differential pertaining to each asset of the investee, including goodwill, must be ascertained. When the equity method is applied, that portion of the differential pertaining to intangible assets or limited-life tangible assets of the investee must be amortized over the remaining economic lives of those assets. The period of amortization for intangible assets may not exceed 40 years, the maximum allowed by **APB Opinion No. 17**, "Intangible Assets." The differential is not amortized under the cost method.

Amortization of the Differential   When the equity method is applied, **APB 18** requires the investor to amortize any portion of the differential that relates to depreciable or amortizable assets held by the investee. Amortization of the differential associated with depreciable or amortizable assets of the investee is necessary on the investor's books to reflect the decline in service potential of those assets during the period. The investee recognizes the reduction in service potential of assets with limited lives as depreciation or amortization expense based on the amount it has invested in those assets. This reduction, in turn, is recognized by the investor through its share of the investee's net income. However, because the cost of the investor's interest in the investee's assets is greater than the investee's cost (given a positive differential), the additional cost must be amortized as well.

The approach to amortizing the differential that is most consistent with the idea of reflecting all aspects of the investment in just one line on the balance sheet and one line on the income statement is to reduce the income recognized by the investor from the investee and the balance of the investment account:

Income from Investee	XXX	
Investment in Common Stock of Investee		XXX

The differential represents the amount paid by the investor in excess of the book value of the investment and is included in the investment amount. Hence, the amortization or reduction of the differential involves the reduction of the investment account. At the same time, the investor's net income must be reduced by an equal amount to recognize that a portion of the amount paid for the investment has expired.

Treatment of the Differential Illustrated   To illustrate the equity method when the cost of the investment exceeds the book value of the underlying net assets, assume that Ajax Corporation purchases 40 percent of the common stock of Barclay Company on January 1, 19X1, for $200,000. Barclay has net assets on that date with a book value of $400,000 and fair value of $465,000. Ajax's share of the book value of Barclay's net assets at acquisition is $160,000 ($400,000 × .40). A $40,000 differential is computed as follows:

Cost of investment to Ajax	$ 200,000
Book value of Ajax's share of Barclay's net assets	(160,000)
Differential	$ 40,000

The $65,000 excess of the fair value over the book value of Barclay's net assets consists of a $15,000 increase in the value of Barclay's land and a $50,000 increase in the value of Barclay's equipment. Ajax's 40 percent share of the increase in the value of Barclay's assets is as follows:

	Total Increase	Ajax's 40% Share
Land	$15,000	$ 6,000
Equipment	50,000	20,000
	$65,000	$26,000

Thus, $26,000 of the differential is assigned to land and equipment, with the remaining $14,000 attributed to goodwill. The allocation of the differential can be illustrated as follows:

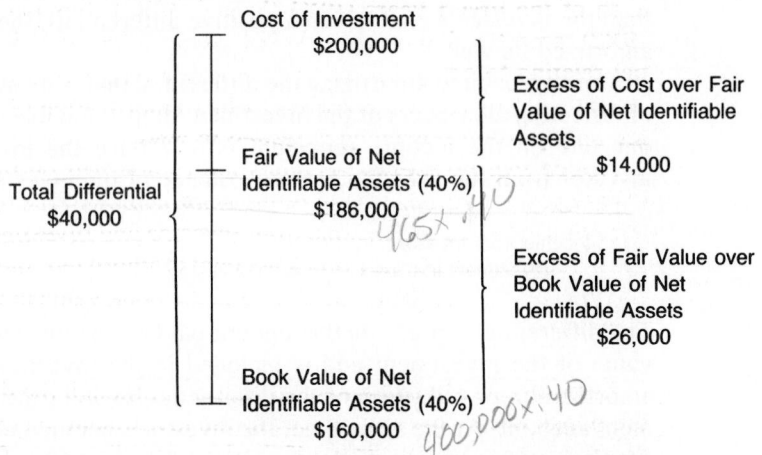

Because land has an unlimited economic life, the portion of the differential related to land is not amortized. The $20,000 portion of the differential related to equipment and the $14,000 portion related to goodwill are amortized over their remaining lives, assumed to be 5 years and 7 years, respectively, as follows:

Equipment ($20,000/5 years)	$4,000
Goodwill ($14,000/7 years)	2,000
Total amortization	$6,000

Barclay reports net income of $80,000 for 19X1 and declares dividends of $20,000. Using the equity method, Ajax records the following entries on its books during 19X1:

(6)	Investment in Barclay Stock	200,000	
	Cash		200,000
	Record purchase of Barclay stock.		
(7)	Investment in Barclay Stock	32,000	
	Income from Investee		32,000
	Record equity-method income: $80,000 × .40		

(8) Cash	8,000	
Investment in Barclay Stock		8,000
Record dividend from Barclay: $20,000 × .40		

(9) Income from Investee	6,000	
Investment in Barclay Stock		6,000
Amortize purchase differential: $4,000 + $2,000		

With these entries, Ajax recognizes $26,000 of income from Barclay and adjusts its investment in Barclay to an ending balance of $218,000.

The amortization of differential on the books of Ajax is the same ($6,000) for each of the first 5 years (19X1 through 19X5). For the next 2 years (19X6 and 19X7), amortization drops to $2,000 per year because the portion of the differential relating to equipment is fully amortized by the beginning of 19X6. After the seventh year (19X7), there is no further amortization of the differential, because the only portion remaining is related to land.

Notice that no special accounts are established on the books of the investor with regard to the differential or the amortization of the differential. The only two accounts involved are Income from Investee and Investment in Barclay Stock. As the Investment in Barclay Stock account is amortized, the differential between the carrying amount of the investment and the book value of the underlying net assets decreases.

Disposal of Differential-Related Assets   Although the differential is included on the books of the investor as part of the investment account, it relates to specific assets of the investee. Thus, if the investee disposes of any asset to which the differential relates, that portion of the differential must be removed from the investment account on the investor's books. When this is done, the investor's share of the investee's gain or loss on disposal of the asset must be adjusted to reflect the fact that the investor paid more for its proportionate share of that asset than did the investee. For example, if in the previous illustration Barclay Company sells the land to which $6,000 of Ajax's differential relates, Ajax does not recognize a full 40 percent of the gain or loss on the sale. Assume that Barclay originally had purchased the land in 19X0 for $75,000 and sells the land in 19X2 for $125,000. Barclay recognizes a gain on the sale of $50,000, and Ajax's share of that gain is 40 percent, or $20,000. The portion of the gain actually recognized by Ajax, however, must be adjusted as follows because of the amount in excess of book value paid by Ajax for its investment in Barclay:

Ajax's share of Barclay's reported gain	$20,000
Portion of Ajax's differential related to the land	(6,000)
Gain to be recognized by Ajax	$14,000

Thus, if Barclay reports net income (including gain on sale of land) of $150,000 for 19X2, Ajax records the following entries (disregarding dividends and amortization of the differential relating to equipment and goodwill):

(10)	Investment in Barclay Stock	60,000	
	Income from Investee		60,000
	Record equity method income: $150,000 × .40		
(11)	Income from Investee	6,000	
	Investment in Barclay Stock		6,000
	Remove differential related to Barclay's land sold.		

The same approach applies when dealing with a limited-life asset. The unamortized portion of the original differential relating to the asset sold is removed from the investment account, and the investor's share of the investee's income is adjusted by that amount.

Note that the investor does not separately report its share of ordinary gains or losses of the investee, such as the gain on the sale of the fixed asset or the write-off of the unamortized purchase differential. Consistent with the idea of using only a single line in the income statement to report the impact of the investee's activities on the investor, all such items are included in the Income from Investee account. **APB 18** does provide for separate disclosure of extraordinary items and prior-period adjustments. The investor's portion of the investee's extraordinary gains or losses and prior-period adjustments are reported separately in the investor's statements, if material to the investor, in the same way that the investor reports its own extraordinary items and prior-period adjustments.

Changes in the Number of Shares Held

Some changes in the number of common shares held by an investor are handled easily under the equity method, while others require a bit more attention. A change resulting from a stock dividend, split, or reverse split is treated in the same way as under the cost method. No formal accounting recognition is required on the books of the investor. On the other hand, purchases and sales of shares do require formal recognition.

Purchases of Additional Shares A purchase of additional shares of a common stock already held by an investor and accounted for using the equity method simply involves adding the cost of the new shares to the investment account and applying the equity method in the normal manner from the date of acquisition forward. The new and old investments in the same stock normally are combined for financial reporting purposes. Income accruing to the new shares can be recognized by the investor only from the date of acquisition forward.

To illustrate, assume that the ABC Company purchases 20 percent of XYZ's common stock on January 2, 19X1, and another 10 percent on July 1, 19X1, and that the stock purchases are at underlying book value. If XYZ Company earns income of $20,000 from January 2 to June 30 and earns $30,000 from July 1 to December 31, the total income recognized in 19X1 by ABC from its investment in XYZ is $13,000, computed as follows:

Income, January 2 to June 30:	$20,000 × .20	$ 4,000
Income, July 1 to December 31:	$30,000 × .30	9,000
Income from investment, 19X1		$13,000

If XYZ declares and pays a $10,000 dividend on January 15 and again on July 15, ABC reduces its investment account by $2,000 ($10,000 × .20) on January 15 and by $3,000 ($10,000 × .30) on July 15.

When an investment in common stock is carried using the cost method and purchases of additional shares give the investor the ability to significantly influence the investee, a retroactive switch from the cost method to the equity method is required. This change to the equity method must be applied retroactively to the date of the first acquisition of the investee's stock.

To illustrate a change to the equity method, assume that Aron Corporation purchases 15 percent of Zenon Company's common stock on January 2, 19X1, and another 10 percent on January 2, 19X4. Further, assume that Aron switches to the equity method on January 2, 19X4, because it gains the ability to significantly influence Zenon. Given the income and dividend data for Zenon as indicated below, and assuming the purchases of stock are at underlying book value, the investment income figures reported by Aron originally and as restated are as follows:

	Zenon		Investment Income Reported by Aron	
Year	Net Income	Dividends	Originally under Cost[a]	Restated under Equity[b]
19X1	$15,000	$10,000	$1,500	$2,250
19X2	18,000	10,000	1,500	2,700
19X3	22,000	10,000	1,500	3,300
	$55,000	$30,000	$4,500	$8,250

[a] 15 percent of Zenon's dividends for the year.
[b] 15 percent of Zenon's net income for the year.

Thus, in Aron's 19X4 financial report, the comparative statements for 19X1, 19X2, and 19X3 are restated to include Aron's 15 percent share of Zenon's profit and to exclude from income Aron's share of dividends recognized under the cost method. In addition, the investment account and retained earnings of Aron are restated as if the equity method had been applied from the date of the original acquisition. This restatement is accomplished on Aron's books with the following journal entry on January 2, 19X4:

(12)	Investment in Zenon Company Stock	3,750	
	Retained Earnings		3,750
	Restate investment account from cost to equity method:		
	$8,250 − $4,500		

In 19X4, if Zenon reports net income of $30,000, Aron's investment income is $7,500 (25 percent of Zenon's net income).

Sales of Shares The sale of all or part of an investment in common stock carried using the equity method is treated the same as the sale of any noncurrent asset. First, the investment account is adjusted to the date of sale for the investor's share of the investee's current earnings. Then, a gain or loss is recognized for the difference between the proceeds received and the carrying amount of the shares sold.

If only part of the investment is sold, the investor must decide whether to continue using the equity method to account for the remaining shares or to change to the cost method. The choice is based on evidence available after the sale as to whether the investor still is able to exercise significant influence over the investee. If the equity method is appropriate after the sale, the carrying amount of the remaining shares continues to be adjusted in the normal manner for the investor's share of the profits or losses and the dividends of the investee from the date of sale. If the equity method no longer is appropriate after the date of sale, the carrying value of the remaining investment is treated as the cost of that investment and the cost method is applied in the normal manner from the date of sale forward. No retroactive restatement of the investment to actual cost is made.

THE COST AND EQUITY METHODS COMPARED

Some of the key features of the cost and equity methods are summarized and compared in Figure 2-2.

The following example illustrates how an investor, Big Company, accounts for its investment in the common stock of another company, Smallco, Inc., under both the cost and equity methods. Big Company purchases 20 percent of Smallco's outstanding common stock on July 1, 19X1, for an amount that is $5,000 more than the book value of the underlying assets; this differential relates to Smallco's equipment having a remaining life of 10 years. Both companies report on a calendar-year basis. The income and dividends of Smallco are:

	Income	Dividends
19X1:		
January 1 to June 30	$ 40,000	
July 1 to December 31	40,000	$50,000
19X2	90,000	50,000
19X3	(10,000)	35,000
19X4	80,000	50,000

Figure 2-3 presents the journal entries that Big Company would use to account for its investment in Smallco if conditions were appropriate (1) for use of the cost method or (2) for use of the equity method.

FIGURE 2-2 Summary comparison of the cost and equity methods.

Item	Cost Method	Equity Method
Recorded amount of investment at date of acquisition	Original cost	Original cost
Usual carrying amount of investment subsequent to acquisition	Original cost	Original cost increased (decreased) by investor's share of investee's income (loss) and decreased by investor's share of investee's dividends and by amortization of the differential
Differential	Not amortized	Amortized if related to limited-life or intangible assets of investee
Income recognition by investor	Investor's share of investee's dividends declared from earnings since acquisition	Investor's share of investee's earnings since acquisition, whether distributed or not, reduced by any amortization of the differential
Investee dividends from earnings since acquisition by investor	Income	Reduction of investment
Investee dividends in excess of earnings since acquisition by investor	Reduction of investment	Reduction of investment

EVALUATION OF THE COST AND EQUITY METHODS

The cost method of accounting for intercorporate investments is consistent with the historical cost basis for most other assets. This method is subject to the usual criticisms leveled against historical cost. In particular, questions arise as to the relevance of reporting the purchase price of an investment acquired some years before. The cost method does conform more closely to the traditional accounting and legal views of the realization of income in that the investee's earnings are not available to the investor until transferred as dividends. Income based on dividend distributions sometimes can be manipulated, however. The significant influence criterion, which must be met to use the equity method, takes into consideration that the declaration of dividends by the investee can be influenced by the investor. Recognizing equity-method income from the investee without regard to investee dividends provides protection against manipulating the investor's net income by influencing investee dividend declarations.

In general, the cost method is considered to be a more conservative approach than the equity method. Income from the investee is not recognized under the cost method until distributed by the investee. The carrying amount of the investment usually is less under the cost method because the investment account is not

FIGURE 2-3 Comparison of journal entries under cost and equity methods.

Event	Cost		Equity	
19X1:				
7/1/X1 — Big Company purchases 20% of Smallco's outstanding common stock for $100,000.	Investment in Smallco Stock Cash	100,000 100,000	Investment in Smallco Stock Cash	100,000 100,000
12/31/X1 — Smallco reports net income of $80,000 for 19X1. Half of that amount was earned after July 1 (.20 × ½ × $80,000).			Investment in Smallco Stock Income from Investee	8,000 8,000
12/31/X1 — Big Company amortizes the differential ($5,000/10 × ½).			Income from Investee Investment in Smallco Stock	250 250
12/31/X1 — Smallco declares and pays its regular dividend of $50,000. (Excess of Big's share of dividends over Big's share of earnings since acquisition is $10,000 − $8,000 = $2,000.)	Cash Dividend Income Investment in Smallco Stock	10,000 8,000 2,000	Cash Investment in Smallco Stock	10,000 10,000
19X2:				
12/31/X2 — Smallco reports net income of $90,000 for 19X2.			Investment in Smallco Stock Income from Investee	18,000 18,000
12/31/X2 — Big Company amortizes the differential ($5,000 ÷ 10).			Income from Investee Investment in Smallco Stock	500 500
12/31/X2 — Smallco declares and pays its regular annual dividend of $50,000.	Cash Dividend Income	10,000 10,000	Cash Investment in Smallco Stock	10,000 10,000
19X3:				
12/31/X3 — Smallco reports a net loss for 19X3 of $10,000.			Loss from Investee Investment in Smallco Stock	2,000 2,000

12/31/X3 Big Company amortizes the differential ($5,000 ÷ 10).

	Debit	Credit
Equity:		
Loss from Investee	500	
Investment in Smallco Stock		500

12/31/X3 Smallco declares and pays a $35,000 dividend. (Excess of Big's share of dividends over Big's share of earnings since 12/31/X1 is $17,000 − $16,000 = $1,000.)

	Debit	Credit
Cost:		
Cash	7,000	
Dividend Income		6,000
Investment in Smallco Stock		1,000
Equity:		
Cash	7,000	
Investment in Smallco Stock		7,000

19X4:

12/31/X4 Smallco reports net income of $80,000 for 19X4.

	Debit	Credit
Equity:		
Investment in Smallco Stock	16,000	
Income from Investee		16,000

12/31/X4 Big Company amortizes the differential ($5,000 ÷ 10).

	Debit	Credit
Equity:		
Income from Investee	500	
Investment in Smallco Stock		500

12/31/X4 Smallco declares and pays its regular annual dividend of $50,000.

	Debit	Credit
Cost:		
Cash	10,000	
Dividend Income		10,000
Equity:		
Cash	10,000	
Investment in Smallco Stock		10,000

Summary

Cost

Dividend Income:

19X1	$ 8,000
19X2	10,000
19X3	6,000
19X4	10,000

(handwritten: 34,000 / 3,000)

Investment in Smallco Stock:

7/1/X1	$100,000
12/31/X1	98,000
12/31/X2	98,000
12/31/X3	97,000
12/31/X4	97,000

Equity

Income (Loss) from Investee:

19X1	$ 7,750
19X2	17,500
19X3	(2,500)
19X4	15,500

Investment in Smallco Stock:

7/1/X1	$100,000
12/31/X1	97,750
12/31/X2	105,250
12/31/X3	95,750
12/31/X4	101,250

adjusted for the investor's share of the investee's earnings. When the investee incurs losses, however, the cost method actually is less conservative than the equity method.

While the equity method avoids the problem of manipulating an investor's income by influencing the dividends paid by an investee, the method is criticized because the asset valuation departs from historical cost but stops short of a market value approach. Instead, the carrying amount of the investment is composed of a number of components and is not similar to the valuation of any other assets.

Over the years there has been considerable criticism of the use of the equity method as a substitute for the consolidation of certain types of subsidiaries. Although the equity method has been viewed as a "one-line consolidation," the amount of detail reported is considerably different under the equity method than with consolidation. For example, an investor would report the same equity-method income from the following two investees even though their income statements are quite different in composition:

	Investee 1	Investee 2
Sales	$ 50,000	$ 500,000
Operating Expenses	(30,000)	(620,000)
Operating Income (Loss)	$ 20,000	$(120,000)
Gain on Sale of Land		140,000
Net Income	$ 20,000	$ 20,000

Similarly, an investment in the stock of another company is reported under the equity method as a single amount in the balance sheet of the investor regardless of the asset and capital structure of the investee. Thus, many companies have borrowed heavily through unconsolidated subsidiaries and have reported their investments in the subsidiaries using the equity method. Because the debt is not reported in these situations, concerns have been raised over the use of the equity method to facilitate "off–balance sheet" financing.

As a result of these concerns, the Financial Accounting Standards Board recently eliminated the use of the equity method for reporting investments in subsidiaries by requiring the consolidation of virtually all majority-owned subsidiaries. The FASB is continuing to study the use of the equity method for investments in corporate joint ventures and other types of investees.

VALUATION OF INTERCORPORATE EQUITY INVESTMENTS

Special treatment is accorded investments in common stock, and other equity investments, when they decline in value. The particular treatment depends on the nature of the decline and the method used to account for the investment on the investor's books.

717-731-7083
412-565-3173

Declines in Value That Are Other than Temporary

When the value of a security held as an investment declines below its carrying amount, and the decline in value is considered material and other than temporary, the carrying amount of the security must be written down to the new lower value. A loss is recognized for the amount of the reduction. This treatment is applicable regardless of the type of security (debt or equity, marketable or nonmarketable) or the method used to account for the security (cost or equity). After such a write-down occurs, the cost or equity method, as appropriate, is applied in the normal manner with the new lower value of the investment serving as the starting point. Once written down, the carrying amount of the investment may not be increased later, except through normal application of the equity method, if appropriate.

Marketable Equity Securities

Those equity securities (for example, preferred and common stock, stock warrants) with price quotations available on a national securities exchange or in the over-the-counter market are considered *marketable equity securities* and fall under the provisions of **FASB Statement No. 12**, "Accounting for Certain Marketable Securities" (FASB 12). This statement requires that marketable equity securities be reported at the lower of their aggregate cost or market value. Securities required by **APB 18** to be reported using the equity method are not included under the provisions of **FASB 12**.

FASB 12 requires investments in marketable equity securities, excluding those reported under the equity method, to be grouped into two portfolios, one current and the other noncurrent. The individual investments within each portfolio generally are carried at cost. When financial statements are prepared, each portfolio is valued at the lower of the aggregate cost of the individual securities in the portfolio or the aggregate market value of those securities at the balance sheet date.

When the aggregate market value of a portfolio at the end of the period is below its aggregate cost, the portfolio is reported at market value. The individual securities in the portfolio are not written down; instead, a contra asset account is used to reduce the net carrying amount of the portfolio. Recoveries in aggregate market value are recognized as decreases in the contra asset account. However, increases in aggregate market value above the aggregate cost of the individual securities are not recognized.

Note that **FASB 12** requires the valuation of portfolios of securities as a whole and does not affect the accounting procedures applied to individual securities. All transactions or events relating to individual securities, including material declines in value that are other than temporary, are recorded in the normal manner without regard to **FASB 12**.

There is an important difference in the way in which the current and the noncurrent marketable equity securities portfolios are treated under **FASB 12**. Changes in the valuation of the current marketable equity securities portfolio are included in the computation of net income in the period in which they occur. They are recognized in the income statement as unrealized losses or recoveries of previously recognized unrealized losses. Changes in the valuation of the noncurrent portfolio are not recognized in income for the period but rather are carried directly to a contra stockholders' equity account. This account, entitled Accumulated Unrealized Loss on Noncurrent Marketable Equity Securities, is reported in the balance sheet as a deduction from stockholders' equity.

All disposals of individual securities are recorded in the normal manner as if there were no valuation accounts regardless of whether the security is classified as current or noncurrent.

Management sometimes may change its investment objectives with respect to a specific security. For example, management may decide that a security originally purchased as a temporary substitute for cash should be held as a long-term investment. If a marketable equity security is transferred from either the current or noncurrent portfolio to the other, the security is valued at the lower of its individual cost or market value at the date of reclassification. If the market value is lower than cost, the market value at the date of reclassification becomes the new cost basis for the security; the reduction to market value is accounted for as a realized loss and is included in the determination of net income in the period of the reclassification.

Valuation of Equity Investments Illustrated

To illustrate the treatment of investments in marketable equity securities under **FASB 12**, assume that Hirsch Company has no investments in securities on January 1, 19X1, but purchases the following marketable equity securities during 19X1:

Security	Cost	Classification
XYZ Common	$ 40,000	Current
ABC Common	50,000	Current
D Company Preferred	100,000	Current
Bud Company Common	500,000	Noncurrent
TUV Preferred	200,000	Noncurrent

All the securities are carried at cost. At the end of 19X1, the securities are valued as follows:

Portfolio	Security	Carrying Amount, 12/31/X1	Market Value, 12/31/X1
Current	XYZ Common	$ 40,000	$ 45,000
	ABC Common	50,000	35,000
	D Company Preferred	100,000	100,000
		$190,000	$180,000
Noncurrent	Bud Company Common	$500,000	$520,000
	TUV Preferred	200,000	160,000
		$700,000	$680,000

Hirsch's balance sheet prepared on December 31, 19X1, reports the current portfolio at $190,000 less a $10,000 Allowance for Decline in Value of Current Marketable Securities. The noncurrent portfolio is reported at $700,000 less a $20,000 allowance. The stockholders' equity section shows a $20,000 contra stockholders' equity account entitled Accumulated Unrealized Loss on Noncurrent Marketable Equity Securities. Hirsch's 19X1 income statement reports a $10,000 unrealized loss on the decline in value of the current marketable securities.

On March 5, 19X2, Hirsch sells the D Company Preferred for $102,000. The value of the TUV Preferred drops to $140,000 by June 30, and the decline in value is considered permanent. Hirsch records the two events as follows:

March 5, 19X2

(13)	Cash	102,000	
	Investment in D Company Preferred		100,000
	Gain on Sale of Securities		2,000
	Record sale of D Company preferred.		

June 30, 19X2

(14)	Loss on Decline in Value of Securities	60,000	
	Investment in TUV Preferred		60,000
	Record permanent decline in value of TUV preferred:		
	$200,000 − $140,000		

At the end of 19X2, Hirsch's marketable equity securities are valued as follows:

Portfolio	Security	Carrying Basis	Carrying Amount, 12/31/X2	Market Value, 12/31/X2
Current	XYZ Common	Cost	$ 40,000	$ 46,000
	ABC Common	Cost	50,000	40,000
			$ 90,000	$ 86,000
Noncurrent	Bud Company Common	Cost	$500,000	$525,000
	TUV Preferred	Reduced cost	140,000	140,000
			$640,000	$665,000

Because there is a $10,000 current allowance and a $20,000 noncurrent allowance from 19X1, the following entries are required to adjust the allowance accounts at the end of 19X2:

December 31, 19X2

(15)	Allowance for Decline in Value of Current Marketable Securities	6,000	
	Recovery in Value of Current Marketable Securities		6,000
	Record recovery in value of current marketable equity securities: $10,000 existing allowance − $4,000 required allowance		

(16)   Allowance for Decline in Value of Noncurrent
            Marketable Securities   20,000
                Accumulated Unrealized Loss on
                Noncurrent Marketable Equity Securities   20,000
            Record recovery in value of noncurrent marketable
            equity securities: $20,000 existing allowance − $0
            required allowance

Thus in Hirsch's 19X2 balance sheet, the current allowance account is reported at $4,000, and there is no noncurrent allowance or contra stockholders' equity account related to marketable securities. The 19X2 income statement reflects a total gain on current marketable securities of $8,000 ($2,000 + $6,000) and a loss on noncurrent marketable securities of $60,000. The $60,000 loss on noncurrent marketable securities is recognized only because the decline is deemed to be other than temporary.

ADDITIONAL CONSIDERATIONS RELATING TO THE EQUITY METHOD

Determination of Significant Influence

The general rule established in **APB 18** is that the equity method is appropriate where the investor, by virtue of its common stock interest in an investee, is able to exercise significant influence over the operating and financial policies of the investee. In the absence of other evidence, common stock ownership of 20 percent or more is viewed as indicating that the investor is able to exercise significant influence over the investee. However, the APB also stated a number of factors that could constitute other evidence of the ability to exercise significant influence:[3]

1. Representation on board of directors
2. Participation in policy-making
3. Material intercompany transactions
4. Interchange of managerial personnel
5. Technological dependency
6. Size of investment in relation to concentration of other shareholdings

FASB Interpretation No. 35, "Criteria for Applying the Equity Method of Accounting for Investments in Common Stock" (FIN 35), provides some examples of evidence that an investor is unable to exercise significant influence over an investee:[4]

1. Opposition by the investee, such as litigation or complaints to governmental regulatory authorities, challenges the investor's ability to exercise significant influence.

---

[3] Ibid., par. 17.

[4] *Financial Accounting Standards Board Interpretation No. 35*, "Criteria for Applying the Equity Method of Accounting for Investments in Common Stock," May 1981, par. 4.

2. The investor and investee sign an agreement under which the investor surrenders significant rights as a shareholder.

3. Majority ownership of the investee is concentrated among a small group of shareholders who operate the investee without regard to the views of the investor.

4. The investor needs or wants more financial information to apply the equity method than is available to the investee's other shareholders (for example, the investor wants quarterly financial information from an investee that publicly reports only annually), tries to obtain that information, and fails.

5. The investor tries and fails to obtain representation on the investee's board of directors.

These lists are not meant to be exhaustive but are intended to indicate the types of factors that must be considered in determining whether the investor has the ability to significantly influence the investee.

Unrealized Intercompany Profits

The equity method as applied under **APB 18** often is referred to as a *one-line consolidation* because (1) the investor's income and stockholders' equity are the same as if the investee were consolidated and (2) all equity method adjustments are made through the investment and related income accounts, which are reported in only a single line in the balance sheet and a single line in the income statement. The view currently taken in consolidation is that intercompany sales do not result in the realization of income until the intercompany profit is confirmed in some way, usually through a transaction with an unrelated third party. For example, if a parent company sells inventory to a subsidiary at a profit, that profit cannot be recognized in the consolidated financial statements until it is confirmed by resale of the inventory to an external party. Because profits from sales to related companies are viewed from a consolidated perspective as being unrealized until there is a resale to unrelated parties, such profits must be eliminated when preparing consolidated financial statements.

The consolidated financial statements are not the only ones affected, however, because **APB 18** requires that the income of an investor that reports an investment using the equity method must be the same as if the investee were consolidated. Therefore, the investor's equity-method income from the investee must be adjusted for unconfirmed profits on intercompany sales as well. The term used in this text to refer to the application of the equity method that includes the adjustment for unrealized profit on sales to affiliates is *fully adjusted equity method*.

Adjusting for Unrealized Intercompany Profits An intercompany sale normally is recorded on the books of the selling affiliate in the same manner as any other sale, including the recognition of profit. In applying the equity method, any intercompany profit remaining unrealized at the end of the period must be deducted from the amount of income that otherwise would be reported.

Under the one-line consolidation approach, the income recognized from the investment and the carrying amount of the investment are reduced to remove the effects of the unrealized intercompany profits:

Income from Investee	XXX	
Investment in Investee		XXX

In future periods when the intercompany profit actually is realized, the entry is reversed.

The equity-method adjusting entries on the investor's books for the amortization of the differential and for the deferral of unrealized profits on intercompany transfers are identical except for the amounts.

Unrealized Profit Adjustments Illustrated   To illustrate the adjustment for unrealized intercompany profits under the equity method, assume that Palit Corporation owns 40 percent of the common stock of Label Manufacturing. During 19X1, Palit sells inventory to Label for $10,000; the inventory originally cost Palit $7,000. Label resells one-third of the inventory to outsiders during 19X1 and retains the other two-thirds in its ending inventory. The amount of unrealized profit is computed as follows:

Total intercompany profit: $10,000 − $7,000 = $3,000
Unrealized portion: $3,000 × ⅔ = $2,000

Assuming that Label reports net income of $60,000 for 19X1 and declares no dividends, the following entries are recorded on Palit's books at the end of 19X1:

December 31, 19X1		
(17) Investment in Label Manufacturing Stock	24,000	
Income from Label Manufacturing		24,000
Record equity-method income:		
$60,000 × .40		
(18) Income from Label Manufacturing	2,000	
Investment in Label Manufacturing Stock		2,000
Remove unrealized intercompany profit.		

If all the remaining inventory is sold in 19X2, the following entry is made on Palit's books at the end of 19X2 to record the realization of the previously unrealized intercompany profit:

December 31, 19X2		
(19) Investment in Label Manufacturing Stock	2,000	
Income from Label Manufacturing		2,000
Recognize realized intercompany profit.		

Additional Requirements of APB 18

APB 18, the governing pronouncement dealing with equity-method reporting, includes several additional requirements:

1. The investor's share of the investee's extraordinary items, prior-period adjustments, and cumulative adjustments due to changes in accounting principles should be reported as such by the investor, if material.

2. The investor should recognize its share of the investee's earnings based on the investee's most recent available financial statements. The time lag from the date of the investee's most recent available financial statements to the end of the investor's fiscal period should be consistent from period to period.

3. If an investor's share of investee losses exceeds the carrying amount of the investment, the equity method should be discontinued once the investment has been reduced to zero. No further losses are to be recognized by the investor unless the investor is committed to provide further financial support for the investee or unless the investee's imminent return to profitability appears assured. If, after the equity method has been suspended, the investee reports net income, the investor again should apply the equity method, but only after the investor's share of net income equals its share of losses not previously recognized.

4. Preferred dividends of the investee should be deducted from the investee's net income if declared or, whether declared or not, if the preferred stock is cumulative, before the investor computes its share of investee earnings.

APB 18 also includes a number of required financial statement disclosures. When using the equity method, the investor must disclose:

1. The name and percentage ownership of each investee, including those in which the investor holds more than 20 percent of the common stock but does not use the equity method and those in which the investor owns less than 20 percent of the common stock and does use the equity method.

2. The investor's accounting policies with respect to its investments in common stock, including the reasons for any departures from the 20 percent criterion established by **APB 18.**

3. The amount and accounting treatment of any differential.

4. The aggregate market value of each identified nonsubsidiary investment where a quoted market price is available.

5. Either separate statements for or summarized information as to assets, liabilities, and results of operations of corporate joint ventures of the investor, if material in the aggregate.

6. Effects on income, if material, of possible conversion, exercise, or contingent issue of the investee's securities.

Tax Allocation Procedures

Intercompany income accruals and dividend transfers must be taken into consideration in computing income tax expense for the period. The impact will depend upon the level of ownership and the filing status of the companies. Because corporations generally are permitted to deduct 80 percent of the dividends received (100 percent if at least 80 percent of all voting stock is owned), they are taxed at relatively low effective tax rates (20 percent times the marginal tax rate) on those dividends.

When an investor and an investee file a consolidated tax return, intercompany dividends and income accruals are eliminated in determining taxable income. Because these items are eliminated, there is no need to provide deferred tax accruals when temporary differences occur between the recognition of investment income by the investor and realization through dividend transfers from the investee. Those situations in which a consolidated return may be filed are relatively limited. The investor must own at least 80 percent of the stock of the investee and must elect to file a consolidated return. In all other cases separate returns must be filed.

If an investor and an investee file separate tax returns, the investor is taxed on the dividends received from the investee rather than on the amount of investment income reported. The amount of tax expense reported in the income statement of the investor each period should be based on income from the investor's own operations as well as on income recognized from its intercompany investments. **FASB Statement No. 109**, "Accounting for Income Taxes" (FASB 109), specifies those situations in which additional deferred tax accruals are required as a result of temporary differences in the recognition of income for financial reporting purposes and that used in determining taxable income.

Tax Expense under the Cost Method   If the investor reports its investment using the cost method, income tax expense recorded by the investor on the investment income and the amount of taxes actually paid both are based on dividends received from the investee. No interperiod income tax allocation is required under the cost method because the income is recognized in the same period for both financial reporting and tax purposes; there are no temporary differences.

Tax Expense under the Equity Method   If the investment is reported using the equity method and separate tax returns are filed, the investor reports its share of the investee's income in the income statement but reports only its share of the investee's dividends in the tax return. When the amount of the investee's dividends is different from its earnings, a temporary difference arises and interperiod tax allocation is required for the investor. In this situation, deferred income taxes must be recognized on the difference between the equity-method income reported by the investor in its income statement and the dividend income reported in its tax return. Current accounting standards generally require that the investor's reported income tax expense be computed as if all the investment income recognized by the investor under the equity method actually had been received. Thus, the investor's tax expense is recorded in excess of the taxes actually paid when the investee's earnings are greater than its dividends and normally is recorded at less than taxes actually paid when dividends are greater than earnings.

FIGURE 2-4 Investor income tax expense computation.

Type of Investee	Computation of Investor's Income Tax Expense Related to Income from Investee
Equity-method investees	Ordinary tax rate × (investor's share of investee net income − dividend deduction)[a]
Cost-method investees	Ordinary tax rate × (dividends received − dividend deduction)

(a) Need not accrue taxes on the undistributed earnings of corporate joint ventures or unconsolidated subsidiaries if there is evidence that the earnings will be reinvested indefinitely in the investee or distributed in a tax-free liquidation.

An exception to the deferred tax requirement is permitted in some cases for investments in corporate joint ventures and unconsolidated subsidiaries.[5] If there is evidence that the earnings of the corporate joint venture or unconsolidated subsidiary are to be reinvested in the investee indefinitely, or if the earnings are to be distributed in a tax-free liquidation, deferred taxes need not be accrued by the investor on the undistributed earnings. This exception is not permitted for equity-method investees other than corporate joint ventures and unconsolidated subsidiaries; deferred taxes must be accrued on the undistributed earnings of the other equity-method investees in all situations. The FASB has considered eliminating this exception to the deferred-tax requirement. Although the Board decided to take no action immediately, future reconsideration is likely.

The requirements for computing the investor's income tax expense on income from intercorporate investments in common stock are summarized in Figure 2-4.

Treatment of Income Taxes Illustrated   As an example of the treatment of income taxes related to intercorporate investments in which the investor and investee each file separate tax returns, assume that T Company owns 20 percent of the common stock of S Company. S reports net income of $100,000 (after deducting its income taxes) for 19X1 and declares dividends of $30,000. T reports income before taxes of $500,000 from its own operations, not including any investment income. Assume that T's effective combined federal and state tax rate is 40 percent. T computes its income taxes payable as follows:

Separate operating income	$500,000
Dividend income: $30,000 × .20	6,000
Total income	$506,000
Dividend deduction: $6,000 × .80	(4,800)
Taxable income	$501,200
Effective tax rate	× .40
Income taxes payable	$200,480

[5] However, majority-owned subsidiaries reported in general-purpose financial statements normally must be consolidated.

The income tax expense to be reported in T Company's income statement for 19X1 is computed as follows:

	Reporting Method	
	Cost	Equity
Computation of T's reported accounting income before taxes:		
Separate operating income	$500,000	$500,000
Income from investee	6,000	20,000
Income before taxes	$506,000	$520,000
Computation of income having no tax consequences:		
Income from investee	$ 6,000	$ 20,000
Dividend deduction	× .80	× .80
Income not taxable	$ 4,800	$ 16,000
Computation of temporary difference:		
Pretax accounting income	$506,000	$520,000
Taxable income	(501,200)	(501,200)
Total difference	$ 4,800	$ 18,800
Income not taxable	(4,800)	(16,000)
Temporary difference	$ -0-	$ 2,800
Computation of income tax expense:		
Income taxes payable	$200,480	$200,480
Tax effect of temporary difference (40%)	-0-	1,120
Income tax expense	$200,480	$201,600

The journal entry on T's books to record income tax expense for 19X1 under equity-method reporting is:

(20) Income Tax Expense	201,600	
Income Taxes Payable		200,480
Deferred Tax Liability		1,120
Record income tax expense for 19X1:		
$1,120 = $2,800 × .40		

Notice that if the investor carries its investment at cost, interperiod tax allocation is not required because the only difference between accounting and taxable income is due to the dividend deduction, which is not a temporary difference. If, however, the investment is carried using the equity method, the investor recognizes its proportionate share of investee income but pays taxes only on the dividends received. A portion of the difference between the equity-method income recognized and the dividends received is viewed as a temporary difference, and in accordance with the general requirements relating to interperiod income tax allocation, the investor's income tax expense for financial reporting purposes is based on its income taxes actually payable for the year plus the tax effects of any temporary differences.

Accounting for Investments in Subsidiaries

Investors that own more than 50 percent of the common stock of other companies normally must, in their general-purpose financial statements, either (1) consolidate the majority-owned investees (subsidiaries) or (2) report them using the cost method if the investor (parent) lacks the ability to control or if control is temporary. While these standards must be followed for financial reporting purposes, companies are free to adopt whatever procedures they wish in accounting for the investments on their books. Because investments in consolidated subsidiaries are eliminated when consolidated statements are prepared, the consolidated statements are not affected by the procedures used to account for the investments on the parent's books.

Three different approaches are followed by companies in practice in accounting for their consolidated subsidiaries:

1. Fully adjusted equity method
2. Modified version of the equity method
3. Cost method

Several modified versions of the equity method are found in practice, and all usually are referred to as the *modified equity method*. Some companies apply the equity method without making adjustments for unrealized intercompany profits and the amortization of the differential. Others adjust for the amortization of the differential but omit the adjustments for unrealized intercompany profits. This latter approach is referred to in this text as the *basic equity method* and is used through many of the later chapters on consolidations. While modified versions of the equity method are not acceptable for financial reporting purposes, they may provide some clerical savings for the parent if used on the books when consolidation of the subsidiary is required.

Accounting for Investments under Pooling of Interests Procedures

For a stock acquisition to qualify as a pooling of interests, a company must exchange its common stock for at least 90 percent of the outstanding common stock of another company. Because the new subsidiary is majority-owned, it normally must be consolidated subsequent to the combination. However, if control does not rest with the parent or control is temporary, the investment is treated in accordance with **APB 18**, which requires that it be reported using the cost method. In other words, the investment would not be reported using the equity method; the subsidiary would either be consolidated or be reported as an investment using the cost method.

While equity-method reporting would be inappropriate for an investment in a subsidiary acquired in a pooling of interests, the parent may choose to use the equity method on its books to account for the investment if the subsidiary is to be consolidated. The parent company records the common stock received in a pooling of interests at the stock's book value. In addition, the parent records on its books its proportionate share of the investee's retained earnings at the date of combination. These procedures contrast with those used in a purchase situation, in which the amounts recorded are based on fair values and the investor's retained earnings balance is unaffected by the combination.

Aside from this difference in the initial recording of the investment, both the cost and the equity methods are applied in exactly the same way under both purchase and pooling of interests accounting. Under the cost method, the investment normally remains unchanged, and dividends received are recorded as income by the investor. Under the equity method, the entries to record the investor's share of investee income and dividends and the adjustments for intercompany profit eliminations, if made, are the same regardless of the method used to record the investment originally. Of course, there is no differential because the investment is recorded at book value under pooling of interests accounting; thus, there is no amortization of differential.

Equity Method under Purchase and Pooling Compared   To compare the application of the equity method under purchase and pooling accounting, assume that X Company exchanges 10,000 shares of its $10 par common stock with a current market value of $350,000 for all the common stock of Y Company. The stock of Y Company has a total book value of $300,000, including retained earnings of $75,000. The $50,000 excess of market value over book value is all attributable to goodwill, with an estimated remaining life of 5 years. Figure 2-5 presents the journal entries recorded on X Company's books during the year of combination, with the investment in Y Company stock carried using the equity method. Comparative entries are presented under both purchase and pooling accounting.

Notice from this illustration that the only differences in applying the equity method under purchase and pooling of interests accounting involve (1) the initial recognition and subsequent disposition of the differential and (2) the initial treatment of retained earnings.

Pooling at an Interim Date   One other difference between purchase and pooling surfaces if a pooling takes place at an interim date. The amount of equity-method income recorded by the investor following a pooling must include the investor's proportionate share of the investee's income for the entire fiscal period, not just the portion subsequent to the combination. Therefore, the entry to record the combination is based on the investee's balances existing at the beginning of the fiscal period, with adjustments to the investment account and retained earnings for the investor's share of any dividends declared by the investee during the fiscal period, but before the combination.

To illustrate, assume that on January 1, Y Company has retained earnings of $75,000 and the total book value of its stockholders' equity is $300,000. Y

FIGURE 2-5 Comparison of equity-method journal entries under purchase and pooling of interests accounting.

Event	Combination Treated as Pooling of Interests		Combination Treated as Purchase	

1/2 X Company exchanges 10,000 shares of its own $10 par common for all of Y Company's common.	Investment in Y Company Stock
	  Common Stock
	  Premium on Common
	  Retained Earnings
		300,000
		100,000
		125,000
		75,000
			Investment in Y Company Stock
			  Common Stock
			  Premium on Common
				350,000
				100,000
				250,000

12/31 Y Company reports income of $40,000 for the year.	Investment in Y Company Stock
	  Income from Investee
		40,000
		40,000
			Investment in Y Company Stock
			  Income from Investee
				40,000
				40,000

12/31 Y Company declares and pays a $15,000 dividend.	Cash
	  Investment in Y Company Stock
		15,000
		15,000
			Cash
			  Investment in Y Company Stock
				15,000
				15,000

12/31 Amortization of $50,000 differential (over 5 years).			Income from Investee Investment in Y Company Stock	10,000 10,000

Summary

	Combination Treated as Pooling of Interests		Combination Treated as Purchase	
	Income from Investee Investment in Y Company Stock, 12/31	$ 40,000 $325,000	Income from Investee Investment in Y Company Stock, 12/31	$ 30,000 $365,000

Company's reporting period is the calendar year, and during the year Y's income, dividends, retained earnings, and book value are as follows:

	Y Company Retained Earnings	Y Company Book Value
Balances, January 1	$ 75,000	$300,000
Income to September 30	28,000	28,000
Dividends to September 30	(15,000)	(15,000)
Balances, September 30	$ 88,000	$313,000
Income from October 1 to December 31	12,000	12,000
Dividends from October 1 to December 31	-0-	-0-
Balances, December 31	$100,000	$325,000

On October 1, X Company exchanges 10,000 shares of its $10 par common stock for all the stock of Y Company in a pooling of interests. The combination is recorded on the books of X Company in the following manner:

(21)	Investment in Y Company Stock	285,000	
	Dividends Declared	15,000	
	Common Stock		100,000
	Additional Paid-In Capital		125,000
	Retained Earnings		75,000

Record the acquisition of Y's stock in a pooling of interests:

$285,000 = $300,000 − $15,000
$100,000 = $10 × 10,000 shares
$125,000 = $285,000 − $100,000
        − ($75,000 − $15,000)

The pooling is recorded as if it had occurred at the beginning of the year. However, X's share of Y's dividend ($15,000 × 1.00) is included in the entry as if X had declared the dividend, and the amount assigned to the investment account is based on the beginning book value of Y Company's net assets of $300,000 less the $15,000 dividend declared by Y prior to the combination. X Company records Y Company's preacquisition dividend as if it had declared the dividend. The reasoning behind this approach is that Y paid the dividend to its pre-pooling stockholders, who then became stockholders of X through the business combination. Because companies combined in a pooling are viewed as always having been combined, the effect is the same as if Y had transferred assets to X and X had then declared a dividend payable to its stockholders who previously had been stockholders of Y.

At the end of the year, X Company records its share (100 percent) of Y's income for the entire year with the following entry:

(22)	Investment in Y Company Stock	40,000	
	Income from Y Company		40,000

SUMMARY OF KEY CONCEPTS AND TERMS

Three main methods of reporting investments in common stock are found in practice: consolidation, the equity method, and the cost method. Consolidation generally is appropriate if the investor controls the investee, usually through majority ownership of the investee's voting stock. The equity method is required when the investor has sufficient stock ownership in the investee to significantly influence the operating and financial policies of the investee but owns less than a majority of the investee's stock. In the absence of other evidence, ownership of 20 percent or more of an investee's voting stock is viewed as giving the investor the ability to exercise significant influence over the investee. The cost method is used when consolidation and the equity method are not appropriate, usually when the investor is unable to exercise significant influence over the investee or when the investment is temporary.

The cost method is similar to the approach used in accounting for other noncurrent assets. The investment is carried at its original cost to the investor. Consistent with the realization concept, income from the investment is recognized when distributed by the investee in the form of dividends.

The equity method is unique in that the carrying value of the investment is adjusted periodically to reflect the investor's changing equity in the underlying investee. Income from the investment is recognized by the investor under the equity method as the investee reports the income rather than when it is distributed.

Basic equity method	Liquidating dividends
Consolidation	Marketable equity securities
Corporate joint venture	Modified equity method
Cost method	One-line consolidation
Differential	Parent
Equity accrual	Significant influence
Equity method	Subsidiary
Fully adjusted equity method	Unconsolidated subsidiary

QUESTIONS

Q2-1 What types of investments in common stock must be reported using (a) the equity method; (b) the cost method?

Q2-2 How is the ability to significantly influence the operating and financial policies of a company normally demonstrated?

Q2-3 When is equity-method reporting considered inappropriate even though sufficient common shares are owned to allow the exercise of significant influence?

Q2-4 When will the balance in the intercorporate investment account be the same under the cost method and the equity method?

Q2-5 Describe an investor's treatment of an investee's prior-period dividends and earnings when the investor acquires significant influence through a purchase of additional stock.

Q2-6 From the point of view of an investor in common stock, what is a liquidating dividend? Is a liquidating dividend viewed in the same way by the investee?

Q2-7   What effect does a liquidating dividend have on the balance in the investment account under the cost method and the equity method?

Q2-8   What is a corporate joint venture? How should an investment in the common stock of a corporate joint venture normally be reported?

Q2-9   What is a differential? How is a differential treated by an investor in computing income from an investee under (a) cost-method and (b) equity-method reporting?

Q2-10   How is the receipt of a dividend recorded under the equity method? Under the cost method?

Q2-11   Turner Manufacturing Corporation owns 40 percent of the common shares of Straight Lace Company. If Straight Lace Company reports net income of $100,000 for 19X5, what factors may cause Turner to report less than $40,000 of income from the investee?

Q2-12   What are marketable equity securities?

Q2-13   Are investments in common stock reported using the equity method also subject to the lower-of-cost-or-market requirements of **FASB Statement No. 12**? Explain.

Q2-14* When must tax allocation procedures be used in recording income tax expense under the equity method?

Q2-15* Will the expected amount of deferred income taxes be larger under the cost method or the equity method? Explain.

Q2-16* How will application of the equity method differ when pooling of interests treatment, rather than purchase treatment, is used in recording a business combination?

Q2-17* How does the fully adjusted equity method differ from the basic equity method?

Q2-18* Explain the concept of a one-line consolidation.

Q2-19* What is the basic equity method? When might a company choose to use the basic equity method rather than the fully adjusted equity method?

Q2-20* How are extraordinary items of the investee disclosed by the investor under equity-method reporting?

CASES

C2-1 Choice of Accounting Method

Slanted Building Supplies purchased 32 percent of the voting shares of Flat Flooring Company in March 19X3. On December 31, 19X3, the officers of Slanted Building Supplies indicated they needed advice on whether to use the equity method or cost method in reporting their ownership in Flat Flooring Company.

Required

   a. What factors should be considered in determining if equity-method reporting is appropriate?

   b. Which of the two methods is likely to show the larger reported contribution to Slanted's earnings in 19X4? Explain.

   c. Why might the use of the equity method become more appropriate as the percentage of ownership increases?

C2-2 Use of the Cost or Equity Method [AICPA Adapted]

Since Boomer Company's inception, Madison Company has owned 18 percent of Boomer's outstanding common stock. Madison provides three key management personnel to Boomer and purchased 25 percent of Boomer's output during 19X7. Boomer is profitable. On January 2, 19X8, Madison purchased additional common stock to finance Boomer's expansion, thereby becoming a 30 percent owner. Boomer's common stock does not have a quoted market price. The stock has always been issued at its book value, which is assumed to approximate its fair value.

Required

*% of stock
sales %
3 people*

a. In general, distinguish between investor-income reporting under the cost method and under the equity method. Which method is more consistent with accrual accounting? Why?

b. Prior to January 2, 19X8, what specific factors should Madison have considered in determining the appropriate method of accounting for its investment in Boomer?

c. For purposes of your answer to **c** only, assume Madison used the cost method in accounting for its investment in Boomer prior to January 2, 19X8. Describe the book adjustments required on January 2, 19X8, when Madison became owner of 30 percent of the outstanding common stock of Boomer. *most go
back to original date &
restate*

C2-3   Marketable Equity Securities [AICPA Adapted]

Brune Company has a portfolio of marketable equity securities that it classifies as a current asset. Brune owns less than 5 percent of the outstanding voting stock of each company's securities in the portfolio. At the beginning of the year, the aggregate market value of the portfolio exceeded its aggregate cost. Cash dividends on these securities were received during the year. All cash dividends received represent distributions of earnings subsequent to Brune's acquisition of these securities. Some of the securities in the portfolio were sold during the year. At the end of the year, the aggregate cost of the portfolio exceeded its aggregate market value.

Brune owns 40 percent of the outstanding voting stock of Joy Company. The remainder of Joy's outstanding voting stock is widely dispersed among unrelated investors.

Required

a. (1) How should Brune report the income statement effects of the cash dividends received during the year on the securities in the portfolio that it classifies as a current asset?

(2) How should Brune report the income statement effects of the securities sold during the year?

b. How should Brune report in its balance sheet as of the end of the year the portfolio of marketable equity securities that it classifies as a current asset? Why? What effect will ownership of these securities have on Brune's income statement for the year? Do not discuss the cash dividends or the securities sold.

c. Identify the method of accounting that Brune should use for its 40 percent investment in the outstanding voting stock of Joy. Why is this method appropriate?

EXERCISES

E2-1   Multiple-Choice Questions on Use of Cost and Equity Methods
[AICPA Adapted]

Select the correct answer for each of the following questions.

1. When the equity method of accounting for an investment in a subsidiary is used, dividends from the subsidiary should be accounted for by the parent corporation as:
   a. Revenue unless paid from retained earnings of the subsidiary earned before the date of acquisition.
   b. Revenue so long as the dividends were declared from retained earnings.
   c. A reduction of the carrying value of the investment account.
   d. A deferred credit.

2. What is the most appropriate basis for recording the acquisition of 40 percent of the stock in another company if the acquisition was a noncash transaction?
   a. At the book value of the consideration given.
   b. At the par value of the stock acquired.
   c. At the book value of the stock acquired.
   d. At the fair value of the consideration given.

3. When an investor uses the cost method to account for investments in common stock, cash dividends received by the investor from the investee should normally be recorded as:
   a. Dividend income.
   b. An addition to the investor's share of the investee's profit.
   c. A deduction from the investor's share of the investee's profit.
   d. A deduction from the investment account.

4. An investor uses the equity method to account for investments in common stock. The purchase price implies a fair value of the investee's depreciable assets in excess of the investee's net asset carrying values. The investor's amortization of the excess:
   a. Decreases the investment account.
   b. Decreases the goodwill account.
   c. Increases the investment revenue account.
   d. Does not affect the investment account.

5. A corporation exercises significant influence over an affiliate in which it holds a 40 percent common stock interest. If its affiliate completed a fiscal year profitably but paid no dividends, how would this affect the investor corporation?
   a. Result in an increased current ratio.
   b. Result in increased earnings per share.
   c. Increase several turnover ratios.
   d. Decrease book value per share.

6. Drab, Inc., owns 40 percent of the outstanding stock of Gloom Company. During 19X5, Drab received a $4,000 cash dividend from Gloom. What effect did this dividend have on Drab's 19X5 financial statements?
   a. Increased total assets.
   b. Decreased total assets.
   c. Increased income.
   d. Decreased the investment account.

7. An investor uses the cost method to account for an investment in common stock. A portion of the dividends received this year was in excess of the investor's share of investee's earnings subsequent to the date of investment. The amount of dividend revenue that should be reported in the investor's income statement for this year would be:

a. Zero.
b. The total amount of dividends received this year.
c. The portion of the dividends received this year that were in excess of the investor's share of investee's earnings subsequent to the date of investment.
d. The portion of the dividends received this year that was not in excess of the investor's share of investee's earnings subsequent to the date of investment.

E2-2   Multiple-Choice Questions on Applying Equity Method [AICPA Adapted]

Select the correct answer for each of the following questions.

1. On January 1, 19X2, Wynn, Inc., bought 15 percent of Parr Corporation's common stock for $60,000. Wynn appropriately accounts for its investment by the cost method. The following data concerning Parr are available for the years ended December 31, 19X2 and 19X3:

	19X2	19X3
Net Income	$30,000	$90,000
Dividends Paid	None	80,000

In its income statement for the year ended December 31, 19X3, how much should Wynn report as income from the investment?
a. $4,500.
b. $9,000.
c. $12,000.
d. $13,500.

2. On January 2, 19X3, Ben Company purchased 40 percent of the outstanding stock of Clarke Company for $1,000. On that date, Clarke's net assets were $2,000, and Ben cannot attribute the excess of the cost of its investment in Clarke over its equity in Clarke's net assets to any particular factor.

   Clarke's 19X3 net income is $250. Ben plans to retain its investment in Clarke indefinitely. Ben accounts for its investment in Clarke by the equity method. The maximum amount that could be included in Ben's 19X3 income before taxes to reflect Ben's "equity in net income of Clarke" is:
a. $95.
b. $100.
c. $200.
d. $245.

3. Investor, Inc., owns 40 percent of Alimand Corporation. During the calendar year 19X5, Alimand had net earnings of $100,000 and paid dividends of $10,000. Investor mistakenly recorded these transactions using the cost method rather than the equity method of accounting. What effect would this have on the investment account, net earnings, and retained earnings, respectively?
a. Understate, overstate, overstate.
b. Overstate, understate, understate.
c. Overstate, overstate, overstate.
d. Understate, understate, understate.

4. On January 1, 19X5, the Swing Company purchased at book value 100,000 shares (20 percent) of the voting common stock of Harpo Instruments, Inc., for $1,200,000. Direct costs associated with the purchase were $50,000. On December 1, 19X5, the board of directors of Harpo declared a dividend of $2 per share payable to holders of record on December 28, 19X5. The net income of Harpo for the year ended December 31, 19X5, was $1,600,000. What should be the balance in Swing's Investment in Harpo Instruments, Inc., account on December 31, 19X5?
   a. $1,200,000.
   b. $1,250,000.
   c. $1,370,000.
   d. $1,520,000.

5. A corporation using the equity method of accounting for its investment in a 40 per-cent–owned investee, which earned $20,000 and paid $5,000 in dividends, made the following entries:

Investment in Investee	8,000	
Equity in Earnings of Investee		8,000
Cash	2,000	
Dividend Revenue		2,000

What effect will these entries have on the investor's statement of financial position?
   a. Financial position will be fairly stated.
   b. Investment in the investee will be overstated, retained earnings understated.
   c. Investment in the investee will be understated, retained earnings understated.
   d. Investment in the investee will be overstated, retained earnings overstated.

6. Cox Company received dividends from its common stock investments during the year ended December 31, 19X4, as follows:

   • A cash dividend of $5,000 from West Corporation, in which Cox owns a 2 percent interest.
   • A cash dividend of $50,000 from Bell Corporation, in which Cox owns a 30 percent interest. A majority of Cox's directors are also directors of Bell.
   • A stock dividend of 300 shares from Mill Corporation, received on December 10, 19X4, on which date the quoted market value of Mill's shares was $10 per share. Cox owns less than 1 percent of Mill's common stock.

   How much dividend income should Cox report in its 19X4 income statement?
   a. $5,000.
   b. $8,000.
   c. $55,000.
   d. $58,000.

E2-3 Multiple Choice Questions on Marketable Equity Securities [AICPA Adapted]

Select the correct answer for each of the following questions.

1. At December 31, 19X7, Bull Corp. had the following marketable equity securities that were purchased during 19X7, its first year of operations:

	Cost	Market	Unrealized Gain (Loss)
In Current Assets:			
Security A	$ 90,000	$ 60,000	$(30,000)
B	15,000	20,000	5,000
Totals	$105,000	$ 80,000	$(25,000)
In Noncurrent Assets:			
Security Y	$ 70,000	$ 80,000	$ 10,000
Z	90,000	45,000	(45,000)
Totals	$160,000	$125,000	$(35,000)

All market declines are considered temporary.

Valuation allowances at December 31, 19X7, should be established with a corresponding charge against

	Income	Stockholders' Equity
a.	$60,000	$0
b.	$30,000	$45,000
c.	$25,000	$35,000
d.	$25,000	$0

2. During 19X5, Pan Company purchased marketable equity securities as a short-term investment. At December 31, 19X5, the balance in the allowance to reduce marketable equity securities to market was $23,000. There were no security transactions during 19X6. Pertinent information at December 31, 19X6 is as follows:

Security	Cost	Market Value
A	$245,000	$230,000
B	180,000	182,000
	$425,000	$412,000

In its 19X6 income statement, Pan should report a (an)
a. Recovery of unrealized loss of $8,000.
b. Recovery of unrealized loss of $10,000.
c. Unrealized loss of $13,000.
d. Unrealized loss of $15,000.

3. During 19X6, Red Company purchased marketable equity securities as a short-term investment. The cost and market value at December 31, 19X6, were as follows:

Security	Cost	Market Value
A— 100 shares	$ 2,800	$ 3,400
B—1,000 shares	17,000	15,300
C—2,000 shares	31,500	29,500
	$51,300	$48,200

Red sold 1,000 shares of Company B stock on January 31, 19X7, for $15 per share, incurring $1,500 in brokerage commission and taxes. On the sale, Red should report a realized loss of:

a. $300.
b. $1,800.
c. $2,000.
d. $3,500.

4. South Co. has a marketable equity securities portfolio classified as noncurrent. None of the holdings enables South to exercise significant influence over an investee. The aggregate cost exceeds its aggregate market value. The decline is considered temporary and should be reported as a (an):

a. Unrealized loss in the income statement.
b. Realized loss in the income statement.
c. Valuation allowance in the noncurrent liability section of the balance sheet.
d. Valuation allowance in the asset section of the balance sheet.

5. On December 29, 19X9, Bro Co. sold a marketable equity security that had been purchased on January 4, 19X8. Bro owned no other marketable equity security. An unrealized loss was reported in the 19X8 income statement. A realized gain was reported in the 19X9 income statement. Was the marketable equity security classified as a noncurrent asset and did its 19X8 market price decline exceed its 19X9 market price recovery?

	Noncurrent	19X8 Market Price Decline Exceeded 19X9 Market Price Recovery
a.	Yes	Yes
b.	Yes	No
c.	No	Yes
d.	No	No

6. On December 31, 19X6, Wells Company purchased marketable equity securities as a temporary investment. Pertinent data are as follows:

Security	Cost	Market Value at 12/31/X7
A	$39,000	$36,000
B	50,000	55,000
C	96,000	85,000

On December 31, 19X7, Wells reclassified its investment in security C from current to noncurrent because Wells intends to retain security C as a long-term investment. What total amount of loss on its securities should be included in Wells's income statement for the year ended December 31, 19X7?

a. $0.
b. $9,000.
c. $11,000.
d. $14,000.

E2-4   Cost versus Equity Reporting

Roller Corporation purchased 20 percent ownership of Steam Company on January 1, 19X5, for $70,000. On that date, the book value of net assets reported by Steam Company was $200,000. The excess over book value paid is attributable to depreciable assets with a remaining useful life of 10 years. Net income and dividend payments of Steam Company in the following periods were:

Year	Net Income	Dividends
19X5	$20,000	$ 5,000
19X6	40,000	15,000
19X7	20,000	35,000

Required

Prepare journal entries on the books of Roller Corporation relating to its investment in Steam Company for each of the 3 years, assuming it accounts for the investment using (a) the cost method and (b) the equity method.

E2-5   Cost versus Equity Reporting

Winston Corporation purchased 40 percent of the stock of Fullbright Company on January 1, 19X2, at underlying book value. The companies reported the following operating results and dividend payments during the first 3 years of intercorporate ownership:

	Winston Corporation		Fullbright Company	
Year	Operating Income	Dividends	Net Income	Dividends
19X2	$100,000	$ 40,000	$70,000	$30,000
19X3	60,000	80,000	40,000	60,000
19X4	250,000	120,000	25,000	50,000

Required

Compute the net income reported by Winston Corporation for each of the 3 years, assuming it accounts for its investment in Fullbright Company using (a) the cost method; (b) the equity method.

E2-6   Acquisition Price

Phillips Company bought 40 percent ownership in Jones Bag Company on January 1, 19X1, at underlying book value. In 19X1, 19X2, and 19X3, Jones Bag reported net income of $8,000, $12,000, $20,000, and dividends of $15,000, $10,000, and $10,000, respectively. The balance in the investment account of Phillips Company on December 31, 19X3, was $54,000.

Required

In each of the following independent cases, determine the amount that Phillips Company paid for its investment in Jones Bag stock assuming that Phillips accounted for its investment using the (a) cost method; (b) equity method.

E2-7 Investment Income

Ravine Corporation purchased 30 percent ownership of Valley Industries for $90,000 on January 1, 19X6, when Valley had capital stock of $240,000 and retained earnings of $60,000. The following data were reported by the companies for the years 19X6 through 19X9:

| | | | Dividends Declared | |
Year	Operating Income, Ravine Corporation	Net Income, Valley Industries	Ravine	Valley
19X6	$140,000	$30,000	$ 70,000	$20,000
19X7	80,000	50,000	70,000	40,000
19X8	220,000	10,000	90,000	40,000
19X9	160,000	40,000	100,000	20,000

Required

a. What net income would have been reported by Ravine Corporation for each of the years, assuming Ravine accounts for the intercorporate investment using (1) the cost method; (2) the equity method?

b. Give all appropriate journal entries for 19X8 made by Ravine Corporation under both the cost and the equity methods.

E2-8 Purchase Differential Assigned to Goodwill

Mastercraft Corporation issued 5,000 shares of its $10 par value stock to acquire 25 percent of the stock of Debt Company on January 1, 19X5. Debt Company net assets had a book value and fair value of $400,000 on that date. The market price of the Mastercraft Corporation shares issued was $160,000. Debt Company reported net income of $35,000 and dividends of $15,000 in 19X5 and a net loss of $20,000 and dividends of $10,000 in 19X6. Any goodwill is to be amortized over the maximum period allowable under generally accepted accounting principles.

Required

Assuming Mastercraft Corporation uses the equity method in accounting for its investment in Debt Company, prepare all journal entries for Mastercraft Corporation for 19X5 and 19X6 that relate to its investment.

E2-9 Purchase Differential Attributable to Depreciable Assets

Capital Corporation purchased 40 percent of the stock of Cook Company on January 1, 19X4, for $136,000. On that date Cook Company reported net assets of $300,000 valued at historical cost and $340,000 stated at fair value. The difference was due to the increased value of buildings with a remaining life of 10 years. During 19X4 and 19X5 Cook Company reported net income of $10,000 and $20,000 and paid dividends of $6,000 and $9,000, respectively.

Required

Assuming Capital Corporation uses (a) the equity method and (b) the cost method in accounting for its ownership of Cook Company, give the journal entries recorded by Capital Corporation in 19X4 and 19X5.

E2-10 Computation of Investment Income

On January 1, 19X7, Soda Corporation purchases 30 percent of the voting common stock of Ace Moving Company for $100,000. On that date Ace Moving Company has assets with a book value of $200,000 and a fair market value of $300,000. Half the increase in fair value is attributable to land, and half to buildings and equipment. The remaining economic life of all depreciable assets is 5 years, and all intangible assets have a remaining life of 10 years.

Required

Assuming that Soda uses the equity method in accounting for its investment in Ace Moving and that Ace Moving reports net income of $80,000 for 19X7 and pays dividends of $10,000, what amount of investment income is reported by Soda Corporation for 19X7?

E2-11 Computation of Purchase Price

Flynn Corporation purchased 40 percent of the common stock of Riverview Company on January 1, 19X5, and paid $10,000 above book value. The full amount of the additional payment is attributed to goodwill with a life of 5 years. During 19X5 and 19X6, Riverview reported net income of $55,000 and $10,000 and paid dividends of $20,000 and $25,000, respectively. Flynn Corporation uses the equity method in accounting for its investment in Riverview and reports a balance in its investment account on December 31, 19X6, of $176,000.

Required

Compute the amount paid by Flynn Corporation to purchase the shares of Riverview Company.

E2-12 Computation of Purchase Price

Scott Company purchased 30 percent of the ownership of Earnest Enterprises on January 1, 19X2, at underlying book value. In 19X2 Earnest Enterprises reported net income of $60,000 and paid dividends of $15,000, and in 19X3 reported a loss of $40,000 and paid dividends of $35,000. Scott Company uses the equity method in accounting for its investment in Earnest Enterprises and reports a balance in its investment account of $135,000 on December 31, 19X3.

Required

Compute the amount paid by Scott Company to purchase the shares of Earnest Enterprises.

E2-13 Correction of Error

During review of the adjusting entries to be recorded on December 31, 19X8, Grand Corporation discovered that it had inappropriately been using the cost method in accounting for its investment in Case Products Corporation. Grand Corporation purchased 40 percent ownership of Case Products on January 1, 19X6, for $56,000, at which time Case Products reported retained earnings of $60,000 and capital stock outstanding of $40,000. The purchase differential was attributable to goodwill with a life of 8 years. Income and dividends of Case Products were:

Year	Net Income	Dividends
19X6	$40,000	$15,000
19X7	60,000	20,000
19X8	80,000	20,000

Required

Give the correcting entry required on December 31, 19X8, to properly report the investment under the equity method assuming the books have not been closed. Case Products dividends were declared in early November and paid in early December each year.

E2-14 Purchase Differential Assigned to Land and Equipment

Rod Corporation purchased 30 percent ownership of Stafford Corporation on January 1, 19X4, for $65,000, which was $10,000 above the underlying book value. Half the additional amount was attributable to an increase in the value of land held by Stafford Corporation, and half was due to an increase in the value of equipment. The equipment had a remaining economic life of 5 years on January 1, 19X4. During 19X4, Stafford Corporation reported net income of $40,000 and paid dividends of $15,000.

Required

Give the journal entries recorded by Rod Corporation during 19X4 related to its investment in Stafford Corporation, assuming Rod Corporation uses the equity method in accounting for its investment.

E2-15 Equity-Method Computations [AICPA Adapted]

The North Company has supplied you with information regarding two investments that were made during 19X5, as follows:

On January 1, 19X5, North purchased for cash 40 percent of the 500,000 shares of voting common stock of the York Company for $2,400,000, representing 40 percent of the net worth of York. York's net income for the year ended December 31, 19X5, was $750,000. York paid dividends of $.50 per share in 19X5. The market value of York's common stock was $14 per share on December 31, 19X5. North exercised significant influence over the operating and financial policies of York.

On July 1, 19X5, North purchased for cash 15,000 shares, representing 5 percent of the voting common stock of the Minor Company for $450,000. Minor's net income for the

6 months ended December 31, 19X5, was $350,000 and for the year ended December 31, 19X5, was $600,000. Minor paid dividends of $.30 per share each quarter during 19X5 to stockholders of record on the last day of each quarter. The market value of Minor's common stock was $32 per share on January 1, 19X5, and $34 per share on December 31, 19X5.

Required

a. As a result of these two investments, what should be the balance in the Investments account for North on December 31, 19X5? Show supporting computations in good form.

b. As a result of these two investments, what should be the income reported by North for the year ended December 31, 19X5? Show supporting computations in good form.

E2-16* Income Reporting

Grandview Company purchased 40 percent of the stock of Spinet Corporation on January 1, 19X8, at underlying book value. Spinet recorded the following income for 19X9:

Income before Extraordinary Gain	$60,000
Extraordinary Gain on Bond Retirement	30,000
Net Income	$90,000

Required

Prepare all journal entries on Grandview's books for 19X9 to account for its investment in Spinet.

E2-17* Investee Preferred Stock

Best Corporation purchased 40 percent ownership of Page Company common stock at underlying book value of $180,000 on January 1, 19X3. The balance sheet of Page Company contained the following summarized data:

Net Assets	$750,000	Preferred Stock	$300,000
		Common Stock	200,000
		Retained Earnings	250,000
	$750,000		$750,000

The preferred stock is $10 par value cumulative preferred with an 8 percent stated dividend rate. At the end of 19X3, Page reported net income of $60,000 and paid dividends of $40,000 for the year.

Required

Give the journal entries recorded on Best Corporation's books for 19X3 related to its investment in Page.

E2-18*   Investment Acquired in a Pooling of Interests

On January 2, 19X9, Cristol Corporation acquired 95 percent of the common stock of Glenco, Inc., in a business combination treated as a pooling of interests. At the date of combination, Glenco had common stock outstanding with a total par value of $400,000, additional paid-in capital of $500,000, and retained earnings of $140,000. Cristol issued 82,000 shares of its $5 par common stock in the combination; the stock had a total market value of $1,200,000 at the date of combination. All the excess of the fair value of the stock issued over the book value of the shares acquired was attributable to goodwill with an estimated life of 10 years.

Glenco continued operating as a separate corporation subsequent to the combination. During 19X9, Glenco reported net income of $68,000 and paid dividends of $20,000.

Required

Present all journal entries that would appear on the books of Cristol Corporation during 19X9 with respect to its investment in Glenco, assuming Cristol accounts for its investment in Glenco using (a) the equity method; (b) the cost method.

E2-19*   Deferred Income Taxes

Denbow Corporation reported a deferred tax liability of $37,800 in its balance sheet dated December 31, 19X1. Denbow's only temporary difference resulted from its use of the equity method to report its 25 percent investment in Crabapple Industries, acquired at underlying book value on December 31, 19X0. During 19X1, Denbow received a dividend of $25,000 from Crabapple, the first dividend ever paid by the company. The dividend qualified for the 80 percent dividend deduction. Denbow's effective tax rate is 45 percent.

Required

Compute Crabapple's net income for 19X1.

PROBLEMS

P2-20   Multiple-Choice Questions on Applying Equity Method [AICPA Adapted]

Select the correct answer for each of the following questions.

1. On July 1, 19X3, Barker Company purchased 20 percent of the outstanding common stock of Acme Company for $400,000 when the fair value of Acme's net assets was $2,000,000. Barker does not have the ability to exercise significant influence over the operating and financial policies of Acme. The following data concerning Acme are available for 19X3:

	Twelve Months Ended December 31, 19X3	Six Months Ended December 31, 19X3
Net income	$300,000	$160,000
Dividends declared and paid	190,000	100,000

In its income statement for the year ended December 31, 19X3, how much income should Barker report from this investment?

a. $20,000.
b. $32,000.
c. $38,000.
d. $60,000.

2. On January 1, 19X3, Miller Company purchased 25 percent of Wall Corporation's common stock; no goodwill resulted from the purchase. Miller appropriately carries this investment at equity, and the balance in Miller's investment account was $190,000 on December 31, 19X3. Wall reported net income of $120,000 for the year ended December 31, 19X3, and paid dividends on its common stock totaling $48,000 during 19X3. How much did Miller pay for its 25 percent interest in Wall?

a. $172,000.
b. $202,000.
c. $208,000.
d. $232,000.

190,000

120,000 X.2
48,000 X.2

3. On January 1, 19X7, the Robohn Company purchased for cash 40 percent of the 300,000 shares of voting common stock of the Lowell Company for $1,800,000 when 40 percent of the underlying equity in the net assets of Lowell was $1,400,000. Robohn amortizes goodwill over a 40-year period with a full year's amortization taken in the year of purchase. The amortization is not deductible for income tax reporting. As a result of this transaction, Robohn has the ability to exercise significant influence over the operating and financial policies of Lowell. Lowell's net income for the year ended December 31, 19X7, was $600,000. During 19X7, Lowell paid $325,000 in dividends to its shareholders. The income reported by Robohn for its investment in Lowell should be:

a. $120,000.
b. $130,000.
c. $230,000.
d. $240,000.

4. On January 1, 19X0, Rey Corporation paid $150,000 for 10,000 shares of Rio Corporation's common stock, representing a 15 percent investment in Rio. Rio declared and paid a dividend of $1 per share to its common stockholders during 19X0. Rio's net income was $130,000 for the year ended December 31, 19X0. At what amount should Rey's investment in Rio appear on Rey's balance sheet as of December 31, 19X0? *original cost*

a. $140,000.
b. $150,000.
c. $159,500.
d. $169,500.

4 hg div. subtract out

5. In January 19X0, Farley Corporation acquired 20 percent of the outstanding common stock of Davis Company for $800,000. This investment gave Farley the ability to exercise significant influence over Davis. The book value of the acquired shares was $600,000. The excess of cost over book value was attributed to an identifiable intangible asset which was undervalued on Davis's balance sheet and which had a remaining economic life of 10 years. For the year ended December 31, 19X0, Davis reported net

income of $180,000 and paid cash dividends of $40,000 on its common stock. What is the proper carrying value of Farley's investment in Davis on December 31, 19X0?

a. $772,000.
b. $780,000.
c. $800,000.
d. $808,000.

P2-21 Cost versus Equity Reporting

Dagger Company purchased 25 percent of the voting common stock of Lurch Corporation on July 1, 19X6, at $10,000 over underlying book value. The excess all relates to goodwill with a remaining life of 10 years. Both companies report on a calendar-year basis and pay dividends at the end of the year. All income is earned evenly throughout the year. The following income and dividend information is provided by the companies at the end of 19X9:

| | | | Dividends Paid | |
Year	Operating Income, Dagger Company	Net Income, Lurch Corporation	Dagger Company	Lurch Corporation
19X6	$50,000	$10,000	$20,000	$ 4,000
19X7	50,000	30,000	10,000	20,000
19X8	50,000	22,000	20,000	30,000
19X9	50,000	40,000	10,000	20,000

Required

Compute net income for Dagger Company for each of the years using (a) the cost method and (b) the equity method.

P2-22 Assignment of Purchase Differential

Excell Corporation purchased 30 percent of the common stock of Glendale Company on January 1, 19X5, by issuing preferred stock with a par value of $50,000 and a market price of $120,000. The following amounts relate to the balance sheet items of Glendale Company at that date:

	Book Value	Fair Value
Cash and Receivables	$200,000	$200,000
Buildings and Equipment	400,000	360,000
Less: Accumulated Depreciation	(100,000)	
	$500,000	
Accounts Payable	$ 50,000	50,000
Bonds Payable	200,000	200,000
Common Stock	100,000	
Retained Earnings	150,000	
	$500,000	

20-5=15yrs·

Buildings and equipment were purchased by Glendale Company on January 1, 19X0, with an expected economic life of 20 years. No change in overall expected economic life occurred as a result of the acquisition of stock by Excell Corporation. During 19X5, Glendale Company reported net income of $40,000 and paid dividends of $10,000. Goodwill is to be amortized over a 40-year period.

Required

Give all journal entries to be recorded on the books of Excell Corporation during 19X5, assuming it uses the equity method in accounting for its ownership of Glendale Company.

P2-23 Computation of Account Balances

Easy Chair Company purchased 40 percent ownership of Stuffy Sofa Corporation on January 1, 19X1, for $150,000. The balance sheet of Stuffy Sofa Corporation at the time of acquisition was as follows:

Stuffy Sofa Corporation
Balance Sheet
January 1, 19X1

Cash		$ 30,000	Current Liabilities	$ 40,000
Accounts Receivable		120,000	Bonds Payable	200,000
Inventory		80,000	Common Stock	200,000
Land		150,000	Additional	
Buildings and Equipment	$300,000		Paid-In Capital	40,000
Less: Accumulated			Retained Earnings	80,000
Depreciation	(120,000)	180,000		
		$560,000		$560,000

During 19X1 Stuffy Sofa Corporation reported net income of $30,000 and paid dividends of $9,000. The fair values of Stuffy Sofa's assets and liabilities were equal to their book values at the date of acquisition, with the exception of buildings and equipment, which had a fair value $35,000 above book. All buildings and equipment had remaining lives of 5 years at the time of the business combination, and all intangible assets had remaining lives of 10 years.

Required

   a. What amount of investment income will Easy Chair Company record during 19X1 under equity-method accounting?
   b. What amount of income will be reported under the cost method?
   c. What will be the balance in the investment account on December 31, 19X1, under (1) cost-method and (2) equity-method accounting?

P2-24 Retroactive Recognition

Idle Corporation has been acquiring shares of Fast Track Enterprises at book value for the last several years. Data provided by Fast Track Enterprises included the following:

	19X2	**19X3**	**19X4**	**19X5**
Net Income	$40,000	$60,000	$40,000	$50,000
Dividends	20,000	20,000	10,000	20,000

Fast Track Enterprises declares and pays its annual dividend on November 15 each year. Its net book value on January 1, 19X2, was $250,000. Idle Corporation purchased shares of Fast Track Enterprises on three occasions:

January 1, 19X2	Purchased 10 percent ownership for $25,000
July 1, 19X3	Purchased 5 percent ownership for $15,000
January 1, 19X5	Purchased 10 percent ownership for $34,000

Required

Give the journal entries to be recorded on the books of Idle Corporation in 19X5 related to its investment in Fast Track Enterprises.

P2-25 Complex Differential Assignment

Northbay Company issued common shares with a par value of $45,000 and a market value of $200,000 in exchange for 35 percent ownership of Offshore Development Corporation on January 1, 19X4. Offshore reported the following balances on that date:

Offshore Development Corporation
Balance Sheet
January 1, 19X4

	Book Value	Fair Value
Assets		
Cash	$ 40,000	$ 40,000
Accounts Receivable	80,000	80,000
Inventory (fifo basis)	120,000	150,000
Land	50,000	65,000
Buildings and Equipment	500,000	
Less: Accumulated Depreciation	(240,000)	320,000
Patent		25,000
	$550,000	
Liabilities and Equities		
Accounts Payable	$ 30,000	30,000
Bonds Payable	100,000	100,000
Common Stock	150,000	
Additional Paid-In Capital	20,000	
Retained Earnings	250,000	
	$550,000	

The estimated economic life of the patents held by Offshore Development is 5 years. The buildings and equipment are expected to last 15 more years on average, and all intangibles other than patents are expected to have 10-year lives. Offshore Development paid dividends of $9,000 during 19X4 and reported net income of $60,000 for the year.

Required

Compute the amount of investment income (loss) reported by Northbay from its investment in Offshore Development Corporation for 19X4 and the balance in the investment account on December 31, 19X4, assuming the equity method is used in accounting for the investment.

P2-26 Equity Entries with Differential

On January 1, 19X0, Hunter Corporation issued 6,000 of its $10 par value shares to acquire 45 percent of the shares of Arrow Manufacturing. The balance sheet of Arrow Manufacturing immediately before the acquisition contained the following items:

Arrow Manufacturing
Balance Sheet
January 1, 19X0

	Book Value	Fair Value
Assets		
Cash and Receivables	$ 30,000	$ 30,000
Land	70,000	80,000
Buildings and Equipment (net)	120,000	150,000
Patent	80,000	80,000
	$300,000	
Liabilities and Equities		
Accounts Payable	$ 90,000	90,000
Common Stock	150,000	
Retained Earnings	60,000	
	$300,000	

On the date of the business combination, Hunter Corporation shares were selling at $35, and the buildings and equipment of Arrow Manufacturing had a remaining economic life of 10 years. The expected economic life of all intangible assets was 5 years. The combination was recorded as a purchase.

In the 2 years following the business combination, Arrow Manufacturing reported net income of $80,000 and $60,000 and paid dividends of $20,000 and $30,000, respectively. Hunter Corporation used the equity method in accounting for its ownership of Arrow Manufacturing.

Required

    a. Give the entry recorded by Hunter Corporation at the time of acquisition.

    b. Give the journal entries recorded by Hunter during 19X0 and 19X1 related to its investment in Arrow Manufacturing.

    c. What balance will be reported in the investment account of Hunter on December 31, 19X1?

P2-27 Multilevel Ownership

Balance sheet data on January 1, 19X2, for Upper Manufacturing Company (Upco), Middle Distributors, Inc. (Midco), and LoCal Cola Corporation (Loco) and income data for 19X2 were as follows:

	Company		
Balance Sheet Item	**Upco**	**Midco**	**Loco**
Cash and Receivables	$ 80,000	$100,000	$ 10,000
Inventory	150,000	40,000	20,000
Land	70,000	20,000	5,000
Buildings and Equipment (net)	450,000	230,000	65,000
Total Assets	$750,000	$390,000	$100,000
Accounts Payable	$ 50,000	$ 90,000	$ 30,000
Common Stock	200,000	100,000	40,000
Additional Paid-In Capital	100,000		10,000
Retained Earnings	400,000	200,000	20,000
Total Liabilities and Equity	$750,000	$390,000	$100,000
19X2 Net Income			$ 15,000
Income from Operations	$100,000	$ 50,000	
Dividends Declared and Paid	30,000	20,000	5,000

On January 1, 19X2, Midco purchased 40 percent ownership of Loco for $28,000 in cash and payables. On January 2, 19X2, Upco issued 5,000 shares of $20 par value preferred stock with a market value of $160,000 in exchange for 30 percent of the voting shares of Midco. On January 1, 19X2, the book values of Midco's net assets were equal to their fair values except for buildings and equipment, which had fair values of $100,000 greater than their book values. The depreciable assets of each company had 5 years of economic life remaining on January 1, 19X2. Goodwill is assumed to have an expected life of 40 years.

Required

    a. Compute the net income reported by Upco for 19X2, assuming the equity method is used by Midco and Upco in accounting for their intercorporate investments.

    b. Give all journal entries recorded by Upco related to its investment in Midco during 19X2.

P2-28 Correction of Recording Error

Flower Company paid $200,000 to acquire 40 percent ownership of Bronze Casting Company on January 1, 19X2. Net book value of Bronze Casting's assets on that date was $300,000. Book values and fair values of net assets held by Bronze Casting were the same, except for equipment, which had a book value of $70,000 and fair value of $120,000. The remaining economic life of all depreciable assets held by Bronze Casting was 5 years, and the life of intangible assets was 20 years.

Net income and dividends of Bronze Casting Company for the 3 years immediately following the purchase of shares were:

Year	Net Income	Dividends
19X2	$40,000	$15,000
19X3	60,000	20,000
19X4	70,000	25,000

The computation of Flower's investment income for 19X4 and entries in its investment account since the date of purchase were as follows:

19X4 Investment Income

Pro rata income accrual ($70,000 × .40)		$28,000
Amortize goodwill ($80,000 ÷ 20 years)	$4,000	
Dividends received ($25,000 × .40)		10,000
19X4 Investment income		$34,000

Investment in Bronze Casting

1/1/X2 Purchase price	$200,000	
19X2 Income accrual	16,000	
Amortize goodwill		$4,000
19X3 Income accrual	24,000	
Amortize goodwill		4,000
19X4 Income accrual	28,000	
Amortize goodwill		4,000
12/31/X4 Balance	$256,000	

Before making closing entries at the end of 19X4, the new controller of Flower Company reviewed the reports and was convinced that the balance in the investment account and investment income reported by Flower Company for 19X4 were in error.

Required

Prepare a correcting entry, along with supporting computations, to properly state the balance in the investment account and all related account balances at the end of 19X4.

P2-29 Correction of Improper Recording Method

On December 31, 19X5, Bailey Company held 35 percent of the common stock of Smart Corporation. The stock had been acquired in several blocks, with 5 percent of Smart's stock purchased on December 31, 19X1; another 20 percent purchased on January 2, 19X4; and 10 percent purchased on January 2, 19X5. All purchases of Smart's stock were at underlying book value except one; the January 2, 19X4, purchase was made at $30,000 over book value, with all of the excess attributable to an office building owned by Smart having a remaining life of 15 years.

Bailey has always used the cost method to account for its investment in Smart, even though Bailey gained significant influence over the financial and operating policies of Smart at the time of its stock purchase on January 2, 19X4. During the time Bailey has held Smart's stock, it has recognized the following dividend income from Smart:

19X2	19X3	19X4	19X5
$2,000	$2,250	$12,500	$21,000

For the years 19X2 through 19X5, Smart reported net income figures of $70,000, $80,000, $85,000, and $75,000, respectively. Bailey's recording error was discovered during its audit at the end of 19X5, after normal adjusting entries had been made but before the books had been closed.

Required

Present the appropriate correcting entry to be made at December 31, 19X5, relating to Bailey's investment in Smart Corporation.

P2-30 Marketable Equity Securities [AICPA Adapted]

At December 31, 19X2, Windsail Corp. properly reported as current assets the following marketable equity securities:

Dea Corp., 1,000 shares, $2.40 convertible preferred stock	$ 40,000
Sha, Inc., 6,000 shares of common stock	60,000
Fey Co., 2,000 shares of common stock	55,000
Marketable equity securities at cost	$155,000
Less: Valuation allowance	(7,000)
Marketable equity securities	$148,000

On January 2, 19X3, Windsail purchased 100,000 shares of Edie Corp. common stock for $1,700,000, representing 30 percent of Edie's outstanding common stock and an underlying equity of $1,400,000 in Edie's net assets at January 2. Windsail, which had no other financial transactions with Edie during 19X3, amortizes goodwill over a 40-year period. As a result of Windsail's 30 percent ownership of Edie, Windsail has the ability to exercise significant influence over Edie's financial and operating policies.

During 19X3, Windsail disposed of the following securities:

- January 18—sold 2,500 shares of Sha for $13 per share.
- June 1—sold 500 shares of Fey, after a 10 percent stock dividend, for $21 per share.
- October 1—converted 500 shares of Dea's preferred stock into 1,500 shares of Dea's common stock, when the market price was $60 per share for the preferred stock and $21 per share for the common stock.

The following 19X3 dividend information pertains to the stock held by Windsail:

- February 14—Fey issued a 10 percent stock dividend, when the market price of Fey's common stock was $22 per share.
- April 5 and October 5—Dea paid dividends of $1.20 per share on its $2.40 preferred stock, to stockholders of record on March 9 and September 9, respectively. Dea did not pay any dividends on its common stock during 19X3.
- June 30—Sha paid a $1.00 per share dividend on its common stock.
- March 1, June 1, September 1, and December 1—Edie paid quarterly dividends of $.50 per share on each of these dates. Edie's net income for the year ended December 31, 19X3, was $1,200,000.

At December 31, 19X3, Windsail's management intended to hold the Edie stock as a long-term investment, with the remaining investments being considered as temporary. Market prices per share of the marketable equity securities were as follows:

	At December 31,	
	19X3	**19X2**
Dea Corp. Preferred	$56	$42
Dea Corp. Common	20	18
Sha, Inc. Common	11	11
Fey Co. Common	22	20
Edie Corp. Common	16	18

All of the foregoing stocks are listed on major stock exchanges. Declines in market value from cost would not be considered as permanent declines.

Required

    a. Prepare a schedule of Windsail's current marketable equity securities at December 31, 19X3, including any information necessary to determine the related valuation allowance and unrealized gross gains and losses.

    b. Prepare a schedule to show the carrying amount of Windsail's noncurrent marketable equity securities at December 31, 19X3.

    c. Prepare a schedule showing all income, gains, and losses (realized and unrealized) relating to Windsail's investments, for the year ended December 31, 19X3.

P2-31* Equity-Method Income Statement

    Wealthy Manufacturing Company purchased 40 percent of the voting shares of Diversified Products Corporation on March 23, 19X4. On December 31, 19X8, the controller of Wealthy Manufacturing Company attempted to prepare income statements and retained earnings statements for the two companies using the following summarized data:

	Wealthy Manufacturing	Diversified Products
Net Sales	$850,000	$400,000
Cost of Goods Sold	670,000	320,000
Other Expenses	90,000	25,000
Dividends Paid	30,000	10,000
Retained Earnings, 12/31/X7	420,000	260,000

Wealthy Manufacturing Company uses the equity method in accounting for its investment in Diversified Products. The controller was also aware of the following specific transactions for Diversified Products in 19X8, which were not included in the preceding data:

1. On June 30, 19X8, Diversified paid $98,500 to repurchase and retire bonds with a book value of $103,500.

2. Diversified sold its entire Health Technologies division on September 30, 19X8, for $375,000. The book value of Health Technologies division's net assets on that date was $331,000. The division incurred an operating loss of $15,000 in the first 9 months of 19X8.

3. On January 1, 19X8, Diversified switched from first-in, first-out inventory costing to the weighted-average method. Had Diversified always used the weighted-average method, prior years' income would have been lower by $20,000.

4. During 19X8, Diversified sold one of its delivery trucks after it was involved in an accident and recorded a gain of $10,000.

Required

a. Prepare an income statement and retained earnings statement for Diversified Products Corporation for 19X8.

b. Prepare an income statement and retained earnings statement for Wealthy Manufacturing Company for 19X8.

P2-32*   Equity-Method Accounts [AICPA Adapted]

Hawkeye Systems, Inc., a chemical processing company, has been operating profitably for many years. On March 1, 19X4, Hawkeye purchased 50,000 shares of Diversified Insurance Company stock for $2,000,000. The 50,000 shares represented 25 percent of Diversified's outstanding stock. Both Hawkeye and Diversified operate on a fiscal year ending August 31.

For the fiscal year ended August 31, 19X4, Diversified reported net income of $800,000 earned uniformly throughout the year. During November 19X3 and February, May, and August 19X4, Diversified paid its regular quarterly cash dividend of $100,000.

Required

Assume that the investment should be classified as a long-term investment in the noncurrent assets section of Hawkeye's balance sheet. The cost of Hawkeye's investment equaled its equity in the recorded values of Diversified's net assets; recorded values were not materially different from fair values (individually or collectively). For the fiscal year ended August 31, 19X4, how did the net income reported and dividends paid by Diversified affect the accounts of Hawkeye (including Hawkeye's income tax accounts)? Indicate each account affected, state whether it increased or decreased, and explain the reason for the change in the account balance (such as Cash, Investment in Diversified, etc.). Organize your answer in the following format:

Account Name	Increase or Decrease	Reason for Change in Account Balance

P2-33* Computing Income Tax Expense

Swan Products, Inc. owns 25 percent of the common stock of Computech Computer Company, purchased December 28, 19X3, at book value. During the 3 years subsequent to the acquisition of its stock by Swan Products, Computech reported the following net income and dividends:

	19X4	19X5	19X6
Net Income	$20,000	$ 8,000	$40,000
Dividends	4,000	10,000	12,000

Swan Products has an effective income tax rate of 40 percent. All dividends received by Swan Products from Computech qualify for the 80 percent dividend deduction.

Required

a. Compute the amount of income tax expense that Swan Products should have reported in its income statement for each of the 3 years with respect to its investment in Computech assuming it reports its investment using (1) the cost method; (2) the equity method.

b. Present all journal entries related to its investment in Computech, including income tax effects, that should have been recorded by Swan Products for each of the 3 years, assuming Swan Products accounts for its investment using the cost method.

c. Present all journal entries related to its investment in Computech, including income tax effects, that should have been recorded by Swan Products for each of the 3 years, assuming Swan Products accounts for its investment using the equity method.

CHAPTER 3

THE REPORTING ENTITY AND CONSOLIDATED FINANCIAL STATEMENTS

Today, nearly all major corporations prepare consolidated financial statements. While people often think of the world's corporate giants as being single companies, closer examination reveals that each actually is composed of a number of separate companies. For example, General Motors Corp. and Ford Motor Company both own hundreds of other companies. Sears, Roebuck and Company consists of one company that owns all or most of the stock of more than 200 other companies, including Sears Roebuck Acceptance Corporation, the Allstate Insurance Group (consisting of many companies), the Coldwell Banker Real Estate Group (consisting of many companies), the Dean Witter Financial Services Group (consisting of many companies), and numerous other companies. Paramount Communications, Inc., (formerly Gulf and Western Industries, Inc.) owns hundreds of other companies, including Famous Players Ltd., Madison Square Garden Corporation, Simon and Schuster, Inc., and Paramount Pictures Corporation. General Motors, Ford, Sears, and Paramount Communications each present consolidated financial statements to the public, as do most corporations that are publicly held.

Consolidated financial statements present the financial position and results of operations for a group of companies, consisting of a parent and one or more subsidiaries, as if the individual companies actually were a single company. The *parent company* is one that owns more than 50 percent of another company's outstanding common stock, the other company being referred to as a *subsidiary*. A parent and subsidiary are considered *related companies* by virtue of the parent's ownership of the subsidiary's stock.

When two or more related companies are viewed as constituting a single economic entity, consolidated financial statements generally are considered to be more useful than the separate financial statements of the individual companies. The accounting principles applied in the preparation of consolidated financial statements are the same accounting principles applied in preparing separate-company financial statements. The process of preparing consolidated financial statements involves bringing together the separate financial statements of related companies to reflect the activities and financial position as if the related companies were actually a single company.

Consolidated financial statements are prepared when there are two or more legally separate but related companies that form a single *economic entity*. Any business combination, whether treated as a purchase or a pooling of interests, results in one of two situations: either (1) the net assets of one or both of the combining companies are transferred to a single company (a merger or statutory consolidation), or (2) the combining companies each remain as *separate legal entities* (a stock acquisition).

In the first case, no consolidation questions arise because only a single corporation emerges from the business combination. The financial statements of the resulting reporting entity are those of a single corporation. The matter of consolidated financial statements arises in the second instance because of the existence of two or more legally separate but related companies. Each individual company maintains its own accounting records, but consolidated statements present the companies together as a single economic entity.

USEFULNESS OF CONSOLIDATED FINANCIAL STATEMENTS

Accounting Research Bulletin No. 51, "Consolidated Financial Statements" (ARB 51), states:[1]

> The purpose of consolidated statements is to present, primarily for the benefit of the shareholders and creditors of the parent company, the results of operations and the financial position of a parent company and its subsidiaries essentially as if the group were a single company with one or more branches or divisions.

Consolidated financial statements often represent the only means of obtaining a clear picture of the total resources of the combined entity that are under the control of the parent company. In fact, when the number of related companies is substantial, there may be no other way of conveniently summarizing the vast amount of information relating to the individual companies. Even when only a few related companies are involved, consolidated statements often provide the best means of presenting information regarding the activities and resources of the overall economic entity.

Long-Term Investors

Consolidated financial statements are most useful to those with a long-run interest in the parent company. Current and prospective stockholders of the parent

---

[1] *Accounting Research Bulletin No. 51*, "Consolidated Financial Statements," August 1959, par. 1.

company generally have the greatest interest in the consolidated entity. Ultimately, the well-being of the parent company is affected by the operations of its subsidiaries. If the subsidiaries are profitable, profits accrue to the parent. On the other hand, the parent cannot avoid feeling the ill effects of unprofitable subsidiaries. By examining the consolidated statements, owners and potential owners are better able to assess the efficiency with which management employs all the resources under its control.

Long-term creditors of the parent company also are concerned with the effects of subsidiary operations on the parent when evaluating the overall health and profitability of the parent company. While the parent and subsidiaries are separate companies, the creditors have an indirect claim on the subsidiaries through the parent's investments. Both the stockholders and the long-term creditors of the parent, as well as others with a continuing interest in the parent, often need to look beyond the parent to the entire group of related companies.

Short-term creditors of the parent company may be more interested in the parent's separate financial statements than in the consolidated financial statements. While the short-term creditors do have an indirect claim on the parent's subsidiaries, these creditors tend to be more concerned with the immediate solvency of the borrower rather than with its long-run profitability. They may find consolidated statements useful, but often are most interested in the parent's separate balance sheet.

Parent Company Management

Management of the parent company has a continuing need for current information both about the combined operations of the consolidated entity and about the individual companies forming the consolidated entity. For example, individual subsidiaries might have substantial volatility in their operations, and not until operating results and balance sheets are combined can the manager be aware of the overall impact of the activities for the period. On the other hand, information about individual companies within the consolidated entity may allow a manager to offset a cash shortfall in one subsidiary with excess cash from another without resorting to costly outside borrowing.

The management of the parent company must be particularly concerned with the consolidated statements because top management generally is evaluated by shareholders, financial analysts, and others outside the company on the basis of the overall performance reflected in the consolidated statements. Also, performance of the overall entity often serves as a basis for executive compensation agreements.

Other Interested Parties

While financial analysts tend to focus on the performance of the overall entity, they often seek information on individual segments to better assess how the entity as a whole will fare under different economic conditions.

Regulatory agencies also are interested in consolidated data. Public utilities commissions often consider consolidated data in deciding on rate requests. Agencies entrusted with enforcement of antitrust or similar types of laws may gather valuable information on the extent of related operations by examining consolidated financial statements. Taxing authorities may be able to gather information on earnings retention or other aspects of operations from the consolidated financial statements.

LIMITATIONS OF CONSOLIDATED FINANCIAL STATEMENTS

While consolidated financial statements are extremely useful, their limitations also must be kept in mind. Some information is lost any time data sets are aggregated; this is particularly true when the information involves an aggregation across companies that have substantially different operating characteristics.

Some of the more important limitations of consolidated financial statements are as follows:

1. Because the operating results and financial position of individual companies included in the consolidation are not disclosed, a poor performance or position of one or more companies may be hidden by the good performance and position of others.

2. Not all the consolidated retained earnings balance is necessarily available for dividends of the parent because a portion may represent the parent's share of undistributed subsidiary earnings. Similarly, because the consolidated statements include the assets of the subsidiary, not all assets shown are available for dividend distributions of the parent company.

3. Because financial ratios based on the consolidated statements are calculated on aggregated information, they are not necessarily representative of any single company in the consolidation, including the parent.

4. Similar accounts of different companies that are combined in the consolidation may not be entirely comparable. For example, the length of operating cycles of different companies may vary, causing receivables of similar length to be classified differently.

5. Additional information about individual companies or groups of companies included in the consolidation often is necessary for a fair presentation; such additional disclosures may require voluminous footnotes.

SUBSIDIARY FINANCIAL STATEMENTS

Some financial statement users may be interested in the separate financial statements of individual subsidiaries, either instead of or in addition to consolidated financial statements. While the management of the parent company is concerned with the entire consolidated entity as well as individual subsidiaries, creditors, preferred stockholders, and noncontrolling common stockholders of subsidiary companies are most interested in the separate financial statements of the subsidiaries in which they have an interest. Because subsidiaries are legally separate from their parents, the creditors and stockholders of a subsidiary generally have no claim on the parent, nor do the stockholders of the subsidiary share in the profits of the parent. Therefore, consolidated financial statements usually are of little use to those interested in obtaining information about the assets, capital, or income of individual subsidiaries.

THE CONSOLIDATED REPORTING DECISION: CONCEPTS AND STANDARDS

Consolidated financial statements are intended to provide a meaningful representation of the overall position and activities of a single economic entity comprising a number of related companies. Under current accounting standards, several factors must be considered in determining whether the presentation of consolidated financial statements is appropriate:

1. Controlling financial interest
2. Ability to exercise control
3. Permanence of control

Controlling Financial Interest

Consolidation normally is appropriate when one company has a controlling financial interest in another. **ARB 51** states that consolidated statements for a group of companies are:[2]

> . . . usually necessary for a fair presentation when one of the companies in the group directly or indirectly has a controlling financial interest in the other companies.

Current standards provide that the usual condition for a controlling financial interest and, hence, for consolidation is ownership by one company, directly or indirectly, of more than 50 percent of the outstanding voting stock of another company. Majority-owned subsidiaries generally must be consolidated unless the parent is precluded from exercising control or unless control is temporary.[3] When consolidation of a subsidiary is not appropriate, the subsidiary is reported as an intercorporate investment.

Although majority ownership is the most common means of acquiring control, a company may be able to control the operating and financing decisions of another with somewhat less than majority ownership. This might be the case, for example, when the remainder of the stock is widely held or when the majority shareholders formally relinquish their right to vote. In past practice in the United States, companies have not been consolidated unless one company controlled more than

[2] Ibid.
[3] *Financial Accounting Standards Board Statement No. 94*, "Consolidation of All Majority-Owned Subsidiaries," October 1987, par. 13.

50 percent of the other's voting stock. The issue of control currently is under study by the FASB.

The traditional view of control includes both direct and indirect control. *Direct control* occurs when one company owns a majority of another company's common stock. *Indirect control* occurs when a majority of a company's common stock is owned by other companies that are all under common control. Examples of the indirect control of Z Company by P Company include the following ownership situations:

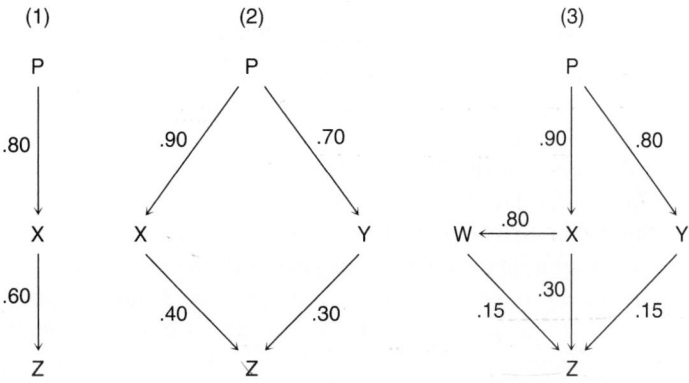

In (1), P owns 80 percent of X, which owns 60 percent of Z.

In (2), P owns 90 percent of X and 70 percent of Y; X owns 40 percent of Z, and Y owns 30 percent of Z.

In (3), P owns 90 percent of X and 80 percent of Y; X owns 80 percent of W and 30 percent of Z; Y owns 15 percent of Z; W owns 15 percent of Z.

In each case, P's control over Z is indirect because it is gained by controlling other companies that control Z.

Ability to Exercise Control

Under certain circumstances, the majority stockholders of a subsidiary may not be able to exercise control even though they hold more than 50 percent of its outstanding voting stock. This might occur, for instance, if the subsidiary was in legal reorganization or in bankruptcy; while the parent might hold majority ownership, control would rest with the courts or a court-appointed trustee. Similarly, if the subsidiary was located in a foreign country and that country had placed restrictions on the subsidiary that prevented the remittance of profits or assets back to the parent company, consolidation of that subsidiary would not be appropriate because of the parent's inability to control important aspects of the subsidiary's operations.

Permanence of Control

If the parent's control of a subsidiary is expected to be temporary, consolidation of that subsidiary is not appropriate. This could occur, for example, when (1) the parent intends to sell a recently acquired investment in a subsidiary in the near future, (2) the political environment of a foreign subsidiary is such that the parent expects to lose control shortly, or (3) an investee's treasury stock transactions cause an investor's stockholdings temporarily to represent a majority of the outstanding common stock.

Differences in Fiscal Periods and Accounting Methods

A difference in the fiscal periods of a parent and subsidiary should not preclude consolidation of that subsidiary. Often the fiscal period of the subsidiary, if different from the parent's, is changed to coincide with that of the parent. Another alternative is to adjust the financial statement data of the subsidiary each period to place the data on a basis consistent with the fiscal period of the parent. **ARB 51** and the SEC permit the consolidation of a subsidiary's financial statements without adjusting the fiscal period of the subsidiary if that period does not differ from the parent's period by more than 3 months and if recognition is given to intervening events that have a material effect on financial position or results of operations.

A difference in accounting methods between a parent and its subsidiary generally should have no effect on the decision to consolidate that subsidiary. In any event, adequate disclosure of the various accounting methods used must be given in the notes to the financial statements.

Consolidated Financial Statements and Securities Regulations

The Securities and Exchange Commission permits companies under its jurisdiction to file consolidated financial statements so long as the consolidated subsidiaries are majority-owned and the difference in the fiscal periods of the parent and an included subsidiary is not more than 93 days. **Regulation S-X** sets forth the specific items and additional disclosures regarding consolidated statements required in annual reports filed with the SEC.

The various national and regional stock exchanges also permit or require the filing of consolidated financial statements. While the exchanges each have their own rules and specific requirements, the general requirements relating to consolidation procedures are similar.

The Changing Concept of the Reporting Entity

For nearly three decades, **ARB 51** served without significant revision as the primary source of consolidation policy. Over those years, there were many changes in the business environment and in the interpretation of the criteria used in determining whether or not to consolidate specific subsidiaries. Now, for the first time in many years, consolidation standards in the United States are undergoing a major change. In particular, the concept of the reporting entity is being broadened in such a way as to view the consolidated financial statements as the primary general-purpose financial statements of a parent and its subsidiaries. Parent company financial statements with subsidiaries reported using the equity method no longer can be considered an alternative to consolidated financial statements. The change in the concept of the reporting entity is most evident with respect to changes in consolidation standards dealing with control and homogeneity of operations.

Control

Control is now the overriding criterion in determining whether or not to include a company in the consolidated financial statements. The reporting entity comprises all companies under common control. In the past, other criteria frequently were used to exclude controlled companies from consolidation. All majority-owned subsidiaries now must be consolidated unless the parent is unable to control the subsidiary or unless control is temporary.

While control in this country has centered on majority ownership of an investee's common stock, this view currently is seen as too restrictive in Europe as well as, increasingly, in the United States. Some accountants feel that the concept of control should be broadened to include not only the traditional view of *de jure control*, a right gained through direct or indirect majority ownership of another company's common stock, but also *de facto control*, control that does in fact exist, even though less than a majority of the common stock is held. De facto control might be gained, for example, by holding a large block of a company's common stock while the majority of the common stock is very widely held, or by entering into an agreement in which one company is given complete operating authority over another. Companies under de facto control would not be consolidated if the benefits of the controlled operations do not accrue to the primary reporting company, such as when an investment advisory company manages a portfolio of securities for the benefit of the investors.

Homogeneity of Operations

As issued, **ARB 51** stated that in deciding whether to consolidate particular subsidiaries, ". . . . the aim should be to make the financial presentation which is most meaningful in the circumstances."[4] This has permitted the accountant and corporate manager to exercise their judgment in deciding whether the result of combining the financial statements of several different companies is more meaningful than providing separate-company data, or whether the separate-company data are more informative without resulting in excessive detail.

[4] Op. cit., par. 3.

When companies are considerably different in nature, a question arises as to the meaningfulness of the consolidated statements. For example, a manufacturing company's balance sheet usually contains large amounts of inventory, equipment, and trade receivables and payables, while the balance sheet of a financial institution usually contains many investments and receivables and payables with maturities considerably different from those of trade receivables and payables. Likewise, the income statement of the manufacturing company contains sales, cost of goods sold, and various operating expenses, while the income statement of the financial institution contains mainly interest and investment income and interest expense. Some argue that combining the financial statements of these two unlike companies could result in a meaningless or even totally misleading presentation.

Under previous consolidation standards, companies that were greatly different in nature from one another generally were not consolidated. No specific rules or guidelines were established to indicate the types of subsidiaries that could be consolidated with one another, and as a result, there was a considerable lack of uniformity in practice. Most commonly, manufacturing and merchandising companies were consolidated with one another even when they were in very different industries and had relatively different operating characteristics. Subsidiaries most frequently omitted from consolidation on the basis of nonhomogeneity were finance, insurance, real estate, and leasing subsidiaries of manufacturing and merchandising companies. In fact, many manufacturing and merchandising companies established financing subsidiaries through which the parents incurred large amounts of debt. These subsidiaries often were excluded from consolidation, leading to widespread concern over off-balance sheet financing.

The FASB recognized that business enterprises have become quite diverse and complex, branching into different lines of business and different geographic areas. For reasons of completeness and uniformity, the Board decided to require consolidation of all majority-owned subsidiaries regardless of the nature of their operations. This was accomplished with the issuance of **FASB Statement No. 94**, "Consolidation of All Majority-Owned Subsidiaries" (FASB 94), which amended **ARB 51** and eliminated homogeneity of operations as a functional criterion. With this change, one of the major causes of inconsistency in consolidation practices has been eliminated.

OVERVIEW OF THE CONSOLIDATION PROCESS

The consolidation process adds together the financial statements of two or more legally separate companies, creating a single set of financial statements. The specific procedures used to produce consolidated financial statements are discussed in considerable detail in the following chapters. An understanding of the procedures is important because they facilitate the accurate and efficient preparation of consolidated statements. However, while these procedures are being learned, the focus should continue to be on the end product, the financial statements. The procedures are intended to produce financial statements that appear as if the consolidated companies are actually a single company.

The separate financial statements of the companies involved serve as the starting point each time consolidated statements are prepared. These separate statements are added together, after some adjustments and eliminations, to get the consolidated statements.

After all the consolidation procedures have been applied, the preparer should review the resulting statements and ask: "Do these statements appear as if the consolidated companies were actually a single company?" To answer this question, two other questions must be answered:

1. "Are there items included in the statements that would not appear, or that would be stated at different amounts, in the statements of a single company?"

2. "Are there items that do not appear in these statements that would appear if the consolidated entity were actually a single company?"

These questions are answered based not on a knowledge of consolidation procedures, but on a thorough knowledge of generally accepted accounting principles. If the statements are not equivalent to those of a single company, additional procedures must be completed to provide statements as they would be presented by a single reporting entity.

THE CONSOLIDATION PROCESS ILLUSTRATED

The basic concepts that apply to the preparation of consolidated financial statements are illustrated in the following example. On January 1, 19X1, Popper Company purchases at book value all the common stock of Sun Corporation. At the end of 19X1, the balance sheets of the two companies appear as follows:

Balance Sheets
December 31, 19X1

	Popper	Sun
Assets		
Cash	$ 5,000	$ 3,000
Receivables (net)	84,000	30,000
Inventory	95,000	60,000
Fixed Assets (net)	375,000	250,000
Other Assets	25,000	15,000
Investment in Sun Stock	300,000	
Total	$884,000	$358,000
Liabilities and Equities		
Short-Term Payables	$ 60,000	$ 8,000
Long-Term Payables	200,000	50,000
Common Stock	500,000	200,000
Retained Earnings	124,000	100,000
Total	$884,000	$358,000

Additional information regarding Popper and Sun is as follows:

1. Popper uses the basic equity method to account for its investment in Sun. The investment account is carried at the book value of Sun's underlying net assets and is adjusted for Popper's share of Sun's earnings and dividends.

2. Sun owes Popper $1,000 on account at the end of the year.

3. Sun purchases $6,000 of inventory from Popper during 19X1. The inventory originally cost Popper $4,000. Sun still holds all the inventory at the end of the year.

The Consolidated Entity

The following diagram can be helpful in understanding the consolidated entity:

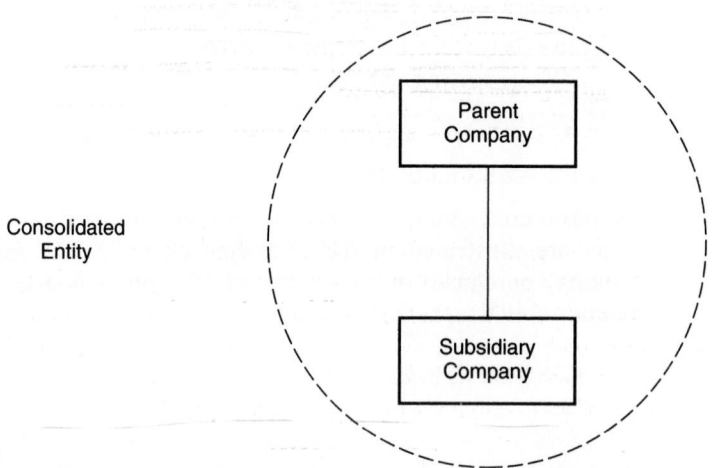

The boxes representing the parent and the subsidiary indicate legal entities. Transactions are recorded in the accounts of these legal entities. The dashed circular line can be viewed as defining the consolidated entity, which encompasses both the parent and the subsidiary. This consolidated entity has no legal existence but is considered to have economic reality. Transactions or ownership relations that cross over the dashed line can be viewed as involving outsiders and are properly reflected in the consolidated financial statements. Those transactions or relations that are entirely within the consolidated entity are not reflected in the consolidated financial statements because they do not involve outsiders. Instead, they are viewed as occurring within a single accounting entity and, therefore, do not qualify for inclusion in the consolidated statements.

FIGURE 3-1 Consolidated balance sheet.

Popper Company
Consolidated Balance Sheet
December 31, 19X1

Assets		Liabilities and Equities	
Cash	$ 8,000[a]	Short-Term Payables	$ 67,000[f]
Receivables (net)	113,000[b]	Long-Term Payables	250,000[g]
Inventory	153,000[c]		
Fixed Assets (net)	625,000[d]	Common Stock	500,000[h]
Other Assets	40,000[e]	Retained Earnings	122,000[i]
	$939,000		$939,000

The consolidated balances were obtained as follows:
(a) Cash: $5,000 + $3,000 = $8,000
(b) Receivables (net): $84,000 + $30,000 − $1,000 = $113,000
(c) Inventory: $95,000 + $60,000 − $2,000 = $153,000
(d) Fixed Assets (net): $375,000 + $250,000 = $625,000
(e) Other Assets: $25,000 + $15,000 = $40,000
(f) Short-Term Payables: $60,000 + $8,000 − $1,000 = $67,000
(g) Long-Term Payables: $200,000 + $50,000 = $250,000
(h) Common Stock: $500,000 + $200,000 − $200,000 = $500,000
(i) Retained Earnings: $124,000 + $100,000 − $100,000 − $2,000 = $122,000

The consolidated balance sheet for Popper and Sun appears in Figure 3-1, along with the computations used in deriving the balances reported. In the case of Popper and Sun, it is possible to determine the consolidated totals in a relatively intuitive manner. The like accounts from the parent and subsidiary financial statements are added together and then adjusted, where appropriate, to remove the effects of intercompany ownership and transactions. For example, the totals reported for cash, fixed assets, other assets, and long-term payables in this example are derived by simply adding together the amounts reported by the two companies. An adjustment is required to reduce receivables (net) and short-term payables for intercompany debt. Similarly, inventory and retained earnings are adjusted to remove the write-up in carrying value which occurred when Sun purchased the inventory from Popper. To remove the effects of intercorporate ownership, only the stockholders' equity balances of Popper, as the parent company, are included in the consolidated balance sheet. A discussion of the rationale for each of the adjustments is presented in the sections that follow.

In the Popper and Sun example, attention needs to be given several items to assure that the consolidated financial statements appear as if they are the statements of a single company:

1. Intercorporate stockholdings
2. Intercompany receivables and payables
3. Profits on intercompany sales

Intercorporate Stockholdings In the example given, Popper Company's common stock is held by those outside the consolidated entity and is properly viewed as the common stock of that entity. The common stock of Sun, on the other hand, is held entirely within the consolidated entity and is not stock outstanding from a consolidated viewpoint. These relationships are illustrated as follows:

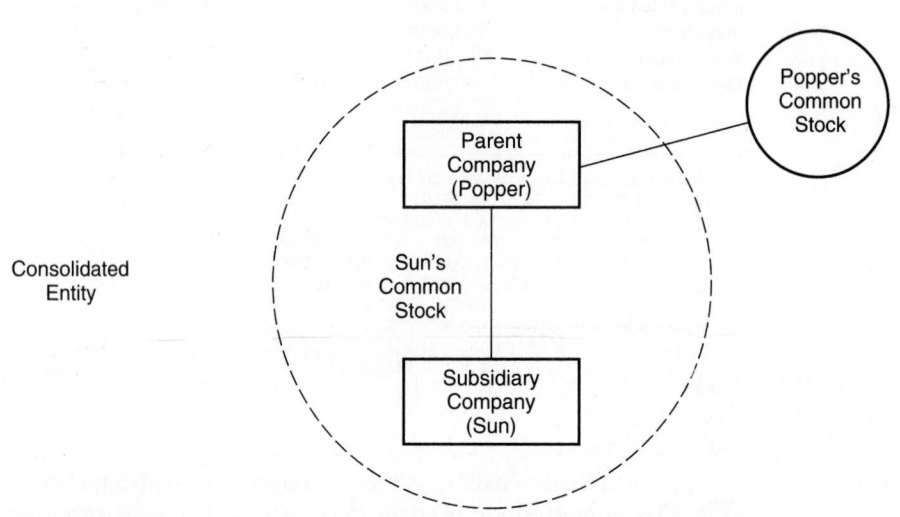

Because a company cannot report in its financial statements an investment in itself, Sun's common stock and Popper's investment in that stock both must be eliminated. Popper's common stock remains as the common stock of the consolidated entity.

Only the retained earnings of Popper Company is included in the consolidated balance sheet shown in Figure 3-1. The retained earnings of Sun is not reported in the consolidated balance sheet because it relates to an ownership interest held entirely within the consolidated entity. The retained earnings of Popper, on the other hand, represents a claim of the parent's shareholders, viewed as the residual owners of the consolidated entity. Popper's retained earnings indicates the amount of undistributed past earnings of the consolidated entity accruing to the stockholders of the parent company and, therefore, is reported as consolidated retained earnings.

Intercompany Receivables and Payables The intercompany receivable/payable can be viewed as follows:

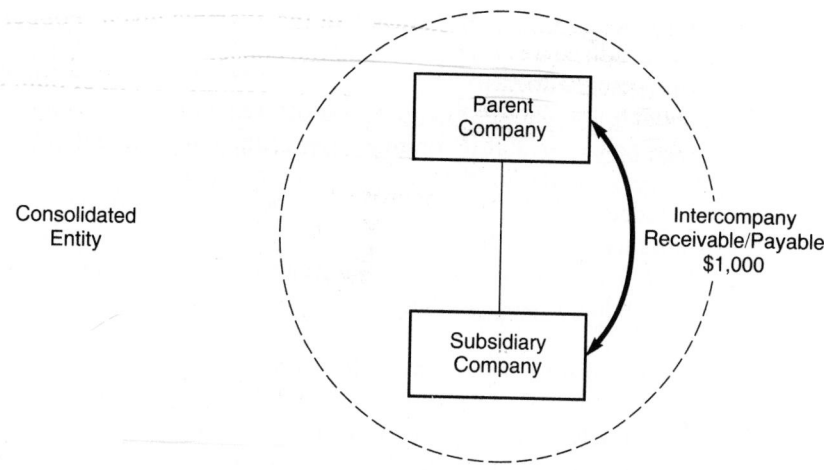

A single company cannot owe itself money. While as separate companies Popper properly reports a $1,000 trade receivable from Sun and Sun properly reports a $1,000 trade payable to Popper, such a receivable/payable does not exist from a consolidated viewpoint. Therefore, the $1,000 is eliminated from both receivables and payables in preparing the consolidated balance sheet.

Profits on Intercompany Sales   The sale of inventory from Popper to Sun also must be viewed in the context of a single entity, as illustrated in the following diagram:

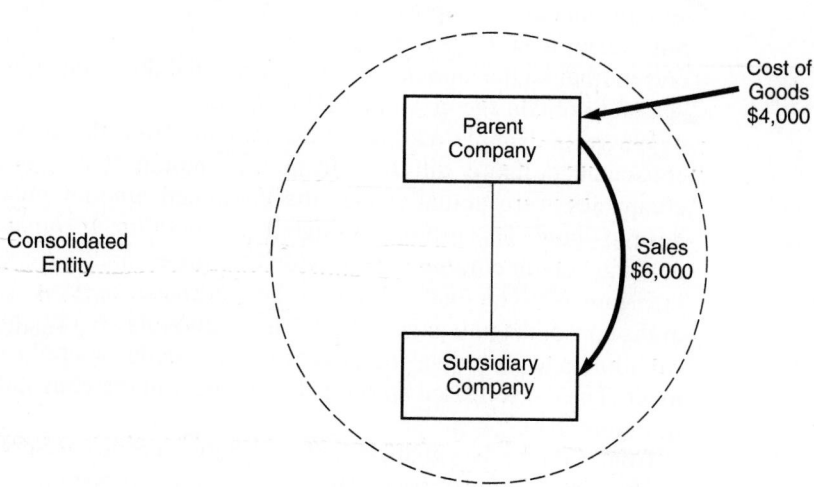

A single company may not recognize a profit and write up its inventory simply because the inventory is transferred from one department or division to another. This also applies to intercompany sales within a consolidated entity. In this example, the intercompany inventory remaining at the end of the period ($6,000) must be restated at its original cost to the consolidated entity, the $4,000 paid by Popper. Similarly, the $2,000 profit recognized on the intercompany sale and included in Popper's retained earnings may not be included in the consolidated amounts. Therefore, both the inventory and the consolidated retained earnings must be reduced by the $2,000 unrealized intercompany profit when preparing the consolidated balance sheet.

Single-Entity Viewpoint   The various adjustments discussed in this simplified example are illustrative of the type of thinking involved in the preparation of consolidated financial statements. In understanding each of the adjustments needed in preparing consolidated statements, the focus should be on (1) identifying the treatment accorded a particular item by each of the separate companies and (2) identifying the amount that would appear in the financial statements with respect to that item if the consolidated entity were actually a single company.

Mechanics of the Consolidation Process

A worksheet is used to facilitate the process of combining and adjusting the account balances involved in a consolidation. While the parent company and the subsidiary each maintain their own books, there are no books for the consolidated entity. Instead, the balances of the accounts are taken at the end of each period from the books of the parent and the subsidiary and entered in the consolidation workpaper.

A consolidation workpaper for the preparation of Popper Company's consolidated balance sheet appears in Figure 3-2. The account balances for Popper and Sun, taken from their separate books, are listed in the first two columns beside one another so the amounts for each asset, liability, and equity item may be added across to obtain the consolidated balances.

Where the simple adding of the amounts from the two companies leads to a consolidated figure different from the amount that would appear if the two companies were actually one, the combined amount must be adjusted to the desired figure. This is done through the preparation of *eliminating entries*. Separate debit and credit columns are provided for the eliminating entries in the workpaper in Figure 3-2. The final column in the workpaper presents the amounts to appear in the consolidated balance sheet. These amounts are obtained by summing across each line and including the effects of each debit or credit elimination or adjustment. The consolidated amounts then appear in the consolidated balance sheet as in Figure 3-1.

Consolidation workpapers and elimination entries are discussed in more detail in the following chapters. The consolidation procedures and workpapers are important because they facilitate the preparation of the consolidated statements,

FIGURE 3-2 Consolidated balance sheet workpaper.

Popper Company
Consolidated Balance Sheet Workpaper
December 31, 19X1

Item	Popper Company	Sun Corpo- ration	Eliminations Debit		Eliminations Credit		Consol- idated
Cash	5,000	3,000					8,000
Receivables (net)	84,000	30,000			(a)	1,000	113,000
Inventory	95,000	60,000			(b)	2,000	153,000
Fixed Assets (net)	375,000	250,000					625,000
Other Assets	25,000	15,000					40,000
Investment in Sun Stock	300,000				(c)	300,000	
	884,000	358,000					939,000
Short-Term Payables	60,000	8,000	(a)	1,000			67,000
Long-Term Payables	200,000	50,000					250,000
Common Stock	500,000	200,000	(c)	200,000			500,000
Retained Earnings	124,000	100,000	(c)	100,000			
			(b)	2,000			122,000
	884,000	358,000		303,000		303,000	939,000

(a) Eliminate intercompany receivable/payable.
(b) Eliminate unrealized intercompany profit included in ending inventory against consolidated retained earnings.
(c) Eliminate intercorporate investment against subsidiary's stockholders' equity.

help assure clerical accuracy, and provide a trail for the verification of the account balances in the consolidated statements. At this point, however, the reader should focus on understanding what numbers appear in the financial statements when adopting a single-entity viewpoint rather than concentrating on specific procedures or workpaper techniques.

NONCONTROLLING INTEREST

When one company acquires the common stock of another in a business combination, it does not always acquire 100 percent of the other company's outstanding shares. For the parent to consolidate the subsidiary, only a majority of the common stock is needed. Those shareholders of the subsidiary other than the parent are referred to as "noncontrolling" or "minority" shareholders. The claim of these shareholders on the income and net assets of the subsidiary is referred to as the *noncontrolling interest* or the *minority interest*.

The noncontrolling shareholders clearly have a claim on the assets and earnings of the subsidiary by virtue of their stock ownership. Because all the assets, liabilities, and earnings of the subsidiary normally are included in the consolidated statements, the noncontrolling shareholders' portion of these items must be reported. The portion of subsidiary net income assigned to the noncontrolling interest normally is deducted from earnings available to all shareholders to arrive at consolidated net income in the consolidated income statement. The noncontrolling shareholders' claim on the net assets of the subsidiary is shown most commonly between liabilities and stockholders' equity in the consolidated balance sheet.

Several different theories of consolidation have been proposed which affect differently the treatment of the noncontrolling interest. These theories are discussed briefly later in the chapter.

In uncomplicated situations, the amount of noncontrolling interest is a simple proportionate share of the relevant subsidiary amounts. For example, if a subsidiary has net income of $150,000 and the noncontrolling shareholders own 10 percent of the subsidiary's common stock, their share of income is $15,000 ($150,000 × .10). Similarly, if the subsidiary's only stockholders' equity accounts are common stock of $600,000 and retained earnings of $200,000, the total noncontrolling interest is computed as follows:

Subsidiary common stock	$600,000
Subsidiary retained earnings	200,000
Book value of subsidiary	$800,000
Noncontrolling stockholders' proportionate share	× .10
Noncontrolling interest	$ 80,000

EFFECT OF PURCHASE VERSUS POOLING ACCOUNTING ON CONSOLIDATION

As discussed in Chapter 1, the purchase and pooling of interests accounting methods often lead to significantly different balances being reported in financial statements prepared after a business combination. While the two accounting methods result in different amounts being reported in the consolidated financial statements, these differences arise because of differences in the amounts at which the balance sheet items were recorded on the date of combination rather than because of any differences in consolidation concepts or procedures. In general, the same consolidation procedures apply whether the combination is treated as a purchase or pooling of interests.

The differences in the consolidated financial statements due to the differences in purchase and pooling accounting fall largely into two areas. First, retained earnings is a residual and, therefore, never can be purchased. The existing retained earnings of a company acquired in a purchase-type business combination cannot become part of consolidated retained earnings. Instead, the amount of the subsidiary's retained earnings at the date of acquisition must be eliminated each time consolidated financial statements are prepared. If the combination originally was accounted for as a pooling of interests, the combining companies are viewed as always having been together and the retained earnings balance of the subsidiary at the date of the combination is included along with the parent's retained earnings.

The second area of difference involves the valuation of the subsidiary's assets and liabilities in the consolidated financial statements. If the subsidiary is purchased, its assets and liabilities must be valued for consolidation purposes at their fair values at the date of combination. When this is not done on the subsidiary's books, the consolidation procedures must provide for this revaluation and any associated amortization of the revalued amounts. For a combination treated as a pooling of interests, no revaluation is needed; instead, the book values of the parent's and subsidiary's assets and liabilities are combined.

In those cases where a subsidiary is purchased and the purchase price exceeds the fair value of the net identifiable assets of the acquired company at the date of combination, the excess is considered as a payment for goodwill. This goodwill normally is not recorded on the subsidiary's books; therefore, the consolidation procedures include recognizing the goodwill in the consolidated balance sheet and amortizing the goodwill in the consolidated income statement. Goodwill never is created as a result of a pooling of interests.

The following chapters emphasize consolidation procedures following a purchase-type business combination because most combinations are treated as purchases. Specific consolidation procedures following a pooling of interests are discussed in Chapter 10.

COMBINED FINANCIAL STATEMENTS

Financial statements sometimes are prepared for a group of companies when no one company in the group owns a majority of the common stock of any other company in the group. Financial statements that include a group of related companies without including the parent company or other owner are referred to as *combined financial statements*.

Combined financial statements are commonly prepared when an individual, rather than a corporation, owns or controls a number of companies and wishes to include them all in a single set of financial statements. In some cases, a parent company may prepare financial statements that include only its subsidiaries and not the parent. In other cases, a parent may prepare financial statements for its subsidiaries by operating group, with all the subsidiaries engaged in a particular type of operation, or those located in a particular geographical region, reported together.

The procedures used to prepare combined financial statements are essentially the same as those used in preparing consolidated financial statements. All intercompany receivables and payables, intercompany transactions, and unrealized intercompany profits and losses must be eliminated in the same manner as in the preparation of consolidated statements. Although no parent company is included in the reporting entity, any intercompany ownership, and the associated portion of stockholders' equity, must be eliminated in the same way as the parent's investment in a subsidiary is eliminated in preparing consolidated financial statements. The remaining stockholders' equity of the companies in the reporting entity is divided into the portions accruing to the controlling and noncontrolling interests.

ADDITIONAL CONSIDERATIONS—THEORIES OF CONSOLIDATION

The previous sections gave a brief overview of the concepts, issues, and procedures to be discussed in Chapters 4 through 10. Before these matters are covered in detail in subsequent chapters, this section addresses the various theories underlying the consolidation process.

Several different theories exist that might serve as a basis for preparing consolidated financial statements. The choice of consolidation theory can have a significant impact on the consolidated financial statements in those cases where the parent company owns less than 100 percent of the subsidiary's common stock. The discussion included in this section of the chapter is intended to provide a basic understanding of the major differences between the theories. An illustration of the effects of these differences on specific balance sheet and income statement totals is presented in Appendix A of this chapter.

This discussion focuses on three alternative theories of consolidation: (1) proprietary, (2) parent company, and (3) entity. The proprietary and entity theories may be viewed as falling near opposite ends of a spectrum, with the parent company theory falling somewhere in between:

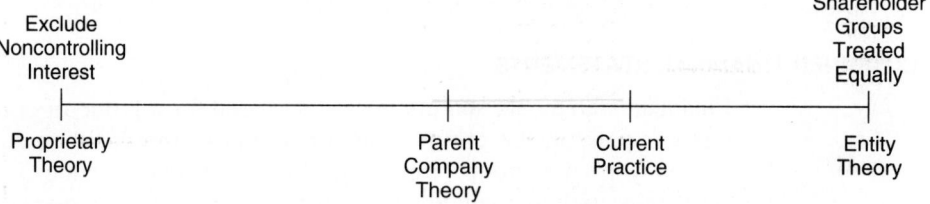

While no one of the three theories has been adopted in its entirety by the accounting profession, the consolidation procedures used in practice seem to come closest to the parent company approach.

Proprietary Theory

The *proprietary theory* of accounting views the firm as an extension of its owners. The assets and liabilities of the firm are considered to be assets and liabilities of the owners themselves. Similarly, revenue of the firm is viewed as increasing the wealth of the owners, while expenses decrease the wealth of the owners.

When applied to the preparation of consolidated financial statements, the proprietary concept results in what is referred to as a *pro rata consolidation*. The parent company consolidates only its proportionate share of the assets and liabilities of the subsidiary. For a subsidiary acquired in a purchase-type business combination, the consolidated amounts are determined at the date of combination by adding the parent's proportionate share of the fair value (book value plus fair value increment) of each of the subsidiary's identifiable assets and liabilities to the book values of the parent's individual assets and liabilities. In addition, the amount paid by the parent in excess of the fair value of the parent's share of the subsidiary's net identifiable assets is reported as goodwill in the consolidated balance sheet. The portion of the subsidiary's identifiable assets and liabilities assignable to the noncontrolling interest is excluded from the consolidated statements, as is any implied goodwill assignable to the noncontrolling interest. The amount of net assets of the subsidiary included in the consolidated financial statements is shown by the shaded area in the left portion of the following diagram:

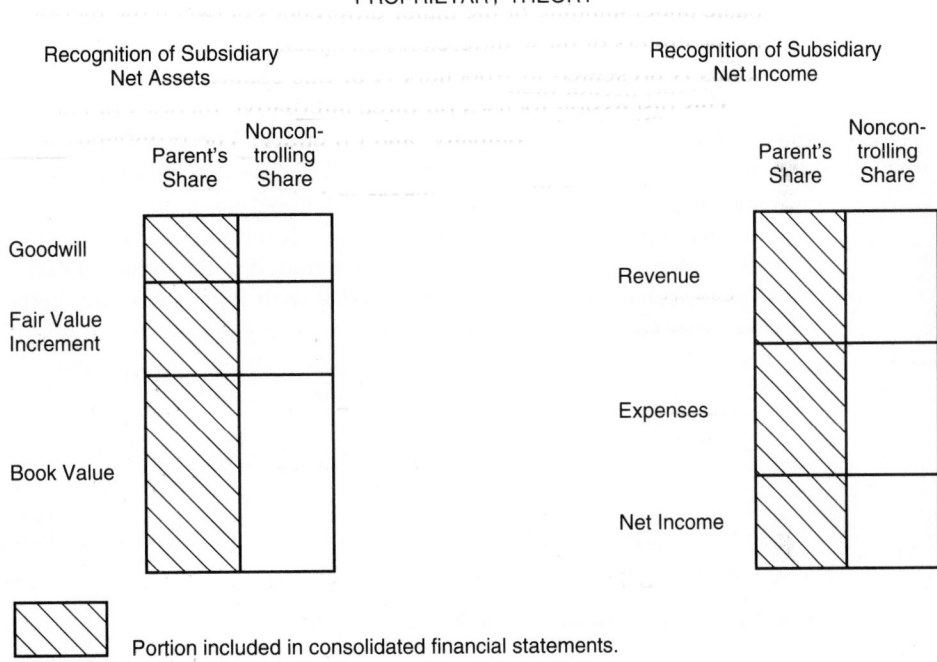

PROPRIETARY THEORY

Portion included in consolidated financial statements.

In a manner similar to the treatment of assets and liabilities, only the parent's share of individual revenues and expenses reported by the subsidiary subsequent to the purchase is combined with the parent's revenues and expenses in preparing the consolidated income statement. As indicated in the diagram, that portion of the subsidiary's revenues and expenses assignable to the noncontrolling shareholders is omitted from the consolidated income statement.

Under each of the consolidation theories, depreciation or other expenses must be adjusted for the write-off of goodwill or fair value increments recognized in the consolidation process, and the effects of intercorporate transactions between the parent and subsidiary during a period must be eliminated. A more detailed comparison of the effects of the different consolidation theories on the consolidated income statement amounts is illustrated in Appendix A.

Parent Company Theory

The *parent company theory* is perhaps better suited to the modern corporation and the preparation of consolidated financial statements than is the proprietary approach. The parent company theory recognizes that although the parent does not have direct ownership of the assets nor direct responsibility for the liabilities of the subsidiary, it has the ability to exercise effective control over all of the subsidiary's assets and liabilities, not simply a proportionate share. Thus, all the assets and liabilities of the subsidiary are reported in the consolidated balance sheet by combining them with the assets and liabilities of the parent. Similarly, all the revenue and expenses of the subsidiary are included in the consolidated income statement. Under this approach, separate recognition is given in the consolidated balance sheet to the noncontrolling interest's claim on the net assets of the subsidiary and in the consolidated income statement to the earnings assigned to the noncontrolling shareholders.

The full amount of the book value of the subsidiary's net assets is included in the consolidated balance sheet when the parent company method is used. In those cases where the parent pays more than book value for its share of the subsidiary's ownership in a purchase-type business combination, the parent's portion of the fair value increment and goodwill is included in the consolidated statements. As a result, subsidiary assets are included at their fair values only in those cases where the parent purchases full ownership. The noncontrolling shareholders are assigned a proportionate share of book value of the subsidiary's net assets in preparing the consolidated balance sheet, as shown in the following diagram:

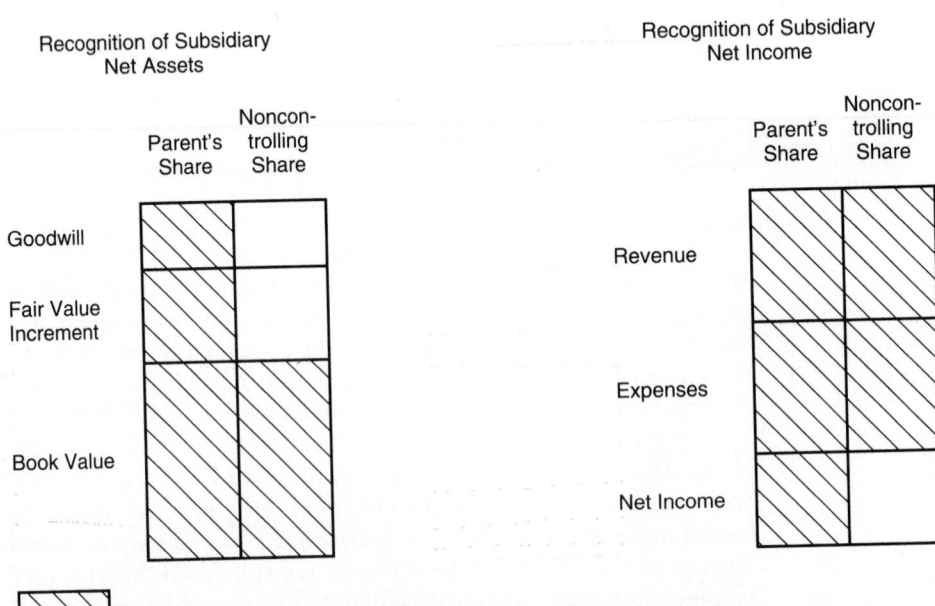

PARENT COMPANY THEORY

Portion included in consolidated financial statements.

While the full book values of the assets of the subsidiary are included in the consolidated balance sheet under this approach, amounts less than the full fair values of identifiable assets and the full amount of goodwill are reported whenever the parent does not purchase all of the subsidiary ownership.

With the parent company theory, the full amounts of subsidiary revenues and expenses are included in the consolidated income statement; however, only the portion of subsidiary income assignable to the parent company is included in consolidated net income. Income assigned to the noncontrolling shareholders is treated as a deduction in the consolidated income statement in arriving at consolidated net income.

Entity Theory

As a general ownership theory, the *entity theory* focuses on the firm as a separate economic entity, rather than on the ownership rights of the shareholders of the parent or subsidiary. Emphasis under the entity approach is on the consolidated entity itself, with the controlling and noncontrolling shareholders viewed as two separate groups, each having an equity in the consolidated entity. Neither of the two groups is emphasized over the other or over the consolidated entity.

Because the parent and subsidiary together are viewed as a single entity under the entity approach, the full amounts of the assets and liabilities of both the parent and subsidiary are combined in the consolidated balance sheet. Assuming the subsidiary was acquired in a business combination accounted for as a purchase, all the assets and liabilities of the subsidiary and any goodwill are reflected in the

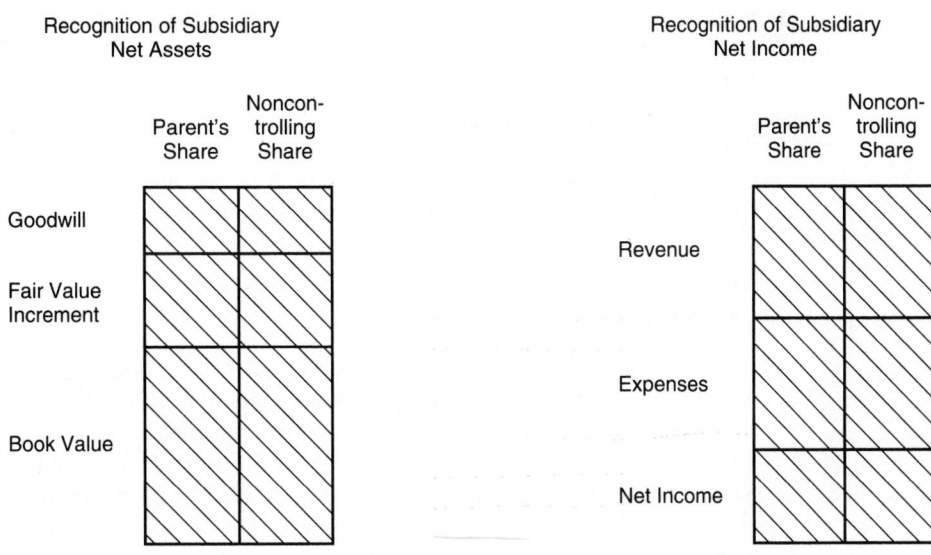

ENTITY THEORY

Recognition of Subsidiary Net Assets

Recognition of Subsidiary Net Income

Portion included in consolidated financial statements.

consolidated balance sheet at their full fair values on the date of combination regardless of the actual percentage of ownership acquired, as shown in the diagram on the preceding page.

The consolidated income statement under the entity approach contains the revenues and expenses of both the parent and the subsidiary companies. Because the parent and subsidiary are viewed as constituting a single entity, consolidated net income is a combined figure that is allocated between the controlling and noncontrolling ownership groups.

Current Practice

The procedures used in practice represent a blending of the parent company and entity approaches. The amount of subsidiary net assets recognized in the consolidated balance sheet at acquisition is the same in practice as under the parent company approach. On the other hand, the determination of consolidated net income is a combination of the entity and parent company approaches.

No specific presentation of noncontrolling (minority) interest is required in the official pronouncements, and there is less than complete uniformity in the presentations found in practice. Most companies deduct the noncontrolling interest's share of subsidiary net income in the consolidated income statement to obtain consolidated net income. This expense-type treatment views the computation of consolidated net income from the parent company's point of view and seems to be consistent with the view of consolidated net income adopted by **APB 18**.

The dollar amount reported as noncontrolling interest in the consolidated balance sheet is presented in any one of three ways. Most companies show the noncontrolling interest either as a part of the liabilities section or between the liabilities and stockholders' equity sections of the balance sheet. The liability treatment is consistent with the parent company approach and with deducting the noncontrolling interest's share of income as an expense. The in-between treatment amounts to no classification at all. A few companies classify the noncontrolling interest as a stockholders' equity item. This presentation is consistent with the entity approach and with the treatment of the noncontrolling interest's share of income as an allocation of consolidated net income rather than as a deduction to obtain consolidated net income.

SUMMARY OF KEY CONCEPTS AND TERMS

Consolidated financial statements present the financial position and results of operations of a parent and one or more subsidiaries as if they were actually a single company. As a result, a group of legally separate companies is portrayed as a single economic entity by the consolidated financial statements. All indications of intercorporate ownership and the effects of all intercompany transactions are excluded from the consolidated statements. The basic approach to the preparation of consolidated financial statements is to combine the separate financial statements of the individual consolidating companies and then to eliminate or adjust those items that would not appear, or that would appear differently, if the companies actually were one.

Current consolidation standards require that the consolidated financial statements include all companies under common control unless control is questionable or temporary. Consolidated financial statements are prepared primarily for those with a long-run interest in the parent company, especially the stockholders and long-term creditors of the parent. While consolidated financial statements allow interested parties to view a group of related companies as a single economic entity, such statements have some limitations. In particular, information about the characteristics and operations of the individual companies within the consolidated entity is lost in the process of combining financial statements.

Several different theories or approaches underlie the preparation of consolidated financial statements, and the approach used can significantly affect the consolidated statements when the subsidiaries are not wholly owned. The proprietary and entity theories can be viewed as lying at opposite ends of a spectrum, with the parent company theory in the middle. Current practice tends to fall closest to the parent company theory, with some characteristics of the entity theory.

Appendix B of this chapter summarizes the accounting treatment of intercorporate investments and much of the discussion in Chapters 1 through 3.

Combined financial statements	Minority interest
Consolidated financial statements	Noncontrolling interest
De facto control	Parent company
De jure control	Parent company theory
Direct control	Proprietary theory
Economic entity	Pro rata consolidation
Eliminating entries	Related companies
Entity theory	Separate legal entities
Indirect control	Subsidiary

APPENDIX A: Theories of Consolidation Illustrated

Chapter 3 provides a general description of the major differences in the theories of consolidation. A better understanding of the impact of selecting a particular theory can be gained by examining the major balance sheet and income statement effects of the theories. Figure 3-3 provides a summary of the procedures used in determining the balance sheet totals at the time of acquisition under each of the theories and current practice, as discussed in the Additional Considerations section of the chapter.

An expansion of the major factors involved in the determination of consolidated net income and income assigned to the noncontrolling (minority) shareholders is presented in Figure 3-4. An understanding of the impact of the amortization of purchase differentials and the apportionment of unrealized profits on intercompany transfers is critical in comparing the income statement effects of the theories of consolidation. A summary of the differences is presented in Figure 3-4.

FIGURE 3-3 The effects of different approaches to the preparation of a consolidated balance sheet at acquisition.

Item	Proprietary Theory	Parent Company Theory	Entity Theory	Current Accounting Practice
Amount of book value of subsidiary net assets included	Parent's proportionate share	Full amount	Full amount	Full amount
Amount of differential recognized:				
Fair value increment	Parent's proportionate share	Parent's proportionate share	Full amount	Parent's proportionate share
Goodwill	Parent's proportionate share	Parent's proportionate share	Full amount	Parent's proportionate share
Amount of noncontrolling interest recognized at acquisition	None recognized	Proportionate share of subsidiary book value	Proportionate share of subsidiary fair value	Proportionate share of subsidiary book value
Financial statement treatment of noncontrolling interest's claim on net assets of subsidiary	None recognized	Liability	Part of stockholders' equity	Liability, part of stockholders' equity, or between liabilities and stockholders' equity

FIGURE 3-4 The effects of different approaches to the preparation of a consolidated income statement.

Item	Proprietary Theory	Parent Company Theory	Entity Theory	Current Accounting Practice
Amount of fair value increment and goodwill amortized	Parent's proportionate share	Parent's proportionate share	Full amount	Parent's proportionate share
Amount of unrealized intercompany gains and losses eliminated:				
Sale from parent to subsidiary	Parent's proportionate share	Parent's proportionate share	100% elimination against parent	100% elimination against parent
Sale from subsidiary to parent	Parent's proportionate share	Parent's proportionate share	100% elimination, proportionate allocation	100% elimination, proportionate allocation
Amount recognized as consolidated net income	Parent's separate income plus a proportionate share of subsidiary net income, with an adjustment for amortization of differential and a proportionate share of unrealized gains and losses on intercompany sales	Parent's separate income plus a proportionate share of subsidiary net income, with an adjustment for amortization of differential and a proportionate share of unrealized gains and losses on intercompany sales	Parent's separate income plus subsidiary net income with an adjustment for amortization of differential and for unrealized gains and losses on intercompany sales	Parent's separate income adjusted for unrealized gains and losses on sales from parent to subsidiary, plus a proportionate share of subsidiary net income adjusted for amortization of differential and unrealized gains and losses on sales from subsidiary to parent
Income assigned to noncontrolling interest in consolidated income statement	None recognized	Proportionate share of subsidiary net income	Proportionate share of subsidiary net income, adjusted for amortization of differential and elimination of unrealized intercompany gains and losses on sales from subsidiary to parent	Proportionate share of subsidiary net income, adjusted for unrealized gains and losses on sales from subsidiary to parent
Income statement treatment of noncontrolling interest	None recognized	Deduction to obtain consolidated net income	Allocation of consolidated net income	Generally a deduction to obtain consolidated net income

ILLUSTRATION OF THE EFFECTS OF DIFFERENT APPROACHES

Figure 3-5 provides a numerical illustration of the different theories of consolidation. The computations in Figure 3-5 assume that P company purchases 80 percent of the stock of S Company on January 1, 19X1, for $96,000. On that date, S Company reports assets with a book value of $100,000 and fair value of $120,000. The assets to which the fair value increment relates have remaining lives of 10 years. For the year 19X1, S Company reports net income of $30,000 and P Company reports income from its separate operations of $200,000. S Company's 19X1 net income includes $4,000 of unrealized profits from intercompany sales of inventory to P Company, and P Company's operating income includes $1,000 of unrealized profits from sales to S Company.

FIGURE 3-5 Illustration of the effects of different approaches to the preparation of consolidated financial statements.

Item	Proprietary	Theory — Parent Company	Theory — Entity	Current Accounting Practice
Value of subsidiary net assets recognized at acquisition:				
Book value:				
$100,000 × .80	$ 80,000			
$100,000 × 1.00		$100,000	$100,000	$100,000
Differential:				
$20,000 × .80	16,000	16,000		16,000
$20,000 × 1.00			20,000	
Total net assets	$ 96,000	$116,000	$120,000	$116,000
Amount of noncontrolling interest recognized at acquisition		$ 20,000	$ 24,000	$ 20,000
Amount of purchase differential amortized	$ 1,600	$ 1,600	$ 2,000	$ 1,600
Elimination of unrealized profit on intercompany sale:				
From parent to subsidiary:				
$1,000 × .80	$ 800	$ 800		
$1,000 × 1.00			$ 1,000	$ 1,000
From subsidiary to parent:				
$4,000 × .80	$ 3,200	$ 3,200		
$4,000 × 1.00			$ 4,000	$ 4,000
Consolidated net income	$218,400^a	$218,400^a	$223,000^b	$218,200^c
Income assigned to noncontrolling interest		$ 6,000^d	$ 4,800^e	$ 5,200^f

^{a} 218,400 = $200,000 + ($30,000 × 0.80) − $1,600* − $800† − $3,200†
^{b} 223,000 = $200,000 + $30,000 − $2,000* − $1,000† − $4,000†
^{c} 218,200 = ($200,000 − $1,000†) + [($30,000 − $4,000†) × 0.80] − $1,600*
^{d} 6,000 = $30,000 × 0.20
^{e} 4,800 = [($30,000 − $4,000†) × 0.20] − $400*
^{f} 5,200 = [($30,000 − $4,000†) × 0.20]

* Amortization of differential using straight-line basis over 10 years
† Elimination of unrealized intercompany profits

NET ASSETS RECOGNIZED AT ACQUISITION

The illustration assumes the parent purchases 80 percent ownership of the subsidiary at fair value ($120,000 × .80 = $96,000). When the proprietary theory is used, only the parent's portion of the book value of the assets reported by the subsidiary ($100,000 × .80) and its portion of the fair value increment ($20,000 × .80) are included in the consolidated financial statements.

The parent company and entity theories differ from the proprietary theory in that they include the full amount of the book value of the subsidiary ($100,000). Only the portion of the fair value increment presumed purchased by the parent company ($20,000 × .80) is included in the consolidated balance sheet under the parent company theory. The entity theory, on the other hand, calls for recognition of both the portion purchased by the parent and the portion attributed to the noncontrolling shareholders. Thus, the full differential or excess of fair value over book value is recognized under the entity theory ($20,000 × 1.00).

As was previously indicated, current accounting practice parallels the parent company method in recognizing total net assets of the subsidiary.

ELIMINATION OF UNREALIZED PROFITS

Profits on intercorporate transfers generally are considered realized at the point when the parent or subsidiary sells the items to a nonaffiliate. Each consolidation theory requires elimination of at least some portion of the profits on intercompany sales when the items have not been resold prior to the end of the period. Under the proprietary and parent company theories, the amount of unrealized intercompany profit eliminated is based on the proportion of ownership held by the parent, while the full amount is eliminated under the entity theory and in current accounting practice.

Only the parent's share of the subsidiary's sales and cost of goods sold is included in the consolidated income statement under the proprietary theory. As a result, $3,200 ($4,000 × .80) of unrealized profit reported by the subsidiary needs to be eliminated to avoid overstating profits of the consolidated enterprise. A proportionate share of unrealized profit or loss also is eliminated in the case of sales made by the parent to the subsidiary. Under the proprietary theory, the noncontrolling shareholders are considered to be independent of the controlling shareholders. That portion of the profit that applies to the noncontrolling shareholders, therefore, is considered realized and does not need to be eliminated. In the sale from P Company to S Company, $1,000 of profit is included in P's income from operations, but only $800 is eliminated. The remaining $200 is viewed as profit from a sale to an outsider.

Under the parent company theory of consolidation, the full amount of the subsidiary's revenue and cost of goods sold is included in the consolidated income statement, unlike under the proprietary theory. The parent's transactions with partially owned subsidiaries are considered to involve outsiders in proportion to the percentage ownership held by noncontrolling shareholders. Only the parent's proportionate share of the unrealized profits and losses is considered unrealized, regardless of whether the sale is from subsidiary to parent or from parent to subsidiary. Thus, $3,200 ($4,000 × .80) is considered unrealized on the sale by S and $800 ($1,000 × .80) is considered unrealized on the sale by P.

The full revenues and expenses of both the parent and the subsidiary also are included in the consolidated income statement under the entity theory. Because all shareholders are considered equivalent under the entity theory, all intercompany transfers and unrealized profits must be eliminated regardless of which affiliate is the seller and which is the purchaser. As shown in Figure 3-5, the full $4,000 of unrealized profit recorded by S Company and the full $1,000 recorded by P Company must be eliminated.

Current accounting practice has adopted the entity approach with regard to unrealized intercompany profit elimination. The amount of the unrealized profit generally is treated as a reduction of income assigned to shareholders of the selling affiliate.

CONSOLIDATED NET INCOME

The amount of net income reported in the consolidated income statement depends on the portion of the subsidiary's net income included and any adjustments for amortization of the purchase differential or elimination of intercompany profit. Under the proprietary and parent company theories, consolidated net income includes both the operating income of the parent ($200,000) and the parent's proportionate share of the reported net income of the subsidiary ($30,000 × .80). However, income must be reduced by amortization of the differential of $1,600 ($16,000/10 years). Consolidated net income also must be reduced by the unrealized profit eliminations discussed in the previous section, so that only realized income is included. In this illustration, the reduction for parent company unrealized profits is $800 ($1,000 × .80) and for subsidiary unrealized profits is $3,200 ($4,000 × .80). Thus, consolidated net income is $218,400.

Consolidated net income under the entity method includes the income to all shareholders. Thus, the full net income of the subsidiary is included along with the separate operating income of the parent. In arriving at consolidated net income, a deduction must be made for $2,000 amortization of the full amount of the excess of fair value over book value at the date of acquisition ($20,000/10 years). The full amounts of the unrealized profits for both the parent ($1,000) and the subsidiary ($4,000) also must be deducted. Consolidated net income is $223,000.

As was previously discussed, consolidated net income in current accounting practice is not computed in strict conformity with any of the three theories of consolidation. Realized operating income of the parent ($200,000 − $1,000 = $199,000) and the parent's portion of the realized net income of the subsidiary [($30,000 − $4,000) × .80 = $20,800] are included. This amount is reduced by the $1,600 amortization of the differential, based on the amount paid by the parent ($16,000/10 years). Consolidated net income is $218,200.

NONCONTROLLING INTEREST

The illustration assumes the net book value of S's assets is $100,000 at January 1, 19X1. The noncontrolling interest is excluded entirely from consolidated financial statements prepared under the proprietary theory. When the parent company approach is used, noncontrolling shareholders are considered outsiders and are assigned a proportionate share of reported subsidiary net assets and income.

Under the entity theory, the noncontrolling interest is assigned a full portion of both the book value of subsidiary net assets ($100,000) and the fair value increase ($20,000) at January 1, 19X1. Income assigned to noncontrolling shareholders for 19X1 is based on a pro rata portion of reported net income of the subsidiary less unrealized profits of the subsidiary [($30,000 − $4,000) × .20 = $5,200]. A proportionate share of the amortization of the purchase differential [($20,000/10 years) × .20 = $400) also must be subtracted.

Under current accounting practice, the amount assigned to the noncontrolling interest in the consolidated balance sheet is equal to a pro rata share of the subsidiary's reported net assets less any unrealized profits of the subsidiary. The January 1, 19X1, claim of the noncontrolling interest is $20,000 ($100,000 $\times$ .20). Income assigned to noncontrolling shareholders in the consolidated income statement is a pro rata share of the subsidiary's reported net income, adjusted for unrealized profits of the subsidiary [($30,000 − $4,000) $\times$ .20 = $5,200].

APPENDIX B: Accounting for Intercorporate Investments

Figure 3-6 is a flow diagram summarizing the accounting treatment of intercorporate investments. Selecting the path in the flow diagram corresponding to the particular type of investment (that is, net assets, common stock, securities other than common stock) reveals the appropriate accounting treatment.

QUESTIONS

Q3-1 What is the basic idea underlying the preparation of consolidated financial statements?

Q3-2 How might consolidated statements help an investor assess the desirability of purchasing shares of the parent company?

Q3-3 Are consolidated financial statements likely to be more useful to the owners of the parent company or to the noncontrolling owners of the subsidiaries? Why?

Q3-4 What is meant by "homogeneity of operations"? What effect does this factor have on consolidation policy?

Q3-5 Are consolidated financial statements likely to be more useful to the creditors of the parent company or to the creditors of the subsidiaries? Why?

Q3-6 Why is ownership of a majority of the common stock of another company considered important in consolidation?

Q3-7 What major criteria must be met before a company is consolidated?

Q3-8 When is consolidation considered inappropriate even though the parent holds a majority of the voting common shares of another company?

Q3-9 What is meant by "indirect control"? Give an illustration.

Q3-10 What means other than majority ownership might be used to gain control over a company? Can consolidation occur if control is gained by other means?

Q3-11 Why must intercompany receivables and payables be eliminated when consolidated financial statements are prepared?

Q3-12 Why are subsidiary shares not reported as stock outstanding in the consolidated balance sheet?

Q3-13 Explain the concept of an economic entity.

Q3-14 What is the noncontrolling interest in a subsidiary?

Q3-15 What is the difference between consolidated and combined financial statements?

Q3-16* How does the proprietary theory of consolidation differ from current accounting practice?

Q3-17* How does the entity theory of consolidation differ from current accounting practice?

Q3-18* Which theory of consolidation is closest to current accounting practice?

FIGURE 3-6 Flow diagram on accounting for intercorporate investments.

Company A Invests in Company B

Acquire Net Assets
- Qualifies as Pooling?
  - Yes → Record Net Assets at Book Value
  - No → Record Net Assets at Fair Value

Acquire Common Stock
- Report as Pooling?
  - Yes → Record Investment in Stock at Book Value
    - Subsidiary Liquidated?
      - No → Subsidiary Qualifies for Consolidation?
        - No → Report as Investment Using Cost Method [a]
        - Yes → Use Cost Method on Books
      - Yes → Record Net Assets at Book Value
  - No → Record Investment in Stock at Fair Value
    - Investee Liquidated?
      - Yes → Record Net Assets at Fair Value
      - No → Investee Qualifies for Consolidation?
        - Yes → Use Equity Method on Books
        - No → Investor Has Ability to Significantly Influence Investee? [c]
          - Yes → Report as Investment Using Equity Method [a]
          - No → Marketable Security?
            - Yes → Report as Investment Using Lower of Cost or Market under SFAS No. 12 [a]
            - No → Report as Investment Using Cost Method [a]

Eliminate Intercorporate Investment and Fully Consolidate

Acquire Securities Other than Common Stock
- Equity Security?
  - Yes → Marketable Security? (see above)
  - No → Temporary Investment?
    - Yes → Report as Investment at Cost [a] or Lower of Cost or Market [b]
    - No → Report as Investment at Cost Adjusted for Amortization of Discount or Premium [a]

[a] If value is less than carrying amount and decline is other than temporary, write down investment.

[b] Although SFAS No. 12 does not apply to debt securities, it is often followed in practice.

[c] If control or significant influence is temporary or does not rest with investor, report at cost or lower market value.

CASES

C3-1 Computation of Total Asset Values

A reader of the consolidated financial statements of Gigantic Company received copies from another source of the financial statements of the individual companies included in the consolidation. He is confused by the fact that the total assets in the consolidated balance sheet differ rather substantially from the sum of the asset totals reported by the individual companies.

Required

Will this relationship always be true? What factors may cause this difference to occur?

C3-2 Accounting Entity [AICPA Adapted]

The concept of the accounting entity often is considered to be the most fundamental of accounting concepts, one that pervades all of accounting.

Required

a. (1) What is an accounting entity? Explain.
  (2) Explain why the accounting entity concept is so fundamental that it pervades all of accounting.
b. For each of the following, indicate whether the accounting concept of the entity is applicable; discuss and give illustrations.
  (1) A unit created by or under law
  (2) The product-line segment of an enterprise
  (3) A combination of legal units
  (4) All the activities of an owner or a group of owners
  (5) The economy of the United States

C3-3 Consolidation Effects

Crumple Car Corporation produces fuel-efficient automobiles and sells them through a vast dealer network. It has two wholly owned subsidiaries. One subsidiary provides financing for approximately 70 percent of all automobile sales of the parent company and its dealers. The other subsidiary purchases approximately 15 percent of the parent company production and leases the cars to other companies. Until recently, the parent company accounted for both subsidiaries using the equity method and reported them in its consolidated financial statements as intercorporate investments. It is now fully consolidating both subsidiaries.

Required

  a. What specific accounts or items within the consolidated financial statements could be expected to be different when both subsidiaries are fully consolidated?
  b. Given that Crumple Car Corporation is a manufacturer and distributor, and its two subsidiaries both are financing-type companies, what arguments can be given for not consolidating either subsidiary? What arguments can be given for consolidating both subsidiaries?

C3-4 Need for Consolidation [AICPA Adapted]

Sharp Company will acquire 90 percent of Moore Company in a business combination. The total consideration has been agreed upon. The nature of Sharp's payment has not been fully agreed upon. Therefore, it is possible that this business combination might be accounted for as either a purchase or a pooling of interests. It is expected that on the date the business combination is to be consummated, the fair value will exceed the book value of Moore's assets minus liabilities. Sharp desires to prepare consolidated financial statements that will include the financial statements of Moore.

Required

a. (1) Would the method of accounting for the business combination (purchase versus pooling of interests) affect whether or not goodwill is reported?
   (2) If goodwill is reported, explain how the amount of goodwill is determined.
   (3) Would the method of accounting for the business combination (purchase versus pooling of interests) affect whether or not a noncontrolling interest is reported? If the amount reported differs, explain why.

b. (1) From a theoretical standpoint, why should consolidated financial statements be prepared?
   (2) From a theoretical standpoint, what is the usual first necessary condition to be met before consolidated financial statements can be prepared?
   (3) From a theoretical standpoint, does the method of accounting for a business combination (purchase versus pooling of interests) affect the decision to prepare consolidated financial statements? Why?

EXERCISES

E3-1 Multiple-Choice Questions on Consolidation Overview [AICPA Adapted]

Select the correct answer for each of the following questions.

1. Consolidated financial statements are prepared when a parent-subsidiary relationship exists in recognition of the accounting concept of:
   a. Materiality.
   b. Entity.
   c. Objectivity.
   d. Going concern.

2. Which of the following is the best theoretical justification for consolidated financial statements?
   a. In form the companies are one entity; in substance they are separate.
   b. In form the companies are separate; in substance they are one entity.
   c. In form and substance the companies are one entity.
   d. In form and substance the companies are separate.

3. At the time Hyman Corporation became a subsidiary of Duane Corporation, Hyman switched depreciation of its plant assets from the straight-line method to the sum-of-the-years'-digits method used by Duane. As to Hyman, this change was a:
   a. Change in an accounting estimate.
   b. Correction of an error.

    c. Change of accounting principle.
    d. Change in the reporting entity.

4. Consolidated statements are proper for Neely, Inc., Randle, Inc., and Walker, Inc., if:
    a. Neely owns 80 percent of the outstanding common stock of Randle and 40 percent of Walker; Randle owns 30 percent of Walker.
    b. Neely owns 100 percent of the outstanding common stock of Randle and 90 percent of Walker; Neely bought the stock of Walker 1 month before the balance sheet date and sold it 7 weeks later.
    c. Neely owns 100 percent of the outstanding common stock of Randle and Walker; Walker is in legal reorganization.
    d. Neely owns 80 percent of the outstanding common stock of Randle and 40 percent of Walker; Reeves, Inc., owns 55 percent of Walker.

E3-2 Multiple-Choice Questions on Consolidation Overview [AICPA Adapted]

Select the correct answer for each of the following questions.

1. How would the retained earnings of a subsidiary acquired in a business combination usually be treated in a consolidated balance sheet prepared immediately after the acquisition?
    a. Excluded for both a purchase and a pooling of interests.
    b. Excluded for a pooling of interests but included for a purchase.
    c. Included for both a purchase and a pooling of interests.
    d. Included for a pooling of interests but excluded for a purchase.

2. Consolidated financial statements are typically prepared when one company has:
    a. Accounted for its investment in another company by the equity method.
    b. Accounted for its investment in another company by the cost method.
    c. Significant influence over the operating and financial policies of another company.
    d. The controlling financial interest in another company.

3. Aaron, Inc., owns 80 percent of the outstanding stock of Belle, Inc. Compare the consolidated net earnings of Aaron and Belle (X) and Aaron's net earnings if it does not consolidate Belle (Y).
    a. X is greater than Y.
    b. X is equal to Y.
    c. X is less than Y.
    d. Cannot be determined.

4. On October 1, X Company acquired for cash all the outstanding common stock of Y Company. Both companies have a December 31 year-end and have been in business for many years. Consolidated net income for the year ended December 31 should include net income of:
    a. X Company for 3 months and Y Company for 3 months.
    b. X Company for 12 months and Y Company for 3 months.
    c. X Company for 12 months and Y Company for 12 months.
    d. X Company for 12 months, but no income from Y Company until Y Company distributes a dividend.

5. A subsidiary may be acquired by issuing common stock in a pooling of interests transaction or by paying cash in a purchase transaction. Regardless of which of these

two approaches is used to effect the combination, which of the following items would be reported in the consolidated financial statements at the same amount?
   a. Noncontrolling interest.
   b. Goodwill.
   c. Retained earnings.
   d. Capital stock.

6. Ownership of 51 percent of the outstanding voting stock of a company would usually result in:
   a. The use of the cost method.
   b. The use of the lower-of-cost-or-market method.
   c. A pooling of interests.
   d. A consolidation.

E3-3   Intercompany Transfers

Route Manufacturing purchased 80 percent of the stock of Hampton Mines, Inc., in 19X3. In preparing the consolidated financial statements at the end of 19X5, the controller of Route discovered that Route Manufacturing had purchased $75,000 of raw materials from Hampton Mines during the year and that the parent company had not paid for the last purchase of $12,000. All the inventory purchased was still on hand at year-end. Hampton Mines had spent $50,000 in producing the items sold to Route Manufacturing.

Required

   a. What effect, if any, will failure to eliminate or adjust for these items have on total current assets reported in the consolidated balance sheet on December 31, 19X5?
   b. What effect, if any, will failure to eliminate or adjust for these items have on net working capital of the consolidated entity?
   c. What effect, if any, will failure to eliminate or adjust for these items have on the computation of income when the inventory is sold in the following period?

E3-4   Subsidiary Acquired for Cash

Fineline Pencil Company purchased 100 percent of the stock of Smudge Eraser Corporation on January 2, 19X3, for $150,000 cash. Summarized balance sheet data for the companies on December 31, 19X2, are as follows:

	Fineline Pencil Company		Smudge Eraser Corporation	
	Book Value	Fair Value	Book Value	Fair Value
Cash	$200,000	$200,000	$ 50,000	$ 50,000
Other Assets	400,000	650,000	120,000	180,000
Total Debits	$600,000		$170,000	
Current Liabilities	$100,000	100,000	$ 80,000	80,000
Common Stock	300,000		50,000	
Retained Earnings	200,000		40,000	
Total Credits	$600,000		$170,000	

Required

Prepare a consolidated balance sheet immediately following the acquisition.

E3-5 Subsidiary Acquired with Bonds

Byte Computer Corporation purchased 100 percent of the stock of Nofail Software Company on January 2, 19X3, by issuing bonds with par value of $140,000 and a fair value of $150,000 in exchange for the shares. Summarized balance sheet data presented for the companies just before the acquisition are as follows:

	Byte Computer Corporation		Nofail Software Company	
	Book Value	Fair Value	Book Value	Fair Value
Cash	$200,000	$200,000	$ 50,000	$ 50,000
Other Assets	400,000	650,000	120,000	180,000
Total Debits	$600,000		$170,000	
Current Liabilities	$100,000	100,000	$ 80,000	80,000
Common Stock	300,000		50,000	
Retained Earnings	200,000		40,000	
Total Credits	$600,000		$170,000	

Required

Prepare a consolidated balance sheet immediately following the acquisition.

E3-6 Subsidiary Acquired with Stock

Jay Manufacturing Company purchased 100 percent of the stock of Safe Products Corporation on January 1, 19X3, by issuing 10,000 shares of preferred stock. At the time of issue the shares had a par value of $10 each and a market value of $18. Summarized balance sheet data for the companies on December 31, 19X2, were as follows:

	Jay Manufacturing Company		Safe Products Corporation	
	Book Value	Fair Value	Book Value	Fair Value
Cash	$200,000	$200,000	$ 70,000	$ 70,000
Other Assets	500,000	750,000	120,000	170,000
Total Debits	$700,000		$190,000	
Current Liabilities	$200,000	200,000	$ 90,000	90,000
Common Stock	100,000		40,000	
Retained Earnings	400,000		60,000	
Total Credits	$700,000		$190,000	

Required

Prepare a consolidated balance sheet immediately following the acquisition.

E3-7 Computation of Subsidiary Net Income

In the consolidated income statement of Hot Sauce Pizza and Greasy Meats, Incorporated, the noncontrolling interest was assigned $16,000 of income for 19X3.

Required

What amount of net income did Greasy Meats apparently report for 19X3 if Hot Sauce owns 80 percent of the stock of Greasy Meats?

E3-8 Incomplete Consolidation

The accountant for Belchfire Motors was called away after completing only half of the consolidated statements at the end of 19X4. The data left behind included the following:

Item	Belchfire Motors	Premium Body Shop	Consolidated
Cash	$ 40,000	$ 20,000	$ 60,000
Accounts Receivable	180,000	30,000	200,000
Inventory	220,000	50,000	270,000
Buildings and Equipment (net)	300,000	290,000	590,000
Investment in Premium Body Shop	150,000		
Total Debits	$890,000	$390,000	$1,120,000
Accounts Payable	$ 30,000	$ 40,000	
Bonds Payable	400,000	200,000	
Common Stock	200,000	100,000	
Retained Earnings	260,000	50,000	
Total Credits	$890,000	$390,000	

Required

a. Belchfire Motors purchased shares of Premium Body Shop at underlying book value on January 1, 19X1. What portion of the ownership of Premium Body Shop does Belchfire apparently hold?

b. Compute the consolidated totals for each of the remaining balance sheet items.

E3-9* Asset Valuation under Alternative Accounting Theories

Spinn Corporation buys 80 percent of the voting stock of Trimble Company on January 1, 19X3. Among its assets, Trimble Company reports land at its historical cost of $200,000. An appraisal, however, gives evidence that the land is actually worth $300,000.

Required

If consolidated statements are prepared, determine the amount at which the land will be reported using the following consolidation alternatives:

a. Entity theory
b. Parent company theory
c. Proprietary theory
d. Current accounting practice

E3-10* Income Measurement under Alternative Accounting Theories

Board Corporation owns 80 percent of the stock of Term Company. Summarized 19X2 income statement data for the separate companies include the following:

	Board Corporation	Term Company
Total Revenue	$210,000	$90,000
Total Expenses	150,000	50,000

Required

Compute the amount of total revenue, total expenses, and net income to be reported in the 19X2 consolidated income statement under the following alternative consolidation approaches:

a. Entity theory
b. Parent company theory
c. Proprietary theory
d. Current accounting practice

PROBLEMS

P3-11 Multiple-Choice Questions on Consolidated and Combined Financial Statements [AICPA Adapted]

Select the correct answer for each of the following questions.

1. What is the theoretically preferred method of presenting a noncontrolling interest in a consolidated balance sheet?
   a. As a separate item within the liability section.
   b. As a deduction from (contra to) goodwill from consolidation, if any.
   c. By means of notes or footnotes to the balance sheet.
   d. As a separate item within the stockholders' equity section.

2. Presenting consolidated financial statements this year when statements of individual companies were presented last year is:
   a. A correction of an error.
   b. An accounting change that should be reported prospectively.
   c. An accounting change that should be reported by restating the financial statements of all prior periods presented.
   d. Not an accounting change.

3. If all other conditions for consolidation are met, how should subsidiaries acquired in a business combination be shown under each of the following methods?

Purchase	Pooling of Interests
a. Consolidated	Not consolidated
b. Consolidated	Consolidated
c. Not consolidated	Consolidated
d. Not consolidated	Not consolidated

4. A subsidiary, acquired for cash in a business combination, owned equipment with a market value in excess of book value as of the date of combination. A consolidated balance sheet prepared immediately after the acquisition would treat this excess as:
   a. Goodwill.
   b. Plant and equipment.
   c. Retained earnings.
   d. Deferred credits.

5. Par Corp. owns 60 percent of Sub Corp.'s outstanding capital stock. On May 1, 19X8, Par advanced Sub $70,000 in cash, which was still outstanding at December 31, 19X8. What portion of this advance should be eliminated in the preparation of the December 31, 19X8, consolidated balance sheet?
   a. $70,000.
   b. $42,000.
   c. $28,000.
   d. $0.

6. When combined financial statements are prepared for a group of related companies, intercompany transactions and intercompany profits or losses should be eliminated when the group is composed of:

	Commonly Controlled Companies	Unconsolidated Subsidiaries
a.	No	No
b.	No	Yes
c.	Yes	Yes
d.	Yes	No

7. Mr. Cord owns four corporations. Combined financial statements are being prepared for these corporations, which have intercompany loans of $200,000 and intercompany profits of $500,000. What amount of these intercompany loans and profits should be included in the combined financial statements?

	Intercompany	
	Loans	Profits
a.	$200,000	$0
b.	$200,000	$500,000
c.	$0	$0
d.	$0	$500,000

P3-12 Intercompany Sales

Knight Corporation owns 100 percent of the voting shares of Spahn Company. During 19X6, Spahn Company purchased inventory items for $20,000 and sold them to Knight Corporation for $50,000. Knight Corporation continues to hold the items in inventory on December 31, 19X6. Sales for the two companies during 19X6 totaled $300,000, and total cost of goods sold was $200,000.

Required

a. If no adjustment is made to eliminate the intercorporate sale when a consolidated income statement is prepared for 19X6, by what amount will consolidated net income be overstated or understated?

b. Prepare a consolidated income statement for 19X6 without any adjustment for the intercorporate sale.

c. Prepare a consolidated income statement for 19X6 adjusted for the intercorporate sale.

d. What items in the consolidated income statements are different in parts **b** and **c**?

P3-13 Intercompany Inventory Transfer

River Products Corporation purchases all its inventory from its wholly owned subsidiary, Clayborn Corporation. In 19X2, Clayborn produced inventory at a cost of $10,000 and sold it to River Products for $25,000. The parent held all the items in inventory on January 1, 19X3. During 19X3, River Products sold all the units for $55,000.

Required

Assuming the companies had no other transactions during either year, indicate the appropriate amounts to be reported in the consolidated financial statements for the following items:

a. Inventory on January 1, 19X3
b. Cost of goods sold for 19X2
c. Cost of goods sold for 19X3
d. Sales for 19X2
e. Sales for 19X3

P3-14 Consolidated Net Income

Learner Company, which owns 80 percent of the stock of Swagger Corporation, reported net income of $72,000 for 19X2. During 19X2 Swagger Corporation reported net income of $40,000 and paid dividends of $15,000. Learner Company accounts for its ownership of Swagger Corporation using the cost method.

Required

Determine the amount of consolidated net income to be reported by Learner Company and its subsidiary for 19X2.

P3-15 Computation of Parent Company Income

Rainbow Corporation and its subsidiary, Westdale Company, reported consolidated net income of $71,000 for 19X3. Rainbow holds 60 percent of the stock of Westdale Company. In the consolidated income statement for 19X3, the noncontrolling interest was assigned $14,000 of income.

Required

Determine the amount of separate operating income of Rainbow Corporation for 19X3.

P3-16 Consolidated Income Statement Data

Slender Products Corporation purchased 80 percent ownership of LoCal Bakeries on January 1, 19X3, for $40,000 more than its portion of LoCal's underlying book value. The full additional payment is assigned to depreciable assets with an 8-year economic life. Income statement data for the two companies for 19X3 included the following:

	Slender Products		LoCal Bakeries	
Sales		$300,000		$200,000
Cost of Goods Sold	$200,000		$130,000	
Depreciation Expense	40,000	(240,000)	30,000	(160,000)
Income before Income from Subsidiary		$ 60,000		
Net Income				$ 40,000

During 19X3 Slender Products Corporation purchased a special imported yeast for $35,000 and resold it to LoCal Bakeries for $50,000. None of the yeast was resold by LoCal Bakeries before year-end.

Required

Determine the amounts to be reported in the consolidated income statement for 19X3 for each of the following items:

a. Sales
b. Investment income from LoCal Bakeries
c. Cost of goods sold
d. Depreciation expense

P3-17 Computation of Consolidated Totals

The following trial balance was prepared by Tripp Corporation on December 31, 19X6:

Item	Debit	Credit
Cash	$ 30,000	
Accounts Receivable	50,000	
Inventory	70,000	
Buildings and Equipment (net)	140,000	
Cost of Goods Sold	35,000	
Interest and Other Expenses	15,000	
Accounts Payable		$ 20,000
Bonds Payable		100,000
Common Stock		50,000
Retained Earnings		90,000
Sales		80,000
Total	$340,000	$340,000

Strand Company purchased 80 percent ownership of Tripp Corporation on December 31, 19X6, at underlying book value.

Required

a. How much did Strand Company pay in purchasing the shares of Tripp Corporation?

b. If consolidated statements are prepared on December 31, 19X6, what amount will be assigned to the noncontrolling interest in the consolidated balance sheet?

c. If Strand's income from its own separate operations is $80,000 for 19X6, what amount of consolidated net income will be reported for the year?

P3-18   Purchase versus Pooling of Interests

Smart Corporation acquires 100 percent of the common stock of Wisner Company on January 1, 19X8, by issuing 50,000 shares of $4 par value common stock. Smart Corporation shares are selling for $11 at the time of issue. Balance sheet data of the two companies just before the acquisition are summarized as follows:

	Smart Corporation		Wisner Company	
	Book Value	**Fair Value**	**Book Value**	**Fair Value**
Total Assets	$800,000	$970,000	$400,000	$610,000
Total Liabilities	$200,000	215,000	$100,000	110,000
Total Stockholders' Equity	600,000		300,000	
Total Liabilities and Stockholders' Equity	$800,000		$400,000	

Required

Indicate the dollar amounts to be reported in the consolidated balance sheet for each of the following items under the alternatives indicated.

a. Acquisition of shares by Smart Corporation recorded as a pooling of interests:
 (1) Total assets
 (2) Total liabilities
 (3) Total stockholders' equity
b. Acquisition of shares by Smart Corporation recorded as a purchase:
 (1) Total assets
 (2) Total liabilities
 (3) Total stockholders' equity

P3-19   Computation of Consolidated and Parent Company Balances

Quality Manufacturing purchased 70 percent of the stock of Purity Mining Corporation on January 1, 19X4, when Purity reported net assets of $450,000. Purity reported the following net income and dividends in the periods following the acquisition:

Year	Net Income	Dividends
19X4	$10,000	$ 5,000
19X5	80,000	15,000
19X6	30,000	20,000

The balance in the investment account of Quality on December 31, 19X6, is $404,600. The excess of the purchase price paid by Quality over the book value of the shares acquired is considered to be goodwill and is being amortized over a 15-year period.

Required

a. What amount of goodwill will be reported in the consolidated balance sheet for December 31, 19X6?

b. How much did Quality Manufacturing pay to purchase the shares of Purity Mining Corporation on January 1, 19X4?

c. What amount will be assigned to noncontrolling shareholders on December 31, 19X6, in the consolidated balance sheet?

P3-20   Fair Value Greater than Cost

Delkart Products Company acquired 100 percent of the common shares of Angel Company on January 1, 19X2, by issuing 6,000 shares of its $10 par common stock. At the time of the business combination, Delkart's stock was selling for $70 per share. Balance sheets for the two companies as of December 31, 19X1, with fair values included, were as follows:

	Delkart Products Co.		Angel Company	
	Book Value	**Fair Value**	**Book Value**	**Fair Value**
Cash and Receivables	$ 80,000	$ 80,000	$ 75,000	$ 75,000
Inventory	240,000	260,000	125,000	145,000
Equipment (net)	480,000	560,000	300,000	340,000
Total Assets	$800,000	$900,000	$500,000	$560,000
Current Payables	$ 50,000	$ 50,000	$ 30,000	$ 30,000
Notes Payable	200,000	220,000	100,000	100,000
Common Stock	300,000		200,000	
Retained Earnings	250,000		170,000	
Total Liabilities and Equity	$800,000		$500,000	

On December 31, 19X1, Angel owed Delkart $25,000 on a 1-year note; although the interest was paid on December 31, the principal was still outstanding on January 1, 19X2.

Required

Prepare a consolidated balance sheet for Delkart Products Company and its subsidiary as of January 1, 19X2:

a. Assuming the combination is treated as a pooling of interests
b. Assuming the combination is treated as a purchase

P3-21   Indirect Ownership

Purple Corporation recently attempted to expand by purchasing ownership in Green Company. The following ownership structure was reported on December 31, 19X9:

Investor	Investee	Percentage of Ownership Held
Purple Corporation	Green Company	70
Green Company	Orange Corporation	10
Orange Corporation	Blue Company	60
Green Company	Yellow Company	40

The following income from operations (excluding investment income) and dividend payments were reported by the companies during 19X9:

Company	Operating Income	Dividends Paid
Purple Corporation	$ 90,000	$60,000
Green Company	20,000	10,000
Orange Corporation	40,000	30,000
Blue Company	100,000	80,000
Yellow Company	60,000	40,000

Required

Compute the amount of consolidated net income reported for 19X9.

P3-22 Comprehensive Problem: Consolidated Financial Statements

Bishop Enterprises purchased 100 percent of the common shares of Mangle Manufacturing Company on January 1, 19X7, for $1,250,000, a price that was $55,000 in excess of the book value of the shares acquired. All of the excess of the cost over book value was related to goodwill except for $25,000 related to equipment with a 5-year remaining life at the date of combination. All intangibles are amortized over 10 years.

Balance sheets for the two companies as of December 31, 19X7, were as follows:

	Bishop Enterprises	Mangle Manufacturing
Cash	$ 71,000	$ 33,000
Receivables (net)	431,000	122,000
Inventory	909,000	370,000
Investment in Mangle Stock (at cost)	1,250,000	—
Land	510,000	100,000
Buildings (net)	1,303,000	250,000
Equipment (net)	1,528,000	475,000
Total Assets	$6,002,000	$1,350,000
Current Payables	$ 227,000	$ 95,000
Bonds Payable	500,000	—
Common Stock	1,000,000	500,000
Additional Paid-In Capital	3,550,000	400,000
Retained Earnings	725,000	355,000
Total Liabilities and Equity	$6,002,000	$1,350,000

For the year 19X7, the separate income statements of Bishop and Mangle included, among other items, the following:

	Bishop Enterprises	Mangle Manufacturing
Sales Revenue	$8,325,000	$2,980,000
Cost of Goods Sold	5,150,000	2,010,000
Depreciation Expense	302,000	85,000

The only intercompany transaction during 19X7 was a sale of inventory at the end of the year from Bishop to Mangle. Bishop originally purchased the goods for $34,000 and sold them to Mangle for $45,000 on account. All of the goods still were in Mangle's inventory at year-end, and the account had not yet been paid by Mangle.

Required

Indicate the amount at which each of the following items would be reported in the 19X7 consolidated financial statements of Bishop Enterprises and its subsidiary:

    a. Cash
    b. Receivables (net)
    c. Inventory
    d. Investment in Mangle Stock
    e. Equipment (net)
    f. Goodwill
    g. Current Payables
    h. Common Stock (par)
    i. Retained Earnings
    j. Sales Revenue
    k. Cost of Goods Sold
    l. Depreciation Expense

P3-23A Inventory Valuation under Alternative Accounting Theories

Mustin Company holds 80 percent of the stock of Staley Corporation. During 19X2, Staley Corporation purchased inventory for $20,000 and sold it to Mustin Company for $50,000. Mustin Company continues to hold the inventory on December 31, 19X2.

Required

Determine the dollar amount of Mustin's inventory purchased from Staley that should be reported in the consolidated balance sheet on December 31, 19X2, under each of the following theories or approaches to consolidation:

    a. Proprietary theory
    b. Parent company theory
    c. Entity theory
    d. Current accounting practice

P3-24A Balance Sheet Data under Alternative Accounting Theories

Expandable Company acquired 60 percent of the voting shares of Rigid Corporation on January 1, 19X2, by issuing 10,000 shares of Expandable Company $10 par value common stock. On that date, the Expandable shares had a market price of $15 per share. Summarized balance sheet data for the two companies on January 1, 19X2, just before the acquisition were as follows:

	Expandable Company		Rigid Corporation	
	Book Value	Fair Value	Book Value	Fair Value
Cash and Accounts Receivable	$150,000	$160,000	$ 20,000	$ 20,000
Other Assets	450,000	630,000	130,000	250,000
Total Assets	$600,000		$150,000	
Accounts Payable	$ 90,000	90,000	$ 70,000	70,000
Common Stock	200,000		30,000	
Retained Earnings	310,000		50,000	
Total Liabilities and Equities	$600,000		$150,000	

Required

Determine the amount to be reported in the consolidated balance sheet for (1) cash and accounts receivable, (2) other assets, (3) goodwill, and (4) accounts payable under each of the following theories or approaches to consolidation:

    a. Proprietary theory
    b. Parent company theory
    c. Entity theory
    d. Current accounting practice

CHAPTER 4

CONSOLIDATION AS OF THE DATE OF ACQUISITION

Consolidated and unconsolidated financial statements are prepared using the same generally accepted accounting principles. The unique aspect of consolidated statements is that they bring together the operating results and financial positions of two or more separate legal entities into a single set of statements for the economic entity as a whole. In order to accomplish this, the consolidation process includes procedures that eliminate all effects of intercorporate ownership and intercompany transactions. Only transactions with parties external to the economic entity are reported in the consolidated financial statements.

The procedures used in accounting for intercorporate investments were discussed in Chapter 2. These procedures are important for the preparation of consolidated statements because the specific consolidation procedures depend on the way in which the parent accounts for its investment in a subsidiary. The consolidated statements, however, are the same regardless of the method used by the parent company to account for its investment.

This chapter and the next provide a thorough introduction to the process by which consolidated financial statements are prepared. After introducing the consolidation workpaper, this chapter provides the foundation for an understanding of the preparation of consolidated financial statements by discussing the preparation of a consolidated balance sheet immediately following the establishment of a parent-subsidiary relationship. The process is extended in Chapter 5 to include the preparation of a full set of consolidated financial statements in subsequent periods. Then, using a building-block approach, Chapters 6 through 10 deal with intercorporate transfers and other more complex issues.

CONSOLIDATION WORKPAPERS

The *consolidation workpaper* provides a mechanism for efficiently combining the accounts of the separate companies involved in the consolidation and for adjusting the combined balances to the amounts that would be reported if all the consolidating companies were actually a single company. Keep in mind that there is no set of books for the consolidated entity. The parent and the subsidiaries, as separate legal and accounting entities, each maintain their own books. When consolidated financial statements are prepared, the account balances are taken from the separate books of the parent and each subsidiary and placed in the consolidation workpaper. The consolidated statements are prepared, after adjustments and eliminations, from the amounts in the consolidation workpaper.

Workpaper Format

The basic form of the consolidation workpaper is shown in Figure 4-1. The titles of the accounts of the consolidating companies are listed in the first column of the workpaper. The account balances from the books or trial balances of the individ-

FIGURE 4-1 Format for consolidation workpaper.

Account Titles	Trial Balance Data		Elimination Entries		Consolidated
	Parent	Subsidiary	Debits	Credits	

Work Flow →

ual companies are listed in the next set of columns, with a separate column for each company included in the consolidation. Entries are made in the columns labeled "Elimination Entries" to adjust or eliminate balances so that the resulting amounts are those that would appear in the financial statements if all the consolidating companies actually formed a single company. The balances in the last column are obtained by summing all amounts algebraically across the workpaper by account. These are the balances that appear in the consolidated financial statements.

Nature of Eliminating Entries

Eliminating entries are used in the consolidation workpaper to adjust the totals of the individual account balances of the separate consolidating companies to reflect the amounts that would appear if all the legally separate companies were actually a single company. Eliminating entries appear only in the consolidating workpapers and do not affect the books of the separate companies.

For the most part, companies that are to be consolidated record their transactions during the period without regard to the consolidated entity. Transactions with related companies tend to be recorded in the same manner as those with unrelated parties, although intercompany transactions may be recorded in separate accounts or other records may be kept to facilitate the later elimination of intercompany transactions. Each of the consolidating companies also prepares its adjusting and closing entries at the end of the period in the normal manner. The resulting balances are entered in the consolidation workpaper and combined to arrive at the consolidated totals. Elimination entries are used to increase or decrease in the workpaper the combined totals for individual accounts so that only transactions with external parties are reflected in the consolidated amounts.

Some eliminating entries are required at the end of one period but not at the end of subsequent periods. For example, a loan from a parent to a subsidiary in December 19X1, repaid in February 19X2, requires an entry to eliminate the intercompany receivable and payable on December 31, 19X1, but not at the end of 19X2. Some other eliminating entries need to be placed in the consolidation workpapers each time consolidated statements are prepared for a period of years. For example, if a parent company sells land to a subsidiary for $5,000 above the cost to the parent, a workpaper entry is needed to reduce the land amount by $5,000 each time a consolidated balance sheet is prepared, for as long as the land is held by an affiliate. It is important to remember that eliminating entries, because they are not made on the books of any company, do not carry over from period to period.

PREPARATION OF CONSOLIDATED BALANCE SHEET IMMEDIATELY FOLLOWING ACQUISITION OF FULL OWNERSHIP

The simplest consolidation setting occurs when the financial statements of related companies are consolidated immediately after a parent-subsidiary relationship is

FIGURE 4-2 Balance sheets of Peerless Products and Special Foods, January 1, 19X1, immediately before combination.

	Peerless Products	Special Foods
Assets		
Cash	$ 350,000	$ 50,000
Accounts Receivable	75,000	50,000
Inventory	100,000	60,000
Land	175,000	40,000
Buildings and Equipment	800,000	600,000
Accumulated Depreciation	(400,000)	(300,000)
Total Assets	$1,100,000	$500,000
Liabilities and Stockholders' Equity		
Accounts Payable	$ 100,000	$100,000
Bonds Payable	200,000	100,000
Common Stock	500,000	200,000
Retained Earnings	300,000	100,000
Total Liabilities and Equity	$1,100,000	$500,000

established through a business combination. A series of examples follows that illustrates the preparation of a consolidated balance sheet in various situations that might arise when the business combination is treated as a purchase. In each example, Peerless Products Corporation purchases all or part of the capital stock of Special Foods, Inc., on January 1, 19X1, and immediately prepares a consolidated balance sheet. The separate balance sheets of the two companies immediately before the combination appear in Figure 4-2.

In the material that follows, all journal entries and workpaper eliminating entries are numbered sequentially throughout the chapter. Eliminating entries appearing in the workpapers also are discussed in the text of the chapter. To avoid confusing the eliminating entries with journal entries that appear on the separate books of the parent or subsidiary, all workpaper eliminating entries appearing in the text are shaded and designated by an entry number preceded by an "E."

Full Ownership Purchased at Book Value

In the first example, Peerless purchases all of Special Foods' outstanding common stock for $300,000. On the date of combination, the fair values of Special Foods' individual assets and liabilities are equal to their book values shown in Figure 4-2. Because Peerless acquires all of Special Foods' common stock and because Special Foods has only the one class of stock outstanding, the total book value of the shares acquired is equal to the total stockholders' equity of Special Foods ($200,000 + $100,000). The purchase price of $300,000 is equal to the book value of the shares acquired. This ownership situation can be characterized as follows:

	P	Investment cost		$300,000
1/1/X1		Book value:		
100%		Common stock—Special Foods	$200,000	
		Retained earnings—Special Foods	100,000	
			$300,000	
	S	Peerless's share	× 1.00	(300,000)
		Difference between cost and book value		$ -0-

Peerless records the acquisition on its books with the following entry on the date of combination:

January 1, 19X1
(1) Investment in Special Foods Stock   300,000
    Cash   300,000
      Record purchase of Special Foods stock.

The separate financial statements of Peerless and Special Foods immediately after the combination appear in Figure 4-3. Special Foods' balance sheet in Figure 4-3 is the same as in Figure 4-2, but the balance sheet of Peerless has changed to reflect the $300,000 reduction in cash and the recording of the investment in Special Foods stock for the same amount.

Consolidation Workpaper   The workpaper for the preparation of a consolidated balance sheet immediately following the acquisition is presented in Figure 4-4. The first two columns of the workpaper in Figure 4-4 are the account balances

FIGURE 4-3 Balance sheets of Peerless Products and Special Foods, January 1, 19X1, immediately after combination.

	Peerless Products	Special Foods
Assets		
Cash	$ 50,000	$ 50,000
Accounts Receivable	75,000	50,000
Inventory	100,000	60,000
Land	175,000	40,000
Buildings and Equipment	800,000	600,000
Accumulated Depreciation	(400,000)	(300,000)
Investment in Special Foods Stock	300,000	
Total Assets	$1,100,000	$500,000
Liabilities and Stockholders' Equity		
Accounts Payable	$ 100,000	$100,000
Bonds Payable	200,000	100,000
Common Stock	500,000	200,000
Retained Earnings	300,000	100,000
Total Liabilities and Equity	$1,100,000	$500,000

taken from the books of Peerless and Special Foods, as shown in Figure 4-3. The balances of like accounts are placed side by side so that they may be added together. If more than two companies were to be consolidated, a separate column would be included in the workpaper for each additional subsidiary.

The accounts are placed in the workpaper so that those having debit balances are in the upper half of the workpaper and those having credit balances are in the lower half. Total debit items must equal total credit items for each of the companies and for the consolidated totals.

The two columns labeled "Eliminations" in Figure 4-4 are used to adjust the amounts reported by the individual companies to the amounts appropriate for the consolidated statement. All eliminations made in the workpapers are made in double-entry form; the debit amounts of each entry must equal the credit amounts. All parts of the same eliminating entry are "keyed" with the same number or other symbol so that whole entries can be identified. When the workpaper is completed, total debits entered in the Debit Eliminations column must equal total credits entered in the Credit Eliminations column. After the appropriate eliminating entries have been entered in the Eliminations columns, summing algebraically across the individual accounts provides the consolidated totals.

The Investment Elimination Entry The only eliminating entry in the workpaper in Figure 4-4 is that needed to eliminate the Investment in Special Foods

FIGURE 4-4 Workpaper for consolidated balance sheet, January 1, 19X1, date of combination; 100 percent purchase at book value.

Item	Peerless Products	Special Foods	Eliminations Debit	Eliminations Credit	Consolidated
Cash	50,000	50,000			100,000
Accounts Receivable	75,000	50,000			125,000
Inventory	100,000	60,000			160,000
Land	175,000	40,000			215,000
Buildings and Equipment	800,000	600,000			1,400,000
Investment in Special Foods Stock	300,000			(2) 300,000	
Total Debits	1,500,000	800,000			2,000,000
Accumulated Depreciation	400,000	300,000			700,000
Accounts Payable	100,000	100,000			200,000
Bonds Payable	200,000	100,000			300,000
Common Stock	500,000	200,000	(2) 200,000		500,000
Retained Earnings	300,000	100,000	(2) 100,000		300,000
Total Credits	1,500,000	800,000	300,000	300,000	2,000,000

Elimination entry:
(2) Eliminate investment balance and stockholders' equity of Special Foods.
(*Note:* Elimination entries are keyed to those in the text; all entries are numbered sequentially throughout the chapter.)

Stock account and the subsidiary's stockholders' equity accounts. This is accomplished through entry E(2) in the workpaper:

E(2)	Common Stock—Special Foods	200,000	
	Retained Earnings	100,000	
	Investment in Special Foods Stock		300,000
	Eliminate investment balance.		

Remember that this entry is made in the consolidation workpaper, not on the books of either the parent or the subsidiary, and is presented here in general journal form only for instructional purposes.

The investment account must be eliminated because, from a single entity viewpoint, a company cannot hold an investment in itself. The subsidiary's stock and the related stockholders' equity accounts also must be eliminated because the stock of the subsidiary is held entirely within the consolidated entity and none represents claims by outsiders.

From a somewhat different viewpoint, the investment account on the parent's books can be thought of as a single account representing the parent's investment in the net assets of the subsidiary, a so-called "one-line consolidation." In a full consolidation, the individual assets and liabilities of the subsidiary are combined with those of the parent. Including both the net assets of the subsidiary, as represented by the balance in the investment account, and the subsidiary's individual assets and liabilities would double-count the same set of assets. Therefore, the investment account is eliminated and not carried to the consolidated balance sheet.

The Consolidated Balance Sheet   The consolidated balance sheet presented in Figure 4-5 is prepared directly from the last column of the consolidation workpaper in Figure 4-4. The total debit and credit balances shown on the balance

FIGURE 4-5 Consolidated balance sheet, January 1, 19X1, date of combination; 100 percent purchase at book value.

Peerless Products Corporation and Subsidiary
Consolidated Balance Sheet
January 1, 19X1

Assets:			Liabilities:	
Cash		$ 100,000	Accounts Payable	$ 200,000
Accounts Receivable		125,000	Bonds Payable	300,000
Inventory		160,000		
Land		215,000	Stockholders' Equity:	
Buildings and Equipment	$1,400,000		Common Stock	500,000
Accumulated Depreciation	(700,000)	700,000	Retained Earnings	300,000
Total Assets		$1,300,000	Total Liabilities and Equity	$1,300,000

sheet differ from the debit and credit totals given in the workpaper because contra asset accounts are included with the credits in the workpaper but are offset against the related assets in the consolidated balance sheet. Because the combination was treated as a purchase and there were no operations between the date of combination and the preparation of the consolidated balance sheet, the stockholders' equity section of the consolidated balance sheet is identical with that of Peerless given in Figure 4-2.

Full Ownership Purchased at More than Book Value

The price of the stock of a company is influenced by many factors, including net asset values, enterprise earning power, and general market conditions. When one company purchases another, there is no reason to expect that the purchase price necessarily will be equal to the book value of the stock acquired. The process used to prepare the consolidated balance sheet is complicated only slightly when 100 percent of the stock of a company is purchased at a price different from its book value.

To illustrate the purchase of a subsidiary at a price greater than book value, assume that Peerless purchases all of Special Foods' outstanding capital stock for $340,000 in cash on January 1, 19X1. In doing so, Peerless pays $40,000 in excess of the book value of that stock. The resulting ownership situation can be viewed as follows:

P	Investment cost			$340,000
	Book value			
1/1/X1	Common stock—Special Foods	$200,000		
100%	Retained earnings—Special Foods	100,000		
		$300,000		
S	Peerless's share	× 1.00	(300,000)	
	Differential			$ 40,000

Peerless records the acquisition by making the following entry:

January 1, 19X1
(3) Investment in Special Foods Stock   340,000
       Cash   340,000
    Record purchase of Special Foods stock.

In a business combination accounted for as a purchase, the purchase price must be allocated to the assets and liabilities acquired. Therefore, the full amount paid by Peerless must be assigned to individual assets and liabilities of Special Foods when preparing consolidated financial statements.

The workpaper procedures used in adjusting to the proper consolidated amounts follow a consistent pattern. The first eliminating entry prepared in each case involves the elimination of the investor's investment account balance and each of the common stockholders' equity accounts of the investee. When the purchase price is above the underlying book value of the stock acquired, the first eliminating entry includes a debit to a workpaper clearing account to balance the entry. This clearing account is referred to as the *purchase differential*, or just differential. The differential represents the difference between the cost of the investment as recorded on the books of the parent and the book value of the shares acquired as determined by the stockholders' equity accounts of the subsidiary.

The workpaper entry to eliminate the investment account of Peerless Products and the stockholders' equity items of Special Foods is as follows:

E(4)	Common Stock—Special Foods	200,000	
	Retained Earnings	100,000	
	Differential	40,000	
	Investment in Special Foods Stock		340,000
	Eliminate investment balance.		

The balance assigned to Differential in this initial eliminating entry is cleared from that account through one or more additional workpaper entries. These additional workpaper entries adjust the various account balances to reflect the fair values of the subsidiary's assets and liabilities at the time the parent acquired the subsidiary.

Treatment of a Positive Differential

There are several reasons why the purchase price of a company's stock might exceed the stock's book value:

1. Errors or omissions on the books of the subsidiary
2. Excess of fair value over the book value of the subsidiary's net identifiable assets
3. Existence of goodwill
4. Other reasons

Errors or Omissions on the Books of the Subsidiary An examination of the books of an acquired company may reveal material errors. In some cases, assets may have been expensed rather than capitalized by the acquired company or, for other reasons, omitted from the books. An acquired company that previously had been closely held may not have followed generally accepted accounting principles in maintaining its accounting records. In some cases, there may simply have been inadequate record keeping.

Where such errors or omissions exist, corrections should be made directly on the books of the subsidiary as of the date of acquisition. These corrections are treated as prior-period adjustments in accordance with **FASB Statement No. 16,**

"Prior Period Adjustments" (FASB 16). Once the books of the subsidiary are stated in accordance with generally accepted accounting principles, that portion of the differential attributable to the errors or omissions would no longer exist.

Excess of Fair Value over Book Value of Subsidiary's Net Identifiable Assets
The fair value of a company's assets is an important factor in the overall determination of the purchase price of the company. In many cases, the fair value of an acquired company's net assets exceeds the book value. Consequently, the purchase price may exceed the book value of the stock acquired. Consistent with the accounting treatment required for purchase-type business combinations, the procedures used in preparing the consolidated balance sheet should lead to reporting all the assets and liabilities of the acquired company based on their fair values on the date of combination. This valuation may be accomplished in one of two ways: (1) the assets and liabilities of the subsidiary may be revalued directly on the books of the subsidiary, or (2) the accounting basis of the subsidiary may be maintained and the revaluations made each period in the consolidation workpaper.

Revaluing the assets and liabilities on the books of the subsidiary generally is the simplest approach if all the common stock of the subsidiary is acquired. On the other hand, it generally is not appropriate to revalue the assets and liabilities on the books of the subsidiary if there is a significant noncontrolling interest in that subsidiary. From a noncontrolling shareholder's point of view, the subsidiary is a continuing company, and the basis of accounting should not change. More difficult to resolve is the situation where the parent acquires all the common stock of the subsidiary but continues to issue separate financial statements of the subsidiary to holders of the subsidiary's bonds or preferred stock. Revaluing the assets and liabilities of the subsidiary directly on the subsidiary's books is referred to as *push-down accounting* and is discussed later in this chapter.

When the assets and liabilities are revalued directly on the subsidiary's books, that portion of the differential no longer exists. However, if the assets and liabilities are not revalued on the subsidiary's books, an entry to revalue those assets and allocate the differential is needed in the consolidation workpaper each time consolidated financial statements are prepared, for as long as the related assets are held.

In the example introduced earlier, Peerless Products acquired all the stock of Special Foods for $340,000, giving rise to a $40,000 debit differential. In a consolidated balance sheet prepared immediately after acquisition, the investment elimination entry appearing in the consolidation workpaper is (as given earlier):

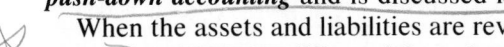

E(4)	Common Stock—Special Foods	200,000	
	Retained Earnings	100,000	
	Differential	40,000	
	Investment in Special Foods Stock		340,000
	Eliminate investment balance.		

If the fair value of Special Foods' land is determined to be $40,000 greater than its book value, and all other assets and liabilities have fair values equal to their book values, the entire amount of the differential is allocated to the subsidiary's land. This allocation of the differential is made in the consolidation workpaper with the following eliminating entry:

E(5)	Land	40,000	
	Differential		40,000
	Assign differential to land.		

The consolidation workpaper reflecting the allocation of the differential to the subsidiary's land is illustrated in Figure 4-6. The workpaper is based on the data in Figure 4-2 and a purchase price of $340,000 for the stock of Special Foods.

The amounts reported in the consolidated balance sheet are those in the consolidated column of the workpaper in Figure 4-6. Land is included in the consolidated balance sheet at $255,000, the amount carried on Peerless's books ($175,000) plus the amount carried on Special Foods' books ($40,000) plus the differential reflecting the increased value of Special Foods' land ($40,000).

FIGURE 4-6 Workpaper for consolidated balance sheet, January 1, 19X1, date of combination; 100 percent purchase at more than book value.

	Peerless Products	Special Foods	Eliminations		Consolidated
Item			Debit	Credit	
Cash	10,000	50,000			60,000
Accounts Receivable	75,000	50,000			125,000
Inventory	100,000	60,000			160,000
Land	175,000	40,000	(5) 40,000		255,000
Buildings and Equipment	800,000	600,000			1,400,000
Investment in Special Foods Stock	340,000			(4) 340,000	
Differential			(4) 40,000	(5) 40,000	
Total Debits	1,500,000	800,000			2,000,000
Accumulated Depreciation	400,000	300,000			700,000
Accounts Payable	100,000	100,000			200,000
Bonds Payable	200,000	100,000			300,000
Common Stock	500,000	200,000	(4) 200,000		500,000
Retained Earnings	300,000	100,000	(4) 100,000		300,000
Total Credits	1,500,000	800,000	380,000	380,000	2,000,000

Elimination entries:
(4) Eliminate investment balance and stockholders' equity of Special Foods.
(5) Assign differential to land.

This example is sufficiently simple that the assignment of the differential to land could be made directly in eliminating entry E(4) rather than through the use of the differential clearing account. In practice, however, the differential often relates to more than a single asset, and the allocation of the differential may be considerably more complex than in this example. The possibilities for clerical errors are reduced in complex situations by making two separate entries rather than one complicated entry.

Existence of Goodwill If a company purchases a subsidiary at a price in excess of the total of the fair values of the subsidiary's net identifiable assets, the additional amount generally is considered to be a payment for the excess earning power of the acquired company, referred to as "goodwill." Thus, once the identifiable assets of the subsidiary are restated to their fair values, any remaining debit differential normally is allocated to goodwill.

If, in the example of Peerless and Special Foods, the fair values of Special Foods' assets and liabilities are equal to their book values, and the $40,000 differential is considered a payment for goodwill, the following elimination entry is needed in the consolidation workpaper:

E(6)	Goodwill	40,000	
	Differential		40,000
	Assign differential to goodwill.		

The consolidation workpaper would appear as in Figure 4-6 except that elimination entry E(6) would replace elimination entry E(5). Goodwill, which does not appear on the books of either Peerless or Special Foods, would appear in the consolidated balance sheet at $40,000.

Other Reasons The amounts assigned to identifiable assets and goodwill should be reasonable when viewed in light of the existing circumstances and the conditions of the purchase. The reason for all or part of a debit differential is not always clear, however. In these cases, management sometimes chooses to carry a portion of the differential directly to the consolidated balance sheet with a title such as "Excess of Purchase Price over Fair Value of Subsidiary's Net Assets."

Cases where the reason for a debit differential is not determinable should be rare. Normally, the management of the parent company is expected to know why they paid a particular price for the subsidiary, and the differential should be allocated accordingly.

In practice, companies sometimes do not attempt to allocate the differential, and simply report the entire amount in the consolidated balance sheet as a deferred charge. Usually this amount is given a title such as "Excess of Purchase

Price over Book Value of Investment in Subsidiary Stock.'' While expedient, such an approach is inappropriate because it is not consistent with the idea of a single economic entity.

Illustration of Treatment of Debit Differential

In many situations, the differential relates to a number of different assets and liabilities. As a means of illustrating the allocation of the differential to various assets and liabilities, assume the book values and fair values of Special Foods' assets and liabilities are as shown in Figure 4-7. The inventory and land have fair values in excess of their book values while the buildings and equipment are worth less than their book values.

Bond prices fluctuate as interest rates change. In this example, the value of Special Foods' bonds payable is greater than the book value. This indicates that the nominal interest rate on the bonds is higher than the current market rate of interest, and, therefore, investors are willing to pay a price higher than par for the bonds. In past practice, book values often were used in place of the fair values of liabilities when recording business combinations using purchase treatment. More recently, however, with the greater fluctuations in interest rates, greater emphasis has been placed on valuing acquired liabilities at their fair values. In determining a purchase price for Special Foods, Peerless must recognize that it is assuming a liability that pays an interest rate higher than the current market rate and will pay a lower price for Special Foods than if the liability carried a lower interest rate. The resulting consolidated financial statements, therefore, should recognize the fair values rather than the book values of Special Foods' liabilities.

FIGURE 4-7 Balance sheet for Special Foods, Inc., January 1, 19X1, date of combination.

		Book Value	Fair Value	Difference between Fair Value and Book Value
Cash		$ 50,000	$ 50,000	
Accounts Receivable		50,000	50,000	
Inventory		60,000	75,000	$ 15,000
Land		40,000	100,000	60,000
Buildings and Equipment	$600,000			
Accumulated Depreciation	(300,000)	300,000	290,000	(10,000)
		$500,000	$565,000	
Accounts Payable		$100,000	$100,000	
Bonds Payable		100,000	135,000	(35,000)
Common Stock		200,000		
Retained Earnings		100,000		
		$500,000	$235,000	$ 30,000

Assume that Peerless Products acquires all Special Foods' capital stock for $400,000 on January 1, 19X1, by issuing $100,000 of 9 percent first mortgage bonds and paying cash of $300,000. The resulting ownership situation can be pictured as follows:

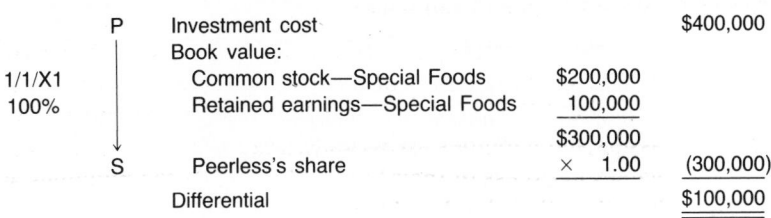

	P	Investment cost		$400,000
		Book value:		
1/1/X1		Common stock—Special Foods	$200,000	
100%		Retained earnings—Special Foods	100,000	
			$300,000	
	S	Peerless's share	× 1.00	(300,000)
		Differential		$100,000

Peerless records the investment on its books with the following entry:

January 1, 19X1
(7)	Investment in Special Foods Stock	400,000	
	Bonds Payable		100,000
	Cash		300,000
	Record purchase of Special Foods stock.		

The relationship between the total purchase price paid for the stock of Special Foods, the fair value of Special Foods' net assets, and the book value of Special Foods' net assets is as follows:

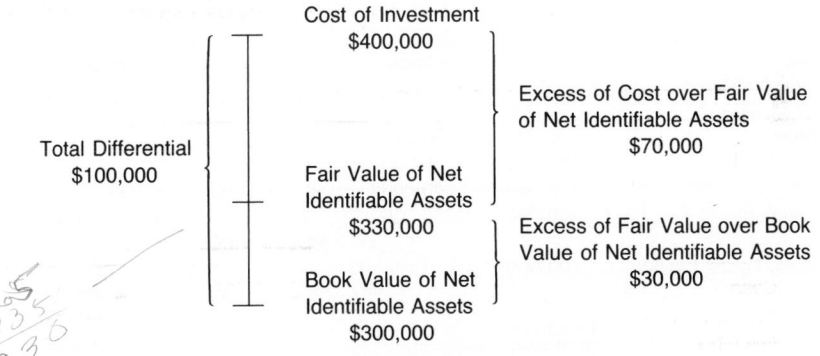

Total Differential $100,000

Cost of Investment $400,000

Fair Value of Net Identifiable Assets $330,000

Book Value of Net Identifiable Assets $300,000

Excess of Cost over Fair Value of Net Identifiable Assets $70,000

Excess of Fair Value over Book Value of Net Identifiable Assets $30,000

The total purchase price of $400,000 exceeds by $100,000 the book value of Special Foods' net assets (assets of $500,000 less liabilities of $200,000). Thus, there is a total purchase differential of $100,000. The total fair value of the net identifiable assets acquired in the combination is $330,000 ($565,000 − $235,000), based on the data in Figure 4-7. The amount by which the total purchase price of $400,000 exceeds the $330,000 fair value of the net identifiable assets is $70,000, and that amount is assigned to goodwill in the consolidated balance sheet.

The eliminations entered in the consolidation workpaper in preparing the consolidated balance sheet immediately after the combination are:

E(8)	Common Stock—Special Foods	200,000	
	Retained Earnings	100,000	
	Differential	100,000	
	Investment in Special Foods Stock		400,000
	Eliminate investment balance.		
E(9)	Inventory	15,000	
	Land	60,000	
	Goodwill	70,000	
	Buildings and Equipment		10,000
	Premium on Bonds Payable		35,000
	Differential		100,000
	Assign differential.		

These entries are reflected in the workpaper in Figure 4-8. While entry E(9) is somewhat more complex than those in the previous examples, there is no conceptual difference. In each case, the end result is a consolidated balance sheet with the assets and liabilities of the subsidiary valued at their fair values at the date of combination.

FIGURE 4-8 Workpaper for consolidated balance sheet, January 1, 19X1, date of combination; 100 percent purchase at more than book value.

Item	Peerless Products	Special Foods	Eliminations Debit	Eliminations Credit	Consolidated
Cash	50,000	50,000			100,000
Accounts Receivable	75,000	50,000			125,000
Inventory	100,000	60,000	(9) 15,000		175,000
Land	175,000	40,000	(9) 60,000		275,000
Buildings and Equipment	800,000	600,000		(9) 10,000	1,390,000
Goodwill			(9) 70,000		70,000
Investment in Special Foods Stock	400,000			(8) 400,000	
Differential			(8) 100,000	(9) 100,000	
Total Debits	1,600,000	800,000			2,135,000
Accumulated Depreciation	400,000	300,000			700,000
Accounts Payable	100,000	100,000			200,000
Bonds Payable	300,000	100,000			400,000
Premium on Bonds Payable				(9) 35,000	35,000
Common Stock	500,000	200,000	(8) 200,000		500,000
Retained Earnings	300,000	100,000	(8) 100,000		300,000
Total Credits	1,600,000	800,000	545,000	545,000	2,135,000

Elimination entries:
(8) Eliminate investment balance and stockholders' equity of Special Foods.
(9) Assign differential.

Full Ownership Purchased at Less than Book Value

There have been numerous cases of companies whose common stock traded in the market at prices less than book value. Often the companies are singled out as prime acquisition targets. When one company acquires the stock of another at less than book value, there may be several reasons for the negative, or credit, differential:

1. Errors or omissions on the books of the subsidiary
2. Excess of book value over the fair value of the subsidiary's net identifiable assets
3. Reduction of previously recorded goodwill
4. Bargain purchase

Errors or Omissions on the Books of the Subsidiary   As in the case of a debit differential, errors or omissions on the subsidiary's books should be corrected directly on those books. Often this involves recognizing previously unrecorded liabilities incurred by the subsidiary. Once these corrections are made on the books of the subsidiary, that portion of the differential no longer will exist.

Excess of Book Value over Fair Value of Subsidiary's Net Identifiable Assets
Because in a purchase-type business combination all assets and liabilities of the acquired company are to be valued at their fair values as of the date of combination, adjustments are needed for any of the acquired company's assets and liabilities carried at amounts other than their current fair values. Assets with fair values less than their book values are written down on the subsidiary's books if push-down accounting is used, or in the consolidation workpaper.

Reduction of Previously Recorded Goodwill   If the subsidiary has goodwill carried on its books from a previous business combination, the credit differential may be an indication that goodwill no longer exists. If that is determined to be the case, the goodwill should be written off the books of the subsidiary.

Bargain Purchase   In some cases the reason for a credit differential may not be clear. One suggestion is the existence of "negative goodwill," indicating that the net assets of the subsidiary are worth less as a going concern than if they were sold individually. If that is the case, the subsidiary may very well be liquidated. Another view is that the acquiring company simply made a *bargain purchase*. This view assumes that for whatever reason (e.g., forced sale, general stock market conditions), the subsidiary was acquired at a price below its estimated value.

Whenever an unallocated credit differential exists, **APB 16** requires that it be allocated against the amounts assigned to the subsidiary's noncurrent assets, excluding marketable securities, in proportion to their fair values. If all the noncurrent assets are reduced to zero and a credit differential remains, the balance should be carried to the consolidated balance sheet as a deferred credit and amortized over the period of time benefited by the bargain purchase, not to

FIGURE 4-9 Balance sheet for Special Foods, Inc., January 1, 19X1, date of combination.

		Book Value	Fair Value	Difference between Fair Value and Book Value
Cash		$ 50,000	$ 50,000	
Accounts Receivable		50,000	50,000	
Inventory		60,000	60,000	
Land		40,000	45,000	$ 5,000
Buildings and Equipment	$ 600,000			
Accumulated Depreciation	(300,000)	300,000	280,000	(20,000)
		$500,000	$485,000	
Accounts Payable		$100,000	$100,000	
Bonds Payable		100,000	100,000	
Common Stock		200,000		
Retained Earnings		100,000		
		$500,000	$200,000	$(15,000)

exceed 40 years. Note that liabilities and current assets are not assigned a portion of an unallocated credit differential under **APB 16**, because other valuation principles take precedence with respect to these items. In particular, liabilities are valued at their present values, while current assets typically have readily determinable net realizable values.

Illustration of Treatment of Credit Differential

Using the example of Peerless Products and Special Foods, assume the book values and fair values of Special Foods' assets and liabilities on January 1, 19X1, are as shown in Figure 4-9. Peerless purchases all Special Foods' stock for $260,000. The resulting ownership situation is as follows:

P	Investment cost		$260,000
	Book value		
1/1/X1	Common stock—Special Foods	$200,000	
100%	Retained earnings—Special Foods	100,000	
		$300,000	
S	Peerless's share	× 1.00	(300,000)
	Differential (credit)		$ (40,000)

Peerless records its investment in Special Foods with the following entry on its books:

January 1, 19X1
    (10) Investment in Special Foods Stock   260,000
              Cash   260,000
          Record purchase of Special Foods stock.

The relationship between the total purchase price of the investment, the fair value of Special Foods' net assets, and the book value of Special Foods' net assets can be shown as follows:

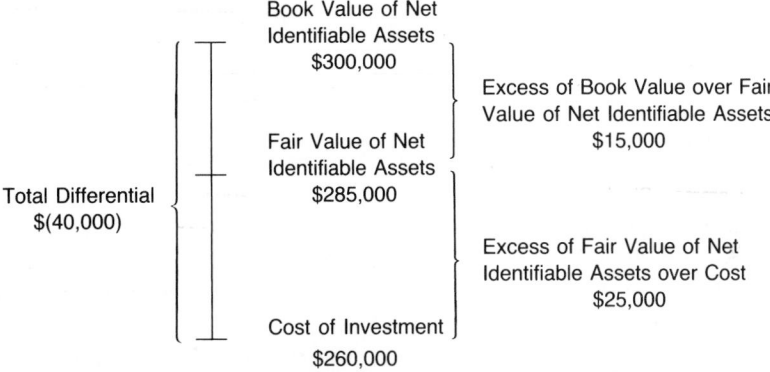

If a consolidated balance sheet is prepared immediately after the combination, the following elimination entries are made in the consolidation workpaper:

E(11)	Common Stock—Special Foods	200,000	
	Retained Earnings	100,000	
	Investment in Special Foods Stock		260,000
	Differential		40,000
	Eliminate investment balance.		
E(12)	Land	5,000	
	Differential	15,000	
	Buildings and Equipment		20,000
	Assign differential to bring land and buildings and equipment of Special Foods to fair values.		
E(13)	Differential	25,000	
	Land		3,462
	Buildings and Equipment		21,538
	Assign remaining credit differential.		

The purchase price ($260,000) of Special Foods' stock is $40,000 less than its book value ($300,000), resulting in a credit differential as shown in eliminating

entry E(11). The assets are revalued to their fair values in eliminating entry E(12), leaving a $25,000 unallocated credit differential. This remaining credit differential is allocated in eliminating entry E(13) against Special Foods' noncurrent assets in proportion to their fair values. The differential allocations in workpaper entries E(12) and E(13) are computed as follows:

Item	Book Value	Initial Adjust-ment to Fair Value	Fair Value	Alloca-tion Ratio	Unallocated Differential	Allocated Reduction
Land	$ 40,000	$ 5,000	$ 45,000	45/325 ×	$(25,000) =	$ (3,462)
Buildings and Equipment	300,000	(20,000)	280,000	280/325 ×	(25,000) =	(21,538)
Totals	$340,000	$(15,000)	$325,000			$(25,000)

Ownership Purchased at More than Book Value and Less than Fair Value

In some cases an investor might purchase the stock of another company at a price higher than the book value of the shares but less than the fair value of the underlying net assets. While this situation gives rise to a debit differential, the excess of the fair value of the subsidiary's net assets over their book values is greater than the differential. In consolidation, the net assets first are revalued to their fair values on the date of combination. Then the difference between the fair value of the net assets acquired and the cost to the parent is treated as a credit differential and assigned to reduce the amounts of the noncurrent assets, excluding marketable securities, in proportion to their fair values.

PREPARATION OF CONSOLIDATED BALANCE SHEET IMMEDIATELY FOLLOWING ACQUISITION OF CONTROLLING INTEREST

In many intercorporate investment situations, the investor may acquire less than full ownership of the investee company. An investor generally is assured of controlling an investee with a simple majority of the voting stock of the investee and can achieve significant influence with an even smaller ownership interest. Thus, an investor usually can attain objectives such as assuring a steady sales distribution channel or a dependable source of raw materials at ownership levels well below 100 percent.

When less than total ownership of a subsidiary is held by the parent, recognition must be given in the consolidated balance sheet to the ownership claim of the subsidiary's noncontrolling shareholders. This is accomplished most frequently by reporting the book value of the noncontrolling shareholders' stock as a single amount in the consolidated balance sheet between liabilities and stockholders' equity or as part of stockholders' equity.

FIGURE 4-10 Workpaper for consolidated balance sheet, January 1, 19X1, date of combination; 80 percent purchase at book value.

Item	Peerless Products	Special Foods	Eliminations		Consolidated
			Debit	Credit	
Cash	110,000	50,000			160,000
Accounts Receivable	75,000	50,000			125,000
Inventory	100,000	60,000			160,000
Land	175,000	40,000			215,000
Buildings and Equipment	800,000	600,000			1,400,000
Investment in Special Foods Stock	240,000			(15) 240,000	
Total Debits	1,500,000	800,000			2,060,000
Accumulated Depreciation	400,000	300,000			700,000
Accounts Payable	100,000	100,000			200,000
Bonds Payable	200,000	100,000			300,000
Common Stock	500,000	200,000	(15) 200,000		500,000
Retained Earnings	300,000	100,000	(15) 100,000		300,000
Noncontrolling Interest				(15) 60,000	60,000
Total Credits	1,500,000	800,000	300,000	300,000	2,060,000

Elimination entry:
(15) Eliminate investment balance and stockholders' equity of Special Foods; establish noncontrolling interest.

Controlling Ownership Purchased at Book Value

Figure 4-10 illustrates a consolidation workpaper for the preparation of a consolidated balance sheet in which the parent company has acquired less than total ownership of the subsidiary. This example is based, once again, on the data in Figure 4-2 and assumes that Peerless Products purchases 80 percent of the outstanding common stock of Special Foods for $240,000 cash. The purchase price represents 80 percent of the book value of Special Foods' stock ($300,000 × .80) on the date of combination, January 1, 19X1. The following diagram reflects the relative ownership interests of the parent company (P) and noncontrolling interest (NCI):

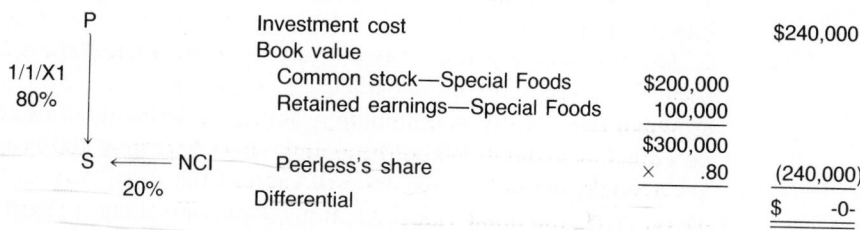

Investment cost		$240,000
Book value		
Common stock—Special Foods	$200,000	
Retained earnings—Special Foods	100,000	
	$300,000	
Peerless's share	× .80	(240,000)
Differential		$ -0-

Peerless records the acquisition of Special Foods' stock with the following entry:

January 1, 19X1
(14) Investment in Special Foods Stock   240,000
              Cash   240,000
       Record purchase of Special Foods stock.

The consolidation workpaper in Figure 4-10, prepared immediately after acquisition, is the same as the workpapers illustrated previously except that it
contains an additional line at the bottom for the noncontrolling interest in the
subsidiary. The amount assigned to the noncontrolling interest in the consolidation workpaper is not assigned in the trial balance of either the parent or the
subsidiary, but through the investment elimination entry each time consolidated
statements are prepared when less than 100 percent ownership is held.

Investment elimination entry E(15) in Figure 4-10 eliminates the full balance of
the investment account and the full balances of all Special Foods' stockholders'
equity accounts, and it establishes the noncontrolling interest amount in the
workpaper:

E(15) Common Stock—Special Foods   200,000
        Retained Earnings   100,000
              Investment in Special Foods Stock   240,000
              Noncontrolling Interest   60,000
        Eliminate investment balance and
        establish noncontrolling interest:
        $60,000 = ($200,000 + $100,000) × .20

The noncontrolling interest amount is calculated by multiplying the noncontrolling stockholders' ownership percentage, 20 percent in this example, times
the stockholders' equity balances of the subsidiary. The stockholders' equity
balances of Special Foods total $300,000 ($200,000 + $100,000), and therefore the
noncontrolling interest is $60,000 ($300,000 × .20). This $60,000 noncontrolling
interest amount is placed in the workpaper as part of the investment elimination
entry E(15) and, when all amounts are summed across, is carried to the consolidated column.

The elimination process is basically the same regardless of whether the parent
owns all or part of the subsidiary's stock. In both cases, all the subsidiary's
stockholders' equity is eliminated, and none is included directly in the consolidated balance sheet. When the parent owns less than 100 percent of the subsidiary's stock, the remaining share of each of the subsidiary's stockholders' equity
accounts is combined in a single item, Noncontrolling Interest, and shown on the
consolidated balance sheet.

Figure 4-11 illustrates a consolidated balance sheet prepared using the data
from the workpaper in Figure 4-10.

FIGURE 4-11 Consolidated balance sheet, January 1, 19X1, date of combination; 80 percent purchase at book value.

Peerless Products Corporation and Subsidiary					
Consolidated Balance Sheet					
January 1, 19X1					

Assets:			Liabilities:		
Cash		$ 160,000	Accounts Payable		$ 200,000
Accounts Receivable		125,000	Bonds Payable		300,000
Inventory		160,000			
Land		215,000	Noncontrolling Interest		60,000
Buildings and Equipment	$1,400,000				
Accumulated Depreciation	(700,000)	700,000	Stockholders' Equity:		
			Common Stock		500,000
			Retained Earnings		300,000
Total Assets		$1,360,000	Total Liabilities and Equity		$1,360,000

Controlling Ownership Purchased at More than Book Value

 When less than 100 percent ownership of a subsidiary is acquired and the stock is purchased at a price greater than book value, a debit differential arises in the workpaper upon elimination of the investment account. The amount of the differential is equal to the difference between the purchase price of the subsidiary's stock and the underlying book value of the shares acquired. This differential is allocated to the assets and liabilities of the subsidiary in the consolidation workpaper in a manner similar to that used when complete ownership is acquired.

When the parent acquires all a subsidiary's common stock and there is a debit differential, that differential is allocated in the consolidation workpaper prepared as of the date of combination so that all the subsidiary's assets and liabilities are reflected at their fair values. When a parent acquires less than 100 percent of the subsidiary's stock and allocates the debit differential in the consolidation work-paper, the assets and liabilities of the subsidiary are reflected at their book values plus the parent's proportionate share of the difference between the fair values and book values; the assets and liabilities are not valued at their full fair values.

Current practice employs a parent company approach toward the differential. Only the parent's share of the excess of the fair value of the subsidiary's assets and liabilities over the book value is reflected in the consolidated balance sheet when less than full ownership is acquired by the parent. If the entity view of consolidated statements discussed in Chapter 3 were adopted, the assets and liabilities of the subsidiary would be adjusted to their full fair values in the consolidation workpaper, even when less than full ownership is acquired by the parent.

Illustration of Treatment of Debit Differential

Using the example developed earlier, assume that Peerless Products purchases 80 percent of Special Foods' outstanding stock on January 1, 19X1, for $272,000. Peerless records the purchase of Special Foods' stock with entry (16):

January 1, 19X1

(16)	Investment in Special Foods Stock	272,000	
	Cash		272,000
	Record purchase of Special Foods stock.		

The stock purchase results in the following ownership situation:

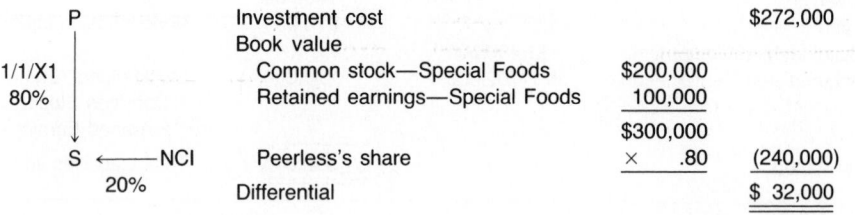

P	Investment cost	$272,000
	Book value	
1/1/X1	Common stock—Special Foods $200,000	
80%	Retained earnings—Special Foods 100,000	
	$300,000	
S ——NCI	Peerless's share × .80	(240,000)
20%	Differential	$ 32,000

A debit differential of $32,000 arises in this case because the book value of an 80 percent interest is $240,000 ($300,000 × .80). Assume that the differential relates to an increase in the value of Special Foods' land and to goodwill. If the fair value of the land is $50,000, or $10,000 greater than its book value, $8,000 ($10,000 × .80) of the differential is allocated to land and the remaining $24,000 to goodwill. The differential can be pictured as follows:

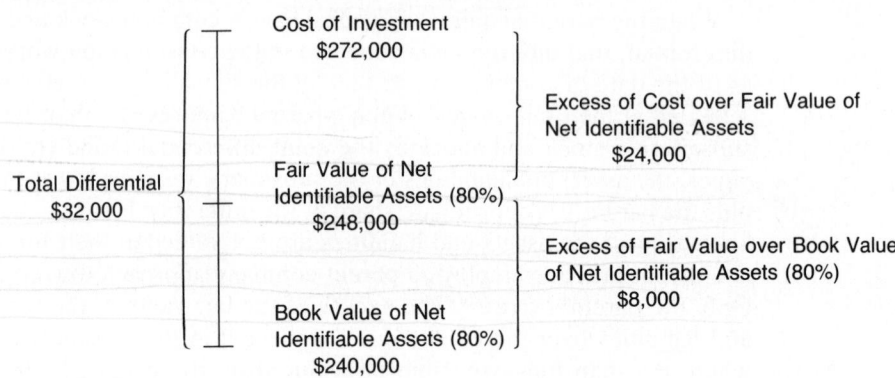

The land is reflected in the consolidated balance sheet at $48,000 because only the parent's share of the increased value of the land is shown. The consolidation workpaper for the date of combination appears as in Figure 4-12.

Entry E(17) in the consolidation workpaper prepared as of January 1, 19X1, eliminates the parent's investment account and each of the stockholders' equity accounts of the subsidiary and establishes the amount assigned to the noncontrolling interest:

FIGURE 4-12 Workpaper for consolidated balance sheet, January 1, 19X1, date of combination; 80 percent purchase at more than book value.

Item	Peerless Products	Special Foods	Eliminations		Consolidated
			Debit	Credit	
Cash	78,000	50,000			128,000
Accounts Receivable	75,000	50,000			125,000
Inventory	100,000	60,000			160,000
Land	175,000	40,000	(18) 8,000		223,000
Buildings and Equipment	800,000	600,000			1,400,000
Goodwill			(18) 24,000		24,000
Investment in Special Foods Stock	272,000			(17) 272,000	
Differential			(17) 32,000	(18) 32,000	
Total Debits	1,500,000	800,000			2,060,000
Accumulated Depreciation	400,000	300,000			700,000
Accounts Payable	100,000	100,000			200,000
Bonds Payable	200,000	100,000			300,000
Common Stock	500,000	200,000	(17) 200,000		500,000
Retained Earnings	300,000	100,000	(17) 100,000		300,000
Noncontrolling Interest				(17) 60,000	60,000
Total Credits	1,500,000	800,000	364,000	364,000	2,060,000

Elimination entries:
(17) Eliminate investment balance and stockholders' equity of Special Foods; establish noncontrolling interest.
(18) Assign differential.

E(17)	Common Stock—Special Foods	200,000	
	Retained Earnings	100,000	
	Differential	32,000	
	Investment in Special Foods Stock		272,000
	Noncontrolling Interest		60,000
	Eliminate investment balance and establish noncontrolling interest.		

The purchase differential is assigned to the appropriate assets by the following entry in the workpaper:

E(18)	Land	8,000	
	Goodwill	24,000	
	Differential		32,000
	Assign differential.		

Controlling Ownership Purchased at Less than Book Value

The procedures discussed previously relating to a credit differential also pertain to situations of less than full ownership. If asset write-downs are not called for on the subsidiary's separate books (as they may be in the case of receivables or inventory, for example), the appropriate assets are reduced by only the parent's proportionate share of the difference between the fair value and book value of the assets. This is consistent with the treatment of debit differentials. As with the case of 100 percent ownership, any credit differential not allocated is applied in the consolidation workpaper against the subsidiary's noncurrent assets, excluding marketable securities, in proportion to their fair values. Any remainder after reducing the subsidiary's noncurrent assets to zero is carried to the consolidated balance sheet as a deferred credit and amortized over the period benefited, not to exceed 40 years.

Effect of Cost versus Equity on Consolidation

The choice of using the cost or equity method to account for an investment in a subsidiary on the parent's books makes no difference in preparing consolidated financial statements as of the date of combination. Under both methods the investment is recorded initially at cost.

Subsequent to acquisition, the amounts on the parent's books usually differ under the two methods. Therefore, different elimination entries are needed to accomplish the consolidation, as will be discussed in Chapter 5. The consolidated financial statements, however, are not affected by the method used to account for the investment because the investment account and related accounts (e.g., income from subsidiary) are eliminated.

Intercorporate Receivables and Payables

All forms of intercorporate receivables and payables need to be eliminated when a consolidated balance sheet is prepared. From a single-company viewpoint, a company cannot owe itself money. If a company owes an affiliate $1,000 on account, one company carries a $1,000 receivable on its separate books and the other has a payable for the same amount. When consolidated financial statements are prepared, the following elimination entry is needed in the consolidation workpaper:

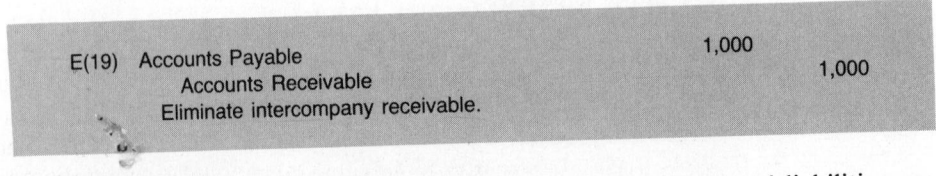

E(19)	Accounts Payable	1,000	
	Accounts Receivable		1,000
	Eliminate intercompany receivable.		

If no eliminating entry is made, both the consolidated assets and liabilities are overstated by an equal amount.

There are many more complex forms of intercorporate claims, such as bonds and leases, that are discussed in subsequent chapters. In all cases, failure to eliminate these claims can distort asset and liability balances. As a result, the magnitude of debt of the combined entity may appear to be greater than it is, working capital ratios may be incorrect, and other types of comparisons may be distorted.

ADDITIONAL CONSIDERATIONS

Asset and Liability Valuation Accounts at Acquisition

 Various asset and liability valuation accounts may appear in a subsidiary's balance sheet. The way these valuation accounts are treated in consolidation depends on the particular type of account. The most common asset valuation accounts are the accumulated depreciation account associated with plant and equipment and the allowance for uncollectible accounts receivable. Companies holding portfolios of marketable equity securities also may have valuation allowances to reduce the portfolios to market value under **FASB 12.**

Accumulated Depreciation on Date of Acquisition   From a theoretical viewpoint, accumulated depreciation at the date of combination on the fixed assets of a subsidiary acquired in a purchase-type business combination should be eliminated when consolidated statements are prepared. As discussed in Chapter 1, accounting for the purchase of a business follows the same general principles as the purchase of any other asset or group of assets. When a partially depreciated asset is purchased from another company, the other company's depreciation accumulated on that asset is not transferred to the books of the purchasing company. Similarly, when one company purchases a subsidiary and then prepares consolidated financial statements, the assets of the subsidiary are viewed as having been purchased by the consolidated entity on the date of combination. The long-term tangible assets of the subsidiary should be reflected in a consolidated balance sheet prepared as of the date of combination at their fair values with no accumulated depreciation. The depreciation begins accumulating from the date of com-bination and is based, from a consolidated viewpoint, on the historical cost of those assets to the consolidated entity, the fair values on the date of combination.

The theoretically correct treatment is to eliminate in the consolidation workpaper the accumulated depreciation of the subsidiary on the date of combination against the assets to which it relates. Those assets then are revalued to their fair values on the date of combination through the assignment of the differential. In the case of Peerless Products and Special Foods, on the basis of the data in Figure 4-2, the accumulated depreciation on Special Foods' buildings and equipment on the date of combination is $300,000. This amount, from a theoretical viewpoint, should be eliminated in the workpaper against the buildings and equipment each time consolidated statements are prepared for as long as those assets are held.

While this treatment is correct in theory, this elimination seldom is made in practice. Eliminating the accumulated depreciation against the asset account has no effect on the net amount of the asset or on total assets, but simply eliminates the overstatement of both the asset and the contra asset accounts. The net amount of the asset is the same ($300,000) whether the accumulated depreciation remains or is eliminated against the asset. In practice, the clerical burden of having to make this eliminating entry each time consolidated statements are prepared seems to outweigh any benefits that might arise from the more technically accurate presentation.

Allowance for Decline in Value of Marketable Securities   As with the accumulated depreciation of the subsidiary, the allowance on the subsidiary's books at the date of combination for valuing marketable equity securities at the lower of cost or market under **FASB 12** theoretically should be eliminated. The marketable equity securities should be viewed as having been purchased by the consolidated entity on the date of combination. Thus, the amount of the contra asset account existing on the date of combination should be netted against the asset in the consolidation workpaper, and the portfolio of marketable securities should be reflected as a single figure at market value in the consolidated balance sheet prepared immediately after the combination.

As with accumulated depreciation, the amount of this valuation account on the date of combination seldom is eliminated in practice.

Allowance for Uncollectible Accounts   Receivables are valued differently than nonmonetary assets. Short-term trade receivables normally are reflected in financial statements at their full legal or face amount with estimated uncollectibles shown in a contra asset account. The difference between the asset and contra asset accounts reflects the expected net realizable value of the receivables. Assuming both the asset and the contra asset accounts are stated correctly on the subsidiary's books, both appropriately are carried to the consolidated balance sheet with no elimination of the contra asset account.

Discount and Premium Accounts   The maturity or face amounts of long-term receivables and payables normally are reflected in the external financial statements issued to the public. When the nominal interest rate on the receivable or payable differs from the effective rate at the time the obligation arises, a valuation account is used to adjust the receivable or payable to its present value. A difference on the date of combination between the fair value and the carrying amount of a long-term receivable or payable requires a workpaper entry to adjust the amount of the receivable or payable to be shown in the consolidated balance sheet. The adjustment is reflected in an asset or liability valuation account, usually labeled as a discount or premium.

Negative Retained Earnings of Subsidiary at Acquisition

A parent company may purchase a subsidiary with a negative or debit balance in its retained earnings account. An accumulated deficit of a subsidiary at acquisition causes no special problems in the consolidation process. The normal investment elimination entry is made in the consolidation workpaper except that the debit balance in the subsidiary's retained earnings account is eliminated with a credit entry. Thus, the investment elimination entry appears as follows:

E(20)	Capital Stock—Subsidiary	XXX	
	Differential	XXX	
	Retained Earnings		XXX
	Investment in Subsidiary		XXX
	Eliminate investment balance.		

Other Stockholders' Equity Accounts

The discussion of consolidated statements up to this point has dealt with companies having stockholders' equity consisting only of retained earnings and a single class of capital stock issued at par. Typically, companies have more complex stockholders' equity structures, often including preferred stock and various types of additional contributed capital. The latter may arise from the issuance of stock in excess of par or stated value, from treasury stock transactions, from the retirement of stock, and from various other sources. The treatment of these accounts in the consolidation process is discussed in detail in Chapter 9.

In general, all those stockholders' equity accounts accruing to the common shareholders receive the same treatment as common stock and are eliminated at the time common stock is eliminated. The proportionate amounts of the noncontrolling shareholders' interests in those accounts are combined as part of the noncontrolling interest in the consolidated balance sheet.

To illustrate, assume that the stockholders' equity accounts of Puro on January 1, 19X1, are as follows:

Common Stock	$100,000
Capital Contributed in Excess of Par	200,000
Capital Contributed from Treasury Stock Transactions	10,000
Retained Earnings	500,000
Total Stockholders' Equity	$810,000

On that date, Marsh Company purchases 90 percent of the stock of Puro for its book value of $729,000 ($810,000 × .90). The consolidation workpaper prepared immediately after the combination includes the following investment elimination entry:

E(21)	Common Stock—Puro	100,000	
	Capital Contributed in Excess of Par	200,000	
	Capital Contributed from Treasury Stock		
	Transactions	10,000	
	Retained Earnings	500,000	
	Investment in Puro Stock		729,000
	Noncontrolling Interest		81,000
	Eliminate investment balance and		
	establish noncontrolling interest.		

All the subsidiary's capital accounts relating to the common stock interest are eliminated in the consolidation workpaper, as is the parent's investment account, and the noncontrolling interest is established at $81,000 ($810,000 × .10).

Push-Down Accounting

The term *push-down accounting* refers to the practice of revaluing the assets and liabilities of a purchased subsidiary directly on the books of that subsidiary at the date of acquisition. If this practice is followed, the revaluations are recorded once on the books of the purchased subsidiary at the date of acquisition and, therefore, are not made in the consolidation workpapers each time consolidated statements are prepared.

Those who favor push-down accounting argue that the change in ownership of the subsidiary in a purchase-type transaction is reason for adopting a new basis of accounting for the subsidiary's assets and liabilities, and this new basis of accounting should be reflected directly on the books of the subsidiary. This argument is most persuasive when the subsidiary is wholly owned and is consolidated or has its separate financial statements included with the statements of the parent.

On the other hand, when there is a significant noncontrolling interest in the subsidiary or the subsidiary has bonds or preferred stock held by the public, push-down accounting may be inappropriate. The use of push-down accounting in the financial statements issued to the noncontrolling shareholders or to those holding bonds or preferred stock results in a new basis of accounting even though, from the perspective of those statement users, the entity has not changed. From their viewpoint, push-down accounting results in the revaluation of the assets and liabilities of a continuing enterprise, a practice that normally is not acceptable.

 Push-down accounting is required by *SEC Staff Accounting Bulletin No. 54* whenever a purchase-type business combination results in the purchased subsidiary becoming substantially wholly owned. The staff accounting bulletin encourages but does not require the use of push-down accounting in situations where the subsidiary is less than wholly owned or where the subsidiary has outstanding debt or preferred stock held by the public.

The revaluation of assets and liabilities on the books of a purchased subsidiary involves making an entry to debit or credit each asset and liability account to be revalued, with the balancing entry to a revaluation capital account. If a consolidated balance sheet is prepared immediately after the revaluation at the date of combination, there is no differential because the subsidiary's assets and liabilities already are revalued to their fair values and any goodwill already is recorded. Instead, the elimination entry in the consolidation workpaper appears as follows:

E(22) Capital Stock—Subsidiary	XXX	
Retained Earnings	XXX	
Revaluation Capital	XXX	
Investment in Subsidiary Stock		XXX
Eliminate investment balance.		

Note that the Revaluation Capital account is eliminated in preparing consolidated statements. A more detailed example of push-down accounting is given in Appendix B in Chapter 5.

SUMMARY OF KEY CONCEPTS AND TERMS

Consolidated financial statements present the financial position and results of operations of two or more separate legal entities as if they were a single company. A consolidated balance sheet prepared on the date a parent acquires a subsidiary appears the same as if the acquired company had been merged into the parent.

A consolidation workpaper provides a means of efficiently developing the data needed to prepare consolidated financial statements. The workpaper includes a separate column for the trial balance data of each of the consolidating companies, a debit and a credit column for the elimination entries, and a column for the consolidated totals that appear in the consolidated financial statements.

Eliminating entries are needed in the consolidation workpaper to remove the effects of intercorporate ownership and intercompany transactions so the consolidated financial statements appear as if the legally separate companies are actually one. In a consolidation workpaper prepared immediately after a purchase-type business combination, elimination entries usually are needed to (1) eliminate the intercorporate investment account of the parent and the stockholders' equity balances of the subsidiary and establish any noncontrolling interest's share of the subsidiary's book value; (2) allocate to the assets and liabilities of the subsidiary, or to goodwill, the difference, if any, between the cost of the investment and the book value of the shares acquired; and (3) eliminate any intercompany receivables and payables.

Bargain purchase   Purchase differential
Consolidation workpaper   Push-down accounting
Eliminating entries

QUESTIONS

Q4-1 How does an elimination entry differ from an adjusting entry?

Q4-2 What is the term *differential* used to indicate?

Q4-3 What is negative goodwill? How is negative goodwill reported in the consolidated balance sheet?

Q4-4 How is it possible for there to be a positive purchase differential but negative goodwill on a purchase of the stock of another company?

Q4-5 What portion of the balances of subsidiary stockholders' equity accounts are included in the consolidated balance sheet?

Q4-6 What portion of the book value of the net assets held by a subsidiary at acquisition is included in the consolidated balance sheet?

Q4-7 What portion of the fair value of the net assets of a subsidiary normally is included in the consolidated balance sheet following a purchase-type business combination?

Q4-8 What is the justification for using a differential clearing account in preparing consolidated statements?

Q4-9 What happens to the purchase differential in the consolidation workpaper prepared as of the date of combination? How is it reestablished so that the proper balances can be reported the following year?

Q4-10 Does a noncontrolling shareholder have access to any information other than the consolidated financial statements to determine how well a subsidiary is doing? Explain.

Q4-11 Explain why consolidated financial statements become increasingly important when the purchase differential is very large.

Q4-12 There is a noncontrolling interest balance reported in the consolidated balance sheet of Worldwide Corporation. Why must the noncontrolling interest be reported in the consolidated balance sheet?

Q4-13 How is the amount assigned to noncontrolling interest in the consolidated balance sheet normally determined?

Q4-14 What does the term *push-down accounting* mean?

Q4-15* Under what conditions is push-down accounting considered appropriate?

Q4-16* What happens to the differential when push-down accounting is used following a business combination?

Q4-17* What effect does a negative retained earnings balance on the subsidiary's books have on the consolidation procedures?

CASES

C4-1   Need for Consolidation Process

At a recent staff meeting, the vice president of marketing appeared confused. He had been assured by the controller that the parent company and each of the subsidiary companies had properly accounted for all transactions during the year. After several other questions, he finally asked, ''If it has been done properly, then why must you spend so much time and make so many changes to the amounts reported by the individual companies when you prepare the consolidated financial statements each month? You should be able just to add the reported balances together.''

Required

Prepare an appropriate response to help the controller answer the question posed by the vice president of marketing.

C4-2 Assigning a Purchase Differential

The owners of Small Corporation recently offered to sell 60 percent of their ownership to Large Corporation for $450,000. The business manager of Large Corporation was told that the book value of Small Corporation was $300,000, and she estimates the fair value of its net assets at approximately $600,000. Small Corporation has relatively old equipment and manufacturing facilities and uses a lifo basis for inventory valuation of some items and a fifo basis for others.

Required

If Large Corporation accepts the offer and purchases Small Corporation, what difficulties are likely to be encountered in assigning the purchase differential?

C4-3* Negative Retained Earnings

Although Sloan Company had good earnings reports in 19X5 and 19X6, it had a negative retained earnings balance on December 31, 19X6. Jacobs Corporation purchased 80 percent of the common stock of Sloan on January 1, 19X7.

Required

a. Indicate how the negative retained earnings balance of Sloan Company is reflected in the consolidated balance sheet immediately following the acquisition.

b. Indicate how the existence of negative retained earnings changes the consolidation workpaper entries.

c. Can goodwill be recorded if Jacobs Corporation pays more than book value for the shares of Sloan Company? Explain.

EXERCISES

E4-1 Multiple-Choice Questions on Consolidation Process

Select the most appropriate answer for each of the following questions.

1. If A Company purchases 80 percent of the stock of B Company on January 1, 19X2, immediately after the acquisition:
   a. Consolidated retained earnings will be equal to the combined retained earnings of the two companies.
   b. Goodwill will be reported in the consolidated balance sheet.
   c. Additional paid-in capital of A Company may be reduced to permit the carryforward of B Company retained earnings.
   d. Consolidated retained earnings and A Company retained earnings will be the same.

2. Goodwill is:
   a. Seldom reported because it is too difficult to measure.
   b. Reported when more than book value is paid in purchasing another company.
   c. Reported when the fair value of the payment made in the purchase is greater than the fair value of the net identifiable assets acquired.
   d. Generally smaller for small companies and increases in amount as the company increases in size.

3. Which of the following is incorrect?
   a. The noncontrolling shareholders' claim on the subsidiary's net assets is based on the book value of the subsidiary's net assets.
   b. Only the parent's portion of the difference between book value and fair value of the subsidiary's assets is assigned to those assets.
   c. Goodwill represents the difference between the book value of the subsidiary's net assets and the amount paid by the parent to buy ownership.
   d. Total assets reported by the parent generally will be less than total assets reported on the consolidated balance sheet.

4. Which of the following statements is correct?
   a. Foreign subsidiaries do not need to be consolidated if they are reported as a separate operating group under segment reporting.
   b. Consolidated retained earnings does not include the noncontrolling interest's claim on the retained earnings of the subsidiary.
   c. The noncontrolling shareholders' claim should be adjusted for changes in the fair value of the subsidiary assets, but should not include goodwill.
   d. Consolidation is expected any time the investor holds significant influence over the investee.

E4-2 Multiple-Choice Questions on Consolidation [AICPA Adapted]

Select the correct answer for each of the following questions.

Items 1 and 2 are based on the following information:

The Nugget Company's balance sheet on December 31, 19X6, is as follows:

Assets		Liabilities and Stockholders' Equity	
Cash	$ 100,000	Current Liabilities	$ 300,000
Accounts Receivable	200,000	Long-Term Debt	500,000
Inventories	500,000	Common Stock (par $1 per share)	100,000
Property, Plant, and		Additional Paid-In Capital	200,000
Equipment (net)	900,000	Retained Earnings	600,000
	$1,700,000		$1,700,000

On December 31, 19X6, the Gold Company purchased all the outstanding common stock of Nugget for $1,500,000 cash. On that date, the fair (market) value of Nugget's inventories was $450,000, and the fair value of Nugget's property, plant, and equipment was $1,000,000. The fair values of all other assets and liabilities of Nugget were equal to their book values.

1. As a result of the acquisition of Nugget by Gold, the consolidated balance sheet of Gold and Nugget should reflect goodwill in the amount of:

a. $500,000.
b. $550,000.
c. $600,000.
d. $650,000.

2. Assuming that the balance sheet of Gold (unconsolidated) on December 31, 19X6, reflected retained earnings of $2,000,000, what amount of retained earnings should be shown in the December 31, 19X6, consolidated balance sheet of Gold and its new subsidiary, Nugget?
a. $2,000,000.
b. $2,600,000.
c. $2,800,000.
d. $3,150,000.

Items 3 and 4 are based on the following information:

Deer Company acquired 70 percent of the outstanding stock of Elk Corporation. The separate balance sheet of Deer immediately after the acquisition and the consolidated balance sheet are as follows:

	Deer	Consolidated
Current Assets	$106,000	$146,000
Investment in Elk (cost)	100,000	
Goodwill		8,100
Fixed Assets (net)	270,000	370,000
	$476,000	$524,100
Current Liabilities	$ 15,000	$ 28,000
Capital Stock	350,000	350,000
Noncontrolling Interest		35,100
Retained Earnings	111,000	111,000
	$476,000	$524,100

Ten thousand dollars of the excess payment for the investment in Elk was ascribed to undervaluation of its fixed assets; the balance of the excess payment was ascribed to goodwill. Current assets of Elk included a $2,000 receivable from Deer that arose before they became related on an ownership basis.

The following two items relate to Elk's separate balance sheet prepared at the time Deer acquired its 70 percent interest in Elk.

3. What was the total of the current assets on Elk's separate balance sheet at the time Deer acquired its 70 percent interest?
a. $38,000.
b. $40,000.
c. $42,000.
d. $104,000.

4. What was the total stockholders' equity on Elk's separate balance sheet at the time Deer acquired its 70 percent interest?
a. $64,900.
b. $70,000.
c. $100,000.
d. $117,000.

E4-3 Basic Elimination Entries

On December 31, 19X3, Broadway Corporation reported common stock outstanding of $200,000, additional paid-in capital of $300,000, and retained earnings of $100,000. On January 1, 19X4, Johe Company acquired control of Broadway in a purchase-type business combination.

a. Give the eliminating entry that would be needed in preparing a consolidated balance sheet immediately following the combination if Johe purchased all of Broadway's outstanding common stock for $600,000.

b. Give the eliminating entry that would be needed in preparing a consolidated balance sheet immediately following the combination if Johe purchased 90 percent of Broadway's outstanding common stock for $540,000.

E4-4 Assigning Differential

Mail Order Sales, Inc., purchased 80 percent ownership of Speedy Delivery Corporation on June 30, 19X4, for $182,000. It was determined that $20,000 of the purchase differential was assignable to depreciable assets and the remainder to land held by Speedy at the time of acquisition. Speedy had retained earnings of $75,000 and stock outstanding of $100,000 on the date of purchase.

Required

Give the appropriate eliminating entry or entries to prepare a consolidated balance sheet as of the date of acquisition.

E4-5 Basic Balance Sheet Workpaper

Bedrock Construction acquired 100 percent of the common stock of Handy Tool Corporation on January 1, 19X2, for $240,000. Data from the balance sheets of the two companies included the following totals as of the date of acquisition:

	Bedrock Construction	Handy Tool Corporation
Cash and Receivables	$150,000	$ 10,000
Inventory	230,000	290,000
Land and Buildings (net)	350,000	80,000
Investment in Handy Tool Corporation	240,000	
Total Assets	$970,000	$380,000
Current Liabilities	$ 95,000	$ 40,000
Bonds Payable	300,000	100,000
Common Stock	100,000	80,000
Retained Earnings	475,000	160,000
Total Liabilities and Stockholders' Equity	$970,000	$380,000

Required

Prepare and complete a consolidated balance sheet workpaper as of January 1, 19X2.

E4-6   Workpaper for Majority-Owned Subsidiary

Glitter Enterprises purchased 60 percent of the stock of Lowtide Builders, Inc., on December 31, 19X4. Balance sheet data for Glitter and Lowtide on January 1, 19X5, are as follows:

	Glitter Enterprises	Lowtide Builders
Cash and Receivables	$ 80,000	$ 30,000
Inventory	150,000	350,000
Buildings and Equipment (net)	430,000	80,000
Investment in Lowtide Stock	90,000	
Total Assets	$750,000	$460,000
Current Liabilities	$100,000	$110,000
Long-Term Debt	400,000	200,000
Common Stock	200,000	140,000
Retained Earnings	50,000	10,000
Total Liabilities and Stockholders' Equity	$750,000	$460,000

Required

a. Give all eliminating entries needed to prepare a consolidated balance sheet on January 1, 19X5.
b. Complete a consolidated balance sheet workpaper.
c. Prepare a consolidated balance sheet in good form.

E4-7   Computation of Consolidated Balances

The balance sheet of Sparkle Corporation at January 1, 19X7, reflected the following balances:

Cash and Receivables	$ 80,000	Accounts Payable	$ 40,000
Inventory	120,000	Income Taxes Payable	60,000
Land	70,000	Bonds Payable	200,000
Buildings and Equipment		Common Stock	250,000
(net)	480,000	Retained Earnings	200,000
		Total Liabilities and	
Total Assets	$750,000	Stockholders' Equity	$750,000

Harrison Corporation, which had just entered into an active acquisition program, purchased 80 percent of the common stock of Sparkle on January 2, 19X7, for $470,000. A careful review of the fair value of the assets and liabilities of Sparkle indicated the following:

	Book Value	Fair Value
Inventory	$120,000	$140,000
Land	70,000	60,000
Buildings and Equipment (net)	480,000	550,000

Required

Compute the appropriate amount to be included in the consolidated balance sheet immediately following the acquisition for each of the following items:

    a. Inventory
    b. Land
    c. Buildings and Equipment (net)
    d. Goodwill
    e. Investment in Sparkle Corporation
    f. Noncontrolling Interest

E4-8   Multiple-Choice Questions on Consolidated Balance Sheet

Balance sheet data for Hobs Corporation and Parkview Company on December 31, 19X3, are given below.

	Hobs Corporation	Parkview Company
Cash and Receivables	$ 70,000	$ 90,000
Inventory	100,000	60,000
Depreciable Assets (net)	500,000	250,000
Investment in Parkview Stock	260,000	
Total Assets	$930,000	$400,000
Current Liabilities	$180,000	$ 60,000
Long-Term Liabilities	200,000	90,000
Common Stock	300,000	100,000
Retained Earnings	250,000	150,000
Total Liabilities and Stockholders' Equity	$930,000	$400,000

Hobs Corporation purchased 80 percent ownership of Parkview Company on December 31, 19X3, for $260,000. On that date, Parkview's depreciable assets had a fair value of $50,000 more than the book value shown above. All other book values approximated fair value.

Required

Indicate in each case the appropriate total that should appear in the consolidated balance sheet on December 31, 19X3.

1. What amount of total depreciable assets will be reported?
    a. $500,000.
    b. $750,000.
    c. $790,000.
    d. $800,000.

2. What amount of goodwill will be reported?
    a. $0.

    b. $20,000.
    c. $25,000.
    d. $60,000.

3. What amount of consolidated retained earnings will be reported?
    a. $250,000.
    b. $280,000.
    c. $370,000.
    d. $400,000.

4. What amount of total stockholders' equity will be reported?
    a. $550,000.
    b. $600,000.
    c. $750,000.
    d. $800,000.

5. What amount of noncontrolling interest will be reported?
    a. $50,000.
    b. $60,000.
    c. $110,000.
    d. $160,000.

6. What amount of total liabilities will be reported?
    a. $240,000.
    b. $290,000.
    c. $380,000.
    d. $530,000.

7. What amount of total assets will be reported?
    a. $930,000.
    b. $1,070,000.
    c. $1,130,000.
    d. $1,330,000.

E4-9* Push-Down Accounting

Jefferson Company purchased all of the common shares of Louis Corporation on January 2, 19X3, for $789,000. At the date of combination, the balance sheet of Louis Corporation appeared as follows:

Assets:		Liabilities:	
Cash and Receivables	$ 34,000	Current Payables	$ 25,000
Inventory	165,000	Notes Payable	100,000
Land	60,000	Stockholders' Equity:	
Buildings (net)	250,000	Common Stock	200,000
Equipment (net)	320,000	Additional Capital	425,000
		Retained Earnings	79,000
Total	$829,000	Total	$829,000

The fair values of all of Louis's assets and liabilities were equal to their book values except for Louis's fixed assets. Louis's land had a fair value of $75,000; the buildings, a fair value of $300,000; and the equipment, a fair value of $340,000.

Jefferson Company decided to employ push-down accounting in accounting for the acquisition of Louis Corporation. Subsequent to the combination, Louis Corporation continued to operate as a separate company.

Required

a. Record the purchase of Louis Corporation's stock on the books of Jefferson Company.

b. Present any entries that would be made on the books of Louis Corporation related to the business combination, assuming push-down accounting is used.

c. Present, in general journal form, all elimination entries that would appear in a consolidation workpaper for Jefferson Company and its subsidiary prepared immediately following the combination.

PROBLEMS

P4-10 Multiple-Choice Questions on Consolidated Balances

Select the correct answer for each of the following questions.

1. Parent Company holds 80 percent of the stock of Subsidiary Company. Parent net assets are $400,000, and Subsidiary net assets are $150,000. Noncontrolling interest in the consolidated balance sheet is reported at:
   a. $30,000.
   b. $50,000.
   c. $80,000.
   d. $110,000.

2. Minor Corporation reports net assets of $300,000 at book value. These assets have an estimated market value of $350,000. If Major Corporation buys 80 percent ownership of Minor for $275,000, goodwill will be reported in the consolidated balance sheet in the amount of:
   a. $0.
   b. $25,000.
   c. $35,000.
   d. $40,000.

3. In question 2, the noncontrolling interest will be reported in the amount of:
   a. $55,000.
   b. $60,000.
   c. $70,000.
   d. None will be reported.

4. Small Company reports total assets of $400,000 and liabilities of $100,000. Big Company reports total assets of $900,000 and liabilities of $200,000. Included in Big Company

assets is its investment of $350,000 in Small Company. When a consolidated balance sheet is prepared, what amount of total assets will be reported if Big holds 100 percent ownership of Small?

a. $900,000.
b. $950,000.
c. $1,000,000.
d. $1,300,000.

5. Computo Corporation recently purchased 80 percent of the stock of Tape Decks, Inc., for $232,000. At the date of purchase the consolidated balance sheet showed $40,000 of goodwill from this acquisition. The underlying book value of Tape Deck's net assets at the time of acquisition was:

a. $192,000.
b. $232,000.
c. $240,000.
d. $290,000.

P4-11   Balance Sheet Workpaper

Shutter Company owns 90 percent of the stock of Pleasantdale Dairy. The balance sheets of the two companies immediately after the acquisition of Pleasantdale showed the following amounts:

	Shutter Company	Pleasantdale Dairy
Cash and Receivables	$ 130,000	$ 70,000
Inventory	210,000	90,000
Land	70,000	40,000
Buildings and Equipment (net)	390,000	220,000
Investment in Pleasantdale Stock	270,000	
Total Assets	$1,070,000	$420,000
Current Payables	$ 80,000	$ 40,000
Long-Term Liabilities	200,000	100,000
Common Stock	400,000	60,000
Retained Earnings	390,000	220,000
Total Liabilities and Stockholders' Equity	$1,070,000	$420,000

At the date of acquisition, Pleasantdale owed Shutter $8,000 plus $900 accrued interest. The accrued interest had been recorded by Pleasantdale, but not by Shutter. Any differential relates to land.

Required

Prepare and complete a consolidated balance sheet workpaper.

P4-12 Consolidated Stockholders' Equity [AICPA Adapted]

On January 1, 19X6, Peters, Inc., issued 200,000 additional shares of its voting common stock in exchange for 100,000 shares of Smith Company's outstanding voting common stock in a business combination appropriately accounted for by the pooling of interests method. The market value of Peters' voting common stock was $40 per share on the date of the business combination. The balance sheets of Peters and Smith immediately before the business combination contained the following information:

Peters, Inc.:	
Common stock, par value $5 per share;	
authorized, 1,000,000 shares; issued	
and outstanding, 600,000 shares	$ 3,000,000
Additional paid-in capital	6,000,000
Retained earnings	11,000,000
Total stockholders' equity	$20,000,000
Smith Company:	
Common stock, par value $10 per share;	
authorized, 250,000 shares; issued	
and outstanding, 100,000 shares	$ 1,000,000
Additional paid-in capital	2,000,000
Retained earnings	4,000,000
Total stockholders' equity	$ 7,000,000

Additional information is as follows:

1. The full amount of any differential at acquisition relates to land.
2. Smith owed $4,000 to Peters on account at the date of combination.

Required

a. Prepare the *consolidated* stockholders' equity section of the balance sheet of Peters, Inc., and its subsidiary, Smith Company, as of January 1, 19X6.

b. What would total stockholders' equity be if the combination were treated as a purchase?

P4-13 Assignment of Differential in Workpaper

Teresa Corporation purchased all the voting shares of Sally Enterprises on January 1, 19X4. Balance sheet totals for the companies on the date of acquisition were as follows:

	Teresa Corporation	Sally Enterprises
Cash and Receivables	$ 40,000	$ 20,000
Inventory	95,000	40,000
Land	80,000	90,000
Buildings and Equipment	400,000	230,000
Investment in Sally Enterprises	290,000	
Total Assets	$905,000	$380,000
Accumulated Depreciation	$175,000	$ 65,000
Accounts Payable	60,000	15,000
Notes Payable	100,000	50,000
Common Stock	300,000	100,000
Retained Earnings	270,000	150,000
Total Liabilities and Stockholders' Equity	$905,000	$380,000

The buildings and equipment reported by Sally Enterprises on January 1, 19X4, were estimated to have a market value of $175,000. All other items appeared to have market values approximating current book values.

Required

a. Complete a consolidated balance sheet workpaper for January 1, 19X4.
b. Prepare a consolidated balance sheet in good form.

P4-14 Computation of Consolidated Balances

Retail Records, Inc., purchased all the voting shares of Decibel Studios on January 1, 19X2, for $280,000. The balance sheet of Retail Records immediately after the combination contained the following balances:

Retail Records, Inc.
Balance Sheet
January 1, 19X2

Cash and Receivables	$120,000	Accounts Payable	$ 75,000
Inventory	110,000	Taxes Payable	50,000
Land	70,000	Notes Payable	300,000
Buildings and Equipment (net)	350,000	Common Stock	400,000
Investment in Decibel Stock	280,000	Retained Earnings	105,000
Total Assets	$930,000	Total Liabilities and Stockholders' Equity	$930,000

The balance sheet of Decibel at acquisition contained the following balances:

Decibel Studios
Balance Sheet
January 1, 19X2

Cash and Receivables	$ 40,000	Accounts Payable	$ 90,000
Inventory	180,000	Notes Payable	250,000
Buildings and Equipment (net)	350,000	Common Stock	100,000
Goodwill	30,000	Additional Paid-In Capital	200,000
		Retained Earnings	(40,000)
		Total Liabilities and	
Total Assets	$600,000	Stockholders' Equity	$600,000

On the date of purchase, the inventory held by Decibel Studios had a fair value of $170,000, and its buildings and recording equipment had a value of $375,000. Goodwill reported by Decibel resulted from a purchase of Sound Stage Enterprises in 19X1. Sound Stage was liquidated and its assets and liabilities were brought onto Decibel's books.

Required

Compute the balances to be reported in the consolidated statements for:

    a. Inventory
    b. Buildings and Equipment (net)
    c. Investment in Decibel Stock
    d. Goodwill
    e. Common Stock
    f. Retained Earnings

P4-15 Consolidation of Majority-Owned Subsidiary

Travel Corporation owns 60 percent of the voting stock of Southern Industries, which it purchased on January 1, 19X1. The balance sheet accounts of the companies on the date of acquisition contained the following balances:

	Travel Corporation	Southern Industries
Cash and Receivables	$ 40,000	$ 20,000
Inventory	80,000	40,000
Land	120,000	90,000
Buildings and Equipment	500,000	300,000
Investment in Southern Industries	150,000	
Total Assets	$890,000	$450,000
Accumulated Depreciation	$165,000	$ 85,000
Accounts Payable	90,000	25,000
Notes Payable	200,000	90,000
Common Stock	100,000	200,000
Retained Earnings	335,000	50,000
Total Liabilities and Stockholders' Equity	$890,000	$450,000

The acquisition was made at book value, and no adjustments to the net assets of Southern Industries are required. On the date of the combination, Travel Corporation was holding land previously purchased from Southern Industries at an amount equal to Southern Industries' cost of $35,000.

Required

a. Give all eliminating entries to prepare a consolidated balance sheet as of the date of acquisition.

b. Prepare a consolidated balance sheet workpaper.

c. Prepare a consolidated balance sheet in good form.

P4-16   Consolidation of Majority-Owned Subsidiary with Differential

Blue Corporation purchased 60 percent of the common stock of Northern Industries on January 1, 19X8, for $185,000. Their balance sheets on the date of acquisition were as follows:

	Blue Corporation	Northern Industries
Cash and Receivables	$ 25,000	$ 20,000
Inventory	80,000	40,000
Land	120,000	90,000
Buildings and Equipment	500,000	300,000
Investment in Northern Industries	185,000	
Total Assets	$910,000	$450,000
Accumulated Depreciation	$165,000	$ 85,000
Accounts Payable	110,000	25,000
Notes Payable	200,000	90,000
Common Stock	100,000	200,000
Retained Earnings	335,000	50,000
Total Liabilities and Stockholders' Equity	$910,000	$450,000

A total of $20,000 of the purchase differential related to Northern Industries inventory, which had increased in value. The fair values and book values of all other assets and liabilities held by Northern at acquisition were approximately equal.

Required

a. Give all eliminating entries to prepare a consolidated balance sheet for January 1, 19X8.

b. Prepare a consolidated balance sheet workpaper.

c. Prepare a consolidated balance sheet in good form.

P4-17 Consolidation of Majority-Owned Subsidiary with Differential

Skyhigh Airlines acquired 80 percent of the stock of Klunker Car Rentals for $285,000 on January 1, 19X2. Summarized balance sheets for the two companies on January 1, 19X2, are presented below.

Klunker Car Rentals
Balance Sheet
January 1, 19X2

Cash and Receivables	$ 90,000	Accounts Payable	$ 60,000
Inventory	60,000	Taxes Payable	30,000
Land	30,000	Notes Payable	100,000
Buildings and Equipment (net)	230,000	Common Stock	200,000
Marketable Securities	80,000	Retained Earnings	100,000
	$490,000		$490,000

Skyhigh Airlines
Balance Sheet
January 1, 19X2

Cash and Receivables	$ 140,000	Accounts Payable	$ 190,000
Inventory	30,000	Taxes Payable	15,000
Land	70,000	Bonds Payable	600,000
Planes and Equipment (net)	790,000	Common Stock	200,000
Investment in Klunker Car Rentals	285,000	Retained Earnings	310,000
	$1,315,000		$1,315,000

At the time of acquisition, Klunker's land had an estimated value of $40,000, its buildings and equipment had a value of $250,000, and its notes payable had a fair value of $108,000. Book values and fair values were approximately equal for all other assets and liabilities.

Required

   a. Give all eliminating entries needed to prepare a consolidated balance sheet for January 1, 19X2.
   b. Complete a consolidated balance sheet workpaper.
   c. Prepare a consolidated balance sheet in good form.

P4-18 Multiple-Choice Questions on Consolidated Balances

Whitehurst Electronics published the following balance sheet for December 31, 19X5:

Whitehurst Electronics
Balance Sheet
December 31, 19X5

Cash	$ 100,000	Accounts Payable	$ 70,000
Accounts Receivable	210,000	Taxes Payable	130,000
Inventory	360,000	Notes Payable	500,000
Buildings and Equipment	800,000	Common Stock	600,000
Less: Accumulated Depreciation	(320,000)	Additional Paid-In Capital	120,000
Goodwill	100,000	Retained Earnings	360,000
Investment in Shocker			
Manufacturing	530,000		
	$1,780,000		$1,780,000

The balance sheet for Shocker Manufacturing for December 31, 19X5, appeared as follows:

Shocker Manufacturing
Balance Sheet
December 31, 19X5

Cash	$ 40,000	Accounts Payable	$ 10,000
Accounts Receivable	80,000	Taxes Payable	60,000
Inventory	120,000	Notes Payable	130,000
Buildings and Equipment	300,000	Common Stock	200,000
Less: Accumulated Depreciation	(90,000)	Retained Earnings	100,000
Marketable Securities	50,000		
	$500,000		$500,000

Whitehurst acquired 80 percent of Shocker's common stock on December 31, 19X5. The fair values of Shocker's identifiable assets and liabilities were equal to book values, except for the following:

	Book Value	Fair Value
Inventory	$120,000	$190,000
Buildings and Equipment (net)	210,000	410,000
Notes Payable	130,000	120,000

Required

Select the correct answer for each of the following questions.

1. What will be the balance reported for consolidated retained earnings on December 31, 19X5?
   a. $360,000.
   b. $380,000.
   c. $440,000.
   d. $460,000.

2. What balance will be reported for common stock in the consolidated balance sheet?
   a. $600,000.
   b. $640,000.
   c. $760,000.
   d. $800,000.

3. What amount of notes payable will be reported by the consolidated entity?
   a. $596,000.
   b. $620,000.
   c. $622,000.
   d. $630,000.

4. What inventory balance will be reported in the consolidated balance sheet?
   a. $480,000.
   b. $512,000.
   c. $536,000.
   d. $550,000.

5. What amount of goodwill will be reported in the consolidated balance sheet?
   a. $100,000.
   b. $166,000.
   c. $330,000.
   d. $390,000.

6. What balance will be reported for the noncontrolling interest?
   a. $0.
   b. $40,000.
   c. $60,000.
   d. $112,000.

7. What amount of accounts payable will be reported in the consolidated balance sheet?
   a. $70,000.
   b. $72,000.
   c. $78,000.
   d. $80,000.

8. Total assets in the consolidated balance sheet will be:
   a. $1,750,000.
   b. $2,032,000.
   c. $2,180,000.
   d. $2,250,000.

9. Total stockholders' equity in the consolidated balance sheet will be:
   a. $1,080,000.
   b. $1,140,000.
   c. $1,320,000.
   d. $1,380,000.

10. Total liabilities reported in the consolidated balance sheet will be:
    a. $200,000.
    b. $700,000.

c. $892,000.
d. $900,000.

P4-19 Intercorporate Receivables and Payables

Astor Corporation acquired 60 percent of the outstanding shares of Shield Company on January 1, 19X7. Balance sheet data for the two companies immediately following the purchase were as follows:

	Astor Corporation	Shield Company
Cash	$ 70,000	$ 35,000
Accounts Receivable	90,000	65,000
Inventory	184,000	80,000
Buildings and Equipment	400,000	300,000
Less: Accumulated Depreciation	(160,000)	(75,000)
Investment in Shield Company Stock	191,000	
Investment in Shield Company Bonds	50,000	
Total Assets	$825,000	$405,000
Accounts Payable	$ 50,000	$ 20,000
Bonds Payable	200,000	100,000
Common Stock	300,000	150,000
Capital in Excess of Par		140,000
Retained Earnings	275,000	(5,000)
Total Liabilities and Equities	$825,000	$405,000

As indicated in the parent company balance sheet, Astor purchased $50,000 of Shield Company bonds from the subsidiary immediately after it purchased the stock. An analysis of intercompany receivables and payables also indicates that the subsidiary owes the parent $10,000. On the date of combination, the book values and fair values of Shield's assets and liabilities were the same.

Required

a. Give all eliminating entries needed to prepare a consolidated balance sheet for January 1, 19X7.
b. Complete a consolidated balance sheet workpaper.
c. Prepare a consolidated balance sheet in good form.

P4-20 Comprehensive Problem: Consolidation of Majority-Owned Subsidiary

On January 2, 19X8, B.N. Counter Corporation purchased 75 percent of the outstanding common stock of Ticken Tie Company. In exchange for Ticken Tie's stock, B.N. Counter issued bonds payable with a par and fair value of $500,000 directly to the selling stockholders of Ticken Tie. The two companies continued to operate as separate entities subsequent to the combination.

Immediately prior to the combination, the book values and fair values of the companies' assets and liabilities were as follows:

	B.N. Counter		Ticken Tie	
	Book Value	Fair Value	Book Value	Fair Value
Cash	$ 12,000	$ 12,000	$ 9,000	$ 9,000
Receivables	41,000	39,000	31,000	30,000
Allowance for Bad Debts	(2,000)		(1,000)	
Inventory	86,000	89,000	68,000	72,000
Land	55,000	200,000	50,000	70,000
Buildings and Equipment	960,000	650,000	670,000	500,000
Accumulated Depreciation	(411,000)		(220,000)	
Patent				40,000
Total Assets	$741,000	$990,000	$607,000	$721,000
Current Payables	$ 38,000	$ 38,000	$ 29,000	$ 29,000
Bonds Payable	200,000	210,000	100,000	90,000
Common Stock	300,000		200,000	
Additional Paid-In Capital	100,000		130,000	
Retained Earnings	103,000		148,000	
Total Liabilities and Equity	$741,000		$607,000	

At the date of combination, Ticken Tie owed B.N. Counter $6,000 plus accrued interest of $500 on a short-term note. These amounts have been properly recorded by both companies.

Required

a. Record the business combination on the books of B.N. Counter Corporation.

b. Present in general journal form all elimination entries that would be needed in a workpaper to prepare a consolidated balance sheet immediately following the business combination on January 2, 19X8.

c. Prepare and complete a consolidated balance sheet workpaper as of January 2, 19X8, immediately following the business combination.

d. Present a consolidated balance sheet for B.N. Counter and its subsidiary as of January 2, 19X8.

CHAPTER 5

CONSOLIDATION
FOLLOWING ACQUISITION

The procedures used to prepare a consolidated balance sheet as of the date of acquisition were introduced in the preceding chapter. More than a consolidated balance sheet, however, is needed to provide a comprehensive picture of the consolidated entity's activities following acquisition. As with a single company, the set of basic financial statements for a consolidated entity consists of a balance sheet, an income statement, a statement of changes in retained earnings, and a statement of cash flows.

The purpose of this chapter is to present the procedures used in the preparation of a consolidated balance sheet, income statement, and retained earnings statement subsequent to the date of combination. The preparation of a consolidated statement of cash flows is discussed in Chapter 10.

This chapter first deals with the important concepts of consolidated net income and consolidated retained earnings, followed by a description of the workpaper format used to facilitate the preparation of a full set of consolidated financial statements. The remainder of the chapter deals with the specific procedures used to prepare consolidated financial statements subsequent to the date of combination.

OVERVIEW OF THE CONSOLIDATION PROCESS

The approach followed to prepare a complete set of consolidated financial statements subsequent to a business combination is quite similar to that used to prepare a consolidated balance sheet as of the date of combination. However, in addition to the assets and liabilities, the revenues and expenses of the consolidating companies must be combined. As the accounts are combined, eliminations must be made in the consolidation workpaper so that the consolidated financial statements appear as if they are the financial statements of a single company.

Because consolidation subsequent to acquisition of a subsidiary involves changes that take place over time, the resulting financial statements rest heavily on the concepts of consolidated net income and consolidated retained earnings. The consolidation approach used in practice in the United States and Canada is essentially the parent company approach, which emphasizes the income and retained earnings of the consolidated entity accruing to the parent.

Consolidated Net Income

All revenues and expenses of the individual consolidating companies arising from transactions with nonaffiliated companies are included in the consolidated income statement. The amount reported as **_consolidated net income_** is that part of the income of the total enterprise that is assigned to the shareholders of the parent company.

Consolidated net income can be calculated by combining the income statement data for individual consolidating companies using either an **_additive_** or a **_residual approach_**. The additive and residual approaches are two different ways of arriving at the same number. Both of these computations will be used in subsequent chapters to verify the results attained through the elimination entry process.

Additive Approach The total income generated from the parent's own operations plus the parent's share of the net income of each subsidiary adjusted for write-off of the differential is equal to consolidated net income. This approach is the same as that used in computing the parent company's equity-method net income and is helpful in reconciling between income from parent company operations and consolidated net income.

Residual Approach The residual approach is important because it represents the manner in which consolidated net income is determined in the consolidation workpaper. When all subsidiaries are wholly owned, all the income accrues to the shareholders of the parent, and consolidated net income is the difference between consolidated revenue and expenses. When a subsidiary is less than wholly owned, a portion of its income accrues to its noncontrolling shareholders. In the consolidation workpaper and resulting income statement, the income assigned to noncontrolling shareholders of consolidated subsidiaries is deducted to arrive at consolidated net income. While revenue and expenses reported in the consolidated income statement are unaffected by the existence of noncontrolling shareholders, consolidated net income is the income of the consolidating companies accruing to the shareholders of the parent company and is reduced as the amount assigned to noncontrolling shareholders of subsidiary companies is increased. Thus, the larger the proportion of noncontrolling ownership, the smaller the reported consolidated net income.

A subsidiary's net income is assigned to its different ownership groups in proportion to the percentage ownership interest held by each group. The subsidiary's income available for common shareholders is divided between the controlling and noncontrolling shareholders based on their relative common stock ownership interests. For example, if a subsidiary earns net income of $100,000, a 20 percent noncontrolling interest is allocated $20,000 of the subsidiary's net income, with the remaining $80,000 included in consolidated net income.

The residual approach begins with the reported net income of each of the separate consolidating companies and eliminates those items that should not be included. Consolidated net income, in simple cases, is equal to the total earnings for all companies consolidated, less any intercorporate investment income recorded by the parent from the consolidating companies and any income assigned to noncontrolling shareholders. Intercorporate investment income included in the parent's net income must be removed in computing consolidated net income in order to avoid double counting.

Computation of Consolidated Net Income Illustrated   To illustrate the computation of consolidated net income under the two approaches, assume that Push Corporation owns 80 percent of the stock of Shove Company, which was purchased at book value. During 19X1, Shove reports net income of $25,000, while Push reports earnings of $100,000 from its own operations and equity-method investment income of $20,000. Consolidated net income for 19X1 is computed as follows:

Additive computation:		
Separate operating income of Push		$100,000
Net income of Shove	$ 25,000	
Push's proportionate share	× .80	20,000
Consolidated net income		$120,000
Residual computation:		
Net income of Push	$120,000	
Less: Income from subsidiary	(20,000)	$100,000
Net income of Shove		25,000
		$125,000
Less: Income to noncontrolling interest	$ 25,000	
	× .20	(5,000)
Consolidated net income		$120,000

Note that both methods of computing consolidated net income lead to the same result; the two methods simply represent different approaches to reaching the same end.

Consolidated Retained Earnings

Consolidated retained earnings must be measured on a basis consistent with that used in determining consolidated net income. *Consolidated retained earnings* is that portion of the undistributed earnings of the consolidated enterprise accruing to the shareholders of the parent company. As with a single company, ending consolidated retained earnings is equal to the beginning consolidated retained earnings balance plus consolidated net income, less consolidated dividends.

Only those dividends paid to the owners of the consolidated entity can be included in the consolidated retained earnings statement. Because the owners of the parent company are considered to be the owners of the consolidated entity, only dividends paid by the parent company to its shareholders are treated as a deduction in the consolidated retained earnings statement; dividends of the subsidiary are not included.

As with consolidated net income, consolidated retained earnings can be computed using either an additive or a residual approach.

Additive Approach   The additive computation is divided into five components:

1. Retained earnings of the parent on date of subsidiary acquisition
2. Plus cumulative earnings of the parent from its own separate operations since date of acquisition
3. Plus the parent's portion of the cumulative earnings of the subsidiary since acquisition
4. Minus total dividends paid by the parent since date of acquisition
5. Plus or minus amortization of the differential since date of acquisition

The additive computation, when taken from the date of acquisition, provides the appropriate retained earnings balance regardless of the method used by the parent to account for its ownership of the subsidiary.

The additive method parallels the computation of the parent's retained earnings when the parent carries its investment in the subsidiary using the equity method. Use of the cost method by the parent, however, leads to a retained earnings balance for the parent that differs from consolidated retained earnings.

Residual Approach   The retained earnings balances of the individual companies are added together as the starting point when the residual approach is used in computing consolidated retained earnings. When the parent uses the equity method to account for its investment in the subsidiary, three deductions are needed to reconcile the combined retained earnings total with the amount to be reported as consolidated retained earnings:

1. Deduct the balance in retained earnings of the subsidiary on the date of purchase. Retained earnings accumulated by a subsidiary before a business combination may not be carried forward when purchase accounting is used.
2. Deduct the parent's portion of retained earnings accumulated by the subsidiary following the acquisition. To the extent that it has been recorded by the parent, the full amount already is included in the parent's retained earnings under the equity method and must not be counted twice.
3. Deduct that portion of earnings retained by the subsidiary since the date of acquisition that accrues to the noncontrolling shareholders of the subsidiary. Only the parent's portion of the subsidiary's retained earnings, already included in the parent's retained earnings under the equity method, is included in the consolidated total.

When the parent uses the cost method to account for its investment in a subsidiary, only items 1 and 3 are deducted; item 2 is not recorded by the parent under the cost method.

Computation of Consolidated Retained Earnings Illustrated Continuing the example of Push and Shove given earlier, assume that on January 1, 19X1, Push has a retained earnings balance of $400,000 and Shove has a retained earnings balance of $250,000. During 19X1, Push reports separate operating earnings of $100,000 and equity-method income from its 80 percent interest in Shove of $20,000; Push declares dividends of $30,000. Shove reports net income of $25,000 and declares dividends of $10,000. On the basis of this information, the ending retained earnings balances for Push and Shove on December 31, 19X1, are computed as follows:

	Push	Shove
Balance, January 1, 19X1	$400,000	$250,000
Net income, 19X1	120,000	25,000
Dividends declared in 19X1	(30,000)	(10,000)
Balance, December 31, 19X1	$490,000	$265,000

Consolidated retained earnings on December 31, 19X1, is computed using the additive approach as follows:

Additive approach:		
Retained earnings of Push at acquisition		$400,000
Cumulative earnings from Push's separate operations		100,000
Cumulative earnings of Shove since acquisition	$25,000	
Percentage ownership held by Push	× .80	20,000
Total		$520,000
Less: Dividends declared by Push		(30,000)
Consolidated retained earnings on December 31, 19X1		$490,000

The same ending consolidated retained earnings balance is obtained using the residual approach:

Residual approach:		
Retained earnings of Push on December 31, 19X1		$490,000
Retained earnings of Shove on December 31, 19X1		265,000
Total		$755,000
Less: Retained earnings of Shove at acquisition		(250,000)
Increase in Shove's retained earnings already recorded by Push	$15,000 × .80	(12,000)
Increase in Shove's retained earnings assigned to noncontrolling interest	$15,000 × .20	(3,000)
Consolidated retained earnings on December 31, 19X1		$490,000

The ending consolidated retained earnings balance can be verified by adding consolidated net income to the beginning balance of consolidated retained earnings and deducting consolidated dividends, as in the consolidated retained earnings statement:

Balance on January 1, 19X1 (at acquisition, equal to retained earnings balance of Push)	$400,000
Add: Consolidated net income	120,000
	$520,000
Deduct: Dividends declared by Push	(30,000)
Consolidated retained earnings on December 31, 19X1	$490,000

Workpaper Format

A number of different workpaper formats for preparing consolidated financial statements are used in practice. One of the most widely used formats is the three-part workpaper, consisting of one part for each of three basic financial statements: the income statement, the statement of retained earnings, and the balance sheet.

Figure 5-1 presents the format for the comprehensive three-part consolidation workpaper. The columns are the same as those for the balance sheet workpaper discussed in Chapters 3 and 4. The final column in the workpaper contains the totals of each line summed algebraically across and is the basis for preparing the consolidated financial statements.

The top portion of the workpaper is used in preparing the consolidated income statement. All income statement accounts with credit balances are listed first, and those with debit balances are listed next. When the income statement portion of the workpaper is completed, a total for each of the columns is entered at the bottom of the income statement portion of the workpaper. The bottom line in this part of the workpaper shows the net income of the parent, the net income of the subsidiary, the totals of the debit and credit eliminations for this section of the workpaper, and consolidated net income. The entire bottom line is carried forward to the retained earnings statement portion of the workpaper immediately below.

The retained earnings statement section of the workpaper is in the same format as a retained earnings statement. Net income and the other totals from the bottom line of the income statement portion of the workpaper are brought down from above. Similarly, the final line in the retained earnings statement section of the workpaper is carried forward in its entirety to the balance sheet section.

The bottom portion of the workpaper reflects the balance sheet amounts at the end of the period. Debits and credits are separated in the same manner as in the consolidated balance sheet workpaper presented earlier. The retained earnings amounts appearing in the balance sheet section of the workpaper are the totals carried forward from the bottom line of the retained earnings statement section.

The series of examples appearing in the following sections of this chapter demonstrate the use of the comprehensive three-part consolidation workpaper.

FIGURE 5-1 Format for comprehensive three-part consolidation workpaper.

Item	Trial Balance Data		Elimination Entries		Consolidated
	Parent	Subsidiary	Debits	Credits	

Credit Accounts:
  Revenues
  Gains
Debit Accounts:
  Contra Revenues
  Expenses
  Losses
Net Income
	INCOME STATEMENT SECTION				

Beginning Retained
  Earnings
Add: Net Income
Deduct: Dividends
Ending Retained
  Earnings
	RETAINED EARNINGS STATEMENT SECTION				

Debit Accounts:
  Assets
  Contra Liabilities
Credit Accounts:
  Contra Assets
  Liabilities
  Stockholders' Equity:
    Capital Stock
    Paid-In Capital
    Retained Earnings
	BALANCE SHEET SECTION				

CONSOLIDATION—100 PERCENT OWNERSHIP

Each of the consolidated financial statements is prepared as if taken from a single set of books that is being used to account for the overall consolidated entity. There is, of course, no set of books for the consolidated entity, and as in the preparation of the consolidated balance sheet, the consolidation process starts with the data recorded on the books of the individual consolidating companies. The account balances from the books of the individual companies are placed in the three-part workpaper, and entries are made to eliminate the effects of intercorporate ownership and transactions.

To view the process of consolidation subsequent to acquisition, assume that on January 1, 19X1, Peerless Products Corporation purchases all the common stock of Special Foods, Inc., for its underlying book value of $300,000. At that time, Special Foods has $200,000 of common stock outstanding and retained earnings of $100,000. The resulting ownership situation is as follows:

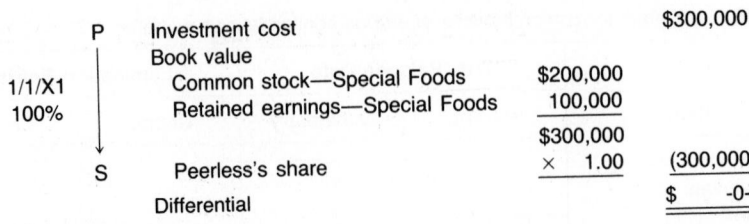

P	Investment cost			$300,000
	Book value			
1/1/X1	Common stock—Special Foods	$200,000		
100%	Retained earnings—Special Foods	100,000		
		$300,000		
S	Peerless's share	× 1.00	(300,000)	
	Differential		$ -0-	

Peerless accounts for its investment in Special Foods stock using the equity method. Information about Peerless and Special Foods as of the date of combination and for the years 19X1 and 19X2 appears in Figure 5-2.

Year of Combination

On January 1, 19X1, Peerless records its purchase of Special Foods common stock with the following entry:

January 1, 19X1
(1)	Investment in Special Foods Stock	300,000	
	Cash		300,000
	Record purchase of Special Foods stock.		

During 19X1, Peerless records operating earnings of $140,000, excluding its income from investing in Special Foods, and declares dividends of $60,000. Special Foods reports 19X1 net income of $50,000 and declares dividends of $30,000.

Parent Company Entries   Peerless records its 19X1 income and dividends from Special Foods under the equity method with the following entries:

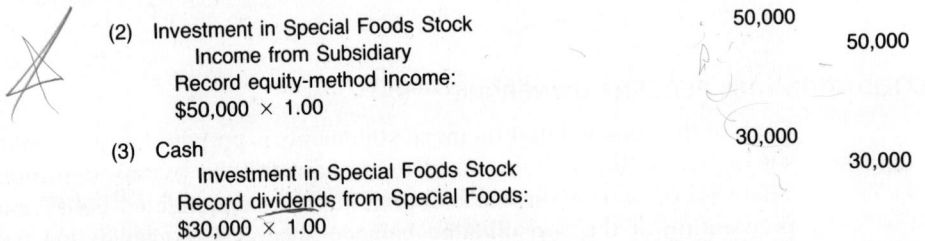

(2)	Investment in Special Foods Stock	50,000	
	Income from Subsidiary		50,000
	Record equity-method income:		
	$50,000 × 1.00		
(3)	Cash	30,000	
	Investment in Special Foods Stock		30,000
	Record dividends from Special Foods:		
	$30,000 × 1.00		

Consolidation Workpaper—Year of Combination   After all appropriate entries, including year-end adjustments, have been made on the books of Peerless and Special Foods, a consolidation workpaper is prepared as in Figure 5-3. The adjusted account balances from the books of Peerless and Special Foods are placed in the first two columns of the workpaper. Then, all amounts that reflect intercorporate transactions or ownership are eliminated in the consolidation process.

FIGURE 5-2 Selected information about Peerless Products and Special Foods on January 1, 19X1, and for the years 19X1 and 19X2.

	Peerless Products	Special Foods
Common Stock, January 1, 19X1	$500,000	$200,000
Retained Earnings, January 1, 19X1	300,000	100,000
19X1:		
Separate Operating Income, Peerless	140,000	
Net Income, Special Foods		50,000
Dividends	60,000	30,000
19X2:		
Separate Operating Income, Peerless	160,000	
Net Income, Special Foods		75,000
Dividends	60,000	40,000

The distinction between journal entries recorded on the books of the individual companies and the eliminating entries recorded only on the consolidation workpaper is an important one. Book entries affect balances on the books and the amounts that are carried to the consolidation workpaper; workpaper eliminating entries affect only those balances carried to the consolidated financial statements in the period. As mentioned previously, the eliminating entries presented in this text are identified with an "E" prefix to the left of the journal entry number whenever they are shown outside the workpaper.

In this example, the accounts which must be eliminated because of intercorporate ownership are the stockholders' equity accounts of Special Foods, including dividends declared, Peerless's investment in Special Foods stock, and Peerless's income from Special Foods. While these accounts can be eliminated in a single entry, two entries often are used to avoid the complexity of a single, large entry.

The first eliminating entry, E(4), removes both the investment income reflected in the parent's income statement and the parent's portion of any dividends declared by the subsidiary during the period:

E(4)	Income from Subsidiary	50,000	
	Dividends Declared		30,000
	Investment in Special Foods Stock		20,000
	Eliminate income from subsidiary.		

Under the equity method, the parent recognized on its separate books its share (100 percent) of the subsidiary's income. In the consolidated income statement, however, the individual revenue and expense accounts of the subsidiary are combined with those of the parent. Income recognized by the parent from all

FIGURE 5-3 December 31, 19X1, equity-method workpaper for consolidated financial statements, year of combination; 100 percent purchase at book value.

Item	Peerless Products	Special Foods	Eliminations Debit	Eliminations Credit	Consolidated
Sales	400,000	200,000			600,000
Income from Subsidiary	50,000		(4) 50,000		
Credits	450,000	200,000			600,000
Cost of Goods Sold	170,000	115,000			285,000
Depreciation and Amortization	50,000	20,000			70,000
Other Expenses	40,000	15,000			55,000
Debits	(260,000)	(150,000)			(410,000)
Net Income, carry forward	190,000	50,000	50,000		190,000
Retained Earnings, January 1	300,000	100,000	(5) 100,000		300,000
Net Income, from above	190,000	50,000	50,000		190,000
	490,000	150,000			490,000
Dividends Declared	(60,000)	(30,000)		(4) 30,000	(60,000)
Retained Earnings, December 31, carry forward	430,000	120,000	150,000	30,000	430,000
Cash	210,000	75,000			285,000
Accounts Receivable	75,000	50,000			125,000
Inventory	100,000	75,000			175,000
Land	175,000	40,000			215,000
Buildings and Equipment	800,000	600,000			1,400,000
Investment in Special Foods Stock	320,000			(4) 20,000	
				(5) 300,000	
Debits	1,680,000	840,000			2,200,000
Accumulated Depreciation	450,000	320,000			770,000
Accounts Payable	100,000	100,000			200,000
Bonds Payable	200,000	100,000			300,000
Common Stock	500,000	200,000	(5) 200,000		500,000
Retained Earnings, from above	430,000	120,000	150,000	30,000	430,000
Credits	1,680,000	840,000	350,000	350,000	2,200,000

Elimination entries:
(4) Eliminate income from subsidiary.
(5) Eliminate beginning investment balance.

consolidated subsidiaries, therefore, must be eliminated to avoid double counting. The subsidiary's dividend declaration related to the parent company must be eliminated when consolidated statements are prepared so that only dividend declarations related to shareholders outside the consolidated entity are treated as dividends.

The investment account is credited for the difference between investment income and the parent's portion of subsidiary dividends. This difference represents the net change in the investment account for the period. The investment account balance increased by $20,000 during 19X1. Entering a $20,000 credit to the investment account in the workpaper takes the account balance back to the $300,000 balance at the start of the period.

The second eliminating entry removes the intercorporate ownership claim and stockholders' equity accounts of the subsidiary as of the start of the period:

E(5)	Common Stock—Special Foods	200,000	
	Retained Earnings, January 1	100,000	
	Investment in Special Foods Stock		300,000
	Eliminate beginning investment balance.		

This entry credits the investment account for its balance at the beginning of the period and, together with entry E(4), fully eliminates the balance of the investment account at the end of the period. Note that the parent's investment in the stock of a consolidated subsidiary never appears in the consolidated balance sheet.

Common stock and retained earnings are debited in entry E(5) for the balances in the accounts at the beginning of the period. Ending retained earnings never is adjusted directly when a three-part workpaper is prepared. Instead, the three components of ending retained earnings are eliminated individually: the beginning retained earnings balance is eliminated by entry E(5) in the retained earnings statement portion of the workpaper, and income (from the subsidiary) and dividends are eliminated by entry E(4).

Workpaper Relationships   Both of the eliminating entries have been entered in Figure 5-3 and the amounts totaled across and down to complete the workpaper. Some specific points to recognize with respect to the full workpaper are as follows:

1. Each of the first two sections of the workpaper "telescopes" into the section below in a logical progression. As part of the normal accounting cycle, net income is closed to retained earnings and reflected in the balance sheet. Similarly, in the consolidation workpaper the net income is carried into the retained earnings statement section of the workpaper, and the ending retained earnings line is carried into the balance sheet section of the workpaper. Note that in both cases the entire line, including total eliminations, is carried forward.

2. Using double-entry bookkeeping, total debits must equal total credits for any single eliminating entry and for the workpaper as a whole. Because some eliminating entries extend to more than one section of the workpaper, however, the totals of the debit and credit eliminations are not likely to be equal in either of the first two sections of the workpaper. The totals of all debits and credits at the very bottom of the balance sheet section are equal because the cumulative balances from the two upper sections are carried forward to the balance sheet section.

3. In the balance sheet portion of the workpaper, total debit balances must equal total credit balances for each company and the consolidated entity.

4. When the parent uses the equity method of accounting for the investment and there are no unrealized profits from intercorporate transactions, consolidated net income should equal the parent's net income and consolidated retained earnings should equal the parent's retained earnings. This means the existing balance in subsidiary retained earnings must be eliminated to avoid double counting.

5. Certain other clerical safeguards are incorporated into the workpaper. The amounts reflected in the bottom line of the income statement section, when summed (algebraically) across, must equal the number reported as consolidated net income. Similarly, the amounts in the last line of the retained earnings statement section must equal consolidated retained earnings when summed across.

Second and Subsequent Years of Ownership

The consolidation procedures employed at the end of the second year, and in periods thereafter, are basically the same as those used at the end of the first year. Adjusted trial balance data of the individual companies are used as the starting point each time consolidated statements are prepared, because no separate books are kept for the consolidated entity. An additional check is needed in each period following the acquisition to assure that the beginning balance in consolidated retained earnings shown in the completed workpaper is equal to the balance reported at the end of the prior period. In all other respects the eliminating entries and workpaper are comparable with those shown for the first year of ownership.

Parent Company Entries Consolidation two years after acquisition is illustrated by continuing the example of Peerless Products and Special Foods, based on the data in Figure 5-2. Peerless's separate income from its own operations for 19X2 is $160,000, and its dividends total $60,000. Special Foods reports net income of $75,000 in 19X2 and pays dividends of $40,000. Equity-method entries recorded by Peerless in 19X2 are as follows:

(6)	Investment in Special Foods Stock	75,000	
	Income from Subsidiary		75,000
	Record equity-method income:		
	$75,000 \times 1.00$		

(7) Cash	40,000	
Investment in Special Foods Stock		40,000
Record dividends from Special Foods:		
$40,000 \times 1.00$		

With these entries, the balance in the investment account reported by Peerless increases from $320,000 on January 1, 19X2, to $355,000 on December 31, 19X2, and reported net income of Peerless totals $235,000 ($160,000 + $75,000).

Consolidation Workpaper—Second Year Following Combination The workpaper to prepare consolidated statements for 19X2 is illustrated in Figure 5-4. Entry E(8) eliminates Peerless's 19X2 income from Special Foods and the dividend payment made to Peerless by Special Foods. The credit to the investment account in entry E(8) removes the change in the investment account recorded by Peerless during the period:

E(8) Income from Subsidiary	75,000	
Dividends Declared		40,000
Investment in Special Foods Stock		35,000
Eliminate income from subsidiary.		

The second workpaper entry eliminates the beginning balance in the investment account and the stockholders' equity accounts of the subsidiary at the beginning of 19X2:

E(9) Common Stock—Special Foods	200,000	
Retained Earnings, January 1	120,000	
Investment in Special Foods Stock		320,000
Eliminate beginning investment balance.		

Because the parent purchased all the common stock of the subsidiary at book value and is accounting for the investment using the equity method, the balance in its investment account will be equal to the stockholders' equity of the subsidiary. The full balance of the retained earnings of the subsidiary must be eliminated each period. Special Foods' retained earnings of $100,000 on the date of combination cannot be purchased by Peerless and therefore must be excluded from consolidated retained earnings. Further, the $20,000 increase in Special Foods' retained earnings during 19X1 already is reflected in the retained earnings of Peerless as a result of using the equity method.

After placement of entries E(8) and E(9) in the consolidation workpaper, the workpaper is completed in the normal manner as shown in Figure 5-4. All

FIGURE 5-4 December 31, 19X2, equity-method workpaper for consolidated financial statements, second year following combination; 100 percent purchase at book value.

Item	Peerless Products	Special Foods	Eliminations Debit	Eliminations Credit	Consolidated
Sales	450,000	300,000			750,000
Income from Subsidiary	75,000		(8) 75,000		
Credits	525,000	300,000			750,000
Cost of Goods Sold	180,000	160,000			340,000
Depreciation and Amortization	50,000	20,000			70,000
Other Expenses	60,000	45,000			105,000
Debits	(290,000)	(225,000)			(515,000)
Net Income, carry forward	235,000	75,000	75,000		235,000
Retained Earnings, January 1	430,000	120,000	(9) 120,000		430,000
Net Income, from above	235,000	75,000	75,000		235,000
	665,000	195,000			665,000
Dividends Declared	(60,000)	(40,000)		(8) 40,000	(60,000)
Retained Earnings, December 31, carry forward	605,000	155,000	195,000	40,000	605,000
Cash	245,000	85,000			330,000
Accounts Receivable	150,000	80,000			230,000
Inventory	180,000	90,000			270,000
Land	175,000	40,000			215,000
Buildings and Equipment	800,000	600,000			1,400,000
Investment in Special Foods Stock	355,000			(8) 35,000	
				(9) 320,000	
Debits	1,905,000	895,000			2,445,000
Accumulated Depreciation	500,000	340,000			840,000
Accounts Payable	100,000	100,000			200,000
Bonds Payable	200,000	100,000			300,000
Common Stock	500,000	200,000	(9) 200,000		500,000
Retained Earnings, from above	605,000	155,000	195,000	40,000	605,000
Credits	1,905,000	895,000	395,000	395,000	2,445,000

Elimination entries:
(8) Eliminate income from subsidiary.
(9) Eliminate beginning investment balance.

the workpaper relationships discussed in conjunction with Figure 5-3 continue in the second year as well. The beginning consolidated retained earnings balance for 19X2, as shown in Figure 5-4, should be compared with the ending consolidated retained earnings balance for 19X1, as shown in Figure 5-3, to assure they are the same.

CONSOLIDATION—CONTROLLING OWNERSHIP PURCHASED AT BOOK VALUE

Total ownership rarely is needed to control and operate another company and often is expensive to acquire. Accordingly, many business combinations involve purchasing less than 100 percent of the stock of another company. Because total ownership of a subsidiary is not needed to present consolidated financial statements, many sets of consolidated financial statements include one or more subsidiaries that are less than wholly owned. Whenever the parent company holds less than total ownership of a subsidiary and consolidated financial statements are prepared, the claim of the noncontrolling shareholders must be reflected in the statements.

When a subsidiary is less than wholly owned, the consolidation procedures must be modified slightly from those discussed previously to include recognition of the noncontrolling interest. To illustrate, assume that on January 1, 19X1, Peerless Products purchases 80 percent of the common stock of Special Foods for $240,000. All other data are the same as those used in the previous example and presented in Figure 5-2. Because Special Foods has stockholders' equity of $300,000 on the date of combination, the purchase of 80 percent of Special Foods' outstanding stock for $240,000 is at underlying book value ($300,000 × .80). The resulting ownership situation can be characterized as follows:

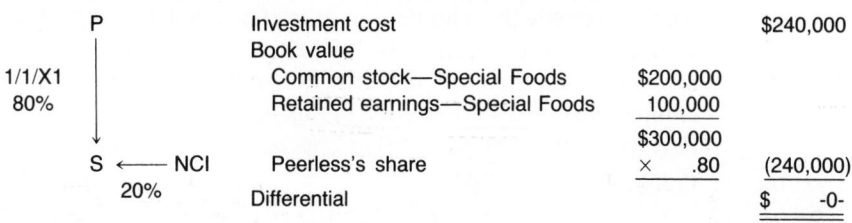

Year of Combination

On January 1, 19X1, Peerless records its purchase of Special Foods common stock with the following entry:

```
January 1, 19X1
  (10)  Investment in Special Foods Stock            240,000
             Cash                                              240,000
        Record purchase of Special Foods stock.
```

During 19X1, Peerless earns $140,000 from its own separate operations and declares dividends of $60,000. Special Foods reports net income of $50,000 and declares dividends of $30,000.

Parent Company Entries Peerless carries its investment in Special Foods stock using the equity method and, therefore, records its 80 percent share of Special Foods' 19X1 income and dividends with the following entries:

(11)	Investment in Special Foods Stock	40,000	
	Income from Subsidiary		40,000
	Record equity-method income:		
	$50,000 × .80		
(12)	Cash	24,000	
	Investment in Special Foods Stock		24,000
	Record dividends from Special Foods:		
	$30,000 × .80		

As a result of the entries recorded on the books of Peerless during 19X1, the balance in the investment account is $256,000 on December 31, 19X1. The trial balance data for Peerless and Special Foods at December 31, 19X1, appear in the workpaper in Figure 5-5. The amounts presented in Figure 5-5 for Peerless Products differ from those presented in Figure 5-3 as a result of the decrease in the percentage of Special Foods stock purchased and the correspondingly lower purchase price. Less cash was used in making the purchase, and a smaller share of income and dividends from Special Foods is recorded during 19X1 by Peerless. The trial balance for Special Foods is unaffected by the level of ownership purchased by Peerless and therefore is the same as in Figure 5-3.

Consolidation Workpaper—Year of Combination   When a subsidiary is not wholly owned, the eliminating entries needed to prepare consolidated financial statements differ from those presented earlier in that these eliminating entries must establish the amount of the noncontrolling interest in the workpaper. Three eliminating entries are needed in this particular case. In the first eliminating entry, Peerless's share (80 percent) of Special Foods' income and dividends is eliminated in the normal manner:

E(13)	Income from Subsidiary	40,000	
	Dividends Declared		24,000
	Investment in Special Foods Stock		16,000
	Eliminate income from subsidiary.		

The difference between income and dividends is credited to the investment account and eliminates the change in the investment balance for 19X1. Except for the difference in the dollar amounts due to the difference in the percentage of ownership, this entry is identical with the entry used in the earlier illustration in which the subsidiary was 100 percent owned.

All three of the consolidated statements are affected by the existence of noncontrolling shareholders. The primary change in the consolidated income statement is that a portion of the income of the subsidiary is assigned to the noncontrolling interest and, in turn, is deducted in computing consolidated net income.

Individual revenue and expense items of the consolidating companies are included in the consolidated income statement at their full amounts regardless of

FIGURE 5-5 December 31, 19X1, equity-method workpaper for consolidated financial statements, year of combination; 80 percent purchase at book value.

Item	Peerless Products	Special Foods	Eliminations				Consolidated
			Debit		Credit		
Sales	400,000	200,000					600,000
Income from Subsidiary	40,000		(13)	40,000			
Credits	440,000	200,000					600,000
Cost of Goods Sold	170,000	115,000					285,000
Depreciation and Amortization	50,000	20,000					70,000
Other Expenses	40,000	15,000					55,000
Debits	(260,000)	(150,000)					(410,000)
							190,000
Income to Noncontrolling Interest			(14)	10,000			(10,000)
Net Income, carry forward	180,000	50,000		50,000			180,000
Retained Earnings, January 1	300,000	100,000	(15)	100,000			300,000
Net Income, from above	180,000	50,000		50,000			180,000
	480,000	150,000					480,000
Dividends Declared	(60,000)	(30,000)			(13)	24,000	
					(14)	6,000	(60,000)
Retained Earnings, December 31, carry forward	420,000	120,000		150,000		30,000	420,000
Cash	264,000	75,000					339,000
Accounts Receivable	75,000	50,000					125,000
Inventory	100,000	75,000					175,000
Land	175,000	40,000					215,000
Buildings and Equipment	800,000	600,000					1,400,000
Investment in Special Foods Stock	256,000				(13)	16,000	
					(15)	240,000	
Debits	1,670,000	840,000					2,254,000
Accumulated Depreciation	450,000	320,000					770,000
Accounts Payable	100,000	100,000					200,000
Bonds Payable	200,000	100,000					300,000
Common Stock	500,000	200,000	(15)	200,000			500,000
Retained Earnings, from above	420,000	120,000		150,000		30,000	420,000
Noncontrolling Interest					(14)	4,000	
					(15)	60,000	64,000
Credits	1,670,000	840,000		350,000		350,000	2,254,000

Elimination entries:
(13) Eliminate income from subsidiary.
(14) Assign income to noncontrolling interest.
(15) Eliminate beginning investment balance.

the percentage ownership held by the parent. Including only the parent's share of revenue and expenses of partially owned subsidiaries would be inconsistent with the idea of a single economic entity. Thus, consolidated revenue and expenses are the same as in Figure 5-3 even though the ownership levels differ. Consolidated net income, on the other hand, is not the same, because it includes only the income assignable to parent company shareholders. Consolidated net income is reduced as the parent's ownership is reduced.

The amount of income assignable to noncontrolling shareholders of the subsidiary must be computed and deducted in arriving at consolidated net income each time consolidated statements are prepared. The share of Special Foods' income accruing to its noncontrolling shareholders is $10,000, the subsidiary's net income times the noncontrolling ownership percentage ($50,000 × .20). This amount is deducted in the workpaper to arrive at consolidated net income.

A separate entry is placed in the workpaper to establish the amount of income allocated to noncontrolling shareholders and to enter the increase in their claim on the net assets of the subsidiary during the period:

E(14)	Income to Noncontrolling Interest	10,000	
	Dividends Declared		6,000
	Noncontrolling Interest		4,000
	Assign income to noncontrolling interest.		

Income is assigned to the noncontrolling shareholders by entering a debit in the income statement portion of the workpaper. After summing across, this amount is subtracted in the consolidated column to arrive at consolidated net income.

Subsidiary dividends do not represent the dividends of the consolidated entity and therefore need to be eliminated fully. Workpaper entry E(13) eliminates only the parent's portion of subsidiary dividends. Entry E(14) eliminates the noncontrolling interest's share of subsidiary dividends. The difference between the noncontrolling stockholders' share of subsidiary income and their share of subsidiary dividends represents the change in their claim on the net assets of the subsidiary for the period and becomes part of the ending balance sheet amount of the noncontrolling interest.

The third workpaper entry in Figure 5-5 eliminates the stockholders' equity accounts of the subsidiary and the investment account balance shown by the parent at the start of the period. This entry also establishes the amount of the noncontrolling interest at the beginning of the period:

E(15)	Common Stock—Special Foods	200,000	
	Retained Earnings, January 1	100,000	
	Investment in Special Foods Stock		240,000
	Noncontrolling Interest		60,000
	Eliminate beginning investment balance.		

Noncontrolling Interest The total credits to noncontrolling interest in the eliminating entries equal $64,000. They consist of the noncontrolling stockholders' share of subsidiary net assets at the beginning of the period, established in entry E(15), and the noncontrolling stockholders' portion of the undistributed 19X1 earnings of the subsidiary, established in entry E(14). This $64,000 amount appears on the consolidated balance sheet prepared as of December 31, 19X1, as the total noncontrolling interest. The noncontrolling interest balance can be verified by multiplying the common stockholders' equity of the subsidiary on December 31, 19X1, by the noncontrolling interest's ownership ratio of 20 percent:

Special Foods common stock, December 31, 19X1	$200,000
Special Foods' retained earnings, December 31, 19X1	120,000
Book value of Special Foods, December 31, 19X1	$320,000
Proportion of stock held by noncontrolling shareholders	× .20
Noncontrolling interest, December 31, 19X1	$ 64,000

Second Year of Ownership

Consolidation in the second year follows the same procedures as in the first year. From the data for Peerless and Special Foods outlined in Figure 5-2, it can be seen that Peerless earns separate operating income of $160,000 and pays dividends of $60,000 in 19X2. Special Foods reports net income of $75,000 and pays dividends of $40,000 in 19X2.

Parent Company Entries Peerless makes the following entries in 19X2 to record its 80 percent share of Special Foods' net income and dividends:

(16)	Investment in Special Foods Stock	60,000	
	Income from Subsidiary		60,000
	Record equity-method income:		
	$75,000 × .80		
(17)	Cash	32,000	
	Investment in Special Foods Stock		32,000
	Record dividends from Special Foods:		
	$40,000 × .80		

These entries increase the balance in Peerless's investment account by $28,000 during 19X2, resulting in an ending balance of $284,000.

Consolidation Workpaper—Second Year Following Combination The three-part workpaper to prepare consolidated financial statements for 19X2 appears in Figure 5-6.

FIGURE 5-6 December 31, 19X2, equity-method workpaper for consolidated financial statements, second year following combination; 80 percent purchase at book value.

Item	Peerless Products	Special Foods	Eliminations Debit		Eliminations Credit		Consolidated
Sales	450,000	300,000					750,000
Income from Subsidiary	60,000		(18)	60,000			
Credits	510,000	300,000					750,000
Cost of Goods Sold	180,000	160,000					340,000
Depreciation and Amortization	50,000	20,000					70,000
Other Expenses	60,000	45,000					105,000
Debits	(290,000)	(225,000)					(515,000)
							235,000
Income to Noncontrolling Interest			(19)	15,000			(15,000)
Net Income, carry forward	220,000	75,000		75,000			220,000
Retained Earnings, January 1	420,000	120,000	(20)	120,000			420,000
Net Income, from above	220,000	75,000		75,000			220,000
	640,000	195,000					640,000
Dividends Declared	(60,000)	(40,000)			(18)	32,000	
					(19)	8,000	(60,000)
Retained Earnings, December 31, carry forward	580,000	155,000		195,000		40,000	580,000
Cash	291,000	85,000					376,000
Accounts Receivable	150,000	80,000					230,000
Inventory	180,000	90,000					270,000
Land	175,000	40,000					215,000
Buildings and Equipment	800,000	600,000					1,400,000
Investment in Special Foods Stock	284,000				(18)	28,000	
					(20)	256,000	
Debits	1,880,000	895,000					2,491,000
Accumulated Depreciation	500,000	340,000					840,000
Accounts Payable	100,000	100,000					200,000
Bonds Payable	200,000	100,000					300,000
Common Stock	500,000	200,000	(20)	200,000			500,000
Retained Earnings, from above	580,000	155,000		195,000		40,000	580,000
Noncontrolling Interest					(19)	7,000	
					(20)	64,000	71,000
Credits	1,880,000	895,000		395,000		395,000	2,491,000

Elimination entries:
 (18) Eliminate income from subsidiary.
 (19) Assign income to noncontrolling interest.
 (20) Eliminate beginning investment balance.

Three eliminating entries are needed to complete the workpaper:

E(18)	Income from Subsidiary	60,000	
	Dividends Declared		32,000
	Investment in Special Foods Stock		28,000
	Eliminate income from subsidiary.		
E(19)	Income to Noncontrolling Interest	15,000	
	Dividends Declared		8,000
	Noncontrolling Interest		7,000
	Assign income to noncontrolling interest.		
E(20)	Common Stock—Special Foods	200,000	
	Retained Earnings, January 1	120,000	
	Investment in Special Foods Stock		256,000
	Noncontrolling Interest		64,000
	Eliminate beginning investment balance.		

The first eliminating entry removes the income that Peerless has recognized from Special Foods, Peerless's share (80 percent) of Special Foods' dividends, and the $28,000 change in the investment account that occurred during 19X2.

Elimination entry E(19) assigns $15,000 of subsidiary income to the non-controlling shareholders, based on subsidiary income of $75,000 and a 20 percent noncontrolling interest. The entry also eliminates the noncontrolling interest's share of Special Foods' dividends because only dividends of Peerless are considered dividends of the consolidated entity. Finally, this entry establishes in the workpaper the increase in the noncontrolling interest for the period.

Entry E(20) eliminates the stockholders' equity accounts of the subsidiary and the investment account balance reported by the parent at the beginning of the year and establishes the amount of the noncontrolling interest's claim on the net assets of the subsidiary at the beginning of the year.

The credits to noncontrolling interest in elimination entries E(19) and E(20) result in a total noncontrolling interest reported in the consolidated balance sheet on December 31, 19X2, of $71,000 ($7,000 + $64,000). This amount is equal to 20 percent of the stockholders' equity balance of Special Foods on that date [($200,000 + $155,000) × .20].

CONSOLIDATION—CONTROLLING OWNERSHIP PURCHASED AT MORE THAN BOOK VALUE

In many cases a controlling investment in another company is purchased at some amount in excess of the book value of the shares acquired. As discussed in Chapter 4, the excess of the purchase price over the book value of the net identifiable assets purchased must be allocated to those assets and liabilities acquired, including any purchased goodwill. If this revaluation is not accomplished on the separate books of the subsidiary through the use of push-down accounting, it must be made in the consolidation workpaper each time consolidated statements are prepared. In addition, if the revaluations relate to assets or liabilities that must be depreciated or amortized, appropriate entries must be made in the consolidation workpaper to reduce consolidated net income accordingly.

When the equity method is applied, as illustrated in Chapter 2, the amount of differential viewed as expiring during the period is recorded by the investor as a reduction in the income recognized from the investee. In consolidation, the purchase differential is assigned to the asset and liability balances, and the amounts expiring during the period are included in the appropriate expense categories (for example, depreciation expense).

Year of Combination

To illustrate the purchase of less than total ownership at an amount greater than book value, assume that Peerless Products purchases 80 percent of the common stock of Special Foods on January 1, 19X1, for $310,000. The resulting ownership situation is as follows:

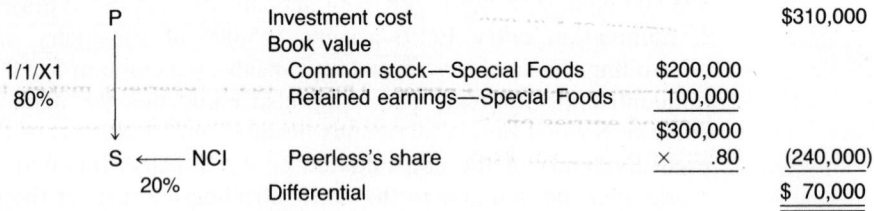

Investment cost		$310,000
Book value		
Common stock—Special Foods	$200,000	
Retained earnings—Special Foods	100,000	
	$300,000	
Peerless's share	× .80	(240,000)
Differential		$ 70,000

The total book value of Special Foods stock on the date of combination is $300,000, and the book value of the stock acquired by Peerless is $240,000 ($300,000 × .80). The difference between the total purchase price of $310,000 and the book value of the shares acquired is $70,000.

On the date of combination, all assets and liabilities of Special Foods have fair values equal to their book values, except as follows:

	Book Value	Fair Value	Fair Value Increment	Peerless's 80% Portion
Inventory	$ 60,000	$ 65,000	$ 5,000	$ 4,000
Land	40,000	50,000	10,000	8,000
Buildings and Equipment	300,000	360,000	60,000	48,000
	$400,000	$475,000	$75,000	$60,000

Of the $70,000 total differential, $60,000 relates to identifiable assets of Special Foods. The remaining $10,000 is attributable to goodwill. The apportionment of the differential appears as follows:

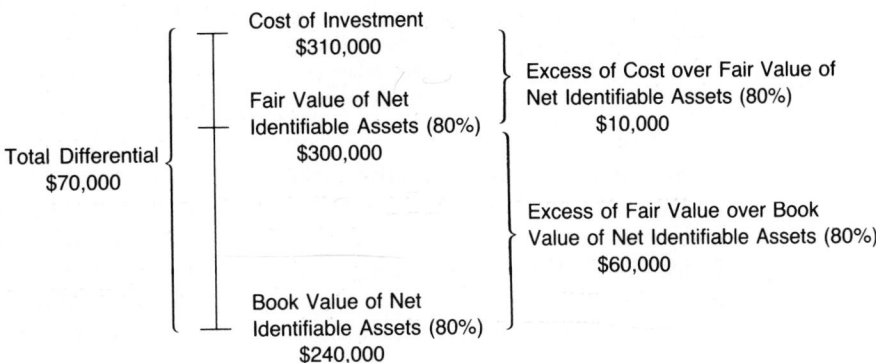

All the inventory to which the differential relates is sold during 19X1; in other words, none is left in ending inventory. The buildings and equipment have a remaining economic life of 10 years from the date of combination, and straight-line depreciation is used. The excess earning power represented by the goodwill is expected to last for 20 years from the date of combination.

For the first year immediately after the date of combination, 19X1, Peerless Products earns income from its own separate operations of $140,000 and pays dividends of $60,000. Special Foods reports net income of $50,000 and pays dividends of $30,000.

Parent Company Entries   During 19X1, Peerless makes the normal equity-method entries on its books to record its purchase of Special Foods stock and its share of Special Foods net income and dividends:

(21)	Investment in Special Foods Stock	310,000	
	Cash		310,000
	Record purchase of Special Foods stock.		
(22)	Investment in Special Foods Stock	40,000	
	Income from Subsidiary		40,000
	Record equity-method income:		
	$50,000 × .80		
(23)	Cash	24,000	
	Investment in Special Foods Stock		24,000
	Record dividends from Special Foods:		
	$30,000 × .80		

Entries (22) and (23) are the same as if Peerless had acquired its 80 percent investment at underlying book value. In addition, however, entries are needed on Peerless's books to recognize the write-off of the differential:

(24)	Income from Subsidiary	4,000	
	Investment in Special Foods Stock		4,000
	Adjust income for differential related to		
	inventory sold: $5,000 × .80		

(25)	Income from Subsidiary	5,300	
	Investment in Special Foods Stock		5,300
	Amortize differential related to		
	buildings and equipment and goodwill:		
	$4,800 + $500		

A portion of the differential, $4,000, relates to inventory of Special Foods that is sold during 19X1. Because the inventory no longer is held by Special Foods, the investment account must be reduced by $4,000 through entry (24). Further, Peerless's income must be reduced by $4,000 to reflect the additional amount paid by Peerless for its share of Special Foods' inventory sold during 19X1.

An additional $48,000 of the differential is attributable to the excess of the fair value over the book value of Special Foods' buildings and equipment with a 10-year remaining life. Use of the equity method requires the matching of the additional cost against the income recognized from the investment, and this is accomplished through annual amortization of $4,800 ($48,000 ÷ 10 years). Similarly, the $10,000 of differential related to goodwill must be amortized over 20 years, resulting in annual amortization of $500 ($10,000 ÷ 20 years). Entry (25) records the total amortization of the differential related to both goodwill and the buildings and equipment.

Consolidation Workpaper—Year of Combination   After the subsidiary income accruals are entered on the books of Peerless, the adjusted trial balance data of the consolidating companies are entered in the three-part consolidation workpaper as shown in Figure 5-7.

As before, the first three workpaper entries eliminate the subsidiary income and dividends recorded by Peerless, eliminate the investment account and the stockholders' equity accounts of Special Foods, and establish the noncontrolling interest:

E(26)	Income from Subsidiary	30,700	
	Dividends Declared		24,000
	Investment in Special Foods Stock		6,700
	Eliminate income from subsidiary.		
E(27)	Income to Noncontrolling Interest	10,000	
	Dividends Declared		6,000
	Noncontrolling Interest		4,000
	Assign income to noncontrolling interest.		
E(28)	Common Stock—Special Foods	200,000	
	Retained Earnings, January 1	100,000	
	Differential	70,000	
	Investment in Special Foods Stock		310,000
	Noncontrolling Interest		60,000
	Eliminate beginning investment balance.		

Entry E(26) removes the net effect of the income accrual recorded by the parent during 19X1 in entries (22), (24), and (25) and removes the parent's portion

FIGURE 5-7 December 31, 19X1, equity-method workpaper for consolidated financial statements, year of combination; 80 percent purchase at more than book value.

Item	Peerless Products	Special Foods	Eliminations Debit		Eliminations Credit		Consolidated
Sales	400,000	200,000					600,000
Income from Subsidiary	30,700		(26)	30,700			
Credits	430,700	200,000					600,000
Cost of Goods Sold	170,000	115,000	(29)	4,000			289,000
Depreciation and Amortization	50,000	20,000	(30)	4,800			
			(31)	500			75,300
Other Expenses	40,000	15,000					55,000
Debits	(260,000)	(150,000)					(419,300)
							180,700
Income to Noncontrolling Interest			(27)	10,000			(10,000)
Net Income, carry forward	170,700	50,000		50,000			170,700
Retained Earnings, January 1	300,000	100,000	(28)	100,000			300,000
Net Income, from above	170,700	50,000		50,000			170,700
	470,700	150,000					470,700
Dividends Declared	(60,000)	(30,000)			(26)	24,000	
					(27)	6,000	(60,000)
Retained Earnings, December 31, carry forward	410,700	120,000		150,000		30,000	410,700
Cash	194,000	75,000					269,000
Accounts Receivable	75,000	50,000					125,000
Inventory	100,000	75,000					175,000
Land	175,000	40,000	(29)	8,000			223,000
Buildings and Equipment	800,000	600,000	(29)	48,000			1,448,000
Investment in Special Foods Stock	316,700				(26)	6,700	
					(28)	310,000	
Goodwill			(29)	10,000	(31)	500	9,500
Differential			(28)	70,000	(29)	70,000	
Debits	1,660,700	840,000					2,249,500
Accumulated Depreciation	450,000	320,000			(30)	4,800	774,800
Accounts Payable	100,000	100,000					200,000
Bonds Payable	200,000	100,000					300,000
Common Stock	500,000	200,000	(28)	200,000			500,000
Retained Earnings, from above	410,700	120,000		150,000		30,000	410,700
Noncontrolling Interest					(27)	4,000	
					(28)	60,000	64,000
Credits	1,660,700	840,000		486,000		486,000	2,249,500

Elimination entries:
(26) Eliminate income from subsidiary.
(27) Assign income to noncontrolling interest.
(28) Eliminate beginning investment balance.
(29) Assign beginning differential.
(30) Amortize differential related to buildings and equipment.
(31) Amortize differential related to goodwill.

of dividends declared by the subsidiary during the period, as recorded in entry (23). Elimination entry E(27) places the noncontrolling interest's share of subsidiary income ($50,000 × .20) in the workpaper, eliminates the noncontrolling interest's share of subsidiary dividends ($30,000 × .20), and recognizes the increase in the noncontrolling interest during 19X1. The $4,000 increase in the claim of the noncontrolling shareholders for the period is included in the balance assigned to the noncontrolling interest in the bottom portion of the balance sheet section of the workpaper.

The third elimination entry, E(28), removes the stockholders' equity balances of the subsidiary and the investment account of the parent as of the beginning of the period and establishes the amount of the noncontrolling shareholders' claim as of the start of the period. Because the purchase price of the investment exceeded its book value, a purchase differential appears as the balancing figure in this entry. The differential established in this entry represents the unamortized amount as of the beginning of the period. Because the combination occurred on the first day of 19X1, the amount is equal to the differential on the date of combination, $70,000. As in Chapter 4, the differential account serves as a clearing account in the workpaper and is entered in the balance sheet portion of the workpaper at the bottom of the asset section.

Noncontrolling interest is credited for $60,000 ($300,000 × .20) in entry E(28), representing 20 percent of Special Foods' stockholders' equity at the start of the year. The noncontrolling interest totals $64,000 at the end of the period as a result of elimination entries E(27) and E(28). The amount assigned to the noncontrolling interest is based on the underlying book value of the subsidiary's net assets and is not affected by the amount paid by the parent in purchasing the subsidiary's stock. Thus, the noncontrolling shareholders' claim in Figure 5-7 is identical with that reported in Figure 5-5.

Three additional eliminating entries are needed in the workpaper in Figure 5-7 to allocate and amortize the differential:

E(29)	Cost of Goods Sold	4,000	
	Land	8,000	
	Buildings and Equipment	48,000	
	Goodwill	10,000	
	Differential		70,000
	Assign beginning differential.		
E(30)	Depreciation and Amortization Expense	4,800	
	Accumulated Depreciation		4,800
	Amortize differential related to buildings and equipment: $48,000 ÷ 10 years		
E(31)	Depreciation and Amortization Expense	500	
	Goodwill		500
	Amortize differential related to goodwill: $10,000 ÷ 20 years		

Entry E(29) assigns the original amount of the differential to the appropriate asset and expense accounts. On the basis of the fair value differences computed previously, $60,000 of the differential is apportioned to identifiable assets of Special Foods: $4,000 to inventory, $8,000 to land, and $48,000 to buildings and equipment.

Because all the inventory on hand on the date of combination has been sold during the year, the $4,000 of differential applicable to inventory is allocated directly to cost of goods sold. The cost of goods sold recorded on the books of Special Foods is correct for that company's separate financial statements. However, the cost of the inventory to the consolidated entity is viewed as being $4,000 higher, and this additional cost must be included in consolidated cost of goods sold.

No workpaper entry is needed in future periods with respect to the inventory because the inventory has been expensed and no longer is on the books of the subsidiary. The portion of the differential related to the inventory no longer exists on Peerless's books after 19X1 because it is removed from the investment account by entry (24).

The difference between the $310,000 total purchase price paid by Peerless and the $300,000 fair value of Peerless's share of the net identifiable assets acquired is assumed to be payment for the excess earning power of Special Foods. This difference is entered in the workpaper with entry E(29) as goodwill of $10,000.

The differential assigned to depreciable assets in entry E(29) must be charged to depreciation expense over the remaining lives of those assets. From a consolidated viewpoint, the parent's additional payment is part of the total cost of the depreciable assets. Depreciation already is recorded on the subsidiary's books based on the original cost of the assets to the subsidiary, and these amounts are carried to the consolidated workpaper as depreciation expense. Depreciation on the additional cost of those assets to the consolidated entity is entered in the consolidation workpaper through entry E(30). Similarly, the $10,000 of goodwill entered in the workpaper in entry E(29) is amortized over its useful life of 20 years with entry E(31).

A distinction must be made between journal entries recorded on the parent's books under equity-method reporting and the eliminating entries needed in the workpaper to prepare the consolidated financial statements. The eliminating entries to record depreciation expense and amortization of goodwill in the workpaper are needed even though Peerless records the amortization of the purchase differential on its books at the end of 19X1 with entry (25). The entry on Peerless's books simply alters the balance in its investment account and the amount of income recognized from Special Foods. Both account balances are eliminated in the consolidation process, thereby removing any effect of entry (25) upon the consolidated totals. Consequently, consolidated income does not reflect the write-off of the differential unless eliminating entries E(30) and E(31) are made.

Once the appropriate eliminating entries are placed in the consolidation workpaper in Figure 5-7, the workpaper is completed by summing each row across, taking into consideration the debit or credit effect of the eliminations.

FIGURE 5-8 Consolidated net income and retained earnings, 19X1; 80 percent purchase at more than book value.

Consolidated net income, 19X1:	
Peerless's separate operating income	$140,000
Peerless's share of Special Foods'	
net income: $50,000 × .80	40,000
Write-off of differential related to inventory sold	
during 19X1	(4,000)
Amortization of differential in 19X1	(5,300)
Consolidated net income, 19X1	$170,700
Consolidated retained earnings, December 31, 19X1:	
Peerless's retained earnings on date of	
combination, January 1, 19X1	$300,000
Peerless's separate operating income, 19X1	140,000
Peerless's share of Special Food's 19X1 net	
income: $50,000 × .80	40,000
Write-off of differential related to inventory sold	(4,000)
Amortization of differential in 19X1	(5,300)
Dividends declared by Peerless, 19X1	(60,000)
Consolidated retained earnings, December 31, 19X1	$410,700

Consolidated Net Income and Retained Earnings   As can be seen from the workpaper, consolidated net income for 19X1 is $170,700 and consolidated retained earnings on December 31, 19X1, is $410,700. These amounts can be computed as shown in Figure 5-8. Note that both consolidated net income and retained earnings are reduced by the write-off of the purchase differential.

Second Year of Ownership

The consolidation procedures employed at the end of the second year, and in periods thereafter, are basically the same as those used at the end of the first year. Consolidation two years after acquisition is illustrated by continuing the example used for 19X1. During 19X2, Peerless Products earns income from its own separate operations of $160,000 and pays dividends of $60,000; Special Foods reports net income of $75,000 and pays dividends of $40,000.

Parent Company Entries   Peerless Products records the following entries on its separate books during 19X2:

(32)	Investment in Special Foods Stock	60,000	
	Income from Subsidiary		60,000
	Record equity-method income:		
	$75,000 × .80		

(33)	Cash	32,000	
	Investment in Special Foods Stock		32,000
	Record dividends from Special Foods:		
	$40,000 × .80		
(34)	Income from Subsidiary	5,300	
	Investment in Special Foods Stock		5,300
	Amortize differential related to buildings		
	and equipment and goodwill:		
	$4,800 + $500		

Entry (34) to record the 19X2 amortization of the purchase differential is identical with the entry recorded in 19X1 because the straight-line method is used.

The changes in the parent's investment account for 19X1 and 19X2 can be summarized as follows:

	19X1		19X2	
Balance at start of year		$310,000		$316,700
Income from subsidiary:				
Parent's share of subsidiary's income	$40,000		$60,000	
Differential write-off for inventory sold	(4,000)			
Amortization of differential	(5,300)		(5,300)	
		30,700		54,700
Less: Dividends received from subsidiary		(24,000)		(32,000)
Balance at end of year		$316,700		$339,400

Consolidation Workpaper—Second Year Following Combination The workpaper to prepare a complete set of consolidated financial statements for the year 19X2 is illustrated in Figure 5-9. Eliminating entries at the end of 19X2 are similar to those at the end of 19X1.

The first workpaper entry, E(35), eliminates Peerless's income from Special Foods and Peerless's share of Special Foods' dividends for 19X2:

E(35)	Income from Subsidiary	54,700	
	Dividends Declared		32,000
	Investment in Special Foods Stock		22,700
	Eliminate income from subsidiary.		

The net credit to the investment account of $22,700 represents the increase in the account balance during the period and takes the account balance back to the amount on January 1, 19X2, the beginning of the second year.

The amount of subsidiary income assigned to the noncontrolling shareholders in 19X2 is $15,000 ($75,000 × .20), and this amount enters the workpaper through entry E(36):

FIGURE 5-9 December 31, 19X2, equity-method workpaper for consolidated financial statements, second year following combination; 80 percent purchase at more than book value.

Item	Peerless Products	Special Foods	Eliminations Debit		Eliminations Credit		Consolidated
Sales	450,000	300,000					750,000
Income from Subsidiary	54,700		(35)	54,700			
Credits	504,700	300,000					750,000
Cost of Goods Sold	180,000	160,000					340,000
Depreciation and Amortization	50,000	20,000	(39)	4,800			
			(40)	500			75,300
Other Expenses	60,000	45,000					105,000
Debits	(290,000)	(225,000)					(520,300)
							229,700
Income to Noncontrolling Interest			(36)	15,000			(15,000)
Net Income, carry forward	214,700	75,000		75,000			214,700
Retained Earnings, January 1	410,700	120,000	(37)	120,000			410,700
Net Income, from above	214,700	75,000		75,000			214,700
	625,400	195,000					625,400
Dividends Declared	(60,000)	(40,000)			(35)	32,000	
					(36)	8,000	(60,000)
Retained Earnings, December 31, carry forward	565,400	155,000		195,000		40,000	565,400
Cash	221,000	85,000					306,000
Accounts Receivable	150,000	80,000					230,000
Inventory	180,000	90,000					270,000
Land	175,000	40,000	(38)	8,000			223,000
Buildings and Equipment	800,000	600,000	(38)	48,000			1,448,000
Investment in Special Foods Stock	339,400				(35)	22,700	
					(37)	316,700	
Goodwill			(38)	9,500	(40)	500	9,000
Differential			(37)	60,700	(38)	60,700	
Debits	1,865,400	895,000					2,486,000
Accumulated Depreciation	500,000	340,000			(38)	4,800	
					(39)	4,800	849,600
Accounts Payable	100,000	100,000					200,000
Bonds Payable	200,000	100,000					300,000
Common Stock	500,000	200,000	(37)	200,000			500,000
Retained Earnings, from above	565,400	155,000		195,000		40,000	565,400
Noncontrolling Interest					(36)	7,000	
					(37)	64,000	71,000
Credits	1,865,400	895,000		521,200		521,200	2,486,000

Elimination entries:
(35) Eliminate income from subsidiary.
(36) Assign income to noncontrolling interest.
(37) Eliminate beginning investment balance.
(38) Assign beginning differential.
(39) Amortize differential related to buildings and equipment.
(40) Amortize differential related to goodwill.

E(36)	Income to Noncontrolling Interest	15,000	
	Dividends Declared		8,000
	Noncontrolling Interest		7,000
	Assign income to noncontrolling interest.		

The $15,000 of subsidiary income assigned to the noncontrolling interest is subtracted to arrive at consolidated net income in the income statement portion of the workpaper. Entry E(36) also includes a credit to Dividends Declared to eliminate the noncontrolling interest's portion of Special Foods' dividends. Entries E(35) and E(36) together totally eliminate the dividends of Special Foods. The $7,000 difference between the noncontrolling stockholders' share of subsidiary income and dividends represents the increase in the noncontrolling interest for 19X2 and is placed in the balance sheet portion of the workpaper.

Entry E(37) eliminates the balances in Peerless's investment account and Special Foods' stockholders' equity accounts as of the beginning of the period:

E(37)	Common Stock—Special Foods	200,000	
	Retained Earnings, January 1	120,000	
	Differential	60,700	
	Investment in Special Foods Stock		316,700
	Noncontrolling Interest		64,000
	Eliminate beginning investment balance.		

Together, entries E(35) and E(37) fully eliminate the ending balance in the parent's investment account. The noncontrolling interest is credited for its proportionate share of the book value of the subsidiary at the start of the period ($320,000 × .20). This amount is added to the 19X2 increase in noncontrolling interest established in entry E(36), and the total is reported in the consolidated balance sheet.

Entry E(37) also establishes the purchase differential as of the beginning of 19X2. The differential at the start of 19X1, the date of combination, was $70,000 and was reduced by the amounts written off during 19X1. During 19X1, Peerless wrote off the $4,000 of the differential related to the inventory that was sold in 19X1 and amortized $5,300 related to buildings and equipment and goodwill. The unamortized balance of the differential at the start of 19X2, therefore, is $60,700 ($70,000 − $4,000 − $5,300).

Allocation of the purchase differential in 19X2 is different from the allocation in the first year in several respects:

1. No allocation is made to inventory or cost of goods sold.
2. Goodwill at the beginning of the year is $9,500 rather than $10,000 as a result of the $500 of amortization taken in 19X1.
3. Accumulated depreciation must be entered to reflect the additional depreciation on the buildings and equipment taken in the 19X1 consolidation workpaper.

Entry E(38) assigns the January 1, 19X2, purchase differential:

E(38)	Land	8,000	
	Buildings and Equipment	48,000	
	Goodwill	9,500	
	Differential		60,700
	Accumulated Depreciation		4,800
	Assign beginning differential.		

Because each year's workpaper is prepared from the trial balance data reported by the separate companies and not from the previous year's workpaper, the $4,800 of accumulated depreciation entered in the consolidation workpaper at the end of 19X1 does not automatically carry over to the 19X2 workpaper. Thus, the workpaper entry to allocate the differential each time also must establish the accumulated depreciation for all prior years on any differential amounts assigned to depreciable assets. The additional accumulated depreciation for the single prior period since the date of combination is $4,800.

The 19X2 depreciation of the portion of the differential assigned to buildings and equipment is given in entry E(39):

E(39)	Depreciation and Amortization Expense	4,800	
	Accumulated Depreciation		4,800
	Amortize differential related to buildings		
	and equipment: $48,000 ÷ 10 years		

The amount written off to expense each period remains the same from year to year unless (1) a depreciation method other than straight-line is used, or (2) some of the underlying assets are sold, or (3) some of the assets become fully depreciated.

Entry E(40) provides for the amortization of the goodwill in the workpaper:

E(40)	Depreciation and Amortization Expense	500	
	Goodwill		500
	Amortize differential related to goodwill:		
	$10,000 ÷ 20 years		

Consolidated Net Income and Retained Earnings The computation of 19X2 consolidated net income and consolidated retained earnings at the end of 19X2 is shown in Figure 5-10.

FIGURE 5-10 Consolidated net income and retained earnings, 19X2; 80 percent purchase at more than book value.

Consolidated net income, 19X2:	
Peerless's separate operating income	$160,000
Peerless's share of Special Foods'	
net income: $75,000 × .80	60,000
Amortization of differential in 19X2	(5,300)
Consolidated net income, 19X2	$214,700
Consolidated retained earnings, December 31, 19X2:	
Consolidated retained earnings, December 31, 19X1	$410,700
Peerless's separate operating income, 19X2	160,000
Peerless's share of Special Foods' 19X2	
net income: $75,000 × .80	60,000
Amortization of differential in 19X2	(5,300)
Dividends declared by Peerless, 19X2	(60,000)
Consolidated retained earnings, December 31, 19X2	$565,400

Consolidated Financial Statements A consolidated income statement and retained earnings statement for the year 19X2 and a consolidated balance sheet as of December 31, 19X2, are presented in Figure 5-11.

CONSOLIDATION FOLLOWING AN INTERIM ACQUISITION

When one company purchases another company's common stock, the subsidiary is viewed as being part of the consolidated entity only from the time the stock is acquired. Consequently, when a subsidiary is purchased during a fiscal period rather than at the beginning or end, the results of the subsidiary's operations are included in the consolidated statements only for the portion of the year that the stock is owned by the parent.

The results of operations for a subsidiary purchased during the fiscal period are included in the consolidated income statement in one of two ways:

1. Include in the consolidated income statement the revenue and expenses of the subsidiary as if it had been acquired at the beginning of the fiscal period, and deduct the subsidiary's preacquisition earnings at the bottom of the consolidated income statement.

2. Include in the consolidated income statement only the subsidiary's revenue earned and expenses incurred subsequent to the date of combination.

While **ARB 51** allows both alternatives, it expresses a preference for the first. The first method is viewed as giving a better indication of the level of activity of the current economic entity and as providing better comparisons with future periods. This alternative is found most often in practice and is illustrated here.

FIGURE 5-11 Consolidated financial statements for Peerless Products Corporation and Special Foods, Inc., 19X2.

Peerless Products Corporation and Subsidiary
Consolidated Income Statement
For the Year Ended December 31, 19X2

Sales		$750,000
Cost of Goods Sold		(340,000)
Gross Margin		$410,000
Expenses:		
Depreciation and Amortization	$ 75,300	
Other Expenses	105,000	
Total Expenses		(180,300)
		$229,700
Income to Noncontrolling Interest		(15,000)
Consolidated Net Income		$214,700

Peerless Products Corporation and Subsidiary
Consolidated Retained Earnings Statement
For the Year Ended December 31, 19X2

Consolidated Retained Earnings, January 1, 19X2	$410,700
Consolidated Net Income, 19X2	214,700
Dividends Declared, 19X2	(60,000)
Consolidated Retained Earnings, December 31, 19X2	$565,400

Peerless Products Corporation and Subsidiary
Consolidated Balance Sheet
December 31, 19X2

Assets:			Liabilities:		
Cash		$ 306,000	Accounts Payable	$200,000	
Accounts Receivable		230,000	Bonds Payable	300,000	
Inventory		270,000			$ 500,000
Land		223,000	Noncontrolling Interest		71,000
Buildings and Equipment	$1,448,000		Stockholders' Equity:		
Accumulated Depreciation	(849,600)		Common Stock	$500,000	
		598,400	Retained Earnings	565,400	
Goodwill		9,000			1,065,400
Total		$1,636,400	Total		$1,636,400

To better understand consolidation following an interim acquisition, assume that on July 1, 19X1, Peerless Products purchases 80 percent of the common stock of Special Foods for its underlying book value of $246,400. During the first half of 19X1, before the combination, Special Foods reports net income of $20,000 and pays dividends of $12,000. For the portion of 19X1 following the combination,

Special Foods reports net income of $30,000 and pays dividends of $18,000. The book value of Special Foods stock on the date of combination is computed as follows:

Book value of Special Foods on January 1, 19X1:	
Common stock	$200,000
Retained earnings	100,000
	$300,000
Net income, January 1 to June 30, 19X1	20,000
Dividends, January 1 to June 30, 19X1	(12,000)
Book value of Special Foods on July 1, 19X1	$308,000
Peerless's ownership interest	× .80
Book value on July 1, 19X1, of shares acquired by Peerless	$246,400

Parent Company Entries

Peerless records the purchase of Special Foods stock with the following entry:

July 1, 19X1			
(41)	Investment in Special Foods Stock	246,400	
	Cash		246,400
	Record purchase of Special Foods stock.		

During the second half of 19X1, Peerless records its share of Special Foods' income and dividends under the equity method:

(42)	Investment in Special Foods Stock	24,000	
	Income from Subsidiary		24,000
	Record equity-method income:		
	$30,000 × .80		
(43)	Cash	14,400	
	Investment in Special Foods Stock		14,400
	Record dividends from Special Foods:		
	$18,000 × .80		

Consolidation Workpaper

The consolidation workpaper reflecting the interim acquisition of Special Foods stock during 19X1 is presented in Figure 5-12. The trial balance of Special Foods for 19X1 is the same as used previously. The trial balance for Peerless is the same as in Figure 5-5 except that the amount of Peerless's cash reflects the interim purchase, as does the income from Special Foods recognized by Peerless.

The elimination entries in the consolidation workpaper prepared as of December 31, 19X1, are as follows:

FIGURE 5-12 December 31, 19X1, equity-method workpaper for consolidated financial statements, year of combination; 80 percent purchase at book value; interim acquisition.

Item	Peerless Products	Special Foods	Eliminations Debit		Eliminations Credit		Consolidated
Sales	400,000	200,000					600,000
Income from Subsidiary	24,000		(44)	24,000			
Credits	424,000	200,000					600,000
Cost of Goods Sold	170,000	115,000					285,000
Depreciation and Amortization	50,000	20,000					70,000
Other Expenses	40,000	15,000					55,000
Debits	(260,000)	(150,000)					(410,000)
							190,000
Preacquisition Subsidiary Income			(46)	16,000			(16,000)
Income to Noncontrolling Interest			(45)	10,000			(10,000)
Net Income, carry forward	164,000	50,000		50,000			164,000
Retained Earnings, January 1	300,000	100,000	(46)	100,000			300,000
Net Income, from above	164,000	50,000		50,000			164,000
	464,000	150,000					464,000
Dividends Declared	(60,000)	(30,000)			(44)	14,400	
					(45)	6,000	
					(46)	9,600	(60,000)
Retained Earnings, December 31, carry forward	404,000	120,000		150,000		30,000	404,000
Cash	248,000	75,000					323,000
Accounts Receivable	75,000	50,000					125,000
Inventory	100,000	75,000					175,000
Land	175,000	40,000					215,000
Buildings and Equipment	800,000	600,000					1,400,000
Investment in Special Foods Stock	256,000				(44)	9,600	
					(46)	246,400	
Debits	1,654,000	840,000					2,238,000
Accumulated Depreciation	450,000	320,000					770,000
Accounts Payable	100,000	100,000					200,000
Bonds Payable	200,000	100,000					300,000
Common Stock	500,000	200,000	(46)	200,000			500,000
Retained Earnings, from above	404,000	120,000		150,000		30,000	404,000
Noncontrolling Interest					(45)	4,000	
					(46)	60,000	64,000
Credits	1,654,000	840,000		350,000		350,000	2,238,000

Elimination entries:
(44) Eliminate income from subsidiary.
(45) Assign income to noncontrolling interest.
(46) Eliminate beginning investment balance.

E(44)	Income from Subsidiary	24,000	
	Dividends Declared		14,400
	Investment in Special Foods Stock		9,600
	Eliminate income from subsidiary.		
E(45)	Income to Noncontrolling Interest	10,000	
	Dividends Declared		6,000
	Noncontrolling Interest		4,000
	Assign income to noncontrolling interest.		
E(46)	Common Stock—Special Foods	200,000	
	Retained Earnings, January 1	100,000	
	Preacquisition Subsidiary Income	16,000	
	Dividends Declared		9,600
	Investment in Special Foods Stock		246,400
	Noncontrolling Interest		60,000
	Eliminate beginning investment balance:		
	$16,000 = $20,000 \times .80$		
	$9,600 = $12,000 \times .80$		

Entry E(44) eliminates the income from Special Foods recognized by Peerless since the date of combination ($30,000 × .80), Peerless's share of Special Foods' dividends declared since the date of combination ($18,000 × .80), and the change in Peerless's investment account since the date of combination. Entry E(45) assigns the noncontrolling interest's share of Special Foods' income for the entire year to the noncontrolling interest, eliminates the noncontrolling interest's share of dividends declared by Special Foods during 19X1, and enters the increase in the noncontrolling interest during the year. Note that the amounts assigned to the noncontrolling interest are not affected by whether the combination takes place at the beginning of the year or during the year.

Entry E(46) eliminates the stockholders' equity accounts of Special Foods, eliminates Peerless's investment account balance as of the date of combination, and establishes the amount of the noncontrolling interest as of the beginning of 19X1. Note that computations relating to the noncontrolling interest consider the entire year 19X1, while those involving the controlling shareholders deal only with the period subsequent to the date of combination.

Entry E(46) also eliminates the dividends declared prior to combination that relate to the Special Foods shares purchased by Peerless on July 1, 19X1. All $30,000 of dividends declared by the subsidiary during 19X1 must be eliminated because none represents dividends paid by the consolidated entity. Entry E(44) eliminates the $14,400 paid to the parent company between July 1, 19X1, and December 31, 19X1. E(45) eliminates the $6,000 paid to the stockholders who did not sell their shares to the parent and who, therefore, are included as noncontrolling stockholders for the entire year. Entry E(46) eliminates the remaining $9,600 of subsidiary dividends paid between January 1, 19X1, and July 1, 19X1, to the stockholders of Special Foods who sold their ownership interests to Peerless on July 1, 19X1.

Entry E(46) also establishes $16,000 of *preacquisition subsidiary income* or purchased net income. This represents the income between January 1, 19X1, and July 1, 19X1, that accrued to the previous stockholders of Special Foods who sold their shares to Peerless on July 1, 19X1. This preacquisition income may not be recognized as income of the consolidated entity because it represents income of Special Foods earned prior to the combination date. Because all Special Foods' revenue and expenses for the entire year 19X1 are included in the consolidated income statement, the preacquisition earnings accruing to the shares purchased by Peerless on July 1, 19X1, must be deducted to obtain consolidated net income.

The consolidated income statement for the year of the interim acquisition is prepared as if the combination had taken place at the beginning of the year, and the controlling stockholders' percentage times Special Food's preacquisition earnings is deducted, along with the income accruing to the noncontrolling interest, at the bottom of the consolidated income statement:

Peerless Products Corporation and Subsidiary
Consolidated Income Statement
For the Year Ended December 31, 19X1

Sales		$600,000
Cost of Goods Sold		(285,000)
Gross Margin		$315,000
Expenses:		
Depreciation and Amortization	$70,000	
Other Expenses	55,000	
Total Expenses		(125,000)
		$190,000
Preacquisition Subsidiary Income		(16,000)
Income to Noncontrolling Interest		(10,000)
Consolidated Net Income		$164,000

The approach described leads to the same result with respect to the controlling shareholders as if the books of Special Foods had been closed immediately before the combination and a new fiscal period started on the date of combination. If the books had been closed, preacquisition earnings and dividends of Special Foods would have been closed into retained earnings. The resulting interim balance of retained earnings would serve as the beginning balance in making the investment elimination entry. As in the normal investment elimination entry, the subsidiary's retained earnings at the beginning of the period, which is the date of combination in this case, would be eliminated.

DISCONTINUANCE OF CONSOLIDATION

A subsidiary that previously has been consolidated but no longer meets the conditions for consolidation normally must be reported as an investment under the cost method in the consolidated financial statements. For example, if a previously consolidated subsidiary declared bankruptcy and the appointment of a receiver by the courts prevented the parent from exercising control, the subsidiary would not qualify for consolidation. A change in the specific companies for which consolidated statements are prepared is viewed as a change in the accounting entity. **Accounting Principles Board Opinion No. 20**, "Accounting Changes" (APB 20), requires financial statements of all prior periods presented for comparative purposes to be restated to exclude from the consolidation the nonqualifying subsidiary and to reflect the new reporting entity. In addition, the financial statements for the period of the change must disclose the nature of the change and the reason for it, and the effect of the change on income before extraordinary items, net income, and related per-share amounts.

ADDITIONAL CONSIDERATIONS RELATING TO THE ASSIGNMENT OF DIFFERENTIAL

Although the assignment of a purchase differential in the consolidation workpaper usually is straightforward, special attention is needed when differential-related assets are sold and when the differential is assigned to liabilities.

Disposal of Differential-Related Assets by Subsidiary

When a subsidiary disposes of an asset, it recognizes a gain or loss on the disposal equal to the difference between the proceeds received and the book value of the asset given up. If the asset is one to which a differential is assigned in the consolidation workpaper, both equity-method income recorded by the parent and consolidated net income are affected. The unamortized portion of the purchase differential that applies to the asset sold or written off must be treated under the equity method as a reduction of both the parent's income from the subsidiary and the investment account. In consolidation, the unamortized part of the purchase differential must be recognized as an adjustment to the gain or loss on the disposal of the asset.

Inventory Any inventory-related differential is assigned to inventory for as long as the inventory units are held by the subsidiary. In the period in which the inventory units are sold, the inventory-related differential is assigned to cost of goods sold, as illustrated previously in Figure 5-7.

The choice of inventory method used by the subsidiary determines the period in which the differential cost of goods sold is recognized. When fifo inventory costing is used by the subsidiary, the inventory units on hand on the date of combination are viewed as being the first units sold after the combination. Therefore, the differential normally is assigned to cost of goods sold in the period immediately after the combination. When the subsidiary uses lifo inventory costing, the inventory units on the date of combination are viewed as remaining in the subsidiary's inventory. Only if the inventory level drops below the level at the date of combination is a portion of the differential assigned to cost of goods sold.

Fixed Assets   A purchase differential related to land held by a subsidiary is added to the land balance in the consolidation workpaper each time a consolidated balance sheet is prepared. If the subsidiary sells the land to which the differential relates, the differential is treated in the consolidation workpaper as an adjustment to the gain or loss on the sale of the land in the period of the sale.

To illustrate, assume that on January 1, 19X1, Bright purchases all the common stock of Star at $10,000 more than book value. All the differential relates to land that Star had purchased earlier for $25,000. So long as Star continues to hold the land, the $10,000 differential is assigned to the land in the consolidation workpaper. If Star sells the land to an unrelated company for $40,000, the following entry is recorded on Star's books:

(47)	Cash	40,000	
	Land		25,000
	Gain on Sale of Land		15,000
	Record sale of land.		

While a gain of $15,000 is appropriate for Star to report, the land cost the consolidated entity $35,000 ($25,000 + $10,000). Therefore, the consolidated enterprise must report a gain of only $5,000. To reduce the $15,000 gain reported by Star to the $5,000 gain that should be reported by the consolidated entity, the following elimination is included in the consolidation workpaper for the year of the sale:

E(48)	Gain on Sale of Land	10,000	
	Differential		10,000
	Assign beginning differential.		

If, instead, Star sells the land for $32,000, the $7,000 ($32,000 − $25,000) gain recorded by Star is eliminated and a loss of $3,000 ($32,000 − $35,000) is recognized in the consolidated income statement. The eliminating entry in this case is:

E(49)	Gain on Sale of Land	7,000	
	Loss on Sale of Land	3,000	
	Differential		10,000
	Assign beginning differential.		

When the equity method is used on the parent's books, the parent must adjust the carrying amount of the investment and its equity-method income in the period of the sale to write off the differential. Thereafter, the $10,000 differential no longer exists.

The sale of differential-related equipment is treated in the same manner as land except that the amortization for the current and previous periods must be considered.

Differential Assigned to Liabilities

With the considerable swings in interest rates over the past decade, companies often find that liabilities assumed in a business combination have fair values different from their book values. As with assets acquired, liabilities assumed in a purchase-type combination must be valued at their fair values. Thus, a portion of the differential arising in the consolidation workpaper often relates to liabilities.

To better understand this, assume that Bright purchases all the common stock of Star on January 1, 19X1, for an amount $19,473 in excess of book value, all relating to Star's 6 percent bonds payable. The bonds were issued 3 years ago at their par value of $100,000 and mature 7 years from the date of combination. The bonds pay interest once each year on December 31. The current market rate of interest is 10 percent. The present value of the bonds on the date of combination is computed as follows:

Present value of $100,000 at 10 percent for 7 years ($100,000 × .51316)	$51,316
Present value at 10 percent of an annuity of seven payments of $6,000 each ($6,000 × 4.86842)	29,211
Present value of bonds	$80,527

The $19,473 difference between the $100,000 book value of the bonds and the $80,527 fair value is considered a discount on the bonds from a consolidated viewpoint. In a consolidation workpaper prepared on the date of combination, the entire $19,473 differential is assigned to the discount on bonds payable. In preparing consolidated statements subsequent to the date of combination, the bond discount differential must be amortized. For 19X1, the amount of amortization to be entered in the consolidation workpaper using effective-interest amortization is computed as follows:

Par value of bonds	$100,000
Imputed discount	(19,473)
Fair value of bonds on January 1, 19X1	$ 80,527
Effective interest rate	× .10
Interest expense for 19X1	$ 8,053
Cash interest payment ($100,000 × .06)	(6,000)
Amortization of bond discount	$ 2,053

The entry to assign the differential in the consolidation workpaper prepared for December 31, 19X1, is:

E(50) Interest Expense	2,053	
Discount on Bonds Payable	17,420	
Differential		19,473
Assign beginning differential.		

Because the differential also is amortized on the parent's books under the equity method, the differential and the amount assigned to the discount will be smaller by $2,053 in the workpaper prepared at the end of 19X2. The remaining $17,420 of discount will be charged to consolidated interest expense over the remaining life of the bonds.

SUMMARY OF KEY CONCEPTS AND TERMS

As with single-corporate reporting entities, a full set of consolidated financial statements includes a balance sheet, income statement, statement of retained earnings, and statement of cash flows. In the preparation of consolidated financial statements subsequent to the date that a company acquires a subsidiary, a comprehensive three-part consolidation workpaper is used. The workpaper is similar to that used in preparing only a consolidated balance sheet, but includes sections for the income statement and retained earnings statement in addition to the section for the balance sheet.

For periods subsequent to the purchase of a subsidiary, workpaper elimination entries are needed to (1) eliminate the parent's intercorporate investment balance and the stockholders' equity accounts of the subsidiary, (2) eliminate income from the subsidiary recognized by the parent during the period and dividends declared by the subsidiary, (3) eliminate intercompany receivables and payables, (4) assign any differential to specific assets and liabilities, and (5) amortize for the period any portion of a differential assigned to limited-life assets or liabilities. In addition, if a noncontrolling interest exists, the noncontrolling shareholders' claim on the income and net assets of the subsidiary must be recognized.

Consolidated net income is computed as the total of the parent's income from its own separate operations and the parent's proportionate share of the net income of the subsidiary. Consolidated retained earnings is computed as the total of the parent's cumulative earnings, excluding any income from the subsidiary, plus the parent's proportionate share of the subsidiary's cumulative net income since acquisition, minus all dividends declared by the parent.

When a subsidiary is purchased *during* a period rather than at the beginning or end, consolidated net income includes the parent's share of the subsidiary's earnings only since the date of combination. The approach usually found in practice is to include in the consolidated income statement the subsidiary's revenue and expenses for the entire year and to deduct an amount equal to the parent's percentage times the subsidiary's preacquisition earnings at the bottom of the statement.

Additive approach to computing consolidated net income and retained earnings
Consolidated net income
Consolidated retained earnings
Preacquisition subsidiary income
Residual approach to computing consolidated net income and retained earnings

APPENDIX A: Consolidation and the Cost Method

Not all parent companies use the equity method to account for their subsidiary invest-ments. When a subsidiary is not to be consolidated because control does not rest with the parent or because control is temporary, the cost method normally must be used by the parent to report its investment in the subsidiary. For those subsidiaries that are consoli-dated, the choice of the cost or equity method has no effect on the consolidated financial statements. This is because the balance in the parent's investment account, the parent's income from the subsidiary, and related items are eliminated in preparing the consolidated statements. Thus, the parent is free to use on its separate books either the cost method or some version of the equity method in accounting for investments in subsidiaries that are to be consolidated.

IMPACT ON THE CONSOLIDATION PROCESS

While the parent's net income and retained earnings under the equity method equal the consolidated amounts, this equality usually does not exist when the cost method is used. Because the cost method requires different parent company entries than the equity method, it also requires different eliminating entries in preparing the consolidation workpaper. Keep in mind that the consolidated financial statements appear the same regardless of whether the parent uses the cost or the equity method on its separate books.

CONSOLIDATION—YEAR OF COMBINATION

To illustrate the preparation of consolidated financial statements when the parent company carries its investment in the subsidiary using the cost method, the Peerless Products and Special Foods example is used once again. Assume that Peerless purchases 80 percent of the common stock of Special Foods on January 1, 19X1, for $310,000. The purchase price is $70,000 in excess of the book value of the stock acquired. Of the total differential, $8,000 relates to land, $48,000 relates to buildings and equipment having a remaining life of 10 years from the date of combination, $4,000 relates to inventory that is sold during 19X1, and $10,000 relates to goodwill with an expected life of 20 years. All other data are the same as that presented in Figure 5-2. Peerless earns income from its own separate operations of $140,000 in 19X1 and declares dividends of $60,000; Special Foods reports net income of $50,000 in 19X1 and pays dividends of $30,000.

Parent Company Cost-Method Entries

When the cost method is used, only two journal entries are recorded by Peerless during 19X1 related to its investment in Special Foods. Entry (51) records Peerless's purchase of Special Foods stock; entry (52) recognizes dividend income based on the $24,000 ($30,000 × .80) of dividends received during the period:

(51)	Investment in Special Foods Stock	310,000	
	Cash		310,000
	Record purchase of Special Foods stock.		
(52)	Cash	24,000	
	Dividend Income		24,000
	Record dividends from Special Foods:		
	$30,000 × .80		

No entries are made on the parent's books to amortize the portion of the purchase differential that expires during 19X1, as would be done under the equity method.

Consolidation Workpaper—Year of Combination

The workpaper to prepare consolidated financial statements for December 31, 19X1, is shown in Figure 5-13. The trial balance data for Peerless and Special Foods included in the workpaper in Figure 5-13 differ from those presented in Figure 5-7 only by the effects of using the cost method rather than the equity method on Peerless's books.

Five eliminating entries are used to prepare the consolidation workpaper:

E(53)	Dividend Income	24,000	
	Dividends Declared		24,000
	Eliminate dividend income from subsidiary.		
E(54)	Income to Noncontrolling Interest	10,000	
	Dividends Declared		6,000
	Noncontrolling Interest		4,000
	Assign income to noncontrolling interest.		
E(55)	Common Stock—Special Foods	200,000	
	Retained Earnings, January 1	100,000	
	Differential	70,000	
	Investment in Special Foods Stock		310,000
	Noncontrolling Interest		60,000
	Eliminate investment balance at date of acquisition.		
E(56)	Cost of Goods Sold	4,000	
	Land	8,000	
	Buildings and Equipment	48,000	
	Goodwill	10,000	
	Differential		70,000
	Assign differential at date of acquisition.		
E(57)	Depreciation and Amortization Expense	5,300	
	Accumulated Depreciation		4,800
	Goodwill		500
	Amortize differential: $4,800 + $500		

FIGURE 5-13 December 31, 19X1, cost-method workpaper for consolidated financial statements, year of combination; 80 percent purchase at more than book value.

Item	Peerless Products	Special Foods	Eliminations Debit		Eliminations Credit		Consolidated
Sales	400,000	200,000					600,000
Dividend Income	24,000		(53)	24,000			
Credits	424,000	200,000					600,000
Cost of Goods Sold	170,000	115,000	(56)	4,000			289,000
Depreciation and Amortization	50,000	20,000	(57)	5,300			75,300
Other Expenses	40,000	15,000					55,000
Debits	(260,000)	(150,000)					(419,300)
							180,700
Income to Noncontrolling Interest			(54)	10,000			(10,000)
Net Income, carry forward	164,000	50,000		43,300			170,700
Retained Earnings, January 1	300,000	100,000	(55)	100,000			300,000
Net Income, from above	164,000	50,000		43,300			170,700
	464,000	150,000					470,700
Dividends Declared	(60,000)	(30,000)			(53)	24,000	
					(54)	6,000	(60,000)
Retained Earnings, December 31, carry forward	404,000	120,000		143,300		30,000	410,700
Cash	194,000	75,000					269,000
Accounts Receivable	75,000	50,000					125,000
Inventory	100,000	75,000					175,000
Land	175,000	40,000	(56)	8,000			223,000
Buildings and Equipment	800,000	600,000	(56)	48,000			1,448,000
Investment in Special Foods Stock	310,000				(55)	310,000	
Goodwill			(56)	10,000	(57)	500	9,500
Differential			(55)	70,000	(56)	70,000	
Debits	1,654,000	840,000					2,249,500
Accumulated Depreciation	450,000	320,000			(57)	4,800	774,800
Accounts Payable	100,000	100,000					200,000
Bonds Payable	200,000	100,000					300,000
Common Stock	500,000	200,000	(55)	200,000			500,000
Retained Earnings, from above	404,000	120,000		143,300		30,000	410,700
Noncontrolling Interest					(54)	4,000	
					(55)	60,000	64,000
Credits	1,654,000	840,000		479,300		479,300	2,249,500

Elimination entries:
  (53) Eliminate dividend income from subsidiary.
  (54) Assign income to noncontrolling interest.
  (55) Eliminate investment balance at date of acquisition.
  (56) Assign differential at date of acquisition.
  (57) Amortize differential.

Entry E(53) eliminates the dividend income recorded by Peerless during the period along with Special Foods' dividend declaration related to the stockholdings of Peerless. Entry E(54) assigns income to the noncontrolling shareholders ($50,000 × .20) and eliminates their portion of the subsidiary dividends ($30,000 × .20). This entry is the same as the one under the equity method and is not affected by the journal entries recorded on the parent's books.

Entry E(55) eliminates the balances in the stockholders' equity accounts of Special Foods and the balance in Peerless's investment account. A differential clearing account is established, representing the $70,000 purchase differential at the start of the year. Entries E(56) and E(57) assign the differential to the appropriate expense and asset categories and charge additional depreciation and amortization expense on that portion of the differential assigned to limited-life assets.

The investment elimination entry, E(55), is the same as the corresponding entry made when using the equity method. This occurs only in the year of acquisition because the balances eliminated are those at the beginning of the year, the date of combination. The balances on the date of combination are the same regardless of the method used to account for the investment subsequent to the combination. In all subsequent years, the investment elimination entries differ according to whether the parent uses the cost or the equity method.

Under the cost method, Peerless's 19X1 net income and ending retained earnings are $6,700 below the consolidated totals in Figure 5-13. This occurs because, using the cost method, Peerless did not include in income its percentage share of the undistributed net income of Special Foods ($20,000 × .80), nor did Peerless reduce its income for the write-off of the portion of the purchase differential assigned to inventory sold during 19X1 ($4,000) and limited-life assets ($4,800 + $500). Under the cost method there is no expectation that the parent's net income and retained earnings will be the same as the consolidated amounts. Consolidated retained earnings in the workpaper includes both the parent's retained earnings and the parent's share of the undistributed earnings of the subsidiary since acquisition.

CONSOLIDATION—SECOND YEAR OF OWNERSHIP

Consolidation differences between cost-method accounting and equity-method accounting tend to be more evident in the second year of ownership. To see this, assume that Peerless earns income from its own separate operations of $160,000 during 19X2 and pays dividends of $60,000; Special Foods reports net income of $75,000 for 19X2 and pays dividends of $40,000.

Parent Company Cost-Method Entry

Only a single entry is recorded by the parent in 19X2 in relation to its subsidiary investment:

(58)	Cash	32,000	
	Dividend Income		32,000
	Record dividends from Special Foods:		
	$40,000 × .80		

Consolidation Workpaper—Second Year Following Combination

The trial balance data for Peerless and Special Foods are entered in the consolidation workpaper at December 31, 19X2, as shown in Figure 5-14.

The first two elimination entries are similar to those used in the first year. Entry E(59) eliminates the dividend income from Special Foods recorded by Peerless and the dividend declaration of Special Foods related to Peerless's investment:

E(59)	Dividend Income	32,000	
	Dividends Declared		32,000
	Eliminate dividend income from subsidiary.		

Entry E(60) assigns to the noncontrolling shareholders their share of the subsidiary's income ($75,000 × .20) and eliminates the noncontrolling interest's portion of subsidiary dividends ($40,000 × .20):

E(60)	Income to Noncontrolling Interest	15,000	
	Dividends Declared		8,000
	Noncontrolling Interest		7,000
	Assign income to noncontrolling interest.		

Under the cost method, the parent company has not recognized its portion of the undistributed earnings of the subsidiary on the parent company's books. Therefore, the parent company's retained earnings at the beginning of the second period is less than consolidated retained earnings and the investment account balance reported by the parent is less than its proportionate share of the subsidiary's net assets at that date. The approach used in completing the consolidation workpaper in Figure 5-14 is to eliminate directly the balances reported by the parent company under the cost method and to carry the parent's portion of the increase in the subsidiary's retained earnings across to the consolidated totals.

An alternative approach would be to convert the accounts of the parent company in the consolidation workpaper to appear as if the parent had used the equity method. This is accomplished by including in the workpaper eliminations an equity-method adjustment, or conversion entry, to add to the parent company's investment account and retained earnings account the amounts that would have been recognized by the parent company if the equity method had been used in the prior years of ownership. If the equity-method conversion entry were used in this illustration, the adjusting entry would be in the amount of $6,700 (income share of $16,000 less $9,300 amortization) and the remaining eliminating entries would be identical to entries E(37) through E(40) presented earlier in the chapter.

The direct elimination approach has been adopted in Figure 5-14 in the belief that it is more consistent with the cost method and that companies may find this approach more efficient. Because all approaches lead to the same set of consolidated statements, there is no reason to believe that companies would wish to convert from the cost method to the equity method so that they can then eliminate those adjusted amounts.

FIGURE 5-14 December 31, 19X2, cost-method workpaper for consolidated financial statements, second year following combination; 80 percent purchase at more than book value.

Item	Peerless Products	Special Foods	Eliminations Debit		Eliminations Credit		Consolidated
Sales	450,000	300,000					750,000
Dividend Income	32,000		(59)	32,000			
Credits	482,000	300,000					750,000
Cost of Goods Sold	180,000	160,000					340,000
Depreciation and Amortization	50,000	20,000	(64)	5,300			75,300
Other Expenses	60,000	45,000					105,000
Debits	(290,000)	(225,000)					(520,300)
							229,700
Income to Noncontrolling Interest			(60)	15,000			(15,000)
Net Income, carry forward	192,000	75,000		52,300			214,700
Retained Earnings, January 1	404,000	120,000	(61)	100,000			
			(62)	4,000			
			(63)	9,300			410,700
Net Income, from above	192,000	75,000		52,300			214,700
	596,000	195,000					625,400
Dividends Declared	(60,000)	(40,000)			(59)	32,000	
					(60)	8,000	(60,000)
Retained Earnings, December 31, carry forward	536,000	155,000		165,600		40,000	565,400
Cash	221,000	85,000					306,000
Accounts Receivable	150,000	80,000					230,000
Inventory	180,000	90,000					270,000
Land	175,000	40,000	(63)	8,000			223,000
Buildings and Equipment	800,000	600,000	(63)	48,000			1,448,000
Investment in Special Foods Stock	310,000				(61)	310,000	
Goodwill			(63)	9,500	(64)	500	9,000
Differential			(61)	70,000	(63)	70,000	
Debits	1,836,000	895,000					2,486,000
Accumulated Depreciation	500,000	340,000			(63)	4,800	
					(64)	4,800	849,600
Accounts Payable	100,000	100,000					200,000
Bonds Payable	200,000	100,000					300,000
Common Stock	500,000	200,000	(61)	200,000			500,000
Retained Earnings, from above	536,000	155,000		165,600		40,000	565,400
Noncontrolling Interest					(60)	7,000	
					(61)	60,000	
					(62)	4,000	71,000
Credits	1,836,000	895,000		501,100		501,100	2,486,000

Elimination entries:
(59) Eliminate dividend income from subsidiary.
(60) Assign income to noncontrolling interest.
(61) Eliminate investment balance at date of acquisition.
(62) Assign undistributed prior earnings of subsidiary to noncontrolling interest.
(63) Assign differential at date of acquisition.
(64) Amortize differential.

Because the balance in the parent's investment account usually remains constant under the cost method, the investment elimination entry also remains constant. Entry E(61) eliminates the balance in Peerless's investment account and the balances in the stockholders' equity accounts of Special Foods as they existed at the date of combination:

E(61)	Common Stock—Special Foods	200,000	
	Retained Earnings, January 1	100,000	
	Differential	70,000	
	Investment in Special Foods Stock		310,000
	Noncontrolling Interest		60,000
	Eliminate investment balance at date of acquisition.		

This entry is exactly the same as investment elimination entry E(55) made in the first year. The investment elimination entry will continue to be the same in each subsequent year unless there is a change in ownership level or a change in the number of subsidiary shares outstanding or unless the subsidiary declares dividends in excess of earnings since acquisition by the parent.

Another workpaper entry is needed to establish the proper balance for noncontrolling shareholders in the consolidated balance sheet. Entry E(60) assigns to the noncontrolling shareholders their share of the increase in the stockholders' equity of the subsidiary during 19X2. Entry E(61) assigns to the noncontrolling interest their share of the subsidiary's stockholders' equity as of the date of combination, January 1, 19X1. An additional entry is needed to assign to the noncontrolling shareholders their share of the increase in the subsidiary's stockholders' equity that occurred between the date of combination and the start of the current period. This increase is computed as follows:

Balance in retained earnings of Special Foods on January 1, 19X2	$120,000
Balance in retained earnings of Special Foods at acquisition	(100,000)
Undistributed earnings	$ 20,000
Noncontrolling interest's share	× .20
Increase assignable to noncontrolling interest	$ 4,000

Entry E(62) assigns to the noncontrolling interest their share of the increase in the stockholders' equity of Special Foods that occurred between the date of combination and the beginning of the current period:

E(62)	Retained Earnings, January 1	4,000	
	Noncontrolling Interest		4,000
	Assign undistributed prior earnings of subsidiary to noncontrolling interest.		

A comparable computation and eliminating entry are necessary each time consolidated statements are prepared.

The final two entries in the consolidation workpaper are related to the differential:

E(63)	Land	8,000	
	Buildings and Equipment	48,000	
	Goodwill	9,500	
	Retained Earnings, January 1	9,300	
	Differential		70,000
	Accumulated Depreciation		4,800
	Assign differential remaining at beginning of year.		
E(64)	Depreciation and Amortization Expense	5,300	
	Accumulated Depreciation		4,800
	Goodwill		500
	Amortize differential.		

Entry E(63) assigns the original amount of the purchase differential so that the subsidiary's asset and contra asset accounts are brought to their appropriate consolidated balances as of the beginning of 19X2. Entry E(64) amortizes the differential for 19X2, leading to the appropriate consolidated balances at year-end.

The assignment of the differential in entry E(63) reflects the reduction in goodwill due to the $500 amortization in 19X1. Similarly, accumulated depreciation is increased for the $4,800 of additional depreciation taken in the consolidation workpaper in 19X1.

Under the cost method, the parent does not recognize the amortization of the differential on its own books. As a result, beginning retained earnings reported by the parent must be reduced by the cumulative write-off of the differential recognized in the consolidated financial statements for all prior years to bring it into agreement with the retained earnings balance reported for the consolidated entity at the end of the prior year. Keep in mind that entries made in the consolidation workpapers of previous years do not carry over to the current year. Therefore, entry E(63) is needed to reduce consolidated retained earnings by the amount of the differential write-off in 19X1, consisting of the following:

Amount related to inventory sold in 19X1	$4,000
Additional depreciation of buildings and equipment	4,800
Amortization of goodwill	500
Reduction in beginning retained earnings	$9,300

Consolidated Retained Earnings

Consolidated retained earnings on January 1, 19X2, is derived in the consolidation workpaper by combining the parent's retained earnings and the subsidiary's retained earnings with the debits and credits from the various eliminating entries. The January 1, 19X2, $410,700 balance computed in this manner is equal to the December 31, 19X1, balance shown in Figure 5-13.

The beginning balance of subsidiary retained earnings is not fully eliminated under the cost method because the parent's retained earnings does not include undistributed earnings of the subsidiary since acquisition. As a result, some portion of subsidiary retained earnings must be carried across and included in consolidated retained earnings.

Consolidated retained earnings on December 31, 19X2, can be reconciled with the balances reported by Peerless and Special Foods, as follows:

Retained earnings of Peerless, December 31, 19X2	$536,000
Retained earnings of Special Foods, December 31, 19X2	155,000
Total	$691,000
Deduct the following:	
Special Foods' retained earnings at acquisition, January 1, 19X1	(100,000)
Noncontrolling interest's share of Special Foods' undistributed earnings since acquisition [($20,000 + $35,000) × .20]	(11,000)
Write-off of differential for 19X1 ($4,000 + $4,800 + $500)	(9,300)
Write-off of differential for 19X2 ($4,800 + $500)	(5,300)
Consolidated retained earnings, December 31, 19X2	$565,400

APPENDIX B: Push-Down Accounting Illustrated

When a subsidiary is acquired in a purchase-type business combination, its assets and liabilities must be revalued to their fair values as of the date of combination for consolidated reporting. Often the books of the subsidiary remain unchanged as a result of the business combination, and the revaluation is made in the consolidation workpaper. As discussed in Chapter 4, however, the revaluations sometimes are recorded directly on the books of the subsidiary, and this approach is referred to as *push-down accounting.*

The following example illustrates the consolidation process when assets and liabilities are revalued directly on a subsidiary's books rather than using consolidation workpaper entries to accomplish the revaluation. Assume that Peerless Products purchases all the common stock of Special Foods on January 1, 19X1, for $370,000 cash. The purchase price is $70,000 in excess of the book value of Special Foods stock, with $10,000 of the differential related to land and $60,000 related to buildings and equipment having a remaining life of 10 years. Peerless accounts for its investment in Special Foods stock using the equity method.

Peerless records the acquisition of stock on its books with the following entry:

January 1, 19X1
    (65) Investment in Special Foods Stock   370,000
            Cash   370,000
            Record purchase of Special Foods stock.

WORKPAPER REVALUATION

To highlight the differences between workpaper revaluations and push-down accounting, assume first that no revaluations are made on Special Foods' books. During the year 19X1, Peerless records $50,000 of equity-method income from Special Foods, $6,000 amortization of the differential ($60,000 ÷ 10 years), and $30,000 of dividends from Special Foods:

(66)	Investment in Special Foods Stock	50,000	
	Income from Subsidiary		50,000
	Record equity-method income.		
(67)	Income from Subsidiary	6,000	
	Investment in Special Foods Stock		6,000
	Amortize purchase differential:		
	$60,000 ÷ 10 years		
(68)	Cash	30,000	
	Investment in Special Foods Stock		30,000
	Record dividends from Special Foods.		

When the assets of Special Foods are not revalued on Special Foods' books, a consolidation workpaper prepared for December 31, 19X1, appears as in Figure 5-15. The following entries appear in the workpaper:

E(69)	Income from Subsidiary	44,000	
	Dividends Declared		30,000
	Investment in Special Foods Stock		14,000
	Eliminate income from subsidiary.		
E(70)	Common Stock—Special Foods	200,000	
	Retained Earnings, January 1	100,000	
	Differential	70,000	
	Investment in Special Foods Stock		370,000
	Eliminate beginning investment balance.		
E(71)	Land	10,000	
	Buildings and Equipment	60,000	
	Differential		70,000
	Assign beginning differential.		
E(72)	Depreciation Expense	6,000	
	Accumulated Depreciation		6,000
	Amortize differential.		

Investment elimination entry E(70) gives rise to a $70,000 differential that is allocated to land and to buildings and equipment. The $60,000 portion of the differential assigned to the buildings and equipment must be amortized over the remaining economic life of 10 years at $6,000 per year.

PUSH-DOWN ACCOUNTING

In contrast to revaluing the assets of Special Foods only in the consolidation workpaper, the use of push-down accounting involves the revaluation of the assets on the separate books of Special Foods and alleviates the need for revaluation entries in the consolidation

FIGURE 5-15 December 31, 19X1, equity-method workpaper for consolidated financial statements, year of combination; 100 percent purchase at more than book value.

Item	Peerless Products	Special Foods	Eliminations Debit	Eliminations Credit	Consolidated
Sales	400,000	200,000			600,000
Income from Subsidiary	44,000		(69) 44,000		
Credits	444,000	200,000			600,000
Cost of Goods Sold	170,000	115,000			285,000
Depreciation and Amortization	50,000	20,000	(72) 6,000		76,000
Other Expenses	40,000	15,000			55,000
Debits	(260,000)	(150,000)			(416,000)
Net Income, carry forward	184,000	50,000	50,000		184,000
Retained Earnings, January 1	300,000	100,000	(70) 100,000		300,000
Net Income, from above	184,000	50,000	50,000		184,000
	484,000	150,000			484,000
Dividends Declared	(60,000)	(30,000)		(69) 30,000	(60,000)
Retained Earnings, December 31, carry forward	424,000	120,000	150,000	30,000	424,000
Cash	140,000	75,000			215,000
Accounts Receivable	75,000	50,000			125,000
Inventory	100,000	75,000			175,000
Land	175,000	40,000	(71) 10,000		225,000
Buildings and Equipment	800,000	600,000	(71) 60,000		1,460,000
Investment in Special Foods Stock	384,000			(69) 14,000	
				(70) 370,000	
Differential			(70) 70,000	(71) 70,000	
Debits	1,674,000	840,000			2,200,000
Accumulated Depreciation	450,000	320,000		(72) 6,000	776,000
Accounts Payable	100,000	100,000			200,000
Bonds Payable	200,000	100,000			300,000
Common Stock	500,000	200,000	(70) 200,000		500,000
Retained Earnings, from above	424,000	120,000	150,000	30,000	424,000
Credits	1,674,000	840,000	490,000	490,000	2,200,000

Elimination entries:
(69) Eliminate income from subsidiary.
(70) Eliminate beginning investment balance.
(71) Assign beginning differential.
(72) Amortize differential.

workpaper. If push-down accounting is used to revalue the assets of Special Foods, the following entry is made directly on the books of Special Foods:

January 1, 19X1		
(73) Land	10,000	
Buildings and Equipment	60,000	
Revaluation Capital		70,000
Revalue assets to reflect purchase-type business combination.		

This entry increases the amount at which the land and the buildings and equipment are shown in the separate financial statements of Special Foods and also gives rise to a revaluation capital account that is shown in the stockholders' equity section of Special Foods' balance sheet. Additional depreciation of $6,000 is recorded by Special Foods on its books to reflect the amortization over 10 years of the $60,000 write-up of buildings and equipment. This additional depreciation decreases Special Foods' reported net income for 19X1 to $44,000.

On its books, Peerless records its income and dividends from Special Foods:

(74) Investment in Special Foods Stock	44,000	
Income from Subsidiary		44,000
Record equity-method income.		
(75) Cash	30,000	
Investment in Special Foods Stock		30,000
Record dividends from Special Foods.		

The equity-method income recorded by Peerless in entry (74) is less than if push-down accounting had not been employed because Special Foods' income is reduced by the additional depreciation on the write-up of the buildings and equipment recorded on Special Foods' books. Because the revaluation is recorded on the books of Special Foods, the book value of the stock purchased by Peerless is equal to the purchase price. Therefore, there is no differential, and Peerless need not record any amortization associated with the investment. The net amount of income from Special Foods recorded by Peerless is the same regardless of whether push-down accounting is employed or not.

Figure 5-16 shows the consolidation workpaper prepared at the end of 19X1 and includes the effects of revaluing Special Foods' assets. Note that Special Foods' Land and its Buildings and Equipment have been increased by $10,000 and $60,000, respectively, and that both its Depreciation Expense and its Accumulated Depreciation are $6,000 higher than in Figure 5-15. Also note the Revaluation Capital account in Special Foods' stockholders' equity.

FIGURE 5-16 December 31, 19X1, equity-method workpaper for consolidated financial statements, year of combination; 100 percent purchase at more than book value; push-down accounting.

Item	Peerless Products	Special Foods	Eliminations Debit	Eliminations Credit	Consolidated
Sales	400,000	200,000			600,000
Income from Subsidiary	44,000		(76) 44,000		
Credits	444,000	200,000			600,000
Cost of Goods Sold	170,000	115,000			285,000
Depreciation and Amortization	50,000	26,000			76,000
Other Expenses	40,000	15,000			55,000
Debits	(260,000)	(156,000)			(416,000)
Net Income, carry forward	184,000	44,000	44,000		184,000
Retained Earnings, January 1	300,000	100,000	(77) 100,000		300,000
Net Income, from above	184,000	44,000	44,000		184,000
	484,000	144,000			484,000
Dividends Declared	(60,000)	(30,000)		(76) 30,000	(60,000)
Retained Earnings, December 31, carry forward	424,000	114,000	144,000	30,000	424,000
Cash	140,000	75,000			215,000
Accounts Receivable	75,000	50,000			125,000
Inventory	100,000	75,000			175,000
Land	175,000	50,000			225,000
Buildings and Equipment	800,000	660,000			1,460,000
Investment in Special Foods Stock	384,000			(76) 14,000	
				(77) 370,000	
Debits	1,674,000	910,000			2,200,000
Accumulated Depreciation	450,000	326,000			776,000
Accounts Payable	100,000	100,000			200,000
Bonds Payable	200,000	100,000			300,000
Common Stock	500,000	200,000	(77) 200,000		500,000
Retained Earnings, from above	424,000	114,000	144,000	30,000	424,000
Revaluation Capital		70,000	(77) 70,000		
Credits	1,674,000	910,000	414,000	414,000	2,200,000

Elimination entries:
(76)   Eliminate income from subsidiary.
(77)   Eliminate beginning investment balance.

Because the revaluation was accomplished directly on the books of Special Foods, only the two investment elimination entries are needed in the workpaper illustrated in Figure 5-16:

E(76)	Income from Subsidiary	44,000	
	Dividends Declared		30,000
	Investment in Special Foods Stock		14,000
	Eliminate income from subsidiary.		
E(77)	Common Stock—Special Foods	200,000	
	Retained Earnings, January 1	100,000	
	Revaluation Capital	70,000	
	Investment in Special Foods Stock		370,000
	Eliminate beginning investment balance.		

QUESTIONS

Q5-1 How does the elimination process change when consolidated statements are prepared after the date of acquisition?

Q5-2 What are the three parts of the consolidation workpaper, and what sequence is used in completing the workpaper parts?

Q5-3 How is the amount of income assigned to a noncontrolling interest determined?

Q5-4 How are dividend declarations of a subsidiary reported in the consolidated retained earnings statement?

Q5-5 Why is the income assigned to the noncontrolling interest treated as a deduction in computing consolidated net income?

Q5-6 Give a definition of consolidated net income.

Q5-7 In an interim acquisition, why is preacquisition subsidiary income shown in the consolidated income statement? How is this amount computed?

Q5-8 How is consolidated net income computed using the additive approach?

Q5-9 How is consolidated net income computed using the residual approach?

Q5-10 Why are there two different approaches to computing consolidated net income? What is the relationship between the additive and residual approaches?

Q5-11 Give a definition of consolidated retained earnings.

Q5-12 How is consolidated retained earnings determined using the additive approach?

Q5-13 How is consolidated retained earnings determined using the residual approach?

Q5-14 Why is the beginning retained earnings balance for each company entered in the three-part consolidation workpaper rather than the ending balance?

Q5-15 When Ajax was preparing its consolidation workpaper, the differential was properly assigned to goodwill. What additional entry must be made in the workpaper?

Q5-16 What determines whether the balance assigned to the differential remains constant or decreases each period?

Q5-17* What type of adjustment must be made in preparing the consolidation workpaper if a differential is assigned to land and the subsidiary disposes of the land in the current period?

Q5-18A Why are the eliminating entries that are used in preparing the consolidation workpaper different when the parent uses the cost method in accounting for its investment rather than the equity method? What is the major difference in the eliminating entries?

CASES

C5-1   Consolidation Workpaper Preparation

The newest clerk in the accounting office recently entered trial balance data for the parent company and its subsidiaries on the new company microcomputer. After a few minutes of additional work needed to eliminate the intercompany investment account balances, he expressed his satisfaction at having completed the consolidation workpaper for 19X5. In reviewing the printout of the consolidation workpaper, other employees raised several questions, and you are asked to respond.

Required

Indicate whether or not each of the following items can be answered by looking at the data in the consolidation workpaper (indicate why or why not):

a. Is it possible to tell if the parent is using the equity method in recording its ownership of each subsidiary?

b. Is it possible to tell if the correct amount of consolidated net income has been reported?

c. One of the employees thought the parent company had paid well above the fair value of net assets for a subsidiary purchased on January 1, 19X5. Is it possible to tell by reviewing the consolidation workpaper?

d. Is it possible to determine from the workpaper the percentage ownership of a subsidiary held by the parent?

C5-2   Elimination Procedures

A new employee has been given responsibility for preparing the consolidated financial statements of Sample Company. After attempting to work alone for some time, the employee seeks assistance in gaining a better overall understanding of the way in which the consolidation process works.

Required

You have been asked to provide assistance in explaining the consolidation process.

a. Why must the eliminating entries be entered in the consolidation workpaper each time consolidated statements are prepared?

b. How is the beginning-of-period noncontrolling interest balance determined?

c. How is the end-of-period noncontrolling interest balance determined?

d. Which of the account balances of the subsidiary always must be eliminated?

e. Which of the account balances of the parent company always must be eliminated?

EXERCISES

E5-1 Multiple-Choice Questions on Consolidation [AICPA Adapted]

Select the correct answer for each of the following questions.

1. On January 1, 19X5, Post Company purchased an 80 percent investment in Stake Company. The acquisition cost was equal to Post's equity in Stake's net assets at that date. On January 1, 19X5, Post and Stake had retained earnings of $500,000 and $100,000, respectively. During 19X5, (1) Post had net income of $200,000, which included its equity in Stake's earnings, and declared dividends of $50,000; (2) Stake had net income of $40,000 and declared dividends of $20,000; and (3) there were no other intercompany transactions between the parent and subsidiary. On December 31, 19X5, the consolidated retained earnings should be:
   a. $650,000.
   b. $666,000.
   c. $766,000.
   d. $770,000.

2. Consolidated financial statements are being prepared for a parent and its four subsidiaries which have intercompany loans of $100,000 and intercompany profits of $300,000. How much of these intercompany loans and profits should be eliminated?

   Intercompany

	Loans	Profits
a.	$0	$0
b.	$0	$300,000
c.	$100,000	$0
d.	$100,000	$300,000

3. How is the portion of consolidated earnings to be assigned to the noncontrolling interest in consolidated financial statements determined?
   a. The net income of the parent is subtracted from the subsidiary's net income to determine the noncontrolling interest.
   b. The subsidiary's net income is extended to the noncontrolling interest.
   c. The amount of the subsidiary's earnings recognized for consolidation purposes is multiplied by the noncontrolling interest's percentage ownership.
   d. The amount of consolidated earnings on the consolidated workpapers is multiplied by the noncontrolling interest percentage on the balance sheet date.

4. On April 1, 19X8, Hart, Inc., paid $1,700,000 for all the issued and outstanding common stock of Ray Corp. On that date, the costs and fair values of Ray's recorded assets and liabilities were as follows:

	Cost	Fair Value
Cash	$ 160,000	$ 160,000
Inventory	480,000	460,000
Property, plant and equipment (net)	980,000	1,040,000
Liabilities	(360,000)	(360,000)
Net assets	$1,260,000	$1,300,000

Hart amortizes goodwill over 40 years. In Hart's March 31, 19X9, consolidated balance sheet, what is the amount of goodwill that should be reported as a result of this business combination?

  a. $390,000.
  b. $400,000.
  c. $429,000.
  d. $440,000.

Items 5 and 6 are based on the following information:

On January 1, 19X8, Ritt Corp. purchased 80 percent of Shaw Corp.'s $10 par common stock for $975,000. On this date, the carrying amount of Shaw's net assets was $1,000,000. The fair values of Shaw's identifiable assets and liabilities were the same as their carrying amounts except for plant assets (net), which were $100,000 in excess of the carrying amount. For the year ended December 31, 19X8, Shaw had net income of $190,000 and paid cash dividends totaling $125,000.

5. In the January 1, 19X8, consolidated balance sheet, goodwill should be reported at:
  a. $0.
  b. $75,000.
  c. $95,000.
  d. $175,000.

6. In the December 31, 19X8, consolidated balance sheet, noncontrolling interest should be reported at:
  a. $200,000.
  b. $213,000.
  c. $220,000.
  d. $233,000.

E5-2 Basic Consolidation Entries for Fully Owned Subsidiary

Amber Corporation reported the following summarized balance sheet data on December 31, 19X6:

Assets	$600,000	Liabilities	$100,000
		Common Stock	300,000
		Retained Earnings	200,000
	$600,000		$600,000

On January 1, 19X7, Purple Company purchased 100 percent of the stock of Amber Corporation for $500,000. Amber Corporation reported net income of $50,000 for 19X7 and paid dividends of $20,000.

Required

  a. Give the journal entries recorded by Purple Company on its books during 19X7 if Purple accounts for its investment in Amber using the equity method.

  b. Give the eliminating entries needed on December 31, 19X7, to prepare consolidated financial statements.

E5-3 Basic Consolidation Entries for Majority-Owned Subsidiary

Farmstead Company reported the following summarized balance sheet data on December 31, 19X8:

Assets	$350,000	Accounts Payable	$ 50,000
		Common Stock	100,000
		Retained Earnings	200,000
	$350,000		$350,000

On January 1, 19X9, Horrigan Corporation purchased 70 percent of the stock of Farmstead Company for $210,000. Farmstead Company reported net income of $20,000 for 19X9 and paid dividends of $5,000.

Required

a. Give the equity-method journal entries recorded by Horrigan Corporation on its books during 19X9 related to its ownership of Farmstead Company.

b. Give the eliminating entries needed on December 31, 19X9, to prepare consolidated financial statements.

E5-4 Differential Assigned to Depreciable Assets

Short Company acquired 75 percent of the common stock of Justice Enterprises on January 1, 19X6, and paid $30,000 more than book value. The entire amount is assigned to equipment with an economic life of 10 years on the date of acquisition.

Required

Give the eliminating entries related to the assignment of the differential that will be made at the end of 19X6 and 19X7 in preparing consolidated statements.

E5-5 Computation of Investment Account Balance

A controlling interest in Turbo Manufacturing was purchased by Major Industries, Inc., on January 1, 19X4. Major paid $60,000 above book value in purchasing 80 percent of the shares of Turbo. It was determined that the full amount of the excess should be assigned to goodwill with a life of 15 years.

Turbo had common stock outstanding of $300,000 and retained earnings of $200,000 on January 1, 19X4. Turbo reported net income of $50,000 and paid dividends of $20,000 in 19X4.

Required

a. What is the balance in the investment account on Major's books on December 31, 19X4, if it uses the equity method in accounting for its investment in Turbo Manufacturing?

b. Give the eliminating entry or entries needed to prepare a consolidated balance sheet on January 1, 19X5.

E5-6 Consolidation after 1 Year of Ownership

Steadry Corporation purchased 80 percent of the stock of Shakey Building Corporation on January 1, 19X2. At that date Shakey reported retained earnings of $80,000 and had $120,000 of stock outstanding. The fair value of its equipment and buildings was $20,000 greater than the book value.

Steadry paid $190,000 to acquire the Shakey shares. The remaining economic life for all Shakey's depreciable assets was 8 years on the date of combination, and the life of all intangible assets was 10 years. Shakey reported net income of $40,000 in 19X2 and declared no dividends.

Required

a. Give the eliminating entries needed to prepare a consolidated balance sheet immediately after Steadry purchased Shakey's stock.

b. Give all eliminating entries needed to prepare a full set of consolidated financial statements for 19X2.

E5-7 Computation of Investment Balance and Noncontrolling Interest

Cameron Corporation has purchased 80 percent of the voting stock of Dorfman Enterprises, Inc. On the date of acquisition, Dorfman reported retained earnings of $200,000 and stock outstanding of $300,000. Cameron Corporation reported $400,000 of retained earnings and $500,000 of stock outstanding.

During the first year of ownership Dorfman reported net income of $50,000 and paid dividends of $30,000. Cameron reported earnings from its separate operations of $120,000 and paid dividends of $80,000. Cameron uses the equity method in accounting for its investment in Dorfman.

Required

a. Assuming Cameron Corporation purchased the Dorfman stock for $400,000, compute:
   (1) Consolidated net income for the year.
   (2) The balance of the investment account at year-end.
   (3) Income to noncontrolling shareholders in the consolidated income statement.
b. Assume that Cameron Corporation purchased the Dorfman stock for $480,000. A total of $20,000 of the differential is attributable to depreciable assets with a life of 10 years remaining. All intangible assets have a life of 20 years. Compute each of the following:
   (1) Consolidated net income for the year.
   (2) The balance of the investment account at year-end.
   (3) Income to noncontrolling shareholders in the consolidated income statement.

E5-8 Computation of Consolidated Balances in Subsequent Period

Bell Corporation holds 60 percent ownership of Champion Company, which it acquired on January 1, 19X1. Bell Corporation paid $218,000 for its ownership of Champion. At acquisition, Champion had retained earnings of $50,000 and $200,000 of stock outstanding. Book values approximated market values on some of Champion's assets and liabilities at the date of combination. However, the following amounts were not in full agreement:

	Book Value	Fair Value
Inventory (fifo basis)	$ 40,000	$ 50,000
Land	40,000	60,000
Buildings and Equipment	150,000	200,000

Champion's depreciable assets should be expensed over 15 years, and the amounts assigned to goodwill amortized over 20 years from the date of combination.

The balance sheets of the companies on December 31, 19X4, included the following amounts:

	Bell Corporation	Champion Company
Cash	$ 10,000	$ 30,000
Accounts Receivable	60,000	100,000
Inventory	230,000	80,000
Land	150,000	40,000
Buildings and Equipment	400,000	240,000
Less: Accumulated Depreciation	(180,000)	(90,000)
Investment in Champion Stock	230,000	
	$900,000	$400,000
Accounts Payable	$ 60,000	$ 10,000
Bonds Payable	300,000	90,000
Common Stock	400,000	200,000
Retained Earnings	140,000	100,000
	$900,000	$400,000

Required

Give the amounts to be reported in the consolidated balance sheet as of December 31, 19X4, for the following accounts:

a. Inventory
b. Land
c. Buildings and Equipment
d. Accumulated Depreciation
e. Investment in Champion Company
f. Goodwill
g. Common Stock
h. Retained Earnings

E5-9 Multiple-Choice Questions on Consolidated Balances

Bumble Corporation acquired 80 percent of the voting stock of Dunwood Enterprises on January 2, 19X2, for $500,000. Other data relevant to the companies are as follows:

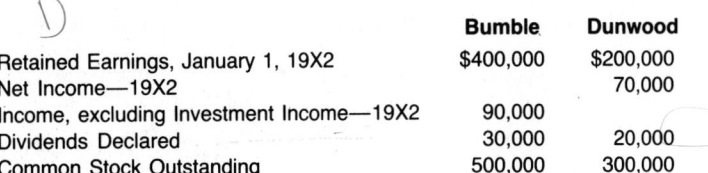

	Bumble	Dunwood
Retained Earnings, January 1, 19X2	$400,000	$200,000
Net Income—19X2		70,000
Income, excluding Investment Income—19X2	90,000	
Dividends Declared	30,000	20,000
Common Stock Outstanding	500,000	300,000

All tangible and intangible assets of the companies are assumed to have remaining economic lives of 10 years from the date of combination.

Required

Choose the correct answer for each of the following questions.

1. What amount of consolidated net income will be reported for 19X2?
   a. $136,000.
   b. $146,000.
   c. $150,000.
   d. $160,000.

2. What will be the balance in the investment account on December 31, 19X2, assuming Bumble uses the equity method in accounting for its investment?
   a. $500,000.
   b. $530,000.
   c. $540,000.
   d. $550,000.

3. What amount of income will be assigned to the noncontrolling interest in the 19X2 consolidated income statement?
   a. $0.
   b. $10,000.
   c. $12,000.
   d. $14,000.

4. What amount of investment income will Bumble recognize for 19X2 if Bumble uses the equity method in accounting for its investment?
   a. $46,000.
   b. $48,000.
   c. $56,000.
   d. $70,000.

5. What amount will be reported as total consolidated retained earnings on January 2, 19X2, immediately following the purchase of Dunwood shares?
   a. $400,000.
   b. $480,000.
   c. $560,000.
   d. $600,000.

6. What amount will be reported in the December 31, 19X2, consolidated balance sheet as stock outstanding?
    a. $500,000.
    b. $640,000.
    c. $740,000.
    d. $800,000.

7. What amount will be reported as dividends declared in the 19X2 consolidated retained earnings statement?
    a. $30,000.
    b. $34,000.
    c. $46,000.
    d. $50,000.

E5-10 Basic Consolidation Workpaper

Blake Corporation acquired 100 percent of the voting shares of Shaw Corporation on January 1, 19X3, at underlying book value. Blake uses the equity method in accounting for its investment in Shaw Corporation. Adjusted trial balances for Blake Corporation and Shaw Corporation on December 31, 19X3, are as follows:

Item	Blake Corporation		Shaw Corporation	
	Debit	Credit	Debit	Credit
Current Assets	$145,000		$105,000	
Depreciable Assets (net)	325,000		225,000	
Investment in Shaw Corporation Stock	170,000			
Depreciation Expense	25,000		15,000	
Other Expenses	105,000		75,000	
Dividends Declared	40,000		10,000	
Current Liabilities		$ 50,000		$ 40,000
Long-Term Debt		100,000		120,000
Common Stock		200,000		100,000
Retained Earnings		230,000		50,000
Sales		200,000		120,000
Income from Subsidiary		30,000		
	$810,000	$810,000	$430,000	$430,000

Required

   a. Give all the eliminating entries required on December 31, 19X3, to prepare consolidated financial statements.
   b. Prepare a three-part consolidation workpaper as of December 31, 19X3.

E5-11 Consolidation Workpaper with Differential

Kennelly Corporation purchased all the common shares of Short Company on January 1, 19X5, for $180,000. On that date, the book value of the net assets reported by Short Company was $150,000. The entire purchase differential was assigned to depreciable assets with a 6-year remaining economic life from January 1, 19X5.

The adjusted trial balances for the two companies on December 31, 19X5, are as follows:

	Kennelly Corporation		Short Company	
Item	**Debit**	**Credit**	**Debit**	**Credit**
Cash	$ 15,000		$ 5,000	
Accounts Receivable	30,000		40,000	
Inventory	70,000		60,000	
Depreciable Assets (net)	325,000		225,000	
Investment in Short				
Company Stock	195,000			
Depreciation Expense	25,000		15,000	
Other Expenses	105,000		75,000	
Dividends Declared	40,000		10,000	
Accounts Payable		$ 50,000		$ 40,000
Notes Payable		100,000		120,000
Common Stock		200,000		100,000
Retained Earnings		230,000		50,000
Sales		200,000		120,000
Income from Subsidiary		25,000		
	$805,000	$805,000	$430,000	$430,000

Kennelly Corporation uses the equity method in accounting for its investment in Short Company. Short Company dividends were declared and paid on December 31, 19X5.

Required

a. Prepare the eliminating entries needed as of December 31, 19X5, to complete a consolidation workpaper.

b. Prepare a three-part consolidation workpaper as of December 31, 19X5.

E5-12 Consolidation Workpaper for Majority-Owned Subsidiary

Proud Corporation purchased 80 percent of the voting stock of Stergis Company on January 1, 19X3, at underlying book value. Proud Corporation uses the equity method in accounting for its ownership of Stergis during 19X3. On December 31, 19X3, the trial balances of the two companies are as follows:

	Proud Corporation		Stergis Company	
Item	Debit	Credit	Debit	Credit
Current Assets	$173,000		$105,000	
Depreciable Assets	500,000		300,000	
Investment in Stergis Company Stock	136,000			
Depreciation Expense	25,000		15,000	
Other Expenses	105,000		75,000	
Dividends Declared	40,000		10,000	
Accumulated Depreciation		$175,000		$ 75,000
Current Liabilities		50,000		40,000
Long-Term Debt		100,000		120,000
Common Stock		200,000		100,000
Retained Earnings		230,000		50,000
Sales		200,000		120,000
Income from Subsidiary		24,000		
	$979,000	$979,000	$505,000	$505,000

Required

a. Give all eliminating entries required as of December 31, 19X3, to prepare consolidated financial statements.

b. Prepare a three-part consolidation workpaper.

c. Prepare a consolidated balance sheet, income statement, and retained earnings statement for 19X3.

E5-13 Interim Acquisition

Blase Company operates on a calendar-year basis, reporting the results of operations quarterly. For the first quarter of 19X6, Blase reported net income of $60,000 and paid a dividend of $10,000. On April 1, Starstruck Theaters, Inc., purchased 85 percent of the common stock of Blase for $750,000; Blase had 100,000 shares of $1 par common stock outstanding, originally issued at $6 per share. Any cost over the book value of the shares acquired by Starstruck Theaters is related to goodwill having a life of 10 years.

Blase's retained earnings statement for the full year 19X6 appears as follows:

Retained Earnings, January 1, 19X6	$150,000
Net Income	175,000
Dividends	(40,000)
Retained Earnings, December 31, 19X6	$285,000

Starstruck Theaters accounts for its investment in Blase using the equity method.

Required

a. Present all entries that would have been recorded by Starstruck Theaters in accounting for its investment in Blase during 19X6.

b. Present all eliminating entries needed in a workpaper to prepare a complete set of consolidated financial statements for the year 19X6.

E5-14* Complex Assignment of Differential

On December 31, 19X4, Holly Corporation purchased 90 percent of the common stock of Brinker, Inc., for $888,000, a price that was $240,000 in excess of the book value of the shares acquired. Of the $240,000 differential, $5,000 related to the increased value of Brinker's inventory, $75,000 related to the increased value of Brinker's land, $60,000 related to the increased value of Brinker's equipment, and $50,000 was associated with a change in the value of Brinker's notes payable due to increasing interest rates. Brinker's equipment had a remaining life of 15 years from the date of combination; intangibles are amortized over 10 years. All of the inventory held by Brinker at the end of 19X4 was sold during 19X5; the land to which the differential related also was sold during the year for a large gain. The amortization of the differential relating to Brinker's notes payable was $7,500 for 19X5.

At the date of combination, Brinker reported retained earnings of $120,000, common stock outstanding of $500,000, and premium on common stock of $100,000. For the year 19X5, Brinker reported net income of $68,000, but paid no dividends. Holly accounts for its investment in Brinker using the equity method.

Required

a. Present all entries that would have been recorded by Holly during 19X5 with respect to its investment in Brinker.

b. Present all elimination entries that would have been included in the workpaper to prepare a full set of consolidated financial statements for the year 19X5.

E5-15A Consolidation Using Cost-Method Accounting

City Touring Company holds 70 percent ownership of Country Playgrounds, Inc., and uses the cost method in accounting for its investment. During 19X5, Country Playgrounds reported net income of $70,000 and paid dividends of $40,000. City Touring reported net income (including dividend income) of $130,000 and paid dividends of $50,000. There was no differential at the time of investment.

Required

a. What amount of consolidated net income will be reported for 19X5?

b. What amount of income will be assigned to the noncontrolling interest in the consolidated income statement?

c. What additional factors must be known to compute consolidated retained earnings for December 31, 19X5?

E5-16A Computation of Consolidated Balances Using Cost Method

Healthcare Products Corporation purchased 60 percent of the stock of Dainty Touch Skin Cream on January 1, 19X2, for $180,000. On that date Dainty reported retained earnings of $100,000 and had $200,000 of stock outstanding. Healthcare's retained earnings was $400,000 at acquisition. Healthcare accounts for its investment in Dainty Touch under the cost method. The companies recorded the following results for 19X2 and 19X3:

	Healthcare	Dainty Touch
19X2:		
Net Income	$70,000	$35,000
Dividends Paid	25,000	30,000
19X3:		
Net Income	90,000	40,000
Dividends Paid	30,000	15,000

Required

   a. What amount of consolidated net income will be reported in 19X3?

   b. What amount of consolidated retained earnings will be reported on December 31, 19X3?

   c. Reconcile the retained earnings balance shown by Healthcare on December 31, 19X3, with consolidated retained earnings on that date.

E5-17A   Basic Cost-Method Workpaper

Blake Corporation purchased 100 percent of the voting shares of Shaw Corporation on January 1, 19X3, at underlying book value. Blake uses the cost method in accounting for its investment in Shaw Corporation. Shaw Corporation retained earnings, as shown in the 19X3 trial balance, was $50,000 on January 1, 19X3. On December 31, 19X3, the trial balance data for the two companies are as follows:

Item	Blake Corporation Debit	Blake Corporation Credit	Shaw Corporation Debit	Shaw Corporation Credit
Current Assets	$145,000		$105,000	
Depreciable Assets (net)	325,000		225,000	
Investment in Shaw Corporation Stock	150,000			
Depreciation Expense	25,000		15,000	
Other Expenses	105,000		75,000	
Dividends Declared	40,000		10,000	
Current Liabilities		$ 50,000		$ 40,000
Long-Term Debt		100,000		120,000
Common Stock		200,000		100,000
Retained Earnings		230,000		50,000
Sales		200,000		120,000
Dividend Income		10,000		
	$790,000	$790,000	$430,000	$430,000

Required

   a. Give all eliminating entries needed to prepare a three-part consolidation workpaper as of December 31, 19X3.

   b. Prepare the workpaper in good form.

E5-18A Cost-Method Workpaper in Subsequent Period

The trial balances for Blake Corporation and Shaw Corporation as of December 31, 19X4, are as follows:

	Blake Corporation		Shaw Corporation	
Item	Debit	Credit	Debit	Credit
Current Assets	$170,000		$110,000	
Depreciable Assets (net)	300,000		210,000	
Investment in Shaw				
Corporation Stock	150,000			
Depreciation Expense	25,000		15,000	
Other Expenses	250,000		160,000	
Dividends Declared	20,000		15,000	
Current Liabilities		$ 30,000		$ 20,000
Long-Term Debt		100,000		120,000
Common Stock		200,000		100,000
Retained Earnings		270,000		70,000
Sales		300,000		200,000
Dividend Income		15,000		
	$915,000	$915,000	$510,000	$510,000

Blake purchased 100 percent ownership of Shaw Corporation on January 1, 19X3, at a cost of $150,000. Shaw reported $50,000 of retained earnings at acquisition. Blake uses the cost method in accounting for its investment in Shaw Corporation.

Required

a. Give all eliminating entries required to prepare a full set of consolidated statements for 19X4.

b. Prepare a three-part consolidation workpaper in good form as of December 31, 19X4.

E5-19A Cost-Method Consolidation for Majority-Owned Subsidiary

Lintner Corporation purchased 80 percent of the voting stock of Knight Company on January 1, 19X6, at underlying book value. Lintner uses the cost method in accounting for its investment in Knight Company. Knight reported $50,000 of retained earnings at the time of acquisition. Trial balance data for the two companies on December 31, 19X7, are as follows:

Item	Lintner Corporation Debit	Lintner Corporation Credit	Knight Company Debit	Knight Company Credit
Current Assets	$ 183,000		$ 80,000	
Depreciable Assets	500,000		300,000	
Investment in Knight Company Stock	120,000			
Depreciation Expense	25,000		15,000	
Other Expenses	251,000		155,000	
Dividends Declared	25,000		20,000	
Accumulated Depreciation		$ 200,000		$ 90,000
Accounts Payable		120,000		110,000
Common Stock		200,000		100,000
Retained Earnings		268,000		70,000
Sales		300,000		200,000
Dividend Income		16,000		
	$1,104,000	$1,104,000	$570,000	$570,000

Required

a. Prepare eliminating entries as of December 31, 19X7, for a full set of consolidated statements.

b. Prepare a three-part consolidation workpaper as of December 31, 19X7.

c. Prepare a consolidated income statement, balance sheet, and retained earnings statement for 19X7.

PROBLEMS

P5-20 Intercorporate Acquisitions [AICPA Adapted]

On January 1, 19X6, Todd Corporation made the following investments:

1. Acquired for cash, 80 percent of the outstanding common stock of Meadow Corporation at $70 per share. The stockholders' equity of Meadow on January 1, 19X6, consisted of the following:

Common stock, par value $50	$50,000
Retained earnings	20,000

2. Acquired for cash, 70 percent of the outstanding common stock of Van Corporation at $40 per share. The stockholders' equity of Van on January 1, 19X6, consisted of the following:

Common stock, par value $20	$60,000
Capital in excess of par value	20,000
Retained earnings	40,000

After these investments were made, Todd was able to exercise significant influence over the operations of both companies.

An analysis of the retained earnings of each company for 19X6 is as follows:

	Todd	Meadow	Van
Balance, 1/1/X6	$240,000	$20,000	$40,000
Net income (loss)	104,000	36,000	(12,000)
Cash dividends paid	(40,000)	(16,000)	(9,000)
Balance, 12/31/X6	$304,000	$40,000	$19,000

Required

a. What entries should have been made on the books of Todd during 19X6 to record the following? Show all supporting computations in good form.
(1) Investments in subsidiaries.
(2) Parent's share of subsidiary income or loss.
(3) Subsidiary dividends received.
b. Using the "parent company theory," compute the amount of noncontrolling interest in each subsidiary's stockholders' equity on December 31, 19X6.
c. What amount should be reported as consolidated retained earnings of Todd Corporation and subsidiaries as of December 31, 19X6?

P5-21 Computation of Ownership Balances

Zone Products Corporation acquired 60 percent ownership of Statler Company on January 1, 19X3, for $350,000. The purchase differential was assignable entirely to depreciable assets with a remaining economic life of 10 years at the date of acquisition. On that date, the following amounts were reported in stockholders' equity by Statler Company:

Common Stock	$200,000
Capital in Excess of Par Value	100,000
Retained Earnings	200,000

In the consolidated balance sheet prepared as of December 31, 19X6, the noncontrolling interest was reported at $232,000. Zone Products reported operating income of $100,000 during the 4-year period and paid dividends of $45,000. Zone had retained earnings of $600,000 on the date of combination.

Required

a. Compute the balance in retained earnings reported by Statler Company on December 31, 19X6.
b. Compute the balance in the investment account reported by Zone on December 31, 19X6, assuming Zone uses the equity method to account for its investment.
c. Compute the balance in consolidated retained earnings on December 31, 19X6.

P5-22 Additive versus Residual Computations

Bolt Corporation is 80 percent owned by Allied Foundries, Inc. The shares of Bolt were acquired by Allied on January 1, 19X2, for $160,000. Selected stockholders' equity balances for the companies are as follows:

	Allied Foundries, Inc.	Bolt Corporation
Common Stock	$400,000	$100,000
Additional Paid-In Capital	150,000	40,000
Retained Earnings, January 1, 19X2	350,000	60,000
Retained Earnings, January 1, 19X4	548,000	130,000
Retained Earnings, December 31, 19X4	642,000	150,000

Allied operates the subsidiary as an independent company and uses the equity method to account for its ownership interest. Operating results for the two enterprises are as follows:

	Allied Foundries, Inc.		Bolt Corporation	
Year	Operating Income	Dividends	Net Income	Dividends
19X2	$100,000	$20,000	$40,000	$10,000
19X3	50,000	20,000	70,000	30,000
19X4	90,000	20,000	30,000	10,000

Operating income for Allied Foundries includes all revenue and expenses except for investment income from Bolt Corporation.

Required

a. Compute consolidated net income for 19X4 using (1) the additive approach and (2) the residual approach.

b. Compute consolidated retained earnings as of December 31, 19X4, using (1) the additive approach and (2) the residual approach.

c. Compute the amount reported as noncontrolling interest in the consolidated balance sheet on December 31, 19X4.

d. Prepare a consolidated retained earnings statement for 19X4.

P5-23 Elimination Entries for Majority-Owned Subsidiary

Mega Corporation purchased 60 percent of the voting shares of National Manufacturing Corporation on January 1, 19X2, when National reported retained earnings of $50,000. The $250,000 purchase price included a differential entirely assignable to buildings and equipment with a remaining economic life of 5 years at the time of the business combination. The balance sheet of National contained the following totals on December 31, 19X5:

National Manufacturing Corporation
Balance Sheet
December 31, 19X5

Cash	$ 40,000	Current Liabilities	$ 50,000
Inventory	140,000	Bonds Payable	100,000
Buildings and Equipment	700,000	Common Stock	300,000
Less: Accumulated Depreciation	(280,000)	Retained Earnings	150,000
	$600,000		$600,000

Required

If the balance in the investment account on the books of Mega Corporation on December 31, 19X5, is $278,000, give all eliminating entries required to prepare a consolidated balance sheet as of December 31, 19X5.

P5-24 Consolidation Workpaper with Differential

Trial balance data for Wacker Corporation and Slade Company on December 31, 19X5, are as follows:

	Wacker Corporation		Slade Company	
Item	**Debit**	**Credit**	**Debit**	**Credit**
Cash	$ 37,000		$ 20,000	
Accounts Receivable	50,000		30,000	
Inventory	70,000		60,000	
Buildings and Equipment	300,000		240,000	
Investment in Slade Company Stock	229,000			
Cost of Goods Sold	210,000		85,000	
Depreciation Expense	25,000		20,000	
Other Expenses	23,000		25,000	
Dividends Declared	20,000		10,000	
Accumulated Depreciation		$105,000		$ 65,000
Accounts Payable		40,000		20,000
Taxes Payable		70,000		55,000
Common Stock		200,000		150,000
Retained Earnings, January 1		230,000		50,000
Sales		300,000		150,000
Income from Subsidiary		19,000		
	$964,000	$964,000	$490,000	$490,000

Wacker Corporation purchased all the shares of Slade Company on January 1, 19X5, for $220,000. The full purchase differential is assigned to goodwill with an expected life of 20 years.

Required

Prepare a consolidation workpaper in good form as of December 31, 19X5, and prepare a consolidated income statement, retained earnings statement, and balance sheet.

P5-25 Consolidation of Majority-Owned Subsidiary

Terrier Corporation was created on January 1, 19X2, and quickly became successful. On January 1, 19X5, the owner sold 75 percent of the stock to Richards Company for $12,000 over book value. The differential was attributed to equipment which had a remaining economic life of 8 years at the date Richards purchased controlling ownership. Richards has continued to operate the subsidiary as a separate legal entity and uses the equity method in recording investment income.

Trial balances for Richards Company and Terrier Corporation on December 31, 19X6, are as follows:

Item	Richards Company Debit	Richards Company Credit	Terrier Corporation Debit	Terrier Corporation Credit
Cash and Receivables	$ 135,500		$ 80,000	
Inventory	240,000		100,000	
Land	80,000		20,000	
Buildings and Equipment	500,000		150,000	
Investment in Terrier Corporation Stock	151,500			
Cost of Goods Sold	500,000		250,000	
Wage Expense	45,000		35,000	
Depreciation Expense	25,000		15,000	
Other Expenses	30,000		40,000	
Dividends Declared	50,000		20,000	
Accumulated Depreciation		$ 155,000		$ 75,000
Accounts Payable		70,000		35,000
Notes Payable		200,000		50,000
Common Stock		300,000		40,000
Additional Paid-In Capital		60,000		35,000
Retained Earnings		228,500		75,000
Sales		700,000		400,000
Income from Subsidiary		43,500		
	$1,757,000	$1,757,000	$710,000	$710,000

Required

a. Prepare a three-part consolidation workpaper for 19X6 in good form.

b. Prepare a consolidated income statement, balance sheet, and statement of changes in retained earnings for 19X6.

P5-26 Balance Sheet Consolidation [AICPA Adapted]

Case, Inc., acquired all the outstanding $25 par common stock of Frey, Inc., on December 31, 19X3, in exchange for 40,000 shares of its $25 par common stock. The business combination was considered to be a purchase transaction. Case's common stock closed at $56.50 per share on a national stock exchange on December 31, 19X3. Both corporations continued to operate as separate businesses maintaining separate accounting records with years ending December 31.

On December 31, 19X4, after year-end adjustments and the closing of nominal accounts, the companies had condensed balance sheet accounts as follows:

	Case	Frey
Assets:		
Cash	$ 825,000	$ 330,000
Accounts and Other Receivables	2,140,000	835,000
Inventories	2,310,000	1,045,000
Land	650,000	300,000
Depreciable Assets (net)	4,575,000	1,980,000
Investment in Frey, Inc.	2,680,000	
Long-Term Investments and Other Assets	865,000	385,000
	$14,045,000	$4,875,000
Liabilities and Stockholders' Equity:		
Accounts Payable and Other Current Liabilities	$ 2,465,000	$1,145,000
Long-Term Debt	1,900,000	1,300,000
Common Stock, $25 Par Value	3,200,000	1,000,000
Additional Paid-In Capital	2,100,000	190,000
Retained Earnings	4,380,000	1,240,000
	$14,045,000	$4,875,000

Additional information is as follows:

1. Case uses the equity method of accounting for its investment in Frey.

2. On December 31, 19X3, Frey's assets and liabilities had fair values equal to the book balances with the exception of land, which had a fair value of $550,000. Frey had no land transactions in 19X4.

3. On June 15, 19X4, Frey paid a cash dividend of $4 per share on its common stock.

4. On December 10, 19X4, Case paid a cash dividend totaling $256,000 on its common stock.

5. On December 31, 19X3, immediately before the combination, the stockholders' equities were:

	Case	Frey
Common Stock	$2,200,000	$1,000,000
Additional Paid-In Capital	1,660,000	190,000
Retained Earnings	3,166,000	820,000
	$7,026,000	$2,010,000

6. The 19X4 net income amounts according to the separate books of Case and Frey were $890,000 (exclusive of equity in Frey's earnings) and $580,000, respectively.

Required

Prepare a consolidated balance sheet workpaper for Case, Inc., and its subsidiary, Frey, Inc., for December 31, 19X4. A formal consolidated balance sheet is not required.

P5-27 Consolidated Balance Sheet

Thompson Company spent $240,000 to buy all the stock of Lake Corporation on January 1, 19X2. The balance sheets of the two companies on December 31, 19X3, showed the following totals:

	Thompson Company	Lake Corporation
Cash	$ 30,000	$ 20,000
Accounts Receivable	100,000	40,000
Land	60,000	50,000
Buildings and Equipment	500,000	350,000
Less: Accumulated Depreciation	(230,000)	(75,000)
Investment in Lake Corporation	252,000	
	$712,000	$385,000
Accounts Payable	$ 80,000	$ 10,000
Taxes Payable	40,000	70,000
Notes Payable	100,000	85,000
Common Stock	200,000	100,000
Retained Earnings	292,000	120,000
	$712,000	$385,000

Lake Corporation reported retained earnings of $100,000 at the date of acquisition. The difference between the purchase price and underlying book value is assigned to buildings and equipment with a remaining economic life of 10 years from the date of acquisition.

Required

a. Give the appropriate eliminating entry or entries needed to prepare a consolidated balance sheet as of December 31, 19X3.

b. Prepare a consolidated balance sheet workpaper as of December 31, 19X3.

P5-28 Comprehensive Problem: Majority-Owned Subsidiary

Pillar Corporation acquired 80 percent ownership of Stanley Wood Products Company on January 1, 19X1, for $160,000. On that date Stanley Wood Products reported retained earnings of $50,000 and had $100,000 of common stock outstanding. Pillar has used the equity method in accounting for its investment in Stanley.

Trial balance data for the two companies on December 31, 19X5, are as follows:

Item	Pillar Corporation		Stanley Wood Products Company	
	Debit	Credit	Debit	Credit
Cash and Receivables	$ 81,000		$ 65,000	
Inventory	260,000		90,000	
Land	80,000		80,000	
Buildings and Equipment	500,000		150,000	
Investment in Stanley Wood Products Stock	188,000			
Cost of Goods Sold	120,000		50,000	
Depreciation Expense	25,000		15,000	
Inventory Losses	15,000		5,000	
Dividends Declared	30,000		10,000	
Accumulated Depreciation		$ 205,000		$105,000
Accounts Payable		60,000		20,000
Notes Payable		200,000		50,000
Common Stock		300,000		100,000
Retained Earnings		314,000		90,000
Sales		200,000		100,000
Income from Subsidiary		20,000		
	$1,299,000	$1,299,000	$465,000	$465,000

Additional information:

1. On the date of combination the fair value of Stanley's depreciable assets was $50,000 above book value. The purchase differential assigned to depreciable assets should be written off over the following 10-year period.

2. There was $10,000 of intercorporate receivables and payables at the end of 19X5.

Required

a. Give all journal entries recorded by Pillar Corporation during 19X5 related to its investment in Stanley Wood Products.

b. Give all eliminating entries needed to prepare consolidated statements for 19X5.

c. Prepare a three-part workpaper as of December 31, 19X5.

P5-29 Comprehensive Problem: Differential Apportionment

Bigelow Corporation purchased 80 percent of Granite Company on January 1, 19X7, for $173,000. The trial balances for the two companies on December 31, 19X7, included the following amounts:

Item	Bigelow Corporation Debit	Bigelow Corporation Credit	Granite Company Debit	Granite Company Credit
Cash	$ 38,000		$ 25,000	
Accounts Receivable	50,000		55,000	
Inventory	240,000		100,000	
Land	80,000		20,000	
Buildings and Equipment	500,000		150,000	
Investment in Granite				
Company Stock	200,000			
Cost of Goods Sold	500,000		250,000	
Depreciation Expense	25,000		15,000	
Other Expense	75,000		75,000	
Dividends Declared	50,000		20,000	
Accumulated Depreciation		$ 155,000		$ 75,000
Accounts Payable		70,000		35,000
Mortgages Payable		200,000		50,000
Common Stock		300,000		50,000
Retained Earnings		290,000		100,000
Sales		700,000		400,000
Income from Subsidiary		43,000		
	$1,758,000	$1,758,000	$710,000	$710,000

Additional information:

1. On January 1, 19X7, Granite Company reported net assets with a book value of $150,000. A total of $20,000 of the purchase price is applied to goodwill with an estimated life of 10 years.

2. Granite Company depreciable assets had an estimated economic life of 11 years on the date of combination. The difference between fair value and book value of tangible assets is related entirely to depreciable assets.

3. Bigelow Corporation used the equity method in accounting for its investment in Granite.

4. Detailed analysis of receivables and payables showed that Granite owed Bigelow Corporation $16,000 on December 31, 19X7.

Required

a. Give all journal entries recorded by Bigelow Corporation with regard to its investment in Granite Company during 19X7.

b. Give all eliminating entries needed to prepare a full set of consolidated financial statements for 19X7.

c. Prepare a three-part consolidation workpaper as of December 31, 19X7.

P5-30   Analyzing Consolidated Data

Buckman Corporation and Eckel Mining Company reported the following balance sheet data as of December 31, 19X3:

Buckman Corporation
Balance Sheet
December 31, 19X3

Current Assets	$ 81,000	Current Liabilities	$ 70,000
Long-Term Assets (net)	400,000	Bonds Payable	100,000
Investment in Eckel		Common Stock	200,000
Mining Company	120,000	Retained Earnings	231,000
	$601,000		$601,000

Eckel Mining Company
Balance Sheet
December 31, 19X3

Current Assets	$ 50,000	Current Liabilities	$ 30,000
Long-Term Assets (net)	200,000	Bonds Payable	50,000
		Common Stock	100,000
		Retained Earnings	70,000
	$250,000		$250,000

Buckman Corporation purchased controlling ownership of Eckel Mining Company on January 1, 19X3. Buckman Corporation uses the equity method in accounting for its ownership in Eckel Mining. Since Buckman has more than 50 percent ownership of Eckel Mining, it prepared consolidated statements for 19X3 as follows:

Buckman Corporation and Subsidiary
Consolidated Balance Sheet
December 31, 19X3

Current Assets	$ 91,000	Current Liabilities	$ 60,000
Long-Term Assets (net)	600,000	Bonds Payable	150,000
Goodwill	18,000	Noncontrolling Interest	68,000
		Common Stock	200,000
		Retained Earnings	231,000
	$709,000		$709,000

Buckman Corporation and Subsidiary
Consolidated Income Statement
For the Year Ended December 31, 19X3

Sales		$400,000
Cost of Goods Sold	$260,000	
Other Expenses	57,000	(317,000)
		$ 83,000
Income to Noncontrolling Interest		(12,000)
Consolidated Net Income		$ 71,000

All intangible assets are amortized over a 10-year life.

Required

    a. What percentage of Eckel Mining Company's common stock does Buckman hold?

    b. Was the stock purchase made at underlying book value or at some other amount? If at another amount, how much more or less than book value was paid?

    c. What amount of net income was reported by Eckel Mining Company for 19X3?

    d. If Eckel Mining Company paid dividends of $10,000 in 19X3, (1) what was the balance of the noncontrolling interest on January 1, 19X3, and (2) what amount did Buckman pay to purchase the Eckel Mining Company shares on January 1, 19X3?

    e. Were there any intercompany receivables or payables on December 31, 19X3? If so, what amount?

P5-31A   Cost-Method Workpaper with Differential

Trial balance data for Wacker Corporation and Slade Company on December 31, 19X5, are as follows:

Item	Wacker Corporation Debit	Wacker Corporation Credit	Slade Company Debit	Slade Company Credit
Cash	$ 37,000		$ 20,000	
Accounts Receivable	50,000		30,000	
Inventory	70,000		60,000	
Buildings and Equipment	300,000		240,000	
Investment in Slade Company Stock	220,000			
Cost of Goods Sold	210,000		85,000	
Depreciation Expense	25,000		20,000	
Other Expenses	23,000		25,000	
Dividends Declared	20,000		10,000	
Accumulated Depreciation		$105,000		$ 65,000
Accounts Payable		40,000		20,000
Taxes Payable		70,000		55,000
Common Stock		200,000		150,000
Retained Earnings, January 1		230,000		50,000
Sales		300,000		150,000
Dividend Income		10,000		
	$955,000	$955,000	$490,000	$490,000

Wacker Corporation purchased all the shares of Slade Company on January 1, 19X5, for $220,000. The full purchase differential is assigned to goodwill with an expected life of 20 years. Wacker uses the cost method in accounting for its investment in Slade.

Required

Present all eliminating entries needed to prepare consolidated financial statements for the year 19X5 and a three-part consolidation workpaper in good form as of December 31, 19X5.

P5-32A Cost-Method Consolidation in Subsequent Period

Trial balance data for Wacker Corporation and Slade Company on December 31, 19X6, are as follows:

Item	Wacker Corporation		Slade Company	
	Debit	Credit	Debit	Credit
Cash	$ 46,000		$ 30,000	
Accounts Receivable	55,000		40,000	
Inventory	75,000		65,000	
Buildings and Equipment	300,000		240,000	
Investment in Slade Company Stock	220,000			
Cost of Goods Sold	270,000		135,000	
Depreciation Expense	25,000		20,000	
Other Expenses	21,000		10,000	
Dividends Declared	20,000		20,000	
Accumulated Depreciation		$ 130,000		$ 85,000
Accounts Payable		20,000		30,000
Taxes Payable		50,000		35,000
Common Stock		200,000		150,000
Retained Earnings, January 1		262,000		60,000
Sales		350,000		200,000
Dividend Income		20,000		
	$1,032,000	$1,032,000	$560,000	$560,000

Wacker Corporation purchased all the shares of Slade Company on January 1, 19X5, for $220,000. The retained earnings balance of Slade Company at the date of acquisition was $50,000. The full purchase differential is assigned to goodwill with an expected life of 20 years. Wacker uses the cost method in accounting for its investment in Slade.

Required

Prepare all eliminating entries needed to prepare consolidated financial statements for the year 19X6 and a three-part consolidation workpaper in good form as of December 31, 19X6.

P5-33A Cost-Method Consolidation of Majority-Owned Subsidiary

Rapid Delivery Corporation was created on January 1, 19X2, and quickly became successful. On January 1, 19X6, the owner sold 80 percent of the stock to Samuelson Company at underlying book value. Samuelson has continued to operate the subsidiary as a separate legal entity and uses the cost method in recording investment income.

Trial balance data for the two companies on December 31, 19X6, consist of the following:

Item	Samuelson Company Debit	Samuelson Company Credit	Rapid Delivery Corporation Debit	Rapid Delivery Corporation Credit
Cash and Receivables	$ 141,000		$ 80,000	
Inventory	240,000		100,000	
Land	80,000		20,000	
Buildings and Equipment	500,000		150,000	
Investment in Rapid Delivery Stock	120,000			
Cost of Goods Sold	500,000		250,000	
Depreciation Expense	25,000		15,000	
Wage Expense	45,000		35,000	
Other Expenses	30,000		40,000	
Dividends Declared	50,000		20,000	
Accumulated Depreciation		$ 155,000		$ 75,000
Accounts Payable		70,000		35,000
Notes Payable		200,000		50,000
Common Stock		300,000		50,000
Retained Earnings		290,000		100,000
Sales		700,000		400,000
Dividend Income		16,000		
	$1,731,000	$1,731,000	$710,000	$710,000

Retained earnings of Rapid Delivery Corporation on the date of acquisition was $100,000.

Required

You have been asked by the controller of Samuelson Company to prepare a three-part consolidation workpaper in good form and to prepare a consolidated income statement, balance sheet, and statement of changes in retained earnings for the year 19X6.

P5-34A Comprehensive Cost-Method Consolidation Problem

Pillar Corporation acquired 80 percent ownership of Stanley Wood Products Company on January 1, 19X1, for $160,000. On that date Stanley Wood Products reported retained earnings of $50,000 and had $100,000 of common stock outstanding. Pillar has used the cost method in recording its investment in Stanley.

Trial balance data for the two companies on December 31, 19X5, are as follows:

Item	Pillar Corporation Debit	Pillar Corporation Credit	Stanley Wood Products Company Debit	Stanley Wood Products Company Credit
Cash and Receivables	$ 81,000		$ 65,000	
Inventory	260,000		90,000	
Land	80,000		80,000	
Buildings and Equipment	500,000		150,000	
Investment in Stanley Wood Products Stock	160,000			
Cost of Goods Sold	120,000		50,000	
Depreciation Expense	25,000		15,000	
Inventory Losses	15,000		5,000	
Dividends Declared	30,000		10,000	
Accumulated Depreciation		$ 205,000		$105,000
Accounts Payable		60,000		20,000
Notes Payable		200,000		50,000
Common Stock		300,000		100,000
Retained Earnings		298,000		90,000
Sales		200,000		100,000
Dividend Income		8,000		
	$1,271,000	$1,271,000	$465,000	$465,000

Additional information:

1. On the date of combination, the fair value of Stanley's depreciable assets was $50,000 above book value. The purchase differential assigned to depreciable assets should be written off over the following 10-year period.

2. There was $10,000 of intercorporate receivables and payables at the end of 19X5.

Required

a. Give all journal entries recorded by Pillar Corporation during 19X5 related to its investment in Stanley Wood Products.

b. Give all eliminating entries needed to prepare consolidated statements for 19X5.

c. Prepare a three-part consolidation workpaper as of December 31, 19X5.

P5-35B Push-Down Accounting

On December 31, 19X6, Greenly Corporation and Lindy Company entered into a business combination in which Greenly acquired all the common stock of Lindy for $935,000. At the date of combination, Lindy had common stock outstanding with a par value of $100,000, additional paid-in capital of $400,000, and retained earnings of $175,000. The fair values and book values of all Lindy's assets and liabilities were equal at the date of combination, except for the following:

	Book Value	Fair Value
Inventory	$ 50,000	$ 55,000
Land	75,000	160,000
Buildings	400,000	500,000
Equipment	500,000	570,000

The buildings had a remaining life of 20 years, while the equipment was expected to last another 10 years. In accounting for the business combination, Greenly decided to use push-down accounting on the books of Lindy Company.

During 19X7, Lindy earned net income of $88,000 and paid a dividend of $50,000. All of the inventory on hand at the end of 19X6 was sold during 19X7. During 19X8, Lindy earned net income of $90,000 and paid a dividend of $50,000.

Required

a. Record the purchase of Lindy Company's stock on the books of Greenly on December 31, 19X6.

b. Record any entries that would be made December 31, 19X6, on the books of Lindy Company related to the business combination if push-down accounting is employed.

c. Present all eliminating entries that would appear in the workpaper to prepare a consolidated balance sheet immediately after the combination.

d. Present all entries that would be recorded by Greenly during 19X7 related to its investment in Lindy if Greenly uses the equity method of accounting for its investment.

e. Present all eliminating entries that would appear in the workpaper to prepare a full set of consolidated financial statements for the year 19X7.

f. Present all eliminating entries that would appear in the workpaper to prepare a full set of consolidated financial statements for the year 19X8.

CHAPTER 6

INTERCORPORATE TRANSFERS: NONCURRENT ASSETS

A parent company and its subsidiaries often engage in a variety of transactions among themselves. For example, manufacturing companies often have subsidiaries that develop raw materials or produce components to be included in the products of affiliated companies. Some companies sell consulting or other services to affiliated companies. A number of major retailers, such as J. C. Penney Company, transfer receivables to their credit subsidiaries in return for operating cash. USX Corporation (formerly United States Steel Corporation) and its subsidiaries engage in numerous transactions with one another, including sales of raw materials, fabricated products, and transportation services. Such transactions often are critical to the operations of the overall consolidated entity. These transactions between related companies are referred to as *intercorporate transfers*.

The central idea of consolidated financial statements is that they report on the activities of the consolidating affiliates as if the separate affiliates actually constitute a single company. Because single companies are not permitted to reflect internal transactions in their financial statements, consolidated entities also must exclude from their financial statements the effects of transactions that are contained totally within the consolidated entity.

Building on the basic consolidation procedures presented in earlier chapters, this chapter and the next two deal with the effects of intercorporate transfers. This chapter deals with intercorporate sales of fixed assets, while intercorporate sales of inventory and intercorporate debt transfers are discussed in Chapters 7 and 8, respectively.

OVERVIEW OF THE CONSOLIDATED ENTITY

The consolidated entity is an aggregation of a number of different companies. The financial statements prepared by the individual affiliates are consolidated into a

FIGURE 6-1 Transactions of affiliated companies.

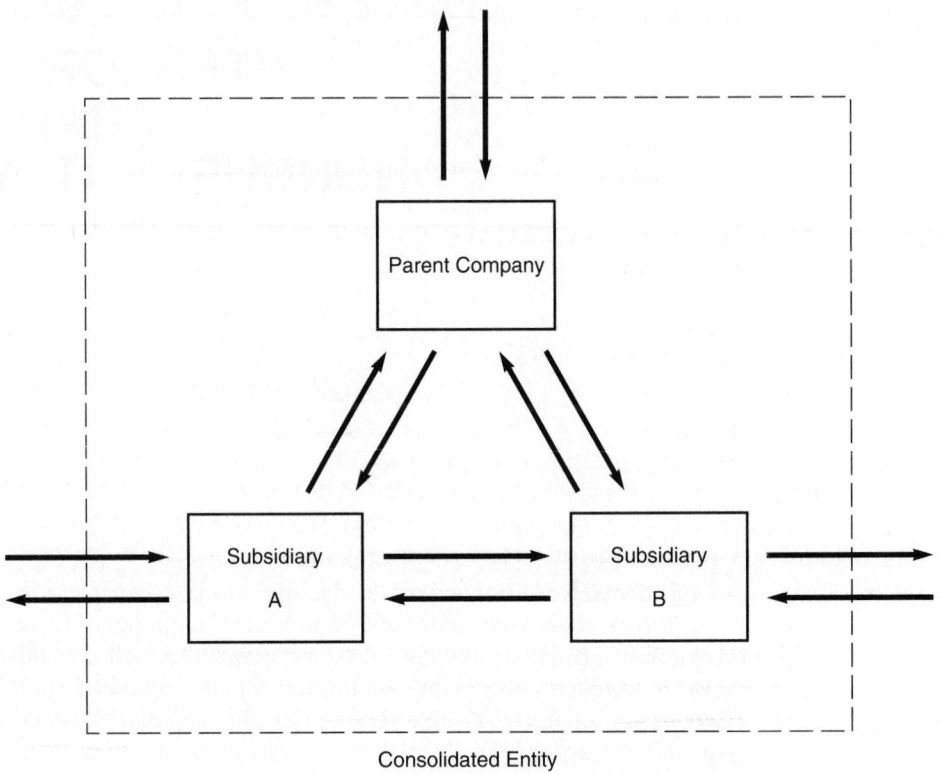

Consolidated Entity

single set of financial statements representing the financial position and operating results of the entire economic entity as if it were a single company.

Figure 6-1 illustrates a consolidated entity with each of the affiliated companies engaging in both intercorporate transfers and transactions with external parties. From a consolidated viewpoint, only transactions with parties outside the economic entity are included in the income statement. Thus, the arrows crossing the perimeter of the consolidated entity in Figure 6-1 represent transactions that are included in the operating results of the consolidated entity for the period. Transfers between the affiliated companies, shown in Figure 6-1 as those arrows not crossing the boundary of the consolidated entity, are equivalent to transfers between operating divisions of a single company and are not reported in the consolidated statements.

Elimination of Intercorporate Transfers

All aspects of intercorporate transfers must be eliminated in preparing consolidated financial statements so that the statements appear as if they were those of a single company. **Accounting Research Bulletin No. 51**, "Consolidated Financial

Statements" (ARB 51), mentions open account balances, security holdings, sales and purchases, and interest and dividends as examples of the intercompany balances and transactions that must be eliminated.[1]

No distinction is made between wholly owned and less than wholly owned subsidiaries with regard to the elimination of intercorporate transfers. The focus in consolidation is on the single-entity concept rather than on the percentage of ownership. Once the conditions for consolidation are met, a company becomes part of a single economic entity and all transactions with related companies become internal transfers that must be eliminated fully, regardless of the level of ownership held.

Elimination of Unrealized Profits and Losses

Companies usually record transactions with affiliates on the same basis as transactions with nonaffiliates, including recognition of profits and losses. Profit or loss from selling an item to a related party normally is considered realized at the time of the sale from the selling company's perspective, but the profit is not considered realized for consolidation purposes until confirmed, usually through resale to an unrelated party. This unconfirmed profit from an intercorporate transfer is referred to as *unrealized intercompany profit*.

The following illustrations provide an overview of the intercompany sale process using land as an example. Figure 6-2 shows a series of transactions involving a parent company and its subsidiary. Land first is purchased by Parent Company from an unrelated party, then sold to a subsidiary of Parent Company, and finally sold by the subsidiary to an unrelated party. The three transactions, and the amounts, are as follows:

T1—Purchase by Parent Company from outsider for $10,000
T2—Sale from Parent Company to Subsidiary Corporation for $15,000
T3—Sale from Subsidiary Corporation to outsider for $25,000

As shown in the following cases, the amount of gain reported by each of the individual companies and by the consolidated entity in a period depends on which of the transactions occur during that period.

Case A All three transactions are completed in the same accounting period. The gain amounts reported on the transactions are:

Parent Company	$ 5,000 ($15,000 − $10,000)
Subsidiary Corporation	10,000 ($25,000 − $15,000)
Consolidated Entity	15,000 ($25,000 − $10,000)

The gain reported by each of the entities is considered to be realized because the land is resold to an unrelated party during the period. The total gain reported by

[1] *Accounting Research Bulletin No. 51*, "Consolidated Financial Statements," August 1959, par. 6.

FIGURE 6-2 Intercorporate sales.

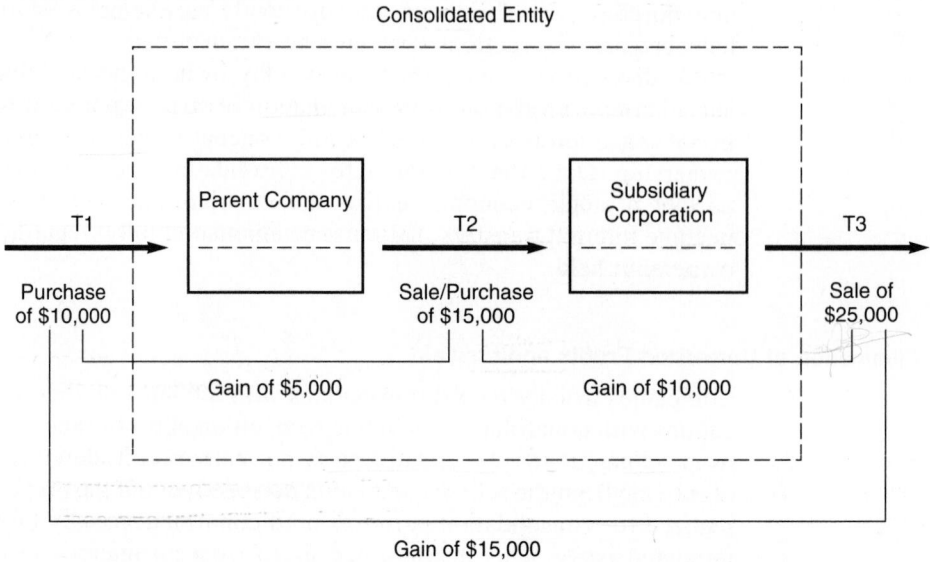

Gain of $15,000

the consolidated entity is the difference between the $10,000 price paid by the consolidated entity and the $25,000 price at which the consolidated entity sold the land to an outsider. This $15,000 gain is reported in the consolidated income statement. From a consolidated viewpoint, the sale from Parent Company to Subsidiary Corporation, transaction T2, is an internal transaction and is not reported in the consolidated financial statements.

Case B   Only transaction T1 is completed during the current period. The gain amounts reported on the transactions are:

Parent Company	$-0-
Subsidiary Corporation	-0-
Consolidated Entity	-0-

No sale has been made by either of the affiliated companies, and no gains are reported or realized. The land is reported both in Parent Company's balance sheet and in the consolidated balance sheet at its cost to Parent which also is the cost to the consolidated entity.

Case C   Only transactions T1 and T2 are completed during the current period. The gain amounts reported on the transactions are:

Parent Company	$5,000 ($15,000 − $10,000)
Subsidiary Corporation	-0-
Consolidated Entity	-0-

The $5,000 gain reported by Parent Company is considered unrealized from a consolidated point of view and is not reported in the consolidated income statement because the land has not been resold to a party outside the consolidated entity. The land is carried on the books of Subsidiary Corporation at $15,000, the cost to Subsidiary. From a consolidated viewpoint, the land is overvalued by $5,000 and must be reported at its $10,000 cost to the consolidated entity.

Case D   Only transaction T3 is completed during the current period, T1 and T2 having occurred in a prior period. The gain amounts reported on the transactions in the current period are:

Parent Company	$ -0-
Subsidiary Corporation	10,000 ($25,000 − $15,000)
Consolidated Entity	15,000 ($25,000 − $10,000)

Subsidiary recognizes a gain equal to the difference between its selling price of $25,000 and cost of $15,000, while the consolidated entity reports a gain equal to the difference between its selling price of $25,000 and cost of $10,000.

From a consolidated viewpoint, the sale of an asset wholly within the consolidated entity involves only a change in the location of the asset and does not represent the culmination of the earning process. To culminate the earning process with respect to the consolidated entity, a sale must be made to a party external to the consolidated entity. The key to deciding when to report a transaction in the consolidated financial statements is to visualize the consolidated entity and determine whether a particular transaction occurs totally within the consolidated entity, in which case its effects must be excluded from the consolidated statements, or involves outsiders and thus constitutes a transaction of the consolidated entity.

ASSET TRANSFERS INVOLVING LAND

When intercorporate transfers of noncurrent assets occur, adjustments often are needed in the preparation of consolidated financial statements for as long as the assets are held by the acquiring company. The simplest example of an intercorporate asset transfer is the intercorporate sale of land.

Overview of the Profit Elimination Process

When land is transferred between related companies at book value, no special adjustments or eliminations are needed in preparing the consolidated statements. If, for example, a company purchases land for $10,000 and sells it to its subsidiary for $10,000, the asset continues to be valued at the $10,000 original cost to the consolidated entity:

	Parent			Subsidiary	
Cash	10,000		Land	10,000	
Land		10,000	Cash		10,000

Further, no gain or loss is recorded by the seller. Thus, both income and assets are stated correctly from a consolidated viewpoint.

Land transfers at more than or less than book value do require special treatment in the consolidation process. The selling entity's gain or loss must be eliminated because the land still is held by the consolidated entity, and no gain or loss may be reported in consolidated financial statements until the land is sold to a party outside the consolidated entity. Likewise, the land must be reported at its original cost in consolidated financial statements as long as it is held within the consolidated entity, regardless of which affiliate holds the land.

As an illustration, assume that Peerless Products Corporation acquires land for $20,000 on January 1, 19X1, and sells the land to its subsidiary, Special Foods, Incorporated, on July 1, 19X1, for $35,000, as follows:

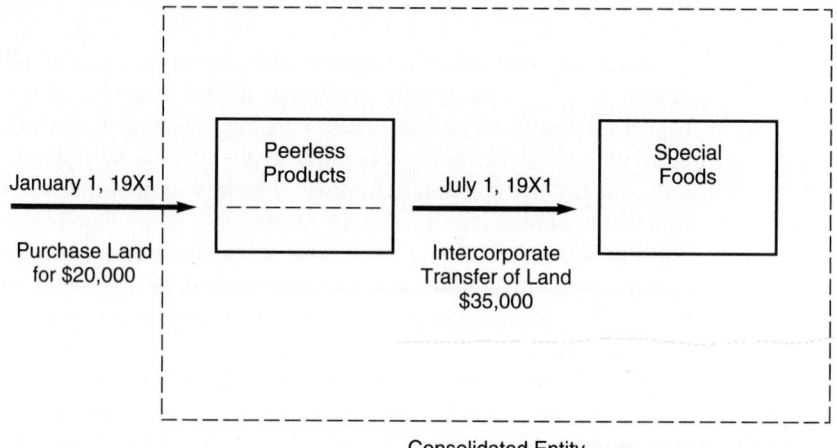

Consolidated Entity

Peerless records the purchase of the land with the following entry:

January 1, 19X1
(1) Land   20,000
         Cash   20,000
     Record purchase of land.

Peerless's entry to record the sale of the land to Special Foods is:

July 1, 19X1
(2) Cash   35,000
         Land   20,000
         Gain on Sale of Land   15,000
     Record sale of land to Special Foods.

Special Foods records the purchase of the land from Peerless as follows:

```
July 1, 19X1
    (3)  Land                                            35,000
             Cash                                                    35,000
         Record purchase of land from Peerless.
```

The intercorporate transfer causes the seller to recognize a $15,000 gain and the carrying value of the land to increase by the same amount. Neither of these amounts may be reported in the consolidated financial statements because the $15,000 intercompany gain is unrealized from a consolidated viewpoint. The land has not been sold to a party outside the consolidated entity but only transferred within; consequently, the land must continue to be reported at its original cost to the consolidated entity. The gain must be eliminated in the preparation of consolidated financial statements and the land restated from the $35,000 recorded on Special Foods' books to its original cost of $20,000. This is accomplished with the following eliminating entry in the consolidation workpaper prepared at the end of 19X1:

```
E(4)  Gain on Sale of Land                               15,000
          Land                                                    15,000
      Eliminate unrealized gain on sale of land.
```

Assignment of Unrealized Profit Elimination

A gain or loss on an intercompany transfer is recognized by the selling affiliate and ultimately accrues to the stockholders of that affiliate. When a sale is from a parent to a subsidiary, referred to as a *downstream sale*, any gain or loss on the transfer accrues to the stockholders of the parent company. When the sale is from a subsidiary to its parent, an *upstream sale*, any gain or loss accrues to the stockholders of the subsidiary. If the subsidiary is wholly owned, all the gain or loss ultimately accrues to the parent company as the sole stockholder. If, however, the selling subsidiary is not wholly owned, the gain or loss is apportioned between the parent company and the noncontrolling shareholders.

No gain or loss is ever considered realized by the consolidated entity until a sale is made to a party outside the consolidated entity. Unrealized gains and losses are eliminated in preparing consolidated financial statements against the interests of those shareholders who recognized the gains and losses in the first place: the shareholders of the selling affiliate. Therefore, the direction of the sale determines which shareholder group absorbs the elimination of unrealized intercompany gains and losses. Specifically, unrealized intercompany gains and losses are eliminated in the following ways:

Sale	Elimination
Downstream (parent to subsidiary)	Against controlling interest
Upstream (subsidiary to parent):	
Wholly owned subsidiary	Against controlling interest
Majority-owned subsidiary	Proportionally against controlling and noncontrolling interests

As an illustration, assume that Purity Company owns 75 percent of the common stock of Southern Corporation. Purity reports income from its own activities, excluding any income from Southern, of $100,000; Southern reports net income of $60,000. Included in the income of the selling affiliate is an unrealized gain of $10,000 on the intercompany transfer of an asset. If the sale is a downstream transfer, all the unrealized profit is eliminated from the controlling interest's share of income when consolidated statements are prepared. Thus, consolidated net income is computed as follows:

Purity's separate income		$100,000
Less: Unrealized intercompany profit on		
downstream asset sale		(10,000)
Purity's separate realized income		$ 90,000
Purity's share of Southern's income:		
Southern's net income	$60,000	
Purity's proportionate share	× .75	45,000
Consolidated net income		$135,000

If, instead, the intercompany transfer is from subsidiary to parent, the unrealized profit on the upstream sale is eliminated proportionately from the interests of the controlling and noncontrolling shareholders. In this situation, consolidated net income is computed as follows:

Purity's separate income		$100,000
Purity's share of Southern's		
realized income:		
Southern's net income	$60,000	
Less: Unrealized intercompany profit		
on upstream asset sale	(10,000)	
Southern's realized income	$50,000	
Purity's proportionate share	× .75	37,500
Consolidated net income		$137,500

Consolidated net income is $2,500 greater in the upstream case because 25 percent of the unrealized profit elimination is deducted from the noncontrolling interest rather than deducting the full amount from the controlling interest as in the downstream case.

Note that unrealized intercompany gains and losses always are fully eliminated in preparing consolidated financial statements. The existence of a noncontrolling interest in a selling subsidiary affects only the allocation of the eliminated unrealized gain or loss and not the amount eliminated.

Income to Noncontrolling Interest   The income assigned to the noncontrolling interest is the noncontrolling interest's proportionate share of the subsidiary's income realized in transactions with parties external to the consolidated entity. The income assigned to the noncontrolling interest is computed as follows:

	Income to Noncontrolling Interest		Subsidiary's Realized Income		Noncontrolling Interest's Ownership Percentage
Downstream	$15,000	=	$60,000	×	.25
Upstream	$12,500	=	$50,000	×	.25

In the downstream example, the $10,000 of unrealized intercompany profit is recognized on the parent company's books; therefore, the noncontrolling interest is not affected by the unrealized gain on the downstream intercompany transaction. The entire $60,000 of the subsidiary's income is realized in transactions with parties external to the consolidated entity. In the upstream example, the subsidiary's income includes $10,000 of unrealized intercompany profit. The amount of the subsidiary's income realized in transactions with external parties is only $50,000 ($60,000 less $10,000 of unrealized intercompany profit).

Downstream Sale

To illustrate the treatment of unrealized intercompany profits, assume the following with respect to the Peerless–Special Foods example used previously:

1. Peerless Products Corporation purchases 80 percent of the stock of Special Foods, Incorporated, on December 31, 19X0, at the stock's book value of $240,000.

2. On July 1, 19X1, Peerless sells land to Special Foods for $35,000. The land originally had been purchased by Peerless on January 1, 19X1, for $20,000. Special Foods continues to hold the land through 19X1 and subsequent years.

3. During 19X1, Peerless reports separate income of $155,000, consisting of income from regular operations of $140,000 and a $15,000 gain on the sale of land; Peerless declares dividends of $60,000. Special Foods reports net income of $50,000 and declares dividends of $30,000.

4. Peerless accounts for its investment in Special Foods using the basic equity method, under which it records its share of Special Foods' net income and dividends but does not adjust for unrealized intercompany profits.

Peerless records the sale of the land and the resulting gain of $15,000 ($35,000 − $20,000) with entry (2), given previously. Special Foods records the purchase of the land for $35,000 with entry (3).

Basic Equity-Method Entries—19X1 During 19X1, Peerless records its share of income and dividends from Special Foods with the usual entries under the basic equity method:

(5)	Investment in Special Foods Stock	40,000	
	Income from Subsidiary		40,000
	Record equity-method income:		
	$50,000 × .80		
(6)	Cash	24,000	
	Investment in Special Foods Stock		24,000
	Record dividends from Special Foods:		
	$30,000 × .80		

On December 31, 19X1, the investment account on Peerless's books appears as follows:

Investment in Special Foods Stock

	Original cost	240,000		
(5)	Equity accrual		(6) Dividends	
	($50,000 × .80)	40,000	($30,000 × .80) 24,000	
	Balance, 12/31/X1	256,000		

Consolidation Workpaper—19X1 The consolidation workpaper used in preparing consolidated financial statements for 19X1 is shown in Figure 6-3. The normal workpaper entries are included:

E(7)	Income from Subsidiary	40,000	
	Dividends Declared		24,000
	Investment in Special Foods Stock		16,000
	Eliminate income from subsidiary.		
E(8)	Income to Noncontrolling Interest	10,000	
	Dividends Declared		6,000
	Noncontrolling Interest		4,000
	Assign income to noncontrolling interest:		
	$10,000 = $50,000 × .20		
	$6,000 = $30,000 × .20		
E(9)	Common Stock—Special Foods	200,000	
	Retained Earnings, January 1	100,000	
	Investment in Special Foods Stock		240,000
	Noncontrolling Interest		60,000
	Eliminate beginning investment balance.		

FIGURE 6-3 December 31, 19X1, consolidation workpaper, period of intercompany sale; downstream sale of land.

Item	Peerless Products	Special Foods	Eliminations Debit		Eliminations Credit		Consolidated
Sales	400,000	200,000					600,000
Gain on Sale of Land	15,000		(10)	15,000			
Income from Subsidiary	40,000		(7)	40,000			
Credits	455,000	200,000					600,000
Cost of Goods Sold	170,000	115,000					285,000
Depreciation and Amortization	50,000	20,000					70,000
Other Expenses	40,000	15,000					55,000
Debits	(260,000)	(150,000)					(410,000)
							190,000
Income to Noncontrolling Interest			(8)	10,000			(10,000)
Net Income, carry forward	195,000	50,000		65,000			180,000
Retained Earnings, January 1	300,000	100,000	(9)	100,000			300,000
Net Income, from above	195,000	50,000		65,000			180,000
	495,000	150,000					480,000
Dividends Declared	(60,000)	(30,000)			(7)	24,000	
					(8)	6,000	(60,000)
Retained Earnings, December 31, carry forward	435,000	120,000		165,000		30,000	420,000
Cash	299,000	40,000					339,000
Accounts Receivable	75,000	50,000					125,000
Inventory	100,000	75,000					175,000
Land	155,000	75,000			(10)	15,000	215,000
Buildings and Equipment	800,000	600,000					1,400,000
Investment in Special Foods Stock	256,000				(7)	16,000	
					(9)	240,000	
Debits	1,685,000	840,000					2,254,000
Accumulated Depreciation	450,000	320,000					770,000
Accounts Payable	100,000	100,000					200,000
Bonds Payable	200,000	100,000					300,000
Common Stock	500,000	200,000	(9)	200,000			500,000
Retained Earnings, from above	435,000	120,000		165,000		30,000	420,000
Noncontrolling Interest					(8)	4,000	
					(9)	60,000	64,000
Credits	1,685,000	840,000		365,000		365,000	2,254,000

Elimination entries:
(7) Eliminate income from subsidiary.
(8) Assign income to noncontrolling interest.
(9) Eliminate beginning investment balance.
(10) Eliminate unrealized gain on sale of land.

Entry E(7) eliminates the changes in Peerless's investment account for the year, the income from Special Foods recognized by Peerless in entry (5), and Peerless's share of Special Foods' income to the noncontrolling stockholders ($50,000 × .20) and eliminates their share of Special Foods' dividends. The noncontrolling interest is not affected by the unrealized intercompany gain, because the transfer was a downstream sale. Entry E(9) eliminates Peerless's beginning investment balance and the beginning stockholders' equity amounts of Special Foods, and establishes the noncontrolling interest as of the beginning of the year.

One additional entry is needed to eliminate the unrealized gain on the intercompany sale of the land:

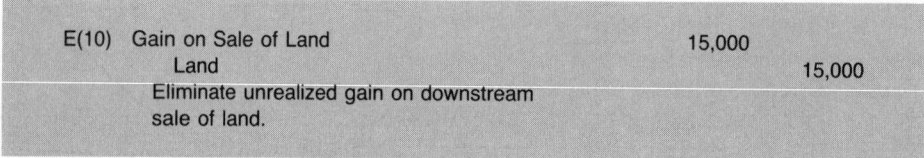

E(10)	Gain on Sale of Land	15,000	
	Land		15,000
	Eliminate unrealized gain on downstream sale of land.		

Because the land still is held within the consolidated entity, the $15,000 gain recognized on Peerless's books must be eliminated in the consolidation workpaper so that it does not appear in the consolidated income statement. Similarly, the land must appear in the consolidated balance sheet at its $20,000 original cost to the consolidated entity and, therefore, must be reduced from the $35,000 amount carried on Special Foods' books.

Consolidated Net Income   The 19X1 consolidated net income is computed as follows:

Peerless's separate income		$155,000
Less: Unrealized intercompany profit on		
downstream land sale		(15,000)
Peerless's separate realized income		$140,000
Peerless's share of Special Foods' income:		
Special Foods' net income	$50,000	
Peerless's proportionate share	× .80	40,000
Consolidated net income, 19X1		$180,000

Noncontrolling Interest   The noncontrolling stockholders' share of the income of the consolidated entity is limited to their proportionate share of the subsidiary's income. Special Foods' net income for 19X1 is $50,000, and the noncontrolling stockholders' ownership interest is 20 percent. Therefore, income of $10,000 ($50,000 × .20) is allocated to the noncontrolling interest.

As shown in Figure 6-3, the total noncontrolling interest at the end of 19X1 is $64,000, which represents the noncontrolling stockholders' proportionate share of the total book value of the subsidiary:

Book value of Special Foods, December 31, 19X1:

Common stock	$200,000
Retained earnings	120,000
Total book value	$320,000
Noncontrolling stockholders' proportionate share	× .20
Noncontrolling interest, December 31, 19X1	$ 64,000

The noncontrolling interest is unaffected by the unrealized gain on the downstream sale.

Upstream Sale

An upstream sale results in the recording of intercompany profits on the books of the subsidiary. If the profits are unrealized from a consolidated viewpoint, they must not be included in the consolidated financial statements. The unrealized intercompany profits are eliminated from the consolidation workpaper in the same manner as in the downstream case. However, the profit elimination reduces both the controlling and the noncontrolling interests in proportion to their ownership.

The treatment of an upstream sale may be illustrated with the same example used to illustrate a downstream sale. In this case, Special Foods recognizes a $15,000 gain from selling the land to Peerless in addition to the $50,000 of income earned from its regular operations; thus, Special Foods' net income for 19X1 is $65,000. Peerless's separate income is $140,000 and comes entirely from its normal operations.

The upstream sale from Special Foods to Peerless is as follows:

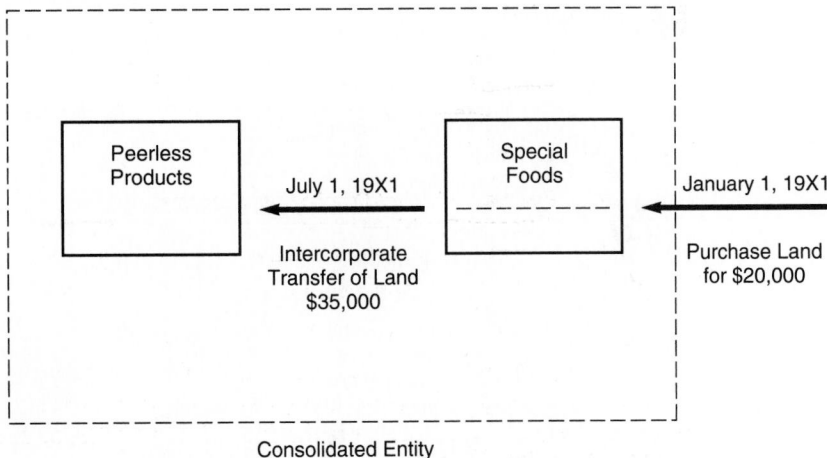

Consolidated Entity

Basic Equity-Method Entries—19X1   During 19X1, Peerless records the normal entries under the basic equity method, reflecting its share of Special Foods' income and dividends:

(11)	Investment in Special Foods Stock	52,000	
	Income from Subsidiary		52,000
	Record equity-method income:		
	$65,000 × .80		
(12)	Cash	24,000	
	Investment in Special Foods Stock		24,000
	Record dividends from Special Foods:		
	$30,000 × .80		

Note that Peerless's equity accrual in entry (11) includes its share of both Special Foods' operating income and Special Foods' gain on the transfer of the land.

The investment account on Peerless's books appears as follows at the end of 19X1:

Investment in Special Foods Stock

	Original cost	240,000			
(11)	Equity accrual		(12)	Dividends	
	($65,000 × .80)	52,000		($30,000 × .80)	24,000
	Balance, 12/31/X1	268,000			

Consolidation Workpaper—19X1 The consolidation workpaper prepared at the end of 19X1 appears in Figure 6-4. The four eliminating entries needed to prepare consolidated statements in the upstream case are nearly identical with those in the downstream case:

E(13)	Income from Subsidiary	52,000	
	Dividends Declared		24,000
	Investment in Special Foods Stock		28,000
	Eliminate income from subsidiary.		
E(14)	Income to Noncontrolling Interest	10,000	
	Dividends Declared		6,000
	Noncontrolling Interest		4,000
	Assign income to noncontrolling interest:		
	$10,000 = ($65,000 − $15,000) × .20		
	$6,000 = $30,000 × .20		
E(15)	Common Stock—Special Foods	200,000	
	Retained Earnings, January 1	100,000	
	Investment in Special Foods Stock		240,000
	Noncontrolling Interest		60,000
	Eliminate beginning investment balance.		
E(16)	Gain on Sale of Land	15,000	
	Land		15,000
	Eliminate unrealized gain on upstream		
	sale of land.		

FIGURE 6-4 December 31, 19X1, consolidation workpaper, period of intercompany sale; upstream sale of land.

Item	Peerless Products	Special Foods	Eliminations Debit		Eliminations Credit		Consolidated
Sales	400,000	200,000					600,000
Gain on Sale of Land		15,000	(16)	15,000			
Income from Subsidiary	52,000		(13)	52,000			
Credits	452,000	215,000					600,000
Cost of Goods Sold	170,000	115,000					285,000
Depreciation and Amortization	50,000	20,000					70,000
Other Expenses	40,000	15,000					55,000
Debits	(260,000)	(150,000)					(410,000)
							190,000
Income to Noncontrolling Interest			(14)	10,000			(10,000)
Net Income, carry forward	192,000	65,000		77,000			180,000
Retained Earnings, January 1	300,000	100,000	(15)	100,000			300,000
Net Income, from above	192,000	65,000		77,000			180,000
	492,000	165,000					480,000
Dividends Declared	(60,000)	(30,000)			(13)	24,000	
					(14)	6,000	(60,000)
Retained Earnings, December 31, carry forward	432,000	135,000		177,000		30,000	420,000
Cash	229,000	110,000					339,000
Accounts Receivable	75,000	50,000					125,000
Inventory	100,000	75,000					175,000
Land	210,000	20,000			(16)	15,000	215,000
Buildings and Equipment	800,000	600,000					1,400,000
Investment in Special Foods Stock	268,000				(13)	28,000	
					(15)	240,000	
Debits	1,682,000	855,000					2,254,000
Accumulated Depreciation	450,000	320,000					770,000
Accounts Payable	100,000	100,000					200,000
Bonds Payable	200,000	100,000					300,000
Common Stock	500,000	200,000	(15)	200,000			500,000
Retained Earnings, from above	432,000	135,000		177,000		30,000	420,000
Noncontrolling Interest					(14)	4,000	
					(15)	60,000	64,000
Credits	1,682,000	855,000		377,000		377,000	2,254,000

Elimination entries:
   (13) Eliminate income from subsidiary.
   (14) Assign income to noncontrolling interest.
   (15) Eliminate beginning investment balance.
   (16) Eliminate unrealized gain on sale of land.

The only difference between these elimination entries and those in the downstream example is in entry E(13). This difference results from the subsidiary's reporting $65,000 as its income in the upstream example rather than the $50,000 reported in the downstream example, with the additional $15,000 being the gain on the sale of the land.

Entry E(14), which assigns income to the noncontrolling interest, is the same as in the downstream example. The assignment of income to the controlling and noncontrolling interests is based on the realized income of the subsidiary, which is the same in both cases, $50,000.

The only procedural difference in the upstream and downstream elimination process is that unrealized intercompany profits of the subsidiary from upstream sales are eliminated proportionately against the controlling and noncontrolling interests, while unrealized intercompany profits of the parent from downstream sales are eliminated totally against the controlling interest. Thus, in the downstream example, the entire $15,000 unrealized intercompany gain was eliminated against the controlling interest's share of income to derive consolidated net income. In the upstream case, $3,000 of the unrealized intercompany gain is subtracted from the noncontrolling stockholders' share of income. The noncontrolling stockholders' share of the subsidiary's total net income is $13,000 ($65,000 × .20), but is reduced by their $3,000 ($15,000 × .20) share of the unrealized gain on the intercompany sale.

Particularly note that the elimination of the unrealized intercompany profit is the same for the upstream case in entry E(16) as for the downstream case, entry E(10). The full amount of the unrealized intercompany profit, $15,000 in this example, always is eliminated. The only difference between the upstream and downstream cases involves how the income reduction for unrealized profit is allocated between the controlling and noncontrolling interests.

Consolidated Net Income   When intercompany profits that are unrealized from a consolidated point of view are included in the income of a subsidiary, consolidated net income and the noncontrolling stockholders' share of income both must be adjusted for the unrealized profits. Consolidated net income for 19X1 is computed as follows:

Peerless's separate income		$140,000
Peerless's share of Special Foods' realized income:		
Special Foods' net income	$65,000	
Less: Unrealized intercompany profit		
on upstream land sale	(15,000)	
Special Foods' realized income	$50,000	
Peerless's proportionate share	× .80	40,000
Consolidated net income, 19X1		$180,000

This amount appears in the workpaper in Figure 6-4 as the result of the income eliminations and the assignment of income to the noncontrolling interest:

Peerless's net income		$192,000
Special Foods' net income		65,000
		$257,000
Eliminations:		
Peerless's income from Special Foods	$52,000	
Unrealized gain on sale of land	15,000	
		(67,000)
		$190,000
Noncontrolling stockholders' share of income		(10,000)
Consolidated net income		$180,000

Consolidated net income in this year is the same whether or not there is an intercompany sale and regardless of whether the sale is upstream or downstream because the gain is unrealized. The unrealized gain must be eliminated fully in all cases, with consolidated net income based only on the realized income of the two affiliates.

Noncontrolling Interest   The income assigned to the noncontrolling shareholders is computed as their proportionate share of the realized income of Special Foods, $10,000 ($50,000 × .20). Total noncontrolling interest is computed as the noncontrolling stockholders' proportionate share of the stockholders' equity of Special Foods, excluding unrealized gains and losses. On December 31, 19X1, noncontrolling interest totals $64,000, computed as follows:

Book value of Special Foods, December 31, 19X1:	
Common stock	$200,000
Retained earnings	135,000
Total book value	$335,000
Unrealized intercompany gain on upstream land sale	(15,000)
Realized book value of Special Foods	$320,000
Noncontrolling stockholders' proportionate share	× .20
Noncontrolling interest, December 31, 19X1	$ 64,000

Eliminating Unrealized Profits after the First Year

In the period in which an intercorporate sale occurs, workpaper eliminating entries are used in the consolidation process to remove the gain or loss recorded by the seller and to adjust the reported amount of the asset back to the price originally paid by the selling affiliate. Each period thereafter while the asset is held by the purchasing affiliate, the reported asset balance and the shareholder claims of the selling affiliate are adjusted to remove the effects of the unrealized gain or loss.

In the case of a downstream sale, the profit on the intercompany transfer is recognized entirely by the parent and is included in the parent's retained earnings in subsequent years. Therefore, the following eliminating entry is needed in the consolidation workpaper each year after the year of the downstream sale of the land, for as long as the land is held by the subsidiary:

E(17)	Retained Earnings, January 1	15,000	
	Land		15,000
	Eliminate unrealized gain on prior-		
	period downstream sale of land.		

This entry reduces beginning consolidated retained earnings and the reported balance of the land to exclude the unrealized intercompany gain.

In the upstream case, the intercompany profit is recognized by the subsidiary. The parent recognizes its proportionate share of the gain, and that amount is included in the parent's beginning retained earnings in subsequent years. In the consolidation workpaper prepared in years subsequent to the intercompany transfer while the land is held by the parent, the unrealized intercompany gain is eliminated from the reported balance of the land and proportionately from the subsidiary ownership interests with the following entry:

E(18)	Retained Earnings, January 1	12,000	
	Noncontrolling Interest	3,000	
	Land		15,000
	Eliminate unrealized gain on prior-		
	period upstream sale of land.		

Thus, in periods subsequent to an upstream intercompany transfer, consolidated retained earnings is reduced by the parent's share of the unrealized intercompany gain, and the noncontrolling interest is reduced by the remainder. All other elimination entries are made as if there is no unrealized intercompany gain.

A comprehensive illustration of consolidation after the year of an intercompany transfer is presented later in this chapter in connection with the discussion of intercorporate sales of depreciable assets.

Subsequent Disposition of Asset

Unrealized profits on intercompany sales of assets are viewed as being realized at the time the assets are resold to external parties. For consolidation purposes, the

gain or loss recognized by the affiliate selling to the external party must be adjusted for the previously unrealized intercompany gain or loss. While the seller's reported profit on the external sale is based on that affiliate's cost, the gain or loss reported by the consolidated entity is based on the cost of the asset to the consolidated entity, which is the cost incurred by the affiliate that purchased the asset originally from an outside party.

When previously unrealized intercompany profits are realized, the effects of the profit elimination process must be reversed. At the time of realization, the full amount of the deferred intercompany profit is added back into the consolidated income computation and assigned to the shareholder interests from which it originally was eliminated.

To illustrate the treatment of unrealized intercompany profits once the transferred asset is resold, assume that Peerless purchases land from an outside party for $20,000 on January 1, 19X1, and sells the land to Special Foods on July 1, 19X1, for $35,000. Special Foods subsequently sells the land to an outside party on March 1, 19X5, for $45,000, as follows:

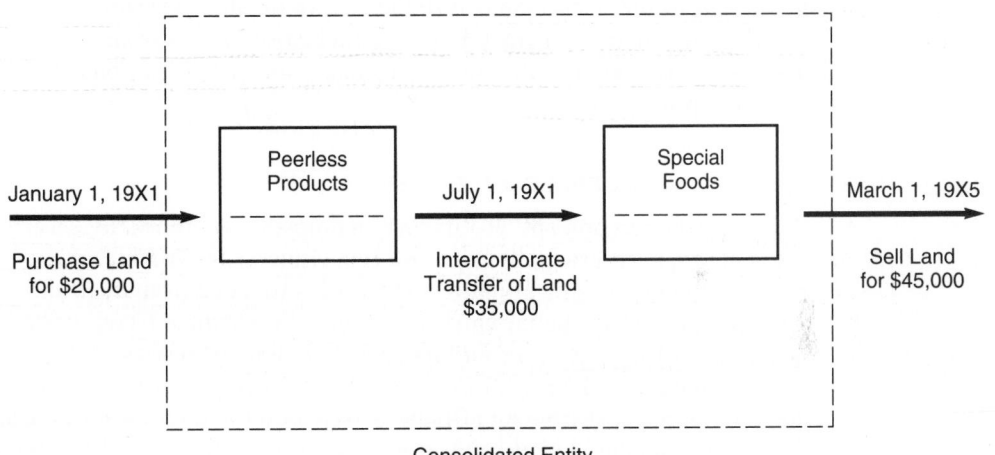

Consolidated Entity

Special Foods recognizes a gain on the sale to the outside party of $10,000 ($45,000 − $35,000). From a consolidated viewpoint, however, the gain is $25,000, the difference between the price at which the land left the consolidated entity ($45,000) and the price at which the land entered the consolidated entity ($20,000) when purchased originally by Peerless.

In the consolidation workpaper, the land no longer needs to be reduced by the unrealized intercompany gain because the gain now is realized and the land no longer is held by the consolidated entity. Instead, the $10,000 gain recognized by Special Foods on the sale of the land to an outsider must be adjusted to reflect a total gain for the consolidated entity of $25,000. Thus, the following eliminating entry is made in the consolidation workpaper prepared at the end of 19X5:

E(19)	Retained Earnings, January 1	15,000	
	Gain on Sale of Land		15,000
	Adjust for previously unrealized		
	intercompany gain on sale of land.		

In addition to adjusting the gain, this entry reduces beginning consolidated retained earnings by the amount of the unrealized intercompany gain previously recognized by Peerless. All other elimination entries are the same as if there were no unrealized intercompany profits at the beginning of the period.

No additional consideration need be given the intercompany transfer in periods subsequent to the external sale. From a consolidated viewpoint, all aspects of the transaction are complete, and the profit is realized once the sale to an external party occurs.

In the example, if the sale to the external party had been made by Peerless following an upstream intercompany transfer from Special Foods, the workpaper treatment would be the same as in the case of the downstream transfer except that the debit in elimination entry E(19) would be prorated between beginning retained earnings ($12,000) and the noncontrolling interest ($3,000) based on the relative ownership interests.

ASSET TRANSFERS INVOLVING DEPRECIABLE ASSETS

Unrealized intercompany profits on a depreciable or amortizable asset are viewed as being realized gradually over the remaining economic life of the asset as it is used by the purchasing affiliate in generating revenue from unaffiliated parties. In effect, a portion of the unrealized gain or loss is realized each period as benefits are derived from the asset and its service potential expires.

The amount of depreciation recognized on a company's books each period on an asset purchased from an affiliate is based on the intercorporate transfer price. From a consolidated viewpoint, however, depreciation must be based on the cost of the asset to the consolidated entity, which is the cost of the asset to the related company that originally purchased it from an outsider. Eliminating entries are needed in the consolidation workpaper to restate the asset, associated accumulated depreciation, and depreciation expense to the amounts that would appear in the financial statements if there had been no intercompany transfer. Because the intercompany sale takes place totally within the consolidated entity, the consolidated financial statements must appear as if the intercompany transfer never had occurred.

Downstream Sale

The example of Peerless Products and Special Foods is modified to illustrate the downstream sale of a depreciable asset. Assume that Peerless sells equipment to Special Foods on December 31, 19X1, for $7,000, as follows:

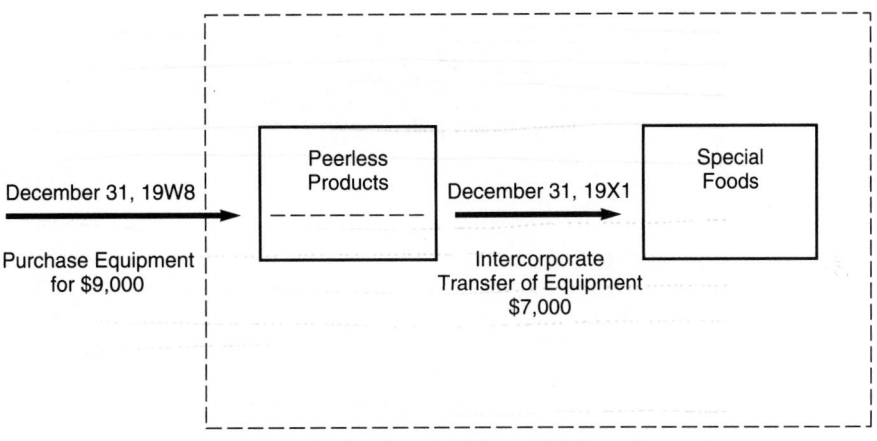

Consolidated Entity

The equipment originally cost Peerless $9,000 when purchased on December 31, 19W8, 3 years before December 31, 19X1, and is being depreciated over a total life of 10 years using straight-line depreciation with no residual value. The book value of the equipment immediately before the sale by Peerless is computed as follows:

Original cost to Peerless		$9,000
Accumulated depreciation on December 31, 19X1:		
Annual depreciation ($9,000 ÷ 10 years)	$900	
Number of years	× 3	
		(2,700)
Book value on December 31, 19X1		$6,300

The gain recognized by Peerless on the intercompany sale of the equipment is:

Sale price of the equipment	$7,000
Book value of the equipment	(6,300)
Gain on sale of the equipment	$ 700

Separate-Company Entries—19X1 Special Foods records the purchase of the equipment at its cost:

December 31, 19X1		
(20) Equipment	7,000	
Cash		7,000
Record purchase of equipment.		

Special Foods does not depreciate the equipment during 19X1 because the equipment is purchased at the very end of 19X1.

Peerless must record depreciation on the equipment for 19X1 because it held the asset until the end of the year:

December 31, 19X1

(21)	Depreciation Expense	900	
	Accumulated Depreciation		900
	Record 19X1 depreciation expense on equipment sold.		

Peerless also records the sale of the equipment at the end of 19X1 and recognizes the $700 ($7,000 − $6,300) gain on the sale:

December 31, 19X1

(22)	Cash	7,000	
	Accumulated Depreciation	2,700	
	Equipment		9,000
	Gain on Sale of Equipment		700
	Record sale of equipment.		

In addition, Peerless records the normal basic equity-method entries to recognize its share of Special Foods' income and dividends for 19X1:

(23)	Investment in Special Foods Stock	40,000	
	Income from Subsidiary		40,000
	Record equity-method income: $50,000 × .80		
(24)	Cash	24,000	
	Investment in Special Foods Stock		24,000
	Record dividends from Special Foods: $30,000 × .80		

Consolidation Workpaper—19X1 The workpaper to prepare consolidated financial statements at the end of 19X1 appears in Figure 6-5. The first three elimination entries in the workpaper are the normal entries to (a) eliminate the income and dividends from Special Foods recognized by Peerless and the change in the investment account for the year, (b) assign income to the noncontrolling interest, and (c) eliminate the stockholders' equity accounts of Special Foods and the investment account as of the beginning of the year:

E(25)	Income from Subsidiary	40,000	
	Dividends Declared		24,000
	Investment in Special Foods Stock		16,000
	Eliminate income from subsidiary.		
E(26)	Income to Noncontrolling Interest	10,000	
	Dividends Declared		6,000
	Noncontrolling Interest		4,000
	Assign income to noncontrolling interest: $10,000 = $50,000 × .20		
E(27)	Common Stock—Special Foods	200,000	
	Retained Earnings, January 1	100,000	
	Investment in Special Foods Stock		240,000
	Noncontrolling Interest		60,000
	Eliminate beginning investment balance.		

FIGURE 6-5 December 31, 19X1, consolidation workpaper, period of intercompany sale; downstream sale of equipment.

Item	Peerless Products	Special Foods	Eliminations Debit		Eliminations Credit		Consolidated
Sales	400,000	200,000					600,000
Gain on Sale of Equipment	700		(28)	700			
Income from Subsidiary	40,000		(25)	40,000			
Credits	440,700	200,000					600,000
Cost of Goods Sold	170,000	115,000					285,000
Depreciation and Amortization	50,000	20,000					70,000
Other Expenses	40,000	15,000					55,000
Debits	(260,000)	(150,000)					(410,000)
							190,000
Income to Noncontrolling Interest			(26)	10,000			(10,000)
Net Income, carry forward	180,700	50,000		50,700			180,000
Retained Earnings, January 1	300,000	100,000	(27)	100,000			300,000
Net Income, from above	180,700	50,000		50,700			180,000
	480,700	150,000					480,000
Dividends Declared	(60,000)	(30,000)			(25)	24,000	
					(26)	6,000	(60,000)
Retained Earnings, December 31, carry forward	420,700	120,000		150,700		30,000	420,000
Cash	271,000	68,000					339,000
Accounts Receivable	75,000	50,000					125,000
Inventory	100,000	75,000					175,000
Land	175,000	40,000					215,000
Buildings and Equipment	791,000	607,000	(28)	2,000			1,400,000
Investment in Special Foods Stock	256,000				(25)	16,000	
					(27)	240,000	
Debits	1,668,000	840,000					2,254,000
Accumulated Depreciation	447,300	320,000			(28)	2,700	770,000
Accounts Payable	100,000	100,000					200,000
Bonds Payable	200,000	100,000					300,000
Common Stock	500,000	200,000	(27)	200,000			500,000
Retained Earnings, from above	420,700	120,000		150,700		30,000	420,000
Noncontrolling Interest					(26)	4,000	
					(27)	60,000	64,000
Credits	1,668,000	840,000		352,700		352,700	2,254,000

Elimination entries:
(25) Eliminate income from subsidiary.
(26) Assign income to noncontrolling interest.
(27) Eliminate beginning investment balance.
(28) Eliminate unrealized gain on equipment.

An additional workpaper entry is needed to eliminate the unrealized intercompany gain on the sale of the equipment from consolidated net income and to restate the equipment to the amounts that would appear in the consolidated statements if there had been no intercompany sale. The amounts in the trial balances of the parent and subsidiary include the effects of the intercompany transfer and need to be adjusted in the consolidation workpaper to the balances immediately before the transfer:

	Amounts from Trial Balances	Elimination	Consolidated Amounts
Buildings and equipment	$7,000	$2,000	$9,000
Accumulated depreciation	-0-	(2,700)	(2,700)
Gain on sale of equipment	(700)	700	-0-

Thus, the following entry is needed in the workpaper:

E(28)	Buildings and Equipment	2,000	
	Gain on Sale of Equipment	700	
	Accumulated Depreciation		2,700
	Eliminate unrealized gain on downstream sale of equipment.		

As a result of this entry, the equipment, stated at $7,000 on Special Foods' books, is reported in the consolidated balance sheet at $9,000 ($7,000 + $2,000), its original cost to Peerless. While Special Foods has not depreciated the equipment, elimination entry E(28) provides for $2,700 of accumulated depreciation ($900 × 3), the amount that would have shown on Peerless's books had the equipment not been sold. Entry E(28) also eliminates the $700 intercompany gain that is unrealized and cannot appear when Peerless and Special Foods are viewed together as a single entity. The overall effect of entry E(28) is to report exactly the same numbers in the consolidated financial statements as if the parent company had continued to own the equipment and there had been no intercompany transfer.

Separate-Company Entries—19X2 During 19X2, Special Foods begins depreciating the $7,000 cost of the equipment acquired from Peerless Products over its remaining life of 7 years using straight-line depreciation. The resulting depreciation is $1,000 per year ($7,000 ÷ 7 years):

(29)	Depreciation Expense	1,000	
	Accumulated Depreciation		1,000
	Record depreciation expense for 19X2.		

Note that this amount is $100 more per year than the depreciation that would have been recorded each year if Peerless had continued to hold the equipment.

Peerless records its normal equity-method entries for 19X2 to reflect its share of Special Foods' $74,000 income and dividends of $40,000:

(30)	Investment in Special Foods Stock	59,200	
	Income from Subsidiary		59,200
	Record equity-method income:		
	$74,000 × .80		
(31)	Cash	32,000	
	Investment in Special Foods Stock		32,000
	Record dividends from Special Foods:		
	$40,000 × .80		

Note that Special Foods' net income is only $74,000 in 19X2 because it has been reduced by the $1,000 of depreciation on the transferred asset. Accordingly, Peerless's share of that income is $59,200 ($74,000 × .80).

Investment Account Balance   The investment account on Peerless's books appears as follows:

Investment in Special Foods Stock

	Original cost	240,000				
(23)	19X1 equity accrual		(24)	19X1 dividends		
	($50,000 × .80)	40,000		($30,000 × .80)	24,000	
	Balance, 12/31/X1	256,000				
(30)	19X2 equity accrual		(31)	19X2 dividends		
	($74,000 × .80)	59,200		($40,000 × .80)	32,000	
	Balance, 12/31/X2	283,200				

Consolidation Workpaper—19X2   The consolidation workpaper for 19X2 is presented in Figure 6-6. The trial balance amounts from the basic example have been adjusted to reflect the intercompany asset sale. The first three elimination entries are the normal entries to eliminate income and dividends from the subsidi-

FIGURE 6-6 December 31, 19X2, consolidation workpaper, next period following intercompany sale; downstream sale of equipment.

Item	Peerless Products	Special Foods	Eliminations Debit		Eliminations Credit		Consolidated
Sales	450,000	300,000					750,000
Income from Subsidiary	59,200		(32)	59,200			
Credits	509,200	300,000					750,000
Cost of Goods Sold	180,000	160,000					340,000
Depreciation and Amortization	49,100	21,000			(36)	100	70,000
Other Expenses	60,000	45,000					105,000
Debits	(289,100)	(226,000)					(515,000)
							235,000
Income to Noncontrolling Interest			(33)	14,800			(14,800)
Net Income, carry forward	220,100	74,000		74,000		100	220,200
Retained Earnings, January 1	420,700	120,000	(34)	120,000			
			(35)	700			420,000
Net Income, from above	220,100	74,000		74,000		100	220,200
	640,800	194,000					640,200
Dividends Declared	(60,000)	(40,000)			(32)	32,000	
					(33)	8,000	(60,000)
Retained Earnings, December 31, carry forward	580,800	154,000		194,700		40,100	580,200
Cash	298,000	78,000					376,000
Accounts Receivable	150,000	80,000					230,000
Inventory	180,000	90,000					270,000
Land	175,000	40,000					215,000
Buildings and Equipment	791,000	607,000	(35)	2,000			1,400,000
Investment in Special Foods Stock	283,200				(32)	27,200	
					(34)	256,000	
Debits	1,877,200	895,000					2,491,000
Accumulated Depreciation	496,400	341,000	(36)	100	(35)	2,700	840,000
Accounts Payable	100,000	100,000					200,000
Bonds Payable	200,000	100,000					300,000
Common Stock	500,000	200,000	(34)	200,000			500,000
Retained Earnings, from above	580,800	154,000		194,700		40,100	580,200
Noncontrolling Interest					(33)	6,800	
					(34)	64,000	70,800
Credits	1,877,200	895,000		396,800		396,800	2,491,000

Elimination entries:
(32) Eliminate income from subsidiary.
(33) Assign income to noncontrolling interest.
(34) Eliminate beginning investment balance.
(35) Eliminate unrealized gain on equipment.
(36) Adjust depreciation for realization of intercompany gain.

ary, the investment account, and the stockholders' equity accounts of the subsidiary, and to establish the noncontrolling interest in the workpaper:

E(32)	Income from Subsidiary	59,200	
	Dividends Declared		32,000
	Investment in Special Foods Stock		27,200
	Eliminate income from subsidiary.		
E(33)	Income to Noncontrolling Interest	14,800	
	Dividends Declared		8,000
	Noncontrolling Interest		6,800
	Assign income to noncontrolling interest:		
	$14,800 = $74,000 × .20		
E(34)	Common Stock—Special Foods	200,000	
	Retained Earnings, January 1	120,000	
	Investment in Special Foods Stock		256,000
	Noncontrolling Interest		64,000
	Eliminate beginning investment balance.		

Entry E(32) eliminates the dividends and income from Special Foods and the change in the investment account for the period based on the amounts recorded on Peerless's books. Entry E(33) assigns the noncontrolling interest its full 20 percent of the $74,000 reported income of Special Foods, given that the unrealized profits are on the books of the parent. Entry E(34) is the normal entry to eliminate the beginning stockholders' equity balances of Special Foods and the investment account balance at the beginning of the year, and to establish the amount of the beginning noncontrolling interest at a proportionate share of the subsidiary's beginning stockholders' equity.

In addition to the normal elimination entries, entry E(35) is needed to eliminate the effects of the 19X1 intercompany transaction as of the beginning of 19X2:

E(35)	Buildings and Equipment	2,000	
	Retained Earnings, January 1	700	
	Accumulated Depreciation		2,700
	Eliminate unrealized gain on equipment.		

Entry E(35) restates the balance of the equipment to $9,000 ($7,000 + $2,000), the original cost to the consolidated entity when purchased by Peerless. Accumulated depreciation on the equipment is credited for $2,700. This is the amount at which accumulated depreciation would have been stated as of January 1, 19X2, if the asset had not been transferred to Special Foods:

Depreciation per year ($9,000 ÷ 10 years)	$ 900
Number of years to December 31, 19X1	× 3
Accumulated depreciation, December 31, 19X1	$2,700

Entry E(35) also reduces beginning retained earnings by the amount of intercompany profit unrealized at the beginning of the year. The full amount of the unrealized gain is included in Peerless's beginning retained earnings. If this amount were reported in consolidated retained earnings, the balance would be overstated because the gain has not been realized from a consolidated viewpoint.

One additional eliminating entry is needed in the December 31, 19X2, consolidation workpaper. Special Foods started depreciating the transferred asset at the beginning of 19X2 and recorded depreciation of $1,000 ($7,000 ÷ 7 years) on its separate books. From a consolidated point of view, however, the depreciation expense for 19X2 should be based on the $6,300 ($9,000 − $2,700) remaining book value of the equipment on Peerless's books immediately before the transfer. This $6,300 is allocated over the remaining 7-year life of the equipment, resulting in depreciation of $900 per year ($6,300 ÷ 7 years) from a consolidated perspective. Therefore, consolidated depreciation expense, and the associated accumulated depreciation, must be reduced by $100 from the amount recorded by Special Foods:

E(36)	Accumulated Depreciation	100	
	Depreciation Expense		100
	Adjust depreciation for realization of		
	intercompany gain.		

Note that this entry increases consolidated net income by $100. The $700 unrealized gain on the intercorporate sale is viewed as being realized at $100 per year over the 7 years following the transfer. After 7 years, the intercompany gain will be fully realized, and no further eliminations of retained earnings will be needed.

The decision to separate entries (35) and (36) is purely a matter of preference. Some prefer to combine the two entries and establish the consolidated balances at the end of the year in a single entry:

E(36a)	Buildings and Equipment	2,000	
	Retained Earnings, January 1	700	
	Depreciation Expense		100
	Accumulated Depreciation		2,600

The $2,600 credit to accumulated depreciation represents the difference between the $3,600 ($900 × 4 years) amount at which consolidated accumulated depreciation should be stated on December 31, 19X2, and the $1,000 amount at which accumulated depreciation is stated on Special Foods' books.

Once all the eliminating entries have been made in the workpaper, the adjusted balances exclude the effects of the intercorporate transfer:

	Subsidiary Trial Balance	Elimination	Consolidated Amounts
Buildings and Equipment	$7,000	$2,000	$9,000
Accumulated Depreciation	(1,000)	(2,600)	(3,600)
Depreciation Expense	1,000	(100)	900

Consolidated Net Income and Retained Earnings   Computation of consolidated net income for 19X2 must include an adjustment for the realization of profit on the 19X1 sale of equipment to Special Foods:

Peerless's separate income		$160,900
Partial realization of intercompany gain on downstream sale of equipment		100
Peerless's separate realized income		$161,000
Peerless's share of Special Foods' income:		
Special Foods' net income	$74,000	
Peerless's proportionate share	× .80	59,200
Consolidated net income, 19X2		$220,200

Consolidated retained earnings on December 31, 19X2, is reduced by the unrealized amount of the gain on the intercompany sale of the equipment:

Peerless's retained earnings on date of combination, December 31, 19X0		$300,000
Peerless's separate income since date of combination ($140,700 + $160,900)	$301,600	
Unrealized 19X1 intercompany gain	(700)	
19X2 partial realization of gain	100	
Peerless's separate realized income since date of combination		301,000
Peerless's share (80 percent) of Special Foods' net income since date of combination ($40,000 + $59,200)		99,200
Peerless's dividends declared since date of combination ($60,000 + $60,000)		(120,000)
Consolidated retained earnings, December 31, 19X2		$580,200

Noncontrolling Interest   Income allocated to the noncontrolling stockholders in 19X2 is equal to their proportionate share of the subsidiary's realized and reported income. Special Foods' net income for 19X2 is $74,000, and the noncontrolling interest's 20 percent share is $14,800 ($74,000 × .20).

The total noncontrolling interest at the end of 19X2 is $70,800, equal to the noncontrolling stockholders' proportionate share of the total book value of the subsidiary:

Book value of Special Foods, December 31, 19X2:	
Common stock	$200,000
Retained earnings	154,000
Total book value	$354,000
Noncontrolling stockholders' proportionate share	× .20
Noncontrolling interest, December 31, 19X2	$ 70,800

Consolidation in Subsequent Years   The consolidation procedures in subsequent years are quite similar to those in 19X2. As long as Special Foods continues to hold and depreciate the equipment, consolidation procedures must include:

1. Restating the asset and accumulated depreciation balances
2. Adjusting depreciation expense for the year
3. Reducing beginning retained earnings by the amount of the intercompany gain unrealized at the beginning of the year

For example, selected entries from the December 31, 19X3, consolidation workpaper for Peerless Products and Special Foods are as follows:

E(37)	Buildings and Equipment	2,000	
	Retained Earnings, January 1	600	
	Accumulated Depreciation		2,600
	Eliminate unrealized gain on equipment.		
E(38)	Accumulated Depreciation	100	
	Depreciation Expense		100
	Adjust depreciation for realization of		
	intercompany gain.		

These entries are the same as entries E(35) and E(36) for 19X2, except that an additional $100 of the intercompany gain is considered realized by the end of 19X2. Therefore, the reduction of beginning retained earnings in entry E(37) is for $600, the $700 original amount of the intercompany gain less the $100 portion of the gain considered realized in 19X2.

The credit to Accumulated Depreciation in entry E(37) is $100 less than in entry E(35) for 19X2 because Special Foods credited $100 more to Accumulated Depreciation on its books in 19X2 than was appropriate for consolidated reporting. Because this amount is brought into the workpaper, the restatement of the beginning accumulated depreciation in entry E(37) is $100 less than in the previous year:

Accumulated depreciation that would have been recorded by Peerless as of December 31, 19X2, if asset had not been transferred [($9,000 ÷ 10) × 4]	$3,600
Accumulated depreciation recorded by Special Foods as of December 31, 19X2 [($7,000 ÷ 7) × 1]	(1,000)
Workpaper adjustment to accumulated depreciation	$2,600

 Both the debit to beginning Retained Earnings and the credit to Accumulated Depreciation will decrease by $100 each year until the asset is fully depreciated and the intercompany gain is fully recognized.

Change in Estimated Life of Asset Sold to Subsidiary

When a depreciable asset is transferred between companies, a change in the remaining estimated economic life may be appropriate. For example, the acquiring company may use the asset in a different type of production process, or the frequency of use may change. New information also may be available on technical obsolescence or regarding the number of years comparable units have been used before replacement was required.

The treatment following a change in estimated life can be illustrated with the previous example of the transfer of a depreciable asset from Peerless to Special Foods at the end of 19X1. If it is assumed that the asset is likely to have only 5, rather than 7, remaining years of useful life following its purchase by Special Foods, the eliminating entries will need to reflect a different pattern of adjustments for income recognition and correction of the balance sheet totals. Entries E(35) and E(36) were used at the end of 19X2 to eliminate the effects of the intercorporate sale when no change in economic life occurred. Use of entries E(35) and E(36) assumes the subsidiary's estimate of the remaining useful life of the transferred asset is the same as the 7-year remaining life based on the parent's original estimate. However, if the subsidiary estimates a different remaining life of the asset, this change in estimate requires that the remaining book value be amortized over the new estimated remaining life. Eliminating entries E(35b) and E(36b) are needed in the December 31, 19X2, consolidation workpaper when the remaining economic life of the transferred equipment is reduced from 7 to 5 years:

E(35b)	Buildings and Equipment	2,000	
	Retained Earnings, January 1	700	
	Accumulated Depreciation		2,700
	Eliminate unrealized gain on equipment.		
E(36b)	Accumulated Depreciation	140	
	Depreciation Expense		140
	Adjust depreciation for realization of intercompany gain.		

Because the asset transfer occurred on the last day of 19X1 and entry E(35b) is used to adjust the balances as of the beginning of 19X2, entry E(35b) is the same as entry E(35). Entry E(36b) corrects for excess depreciation in the amount of $140 ($700 ÷ 5 years), rather than $100 ($700 ÷ 7 years).

In a similar manner, entries E(37b) and E(38b) are needed at December 31, 19X3, in place of entries E(37) and E(38):

E(37b)	Buildings and Equipment	2,000	
	Retained Earnings, January 1	560	
	Accumulated Depreciation		2,560
	$560 = $700 − $140		
E(38b)	Accumulated Depreciation	140	
	Depreciation Expense		140

The additional depreciation charge of $40 per period recorded by Special Foods results in a more rapid realization of the unrealized profits from a consolidated perspective and, therefore, a smaller adjustment to retained earnings at the start of the period and to accumulated depreciation.

Upstream Sale

The treatment of unrealized profits arising from upstream intercompany sales is identical to that of downstream sales except that the unrealized profit, and subsequent realization, must be allocated between the controlling and non-controlling interests. The case of an upstream sale can be illustrated using the same example as for the downstream sale. Assume that Special Foods sells equipment to Peerless Products for $7,000 on December 31, 19X1, and reports total income for 19X1 of $50,700, including the $700 gain on the sale of the equipment. The equipment originally was purchased for $9,000 by Special Foods

3 years before the intercompany sale.[2] The book value of the equipment at the date of sale is as follows:

Original cost to Special Foods		$9,000
Accumulated depreciation on December 31, 19X1:		
Annual depreciation ($9,000 ÷ 10 years)	$900	
Number of years	× 3	
		(2,700)
Book value on December 31, 19X1		$6,300

Separate-Company Entries—19X1 Special Foods records depreciation on the equipment for the year and the sale of the equipment to Peerless on December 31, 19X1, with the following entries:

December 31, 19X1

(39)	Depreciation Expense	900	
	Accumulated Depreciation		900
	Record 19X1 depreciation expense on		
	equipment sold.		
(40)	Cash	7,000	
	Accumulated Depreciation	2,700	
	Equipment		9,000
	Gain on Sale of Equipment		700
	Record sale of equipment.		

Peerless records the purchase of the equipment from Special Foods with the following entry:

December 31, 19X1

(41)	Equipment	7,000	
	Cash		7,000
	Record purchase of equipment.		

In addition, Peerless records the following basic equity-method entries to recognize its share of Special Foods' reported income and dividends:

(42)	Investment in Special Foods Stock	40,560	
	Income from Subsidiary		40,560
	Record equity-method income:		
	($50,000 + $700) × .80		
(43)	Cash	24,000	
	Investment in Special Foods Stock		24,000
	Record dividends from Special Foods:		
	$30,000 × .80		

[2] To avoid additional complexity, the fair value of the equipment is assumed to be equal to its book value on the date of combination; there is, therefore, no purchase differential related to the equipment.

Consolidation Workpaper—19X1 The consolidation workpaper for 19X1 is presented in Figure 6-7. It is the same as that presented in Figure 6-5 except where modified to reflect the upstream sale of the equipment.

Four eliminating entries appear in the consolidation workpaper for 19X1:

E(44)	Income from Subsidiary	40,560	
	Dividends Declared		24,000
	Investment in Special Foods Stock		16,560
	Eliminate income from subsidiary.		
E(45)	Income to Noncontrolling Interest	10,000	
	Dividends Declared		6,000
	Noncontrolling Interest		4,000
	Assign income to noncontrolling interest:		
	$10,000 = ($50,700 − $700) × .20		
E(46)	Common Stock—Special Foods	200,000	
	Retained Earnings, January 1	100,000	
	Investment in Special Foods Stock		240,000
	Noncontrolling Interest		60,000
	Eliminate beginning investment balance.		
E(47)	Buildings and Equipment	2,000	
	Gain on Sale of Equipment	700	
	Accumulated Depreciation		2,700
	Eliminate unrealized gain on equipment.		

Entry E(44) is the normal workpaper entry to eliminate the income and dividends from Special Foods recorded by Peerless and is based on the amounts recorded by Peerless on its books during 19X1. Entry E(45) assigns income to the noncontrolling shareholders based on their share of Special Foods' realized income, computed as follows:

Net income of Special Foods for 19X1	$50,700
Unrealized gain on intercompany sale	(700)
Realized net income of Special Foods for 19X1	$50,000
Noncontrolling stockholders' proportionate share	× .20
Income to noncontrolling interest, 19X1	$10,000

In the upstream case, unrealized profits are allocated against both Peerless Products and the noncontrolling shareholders, both being owners of Special Foods.

FIGURE 6-7 December 31, 19X1, consolidation workpaper, period of intercompany sale; upstream sale of equipment.

Item	Peerless Products	Special Foods	Eliminations		Consolidated
			Debit	Credit	
Sales	400,000	200,000			600,000
Gain on Sale of Equipment		700	(47) 700		
Income from Subsidiary	40,560		(44) 40,560		
Credits	440,560	200,700			600,000
Cost of Goods Sold	170,000	115,000			285,000
Depreciation and Amortization	50,000	20,000			70,000
Other Expenses	40,000	15,000			55,000
Debits	(260,000)	(150,000)			(410,000)
					190,000
Income to Noncontrolling Interest			(45) 10,000		(10,000)
Net Income, carry forward	180,560	50,700	51,260		180,000
Retained Earnings, January 1	300,000	100,000	(46) 100,000		300,000
Net Income, from above	180,560	50,700	51,260		180,000
	480,560	150,700			480,000
Dividends Declared	(60,000)	(30,000)		(44) 24,000	
				(45) 6,000	(60,000)
Retained Earnings, December 31, carry forward	420,560	120,700	151,260	30,000	420,000
Cash	257,000	82,000			339,000
Accounts Receivable	75,000	50,000			125,000
Inventory	100,000	75,000			175,000
Land	175,000	40,000			215,000
Buildings and Equipment	807,000	591,000	(47) 2,000		1,400,000
Investment in Special Foods Stock	256,560			(44) 16,560	
				(46) 240,000	
Debits	1,670,560	838,000			2,254,000
Accumulated Depreciation	450,000	317,300		(47) 2,700	770,000
Accounts Payable	100,000	100,000			200,000
Bonds Payable	200,000	100,000			300,000
Common Stock	500,000	200,000	(46) 200,000		500,000
Retained Earnings, from above	420,560	120,700	151,260	30,000	420,000
Noncontrolling Interest				(45) 4,000	
				(46) 60,000	64,000
Credits	1,670,560	838,000	353,260	353,260	2,254,000

Elimination entries:
(44) Eliminate income from subsidiary.
(45) Assign income to noncontrolling interest.
(46) Eliminate beginning investment balance.
(47) Eliminate unrealized gain on equipment.

Assigning income of $10,000 to the noncontrolling interest in the Figure 6-7 workpaper leaves $180,000 as consolidated net income. Thus, consolidated net income is equal to Peerless's income from its own separate operations plus Peerless's share of Special Foods' realized net income:

Peerless's separate operating income	$140,000
Peerless's share of Special Foods' realized income [($50,700 − $700) × .80]	40,000
Consolidated net income, 19X1	$180,000

Eliminating entries E(46) and E(47) are identical to those used in the downstream case. Entry E(46) eliminates the investment account balance and subsidiary stockholders' equity balances on January 1, 19X1, and is not affected by the transfer. Entry E(47) eliminates the gain on the sale of the equipment and adjusts related account balances to their appropriate consolidated totals. This entry is not affected by the direction of the sale in the period in which the sale occurs and therefore is identical to E(28) in Figure 6-5.

Separate-Company Books—19X2   In the year following the intercorporate transfer, Special Foods reports net income of $75,900 (with the $900 of depreciation expense on the transferred asset now excluded). Peerless records the normal basic equity-method entries on its books to recognize its share of Special Foods' 19X2 income and dividends. At the end of 19X2, the investment account on Peerless's books appears as follows:

Investment in Special Foods Stock

	Original cost	240,000				
(42)	19X1 equity accrual ($50,700 × .80)	40,560	(43)	19X1 dividends ($30,000 × .80)	24,000	
	Balance, 12/31/X1	256,560				
	19X2 equity accrual ($75,900 × .80)	60,720		19X2 dividends ($40,000 × .80)	32,000	
	Balance, 12/31/X2	285,280				

Consolidation Elimination Entries—19X2   The elimination entries used in the preparation of consolidated financial statements for 19X2 are as follows:

E(48)	Income from Subsidiary	60,720	
	Dividends Declared		32,000
	Investment in Special Foods Stock		28,720
	Eliminate income from subsidiary:		
	$60,720 = $75,900 × .80		
E(49)	Income to Noncontrolling Interest	15,200	
	Dividends Declared		8,000
	Noncontrolling Interest		7,200
	Assign income to noncontrolling interest:		
	$15,200 = ($75,900 + $100) × .20		
E(50)	Common Stock—Special Foods	200,000	
	Retained Earnings, January 1	120,700	
	Investment in Special Foods Stock		256,560
	Noncontrolling Interest		64,140
	Eliminate beginning investment balance:		
	$256,560 = ($200,000 + $120,700) × .80		
	$64,140 = ($200,000 + $120,700) × .20		
E(51)	Buildings and Equipment	2,000	
	Retained Earnings, January 1	560	
	Noncontrolling Interest	140	
	Accumulated Depreciation		2,700
	Eliminate unrealized gain on upstream		
	sale of equipment.		
E(52)	Accumulated Depreciation	100	
	Depreciation Expense		100
	Adjust depreciation for realization of		
	intercompany gain.		

There is little difference between the elimination entries in the upstream and downstream cases in the second year, except that the amount of the unrealized intercompany gain at the beginning of the period is allocated proportionally between the controlling interest (retained earnings) and the noncontrolling interest in entry E(51); it was allocated entirely to the controlling interest in entry E(35) for the downstream case. The $700 unrealized gain on the upstream sale was eliminated proportionally against both the controlling and the noncontrolling interests at the end of 19X1. Therefore, the subsequent realization of the gain increases the interests of both the controlling interest and the noncontrolling shareholders.

The difference in the annual depreciation recorded by the purchasing affiliate, Peerless in this case, and the amount that would have been recorded by the selling affiliate, Special Foods, is $100:

Depreciation recorded by Peerless ($7,000 ÷ 7 years)	$1,000
Depreciation that would have been recorded by Special	
Foods if asset had not been transferred ($9,000 ÷ 10 years)	(900)
	$ 100

Entry E(52) adjusts depreciation expense and accumulated depreciation for this difference and has the effect of increasing total income by $100.

The $100 increase in income is viewed as resulting from the realization of a portion of the gain on the intercompany transfer. The $700 unrealized gain is considered realized at $100 per year over the 7-year period following the intercorporate transfer. As $100 of the gain is realized each year, the controlling interest is increased by $80, its 80 percent share, and the noncontrolling interest is increased by $20, its 20 percent share. Entry E(49) allocates a proportionate share of Special Foods' income to the noncontrolling interest and is based on Special Foods' reported income ($75,900) plus the portion of the intercompany gain considered realized during 19X2 ($100). The remaining $80 of realized gain accrues to the controlling interest and increases consolidated net income.

Entry E(50) is the normal entry to eliminate the investment account and subsidiary stockholders' equity balances as of the beginning of the year. The entry also assigns to the noncontrolling interest a pro rata portion of the subsidiary stockholders' equity balances ($320,700 × .20) as of the beginning of the year. This amount ($64,140), however, is greater than the actual amount assigned to the noncontrolling interest at the end of last period (Figure 6-7) by the $140 noncontrolling stockholders' share of the unrealized intercompany profit at the beginning of the period ($700 × .20). Entry E(51) reduces the noncontrolling interest by a proportionate share of the unrealized intercompany profit at the beginning of the year, and the two entries together establish the correct beginning balance of the noncontrolling interest.

Consolidated Net Income   Peerless Products' separate income for 19X2 is $159,000 after deducting an additional $1,000 for the depreciation on the transferred asset. Consolidated net income for 19X2 can be computed as follows:

Peerless's separate operating income		$159,000
Peerless's share of Special Foods' realized income:		
Special Foods' net income	$75,900	
Partial realization of intercompany gain on upstream sale	100	
Special Foods' realized income	$76,000	
Peerless's proportionate share	× .80	60,800
Consolidated net income, 19X2		$219,800

Noncontrolling Interest   The noncontrolling interest's share of income is $15,200 for 19X2, computed as the noncontrolling stockholders' proportionate share of the realized income of Special Foods ($76,000 × .20). Total noncontrolling interest is computed as the noncontrolling stockholders' proportionate share of the stockholders' equity of Special Foods, excluding unrealized gains and losses. On December 31, 19X2, the noncontrolling interest totals $71,200, computed as follows:

Book value of Special Foods, December 31, 19X2:

Common stock	$200,000
Retained earnings ($120,700 + $75,900 − $40,000)	156,600
Total book value	$356,600
Unrealized 19X1 intercompany gain on upstream sale	(700)
Intercompany gain realized in 19X2	100
Realized book value of Special Foods	$356,000
Noncontrolling stockholders' share	× .20
Noncontrolling interest, December 31, 19X2	$ 71,200

Asset Transfers before Year-End

In those cases where an intercorporate asset transfer occurs during a period rather than at the end, a portion of the intercompany gain or loss is considered realized in the period of the transfer. When this occurs, the workpaper eliminating entries at the end of the year must include an adjustment of depreciation expense and accumulated depreciation. The amount of this adjustment is equal to the difference between the depreciation recorded by the purchaser and that which would have been recorded by the seller during the portion of the year elapsing after the intercorporate sale.

If, for example, the upstream sale of equipment from Special Foods to Peerless occurred on January 1, 19X1, rather than on December 31, 19X1, an additional eliminating entry identical to E(52) would be needed in the consolidation workpaper prepared for December 31, 19X1.

ASSET TRANSFERS INVOLVING AMORTIZABLE ASSETS

Production rights, patents, and other types of intangible assets may be sold to affiliated enterprises. Intangible assets differ from tangible assets in two respects: (1) all intangible assets must be amortized over a period not in excess of 40 years, and (2) intangibles normally are reported at the remaining unamortized balance without the use of a contra account. Other than netting the accumulated amortization on an intangible asset against the asset cost, the intercompany sale of intangibles is treated the same in consolidation as the intercompany sale of tangible assets.

SUMMARY OF KEY CONCEPTS AND TERMS

Transactions between affiliated companies within a consolidated entity must be viewed as if they occurred within a single company. Under generally accepted accounting principles, the effects of transactions that are internal to an enterprise may not be included in external accounting reports. Therefore, the effects of all transactions between companies within the consolidated entity must be eliminated in preparing consolidated financial statements.

The elimination of intercompany transactions must include the removal of unrealized intercompany profits. When one company sells an asset to an affiliate within the consolidated entity, any intercompany profit is not considered realized until confirmed by subsequent events. If the asset has an unlimited life, as with land, the unrealized intercompany gain or loss is realized at the time the asset is resold to a party outside the consolidated entity. If the asset has a limited life, the unrealized intercompany gain or loss is considered to be realized over the remaining life of the asset as the asset is used and depreciated or amortized.

Consolidation procedures relating to unrealized gains and losses on intercompany transfers of assets involve workpaper adjustments to restate the assets and associated accounts, such as accumulated depreciation, to the balances that would be reported if there had been no intercompany transfer. In the period of transfer, the income assigned to the shareholders of the selling affiliate must be reduced by their share of the unrealized intercompany profit. If the sale is a downstream sale, the unrealized intercompany gain or loss is eliminated against the controlling interest. When an upstream sale occurs, the unrealized intercompany gain or loss is eliminated proportionately against the controlling and noncontrolling interests.

Downstream sale
Intercorporate transfers

Unrealized intercompany profit
Upstream sale

APPENDIX: Intercorporate Transfers of Noncurrent Assets—Fully Adjusted Equity Method and Cost Method

A parent company may account for a subsidiary using any of several methods. So long as the subsidiary is to be consolidated, the method of accounting for the subsidiary on the parent's books will have no impact on the consolidated financial statements. While the primary focus of Chapter 6 is on consolidation following use of the basic equity method on the parent's books, two other methods are used in practice with some frequency as well. These methods are the fully adjusted equity method and the cost method.

FULLY ADJUSTED EQUITY METHOD

A company that chooses to account for an investment using the fully adjusted equity method records its proportionate share of subsidiary income and dividends in the same manner as under the basic equity method. In addition, the investor's share of any unrealized profits from intercompany transactions is removed from the parent's income in the period of intercompany sale by reducing both the investment account and the income recognized from the investee. When the intercompany profits subsequently are realized, the investor increases both the investment account and the income recognized from the investee. With these adjustments, parent company net income will always equal consolidated net income.

To illustrate this, assume the same facts as in the upstream sale of equipment discussed previously and reflected in Figure 6-7. Special Foods sells equipment to Peerless Products for $7,000 on December 31, 19X1, and reports total income for 19X1 of $50,700, including the $700 gain on the sale of the equipment. The equipment originally was purchased for $9,000 by Special Foods 3 years before the intercompany sale. Both companies use straight-line depreciation.

As illustrated previously, Special Foods records 19X1 depreciation on the equipment and the gain on the December 31, 19X1, sale of the equipment to Peerless with the following entries:

December 31, 19X1
(53)	Depreciation Expense	900	
	Accumulated Depreciation		900
	Record 19X1 depreciation expense on equipment sold.		
(54)	Cash	7,000	
	Accumulated Depreciation	2,700	
	Equipment		9,000
	Gain on Sale of Equipment		700
	Record sale of equipment.		

Peerless records the purchase of the equipment from Special Foods with the following entry:

December 31, 19X1
(55)	Equipment	7,000	
	Cash		7,000
	Record purchase of equipment.		

Fully Adjusted Equity-Method Entries—19X1

In applying the fully adjusted equity method, Peerless recognizes its 80 percent share of Special Foods' income and dividends for 19X1 in the same way as under the basic equity method:

(56)	Investment in Special Foods Stock	40,560	
	Income from Subsidiary		40,560
	Record equity-method income:		
	$50,700 \times .80$		
(57)	Cash	24,000	
	Investment in Special Foods Stock		24,000
	Record dividends from Special Foods:		
	$30,000 \times .80$		

An additional entry is needed under the fully adjusted equity method to reduce income by Peerless's proportionate share of the $700 unrealized intercompany gain:

(58)   Income from Subsidiary   560
      Investment in Special Foods Stock   560
      Remove unrealized gain on sale of
      equipment: $700 × .80

This entry is consistent with the idea of a "one-line consolidation" and assures that the parent's equity-method net income is equal to consolidated net income.

Entries (56) and (58) together record total income from Special Foods of $40,000. This amount is equal to Peerless's share of the realized net income of Special Foods, computed as follows:

Reported net income of Special Foods for 19X1	$50,700
Unrealized gain on intercompany sale	(700)
Realized net income of Special Foods for 19X1	$50,000
Peerless's proportionate share	× .80
Peerless's income from Special Foods, 19X1	$40,000

Because the intercompany sale is an upstream sale, only the parent's share of the unrealized gain is deducted in deriving equity-method net income. If the sale were downstream, the full $700 amount of the unrealized gain would be deducted from the parent's income.

After the equity-method adjustments for December 31, 19X1, the investment account has a balance of $256,000:

Original purchase price of Special Foods stock	$240,000
Peerless's proportionate share of Special Foods' income ($50,700 × .80)	40,560
Peerless's share of Special Foods' dividends ($30,000 × .80)	(24,000)
Peerless's share of unrealized gain ($700 × .80)	(560)
Balance of investment account, December 31, 19X1	$256,000

It is important to note that at the end of 19X1 Peerless's income and the investment account both are lower than if the basic equity method had been used to account for the investment in Special Foods. The $560 difference is equal to Peerless's share of the unrealized intercompany gain ($700 × .80).

Consolidation Workpaper—19X1

The consolidation workpaper prepared as of December 31, 19X1, is presented in Figure 6-8. It is the same as that presented in Figure 6-7, except where modified to reflect use of the fully adjusted equity method.

FIGURE 6-8 December 31, 19X1, fully adjusted equity-method consolidation workpaper, period of intercompany sale; upstream sale of equipment.

Item	Peerless Products	Special Foods	Eliminations Debit	Eliminations Credit	Consolidated
Sales	400,000	200,000			600,000
Gain on Sale of Equipment		700	(62) 700		
Income from Subsidiary	40,000		(59) 40,000		
Credits	440,000	200,700			600,000
Cost of Goods Sold	170,000	115,000			285,000
Depreciation and Amortization	50,000	20,000			70,000
Other Expenses	40,000	15,000			55,000
Debits	(260,000)	(150,000)			(410,000)
					190,000
Income to Noncontrolling Interest			(60) 10,000		(10,000)
Net Income, carry forward	180,000	50,700	50,700		180,000
Retained Earnings, January 1	300,000	100,000	(61) 100,000		300,000
Net Income, from above	180,000	50,700	50,700		180,000
	480,000	150,700			480,000
Dividends Declared	(60,000)	(30,000)		(59) 24,000	
				(60) 6,000	(60,000)
Retained Earnings, December 31, carry forward	420,000	120,700	150,700	30,000	420,000
Cash	257,000	82,000			339,000
Accounts Receivable	75,000	50,000			125,000
Inventory	100,000	75,000			175,000
Land	175,000	40,000			215,000
Buildings and Equipment	807,000	591,000	(62) 2,000		1,400,000
Investment in Special Foods Stock	256,000			(59) 16,000	
				(61) 240,000	
Debits	1,670,000	838,000			2,254,000
Accumulated Depreciation	450,000	317,300		(62) 2,700	770,000
Accounts Payable	100,000	100,000			200,000
Bonds Payable	200,000	100,000			300,000
Common Stock	500,000	200,000	(61) 200,000		500,000
Retained Earnings, from above	420,000	120,700	150,700	30,000	420,000
Noncontrolling Interest				(60) 4,000	
				(61) 60,000	64,000
Credits	1,670,000	838,000	352,700	352,700	2,254,000

Elimination entries:
(59) Eliminate income from subsidiary.
(60) Assign income to noncontrolling interest.
(61) Eliminate beginning investment balance.
(62) Eliminate unrealized gain on equipment.

Four eliminating entries appear in the consolidation workpaper prepared as of December 31, 19X1:

E(59)	Income from Subsidiary	40,000	
	Dividends Declared		24,000
	Investment in Special Foods Stock		16,000
	Eliminate income from subsidiary.		
E(60)	Income to Noncontrolling Interest	10,000	
	Dividends Declared		6,000
	Noncontrolling Interest		4,000
	Assign income to noncontrolling interest:		
	$10,000 = ($50,700 − $700) × .20$		
E(61)	Common Stock—Special Foods	200,000	
	Retained Earnings, January 1	100,000	
	Investment in Special Foods Stock		240,000
	Noncontrolling Interest		60,000
	Eliminate beginning investment balance.		
E(62)	Buildings and Equipment	2,000	
	Gain on Sale of Equipment	700	
	Accumulated Depreciation		2,700
	Eliminate unrealized gain on equipment.		

All these entries are the same as those in Figure 6-7 prepared following use of the basic equity method, except for entry E(59). This entry eliminates the income recorded by Peerless under the equity method and differs from entry E(44) in Figure 6-7 by the amount of the unrealized profit adjustment recorded by Peerless with entry (58). The remainder of the workpaper is completed the same way as when the basic equity method is used.

Although entry (58) removed a pro rata share of the unrealized gain from the income reported on Peerless's books, it did not eliminate the gain from consolidated net income. Entry (58) changes only the amount of income from the subsidiary recognized by Peerless and the balance in the investment account. These balances, in turn, are eliminated by entries E(59) and E(61). The gain account entered on Special Foods' books at the time the equipment is sold is unaffected by the entries recorded by Peerless and, therefore, carries over to the consolidation workpaper unless eliminated. Entry E(62) is needed to prevent the gain from appearing in the consolidated income statement.

Note that in the workpaper shown in Figure 6-8, the parent's net income is equal to consolidated net income and the parent's retained earnings is equal to consolidated retained earnings.

Fully Adjusted Equity-Method Entries—19X2

In 19X2, Peerless records its share of Special Foods' $75,900 income and $40,000 of dividends with the following entries:

(63)	Investment in Special Foods Stock	60,720	
	Income from Subsidiary		60,720
	Record equity-method income:		
	$75,900 × .80		
(64)	Cash	32,000	
	Investment in Special Foods Stock		32,000
	Record dividends from Special Foods:		
	$40,000 × .80		

An additional entry is recorded by Peerless under the fully adjusted equity method to increase income for the partial realization of the unrealized intercompany gain:

(65)	Investment in Special Foods Stock	80	
	Income from Subsidiary		80
	Recognize portion of gain on sale of		
	equipment: ($700 ÷ 7 years) × .80		

The gain on the 19X1 intercompany transfer is viewed as being realized over a 7-year period. The $100 of intercompany gain realized each year is equal to the difference between the amount of depreciation recorded by Peerless for 19X2 ($1,000) and the amount that would have been recorded by Special Foods had there been no intercompany transfer ($900). Because depreciation expense will be adjusted in the preparation of consolidated financial statements to the amount that would have been reported if there had been no intercompany transfer, total income in the workpaper will be increased by $100. This increase will be allocated between the controlling and noncontrolling interests in the upstream case, leading to an increase of $80 ($100 × .80) in consolidated net income.

Entry (65) adds into Peerless's equity-method income a proportionate share of the part of the gain considered realized during 19X2. Recall that Peerless's 19X1 income was reduced by a proportionate share of the unrealized gain. Therefore, Peerless's portion of the realized part of the gain ($100 × .80) is put back into Peerless's income and the investment account in 19X2. Consistent with the idea of a one-line consolidation, entry (65) makes Peerless's fully adjusted equity-method net income equal to consolidated net income.

Consolidation Workpaper—19X2

The consolidation workpaper for 19X2 is shown in Figure 6-9. The following elimination entries are included in the workpaper:

FIGURE 6-9 December 31, 19X2, fully adjusted equity-method consolidation workpaper, next period following intercompany sale; upstream sale of equipment.

Item	Peerless Products	Special Foods	Eliminations Debit		Eliminations Credit		Consolidated
Sales	450,000	300,000					750,000
Income from Subsidiary	60,800		(66)	60,800			
Credits	510,800	300,000					750,000
Cost of Goods Sold	180,000	160,000					340,000
Depreciation and Amortization	51,000	19,100			(70)	100	70,000
Other Expenses	60,000	45,000					105,000
Debits	(291,000)	(224,100)					(515,000)
							235,000
Income to Noncontrolling Interest			(67)	15,200			(15,200)
Net Income, carry forward	219,800	75,900		76,000		100	219,800
Retained Earnings, January 1	420,000	120,700	(68)	120,700			420,000
Net Income, from above	219,800	75,900		76,000		100	219,800
	639,800	196,600					639,800
Dividends Declared	(60,000)	(40,000)			(66)	32,000	
					(67)	8,000	(60,000)
Retained Earnings, December 31, carry forward	579,800	156,600		196,700		40,100	579,800
Cash	284,000	92,000					376,000
Accounts Receivable	150,000	80,000					230,000
Inventory	180,000	90,000					270,000
Land	175,000	40,000					215,000
Buildings and Equipment	807,000	591,000	(69)	2,000			1,400,000
Investment in Special Foods Stock	284,800		(69)	560	(66)	28,800	
					(68)	256,560	
Debits	1,880,800	893,000					2,491,000
Accumulated Depreciation	501,000	336,400	(70)	100	(69)	2,700	840,000
Accounts Payable	100,000	100,000					200,000
Bonds Payable	200,000	100,000					300,000
Common Stock	500,000	200,000	(68)	200,000			500,000
Retained Earnings, from above	579,800	156,600		196,700		40,100	579,800
Noncontrolling Interest			(69)	140	(67)	7,200	
					(68)	64,140	71,200
Credits	1,880,800	893,000		399,500		399,500	2,491,000

Elimination entries:
(66) Eliminate income from subsidiary.
(67) Assign income to noncontrolling interest.
(68) Eliminate beginning investment balance.
(69) Eliminate unrealized gain on equipment.
(70) Adjust depreciation for realization of intercompany gain.

E(66)	Income from Subsidiary	60,800	
	Dividends Declared		32,000
	Investment in Special Foods Stock		28,800
	Eliminate income from subsidiary:		
	$60,800 = ($75,900 + $100) \times .80$		
E(67)	Income to Noncontrolling Interest	15,200	
	Dividends Declared		8,000
	Noncontrolling Interest		7,200
	Assign income to noncontrolling interest:		
	$15,200 = ($75,900 + $100) \times .20$		
E(68)	Common Stock—Special Foods	200,000	
	Retained Earnings, January 1	120,700	
	Investment in Special Foods Stock		256,560
	Noncontrolling Interest		64,140
	Eliminate beginning investment balance:		
	$256,560 = ($200,000 + $120,700) \times .80$		
	$64,140 = ($200,000 + $120,700) \times .20$		
E(69)	Buildings and Equipment	2,000	
	Investment in Special Foods Stock	560	
	Noncontrolling Interest	140	
	Accumulated Depreciation		2,700
	Eliminate unrealized gain on upstream sale of equipment.		
E(70)	Accumulated Depreciation	100	
	Depreciation Expense		100
	Adjust depreciation for realization of intercompany gain.		

These entries are the same as the eliminating entries used following application of the basic equity method, with two differences. First, entry E(66) eliminates Special Foods' income and dividends recognized by Peerless. Because the income recognized by Peerless under the fully adjusted equity method includes Peerless's share of the realized 19X1 intercompany gain, which is not included when using the basic equity method, the income elimination is $80 ($100 \times .80$) greater following use of the fully adjusted equity method.

The second difference is in entry E(69). When the basic equity method is used, the parent's share of the intercompany gain unrealized at the beginning of 19X2 is included in its retained earnings and must be eliminated when consolidating. This was accomplished in the basic equity illustration through entry E(51). When the fully adjusted equity method is used, however, the parent's share of the unrealized gain is deducted from income on the parent's books in the year of the intercompany transfer and subsequently is not included in retained earnings. Therefore, no additional elimination of retained earnings is needed.

Replacing the debit to Retained Earnings in entry E(51) is a debit to the investment account in entry E(69). Because the investment account is reduced at the same time that the unrealized income is deducted from the parent's income, eliminating entry E(68), which credits the investment account for an amount equal to the parent's proportionate share of the beginning subsidiary stockholders' equity balances, eliminates an amount greater than the actual beginning investment account balance. The additional amount is equal to the parent's share of the intercompany gain unrealized at the beginning of the year. Entry E(69) debits the investment account for that amount, and the two entries together, E(68) and E(69), fully eliminate the beginning balance of the investment.

All other eliminations are the same under both the basic and the fully adjusted equity methods.

COST METHOD

When using the cost method of accounting for an investment in a subsidiary, the parent records dividends received from the subsidiary during the period as income. No entries are made under the cost method to record the parent's share of undistributed subsidiary earnings, to amortize differential, or to remove unrealized intercompany profits.

To illustrate consolidation following an intercompany sale of equipment when the parent accounts for its subsidiary investment using the cost method, assume the same facts as in previous illustrations of an upstream sale.

Consolidation Workpaper—19X1

The workpaper illustrated in Figure 6-10 is used in preparing consolidated financial statements for 19X1 following the upstream sale of equipment to Peerless by Special Foods. The following elimination entries appear in the workpaper, assuming Peerless uses the cost method to account for its investment:

E(71)	Dividend Income	24,000	
	Dividends Declared		24,000
	Eliminate dividend income from subsidiary:		
	$30,000 \times .80$		
E(72)	Income to Noncontrolling Interest	10,000	
	Dividends Declared		6,000
	Noncontrolling Interest		4,000
	Assign income to noncontrolling interest:		
	$10,000 = (\$50,700 - \$700) \times .20$		
E(73)	Common Stock—Special Foods	200,000	
	Retained Earnings, January 1	100,000	
	Investment in Special Foods Stock		240,000
	Noncontrolling Interest		60,000
	Eliminate investment balance at date of acquisition.		
E(74)	Buildings and Equipment	2,000	
	Gain on Sale of Equipment	700	
	Accumulated Depreciation		2,700
	Eliminate unrealized gain on equipment.		

Entry E(71) eliminates Peerless's share of Special Foods' 19X1 dividends. All other eliminating entries are the same as under the basic equity method.

FIGURE 6-10 December 31, 19X1, cost-method consolidation workpaper, period of intercompany sale; upstream sale of equipment.

Item	Peerless Products	Special Foods	Eliminations Debit		Eliminations Credit		Consolidated
Sales	400,000	200,000					600,000
Gain on Sale of Equipment		700	(74)	700			
Dividend Income	24,000		(71)	24,000			
Credits	424,000	200,700					600,000
Cost of Goods Sold	170,000	115,000					285,000
Depreciation and Amortization	50,000	20,000					70,000
Other Expenses	40,000	15,000					55,000
Debits	(260,000)	(150,000)					(410,000)
							190,000
Income to Noncontrolling Interest			(72)	10,000			(10,000)
Net Income, carry forward	164,000	50,700		34,700			180,000
Retained Earnings, January 1	300,000	100,000	(73)	100,000			300,000
Net Income, from above	164,000	50,700		34,700			180,000
	464,000	150,700					480,000
Dividends Declared	(60,000)	(30,000)			(71)	24,000	
					(72)	6,000	(60,000)
Retained Earnings, December 31, carry forward	404,000	120,700		134,700		30,000	420,000
Cash	257,000	82,000					339,000
Accounts Receivable	75,000	50,000					125,000
Inventory	100,000	75,000					175,000
Land	175,000	40,000					215,000
Buildings and Equipment	807,000	591,000	(74)	2,000			1,400,000
Investment in Special Foods Stock	240,000				(73)	240,000	
Debits	1,654,000	838,000					2,254,000
Accumulated Depreciation	450,000	317,300			(74)	2,700	770,000
Accounts Payable	100,000	100,000					200,000
Bonds Payable	200,000	100,000					300,000
Common Stock	500,000	200,000	(73)	200,000			500,000
Retained Earnings, from above	404,000	120,700		134,700		30,000	420,000
Noncontrolling Interest					(72)	4,000	
					(73)	60,000	64,000
Credits	1,654,000	838,000		336,700		336,700	2,254,000

Elimination entries:
(71) Eliminate dividend income from subsidiary.
(72) Assign income to noncontrolling interest.
(73) Eliminate investment balance at date of acquisition.
(74) Eliminate unrealized gain on equipment.

Consolidation Workpaper—19X2

The consolidation workpaper prepared for December 31, 19X2, is presented in Figure 6-11. The following eliminating entries are needed in the workpaper:

E(75)	Dividend Income	32,000	
	Dividends Declared		32,000
	Eliminate dividend income from subsidiary:		
	$40,000 × .80		
E(76)	Income to Noncontrolling Interest	15,200	
	Dividends Declared		8,000
	Noncontrolling Interest		7,200
	Assign income to noncontrolling interest:		
	$15,200 = ($75,900 + $100) × .20		
E(77)	Common Stock—Special Foods	200,000	
	Retained Earnings, January 1	100,000	
	Investment in Special Foods Stock		240,000
	Noncontrolling Interest		60,000
	Eliminate investment balance at date of		
	acquisition.		
E(78)	Retained Earnings, January 1	4,140	
	Noncontrolling Interest		4,140
	Assign undistributed prior earnings		
	of subsidiary to noncontrolling		
	interest: ($120,700-$100,000) × .20		
E(79)	Buildings and Equipment	2,000	
	Retained Earnings, January 1	560	
	Noncontrolling Interest	140	
	Accumulated Depreciation		2,700
	Eliminate unrealized gain on equipment.		
E(80)	Accumulated Depreciation	100	
	Depreciation Expense		100
	Adjust depreciation for realization of		
	intercompany gain.		

Entry E(75) eliminates Peerless's share of Special Foods' dividends. Entry E(76) assigns income to the noncontrolling interest in the normal manner, taking into consideration a proportionate share of the $100 of intercompany gain considered realized during 19X2. The investment elimination entry normally does not change under the cost method, because the carrying amount of the investment does not change. Therefore, entry E(77) is the same as the investment elimination entry in 19X1. However, an additional entry, E(78), is needed to assign a proportionate share of Special Foods' undistributed prior years' income since the date of combination to the noncontrolling interest [($50,700 − $30,000) × .20]. The portion of beginning retained earnings that is neither eliminated nor assigned to the noncontrolling interest carries over in the workpaper to the consolidated column as the beginning balance of consolidated retained earnings.

Entries E(79) and E(80) eliminate the effects of the intercompany transfer and are the same as when consolidation follows use of the basic equity method.

FIGURE 6-11 December 31, 19X2, cost-method consolidation workpaper, next period following intercompany sale; upstream sale of equipment.

Item	Peerless Products	Special Foods	Eliminations		Consolidated
			Debit	Credit	
Sales	450,000	300,000			750,000
Dividend Income	32,000		(75) 32,000		
Credits	482,000	300,000			750,000
Cost of Goods Sold	180,000	160,000			340,000
Depreciation and Amortization	51,000	19,100		(80) 100	70,000
Other Expenses	60,000	45,000			105,000
Debits	(291,000)	(224,100)			(515,000)
					235,000
Income to Noncontrolling Interest			(76) 15,200		(15,200)
Net Income, carry forward	191,000	75,900	47,200	100	219,800
Retained Earnings, January 1	404,000	120,700	(77) 100,000		
			(78) 4,140		
			(79) 560		420,000
Net Income, from above	191,000	75,900	47,200	100	219,800
	595,000	196,600			639,800
Dividends Declared	(60,000)	(40,000)		(75) 32,000	
				(76) 8,000	(60,000)
Retained Earnings, December 31, carry forward	535,000	156,600	151,900	40,100	579,800
Cash	284,000	92,000			376,000
Accounts Receivable	150,000	80,000			230,000
Inventory	180,000	90,000			270,000
Land	175,000	40,000			215,000
Buildings and Equipment	807,000	591,000	(79) 2,000		1,400,000
Investment in Special Foods Stock	240,000			(77) 240,000	
Debits	1,836,000	893,000			2,491,000
Accumulated Depreciation	501,000	336,400	(80) 100	(79) 2,700	840,000
Accounts Payable	100,000	100,000			200,000
Bonds Payable	200,000	100,000			300,000
Common Stock	500,000	200,000	(77) 200,000		500,000
Retained Earnings, from above	535,000	156,600	151,900	40,100	579,800
Noncontrolling Interest			(79) 140	(76) 7,200	
				(77) 60,000	
				(78) 4,140	71,200
Credits	1,836,000	893,000	354,140	354,140	2,491,000

Elimination entries:
(75) Eliminate dividend income from subsidiary.
(76) Assign income to noncontrolling interest.
(77) Eliminate investment balance at date of acquisition.
(78) Assign undistributed prior earnings of subsidiary to noncontrolling interest.
(79) Eliminate unrealized gain on equipment.
(80) Adjust depreciation for realization of intercompany gain.

QUESTIONS

Q6-1   When are profits on intercorporate sales considered to be realized?

Q6-2   What is an upstream sale? Which company may have unrealized profits on its books in an upstream sale?

Q6-3   How are unrealized profits on current-period intercorporate sales treated in preparing the income statement for **(a)** the selling company and **(b)** the consolidated entity?

Q6-4   How are unrealized profits treated in the consolidated income statement if the intercorporate sale occurred in a prior period and the transferred item is sold to a nonaffiliate in the current period?

Q6-5   How are unrealized intercorporate profits treated in the consolidated statements if the intercorporate sale occurred in a prior period and the profits have not been realized by the end of the current period?

Q6-6   What is a downstream sale? Which company may have unrealized profits on its books in a downstream sale?

Q6-7   What portion of the unrealized intercorporate profit is eliminated in a downstream sale? In an upstream sale?

Q6-8   How is the effect of unrealized intercorporate profits on consolidated net income different between an upstream and a downstream sale?

Q6-9   Unrealized profits from a prior-year upstream sale were realized in the current period. What effect will this event have on income assigned to the noncontrolling interest in the consolidated income statement for the current period?

Q6-10   A subsidiary sold a depreciable asset to the parent company at a profit in the current period. Will the income assigned to the noncontrolling interest in the consolidated income statement for the current period be greater than, less than, or equal to a proportionate share of the reported net income of the subsidiary? Why?

Q6-11   A subsidiary sold a depreciable asset to the parent company at a profit of $1,000 in the current period. Will the income assigned to the noncontrolling interest in the consolidated income statement for the current period be larger if the intercorporate sale occurs on January 1 or on December 31? Why?

Q6-12   If a company sells a depreciable asset to its subsidiary at a profit on December 31, 19X3, what account balances must be eliminated or adjusted in preparing the consolidated income statement for 19X3?

Q6-13   If the sale in the preceding question occurs on January 1, 19X3, what additional account will require adjustment in preparing the consolidated income statement?

Q6-14   In the period in which an intercorporate sale occurs, how do the consolidation eliminating entries differ when unrealized profits pertain to an intangible asset rather than a tangible asset?

Q6-15   When is unrealized profit on an intercompany sale of land considered realized? When is profit on an intercompany sale of equipment considered realized? Why do the treatments differ?

Q6-16   In the elimination of a prior-period unrealized intercorporate gain on depreciable assets, why does the debit to retained earnings decrease over time?

Q6-17A A parent company may use on its books one of several different methods of accounting for its ownership of a subsidiary: **(a)** cost method, **(b)** basic equity method, or **(c)** fully adjusted equity method. How will the choice of method affect the reported balance in the investment account when there are unrealized intercorporate profits on the parent's books at the end of the period?

CASES

C6-1   Historical Cost Model

The consolidation process is intended to adjust the reported amounts of items transferred between related companies back to their original acquisition costs. Such procedures are appropriate so long as original acquisition cost is the primary basis of asset valuation.

Required

How might the elimination of profit on an intercorporate sale of land or depreciable assets change if replacement cost accounting was substituted for the original acquisition cost basis currently in use?

C6-2   Impact of the Elimination Process

The elimination process used in consolidation is intended to remove all unrealized intercorporate profits from the various asset categories.

Required

a. How might companies determine if there are unrealized intercorporate profits at year-end?

b. What problems occur if unrealized intercorporate profits are not eliminated?

c. Will the adjustment process for unrealized intercorporate profits always result in a reduction of net income? Explain.

C6-3   Noncontrolling Interest

Current reporting standards require the consolidated entity to include all the revenue, expenses, assets, and liabilities of the parent and its subsidiaries in the consolidated financial statements. In those cases where the parent does not own all of a subsidiary's shares, various rules and procedures exist with regard to the assignment of income and net assets to noncontrolling shareholders and the way in which the noncontrolling interest is to be reported.

Required

a. How is the amount of income assigned to noncontrolling shareholders in the consolidated income statement computed if there are no unrealized intercorporate profits on the subsidiary's books?

b. How is the amount reported for the noncontrolling interest in the consolidated balance sheet computed if there are no unrealized intercorporate profits on the subsidiary's books?

c. What effect do unrealized intercorporate profits have on the computation of income assigned to the noncontrolling interest if the profits arose from a transfer of (**1**) land or (**2**) equipment?

d. Are the noncontrolling shareholders of a subsidiary likely to find the amounts assigned to them in the consolidated financial statements useful? Explain.

C6-4 Intercompany Sale of Services

Diamond Manufacturing Company regularly purchases janitorial and maintenance services from its wholly owned subsidiary, Schwartz Maintenance Services, Inc. Schwartz bills Diamond monthly at its regular rates for the services provided, with the services consisting primarily of cleaning, groundskeeping, and small repairs. The cost of providing the services that Schwartz sells consists mostly of salaries and associated labor costs that total about 60 percent of the amount billed. Diamond issues consolidated financial statements annually.

Required

a. When Diamond prepares consolidated financial statements, what account balances of Diamond and Schwartz related to the intercompany sales of services must be adjusted or eliminated in the consolidation workpaper? What impact do these adjustments or eliminations have on consolidated net income?

b. In the case of intercompany sales of services at a profit, at what point in time are the intercompany profits considered to be realized? Explain.

EXERCISES

E6-1 Multiple-Choice Questions on Intercompany Transactions

Select the correct answer for each of the following questions.

1. Upper Company holds 60 percent of the voting shares of Lower Company. During the preparation of consolidated financial statements for 19X5, the following eliminating entry was made:

Retained Earnings, January 1	10,000	
Land		10,000

Which of the following statements is correct?
a. Upper Company purchased land from Lower Company during 19X5.
b. Upper Company purchased land from Lower Company before January 1, 19X5.
c. Lower Company purchased land from Upper Company during 19X5.
d. Lower Company purchased land from Upper Company before January 1, 19X5.

2. Middle Company holds 60 percent of the voting shares of Bottom Corporation. Bottom Corporation has developed a new type of production equipment that appears to be quite marketable. Bottom Corporation spent $40,000 in developing the equipment; however, Middle Company agreed to purchase the production rights for the machine for $100,000. If the intercompany sale occurred on January 1, 19X2, and the production rights are expected to have value for 5 years, at what amount should the rights be reported in the consolidated balance sheet for December 31, 19X2?
a. $0.
b. $32,000.
c. $80,000.
d. $100,000.

Questions 3 through 6 are based on the following information:

On January 1, 19X4, Gold Company purchased a computer with an expected economic life of 5 years. On January 1, 19X6, Gold Company sold the computer to Silver Corporation and recorded the following entry:

Cash	39,000	
Accumulated Depreciation	16,000	
Computer Equipment		40,000
Gain on Sale of Equipment		15,000

Silver Corporation holds 60 percent of the voting shares of Gold Company. Gold Company reported net income of $45,000, and Silver Corporation reported income from its own operations of $85,000 for 19X6. There is no change in the estimated economic life of the equipment as a result of the intercorporate transfer.

3. In the preparation of the 19X6 consolidated income statement, depreciation expense will be:
   a. Debited for $5,000 in the eliminating entries.
   b. Credited for $5,000 in the eliminating entries.
   c. Debited for $13,000 in the eliminating entries.
   d. Credited for $13,000 in the eliminating entries.

4. In the preparation of the 19X6 consolidated balance sheet, computer equipment will be:
   a. Debited for $1,000.
   b. Debited for $15,000.
   c. Credited for $24,000.
   d. Debited for $40,000.

5. Income assigned to the noncontrolling interest in the 19X6 consolidated income statement will be:
   a. $12,000.
   b. $14,000.
   c. $18,000.
   d. $52,000.

6. Consolidated net income for 19X6 will be:
   a. $103,000.
   b. $106,000.
   c. $112,000.
   d. $130,000.

E6-2 Elimination Entries for Land Transfer

Huckster Corporation purchased land on January 1, 19X1, for $20,000. On June 10, 19X4, Huckster sold the land to its subsidiary, Lowly Corporation, for $30,000. Huckster Corporation owns 60 percent of the voting shares of Lowly Corporation.

Required

a. Give the workpaper eliminating entries needed to remove the effects of the intercompany sale of land in preparing the consolidated financial statements for 19X4 and 19X5.

b. Give the workpaper eliminating entries needed on December 31, 19X4 and 19X5, if the land had initially been purchased by Lowly Corporation for $20,000 and sold to Huckster Corporation on June 10, 19X4, for $30,000.

E6-3 Elimination Entries for Depreciable Asset Transfer: Year-End Sale

Sparkle Corporation holds 70 percent ownership of Playtime Enterprises. On December 31, 19X6, Playtime paid Sparkle $40,000 for a truck that had been purchased by Sparkle for $45,000 on January 1, 19X2. The truck was considered to have a 15-year life from January 1, 19X2, and no residual value. Both companies depreciate equipment using the straight-line method.

Required

a. Give the workpaper eliminating entry or entries needed on December 31, 19X6, to remove the effects of the intercompany sale.

b. Give the workpaper eliminating entry or entries needed on December 31, 19X7, to remove the effects of the intercompany sale.

E6-4 Elimination Entries for Depreciable Asset Transfer: Beginning-of-Year Sale

Sparkle Corporation holds 70 percent ownership of Playtime Enterprises. On January 1, 19X6, Playtime Enterprises paid Sparkle Corporation $40,000 for a truck that Sparkle Corporation had purchased for $45,000 on January 1, 19X2. The truck has a 15-year total economic life and no residual value. Both companies use straight-line depreciation.

Required

a. Give the eliminating entry or entries in the consolidation workpaper prepared as of December 31, 19X6, to remove the effects of the intercompany sale.

b. Give the eliminating entry or entries in the consolidation workpaper prepared as of December 31, 19X7, to remove the effects of the intercompany sale.

E6-5 Elimination Entries for Midyear Depreciable Asset Transfer

Albion Corporation holds 90 percent ownership of Andrews Company. On July 1, 19X3, Albion Corporation sold equipment that it had purchased for $30,000 on January 1, 19X1, to Andrews Company for $28,000. The original 6-year estimated total economic life of the equipment remains unchanged. Both companies use straight-line depreciation. The residual value of the equipment is considered negligible.

Required

a. Give the eliminating entry or entries in the consolidation workpaper prepared as of December 31, 19X3, to remove the effects of the intercompany sale.

b. Give the eliminating entry or entries in the consolidation workpaper prepared as of December 31, 19X4, to remove the effects of the intercompany sale.

E6-6 Computation of Consolidated Net Income

Redburn Corporation reported income on sales to customers of $350,000 in 19X8. In addition, Redburn owns 60 percent of the stock of Sundale Corporation, which reported income for 19X8 of $70,000 from its manufacturing activities. On November 10, 19X8, Sundale Corporation sold land costing $40,000 to Redburn Corporation for $90,000 for use as a new plant site.

Required

a. Compute consolidated net income for 19X8.

b. If Redburn Corporation had purchased the land for $40,000 and sold it to Sundale Corporation for $90,000, what amount of consolidated net income would be reported for 19X8?

E6-7 Elimination Entries for Intercompany Transfers

Speedy Delivery Service owns 80 percent of the voting shares of Acme Real Estate Company. During 19X3 Speedy Delivery provided courier services for Acme Real Estate in the amount of $15,000. Also during 19X3, Acme Real Estate purchased land for $1,000. The land was then sold to Speedy Delivery Service for $26,000 so that Speedy Delivery could proceed with building a new transportation center. Speedy Delivery reported $65,000 of operating income from its delivery operations in 19X3. Acme Real Estate reported net income of $40,000 and paid dividends of $10,000 in 19X3.

Required

a. Compute consolidated net income for 19X3.

b. Give all journal entries recorded by Speedy Delivery Service related to its investment in Acme Real Estate assuming Speedy uses the basic equity method in accounting for the investment.

c. Give all eliminating entries required in preparing a consolidation workpaper as of December 31, 19X3.

E6-8 Transfers through Multiple Entities

Bannister Corporation exercises control of the following companies:

Subsidiary	Level of Ownership	19X8 Net Income
Smith Company	75 percent	$100,000
Jones Corporation	60 percent	150,000
Olson Corporation	80 percent	50,000

As best the management of Bannister Corporation can ascertain, the following land transfers occurred in 19X8. On January 3, 19X8, Smith Company purchased a plot of land for $50,000 and sold it to Jones Corporation for $90,000 the following week. In March 19X8, Olson Corporation purchased the land from Jones Corporation for $160,000. On November 30, 19X8, Olson Corporation sold the land to Bannister Corporation for $130,000.

Required

    a. What amount of gain or loss on the sale of land should be reported in the 19X8 consolidated income statement?

    b. At what amount, if any, should land be reported in the consolidated balance sheet as of December 31, 19X8?

    c. If Bannister Corporation reported income from its separate operations of $200,000 for 19X8, what amount of consolidated net income should be reported for the year?

    d. Give any elimination entries related to the land that should appear in the workpaper used to prepare consolidated financial statements for 19X8.

E6-9 Elimination Entry Computation

Stern Manufacturing purchased an ultrasound drilling machine with a remaining economic life of 10 years from a 70 percent–owned subsidiary for $360,000 on January 1, 19X6. Both companies use straight-line depreciation. The subsidiary recorded the following entry when it sold the machine to Stern Manufacturing:

Cash	360,000	
Accumulated Depreciation	150,000	
Equipment		450,000
Gain on Sale of Equipment		60,000

Required

Give the workpaper elimination entry or entries needed to remove the effects of the intercorporate sale of equipment when consolidated financial statements are prepared as of **(a)** December 31, 19X6, and **(b)** December 31, 19X7.

E6-10 Intercompany Sale of Services

Norgaard Corporation is provided with management consulting services by its 75 percent–owned subsidiary, Bline, Inc. During 19X3, Bline billed Norgaard $123,200 for the services provided. For the year 19X4, Bline billed Norgaard $138,700 for such services and collected all but $6,600 by year-end. Bline's labor cost and other associated costs for the employees providing services to Norgaard totaled $91,000 in 19X3 and $112,000 in 19X4. Norgaard reported $2,342,000 of income from its own separate operations for 19X4, and Bline reported net income of $631,000.

Required

    a. Present all elimination entries related to the intercompany sale of services that would be needed in the consolidation workpaper used to prepare a complete set of consolidated financial statements for 19X4.

    b. Compute consolidated net income for 19X4.

E6-11A Fully Adjusted Equity Method and Cost Method

Newtime Products purchased 65 percent of TV Sales Company's stock at underlying book value on January 1, 19X3. At that time, TV Sales reported shares outstanding of $300,000 and retained earnings of $100,000. During 19X3, TV Sales reported net income of $50,000 and paid dividends of $5,000. In 19X4, TV Sales reported net income of $70,000 and paid dividends of $20,000.

The following transactions occurred between Newtime Products and TV Sales in 19X3 and 19X4:

1. TV Sales sold camera equipment to Newtime Products for a profit of $40,000 on December 31, 19X3. The equipment had a 5-year estimated economic life remaining at the time of intercompany transfer and is depreciated on a straight-line basis.

2. Newtime Products sold land costing $30,000 to TV Sales on June 30, 19X4, for $41,000.

Required

a. Assuming Newtime Products uses the fully adjusted equity method to account for its investment in TV Sales Company:
  (1) Give the journal entries recorded on Newtime's books in 19X4 related to its investment in TV Sales.
  (2) Give all eliminating entries needed to prepare a consolidation workpaper for 19X4.
b. Assuming Newtime Products uses the cost method to account for its investment in TV Sales Company:
  (1) Give the journal entries recorded on Newtime's books in 19X4 related to its investment in TV Sales.
  (2) Give all eliminating entries needed to prepare a consolidation workpaper for 19X4.

PROBLEMS

P6-12 Computation of Subsidiary Net Income

Riverboat Enterprises owns 60 percent of the voting common stock of Sandbar Hotel, which it purchased for $50,000 above the underlying book value of $720,000 on December 31, 19X2. For the year 19X5, Sandbar included in its net income $90,000 of unrealized gain on a year-end sale of depreciable assets to Riverboat Enterprises. The noncontrolling interest of Sandbar was assigned $12,000 of income in the 19X5 consolidated financial statements. The purchase differential is amortized over 20 years.

Required

Compute the amount of net income reported by Sandbar for 19X5.

P6-13 Computation of Consolidated Net Income

United Grain Company is 90 percent owned by Petime Corporation. Petime Corporation paid $9,000 in excess of underlying book value to purchase the shares of United Grain Company and is amortizing the balance over a 10-year period. During 19X4, United Grain Company sold land to Petime Corporation at a profit of $7,000. United Grain reported net income of $19,000 and paid dividends of $4,000 in 19X4. Petime Corporation reported income, exclusive of its income from United Grain, of $34,000 and paid dividends of $15,000 in 19X4.

Required

 a. Compute consolidated net income for 19X4.

 b. By what amount would consolidated net income for 19X4 increase or decrease if the sale of land had been from Petime Corporation to United Grain Company, and the gain on the sale of the land was included in Petime's income of $34,000?

P6-14 Transfer of Asset from One Subsidiary to Another

A total of 70 percent of Bugle Corporation and 80 percent of Cook Products Corporation stock is held by Smelts Company. Bugle Corporation purchased a warehouse with an expected life of 20 years on January 1, 19X1, for $40,000. On January 1, 19X6, Bugle Corporation sold the warehouse to Cook Products Corporation for $45,000.

Required

Complete the following table showing selected information that would appear in the separate 19X6 income statements and balance sheets of Bugle Corporation and Cook Products Corporation, and in the 19X6 consolidated financial statements.

	Bugle Corporation	Cook Products Corporation	Consolidated Entity
Depreciation expense			
Fixed assets—warehouse			
Accumulated depreciation			
Gain on sale of warehouse			

P6-15 Computation of Consolidated and Subsidiary Balances

Grafton Corporation is 80 percent owned by Pushon, Inc. On January 1, 19X1, Grafton paid $100,000 for a truck with an expected economic life of 10 years and no anticipated residual value. Grafton sold the truck to Pushon, Inc., on January 1, 19X7. During preparation of the consolidation workpaper for 19X7, the following workpaper entry was made to eliminate the effects of the intercompany truck sale:

Truck	48,000	
Gain on Sale of Truck	12,000	
Depreciation Expense		3,000
Accumulated Depreciation		57,000

Required

 a. What was the amount of accumulated depreciation on the books of Grafton at the time of the intercompany sale?

 b. What amount did Pushon, Inc., pay Grafton for the truck?

 c. What amount of depreciation expense was recorded by Pushon during 19X7?

 d. What amount will be reported for (1) trucks and (2) accumulated depreciation in the December 31, 19X7, consolidated balance sheet?

e. If Grafton reports net income of $50,000 in 19X7, what amount of income will be assigned to the noncontrolling interest in the 19X7 consolidated income statement?

f. If Grafton reports net income of $60,000 in 19X8, what amount of income will be assigned to the noncontrolling interest in the 19X8 consolidated income statement?

P6-16 Multiple-Choice Questions

Select the correct answer for each of the following questions.

1. During 19X7, subsidiary A charged subsidiary B $8,000 for janitorial services provided during the year. The cost incurred by subsidiary A in providing the services was $5,000. If both subsidiaries are fully consolidated, which of the following statements is correct?
   a. Consolidated net income will be reduced by $8,000 when the intercompany services are eliminated.
   b. Consolidated net income will be reduced by $3,000 when the intercompany services are eliminated.
   c. Consolidated net income will be unaffected by the elimination of the intercompany services.
   d. Income assigned to the noncontrolling shareholders of subsidiary A must be reduced by a pro rata portion of the $3,000 profit earned.

2. In the preparation of a consolidated income statement:
   a. Income assigned to noncontrolling shareholders always is computed as a pro rata portion of the reported net income of the consolidated entity.
   b. Income assigned to noncontrolling shareholders always is computed as a pro rata portion of the reported net income of the subsidiary.
   c. Income assigned to noncontrolling shareholders in the current period is likely to be less than a pro rata portion of the reported net income of the subsidiary in the current period if the subsidiary had an unrealized gain on an intercorporate sale of depreciable assets in the preceding period.
   d. Income assigned to noncontrolling shareholders in the current period is likely to be more than a pro rata portion of the reported net income of the subsidiary in the current period if the subsidiary had an unrealized gain on an intercorporate sale of depreciable assets in the preceding period.

3. When a 90 percent–owned subsidiary records a gain on a sale of land to an affiliate during the current period and the land is not resold before the end of the period:
   a. The full amount of the gain will be excluded from consolidated net income.
   b. Consolidated net income will be increased by the full amount of the gain.
   c. A proportionate share of the unrealized gain will be excluded from income assigned to noncontrolling interest.
   d. The full amount of the unrealized gain will be excluded from income assigned to noncontrolling interest.

4. During 19X5, Subsidiary Corporation sells land to Parent Corporation and records a gain of $15,000 on the sale. Subsidiary Corporation reports 19X5 net income of $55,000. Parent Corporation holds 60 percent of the voting shares of Subsidiary Corporation. Parent Corporation plans to build a new general headquarters on the land in 19X7. If there is no adjustment made for unrealized profits in preparing the consolidated financial statements as of December 31, 19X5:

a. Consolidated net income will be overstated by $15,000.
b. Consolidated retained earnings will be overstated by $15,000.
c. Income assigned to the noncontrolling interest in the consolidated income statement will be overstated by $9,000.
d. Consolidated net income will be overstated by $9,000.
e. Both a and b are correct.

5. Minor Company sold land to Major Company on November 15, 19X4, and recorded a gain of $30,000 on the sale. Major Company owns 80 percent of the common shares of Minor Company. Which of the following statements is correct?
   a. A proportionate share of the $30,000 must be treated as a reduction of income assigned to the noncontrolling interest in the consolidated income statement unless the land is resold to a nonaffiliate in 19X4.
   b. The $30,000 will not be treated as an adjustment in computing income assigned to the noncontrolling interest in the consolidated income statement in 19X4 unless the land is resold to a nonaffiliate in 19X4.
   c. In computing consolidated net income it does not matter whether the land is or is not resold to a nonaffiliate before the end of the period; the $30,000 will not affect the computation of consolidated net income in 19X4 because the profits are on the subsidiary's books.
   d. The trial balance of Minor Company as of December 31, 19X4, should be adjusted to remove the $30,000 gain since the gain is not yet realized.

6. Lewis Company owns 80 percent of the stock of Tomassini Corporation. You are told that Tomassini Corporation has sold equipment to Lewis Company and that the following journal entry is needed to prepare consolidated statements for 19X9:

Equipment	20,000	
Gain on Sale of Equipment	40,000	
Depreciation Expense		5,000
Accumulated Depreciation		55,000

Which of the following is incorrect?
   a. The parent paid $40,000 in excess of the subsidiary's carrying amount to acquire the asset.
   b. From a consolidated viewpoint, depreciation expense as recorded by Lewis is overstated.
   c. The asset transfer occurred in 19X9 before the end of the year.
   d. Consolidated net income will be reduced by $40,000 when this entry is used as an eliminating entry.

P6-17 Consolidated Net Income with Intercorporate Transfers

In its 19X7 consolidated income statement, Skekel Development Company reported consolidated net income of $921,000 and $45,000 of income assigned to the 30 percent noncontrolling interest in its only subsidiary, Subsidence Mining, Inc. During the year, Subsidence had sold a previously mined parcel of land to Skekel for a new housing development; the sales price to Skekel was $500,000 and the land had a carrying amount at the time of sale of $560,000. At the beginning of the previous year, Skekel had sold excavation and grading equipment to Subsidence for $240,000; the equipment had a remaining life of 6 years as of the date of sale and a book value of $210,000. The equipment originally had cost $350,000 when purchased by Skekel on January 2, 19X2. The equipment never was expected to have any salvage value.

Skekel had purchased its investment in Subsidence Mining 12 years ago for a price that was $300,000 in excess of the book value of the shares acquired; all the excess over the book value was attributable to goodwill with a remaining life of 20 years from the date of combination. Both parent and subsidiary use straight-line amortization and depreciation.

Required

  a. Present the journal entry made by Skekel to record the sale of equipment in 19X6 to Subsidence Mining.

  b. Present all elimination entries related to the intercompany transfers of land and equipment that should appear in the consolidation workpaper used to prepare a complete set of consolidated financial statements for 19X7.

  c. Compute Subsidence Mining's 19X7 net income.

  d. Compute Skekel's 19X7 income from its own separate operations, excluding any investment income from its investment in Subsidence Mining.

P6-18 Preparation of Consolidated Balance Sheet

Lofton Company owns 60 percent of the voting shares of Temple Corporation, purchased on May 17, 19X1, at underlying book value. The permanent accounts of the companies on December 31, 19X6, contained the following balances:

	Lofton Company	Temple Corporation
Cash and Receivables	$101,000	$ 20,000
Inventory	80,000	40,000
Land	150,000	90,000
Buildings and Equipment	400,000	300,000
Investment in Temple Corporation Stock	150,000	
	$881,000	$450,000
Accumulated Depreciation	$135,000	$ 85,000
Accounts Payable	90,000	25,000
Notes Payable	200,000	90,000
Common Stock	100,000	200,000
Retained Earnings	356,000	50,000
	$881,000	$450,000

On January 1, 19X2, Lofton Company paid $100,000 for equipment with an expected total economic life of 10 years. The equipment was depreciated on a straight-line basis with no residual value. Temple Corporation purchased the equipment from Lofton Company on December 31, 19X4, for $91,000.

Temple Corporation sold land it had purchased for $30,000 on February 23, 19X4, to Lofton Company for $20,000 on October 14, 19X5.

Required

  a. Prepare a consolidated balance sheet workpaper in good form as of December 31, 19X6.

  b. Prepare a consolidated balance sheet as of December 31, 19X6.

P6-19 Consolidation Workpaper

Streamline Manufacturing purchased 75 percent ownership of Yardley Corporation on January 1, 19X1, at underlying book value. The balance sheets and income statements for the companies on December 31, 19X4, are as follows:

Streamline Manufacturing and Yardley Corporation
Balance Sheets
December 31, 19X4

	Streamline Manufacturing	Yardley Corporation
Cash and Receivables	$153,500	$ 71,500
Inventory	100,000	60,000
Land, Buildings, and Equipment (net)	274,000	88,500
Investment in Yardley Corporation Stock	127,500	
Total Assets	$655,000	$220,000
Liabilities	$160,000	$ 50,000
Common Stock	200,000	60,000
Retained Earnings	295,000	110,000
Total Liabilities and Stockholders' Equity	$655,000	$220,000

Streamline Manufacturing and Yardley Corporation
Combined Income and Retained Earnings Statements
Year Ended December 31, 19X4

	Streamline Manufacturing		Yardley Corporation	
Sales and Service Revenue		$400,000		$200,000
Gain on Sale of Land		7,500		
Gain on Sale of Equipment				10,000
Income from Subsidiary		22,500		
		$430,000		$210,000
Cost of Goods Sold	$245,000		$130,000	
Depreciation Expense	40,000		15,000	
Other Expenses	62,500	(347,500)	35,000	(180,000)
Net Income		$ 82,500		$ 30,000
Dividends Paid		(25,000)		(10,000)
Change in Retained Earnings		$ 57,500		$ 20,000

Additional information:

1. Streamline Manufacturing uses the basic equity method in accounting for its investment in Yardley Corporation.

2. On January 1, 19X4, Yardley Corporation sold to Streamline Manufacturing equipment with a book value of $35,000. Streamline Manufacturing paid Yardley Corporation $45,000. The equipment had a remaining economic life of 5 years at the time of the intercorporate sale.

3. On December 31, 19X4, Streamline Manufacturing sold land costing $31,000 to Yardley Corporation for $38,500.

Upstream

4. During 19X4, Yardley Corporation personnel provided janitorial and other services to Streamline Manufacturing for $40,000. Yardley Corporation paid the employees providing the services $27,000.

Required

a. Give all workpaper elimination entries needed to prepare a full set of consolidated financial statements for 19X4.

b. Prepare a consolidation workpaper in good form for 19X4.

c. Prepare the 19X4 consolidated balance sheet, income statement, and retained earnings statement.

P6-20 Consolidation Workpaper in Year of Intercompany Transfer

Blasto Furnace Company holds 80 percent of the stock of Lumpy Coal Works, acquired on January 1, 19X2, for $160,000. On the date of acquisition, Lumpy Coal reported retained earnings of $50,000 and had $100,000 of common stock outstanding. Blasto uses the basic equity method in accounting for its investment in Lumpy Coal.

Trial balance data for the two companies on December 31, 19X6, are as follows:

	Blasto Furnace Company		Lumpy Coal Works	
Item	**Debit**	**Credit**	**Debit**	**Credit**
Cash and Accounts Receivable	$ 113,000		$ 35,000	
Inventory	260,000		90,000	
Land	80,000		80,000	
Buildings and Equipment	500,000		150,000	
Investment in Lumpy Coal Stock	212,000			
Cost of Goods Sold	140,000		60,000	
Depreciation and Amortization	25,000		15,000	
Other Expenses	15,000		5,000	
Dividends Declared	30,000		5,000	
Accumulated Depreciation		$ 205,000		$ 45,000
Accounts Payable		60,000		20,000
Bonds Payable		200,000		50,000
Common Stock		300,000		100,000
Retained Earnings		322,000		105,000
Sales		240,000		120,000
Gain on Sale of Equipment		20,000		
Income from Subsidiary		28,000		
Total	$1,375,000	$1,375,000	$440,000	$440,000

Additional information:

1. At the date of combination, the book values and fair values of all separately identifiable assets of Lumpy Coal Works were the same. Any intangible asset has an estimated life of 10 years.

2. On January 1, 19X5, Lumpy Coal Works sold land that had cost $8,000 to Blasto Furnace Company for $18,000.

3. On January 1, 19X6, Blasto Furnace Company sold to Lumpy Coal Works equipment that it had purchased for $75,000 on January 1, 19X1. The equipment has a total economic life of 15 years and was sold to Lumpy Coal Works for $70,000. Both companies use straight-line depreciation.

4. There was $7,000 of intercompany receivables and payables on December 31, 19X6.

Required

a. Give all eliminating entries needed to prepare a consolidation workpaper for 19X6.
b. Prepare a three-part workpaper for 19X6, in good form.
c. Prepare a consolidated balance sheet, income statement, and retained earnings statement for 19X6.

P6-21 Consolidation Workpaper in Year following Intercompany Transfer

Blasto Furnace Company holds 80 percent of the stock of Lumpy Coal Works, acquired on January 1, 19X2, for $160,000. On the date of acquisition, Lumpy Coal reported retained earnings of $50,000 and $100,000 of common stock outstanding. Blasto uses the basic equity method in accounting for its investment in Lumpy Coal.

Trial balance data for the two companies on December 31, 19X7, are as follows:

Item	Blasto Furnace Company Debit	Blasto Furnace Company Credit	Lumpy Coal Works Debit	Lumpy Coal Works Credit
Cash and Accounts Receivable	$ 151,000		$ 55,000	
Inventory	240,000		100,000	
Land	100,000		80,000	
Buildings and Equipment	500,000		150,000	
Investment in Lumpy Coal Stock	216,000			
Cost of Goods Sold	160,000		80,000	
Depreciation and Amortization	25,000		15,000	
Other Expenses	20,000		10,000	
Dividends Declared	60,000		35,000	
Accumulated Depreciation		$ 230,000		$ 60,000
Accounts Payable		60,000		25,000
Bonds Payable		200,000		50,000
Common Stock		300,000		100,000
Retained Earnings		400,000		140,000
Sales		250,000		150,000
Income from Subsidiary		32,000		
Total	$1,472,000	$1,472,000	$525,000	$525,000

Additional information:

1. At the date of combination, the book values and fair values of all separably identifiable assets of Lumpy Coal Works were the same. Any intangible asset has an estimated life of 10 years.

2. On January 1, 19X5, Lumpy Coal Works sold land that had cost $8,000 to Blasto Furnace Company for $18,000.

3. On January 1, 19X6, Blasto Furnace Company sold to Lumpy Coal Works equipment

that it had purchased for $75,000 on January 1, 19X1. The equipment has a total economic life of 15 years and was sold to Lumpy Coal Works for $70,000. Both companies use straight-line depreciation.

4. Intercorporate receivables and payables total $4,000 on December 31, 19X7.

Required

a. Show how Blasto's income from its subsidiary is computed for 19X7.

b. Prepare a reconciliation between the balance in the investment in subsidiary account reported by Blasto Furnace Company on December 31, 19X7, and the underlying book value of Lumpy Coal Works.

c. Prepare all workpaper eliminating entries needed as of December 31, 19X7, and complete a three-part consolidation workpaper for 19X7.

P6-22 Multiple-Choice Questions—Computation of Various Account Balances

Kendel Manufacturing Corporation purchased 60 percent of the outstanding stock of Trendy Products Corporation on January 1, 19X2. Trendy reported retained earnings of $120,000 at the date of acquisition. The price paid for Trendy's stock included $30,000 for goodwill arising as a result of the combination. The goodwill is being amortized over a 10-year period. Summarized balance sheet data for December 31, 19X4, are as follows:

	Kendel Manufacturing	Trendy Products
Current Assets	$200,000	$100,000
Land	120,000	80,000
Buildings and Equipment (net)	300,000	200,000
Investment in Trendy Products Corporation Stock	201,000	
Total Assets	$821,000	$380,000
Liabilities	$150,000	$ 80,000
Common Stock	150,000	90,000
Additional Paid-In Capital	100,000	10,000
Retained Earnings	421,000	200,000
Total Liabilities and Equity	$821,000	$380,000

Kendel Manufacturing uses the basic equity method in accounting for its investment in Trendy Products. For the year ended December 31, 19X4, Trendy Products reported net income of $40,000 and paid dividends of $15,000; Kendel Manufacturing reported income from its separate operations of $75,000 and paid dividends of $55,000.

Kendel Manufacturing sold land that it had purchased for $25,000 to Trendy Products for $45,000 on December 31, 19X3. On January 1, 19X4, Trendy Products sold equipment with a book value of $48,000 to Kendel Manufacturing for $58,000. The equipment had an estimated economic life of 5 years at the time of intercorporate transfer.

Required

1. What amount of income will be assigned to noncontrolling shareholders in the 19X4 consolidated income statement?
   a. $4,000.
   b. $12,000.

c. $12,800.
d. $16,800.

2. What amount of goodwill will be reported in the consolidated balance sheet on December 31, 19X4?
   a. $12,600.
   b. $21,000.
   c. $24,000.
   d. $30,000.

3. What amount of buildings and equipment (net) will be reported in the consolidated balance sheet on December 31, 19X4?
   a. $490,000.
   b. $492,000.
   c. $494,000.
   d. $495,000.
   e. $500,000.

4. What amount of land will be reported in the consolidated balance sheet on December 31, 19X4?
   a. $120,000.
   b. $180,000.
   c. $188,000.
   d. $200,000.

5. What amount of consolidated net income will be reported for 19X4?
   a. $91,200.
   b. $99,000.
   c. $104,000.
   d. $112,000.
   e. $115,000.

6. What amount of consolidated retained earnings will be reported in the consolidated balance sheet on December 31, 19X4?
   a. $396,200.
   b. $516,200.
   c. $566,200.
   d. $568,200.
   e. $596,200.

7. What balance will be reported for the noncontrolling interest in the December 31, 19X4, consolidated balance sheet?
   a. $108,000.
   b. $116,000.
   c. $116,800.
   d. $120,000.

8. What amount was reported as noncontrolling interest in the consolidated balance sheet prepared as of December 31, 19X3?
   a. $102,000.
   b. $110,000.
   c. $120,000.
   d. $122,000.

P6-23 Comprehensive Problem: Intercorporate Transfers

Rossman Corporation holds 75 percent of the common stock of Schmid Distributors, Inc. The stock originally was purchased on December 31, 19X1, for $2,340,000. At the date of acquisition, Schmid reported common stock with a par value of $1,000,000, additional paid-in capital of $1,350,000, and retained earnings of $620,000. The differential at acquisition was attributable to the following items:

Inventory (sold in 19X2)	$ 22,500
Land	40,000
Goodwill (10-year life)	50,000
Total Differential	$112,500

During 19X2, Rossman sold to Schmid at a gain of $23,000 a piece of land that it had purchased several years before; Schmid continues to hold the land. Also in 19X2, Rossman and Schmid entered into a 10-year contract under which Rossman provides management consulting services to Schmid on a continuing basis; Schmid pays Rossman a fixed fee of $80,000 per year for these services. At December 31, 19X8, Schmid owed Rossman $20,000 as the final 19X8 quarterly payment under the contract.

On January 2, 19X8, Rossman purchased from Schmid for $250,000 equipment that Schmid was then carrying at $290,000. That equipment had been purchased by Schmid on December 27, 19X2, for $435,000. The equipment is expected to have a total life of 15 years and no salvage value.

At December 31, 19X8, trial balances for Rossman and Schmid appeared as follows:

Item	Rossman Corporation Debit	Rossman Corporation Credit	Schmid Distributors Debit	Schmid Distributors Credit
Cash	$ 50,700		$ 38,000	
Current Receivables	101,800		89,400	
Inventory	286,000		218,900	
Investment in Schmid Stock	2,935,000			
Land	400,000		1,200,000	
Buildings and Equipment	2,400,000		2,990,000	
Cost of Goods Sold	2,193,000		525,000	
Depreciation and Amortization	202,000		88,000	
Other Expenses	1,381,000		227,000	
Dividends Declared	50,000		20,000	
Accumulated Depreciation		$1,105,000		$ 420,000
Current Payables		86,200		76,300
Bonds Payable		1,000,000		200,000
Common Stock		100,000		1,000,000
Additional Paid-In Capital		1,272,000		1,350,000
Retained Earnings, January 1		1,467,800		1,400,000
Sales		4,801,000		985,000
Other Income or Less		90,000	35,000	
Income from Subsidiary		77,500		
	$9,999,500	$9,999,500	$5,431,300	$5,431,300

As of December 31, 19X8, Schmid had declared but not yet paid its fourth-quarter dividend of $5,000. Both companies use straight-line depreciation and amortization. Rossman uses the basic equity method to account for its investment in Schmid Distributors.

Required

    a. Compute the amount of the differential as of January 1, 19X8.

    b. Verify the balance in Rossman's Investment in Schmid Stock account as of December 31, 19X8.

    c. Present all elimination entries that would appear in a three-part consolidation workpaper as of December 31, 19X8.

    d. Prepare and complete a three-part workpaper for the preparation of consolidated financial statements for 19X8.

P6-24A Fully Adjusted Equity Method

On December 31, 19X7, Blasto Furnace Company recorded the following entry on its books to adjust from the basic equity method to the fully adjusted equity method on its investment in Lumpy Coal Works:

Retained Earnings	26,000	
Income from Subsidiary		2,000
Investment in Lumpy Coal Stock		24,000

Required

    a. Adjust the data reported by Blasto Furnace Company in the trial balance contained in Problem 6-21 for the effects of the adjusting entry presented above.

    b. Prepare the journal entries that would have been recorded on the books of Blasto Furnace Company during 19X7 under the fully adjusted equity method.

    c. Prepare all eliminating entries needed to complete a consolidation workpaper as of December 31, 19X7, assuming Blasto has used the fully adjusted equity method.

    d. Complete a three-part consolidation workpaper as of December 31, 19X7.

P6-25A Cost Method

The trial balance data presented in Problem 6-21 can be converted to reflect use of the cost method by inserting the following amounts in place of those presented for Blasto Furnace Company:

Investment in Lumpy Coal Stock	$160,000
Retained Earnings	348,000
Income from Subsidiary	-0-
Dividend Income	28,000

Required

a. Prepare the journal entries that would have been recorded on the books of Blasto Furnace Company during 19X7 under the cost method.

b. Prepare all eliminating entries needed to complete a consolidation workpaper as of December 31, 19X7, assuming Blasto has used the cost method.

c. Complete a three-part consolidation workpaper as of December 31, 19X7.

CHAPTER 7

INTERCOMPANY INVENTORY TRANSACTIONS

Inventory transactions are the most common form of intercorporate exchange. Conceptually, the elimination of inventory transfers between related companies is no different than for other types of intercompany transactions. All revenue and expense items recorded by the participants must be eliminated fully in preparing the consolidated income statement, and all gains and losses recorded on the transfers are deferred until the items are sold to a nonaffiliate.

The record-keeping process for intercorporate transfers of inventory may be more complex than for other forms of transfers. There often are many different types of inventory items, and some may be transferred from affiliate to affiliate. Also, the problems of keeping tabs on which items have been resold and which items still are on hand are greater in the case of inventory transactions because part of a shipment may be sold immediately by the purchasing company and other units may remain on hand for several accounting periods. Nevertheless, the consolidation procedures relating to inventory transfers are quite similar to those discussed in Chapter 6 relating to fixed assets.

This chapter discusses the procedures for preparing consolidated financial statements when there have been intercompany transfers of inventory. Examples are given to illustrate both perpetual and periodic inventory control systems.

GENERAL OVERVIEW

The workpaper eliminating entries used in preparing consolidated financial statements must eliminate fully the effects of all intercorporate transactions. When there have been intercompany inventory transactions, eliminating entries are needed to remove the revenue and expenses related to the intercompany transfers recorded by the individual companies. The eliminations assure that only the historical cost of the inventory to the consolidated entity is included in the consolidated balance sheet when the inventory is still on hand and is charged to cost of goods sold in the period the inventory is resold to nonaffiliates.

Transfers at Cost

Merchandise sometimes is sold to related companies at the seller's cost or carrying value. When an intercorporate sale includes no profit or loss, the balance sheet inventory amounts at the end of the period require no adjustment for consolidation because the carrying amount of the inventory for the purchasing affiliate is the same as the cost to the transferring affiliate and the consolidated entity. At the time the inventory is resold to a nonaffiliate, the amount charged to cost of goods sold by the affiliate making the outside sale is the cost to the consolidated entity.

Even when the intercorporate sale includes no profit or loss, however, an eliminating entry is needed to remove both the revenue from the intercorporate sale and the related cost of goods sold recorded by the seller. This avoids overstating these two accounts. Consolidated net income is not affected by the eliminating entry when the transfer is made at cost because both revenue and cost of goods sold are reduced by the same amount.

Transfers at a Profit or Loss

Companies use many different approaches in setting intercorporate transfer prices. In some companies, the sale price to an affiliate is the same as the price to any other customer. Some companies routinely mark up inventory transferred to affiliates by a certain percentage of cost. For example, a company might mark up inventory transferred to affiliates by 50 percent of cost, selling inventory that cost $2,000 to an affiliate for $3,000. Other companies have elaborate transfer pricing policies designed to encourage internal sales. Regardless of the method used in setting intercorporate transfer prices, the elimination process must remove the effects of such sales from the consolidated statements.

When intercorporate sales include profits or losses, there are two aspects of the workpaper eliminations needed in the period of transfer to prepare consolidated financial statements:

1. Elimination of the income statement effects of the intercorporate sale in the period in which the sale occurs, including the sales revenue from the intercorporate sale and the related cost of goods sold recorded by the transferring affiliate.

2. Elimination from the inventory on the balance sheet of any profit or loss on the intercompany sale that has not been confirmed by resale of the inventory to outsiders.

Inventory reported in the consolidated balance sheet must be reported at the cost to the consolidated entity. Therefore, if profits or losses have been recorded on inventory acquired in an intercompany transfer, those profits or losses must be eliminated to state the inventory in the consolidated balance sheet at its cost to the consolidated entity. The result is the same as if the intercompany transfer had not occurred.

Effect of Type of Inventory System

Most companies use either a ***perpetual*** or a ***periodic inventory control system*** to keep track of inventory and cost of goods sold. Under a perpetual inventory system, a purchase of merchandise is debited directly to the inventory account; a sale requires a debit to cost of goods sold and a credit to inventory for the cost of the item. When a periodic system is used, a purchase of merchandise is debited to a purchases account rather than to inventory, and no entry is made to recognize cost of goods sold until the end of the accounting period.

The choice between periodic and perpetual inventory systems results in different entries on the books of the individual companies and, therefore, slightly different workpaper eliminating entries in preparing consolidated financial statements.

DOWNSTREAM SALE—PERPETUAL INVENTORY SYSTEM

For consolidation purposes, profits recorded on an intercorporate inventory sale are recognized in the period in which the inventory is resold to an unrelated party. Until the point of resale, all intercorporate profits must be deferred. Consolidated net income must be based on the realized income of the transferring affiliate. Because intercompany profits from downstream sales are on the books of the parent, consolidated net income and the overall claim of parent company shareholders must be reduced by the full amount of the unrealized profits.

When a company sells an inventory item to an affiliate, one of three situations results: (1) the item is resold to a nonaffiliate during the same period, (2) the item is resold to a nonaffiliate during the next period, or (3) the item is held for two or more periods by the purchasing affiliate. The continuing example of Peerless Products Corporation and Special Foods, Incorporated, is used to illustrate the consolidation process under each of the alternatives. As in Chapter 6, assume that Peerless Products purchases 80 percent of the common stock of Special Foods on December 31, 19X0, for its book value of $240,000.

As an illustration of the effects of a downstream sale, assume that on March 1, 19X1, Peerless buys inventory for $7,000 and resells it to Special Foods for $10,000 on April 1. Peerless records the following entries on its books:

```
March 1, 19X1
   (1)  Inventory                         7,000
             Cash                                   7,000
        Purchase of inventory.
```

```
April 1, 19X1
    (2)  Cash                                              10,000
            Sales                                                        10,000
         Sale of inventory to Special Foods.

    (3)  Cost of Goods Sold                                7,000
            Inventory                                                    7,000
         Cost of inventory sold to Special Foods.
```

Special Foods records the purchase of the inventory from Peerless with the following entry:

```
April 1, 19X1
    (4)  Inventory                                         10,000
            Cash                                                         10,000
         Purchase of inventory from Peerless.
```

Resale in Period of Intercorporate Transfer

To illustrate consolidation when inventory is sold to an affiliate and then resold to a nonaffiliate during the same period, assume that on November 5, 19X1, Special Foods sells the inventory purchased from Peerless to Nonaffiliated Corporation for $15,000, as follows:

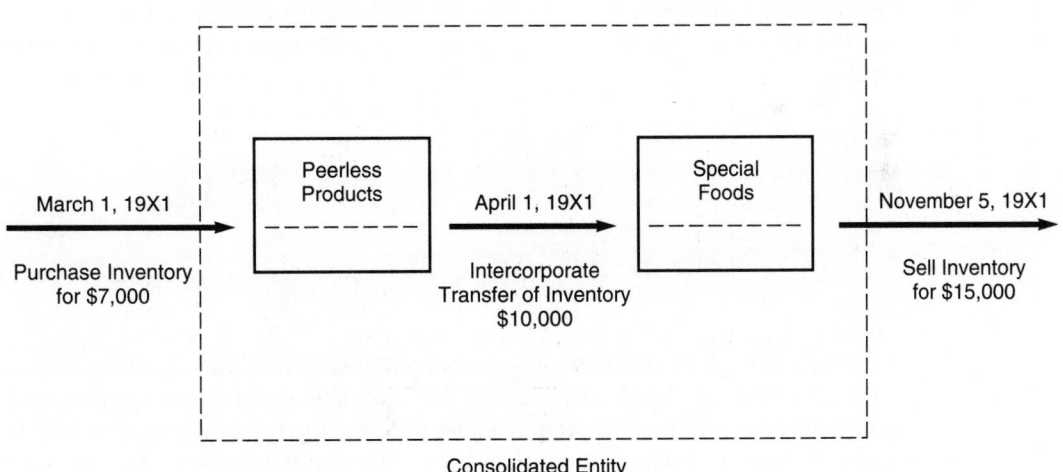

Consolidated Entity

Special Foods records the sale to Nonaffiliated with the following entries:

```
November 5, 19X1
    (5)  Cash                                              15,000
            Sales                                                        15,000
         Sale of inventory to Nonaffiliated.
```

(6) Cost of Goods Sold   10,000
     Inventory   10,000
     Cost of inventory sold to Nonaffiliated.

A review of all entries recorded by the individual companies indicates that incorrect balances will be reported in the consolidated income statement if the effects of the intercorporate sale are not removed:

Item	Peerless Products	Special Foods	Unadjusted Totals	Consolidated Amounts
Sales	$10,000	$15,000	$25,000	$15,000
Cost of Goods Sold	(7,000)	(10,000)	(17,000)	(7,000)
Gross Profit	$ 3,000	$ 5,000	$ 8,000	$ 8,000

While consolidated gross profit is correct even if no adjustments are made, the totals for sales and cost of goods sold derived by simply adding the amounts on the books of Peerless and Special Foods are overstated for the consolidated entity. The selling price of the inventory to Nonaffiliated Corporation is $15,000, and the original cost to Peerless Products is $7,000. Thus, gross profit of $8,000 is correct from a consolidated viewpoint, but consolidated sales and cost of goods sold should be $15,000 and $7,000, respectively, rather than $25,000 and $17,000. In the consolidation workpaper, the amount of the intercompany sale must be eliminated from both sales and cost of goods sold to correctly state the consolidated totals:

E(7) Sales   10,000
     Cost of Goods Sold   10,000
     Eliminate intercompany inventory sale.

Note that this entry does not affect consolidated net income because sales and cost of goods sold both are reduced by the same amount. No elimination of intercompany profit is needed because all the intercompany profit has been realized through resale of the inventory to the external party.

Resale in Period following Intercorporate Transfer

When inventory is sold to an affiliate at a profit, appropriate adjustments are needed to prepare consolidated financial statements in the period of the intercompany sale and in each subsequent period until the inventory is sold to a nonaffiliate. By way of illustration, assume that Peerless Products purchases inventory in 19X1 for $7,000 and sells the inventory during the year to Special Foods for

$10,000. Special Foods sells the inventory to Nonaffiliated Corporation for $15,000 on January 2, 19X2, as follows:

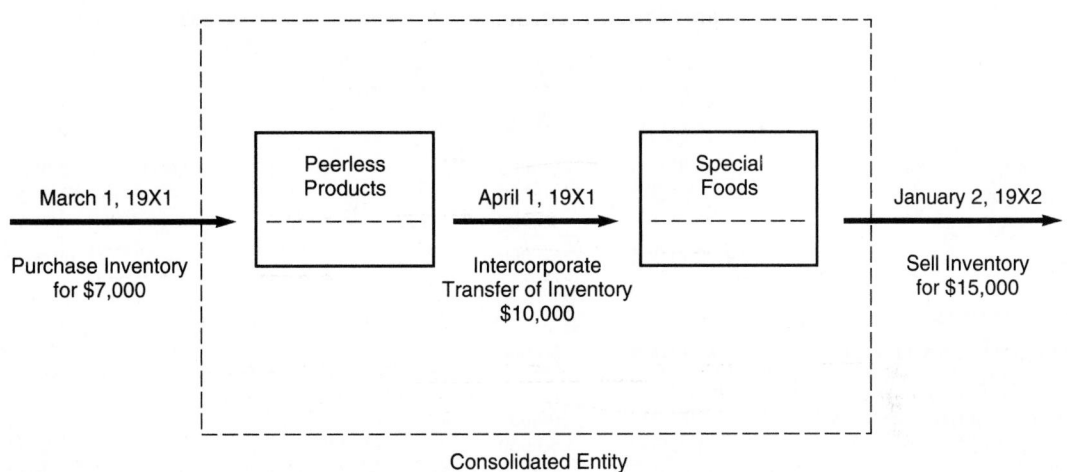

Consolidated Entity

During 19X1, Peerless records the purchase of the inventory and the sale to Special Foods with journal entries (1) through (3), given previously; Special Foods records the purchase of the inventory from Peerless with entry (4). In 19X2, Special Foods records the sale of the inventory to Nonaffiliated with entries (5) and (6), given earlier.

Basic Equity-Method Entries—19X1   Using the basic equity method, Peerless records its share of Special Foods' income and dividends for 19X1 in the normal manner:

(8)	Investment in Special Foods Stock	40,000	
	Income from Subsidiary		40,000
	Record equity-method income:		
	$50,000 × .80		
(9)	Cash	24,000	
	Investment in Special Foods Stock		24,000
	Record dividends from Special Foods:		
	$30,000 × .80		

As a result of these entries, the ending balance of the investment account is $256,000 ($240,000 + $40,000 − $24,000).

Consolidation Workpaper—19X1   The consolidation workpaper prepared at the end of 19X1 appears in Figure 7-1. Four elimination entries are included in the workpaper:

FIGURE 7-1 December 31, 19X1, consolidation workpaper, period of intercompany sale; downstream inventory sale, perpetual inventory.

Item	Peerless Products	Special Foods	Eliminations Debit		Eliminations Credit		Consolidated
Sales	400,000	200,000	(13)	10,000			590,000
Income from Subsidiary	40,000		(10)	40,000			
Credits	440,000	200,000					590,000
Cost of Goods Sold	170,000	115,000			(13)	7,000	278,000
Depreciation and Amortization	50,000	20,000					70,000
Other Expenses	40,000	15,000					55,000
Debits	(260,000)	(150,000)					(403,000)
							187,000
Income to Noncontrolling Interest			(11)	10,000			(10,000)
Net Income, carry forward	180,000	50,000		60,000		7,000	177,000
Retained Earnings, January 1	300,000	100,000	(12)	100,000			300,000
Net Income, from above	180,000	50,000		60,000		7,000	177,000
	480,000	150,000					477,000
Dividends Declared	(60,000)	(30,000)			(10)	24,000	
					(11)	6,000	(60,000)
Retained Earnings, December 31, carry forward	420,000	120,000		160,000		37,000	417,000
Cash	264,000	75,000					339,000
Accounts Receivable	75,000	50,000					125,000
Inventory	100,000	75,000			(13)	3,000	172,000
Land	175,000	40,000					215,000
Buildings and Equipment	800,000	600,000					1,400,000
Investment in Special Foods Stock	256,000				(10)	16,000	
					(12)	240,000	
Debits	1,670,000	840,000					2,251,000
Accumulated Depreciation	250,000	220,000					470,000
Accounts Payable	100,000	100,000					200,000
Bonds Payable	400,000	200,000					600,000
Common Stock	500,000	200,000	(12)	200,000			500,000
Retained Earnings, from above	420,000	120,000		160,000		37,000	417,000
Noncontrolling Interest					(11)	4,000	
					(12)	60,000	64,000
Credits	1,670,000	840,000		360,000		360,000	2,251,000

Elimination entries:
(10) Eliminate income from subsidiary.
(11) Assign income to noncontrolling interest.
(12) Eliminate beginning investment balance.
(13) Eliminate intercompany downstream sale of inventory.

E(10)	Income from Subsidiary	40,000	
	Dividends Declared		24,000
	Investment in Special Foods Stock		16,000
	Eliminate income from subsidiary.		
E(11)	Income to Noncontrolling Interest	10,000	
	Dividends Declared		6,000
	Noncontrolling Interest		4,000
	Assign income to noncontrolling interest:		
	$10,000 = $50,000 × .20		
E(12)	Common Stock—Special Foods	200,000	
	Retained Earnings, January 1	100,000	
	Investment in Special Foods Stock		240,000
	Noncontrolling Interest		60,000
	Eliminate beginning investment balance.		
E(13)	Sales	10,000	
	Cost of Goods Sold		7,000
	Inventory		3,000
	Eliminate intercompany downstream sale of inventory.		

Only entry E(13) relates to the elimination of unrealized inventory profits; the other entries are the type normally found in the workpaper.

Entry E(10) is based on entries (8) and (9) on Peerless's books and eliminates Peerless's share of Special Foods' income and dividends. This entry also eliminates the change in the investment account for the period and returns the investment account balance in the workpaper to the beginning balance of $240,000.

The noncontrolling interest is not affected by the downstream inventory transfer and is assigned a pro rata portion ($50,000 × .20) of the net income of Special Foods in workpaper entry E(11). This entry also eliminates the noncontrolling stockholders' share of Special Foods' dividends ($30,000 × .20) and establishes the $4,000 increase in the noncontrolling interest for the period due to the excess of Special Foods' net income over its dividends [($50,000 − $30,000) × .20].

Entry E(12) eliminates the beginning balances of Special Foods' stockholders' equity accounts and Peerless's investment account. This entry also establishes the amount of the noncontrolling interest at the beginning of the period. The intercompany inventory sale has no effect on this entry because the entry eliminates balances as of the beginning of the year, while the intercompany transaction occurred during the year.

Entry E(13) is needed to eliminate the effects of the intercompany sale of inventory. The journal entries recorded by Peerless Products and Special Foods in 19X1 on their separate books will result in an overstatement of consolidated gross profit for 19X1 and the consolidated inventory balance at year-end unless the amounts are adjusted in the consolidation workpaper. The amounts resulting from the intercompany inventory transactions from the separate books of Peerless

Products and Special Foods, and the appropriate consolidated amounts, are as follows:

Item	Peerless Products	Special Foods	Unadjusted Totals	Consolidated Amounts
Sales	$10,000	$ -0-	$10,000	$ -0-
Cost of Goods Sold	(7,000)	-0-	(7,000)	-0-
Gross Profit	$ 3,000	$ -0-	$ 3,000	$ -0-
Inventory	$ -0-	$10,000	$10,000	$7,000

Eliminating entry E(13) corrects the unadjusted totals to the appropriate consolidated amounts. Both sales and cost of goods sold taken from the trial balance of Peerless Products are reduced in preparing the consolidated income statement. In doing so, income is reduced by the difference of $3,000 ($10,000 − $7,000). In addition, ending inventory reported on the books of Special Foods is stated at the intercompany exchange price rather than the historical cost to the consolidated entity. Until resold to an external party by Special Foods, the inventory must be reduced by the amount of unrealized intercompany profit each time consolidated statements are prepared.

Consolidated Net Income—19X1   Consolidated net income for 19X1 is shown as $177,000 in the Figure 7-1 workpaper. This amount is verified as follows:

Peerless's separate operating income		$140,000
Less: Unrealized intercompany profit on		
downstream inventory sale		(3,000)
Peerless's separate realized income		$137,000
Peerless's share of Special Foods' income:		
Special Foods' net income	$50,000	
Peerless's proportionate share	× .80	40,000
Consolidated net income, 19X1		$177,000

Basic Equity-Method Entries—19X2   During 19X2, Special Foods receives $15,000 when it sells to Nonaffiliated Corporation the inventory that it had purchased for $10,000 from Peerless in 19X1. Also, Peerless records its pro rata portion of Special Foods' net income and dividends for 19X2 with the normal basic equity-method entries:

(14) Investment in Special Foods Stock	60,000	
Income from Subsidiary		60,000
Record equity-method income:		
$75,000 × .80		
(15) Cash	32,000	
Investment in Special Foods Stock		32,000
Record dividends from Special Foods:		
$40,000 × .80		

Investment Account Balance The investment account on Peerless's books appears as follows:

Investment in Special Foods Stock

	Original cost	240,000		
(8)	19X1 equity accrual		(9) 19X1 dividends	
	($50,000 × .80)	40,000	($30,000 × .80)	24,000
	Balance, 12/31/X1	256,000		
(14)	19X2 equity accrual		(15) 19X2 dividends	
	($75,000 × .80)	60,000	($40,000 × .80)	32,000
	Balance, 12/31/X2	284,000		

Consolidation Workpaper—19X2 The consolidation workpaper prepared at the end of 19X2 is shown in Figure 7-2. Four elimination entries are needed:

E(16)	Income from Subsidiary	60,000	
	Dividends Declared		32,000
	Investment in Special Foods Stock		28,000
	Eliminate income from subsidiary.		
E(17)	Income to Noncontrolling Interest	15,000	
	Dividends Declared		8,000
	Noncontrolling Interest		7,000
	Assign income to noncontrolling interest:		
	$15,000 = $75,000 × .20		
E(18)	Common Stock—Special Foods	200,000	
	Retained Earnings, January 1	120,000	
	Investment in Special Foods Stock		256,000
	Noncontrolling Interest		64,000
	Eliminate beginning investment balance.		
E(19)	Retained Earnings, January 1	3,000	
	Cost of Goods Sold		3,000
	Eliminate beginning inventory profit.		

Entry E(16) eliminates the effects of basic equity-method entries (14) and (15) recorded by Peerless Products during 19X2. Entry E(17) assigns the noncontrolling shareholders their share of income ($75,000 × .20) and establishes in the workpaper the 19X2 increase in the claim of the noncontrolling shareholders on the net assets of Special Foods. Because the sale is downstream, the amount of income assigned to noncontrolling shareholders and the balance of the noncontrolling interest are not affected by the intercompany profit.

Workpaper entry E(18) eliminates the beginning stockholders' equity balances of Special Foods and Peerless's beginning investment balance. The investment account is credited for 80 percent of Special Foods' book value at the start of the

FIGURE 7-2 December 31, 19X2, consolidation workpaper, next period following intercompany sale; downstream inventory sale, perpetual inventory.

Item	Peerless Products	Special Foods	Eliminations Debit		Eliminations Credit		Consolidated
Sales	450,000	300,000					750,000
Income from Subsidiary	60,000		(16)	60,000			
Credits	510,000	300,000					750,000
Cost of Goods Sold	180,000	160,000			(19)	3,000	337,000
Depreciation and Amortization	50,000	20,000					70,000
Other Expenses	60,000	45,000					105,000
Debits	(290,000)	(225,000)					(512,000)
							238,000
Income to Noncontrolling Interest			(17)	15,000			(15,000)
Net Income, carry forward	220,000	75,000		75,000		3,000	223,000
Retained Earnings, January 1	420,000	120,000	(18)	120,000			
			(19)	3,000			417,000
Net Income, from above	220,000	75,000		75,000		3,000	223,000
	640,000	195,000					640,000
Dividends Declared	(60,000)	(40,000)			(16)	32,000	
					(17)	8,000	(60,000)
Retained Earnings, December 31, carry forward	580,000	155,000		198,000		43,000	580,000
Cash	291,000	85,000					376,000
Accounts Receivable	150,000	80,000					230,000
Inventory	180,000	90,000					270,000
Land	175,000	40,000					215,000
Buildings and Equipment	800,000	600,000					1,400,000
Investment in Special Foods Stock	284,000				(16)	28,000	
					(18)	256,000	
Debits	1,880,000	895,000					2,491,000
Accumulated Depreciation	300,000	240,000					540,000
Accounts Payable	100,000	100,000					200,000
Bonds Payable	400,000	200,000					600,000
Common Stock	500,000	200,000	(18)	200,000			500,000
Retained Earnings, from above	580,000	155,000		198,000		43,000	580,000
Noncontrolling Interest					(17)	7,000	
					(18)	64,000	71,000
Credits	1,880,000	895,000		398,000		398,000	2,491,000

Elimination entries:
(16) Eliminate income from subsidiary.
(17) Assign income to noncontrolling interest.
(18) Eliminate beginning investment balance.
(19) Eliminate beginning inventory profit.

period, while the noncontrolling interest is credited with a starting balance equal to 20 percent of Special Foods' book value.

Entry E(19) is needed to adjust cost of goods sold to the proper consolidated balance and to reduce beginning retained earnings. The unrealized intercompany profit included in Special Foods' beginning inventory was charged to Cost of Goods Sold when Special Foods sold the inventory during the period. Thus, consolidated cost of goods sold will be overstated for 19X2 if it is reported in the consolidated income statement at the unadjusted total from the books of Peerless and Special Foods:

Item	Peerless Products	Special Foods	Unadjusted Totals	Consolidated Amounts
Sales	$ -0-	$15,000	$15,000	$15,000
Cost of Goods Sold	$ -0-	(10,000)	(10,000)	(7,000)
Gross Profit	$ -0-	$ 5,000	$ 5,000	$ 8,000

Unlike the period in which the intercompany transfer occurs, no adjustment to sales is required in a subsequent period when the inventory is sold to a nonaffiliate. The amount reported by Special Foods reflects the sale outside the economic entity and is the appropriate amount to be reported for consolidation. By removing the $3,000 of intercorporate profit from Cost of Goods Sold in entry E(19), the original acquisition price paid by Peerless Products is reported, and $8,000 of gross profit is correctly reported in the consolidated income statement.

Elimination entry E(19) also reduces the beginning balance of retained earnings by the amount of the intercompany profit unrealized at the beginning of 19X2. Because all the intercompany profit on the downstream sale had been recognized by Peerless in 19X1 and is included in Peerless's beginning retained earnings balance, beginning consolidated retained earnings will be overstated if the full balance reported by Peerless is carried to the consolidated financial statements. Entry E(19) results in the reporting of beginning consolidated retained earnings and cost of goods sold for the year as if there had been no unrealized intercompany profit at the beginning of the year.

Once the sale is made to an external party, the transaction is complete and no adjustments or eliminations related to the intercompany transaction are needed in future periods.

Consolidated Net Income—19X2   Consolidated net income for 19X2 is shown as $223,000 in the Figure 7-2 workpaper. This amount is verified as follows:

Peerless's separate operating income		$160,000
Realization of deferred intercompany profit		3,000
Peerless's separate realized income		$163,000
Peerless's share of Special Foods' income:		
Special Foods' net income	$75,000	
Peerless's proportionate share	× .80	60,000
Consolidated net income, 19X2		$223,000

Inventory Held Two or More Periods

Companies may carry the cost of inventory purchased from an affiliate for more than one accounting period. For example, the cost of an item may be in a lifo inventory layer and would be included as a part of the inventory balance until the layer is liquidated. Prior to liquidation, an eliminating entry is needed in the consolidation workpaper each time consolidated statements are prepared to restate the inventory to its cost to the consolidated entity.

As an example, assume that Special Foods continues to carry the inventory purchased from Peerless Products in its inventory, as follows:

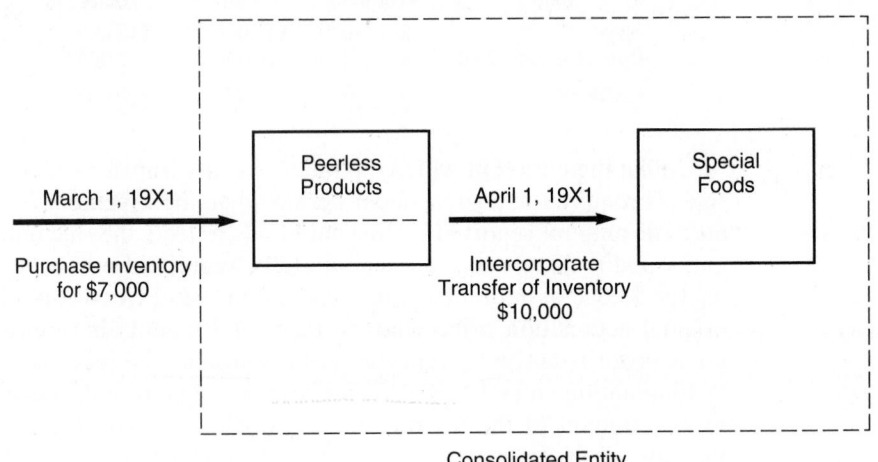

Consolidated Entity

Under a perpetual inventory system, the following eliminating entry is needed in the consolidation workpaper each time a consolidated balance sheet is prepared for years following the year of intercompany sale, for as long as the inventory is held:

E(20)	Retained Earnings, January 1	3,000	
	Inventory		3,000
	Eliminate beginning inventory profit.		

No income statement adjustments are needed in the periods following the intercorporate sale until the inventory is resold to parties external to the consolidated entity.

UPSTREAM SALE—PERPETUAL INVENTORY SYSTEM

When an upstream sale of inventory occurs and the inventory is resold by the parent to a nonaffiliate during the same period, all the parent's equity-method entries and the eliminating entries in the consolidation workpaper are identical to those in the downstream case.

When the inventory is not resold to a nonaffiliate before the end of the period, workpaper eliminating entries are different from the downstream case only by the apportionment of the unrealized intercompany profit to both the controlling and noncontrolling interests. The intercompany profit in an upstream sale is recognized by the subsidiary and shared between the controlling and noncontrolling stockholders of the subsidiary. Therefore, the elimination of the unrealized intercompany profit must reduce the interests of both ownership groups each period until the profit is confirmed by resale of the inventory to a nonaffiliated party.

An upstream sale can be illustrated using the same example as used for the downstream sale. Assume an intercompany sale of inventory from Special Foods to Peerless Products, as follows:

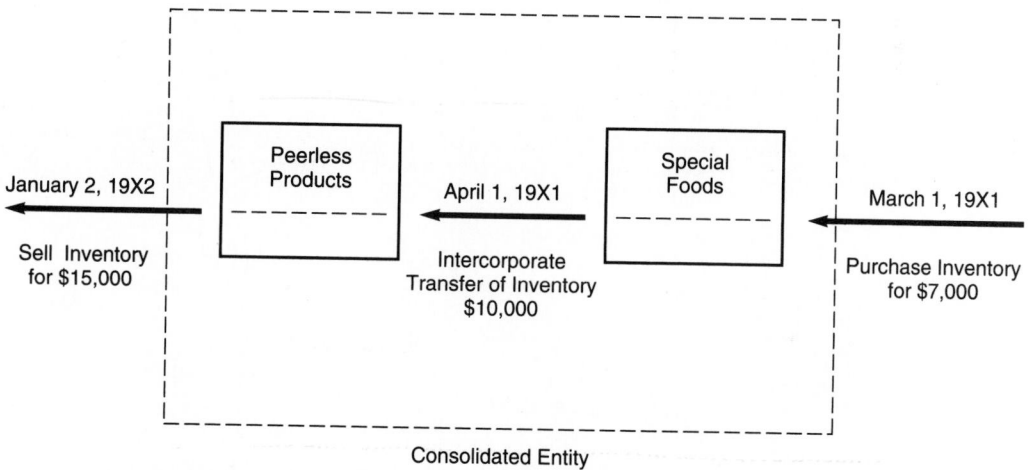

Consolidated Entity

Special Foods purchases the inventory on March 1, 19X1, for $7,000 and sells it to Peerless for $10,000 during the same year. Peerless holds the inventory until January 2 of the following year, at which time Peerless sells it to Nonaffiliated Corporation for $15,000.

Basic Equity-Method Entries—19X1

The following basic equity-method entries are recorded by Peerless Products in 19X1:

(21)	Investment in Special Foods Stock	40,000	
	Income from Subsidiary		40,000
	Record equity-method income:		
	$50,000 × .80		

(22)	Cash	24,000	
	Investment in Special Foods Stock		24,000
	Record dividends from Special Foods:		
	$30,000 × .80		

These entries are the same as in the illustration of the downstream sale.

Consolidation Workpaper—19X1

The workpaper for the preparation of the 19X1 consolidated financial statements is shown in Figure 7-3. Four eliminating entries are included in the workpaper:

E(23)	Income from Subsidiary	40,000	
	Dividends Declared		24,000
	Investment in Special Foods Stock		16,000
	Eliminate income from subsidiary.		
E(24)	Income to Noncontrolling Interest	9,400	
	Dividends Declared		6,000
	Noncontrolling Interest		3,400
	Assign income to noncontrolling interest:		
	$9,400 = ($50,000 − $3,000) × .20		
E(25)	Common Stock—Special Foods	200,000	
	Retained Earnings, January 1	100,000	
	Investment in Special Foods Stock		240,000
	Noncontrolling Interest		60,000
	Eliminate beginning investment balance.		
E(26)	Sales	10,000	
	Cost of Goods Sold		7,000
	Inventory		3,000
	Eliminate intercompany upstream		
	sale of inventory.		

All the workpaper eliminating entries in the year of the intercorporate transfer are the same in the upstream case as in the downstream case except for entry E(24). Because the intercompany profit recognized by Special Foods on the upstream sale was shared by both the controlling and noncontrolling interests, both must be reduced by the unrealized profit elimination. Income assigned to the noncontrolling interest in entry E(24) is based on the realized income of Special Foods ($50,000 − $3,000), and therefore is reduced by the noncontrolling stockholders' share of the unrealized intercompany profit.

Because the unrealized profit elimination is allocated proportionately between the controlling and noncontrolling interests in the upstream case, the income assigned to the noncontrolling shareholders is $600 ($3,000 × .20) less in Figure

FIGURE 7-3 December 31, 19X1, consolidation workpaper, period of intercompany sale; upstream inventory sale, perpetual inventory.

Item	Peerless Products	Special Foods	Eliminations Debit		Eliminations Credit		Consolidated
Sales	400,000	200,000	(26)	10,000			590,000
Income from Subsidiary	40,000		(23)	40,000			
Credits	440,000	200,000					
							590,000
Cost of Goods Sold	170,000	115,000			(26)	7,000	278,000
Depreciation and Amortization	50,000	20,000					70,000
Other Expenses	40,000	15,000					55,000
Debits	(260,000)	(150,000)					(403,000)
							187,000
Income to Noncontrolling Interest			(24)	9,400			(9,400)
Net Income, carry forward	180,000	50,000		59,400		7,000	177,600
Retained Earnings, January 1	300,000	100,000	(25)	100,000			300,000
Net Income, from above	180,000	50,000		59,400		7,000	177,600
	480,000	150,000					477,600
Dividends Declared	(60,000)	(30,000)			(23)	24,000	
					(24)	6,000	(60,000)
Retained Earnings, December 31, carry forward	420,000	120,000		159,400		37,000	417,600
Cash	264,000	75,000					339,000
Accounts Receivable	75,000	50,000					125,000
Inventory	100,000	75,000			(26)	3,000	172,000
Land	175,000	40,000					215,000
Buildings and Equipment	800,000	600,000					1,400,000
Investment in Special Foods Stock	256,000				(23)	16,000	
					(25)	240,000	
Debits	1,670,000	840,000					2,251,000
Accumulated Depreciation	250,000	220,000					470,000
Accounts Payable	100,000	100,000					200,000
Bonds Payable	400,000	200,000					600,000
Common Stock	500,000	200,000	(25)	200,000			500,000
Retained Earnings, from above	420,000	120,000		159,400		37,000	417,600
Noncontrolling Interest					(24)	3,400	
					(25)	60,000	63,400
Credits	1,670,000	840,000		359,400		359,400	2,251,000

Elimination entries:
(23) Eliminate income from subsidiary.
(24) Assign income to noncontrolling interest.
(25) Eliminate beginning investment balance.
(26) Eliminate intercompany upstream sale of inventory.

7-3 for the upstream case than in Figure 7-1 for the downstream case. Accordingly, consolidated net income is $600 higher. All other consolidated income statement amounts are identical in the two cases.

Workpaper entry E(25) eliminates the beginning investment account balance and establishes the noncontrolling interest at net book value at the beginning of 19X1. This entry is not affected by the inventory transfer, because the transfer occurred after the start of the year. Eliminating entry E(26) is the same as in the downstream case: 100 percent of all intercorporate revenue and expenses must be eliminated. The direction of the sale has no effect on the amount of intercompany profit eliminated, only on the allocation of the amount between the controlling and noncontrolling interests.

Consolidated Net Income—19X1

Consolidated net income for 19X1 is shown in the workpaper as $177,600 after deducting the noncontrolling stockholders' share of income. This amount may be verified as follows:

Peerless's separate operating income		$140,000
Peerless's share of Special Foods' income:		
Special Foods' net income	$50,000	
Less: Unrealized intercompany profit		
on upstream inventory sale	(3,000)	
Special Foods' realized income	$47,000	
Peerless's proportionate share	× .80	37,600
Consolidated net income, 19X1		$177,600

Basic Equity-Method Entries—19X2

Peerless recognizes its share of Special Foods' income and dividends for 19X2 with the normal basic equity-method entries:

(27)	Investment in Special Foods Stock	60,000	
	Income from Subsidiary		60,000
	Record equity-method income:		
	$75,000 × .80		
(28)	Cash	32,000	
	Investment in Special Foods Stock		32,000
	Record dividends from Special Foods:		
	$40,000 × .80		

As in the downstream illustration, the investment account balance at the end of 19X2 is $284,000.

Consolidation Workpaper—19X2

The consolidation workpaper used to prepare consolidated financial statements at the end of 19X2 appears in Figure 7-4. The workpaper includes the following elimination entries:

E(29)	Income from Subsidiary	60,000	
	Dividends Declared		32,000
	Investment in Special Foods Stock		28,000
	Eliminate income from subsidiary.		
E(30)	Income to Noncontrolling Interest	15,600	
	Dividends Declared		8,000
	Noncontrolling Interest		7,600
	Assign income to noncontrolling interest:		
	$15,600 = ($75,000 + $3,000) × .20		
E(31)	Common Stock—Special Foods	200,000	
	Retained Earnings, January 1	120,000	
	Investment in Special Foods Stock		256,000
	Noncontrolling Interest		64,000
	Eliminate beginning investment balance.		
E(32)	Retained Earnings, January 1	2,400	
	Noncontrolling Interest	600	
	Cost of Goods Sold		3,000
	Eliminate beginning inventory profit:		
	$2,400 = $3,000 × .80		
	$600 = $3,000 × .20		

Peerless's equity-method income and dividends received from Special Foods are eliminated in entry E(29). Entry E(30) assigns income of $15,600 [($75,000 + $3,000) × .20] to the noncontrolling stockholders based on the realized net income of the subsidiary. The income assigned to the noncontrolling interest consists of a proportionate share of both the $75,000 reported net income of Special Foods and the $3,000 of intercompany inventory profit realized in 19X2.

Workpaper entry E(32) deals explicitly with the elimination of the inventory profit on the upstream sale. In the preparation of the 19X1 consolidated financial statements, the unrealized profit was deducted proportionately from consolidated net income and the income assigned to the noncontrolling interest. The unrealized profit at the beginning of 19X2 is apportioned against both controlling and noncontrolling shareholders in entry E(32). As in the downstream case, cost of goods sold must be credited in the consolidation workpaper to reflect the original cost to the consolidated entity ($7,000) of the inventory sold.

Consolidated Net Income—19X2

Consolidated net income for 19X2 is shown as $222,400 in the Figure 7-4 workpaper. This amount is verified as follows:

FIGURE 7-4 December 31, 19X2, consolidation workpaper, next period following intercompany sale; upstream inventory sale, perpetual inventory.

Item	Peerless Products	Special Foods	Eliminations Debit		Eliminations Credit		Consolidated
Sales	450,000	300,000					750,000
Income from Subsidiary	60,000		(29)	60,000			
Credits	510,000	300,000					750,000
Cost of Goods Sold	180,000	160,000			(32)	3,000	337,000
Depreciation and Amortization	50,000	20,000					70,000
Other Expenses	60,000	45,000					105,000
Debits	(290,000)	(225,000)					(512,000)
							238,000
Income to Noncontrolling Interest			(30)	15,600			(15,600)
Net Income, carry forward	220,000	75,000		75,600		3,000	222,400
Retained Earnings, January 1	420,000	120,000	(31)	120,000			
			(32)	2,400			417,600
Net Income, from above	220,000	75,000		75,600		3,000	222,400
	640,000	195,000					640,000
Dividends Declared	(60,000)	(40,000)			(29)	32,000	
					(30)	8,000	(60,000)
Retained Earnings, December 31, carry forward	580,000	155,000		198,000		43,000	580,000
Cash	291,000	85,000					376,000
Accounts Receivable	150,000	80,000					230,000
Inventory	180,000	90,000					270,000
Land	175,000	40,000					215,000
Buildings and Equipment	800,000	600,000					1,400,000
Investment in Special Foods Stock	284,000				(29)	28,000	
					(31)	256,000	
Debits	1,880,000	895,000					2,491,000
Accumulated Depreciation	300,000	240,000					540,000
Accounts Payable	100,000	100,000					200,000
Bonds Payable	400,000	200,000					600,000
Common Stock	500,000	200,000	(31)	200,000			500,000
Retained Earnings, from above	580,000	155,000		198,000		43,000	580,000
Noncontrolling Interest			(32)	600	(30)	7,600	
					(31)	64,000	71,000
Credits	1,880,000	895,000		398,600		398,600	2,491,000

Elimination entries:
(29) Eliminate income from subsidiary.
(30) Assign income to noncontrolling interest.
(31) Eliminate beginning investment balance.
(32) Eliminate beginning inventory profit.

Peerless's separate operating income		$160,000
Peerless's share of Special Foods' income:		
Special Foods' net income	$75,000	
Realized intercompany profit		
on upstream inventory sale	3,000	
Special Foods' realized income	$78,000	
Peerless's proportionate share	× .80	62,400
Consolidated net income, 19X2		$222,400

INTERCOMPANY TRANSFERS UNDER A PERIODIC INVENTORY SYSTEM

When the affiliates involved in an intercompany sale of inventory use periodic rather than perpetual inventory systems, only the cost of goods sold section of the income statement is different. None of the other income statement and balance sheet amounts are affected by the choice of inventory systems.

The example presented earlier in the chapter is revised to illustrate the use of periodic inventory systems. As before, assume that Peerless Products purchases inventory from an outside party for $7,000 and sells it to Special Foods for $10,000. Special Foods then sells the inventory to Nonaffiliated Corporation for $15,000. Peerless Products records the inventory purchase and downstream sale to Special Foods with the following entries:

```
March 1, 19X1
     (33)  Purchases                              7,000
              Cash                                          7,000
           Purchase of inventory.

April 1, 19X1
     (34)  Cash                                   10,000
              Sales                                         10,000
           Sale of inventory to Special Foods.
```

Special Foods records the purchase of inventory from Peerless as follows:

```
April 1, 19X1
     (35)  Purchases                             10,000
              Cash                                         10,000
           Purchase of inventory from Peerless.
```

Subsequently, Special Foods resells the inventory to Nonaffiliated Corporation and records the sale with the following entry:

```
     (36)  Cash                                   15,000
              Sales                                         15,000
           Sale of inventory to Nonaffiliated.
```

Resale in Period of Intercorporate Transfer

If the inventory is resold by Special Foods to Nonaffiliated during 19X1, all four entries (33) through (36) are made during the year. With respect to the intercompany inventory, the gross profit and cost of goods sold computations for 19X1 are as follows:

Item	Peerless Products	Special Foods	Unadjusted Totals	Consolidated Amounts
Sales	$10,000	$ 15,000	$ 25,000	$15,000
Beginning Inventory	$ -0-	$ -0-	$ -0-	$ -0-
Purchases	7,000	10,000	17,000	7,000
Goods Available	$ 7,000	$ 10,000	$ 17,000	$ 7,000
Ending Inventory	-0-	-0-	-0-	-0-
Cost of Goods Sold	$ (7,000)	$(10,000)	$(17,000)	$ (7,000)
Gross Profit	$ 3,000	$ 5,000	$ 8,000	$ 8,000

As can be seen by comparing the unadjusted totals with the consolidated amounts, consolidated net income will be correctly stated even if no adjustments are made, as long as the sale to an outside party occurs in the same period as the intercompany transfer. However, both sales and purchases will be overstated from a consolidated point of view unless the intercompany sale is eliminated. Therefore, the following workpaper entry is needed to eliminate the intercompany sale by Peerless and the intercompany purchase by Special Foods:

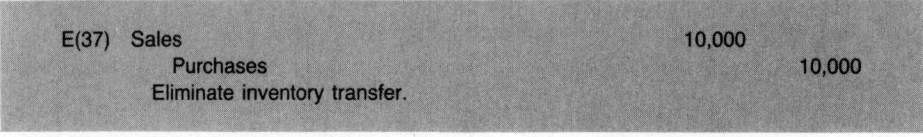

E(37) Sales	10,000	
Purchases		10,000
Eliminate inventory transfer.		

Entry E(37) is needed only in the 19X1 consolidation workpaper. No eliminating entries related to the transfer are needed in preparing consolidated financial statements in future years.

Resale in Period following Intercorporate Transfer

When inventory acquired in an intercompany transfer is held at the end of the period, the effects of the intercompany sale and any intercompany profit included in the carrying amount of the unsold inventory must be eliminated. For example, assume that Special Foods does not resell the inventory acquired from Peerless in 19X1 until 19X2. In that case, Special Foods records only entry (35) during 19X1.

Basic Equity-Method Entries—19X1   Peerless records the purchase and sale of inventory with entries (33) and (34). In addition, Peerless makes the normal equity-method entries during 19X1. The equity-method entries are not affected by the choice of inventory control systems and are identical with entries (8) and (9) presented in the earlier illustration of the perpetual inventory system:

(38)	Investment in Special Foods Stock	40,000	
	Income from Subsidiary		40,000
	Record equity-method income:		
	$50,000 × .80		
(39)	Cash	24,000	
	Investment in Special Foods Stock		24,000
	Record dividends from Special Foods:		
	$30,000 × .80		

Consolidation Workpaper—19X1   The consolidation workpaper prepared at the end of 19X1 using a periodic inventory system is shown in Figure 7-5. The following elimination entries are needed:

E(40)	Income from Subsidiary	40,000	
	Dividends Declared		24,000
	Investment in Special Foods Stock		16,000
	Eliminate income from subsidiary.		
E(41)	Income to Noncontrolling Interest	10,000	
	Dividends Declared		6,000
	Noncontrolling Interest		4,000
	Assign income to noncontrolling interest:		
	$10,000 = $50,000 × .20		
E(42)	Common Stock—Special Foods	200,000	
	Retained Earnings, January 1	100,000	
	Investment in Special Foods Stock		240,000
	Noncontrolling Interest		60,000
	Eliminate beginning investment balance.		
E(43)	Sales	10,000	
	Purchases		10,000
	Eliminate inventory transfer.		
E(44)	Ending Inventory (Income Statement)	3,000	
	Inventory (Ending, Balance Sheet)		3,000
	Eliminate unrealized profit on		
	downstream sale of inventory.		

FIGURE 7-5 December 31, 19X1, consolidation workpaper, period of intercompany sale; downstream inventory sale, periodic inventory.

Item	Peerless Products	Special Foods	Eliminations Debit		Eliminations Credit		Consolidated
Sales	400,000	200,000	(43)	10,000			590,000
Income from Subsidiary	40,000		(40)	40,000			
Ending Inventory	100,000	75,000	(44)	3,000			172,000
Credits	540,000	275,000					762,000
Purchases	170,000	130,000			(43)	10,000	290,000
Beginning Inventory	100,000	60,000					160,000
Depreciation and Amortization	50,000	20,000					70,000
Other Expenses	40,000	15,000					55,000
Debits	(360,000)	(225,000)					(575,000)
							187,000
Income to Noncontrolling Interest			(41)	10,000			(10,000)
Net Income, carry forward	180,000	50,000		63,000		10,000	177,000
Retained Earnings, January 1	300,000	100,000	(42)	100,000			300,000
Net Income, from above	180,000	50,000		63,000		10,000	177,000
	480,000	150,000					477,000
Dividends Declared	(60,000)	(30,000)			(40)	24,000	
					(41)	6,000	(60,000)
Retained Earnings, December 31, carry forward	420,000	120,000		163,000		40,000	417,000
Cash	264,000	75,000					339,000
Accounts Receivable	75,000	50,000					125,000
Inventory	100,000	75,000			(44)	3,000	172,000
Land	175,000	40,000					215,000
Buildings and Equipment	800,000	600,000					1,400,000
Investment in Special Foods Stock	256,000				(40)	16,000	
					(42)	240,000	
Debits	1,670,000	840,000					2,251,000
Accumulated Depreciation	250,000	220,000					470,000
Accounts Payable	100,000	100,000					200,000
Bonds Payable	400,000	200,000					600,000
Common Stock	500,000	200,000	(42)	200,000			500,000
Retained Earnings, from above	420,000	120,000		163,000		40,000	417,000
Noncontrolling Interest					(41)	4,000	
					(42)	60,000	64,000
Credits	1,670,000	840,000		363,000		363,000	2,251,000

Elimination entries:
(40) Eliminate income from subsidiary.
(41) Assign income to noncontrolling interest.
(42) Eliminate beginning investment balance.
(43) Eliminate inventory transfer.
(44) Eliminate unrealized profit on downstream sale of inventory.

The first three eliminating entries are identical to those used in preparing the workpaper in Figure 7-1 under a perpetual inventory system. The change from a perpetual to a periodic inventory system has no effect on these entries.

Two eliminating entries are used to eliminate the inventory transfer and the unrealized intercompany profit in the periodic inventory case. Entry E(43) adjusts the balances in Purchases and Sales for 19X1 to eliminate the effects of the intercompany sale. Entry E(44) eliminates the unrealized intercompany profit included in the ending inventory.

Eliminating entry E(44) is unique to the use of a periodic inventory system and is needed because of the role of the ending inventory figure in such a system. The ending inventory amount not only appears in the balance sheet but also is used in the computation of cost of goods sold in the income statement. For Peerless Products, this computation is as follows:

Beginning inventory	$100,000	(debit balance)
Purchases	170,000	(debit balance)
Goods available for sale	$270,000	
Less: Ending inventory	(100,000)	(credit balance)
Cost of goods sold	$170,000	

When ending inventory includes unrealized intercompany profits, it is overstated from a consolidated viewpoint. The overstatement is not limited to the balance sheet, however. If the ending inventory subtracted in arriving at consolidated cost of goods sold in the income statement is overstated, cost of goods sold will be understated and consolidated net income will be overstated. Therefore, unrealized intercompany inventory profits must be eliminated from both the ending inventory figure shown in the consolidated balance sheet and the ending inventory figure used in computing cost of goods sold in the consolidated income statement.

The amounts included in the income statement portion of the consolidation workpaper shown in Figure 7-5 are separated into debit and credit amounts, as in all three-part workpapers illustrated previously. When a company uses a periodic inventory system, the amounts used in the computation of cost of goods sold are included in the appropriate debit or credit part of the income statement section of the workpaper. Specifically, the beginning inventory and purchases are included as debits, and ending inventory is included as a credit. Note that all these amounts are simply components in the computation of cost of goods sold and could be collapsed into a single cost of goods sold figure.

Workpaper entry E(44) corrects the ending inventory balances in the two locations in the workpaper by debiting the balance in the income statement portion of the workpaper and crediting the amount in the balance sheet portion of the workpaper. Entries E(43) and E(44) together eliminate the effects of the intercompany transaction and the unrealized intercompany profit remaining in ending inventory, providing the correct consolidated balances. With regard to the inventory transferred from Peerless to Special Foods, the 19X1 amounts from the books of the separate companies and the appropriate consolidated amounts are:

Item	Peerless Products	Special Foods	Unadjusted Totals	Consolidated Amounts
Sales	$10,000	$ -0-	$10,000	$ -0-
Beginning Inventory	$ -0-	$ -0-	$ -0-	$ -0-
Purchases	7,000	10,000	17,000	7,000
Goods Available	$ 7,000	$10,000	$17,000	$7,000
Ending Inventory	-0-	10,000	10,000	7,000
Cost of Goods Sold	$ (7,000)	$ -0-	$ (7,000)	$ -0-
Gross Profit	$ 3,000	$ -0-	$ 3,000	$ -0-
Inventory	$ -0-	$10,000	$10,000	$7,000

With the exception of the items used to compute cost of goods sold in Figure 7-5, all the data shown in Figures 7-5 and 7-1 for the consolidated entity are identical. Note that total cost of goods sold is not changed by the choice of a perpetual or periodic inventory system.

Basic Equity-Method Entries—19X2   The basic equity-method entries recorded by Peerless during 19X2 are identical to entries (14) and (15) presented in the earlier illustration of the perpetual inventory system:

(45) Investment in Special Foods Stock	60,000	
Income from Subsidiary		60,000
Record equity-method income:		
$75,000 × .80		
(46) Cash	32,000	
Investment in Special Foods Stock		32,000
Record dividends from Special Foods:		
$40,000 × .80		

As in the earlier illustration, the investment account balance at the end of 19X2 is $284,000.

Consolidation Workpaper—19X2   The workpaper to prepare consolidated financial statements at the end of 19X2 is presented in Figure 7-6. The workpaper elimination entries are as follows:

FIGURE 7-6 December 31, 19X2, consolidation workpaper, next period following intercompany sale; downstream inventory sale, periodic inventory.

Item	Peerless Products	Special Foods	Eliminations Debit		Eliminations Credit		Consolidated
Sales	450,000	300,000					750,000
Income from Subsidiary	60,000		(47)	60,000			
Ending Inventory	180,000	90,000					270,000
Credits	690,000	390,000					1,020,000
Purchases	260,000	175,000					435,000
Beginning Inventory	100,000	75,000			(50)	3,000	172,000
Depreciation and Amortization	50,000	20,000					70,000
Other Expenses	60,000	45,000					105,000
Debits	(470,000)	(315,000)					(782,000)
Income to Noncontrolling Interest			(48)	15,000			238,000
							(15,000)
Net Income, carry forward	220,000	75,000		75,000		3,000	223,000
Retained Earnings, January 1	420,000	120,000	(49)	120,000			
			(50)	3,000			417,000
Net Income, from above	220,000	75,000		75,000		3,000	223,000
	640,000	195,000					640,000
Dividends Declared	(60,000)	(40,000)			(47)	32,000	
					(48)	8,000	(60,000)
Retained Earnings, December 31, carry forward	580,000	155,000		198,000		43,000	580,000
Cash	291,000	85,000					376,000
Accounts Receivable	150,000	80,000					230,000
Inventory	180,000	90,000					270,000
Land	175,000	40,000					215,000
Buildings and Equipment	800,000	600,000					1,400,000
Investment in Special Foods Stock	284,000				(47)	28,000	
					(49)	256,000	
Debits	1,880,000	895,000					2,491,000
Accumulated Depreciation	300,000	240,000					540,000
Accounts Payable	100,000	100,000					200,000
Bonds Payable	400,000	200,000					600,000
Common Stock	500,000	200,000	(49)	200,000			500,000
Retained Earnings, from above	580,000	155,000		198,000		43,000	580,000
Noncontrolling Interest					(48)	7,000	
					(49)	64,000	71,000
Credits	1,880,000	895,000		398,000		398,000	2,491,000

Elimination entries:
(47) Eliminate income from subsidiary.
(48) Assign income to noncontrolling interest.
(49) Eliminate beginning investment balance.
(50) Eliminate beginning inventory profit.

E(47)	Income from Subsidiary	60,000	
	Dividends Declared		32,000
	Investment in Special Foods Stock		28,000
	Eliminate income from subsidiary.		
E(48)	Income to Noncontrolling Interest	15,000	
	Dividends Declared		8,000
	Noncontrolling Interest		7,000
	Assign income to noncontrolling interest:		
	$15,000 = $75,000 × .20		
E(49)	Common Stock—Special Foods	200,000	
	Retained Earnings, January 1	120,000	
	Investment in Special Foods Stock		256,000
	Noncontrolling Interest		64,000
	Eliminate beginning investment balance.		
E(50)	Retained Earnings, January 1	3,000	
	Beginning Inventory (Income Statement)		3,000
	Eliminate beginning inventory profit.		

Entries E(47), E(48), and E(49) are the normal workpaper entries to eliminate the parent's income and dividends from the subsidiary, assign income to the noncontrolling interest, establish the beginning balance of the noncontrolling interest, and eliminate the stockholders' equity accounts of the subsidiary and the parent's investment account. These entries are not affected by the use of a periodic inventory system and are identical with entries E(16), E(17), and E(18) used in the perpetual inventory illustration.

Entry E(50) eliminates from beginning inventory the intercompany profit that had been unrealized at the end of 19X1. From a consolidated viewpoint, the beginning inventory amount taken from Special Foods' books is overstated by the intercompany profit included therein. To avoid understating 19X2 consolidated net income, the intercompany profit must be eliminated before the beginning inventory figure is used in the computation of consolidated cost of goods sold. The effect of entry E(50) on consolidated cost of goods sold related to the intercompany inventory can be seen as follows:

Item	Peerless Products	Special Foods	Unadjusted Totals	Consolidated Amounts
Sales	$ -0-	$ 15,000	$ 15,000	$15,000
Beginning Inventory	$ -0-	$ 10,000	$ 10,000	$ 7,000
Purchases	-0-	-0-	-0-	-0-
Goods Available	$ -0-	$ 10,000	$ 10,000	$ 7,000
Ending Inventory	-0-	-0-	-0-	-0-
Cost of Goods Sold	$ -0-	$(10,000)	$(10,000)	$ (7,000)
Gross Profit	$ -0-	$ 5,000	$ 5,000	$ 8,000
Inventory	$ -0-	$ -0-	$ -0-	$ -0-

Entry E(50) also reduces beginning consolidated retained earnings by the amount of the unrealized intercompany profit recognized by Peerless in 19X1 and included in its beginning retained earnings balance for 19X2.

Inventory Held Two or More Periods

If inventory is purchased from an affiliate in a prior period and still is held by the purchasing affiliate, an adjustment for the unrealized intercompany profit is needed each time consolidated statements are prepared. The unrealized intercompany profit must be eliminated from the beginning retained earnings balance, from the inventory shown in the consolidated balance sheet, and from the beginning and ending inventory amounts used to compute cost of goods sold in the consolidated income statement:

E(51)	Retained Earnings, January 1	3,000	
	Beginning Inventory (Income Statement)		3,000
	Eliminate beginning inventory profit.		
E(52)	Ending Inventory (Income Statement)	3,000	
	Inventory (Ending, Balance Sheet)		3,000
	Eliminate unrealized inventory profit		
	in ending inventory.		

SUMMARY COMPARISON OF INTERCOMPANY INVENTORY TRANSACTIONS

To summarize and compare, Figures 7-7 and 7-8 show the entries discussed earlier in the chapter for the $10,000 sale of inventory between Peerless Products and Special Foods at a $3,000 profit. Figure 7-7 shows the entries for 19X1, the year of the intercompany sale. Figure 7-8 shows the entries for 19X2, the year the inventory is resold to external parties. Entries are shown for both downstream and upstream sales under both the perpetual and periodic inventory systems.

ADDITIONAL CONSIDERATIONS

The frequency of intercompany inventory transfers and the varied circumstances under which they may occur raise a number of additional implementation issues. Several of these are discussed briefly in this section.

Sale from One Subsidiary to Another

Transfers of inventory often occur between companies that are under common control or ownership. When one subsidiary sells merchandise to another subsidiary, the eliminating entries are identical to those presented earlier for sales from a subsidiary to its parent. The full amount of any unrealized intercompany profit is

FIGURE 7-7 Comparison of elimination entries in December 31, 19X1, consolidation workpaper for year of (1) downstream sale and (2) upstream sale of inventory, using (a) perpetual and (b) periodic inventory system.

Downstream Sale

Perpetual Inventory System

Income from Subsidiary	40,000	
Dividends Declared		24,000
Investment in Special Foods Stock		16,000
Income to Noncontrolling Interest	10,000	
Dividends Declared		6,000
Noncontrolling Interest		4,000
Common Stock—Special Foods	200,000	
Retained Earnings, January 1	100,000	
Investment in Special Foods Stock		240,000
Noncontrolling Interest		60,000
Sales	10,000	
Cost of Goods Sold		7,000
Inventory		3,000

Periodic Inventory System

Income from Subsidiary	40,000	
Dividends Declared		24,000
Investment in Special Foods Stock		16,000
Income to Noncontrolling Interest	10,000	
Dividends Declared		6,000
Noncontrolling Interest		4,000
Common Stock—Special Foods	200,000	
Retained Earnings, January 1	100,000	
Investment in Special Foods Stock		240,000
Noncontrolling Interest		60,000
Sales	10,000	
Purchases		10,000
Ending Inventory (Income Statement)	3,000	
Inventory (Ending, Balance Sheet)		3,000

Upstream Sale

Perpetual Inventory System

Income from Subsidiary	40,000	
Dividends Declared		24,000
Investment in Special Foods Stock		16,000
Income to Noncontrolling Interest	9,400	
Dividends Declared		6,000
Noncontrolling Interest		3,400
Common Stock—Special Foods	200,000	
Retained Earnings, January 1	100,000	
Investment in Special Foods Stock		240,000
Noncontrolling Interest		60,000
Sales	10,000	
Cost of Goods Sold		7,000
Inventory		3,000

Periodic Inventory System

Income from Subsidiary	40,000	
Dividends Declared		24,000
Investment in Special Foods Stock		16,000
Income to Noncontrolling Interest	9,400	
Dividends Declared		6,000
Noncontrolling Interest		3,400
Common Stock—Special Foods	200,000	
Retained Earnings, January 1	100,000	
Investment in Special Foods Stock		240,000
Noncontrolling Interest		60,000
Sales	10,000	
Purchases		10,000
Ending Inventory (Income Statement)	3,000	
Inventory (Ending, Balance Sheet)		3,000

FIGURE 7-8 Comparison of elimination entries in December 31, 19X2, consolidation workpaper for year following (1) downstream sale and (2) upstream sale of inventory, using (a) perpetual and (b) periodic inventory system.

Downstream Sale

Perpetual Inventory System

Account	Debit	Credit
Income from Subsidiary	60,000	
Dividends Declared		32,000
Investment in Special Foods Stock		28,000
Income to Noncontrolling Interest	15,000	
Dividends Declared		8,000
Noncontrolling Interest		7,000
Common Stock—Special Foods	200,000	
Retained Earnings, January 1	120,000	
Investment in Special Foods Stock		256,000
Noncontrolling Interest		64,000
Retained Earnings, January 1	3,000	
Cost of Goods Sold		3,000

Periodic Inventory System

Account	Debit	Credit
Income from Subsidiary	60,000	
Dividends Declared		32,000
Investment in Special Foods Stock		28,000
Income to Noncontrolling Interest	15,000	
Dividends Declared		8,000
Noncontrolling Interest		7,000
Common Stock—Special Foods	200,000	
Retained Earnings, January 1	120,000	
Investment in Special Foods Stock		256,000
Noncontrolling Interest		64,000
Retained Earnings, January 1	3,000	
Beginning Inventory (Income Statement)		3,000

Upstream Sale

Perpetual Inventory System

Account	Debit	Credit
Income from Subsidiary	60,000	
Dividends Declared		32,000
Investment in Special Foods Stock		28,000
Income to Noncontrolling Interest	15,600	
Dividends Declared		8,000
Noncontrolling Interest		7,600
Common Stock—Special Foods	200,000	
Retained Earnings, January 1	120,000	
Investment in Special Foods Stock		256,000
Noncontrolling Interest		64,000
Retained Earnings, January 1	2,400	
Noncontrolling Interest	600	
Cost of Goods Sold		3,000

Periodic Inventory System

Account	Debit	Credit
Income from Subsidiary	60,000	
Dividends Declared		32,000
Investment in Special Foods Stock		28,000
Income to Noncontrolling Interest	15,600	
Dividends Declared		8,000
Noncontrolling Interest		7,600
Common Stock—Special Foods	200,000	
Retained Earnings, January 1	120,000	
Investment in Special Foods Stock		256,000
Noncontrolling Interest		64,000
Retained Earnings, January 1	2,400	
Noncontrolling Interest	600	
Beginning Inventory (Income Statement)		3,000

eliminated, with the profit elimination allocated proportionately against the ownership interests of the selling subsidiary.

As an illustration, assume that Peerless Products owns 90 percent of the outstanding stock of Super Industries in addition to its 80 percent interest in Special Foods. If Special Foods sells inventory at a $3,000 profit to Super Industries for $10,000 and all the inventory is held by Super Industries at the end of the period, the following elimination entry is among those needed in the consolidation workpaper prepared at the end of the period:

E(53)	Sales	10,000	
	Cost of Goods Sold		7,000
	Inventory		3,000
	Eliminate intercompany sale of inventory.		

The $3,000 elimination of unrealized intercompany profit is allocated proportionately between the two shareholder groups of the selling affiliate. Thus, consolidated net income is reduced by Peerless's 80 percent share of the intercompany profit, or $2,400, and Special Foods' noncontrolling interest is reduced by its 20 percent share, or $600.

Costs Associated with Transfers

When inventory is transferred from one affiliate to another, there often is some additional cost, such as freight, incurred in the transfer. This cost should be treated in the same way as if the affiliates were operating divisions of a single company. If the additional cost would be inventoried in transferring the units from one location to another within the same company, that treatment also would be appropriate for consolidation.

Lower of Cost or Market

Inventory purchased from an affiliate might be written down by the purchasing affiliate under the lower-of-cost-or-market rule if the market value is less than the intercompany transfer price. Such a situation can be illustrated by assuming that a parent company purchases inventory for $20,000 and sells it to its subsidiary for $35,000. The subsidiary still holds the inventory at year-end and determines that its market value (replacement cost) is $25,000 at that time.

The subsidiary must write the inventory down from $35,000 to its lower market value of $25,000 at the end of the year and record the following entry:

(54)	Loss on Decline in Value of Inventory	10,000	
	Inventory		10,000
	Write inventory down to market value.		

While this entry revalues the inventory to $25,000 on the books of the subsidiary, the appropriate valuation from a consolidated viewpoint is the $20,000 original cost of the inventory to the parent. Therefore, the following eliminating entry is needed in the consolidation workpaper:

E(55)	Sales	35,000	
	Cost of Goods Sold		20,000
	Inventory		5,000
	Loss on Decline in Value of Inventory		10,000
	Eliminate intercompany sale of		
	inventory.		

The inventory loss recorded by the subsidiary must be eliminated because the $20,000 inventory valuation for consolidation purposes is below the $25,000 market value of the inventory.

Sales and Purchases before Affiliation

Sometimes companies that have sold inventory to one another later join together in a business combination. The consolidation treatment of profits on inventory transfers that occurred before the business combination depends on the circumstances and the type of business combination consummated.

As a general rule, the effects of transactions that are not considered to be the result of arm's-length bargaining should be eliminated. However, the combining of two companies does not necessarily mean that their prior transactions with one another were not arm's-length. The attendant circumstances, such as the price and quantity of units transferred, would have to be examined.

For arm's-length transactions, the type of business combination has a bearing on the treatment of prior transfers. Companies that combine in purchase-type business combinations are considered as having been separate companies before the combination. Therefore, any sales between the combining companies before the combination are considered as sales between separate companies. No elimination or adjustment is needed in preparing consolidated statements subsequent to the combination, even if the inventory still is held by an affiliate.

Companies that combine in a pooling of interests are viewed as if they always had been combined. Any transactions between the combining companies that occurred before the combination are viewed after the combination as if they had occurred within the consolidated entity. Therefore, the transactions require elimination when preparing consolidated statements in the same manner as if the companies already had been combined at the time they occurred. Consolidation following a combination treated as a pooling of interests is discussed in greater detail in Chapter 10.

SUMMARY OF KEY CONCEPTS AND TERMS

Consolidated financial statements are prepared for the consolidated entity as if it were a single company. Therefore, the effects of all transactions between companies within the entity must be eliminated in preparing consolidated financial statements.

The treatment of intercompany inventory transactions is similar to the treatment of intercompany transfers of noncurrent assets discussed in Chapter 6. Each time consolidated statements are prepared, all effects of intercompany transactions occurring that period, and the effects of unrealized profits from transactions in prior periods, must be eliminated. For intercompany inventory transactions, the intercompany sale and cost of goods sold must be eliminated. In addition, the intercompany profit may not be recognized in consolidation until it is confirmed by resale of the inventory to an external party. Unrealized intercompany profits must be eliminated fully and are allocated proportionately against the stockholder groups of the selling affiliate. If inventory that includes unrealized intercompany profits is held from one period to the next, both the ending inventory of the first period and the beginning inventory of the second must be reduced to eliminate the unrealized intercompany profits for consolidation.

Periodic inventory control system   Perpetual inventory control system

APPENDIX A: Comprehensive Example of Intercompany Inventory Transactions

The example of Peerless Products and Special Foods is used for the year 19X2 to provide a comprehensive illustration of the elimination process in which there are transfers of inventories between related companies. Assume the following information regarding the intercompany transactions between Peerless and Special Foods:

1. During 19X1, Peerless Products purchases inventory for $44,000 and sells it to Special Foods for $80,000. Special Foods sells two-thirds of the inventory in 19X1 and one-third in 19X2.

2. During 19X1, Special Foods purchases inventory for $30,000 and sells it to Peerless Products for $42,500. Peerless Products sells two-fifths of the inventory in 19X1 and three-fifths in 19X2.

3. Peerless Products purchases inventory for $16,000 during 19X2 and sells it to Special Foods for $20,000. Special Foods continues to hold all this inventory at the end of 19X2.

4. Special Foods purchases inventory for $20,000 during 19X2 and sells it to Peerless Products for $38,000. Peerless resells one-quarter of the inventory in 19X2.

5. On December 31, 19X2, there is $15,000 of intercorporate receivables and payables resulting from 19X2 inventory transfers.

An overview of the intercompany inventory transactions is presented in the following table:

	Intercompany Sales	Total Intercompany Profit	Goods in Inventory at Year-End	Intercompany Profit Unrealized at Year-End
Downstream:				
19X1	$80,000	$36,000	$26,667 (33⅓%)	$12,000
19X2	20,000	4,000	20,000 (100%)	4,000
Upstream:				
19X1	42,500	12,500	25,500 (60%)	7,500
19X2	38,000	18,000	28,500 (75%)	13,500

BASIC EQUITY METHOD—19X2

During 19X2, Peerless Products recognizes its $60,000 share of Special Foods' net income and its dividends received of $32,000 with the normal basic equity-method entries. The investment account on Peerless's books appears as follows:

Investment in Special Foods Stock

Original cost	240,000		
19X1 equity accrual		19X1 dividends	
($50,000 × .80)	40,000	($30,000 × .80)	24,000
Balance, 12/31/X1	256,000		
19X2 equity accrual		19X2 dividends	
($75,000 × .80)	60,000	($40,000 × .80)	32,000
Balance, 12/31/X2	284,000		

INCOME ASSIGNED TO NONCONTROLLING INTEREST—19X2

Income assigned to noncontrolling shareholders in the 19X2 consolidated income statement is based on the realized net income of Special Foods for 19X2. Intercompany profits deferred in 19X1 and realized in 19X2 are added to reported earnings. Similarly, Special Foods' unrealized 19X2 intercompany profits are deducted from its net income in computing the amount assigned to noncontrolling shareholders. The noncontrolling stockholders' share of income is computed as follows:

Special Foods' reported net income, 19X2	$75,000
Add: 19X1 profits realized in 19X2	
[($42,500 − $30,000) × ⅗]	7,500
Less: 19X2 profits not realized by year-end	
[($38,000 − $20,000) × ¾]	(13,500)
Realized income of Special Foods, 19X2	$69,000
Percentage ownership held by noncontrolling shareholders	× .20
Income assigned to noncontrolling interest, 19X2	$13,800

BALANCE OF NONCONTROLLING INTEREST—DECEMBER 31, 19X2

The balance of the noncontrolling stockholders' claim on the net assets of Special Foods on December 31, 19X2, must exclude the noncontrolling stockholders' share of the unrealized intercompany profits:

Book value of Special Foods, December 31, 19X2	$355,000
Less: Unrealized profits on December 31, 19X2	
[($38,000 − $20,000) × $\frac{3}{4}$]	(13,500)
Realized book value of Special Foods, December 31, 19X2	$341,500
Percentage ownership held by noncontrolling shareholders	× .20
Noncontrolling interest, December 31, 19X2	$ 68,300

CONSOLIDATION WORKPAPER, 19X2—PERPETUAL INVENTORY SYSTEM

The workpaper to prepare consolidated financial statements for 19X2 using a perpetual inventory system is presented in Figure 7-9. The following elimination entries are included in the workpaper:

E(56)	Income from Subsidiary	60,000	
	Dividends Declared		32,000
	Investment in Special Foods Stock		28,000
	Eliminate income from subsidiary.		
E(57)	Income to Noncontrolling Interest	13,800	
	Dividends Declared		8,000
	Noncontrolling Interest		5,800
	Assign income to noncontrolling interest.		
E(58)	Common Stock—Special Foods	200,000	
	Retained Earnings, January 1	120,000	
	Investment in Special Foods Stock		256,000
	Noncontrolling Interest		64,000
	Eliminate beginning investment balance.		
E(59)	Accounts Payable	15,000	
	Accounts Receivable		15,000
	Eliminate intercompany receivable/payable.		
E(60)	Retained Earnings, January 1	12,000	
	Cost of Goods Sold		12,000
	Eliminate beginning inventory profit recognized by Peerless: ($80,000 − $44,000) × $\frac{1}{3}$		

E(61)	Retained Earnings, January 1	6,000	
	Noncontrolling Interest	1,500	
	Cost of Goods Sold		7,500
	Eliminate beginning inventory profit		
	recognized by Special Foods:		
	$6,000 = ($42,500 - $30,000) \times \frac{3}{5} \times .80$		
	$1,500 = ($42,500 - $30,000) \times \frac{3}{5} \times .20$		
E(62)	Sales	20,000	
	Cost of Goods Sold		16,000
	Inventory		4,000
	Eliminate intercompany downstream sale		
	of inventory.		
E(63)	Sales	38,000	
	Cost of Goods Sold		24,500
	Inventory		13,500
	Eliminate intercompany upstream sale		
	of inventory:		
	$24,500 = ($20,000 \times \frac{3}{4}) + ($38,000 \times \frac{1}{4})$		
	$13,500 = ($38,000 - $20,000) \times \frac{3}{4}$		

The first three elimination entries are the normal entries to eliminate the investment and establish the noncontrolling interest. The fourth entry eliminates the intercompany receivable/payable at the end of 19X2. These four entries are the same regardless of the inventory control system used by the companies. Entries E(60) through E(63) eliminate the intercompany sales and unrealized intercompany profits.

CONSOLIDATION WORKPAPER, 19X2—PERIODIC INVENTORY SYSTEM

The 19X2 consolidation workpaper prepared using a periodic inventory system is presented in Figure 7-10. With the exception of the change in format in the income statement portion of the workpaper caused by adding the purchases account and beginning and ending inventory totals, all the consolidated totals are identical to those shown in Figure 7-9.

Entries E(60a) through E(63b) in Figure 7-10 replace entries E(60) through E(63) in Figure 7-9. In the Figure 7-10 periodic inventory workpaper, entries E(62a) and E(62b) together eliminate a total of $16,000 from cost of goods sold when purchases and ending inventory (income statement) are reduced. This is the same amount eliminated from cost of goods sold by entry E(62) in Figure 7-9 under the perpetual inventory system. Similarly, entries E(63a) and E(63b) eliminate a total of $24,500 from cost of goods sold, the same amount as entry E(63).

FIGURE 7-9 December 31, 19X2, consolidation workpaper for comprehensive inventory illustration; perpetual inventory.

Item	Peerless Products	Special Foods	Eliminations Debit		Eliminations Credit		Consolidated
Sales	450,000	300,000	(62)	20,000			
			(63)	38,000			692,000
Income from Subsidiary	60,000		(56)	60,000			
Credits	510,000	300,000					692,000
Cost of Goods Sold	180,000	160,000			(60)	12,000	
					(61)	7,500	
					(62)	16,000	
					(63)	24,500	280,000
Depreciation and Amortization	50,000	20,000					70,000
Other Expenses	60,000	45,000					105,000
Debits	(290,000)	(225,000)					(455,000)
							237,000
Income to Noncontrolling Interest			(57)	13,800			(13,800)
Net Income, carry forward	220,000	75,000		131,800		60,000	223,200
Retained Earnings, January 1	420,000	120,000	(58)	120,000			
			(60)	12,000			
			(61)	6,000			402,000
Net Income, from above	220,000	75,000		131,800		60,000	223,200
	640,000	195,000					625,200
Dividends Declared	(60,000)	(40,000)			(56)	32,000	
					(57)	8,000	(60,000)
Retained Earnings, December 31, carry forward	580,000	155,000		269,800		100,000	565,200
Cash	291,000	85,000					376,000
Accounts Receivable	150,000	80,000			(59)	15,000	215,000
Inventory	180,000	90,000			(62)	4,000	
					(63)	13,500	252,500
Land	175,000	40,000					215,000
Buildings and Equipment	800,000	600,000					1,400,000
Investment in Special Foods Stock	284,000				(56)	28,000	
					(58)	256,000	
Debits	1,880,000	895,000					2,458,500
Accumulated Depreciation	300,000	240,000					540,000
Accounts Payable	100,000	100,000	(59)	15,000			185,000
Bonds Payable	400,000	200,000					600,000
Common Stock	500,000	200,000	(58)	200,000			500,000
Retained Earnings, from above	580,000	155,000		269,800		100,000	565,200
Noncontrolling Interest			(61)	1,500	(57)	5,800	
					(58)	64,000	68,300
Credits	1,880,000	895,000		486,300		486,300	2,458,500

Elimination entries:
(56) Eliminate income from subsidiary.
(57) Assign income to noncontrolling interest.
(58) Eliminate beginning investment balance.
(59) Eliminate intercompany receivable/payable.
(60) Eliminate beginning inventory profit recognized by Peerless.
(61) Eliminate beginning inventory profit recognized by Special Foods.
(62) Eliminate intercompany downstream sale of inventory.
(63) Eliminate intercompany upstream sale of inventory.

FIGURE 7-10 December 31, 19X2, consolidation workpaper for comprehensive inventory illustration; periodic inventory.

Item	Peerless Products	Special Foods	Eliminations Debit		Eliminations Credit		Consolidated
Sales	450,000	300,000	(62a)	20,000			
			(63a)	38,000			692,000
Income from Subsidiary	60,000		(56)	60,000			
Ending Inventory	180,000	90,000	(62b)	4,000			
			(63b)	13,500			252,500
Credits	690,000	390,000					944,500
Purchases	260,000	175,000			(62a)	20,000	
					(63a)	38,000	377,000
Beginning Inventory	100,000	75,000			(60a)	12,000	
					(61a)	7,500	155,500
Depreciation and Amortization	50,000	20,000					70,000
Other Expenses	60,000	45,000					105,000
Debits	(470,000)	(315,000)					(707,500)
							237,000
Income to Noncontrolling Interest			(57)	13,800			(13,800)
Net Income, carry forward	220,000	75,000		149,300		77,500	223,200
Retained Earnings, January 1	420,000	120,000	(58)	120,000			
			(60a)	12,000			
			(61a)	6,000			402,000
Net Income, from above	220,000	75,000		149,300		77,500	223,200
	640,000	195,000					625,200
Dividends Declared	(60,000)	(40,000)			(56)	32,000	
					(57)	8,000	(60,000)
Retained Earnings, December 31, carry forward	580,000	155,000		287,300		117,500	565,200
Cash	291,000	85,000					376,000
Accounts Receivable	150,000	80,000			(59)	15,000	215,000
Inventory	180,000	90,000			(62b)	4,000	
					(63b)	13,500	252,500
Land	175,000	40,000					215,000
Buildings and Equipment	800,000	600,000					1,400,000
Investment in Special Foods Stock	284,000				(56)	28,000	
					(58)	256,000	
Debits	1,880,000	895,000					2,458,500
Accumulated Depreciation	300,000	240,000					540,000
Accounts Payable	100,000	100,000	(59)	15,000			185,000
Bonds Payable	400,000	200,000					600,000
Common Stock	500,000	200,000	(58)	200,000			500,000
Retained Earnings, from above	580,000	155,000		287,300		117,500	565,200
Noncontrolling Interest			(61a)	1,500	(57)	5,800	
					(58)	64,000	68,300
Credits	1,880,000	895,000		503,800		503,800	2,458,500

Elimination entries:
(56) Eliminate income from subsidiary.
(57) Assign income to noncontrolling interest.
(58) Eliminate beginning investment balance.
(59) Eliminate intercompany receivable/payable.
(60a) Eliminate beginning inventory profit recognized by Peerless.

(61a) Eliminate beginning inventory profit recognized by Special Foods.
(62a) Eliminate inventory transfer from Peerless to Special Foods.
(62b) Eliminate unrealized inventory profit recognized by Peerless.
(63a) Eliminate inventory transfer from Special Foods to Peerless.
(63b) Eliminate unrealized inventory profit recognized by Special Foods.

APPENDIX B: Intercompany Inventory Transactions—Fully Adjusted Equity Method and Cost Method

Consolidation procedures following use of first the fully adjusted equity method and then the cost method are illustrated with the example of the upstream sale of inventory presented earlier. Assume that Special Foods purchases inventory for $7,000 in 19X1 and, in the same year, sells the inventory to Peerless Products for $10,000. Peerless Products sells the inventory to external parties in 19X2. Both companies use perpetual inventory control systems.

FULLY ADJUSTED EQUITY METHOD

The journal entries on the books of Peerless and the elimination entries in the consolidation workpaper are the same under the fully adjusted equity method as under the basic equity method except for differences related to unrealized intercompany profits. When using the fully adjusted equity method, the parent reduces its income and the balance of the investment account for its share of unrealized intercompany profits that arise during the period. Subsequently, the parent increases its income and the carrying amount of the investment account when the intercompany profits are realized through transactions with external parties.

Fully Adjusted Equity-Method Entries—19X1

In 19X1, Peerless Products records the normal equity-method entries reflecting its share of Special Foods' income and dividends, and an additional entry to reduce income and the investment account by the parent's share of the unrealized intercompany profit arising during the year:

(64)	Investment in Special Foods Stock	40,000	
	Income from Subsidiary		40,000
	Record equity-method income:		
	$50,000 × .80		
(65)	Cash	24,000	
	Investment in Special Foods Stock		24,000
	Record dividends from Special Foods:		
	$30,000 × .80		
(66)	Income from Subsidiary	2,400	
	Investment in Special Foods Stock		2,400
	Remove unrealized profit on upstream		
	sale of inventory: $3,000 × .80		

Entry (66) is used under the fully adjusted equity method to reduce the parent's income and the investment account by the parent's share of unrealized profits and, consequently, to bring the parent's net income into agreement with consolidated net income.

Consolidation Elimination Entries—19X1

Four eliminating entries are needed in the workpaper to prepare consolidated financial statements for 19X1:

E(67)	Income from Subsidiary	37,600	
	Dividends Declared		24,000
	Investment in Special Foods Stock		13,600
	Eliminate income from subsidiary.		
E(68)	Income to Noncontrolling Interest	9,400	
	Dividends Declared		6,000
	Noncontrolling Interest		3,400
	Assign income to noncontrolling interest:		
	$9,400 = ($50,000 − $3,000) × .20		
E(69)	Common Stock—Special Foods	200,000	
	Retained Earnings, January 1	100,000	
	Investment in Special Foods Stock		240,000
	Noncontrolling Interest		60,000
	Eliminate beginning investment balance.		
E(70)	Sales	10,000	
	Cost of Goods Sold		7,000
	Inventory		3,000
	Eliminate intercompany upstream		
	sale of inventory.		

All these workpaper entries are the same as those following use of the basic equity method except for entry E(67). Because the parent's recorded income from Special Foods is $2,400 less under the fully adjusted equity method than under the basic equity method, the elimination of that income in entry E(67) is for the lesser amount. Similarly, the increase in the investment account on the parent's books during 19X1 under the fully adjusted equity method is reduced by the parent's share of the unrealized intercompany profit, and that difference is reflected in elimination entry E(67).

Fully Adjusted Equity-Method Entries—19X2

With resale of the inventory to an external party in 19X2, the parent company recognizes its portion of the $3,000 of deferred inventory profit in addition to its pro rata portion of the reported net income of the subsidiary:

(71)	Investment in Special Foods Stock	60,000	
	Income from Subsidiary		60,000
	Record equity-method income:		
	$75,000 × .80		
(72)	Cash	32,000	
	Investment in Special Foods Stock		32,000
	Record dividends from Special Foods:		
	$40,000 × .80		
(73)	Investment in Special Foods Stock	2,400	
	Income from Subsidiary		2,400
	Recognize deferred profit on upstream		
	sale of inventory: $3,000 × .80		

Once the inventory is sold to a nonaffiliate, the intercompany profit is considered realized by the consolidated entity and is included in consolidated net income. Entry (73) is recorded by Peerless to bring its equity-method net income into agreement with consolidated net income.

Investment Account Balance

The investment account on Peerless's books appears as follows:

Investment in Special Foods Stock

	Original cost	240,000			
(64)	19X1 equity accrual		(65)	19X1 dividends	
	($50,000 × .80)	40,000		($30,000 × .80)	24,000
			(66)	Unrealized profit on upstream sale	
				($3,000 × .80)	2,400
	Balance, 12/31/X1	253,600			
(71)	19X2 equity accrual		(72)	19X2 dividends	
	($75,000 × .80)	60,000		($40,000 × .80)	32,000
(73)	Realized profit from upstream sale in prior period				
	($3,000 × .80)	2,400			
	Balance, 12/31/X2	284,000			

Consolidation Elimination Entries—19X2

Workpaper eliminating entries needed for the preparation of consolidated financial statements at the end of 19X2 are as follows:

E(74)	Income from Subsidiary	62,400	
	Dividends Declared		32,000
	Investment in Special Foods Stock		30,400
	Eliminate income from subsidiary.		
E(75)	Income to Noncontrolling Interest	15,600	
	Dividends Declared		8,000
	Noncontrolling Interest		7,600
	Assign income to noncontrolling interest:		
	$15,600 = ($75,000 + $3,000) × .20		
E(76)	Common Stock—Special Foods	200,000	
	Retained Earnings, January 1	120,000	
	Investment in Special Foods Stock		256,000
	Noncontrolling Interest		64,000
	Eliminate beginning investment balance.		
E(77)	Investment in Special Foods Stock	2,400	
	Noncontrolling Interest	600	
	Cost of Goods Sold		3,000
	Eliminate beginning inventory profit.		

Peerless's equity-method income and dividends received from Special Foods are eliminated in entry E(74). Just as the equity-method entries on the parent's books include the parent's share of the realized inventory profit, income assigned to noncontrolling shareholders for 19X2 in entry E(75) must include 20 percent of both the $75,000 reported net income of Special Foods and the $3,000 deferred intercompany inventory profit realized in 19X2. Thus, income assigned to the noncontrolling interest in the 19X2 income statement is $15,600 [($75,000 + $3,000) × .20].

Entry E(76) is the normal workpaper entry to eliminate the beginning balances of the subsidiary's stockholders' equity accounts and the investment account. The credit to the investment account is for Peerless's share of the book value of Special Foods. Because Peerless reduced the balance of the investment account in 19X1 with entry (66) to remove unrealized intercompany profits, entry E(76) credits the investment account for $2,400 more than its beginning balance.

Workpaper entry E(77) deals explicitly with the elimination of the inventory profit on the upstream sale. Cost of Goods Sold is credited in the consolidation workpaper to reflect the original cost to the consolidated entity ($7,000) of the inventory sold. The unrealized profit at the beginning of the period is allocated against both controlling and noncontrolling shareholders. The parent's share of the unrealized intercompany profit already has been removed from its beginning retained earnings by entry (66) in 19X1. This entry reduced Peerless's income and ending retained earnings for 19X1 and brought Peerless's retained earnings into agreement with consolidated retained earnings on December 31, 19X1. Thus, Peerless's 19X2 beginning retained earnings is equal to consolidated retained earnings at the beginning of 19X2 and may be included in the 19X2 consolidation workpaper without additional adjustment.

The debit to the investment account for $2,400 in entry E(77) is needed because entry E(76) overeliminates the investment account owing to the reduction by entry (66). Together, entries E(74), E(76), and E(77) fully eliminate the balance in the investment account.

COST METHOD

When using the cost method, the parent records dividends received from the subsidiary as income but makes no adjustments with respect to undistributed income of the subsidiary or unrealized intercompany profits. As an example of consolidation following an upstream intercompany sale of inventory when the parent accounts for its investment in the subsidiary using the cost method, assume the same facts as in previous illustrations dealing with an upstream sale.

Consolidation Elimination Entries—19X1

The following eliminating entries are needed in the workpaper used to prepare consolidated financial statements for 19X1:

E(78)	Dividend Income	24,000	
	Dividends Declared		24,000
	Eliminate dividend income from subsidiary:		
	$30,000 × .80		

E(79)	Income to Noncontrolling Interest	9,400	
	Dividends Declared		6,000
	Noncontrolling Interest		3,400
	Assign income to noncontrolling interest:		
	$9,400 = (\$50,000 - \$3,000) \times .20$		
E(80)	Common Stock—Special Foods	200,000	
	Retained Earnings, January 1	100,000	
	Investment in Special Foods Stock		240,000
	Noncontrolling Interest		60,000
	Eliminate investment balance at date of acquisition.		
E(81)	Sales	10,000	
	Cost of Goods Sold		7,000
	Inventory		3,000
	Eliminate intercompany upstream sale of inventory.		

These eliminating entries are the same as those following use of the basic equity method, except for entry E(78). This entry eliminates the parent's dividend income from Special Foods rather than its share of Special Foods' net income.

Consolidation Elimination Entries—19X2

Elimination entries needed in the consolidation workpaper prepared at the end of 19X2 are as follows:

E(82)	Dividend Income	32,000	
	Dividends Declared		32,000
	Eliminate dividend income from subsidiary:		
	$40,000 \times .80$		
E(83)	Income to Noncontrolling Interest	15,600	
	Dividends Declared		8,000
	Noncontrolling Interest		7,600
	Assign income to noncontrolling interest:		
	$15,600 = (\$75,000 + \$3,000) \times .20$		
E(84)	Common Stock—Special Foods	200,000	
	Retained Earnings, January 1	100,000	
	Investment in Special Foods Stock		240,000
	Noncontrolling Interest		60,000
	Eliminate investment balance at date of acquisition.		

E(85)	Retained Earnings, January 1	4,000	
	Noncontrolling Interest		4,000
	Assign undistributed prior earnings of subsidiary to noncontrolling interest:		
	$20,000 × .20		
E(86)	Retained Earnings, January 1	2,400	
	Noncontrolling Interest	600	
	Cost of Goods Sold		3,000
	Eliminate beginning inventory profit.		

Entries E(83) and E(86) are the same as those following use of the basic equity method. Entry E(82) eliminates the dividend income recorded by Peerless in 19X2. Entry E(84) eliminates the balances at the date of combination of Special Foods' stockholders' equity accounts and the investment account. This entry is the same each year. Because this entry does not change, it assigns to the noncontrolling stockholders only their share of Special Foods' book value at the date of combination. Therefore, entry E(85) is needed to assign to the noncontrolling interest a proportionate share of the undistributed earnings of Special Foods from the date of combination to the beginning of the current year.

QUESTIONS

Q7-1 Why must inventory transfers to related companies be eliminated in preparing consolidated financial statements?

Q7-2 Why is there need for an eliminating entry when an intercompany inventory transfer is made at cost?

Q7-3 Distinguish between an upstream sale of inventory and a downstream sale. Why is it important to know whether a sale is upstream or downstream?

Q7-4 How do unrealized intercompany profits on a downstream sale of inventory made during the current period affect the computation of consolidated net income?

Q7-5 How do unrealized intercompany profits on an upstream sale of inventory made during the current period affect the computation of consolidated net income?

Q7-6 Will the elimination of unrealized intercompany profits on an upstream sale or on a downstream sale in the current period have a greater effect on income assigned to the noncontrolling interest? Why?

Q7-7 What is the basic eliminating entry needed when inventory is sold to an affiliate at a profit and is resold to an unaffiliated party before the end of the period, if perpetual inventory systems are used by both affiliates?

Q7-8 What is the basic eliminating entry needed when inventory is sold to an affiliate at a profit and is not resold before the end of the period, if perpetual inventory systems are used by both affiliates?

Q7-9 What are the major differences in journal entries recorded by a company under perpetual and periodic inventory systems when inventory is purchased and resold in the same period?

Q7-10 What are the basic eliminating entries needed when inventory is sold to an affiliate at a profit and is not resold before the end of the period if periodic inventory systems are used by both affiliates?

Q7-11 What is the basic eliminating entry needed when inventory is sold to an affiliate at a profit and is resold to an unaffiliated party before the end of the period if periodic inventory systems are used by both affiliates?

Q7-12 How do unrealized intercompany inventory profits from a prior period affect the computation of consolidated net income when the inventory is resold in the current period? Is it important to know if the sale was upstream or downstream? Why, or why not?

Q7-13 What is the basic eliminating entry needed under a periodic inventory system when intercompany inventory profits that are unrealized at the beginning of the period are realized during the year?

Q7-14 How will the elimination of unrealized intercompany inventory profits recorded on the parent's books affect consolidated retained earnings?

Q7-15 How will the elimination of unrealized intercompany inventory profits recorded on the subsidiary's books affect consolidated retained earnings?

Q7-16* Is an inventory sale from one subsidiary to another treated in the same manner as an upstream sale or a downstream sale? Why?

Q7-17* Par Company regularly purchased inventory from Eagle Company. Recently, Par Company purchased a majority of the voting shares of Eagle Company. How should it treat inventory profits recorded by Eagle Company before the day of acquisition? Following the day of acquisition?

CASES

C7-1 Measuring Cost of Goods Sold

Shortcut Charlie usually manages to develop some simple rule to handle even the most complex situations. In providing for the elimination of the effects of inventory transfers between the parent company and a subsidiary or between subsidiaries, Shortcut started with the following rules:

1. When the buyer continues to hold the inventory at the end of the period, credit cost of goods sold for the amount recorded as cost of goods sold by the company that made the intercompany sale.

2. When the buyer resells the inventory before the end of the period, credit cost of goods sold for the amount recorded as cost of goods sold by the company that made the intercompany sale plus the profit recorded by that company.

3. Debit sales for the total amount credited in rule 1 or 2 above.

One of the new employees is seeking some assistance in understanding how the rules work and why.

Required

a. Explain why rule 1 is needed when consolidated statements are prepared.

b. Explain what is missing from rule 1, and prepare an alternative or additional statement for the elimination of unrealized profit when the purchasing affiliate does not resell to an unaffiliated company in the period in which it purchases inventory from an affiliate.

c. Does rule 2 lead to the correct result? Explain your answer.

d. The rules do not provide assistance in determining how much profit was recorded by either of the two companies. Where should the employee look to determine the amount of profit referred to in rule 2?

C7-2 Unrealized Inventory Profits

Morrison Company owns 80 percent of the stock of Bloom Corporation. The companies frequently engage in intercompany inventory transactions.

Required

Name the conditions that would make it possible for each of the following statements to be true. Treat each statement independently.

a. Income assigned to the noncontrolling interest in the consolidated income statement for 19X3 is greater than a pro rata share of the reported net income of Bloom Corporation.

b. Income assigned to the noncontrolling interest in the consolidated income statement for 19X3 is greater than a pro rata share of Bloom's reported net income, but consolidated net income is reduced as a result of the elimination of intercompany inventory transfers.

c. Cost of goods sold reported in the income statement of Morrison is greater than consolidated cost of goods sold for 19X3.

d. Ending inventory is not included in the December 31, 19X3, trial balance of Bloom Corporation.

C7-3 Intercompany Profit Elimination Alternatives

Rockness Corporation purchases much of its inventory from its 90 percent–owned subsidiary, Mauch Company. Mauch prices its sales to Rockness to earn a 40 percent gross profit on the sales. During 19X4, Rockness purchases $400,000 of inventory from Mauch and resells all of the inventory to unrelated parties, except for $40,000 left in ending inventory.

In reviewing the preparation of consolidated financial statements for the year, the controller of Rockness Corporation, Liz Weber, notes that all the unrealized intercompany profit remaining in ending inventory is eliminated proportionately against the controlling and noncontrolling interests. This proportionate elimination is reflected in the amounts reported for consolidated net income and the income assigned to the noncontrolling interest. Liz recalls that several alternatives exist when preparing consolidated financial statements for dealing with unrealized intercompany profits on transfers from less-than-wholly-owned subsidiaries to the parent, but not all are considered currently acceptable. She remembers, for example, that proportionate elimination has been suggested, where only the parent's proportionate share (based on the extent to which the parent shares in the subsidiary's profits) would be eliminated. Also, she has heard that some companies eliminate all of the unrealized intercompany profit against the controlling interest.

Having been impressed previously with your knowledge of accounting theory, Liz asks you to provide her with some additional information about different approaches to the elimination of unrealized intercompany profits on upstream sales.

Required

a. Compute the amount at which Rockness's inventory purchased from Mauch would be reported in the consolidated balance sheet at December 31, 19X4, under each of the following three approaches to the elimination of unrealized intercompany profits:
   (1) Proportionate or pro rata (90 percent) elimination
   (2) Full elimination against the controlling interest
   (3) Full elimination, with proportionate allocation against the controlling and non-controlling interests

b. What amount of unrealized intercompany profit would be eliminated from consolidated net income and from the income assigned to the noncontrolling interest for 19X4 under each of the three approaches listed in part **a**?

c. Provide supporting arguments for the use of each of the three methods listed in part **a**, and indicate which are acceptable in practice based on current authoritative standards.

EXERCISES

E7-1 Multiple-Choice Questions—Consolidated Income Statement

Select the correct answer for each of the following questions.

Collins Company holds 80 percent ownership of Stone Corporation. On January 10, 19X3, Collins Company sold inventory costing $40,000 to Stone Corporation for $50,000. Stone Corporation resold all the inventory to an unaffiliated company before December 31, 19X3, for $75,000. The companies had no other transactions during 19X3.

1. Sales will be reported in the 19X3 consolidated income statement at:
   a. $40,000.
   b. $75,000.
   c. $100,000.
   d. $115,000.

2. Cost of goods sold will be reported in the 19X3 consolidated income statement at:
   a. $40,000.
   b. $50,000.
   c. $80,000.
   d. $90,000.

3. Consolidated net income for 19X3 will be reported as:
   a. $10,000.
   b. $25,000.
   c. $30,000.
   d. $35,000.

E7-2 Multiple-Choice Questions—Consolidated Balances

Select the correct answer for each of the following questions.

The Derby Hat Company owns 60 percent of the voting shares of Acme Shirt Works. During 19X2, Acme sold inventory costing $20,000 to the Derby Hat Company for $28,000. The Derby Hat Company received a total of $40,000 when it resold 75 percent of the inventory to unaffiliated companies before the end of 19X2. The remaining 25 percent was held as inventory by the Derby Hat Company on December 31, 19X2. The companies had no other transactions during 19X2.

1. What amount of sales will be reported by the consolidated entity for 19X2?
   a. $28,000.
   b. $40,000.
   c. $61,000.
   d. $68,000.

2. What amount of cost of goods sold will be reported by the consolidated entity for 19X2?
   a. $15,000.
   b. $20,000.
   c. $21,000.
   d. $28,000.

3. What amount of net income will be reported by the consolidated entity for 19X2?
   a. $8,000.
   b. $18,750.
   c. $22,600.
   d. $25,000.

4. What inventory balance will be reported by the consolidated entity on December 31, 19X2?
   a. $5,000.
   b. $5,800.
   c. $7,000.
   d. $12,000.

E7-3 Multiple-Choice Questions—Consolidated Income Statement

Select the correct answer for each of the following questions.

Showtime Corporation holds 80 percent of the stock of Movie Productions, Inc. During 19X4, Showtime purchased an inventory of snack bar items for $40,000 and resold $30,000 to Movie Productions, Inc., for $48,000. Movie Productions, Inc., reported sales of $67,000 in 19X4 and had inventory of $16,000 on December 31, 19X4. The companies held no beginning inventory and had no other transactions in 19X4.

1. What amount of cost of goods sold will be reported in the 19X4 consolidated income statement?
   a. $20,000.
   b. $30,000.
   c. $32,000.
   d. $52,000.
   e. $62,000.

2. What amount of net income will be reported in the 19X4 consolidated income statement?
   a. $12,000.
   b. $18,000.
   c. $40,000.
   d. $47,000.
   e. $53,000.

3. What amount of income will be assigned to the noncontrolling interest in the 19X4 consolidated income statement?
   a. $7,000.
   b. $8,000.
   c. $9,400.
   d. $10,200.
   e. $13,400.

E7-4 Intercompany Sales

Amalgamated Bolt Works holds 70 percent of the voting shares of stock of Lockright Washer Company. During 19X2, Lockright sold washers costing $60,000 to Amalgamated Bolt Works for $80,000. By the end of 19X2, Amalgamated Bolt sold all the washers at a profit of $15,000. Both companies use perpetual inventory systems.

Required

a. Give the journal entries recorded by Lockright Washer Company and Amalgamated Bolt Works during 19X2 relating to the initial purchase, intercorporate sale, and resale of the washers.

b. Give the workpaper eliminating entries needed in preparing consolidated financial statements for 19X2 to remove all effects of the intercompany transfer.

E7-5 Unrealized Inventory Profit

Plainview Manufacturing produced 10,000 kitchen clocks in 19X6 for $5 each and sold them to Snider Sales Corporation at $15 each. Snider Sales resold 8,000 units at $22 each in 19X6 and held the remaining units in inventory on December 31, 19X6. Snider Sales owns 70 percent of the stock of Plainview Manufacturing.

Required

a. Give all journal entries recorded by Plainview Manufacturing and Snider Sales Corporation during 19X6 relating to the intercorporate sale and the resale of the clocks.

b. Give all workpaper eliminating entries needed in preparing consolidated financial statements for 19X6 to remove the effects of the intercorporate sale.

E7-6 Income Statement Effects of Unrealized Profit

Holiday Bakery owns 60 percent of the stock of Farmco Products Company. During 19X8, Farmco Products produced 100,000 bags of flour, which it sold to Holiday Bakery for

$900,000. On December 31, 19X8, Holiday Bakery had 20,000 bags of flour purchased from Farmco Products on hand. Farmco prices its sales at cost plus 50 percent of cost for profit. Holiday Bakery, which purchased all its flour from Farmco Products in 19X8, had no inventory on hand on January 1, 19X8.

Holiday Bakery reported income from its baking operations of $400,000, and Farmco Products reported net income of $150,000 for 19X8.

Required

a. Compute the amount reported as cost of goods sold in the 19X8 consolidated income statement.

b. Give the workpaper eliminating entry or entries required to remove the effects of the intercompany sale in preparing consolidated statements at the end of 19X8.

c. Compute the amount reported as consolidated net income for 19X8.

E7-7 Prior-Period Unrealized Inventory Profit

Holiday Bakery owns 60 percent of the stock of Farmco Products. On January 1, 19X9, inventory reported by Holiday Bakery included 20,000 bags of flour purchased from Farmco Products at $9 per bag. By December 31, 19X9, all the beginning inventory purchased from Farmco Products had been baked into products and sold to customers by Holiday Bakery. There were no transactions between Holiday Bakery and Farmco Products during 19X9.

Both Holiday Bakery and Farmco Products price their sales at cost plus 50 percent markup for profit. Holiday Bakery reported income from its baking operations of $300,000, and Farmco Products reported net income of $250,000 for 19X9.

Required

a. Compute the amount reported as cost of goods sold in the 19X9 consolidated income statement for the flour purchased from Farmco Products in 19X8.

b. Give the eliminating entry or entries required to remove the effects of the unrealized profit in beginning inventory in preparing the consolidation workpaper as of December 31, 19X9.

c. Compute the amount reported as consolidated net income for 19X9.

E7-8 Computation of Consolidated Income Statement Data

Bass Company purchased 60 percent of the voting shares of Cooper Company for $260,000 on January 1, 19X2. Cooper Company reported total stockholders' equity of $400,000 at the time of acquisition. The purchase differential is assigned to patents with an expected economic life of 20 years from the date of combination.

During 19X5, Bass Company purchased inventory for $20,000 and sold the full amount to Cooper Company for $30,000. On December 31, 19X5, Cooper's ending inventory included $6,000 of items purchased from Bass Company. Also in 19X5, Cooper Company purchased inventory for $50,000 and sold the units to Bass Company for $80,000. Bass included $20,000 of its purchase from Cooper in ending inventory on December 31, 19X5.

Summary income statement data for the two companies revealed the following:

	Bass Company	Cooper Company
Sales	$ 400,000	$ 200,000
Income from Subsidiary	26,000	
	$ 426,000	$ 200,000
Cost of Goods Sold	$ 250,000	$ 120,000
Other Expenses	70,000	35,000
Total Expenses	$(320,000)	$(155,000)
Net Income	$ 106,000	$ 45,000

Required

a. Compute the amount to be reported as sales in the 19X5 consolidated income statement.

b. Compute the amount to be reported as cost of goods sold in the 19X5 consolidated income statement.

c. What amount of income will be assigned to the noncontrolling shareholders in the 19X5 consolidated income statement?

d. What amount of consolidated net income will be reported for 19X5?

E7-9   Inventory Sales under Periodic Inventory System

Herb Corporation holds 60 percent ownership of Spice Company. Each year, Spice Company purchases large quantities of a gnarl root used in producing health drinks. Spice purchased $150,000 of roots in 19X7 and sold $40,000 of these purchases to Herb Corporation for $60,000. By the end of 19X7, Herb Corporation had resold all but $15,000 of its purchase from Spice. Herb Corporation generated $90,000 on the sale of roots to various health stores during the year. Both Herb Corporation and Spice Company use periodic inventory systems in accounting for inventory.

Required

a. Give the journal entries recorded by Herb Corporation and Spice Company during 19X7 relating to the initial purchase, intercorporate sale, and resale of gnarl roots.

b. Give the workpaper eliminating entries needed as of December 31, 19X7, to remove all effects of the intercompany transfer in preparing the 19X7 consolidated financial statements.

E7-10   Prior-Period Profits under Periodic Inventory System

Home Products Corporation sells a broad line of home detergent products. Home Products owns 75 percent of the stock of Level Brothers Soap Company. During 19X8, Level

Brothers sold soap products to Home Products for $180,000, which it had produced for $120,000. Home Products sold $150,000 of its purchase from Level Brothers in 19X8 and the remainder in 19X9. In addition, Home Products purchased $240,000 of inventory from Level Brothers in 19X9 and resold $90,000 of the items before year-end. The cost to Level Brothers of producing the items sold to Home Products in 19X9 was $160,000. Both companies use periodic inventory systems.

Required

a. Give all workpaper eliminating entries needed for December 31, 19X9, to remove the effects of the intercompany inventory transfers in 19X8 and 19X9.

b. Compute the amount of income assigned to noncontrolling shareholders in the 19X8 and 19X9 consolidated income statements if Level Brothers reported net income of $350,000 for 19X8 and $420,000 in 19X9.

E7-11   Upstream and Downstream Sales

Brown Company purchased 90 percent ownership of Green Company on January 1, 19X1, at underlying book value. While each company has its own sales forces and independent product lines, there are substantial intercorporate sales of inventory each period. The following intercorporate sales occurred during 19X3 and 19X4:

Year	Producer	Production Cost	Buyer	Sale Price	Unsold at End of Year	Year Sold
19X3	Green Co.	$64,000	Brown Co.	$80,000	$20,000	19X4
19X4	Green Co.	36,000	Brown Co.	44,000	11,000	19X5
19X4	Brown Co.	40,000	Green Co.	60,000	9,000	19X5

Green reported net income of $20,000 for 19X4, and Brown reported operating income (excluding income from its Green Company investment) of $45,000.

Required

a. Compute the amount of consolidated net income reported for 19X4.

b. Compute the inventory amount included in the December 31, 19X4, consolidated balance sheet for the items shown above.

c. Compute the amount included in consolidated cost of goods sold for 19X4 relating to the transactions shown above.

E7-12   Consolidated Balance Sheet Workpaper

The December 31, 19X8, balance sheets for Doorst Corporation and its 70 percent–owned subsidiary Hingle Company contained the following summarized amounts:

Doorst Corporation and Hingle Company
Balance Sheets
December 31, 19X8

	Doorst Corporation	Hingle Company
Cash and Receivables	$ 98,000	$ 40,000
Inventory	150,000	100,000
Buildings and Equipment (net)	310,000	280,000
Investment in Hingle Company Stock	280,000	
Total Assets	$838,000	$420,000
Accounts Payable	$ 70,000	$ 20,000
Common Stock	200,000	150,000
Retained Earnings	568,000	250,000
Total Liabilities and Equity	$838,000	$420,000

Doorst purchased the shares of Hingle Company at underlying book value on January 1, 19X7. On December 31, 19X8, the balance sheet of Doorst contains inventory items purchased from Hingle for $95,000. The items cost Hingle $55,000 to produce. In addition, Hingle's inventory contains goods it purchased from Doorst for $25,000 that Doorst had produced for $15,000.

Required

a. Prepare all eliminating entries needed to complete a consolidated balance sheet workpaper as of December 31, 19X8.

b. Prepare a consolidated balance sheet workpaper as of December 31, 19X8.

PROBLEMS

P7-13 Consolidated Income Statement Data

Sweeny Corporation owns 60 percent of the shares of Bitner Company. Partial 19X2 financial data for the companies and consolidated entity were as follows:

	Sweeny Corporation	Bitner Company	Consolidated Totals
Sales	$550,000	$450,000	$820,000
Cost of Goods Sold	310,000	300,000	420,000
Inventory, Dec. 31	180,000	210,000	375,000

On January 1, 19X2, the inventory of Sweeny Corporation contained items purchased from Bitner Company for $75,000. The cost of the units to Bitner Company was $50,000. All intercorporate sales during 19X2 were made by Bitner Company to Sweeny Corporation.

Required

   a. What amount of intercorporate sales occurred in 19X2?

   b. How much unrealized intercompany profit existed on January 1, 19X2? On December 31, 19X2?

   c. Give the workpaper eliminating entries relating to inventory and cost of goods sold needed to prepare consolidated financial statements for 19X2.

   d. If Bitner Company reports net income of $90,000 for 19X2, what amount of income is assigned to the noncontrolling interest in the 19X2 consolidated income statement?

P7-14 Unrealized Profit on Upstream Sales

Andover Company sells all its output at 40 percent above cost. Standard Dairies purchases all its inventory from its subsidiary, Andover Company. Selected information on the operations of the companies over the past 3 years is as follows:

	Andover Company		Standard Dairies	
Year	Sales to Standard Dairies	Net Income	Inventory, Dec. 31	Operating Income
19X3	$360,000	$ 80,000	$17,500	$200,000
19X4	560,000	140,000	70,000	310,000
19X5	480,000	60,000	28,000	150,000

Andover Company was started in 19X1. Standard purchased 70 percent ownership at book value on January 1, 19X3.

Required

Compute consolidated net income and income assigned to the noncontrolling interest for each of the years 19X3 through 19X5.

P7-15 Consolidated Net Income

Alpine Corporation purchased 80 percent of the stock of Hillside Company for $210,000 on January 1, 19X3, when Hillside had retained earnings of $125,000 and common stock outstanding of $100,000. The differential is assigned to equipment with an expected life of 10 years from the date of combination.

   On December 31, 19X5, Hillside had $5,000 of unrealized profits on its books from inventory sales to Alpine, and Alpine had $7,000 of unrealized profits on its books from sales to Hillside. All inventory held by the two companies on December 31, 19X5, was resold during 19X6. On December 31, 19X6, Alpine Corporation held inventory purchased from Hillside on which Hillside had recognized a profit of $15,000.

   Alpine Corporation reported income from its separate operations of $140,000 and paid dividends of $80,000 in 19X6. Hillside Company reported net income of $40,000 and paid dividends of $15,000 in 19X6.

Required

Compute consolidated net income for 19X6.

P7-16 Eliminations for Upstream Sales

Clean Air Products owns 80 percent of the stock of Superior Filter Company, which it acquired at underlying book value on August 30, 19X6. Summarized trial balance data for the two companies as of December 31, 19X8, are as follows:

	Clean Air Products		Superior Filter Company	
Cash and Accounts Receivable	$ 145,000		$ 90,000	
Inventory	220,000		110,000	
Buildings and Equipment (net)	270,000		180,000	
Investment in Superior Filter Stock	280,000			
Cost of Goods Sold	175,000		140,000	
Depreciation Expense	30,000		20,000	
Current Liabilities		$ 150,000		$ 30,000
Common Stock		200,000		90,000
Retained Earnings		488,000		220,000
Sales		250,000		200,000
Income from Subsidiary		32,000		
Total	$1,120,000	$1,120,000	$540,000	$540,000

On January 1, 19X8, the inventory held by Clean Air Products contained filters purchased for $60,000 from Superior Filter Company. Superior had produced the filters for $40,000. In 19X8, Superior Filter spent $100,000 to produce additional filters, which it sold to Clean Air for $150,000. By December 31, 19X8, Clean Air had sold all the filters that had been on hand January 1, 19X8, but continued to hold in inventory $45,000 of the 19X8 purchase from Superior Filter.

Required

a. Prepare all eliminating entries needed to complete a consolidation workpaper for 19X8.

b. Compute consolidated net income for 19X8.

c. Compute the balance assigned to the noncontrolling interest in the consolidated balance sheet as of December 31, 19X8.

P7-17 Multiple Inventory Transfers

Ajax Corporation purchased at book value 70 percent of the ownership of Beta Corporation and 90 percent of the ownership of Cole Corporation in 19X5. There are frequent intercompany transfers among the companies. Activity relevant to 19X8 is presented below.

Year	Producer	Production Cost	Buyer	Transfer Price	Unsold at End of Year	Year Sold
19X7	Beta Corp.	$24,000	Ajax Corp.	$30,000	$10,000	19X8
19X7	Cole Corp.	60,000	Beta Corp.	72,000	18,000	19X8
19X8	Ajax Corp.	15,000	Beta Corp.	35,000	7,000	19X9
19X8	Beta Corp.	63,000	Cole Corp.	72,000	12,000	19X9
19X8	Cole Corp.	27,000	Ajax Corp.	45,000	15,000	19X9

For the year ended December 31, 19X8, Ajax Corporation reported $80,000 of income from its separate operations (excluding income from intercorporate investments), Beta Corporation reported net income of $37,500, and Cole Corporation reported net income of $20,000.

Required

a. Compute the amount to be reported as consolidated net income for 19X8.

b. Compute the amount to be reported as inventory in the December 31, 19X8, consolidated balance sheet for the items shown above.

c. Compute the amount to be reported as income assigned to noncontrolling shareholders in the 19X8 consolidated income statement.

P7-18   Consolidation Workpaper

Bear Construction Corporation holds 70 percent of the stock of Marshall Company. Bear Construction acquired the shares of Marshall Company on December 31, 19X5, at underlying book value. Trial balance data for the two companies as of December 31, 19X9, are summarized as follows:

Bear Construction Corporation and Marshall Company
Trial Balance Data
December 31, 19X9

	Bear Construction Corporation		Marshall Company	
Cash and Receivables	$ 106,500		$ 85,000	
Inventory	200,000		110,000	
Buildings and Equipment (net)	270,000		250,000	
Investment in Marshall Company Stock	290,500			
Cost of Goods and Services	200,000		150,000	
Depreciation Expense	40,000		30,000	
Dividends Declared	35,000		5,000	
Sales and Service Revenue		$ 300,000		$200,000
Income from Subsidiary		14,000		
Accounts Payable		60,000		30,000
Common Stock		200,000		150,000
Retained Earnings		568,000		250,000
Total	$1,142,000	$1,142,000	$630,000	$630,000

On January 1, 19X9, the inventory of Bear Construction contained unrealized intercompany profits recorded by Marshall Company in the amount of $40,000. The inventory of Marshall Company on that date contained $10,000 of unrealized intercompany profits recorded on the books of Bear Construction. Both companies sold their ending 19X8 inventories in 19X9.

During 19X9, Marshall Company sold inventory costing $37,000 to Bear Construction for $67,000. All the inventory purchased from Marshall Company during 19X9 is held by Bear Construction on December 31, 19X9. Also during 19X9, Bear Construction sold goods costing $54,000 to Marshall Company for $90,000. Marshall Company continues to hold $30,000 of its purchase from Bear Construction on December 31, 19X9.

Required

  a. Prepare all eliminating entries needed to complete a consolidation workpaper as of December 31, 19X9.
  b. Prepare a consolidation workpaper as of December 31, 19X9.
  c. Prepare a reconciliation between the balance in retained earnings reported by Bear Construction Corporation on December 31, 19X9, and consolidated retained earnings.

P7-19 Computation of Consolidated Totals

Bunker Corporation owns 80 percent of the stock of Harrison Company. At the end of 19X8, Bunker Corporation and Harrison Company reported the following partial operating results and inventory balances:

	Bunker Corporation	Harrison Company
Total sales	$660,000	$510,000
Sales to Harrison Company	140,000	
Sales to Bunker Corporation		240,000
Net income		20,000
Operating income (excluding income from Harrison Company)	70,000	
Inventory on hand, December 31, 19X8, purchased from:		
Harrison Company	48,000	
Bunker Corporation		42,000

Bunker Corporation regularly prices its products at cost plus a 40 percent markup for profit. Harrison Company prices its sales at cost plus a 20 percent markup. The total sales reported by Bunker and Harrison include both intercompany sales and sales to nonaffiliates.

Required

  a. What amount of sales will be reported in the consolidated income statement for 19X8?
  b. What amount of cost of goods sold will be reported in the 19X8 consolidated income statement?
  c. What amount of consolidated net income will be reported for 19X8?
  d. What balance will be reported for inventory in the consolidated balance sheet for December 31, 19X8?

P7-20 Consolidation Using Financial Statement Data

Direct Sales Corporation purchased 60 percent of the stock of Concerto Company on January 1, 19X3, for $24,000 in excess of the underlying book value. The difference relates to goodwill and is being amortized over an 8-year period.

Balance sheet data for January 1, 19X6, and December 31, 19X6, and income statement data for 19X6 for the two companies are as follows:

Direct Sales Corporation and Concerto Company
Balance Sheet Data
January 1, 19X6

	Direct Sales Corporation		Concerto Company	
Cash	$ 9,800		$ 10,000	
Accounts Receivable	60,000		50,000	
Inventory	100,000		80,000	
Total Current Assets		$169,800		$140,000
Land		70,000		20,000
Buildings and Equipment	$300,000		$200,000	
Less: Accumulated Depreciation	(140,000)	160,000	(70,000)	130,000
Investment in Concerto Company Stock		135,000		
Total Assets		$534,800		$290,000
Accounts Payable		$ 30,000		$ 20,000
Bonds Payable		120,000		70,000
Common Stock	$100,000		$ 50,000	
Retained Earnings	284,800	384,800	150,000	200,000
Total Liabilities and Stockholders' Equity		$534,800		$290,000

Direct Sales Corporation and Concerto Company
Balance Sheet Data
December 31, 19X6

	Direct Sales Corporation		Concerto Company	
Cash	$ 26,800		$ 35,000	
Accounts Receivable	80,000		40,000	
Inventory	120,000		90,000	
Total Current Assets		$226,800		$165,000
Land		70,000		20,000
Buildings and Equipment	$340,000		$200,000	
Less: Accumulated Depreciation	(165,000)	175,000	(85,000)	115,000
Investment in Concerto Company Stock		141,000		
Total Assets		$612,800		$300,000
Accounts Payable		$ 80,000		$ 15,000
Bonds Payable		120,000		70,000
Common Stock	$100,000		$ 50,000	
Retained Earnings	312,800	412,800	165,000	215,000
Total Liabilities and Stockholders' Equity		$612,800		$300,000

Direct Sales Corporation and Concerto Company
Income Statement Data
Year Ended December 31, 19X6

Sales		$400,000		$200,000
Income from Subsidiary		18,000		
		$418,000		$200,000
Cost of Goods Sold	$280,000		$120,000	
Depreciation and Amortization				
Expense	25,000		15,000	
Other Expenses	35,000	(340,000)	30,000	(165,000)
Net Income		$ 78,000		$ 35,000

In 19X4, Concerto Company purchased a piece of land for $35,000 and later in the year sold it to Direct Sales Corporation for $45,000. Direct Sales Corporation is still using the land in its operations.

On January 1, 19X6, Direct Sales Corporation held inventory purchased from Concerto Company for $48,000. During 19X6, Direct Sales purchased an additional $90,000 of goods from Concerto Company and held $54,000 of its purchases on December 31, 19X6. Concerto Company sells inventory to the parent at 20 percent above cost.

Concerto Company also purchases inventory from Direct Sales Corporation. On January 1, 19X6, Concerto held inventory purchased from Direct Sales for $14,000, and on December 31, 19X6, it held inventory purchased from Direct Sales for $7,000. Concerto's total purchases from Direct Sales Corporation were $22,000 in 19X6. Direct Sales Corporation sells items to Concerto Company at 40 percent above cost.

During 19X6, Direct Sales Corporation paid dividends of $50,000, and Concerto Company paid dividends of $20,000.

Required

a. Prepare all eliminating entries needed to complete a consolidation workpaper as of December 31, 19X6.

b. Prepare a three-part consolidation workpaper as of December 31, 19X6.

P7-21 Comprehensive Multiple-Choice Problem

Mega Retail Corporation purchased 80 percent of the voting shares of Dime Store Enterprises on January 1, 19X4, for $240,000. On that date Dime Store Enterprises reported retained earnings of $50,000 and common stock outstanding of $200,000.

Partial balance sheets and income statements for the companies are available at December 31, 19X6, as follows:

Mega Retail Corporation and Dime Store Enterprises
Balance Sheets
December 31, 19X6

	Mega Retail Corporation		Dime Store Enterprises
Cash	$?		$163,000
Inventory	200,000		200,000
Land	50,000		30,000
Buildings and Equipment	$500,000		$400,000
Less: Accumulated Depreciation	(250,000)	250,000	(180,000) 220,000
Investment in Smith Company Bonds		106,400	
Investment in Dime Store Stock		?	
Total Assets		$1,080,000	$613,000
Current Liabilities		$ 150,000	$ 80,000
Bonds Payable		400,000	$200,000
Bond Premium			8,000 208,000
Common Stock		300,000	200,000
Retained Earnings		230,000	125,000
Total Liabilities and Equities		$1,080,000	$613,000

Mega Retail Corporation and Dime Store Enterprises
Income Statements
Year Ended December 31, 19X6

	Mega Retail Corporation		Dime Store Enterprises
Sales	$300,000		$200,000
Other Income	34,000		
Income from Subsidiary	?		
	$?		$200,000
Cost of Goods Sold	$220,000		$100,000
Depreciation and Amortization	50,000		20,000
Interest Expense	24,000		14,000
Other Expenses	16,000	(310,000)	26,000 (160,000)
Net Income		$?	$ 40,000

On the date of combination, all Dime Store's assets were carried at book values that were equal to their market values except for buildings, which had a fair value of $30,000 greater than book value. The buildings had an expected 10-year remaining life on that date. Goodwill is amortized over the maximum period permitted by authoritative standards.

Dime Store sells part of its inventory to Mega Retail each year. During 19X5, Dime Store sold goods costing $30,000 to Mega Retail for $35,000. Mega resold 60 percent of the inventory in 19X5 and 40 percent in 19X6. In 19X6, Dime Store sold goods costing $50,000 to Mega Retail for $70,000, and Mega resold 70 percent of the goods during 19X6.

During 19X6, Mega Retail Corporation paid dividends of $20,000, and Dime Store Enterprises paid dividends of $15,000.

Required

Select the correct answer for each of the following questions.

1. What total amount of depreciation and amortization will be reported in the 19X6 consolidated income statement?
   a. $70,000.
   b. $72,800.
   c. $73,000.
   d. $73,250.

2. What amount of inventory will be reported in the consolidated balance sheet of December 31, 19X6?
   a. $380,000.
   b. $394,000.
   c. $396,000.
   d. $400,000.

3. What amount of cost of goods sold will be reported in the 19X6 consolidated income statement?
   a. $248,000.
   b. $254,000.
   c. $256,000.
   d. $320,000.

4. What was the amount of unamortized purchase differential on January 1, 19X6?
   a. $30,250.
   b. $31,600.
   c. $33,500.
   d. $34,400.
   e. $40,000.

5. What amount of goodwill will be reported in the December 31, 19X6, consolidated balance sheet?
   a. $14,800.
   b. $16,000.
   c. $16,800.
   d. $24,000.
   e. $40,000.

6. What amount of income will be assigned to the noncontrolling interest in the 19X6 consolidated income statement?
   a. $6,800.
   b. $7,200.
   c. $8,000.
   d. $8,400.

7. What amount will be reported as the noncontrolling shareholders' claim in the consolidated balance sheet as of December 31, 19X6?
   a. $59,000.
   b. $63,800.
   c. $64,200.
   d. $65,000.

8. What is consolidated net income for 19X6?
   a. $48,400.
   b. $50,000.
   c. $51,200.
   d. $56,000.

P7-22 Consolidated Balance Sheet Workpaper [AICPA Adapted]

The December 31, 19X6, condensed balance sheets of Pine Corp. and its 90 percent–owned subsidiary, Slim Corp., are presented in the accompanying worksheet.
Additional information is as follows:

• Pine's investment in Slim was purchased for $1,200,000 cash on January 1, 19X6, and is accounted for by the basic equity method.
• At January 1, 19X6, Slim's retained earnings amounted to $600,000, and its common stock amounted to $200,000.
• Slim declared a $1,000 cash dividend in December 19X6, payable in January 19X7.
• As of December 31, 19X6, Pine had not recorded any portion of Slim's 19X6 net income or dividend declaration.
• Slim borrowed $100,000 from Pine on June 30, 19X6, with the note maturing on June 30, 19X7, at 10 percent interest. Correct accruals have been recorded by both companies.
• During 19X6, Pine sold merchandise to Slim at an aggregate invoice price of $300,000, which included a profit of $60,000. At December 31, 19X6, Slim had not paid Pine for $90,000 of these purchases, and 5 percent of the total merchandise purchased from Pine still remained in Slim's inventory.
• Pine's excess cost over book value of its investment in Slim has appropriately been identified as goodwill and is to be amortized over 10 years.

Required

Complete the accompanying workpaper for Pine Corp. and its subsidiary, Slim Corp., at December 31, 19X6.

Pine Corp. and Subsidiary
Consolidated Balance Sheet Workpaper
December 31, 19X6

	Pine Corp.	Slim Corp.	Adjustments and Eliminations Debit	Adjustments and Eliminations Credit	Consolidated
Assets:					
Cash	75,000	15,000			
Accounts and Other Current Receivables	410,000	120,000			
Merchandise Inventory	920,000	670,000			
Plant and Equipment, Net	1,000,000	400,000			
Investment in Slim	1,200,000				
Totals	3,605,000	1,205,000			
Liabilities and Stockholders' Equity:					
Accounts Payable and Other Current Liabilities	140,000	305,000			
Common Stock ($10 par)	500,000	200,000			
Retained Earnings	2,965,000	700,000			
Totals	3,605,000	1,205,000			

P7-23 Comprehensive Worksheet Problem—Perpetual Inventories

Randall Corporation acquired 80 percent of the voting shares of Sharp Company on January 1, 19X4, for $280,000 in cash and marketable securities. At the time of acquisition, Sharp Company reported net assets of $300,000. Trial balances for the two companies on December 31, 19X7, are as follows:

Item	Randall Corporation Debit	Randall Corporation Credit	Sharp Company Debit	Sharp Company Credit
Cash	$ 130,300		$ 10,000	
Accounts Receivable	80,000		70,000	
Inventory	170,000		110,000	
Buildings and Equipment	600,000		400,000	
Investment in Sharp Company Stock	304,000			
Cost of Goods Sold	416,000		202,000	
Depreciation and Amortization	30,000		20,000	
Other Expenses	24,000		18,000	
Dividends Declared	50,000		25,000	
Accumulated Depreciation		$ 310,000		$120,000
Accounts Payable		100,000		15,200
Bonds Payable		300,000		100,000
Bond Premium				4,800
Common Stock		200,000		100,000
Additional Paid-In Capital				20,000
Retained Earnings		345,900		215,000
Sales		500,000		250,000
Other Income		20,400		30,000
Income from Subsidiary		28,000		
	$1,804,300	$1,804,300	$855,000	$855,000

Additional information:

1. The purchase differential is appropriately assigned to buildings and equipment that had a remaining 10-year economic life at the date of combination.

2. Randall Corporation and Sharp Company regularly purchase inventory from each other. During 19X6, Sharp sold inventory costing $40,000 to Randall Corporation for $60,000, and Randall resold 60 percent of the inventory in 19X6 and 40 percent in 19X7. Also in 19X6, Randall sold inventory costing $20,000 to Sharp for $26,000. Sharp resold two-thirds of the inventory in 19X6 and one-third in 19X7.

3. During 19X7, Sharp sold inventory costing $30,000 to Randall Corporation for $45,000, and Randall sold items purchased for $9,000 to Sharp for $12,000. Randall resold before the end of the year one-third of the inventory it purchased from Sharp in 19X7. Sharp continues to hold all the units purchased from Randall during 19X7.

4. Randall Corporation sold equipment originally purchased for $75,000 to Sharp for $50,000 on December 31, 19X5. Accumulated depreciation over the 12 years of use before the intercorporate sale was $45,000. The estimated remaining life at the time of transfer was 8 years. Straight-line depreciation is used by both companies.

5. Sharp owes Randall $10,000 on account on December 31, 19X7.

Required

a. Prepare the 19X7 journal entries recorded on the books of Randall Corporation related to its investment in Sharp Company if Randall uses the basic equity method.

b. Prepare all eliminating entries needed to complete a consolidation workpaper as of December 31, 19X7.

c. Prepare a three-part consolidation workpaper as of December 31, 19X7.

d. Prepare, in good form, a consolidated income statement, balance sheet, and retained earnings statement for 19X7.

P7-24 Comprehensive Worksheet Problem—Periodic Inventories

Randall Corporation acquired 80 percent of the voting shares of Sharp Company on January 1, 19X4, for $280,000 in cash and marketable securities. At the time of acquisition, Sharp Company reported net assets of $300,000. Trial balances for the two companies on December 31, 19X7, are as follows:

	Randall Corporation		Sharp Company	
Item	**Debit**	**Credit**	**Debit**	**Credit**
Cash	$ 130,300		$ 10,000	
Accounts Receivable	80,000		70,000	
Inventory	150,000		120,000	
Buildings and Equipment	600,000		400,000	
Investment in Sharp Company Stock	304,000			
Purchases	436,000		192,000	
Depreciation and Amortization	30,000		20,000	
Other Expenses	24,000		18,000	
Dividends Declared	50,000		25,000	
Accumulated Depreciation		$ 310,000		$120,000
Accounts Payable		100,000		15,200
Bonds Payable		300,000		100,000
Bond Premium				4,800
Common Stock		200,000		100,000
Additional Paid-In Capital				20,000
Retained Earnings		345,900		215,000
Sales		500,000		250,000
Other Income		20,400		30,000
Income from Subsidiary		28,000		
	$1,804,300	$1,804,300	$855,000	$855,000

Additional information:

1. Both companies use periodic inventory systems. At December 31, 19X7, Sharp Company reported ending inventory of $110,000, and Randall Corporation reported ending inventory of $170,000.

2. The purchase differential is appropriately assigned to buildings and equipment that had a remaining 10-year economic life at the date of combination.

3. Randall Corporation and Sharp Company regularly purchase inventory from each other. During 19X6, Sharp sold inventory costing $40,000 to Randall Corporation for $60,000, and Randall resold 60 percent of the inventory in 19X6 and 40 percent in 19X7. Also in 19X6, Randall sold inventory costing $20,000 to Sharp for $26,000. Sharp resold two-thirds of the inventory in 19X6 and one-third in 19X7.

4. During 19X7, Sharp sold inventory costing $30,000 to Randall Corporation for $45,000, and Randall sold items purchased for $9,000 to Sharp for $12,000. Randall resold before the end of the year one-third of the inventory it purchased from Sharp in 19X7. Sharp continues to hold all the units purchased from Randall during 19X7.

5. Randall Corporation sold equipment originally purchased for $75,000 to Sharp for $50,000 on December 31, 19X5. Accumulated depreciation over the 12 years of use before the intercorporate sale was $45,000. The estimated remaining life at the time of transfer was 8 years. Straight-line depreciation is used by both companies.

6. Sharp owes Randall $10,000 on account on December 31, 19X7.

Required

a. Prepare the 19X7 journal entries recorded on the books of Randall Corporation related to its investment in Sharp Company if Randall uses the basic equity method.

b. Prepare all eliminating entries needed to complete a consolidation workpaper as of December 31, 19X7.

c. Prepare a three-part consolidation workpaper as of December 31, 19X7.

d. Prepare, in good form, a consolidated income statement, balance sheet, and retained earnings statement for 19X7.

P7–25 Comprehensive Consolidation Workpaper; Equity Method [AICPA Adapted]

Fran Corp. acquired all the outstanding $10 par value voting common stock of Brey, Inc. on January 1, 19X9, in exchange for 25,000 shares of its $20 par value voting common stock. On December 31, 19X8, Fran's common stock had a closing market price of $30 per share on a national stock exchange. The acquisition was appropriately accounted for as a purchase. Both companies continued to operate as separate business entities maintaining separate accounting records with years ending December 31. Fran accounts for its investment in Brey stock using the equity method without adjusting for unrealized intercompany profits.

On December 31, 19X9, the companies had condensed financial statements as follows:

	Fran Corp. Dr (Cr)	Brey, Inc. Dr (Cr)
Income Statement		
Net Sales	$(3,800,000)	$(1,500,000)
Equity in Brey's Income	(178,000)	
Gain on Sale of Warehouse	(30,000)	
Cost of Goods Sold	2,360,000	870,000
Operating Expenses (Including Depreciation)	1,100,000	440,000
Net Income	$ (548,000)	$ (190,000)
Retained Earnings Statement		
Balance, 1/1/X9	$ (440,000)	$ (156,000)
Net Income	(548,000)	(190,000)
Dividends Paid		40,000
Balance, 12/31/X9	$ (988,000)	$ (306,000)
Balance Sheet		
Assets:		
Cash	$ 570,000	$ 150,000
Accounts Receivable (net)	860,000	350,000
Inventories	1,060,000	410,000
Land, Plant, and Equipment	1,320,000	680,000
Accumulated Depreciation	(370,000)	(210,000)
Investment in Brey	888,000	
Total Assets	$ 4,328,000	$ 1,380,000
Liabilities and Stockholders' Equity:		
Accounts Payable and Accrued Expenses	$(1,340,000)	$ (594,000)
Common Stock	(1,700,000)	(400,000)
Additional Paid-in Capital	(300,000)	(80,000)
Retained Earnings	(988,000)	(306,000)
Total Liabilities and Equity	$(4,328,000)	$(1,380,000)

Additional information:

• There were no changes in the Common Stock and Additional Paid-In Capital accounts during 19X9 except the one necessitated by Fran's acquisition of Brey.

• At the acquisition date, the fair value of Brey's machinery exceeded its book value by $54,000. The excess cost will be amortized over the estimated average remaining life of 6 years. The fair values of all of Brey's other assets and liabilities were equal to their book values. Any goodwill resulting from the acquisition will be amortized over a 20-year period.

• On July 1, 19X9, Fran sold a warehouse facility to Brey for $129,000 cash. At the date of sale, Fran's book values were $33,000 for the land and $66,000 for the undepreciated cost of the building. Based on a real estate appraisal, Brey allocated $43,000 of the purchase price to land and $86,000 to building. Brey is depreciating the building over its estimated 5-year remaining useful life by the straight-line method with no salvage value.

• During 19X9, Fran purchased merchandise from Brey at an aggregate invoice price of $180,000, which included a 100 percent markup on Brey's cost. At December 31, 19X9, Fran owed Brey $86,000 on these purchases, and $36,000 of this merchandise remained in Fran's inventory.

Required

Develop and complete a consolidation workpaper that would be used to prepare a consolidated income statement and a consolidated retained earnings statement for the year ended December 31, 19X9, and a consolidated balance sheet as of December 31, 19X9. List the accounts in the workpaper in the same order as they are listed in the financial statements provided. Formal consolidated statements are not required. Ignore income tax considerations. Supporting computations should be in good form.

P7-26B Fully Adjusted Equity Method

On December 31, 19X7, Randall Corporation recorded the following entry on its books to adjust from the basic equity method to the fully adjusted equity method on its investment in Sharp Company stock:

Retained Earnings	25,900	
Income from Subsidiary	100	
Investment in Sharp Company Stock		26,000

Required

a. Adjust the data reported by Randall Corporation in the trial balance contained in Problem 7–23 for the effects of the adjusting entry presented above.

b. Prepare the journal entries that would have been recorded on the books of Randall Corporation during 19X7 under the fully adjusted equity method.

c. Prepare all eliminating entries needed to complete a consolidation workpaper at December 31, 19X7, assuming Randall has used the fully adjusted equity method.

d. Complete a three-part consolidation workpaper as of December 31, 19X7.

P7-27B Comprehensive Consolidation Workpaper; Cost Method [AICPA Adapted]

Fran Corp. acquired all the outstanding $10 par value voting common stock of Brey, Inc. on January 1, 19X9, in exchange for 25,000 shares of its $20 par value voting common stock. On December 31, 19X8, Fran's common stock had a closing market price of $30 per share on a national stock exchange. The acquisition was appropriately accounted for as a purchase. Both companies continued to operate as separate business entities maintaining separate accounting records with years ending December 31.

On December 31, 19X9, the companies had condensed financial statements as follows:

	Fran Corp. Dr (Cr)	Brey, Inc. Dr (Cr)
Income Statement		
Net Sales	$(3,800,000)	$(1,500,000)
Dividends from Brey	(40,000)	
Gain on Sale of Warehouse	(30,000)	
Cost of Goods Sold	2,360,000	870,000
Operating Expenses (Including Depreciation)	1,100,000	440,000
Net Income	$ (410,000)	$ (190,000)
Retained Earnings Statement		
Balance, 1/1/X9	$ (440,000)	$ (156,000)
Net Income	(410,000)	(190,000)
Dividends Paid		40,000
Balance, 12/31/X9	$ (850,000)	$ (306,000)
Balance Sheet		
Assets:		
Cash	$ 570,000	$ 150,000
Accounts Receivable (net)	860,000	350,000
Inventories	1,060,000	410,000
Land, Plant, and Equipment	1,320,000	680,000
Accumulated Depreciation	(370,000)	(210,000)
Investment in Brey (at cost)	750,000	
Total Assets	$ 4,190,000	$ 1,380,000
Liabilities and Stockholders' Equity:		
Accounts Payable and Accrued Expenses	$(1,340,000)	$ (594,000)
Common Stock	(1,700,000)	(400,000)
Additional Paid-in Capital	(300,000)	(80,000)
Retained Earnings	(850,000)	(306,000)
Total Liabilities and Equity	$(4,190,000)	$(1,380,000)

Additional information:

• There were no changes in the Common Stock and Additional Paid-In Capital accounts during 19X9 except the one necessitated by Fran's acquisition of Brey.

• At the acquisition date, the fair value of Brey's machinery exceeded its book value by $54,000. The excess cost will be amortized over the estimated average remaining life of 6 years. The fair values of all of Brey's other assets and liabilities were equal to their book values. Any goodwill resulting from the acquisition will be amortized over a 20-year period.

• On July 1, 19X9, Fran sold a warehouse facility to Brey for $129,000 cash. At the date of sale, Fran's book values were $33,000 for the land and $66,000 for the undepreciated cost of the building. Based on a real estate appraisal, Brey allocated $43,000 of the purchase price to land and $86,000 to building. Brey is depreciating the building over its estimated 5-year remaining useful life by the straight-line method with no salvage value.

• During 19X9, Fran purchased merchandise from Brey at an aggregate invoice price of $180,000, which included a 100 percent markup on Brey's cost. At December 31, 19X9, Fran owed Brey $86,000 on these purchases, and $36,000 of this merchandise remained in Fran's inventory.

Required

Develop and complete a consolidation workpaper that would be used to prepare a consolidated income statement and a consolidated retained earnings statement for the year ended December 31, 19X9, and a consolidated balance sheet as of December 31, 19X9. Formal consolidated statements are not required. Ignore income tax considerations. Supporting computations should be in good form.

P7-28B Cost Method

The trial balance data presented in Problem 7–23 can be converted to reflect use of the cost method by inserting the following amounts in place of those presented for Randall Corporation:

Investment in Sharp Company Stock	$280,000
Retained Earnings	329,900
Income from Subsidiary	-0-
Dividend Income	20,000

Required

a. Prepare the journal entries that would have been recorded on the books of Randall Corporation during 19X7 under the cost method.

b. Prepare all eliminating entries needed to complete a consolidation workpaper as of December 31, 19X7, assuming Randall uses the cost method.

c. Complete a three-part consolidation workpaper as of December 31, 19X7.

CHAPTER 8

INTERCOMPANY INDEBTEDNESS

One advantage of having control over other companies is that management has the ability to transfer resources from one legal entity to another as needed by the individual companies. Companies often find it beneficial to lend excess funds to affiliates and to borrow from affiliates when cash shortages arise. The borrower often benefits from lower borrowing rates, less restrictive credit terms, and the informality and lower debt issue costs of intercompany borrowing relative to public debt offerings. The lending affiliate may benefit by being able to invest excess funds in a company about which it has considerable knowledge, perhaps allowing it to earn a given return on the funds invested while incurring less risk than if it invested in unrelated companies. Also, the combined entity may find it advantageous for the parent company or another affiliate to borrow funds for the entire enterprise rather than having each affiliate going directly to the capital markets.

CONSOLIDATION OVERVIEW

Figure 8-1 illustrates two types of intercorporate debt transfers. A *direct intercompany debt transfer* involves a loan from one affiliate to another without the participation of an unrelated party, as in Figure 8-1a. Examples include a trade receivable/payable arising from an intercompany sale of inventory on credit, and the issuance of a note payable by one affiliate to another in exchange for operating funds.

An *indirect intercompany debt transfer* involves the issuance of debt to an unrelated party and the subsequent purchase of the debt instrument by an affiliate of the issuer. For example, in Figure 8-1b, Special Foods borrows funds by issuing

FIGURE 8-1 Intercompany debt transactions.

(*a*) Direct Intercompany Debt Transfer

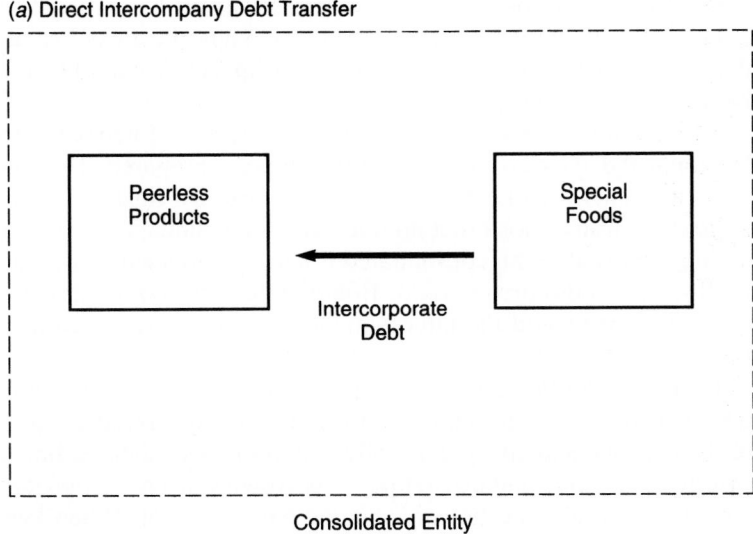

Consolidated Entity

(*b*) Indirect Intercompany Debt Transfer

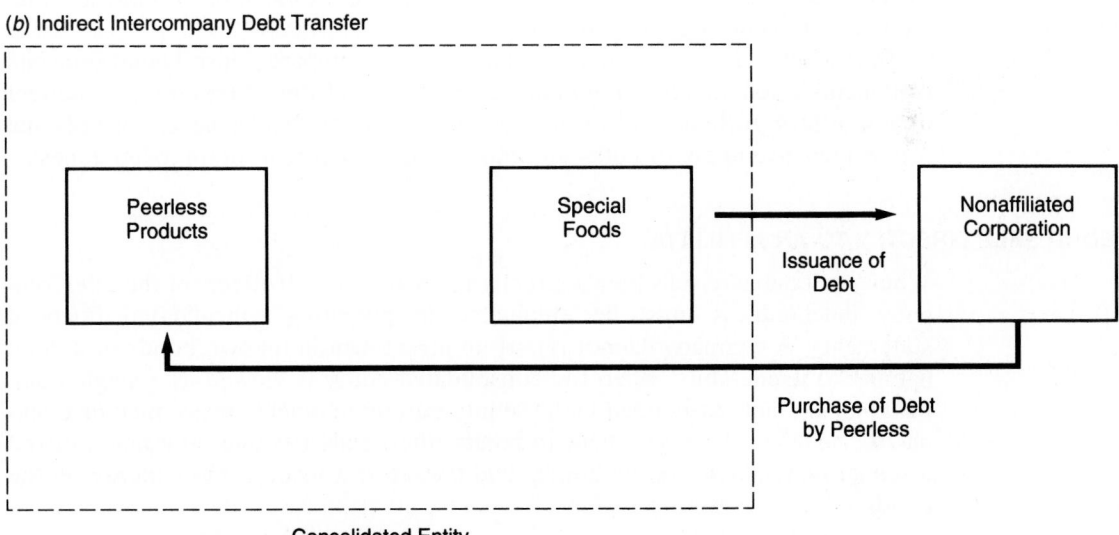

Consolidated Entity

a debt instrument, such as a note or a bond, to Nonaffiliated Corporation. The debt instrument subsequently is purchased from Nonaffiliated Corporation by Special Foods' parent, Peerless Products. Thus, Peerless Products acquires the debt of Special Foods, not directly from Special Foods, but indirectly through Nonaffiliated Corporation.

All account balances arising from intercorporate financing arrangements must be eliminated when consolidated statements are prepared. The consolidated financial statements portray the consolidated entity as a single company. Therefore, in Figure 8-1, transactions that do not cross the boundary of the consolidated entity are not reported in the consolidated financial statements. Although in illustration (a) Special Foods borrows funds from Peerless, the consolidated entity as a whole does not borrow and the intercompany loan is not reflected in the consolidated financial statements.

In illustration (b), Special Foods borrows funds from Nonaffiliated Corporation. Because this transaction is with an unrelated party and crosses the boundary of the consolidated entity, it is reflected in the consolidated financial statements. In effect, the consolidated entity is borrowing from an outside party, and the liability is included in the consolidated balance sheet. When Peerless purchases Special Foods' debt instrument from Nonaffiliated, this transaction also crosses the boundary of the consolidated entity. In effect, the consolidated entity repurchases its debt, and needs to report the purchase as a debt retirement. As with most retirements of debt before maturity, a purchase of an affiliate's bonds usually gives rise to a gain or loss on the retirement; the gain or loss is reported in the consolidated income statement even though it does not appear in the separate income statement of either affiliate.

This chapter discusses the procedures used to prepare consolidated financial statements when intercorporate indebtedness arises from either direct or indirect debt transfers. Although the discussion focuses on bonds, the same concepts and procedures also apply to notes and other types of intercorporate indebtedness.

BOND SALE DIRECTLY TO AN AFFILIATE

When one company sells bonds directly to an affiliate, all effects of the intercompany indebtedness must be eliminated in preparing consolidated financial statements. A company cannot report an investment in its own bonds or a bond liability to itself. Thus, when the consolidated entity is viewed as a single company, all amounts associated with the intercorporate indebtedness must be eliminated, including the investment in bonds, the bonds payable, any unamortized discount or premium on the bonds, and the interest income and expense on the bonds.

Transfer at Par Value

When a note or bond payable is sold directly to an affiliate at par value, the entries recorded by the investor and the issuer should be mirror images of each other. To illustrate, assume that on January 1, 19X1, Special Foods borrows $100,000 from Peerless Products by issuing to Peerless $100,000 par value, 12 percent, 10-year bonds. This transaction is represented by Figure 8-1a. During 19X1, Special Foods records interest expense on the bonds of $12,000 ($100,000 × .12), and Peerless records an equal amount of interest income.

In the preparation of consolidated financial statements for 19X1, two elimination entries are needed in the consolidation workpaper to remove the effects of the intercompany indebtedness:

E(1)	Bonds Payable	100,000	
	Investment in Special Foods Bonds		100,000
	Eliminate intercorporate bond holdings.		
E(2)	Interest Income	12,000	
	Interest Expense		12,000
	Eliminate intercompany interest.		

These entries eliminate from the consolidated statements the bond investment and associated income recorded on Peerless's books and the liability and related interest expense recorded on Special Foods' books. The resulting statements appear as if the indebtedness does not exist, which from a consolidated viewpoint it does not.

Note that these entries have no effect on consolidated net income because they reduce interest income and interest expense by the same amount. Eliminating entries E(1) and E(2) are required at the end of each period for as long as the intercorporate indebtedness continues.

Transfer at a Discount or Premium

When the coupon or nominal interest rate on a bond is different from the yield demanded by those who lend funds, a bond will sell at a discount or premium. In such cases, the amount of bond interest income or expense recorded no longer is equal to the cash interest payments. Instead, interest income and expense amounts are adjusted for the amortization of the discount or premium.

As an illustration of the treatment of intercompany bond transfers at other than par, assume that on January 1, 19X1, Peerless Products purchases $100,000 par value, 12 percent, 10-year bonds from Special Foods for $90,000. Interest on the bonds is payable on January 1 and July 1. The interest expense recognized by Special Foods and the interest income recognized by Peerless each year include straight-line amortization of the discount, as follows:

Cash interest ($100,000 × .12)	$12,000
Amortization of discount	
($10,000 ÷ 20 semiannual interest periods) × 2 periods	1,000
Interest expense or income	$13,000

Half these amounts are recognized in each of the two interest payment periods during a year. Although the effective-interest method of amortization usually is required for amortizing discounts and premiums, the straight-line method is acceptable where it does not depart materially from the effective-interest method and where transactions are between parent and subsidiary companies or between subsidiaries of a common parent.

Entries by the Debtor   Special Foods records the issuance of the bonds on January 1 at a discount of $10,000. Interest expense is recognized on July 1, when the first semiannual interest payment is made, and on December 31, when interest is accrued for the second half of the year. The amortization of the bond discount causes interest expense to be greater than the cash interest payment and causes the balance of the discount to decrease. The following entries related to the bonds are recorded by Special Foods during 19X1:

January 1, 19X1
(3)	Cash	90,000	
	Discount on Bonds Payable	10,000	
	Bonds Payable		100,000
	Issue bonds to Peerless Products.		

July 1, 19X1
(4)	Interest Expense	6,500	
	Discount on Bonds Payable		500
	Cash		6,000
	Semiannual payment of interest.		

December 31, 19X1
(5)	Interest Expense	6,500	
	Discount on Bonds Payable		500
	Interest Payable		6,000
	Accrue interest expense at year-end.		

Entries by the Bond Investor   Peerless Products records the purchase of the bonds and the interest income derived from the bonds during 19X1 with the following entries:

January 1, 19X1
(6)	Investment in Special Foods Bonds	90,000	
	Cash		90,000
	Purchase of bonds from Special Foods.		

July 1, 19X1
(7)	Cash	6,000	
	Investment in Special Foods Bonds	500	
	Interest Income		6,500
	Receive interest on bond investment.		

December 31, 19X1

(8)	Interest Receivable	6,000	
	Investment in Special Foods Bonds	500	
	Interest Income		6,500
	Accrue interest income at year-end.		

The amortization of the discount by Peerless increases interest income to an amount greater than the cash interest payment and causes the balance of the bond investment account to increase.

Elimination Entries at Year-End The December 31, 19X1, bond-related amounts taken from the books of Peerless Products and Special Foods, and the appropriate consolidated amounts, are as follows:

Item	Peerless Products	Special Foods	Unadjusted Totals	Consolidated Amounts
Bonds Payable	–0–	$(100,000)	$(100,000)	–0–
Discount on Bonds Payable	–0–	9,000	9,000	–0–
Interest Payable	–0–	(6,000)	(6,000)	–0–
Investment in Bonds	$ 91,000	–0–	91,000	–0–
Interest Receivable	6,000	–0–	6,000	–0–
Interest Expense	–0–	$ 13,000	$ 13,000	–0–
Interest Income	$(13,000)	–0–	(13,000)	–0–

All account balances relating to the intercorporate bond holdings must be eliminated in the preparation of consolidated financial statements. Toward that end, the consolidation workpaper prepared on December 31, 19X1, includes the following eliminating entries related to the intercompany bond holdings:

E(9)	Bonds Payable	100,000	
	Investment in Special Foods Bonds		91,000
	Discount on Bonds Payable		9,000
	Eliminate intercorporate bond holdings.		
E(10)	Interest Income	13,000	
	Interest Expense		13,000
	Eliminate intercompany interest.		
E(11)	Interest Payable	6,000	
	Interest Receivable		6,000
	Eliminate intercompany interest receivable/payable.		

Entry E(9) eliminates the bonds payable and associated discount against the investment in bonds. The book value of the bond liability on Special Foods' books and the investment in bonds on Peerless's books will be the same so long as both companies amortize the discount in the same way.

Entry E(10) eliminates the bond interest income recognized by Peerless during 19X1 against the bond interest expense recognized by Special Foods. Because the interest for the second half of 19X1 was accrued and not paid, an intercompany receivable/payable exists at the end of the year. Entry E(11) eliminates the interest receivable against the interest payable.

Consolidation at the end of 19X2 requires elimination entries similar to those at the end of 19X1. Because $1,000 of the discount is amortized each year, the bond investment balance on Peerless's books increases to $92,000 ($90,000 + $1,000 + $1,000). Similarly, the bond discount on Special Foods' books decreases to $8,000, resulting in an effective bond liability of $92,000. The consolidation elimination entries related to the bonds at the end of 19X2 are as follows:

E(12)	Bonds Payable	100,000	
	Investment in Special Foods Bonds		92,000
	Discount on Bonds Payable		8,000
	Eliminate intercorporate bond holdings.		
E(13)	Interest Income	13,000	
	Interest Expense		13,000
	Eliminate intercompany interest.		
E(14)	Interest Payable	6,000	
	Interest Receivable		6,000
	Eliminate intercompany interest receivable/payable.		

BONDS OF AFFILIATE PURCHASED FROM A NONAFFILIATE

A more complex situation occurs when bonds that were issued to an unrelated party are acquired later by an affiliate of the issuer. From the viewpoint of the consolidated entity, an acquisition of an affiliate's bonds retires the bonds at the time they are purchased. The bonds no longer are held outside the consolidated entity once they are purchased by another company within the consolidated entity, and they must be treated as if repurchased by the debtor. Acquisition of the bonds of an affiliate by another company within the consolidated entity is referred to as *constructive retirement*. Although the bonds actually are not retired, they are treated as if they were retired in preparing consolidated financial statements.

When a constructive retirement occurs, the consolidated income statement for the period reports a gain or loss on debt retirement based on the difference between the carrying value of the bonds on the books of the debtor and the purchase price paid by the affiliate in acquiring the bonds. Neither the bonds payable nor the purchaser's investment in the bonds is reported in the consolidated balance sheet because the bonds no longer are considered outstanding.

Purchase at Book Value

In the event that a company purchases the debt of an affiliate from an unrelated party at a price equal to the liability reported by the debtor, the elimination entries required in preparing the consolidated financial statements are identical to those used in eliminating a direct intercorporate debt transfer. In this case, the total of the bond liability and the related premium or discount reported by the debtor will equal the balance in the investment account shown by the bondholder, and the interest income reported by the bondholder each period will equal the interest expense reported by the debtor. All these amounts need to be eliminated to avoid misstating the accounts in the consolidated financial statements.

Purchase at an Amount Less than Book Value

Continuing movement in the level of interest rates and the volatility of other factors influencing the securities markets make it unlikely that a company's bonds will sell after issuance at a price identical to their book value. When the price paid to acquire the bonds of an affiliate differs from the liability reported by the debtor, a gain or loss is reported in the consolidated income statement in the period of constructive retirement. In addition, the bond interest income and interest expense reported by the two affiliates subsequent to the purchase must be eliminated in preparing consolidated statements. Interest income reported by the investing affiliate and interest expense reported by the debtor are not equal in this case because of the different bond carrying amounts on the books of the two companies. The difference in the bond carrying amounts is reflected in the amortization of the discount or premium and, in turn, causes interest income and expense to differ.

As an example of consolidation following the purchase of an affiliate's bonds at less than book value, assume Peerless Products Corporation purchases 80 percent of the common stock of Special Foods, Inc., on December 31, 19X0, for its underlying book value of $240,000. In addition, the following conditions occur:

1. On January 1, 19X1, Special Foods issues 10-year, 12 percent bonds payable with a par value of $100,000; the bonds are issued at 102. The bonds are purchased from Special Foods by Nonaffiliated Corporation.

2. The bonds pay interest on June 30 and December 31.

3. Both Peerless Products and Special Foods amortize bond discount and premium using the straight-line method.

4. On December 31, 19X1, Peerless Products purchases the bonds from Nonaffiliated for $91,000.

5. Special Foods reports net income of $50,000 for 19X1 and $75,000 for 19X2. Special Foods declares dividends of $30,000 in 19X1 and $40,000 in 19X2.

6. Peerless earns $140,000 in 19X1 and $160,000 in 19X2 from its own separate operations. Peerless declares dividends of $60,000 in both 19X1 and 19X2.

The bond transactions of Special Foods and Peerless appear as follows:

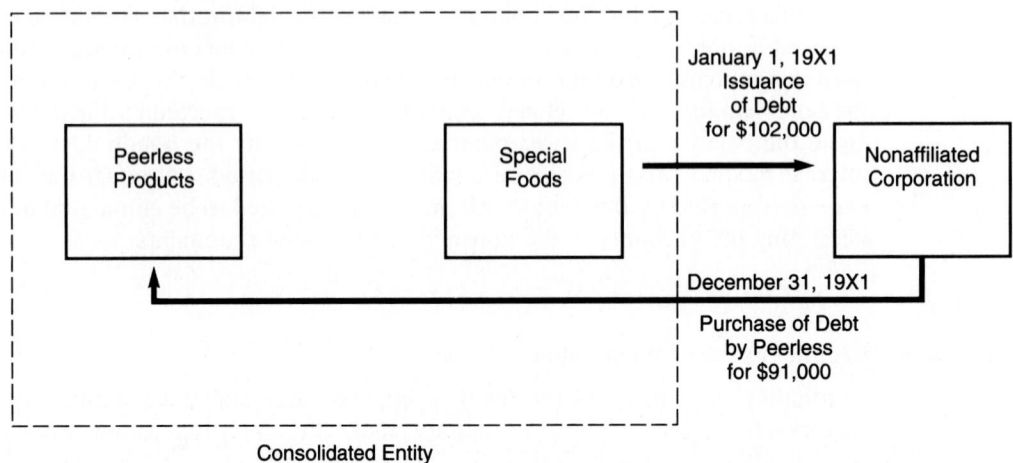

Consolidated Entity

Bond Liability Entries—19X1 Special Foods records the following entries related to its bonds during 19X1:

```
January 1, 19X1
    (15)  Cash                                      102,000
             Bonds Payable                                      100,000
             Premium on Bonds Payable                             2,000
          Sale of bonds to Nonaffiliated.

June 30, 19X1
    (16)  Interest Expense                            5,900
          Premium on Bonds Payable                      100
             Cash                                               6,000
          Semiannual payment of interest:
          $5,900 = $6,000 − $100
          $100 = $2,000 ÷ 20 interest periods
          $6,000 = $100,000 × .12 × 6/12

December 31, 19X1
    (17)  Interest Expense                            5,900
          Premium on Bonds Payable                      100
             Cash                                               6,000
          Semiannual payment of interest.
```

Entry (15) records the issuance of the bonds to Nonaffiliated Corporation for $102,000. Entries (16) and (17) record the payment of interest and the amortization of the bond premium at each of the two interest payment dates during 19X1. Total interest expense for 19X1 is $11,800 ($5,900 × 2), and the book value of the bonds on December 31, 19X1, is as follows:

Book value of bonds at issuance	$102,000
Amortization of premium, 19X1	(200)
Book value of bonds, December 31, 19X1	$101,800

Bond Investment Entries—19X1 Peerless Products records the purchase of Special Foods' bonds from Nonaffiliated with the following entry:

December 31, 19X1
   (18) Investment in Special Foods Bonds   91,000
          Cash   91,000
          Purchase of Special Foods bonds from
          Nonaffiliated Corporation.

This entry is the same as if the bonds purchased were those of an unrelated company. The bonds are purchased by Peerless at the very end of the year, after payment of the interest to Nonaffiliated; therefore, Peerless earns no interest on the bonds during 19X1, nor is there any interest accrued on the bonds at the date of purchase.

Computation of Gain on Constructive Retirement of Bonds From a consolidated viewpoint, the purchase of Special Foods' bonds by Peerless is considered a retirement of the bonds by the consolidated entity. Therefore, in the preparation of consolidated financial statements, a gain or loss must be recognized for the difference between the book value of the bonds on the date of repurchase and the amount paid by the consolidated entity in reacquiring the bonds:

Book value of Special Foods' bonds, December 31, 19X1	$101,800
Price paid by Peerless to purchase bonds	(91,000)
Gain on constructive retirement of bonds	$ 10,800

This gain is included in the consolidated income statement as a gain on the retirement of bonds. Gains and losses on the retirement of debt, if material, are required to be treated as extraordinary by **FASB Statement No. 4**, "Reporting Gains and Losses from Extinguishment of Debt" (FASB 4).

Assignment of Gain on Constructive Retirement Four approaches have been used in practice for assigning the gain or loss on the constructive retirement of the bonds of an affiliate to the shareholders of the participating companies:

   1. To the affiliate issuing the bonds
   2. To the affiliate purchasing the bonds
   3. To the parent company
   4. To the issuing and purchasing companies based on the difference between the carrying amounts of the bonds on their books at the date of purchase and the par value of the bonds

There do not seem to be compelling reasons for choosing one of these methods over the others, and in practice the choice often is based on expediency and lack of materiality. The approach used in this text is to assign the gain or loss to the issuing company. In previous chapters, gains and losses on intercompany transactions were viewed as accruing to the shareholders of the selling affiliate. When this approach is applied in the case of intercorporate debt transactions, gains and losses arising from the intercompany debt transactions are viewed as accruing to the shareholders of the selling or issuing affiliate. In effect, the purchasing affiliate is viewed as acting on behalf of the issuing affiliate by acquiring the bonds.

An important difference exists between the intercompany gains and losses discussed in previous chapters and the gains and losses arising from intercorporate debt transactions. Gains and losses from intercorporate transfers of assets are recognized by the individual affiliates and are eliminated in consolidation. Gains and losses from intercorporate debt transactions are not recognized by the individual affiliates, but must be included in consolidation.

When the subsidiary is the issuing affiliate, the gain or loss on constructive retirement of the bonds is viewed as accruing to the shareholders of the subsidiary. Thus, the gain or loss is apportioned between consolidated net income and the noncontrolling interest based on the relative ownership interests in the common stock. If the parent is the issuing affiliate, the entire gain on the constructive retirement accrues to the controlling interest, and none is apportioned to the noncontrolling interest.

As a result of the entries recorded annually by the companies involved, the amount of the unrecognized gain or loss decreases each period and is fully amortized at the time the bond matures. Thus, no permanent gain or loss is assigned to the shareholders of the debtor company.

Basic Equity-Method Entries—19X1 In addition to recording the bond investment with entry (18), Peerless records the following basic equity-method entries during 19X1 to account for its investment in Special Foods stock:

(19)	Investment in Special Foods Stock	40,000	
	Income from Subsidiary		40,000
	Record equity-method income:		
	$50,000 × .80		
(20)	Cash	24,000	
	Investment in Special Foods Stock		24,000
	Record dividends from Special Foods:		
	$30,000 × .80		

These entries result in a balance of $256,000 in the investment account at the end of 19X1.

Consolidation Workpaper—19X1 The December 31, 19X1, workpaper to prepare consolidated financial statements for Peerless Products and Special Foods is presented in Figure 8-2. The following eliminating entries are included in the workpaper:

E(21)	Income from Subsidiary	40,000	
	Dividends Declared		24,000
	Investment in Special Foods Stock		16,000
	Eliminate income from subsidiary.		
E(22)	Income to Noncontrolling Interest	12,160	
	Dividends Declared		6,000
	Noncontrolling Interest		6,160
	Assign income to noncontrolling interest:		
	$12,160 = ($50,000 + $10,800) × .20		
E(23)	Common Stock—Special Foods	200,000	
	Retained Earnings, January 1	100,000	
	Investment in Special Foods Stock		240,000
	Noncontrolling Interest		60,000
	Eliminate beginning investment balance.		
E(24)	Bonds Payable	100,000	
	Premium on Bonds Payable	1,800	
	Investment in Special Foods Bonds		91,000
	Gain on Bond Retirement		10,800
	Eliminate intercorporate bonds payable.		

Workpaper entry E(21) eliminates the changes in the investment account during 19X1, the parent's share of the subsidiary's net income, and the dividends recognized by Peerless during the year. Income of $12,160 is assigned to the noncontrolling interest in entry E(22), computed as follows:

Net income of Special Foods	$50,000
Gain on constructive retirement of bonds	10,800
Realized net income of Special Foods	$60,800
Noncontrolling stockholders' share	× .20
Noncontrolling interest's share of income	$12,160

The gain on the constructive retirement of the bonds is viewed as accruing to the shareholders of the issuing company, Special Foods. Therefore, a proportionate share of the gain ($10,800 × .20) is assigned to the noncontrolling interest along with a proportionate share of Special Foods' reported net income. If Peerless had been the issuing affiliate, all the gain would be included in consolidated net income and none would be allocated to the noncontrolling interest.

Entry E(22) also eliminates the noncontrolling interest's share of Special Foods' dividends declared during 19X1 and recognizes the increase in the noncontrolling interest's claim on the net assets of the subsidiary. Entry E(23)

FIGURE 8-2 December 31, 19X1, consolidation workpaper; repurchase of bonds at less than book value.

Item	Peerless Products	Special Foods	Eliminations Debit		Eliminations Credit		Consolidated
Sales	400,000	200,000					600,000
Income from Subsidiary	40,000		(21)	40,000			
Gain on Bond Retirement					(24)	10,800	10,800
Credits	440,000	200,000					610,800
Cost of Goods Sold	170,000	115,000					285,000
Depreciation and Amortization	50,000	20,000					70,000
Other Expenses	20,000	3,200					23,200
Interest Expense	20,000	11,800					31,800
Debits	(260,000)	(150,000)					(410,000)
							200,800
Income to Noncontrolling Interest			(22)	12,160			(12,160)
Net Income, carry forward	180,000	50,000		52,160		10,800	188,640
Retained Earnings, January 1	300,000	100,000	(23)	100,000			300,000
Net Income, from above	180,000	50,000		52,160		10,800	188,640
	480,000	150,000					488,640
Dividends Declared	(60,000)	(30,000)			(21)	24,000	
					(22)	6,000	(60,000)
Retained Earnings, December 31, carry forward	420,000	120,000		152,160		40,800	428,640
Cash	173,000	76,800					249,800
Accounts Receivable	75,000	50,000					125,000
Inventory	100,000	75,000					175,000
Land	175,000	40,000					215,000
Buildings and Equipment	800,000	600,000					1,400,000
Investment in Special Foods Bonds	91,000				(24)	91,000	
Investment in Special Foods Stock	256,000				(21)	16,000	
					(23)	240,000	
Debits	1,670,000	841,800					2,164,800
Accumulated Depreciation	450,000	320,000					770,000
Accounts Payable	100,000	100,000					200,000
Bonds Payable	200,000	100,000	(24)	100,000			200,000
Premium on Bonds Payable		1,800	(24)	1,800			
Common Stock	500,000	200,000	(23)	200,000			500,000
Retained Earnings, from above	420,000	120,000		152,160		40,800	428,640
Noncontrolling Interest					(22)	6,160	
					(23)	60,000	66,160
Credits	1,670,000	841,800		453,960		453,960	2,164,800

Elimination entries:
- (21) Eliminate income from subsidiary.
- (22) Assign income to noncontrolling interest.
- (23) Eliminate beginning investment balance.
- (24) Eliminate intercorporate bonds payable.

eliminates Peerless's investment account and the stockholders' equity balances of Special Foods at the beginning of the year, and establishes in the workpaper the amount of the noncontrolling interest at the beginning of the year.

The final entry in the workpaper, E(24), eliminates the intercompany bond holdings and recognizes the gain on constructive retirement of the bonds. The appropriate consolidated balances and the amounts recorded on the books of Peerless and Special Foods are as follows:

Item	Peerless Products	Special Foods	Unadjusted Totals	Consolidated Amounts
Bonds Payable	–0–	$(100,000)	$(100,000)	–0–
Premium on Bonds Payable	–0–	(1,800)	(1,800)	–0–
Investment in Bonds	$91,000	–0–	91,000	–0–
Interest Expense	–0–	$ 11,800	$ 11,800	$11,800
Interest Income	–0–	–0–	–0–	–0–
Gain on Bond Retirement	–0–	–0–	–0–	(10,800)

Special Foods' bonds payable and Peerless's investment in Special Foods' bonds cannot appear in the consolidated balance sheet because the bond holdings involve parties totally within the single economic entity. Note that the gain recognized on the constructive retirement of the bonds does not appear on the books of either Peerless or Special Foods because the bonds still are outstanding from the perspective of the separate companies. From the viewpoint of the consolidated entity, the bonds are retired at the end of 19X1, and a gain must be entered in the consolidation workpaper so that it appears in the consolidated income statement.

No eliminations are needed with respect to interest income or interest expense in preparing the consolidated statements for December 31, 19X1. Because Peerless purchased the bonds at the end of the year, no interest income is recorded by Peerless until 19X2. The interest expense of $11,800 ($12,000 − $200) recorded by Special Foods is viewed appropriately as interest expense of the consolidated entity because the bonds were held by an unrelated party during all of 19X1.

Consolidated Net Income—19X1 Consolidated net income of $188,640 is shown in the workpaper in Figure 8-2. This amount is verified as follows:

Peerless's separate operating income		$140,000
Peerless's share of Special Foods' income:		
Special Foods' net income	$50,000	
Gain on constructive retirement of bonds	10,800	
Special Foods' realized income	$60,800	
Peerless's proportionate share	× .80	48,640
Consolidated net income, 19X1		$188,640

Consolidated net income is $8,640 higher ($10,800 × .80) than if the bonds had not been purchased by Peerless.

Noncontrolling Interest—December 31, 19X1   Total noncontrolling interest on December 31, 19X1, includes a proportionate share of both the reported book value of Special Foods and the gain on constructive bond retirement. The balance of the noncontrolling interest on December 31, 19X1, is computed as follows:

Book value of Special Foods, December 31, 19X1:	
Common stock	$200,000
Retained earnings	120,000
Total reported book value	$320,000
Gain on constructive retirement of bonds	10,800
Realized book value of Special Foods	$330,800
Noncontrolling stockholders' share	× .20
Noncontrolling interest, December 31, 19X1	$ 66,160

Bond Liability Entries—19X2   Special Foods records interest on its bonds during 19X2 with the following entries:

```
June 30, 19X2
   (25)  Interest Expense                       5,900
         Premium on Bonds Payable                 100
            Cash                                          6,000
         Semiannual payment of interest.

December 31, 19X2
   (26)  Interest Expense                       5,900
         Premium on Bonds Payable                 100
            Cash                                          6,000
         Semiannual payment of interest.
```

Bond Investment Entries—19X2   Peerless Products accounts for its investment in Special Foods' bonds in the same way as if the bonds were those of a nonaffiliate. The $91,000 purchase price paid by Peerless reflects a $9,000 ($100,000 − $91,000) discount from the par value of the bonds. This discount is amortized over the 9-year remaining term of the bonds at $1,000 per year ($9,000 ÷ 9 years), or $500 per 6-month interest payment period. Peerless's entries to record interest income for 19X2 are as follows:

```
June 30, 19X2
   (27)  Cash                                   6,000
         Investment in Special Foods Bonds        500
            Interest Income                                6,500
         Record receipt of bond interest.
```

December 31, 19X2
   (28) Cash   6,000
           Investment in Special Foods Bonds   500
               Interest Income   6,500
           Record receipt of bond interest.

Subsequent Recognition of Gain on Constructive Retirement   In the year of the constructive bond retirement, 19X1, the entire $10,800 gain on the retirement was recognized in the consolidated income statement but not on the books of either Peerless or Special Foods. The total gain on the constructive bond retirement in 19X1 was equal to the sum of the discount on Peerless's bond investment and the premium on Special Foods' bond liability at the time of the constructive retirement:

Peerless's discount on bond investment	$ 9,000
Special Foods' premium on bond liability	1,800
Total gain on constructive retirement of bonds	$10,800

This can be visualized as in the following figure:

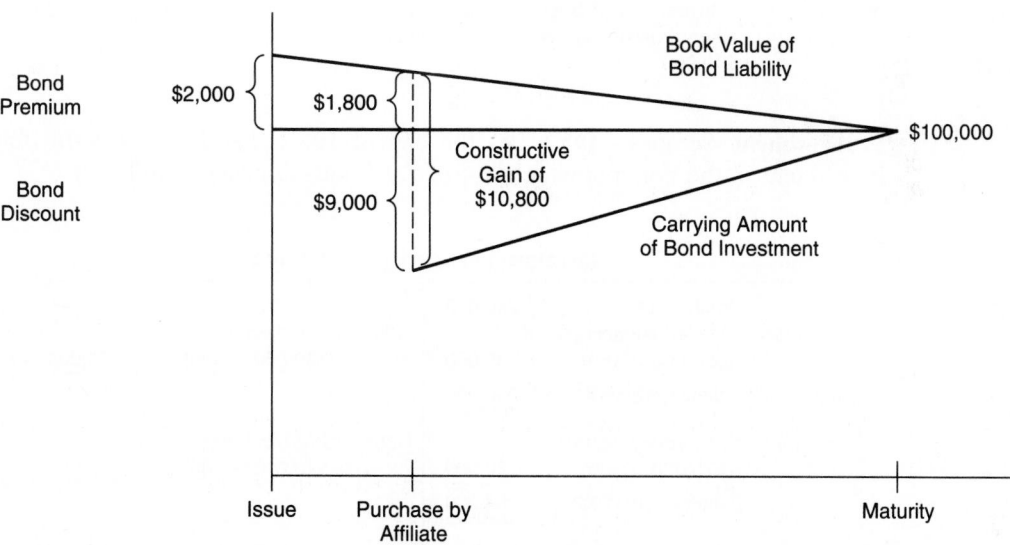

In each year subsequent to 19X1, both Peerless and Special Foods recognize a portion of the constructive gain as they amortize the discount on the bond investment and the premium on the bond liability:

Peerless's amortization of discount on bond investment ($9,000 ÷ 9 years)	$1,000
Special Foods' amortization of premium on bonds payable ($1,800 ÷ 9 years)	200
Annual increase in combined incomes of separate companies	$1,200

Thus, the $10,800 gain on constructive bond retirement, previously recognized in the consolidated income statement, is recognized on the books of Peerless and Special Foods at the rate of $1,200 each year. Over the remaining 9-year term of the bonds, the full $10,800 gain will be recognized by Peerless and Special Foods ($1,200 × 9).

Basic Equity-Method Entries—19X2 In addition to the entries related to its investment in Special Foods' bonds, Peerless records the following entries during 19X2 under the basic equity method:

(29)	Investment in Special Foods Stock	60,000	
	Income from Subsidiary		60,000
	Record equity-method income:		
	$75,000 × .80		
(30)	Cash	32,000	
	Investment in Special Foods Stock		32,000
	Record dividends from Special Foods:		
	$40,000 × .80		

Investment Account—19X2 At the end of 19X2, Peerless's account for its investment in the common stock of Special Foods appears as follows:

Investment in Special Foods Stock

	Original cost	240,000				
(19)	19X1 equity accrual			(20)	19X1 dividends	
	($50,000 × .80)	40,000			($30,000 × .80)	24,000
	Balance, 12/31/X1	256,000				
(29)	19X2 equity accrual			(30)	19X2 dividends	
	($75,000 × .80)	60,000			($40,000 × .80)	32,000
	Balance, 12/31/X2	284,000				

Consolidation Workpaper—19X2 The consolidation workpaper prepared for December 31, 19X2, is presented in Figure 8-3. The following elimination entries are needed in the workpaper:

FIGURE 8-3 December 31, 19X2, consolidation workpaper; next year following repurchase of bonds at less than book value.

Item	Peerless Products	Special Foods	Eliminations Debit		Eliminations Credit		Consolidated
Sales	450,000	300,000					750,000
Interest Income	13,000		(34)	13,000			
Income from Subsidiary	60,000		(31)	60,000			
Credits	523,000	300,000					750,000
Cost of Goods Sold	180,000	160,000					340,000
Depreciation and Amortization	50,000	20,000					70,000
Other Expenses	40,000	33,200					73,200
Interest Expense	20,000	11,800			(34)	11,800	20,000
Debits	(290,000)	(225,000)					(503,200)
							246,800
Income to Noncontrolling Interest			(32)	14,760			(14,760)
Net Income, carry forward	233,000	75,000		87,760		11,800	232,040
Retained Earnings, January 1	420,000	120,000	(33)	120,000	(34)	8,640	428,640
Net Income, from above	233,000	75,000		87,760		11,800	232,040
	653,000	195,000					660,680
Dividends Declared	(60,000)	(40,000)			(31)	32,000	
					(32)	8,000	(60,000)
Retained Earnings, December 31, carry forward	593,000	155,000		207,760		60,440	600,680
Cash	212,000	86,600					298,600
Accounts Receivable	150,000	80,000					230,000
Inventory	180,000	90,000					270,000
Land	175,000	40,000					215,000
Buildings and Equipment	800,000	600,000					1,400,000
Investment in Special Foods Bonds	92,000				(34)	92,000	
Investment in Special Foods Stock	284,000				(31)	28,000	
					(33)	256,000	
Debits	1,893,000	896,600					2,413,600
Accumulated Depreciation	500,000	340,000					840,000
Accounts Payable	100,000	100,000					200,000
Bonds Payable	200,000	100,000	(34)	100,000			200,000
Premium on Bonds Payable		1,600	(34)	1,600			
Common Stock	500,000	200,000	(33)	200,000			500,000
Retained Earnings, from above	593,000	155,000		207,760		60,440	600,680
Noncontrolling Interest					(32)	6,760	
					(33)	64,000	
					(34)	2,160	72,920
Credits	1,893,000	896,600		509,360		509,360	2,413,600

Elimination entries:
(31) Eliminate income from subsidiary.
(32) Assign income to noncontrolling interest.
(33) Eliminate beginning investment balance.
(34) Eliminate intercorporate bonds payable.

E(31)	Income from Subsidiary	60,000	
	Dividends Declared		32,000
	Investment in Special Foods Stock		28,000
	Eliminate income from subsidiary.		

E(32)	Income to Noncontrolling Interest	14,760	
	Dividends Declared		8,000
	Noncontrolling Interest		6,760
	Assign income to noncontrolling interest:		
	$14,760 = ($75,000 − $1,200) × .20		

E(33)	Common Stock—Special Foods	200,000	
	Retained Earnings, January 1	120,000	
	Investment in Special Foods Stock		256,000
	Noncontrolling Interest		64,000
	Eliminate beginning investment balance.		

E(34)	Bonds Payable	100,000	
	Premium on Bonds Payable	1,600	
	Interest Income	13,000	
	Investment in Special Foods Bonds		92,000
	Interest Expense		11,800
	Retained Earnings, January 1		8,640
	Noncontrolling Interest		2,160
	Eliminate intercorporate bonds payable:		
	$1,600 = $2,000 − $200 − $200		
	$13,000 = ($100,000 × .12) + $1,000		
	$92,000 = $91,000 + $1,000		
	$11,800 = ($100,000 × .12) − $200		
	$8,640 = $10,800 × .80		
	$2,160 = $10,800 × .20		

Entry E(31) eliminates the net effect of the 19X2 equity-method entries recorded on Peerless's books. Entry E(32) assigns income to the noncontrolling interest, as follows:

Net income of Special Foods, 19X2	$75,000
Less: 19X1 gain on constructive retirement of debt	
recognized currently by affiliates:	
Amortization of Peerless's bond discount	(1,000)
Amortization of Special Foods' bond premium	(200)
Income as a basis for apportionment	$73,800
Noncontrolling interest's proportionate share	× .20
Noncontrolling interest's share of income	$14,760

In 19X1, the gain on the constructive retirement of the bonds was included in consolidated net income and in the computation of income assigned to noncontrolling shareholders. As the gain is recognized on the books of the two affiliates through their amortization of the bond discount and premium, its effect must be eliminated from consolidated net income and from the amount of income assigned to the noncontrolling interest in entry E(32).

Entry E(33) is the normal entry to eliminate the 19X2 beginning balances of Special Foods' stockholders' equity accounts and the beginning balance of Peerless's investment in Special Foods stock account and to establish the amount of the noncontrolling interest at the beginning of 19X2. Entry E(33) establishes the beginning amount of the noncontrolling interest as if there were no constructive gain. The entries to the investment account and to noncontrolling interest are based on each shareholder group's proportionate share of the book value of Special Foods at the beginning of the period:

Book value of Special Foods, January 1, 19X2:		
Common stock		$200,000
Retained earnings		120,000
Total book value		$320,000
Controlling interest's share of book value		
($320,000 × .80)		$256,000
Noncontrolling interest's share of book value		
($320,000 × .20)		64,000
Total assigned		$320,000

The impact of the constructive gain on the beginning noncontrolling interest balance, and on the beginning consolidated retained earnings balance, is reflected in entry E(34) in the workpaper. Entry E(34) increases the beginning balance of consolidated retained earnings by Peerless's $8,640 share ($10,800 × .80) of the gain on constructive retirement of the bonds that has not been recorded on the books of the affiliates as of the beginning of the period. Similarly, the noncontrolling interest is increased by its $2,160 proportionate share ($10,800 × .20) of the unrecorded gain. Because the gain on constructive retirement of the bonds was recognized in the 19X1 consolidated income statement but not on the separate books of Peerless and Special Foods, the beginning balances of consolidated retained earnings and the noncontrolling interest will be understated unless the gain amount is added into the workpaper in 19X2 and apportioned to each.

Entry E(34) also eliminates all aspects of the intercorporate bond holdings, including (1) Peerless's investment in bonds, (2) Special Foods' bonds payable and the associated premium, (3) Peerless's bond interest income, and (4) Special Foods' bond interest expense. The amounts related to the bonds from the books of Peerless and Special Foods, and the appropriate consolidated amounts, are as follows:

Item	Peerless Products	Special Foods	Unadjusted Totals	Consolidated Amounts
Bonds Payable	-0-	$(100,000)	$(100,000)	-0-
Premium on Bonds Payable	-0-	(1,600)	(1,600)	-0-
Investment in Bonds	$ 92,000	-0-	92,000	-0-
Interest Expense	-0-	$ 11,800	$ 11,800	-0-
Interest Income	$(13,000)	-0-	(13,000)	-0-

All balances related to the intercompany bond holdings are eliminated in entry E(34) so that none of the unadjusted totals appear in the consolidated financial statements.

Consolidated Net Income—19X2 Consolidated net income of $232,040 is shown in the workpaper in Figure 8-3. This amount is verified as follows:

Peerless's separate income		$173,000
Peerless's share of Special Foods' income:		
Special Foods' net income	$75,000	
Peerless's amortization of bond discount	(1,000)	
Special Foods' amortization of bond premium	(200)	
Income as a basis for apportionment	$73,800	
Peerless's proportionate share	× .80	59,040
Consolidated net income, 19X2		$232,040

Noncontrolling Interest—December 31, 19X2 Total noncontrolling interest on December 31, 19X2, includes a proportionate share of both the reported book value of Special Foods and the portion of the gain on constructive bond retirement not yet recognized by the affiliates:

Book value of Special Foods, December 31, 19X2:		
Common stock		$200,000
Retained earnings		155,000
Total book value		$355,000
Gain on constructive retirement of bonds	$10,800	
Less: Portion recognized by affiliates during 19X2	(1,200)	
Constructive gain not yet recognized by affiliates		9,600
Realized book value of Special Foods		$364,600
Noncontrolling stockholders' share		× .20
Noncontrolling interest, December 31, 19X2		$ 72,920

Bond Elimination Entry in Subsequent Years In years after 19X2, the workpaper entry to eliminate the intercompany bonds and to adjust for the gain on constructive retirement of the bonds is similar to entry E(34). The unamortized bond discount and premium decrease each year by $1,000 and $200, respectively. As of the beginning of 19X3, $9,600 of the gain on the constructive retirement of the bonds remains unrecognized by the affiliates, computed as follows:

Gain on constructive retirement of bonds		$10,800
Less: Portion recognized by affiliates during 19X2:		
Peerless's amortization of bond discount	$1,000	
Special Foods' amortization of bond premium	200	
Total gain recognized by affiliates		(1,200)
Unrecognized gain on constructive retirement of bonds, January 1, 19X3		$ 9,600

This amount is allocated between beginning retained earnings and the noncontrolling interest in the bond elimination entry in the consolidation workpaper prepared at the end of 19X3:

E(35)	Bonds Payable	100,000	
	Premium on Bonds Payable	1,400	
	Interest Income	13,000	
	Investment in Special Foods Bonds		93,000
	Interest Expense		11,800
	Retained Earnings, January 1		7,680
	Noncontrolling Interest		1,920

Eliminate intercorporate bonds payable:

$1,400 = $2,000 − $200 − $200 − $200
$13,000 = ($100,000 × .12) + $1,000
$93,000 = $91,000 + $1,000 + $1,000
$11,800 = ($100,000 × .12) − $200
$7,680 = ($10,800 − $1,200) × .80
$1,920 = ($10,800 − $1,200) × .20

Purchase at an Amount Greater than Book Value

When an affiliate's bonds are purchased from a nonaffiliate at an amount greater than their book value, the consolidation procedures are virtually the same as previously illustrated except that a loss is recognized on the constructive retirement of the debt. For example, assume that Special Foods issues 10-year, 12 percent bonds on January 1, 19X1, at par of $100,000. The bonds are purchased from Special Foods by Nonaffiliated Corporation, which sells the bonds to Peerless Products on December 31, 19X1, for $104,500. Special Foods recognizes $12,000 ($100,000 × .12) of interest expense each year. Peerless recognizes interest income of $11,500 in each year after 19X1, computed as follows:

Annual cash interest payment ($100,000 × .12)	$12,000
Less: Amortization of premium on bond investment	
($4,500 ÷ 9 years)	(500)
Interest income	$11,500

Because the bonds were issued at par, the carrying amount on Special Foods' books remains at $100,000. Thus, once the bonds are purchased from Nonaffiliated Corporation by Peerless for $104,500, a loss on the constructive retirement must be recognized in the consolidated income statement for $4,500 ($104,500 − $100,000). The bond elimination entry in the consolidation workpaper prepared at the end of 19X1 removes the bonds payable and the bond investment and recognizes the loss on the constructive retirement:

E(36)	Bonds Payable	100,000	
	Loss on Bond Retirement	4,500	
	Investment in Special Foods Bonds		104,500
	Eliminate intercorporate bonds payable.		

In subsequent years, the premium on the bond investment is amortized by Peerless, reducing interest income and the bond investment balance by $500 each year. This, in effect, recognizes a portion of the loss on the constructive retirement. When consolidated statements are prepared, the amount of the loss on constructive retirement that has not been recognized by the separate affiliates at the beginning of the period is allocated proportionately against the ownership interests of the issuing affiliate. The bond elimination entry needed in the consolidation workpaper prepared at the end of 19X2 is as follows:

E(37)	Bonds Payable	100,000	
	Interest Income	11,500	
	Retained Earnings, January 1	3,600	
	Noncontrolling Interest	900	
	Investment in Special Foods Bonds		104,000
	Interest Expense		12,000
	Eliminate intercorporate bonds payable:		
	$11,500 = ($100,000 × .12) − $500		
	$3,600 = $4,500 × .80		
	$900 = $4,500 × .20		
	$104,000 = $104,500 − $500		
	$12,000 = $100,000 × .12		

Entry E(38) is needed in the consolidation workpaper at the end of 19X3:

E(38)	Bonds Payable	100,000	
	Interest Income	11,500	
	Retained Earnings, January 1	3,200	
	Noncontrolling Interest	800	
	Investment in Special Foods Bonds		103,500
	Interest Expense		12,000
	Eliminate intercorporate bonds payable:		
	$3,200 = ($4,500 − $500) × .80		
	$800 = ($4,500 − $500) × .20		
	$103,500 = $104,500 − $500 − $500		

ADDITIONAL CONSIDERATIONS—INTERCORPORATE LEASING TRANSACTIONS

Leasing has become extremely common in the business world, often providing an attractive alternative to bonds or notes as a means of financing asset acquisitions.

Leasing arrangements vary from a simple rental of an office suite to complex situations involving transfers of depreciation deductions and tax credits among three or more parties.

Intercorporate leases also are common and often are significant in amount. Consolidation requires full elimination of all leasing transactions between affiliated companies. The remainder of this chapter illustrates the consolidation procedures that apply when there are intercorporate leasing arrangements. Three types of leasing arrangements are discussed: (1) operating leases, (2) direct financing leases, and (3) sales-type leases.

Operating Leases

The only consolidation eliminations needed in the case of an operating lease between affiliated companies are those to remove the rent expense recorded by the lessee and rental income recorded by the lessor. If the affiliates have recorded accrued rent, that also must be eliminated. The amount paid by the lessor in acquiring the leased asset and the lessor's depreciation charge represent the proper totals for consolidation.

Direct Financing Leases

With a direct financing lease, the lessor normally purchases an asset and enters into a long-term lease that provides the lessee with use of the asset and allows the lessor to earn an acceptable rate of return on its investment. For example, assume that Special Foods purchases equipment for $330,000 on January 1, 19X1, and immediately leases it to Peerless Products for 3 years at an annual rental of $133,000 due at the end of the year. The equipment has a 3-year expected life. The lease provides Special Foods with an annual return of about 10 percent on its unrecovered investment. The lease-related journal entries for both the lessee and the lessor for the first year of the lease are given in Figure 8-4.

For consolidation purposes, three eliminating entries are needed to remove the financial statement effects of the lease as of December 31, 19X1:

E(39)	Equipment	330,000	
	Leased Equipment		330,000
	Establish owned equipment.		
E(40)	Capital Lease Obligation	230,000	
	Unearned Interest	36,000	
	Lease Payments Receivable		266,000
	Eliminate intercompany lease obligation.		
E(41)	Interest Income	33,000	
	Interest Expense		33,000
	Eliminate intercompany interest.		

Entry E(39) adds back into the consolidated workpaper the equipment owned by the consolidated entity and eliminates the lease rights to the asset (leased equip-

FIGURE 8-4 Journal entries recorded by lessor and lessee under direct financing capital lease.

Date	Entries Recorded by Special Foods (Lessor)		Entries Recorded by Peerless Products (Lessee)	
January 1, 19X1	Equipment	330,000		
	Cash	330,000		
			Leased Equipment	330,000
			Capital Lease Obligation	330,000
January 1, 19X1	Lease Payments Receivable	399,000		
	Unearned Interest	69,000		
	Equipment	330,000		
December 31, 19X1	Cash	133,000	Interest Expense	33,000
	Lease Payments Receivable	133,000	Capital Lease Obligation	100,000
			Cash	133,000
	Unearned Interest	33,000	($33,000 = $330,000 × .10)	
	Interest Income	33,000		
	($33,000 = $330,000 × .10)		Depreciation Expense	110,000
			Accumulated Depreciation	110,000
			($110,000 = $330,000 ÷ 3 years)	

ment). Entry E(40) eliminates the intercompany receivable/payable. Entry E(41) eliminates the income and expense related to the intercompany transaction; because this transaction did not involve a party external to the consolidated entity, the income and expense are viewed as arising within the entity and must be eliminated.

Note that from a consolidated viewpoint, the consolidated entity has purchased and held an asset. No adjustment to depreciation expense is needed because the annual depreciation of $110,000 is reflected in the amount taken from Peerless's books and is equal to one-third of the original $330,000 cost of the equipment to the consolidated entity.

Sales-Type Leases

A sales-type lease is one in which the lessor earns some amount of profit from the lease in addition to the interest from financing the transaction. As an illustration of the treatment of a sales-type lease, assume the following:

1. Special Foods purchases equipment on January 1, 19X1, for $450,000. The equipment has an expected economic life of 5 years, with no residual value.

2. Special Foods uses the equipment for 2 years and depreciates the equipment at the rate of $90,000 ($450,000 ÷ 5 years) per year over the 2-year period.

3. On January 1, 19X3, Special Foods leases the equipment to Peerless Products for 3 years with rental payments of $133,000 due at the end of each year.

Special Foods recognizes a $60,000 gain at the inception of the sales-type lease, equal to the difference between the $330,000 present value of the lease payments discounted at 10 percent and the $270,000 ($450,000 − $180,000) book value of the equipment. The lease-related journal entries recorded by the lessee and the lessor in 19X1 through 19X4 are shown in Figure 8-5.

Eliminations in First Year of Lease The following eliminating entries are among those needed in the consolidation workpaper prepared at the end of 19X3:

E(42)	Equipment	450,000	
	Gain on Sale of Equipment	60,000	
	Leased Equipment		330,000
	Accumulated Depreciation		160,000
	Depreciation Expense		20,000
	Eliminate gain on sales-type lease and establish owned equipment.		
E(43)	Capital Lease Obligation	230,000	
	Unearned Interest	36,000	
	Lease Payments Receivable		266,000
	Eliminate intercompany lease obligation.		
E(44)	Interest Income	33,000	
	Interest Expense		33,000
	Eliminate intercompany interest.		

FIGURE 8-5 Journal entries recorded by lessor and lessee under sales-type capital lease.

Date	Entries Recorded by Special Foods (Lessor)			Entries Recorded by Peerless Products (Lessee)		
January 1, 19X1	Equipment Cash	450,000	450,000			

December 31, 19X1	Depreciation Expense
	  Accumulated Depreciation
	    ($90,000 = $450,000 ÷ 5 years)
		90,000	90,000			

December 31, 19X2	Depreciation Expense Accumulated Depreciation	90,000	90,000			

January 1, 19X3	Lease Payments Receivable
	Accumulated Depreciation
	  Unearned Interest
	  Equipment
	  Gain on Sale of Equipment
	    ($180,000 = $90,000 + $90,000)
		399,000
		180,000
			69,000
			450,000
			60,000
				Leased Equipment
				  Capital Lease Obligation
					330,000	330,000

December 31, 19X3	Cash
	  Lease Payments Receivable
	Unearned Interest
	  Interest Income
	    ($33,000 = $330,000 × .10)
		133,000
		
		33,000
			133,000
			
			33,000
				Interest Expense
				Capital Lease Obligation
				  Cash
				    ($33,000 = $330,000 × .10)
				Depreciation Expense
				  Accumulated Depreciation
				    ($110,000 = $330,000 ÷ 3 years)
					33,000
					100,000
					
					110,000
						133,000
						
						110,000

December 31, 19X4	Cash
	  Lease Payments Receivable
	Unearned Interest
	  Interest Income
	    ($23,000 = $230,000 × .10)
		133,000
		
		23,000
			133,000
			
			23,000
				Interest Expense
				Capital Lease Obligation
				  Cash
				    ($23,000 = $230,000 × .10)
				Depreciation Expense
				  Accumulated Depreciation
				    ($110,000 = $330,000 ÷ 3 years)
					23,000
					110,000
					
					110,000
						133,000
						
						110,000

Entry E(42) establishes the equipment in the workpaper at its original cost of $450,000 and eliminates the lease rights to the asset (leased equipment). This entry also eliminates the unrealized gain on the intercompany sales-type lease. In addition, entry E(42) reduces depreciation expense from the $110,000 ($330,000 ÷ 3 years) recorded on Peerless's books to the $90,000 ($450,000 ÷ 5 years) that would be shown if there had been no intercompany transfer. Finally, this entry increases accumulated depreciation from the $110,000 ($110,000 × 1 year) recorded on Peerless's books to the $270,000 ($90,000 × 3) that would be shown if Special Foods still held the equipment.

The elimination of the gain on the sale of the equipment ($60,000) and the reduction of depreciation expense ($20,000) in E(42) reduce income available to the combined shareholder group by $40,000 for 19X3. In this upstream illustration, the result is to reduce income assigned to noncontrolling shareholders by $8,000 ($40,000 × .20) and consolidated net income by $32,000 ($40,000 × .80).

Entry E(43) eliminates the intercompany receivable/payable, and entry E(44) eliminates the interest income and interest expense recorded during the year. Note that these two entries have no net effect on the income of the consolidated entity.

Eliminations in Second Year of Lease   Eliminations in the consolidation workpaper prepared as of December 31, 19X4, include the following:

E(45)	Equipment	450,000	
	Retained Earnings, January 1	32,000	
	Noncontrolling Interest	8,000	
	Leased Equipment		330,000
	Accumulated Depreciation		140,000
	Depreciation Expense		20,000
	Eliminate gain on lease and		
	establish owned equipment:		
	$32,000 = ($60,000 − $20,000) × .80		
	$8,000 = ($60,000 − $20,000) × .20		
E(46)	Capital Lease Obligation	120,000	
	Unearned Interest	13,000	
	Lease Payments Receivable		133,000
	Eliminate intercompany lease obligation.		
E(47)	Interest Income	23,000	
	Interest Expense		23,000
	Eliminate intercompany interest.		

Entry E(45) apportions the remaining unrealized intercompany gain included on Peerless's books in 19X3 against the beginning consolidated retained earnings balance ($40,000 × .80) and the noncontrolling interest ($40,000 × .20). Accumulated Depreciation is credited for $140,000 at the end of 19X4 to increase the reported balance from the $220,000 ($110,000 × 2 years) on Peerless's books to the $360,000 ($90,000 × 4 years) that would be reported if Special Foods continued to hold the equipment. As in 19X3, depreciation expense must be reduced from the $110,000 recorded by Peerless to the $90,000 that would be reported if Special Foods still held the equipment.

Each year over the 3-year term of the lease, one-third of the original $60,000 intercompany gain is realized. Thus, the increase in income resulting from the $20,000 reduction in depreciation expense in entry E(45) increases the non-controlling interest's share of income by $4,000 ($20,000 × .20) and consolidated net income by $16,000 ($20,000 × .80).

Entries E(46) and E(47) eliminate the remaining intercompany receivable/payable and the intercompany income and expense.

SUMMARY OF KEY CONCEPTS AND TERMS

The effects of intercompany debt transactions must be eliminated completely in preparing consolidated financial statements, just as with other types of intercompany transactions. Only debt transactions between the consolidated entity and unaffiliated parties are reported in the consolidated statements.

When one affiliate issues bonds that are purchased directly by another affiliate, the bonds are viewed as never having been issued, from a consolidated point of view. Thus, all aspects of the intercompany bond holding are eliminated in consolidation. Items requiring elimination include (1) the bond investment from the purchasing affiliate's books, (2) the bond liability and any associated discount or premium from the issuer's books, (3) the interest income recognized by the investing affiliate and the interest expense recognized by the issuer, and (4) any intercompany interest receivable/payable as of the date of the consolidated statements.

When a company purchases the bonds of an affiliate from a nonaffiliate, the bonds are treated in consolidation as if they had been issued and subsequently repurchased by the consolidated entity. If the price paid by the purchasing affiliate is different from the issuer's book value of the bonds, a gain or loss from retirement of the bonds is recognized in the consolidated income statement. In addition, all aspects of the intercompany bond holding are eliminated because the bonds are treated as if they had been retired by the consolidated entity.

Intercorporate leasing transactions have become extremely common. As with other types of intercompany transactions, consolidation requires the complete elimination of all aspects of the intercompany lease arrangement, including any intercompany receivable/payable and intercompany income and expense. The leased asset must be reported based on the lessor's cost.

Constructive retirement   Indirect intercompany debt transfer
Direct intercompany debt transfer

APPENDIX: Intercompany Indebtedness—Fully Adjusted Equity Method and Cost Method

Consolidation procedures following use of (1) the fully adjusted equity method and (2) the cost method are illustrated with the example of the intercompany bond transaction presented earlier. Assume that Special Foods issues bonds with a par value of $100,000 and a term of 10 years to Nonaffiliated Corporation for $102,000 on January 1, 19X1. Peerless Products purchases the bonds from Nonaffiliated Corporation on December 31, 19X1, for $91,000.

FULLY ADJUSTED EQUITY METHOD

The accounting procedures under the fully adjusted equity method are the same as under the basic equity method except that the parent (1) adjusts its income and the investment account by its proportionate share of the gain or loss on the constructive retirement of the bonds in the year of repurchase and (2) adjusts for the implicit recognition of the gain or loss by it and its subsidiary as they amortize the discount and premium in subsequent years.

The 19X1 gain on the constructive retirement in this illustration is $10,800, computed as follows:

Book value of Special Foods' bonds, December 31, 19X1 ($102,000 − $200)	$101,800
Price paid by Peerless to purchase bonds	(91,000)
Gain on constructive retirement of bonds	$ 10,800

Fully Adjusted Equity-Method Entries—19X1

Peerless records the following entries under the fully adjusted equity method during 19X1 to account for its investment in Special Foods stock:

(48)	Investment in Special Foods Stock	40,000	
	Income from Subsidiary		40,000
	Record equity-method income:		
	$50,000 × .80		
(49)	Cash	24,000	
	Investment in Special Foods Stock		24,000
	Record dividends from Special Foods:		
	$30,000 × .80		
(50)	Investment in Special Foods Stock	8,640	
	Income from Subsidiary		8,640
	Recognize income from bond retirement:		
	($101,800 − $91,000) × .80		

Entry (50) adjusts equity-method net income by a proportionate share of the gain on the constructive retirement of Special Foods' bonds. Although the gain itself is not recognized by Peerless, its net income under the fully adjusted equity method must equal consolidated net income. In keeping with the concept of a one-line consolidation, Peerless's share of the gain on constructive retirement of Special Foods' bonds is included in its share of income from Special Foods.

Entries (48), (49), and (50) record income from Special Foods of $48,640 and increase the carrying amount of the investment on Peerless's books to $264,640 as of December 31, 19X1.

Consolidation Elimination Entries—19X1

The December 31, 19X1, workpaper to prepare consolidated financial statements for Peerless Products and Special Foods contains the following eliminating entries:

E(51)	Income from Subsidiary	48,640	
	Dividends Declared		24,000
	Investment in Special Foods Stock		24,640
	Eliminate income from subsidiary.		
E(52)	Income to Noncontrolling Interest	12,160	
	Dividends Declared		6,000
	Noncontrolling Interest		6,160
	Assign income to noncontrolling interest:		
	$12,160 = ($50,000 + $10,800) \times .20$		
E(53)	Common Stock—Special Foods	200,000	
	Retained Earnings, January 1	100,000	
	Investment in Special Foods Stock		240,000
	Noncontrolling Interest		60,000
	Eliminate beginning investment balance.		
E(54)	Bonds Payable	100,000	
	Premium on Bonds Payable	1,800	
	Investment in Special Foods Bonds		91,000
	Gain on Bond Retirement		10,800
	Eliminate intercorporate bonds payable.		

Fully Adjusted Equity-Method Entries—19X2

In addition to the entries related to its investment in Special Foods' bonds, Peerless records the following entries during 19X2 under the fully adjusted equity method:

(55)	Investment in Special Foods Stock	60,000	
	Income from Subsidiary		60,000
	Record equity-method income:		
	$75,000 \times .80$		
(56)	Cash	32,000	
	Investment in Special Foods Stock		32,000
	Record dividends from Special Foods:		
	$40,000 \times .80$		

(57)	Income from Subsidiary	960	
	Investment in Special Foods Stock		960

Adjust for portion of gain on constructive
bond retirement recognized:
($10,800 ÷ 9) × .80

Entry (57) adjusts for Peerless's portion of the gain on the constructive bond retirement recognized on the separate books of Peerless and Special Foods during 19X2. While neither Peerless nor Special Foods recognized any of the gain from the constructive bond retirement on their separate books in 19X1, Peerless adjusted its equity-method income from Special Foods for its 80 percent share of the $10,800 gain, $8,640. Therefore, as the gain is recognized over the remaining term of the bonds by Peerless and Special Foods, Peerless must reverse its 19X1 entry for its share of the gain. This adjustment is needed to avoid double-counting Peerless's share of the gain. Thus, the original adjustment of $8,640 is reversed by $960 ($8,640 ÷ 9 years) each year. This is accomplished in 19X2 through entry (57).

The amount of entry (57) also is equal to Peerless's 80 percent share of the difference in interest expense and interest income to be eliminated in consolidation:

Elimination of Peerless's interest income	$13,000
Elimination of Special Foods' interest expense	(11,800)
Net reduction in income	$ 1,200
Peerless's proportionate share	.80
Reduction in consolidated net income	$ 960

When the bond interest expense and bond interest income are eliminated in the preparation of consolidated financial statements, consolidated net income will be reduced by $960. Entry (57) adjusts Peerless's equity-method income to be equal to consolidated net income.

Investment Account—19X2

Peerless's account relating to its investment in the common stock of Special Foods appears as follows at the end of 19X2:

Investment in Special Foods Stock

	Original cost	240,000			
(48)	19X1 equity accrual		(49)	19X1 dividends	
	($50,000 × .80)	40,000		($30,000 × .80)	24,000
(50)	Gain on constructive				
	bond retirement				
	($10,800 × .80)	8,640			
	Balance, 12/31/X1	264,640			
(55)	19X2 equity accrual		(56)	19X2 dividends	
	($75,000 × .80)	60,000		($40,000 × .80)	32,000
			(57)	Recognized portion	
				of constructive gain	
				($8,640 ÷ 9 years)	960
	Balance, 12/31/X2	291,680			

Consolidation Elimination Entries—19X2

The following elimination entries are needed in the workpaper to prepare consolidated financial statements for 19X2:

E(58)	Income from Subsidiary	59,040	
	Dividends Declared		32,000
	Investment in Special Foods Stock		27,040
	Eliminate income from subsidiary.		
E(59)	Income to Noncontrolling Interest	14,760	
	Dividends Declared		8,000
	Noncontrolling Interest		6,760
	Assign income to noncontrolling interest:		
	$14,760 = ($75,000 − $1,200) × .20		
E(60)	Common Stock—Special Foods	200,000	
	Retained Earnings, January 1	120,000	
	Investment in Special Foods Stock		256,000
	Noncontrolling Interest		64,000
	Eliminate beginning investment balance.		
E(61)	Bonds Payable	100,000	
	Premium on Bonds Payable	1,600	
	Interest Income	13,000	
	Investment in Special Foods Bonds		92,000
	Interest Expense		11,800
	Investment in Special Foods Stock		8,640
	Noncontrolling Interest		2,160
	Eliminate intercorporate bonds payable:		
	$1,600 = $2,000 − $200 − $200		
	$13,000 = ($100,000 × .12) + $1,000		
	$92,000 = $91,000 + $1,000		
	$11,800 = ($100,000 × .12) − $200		
	$8,640 = $10,800 × .80		
	$2,160 = $10,800 × .20		

COST METHOD

Preparation of consolidated financial statements when the cost method has been used is illustrated with the same example employed for the fully adjusted equity method. Peerless recognizes dividend income of $24,000 ($30,000 × .80) in 19X1 and $32,000 ($40,000 × .80) in 19X2 under the cost method. Peerless makes no adjustments with respect to the undistributed earnings of Special Foods or the gain on the constructive bond retirement.

Consolidation Elimination Entries—19X1

The following eliminating entries are needed in the consolidation workpaper prepared at the end of 19X1, following use of the cost method:

E(62)	Dividend Income	24,000	
	Dividends Declared		24,000
	Eliminate dividend income from subsidiary: $30,000 \times .80$		

E(63)	Income to Noncontrolling Interest	12,160	
	Dividends Declared		6,000
	Noncontrolling Interest		6,160
	Assign income to noncontrolling interest: $12,160 = (\$50,000 + \$10,800) \times .20$		

E(64)	Common Stock—Special Foods	200,000	
	Retained Earnings, January 1	100,000	
	Investment in Special Foods Stock		240,000
	Noncontrolling Interest		60,000
	Eliminate investment balance at date of acquisition.		

E(65)	Bonds Payable	100,000	
	Premium on Bonds Payable	1,800	
	Investment in Special Foods Bonds		91,000
	Gain on Bond Retirement		10,800
	Eliminate intercorporate bonds payable.		

Consolidation Elimination Entries—19X2

Elimination entries needed in the consolidation workpaper at the end of 19X2 are as follows:

E(66)	Dividend Income	32,000	
	Dividends Declared		32,000
	Eliminate dividend income from subsidiary: $40,000 \times .80$		

E(67)	Income to Noncontrolling Interest	14,760	
	Dividends Declared		8,000
	Noncontrolling Interest		6,760
	Assign income to noncontrolling interest: $14,760 = (\$75,000 - \$1,200) \times .20$		

E(68)	Common Stock—Special Foods	200,000	
	Retained Earnings, January 1	100,000	
	Investment in Special Foods Stock		240,000
	Noncontrolling Interest		60,000
	Eliminate investment balance at date of acquisition.		

E(69)	Retained Earnings, January 1	4,000	
	Noncontrolling Interest		4,000
	Assign undistributed prior earnings of subsidiary to noncontrolling interest: $20,000 \times .20$		

E(70)	Bonds Payable	100,000	
	Premium on Bonds Payable	1,600	
	Interest Income	13,000	
	Investment in Special Foods Bonds		92,000
	Interest Expense		11,800
	Retained Earnings, January 1		8,640
	Noncontrolling Interest		2,160

Eliminate intercorporate bonds payable:
$1,600 = $2,000 − $200 − $200
$13,000 = ($100,000 × .12) + $1,000
$92,000 = $91,000 + $1,000
$11,800 = ($100,000 × .12) − $200
$8,640 = $10,800 × .80
$2,160 = $10,800 × .20

QUESTIONS

Q8-1 When is a gain or loss on bond retirement included in the consolidated income statement?

Q8-2 What is meant by a constructive bond retirement in a multicorporate setting? How does a constructive bond retirement differ from an actual bond retirement?

Q8-3 When a bond issue has been placed directly with an affiliate, what account balances will be stated incorrectly in the consolidated statements if the intercompany bond ownership is not eliminated in preparing the consolidation workpaper?

Q8-4 When bonds of an affiliate are purchased from a nonaffiliate during the period, what balances will be stated incorrectly in the consolidated financial statements if the intercompany bond ownership is not eliminated in preparing the consolidation workpaper?

Q8-5 For a multicorporate entity, how is the recognition of gains or losses on bond retirement changed when emphasis is placed on the economic entity rather than the legal entity?

Q8-6 When a parent company sells land to a subsidiary at more than book value, the consolidation eliminating entries at the end of the period include a debit to the gain on the sale of land. When a parent purchases the bonds of a subsidiary from a nonaffiliate at less than book value, the eliminating entries at the end of the period contain a credit to a gain on bond retirement. Why are these two situations not handled in the same manner in the consolidation workpaper?

Q8-7 What is the effect on consolidated net income of eliminating intercompany interest income and interest expense when there has been a direct sale of bonds to an affiliate? Why?

Q8-8 What is the effect on consolidated net income of eliminating intercompany interest income and interest expense when a loss on bond retirement has been reported in a prior year's consolidated financial statements as a result of a constructive retirement of an affiliate's bonds? Why?

Q8-9 If the bonds of an affiliate are purchased from a nonaffiliate at the beginning of the current year, how can the amount of the gain or loss on constructive retirement be computed by looking at the year-end trial balances of the two companies?

Q8-10 When the parent company purchases the bonds of a subsidiary from a nonaffiliate for more than book value, what income statement accounts will be affected in preparing consolidated financial statements? What will be the effect of the purchase upon consolidated net income? Explain.

Q8-11 When a subsidiary purchases the bonds of its parent from a nonaffiliate for less than book value, what will be the effect on consolidated net income?

Q8-12 How is the amount of income assigned to the noncontrolling interest affected by the direct placement of a subsidiary's bonds with the parent company?

Q8-13 How is the amount of income assigned to the noncontrolling interest affected when bonds of the subsidiary are purchased by the parent from an unaffiliated company for less than book value?

Q8-14 How would the relationship between interest income recorded by a subsidiary and interest expense recorded by the parent be expected to change when a direct placement of the parent's bonds with the subsidiary is compared with a constructive retirement in which the subsidiary purchases the bonds of the parent from a nonaffiliate?

Q8-15 A subsidiary purchased bonds of the parent company from a nonaffiliate in the preceding period, and a gain on bond retirement was reported in the consolidated income statement as a result of the purchase. What effect will that event have on the amount of consolidated net income reported in the current period?

Q8-16 A parent company purchased bonds of its subsidiary from a nonaffiliate in the preceding year, and a loss on bond retirement was reported in the consolidated income statement. How will income assigned to the noncontrolling interest be affected in the year following the constructive retirement?

Q8-17 A parent purchases bonds of a subsidiary directly from the subsidiary. The parent later sells the bonds to a nonaffiliate. From a consolidated viewpoint, what occurs when the parent sells the bonds? Is a gain or loss reported in the consolidated income statement when the parent sells the bonds? Why?

Q8-18 Shortly after a parent company purchased its subsidiary's bonds from a nonaffiliate, the subsidiary retired the entire issue. How is the gain or loss on bond retirement that is reported by the subsidiary treated for consolidation purposes?

Q8-19* Describe the consolidation procedures needed to deal with intercorporate leasing arrangements for the following types of leases: **(a)** operating, **(b)** direct financing, and **(c)** sales-type.

CASES

C8-1 Recognition of Retirement Gains and Losses

Bradley Corporation sold bonds to Flood Company in 19X2 at 90. At the end of 19X4, Century Corporation purchased the bonds from Flood Company at 105. Bradley Corporation then retired the full bond issue on December 31, 19X7, at 101. Century Corporation holds 80 percent of the voting stock of Bradley Corporation. Neither Century Corporation nor Bradley Corporation owns stock of Flood Company.

Required

a. Indicate how each of the three bond transactions should be recorded by the companies involved.

b. Indicate when, if at all, the consolidated entity headed by Century Corporation should recognize a gain or loss on bond retirement and indicate whether a gain or a loss should be recognized.

c. Will income assigned to the noncontrolling shareholders of Bradley Corporation be affected by the bond transactions? If so, in which years?

C8-2 Interest Income and Expense

The controller of Snerd Corporation is experiencing difficulty in explaining the impact of several of the company's intercorporate bond transactions.

Required

a. Snerd receives interest payments in excess of the amount of interest income it records on its investment in Snort bonds. Did Snerd purchase the bonds at par value, at a premium, or at a discount? How can you tell?

b. The 19X3 consolidated income statement reported a gain on the retirement of a subsidiary's bonds. If Snerd purchased the bonds from a nonaffiliate at par value:

(1) Were the bonds of the subsidiary originally sold at a premium or a discount? How can you tell?

(2) Will the annual interest payments received by Snerd be greater or less than the interest expense recorded by the subsidiary? Explain why.

(3) How is the difference between the interest income recorded by Snerd and the interest expense recorded by the subsidiary treated in preparing consolidated financial statements at the end of each period?

EXERCISES

E8-1 Bond Sale from Subsidiary to Parent

On January 1, 19X3, Circle Company sold $100,000 par value, 8 percent, first mortgage bonds to Chicago Tire Corporation for $120,000. The bonds mature in 10 years and pay interest semiannually on January 1 and July 1. Chicago Tire Corporation holds ownership to 80 percent of the voting shares of Circle Company.

Required

a. Prepare the 19X3 journal entries on the books of Chicago Tire Corporation related to its ownership of Circle Company bonds.

b. Prepare the journal entries recorded by Circle Company in 19X3 related to the bonds.

c. Prepare the workpaper eliminating entry needed on December 31, 19X3, to remove the effects of the intercorporate ownership of bonds.

E8-2 Computation of Transfer Price

Nettle Corporation sold $100,000 par value, 10-year, first mortgage bonds to Timberline Corporation on January 1, 19X5. The bonds, which bear a nominal interest rate of 12 percent, pay interest semiannually on January 1 and July 1. The entry to record interest income by Timberline Corporation on December 31, 19X7, was as follows:

Interest Receivable	6,000	
Interest Income		5,750
Investment in Nettle Company Bonds		250

Timberline Corporation owns 65 percent of the voting stock of Nettle Corporation, and consolidated statements are prepared on December 31, 19X7.

Required

a. What was the original purchase price of the bonds to Timberline Corporation?

b. What is the balance in Timberline's bond investment account on December 31, 19X7?

c. Give the workpaper eliminating entry or entries needed to remove the effects of the intercompany ownership of bonds in preparing consolidated financial statements for 19X7.

E8-3 Bond Sale at Discount

Altar Corporation sold $500,000 par value, 10 percent bonds on January 1, 19X2, at 90. Ron's Concrete Products Company, which owns 60 percent of the voting shares of Altar Corporation, purchased one-fifth of the bonds at the time of sale. The bonds mature in 10 years and pay interest semiannually on January 1 and July 1.

Required

a. What amount of interest expense should be reported in the 19X3 consolidated income statement?

b. Give the journal entries recorded on the books of Ron's Concrete Products Company during 19X3 with regard to its investment in Altar Corporation bonds.

c. Give all workpaper eliminating entries needed to remove the effects of the intercorporate bond ownership in preparing consolidated financial statements for 19X3.

E8-4 Multiple-Choice Questions

Parent Company paid a nonaffiliate $95,000 in 19X4 to purchase bonds that are recorded as a liability of $105,000 on the books of Subsidiary Company. Parent Company owns 60 percent of the shares of Subsidiary Company stock. The bonds have 5 years remaining to maturity from the date of purchase by Parent Company. Subsidiary Company reports net income of $40,000 in 19X4 and $60,000 in 19X5. Parent Company reports income, excluding investment income from Subsidiary Company stock, of $200,000 in both 19X4 and 19X5.

Required

Select the correct answer for each of the following questions.

1. If the bond purchase occurred on December 31, 19X4, what amount of consolidated net income should be reported for 19X4?

    a. $228,800.
    b. $230,000.
    c. $232,000.
    d. $234,000.

2. If the bond purchase occurred on January 1, 19X4, what amount of consolidated net income should be reported for 19X4?
    a. $228,800.
    b. $230,800.
    c. $232,000.
    d. $234,000.

3. What amount of consolidated net income should be reported for 19X5 if the bond purchase occurred on January 1, 19X4?
    a. $234,000.
    b. $234,800.
    c. $237,200.
    d. $238,000.

4. What amount of consolidated net income should be reported for 19X5 if the bond purchase occurred on December 31, 19X4?
    a. $234,000.
    b. $234,800.
    c. $237,200.
    d. $238,000.

5. Suppose the bond liability had been recorded on the books of Parent Company and Subsidiary Company purchased the bonds under the conditions indicated. What amount of consolidated net income would be reported for 19X4 if the purchase occurred on December 31, 19X4?
    a. $228,800.
    b. $230,000.
    c. $232,000.
    d. $234,000.

6. Suppose the bond liability had been recorded on the books of Parent Company and Subsidiary Company purchased the bonds under the conditions indicated. What amount of consolidated net income would be reported for 19X4 if the purchase occurred on January 1, 19X4?
    a. $228,800.
    b. $230,000.
    c. $232,000.
    d. $234,000.

E8-5   Multiple-Choice Questions

Kruse Corporation holds 60 percent of the voting common shares of Gary's Ice Cream Parlors. On January 1, 19X6, Gary's Ice Cream Parlors purchased $50,000 par value, 10 percent, first mortgage bonds of Kruse Corporation from Cane Corporation for $58,000.

Kruse Corporation originally issued the bonds to Cane Corporation on January 1, 19X4, for $53,000. The bonds have a 10-year maturity from the date of issue.

Gary's Ice Cream Parlors reported net income of $20,000 for 19X6, and Kruse Corporation reported income (excluding income from ownership of Gary's Ice Cream Parlors stock) of $40,000.

Required

Select the correct answer for each of the following questions.

1. What amount of interest expense is recorded annually by Kruse Corporation?
   a. $4,000.
   b. $4,700.
   c. $5,000.
   d. $10,000.

2. What amount of interest income is recorded by Gary's Ice Cream Parlors for 19X6?
   a. $4,000.
   b. $5,000.
   c. $9,000.
   d. $10,000.

3. What gain or loss on the retirement of bonds should be reported in the 19X6 consolidated income statement?
   a. $2,400 gain.
   b. $5,600 gain.
   c. $5,600 loss.
   d. $8,000 loss.

4. What amount of consolidated net income should be reported for 19X6?
   a. $47,100.
   b. $52,000.
   c. $54,400.
   d. $60,000.

E8-6 Multiple-Choice Questions

On January 1, 19X4, Passive Heating Corporation paid $104,000 for $100,000 par value, 9 percent bonds of Solar Energy Corporation. Solar Energy Corporation had issued $300,000 of the 10-year bonds on January 1, 19X2, for $360,000. Passive previously had purchased 80 percent of the common stock of Solar on January 1, 19X1, at underlying book value.

Passive Heating Corporation reported operating income (excluding income from subsidiary) of $50,000, and Solar Energy Corporation reported net income of $30,000 for 19X4.

Required

Select the correct answer for each of the following questions.

1. What amount of interest expense should be included in the 19X4 consolidated income statement?
   a. $14,000.
   b. $18,000.
   c. $21,000.
   d. $27,000.

2. What amount of interest income should be included in Passive Heating Corporation's 19X4 income statement?
   a. $7,000.
   b. $8,500.
   c. $9,000.
   d. $9,500.

3. What amount of gain or loss on bond retirement should be included in the 19X4 consolidated income statement?
   a. $4,000 gain.
   b. $4,000 loss.
   c. $12,000 gain.
   d. $16,000 loss.

4. Consolidated net income for 19X4 should be:
   a. $80,000.
   b. $82,400.
   c. $88,400.
   d. $92,000.

5. Income assigned to the noncontrolling interest in the 19X4 consolidated income statement should be:
   a. $6,000.
   b. $8,100.
   c. $8,400.
   d. $16,000.

E8-7 Constructive Retirement at End of Year

Debtor Corporation issued $400,000 of 7 percent, 10-year, first mortgage bonds on January 1, 19X2, at 120. Creditor Corporation holds 80 percent of the common shares of Debtor Corporation and on December 31, 19X5, purchased $100,000 of Debtor Corporation bonds from the original purchaser for $94,000 plus accrued interest. Interest is paid semiannually on January 1 and July 1.

Required

a. Prepare the workpaper eliminating entry or entries needed to remove the effects of the intercorporate bond ownership in preparing consolidated financial statements for 19X5.

b. Prepare the workpaper eliminating entry or entries needed to remove the effects of the intercorporate bond ownership in preparing consolidated financial statements for 19X6.

E8-8   Constructive Retirement at Beginning of Year

Armstrong Siding Corporation issued $400,000 of 7 percent, 10-year, first mortgage bonds on January 1, 19X2, at 120. Pilot Company holds 80 percent of the common shares of Armstrong Siding Corporation and on January 1, 19X5, purchased $100,000 of Armstrong Siding bonds from the original purchaser for $93,000. Interest is paid semiannually on January 1 and July 1.

Required

a. Prepare the workpaper eliminating entry or entries needed to remove the effects of the intercompany bond ownership in preparing consolidated financial statements for 19X5.
b. Prepare the workpaper eliminating entry or entries needed to remove the effects of the intercompany bond ownership in preparing consolidated financial statements for 19X6.

E8-9   Loss on Constructive Retirement

Apple Corporation holds 60 percent of the voting shares of Shortway Publishing Company. Apple Corporation issued $500,000 of 10 percent bonds with a 10-year maturity on January 1, 19X2, at 90. On January 1, 19X8, Shortway Publishing Company purchased $100,000 of the Apple Corporation bonds for $108,000. Partial trial balances for the two companies on December 31, 19X8, are as follows:

	Apple Corporation	Shortway Publishing Company
Investment in Shortway Publishing Company Stock	$141,000	
Investment in Apple Corporation Bonds		$106,000
Bonds Payable	500,000	
Discount on Bonds Payable	15,000	
Interest Expense	55,000	
Interest Income		8,000
Interest Payable	25,000	
Interest Receivable		5,000

Required

Prepare the workpaper eliminating entry or entries needed on December 31, 19X8, to remove the effects of the intercorporate bond ownership in preparing consolidated financial statements.

E8-10   Determining the Amount of Retirement Gain or Loss

Downlink Corporation is 95 percent owned by Online Enterprises. On January 1, 19X1, Downlink Corporation issued $200,000 of 5-year bonds at 115. Annual interest of 12 percent is paid semiannually on January 1 and July 1. Online Enterprises purchased $100,000 of the bonds on August 31, 19X3, at par value. The following balances are taken from the separate 19X3 financial statements of the two companies:

	Online Enterprises	Downlink Corporation
Investment in Downlink Corporation Bonds	$100,000	
Interest Income	4,000	
Interest Receivable	6,000	
Bonds Payable		$200,000
Bond Premium		12,000
Interest Expense		18,000
Interest Payable		12,000

Required

a. Compute the amount of interest expense that should be reported in the consolidated income statement for 19X3.

b. Compute the gain or loss on constructive bond retirement that should be reported in the 19X3 consolidated income statement.

c. Prepare the consolidation workpaper eliminating entry or entries as of December 31, 19X3, to remove the effects of the intercorporate bond ownership.

E8-11* Intercorporate Leases

Thomas Company owns 95 percent of the common stock of Bradley Financial Corporation, from which Thomas leases some of the assets it uses in its operations. On November 7, 19X8, Thomas entered into an operating lease with Bradley under which Thomas leases several delivery trucks for $38,000 per year; the lease payments are made at the end of each calendar year. Bradley recognizes $21,000 of depreciation per year on the trucks.

On January 2, 19X9, Thomas leased some heavy-duty lifting equipment from Bradley under a 10-year direct financing lease. The terms of the lease call for Thomas to pay $100,000 on signing the lease and to make payments of $59,612 on December 31 of each year. The present value of the 10 end-of-year lease payments of $59,612 each is $400,000. The equipment has an estimated life of 10 years, with no residual value. An interest rate of 8 percent is implicit in the terms of the lease. The equipment had been purchased by Bradley on December 31, 19X8, for $500,000. Both companies use straight-line depreciation.

Required

a. Present all entries recorded by Thomas during 19X9 with respect to (1) the operating lease and (2) the capital lease.

b. Present all entries recorded by Bradley during 19X9 with respect to (1) the operating lease and (2) the direct financing lease.

c. Present all eliminating entries regarding the intercompany leases that should appear in the workpaper to prepare a complete set of consolidated financial statements for 19X9.

PROBLEMS

P8-12 Direct Sale of Bonds at Premium

Premium Pipe Company holds 70 percent ownership of Dryleaf Tobacco Corporation, which it acquired on January 1, 19X3, at underlying book value. At that time, Premium

Pipe Company also purchased $50,000 of Dryleaf Tobacco bonds directly from Dryleaf for a total price of $55,000. The Dryleaf bonds have an 8 percent coupon rate and pay interest on January 1 and July 1. The bonds have a 10-year maturity from the date of issue.

Trial balances for the companies as of December 31, 19X4, are as follows:

Item	Premium Pipe Company Debit	Premium Pipe Company Credit	Dryleaf Tobacco Corporation Debit	Dryleaf Tobacco Corporation Credit
Cash and Receivables	$ 62,000		$ 60,000	
Inventory	170,000		70,000	
Buildings and Equipment (net)	320,000		180,000	
Investment in Dryleaf Corporation Bonds	54,000			
Investment in Dryleaf Corporation Stock	119,000			
Operating Expenses	197,500		163,000	
Interest Expense	27,000		7,000	
Dividends Declared	60,000		10,000	
Current Liabilities		$ 35,000		$ 32,000
Bonds Payable		300,000		100,000
Bond Premium				8,000
Common Stock		100,000		50,000
Retained Earnings		250,000		100,000
Sales		300,000		200,000
Interest Income		3,500		
Income from Subsidiary		21,000		
Total	$1,009,500	$1,009,500	$490,000	$490,000

Required

a. Record the 19X4 journal entries on the books of Dryleaf Tobacco Corporation related to its bonds outstanding.

b. Record the 19X4 journal entries on the books of Premium Pipe Company relating to its investment in the bonds of Dryleaf.

c. Prepare the elimination entries needed to complete a consolidation workpaper for 19X4.

P8-13 Consolidation Workpaper

Using the data presented in Problem 8-12, prepare a three-part consolidation workpaper for 19X4.

P8-14 Direct Sale of Bonds to Parent

On January 1, 19X1, Tower Cable Corporation purchased 70 percent of the stock of Underground Power Company at underlying book value and $50,000 of Underground Power bonds. The 8 percent, 10-year bonds were purchased directly from Underground Power for $45,000. Interest payments are made on January 1 and July 1.

Trial balances for the two companies as of December 31, 19X3, are as follows:

Item	Tower Cable Corporation Debit	Tower Cable Corporation Credit	Underground Power Company Debit	Underground Power Company Credit
Cash and Accounts Receivable	$ 69,500		$ 46,000	
Inventory	170,000		70,000	
Buildings and Equipment (net)	320,000		180,000	
Investment in Underground Power Bonds	46,500			
Investment in Underground Power Stock	119,000			
Discount on Bonds Payable			7,000	
Operating Expenses	198,500		161,000	
Interest Expense	27,000		9,000	
Dividends Declared	60,000		10,000	
Current Liabilities		$ 35,000		$ 33,000
Bonds Payable		300,000		100,000
Common Stock		100,000		50,000
Retained Earnings		250,000		100,000
Sales		300,000		200,000
Interest Income		4,500		
Income from Subsidiary		21,000		
Total	$1,010,500	$1,010,500	$483,000	$483,000

Required

a. Record the journal entries for 19X3 on the books of Tower Cable Corporation related to its investments in Underground Power Company's stock and bonds.

b. Record the entries for 19X3 on the books of Underground Power Company related to its bond issue.

c. Prepare elimination entries needed to complete a consolidation workpaper for 19X3.

P8-15 Consolidation Workpaper

Using the data presented in Problem 8-14, prepare a three-part consolidation workpaper for 19X3.

P8-16 Incomplete Data

Ballard Corporation purchased 70 percent of the voting shares of Condor Company on January 1, 19X4, at underlying book value. It also purchased $100,000 par value, 12 percent Condor Company bonds on that date. The bonds had been issued on January 1, 19X1, with a 10-year maturity.

During preparation of the consolidated financial statements for December 31, 19X4, the following eliminating entry was made on the workpaper:

Bonds Payable	100,000	
Bond Premium	6,000	
Loss on Bond Retirement	3,500	
Interest Income	?	
Investment in Condor Company Bonds		109,000
Interest Expense		?

Required

    a. What was the price paid by Ballard Corporation to purchase the Condor bonds?

    b. What was the carrying amount of the bonds on the books of Condor Company on the date of purchase?

    c. If Condor Company reports net income of $30,000 in 19X5, what amount of income should be assigned to the noncontrolling interest in the 19X5 consolidated income statement?

P8-17 Balance Sheet Eliminations

Perth Corporation purchased 80 percent of the stock of Hearty Brewing Company on January 1, 19X1, at underlying book value. On that date, Hearty Brewing Company issued $300,000 par value, 8 percent, 10-year bonds to Keller Paving Company. Perth Corporation subsequently purchased $100,000 of the bonds from Keller Paving for $102,000 on January 1, 19X3. Interest is paid semiannually on January 1 and July 1.

    Summarized balance sheets for Perth Corporation and Hearty Brewing Company as of December 31, 19X4, are as follows:

Perth Corporation
Balance Sheet
December 31, 19X4

Cash and Receivables	$122,500	Accounts Payable	$ 40,000
Inventory	200,000	Bonds Payable	400,000
Buildings and Equipment (net)	320,000	Common Stock	200,000
Investment in Hearty Brewing:		Retained Earnings	320,000
Bonds	101,500		
Stock	216,000		
		Total Liabilities	
Total Assets	$960,000	and Owners' Equity	$960,000

Hearty Brewing Company
Balance Sheet
December 31, 19X4

Cash and Receivables	$124,000	Accounts Payable	$ 28,000
Inventory	150,000	Bonds Payable	300,000
Buildings and Equipment (net)	360,000	Bond Premium	36,000
		Common Stock	100,000
		Retained Earnings	170,000
		Total Liabilities	
Total Assets	$634,000	and Owners' Equity	$634,000

Required

    a. Prepare all elimination entries needed on December 31, 19X4, to complete a consolidation balance sheet workpaper.

    b. Prepare a consolidation balance sheet workpaper as of December 31, 19X4.

    c. Prepare a consolidated balance sheet in good form.

P8-18 Computations Relating to Bond Purchase from Nonaffiliate

Bliss Perfume Company issued $300,000 of 10 percent bonds on January 1, 19X2, at 110. The bonds mature 10 years from issue and have semiannual interest payments on January 1 and July 1. Parsons Corporation owns 80 percent of the stock of Bliss Perfume Company. On April 1, 19X4, Parsons Corporation purchased $100,000 par value of Bliss Perfume bonds in the securities markets.

Partial trial balances for the two companies on December 31, 19X4, are as follows:

	Parsons Corporation	Bliss Perfume Company
Investment in Bliss Perfume Company Bonds	$105,600	
Interest Income	6,900	
Interest Receivable	5,000	
Bonds Payable		$300,000
Bond Premium		21,000
Interest Expense		27,000
Interest Payable		15,000

Required

a. What was the purchase price of the Bliss Perfume Company bonds to Parsons Corporation?

b. What amount of gain or loss on bond retirement should be reported in the consolidated income statement for 19X4?

c. Prepare the necessary workpaper eliminating entries as of December 31, 19X4, to remove the effects of the intercorporate bond ownership.

P8-19 Determination of Consolidated Net Income

Parker Chemical Corporation purchased 60 percent ownership of Jones Supply Company on January 1, 19X1, for $99,000. At that time Jones Supply Company reported stock outstanding of $100,000 and retained earnings of $50,000. The retained earnings balance of Jones Supply Company increased to $70,000 by January 1, 19X4.

Net income of Jones Supply Company and the separate operating income of Parker Chemical Corporation were:

	Parker Chemical Operating Income	Jones Supply Net Income
19X4	$100,000	$40,000
19X5	120,000	30,000

Jones Supply Company frequently purchases inventory from Parker Chemical Corporation. On December 31, 19X4, Jones Supply Company inventory contained $2,000 of unrealized intercompany profit, and on December 31, 19X5, $5,500 of unrealized intercompany profit.

On January 1, 19X2, Jones Supply Company issued $300,000 of 12 percent, 10-year bonds at 92. Parker Chemical Corporation paid $97,600 to acquire $100,000 of the bonds on January 1, 19X4.

On January 1, 19X1, the buildings of Jones Supply Company had a book value of $230,000 and fair value of $245,000, with a 9-year economic life remaining on that date.

Required

Compute consolidated net income for 19X4 and 19X5.

P8-20 Computations following Parent's Acquisition of Subsidiary Bonds

Mainstream Corporation holds 80 percent of the voting shares of Offenberg Company, acquired on January 1, 19X1, at underlying book value. On January 1, 19X4, Mainstream purchased Offenberg Company bonds with a par value of $40,000. The bonds pay 10 percent interest annually on December 31 and mature on December 31, 19X8. Mainstream uses the basic equity method in accounting for its ownership in Offenberg Company. Partial balance sheet data for the two companies on December 31, 19X5, are as follows:

	Mainstream Corporation	Offenberg Company
Investment in Offenberg Company Stock	$120,000	
Investment in Offenberg Company Bonds	42,400	
Interest Income	3,200	
Bonds Payable		$100,000
Bond Premium		11,250
Interest Expense		6,250
Common Stock	300,000	100,000
Retained Earnings, December 31, 19X5	500,000	50,000

Required

a. Compute the gain or loss on bond retirement reported in the 19X4 consolidated income statement.

b. Prepare the eliminating entry needed to remove the effects of the intercorporate bond ownership in completing the consolidation workpaper for 19X5.

c. What balance should be reported as consolidated retained earnings on December 31, 19X5?

P8-21 Consolidation Workpaper—Year of Retirement

Snyder Manufacturing purchased 60 percent ownership of Knudtson Corporation stock on January 1, 19X1, at underlying book value. Snyder also purchased $50,000 of Knudtson Corporation bonds at par value on December 31, 19X3. The bonds were sold by Knudtson Corporation on January 1, 19X1, at 120 and have a stated interest rate of 12 percent. Interest is paid semiannually on June 30 and December 31. Trial balances for the two companies on December 31, 19X3, are as follows:

	Snyder Manufacturing		Knudtson Corporation	
Item	**Debit**	**Credit**	**Debit**	**Credit**
Cash	$ 68,000		$ 55,000	
Accounts Receivable	100,000		75,000	
Inventory	120,000		110,000	
Investment in Knudtson Bonds	50,000			
Investment in Knudtson Stock	102,000			
Other Assets	360,000		210,000	
Interest Expense	20,000		20,000	
Other Expenses	302,200		150,000	
Dividends Declared	40,000		10,000	
Accounts Payable		$ 94,200		$ 52,000
Bonds Payable		200,000		200,000
Bond Premium				28,000
Common Stock		300,000		100,000
Retained Earnings		150,000		50,000
Sales		400,000		200,000
Income from Subsidiary		18,000		
Total	$1,162,200	$1,162,200	$630,000	$630,000

Required

  a. Prepare a consolidation workpaper for 19X3, in good form.

  b. Prepare a consolidated balance sheet, income statement, and statement of changes in retained earnings for 19X3.

P8-22 Consolidation Workpaper—Year after Retirement

Bennett Corporation owns 60 percent of the stock of Stone Container Company, which it acquired at book value in 19X1. On December 31, 19X3, Bennett Corporation purchased $100,000 par value bonds of Stone Container. The bonds originally were issued by Stone Container Company at par value. The coupon rate on the bonds is 9 percent. Interest is paid semiannually on June 30 and December 31. Trial balances for the two companies on December 31, 19X4, are as follows:

Item	Bennett Corporation Debit	Bennett Corporation Credit	Stone Container Company Debit	Stone Container Company Credit
Cash	$ 61,600		$ 20,000	
Accounts Receivable	100,000		80,000	
Inventory	120,000		110,000	
Other Assets	340,000		250,000	
Investment in Stone Container Bonds	106,000			
Investment in Stone Container Stock	126,000			
Interest Expense	20,000		18,000	
Other Expenses	368,600		182,000	
Dividends Declared	40,000		10,000	
Accounts Payable		$ 80,000		$ 50,000
Bonds Payable		200,000		200,000
Common Stock		300,000		100,000
Retained Earnings		214,200		70,000
Sales		450,000		250,000
Interest Income		8,000		
Income from Subsidiary		30,000		
Total	$1,282,200	$1,282,200	$670,000	$670,000

All the interest income recognized by Bennett is related to its investment in Stone Container bonds.

Required

  a. Prepare a consolidation workpaper for 19X4 in good form.
  b. Prepare a consolidated balance sheet, income statement, and retained earnings statement for 19X4.

P8-23 Comprehensive Multiple-Choice Questions

Blackwood Enterprises owns 80 percent of the voting stock of Grange Corporation. Blackwood purchased the shares on January 1, 19X4, for $240,000, at which time Grange reported common stock outstanding of $200,000 and retained earnings of $50,000. The book values of all Grange's assets were equal to their market values, except for buildings with a fair value $30,000 greater than book value at the date of combination. The buildings had an expected 10-year remaining economic life from the date of combination. All intangible assets are amortized over a 40-year period.

The following trial balances were prepared by the companies on December 31, 19X6:

Item	Blackwood Enterprises Debit	Blackwood Enterprises Credit	Grange Corporation Debit	Grange Corporation Credit
Cash	$ 188,720		$183,000	
Inventory	200,000		180,000	
Buildings and Equipment	500,000		400,000	
Investment in Grange Corporation Bonds	106,400			
Investment in Grange Corporation Stock	291,600			
Cost of Goods Sold	220,000		140,000	
Depreciation and Amortization	50,000		30,000	
Interest Expense	24,000		16,000	
Other Expenses	16,000		14,000	
Dividends Declared	20,000		15,000	
Accumulated Depreciation		$ 250,000		$180,000
Current Liabilities		100,000		50,000
Bonds Payable		400,000		200,000
Bond Premium				8,000
Common Stock		300,000		200,000
Retained Earnings		201,600		100,000
Sales		300,000		240,000
Other Income		35,920		
Income from Subsidiary		29,200		
Total	$1,616,720	$1,616,720	$978,000	$978,000

Blackwood purchases much of its inventory from Grange. The inventory held by Blackwood on January 1, 19X6, contained $2,000 of unrealized intercompany profit. During 19X6, Grange sold goods costing $50,000 to Blackwood for $70,000. Blackwood resold 70 percent of the inventory in 19X6 and the remaining 30 percent in 19X7.

On January 1, 19X6, Blackwood Enterprises purchased from Kirkwood Corporation $100,000 par value bonds of Grange Corporation. The bonds had been sold to Kirkwood Corporation on January 1, 19X1, with a 10-year maturity. The coupon rate is 9 percent, and interest is paid annually on December 31.

Required

Select the correct answer for each of the following questions.

1. What should be the total amount of inventory reported in the consolidated balance sheet as of December 31, 19X6?
   a. $360,000.
   b. $374,000.
   c. $375,200.
   d. $380,000.

2. What amount of cost of goods sold should be reported in the 19X6 consolidated income statement?
   a. $288,000.
   b. $294,000.
   c. $296,000.
   d. $360,000.

3. What amount of interest income did Blackwood Enterprises record from its investment in Grange Corporation bonds during 19X6?
   a. $7,400.
   b. $7,720.
   c. $9,000.
   d. $10,600.

4. What amount of interest expense should be reported in the 19X6 consolidated income statement?
   a. $24,000.
   b. $32,000.
   c. $33,000.
   d. $40,000.

5. What is the unamortized balance of the purchase differential as of January 1, 19X6?
   a. $31,600.
   b. $33,500.
   c. $34,400.
   d. $40,000.

6. What amount of depreciation and amortization should be reported in the 19X6 consolidated income statement?
   a. $80,000.
   b. $82,400.
   c. $82,800.
   d. $83,250.

7. What amount of gain or loss on bond retirement should be included in the 19X6 consolidated income statement?
   a. $2,400.
   b. $3,000.
   c. $4,000.
   d. $6,400.

8. What amount of income should be assigned to the noncontrolling interest in the 19X6 consolidated income statement?
   a. $6,720.
   b. $7,200.
   c. $8,000.
   d. $8,400.

9. What amount should be assigned to the noncontrolling interest in the consolidated balance sheet as of December 31, 19X6?
   a. $63,200.
   b. $63,320.
   c. $63,800.
   d. $65,000.

10. What amount of goodwill, if any, should be reported in the consolidated balance sheet as of December 31, 19X6?
    a. $9,250.
    b. $14,800.
    c. $15,200.
    d. $37,000.

P8-24 Comprehensive Problem: Intercorporate Transfers

Berry Manufacturing Company purchased 90 percent of the outstanding common stock of Bussman Corporation on December 31, 19X5, for $1,150,000. On that date, Bussman reported common stock of $500,000, premium on common stock of $280,000, and retained earnings of $420,000. The fair values of all of Bussman's assets and liabilities were equal to their book values on the date of combination, except for land, which was worth more than its book value. Berry estimated that its 90 percent share of the increase in the value of Bussman's land was $30,000.

On April 1, 19X6, Berry issued at par $200,000 of 10 percent bonds directly to Bussman; interest on the bonds is payable March 31 and September 30. On January 2, 19X7, Berry purchased all of Bussman's outstanding 10-year, 12 percent bonds from an unrelated institutional investor at 98. The bonds originally had been issued on January 2, 19X1, for 101. Interest on the bonds is payable December 31 and June 30.

Since the date it was acquired by Berry Manufacturing, Bussman has sold inventory to Berry on a regular basis. The amount of such intercompany sales totaled $64,000 in 19X6 and $78,000 in 19X7, including a 30 percent gross profit. All the inventory transferred in 19X6 had been resold by December 31, 19X6, except inventory for which Berry paid $15,000 and which was not resold until January 19X7. All the inventory transferred in 19X7 had been resold at December 31, 19X7, except merchandise for which Berry had paid $18,000.

At December 31, 19X7, trial balances for Berry Manufacturing and Bussman Corporation appeared as follows:

	Berry Manufacturing		Bussman Corporation	
Item	Debit	Credit	Debit	Credit
Cash	$ 41,500		$ 29,000	
Current Receivables	112,500		85,100	
Inventory	301,000		348,900	
Investment in Bussman Stock	1,241,000			
Investment in Bussman Bonds	985,000			
Investment in Berry Bonds			200,000	
Land	1,231,000		513,000	
Buildings and Equipment	2,750,000		1,835,000	
Cost of Goods Sold	2,009,000		430,000	
Depreciation and Amortization	195,000		85,000	
Other Expenses	643,000		206,000	
Dividends Declared	50,000		40,000	
Accumulated Depreciation		$1,210,000		$ 619,000
Current Payables		98,000		79,000
Bonds Payable		200,000		1,000,000
Premium on Bonds Payable				3,000
Common Stock		1,000,000		500,000
Premium on Common Stock		700,000		280,000
Retained Earnings, January 1		3,029,000		470,000
Sales		3,101,000		790,000
Other Income		135,000		31,000
Income from Subsidiary		86,000		
	$9,559,000	$9,559,000	$3,772,000	$3,772,000

As of December 31, 19X7, Bussman had declared but not yet paid its fourth-quarter dividend of $10,000. Both Berry Manufacturing and Bussman use straight-line depreciation and amortization, including the amortization of bond discount and premium; all intangibles are amortized over 10 years. Berry Manufacturing uses the basic equity method to account for its investment in Bussman Corporation.

Required

   a. Compute the amount of the differential as of January 1, 19X7.
   b. Compute the balance of Berry Manufacturing's Investment in Bussman Stock account as of January 1, 19X7.
   c. Compute the gain or loss on the constructive retirement of Bussman's bonds that should appear in the 19X7 consolidated income statement.
   d. Compute the income that should be assigned to the noncontrolling interest in the 19X7 consolidated income statement.
   e. Compute the total noncontrolling interest as of December 31, 19X6.
   f. Present all elimination entries that would appear in a three-part consolidation workpaper as of December 31, 19X7.
   g. Prepare and complete a three-part workpaper for the preparation of consolidated financial statements for 19X7.

P8-25* Intercorporate Leases

Johnson Company owns 75 percent of the voting shares of Hall Leasing Corporation. On January 1, 19X3, Hall Leasing Corporation purchased a fleet of small delivery trucks with an expected economic life of 6 years and no anticipated residual value. Hall Leasing Corporation leased the trucks to Chech Corporation for 2 years and on January 1, 19X5, leased the fleet to Johnson Company. The vehicles had a remaining estimated economic life of 4 years at the time they were leased to Johnson Company. Both Johnson Company and Hall Leasing record depreciation on a straight-line basis.

Required

Give the eliminating entries needed to remove the effects of the intercorporate lease in preparing the consolidated financial statements for 19X5 in each of the following situations:

a. Assume Hall purchased the trucks for $720,000 and leases them to Johnson under an operating lease at an annual rental of $175,000.

b. Assume Hall purchased the trucks for $696,000 and leases them to Johnson for their remaining 4-year life under a direct financing lease. An annual payment of $146,400 is made at the end of each year. The lease with Johnson provides approximately a 10 percent return on the unrecovered investment balance.

c. Assume Hall purchased the trucks for $600,000 and leases them to Johnson for their remaining 4-year life on a sales-type lease. An annual payment of $146,400 is made at the end of each year. The present value of the lease payments on January 1, 19X5, using a 10 percent discount rate was approximately $464,000.

P8-26A Fully Adjusted Equity Method

On December 31, 19X4, Bennett Corporation recorded the following entry on its books to adjust from the basic equity method to the fully adjusted equity method on its investment in Stone Container Company stock:

Retained Earnings	4,200	
Income from Subsidiary		600
Investment in Stone Container Company Stock		3,600

Required

a. Adjust the data reported by Bennett Corporation in the trial balance contained in Problem 8-22 for the effects of the adjusting entry presented above.

b. Prepare the journal entries that would have been recorded on the books of Bennett Corporation during 19X4 under the fully adjusted equity method.

c. Prepare all eliminating entries needed to complete a consolidation workpaper as of December 31, 19X4, assuming Bennett has used the fully adjusted equity method.

d. Complete a three-part consolidation workpaper as of December 31, 19X4.

P8-27A Cost Method

The trial balance data presented in Problem 8-22 can be converted to reflect use of the cost method by inserting the following amounts in place of those presented for Bennett Corporation:

Investment in Stone Container Stock	$ 75,000
Retained Earnings	187,200
Income from Subsidiary	-0-
Dividend Income	6,000

Stone Container Company reported retained earnings of $25,000 on the date Bennett Corporation purchased 60 percent of the stock.

Required

   a. Prepare the journal entries that would have been recorded on the books of Bennett Corporation during 19X4 under the cost method.

   b. Prepare all eliminating entries needed to complete a consolidation workpaper as of December 31, 19X4, assuming Bennett uses the cost method.

   c. Complete a three-part consolidation workpaper as of December 31, 19X4.

CHAPTER 9

CONSOLIDATION OWNERSHIP ISSUES

Only simple ownership situations have been presented in the preceding chapters. In practice, however, relatively complex ownership structures often are found. For example, a subsidiary may have preferred stock outstanding in addition to its common stock, and in some cases a parent may acquire shares of both the common and the preferred stock of a subsidiary. Other times, one or more subsidiaries may acquire stock of the parent or of other related companies. Sometimes the parent's ownership claim on a subsidiary may change through its purchase or sale of subsidiary shares or through stock transactions of the subsidiary.

The discussion in this chapter is intended to provide a basic understanding of some of the consolidation problems arising from complex ownership situations commonly encountered in practice. The following topics are discussed:

1. Subsidiary preferred stock outstanding
2. Changes in the parent's ownership interest in the subsidiary
3. Multiple ownership levels
4. Reciprocal ownership
5. Subsidiary stock dividends

SUBSIDIARY PREFERRED STOCK OUTSTANDING

Many companies have more than one type of stock outstanding. Each type of security typically serves a particular function, and each has a different set of rights and features. Preferred stockholders normally have preference over common shareholders with respect to dividends and the distribution of assets in a liquidation. The right to vote usually is withheld from preferred shareholders, so that preferred stock ownership normally does not convey control, regardless of the number of shares owned.

Because preferred shareholders of a subsidiary do have a claim on the net assets of the subsidiary, special attention must be given to that claim in the preparation of consolidated financial statements.

Consolidation with Subsidiary Preferred Stock Outstanding

During preparation of consolidated financial statements, the amount of subsidiary stockholders' equity accruing to preferred shareholders must be determined before dealing with the elimination of the intercorporate common stock ownership. If the parent holds some of the subsidiary's preferred stock, its portion of the preferred stock interest must be eliminated. Any portion of the subsidiary's preferred stock interest not held by the parent is assigned to the noncontrolling interest.

As an illustration of the preparation of consolidated financial statements with subsidiary preferred stock outstanding, recall the following information from the example of Peerless Products Corporation and Special Foods, Incorporated, used in previous chapters:

1. Peerless Products purchases 80 percent of the common stock of Special Foods on December 31, 19X0, at its underlying book value of $240,000 and accounts for the investment using the basic equity method.

2. Peerless Products earns income from its own operations of $140,000 in 19X1 and declares dividends of $60,000.

3. Special Foods reports net income of $50,000 in 19X1 and declares common dividends of $30,000.

Also assume that on January 1, 19X1, Special Foods issues $100,000 of 12 percent preferred stock at par value, none of which is purchased by Peerless. The regular $12,000 preferred dividend is paid in 19X1.

Allocation of Special Foods' Net Income Of the total $50,000 of net income reported by Special Foods for 19X1, $12,000 ($100,000 × .12) is assigned to the preferred shareholders as their current dividend. Peerless Products records its share of the remaining amount, computed as follows:

Special Foods' net income, 19X1	$50,000
Less: Preferred dividends ($100,000 × .12)	(12,000)
Special Foods' income accruing to common shareholders	$38,000
Peerless's proportionate share	× .80
Peerless's income from Special Foods	$30,400

Income assigned to the noncontrolling interest for 19X1 is the total of Special Foods' preferred dividends and the noncontrolling common stockholders' 20 percent share of Special Foods' $38,000 of income remaining after preferred dividends are deducted:

Preferred dividends of Special Foods	$12,000
Income assigned to Special Foods' noncontrolling common shareholders ($38,000 × .20)	7,600
Income to noncontrolling interest	$19,600

Consolidation Workpaper   The workpaper to prepare consolidated financial statements at the end of 19X1 appears in Figure 9-1. The following elimination entries are included in the workpaper:

E(1)	Income from Subsidiary	30,400	
	Dividends Declared—Common		24,000
	Investment in Special Foods Common		6,400
	Eliminate income from subsidiary.		
E(2)	Income to Noncontrolling Interest	19,600	
	Dividends Declared—Preferred		12,000
	Dividends Declared—Common		6,000
	Noncontrolling Interest		1,600
	Assign income to noncontrolling interest.		
E(3)	Common Stock—Special Foods	200,000	
	Retained Earnings, January 1	100,000	
	Investment in Special Foods Common		240,000
	Noncontrolling Interest		60,000
	Eliminate beginning investment in common stock.		
E(4)	Preferred Stock—Special Foods	100,000	
	Noncontrolling Interest		100,000
	Eliminate subsidiary preferred stock.		

In consolidation, the $12,000 preferred dividend is treated as income assigned to the noncontrolling interest. Because none of Special Foods' preferred stock is held by Peerless, all of it is classified as part of the noncontrolling interest.

Subsidiary Preferred Stock Held by Parent

Occasionally a parent company will hold preferred stock of a subsidiary in addition to its investment in the subsidiary's common stock. Because the preferred stock held by the parent is within the consolidated entity, it must be eliminated when consolidated financial statements are prepared. Likewise, any income from the preferred stock recorded by the parent also must be eliminated.

As an illustration of the treatment of subsidiary preferred stock held by the parent, assume that Peerless Products purchases 60 percent of Special Foods'

FIGURE 9-1 December 31, 19X1, consolidation workpaper, first year following combination; 80 percent purchase at book value.

Item	Peerless Products	Special Foods	Eliminations Debit	Eliminations Credit	Consolidated
Sales	400,000	200,000			600,000
Income from Subsidiary	30,400		(1) 30,400		
Credits	430,400	200,000			600,000
Cost of Goods Sold	170,000	115,000			285,000
Depreciation and Amortization	50,000	20,000			70,000
Other Expenses	40,000	15,000			55,000
Debits	(260,000)	(150,000)			(410,000)
					190,000
Income to Noncontrolling Interest			(2) 19,600		(19,600)
Net Income, carry forward	170,400	50,000	50,000		170,400
Retained Earnings, January 1	300,000	100,000	(3) 100,000		300,000
Net Income, from above	170,400	50,000	50,000		170,400
	470,400	150,000			470,400
Dividends Declared: Preferred		(12,000)		(2) 12,000	
Common	(60,000)	(30,000)		(1) 24,000	
				(2) 6,000	(60,000)
Retained Earnings, December 31, carry forward	410,400	108,000	150,000	42,000	410,400
Cash	264,000	163,000			427,000
Accounts Receivable	75,000	50,000			125,000
Inventory	100,000	75,000			175,000
Land	175,000	40,000			215,000
Buildings and Equipment	800,000	600,000			1,400,000
Investment in Special Foods Common	246,400			(1) 6,400	
				(3) 240,000	
Debits	1,660,400	928,000			2,342,000
Accumulated Depreciation	250,000	220,000			470,000
Accounts Payable	100,000	100,000			200,000
Bonds Payable	400,000	200,000			600,000
Preferred Stock		100,000	(4) 100,000		
Common Stock	500,000	200,000	(3) 200,000		500,000
Retained Earnings, from above	410,400	108,000	150,000	42,000	410,400
Noncontrolling Interest				(2) 1,600	
				(3) 60,000	
				(4) 100,000	161,600
Credits	1,660,400	928,000	450,000	450,000	2,342,000

Elimination entries:
(1) Eliminate income from subsidiary.
(2) Assign income to noncontrolling interest.
(3) Eliminate beginning investment in common stock.
(4) Eliminate subsidiary preferred stock.

$100,000 par value, 12 percent preferred stock for $60,000 when issued on January 1, 19X1. During 19X1, dividends of $12,000 are declared on the preferred stock. Peerless recognizes $7,200 ($12,000 × .60) of dividend income from its investment in Special Foods' preferred stock, and the remaining $4,800 ($12,000 × .40) is paid to the holders of the other preferred shares.

In consolidation, the total income assigned to the noncontrolling interest includes the portion of the preferred dividend paid on the shares not held by Peerless:

Noncontrolling interest's share of preferred dividends ($12,000 × .40)	$ 4,800
Income assigned to Special Foods' noncontrolling common shareholders ($38,000 × .20)	7,600
Income to noncontrolling interest	$12,400

The eliminating entries needed in the consolidation workpaper prepared at the end of 19X1 are as follows:

E(5)	Income from Subsidiary	30,400	
	Dividends Declared—Common		24,000
	Investment in Special Foods Common		6,400
	Eliminate income from subsidiary:		
	$30,400 = ($50,000 − $12,000) × .80		
E(6)	Dividend Income—Preferred	7,200	
	Dividends Declared—Preferred		7,200
	Eliminate dividend income from		
	subsidiary preferred: $12,000 × .60		
E(7)	Income to Noncontrolling Interest	12,400	
	Dividends Declared—Preferred		4,800
	Dividends Declared—Common		6,000
	Noncontrolling Interest		1,600
	Assign income to noncontrolling interest:		
	$12,400 = $4,800 + $7,600		
	$4,800 = $12,000 × .40		
E(8)	Common Stock—Special Foods	200,000	
	Retained Earnings, January 1	100,000	
	Investment in Special Foods Common		240,000
	Noncontrolling Interest		60,000
	Eliminate beginning investment in		
	common stock.		
E(9)	Preferred Stock—Special Foods	100,000	
	Investment in Special Foods Preferred		60,000
	Noncontrolling Interest		40,000
	Eliminate subsidiary preferred stock.		

Several points should be noted regarding these elimination entries:

1. Peerless's 60 percent share of Special Foods' preferred stock is eliminated against the preferred stock investment account. The remaining preferred stock is included in the noncontrolling interest.

2. Peerless's dividend income from its investment in Special Foods' preferred stock is eliminated against its share of Special Foods' dividends declared.

3. The income assigned to the noncontrolling interest includes income of Special Foods accruing to both preferred and common shareholders other than Peerless Products. Similarly, the total noncontrolling interest includes Special Foods' stockholders' equity amounts accruing to both preferred and common stockholders other than Peerless.

Subsidiary Preferred Stock with Special Provisions

Many different features of preferred stocks are found in practice. For example, most preferred stocks are cumulative, a few are participating, and many are callable at some price other than par value. When a subsidiary with preferred stock outstanding is consolidated, the provisions of the preferred stock agreement must be examined to determine the portion of the subsidiary's stockholders' equity to be assigned to the preferred stock interest.

A cumulative dividend provision provides some degree of protection for preferred shareholders by requiring the company to pay both current and omitted past preferred dividends before any dividend can be given to common shareholders. If a subsidiary has cumulative preferred stock outstanding, an amount of income equal to the current year's preferred dividend is assigned to the preferred stock interest in consolidation whether or not the preferred dividend is declared. When there are dividends in arrears on a subsidiary's cumulative preferred stock, recognition is given in consolidation to the claim of the preferred shareholders by assigning to the preferred stock interest an amount of subsidiary retained earnings equal to the passed dividends. On the other hand, when a subsidiary's preferred stock is noncumulative, the subsidiary has no obligation to pay undeclared dividends of prior periods. Consequently, no special consolidation procedures are needed with respect to undeclared dividends on noncumulative subsidiary preferred stock.

Preferred stock participation features allow the preferred stockholders to receive a share of income distributions that exceed the preferred stock base dividend rate. Although few preferred stocks are participating, many different types of participation arrangements are possible. Once the degree of participation has been determined, the appropriate share of subsidiary income and net assets is assigned to the preferred stock interest in the consolidated financial statements.

Many preferred stocks are callable, often at prices that exceed the par value. The amount to be paid to retire a subsidiary's callable preferred stock under the preferred stock agreement is viewed as the preferred stockholders' claim on the subsidiary's assets, and that amount of subsidiary stockholders' equity is assigned to the preferred stock interest in preparing the consolidated balance sheet.

Illustration of Subsidiary Preferred Stock with Special Features

To examine the consolidation treatment of subsidiary preferred stock with the most common special features, assume that Special Foods issues $100,000 par value, 12 percent preferred stock on January 1, 19X0, and that the stock is cumulative, nonparticipating, and callable at 105. No dividends are declared on the preferred stock during 19X0. On December 31, 19X0, Peerless Products purchases 80 percent of the common stock of Special Foods for $240,000, and on January 1, 19X1, Peerless purchases 60 percent of the preferred stock for $61,000. The following are the stockholders' equity accounts of Special Foods on December 31, 19X0:

Preferred Stock	$100,000
Common Stock	200,000
Retained Earnings	100,000
Total Stockholders' Equity	$400,000

The amount assigned to the preferred stock interest in the preparation of a consolidated balance sheet on January 1, 19X1, is computed as follows:

Par value of Special Foods' preferred stock	$100,000
Call premium	5,000
Dividends in arrears for 19X0	12,000
Total preferred stock interest, January 1, 19X1	$117,000

This amount is apportioned between Peerless and the noncontrolling shareholders:

Peerless's share of preferred stock interest ($117,000 × .60)	$ 70,200
Noncontrolling stockholders' share of preferred stock interest ($117,000 × .40)	46,800
Total preferred stock interest, January 1, 19X1	$117,000

Because the preferred stock interest exceeds the par value of the preferred stock by $17,000, the portion of Special Foods' retained earnings accruing to the common shareholders is reduced by that amount. Therefore, the total claim on net assets of Special Foods' common stockholders is as follows:

Common stock	$200,000
Retained earnings ($100,000 − $17,000)	83,000
Total common stock interest, January 1, 19X1	$283,000

Special Foods' common stock interest is apportioned between Peerless Products and the noncontrolling shareholders in the following manner:

Peerless's share of common stock interest ($283,000 × .80)	$226,400
Noncontrolling stockholders' share of common stock interest ($283,000 × .20)	56,600
Total common stock interest, January 1, 19X1	$283,000

Eliminating entries needed in the consolidation workpaper to prepare a consolidated balance sheet as of January 1, 19X1, are as follows:

E(10)	Common Stock—Special Foods	200,000	
	Retained Earnings	83,000	
	Differential	13,600	
	Investment in Special Foods Common		240,000
	Noncontrolling Interest		56,600
	Eliminate investment in common stock:		
	$83,000 = $100,000 − $17,000		
	$13,600 = $240,000 − ($283,000 × .80)		
	$56,600 = $283,000 × .20		
E(11)	Preferred Stock—Special Foods	100,000	
	Retained Earnings	17,000	
	Investment in Special Foods Preferred		61,000
	Additional Paid-In Capital		9,200
	Noncontrolling Interest		46,800
	Eliminate subsidiary preferred stock:		
	$17,000 = $117,000 − $100,000		
	$9,200 = ($117,000 × .60) − $61,000		
	$46,800 = $117,000 × .40		

The following points should be noted with respect to eliminating entries E(10) and E(11):

1. Only the $83,000 portion of Special Foods' retained earnings relating to the common stock interest is eliminated in entry E(10). The remaining $17,000 of retained earnings related to the preferred stock interest is eliminated in entry E(11).

2. Because Peerless's share of Special Foods' common stock interest is $226,400 ($283,000 × .80) and the cost of the investment was $240,000, a $13,600 differential arises in consolidation. This differential would be assigned to the appropriate assets and liabilities in the workpaper.

3. The total noncontrolling interest on January 1, 19X1, consists of both preferred and common stock interests, as follows:

Preferred stock interest ($117,000 × .40)	$ 46,800
Common stock interest ($283,000 × .20)	56,600
Total noncontrolling interest, January 1, 19X1	$103,400

4. The difference between the cost of Peerless's investment in Special Foods' preferred stock and the underlying claim on Special Foods' net assets is computed as follows:

Claim on Special Foods' net assets ($117,000 × .60)	$70,200
Cost of preferred stock investment	(61,000)
Difference	$ 9,200

From a consolidated viewpoint, the purchase of the preferred stock by Peerless is considered a retirement of a noncontrolling ownership interest by the consolidated entity. Because this retirement occurred at less than book value and gains and losses are not recognized on capital transactions, this excess is considered to be additional paid-in capital of the consolidated entity and is credited to that account in entry E(11).

CHANGES IN PARENT COMPANY OWNERSHIP

Although preceding chapters have treated the parent company's subsidiary ownership interest as remaining constant over time, in actuality ownership levels sometimes vary. Changes in ownership levels may result from actions of either the parent or the subsidiary. The parent company can change ownership ratios by purchasing or selling shares of the subsidiary in transactions with unaffiliated companies. A subsidiary can change the ownership percentage of the parent by selling additional shares to or repurchasing shares from unaffiliated parties, or through stock transactions with the parent (if the subsidiary is less than wholly owned).

Parent's Purchase of Additional Shares from Nonaffiliate

A parent company may purchase the common stock of a subsidiary at different points in time. When consolidated statements are prepared, the cost of each block of stock purchased is compared with the stock's book value at the date of purchase and the difference is treated as part of the purchase differential to be assigned.

Purchases of additional shares of an investee's common stock were discussed in the context of accounting for intercorporate investments in Chapter 2, and interim purchases of a subsidiary were discussed briefly in Chapter 5. Additional effects of multiple purchases of a subsidiary's stock on the consolidation process are illustrated in the following example.

Assume that on January 1, 19X0, Special Foods has $200,000 of common stock outstanding and retained earnings of $60,000. During 19X0 and 19X1, Special Foods reports the following information:

Period	Net Income	Dividends	Ending Book Value
19X0	$40,000	-0-	$300,000
19X1:			
January 1–June 30	20,000	$12,000	308,000
July 1–December 31	30,000	18,000	320,000

Peerless Products purchases its 80 percent interest in Special Foods in several blocks, as follows:

Purchase Date	Ownership Percentage	Cost	Book Value	Differential
January 1, 19X0	20	$ 56,000	$ 52,000	$ 4,000
December 31, 19X0	10	35,000	30,000	5,000
June 30, 19X1	50	179,000	154,000	25,000
	80	$270,000	$236,000	$34,000

All the differential relates to land held by Special Foods. Note that Peerless does not gain control of Special Foods until June 30, 19X1.

The investment account on Peerless's books appears as follows:

Investment in Special Foods Stock

1/1/X0 purchase	56,000		
19X0 equity accrual ($40,000 × .20)	8,000		
12/31/X0 purchase	35,000		
Balance, 12/31/X0	99,000		
6/30/X1 equity accrual ($20,000 × .30)	6,000	Dividends to 6/30/X1 ($12,000 × .30)	3,600
6/30/X1 purchase	179,000	Dividends to 12/31/X1 ($18,000 × .80)	14,400
12/31/X1 equity accrual ($30,000 × .80)	24,000		
Balance, 12/31/X1	290,000		

Because Peerless Products gains control over Special Foods on June 30, 19X1, consolidated statements are prepared for the year 19X1. The consolidation workpaper prepared at the end of the year includes the following entries:

E(12)	Income from Subsidiary	30,000	
	Dividends Declared		18,000
	Investment in Special Foods Stock		12,000

Eliminate income from subsidiary:
$30,000 = $6,000 + $24,000
$18,000 = $3,600 + $14,400
$12,000 = $30,000 − $18,000

E(13)	Income to Noncontrolling Interest	10,000	
	Dividends Declared		6,000
	Noncontrolling Interest		4,000

Assign income to noncontrolling shareholders:
$10,000 = $50,000 × .20
$6,000 = $30,000 × .20
$4,000 = $10,000 − $6,000

E(14)	Common Stock—Special Foods	200,000	
	Retained Earnings, January 1	100,000	
	Land	34,000	
	Preacquisition Subsidiary Income	10,000	
	Dividends Declared		6,000
	Investment in Special Foods Stock		278,000
	Noncontrolling Interest		60,000

Eliminate investment in common stock:
$10,000 = $20,000 × .50
$6,000 = $12,000 × .50
$278,000 = $99,000 + $179,000
$60,000 = $300,000 × .20

Entry E(12) eliminates the income from Special Foods recognized by Peerless during 19X1. This includes the $6,000 ($20,000 × .30) from the first half of the year when Peerless held a 30 percent interest in Special Foods and $24,000 ($30,000 × .80) from the second half of the year when Peerless held an 80 percent interest. This entry also eliminates the dividends from Special Foods recognized by Peerless in 19X1, consisting of $3,600 ($12,000 × .30) from the first half of the year and $14,400 ($18,000 × .80) from the second half.

Entry E(13) assigns income to the noncontrolling shareholders and eliminates their share of Special Foods' dividends based on the 20 percent noncontrolling ownership interest at the end of 19X1. The eliminating entries related to the noncontrolling interest are the same whether the parent's additional purchase of shares in 19X1 occurred at the beginning, end, or middle of the year.

Entry E(14) eliminates the beginning stockholders' equity balances of Special Foods, establishes the noncontrolling interest based on the ending ownership percentage, and eliminates the investment account balance of Peerless. The amount of the investment eliminated in entry E(14) is the 19X1 beginning balance of $99,000 plus the $179,000 cost of the additional shares purchased by Peerless in

19X1. This entry, together with entry E(12), fully eliminates the $290,000 balance of the investment account.

Because Peerless purchased a 50 percent additional interest in Special Foods during 19X1, entry E(14) eliminates the $10,000 ($20,000 × .50) of preacquisition earnings of Special Foods purchased by Peerless. Peerless presents consolidated financial statements as if it had owned 80 percent of Special Foods' stock for the entire year 19X1, but must deduct from consolidated net income the portion of Special Foods' income accruing to the shares purchased in 19X1 because that income was earned by Special Foods before the acquisition of control by Peerless. Also, the $6,000 ($12,000 × .50) of dividends paid by Special Foods to the shareholders who sold their ownership interests to Peerless is eliminated with this entry.

Parent's Sale of Subsidiary Shares to Nonaffiliate

A gain or loss normally occurs and is recorded on the books of the seller when a company disposes of all or part of an investment. **APB 18** deals explicitly with sales of stock of an investee, requiring recognition of a gain or loss on the difference between the selling price and the carrying amount of the stock.[1] A question arises, however, when the shares sold are those of a subsidiary and the subsidiary continues to qualify for consolidation. When a parent sells some of the shares of a subsidiary but continues to hold a controlling interest, the question is whether the gain or loss on the sale of shares should be carried to the consolidated income statement or eliminated in consolidation.

Recognizing a gain or loss in the consolidated income statement on a sale of subsidiary shares while continuing to consolidate the subsidiary seems inconsistent with the concept of a single economic entity. From a consolidated viewpoint, the subsidiary shares become part of the noncontrolling interest outstanding at the point they are sold to a nonaffiliate. If no gains or losses are recognized when stock is issued by the subsidiary to nonaffiliates, none should be recognized when the parent sells subsidiary shares to a nonaffiliate. The difference between the carrying value on the books of the parent before the sale and the sale price is better represented in the consolidated financial statements as an adjustment to additional paid-in capital rather than as a gain or loss.

As an illustration of the sale of subsidiary stock to a nonaffiliate, assume that on December 31, 19X0, Special Foods has 20,000 common shares outstanding with a total par value of $200,000 and retained earnings of $100,000. On that date, Peerless acquires an 80 percent interest in Special Foods by purchasing 16,000 shares of its $10 par common stock at book value of $240,000 ($300,000 × .80). Special Foods reports net income of $50,000 for 19X1 and pays dividends of $30,000. On January 1, 19X2, Peerless sells 1,000 shares of its Special Foods common stock to a nonaffiliate for $19,000, leaving it with a 75 percent interest

---

[1] *Accounting Principles Board Opinion No. 18,* "The Equity Method of Accounting for Investments in Common Stock," March 1971, par. 19(f).

(15,000 ÷ 20,000) in Special Foods. On the date of sale, Special Foods has total stockholders' equity of $320,000, consisting of common stock of $200,000 and retained earnings of $120,000.

Difference between Carrying Amount and Sales Price of Investment The equity-method carrying amount of Peerless's investment in Special Foods on the date of sale reflects Peerless's share of Special Foods' 19X1 net income and dividends, as follows:

Cost of investment, December 31, 19X0	$240,000
Peerless's share of Special Foods' 19X1 net income ($50,000 × .80)	40,000
Peerless's share of Special Foods' 19X1 dividends ($30,000 × .80)	(24,000)
Investment balance, January 1, 19X2	$256,000

Because there is no differential, the balance of the investment account is equal to 80 percent of the total stockholders' equity of Special Foods on January 1, 19X1.

Peerless records the sale of the Special Foods stock with the following entry:

January 1, 19X2

(15) Cash	19,000	
Investment in Special Foods Stock		16,000
Gain on Sale of Investment		3,000
Record sale of x35.4investment:		
$16,000 = $256,000 × $\frac{1}{16}$		

Peerless recognizes a gain of $3,000 on the sale for the difference between the $16,000 carrying amount of the shares ($256,000 × $\frac{1}{16}$) and the selling price of $19,000.

Consolidation Workpaper—19X2 If recognition of the gain on the sale of the stock is considered appropriate in the consolidated income statement, no adjustment is needed in preparing consolidated statements for December 31, 19X2, or in the periods that follow. On the other hand, excluding the gain from the consolidated income statement is more consistent with the view of a single economic entity. In that case, the gain is eliminated and additional paid-in capital is established in the December 31, 19X2, consolidation workpaper with the following entry:

E(16) Gain on Sale of Investment	3,000	
Additional Paid-In Capital		3,000
Eliminate gain on transaction involving subsidiary stock.		

This entry treats the stock transaction as the issuance of stock by the consolidated entity to the noncontrolling interest.

The consolidation workpaper prepared as of December 31, 19X2, is shown in Figure 9-2. In addition to entry E(16), the workpaper includes the normal entries to eliminate a 75 percent investment in Special Foods:

E(17)	Income from Subsidiary	56,250	
	Dividends Declared		30,000
	Investment in Special Foods Stock		26,250
	Eliminate income from subsidiary:		
	$56,250 = \$75,000 \times .75$		
	$30,000 = \$40,000 \times .75$		
	$26,250 = \$56,250 - \$30,000$		
E(18)	Income to Noncontrolling Interest	18,750	
	Dividends Declared		10,000
	Noncontrolling Interest		8,750
	Assign income to noncontrolling interest:		
	$18,750 = \$75,000 \times .25$		
	$10,000 = \$40,000 \times .25$		
	$8,750 = \$18,750 - \$10,000$		
E(19)	Common Stock—Special Foods	200,000	
	Retained Earnings, January 1	120,000	
	Investment in Special Foods Stock		240,000
	Noncontrolling Interest		80,000
	Eliminate beginning investment in common stock:		
	$240,000 = \$320,000 \times .75$		
	$80,000 = \$320,000 \times .25$		

Entry E(17) eliminates Peerless's 75 percent share of Special Foods' income and dividends. Entry E(18) assigns income to the noncontrolling stockholders based on their 25 percent ownership interest.

The balance in Peerless's investment account shown in the consolidation workpaper is $266,250. This amount is the result of the following entries in the investment account:

Investment in Special Foods Stock

Original cost	240,000				
19X1 equity accrual			19X1 dividends		
($50,000 × .80)	40,000		($30,000 × .80)		24,000
Balance, 12/31/X1	256,000				
		(15)	Sale of 1,000 shares		
			($256,000 × $\frac{1}{16}$)		16,000
19X2 equity accrual			19X2 dividends		
($75,000 × .75)	56,250		($40,000 × .75)		30,000
Balance, 12/31/X2	266,250				

FIGURE 9-2 December 31, 19X2, consolidation workpaper, second year following combination; 75 percent ownership, purchased at book value.

Item	Peerless Products	Special Foods	Eliminations Debit		Eliminations Credit		Consolidated
Sales	450,000	300,000					750,000
Gain on Sale of Investment	3,000		(16)	3,000			
Income from Subsidiary	56,250		(17)	56,250			
Credits	509,250	300,000					750,000
Cost of Goods Sold	180,000	160,000					340,000
Depreciation and Amortization	50,000	20,000					70,000
Other Expenses	60,000	45,000					105,000
Debits	(290,000)	(225,000)					(515,000)
							235,000
Income to Noncontrolling Interest			(18)	18,750			(18,750)
Net Income, carry forward	219,250	75,000		78,000			216,250
Retained Earnings, January 1	420,000	120,000	(19)	120,000			420,000
Net Income, from above	219,250	75,000		78,000			216,250
	639,250	195,000					636,250
Dividends Declared	(60,000)	(40,000)			(17)	30,000	
					(18)	10,000	(60,000)
Retained Earnings, December 31, carry forward	579,250	155,000		198,000		40,000	576,250
Cash	308,000	85,000					393,000
Accounts Receivable	150,000	80,000					230,000
Inventory	180,000	90,000					270,000
Land	175,000	40,000					215,000
Buildings and Equipment	800,000	600,000					1,400,000
Investment in Special Foods Stock	266,250				(17)	26,250	
					(19)	240,000	
Debits	1,879,250	895,000					2,508,000
Accumulated Depreciation	300,000	240,000					540,000
Accounts Payable	100,000	100,000					200,000
Bonds Payable	400,000	200,000					600,000
Common Stock	500,000	200,000	(19)	200,000			500,000
Additional Paid-In Capital					(16)	3,000	3,000
Retained Earnings, from above	579,250	155,000		198,000		40,000	576,250
Noncontrolling Interest					(18)	8,750	
					(19)	80,000	88,750
Credits	1,879,250	895,000		398,000		398,000	2,508,000

Elimination entries:
  (16) Eliminate gain on transaction involving subsidiary stock.
  (17) Eliminate income from subsidiary.
  (18) Assign income to noncontrolling interest.
  (19) Eliminate beginning investment in common stock.

The amount of Peerless's investment eliminated in entry E(19) is the balance at the beginning of 19X2 immediately after Peerless sold the 1,000 shares; this amount is equal to Peerless's 75 percent share of the $320,000 beginning book value of Special Foods. Entries E(17) and E(19) together eliminate the total investment balance reported by Peerless on December 31, 19X2.

The amount assigned to the noncontrolling interest in entry E(19) is 25 percent of Special Foods' beginning book value. The total noncontrolling interest established in entries E(18) and E(19) together is $88,750, equal to 25 percent of Special Foods' $355,000 book value on December 31, 19X2.

Consolidation Subsequent to 19X2 In preparing consolidated financial statements each year after 19X2, a workpaper entry similar to E(16) is needed to reestablish the $3,000 increase in additional paid-in capital. Because the gain recognized by Peerless in 19X2 has been closed to retained earnings, beginning retained earnings must be reduced to eliminate the effects of the gain. The entry that would be included in the consolidation workpaper each year after 19X2 is as follows:

E(20) Retained Earnings, January 1	3,000	
Additional Paid-In Capital		3,000
Eliminate effects of gain on transaction involving subsidiary stock.		

Subsidiary's Sale of Additional Shares to Nonaffiliate

Additional funds are generated for the consolidated enterprise when a subsidiary sells new shares to parties outside the economic entity. A sale of additional shares to an unaffiliated party increases the total shares of the subsidiary outstanding and, consequently, reduces the percentage ownership held by the parent company. At the same time, the dollar amount assigned to the noncontrolling interest in the consolidated financial statements increases. The resulting amounts of the controlling and noncontrolling interests are affected by two factors:

1. The number of shares sold to nonaffiliates
2. The price at which the shares are sold to nonaffiliates

Difference between Book Value and Sale Price of Subsidiary Shares If the sale price of new shares equals the book value of outstanding shares, there is no change in the claim of the existing shareholders. If the stockholders' equity of the subsidiary is viewed as a pie, the overall size of the pie increases. While the parent's share of the pie decreases, the size of the parent's slice remains the same because of the increase in the overall size of the pie. The eliminating entries used in consolidation simply are changed to recognize the increase in the claim of the noncontrolling shareholders and the corresponding increase in the stockholders' equity balances of the subsidiary.

Most sales, however, do not occur at book value. When the sale price and book value are not the same, all common shareholders are assigned a pro rata portion of the difference.

In this situation, the book value of the subsidiary's shares held by the parent changes even though the number remains constant. Both the size of the pie and the size of the parent's share of the pie change; the size of the parent's slice changes because the increase in the size of the pie and the decrease in the parent's share do not exactly offset one another.

The change in book value of the shares held by the parent company can be reported in the consolidated statements in one of two ways under current reporting standards:

1. An adjustment to paid-in capital
2. A gain or loss in the consolidated income statement

At present, support for both alternatives can be found in the accounting literature. In 1983, the SEC issued a *Staff Accounting Bulletin* allowing recognition of a nonoperating gain or loss.[2] The SEC continues to permit the paid-in capital approach, as well. The FASB, on the other hand, has not explicitly approved income statement recognition and appears to favor an adjustment to paid-in capital.

From a consolidated viewpoint, the sale of additional shares to unaffiliated parties by a subsidiary and a sale of subsidiary shares by the parent are similar transactions: in both cases the consolidated entity sells shares to the noncontrolling interest. Because the participants in a consolidation are regarded as members of a single economic entity, the sale of subsidiary shares to the noncontrolling interest should be treated in the same way regardless of whether the shares are sold by the parent or the subsidiary. The recognition of a gain or loss on such a transaction seems inappropriate because the sale of stock to unaffiliated parties by the consolidated entity is a capital transaction from a single-entity viewpoint.

Illustration of Sale of Subsidiary Stock to Nonaffiliate To examine the sale of additional shares by a subsidiary to a nonaffiliate, assume that Peerless Products acquires an 80 percent interest in Special Foods by purchasing 16,000 shares of Special Foods' $10 par common stock on December 31, 19X0, at book value of $240,000. Special Foods has only common stock outstanding. All other information is the same as that used previously. On January 1, 19X2, Special Foods sells 5,000 additional shares of stock to nonaffiliates for $20 per share, a total of $100,000. After the sale, Special Foods has 25,000 shares outstanding, and Peerless has a 64 percent interest (16,000 ÷ 25,000) in Special Foods.

---

[2] *SEC Staff Accounting Bulletin No. 51*, 1983.

The January 1, 19X2, sale of additional shares results in the following change in Special Foods' balance sheet:

	Before Sale	Following Sale
Common Stock, $10 par value	$200,000	$250,000
Additional Paid-In Capital		50,000
Retained Earnings	120,000	120,000
Total Stockholders' Equity	$320,000	$420,000

The book value of Peerless's investment in Special Foods changes as a result of the sale of additional shares as follows:

	Before Sale	Following Sale
Special Foods' total stockholders' equity	$320,000	$420,000
Peerless's proportionate share	× .80	× .64
Book value of Peerless's investment in Special Foods	$256,000	$268,800

Note that, while Peerless's ownership percentage decreases from 80 percent to 64 percent, the book value of Peerless's investment increases by $12,800. The increase in book value occurs because the $20 selling price of the additional shares exceeds the $16 ($320,000 ÷ 20,000 shares) book value of the outstanding shares before the sale:

Selling price of additional shares	$ 20
Book value of shares before sale ($320,000 ÷ 20,000 shares)	(16)
Excess of selling price over book value	$ 4
Number of shares sold	× 5,000
Excess book value added	$20,000
Peerless's proportionate share	× .64
Increase in Peerless's equity	$12,800

The increase in Peerless's equity in the net assets of Special Foods may be recorded on Peerless's books with the following entry:

(21) Investment in Special Foods Stock	12,800	
Additional Paid-In Capital		12,800
Record increase in equity in subsidiary		
resulting from subsidiary sale of shares.		

Not everyone agrees that Additional Paid-In Capital should be credited in entry (21). Some would recognize a gain or loss on the change in equity. The approach used here, however, avoids recognizing a gain or loss because the change results from the capital transactions of a related company.

The investment elimination entry needed to prepare a consolidated balance sheet on January 1, 19X2, immediately after the sale of the additional shares, is as follows:

E(22)	Common Stock—Special Foods	250,000	
	Additional Paid-In Capital—Special Foods	50,000	
	Retained Earnings	120,000	
	Investment in Special Foods Stock		268,800
	Noncontrolling Interest		151,200
	Eliminate investment in common stock:		
	$268,800 = $420,000 × .64		
	$151,200 = $420,000 × .36		

Additional paid-in capital recorded by Special Foods from the sale of the additional shares is eliminated in the preparation of consolidated financial statements, as are all the subsidiary's stockholders' equity accounts. The noncontrolling interest's share of the increase in the book value of Special Foods' stock resulting from the sale of additional shares is reflected in the balance of the noncontrolling interest in the consolidated balance sheet. The $151,200 balance of the noncontrolling interest is 36 percent of the $420,000 total book value of Special Foods after the sale of the additional shares. Peerless's $12,800 share of the increase in Special Foods' book value is included in the consolidated balance sheet by carrying over the additional paid-in capital recorded by Peerless in entry (21).

Sale of Subsidiary Stock at Less than Book Value   A sale of stock by a subsidiary to a nonaffiliate at less than existing book value has an effect opposite to that just illustrated. The claim of the parent company is diminished as a result of selling additional shares at less than existing book value. A reduction in the book value of the shares held by the parent normally is treated as a debit to additional paid-in capital and a credit to the investment account. In the absence of additional paid-in capital, retained earnings is reduced.

Subsidiary's Sale of Additional Shares to Parent

A sale of additional shares directly from a less than wholly owned subsidiary to its parent increases the parent's ownership percentage. If the sale is at a price equal to the book value of the existing shares, the increase in the investment account of the parent equals the increase in the stockholders' equity of the subsidiary. The net book value assigned to the noncontrolling interest remains unchanged. In preparing consolidated financial statements, the normal elimination entries are made based on the parent's new ownership percentage.

When the parent purchases shares directly from a subsidiary at an amount other than the book value of the subsidiary's shares already outstanding, a differential is measured as the difference between the price paid and the resulting increase in the total underlying book value of all shares owned by the parent. This increase in book value includes both the amount assigned to the new shares just acquired from the subsidiary and the increase or decrease in the book value of shares previously held by the parent. Once determined, the differential is treated in preparing consolidated financial statements in the same manner as a differential arising on a purchase from a nonaffiliate. However, because the parent may be able to influence the purchase price of the shares in this case, the amount of differential may or may not have an obvious connection to changes in the value of identifiable assets or liabilities and must be reviewed carefully in determining how it is to be assigned.

As an illustration of the sale of additional shares from a subsidiary to its parent, assume that in the example of Peerless Products and Special Foods, Peerless purchases in the market 16,000 shares of Special Foods $10 par common stock at book value of $240,000 on December 31, 19X0, giving Peerless an 80 percent interest. By December 31, 19X1, the equity-method carrying amount of the investment on Peerless's books is $256,000. On January 1, 19X2, Peerless purchases an additional 5,000 shares of common directly from Special Foods for $20 per share. This additional $100,000 investment gives Peerless a total ownership interest in Special Foods of 84 percent (21,000 ÷ 25,000).

The sale of additional shares by the subsidiary to the parent results in the following change in Special Foods' balance sheet:

	Before Sale	Following Sale
Common Stock, $10 par value	$200,000	$250,000
Additional Paid-In Capital		50,000
Retained Earnings	120,000	120,000
Total Stockholders' Equity	$320,000	$420,000

The book value of Peerless's investment in Special Foods changes as a result of the sale of additional shares, as follows:

	Before Sale	Following Sale
Special Foods' total stockholders' equity	$320,000	$420,000
Peerless's proportionate share	× .80	× .84
Book value of Peerless's investment in Special Foods	$256,000	$352,800

If Special Foods' stockholders' equity is viewed as a pie, both the size of the pie and Peerless's percentage share of the pie increase. Therefore, the size of Peerless's slice of the pie increases by $96,800.

The new book value per share of Special Foods' stock is $16.80 ($420,000 ÷ 25,000 shares) as compared with the $16.00 ($320,000 ÷ 20,000 shares) book value before the sale of additional shares. The book value is higher because the price paid by Peerless for the additional shares is greater than the stock's previous book value.

Because Peerless paid a price for the additional shares that is in excess of their book value, a differential arises, as follows:

Price paid by Peerless for additional shares		$100,000
Increase in book value of Peerless's investment:		
Book value following acquisition		
($420,000 × .84)	$352,800	
Book value before acquisition		
($320,000 × .80)	(256,000)	
Increase in book value		(96,800)
Differential		$ 3,200

The investment elimination entry needed to prepare a consolidated balance sheet immediately following the sale of additional shares to Peerless on January 1, 19X2, is as follows:

E(23)	Common Stock—Special Foods	250,000	
	Additional Paid-In Capital	50,000	
	Retained Earnings	120,000	
	Differential	3,200	
	Investment in Special Foods Stock		356,000
	Noncontrolling Interest		67,200
	Eliminate investment in common stock:		
	$356,000 = $256,000 + $100,000		
	$67,200 = $420,000 × .16		

The balance eliminated from Peerless's investment account is equal to the previous balance of $256,000 plus the $100,000 cost of the additional shares. The amount of the noncontrolling interest is established at 16 percent of the $420,000 book value of Special Foods.

Subsidiary's Purchase of Shares from Nonaffiliate

Treasury shares sometimes are purchased by a subsidiary from noncontrolling shareholders. Noncontrolling shareholders frequently find they have little opportunity for input into the activities and operations of the subsidiary and often are willing sellers. The parent company may prefer not to be concerned with outside shareholders and may direct the subsidiary to reacquire any of the noncontrolling shares that become available.

Although the parent is not a direct participant when a subsidiary purchases treasury stock from noncontrolling shareholders, the parent's equity in the net assets of the subsidiary may change as a result of the transaction. When this occurs, the amount of the change must be recognized in preparing the consolidated statements.

For example, assume that Peerless Products owns 80 percent of Special Foods' 20,000 shares of $10 par common stock. On January 1, 19X2, Special Foods purchases 1,000 treasury shares from a nonaffiliate for $20 per share. Peerless's interest in Special Foods increases to 84.21 percent (16,000 ÷ 19,000) as a result of the reacquisition of shares by Special Foods, and the noncontrolling interest decreases to 15.79 percent (3,000 ÷ 19,000). The stockholders' equity of Special Foods before and after the reacquisition of shares is as follows:

	Before Purchase	Following Purchase
Common Stock, $10 par value	$200,000	$200,000
Retained Earnings	120,000	120,000
Total	$320,000	$320,000
Less: Treasury Stock		(20,000)
Total Stockholders' Equity	$320,000	$300,000

The underlying book value of Special Foods' shares held by Peerless changes as a result of the stock reacquisition, as follows:

	Before Purchase	Following Purchase
Special Foods' total stockholders' equity	$320,000	$300,000
Peerless's proportionate share	× .80	× .8421
Book value of Peerless's investment in Special Foods	$256,000	$252,630

The reacquisition of shares by Special Foods at an amount greater than book value results in a decrease in the book value of Peerless's investment of $3,370 ($256,000 − $252,630). Peerless recognizes the decrease with the following entry:

(24)	Retained Earnings	3,370	
	Investment in Special Foods Stock		3,370
	Record decrease in equity in subsidiary		
	from subsidiary stock reacquisition.		

As with the sale of additional shares to a nonaffiliate, an adjustment to additional paid-in capital seems to be the most appropriate way of recognizing the change in the parent's equity in the net assets of the subsidiary. Peerless reduces retained earnings in this situation because it has no additional paid-in capital on its books.

The investment elimination entry needed in a consolidation workpaper prepared immediately after the stock reacquisition on January 1, 19X2, is as follows:

E(25)	Common Stock—Special Foods	200,000	
	Retained Earnings	120,000	
	Treasury Stock		20,000
	Investment in Special Foods Stock		252,630
	Noncontrolling Interest		47,370
	Eliminate investment in common stock:		
	$252,630 = $256,000 − $3,370		
	$47,370 = $300,000 × .1579		

Note that this entry eliminates all the common stockholders' equity balances of the subsidiary, including the treasury stock.

Subsidiary's Purchase of Shares from Parent

A subsidiary can reduce the number of shares it has outstanding through purchases from the parent as well as from noncontrolling shareholders. In practice, stock repurchases from the parent occur infrequently. A parent reducing its ownership interest in a subsidiary usually does so by selling some of its holdings to nonaffiliates to generate additional funds.

When a subsidiary reacquires some of its shares from its parent, the parent records a gain or loss on the difference between the selling price and the change in the carrying amount of its investment. There is some question as to whether a transaction of this type between a parent and its subsidiary can be regarded as arm's-length, and consequently the reporting of the gain or loss in the parent's income statement can be questioned. From a consolidated viewpoint, when a subsidiary reacquires its shares from the parent, the transaction represents an internal transfer and does not give rise to a gain or loss.

As an example of the reacquisition of a subsidiary's shares from its parent, assume that Peerless Products purchases in the market 16,000 of Special Foods' 20,000 shares of $10 par common stock on December 31, 19X0, at book value of $240,000. On January 1, 19X2, Special Foods repurchases 4,000 shares from Peerless at $20 per share, leaving Peerless with a 75 percent interest (12,000 ÷ 16,000) in Special Foods. The stockholders' equity of Special Foods before and after the reacquisition of shares is as follows:

	Before Purchase	Following Purchase
Common Stock, $10 par value	$200,000	$200,000
Retained Earnings	120,000	120,000
Total	$320,000	$320,000
Less: Treasury Stock		(80,000)
Total Stockholders' Equity	$320,000	$240,000

The carrying amount of Peerless's investment in Special Foods' stock is equal to the underlying book value of the shares in this example. The book value of the shares changes as a result of the reacquisition, as follows:

	Before Purchase	Following Purchase
Special Foods' total stockholders' equity	$320,000	$240,000
Peerless's proportionate share	× .80	× .75
Book value of Peerless's investment in Special Foods	$256,000	$180,000

Peerless records the sale of 25 percent (4,000 ÷ 16,000) of its investment in Special Foods with the following entry:

January 1, 19X2		
(26) Cash	80,000	
Investment in Special Foods Stock		76,000
Gain on Sale of Investment		4,000
Record sale of investment:		
$80,000 = $20 × 4,000 shares		
$76,000 = $256,000 − $180,000		
$4,000 = $80,000 − $76,000		

The new carrying value of the investment is $180,000 ($256,000 − $76,000) and, because there is no differential in this case, is equal to 75 percent of Special Foods' total stockholders' equity of $240,000 following the reacquisition. The $76,000 decrease in the carrying value includes both the reduction resulting from the decrease in the number of shares held and the reduction in the book value of those shares still held.

During preparation of consolidated financial statements for 19X2, the gain must be reclassified as additional paid-in capital, and the stockholders' equity balances of Special Foods, including the treasury stock, must be eliminated. The following eliminating entries are included, along with the other usual entries, in a consolidation workpaper prepared as of December 31, 19X2:

E(27) Gain on Sale of Investment	4,000	
Additional Paid-In Capital		4,000
Eliminate gain on transaction involving subsidiary stock.		
E(28) Common Stock—Special Foods	200,000	
Retained Earnings, January 1	120,000	
Treasury Stock		80,000
Investment in Special Foods Stock		180,000
Noncontrolling Interest		60,000
Eliminate investment in common stock:		
$180,000 = $240,000 × .75		
$60,000 = $240,000 × .25		

COMPLEX OWNERSHIP STRUCTURES

Current reporting standards call for the preparation of consolidated financial statements whenever one company has direct or indirect control over another. The discussion to this point has focused on a simple, direct parent-subsidiary relationship. Many companies, however, have substantially more complex organizational schemes.

Figure 9-3 shows three different types of ownership structures. A ***direct ownership*** situation of the type discussed in preceding chapters is shown in Figure 9-3*a*; the parent has controlling interest in each of the subsidiaries. In the ***multilevel ownership*** case, shown in Figure 9-3*b*, the parent has only ***indirect control*** over the company controlled by its subsidiary. While the eliminating entries used in preparing consolidated financial statements in this situation are similar to those used in a simple ownership situation, careful attention must be given to the sequence in which the data are brought together.

Figure 9-3*c* reflects ***reciprocal ownership***, where the subsidiary has an ownership interest in the parent. If mutual shareholdings are ignored in the preparation of consolidated financial statements, some of the reported amounts may be materially overstated.

Multilevel Ownership and Control

In many cases, companies establish multiple corporate levels through which they carry out diversified operations. For example, a company may have a number of

FIGURE 9-3 Alternative ownership structures.

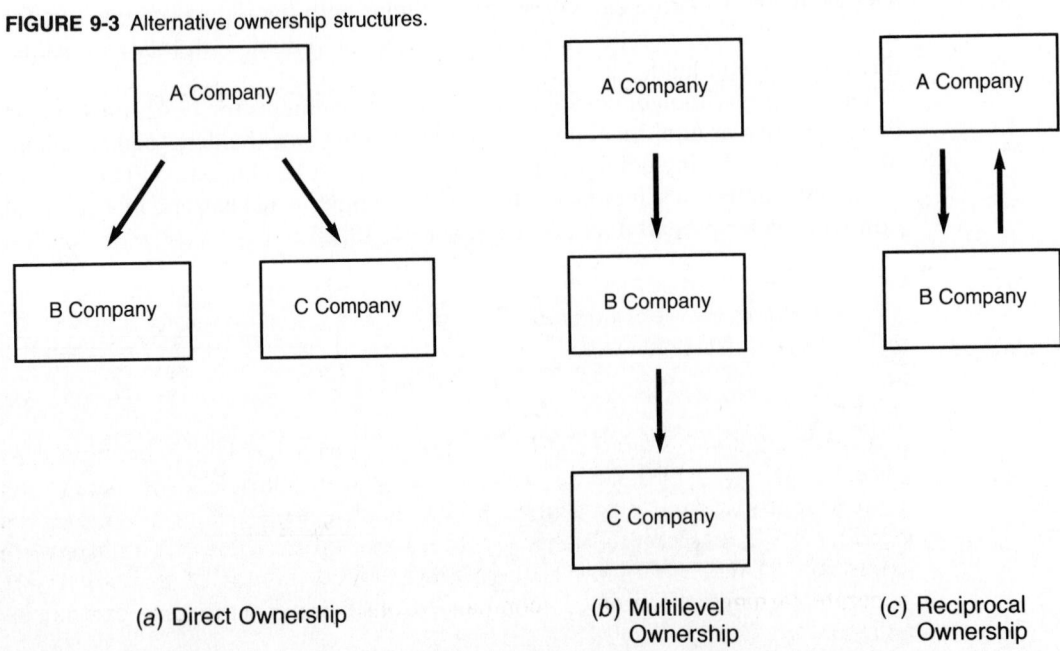

(*a*) Direct Ownership

(*b*) Multilevel Ownership

(*c*) Reciprocal Ownership

subsidiaries, one of which is a retailer. The retail subsidiary may in turn have a finance subsidiary, a real estate subsidiary, an insurance subsidiary, and perhaps other subsidiaries. This means that when consolidated statements are prepared, the statements will include companies in which the parent has only an indirect investment along with those in which direct ownership is held.

The complexity of the consolidation process increases as additional ownership levels are included. The amount of income and net assets to be assigned to the controlling and noncontrolling shareholders, and the amount of unrealized profits and losses to be eliminated, must be determined at each level of ownership.

When there are a number of different levels of ownership, the first step normally is to consolidate the bottom, or most remote, subsidiaries with the companies at the next higher level. This sequence is continued up through the ownership structure until the subsidiaries owned directly by the parent are consolidated with the parent company. Income is apportioned between the controlling and noncontrolling shareholders of the companies at each level.

As an illustration of consolidation when there are multiple ownership levels, assume the following:

1. Peerless Products purchases 80 percent of the common stock of Special Foods on December 31, 19X0, at book value of $240,000.

2. Special Foods purchases 90 percent of the common stock of Bottom Company on January 1, 19X1, at book value of $162,000. On the date of acquisition, Bottom Company has common stock of $100,000 and retained earnings of $80,000.

3. During 19X1, Bottom Company reports net income of $10,000 and declares dividends of $8,000; Special Foods reports separate operating income of $50,000 and declares dividends of $30,000.

All other data are the same as in the Peerless Products–Special Foods examples used throughout previous chapters. The ownership structure is as follows:

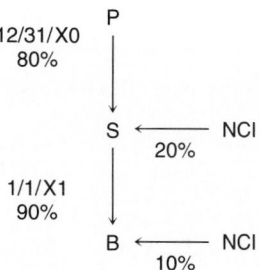

Computation of Net Income   In the case of a three-tiered structure involving a parent company, its subsidiary, and the subsidiary's subsidiary, the parent company's equity-method net income is computed by first adding an appropriate portion of the income of the bottom subsidiary to the separate earnings of the parent's subsidiary and then adding an appropriate portion of that total to the separate earnings of the parent company. Consolidated net income can be computed in the same way.

Peerless's net income is computed as follows:

	Peerless Products	Special Foods	Bottom Company	Noncontrolling Interest
Operating income	$140,000	$50,000	$10,000	
Allocation of income:				
Bottom Company		9,000	(10,000)	$ 1,000
Special Foods	47,200	(59,000)		11,800
Net income	$187,200	$ -0-	$ -0-	$12,800

Consolidated net income is equal to Peerless's equity-method net income and can be verified by totaling the operating incomes of the three companies and deducting the noncontrolling interest:

Operating income:		
Peerless Products		$140,000
Special Foods		50,000
Bottom Company		10,000
Total separate income		$200,000
Noncontrolling interest in:		
Bottom Company ($10,000 × .10)	$ 1,000	
Special Foods ($59,000 × .20)	11,800	
Total noncontrolling interest		(12,800)
Consolidated net income		$187,200

Consolidation Workpaper   The 19X1 workpaper used in consolidating Peerless Products, Special Foods, and Bottom Company is shown in Figure 9-4.

The eliminations related to Special Foods' investment in Bottom Company are entered first:

E(29)	Income from Bottom Company	9,000	
	Dividends Declared		7,200
	Investment in Bottom Company Stock		1,800
	Eliminate income from Bottom Company:		
	$9,000 = $10,000 × .90		
	$7,200 = $8,000 × .90		
	$1,800 = $9,000 − $7,200		
E(30)	Income to Noncontrolling Interest	1,000	
	Dividends Declared		800
	Noncontrolling Interest		200
	Assign income to noncontrolling		
	shareholders of Bottom Company:		
	$1,000 = $10,000 × .10		
	$800 = $8,000 × .10		
	$200 = $1,000 − $800		

E(31)	Common Stock—Bottom Company	100,000	
	Retained Earnings, January 1	80,000	
	Investment in Bottom Company Stock		162,000
	Noncontrolling Interest		18,000
	Eliminate investment		
	in Bottom Company Stock:		
	$162,000 = $180,000 × .90		
	$18,000 = $180,000 × .10		

Next, the eliminations related to Peerless's investment in Special Foods are entered in the workpaper:

E(32)	Income from Special Foods	47,200	
	Dividends Declared		24,000
	Investment in Special Foods Stock		23,200
	Eliminate income from Special Foods:		
	$47,200 = $59,000 × .80		
	$24,000 = $30,000 × .80		
	$23,200 = $47,200 − $24,000		
E(33)	Income to Noncontrolling Interest	11,800	
	Dividends Declared		6,000
	Noncontrolling Interest		5,800
	Assign income to noncontrolling		
	shareholders of Special Foods:		
	$11,800 = $59,000 × .20		
	$6,000 = $30,000 × .20		
	$5,800 = $11,800 − $6,000		
E(34)	Common Stock—Special Foods	200,000	
	Retained Earnings, January 1	100,000	
	Investment in Special Foods Stock		240,000
	Noncontrolling Interest		60,000
	Eliminate investment in Special Foods		
	stock:		
	$240,000 = $300,000 × .80		
	$60,000 = $300,000 × .20		

Order of Acquisition   In the preceding example, Peerless acquired its investment in Special Foods before Special Foods acquired its investment in Bottom Company. If, however, Special Foods had already owned its interest in Bottom Company when Peerless purchased its interest in Special Foods, a portion of Bottom Company's undistributed income since its acquisition would have accrued to Special Foods. So long as Special Foods accounts for its investment in Bottom Company using the equity method, no special problems arise; the normal consolidation procedures are followed. If Special Foods uses the cost method in accounting for its investment in Bottom Company, a workpaper conversion to the equity method must be made so that Special Foods' retained earnings at the date

FIGURE 9-4 December 31, 19X1, consolidation workpaper, first year following combination; direct and indirect holdings.

Item	Peerless Products	Special Foods	Bottom Company	Eliminations Debit		Eliminations Credit		Consolidated
Sales	400,000	200,000	150,000					750,000
Income from Bottom Company		9,000		(29)	9,000			
Income from Special Foods	47,200			(32)	47,200			
Credits	447,200	209,000	150,000					750,000
Cost of Goods Sold	170,000	115,000	80,000					365,000
Depreciation and Amortization	50,000	20,000	35,000					105,000
Other Expenses	40,000	15,000	25,000					80,000
Debits	(260,000)	(150,000)	(140,000)					(550,000)
								200,000
Income to Noncontrolling Interest				(30)	1,000			(12,800)
				(33)	11,800			
Net Income, carry forward	187,200	59,000	10,000		69,000			187,200
Retained Earnings, January 1	300,000	100,000	80,000	(31)	80,000			300,000
				(34)	100,000			
Net Income, from above	187,200	59,000	10,000		69,000			187,200
	487,200	159,000	90,000					487,200
Dividends Declared	(60,000)	(30,000)	(8,000)			(29)	7,200	(60,000)
						(30)	800	
						(32)	24,000	
						(33)	6,000	
Retained Earnings, December 31, carry forward	427,200	129,000	82,000		249,000		38,000	427,200

				Eliminations Debit	Eliminations Credit	
Cash	264,000	20,200	25,000			309,200
Accounts Receivable	75,000	50,000	30,000			155,000
Inventory	100,000	75,000	40,000			215,000
Land	175,000	40,000	50,000			265,000
Buildings and Equipment	800,000	600,000	75,000			1,475,000
Investment in Bottom Company Stock		163,800			(29) 1,800; (31) 162,000	
Investment in Special Foods Stock	263,200				(32) 23,200; (34) 240,000	
Debits	1,677,200	949,000	220,000			2,419,200
Accumulated Depreciation	250,000	220,000	20,000			490,000
Accounts Payable	100,000	100,000	18,000			218,000
Bonds Payable	400,000	300,000				700,000
Common Stock	500,000	200,000	100,000	(31) 100,000; (34) 200,000		500,000
Retained Earnings, from above	427,200	129,000	82,000	249,000		427,200
Noncontrolling Interest					(30) 38,000; (31) 200; (33) 18,000; (34) 5,800; 60,000	84,000
Credits	1,677,200	949,000	220,000	549,000	549,000	2,419,200

Elimination entries:
(29) Eliminate income from Bottom Company.
(30) Assign income to noncontrolling shareholders of Bottom Company.
(31) Eliminate investment in Bottom Company stock.
(32) Eliminate income from Special Foods.
(33) Assign income to noncontrolling shareholders of Special Foods.
(34) Eliminate investment in Special Foods stock.

of the combination includes the appropriate share of Bottom Company's earnings since acquisition and so that the differential is correctly determined.

Unrealized Intercompany Profits   When there are intercompany sales between multilevel affiliates, unrealized intercompany profits must be eliminated against the appropriate ownership interests. The most convenient way of doing this is to compute the amount of realized income each company contributes before apportioning income between controlling and noncontrolling interests.

For example, the realized income accruing to the ownership interests of each affiliate is computed in the following manner given the unrealized profit amounts indicated:

	Peerless Products	Special Foods	Bottom Company	Noncontrolling Interest
Operating income	$140,000	$50,000	$10,000	
Unrealized profit	(5,000)	(10,000)	(3,000)	
Realized operating profit	$135,000	$40,000	$ 7,000	
Allocation of income:				
Bottom Company		6,300	(7,000)	$ 700
Special Foods	37,040	(46,300)		9,260
Realized net income	$172,040	$ -0-	$ -0-	$9,960

Consolidated net income is equal to the $172,040 realized net income listed for Peerless Products. The normal workpaper entries to eliminate unrealized intercompany profits, as discussed in Chapters 6 and 7, are entered in the workpaper for each company involved.

Reciprocal Ownership

A reciprocal relationship exists when two companies hold stock in each other. Reciprocal relationships are relatively rare in practice, and their accounting impact often is immaterial. Accordingly, the discussion of this aspect of intercorporate ownership is brief.

There are two different approaches to the treatment of reciprocal relationships. The *treasury stock method* is used most frequently in practice and treats shares of the parent held by a subsidiary as if they had been repurchased by the parent. The *entity approach* views the parent and subsidiary as a single entity with income shared between the different ownership groups, explicitly taking into consideration the reciprocal relationship.

Treasury Stock Method   Under the treasury stock method, purchases of a parent's stock by a subsidiary are treated in the same way as if the parent had repurchased its own stock and was holding it in the treasury. The subsidiary normally accounts for the investment in the parent's stock using the cost method because such investments usually are small and almost never confer the ability to significantly influence the parent.

Income assigned to the noncontrolling interest in the subsidiary usually is based on the subsidiary's net income, which includes the dividend income from the investment in the parent. The parent, however, normally bases its equity-method share of the subsidiary's income on the subsidiary's income excluding the dividend income from the parent.

As an example of the treasury stock method, assume the following:

1. Peerless Products purchases 80 percent of the common stock of Special Foods on December 31, 19X0, at book value of $240,000.

2. Special Foods purchases 10 percent of the common stock of Peerless Products on January 1, 19X1, at book value of $80,000.

3. For 19X1, the two companies report the following separate operating income and dividends:

	Operating Income	Dividends
Peerless Products	$140,000	$60,000
Special Foods	50,000	30,000
Total operating income	$190,000	

The reciprocal ownership relationship between Peerless and Special Foods is as follows:

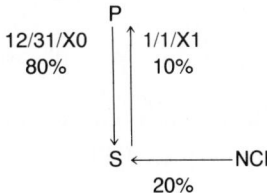

Special Foods records the purchase of its investment in the common stock of Peerless Products with the following entry:

January 1, 19X1
(35)	Investment in Peerless Products Stock	80,000	
	Cash		80,000
	Record purchase of Peerless Products stock.		

Because Special Foods does not gain the ability to significantly influence Peerless, it accounts for the investment using the cost method. During 19X1, Special Foods records the receipt of dividends from Peerless with the following entry:

(36)	Cash	6,000	
	Dividend Income		6,000
	Record dividend income from Peerless:		
	$60,000 × .10		

The consolidation workpaper prepared at the end of 19X1 includes the following entries to eliminate the intercompany dividend income and to report Special Foods' investment in Peerless as if it were treasury stock:

E(37)	Dividend Income	6,000	
	Dividends Declared		6,000
	Eliminate dividend income from Peerless.		
E(38)	Treasury Stock	80,000	
	Investment in Peerless Products Stock		80,000
	Reclassify investment in Peerless stock as treasury stock.		

All of Peerless's common stock is shown in the consolidated balance sheet as outstanding. The treasury stock is shown at cost as an $80,000 deduction from total stockholders' equity, just as treasury stock is shown in the balance sheet of a single company at cost. Note that entry E(37) reduces the amount shown in the consolidated retained earnings statement as dividends paid to those outside the consolidated entity.

The remaining entries needed in the 19X1 consolidation workpaper are the normal entries to eliminate Peerless's investment in Special Foods and income from Special Foods recognized by Peerless. The income from Special Foods recognized by Peerless is based on Special Foods' separate income excluding dividend income from Peerless. Therefore, the income elimination is for $40,000, Peerless's 80 percent share of Special Foods' separate operating income of $50,000.

Note that the parent's equity-method income and consolidated net income may not be equal under this approach. Peerless's income is computed as follows:

Peerless's separate operating income	$140,000
Peerless's share of Special Foods' operating income ($50,000 × .80)	40,000
Peerless's net income	$180,000

Consolidated net income is computed as follows:

Peerless's separate operating income		$140,000
Special Foods' separate operating income		50,000
Total separate income		$190,000
Less noncontrolling interest:		
Special Foods' net income		
($50,000 + $6,000)	$56,000	
Noncontrolling stockholders' share	× .20	
		(11,200)
Consolidated net income		$178,800

The difference occurs because the $6,000 of Peerless's dividends paid to Special Foods is considered when computing the noncontrolling interest but not when computing the parent's net income.

There is some question about the appropriate amount of income to assign to the noncontrolling interest under the treasury stock approach and, therefore, the amount of consolidated net income. Income assigned to the noncontrolling interest normally is computed as the noncontrolling stockholders' proportionate share of the subsidiary's net income. In the computation shown, the subsidiary's net income includes dividend income from Special Foods' investment in Peerless. The noncontrolling interest is credited with its full share of subsidiary net income.

Two other treatments also are found. Under one, income assigned to the noncontrolling interest is computed based on the subsidiary's income from its own operations, excluding the income from Peerless's dividends. Under the second treatment, income is assigned to the noncontrolling interest as if all the parent's income were distributed during the period. The amount of the noncontrolling interest in this second case indicates the claim of the noncontrolling shareholders in the event that the parent is liquidated. The differences between the treatments typically are small.

Entity Approach   The entity approach to dealing with reciprocal stock holdings, often referred to as the "traditional" or "conventional approach," is more consistent with the entity theory of consolidation than is the treasury stock method. Under this approach, the total of the separate incomes of the consolidating companies is viewed as the total income of the consolidated entity and is apportioned between the controlling and noncontrolling shareholders. In assigning income to the shareholder groups, recognition is given to the reciprocal nature of the relationship created when a subsidiary acquires shares of the parent company. A set of simultaneous equations normally is used in computing a reciprocal income total for each company. The resulting amounts then are used in apportioning income to the controlling and noncontrolling interests.

The balance sheet presentation under the entity approach is quite different than under the treasury stock method. The parent's shares held by the subsidiary are not reported as treasury stock; instead, the balance in the subsidiary's investment in the parent is eliminated in the same manner as the parent's investment in the common stock of the subsidiary. A proportionate amount of the parent's common stock, additional paid-in capital, and retained earnings is eliminated against the subsidiary's investment account in preparing the consolidated statements.

The apportionment of income under the entity approach is illustrated with the same example used to illustrate the treasury stock method. Total income assigned to each of the two companies is equal to the company's separate operating income plus its share of the other company's total income. For example, let

$$P = \text{Peerless Products' total income}$$
$$S = \text{Special Foods' total income}$$

The total incomes of Peerless and Special Foods can be stated as follows:

$$P = \$140,000 + .80S$$
$$S = \$50,000 + .10P$$

Total income assigned to each of the two companies can be determined by solving these equations simultaneously:

$$P = \$140,000 + .80S$$
$$P = \$140,000 + .80(\$50,000 + .10P)$$
$$P = \$140,000 + \$40,000 + .08P$$
$$.92P = \$180,000$$
$$P = \underline{\underline{\$195,652}}$$

$$S = \$50,000 + .10P$$
$$S = \$50,000 + .10(\$195,652)$$
$$S = \$50,000 + \$19,565$$
$$S = \underline{\underline{\$69,565}}$$

These income figures serve as a basis for determining the amount of income to be assigned to the controlling and noncontrolling interests. However, none of the computed totals can be reported without adjustment because each company has some portion of its shares held by an affiliate. The balances assigned are based on the portion of ownership held by shareholders outside the consolidated entity:

Consolidated net income:		
Peerless's income	$195,652	
Proportion of shares held outside		
consolidated entity	× .90	
		$176,087
Income to noncontrolling interest:		
Special Foods' income	$ 69,565	
Proportion of shares held by		
noncontrolling stockholders	× .20	
		13,913
Total income assigned		$190,000

Note that consolidated net income is not the amount of income assigned to Peerless; rather, it is the assigned amount adjusted for the percentage of total shares held by the stockholders of the consolidated entity. That is, 90 percent of Peerless's shares are held by those deemed to be the stockholders of the consolidated entity, while the other 10 percent are held within the consolidated entity.

The total of the amounts reported as consolidated net income and income assigned to noncontrolling shareholders of the consolidated subsidiaries always should equal the sum of the separate operating incomes of the individual companies:

Reported operating income:	
Peerless Products	$140,000
Special Foods	50,000
Total income reported	$190,000

An illustration of the entity approach applied to the assignment of income in a more complex ownership situation is given in the appendix to this chapter.

SUBSIDIARY STOCK DIVIDENDS

Subsidiary dividends payable in shares of the subsidiary's common stock require slight changes in the elimination entries used in preparing consolidated financial statements. Because stock dividends are issued proportionally to all common stockholders, the relative interests of the controlling and noncontrolling stockholders do not change as a result of the stock dividend. The carrying amount of the investment on the books of the parent also is unaffected by a stock dividend. On the other hand, the stockholders' equity accounts of the subsidiary do change, although total stockholders' equity does not. The stock dividend represents a permanent capitalization of retained earnings, thus decreasing retained earnings and increasing capital stock and, perhaps, additional paid-in capital.

In the preparation of consolidated financial statements for the period in which a stock dividend is declared by the subsidiary, the stock dividend declaration must be eliminated along with the increased common stock and increased additional paid-in capital, if any. The stock dividend declared cannot appear in the consolidated retained earnings statement because only the parent's dividends are viewed as dividends of the consolidated entity.

In subsequent years, the balances in the subsidiary's stockholders' equity accounts are eliminated in the normal manner. Keep in mind that stock dividends do not change the total stockholders' equity of a company; they only realign the individual accounts within stockholders' equity. Therefore, the full balances of all the subsidiary's stockholders' equity accounts must be eliminated in consolidation, as is the usual procedure, even though amounts have been shifted from one account to another.

Illustration of Subsidiary Stock Dividends

As an illustration of the treatment of a subsidiary's stock dividend, assume that in the Peerless Products and Special Foods example, Special Foods declares a 25 percent stock dividend in 19X1 on its $200,000 of common stock and elects to capitalize the par value of the shares. Special Foods records the stock dividend with the following entry:

(39)	Stock Dividends Declared	50,000	
	Common Stock		50,000
	Record 25 percent stock dividend:		
	$200,000 × .25		

Only a memo entry is made by the investors to record the receipt of the stock dividend.

When consolidated financial statements are prepared at the end of 19X1, the normal elimination entries are made in the workpaper. If the subsidiary had declared no stock dividend, the entry for the elimination of the investment account and subsidiary stockholders' equity balances at the beginning of the period would have been:

E(40)	Common Stock—Special Foods	200,000	
	Retained Earnings, January 1	100,000	
	Investment in Special Foods Stock		240,000
	Noncontrolling Interest		60,000
	Eliminate beginning investment balance.		

With the subsidiary having declared the stock dividend, all elimination entries are the same except for the investment elimination entry. Entry E(40) is altered as follows:

E(41)	Common Stock—Special Foods	250,000	
	Retained Earnings, January 1	100,000	
	Investment in Special Foods Stock		240,000
	Noncontrolling Interest		60,000
	Stock Dividends Declared		50,000
	Eliminate beginning investment balance:		
	$250,000 = $200,000 + $50,000$		
	$50,000 = $200,000 \times .25$		

Note that while the common stock balance has increased by the $50,000 amount of the stock dividend, the elimination of retained earnings is not changed in the year of the stock dividend because dividends declared have not been closed to retained earnings; it is the beginning balance of retained earnings that is eliminated. Just as with other dividends of the subsidiary, stock dividends must be eliminated because they are not viewed as dividends of the consolidated entity.

Impact on Subsequent Periods

At the end of 19X1, the stock dividend declaration is closed into the subsidiary's retained earnings and does not separately appear in the financial statements of future periods. The stock dividend results in a common stock balance $50,000 higher and a retained earnings balance $50,000 lower on the books of the subsidiary than if there had been no stock dividend. The investment elimination entry in the consolidation workpaper must consider these changed balances.

Thus, assume that the appropriate investment elimination entry on December 31, 19X2, is as follows if Special Foods declares no stock dividend:

E(42)	Common Stock—Special Foods	200,000	
	Retained Earnings, January 1	120,000	
	Investment in Special Foods Stock		256,000
	Noncontrolling Interest		64,000
	Eliminate beginning investment balance.		

The following entry would replace entry E(42) in the consolidation workpaper prepared as of December 31, 19X2, if Special Foods had declared the stock dividend during 19X1:

E(43)	Common Stock—Special Foods	250,000	
	Retained Earnings, January 1	70,000	
	Investment in Special Foods Stock		256,000
	Noncontrolling Interest		64,000
	Eliminate beginning investment balance.		

Entry E(43) is identical to entry E(42) except that the elimination of common stock is $50,000 higher and the elimination of retained earnings is $50,000 lower, reflecting the differences in the balances of those accounts due to the stock dividend.

SUMMARY OF KEY CONCEPTS AND TERMS

A number of stockholders' equity issues arise in the preparation of consolidated financial statements. When subsidiaries have preferred stock outstanding, any of the preferred stock held by the parent must be eliminated because it is held within the consolidated entity. The remaining preferred stock is treated as part of the noncontrolling interest. In the assessment of the preferred shareholders' claim, consideration must be given to all the features of the preferred stock, including cumulative dividends in arrears, dividend participation features, and retirement premiums.

Transactions involving subsidiary common stock may affect the percentage ownership of the controlling shareholders. Although existing accounting standards permit some degree of diversity in practice, the concept of a single economic entity implies that subsidiary stock transactions should be viewed as transactions of the consolidated entity. Thus, no gains or losses should be reported in the consolidated income statement when a subsidiary issues new shares or purchases treasury stock. For example, a gain or loss recognized by a parent on a sale of subsidiary shares back to the subsidiary should be eliminated in preparing consolidated statements because the transfer is entirely within the consolidated entity.

The organizational structure of some consolidated entities may be more complex than just a parent and one or more subsidiaries. In some cases, subsidiaries hold controlling interests in other companies, thus giving the parent an indirect interest. Consolidation proceeds from the lowest level to the highest in these cases. In a relatively few cases, a subsidiary may own common shares of its parent. Usually those common shares are treated as treasury stock in consolidated financial statements.

Stock dividends declared by a subsidiary result in only minor changes in the eliminations needed to prepare consolidated financial statements. In the year the stock dividend is declared, the stock dividend declaration and the higher balance of the common stock must be eliminated in preparing consolidated statements. In subsequent years, the investment elimination entry reflects the higher amount of the subsidiary's common stock and the lower amount of retained earnings.

Direct ownership	Multilevel ownership
Entity approach	Reciprocal ownership
Indirect control	Treasury stock method

APPENDIX: Illustration of Consolidated Net Income Computation in a Complex Ownership Situation

As an illustration of the entity approach to computing consolidated net income in a complex ownership situation, assume the following ownership relations between A Company, B Company, and C Company:

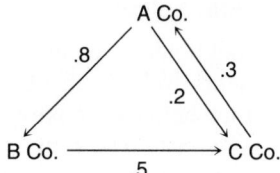

The income accruing to each company is defined as:

A = the net income of A Company on an equity basis
B = the net income of B Company on an equity basis
C = the net income of C Company on an equity basis

If the separate operating incomes of A, B, and C Companies are $122,000, $80,000, and $100,000, respectively, the algebraic equations to determine the appropriate balances are:

$$A = \$122,000 + .8B + .2C$$

$$B = \$80{,}000 + .5C$$
$$C = \$100{,}000 + .3A$$

$$
\begin{aligned}
A &= \$122{,}000 + .8[\$80{,}000 + .5(\$100{,}000 + .3A)] + .2(\$100{,}000 + .3A) \\
&= \$122{,}000 + .8(\$80{,}000 + \$50{,}000 + .15A) + \$20{,}000 + .06A \\
&= \$122{,}000 + \$64{,}000 + \$40{,}000 + .12A + \$20{,}000 + .06A \\
&= \$246{,}000 + .18A
\end{aligned}
$$
$$.82A = \$246{,}000$$
$$A = \$300{,}000$$

$$
\begin{aligned}
C &= \$100{,}000 + .3(\$300{,}000) \\
&= \$100{,}000 + \$90{,}000 = \$190{,}000
\end{aligned}
$$

$$
\begin{aligned}
B &= \$80{,}000 + .5(\$190{,}000) \\
&= \$80{,}000 + \$95{,}000 = \$175{,}000
\end{aligned}
$$

These income figures provide the basis for determining the amount to be reported as consolidated net income and the amount to be assigned to the noncontrolling shareholders of each company. However, none of the computed totals can be reported without adjustment in this case because each company has some portion of its shares held by an affiliate. The income amounts assigned are based on the portion of ownership held by outside shareholders, as follows:

Consolidated net income:		
A's income	$300,000	
Proportion of shares held outside consolidated entity	× .70	
		$210,000
Income to noncontrolling interest:		
B's income	$175,000	
Proportion of shares held by noncontrolling stockholders	× .20	
		35,000
C's income	$190,000	
Proportion of shares held by noncontrolling stockholders	× .30	
		57,000
Total income assigned		$302,000

Consolidated net income in this situation is not the amount of income computed for A Company; rather, it is the computed amount adjusted for the percentage of total shares held outside the consolidated entity itself. The total of the amounts reported as consolidated net income and income assigned to noncontrolling shareholders of the subsidiaries should always equal the sum of the separate operating incomes of the individual companies:

Separate operating income:	
A Company	$122,000
B Company	80,000
C Company	100,000
Total operating income	$302,000

QUESTIONS

Q9-1 How does the consolidation process deal with preferred stock of a subsidiary?

Q9-2 What portion of subsidiary preferred stock outstanding is reported as part of the noncontrolling interest in the consolidated balance sheet?

Q9-3 Why are subsidiary preferred dividends that are paid to nonaffiliates normally deducted from earnings in arriving at consolidated net income? When is it not appropriate to deduct subsidiary preferred dividends in computing consolidated net income?

Q9-4 How does a call feature on subsidiary preferred stock affect the claim of the noncontrolling interest reported in the consolidated balance sheet?

Q9-5 Explain how the existence of a subsidiary's preferred shares might affect the amount of goodwill reported following the purchase of the subsidiary.

Q9-6 A parent company sells common shares of one of its subsidiaries to a nonaffiliate for more than their carrying value on the parent's books. How should the sale be reported by the parent company? How should the sale be reported in the consolidated financial statements?

Q9-7 A subsidiary sells additional shares of its common stock to a nonaffiliate at a price that is greater than the previous book value per share. How does the sale benefit the existing shareholders?

Q9-8 A parent company purchases additional common shares of one of its subsidiaries from a nonaffiliate at $10 per share above underlying book value. Explain how this purchase is reflected in the consolidated financial statements for the year.

Q9-9 How are treasury shares held by a subsidiary reported in the consolidated financial statements?

Q9-10 What is indirect ownership? How does one company gain control of another through indirect ownership?

Q9-11 Explain how a reciprocal ownership arrangement between two subsidiaries could lead the parent company to overstate its income if no adjustment is made for the reciprocal relationship.

Q9-12 How will parent company shares held by a subsidiary be reflected in the consolidated balance sheet when the treasury stock method is used?

Q9-13 How does the entity method differ from the treasury stock method in computing consolidated net income when there is reciprocal ownership between the parent and the subsidiary?

Q9-14 Parent Company holds 80 percent ownership of Subsidiary Company, and Subsidiary Company owns 90 percent of the stock of Tiny Corporation. What effect will $100,000 of unrealized intercompany profits on the books of Tiny Corporation on December 31, 19X5, have on the amount of consolidated net income reported for the year?

Q9-15 Snapper Corporation holds 70 percent ownership of Bit Company, and Bit Company holds 60 percent ownership of Slide Company. Should Slide Company be consolidated with Snapper Corporation? Why?

Q9-16 What effect will a subsidiary's 15 percent stock dividend have on the consolidated financial statements?

Q9-17 What effect will a subsidiary's 15 percent stock dividend have on the elimination entries used in preparing a consolidated balance sheet at the end of the year in which the dividend is distributed?

Q9-18 When there are multilevel affiliations, explain why it generally is best to prepare consolidated financial statements by completing the eliminating entries for companies furthest from parent company ownership first and completing the eliminating entries for those owned directly by the parent company last.

CASES

C9-1 Effect of Subsidiary Preferred Stock

Snow Corporation issued common stock with a par value of $100,000 and preferred stock with a par value of $80,000 on January 1, 19X5, when the company was created. Klammer Corporation acquired a controlling interest in Snow Corporation on January 1, 19X6.

Required

What does the controller of Klammer Corporation need to know about the preferred stock in order to determine consolidated net income for 19X6?

C9-2 Sale of Subsidiary Shares

Hardcore Mining Company acquired 88 percent of the common stock of Mountain Trucking Company on January 1, 19X2, at a cost of $30 per share. On December 31, 19X7, when the book value of Mountain Trucking stock was $70 per share, Hardcore sold one-quarter of its investment in Mountain Trucking to Basic Manufacturing Company for $90 per share.

Required

What effect will the sale have on the 19X7 consolidated financial statements of Hardcore mining if (a) Basic Manufacturing is an unrelated company; (b) Hardcore Mining holds 60 percent of the voting shares of Basic Manufacturing?

C9-3 Reciprocal Ownership

Strong Manufacturing Company holds 94 percent ownership of Thorson Farm Products and 68 percent ownership of Kenwood Distributors. Thorson Farm Products has excess cash at the end of 19X4 and is considering buying shares of its own stock, shares of Strong Manufacturing, or shares of Kenwood Distributors.

Required

If Thorson Farm Products wishes to take the action that will be best for the consolidated entity, what factors will it need to consider in making its decision? How can it maximize consolidated net income?

EXERCISES

E9-1   Multiple-Choice Questions on Preferred Stock Ownership

Blank Corporation prepared the following summarized balance sheet on January 1, 19X7:

Assets	$150,000	Liabilities	$ 20,000
		Preferred Stock	30,000
		Common Stock	40,000
		Retained Earnings	60,000
	$150,000		$150,000

Required

Select the correct answer for each of the following questions.

1. If Shepard Company purchases 80 percent of the common shares of Blank Corporation for $90,000, the amount reported as noncontrolling interest in the consolidated balance sheet is:
   a. $20,000.
   b. $26,000.
   c. $30,000.
   d. $50,000.

2. Shepard Company purchases 80 percent of the common shares of Blank Corporation for $90,000 and 70 percent of the preferred shares of Blank Corporation for $21,000. The amount reported as noncontrolling interest in the consolidated balance sheet of Shepard Company is:
   a. $9,000.
   b. $20,000.
   c. $29,000.
   d. $50,000.

3. Shepard Company purchases 80 percent of the common shares of Blank Corporation for $90,000 and 70 percent of the preferred shares of Blank Corporation for $21,000 on January 1, 19X7. If Shepard Company's retained earnings is $150,000 on December 31, 19X6, the consolidated retained earnings reported immediately after the stock purchases is:
   a. $48,000.
   b. $150,000.
   c. $198,000.
   d. $210,000.

4. Shepard Company purchases 80 percent of the common shares of Blank Corporation for $90,000 and 70 percent of the preferred shares of Blank Corporation for $21,000 on January 1, 19X7. Shepard Company has no preferred shares outstanding. The amount of preferred stock reported in the consolidated balance sheet immediately after the stock purchases is:
   a. $0.
   b. $9,000.
   c. $21,000.
   d. $30,000.

E9-2 Multiple-Choice Questions on Multilevel Ownership

Musial Corporation purchases 80 percent of the common shares of Dustin Corporation on January 1, 19X5. On January 2, 19X5, Dustin Corporation purchases 60 percent of the common stock of Rustic Corporation. Information on company book values on the date of purchase and operating results for 19X5 is as follows:

Company	Book Value	Purchase Price	19X5 Operating Income
Musial Corporation	$800,000		$100,000
Dustin Corporation	300,000	$240,000	80,000
Rustic Corporation	200,000	120,000	50,000

Required

Select the correct answer for each of the following questions.

1. Consolidated net income for 19X5 is:
   a. $180,000.
   b. $188,000.
   c. $194,000.
   d. $234,000.

2. The amount of 19X5 income assigned to the noncontrolling interest of Rustic Corporation is:
   a. $0.
   b. $20,000.
   c. $30,000.
   d. $50,000.

3. The amount of 19X5 income assigned to the noncontrolling interest of Dustin Corporation is:
   a. $10,000.
   b. $16,000.
   c. $22,000.
   d. $26,000.

4. The amount of income assigned to the noncontrolling interest in the 19X5 consolidated income statement is:
   a. $20,000.
   b. $22,000.
   c. $42,000.
   d. $46,000.

5. Assume that Dustin Corporation pays $160,000, rather than $120,000, to purchase 60 percent of the common stock of Rustic Corporation. If the purchase differential is amortized over 10 years, the effect on 19X5 consolidated net income will be a decrease of:
   a. $0.
   b. $2,400.
   c. $3,200.
   d. $4,000.

E9-3 Acquisition of Preferred Shares

The summarized balance sheet of Separate Company on January 1, 19X3, contained the following amounts:

Total Assets	$350,000	Total Liabilities	$ 50,000
		Preferred Stock	100,000
		Common Stock	50,000
		Retained Earnings	150,000
	$350,000		$350,000

On January 1, 19X3, Joint Corporation purchased 70 percent of the common shares and 60 percent of the preferred shares of Separate Company at underlying book value.

Required

Give the workpaper elimination entries needed to prepare a consolidated balance sheet immediately following the purchase of shares by Joint Corporation.

E9-4 Preferred Dividends and Call Premium

On January 1, 19X9, Fischer Corporation purchased 90 percent of the common shares and 60 percent of the preferred shares of Culbertson Company at underlying book value. The balance sheet of Culbertson Company at the time of purchase contained the following balances:

Total Assets	$860,000	Total Liabilities	$ 80,000
		Preferred Stock	100,000
		Common Stock	300,000
		Retained Earnings	380,000
	$860,000		$860,000

The preferred shares are cumulative with regard to dividends. The shares have a 12 percent annual dividend rate and are 5 years in arrears on January 1, 19X9. All the $10 par value preferred shares are callable at $12 per share after December 31, 19X7. During 19X9, Culbertson Company reported net income of $70,000 and paid no dividends.

Required

a. Compute the contribution of Culbertson Company to consolidated net income for 19X9.

b. Compute the amount of income to be assigned to the noncontrolling interest in the 19X9 consolidated income statement.

c. Compute the portion of the retained earnings of Culbertson Company assignable to its preferred shareholders on January 1, 19X9.

d. Compute the book value of the common stock on January 1, 19X9.

e. Compute the amount to be reported as the noncontrolling interest in the consolidated balance sheet on January 1, 19X9.

E9-5   Reciprocal Ownership

Grower Supply Corporation holds 85 percent of the voting common stock of Schultz Company. At the end of 19X4, Schultz Company had funds to invest and purchased 30 percent of the stock of Grower Supply Corporation. Schultz Company records dividends received from Grower Supply Corporation as dividend income. In 19X5, Grower Supply Corporation and Schultz Company reported income from their separate operations of $112,000 and $50,000 and paid dividends of $70,000 and $30,000, respectively.

Required

Compute the amount reported as consolidated net income and as income assigned to the noncontrolling interest for 19X5 under (a) the treasury stock method and (b) the entity approach.

E9-6   Consolidated Balance Sheet with Reciprocal Ownership

The Talbott Company purchased 80 percent of the stock of Short Company on January 1, 19X8, at underlying book value. On December 31, 19X9, Short Company purchased 10 percent of the stock of Talbott Company. Balance sheets for the two companies on December 31, 19X9, are as follows:

Talbott Company
Condensed Balance Sheet
December 31, 19X9

Cash	$ 78,000	Accounts Payable	$ 90,000
Accounts Receivable	120,000	Bonds Payable	400,000
Inventory	150,000	Common Stock	300,000
Buildings and Equipment (net)	400,000	Retained Earnings	310,000
Investment in Short Company			
Common Stock	352,000		
	$1,100,000		$1,100,000

Short Company
Condensed Balance Sheet
December 31, 19X9

Cash	$ 39,000	Accounts Payable	$ 60,000
Accounts Receivable	80,000	Bonds Payable	100,000
Inventory	120,000	Common Stock	200,000
Buildings and Equipment (net)	300,000	Retained Earnings	240,000
Investment in Talbott Company			
Common Stock	61,000		
	$600,000		$600,000

Required

Assuming the treasury stock method is used in reporting the shares of Talbott Company held by Short Company, prepare a consolidated balance sheet workpaper and consolidated balance sheet for December 31, 19X9.

E9-7 Subsidiary Stock Dividend

Lake Company reported the following summarized balance sheet data as of December 31, 19X6:

Cash	$ 30,000	Accounts Payable	$ 50,000
Accounts Receivable	80,000	Common Stock	100,000
Inventory	90,000	Retained Earnings	200,000
Buildings and Equipment	270,000		
Less: Accumulated Depreciation	(120,000)		
	$ 350,000		$350,000

Lake Company issues 4,000 additional shares of its $10 par value stock to its shareholders as a stock dividend on April 20, 19X7. The market price of Lake Company's shares at the time of the stock dividend is $40. Lake Company reports net income of $25,000 and pays a $10,000 cash dividend in 19X7. Lindale Company purchased 70 percent of the common shares of Lake Company at underlying book value on January 1, 19X4, and uses the basic equity method in accounting for its investment in Lake Company.

Required

a. Give the journal entries recorded by Lake Company and Lindale Company at the time the stock dividend is declared and distributed.

b. Give the workpaper elimination entries needed to prepare consolidated financial statements for 19X7.

c. Give the workpaper elimination entry needed to prepare a consolidated balance sheet on January 1, 19X8.

E9-8 Sale of Subsidiary Shares by Parent

Stable Home Builders, Inc., purchased 80 percent of the stock of Acme Concrete Works on January 1, 19X3, for $360,000. The balance sheet of Acme Concrete contained the following amounts at the time of the combination:

Cash	$ 30,000	Accounts Payable	$ 50,000
Accounts Receivable	65,000	Bonds Payable	300,000
Inventory	15,000	Common Stock	200,000
Construction Work in Progress	470,000	Retained Earnings	250,000
Other Assets (net)	220,000		
	$800,000		$800,000

During each of the next 3 years, Acme Concrete reported net income of $50,000 and paid dividends of $20,000. On January 1, 19X5, Stable Home Builders sold 4,000 of the $10 par value shares of Acme for $120,000 in cash. Stable Home Builders used the basic equity method in accounting for its ownership of Acme Concrete.

Required

a. Compute the balance in the investment account reported by Stable Home Builders on January 1, 19X5, before its sale of shares.

b. Prepare the entry recorded by Stable Home Builders when it sold the Acme Concrete shares.

c. Prepare the appropriate elimination entries to complete a full consolidation workpaper for 19X5.

E9-9 Purchase of Additional Shares from Nonaffiliate

Weal Corporation purchased 60 percent of the shares of Modern Products Company on December 31, 19X7, for $240,000 and 20 percent on January 1, 19X9, for $96,000. Summarized balance sheets for Modern Products Company on the dates indicated are as follows:

	December 31		
	19X7	**19X8**	**19X9**
Cash	$ 40,000	$ 70,000	$ 90,000
Accounts Receivable	50,000	90,000	120,000
Inventory	70,000	100,000	160,000
Buildings and Equipment (net)	340,000	320,000	300,000
	$500,000	$580,000	$670,000
Accounts Payable	$ 50,000	$100,000	$140,000
Bonds Payable	100,000	100,000	100,000
Common Stock	150,000	150,000	150,000
Retained Earnings	200,000	230,000	280,000
	$500,000	$580,000	$670,000

Modern Products Company paid dividends of $20,000 in each of the 3 years. Weal Corporation uses the basic equity method in accounting for its investment in Modern Products Company and amortizes all purchase differentials over 10 years against the related investment income. All differentials are assigned to goodwill in the consolidated financial statements.

Required

a. Compute the balance in Weal's Investment in Modern Products Company Stock account on December 31, 19X8.

b. Compute the balance in Weal's Investment in Modern Products Company Stock account on December 31, 19X9.

c. Prepare the eliminating entries needed as of December 31, 19X9, to complete a three-part consolidation workpaper.

E9-10 Purchase of Shares by Subsidiary from Nonaffiliate

Blatant Advertising Corporation acquired 60 percent of the shares of Quinn Manufacturing Company on December 31, 19X1, at underlying book value of $180,000. The balance sheet of Quinn Manufacturing Company on January 1, 19X7, contained the following balances:

Cash	$ 80,000	Accounts Payable	$ 60,000
Accounts Receivable	100,000	Bonds Payable	240,000
Inventory	160,000	Common Stock	100,000
Buildings and Equipment	700,000	Additional Paid-In Capital	150,000
Less: Accumulated Depreciation	(240,000)	Retained Earnings	250,000
	$800,000		$800,000

On January 1, 19X7, Quinn Manufacturing Company purchased 2,000 of its own $10 par value common shares from Nonaffiliated Corporation for $42 per share.

Required

a. Compute the change in the book value of the shares held by Blatant Advertising as a result of the repurchase of shares by Quinn Manufacturing.

b. Give the entry to be recorded on the books of Blatant Advertising to recognize the change in the book value of the shares it holds.

c. Give the eliminating entry needed in preparing a consolidated balance sheet immediately following the purchase of shares by Quinn Manufacturing.

E9-11 Sale of Shares by Subsidiary to Nonaffiliate

Browne Corporation purchased 11,000 shares of Schroeder Corporation on January 1, 19X3, at underlying book value. On December 31, 19X8, Schroeder Corporation reported the following balance sheet amounts:

Cash	$ 80,000	Accounts Payable	$ 50,000
Accounts Receivable	120,000	Bonds Payable	100,000
Inventory	200,000	Common Stock	150,000
Buildings and Equipment	600,000	Additional Paid-In Capital	50,000
Less: Accumulated Depreciation	(250,000)	Retained Earnings	400,000
	$750,000		$750,000

On January 1, 19X9, Schroeder Corporation issued an additional 5,000 shares of its $10 par value common stock to Nonaffiliated Company for $80 per share.

Required

a. Compute the change in book value of the shares held by Browne Corporation as a result of the issuance of additional shares by Schroeder Corporation.

b. Give the entry to be recorded on the books of Browne Corporation to recognize the change in book value of the shares it holds, assuming the change in book value is to be treated as an adjustment to additional paid-in capital.

   c. Record the eliminating entry needed to prepare a consolidated balance sheet immediately after the sale of additional shares by Schroeder Corporation.

PROBLEMS

P9-12 Multiple-Choice Questions on Preferred Stock Ownership

Stacey Corporation owns 80 percent of the common shares and 70 percent of the preferred shares of Upland Company, all purchased at underlying book value on January 1, 19X2. The balance sheets of Stacey Corporation and Upland Company immediately after the acquisition contained the following balances:

	Stacey Corporation	Upland Company
Cash and Receivables	$150,000	$ 80,000
Inventory	200,000	100,000
Buildings and Equipment (net)	250,000	220,000
Investment in Upland Preferred Stock	70,000	
Investment in Upland Common Stock	200,000	
Total Assets	$870,000	$400,000
Liabilities	$220,000	$ 50,000
Preferred Stock		100,000
Common Stock	300,000	200,000
Retained Earnings	350,000	50,000
Total Liabilities and Equities	$870,000	$400,000

The preferred stock issued by Upland Company pays a 10 percent dividend and is cumulative. For 19X2 Upland Company reports net income of $30,000 and pays no dividends. Stacey Corporation reports income from its separate operations of $100,000 and pays dividends of $40,000 during 19X2.

Required

Select the correct answer for each of the following questions.

1. Total noncontrolling interest reported in the consolidated balance sheet as of January 1, 19X2, is:
   a. $30,000.
   b. $50,000.
   c. $70,000.
   d. $80,000.

2. Income assigned to the noncontrolling interest in the 19X2 consolidated income statement is:

    a. $6,000.
    b. $7,000.
    c. $9,000.
    d. $14,000.

3. Consolidated net income for 19X2 is:
    a. $116,000.
    b. $123,000.
    c. $124,000.
    d. $130,000.

4. Excluding the noncontrolling interest, total stockholders' equity reported in the consolidated balance sheet as of January 1, 19X2, is:
    a. $650,000.
    b. $750,000.
    c. $850,000.
    d. $900,000.

5. Preferred stock outstanding reported in the consolidated balance sheet as of January 1, 19X2, is:
    a. $0.
    b. $30,000.
    c. $70,000.
    d. $100,000.

P9-13   Multiple-Choice Questions on Reciprocal Ownership [AICPA Adapted]

Akron, Inc., owns 80 percent of the capital stock of Benson Company and 70 percent of the capital stock of Cashin, Inc. Benson Company owns 15 percent of the capital stock of Cashin, Inc. Cashin, Inc., in turn, owns 25 percent of the capital stock of Akron, Inc. These ownership interrelationships are illustrated in the following diagram:

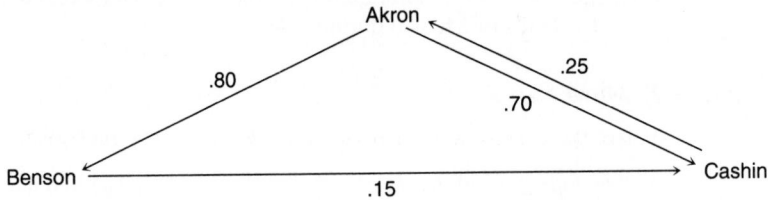

Income from the separate operations of each corporation is as follows:

Akron, Inc.	$190,000
Benson Company	170,000
Cashin, Inc.	230,000

The following notations relate to items 1 through 4. Ignore all income tax considerations.

A = Akron's consolidated net income; that is, its income plus its share of the consolidated net incomes of Benson and Cashin

B = Benson's consolidated net income; that is, its income plus its share of the consolidated net income of Cashin

C = Cashin's consolidated net income; that is, its income plus its share of the consolidated net income of Akron

Select the correct answer for each of the following questions.

1. The equation, in a set of simultaneous equations, that computes A is:
   a. $A = .75(\$190,000 + .8B + .7C)$.
   b. $A = \$190,000 + .8B + .7C$.
   c. $A = .75(\$190,000) + .8(\$170,000) + .7(\$230,000)$.
   d. $A = .75(\$190,000) + .8B + .7C$.

2. The equation, in a set of simultaneous equations, that computes B is:
   a. $B = \$170,000 + .15C - .75A$.
   b. $B = \$170,000 + .15C$.
   c. $B = .2(\$170,000) + .15(\$230,000)$.
   d. $B = .2(\$170,000) + .15C$.

3. Cashin's noncontrolling interest in consolidated net income is:
   a. $.15(\$230,000)$.
   b. $\$230,000 + .25A$.
   c. $.15(\$230,000) + .25A$.
   d. $.15C$.

4. Benson's noncontrolling interest in consolidated net income is:
   a. $25,500.
   b. $30,675.
   c. $34,316.
   d. $45,755.

P9-14 Subsidiary Stock Dividend

Pound Manufacturing Corporation prepared the following balance sheet as of January 1, 19X8:

Cash	$ 40,000	Accounts Payable	$ 50,000
Accounts Receivable	90,000	Bonds Payable	200,000
Inventory	180,000	Common Stock	100,000
Buildings and Equipment	500,000	Additional Paid-In Capital	70,000
Less: Accumulated Depreciation	(110,000)	Retained Earnings	280,000
	$700,000		$700,000

The company is considering a 2 for 1 stock split, a stock dividend of 4,000 shares, or a stock dividend of 1,500 shares on its $10 par value common stock. The current market price per share of Pound Manufacturing stock on January 1, 19X8, is $50. Quick Sales Corporation acquired 68 percent of the common shares of Pound Manufacturing on January 1, 19X4, at underlying book value.

Required

Give the investment elimination entry required to prepare a consolidated balance sheet at the close of business on January 1, 19X8, for each of the alternative transactions under consideration by Pound Manufacturing.

P9-15 Subsidiary Preferred Stock Outstanding

Emerald Corporation purchased 10,500 shares of the common stock and 800 shares of the 8 percent preferred stock of Pert Company on December 31, 19X4, at underlying book value. Pert Company reported the following balance sheet amounts on January 1, 19X5:

Cash	$ 30,000	Accounts Payable	$ 20,000
Accounts Receivable	70,000	Bonds Payable	100,000
Inventory	120,000	Preferred Stock	200,000
Buildings and Equipment	600,000	Common Stock	150,000
Less: Accumulated Depreciation	(150,000)	Retained Earnings	200,000
	$670,000		$670,000

The preferred stock of Pert Company is $100 par value, and the common stock is $10 par value. The preferred dividends are cumulative and are 2 years in arrears on January 1, 19X5. Pert Company reports net income of $34,000 for 19X5 and pays no dividends.

Required

a. Present the workpaper eliminating entries needed to prepare a consolidated balance sheet on January 1, 19X5.

b. Assuming Emerald Corporation reported income from its separate operations of $80,000 in 19X5, compute the amount of consolidated net income and the amount of income to be assigned to noncontrolling shareholders in the 19X5 consolidated income statement.

P9-16 Ownership of Subsidiary Preferred Stock

Presley Pools, Inc., purchased 60 percent of the common stock of Jacobs Jacuzzi Company on December 31, 19X6, for $1,800,000. All the excess of the cost of the investment over the book value of the shares acquired was attributable to goodwill with a life of 10 years. On January 2, 19X7, Presley purchased 20 percent of the outstanding preferred shares of Jacobs for $42,000.

In its 19X6 annual report, Jacobs reported the following stockholders' equity balances at the end of the year:

Preferred Stock (10 percent, $100 par)	$ 200,000
Premium on Preferred Stock	5,000
Common Stock	500,000
Additional Paid-In Capital—Common	800,000
Retained Earnings	1,650,000
Total Stockholders' Equity	$3,155,000

The preferred stock is cumulative and has a liquidation value equal to its call price of $101 per share. Because of cash flow problems, Jacobs declared no dividends during 19X6, the first time a preferred dividend had been missed. With the improvement in operations during 19X7, Jacobs declared the current stated preferred dividend as well as preferred dividends in arrears; Jacobs also declared a common dividend for 19X7 of $10,000. Jacobs' reported net income for 19X7 was $280,000.

Required

   a. Compute the amount of the preferred stockholders' claim on the net assets of Jacobs Jacuzzi on December 31, 19X6.
   b. Compute the December 31, 19X6, book value of the Jacobs common shares purchased by Presley.
   c. Compute the amount of goodwill associated with Presley's purchase of Jacobs common stock at the date of acquisition.
   d. Compute the amount of income that should be assigned to the noncontrolling interest in the 19X7 consolidated income statement.
   e. Compute the amount of income from its subsidiary that Presley should have recorded during 19X7 using the basic equity method.
   f. Compute the total amount that should be reported as noncontrolling interest in the December 31, 19X7, consolidated balance sheet.
   g. Present all elimination entries that should appear in a consolidation workpaper to prepare a complete set of 19X7 consolidated financial statements for Presley Pools and its subsidiary.

P9-17 Consolidation Workpaper with Subsidiary Preferred Stock

Brown Company owns 90 percent of the common stock and 60 percent of the preferred stock of White Corporation, both acquired at underlying book value on January 1, 19X1. Trial balances for the companies on December 31, 19X6, are as follows:

	Brown Company		White Corporation	
	Debit	**Credit**	**Debit**	**Credit**
Cash	$ 58,000		$100,000	
Accounts Receivable	80,000		120,000	
Dividends Receivable	9,000			
Inventory	100,000		200,000	
Buildings and Equipment (net)	360,000		270,000	
Investment in White Corporation:				
Preferred Stock	120,000			
Common Stock	364,500			
Cost of Goods Sold	280,000		170,000	
Depreciation and Amortization	40,000		30,000	
Other Expenses	131,000		20,000	
Dividends Declared:				
Preferred Stock			15,000	
Common Stock	60,000		10,000	
Accounts Payable		$ 100,000		$ 70,000
Bonds Payable		300,000		
Dividends Payable				15,000
Preferred Stock				200,000
Common Stock		200,000		100,000
Retained Earnings		435,000		250,000
Sales		500,000		300,000
Dividend Income		9,000		
Income from Subsidiary		58,500		
	$1,602,500	$1,602,500	$935,000	$935,000

White Corporation's preferred shares pay a 7.5 percent annual dividend and are cumulative. Preferred dividends for 19X6 were declared on December 31, 19X6, and are to be paid January 1, 19X7.

Required

a. Prepare the eliminating entries needed to complete a full consolidation workpaper for 19X6.

b. Prepare a consolidation workpaper as of December 31, 19X6.

P9-18   Subsidiary Stock Transactions

Apex Corporation acquired 75 percent of the common stock of Beta Company on May 15, 19X3, at underlying book value. The balance sheet of Beta Company on December 31, 19X6, contained the following amounts:

Cash	$ 55,000	Accounts Payable	$ 30,000
Accounts Receivable	70,000	Bonds Payable	200,000
Inventory	125,000	Common Stock ($10 par)	100,000
Buildings and Equipment	700,000	Additional Paid-In Capital	80,000
Less: Accumulated Depreciation	(220,000)	Retained Earnings	320,000
	$730,000		$730,000

During 19X7, Apex earned operating income of $90,000, and Beta reported net income of $45,000. Neither company declared any dividends during 19X7.

Beta Company is considering repurchasing 1,000 of its outstanding shares as treasury stock at a price of $68 each.

Required

a. Assuming the shares are purchased from Nonaffiliated Company on January 1, 19X7:
   (1) Compute the effect on the book value of the shares held by Apex Corporation.
   (2) Give the entry on the books of Apex Corporation to record the change in the book value of its investment in Beta's shares.
   (3) Prepare the eliminating entries needed on December 31, 19X7, to complete a consolidation workpaper.
b. Assuming the shares are purchased directly from Apex Corporation on January 1, 19X7:
   (1) Compute the effect on the book value of the shares held by Apex Corporation.
   (2) Give the entry on the books of Apex Corporation to record its sale of Beta Corporation shares to Beta.
   (3) Prepare the eliminating entries needed on December 31, 19X7, to complete a consolidation workpaper.

P9-19 Sale of Subsidiary Shares

Penn Corporation purchased 80 percent ownership of ENC Company on January 1, 19X2, at underlying book value. On January 1, 19X4, Penn Corporation sold 2,000 shares of ENC Company stock for $60,000 to American School Products. Trial balances for the companies on December 31, 19X4, contain the following data:

	Penn Corporation		ENC Company	
	Debit	**Credit**	**Debit**	**Credit**
Cash	$ 30,000		$ 35,000	
Accounts Receivable	70,000		50,000	
Inventory	120,000		100,000	
Buildings and Equipment	650,000		230,000	
Investment in ENC Company	162,000			
Cost of Goods Sold	210,000		100,000	
Depreciation Expense	20,000		15,000	
Other Expenses	21,000		25,000	
Dividends Declared	15,000		10,000	
Accumulated Depreciation		$ 170,000		$ 95,000
Accounts Payable		50,000		20,000
Bonds Payable		200,000		30,000
Common Stock ($10 par)		200,000		100,000
Additional Paid-In Capital		50,000		20,000
Retained Earnings		320,000		130,000
Sales		280,000		170,000
Gain on Sale of ENC Company Stock		10,000		
Income from Subsidiary		18,000		
	$1,298,000	$1,298,000	$565,000	$565,000

ENC Company net income was earned evenly throughout the year. Both companies declared and paid their dividends on December 31, 19X4. Penn Corporation uses the basic equity method in accounting for its investment in ENC Company.

Required

a. Prepare the elimination entries needed to complete a full consolidation workpaper for 19X4.

b. Prepare a consolidation workpaper for 19X4.

P9-20 Sale of Shares by Subsidiary to Nonaffiliate

Craft Corporation held 80 percent of the outstanding common shares of Delta Corporation on December 31, 19X2. Balance sheets for the two companies on that date were as follows:

Craft Corporation
Balance Sheet
December 31, 19X2

Cash	$ 50,000	Accounts Payable	$ 70,000
Accounts Receivable	90,000	Mortgages Payable	250,000
Inventory	180,000	Common Stock	300,000
Buildings and Equipment	700,000	Additional Paid-In	
Less: Accumulated		Capital	180,000
Depreciation	(200,000)	Retained Earnings	500,000
Investment in			
Delta Corporation	480,000		
	$1,300,000		$1,300,000

Delta Corporation
Balance Sheet
December 31, 19X2

Cash	$ 50,000	Accounts Payable	$ 70,000
Accounts Receivable	120,000	Taxes Payable	80,000
Inventory	200,000	Common Stock	200,000
Buildings and Equipment	600,000	Additional Paid-In	
Less: Accumulated		Capital	50,000
Depreciation	(220,000)	Retained Earnings	350,000
	$750,000		$750,000

On January 1, 19X3, Delta Corporation issued 4,000 additional shares of its $10 par value common stock to Nonaffiliated Corporation for $45 per share. The change in the book value of the Delta Corporation shares held by Craft Corporation was recorded by Craft as an adjustment to its investment in Delta and to its additional paid-in capital.

Required

    a. Give the workpaper elimination entry needed in preparing a consolidated balance sheet as of January 1, 19X3, immediately following the sale of shares by Delta Corporation.

    b. Prepare a consolidated balance sheet workpaper in good form as of the close of business on January 1, 19X3.

    c. Prepare a consolidated balance sheet as of the close of business on January 1, 19X3.

P9-21 Sale of Additional Shares to Parent

    Shady Lane Manufacturing Company holds 75 percent of the common stock of Tin Products Corporation. The balance sheets of the two companies for January 1, 19X9, are as follows:

Shady Lane Manufacturing Company
Balance Sheet
January 1, 19X9

Cash	$ 227,500	Accounts Payable	$ 50,000
Accounts Receivable	60,000	Bonds Payable	400,000
Inventory	100,000	Common Stock	200,000
Buildings and Equipment	600,000	Additional Paid-In	
Less: Accumulated		Capital	50,000
Depreciation	(150,000)	Retained Earnings	400,000
Investment in			
Tin Products	262,500		
	$1,100,000		$1,100,000

Tin Products Corporation
Balance Sheet
January 1, 19X9

Cash	$ 60,000	Accounts Payable	$ 50,000
Accounts Receivable	100,000	Bonds Payable	300,000
Inventory	180,000	Common Stock ($10 par)	100,000
Buildings and Equipment	600,000	Additional Paid-In	
Less: Accumulated		Capital	50,000
Depreciation	(240,000)	Retained Earnings	200,000
	$700,000		$700,000

On January 2, 19X9, Shady Lane purchased an additional 2,500 shares of common stock directly from Tin Products for $150,000. Any purchase differential is assigned to buildings and equipment.

Required

    a. Prepare the eliminating entry or entries needed to complete a consolidated balance sheet workpaper immediately following the issuance of additional shares to Shady Lane.

b. Prepare a consolidated balance sheet workpaper immediately following the issuance of additional shares to Shady Lane.

P9-22 Complex Ownership Structure

First Boston Corporation purchased 80 percent of the common stock of Gulfside Corporation on January 1, 19X5. Gulfside Corporation holds 60 percent of the voting shares of Paddock Company, and Paddock Company owns 10 percent of the stock of First Boston Corporation. All purchases were made at underlying book value. During 19X7, income from the separate operations of First Boston Corporation, Gulfside Corporation, and Paddock Company was $44,000, $34,000, and $50,000, respectively, and dividends of $30,000, $20,000, and $10,000, respectively, were paid. The companies use the cost method of accounting for intercorporate investments and, accordingly, record dividends received as other (nonoperating) income.

Required

Compute the amount of consolidated net income and the income to be assigned to the noncontrolling shareholders of Gulfside Corporation and Paddock Company for 19X7 using (a) the entity approach and (b) the treasury stock approach.

P9-23 Reciprocal Ownership

The following ownership relations exist between Black Corporation and its affiliates:

Owner	Investee	Ownership Percentage	Investor's 19X3 Operating Income
Black Corporation	Red Corporation	80	$66,000
Black Corporation	Green Company	30	66,000
Red Corporation	Green Company	50	35,000
Green Company	Black Corporation	20	50,000

The 19X3 operating income given for each investor excludes income from intercorporate investments. Dividends of $40,000, $15,000 and $20,000, respectively, were paid by Black Corporation, Red Corporation, and Green Company in 19X3. The companies record dividends received as nonoperating income.

Required

Compute consolidated net income for 19X3 and the income to be assigned to the noncontrolling shareholders of Red Corporation and Green Company under (a) the entity approach and (b) the treasury stock method.

CHAPTER 10

ADDITIONAL CONSOLIDATION REPORTING ISSUES

The financial statements of a consolidated entity must be prepared in conformity with generally accepted accounting principles in the same manner as for any individual enterprise. Standards of reporting and presentation are no different for a consolidated entity than for a single-corporate entity. In preparing consolidated statements there are, however, a number of special issues that have not been discussed in earlier chapters. This chapter discusses the following additional consolidation issues:

1. The consolidated statement of cash flows
2. Consolidation following a pooling of interests
3. Consolidation tax considerations
4. Consolidated earnings per share

CONSOLIDATED STATEMENT OF CASH FLOWS

Companies must present a *statement of cash flows* when they issue a complete set of financial statements. The cash flow statement replaces the previously required statement of changes in financial position.

Preparation of a Consolidated Cash Flow Statement

Although a consolidated statement of cash flows normally must be presented whenever consolidated statements are issued, the three-part workpaper typically is not expanded to include such a statement. Instead, a cash flow statement for the consolidated entity is prepared after the other statements are completed. Usually, the consolidated balance sheet, income statement, and retained earnings statement are prepared using the consolidation workpaper, and information from these statements is used in preparing the consolidated statement of cash flows. Unrealized profits on intercompany transfers are eliminated in preparing the consolidated balance sheet and income statement, and therefore no additional action need be taken to eliminate unrealized profits in preparing the workpaper for the consolidated cash flow statement. When net income is used as the starting point for the cash flow statement, all noncash charges, including depreciation and amortization expense resulting from the write-off of a purchase differential, must be added to net income in computing the cash flow derived from operations.

As in the other consolidated financial statements, all transfers between affiliates should be eliminated in preparing the consolidated statement of cash flows. While the sale or purchase of assets is a source or use of cash to an individual company, if such activities occur entirely within the consolidated entity, they should not be included in the statement of cash flows.

Receipts from and payments to noncontrolling shareholders usually are included in the consolidated cash flow statement as cash flows related to financing activities. For example, dividend payments to noncontrolling shareholders normally are included along with dividend payments to parent company shareholders as a use of cash. A sale of additional shares to noncontrolling shareholders or a repurchase of shares from them is considered to be a transaction with a nonaffiliate and is reported as a source or use of cash.

When there is a noncontrolling interest, the income assigned to the noncontrolling stockholders is treated as an adjustment in deriving the amount of cash generated from operating activities. Income assigned to the noncontrolling interest is deducted in computing consolidated net income but does not represent an outflow of cash. Therefore, income assigned to the noncontrolling interest is added back to consolidated net income in the consolidated statement of cash flows to derive the cash flow from operating activities.

Consolidated Cash Flow Statement Illustrated

As an example of the preparation of a consolidated cash flow statement, assume the following:

1. Peerless Products purchases 80 percent of the common stock of Special Foods on December 31, 19X0, for $66,000 above book value.

2. Of the $66,000 differential at acquisition, $8,000 is assigned to land, $48,000 to equipment with a 10-year remaining life, and $10,000 to goodwill with a 20-year expected life.

3. During 19X2, Peerless pays dividends of $60,000; Special Foods reports net income of $75,000 and pays dividends of $40,000.

4. During 19X2, Peerless sells land to a nonaffiliate for $70,000; Peerless had purchased the land in 19X1 for $40,000.

5. Special Foods purchases additional equipment from an unrelated company at the end of 19X2 for $100,000.

Consolidated balance sheets as of December 31, 19X1 and 19X2, are as follows:

	December 31	
	19X1	**19X2**
Cash	$ 269,000	$ 276,000
Accounts Receivable	125,000	230,000
Inventories	175,000	270,000
Land	223,000	183,000
Buildings and Equipment	1,448,000	1,548,000
Goodwill	9,500	9,000
Total Debits	$2,249,500	$2,516,000
Accumulated Depreciation	$ 774,800	$ 849,600
Accounts Payable	200,000	230,000
Bonds Payable	300,000	300,000
Common Stock	500,000	500,000
Retained Earnings	410,700	565,400
Noncontrolling Interest	64,000	71,000
Total Credits	$2,249,500	$2,516,000

Information from the consolidated income statement for 19X2 is as follows:

Sales		$720,000
Gain on Sale of Land		30,000
		$750,000
Less: Cost of Goods Sold	$340,000	
Depreciation Expense	74,800	
Amortization Expense	500	
Other Expenses	105,000	(520,300)
Income Available to All Shareholders		$229,700
Income to Noncontrolling Interest		(15,000)
Consolidated Net Income		$214,700

A workpaper to prepare a consolidated statement of cash flows is presented in Figure 10-1. While a number of different workpaper formats are used in preparing statements of cash flows, the essential workpaper entries can be seen in Figure 10-1. The consolidated statement of cash flows is prepared from the bottom portion of the workpaper.

Peerless's consolidated statement of cash flows for 19X2 is shown in Figure 10-2. The statement is similar to one that would be prepared for a single company. However, two items unique to consolidated statements are included in Figure 10-2. First, income assigned to the noncontrolling interest is added back to cash generated from operating activities because it was subtracted to arrive at consolidated net income but did not reduce the cash generated from operations. Second, dividends paid to noncontrolling shareholders result in an outflow of cash even though they are not shown as dividends declared in the consolidated retained earnings statement. Although not viewed as distributions of consolidated retained

FIGURE 10-1 Workpaper for Peerless Products and subsidiary consolidated statement of cash flows, 19X2.

Item	Balance 1/1/X2	Debits	Credits	Balance 12/31/X2
Cash	269,000	7,000 (a)		276,000
Accounts Receivable	125,000	105,000 (b)		230,000
Inventory	175,000	95,000 (c)		270,000
Land	223,000		40,000 (d)	183,000
Buildings and Equipment	1,448,000	100,000 (e)		1,548,000
Goodwill	9,500		500 (f)	9,000
	2,249,500			2,516,000
Accumulated Depreciation	774,800		74,800 (g)	849,600
Accounts Payable	200,000		30,000 (h)	230,000
Bonds Payable	300,000			300,000
Common Stock	500,000			500,000
Retained Earnings	410,700	60,000 (i)	214,700 (j)	565,400
Noncontrolling Interest	64,000	8,000 (k)	15,000 (l)	71,000
	2,249,500	375,000	375,000	2,516,000
Cash Flows from Operating Activities:				
Net Income		214,700 (j)		
Depreciation Expense		74,800 (g)		
Amortization of Goodwill		500 (f)		
Income to Noncontrolling Interest		15,000 (l)		
Gain on Sale of Land			30,000 (d)	
Increase in Accounts Receivable			105,000 (b)	
Increase in Inventory			95,000 (c)	
Increase in Accounts Payable		30,000 (h)		
Cash Flows from Investing Activities:				
Acquisition of Equipment			100,000 (e)	
Sale of Land		70,000 (d)		
Cash Flows from Financing Activities:				
Dividends to Parent Company Shareholders			60,000 (i)	
Dividends to Noncontrolling Shareholders			8,000 (k)	
Increase in Cash			7,000 (a)	
		405,000	405,000	

(a) Increase in cash balance.
(b) Increase in accounts receivable.
(c) Increase in inventory.
(d) Sale of land.
(e) Purchase of buildings and equipment.
(f) Amortization of goodwill for 19X2.
(g) Depreciation charges for 19X2.
(h) Increase in accounts payable.
(i) Peerless dividends, $60,000.
(j) Consolidated net income, $214,700.
(k) Special Foods' dividends to noncontrolling interest ($40,000 × .20).
(l) Income to noncontrolling interest ($75,000 × .20).

FIGURE 10-2 Consolidated statement of cash flows, 19X2.

Peerless Products Corporation and Subsidiary
Consolidated Statement of Cash Flows
For the Year 19X2

Cash Flows from Operating Activities:		
Consolidated Net Income	$ 214,700	
Noncash Expenses, Revenues, Losses, and Gains Included in Income:		
Depreciation Expense	74,800	
Amortization of Goodwill	500	
Income Assigned to Noncontrolling Interest	15,000	
Gain on Sale of Land	(30,000)	
Increase in Accounts Receivable	(105,000)	
Increase in Inventory	(95,000)	
Increase in Accounts Payable	30,000	
Net Cash Provided by Operating Activities		$105,000
Cash Flows from Investing Activities:		
Acquisition of Equipment	$(100,000)	
Sale of Land	70,000	
Net Cash Used in Investing Activities		(30,000)
Cash Flows from Financing Activities:		
Dividends Paid:		
To Parent Company Shareholders	$ (60,000)	
To Noncontrolling Shareholders	(8,000)	
Net Cash Used in Financing Activities		(68,000)
Net Increase in Cash		$ 7,000

earnings, dividends to the noncontrolling shareholders use cash in reducing the noncontrolling interest.

CONSOLIDATION FOLLOWING A POOLING OF INTERESTS

When two companies combine in a **pooling of interests,** they are viewed as always having been a single company. This is true whether one company acquires the assets and liabilities of another and merges them with its own, or acquires a common stock investment in another company and continues to operate the other company as a separate legal entity.

When consolidated financial statements are prepared for companies that remain as separate legal entities following a pooling of interests, the balances reported should be the same as if the subsidiary had been liquidated at the date of the pooling and its assets and liabilities transferred to the parent company. For the most part, consolidation following a pooling of interests involves bringing together the book values of the assets and liabilities of the parent and subsidiary and eliminating the parent company investment account against the stockholders' equity accounts of the subsidiary.

Carryforward of Account Balances

When a business combination qualifies as a pooling of interests, the consolidation process is simplified. While a new basis of accountability is established in a purchase-type business combination, such is not the case with a pooling; previous book values, rather than current fair values, are carried forward to the combined entity in a pooling of interests.

The acquiring company in a pooling of interests combination records its investment in the acquired company at the book value of the shares acquired. Thus, no differential arises in consolidation, and the problems associated with the assignment of a differential are avoided.

To arrive at the proper consolidated totals, the book values of all assets and liabilities of the combining companies, except for related-company claims, are added across the consolidation workpaper. As in any consolidation, the effects of transactions between affiliates must be eliminated. In a pooling of interests, the companies are viewed as always having been combined. Therefore, the effects of all transactions between affiliates, whether the transactions occurred before or after the combination, must be eliminated when preparing consolidated financial statements following a pooling. When one combining company has recorded a gain or loss on a sale of an item to another combining company and the item still is held by the purchaser, the unrealized profit on the sale must be removed.

Contra accounts reported by the subsidiary at acquisition normally are carried forward in a pooling of interests. For example, the balance in the subsidiary's accumulated depreciation account on the date of combination is combined with that of the parent and carried to the consolidated balance sheet. A subsidiary's treasury stock account, if there is one, normally is the only contra account eliminated in preparing consolidated statements under pooling of interests treatment.

Consolidated Stockholders' Equity after a Pooling of Interests

A business combination treated as a pooling of interests always involves an exchange of common stock for common stock if the combining companies are to remain as separate legal entities. The impact of a pooling on the combined stockholders' equity was discussed in Chapter 1. As illustrated in the first chapter, the credits to the stockholders' equity accounts on the books of the acquiring company on the date of acquisition are the same whether the acquired company is dissolved and the assets are transferred to the acquiring company or the assets and liabilities remain with the acquired company and it is operated as a subsidiary.

When the assets and liabilities are transferred to the acquiring company's books, all assets and equities of the combined enterprise are recorded on the books of a single company and consolidation is not needed. However, when the acquired company is not liquidated, part of the consolidated assets and liabilities are carried on the books of the parent and part on the books of the subsidiary. Consolidated statements are needed to reflect the assets, liabilities, and equity for the enterprise as a whole. When complete ownership of another company is acquired, the consolidated financial statements are identical with the statements that would have been prepared had the two companies merged.

Consolidation at Date of Combination

As an illustration of consolidation following a pooling of interests combination, assume that on December 31, 19X0, Peerless Products Corporation exchanges 12,000 shares of its $10 par common stock for 90 percent of the 10,000 outstanding shares of Special Foods. The combination qualifies as a pooling of interests because Peerless acquires 90 percent of Special Foods' common stock in exchange for its own $10 par common stock (assuming all other pooling conditions are met). At the time of the combination, Special Foods' stockholders' equity accounts are as follows:

Common Stock	$200,000
Retained Earnings	100,000
Total Stockholders' Equity	$300,000

Peerless records the acquisition with the following entry:

December 31, 19X0:		
(1) Investment in Special Foods Stock	270,000	
Common Stock		120,000
Additional Paid-In Capital		60,000
Retained Earnings		90,000

    Record acquisition of Special Foods stock:
    $270,000 = $300,000 × .90
    $120,000 = $10 × 12,000 shares
    $60,000 = ($200,000 × .90) − $120,000
    $90,000 = $100,000 × .90

The investment is recorded at $270,000, Peerless's 90 percent share of Special Foods' $300,000 book value. Additional paid-in capital is recorded for the $60,000 difference between the $180,000 par value of Special Foods' shares acquired ($200,000 × .90) and the $120,000 par value of Peerless's shares issued in the exchange. A proportionate share of Special Foods' retained earnings ($100,000 × .90) is recorded by Peerless on the date of combination.

A workpaper to prepare a consolidated balance sheet immediately after the pooling of interests is shown in Figure 10-3. A single eliminating entry is needed:

E(2) Common Stock—Special Foods	200,000	
Retained Earnings	100,000	
Investment in Special Foods Stock		270,000
Noncontrolling Interest		30,000
Eliminate investment balance.		

FIGURE 10-3 December 31, 19X0, workpaper for consolidated balance sheet, date of combination; 90 percent, pooling of interests.

Item	Peerless Products	Special Foods	Eliminations Debit	Eliminations Credit	Consolidated
Cash	350,000	50,000			400,000
Accounts Receivable	75,000	50,000			125,000
Inventory	100,000	60,000			160,000
Land	175,000	40,000			215,000
Buildings and Equipment	800,000	600,000			1,400,000
Investment in Special Foods Stock	270,000			(2) 270,000	
Total Debits	1,770,000	800,000			2,300,000
Accumulated Depreciation	400,000	300,000			700,000
Accounts Payable	100,000	100,000			200,000
Bonds Payable	200,000	100,000			300,000
Common Stock	620,000	200,000	(2) 200,000		620,000
Additional Paid-In Capital	60,000				60,000
Retained Earnings	390,000	100,000	(2) 100,000		390,000
Noncontrolling Interest				(2) 30,000	30,000
Total Credits	1,770,000	800,000	300,000	300,000	2,300,000

Elimination entry:
  (2) Eliminate investment balance.

As in workpapers illustrated previously, the stockholders' equity balances of the subsidiary are eliminated and those of the parent are carried to the consolidated balance sheet. Unlike the purchase situation, no differential is created, and none of the assets or liabilities are revalued.

Note that although the subsidiary's retained earnings balance is eliminated, the parent company's retained earnings includes the parent's share of the subsidiary's retained earnings. The parent's entry (1) recording its share of subsidiary retained earnings on the date of the combination results in the same retained earnings balance that would have been reported if the companies had always been together. Therefore, parent company retained earnings is equal to consolidated retained earnings, and the full amount of subsidiary retained earnings is eliminated. The noncontrolling shareholders' claim following a pooling is computed in the same way as following a purchase.

Consolidation Subsequent to Date of Combination

Entries recorded by the parent company to account for its investment in Special Foods during 19X1 are the same as under purchase accounting, with the exception that there is no purchase differential and, consequently, no additional depreciation or amortization to be recognized. Unrealized profits on intercompany transfers are eliminated in the same way under both purchase and pooling of interests accounting.

As an illustration of the preparation of a three-part consolidation workpaper for a period following a pooling of interests combination, assume the following additional information with respect to Peerless and Special Foods:

1. Special Foods reports net income of $50,000 for 19X1 and declares dividends of $30,000.

2. During 19X1, Peerless sells inventory that it purchased for $7,000 to Special Foods for $10,000. Special Foods still holds all the inventory at the end of the year.

Peerless recognizes 19X1 income from Special Foods of $45,000 ($50,000 × .90) under the basic equity method. The balance in Peerless's investment account at the end of 19X1 is computed as follows:

Original amount recorded	$270,000
Income from subsidiary	45,000
Peerless's share of subsidiary dividends	
($30,000 × .90)	(27,000)
Balance of investment, December 31, 19X1	$288,000

The workpaper to prepare consolidated financial statements for 19X1 is shown in Figure 10-4. The following elimination entries are needed in the workpaper:

E(3)	Income from Subsidiary	45,000	
	Dividends Declared		27,000
	Investment in Special Foods Stock		18,000
	Eliminate income from subsidiary.		
E(4)	Income to Noncontrolling Interest	5,000	
	Dividends Declared		3,000
	Noncontrolling Interest		2,000
	Assign income to noncontrolling interest:		
	$5,000 = $50,000 × .10		
	$3,000 = $30,000 × .10		
E(5)	Common Stock—Special Foods	200,000	
	Retained Earnings, January 1	100,000	
	Investment in Special Foods Stock		270,000
	Noncontrolling Interest		30,000
	Eliminate beginning investment balance.		
E(6)	Sales	10,000	
	Cost of Goods Sold		7,000
	Inventory		3,000
	Eliminate intercompany downstream sale of inventory.		

Other than those differences arising because of the initial recording of the business combination, the consolidation procedures are the same whether the combination is treated as a purchase or a pooling of interests.

FIGURE 10-4 December 31, 19X1, consolidation workpaper, first year following combination; 90 percent, pooling of interests.

Item	Peerless Products	Special Foods	Eliminations Debit	Eliminations Credit	Consolidated
Sales	400,000	200,000	(6) 10,000		590,000
Income from Subsidiary	45,000		(3) 45,000		
Credits	445,000	200,000			590,000
Cost of Goods Sold	170,000	115,000		(6) 7,000	278,000
Depreciation and Amortization	50,000	20,000			70,000
Other Expenses	40,000	15,000			55,000
Debits	(260,000)	(150,000)			(403,000)
					187,000
Income to Noncontrolling Interest			(4) 5,000		(5,000)
Net Income, carry forward	185,000	50,000	60,000	7,000	182,000
Retained Earnings, January 1	390,000	100,000	(5) 100,000		390,000
Net Income, from above	185,000	50,000	60,000	7,000	182,000
	575,000	150,000			572,000
Dividends Declared	(60,000)	(30,000)		(3) 27,000	
				(4) 3,000	(60,000)
Retained Earnings, December 31, carry forward	515,000	120,000	160,000	37,000	512,000
Cash	507,000	75,000			582,000
Accounts Receivable	75,000	50,000			125,000
Inventory	100,000	75,000		(6) 3,000	172,000
Land	175,000	40,000			215,000
Buildings and Equipment	800,000	600,000			1,400,000
Investment in Special Foods Stock	288,000			(3) 18,000	
				(5) 270,000	
Debits	1,945,000	840,000			2,494,000
Accumulated Depreciation	450,000	320,000			770,000
Accounts Payable	100,000	100,000			200,000
Bonds Payable	200,000	100,000			300,000
Common Stock	620,000	200,000	(5) 200,000		620,000
Additional Paid-In Capital	60,000				60,000
Retained Earnings, from above	515,000	120,000	160,000	37,000	512,000
Noncontrolling Interest				(4) 2,000	
				(5) 30,000	32,000
Credits	1,945,000	840,000	360,000	360,000	2,494,000

Elimination entries:
(3) Eliminate income from subsidiary.
(4) Assign income to noncontrolling interest.
(5) Eliminate beginning investment balance.
(6) Eliminate intercompany downstream sale of inventory.

Consolidation following an Interim Acquisition

Business combinations usually occur during an accounting period rather than at the beginning or end of the period. When the combination is treated as a pooling of interests, the consolidated financial statements appear as if the companies always have been a single company, regardless of when the combination actually occurs.

In the year of a purchase-type business combination, the parent records its share of the subsidiary's income and dividends from the date of combination to the end of the year. Under pooling accounting, however, the parent records income and dividends from the subsidiary for the entire period as if the companies had always been together.

To examine a midyear acquisition under pooling of interests accounting, assume that the combination of Peerless Products and Special Foods occurs on September 1, 19X1. Special Foods reports income and dividends for 19X1 as follows:

	Before Combination (January 1–August 31)	After Combination (September 1–December 31)
Net Income	$35,000	$15,000
Dividends	25,000	5,000

All other conditions are identical with those illustrated in Figure 10-4. Peerless records the pooling with the following entry:

```
September 1, 19X1
  (7)   Investment in Special Foods Stock            270,000
              Common Stock                                      120,000
              Additional Paid-In Capital                         60,000
              Retained Earnings                                  90,000
         Record acquisition of Special Foods stock.
```

Although the combination occurred on September 1, entry (7) records the pooling as though it occurred on the first day of 19X1 and, therefore, is identical to entry (1). The $270,000 initial balance recorded in the investment account equals the book value at the beginning of the period ($300,000 × .90) of the shares acquired.

At the date of combination, Peerless also must record an adjustment for the preacquisition dividend paid by Special Foods. Because a pooling is recorded on a retroactive basis and 90 percent of Special Foods' pre-pooling dividend was paid to stockholders who subsequently became stockholders of Peerless through the pooling, Peerless records its proportionate amount of the dividend ($25,000 × .90) as if it declared the dividend. At the same time, Peerless must reduce the recorded amount of the investment account to reflect the reduction in Special Foods' net assets due to the dividend. The effect is the same as if Special Foods had transferred assets to Peerless and Peerless then had declared a dividend payable to those stockholders who previously had held shares of Special Foods. The dividend is recorded and the investment account adjusted with the following entry:

```
September 1, 19X1
   (8)  Dividends Declared                              22,500
            Investment in Special Foods Stock                      22,500
            Record proportionate amount of subsidiary's
            preacquisition dividends: $25,000 × .90
```

Dividends received by Peerless from Special Foods subsequent to the combination are recorded in the normal manner:

```
   (9)  Cash                                            4,500
            Investment in Special Foods Stock                       4,500
            Record dividends from Special Foods:
            $5,000 × .90
```

At the end of 19X1, Peerless records its share of Special Foods' net income. Because under pooling accounting the two companies are viewed as always having been combined, Peerless recognizes its 90 percent share of Special Foods' $50,000 net income for the entire year rather than just from the date of acquisition:

```
  (10)  Investment in Special Foods Stock               45,000
            Income from Subsidiary                                 45,000
            Record equity-method income:
            $50,000 × .90
```

Peerless's Investment in Special Foods Stock account appears as follows at the end of 19X1:

Investment in Special Foods Stock

(7) Original amount	270,000	(8) 19X1 dividends before combination		
(10) 19X1 equity accrual ($50,000 × .90)	45,000	($25,000 × .90)	22,500	
		(9) 19X1 dividends after combination		
		($5,000 × .90)	4,500	
Balance, 12/31/X1	288,000			

Figure 10-5 shows a consolidation workpaper for Peerless Products and Special Foods on December 31, 19X1. The eliminating entries included in the workpaper following a midyear combination are identical to those used in preparing the workpaper in Figure 10-4 following a beginning-of-year combination. The only differences in the two workpapers involve Special Foods' dividends. In Figure 10-5, the dividends Special Foods paid before acquisition are viewed as being paid

FIGURE 10-5 December 31, 19X1, consolidation workpaper, year of combination; 90 percent, pooling of interests; interim acquisition.

Item	Peerless Products	Special Foods	Eliminations		Consolidated
			Debit	**Credit**	
Sales	400,000	200,000	(6) 10,000		590,000
Income from Subsidiary	45,000		(3) 45,000		
Credits	445,000	200,000			590,000
Cost of Goods Sold	170,000	115,000		(6) 7,000	278,000
Depreciation and Amortization	50,000	20,000			70,000
Other Expenses	40,000	15,000			55,000
Debits	(260,000)	(150,000)			(403,000)
					187,000
Income to Noncontrolling Interest			(4) 5,000		(5,000)
Net Income, carry forward	185,000	50,000	60,000	7,000	182,000
Retained Earnings, January 1	390,000	100,000	(5) 100,000		390,000
Net Income, from above	185,000	50,000	60,000	7,000	182,000
	575,000	150,000			572,000
Dividends Declared	(82,500)	(30,000)		(3) 27,000	
				(4) 3,000	(82,500)
Retained Earnings, December 31, carry forward	492,500	120,000	160,000	37,000	489,500
Cash	484,500	75,000			559,500
Accounts Receivable	75,000	50,000			125,000
Inventory	100,000	75,000		(6) 3,000	172,000
Land	175,000	40,000			215,000
Buildings and Equipment	800,000	600,000			1,400,000
Investment in Special Foods Stock	288,000			(3) 18,000	
				(5) 270,000	
Debits	1,922,500	840,000			2,471,500
Accumulated Depreciation	450,000	320,000			770,000
Accounts Payable	100,000	100,000			200,000
Bonds Payable	200,000	100,000			300,000
Common Stock	620,000	200,000	(5) 200,000		620,000
Additional Paid-In Capital	60,000				60,000
Retained Earnings, from above	492,500	120,000	160,000	37,000	489,500
Noncontrolling Interest				(4) 2,000	
				(5) 30,000	32,000
Credits	1,922,500	840,000	360,000	360,000	2,471,500

Elimination entries:
  (3) Eliminate income from subsidiary.
  (4) Assign income to noncontrolling interest.
  (5) Eliminate beginning investment balance.
  (6) Eliminate intercompany downstream sale of inventory.

to shareholders of Peerless rather than to Peerless; consequently, the consolidated statements show higher dividends declared, lower ending retained earnings, and less cash than in Figure 10-4.

CONSOLIDATION INCOME TAX ISSUES

A parent company and its subsidiaries may file a *consolidated income tax return,* or they may choose to file separate returns. For a subsidiary to be eligible to be included in a consolidated tax return, at least 80 percent of its stock must be held by companies included in the consolidated return.

A major advantage of filing a consolidated return is the ability to offset the losses of one company against the profits of another. In addition, dividends and other transfers between the affiliated companies are tax-exempt. Thus, tax payments on profits from intercompany transfers can be delayed until the intercompany profits are realized through transactions with nonaffiliates. When separate returns are filed, the selling company is required to pay tax on intercompany profits it has recognized, whether or not the profits are realized from a consolidated viewpoint. Filing a consolidated return also may make it possible to avoid limits on the use of certain items such as foreign tax credits and charitable contributions.

An election to file a consolidated income tax return carries with it some limitations. Once an election is made to include a subsidiary in the consolidated return, the company cannot file separate tax returns in the future unless it receives approval from the Internal Revenue Service. The subsidiary's tax year also must be brought into conformity with the parent's tax year. In addition, preparing a consolidated tax return can become quite difficult when numerous companies are involved and complex ownership arrangements exist between the companies.

The income tax aspects associated with equity-method reporting for unconsolidated investees were discussed in Chapter 2. Two additional income tax considerations are discussed in this chapter, both relating to consolidation:

1. Allocation of income tax amounts from a consolidated tax return to the individual companies
2. The tax effects of unrealized intercompany profit eliminations

Allocating Tax Expense when a Consolidated Return Is Filed

A consolidated tax return portrays the companies included in the return as if they actually were a single legal entity. All intercorporate transfers of goods and services and intercompany dividends are eliminated and a single income tax figure is assessed when a consolidated return is prepared.

Consolidated companies sometimes need to prepare separate financial statements for noncontrolling shareholders and creditors. Because only a single income tax amount is determined for the consolidated entity when a consolidated tax return is filed, income tax expense must be assigned to the individual companies included in the return in some manner. The way in which the consolidated income tax amount is allocated to the individual companies can affect the amounts reported in the income statements of both the separate companies and the consolidated entity. When a subsidiary is less than 100 percent owned by the parent, income tax expense assigned to the subsidiary reduces proportionately the income assigned to the parent and the noncontrolling interest. Therefore, as a larger part of the tax expense is assigned to such a subsidiary, the income to noncontrolling interest becomes smaller and consolidated net income becomes greater.

While no authoritative pronouncements specify the assignment of consolidated income tax expense to the individual companies included in the consolidated tax return, a reasonable approach is to allocate consolidated income tax expense among the companies on the basis of their relative contributions to income before taxes. As an example, assume that Peerless Products owns 80 percent of the stock of Special Foods, purchased at book value, and the two companies elect to file a consolidated tax return for 19X1. Peerless Products reports operating earnings before taxes of $140,000, excluding income from Special Foods, and Special Foods reports income before taxes of $50,000. If there is a 40 percent corporate tax rate, consolidated income taxes are $76,000 ($190,000 × .40). Tax expense of $56,000 is assigned to Peerless Products, and $20,000 is assigned to Special Foods, determined as follows:

Peerless Products:	($140,000/$190,000) × $76,000 =	$56,000
Special Foods:	($50,000/$190,000) × $76,000 =	20,000
Consolidated tax expense		$76,000

The consolidated income statement for 19X1 shows the following totals:

Consolidated Operating Income	$190,000
Less: Income Tax Expense	(76,000)
Income Available to All Shareholders	$114,000
Less: Income Assigned to Noncontrolling Interest	(6,000)
Consolidated Net Income	$108,000

Income assigned to the noncontrolling interest is computed as follows:

Special Foods' income before tax	$50,000
Income tax expense assigned to Special Foods	(20,000)
Special Foods' net income	$30,000
Noncontrolling stockholders' proportionate share	× .20
Income assigned to noncontrolling interest	$ 6,000

Other allocation bases may be preferred when affiliates have significantly different tax characteristics, such as when only one of the companies qualifies for special tax exemptions or credits.

Tax Effects of Unrealized Intercompany Profit Eliminations

The income tax effects of unrealized intercompany profit eliminations depend on whether the companies within the consolidated entity file a consolidated tax return or separate tax returns.

Unrealized Profits when a Consolidated Return Is Filed   Intercompany transfers are eliminated in computing both consolidated net income and taxable income when a consolidated tax return is filed. Only sales outside the consolidated entity are recognized, both for tax and for financial reporting purposes. Because profits are taxed in the same period they are recognized for financial reporting purposes, no *temporary differences* arise and no additional tax accruals are needed in preparing the consolidated financial statements.

Unrealized Profits when Separate Returns Are Filed   When the companies within a consolidated entity each file separate income tax returns, they are taxed individually on the profits from intercompany sales. The focus in separate tax returns is on the transactions of the separate companies, and no consideration is given to whether the intercompany profits are realized from a consolidated viewpoint. Thus, the profit from an intercompany sale is taxed when the intercompany transfer occurs, without waiting for confirmation through sale to a nonaffiliate. For consolidated financial reporting purposes, however, unrealized intercompany profits must be eliminated. While the separate company may pay income taxes on the unrealized intercompany profit, the tax expense must be eliminated when the unrealized intercompany profit is eliminated in the preparation of consolidated financial statements. This difference in the timing of the income tax expense recognition results in the recording of *deferred income taxes.*

For example, if Special Foods sells inventory costing $23,000 to Peerless Products for $28,000, and none is resold before year-end, the entry to eliminate the intercorporate transfer when consolidated statements are prepared is:

E(11)	Sales	28,000	
	Cost of Goods Sold		23,000
	Inventory		5,000
	Eliminate intercompany upstream		
	sale of inventory.		

Income assigned to the shareholders of Special Foods is reduced by $5,000 as a result of entry E(11). An adjustment to tax expense also is required in preparing consolidated statements if Special Foods files a separate tax return. With a 40 percent corporate income tax rate, eliminating entry E(12) adjusts income tax expense of the consolidated entity downward by $2,000 ($5,000 × .40) to reflect the reduction of reported profits:

E(12)	Deferred Tax Asset	2,000	
	Income Tax Expense		2,000
	Eliminate tax expense on unrealized intercompany profit.		

The debit to the deferred tax asset in entry E(12) reflects the tax effect of a temporary difference between the income reported in the consolidated income statement and that reported in the separate tax returns of the companies within the consolidated entity. Consistent with the treatment accorded other temporary differences, this tax effect normally is carried to the consolidated balance sheet as an asset. If the intercompany profit is expected to be recognized in the consolidated income statement in the next year, the deferred taxes are classified as current.

Unrealized Profit in Separate Tax Return Illustrated   Figure 10-6 illustrates the workpaper used to prepare consolidated financial statements when income taxes are included and Peerless and Special Foods file separate tax returns. The illustration is based on the following information:

1. Peerless owns 80 percent of the common stock of Special Foods, purchased at book value.

2. During 19X1, Special Foods purchases inventory for $23,000 and sells it to Peerless for $28,000. Peerless continues to hold all the inventory at the end of 19X1.

3. The effective combined federal and state tax rate for both Peerless and Special Foods is 40 percent.

While the trial balance of Special Foods includes $50,000 of income before taxes and tax expense of $20,000 ($50,000 $\times$ .40), consolidated net income and income assigned to noncontrolling shareholders are based on realized net income of $27,000, computed as follows:

Special Foods' net income	$30,000
Add back income tax expense	20,000
Special Foods' income before taxes	$50,000
Unrealized profit on upstream sale	(5,000)
Special Foods' realized income before taxes	$45,000
Income taxes on realized income (40%)	(18,000)
Special Foods' realized net income	$27,000
Special Foods' realized net income assigned to:	
Controlling interest ($27,000 $\times$ .80)	$21,600
Noncontrolling interest ($27,000 $\times$ .20)	5,400
Special Foods' realized net income	$27,000

FIGURE 10-6 December 31, 19X1, consolidation workpaper; deferred income tax illustration.

Item	Peerless Products	Special Foods	Debit		Credit		Consolidated
			Eliminations				
Sales	400,000	200,000	(16)	28,000			572,000
Income from Subsidiary	24,000		(13)	24,000			
Credits	424,000	200,000					572,000
Cost of Goods Sold	170,000	115,000			(16)	23,000	262,000
Depreciation and Amortization	50,000	20,000					70,000
Other Expenses	40,000	15,000					55,000
Income Tax Expense	57,920 *a*	20,000			(17)	2,000	75,920
Debits	(317,920)	(170,000)					(462,920)
							109,080
Income to Noncontrolling Interest			(14)	5,400			(5,400)
Net Income, carry forward	106,080	30,000		57,400		25,000	103,680
Retained Earnings, January 1	300,000	100,000	(15)	100,000			300,000
Net Income, from above	106,080	30,000		57,400		25,000	103,680
	406,080	130,000					403,680
	(60,000)	(30,000)			(13)	24,000	
					(14)	6,000	(60,000)
Retained Earnings, December 31, carry forward	346,080	100,000		157,400		55,000	343,680
Cash	206,080	55,000					261,080
Accounts Receivable	75,000	50,000					125,000
Inventory	100,000	75,000			(16)	5,000	170,000
Deferred Tax Asset			(17)	2,000			2,000
Land	175,000	40,000					215,000
Buildings and Equipment	800,000	600,000					1,400,000
Investment in Special Foods Stock	240,000				(15)	240,000	
Debits	1,596,080	820,000					2,173,080
Accumulated Depreciation	450,000	320,000					770,000
Accounts Payable	100,000	100,000					200,000
Bonds Payable	200,000	100,000					300,000
Common Stock	500,000	200,000	(15)	200,000			500,000
Retained Earnings, from above	346,080	100,000		157,400		55,000	343,680
Noncontrolling Interest			(14)	600	(15)	60,000	59,400
Credits	1,596,080	820,000		360,000		360,000	2,173,080

a [$424,000 − $260,000 − ($24,000 × .80 dividend deduction)] × .40

Elimination entries:
(13) Eliminate income from subsidiary.
(14) Assign income to noncontrolling interest.
(15) Eliminate beginning investment balance.
(16) Eliminate intercompany upstream sale of inventory.
(17) Eliminate tax expense on unrealized intercompany profit.

If Peerless accounts for its investment in Special Foods using the basic equity method, the eliminating entries needed for the preparation of a consolidation workpaper as of December 31, 19X1, are as follows:

E(13)	Income from Subsidiary	24,000	
	Dividends Declared		24,000
	Eliminate income from subsidiary:		
	$30,000 × .80		
E(14)	Income to Noncontrolling Interest	5,400	
	Noncontrolling Interest	600	
	Dividends Declared		6,000
	Assign income to noncontrolling interest:		
	$5,400 = $27,000 × .20		
	$600 = $6,000 − $5,400		
	$6,000 = $30,000 × .20		
E(15)	Common Stock—Special Foods	200,000	
	Retained Earnings, January 1	100,000	
	Investment in Special Foods Stock		240,000
	Noncontrolling Interest		60,000
	Eliminate beginning investment balance.		
E(16)	Sales	28,000	
	Cost of Goods Sold		23,000
	Inventory		5,000
	Eliminate intercompany upstream sale		
	of inventory.		
E(17)	Deferred Tax Asset	2,000	
	Income Tax Expense		2,000
	Eliminate tax expense on unrealized		
	intercompany profit: $5,000 × .40		

Entries E(13), E(14), and E(15) are the normal entries to eliminate the dividends declared and beginning stockholders' equity accounts of the subsidiary, the investment account of the parent, and income from the subsidiary recognized by the parent, and to establish the noncontrolling interest. As can be seen from entry E(13), Special Foods distributed its entire 19X1 reported net income as dividends. Thus, the balance of the investment account remains at the original cost. Because the realized net income of Special Foods ($27,000) was less than dividends paid ($30,000), entry E(14) contains a debit to noncontrolling interest indicating a reduction in the claim of the noncontrolling shareholders during the period. Entries E(16) and E(17) eliminate the effects of the intercompany transaction, establish the tax effects of the temporary difference, and reduce consolidated net income by the unrealized intercompany profit net of taxes.

Another temporary difference normally would be included in the consolidated balance sheet and in the computation of consolidated income tax expense. In addition to temporary differences arising from unrealized profits, there normally are differences between subsidiary net income and dividend distributions. Peerless pays income taxes for the period based on its reported dividends from Special Foods but includes in consolidated net income for financial reporting its proportionate share of Special Foods' realized net income. This difference between the amount of income reported in the consolidated income statement and the amount reported in the tax return is considered a temporary difference, and deferred taxes normally must be recognized on this difference. In this example, Special Foods distributes all its income as dividends, and the only temporary difference relates to the unrealized intercompany profit.

Subsequent Profit Realization when Separate Returns Are Filed   When unrealized intercompany profits at the end of one period subsequently are recognized in another period, the tax effects of the temporary difference must again be considered.

If income taxes were ignored, eliminating entry E(18) would be used in preparing consolidated statements as of December 31, 19X2, assuming Special Foods had $5,000 of unrealized inventory profit on its books on January 1, 19X2, and the inventory was resold in 19X2:

E(18)	Retained Earnings, January 1	4,000	
	Noncontrolling Interest	1,000	
	Cost of Goods Sold		5,000
	Eliminate beginning inventory profit.		

On the other hand, if the 40 percent tax rate is considered, eliminating entry E(19) is used in place of entry E(18):

E(19)	Retained Earnings, January 1	2,400	
	Noncontrolling Interest	600	
	Income Tax Expense	2,000	
	Cost of Goods Sold		5,000
	Eliminate beginning inventory profit:		
	$2,400 = ($5,000 − $2,000) × .80		
	$600 = ($5,000 − $2,000) × .20		
	$2,000 = $5,000 × .40		

Unrealized profit of $3,000 rather than $5,000 is apportioned between the controlling and noncontrolling shareholders in this case. Tax expense of $2,000 is recognized for financial reporting purposes in 19X2 even though the $5,000 of intercompany profit was reported on Special Foods' separate tax return and the $2,000 of taxes was paid on the profit in 19X1. Entry E(19) recognizes the tax expense in the consolidated income statement in the same year as the income is recognized from a consolidated viewpoint.

Note that no workpaper adjustment to the Deferred Tax Asset account is needed at the end of 19X2. Because the deferred tax asset was entered only in the consolidation workpaper at the end of 19X1 and not on the books of either company, it does not carry over to 19X2. It is not reestablished in the 19X2 workpaper because the temporary difference has completely reversed by the end of 19X2.

CONSOLIDATED EARNINGS PER SHARE

The procedures for computing earnings per share (EPS) are prescribed in **APB Opinion No. 15,** "Earnings per Share" (APB 15). In general, *consolidated earnings per share* is calculated in the same way as earnings per share for a single corporation. The numerator of the EPS computation is based on income available to common shareholders and common shareholder equivalents. The denominator includes shares actually outstanding and, when appropriate, the additional shares that would be issued if convertible securities were converted and existing rights, warrants, and options were exercised.

Consolidated net income normally is the starting point in the computation of consolidated EPS and is adjusted for items that are treated differently in computing consolidated net income and consolidated EPS. Because there may be different assumptions underlying the computation of reported net income and EPS, a subsidiary's contribution to consolidated EPS may not be the same as its contribution to consolidated net income. Both the percentage of ownership held within the consolidated entity and the total amount of subsidiary income available to common shareholders may be different. In the computation of EPS, the parent's percentage of ownership frequently is changed when a subsidiary's convertible bonds and preferred stock are treated as common stock and its options and warrants are treated as if they had been exercised. In addition, income available to common shareholders of the subsidiary changes when bonds and preferred stock are treated as common stock for purposes of computing EPS. Interest expense or preferred dividends, if already deducted, must be added back in computing income available to common shareholders when the securities are considered to be common stock.

Computation of Consolidated Earnings per Share

The following formulation can be used in computing consolidated EPS:

$$
\text{Consolidated EPS} = \frac{
\begin{array}{c}
\text{consol-} \\
\text{idated} \\
\text{net} \\
\text{income}
\end{array}
\genfrac{}{}{0pt}{}{+}{-}
\begin{array}{c}
\text{adjustment} \\
\text{for parent} \\
\text{securities}
\end{array}
-
\left(
\begin{array}{c}
\text{percent} \\
\text{ownership} \\
\text{held by} \\
\text{parent}
\end{array}
\times
\begin{array}{c}
\text{income} \\
\text{available} \\
\text{to common} \\
\text{shareholders} \\
\text{of subsidiary}
\end{array}
\right)
+
\left(
\begin{array}{c}
\text{shares} \\
\text{held} \\
\text{by} \\
\text{parent}
\end{array}
\times
\begin{array}{c}
\text{subsid-} \\
\text{iary} \\
\text{EPS}
\end{array}
\right)
}{
\begin{array}{c}
\text{weighted average of} \\
\text{parent company shares} \\
\text{outstanding}
\end{array}
\quad + \quad
\begin{array}{c}
\text{shares of parent to be issued} \\
\text{if dilutive securities are} \\
\text{converted and options exercised}
\end{array}
}
$$

This formula shows the adjustments to consolidated net income and to common shares outstanding needed in computing consolidated EPS. In general, securities of the parent company that are convertible or exercisable into parent company shares must be included as shares outstanding if they are dilutive. When convertible bonds are treated as common stock and the additional shares are added in the denominator, the after-tax interest savings must be added back into the numerator. Dividends on preferred stock that continues to be classified as preferred stock are deducted from the numerator, while no deduction is made for dividends on preferred stock considered to be common stock.

The two other adjustments in the numerator relate to the amount of subsidiary income to be included in computing consolidated EPS. First, the parent's portion of the income of the subsidiary available to common shareholders is deducted so that an adjusted income number can be substituted. The amount deducted from consolidated net income is computed by multiplying the parent's ownership percentage of subsidiary common shares outstanding times the income of the subsidiary after preferred dividends have been deducted. The subsidiary's contribution to consolidated EPS is determined by multiplying the number of shares of the subsidiary that are held by the parent and other affiliates (or that would be held after exercise or conversion of other subsidiary securities held) times the EPS computed for the subsidiary. In this way, the effect of the subsidiary's dilutive securities is considered in computing consolidated EPS.

No additional adjustments need be made for unrealized intercompany profits or amortization of differential. Such adjustments already are included, if appropriate, in the computation of consolidated net income, the first term in the numerator.

Occasionally a subsidiary is permitted to issue rights, warrants, or options to purchase the common stock of the parent or to issue a security convertible into common stock of the parent. Such rights, warrants, and options of the subsidiary are treated in the same way as if the parent had issued them.

Subsidiary bonds or preferred stock convertible into the parent's common stock are treated in a slightly different manner. If the securities are treated as if converted, income available to common shareholders of the subsidiary is increased as a result of the reduction in interest expense, net of tax, or preferred dividends. The parent's portion of the earnings increase is included in the consolidated EPS computation through the subsidiary EPS component. The number of parent company shares into which the security is convertible is added to the denominator of the consolidated EPS computation.

Computation of Consolidated Earnings per Share Illustrated

As an illustration of the computation of consolidated earnings per share for Peerless Products and Special Foods, assume the following:

1. Peerless Products purchases 80 percent of the stock of Special Foods on December 31, 19X0, at book value.

2. Both Special Foods and Peerless Products have effective income tax rates of 40 percent and file a consolidated tax return.

3. Special Foods has 19X1 income before taxes of $50,000, an allocated share of consolidated income taxes of $20,000, and net income of $30,000.

4. Consolidated net income for 19X1 is $108,000, computed as follows:

Peerless's separate operating income	$140,000
Special Foods' income before taxes	50,000
Total entity income before taxes	$190,000
Consolidated income taxes (40%)	(76,000)
Total entity income after taxes	$114,000
Less: Income to noncontrolling shareholders	
($30,000 × .20)	(6,000)
Consolidated net income	$108,000

5. Peerless's capital structure consists of 100,000 shares of $5 par value common stock and 10,000 shares of $10 par, 10 percent convertible preferred stock. The preferred stock, which is convertible into 25,000 shares of Peerless's common, is not a common stock equivalent.

6. Special Foods has 20,000 shares of $10 par value common stock and $100,000 of 6 percent convertible bonds outstanding. The bonds, issued at par, are convertible into 4,000 shares of Special Foods' common stock and are common stock equivalents.

7. On January 1, 19X1, Special Foods grants its officers options to purchase 9,000 shares of common stock of Peerless Products at $26 per share at any time during the 5 years following the date of the grant. None are exercised during 19X1. The average market price of Peerless's common stock during 19X1 is $29 per share, and the closing price on December 31, 19X1, is $30 per share.

Special Foods' Earnings per Share   Before consolidated EPS can be calculated, the EPS totals for each subsidiary must be computed. Primary and fully diluted EPS for Special Foods are the same for 19X1 because the only potentially dilutive securities that Special Foods has outstanding are the convertible bonds. The bonds are dilutive common stock equivalents and therefore are treated as converted for both primary and fully diluted EPS.

Special Foods' EPS for 19X1 is $1.40, computed as follows:

Special Foods' net income	$30,000
Interest effect of assumed conversion of bonds,	
net of taxes ($100,000 × .06) × (1 − .40)	3,600
Income accruing to common shares and equivalents	$33,600
Weighted-average common shares outstanding in 19X1	20,000
Additional shares from assumed bond conversion	4,000
Weighted-average shares and share equivalents	24,000
Earnings per share: $33,600/24,000 shares	$1.40

The assumed conversion of the bonds reduces Special Foods' EPS from $1.50 ($30,000/20,000 shares) to $1.40.

Consolidated Earnings per Share   Consolidated earnings per share for 19X1 is $.96 based on common stock and common stock equivalents, and $.84 assuming full dilution. The computations are shown in Figure 10-7 and are based on the formula presented earlier.

In the numerator, consolidated net income of $108,000 is reduced by Peerless's $24,000 share ($30,000 × .80) of Special Foods' net income. Special Foods' $22,400 contribution ($1.40 × 16,000 shares) to consolidated earnings per share then is added back. The amount of subsidiary earnings added back into the numerator also can be computed by multiplying the revised ownership ratio times the revised earnings contribution. Earnings available to Special Foods' common

FIGURE 10-7 Computation of Peerless Products and subsidiary consolidated earnings per share for 19X1.

	Primary Earnings per Share	Fully Diluted Earnings per Share
Numerator:		
Consolidated net income	$108,000	$108,000
Less: Peerless's share of Special Foods' net income ($30,000 × .80)	(24,000)	(24,000)
Add: Peerless's share of Special Foods' income based on EPS ($1.40 × 16,000 shares)	22,400	22,400
Less: Preferred dividends	(10,000)	
Total	$ 96,400	$106,400
Denominator:		
Weighted-average shares outstanding	100,000	100,000
Assumed exercise of stock options[a]	931	1,200
Preferred stock assumed converted		25,000
Total	100,931	126,200
Earnings per Share:		
$96,400/100,931 shares	$.96	
$106,400/126,200 shares		$.84

[a] Treasury stock method of assuming exercise of stock options:

	Primary	Fully Diluted
Proceeds from issue of shares:		
9,000 shares × $26	$234,000	$234,000
Shares repurchased:		
$234,000 ÷ $29 average price	8,069	
$234,000 ÷ $30 ending price		7,800
Increase in shares outstanding:		
9,000 − 8,069	931	
9,000 − 7,800		1,200

shareholders increases to $33,600 ($30,000 + $3,600) with the assumed bond conversion, and shares outstanding increases by 4,000. As a result, the revised ownership ratio is reduced to $66\frac{2}{3}$ percent (16,000 shares ÷ 24,000 shares). The earnings contribution computed in this manner is $22,400 ($33,600 × $.66\frac{2}{3}$).

Peerless's preferred stock is classified as a senior security rather than a common stock equivalent. Therefore, it is treated as preferred stock in computing primary EPS, and preferred dividends are deducted in determining the income accruing to common shareholders in the numerator. In computing fully diluted earnings per share, the preferred stock is treated as common stock outstanding because it is convertible and dilutive. Therefore, no dividends are deducted in the numerator, and 25,000 shares of common are added into the denominator.

Stock options for 9,000 shares of parent company stock can be exercised at any time and must be reflected in the computation of consolidated EPS. As computed in Figure 10-7 using the treasury stock method, an additional 931 shares are added to the denominator in computing primary earnings per share, and 1,200 shares are added in computing fully diluted EPS.

SUMMARY OF KEY CONCEPTS AND TERMS

In addition to an income statement, balance sheet, and statement of retained earnings, a full set of consolidated financial statements must include a consolidated statement of cash flows. The consolidated statement of cash flows is prepared from the other three consolidated statements in the same way as the statement of cash flows is prepared for a single company. However, certain additional adjustments are needed. For example, income assigned to the noncontrolling interest reduces consolidated net income but does not use cash; it therefore must be added back to net income in deriving cash generated from operating activities. Also, dividends to noncontrolling shareholders must be included as a financing use of cash because, while they are not viewed as dividends of the consolidated entity, they do require the use of cash.

The procedures for consolidation following a pooling of interests are virtually identical to those used following a purchase-type business combination. Differences between consolidated statements prepared following a pooling and those prepared following a purchase stem from differences in the initial recording procedures rather than in the consolidation procedures. With a pooling of interests, the initial investment in the stock of the subsidiary is recorded at its book value; therefore, no differential arises in consolidation. Also, the parent's share of the subsidiary's retained earnings on the date of combination is recorded on the parent's books when the initial investment is recorded, and this amount is carried over to the consolidated balance sheet. The general view taken in a pooling of interests is that the combining companies always have been combined.

Two major income tax issues arise in consolidation. The first is concerned with how to allocate income tax expense to individual companies included in a consolidated income tax return. One approach is to allocate the total tax based on the contributions of the individual companies to the total entity income. The issue is important because the allocation impacts the separate financial statements and the amounts assigned to the noncontrolling interests in the consolidated statements. The second tax issue involves the income tax effects of intercorporate transactions. For consolidating companies filing separate tax returns, income tax expense is recognized in the consolidated income statement when the associated transaction is recognized by the consolidated entity, not necessarily when it is reported by an individual company. If an intercompany gain or loss is included in an individual company's tax return in a different period from the one in which it is included in the consolidated income statement, deferred income taxes should be recognized on the temporary difference.

Consolidated earnings per share is calculated largely in the same way as for a single company. The numerator of the EPS computation is based on earnings available to the holders of the parent's common stock and to holders of securities treated as if converted into the parent's common stock. The denominator is based on the number of the parent's common shares outstanding as well as the number of shares that would be issued if other dilutive securities requiring the issuance of additional shares of the parent's common stock were converted or exercised.

Consolidated earnings per share	Pooling of interests
Consolidated income tax return	Statement of cash flows
Deferred income taxes	Temporary differences

QUESTIONS

Q10-1 How does the effect of pooling of interests accounting for a business combination differ from that of purchase accounting with respect to the elimination of the parent's investment in subsidiary account in periods following the combination?

Q10-2 When common shares are exchanged in a pooling of interests, how is the amount of additional paid-in capital of the combined entity determined?

Q10-3 Is it possible to have a noncontrolling interest reported on the consolidated balance sheet when one company has acquired substantially all of another's common stock in a pooling of interests? Explain.

Q10-4 How do purchase and pooling of interests accounting differ with regard to the treatment of profits on inventory transfers that occurred before the time of the business combination?

Q10-5 Parent Company has no goodwill recorded before combining with Subsidiary Company in a pooling of interests. How is it possible for there to be goodwill reported on the consolidated balance sheet immediately following the combination?

Q10-6 What portion of the 19X5 net income of Green Company is included in consolidated net income under (1) purchase and (2) pooling of interests accounting if Brown Company acquires ownership of Green Company on October 18, 19X5?

Q10-7 How is it possible to eliminate a subsidiary's retained earnings balance when the parent company investment account is eliminated in the consolidation workpaper and still provide for the carryforward of retained earnings following a pooling of interests?

Q10-8 Why not simply add a fourth part to the three-part consolidation workpaper to permit preparation of a consolidated cash flow statement?

Q10-9 Why is income that is assigned to the noncontrolling interest added back to consolidated net income to compute net cash flow from operating activities in a consolidated statement of cash flows?

Q10-10 Why are dividend payments to noncontrolling shareholders treated as an outflow of cash in the consolidated cash flow statement but not included as dividends paid in the consolidated retained earnings statement?

Q10-11 What balances, if any, are likely to be different in the consolidated cash flow statement if pooling of interests accounting is used in recording a company's acquisition of a subsidiary rather than purchase accounting?

Q10-12 Why do companies that file consolidated tax returns often feel the need to allocate tax expense to the individual affiliates?

Q10-13 How do unrealized profits on intercompany transfers affect the amount reported as income tax expense in the consolidated financial statements?

Q10-14 How do interperiod income tax allocation procedures affect consolidation eliminating entries in the period in which unrealized intercompany profits arise?

Q10-15 How do interperiod income tax allocation procedures affect consolidation eliminating entries in the period in which intercompany profits unrealized as of the beginning of the period are realized?

Q10-16 How does the use of interperiod tax allocation procedures affect the amount of income assigned to noncontrolling shareholders in the period in which unrealized intercompany profits are recorded by the subsidiary?

Q10-17 Why is it not possible simply to add together the separately computed earnings per share amounts of individual affiliates in deriving consolidated earnings per share?

Q10-18 How are dividends that are paid to preferred shareholders of the parent and to preferred shareholders of the subsidiary treated in computing consolidated earnings per share?

Q10-19 What factors may cause a subsidiary's income contribution to consolidated earnings per share to be different from its contribution to consolidated net income?

Q10-20 When a convertible bond of a subsidiary is treated as common stock in computing the subsidiary's earnings per share, how is the interest on the bond treated in the computation of consolidated earnings per share?

Q10-21 How are rights, warrants, and options of subsidiary companies treated in the computation of consolidated earnings per share?

Q10-22 What effect does the presence of a noncontrolling interest have on the computation of consolidated earnings per share?

CASES

C10-1 The Effect of Security Type on Earnings per Share

Stage Corporation has both convertible preferred stock and convertible debentures outstanding at the end of 19X3. The annual cash payment to the preferred shareholders and to the bondholders is the same, and the two issues convert into the same number of common shares.

Required

a. If neither issue is a common stock equivalent and both issues are dilutive and are converted into common stock, which issue will cause the greater reduction in primary earnings per share when converted? Why?

b. If both issues are converted into common stock, which issue will cause the greater increase in consolidated net income when converted?

c. If the preferred shares remain outstanding, what conditions must exist for them to be excluded entirely from the computation of primary earnings per share?

d. Stage Corporation is a subsidiary of Prop Company. How will these securities affect the earnings per share reported for the consolidated enterprise?

C10-2 Income Tax Expense

Johnson Corporation purchased 100 percent ownership of Freelance Company at underlying book value on March 3, 19X2. Johnson Corporation makes frequent inventory purchases from Freelance Company. Johnson uses the equity method in accounting for its investment in Freelance. Both companies are subject to 40 percent income tax rates and file separate tax returns.

Required

a. If there were no intercompany inventory transfers, what would cause consolidated tax expense to be less than the amount paid?

b. When will an inventory transfer cause consolidated income tax expense to be greater than the amount paid?

c. When tax payments are greater than tax expense, how is the overpayment reported in the consolidated financial statements?

d. What types of transfers other than inventory transfers will cause consolidated income tax expense to be less than income taxes paid?

e. What types of transfers other than inventory transfers will cause consolidated income tax expense to be greater than income taxes paid?

C10-3 Consolidation following a Pooling of Interests

Northland Company acquires 90 percent of the voting shares of United Nurseries Corporation in a pooling of interests accomplished through an exchange of common shares. Consolidated earnings per share for the period in which the business combination occurs is lower than earnings per share that would have been reported by Northland Company if it had not acquired the shares of United Nurseries.

Required

a. What factors might cause earnings per share to decrease as a result of the combination?

b. Is the reported retained earnings balance for the consolidated entity at the end of the period in which the business combination occurs greater or less than the sum of the retained earnings balances of Northland Company and United Nurseries Corporation before the business combination?

c. If United Nurseries sells additional shares of convertible securities following the business combination, what impact will the new securities have on consolidated earnings per share?

d. What portion of consolidated net income will be assigned to noncontrolling interest in the period following the business combination?

C10-4 Consolidated Cash Flows

The consolidated cash flows from operations of Jones Corporation and Short Manufacturing for 19X7 decreased quite substantially from 19X6 despite the fact that consolidated net income increased slightly in 19X7.

Required

a. What factors included in the computation of consolidated net income may explain this difference between cash flows from operations and net income?

b. How might a change in credit terms extended by Short Manufacturing explain a part of the difference?

c. How would an inventory write-off affect this difference?

d. How would a write-off of uncollectible accounts receivable affect this difference?

e. How does the preparation of a statement of cash flows differ for a consolidated entity compared with a single corporate entity?

EXERCISES

E10-1 Elimination Entries—Pooling of Interests

Swan Corporation acquired 90 percent of the stock of United Mining Company in a business combination recorded as a pooling of interests on January 1, 19X3. United Mining Company reports the following balances on January 1, 19X6:

Cash	$ 60,000	Accounts Payable	$ 40,000
Accounts Receivable	90,000	Bonds Payable	200,000
Inventory	140,000	Common Stock	100,000
Buildings and Equipment	600,000	Additional Paid-In	
Less: Accumulated		Capital	50,000
Depreciation	(250,000)	Retained Earnings	250,000
	$640,000		$640,000

Swan Corporation uses the basic equity method in accounting for its investment in United Mining and reports a balance of $360,000 as its investment on January 1, 19X6.

Required

a. Give the workpaper elimination entry or entries needed to prepare a consolidated balance sheet as of January 1, 19X6.

b. If the parent company had $400,000 of accumulated retained earnings on December 31, 19X5, compute the total balance of retained earnings to be reported in the consolidated balance sheet as of January 1, 19X6.

E10-2 Pooling of Interests Financial Statement Data

Crandic Company and Modest Corporation joined together on January 1, 19X8, in a business combination treated as a pooling of interests. Simplified trial balances for the two companies on December 31, 19X8, are as follows:

	Crandic Company		Modest Corporation	
	Debit	Credit	Debit	Credit
Current Assets	$136,000		$110,000	
Noncurrent Assets	400,000		150,000	
Investment in				
Modest Corporation	210,000			
Cost of Goods Sold	60,000		30,000	
Other Expenses	18,000		10,000	
Dividends Declared	15,000		10,000	
Current Liabilities		$159,000		$ 50,000
Common Stock		270,000		100,000
Additional Paid-In Capital		112,000		20,000
Retained Earnings		188,000		80,000
Sales		90,000		60,000
Income from Subsidiary		20,000		
	$839,000	$839,000	$310,000	$310,000

The pooling of interests was accomplished by Crandic Company's issuing 3,500 shares of its $20 par value stock to acquire 100 percent of the $10 par value shares of Modest Corporation.

Required

a. Determine the amounts to be reported in the consolidated balance sheet immediately following the business combination for each of the following:
   (1) Common stock
   (2) Additional paid-in capital
   (3) Retained earnings
   (4) Investment in Modest Corporation
b. What amount of total assets will be reported in the consolidated balance sheet as of December 31, 19X8?
c. If comparative statements for 19X7 and 19X8 are prepared, what portion of the 19X7 income statement data for Modest Corporation will be included in the consolidated income statement? Explain.

E10-3 Balance Sheet Consolidation

Summarized balance sheets for Blue Star Corporation and Select Soup Company as of December 31, 19X8, are presented below. The two companies plan to join together in a pooling of interests involving an exchange of 5,000 shares of Blue Star Corporation $10 par value stock for 18,000 shares of Select Soup Company $5 par value stock on January 1, 19X9.

Blue Star Corporation
Balance Sheet
December 31, 19X8

Cash	$ 30,000	Accounts Payable	$ 40,000
Accounts Receivable	90,000	Bonds Payable	100,000
Inventory	150,000	Common Stock	150,000
Land	90,000	Additional Paid-In Capital	80,000
Buildings and Equipment	400,000	Retained Earnings	270,000
Less: Accumulated			
Depreciation	(120,000)		
	$640,000		$640,000

Select Soup Company
Balance Sheet
December 31, 19X8

Cash	$ 10,000	Accounts Payable	$ 20,000
Accounts Receivable	50,000	Bonds Payable	50,000
Inventory	80,000	Common Stock	100,000
Buildings and Equipment	250,000	Retained Earnings	130,000
Less: Accumulated			
Depreciation	(90,000)		
	$300,000		$300,000

Required

a. Prepare the journal entry or entries recorded by Blue Star Corporation in completing the business combination on January 1, 19X9.

b. Prepare a consolidated balance sheet workpaper as of January 1, 19X9, immediately after the combination is effected.

c. Prepare a consolidated balance sheet as of January 1, 19X9.

E10-4 Midyear Acquisition

Yarn Manufacturing Corporation issued stock with a par value of $67,000 to acquire 95 percent of the stock of Spencer Corporation in a pooling of interests completed on August 30, 19X7. On January 1, 19X7, Spencer Corporation reported the following stockholders' equity balances:

Common Stock ($10 par value)	$150,000
Additional Paid-In Capital	50,000
Retained Earnings	300,000
	$500,000

Spencer Corporation reported net income of $60,000 in 19X7, earned uniformly throughout the year. Spencer declared and paid dividends of $10,000 on June 30 and $25,000 on December 31, 19X7. Yarn Manufacturing accounts for its investment in Spencer Corporation using the equity method.

Yarn Manufacturing reported retained earnings of $400,000 on January 1, 19X7, and had 19X7 income from its separate operations of $140,000. Dividends of $80,000 were paid by Yarn Manufacturing on December 31, 19X7.

Required

a. Compute consolidated retained earnings as of January 1, 19X7, as it would appear in comparative consolidated financial statements presented at the end of 19X7.

b. Compute consolidated net income reported for 19X7.

c. Compute consolidated retained earnings as of December 31, 19X7.

d. Give the December 31, 19X7, balance of Yarn Manufacturing's investment in Spencer Corporation.

E10-5 Preparation of Statement of Cash Flows

The accountant for Consolidated Enterprises, Inc., has just finished preparing a consolidated balance sheet, income statement, and statement of changes in retained earnings for 19X3. The accountant has asked for assistance in preparing a statement of cash flows for the consolidated entity. Consolidated Enterprises holds 80 percent of the stock of Separate Way Manufacturing. The following items are proposed for inclusion in the consolidated cash flow statement:

Decrease in accounts receivable	$ 23,000
Increase in accounts payable	5,000
Increase in inventory	15,000
Increase in bonds payable	120,000
Equipment purchased	380,000
Common stock repurchased	35,000
Depreciation reported for current period	73,000
Gain recorded on sale of equipment	8,000
Book value of equipment sold	37,000
Goodwill amortized	3,000
Accounts receivable collected during year	195,000
Payments made on accounts payable	150,000
Dividends paid by parent	60,000
Dividends paid by subsidiary	30,000
Consolidated net income for the year	450,000
Income assigned to the noncontrolling interest	14,000

Required

Prepare in good form a statement of cash flows for Consolidated Enterprises, Inc.

E10-6 Analysis of Consolidated Cash Flow Statement

The following 19X3 consolidated statement of cash flows is presented for Acme Printing Company and its subsidiary, Jones Delivery:

Acme Printing Company and Subsidiary
Consolidated Statement of Cash Flows
For the Year 19X3

Cash Flows from Operating Activities:		
Consolidated Net Income	$ 120,000	
Noncash Items Included in Income:		
Depreciation Expense	45,000	
Amortization of Goodwill	1,000	
Amortization of Bond Premium	(2,000)	
Income to Noncontrolling Interest	10,000	
Loss on Sale of Equipment	23,000	
Decrease in Inventory	20,000	
Increase in Accounts Receivable	(12,000)	
Net Cash Provided by Operating Activities		$205,000
Cash Flows from Investing Activities:		
Purchase of Buildings	$(150,000)	
Sale of Equipment	60,000	
Net Cash Used in Investing Activities		(90,000)
Cash Flows from Financing Activities:		
Dividends Paid:		
To Acme Printing Shareholders	$ (50,000)	
To Noncontrolling Shareholders	(6,000)	
Sale of Bonds	100,000	
Repurchase of Acme Printing Stock	(120,000)	
Net Cash Used in Financing Activities		(76,000)
Net Increase in Cash		$ 39,000

Acme Printing Company purchased 60 percent of the voting shares of Jones Delivery in 19X1 for $40,000 above book value.

Required

a. Determine the net income of Jones Delivery for 19X3.

b. Determine the amount of dividends paid by Jones Delivery in 19X3.

c. Explain why the amortization of bond premium is treated as a deduction from net income in arriving at net cash flow from operating activities.

d. Explain why an increase in accounts receivable is treated as a deduction from net income in arriving at net cash flows from operating activities.

e. Explain why dividends to noncontrolling stockholders are not shown as a dividend payment in the retained earnings statement but are shown as a distribution of cash in the consolidated cash flow statement.

f. Did the loss on the sale of equipment included in the consolidated statement of cash flows result from a sale to an affiliate or a nonaffiliate? How do you know?

E10-7 Tax Deferral on Gains and Losses

Springdale Corporation holds 75 percent of the voting shares of Holiday Services Company. During 19X7 Springdale sold inventory costing $60,000 to Holiday Services for

$90,000, and Holiday Services resold one-third of the inventory in 19X7. Also in 19X7, Holiday Services sold land with a book value of $140,000 to Springdale Corporation for $240,000. The companies file separate tax returns and are subject to a 40 percent tax rate.

Required

Give the eliminating entries relating to the intercorporate sale of inventories and land to be entered in the consolidation workpaper prepared at the end of 19X7.

E10-8 Unrealized Profits in Prior Year

Springdale Corporation holds 75 percent of the voting shares of Holiday Services Company. During 19X7 Springdale sold inventory costing $60,000 to Holiday Services for $90,000, and Holiday Services resold one-third of the inventory in 19X7. The remaining inventory was resold in 19X8. Also in 19X7, Holiday Services sold land with a book value of $140,000 to Springdale Corporation for $240,000. Springdale Corporation continues to hold the land at the end of 19X8. The companies file separate tax returns and are subject to a 40 percent tax rate.

Required

Give the eliminating entries relating to the intercorporate sale of inventories and land needed in the consolidation workpaper at the end of 19X8. Assume Springdale uses the basic equity method in accounting for its investment in Holiday Services.

E10-9 Allocation of Income Tax Expense

Winter Corporation owns 80 percent of the stock of Ray Guard Corporation and 90 percent of the stock of Block Company. The companies file a consolidated tax return each year and in 19X5 paid a total tax of $80,000. Each of the companies is involved in a number of intercompany inventory transfers each period. Information on the activities of the companies for 19X5 is as follows:

Company	Reported Operating Income	19X4 Intercompany Profit Realized in 19X5	19X5 Intercompany Profit Not Realized in 19X5
Winter Corporation	$100,000	$40,000	$10,000
Ray Guard Corporation	50,000		20,000
Block Company	30,000	20,000	10,000

Required

a. Determine the amount of income tax expense that should be assigned to each company.

b. Compute consolidated net income for 19X5. (*Note:* Winter Corporation does not record income tax expense on income from subsidiaries because a consolidated tax return is filed.)

E10-10   Effect of Preferred Stock on Earnings per Share

Crestwood Corporation holds 80 percent of the voting common shares of Dennison Company, but none of its preferred shares. Summary balance sheets for the companies on December 31, 19X6, are as follows:

	Crestwood Corporation	Dennison Company
Cash	$ 50,000	$ 40,000
Accounts Receivable	80,000	60,000
Inventory	140,000	90,000
Buildings and Equipment	700,000	300,000
Less: Accumulated Depreciation	(280,000)	(140,000)
Investment in Dennison Company Stock	160,000	
	$850,000	$350,000
Accounts Payable	$120,000	$ 50,000
Taxes Payable	80,000	
Preferred Stock	200,000	100,000
Common Stock ($10 par value)	100,000	50,000
Retained Earnings	350,000	150,000
	$850,000	$350,000

Neither of the preferred issues is convertible. Crestwood Corporation preferred pays a 12 percent annual dividend, and Dennison Company preferred pays a 10 percent dividend. Dennison Company reported net income of $50,000 and paid a total of $20,000 of dividends in 19X6. Crestwood Corporation reported income from its separate operations of $60,000 and paid total dividends of $45,000 in 19X6.

Required

Compute 19X6 consolidated earnings per share. Ignore any tax consequences.

E10-11   Effect of Convertible Bonds on Earnings per Share

Crystal Corporation owns 60 percent of the common shares of Evans Company. Balance sheet data for the companies on December 31, 19X2, are as follows:

	Crystal Corporation	Evans Company
Cash	$ 85,000	$ 30,000
Accounts Receivable	80,000	50,000
Inventory	120,000	100,000
Buildings and Equipment	700,000	400,000
Less: Accumulated Depreciation	(240,000)	(80,000)
Investment in Evans Company Stock	150,000	
	$895,000	$500,000
Accounts Payable	$145,000	$ 50,000
Bonds Payable	250,000	200,000
Common Stock ($10 par value)	300,000	100,000
Retained Earnings	200,000	150,000
	$895,000	$500,000

The bonds of Crystal Corporation and Evans Company pay annual interest of 12 percent and 10 percent, respectively. The bonds of Crystal Corporation are not convertible. Although the bonds of Evans Company can be converted into 10,000 shares of Evans Company stock anytime after January 1, 19X1, they are not common stock equivalents. A federal income tax rate of 40 percent is applicable to both companies. Evans Company reports net income of $30,000 for 19X2 and pays dividends of $15,000, while Crystal Corporation reports income from its separate operations of $45,000 and pays dividends of $25,000.

Required

Compute primary and fully diluted earnings per share for the consolidated entity for 19X2.

E10-12 Effect of Convertible Preferred Stock on Earnings per Share

Eagle Corporation holds 80 percent of the common shares of Standard Company. The following balance sheet data are reported by the companies for December 31, 19X8:

	Eagle Corporation	Standard Company
Cash	$ 50,000	$ 40,000
Accounts Receivable	80,000	60,000
Inventory	140,000	90,000
Buildings and Equipment	700,000	300,000
Less: Accumulated Depreciation	(280,000)	(140,000)
Investment in Standard Company Stock	160,000	
	$850,000	$350,000
Accounts Payable	$120,000	$ 50,000
Taxes Payable	80,000	
Preferred Stock ($10 par value)	200,000	100,000
Common Stock:		
$10 par value	100,000	
$5 par value		50,000
Retained Earnings	350,000	150,000
	$850,000	$350,000

An 8 percent annual dividend is paid on the Eagle Corporation preferred stock and a 12 percent dividend is paid on the Standard Company preferred stock. The preferred shares of Eagle are not convertible. While the Standard Company preferred shares can be converted into 15,000 shares of common stock at any time, they are not common stock equivalents. For 19X8, Standard Company reports net income of $45,000 and pays total dividends of $20,000, and Eagle Corporation reports income from its separate operations of $60,000 and pays total dividends of $35,000.

Required

Compute primary and fully diluted earnings per share for the consolidated entity for 19X8.

PROBLEMS

P10-13   Consolidation Workpaper under Pooling of Interests

Proud Corporation acquired 90 percent of the voting shares of Allied Products Company in a business combination recorded as a pooling of interests on January 1, 19X2. Proud Corporation uses the equity method in accounting for its ownership of Allied Products. On December 31, 19X3, the trial balances of the two companies are as follows:

	Proud Corporation		Allied Products Company	
	Debit	Credit	Debit	Credit
Current Assets	$159,000		$105,000	
Depreciable Assets	500,000		300,000	
Investment in Allied Products Company Stock	153,000			
Operating Expenses	105,000		75,000	
Depreciation Expense	25,000		15,000	
Dividends Declared	40,000		10,000	
Accumulated Depreciation		$175,000		$ 75,000
Current Liabilities		50,000		40,000
Long-Term Debt		100,000		120,000
Common Stock		200,000		100,000
Retained Earnings		230,000		50,000
Sales		200,000		120,000
Income from Subsidiary		27,000		
	$982,000	$982,000	$505,000	$505,000

Required

   a. Give all workpaper eliminating entries required as of December 31, 19X3, to prepare consolidated financial statements.
   b. Prepare and complete a three-part consolidation workpaper.

P10-14   Consolidation Workpaper under Pooling of Interests

Blackburn Corporation acquired 100 percent ownership of MDK Company on May 13, 19X3, in a business combination recorded as a pooling of interests. Trial balances for the companies on December 31, 19X8, are as follows:

	Blackburn Corporation		MDK Company	
	Debit	**Credit**	**Debit**	**Credit**
Cash	$ 97,000		$ 45,000	
Accounts Receivable	80,000		50,000	
Inventory	100,000		80,000	
Buildings and Equipment	380,000		350,000	
Investment in MDK Company	260,000			
Cost of Goods Sold	110,000		90,000	
Depreciation Expense	20,000		15,000	
Other Expenses	28,000		25,000	
Dividends Declared	15,000		10,000	
Accumulated Depreciation		$ 240,000		$155,000
Accounts Payable		20,000		10,000
Bonds Payable		200,000		100,000
Common Stock		100,000		50,000
Additional Paid-In Capital		5,000		
Retained Earnings		305,000		200,000
Sales		200,000		150,000
Income from Subsidiary		20,000		
	$1,090,000	$1,090,000	$665,000	$665,000

Blackburn Corporation uses the equity method in accounting for its ownership of MDK Company. Dividends were declared and paid on November 15, 19X8, by Blackburn Corporation and on December 20, 19X8, by MDK Company.

Required

a. Prepare all eliminating entries needed to complete a three-part consolidation work-paper as of December 31, 19X8.
b. Prepare a consolidation workpaper as of December 31, 19X8.

P10-15   Consolidation with Controlling Ownership

Richardson Corporation was created on January 1, 19X2, to develop computer software. On January 1, 19X6, Wealthy Company acquired 90 percent of the common stock of Richardson Corporation in a business combination recorded as a pooling of interests. Wealthy Company continued to operate Richardson Corporation as a separate legal entity and used the basic equity method in accounting for its investment.

Trial balances for Wealthy Company and Richardson Corporation on December 31, 19X6, are as follows:

Item	Wealthy Company Debit	Wealthy Company Credit	Richardson Corporation Debit	Richardson Corporation Credit
Cash	$ 48,000		$ 30,000	
Accounts Receivable	80,000		50,000	
Inventory	240,000		100,000	
Buildings and Equipment	500,000		250,000	
Land	80,000		20,000	
Investment in Richardson Stock	171,000			
Cost of Goods Sold	500,000		250,000	
Depreciation Expense	25,000		15,000	
Other Expenses	95,000		75,000	
Dividends Declared	50,000		20,000	
Accumulated Depreciation		$ 155,000		$ 75,000
Accounts Payable		70,000		35,000
Bonds Payable		200,000		150,000
Common Stock		300,000		50,000
Retained Earnings		290,000		100,000
Sales		700,000		400,000
Gain on Sale of Equipment		20,000		
Income from Subsidiary		54,000		
	$1,789,000	$1,789,000	$810,000	$810,000

During 19X6, Richardson Corporation purchased inventory costing $20,000 and sold it to Wealthy Company for $30,000. Wealthy Company resold 60 percent of the inventory in 19X6.

On January 2, 19X6, Wealthy Company sold equipment to Richardson Corporation for $120,000. The equipment had been purchased for $150,000 on January 1, 19X1, by Wealthy Company and was depreciated on a straight-line basis with an expected life of 15 years. Richardson Corporation is depreciating the equipment over an expected 10-year life on a straight-line basis, with no expected residual value.

Required

a. Prepare a three-part consolidation workpaper in good form as of December 31, 19X6.

b. Prepare a consolidated income statement, balance sheet, and statement of changes in retained earnings for 19X6.

P10-16   Comprehensive Pooling of Interests Balance Sheet [AICPA Adapted]

Emma, Inc., acquired all the outstanding $25 par value common stock of Steed, Inc., on June 30, 19X7, in exchange for 40,000 shares of its $25 par value common stock. The business combination meets all conditions for a pooling of interests. On June 30, 19X7, Emma's common stock closed at $65 per share on a national stock exchange. Both corporations continued to operate as separate businesses maintaining separate accounting records with years ending December 31.

On December 31, 19X7, after year-end adjustments and closing nominal accounts, the companies had condensed balance sheet accounts as follows:

	Emma, Inc.	Steed, Inc.
Assets		
Cash	$ 925,000	$ 300,000
Accounts and Other Receivables	2,140,000	835,000
Inventories	2,310,000	1,045,000
Land	600,000	330,000
Depreciable Assets (net)	4,525,000	1,980,000
Investment in Steed, Inc.	2,430,000	
Long-Term Investments and Other Assets	865,000	385,000
Total	$13,795,000	$4,875,000
Liabilities and Stockholders' Equity		
Accounts Payable and Other Current Liabilities	$ 2,465,000	$1,145,000
Long-Term Debt	1,900,000	1,300,000
Common Stock ($25 par value)	3,200,000	1,000,000
Additional Paid-In Capital	1,850,000	190,000
Retained Earnings	4,380,000	1,240,000
Total	$13,795,000	$4,875,000

Additional information:

1 Emma uses the equity method of accounting for its investment in Steed. The investment in Steed has not been adjusted for any intercompany transactions.

2. On June 30, 19X7, Steed's assets and liabilities had fair values equal to the book balances, with the exception of land, which had a fair value of $550,000.

3. On June 15, 19X7, Steed paid a cash dividend of $4 per share on its common stock.

4. On December 10, 19X7, Emma paid a cash dividend totaling $256,000 on its common stock.

5. On June 30, 19X7, immediately before the combination, the stockholders' equities were:

	Emma, Inc.	Steed, Inc.
Common Stock	$2,200,000	$1,000,000
Additional Paid-In Capital	1,660,000	190,000
Retained Earnings	3,036,000	980,000
	$6,896,000	$2,170,000

6. Steed's long-term debt consisted of 10 percent 10-year bonds issued at face value on March 31, 19X1. Interest is payable semiannually on March 31 and September 30. Emma had purchased Steed's bonds at face value of $320,000 in 19X1, and there was no change in ownership through December 31, 19X7.

7. During October 19X7, Emma sold merchandise to Steed at an aggregate invoice price of $720,000, which included a profit of $180,000. At December 31, 19X7, one-half of the merchandise remained in Steed's inventory, and Steed had not paid Emma for the merchandise purchased.

8. Steed's 19X7 net income was $580,000. Emma's 19X7 income before considering equity in Steed's net income was $890,000.

9. The balances in retained earnings at December 31, 19X6, were $2,506,000 and $820,000 for Emma and Steed, respectively.

Required

a. Develop and complete a workpaper for the preparation of a consolidated balance sheet of Emma, Inc., and its subsidiary, Steed, Inc., at December 31, 19X7. A formal consolidated balance sheet and journal entries are not required.

b. Prepare a formal consolidated statement of retained earnings for the year ended December 31, 19X7.

P10-17   Consolidation Involving a Midyear Pooling of Interests

Buster Products Corporation acquired 90 percent ownership of Sanford Company on October 20, 19X5, through an exchange of voting shares in a transaction qualifying as a pooling of interests. Buster Products issued 8,000 shares of its $10 par stock to acquire 27,000 shares of Sanford Company $5 par stock. Trial balances of the two companies on December 31, 19X5, are as follows:

Item	Buster Products Corporation Debit	Buster Products Corporation Credit	Sanford Company Debit	Sanford Company Credit
Cash	$ 85,000		$ 50,000	
Accounts Receivable	100,000		60,000	
Inventory	150,000		100,000	
Buildings and Equipment	400,000		340,000	
Investment in Sanford Stock	252,000			
Cost of Goods Sold	305,000		145,000	
Depreciation Expense	25,000		20,000	
Other Expenses	14,000		25,000	
Dividends Declared	58,000		30,000	
Accumulated Depreciation		$ 105,000		$ 65,000
Accounts Payable		40,000		50,000
Taxes Payable		70,000		55,000
Bonds Payable		250,000		100,000
Common Stock		200,000		150,000
Additional Paid-In Capital		55,000		
Retained Earnings		225,000		100,000
Sales		390,000		250,000
Income from Subsidiary		54,000		
	$1,389,000	$1,389,000	$770,000	$770,000

In 19X5, Sanford Company reported net income of $45,000 before its acquisition by Buster Products and $15,000 after acquisition. Sanford Company paid dividends of $20,000 in April and $10,000 in November of 19X5. Buster Products Corporation paid dividends of $40,000 in 19X5. Buster Products uses the equity method in accounting for its investment in Sanford.

Required

a. Give all journal entries recorded by Buster Products Corporation during 19X5 that relate to its investment in Sanford Company.

b. Give the workpaper elimination entries needed on December 31, 19X5, to prepare consolidated financial statements.

c. Prepare a three-part consolidation workpaper as of December 31, 19X5.

P10-18 Midyear Pooling of Interests [AICPA Adapted]

Pico Corporation issued 200,000 shares of its $10 par common stock on March 31, 19X0, to acquire all the outstanding $25 par value common stock of Strata, Inc. The business combination meets all conditions for a pooling of interests. On March 31, 19X0, the market price of Pico's common stock was $35 a share. Both corporations continued to operate as separate businesses, maintaining separate accounting records with years ending December 31.

On March 31, 19X0, immediately before the combination, the stockholders' equities were:

	Pico Corporation	Strata, Inc.
Common Stock	$ 5,500,000	$2,500,000
Additional Paid-In Capital	4,200,000	470,000
Retained Earnings	7,360,000	2,430,000
	$17,060,000	$5,400,000

Additional information:

1. During March 19X0, Pico paid $720,000 for expenditures relating to the business combination with Strata.

2. Pico accounts for its investment in Strata using the equity method.

3. On March 31, 19X0, the fair values of Strata's assets and liabilities equaled their book values, except for its long-term investment in marketable equity securities, for which the aggregate market value exceeded aggregate cost by $600,000.

4. On March 10, 19X0, Strata paid a cash dividend totaling $250,000 on its common stock.

5. On November 15, 19X0, Pico paid a cash dividend totaling $1,500,000 on its common stock.

6. During August 19X0, Pico sold merchandise to Strata at a profit of $800,000. On December 31, 19X0, one-fourth of this merchandise remained in Strata's inventory.

7. For the period April 1 through December 31, 19X0, Strata paid Pico management fees totaling $150,000.

8. Strata's 19X0 net income was $1,450,000. Pico's income was $2,240,000, before considering equity in Strata's net income.

9. The balances in retained earnings at January 1, 19X0, were $6,820,000 and $2,290,000 for Pico and Strata, respectively.

Required

   a. Prepare Pico Corporation's journal entries to record the business combination with Strata, Inc. and the expenditures relating to the business combination.

   b. Prepare a schedule to compute the investment in Strata, Inc., at equity, at December 31, 19X0.

   c. Prepare a formal consolidated statement of changes in retained earnings of Pico Corporation and its subsidiary Strata, Inc., for the year ended December 31, 19X0.

P10-19 Consolidated Statement of Cash Flows

Blue Spruce Company holds 80 percent ownership of Wilderness Land Company. The consolidated balance sheets as of December 31, 19X3, and December 31, 19X4, are as follows:

	Dec. 31, 19X3	Dec. 31, 19X4
Cash	$ 83,000	$ 181,000
Accounts Receivable	210,000	175,000
Inventory	320,000	370,000
Land	190,000	160,000
Buildings and Equipment	850,000	980,000
Less: Accumulated Depreciation	(280,000)	(325,000)
Goodwill	32,000	28,000
Total Debits	$1,405,000	$1,569,000
Accounts Payable	$ 52,000	$ 74,000
Taxes Payable	45,000	30,000
Bonds Payable	400,000	500,000
Bond Premium	18,000	16,000
Noncontrolling Interest	40,000	44,000
Common Stock	300,000	300,000
Additional Paid-In Capital	70,000	70,000
Retained Earnings	480,000	535,000
Total Credits	$1,405,000	$1,569,000

The 19X4 consolidated income statement contained the following amounts:

Sales		$600,000
Cost of Goods Sold	$375,000	
Depreciation Expense	45,000	
Interest Expense	69,000	
Loss on Sale of Land	20,000	
Amortization of Goodwill	4,000	(513,000)
		$ 87,000
Income to Noncontrolling Interest		(7,000)
Consolidated Net Income		$ 80,000

Blue Spruce purchased its investment in Wilderness Land on January 1, 19X2, for $190,000. At that time, Wilderness Land reported net assets of $150,000. A total of $40,000 of the purchase differential was assigned to goodwill with an estimated life of 10 years, and the remainder of the differential was assigned to equipment with a remaining life of 20 years from the date of combination.

Blue Spruce Company sold $100,000 of bonds on December 31, 19X4, to assist in generating additional funds. Wilderness Land reported net income of $35,000 for 19X4 and paid dividends of $15,000. Blue Spruce reported 19X4 equity-method net income of $80,000 and paid dividends of $25,000.

Required

a. Prepare a workpaper to develop a consolidated statement of cash flows for 19X4.
b. Prepare a consolidated statement of cash flows for 19X4.

P10-20 Consolidated Statement of Cash Flows

Sun Corporation was created on January 1, 19X2, and quickly became successful. On January 1, 19X6, the owner sold 80 percent of the stock to Weatherbee Company at underlying book value. Weatherbee continued to operate the subsidiary as a separate legal entity and used the equity method in accounting for its investment in Sun Corporation. The following consolidated financial statements have been prepared as of December 31, 19X6:

Weatherbee Company and Subsidiary
Consolidated Balance Sheets

	January 1, 19X6	December 31, 19X6
Cash	$ 54,000	$ 75,000
Accounts Receivable	121,000	111,000
Inventory	230,000	360,000
Land	95,000	100,000
Buildings and Equipment	800,000	650,000
Less: Accumulated Depreciation	(290,000)	(230,000)
Total Debits	$1,010,000	$1,066,000
Accounts Payable	$ 90,000	$ 105,000
Bonds Payable	300,000	250,000
Noncontrolling Interest	30,000	38,000
Common Stock	300,000	300,000
Retained Earnings	290,000	373,000
Total Credits	$1,010,000	$1,066,000

**Weatherbee Company and Subsidiary
Consolidated Income Statement
Year Ended December 31, 19X6**

Sales	$1,070,000
Gain on Sale of Equipment	30,000
	$1,100,000
Cost of Goods Sold	$ 750,000
Depreciation Expense	40,000
Other Expenses	150,000
Total Expenses	$ (940,000)
	$ 160,000
Income to Noncontrolling Interest	(12,000)
Consolidated Net Income	$ 148,000

**Weatherbee Company and Subsidiary
Consolidated Retained Earnings Statement
Year Ended December 31, 19X6**

Balance, January 1, 19X6	$290,000
19X6 Net Income	148,000
	$438,000
Dividends Paid in 19X6	(65,000)
Balance, December 31, 19X6	$373,000

During 19X6, Sun Corporation reported net income of $60,000 and paid dividends of $20,000; Weatherbee Company reported net income of $148,000 and paid dividends of $65,000. There were no intercompany transfers during the period.

Required

Prepare a workpaper for a consolidated statement of cash flows for 19X6.

P10-21 Consoldiated Statement of Cash Flows [AICPA Adapted]

Presented below are the consolidated balance sheet accounts of Brimer, Inc., and its subsidiary, Dore Corporation, as of December 31, 19X6 and 19X5.

	19X6	19X5	Net Increase (Decrease)
Assets			
Cash	$ 313,000	$ 195,000	$118,000
Marketable Equity Securities, at cost	175,000	175,000	–0–
Allowance to Reduce Marketable Equity Securities to Market	(13,000)	(24,000)	11,000
Accounts Receivable, net	418,000	440,000	(22,000)
Inventories	595,000	525,000	70,000
Land	385,000	170,000	215,000
Plant and Equipment	755,000	690,000	65,000
Accumulated Depreciation	(199,000)	(145,000)	(54,000)
Goodwill, net	57,000	60,000	(3,000)
Total Assets	$2,486,000	$2,086,000	$400,000
Liabilities and Stockholders' Equity			
Current Portion of Long-Term Note	$ 150,000	$ 150,000	$ –0–
Accounts Payable and Accrued Liabilities	595,000	474,000	121,000
Note Payable, Long-Term	300,000	450,000	(150,000)
Deferred Income Taxes	44,000	32,000	12,000
Minority Interest in Net Assets of Subsidiary	179,000	161,000	18,000
Common Stock, par $10	580,000	480,000	100,000
Additional Paid-In Capital	303,000	180,000	123,000
Retained Earnings	335,000	195,000	140,000
Treasury Stock, at cost	–0–	(36,000)	36,000
Total Liabilities and Stockholders' Equity	$2,486,000	$2,086,000	$400,000

Additional information:

1. On January 20, 19X6, Brimer, Inc., issued 10,000 shares of its common stock for land having a fair value of $215,000.

2. On February 5, 19X6, Brimer, Inc., reissued all of its treasury stock for $44,000.

3. On May 15, 19X6, Brimer, Inc., paid a cash dividend of $58,000 on its common stock.

4. On August 8, 19X6, equipment was purchased for $127,000.

5. On September 30, 19X6, equipment was sold for $40,000. The equipment cost $62,000 and had a carrying amount of $34,000 on the date of sale.

6. On December 15, 19X6, Dore Corporation paid a cash dividend of $50,000 on its common stock.

7. Deferred income taxes represent temporary differences relating to the use of accelerated depreciation methods for income tax reporting and the straight-line method for financial reporting.

8. Net income for 19X6 was as follows:

Consolidated net income	$198,000
Dore Corporation	110,000

9. Brimer, Inc., owns 70 percent of its subsidiary, Dore Corporation. There was no change in the ownership interest in Dore Corporation during 19X5 and 19X6. There were no intercompany transactions other than the dividend paid to Brimer, Inc., by its subsidiary.

Required

Prepare a consolidated statement of cash flows for Brimer, Inc., and Subsidiary for the year ended December 31, 19X6.

P10-22 Statement of Cash Flows Prepared from Consolidation Workpaper

Detecto Corporation purchased 60 percent of the outstanding shares of Strand Company on January 1, 19X4, for $24,000 more than book value. The full amount of the excess payment is considered related to goodwill and is being amortized over an 8-year period. In 19X4, Strand Company purchased a piece of land for $35,000 and later in the year sold it to Detecto Corporation for $45,000. Detecto Corporation is still holding the land as an investment. During 19X6, Detecto bonds with a value of $100,000 were exchanged for equipment valued at $100,000.

On January 1, 19X6, Detecto Corporation held inventory purchased previously from Strand Company for $48,000. During 19X6 Detecto Corporation purchased an additional $90,000 of goods from Strand Company and held $54,000 of this inventory on December 31, 19X6. Strand Company sells merchandise to the parent at cost plus a 20 percent markup.

Strand Company also purchases inventory items from Detecto Corporation. On January 1, 19X6, Strand Company held inventory it previously purchased from Detecto Corporation for $14,000, and on December 31, 19X6, it held goods it purchased from Detecto for $7,000 during 19X6. Strand's total purchases from Detecto Corporation in 19X6 were $22,000. Detecto Corporation sells inventory to Strand Company at cost plus a 40 percent markup.

The consolidated balance sheet at December 31, 19X5, contained the following amounts:

	Debit	Credit
Cash	$ 92,000	
Accounts Receivable	135,000	
Inventory	140,000	
Land	75,000	
Buildings and Equipment	400,000	
Goodwill	18,000	
Accumulated Depreciation		$210,000
Accounts Payable		114,200
Bonds Payable		90,000
Noncontrolling Interest		72,800
Common Stock		100,000
Retained Earnings		273,000
	$860,000	$860,000

The consolidation workpaper on page 604 was prepared on December 31, 19X6. All eliminating entries and adjustments have been entered properly in the workpaper. Detecto Corporation accounts for its investment in Strand Company using the basic equity method.

Required

a. Prepare a workpaper for a consolidated statement of cash flows for 19X6.
b. Prepare a consolidated statement of cash flows for 19X6.

Detecto Corporation and Strand Company
Consolidation Workpaper
December 31, 19X6

Item	Detecto Corporation	Strand Company	Eliminations Debit		Eliminations Credit		Consolidated
Sales	400,000	200,000	(8)	22,000			
			(9)	90,000			488,000
Income from Subsidiary	18,000		(1)	18,000			
Credits	418,000	200,000					488,000
Cost of Goods Sold	280,000	120,000			(6)	4,000	
					(7)	8,000	
					(8)	20,000	
					(9)	81,000	287,000
Amortization Expense			(4)	3,000			3,000
Depreciation Expense	25,000	15,000					40,000
Other Expenses	35,000	30,000					65,000
Debits	(340,000)	(165,000)					(395,000)
							93,000
Income to Noncontrolling Interest			(2)	13,600			(13,600)
Net Income, carry forward	78,000	35,000		146,600		113,000	79,400
Retained Earnings, January 1	287,800	150,000	(3)	150,000			
			(5)	6,000			
			(6)	4,000			
			(7)	4,800			273,000
Net Income, from above	78,000	35,000		146,600		113,000	79,400
	365,800	185,000					352,400
Dividends Declared	(50,000)	(20,000)			(1)	12,000	
					(2)	8,000	(50,000)
Retained Earnings, December 31, carry forward	315,800	165,000		311,400		133,000	302,400
Cash	26,800	35,000					61,800
Accounts Receivable	80,000	40,000					120,000
Inventory	120,000	90,000			(8)	2,000	
					(9)	9,000	199,000
Land	70,000	20,000			(5)	10,000	80,000
Buildings and Equipment	340,000	200,000					540,000
Investment in Strand Company Stock	144,000				(1)	6,000	
					(3)	138,000	
Differential			(3)	18,000	(4)	18,000	
Goodwill			(4)	15,000			15,000
Debits	780,800	385,000					1,015,800
Accumulated Depreciation	165,000	85,000					250,000
Accounts Payable	80,000	15,000					95,000
Bonds Payable	120,000	70,000					190,000
Common Stock	100,000	50,000	(3)	50,000			100,000
Retained Earnings, from above	315,800	165,000		311,400		133,000	302,400
Noncontrolling Interest			(5)	4,000	(2)	5,600	
			(7)	3,200	(3)	80,000	78,400
Credits	780,800	385,000		401,600		401,600	1,015,800

P10-23 Tax Allocation in Consolidated Balance Sheet

Acme Powder Corporation purchased 70 percent of the stock of Brown Company on December 31, 19X7, at underlying book value. The balance sheets of the two companies on December 31, 19X9, are as follows:

Acme Powder Corporation and Brown Company
Balance Sheets
December 31, 19X9

	Acme Powder Corporation	Brown Company
Cash	$ 44,400	$ 20,000
Accounts Receivable	120,000	60,000
Inventory	170,000	120,000
Land	90,000	30,000
Buildings and Equipment	500,000	300,000
Less: Accumulated Depreciation	(180,000)	(80,000)
Investment in Brown Company Stock	280,000	
	$1,024,400	$450,000
Accounts Payable	$ 70,000	$ 20,000
Wages Payable	80,000	30,000
Bonds Payable	200,000	
Common Stock	100,000	150,000
Retained Earnings	574,400	250,000
	$1,024,400	$450,000

On December 31, 19X9, Acme Powder Corporation holds inventory purchased from Brown Company for $70,000. Brown's cost of producing the merchandise was $50,000. Brown Company had purchased inventory from Acme Powder also. Brown's ending inventory contains $85,000 of purchases that had cost Acme Powder $60,000 to produce.

On December 30, 19X9, Brown Company sold equipment to Acme Powder for $90,000. The equipment was purchased by Brown Company for $120,000 several years earlier and had a book value of $40,000 at the time of sale to Acme. The two companies file separate tax returns and are subject to a 40 percent tax rate. Acme Powder does not record tax expense on its share of the undistributed earnings of Brown Company.

Required

a. Complete a consolidated balance sheet workpaper as of December 31, 19X9.
b. Prepare a consolidated balance sheet as of December 31, 19X9.

P10-24 Computations Involving Tax Allocation

Broom Manufacturing used cash to purchase 75 percent of the voting stock of Satellite Industries on January 1, 19X3, at underlying book value. Broom accounts for its investment in Satellite using the basic equity method.

Broom Manufacturing had no inventory on hand on January 1, 19X5. During 19X5 Broom purchased $300,000 of goods from Satellite and had $100,000 remaining on hand at the end of 19X5. Satellite normally prices its items so that their cost is 70 percent of sale price. On January 1, 19X5, Satellite held inventory that it purchased from Broom for $50,000. Broom's cost of producing the items was $30,000. Satellite sold all the merchandise in 19X5 and made no inventory purchases from Broom during 19X5.

On July 15, 19X5, Satellite sold land that it had purchased for $240,000 to Broom for $360,000. The companies file separate tax returns and have a 40 percent income tax rate. Broom does not record tax expense on its portion of the undistributed earnings of Satellite. Tax expense recorded by Broom in 19X5 with regard to its investment in Satellite is based on dividends received from Satellite in 19X5. In computing taxable income, 80 percent of intercorporate dividend payments are exempt from tax.

Satellite reported net income of $190,000 for 19X5 and net assets of $900,000 on December 31, 19X5. Broom's reported income before investment income from Satellite and income tax expense was $700,000 for 19X5. Dividends of $150,000 and $400,000 were paid by Satellite and Broom, respectively, in 19X5.

Required

a. Give the journal entries recorded on the books of Broom Manufacturing during 19X5 to reflect its ownership of Satellite Industries.

b. Compute consolidated net income for 19X5.

c. Compute the income assigned to the noncontrolling interest in the 19X5 consolidated income statement.

d. Compute the amount assigned to the noncontrolling interest in the consolidated balance sheet prepared as of December 31, 19X5.

P10-25 Workpaper Involving Tax Allocation

Hardtack Bread Company holds 70 percent of the common shares of Custom Pizza Corporation. Trial balances for the two companies on December 31, 19X7, are as follows:

Item	Hardtack Bread Company		Custom Pizza Corporation	
	Debit	Credit	Debit	Credit
Cash	$ 35,800		$ 56,000	
Accounts Receivable	130,000		40,000	
Inventory	220,000		60,000	
Land	60,000		20,000	
Buildings and Equipment	450,000		400,000	
Patents	70,000			
Investment in Custom Pizza Common Stock	158,200			
Cost of Goods Sold	435,000		210,000	
Depreciation and Amortization	40,000		20,000	
Tax Expense	44,000		24,000	
Other Expenses	11,400		10,000	
Dividends Declared	20,000		10,000	
Accumulated Depreciation		$ 150,000		$160,000
Accounts Payable		40,000		30,000
Wages Payable		70,000		20,000
Bonds Payable		200,000		100,000
Deferred Income Taxes		120,000		40,000
Common Stock ($10 par value)		100,000		50,000
Retained Earnings		374,200		150,000
Sales		580,000		300,000
Income from Subsidiary		25,200		
Gain on Sale of Equipment		15,000		
	$1,674,400	$1,674,400	$850,000	$850,000

At the beginning of 19X7, Hardtack held inventory purchased from Custom Pizza Corporation containing unrealized profits of $10,000. During 19X7, Hardtack purchased $120,000 of inventory from Custom Pizza and had goods on hand on December 31, 19X7, containing $25,000 of unrealized intercompany profit. On December 31, 19X7, Hardtack sold equipment to Custom Pizza for $65,000. Hardtack had purchased the equipment for $150,000 and had accumulated depreciation of $100,000 on it at the time of sale. The companies file separate tax returns and are subject to a 40 percent income tax rate on all taxable income. Intercompany dividends are 80 percent exempt from taxation.

Required

a. Prepare all eliminating entries needed as of December 31, 19X7, to prepare consolidated financial statements for Hardtack Bread Company and its subsidiary.
b. Prepare a three-part consolidation workpaper for 19X7.

P10-26 Earnings per Share with Convertible Securities

Branch Manufacturing Corporation owns 80 percent of the common shares of Short Retail Stores. The balance sheets of the companies as of December 31, 19X4, were as follows:

	Branch Manufacturing Corporation	Short Retail Stores
Cash	$ 50,000	$ 30,000
Accounts Receivable	100,000	80,000
Inventory	180,000	120,000
Land	90,000	60,000
Buildings and Equipment	500,000	300,000
Less: Accumulated Depreciation	(220,000)	(120,000)
Investment in Short Retail Stores Stock	200,000	
	$900,000	$470,000
Accounts Payable	$ 40,000	$ 20,000
Bonds Payable	300,000	200,000
Preferred Stock ($10 par value)	200,000	100,000
Common Stock:		
$10 par value	150,000	
$5 par value		100,000
Retained Earnings	210,000	50,000
	$900,000	$470,000

The 8 percent preferred stock of Short Retail is convertible into 12,000 shares of common stock, and Short's 10 percent bonds are convertible into 8,000 shares of common stock. Short Retail reported net income of $49,200 for 19X4 and paid dividends of $30,000.

Branch Manufacturing has 11 percent preferred stock and 12 percent bonds outstanding, neither of which is convertible. Branch Manufacturing reported after-tax income, excluding investment income from Short Retail, of $100,000 in 19X4 and paid dividends of $60,000. The companies file separate tax returns and are subject to a 40 percent income tax.

Required

a. Compute primary and fully diluted earnings per share for the consolidated entity assuming the bonds of Short Retail are common stock equivalents and the preferred shares are not.

b. Compute primary and fully diluted earnings per share for the consolidated entity assuming both the bonds and the preferred shares of Short Retail are common stock equivalents.

P10-27 Comprehensive Earnings per Share

Mighty Corporation holds 80 percent of the common stock of Longfellow Company. The following balance sheet data are presented for December 31, 19X7:

	Mighty Corporation	Longfellow Company
Cash	$ 100,000	$ 90,000
Accounts Receivable	150,000	220,000
Inventory	300,000	300,000
Land	100,000	290,000
Buildings and Equipment	2,400,000	900,000
Less: Accumulated Depreciation	(850,000)	(250,000)
Investment in Longfellow Company Stock	450,000	
	$2,650,000	$1,550,000
Accounts Payable	$ 200,000	$ 100,000
Bonds Payable	800,000	500,000
Preferred Stock ($100 par value)		200,000
Common Stock ($10 par value)	1,000,000	400,000
Retained Earnings	650,000	350,000
	$2,650,000	$1,550,000

Longfellow Company reported net income of $115,000 in 19X7 and paid dividends of $60,000. The Longfellow Company bonds have an annual interest rate of 8 percent and are convertible into 30,000 common shares. The preferred shares of Longfellow Company pay an 11 percent annual dividend and convert into 20,000 shares of common stock. The bonds are common stock equivalents, but the preferred shares are not. In addition, Longfellow Company has warrants outstanding for 10,000 shares of common stock at $8 per share. The 19X7 average price of Longfellow Company common shares was $40, and the price at year-end is $50.

Mighty Corporation reported income from its own operations for 19X7 of $300,000 and paid dividends of $200,000. Its 10 percent bonds are not common stock equivalents. They convert into 25,000 shares of Mighty Corporation common stock. The companies file separate tax returns and are subject to income taxes of 40 percent.

Required

Compute primary and fully diluted earnings per share for the consolidated entity for 19X7.

CHAPTER 11

ACCOUNTING FOR BRANCH OPERATIONS

One route to corporate expansion is the external approach of acquiring other companies in business combinations. The specific procedures used to account and report for business combinations and for operations subsequent to a business combination depend on whether the companies merge into a single legal entity or remain as separate legal entities under common ownership. Business combinations were discussed in Chapter 1, and the procedures used in reporting for multiple affiliated companies were discussed in Chapters 2 through 10.

Another approach to expansion is through internal growth. While such growth can occur at a single location, companies often expand by establishing additional locations. For example, Wal-Mart's phenomenal growth would have been impossible had the company not established many new stores at various locations throughout much of the country.

When operations are conducted at more than a single location, the different locations may be referred to as sales agencies, branches, plants, or by numerous other terms. Unfortunately, terminology referring to multiple operating locations is not standardized. In addition, many different approaches are taken in establishing internal accounting and reporting systems for companies operating through outlying locations.

DISTINCTION BETWEEN SALES AGENCY AND BRANCH

The difference between a sales agency and a branch most often has to do with the degree of autonomy. A *sales agency*, sometimes referred to simply as an "agency," usually is not an autonomous operation but acts on behalf of the *home office*. The agency may display and demonstrate sample merchandise, take orders, and arrange for delivery. The orders typically are filled by the home office because a sales agency usually does not stock inventory. Merchandise selection, advertising, granting of credit, collection on accounts, and other aspects of operating the business usually are conducted by the home office. As an example, Montgomery Ward and Company for many years had numerous catalog stores across the country that took orders but did not stock merchandise.

A *branch office* usually has more autonomy and provides a greater range of services than a sales agency does, although the degree differs with the individual company. A branch typically stocks merchandise and fills customers' orders. For some companies the branches perform their own credit function, while for other companies credit is handled by the home office.

Many different types of companies operate through branches. Nearly everyone has visited branches of major department store chains such as J. C. Penney Company and Sears Roebuck and Company. In states that permit branch banking, some banks, such as the Bank of America in California, have expanded throughout the state with extensive networks of branch banks. Some manufacturing companies also conduct business through a comparable system of operating locations, usually referred to as "plants." For example, General Motors operates assembly plants at many different sites, including locations in or near Detroit, St. Louis, Los Angeles, and Nashville.

There typically is little management decision making in a sales agency; decisions are made at the home office, and the agency conducts routine operations. The degree of management decision making in branches usually is greater than in sales agencies but differs considerably from company to company.

Some branch managers may be permitted few choices, while other branch managers may operate with relative independence from the home office. The manager of an automobile assembly plant, for example, may have no discretion over the quantity and type of units produced and little discretion in the choice of vendors. On the other hand, the manager of a branch grocery store may have considerable discretion in the types and quantities of products to stock and in the choice of vendors. In some banks, loans may be approved by branch management, at least up to a certain limit, while in other banks, all loans must be approved by a centralized loan committee. In large department store chains, branch stores normally are required to stock certain items chosen by the home office, but local management has a choice of other items from a large number specified by central management. In some cases, local management may be free to make purchases entirely on its own.

ACCOUNTING SYSTEMS AND THE ACCOUNTING ENTITY

A sales agency usually does not maintain a financial accounting system but only keeps sufficient records to conduct its business. The home office maintains the accounting system, and transactions of the agency are recorded by the home office. A branch, on the other hand, does maintain a complete financial accounting system in most cases. The maintenance of separate accounting systems for the home office and each branch often provides better control over operations and allows top management to assess the performance of individual branches.

Neither sales agencies nor branches are separate legal or accounting entities; they do not prepare separate external accounting reports. Whether the accounting system is centralized in the home office or separate accounting systems are maintained by individual branches, the external reporting entity is the company as a whole. When separate branch accounting records are maintained for internal purposes, such as responsibility accounting and performance evaluation, the accounts of the branches and the home office must be combined in preparing external accounting reports.

ACCOUNTING FOR SALES AGENCIES

Because a sales agency normally does not have an accounting system, all transactions involving the agency are recorded by the home office. For some types of transactions, the entries recorded by the home office are based on source documents generated by the agency. For example, the home office may record agency transactions based on sales invoices, payroll records, and documented petty cash vouchers provided by a sales agency. Other transactions may be recorded based on source documents provided by external parties directly to the home office. For example, the utility companies providing gas, electricity, water, and phone service to the agency might bill the home office directly.

The home office normally accounts for the assets, revenues, and expenses of each agency separately. This allows the home office to maintain control over the assets and provides information for assessing the performance of each agency.

As an example of home office accounting for a sales agency, assume that Carver Enterprises, a manufacturer of modular structures and partitions based in Atlanta, establishes a sales agency in San Diego. The journal entries to record typical sales agency transactions on the home office books are illustrated in Figure 11-1. Note that the entries are recorded in the same way as if the home office had engaged in the transactions except that the assets, revenues, and expenses are specifically designated as relating to the San Diego branch.

ACCOUNTING FOR BRANCH OPERATIONS

Occasionally, accounting for branch operations is centralized at the home office, and the procedures followed are similar to those for a sales agency. If such an approach is used, the branch maintains only limited accounting records and submits source documents for transactions to the home office for entry in the centralized accounting system.

Normally, however, and especially with larger branches, the home office and branch maintain separate accounting systems. Each maintains a full set of books with a complete self-balancing set of accounts. Each records its transactions with external parties in its own accounting system. These transactions are recorded in the normal manner, and no special treatment is needed. In addition, the home

FIGURE 11-1 Home office journal entries for sales agency transactions.

Transactions	Journal Entries on Home Office Books		
Rent land for sales facility.	Prepaid Rent—San Diego Agency	50,000	
	Cash		50,000
Construct and furnish building for sales facility.	Leasehold Improvements—San Diego Agency	80,000	
	Furniture and Fixtures—San Diego Agency	21,000	
	Equipment—San Diego Agency	16,000	
	Cash		117,000
Transfer cash to agency for petty cash fund.	Petty Cash—San Diego Agency	2,500	
	Cash		2,500
Transfer inventory to be used for demonstrations at sales agency.	Demonstration Inventory—San Diego Agency	135,000	
	Inventory		135,000
Pay bills received by home office for expenses of sales agency.	Utilities Expense—San Diego Agency	1,100	
	Office Expense—San Diego Agency	800	
	Insurance Expense—San Diego Agency	2,000	
	Travel Expense—San Diego Agency	1,400	
	Advertising Expense—San Diego Agency	2,700	
	Cash		8,000
Disburse payroll for sales agency employees.	Wage Expense—San Diego Agency	31,000	
	Cash		31,000
Fill sales orders from sales agency.	Accounts Receivable	88,000	
	Sales—San Diego Agency		88,000
	Cost of Goods Sold—San Diego Agency	56,000	
	Inventory		56,000
Replenish sales agency petty cash fund.	Office Expense—San Diego Agency	420	
	Travel Expense—San Diego Agency	1,200	
	Casual Labor Expense—San Diego Agency	750	
	Cash		2,370
Record end-of-period adjusting entries.	Rent Expense—San Diego Agency	25,000	
	Depreciation Expense—San Diego Agency	14,500	
	Wage Expense—San Diego Agency	1,900	
	Prepaid Rent—San Diego Agency		25,000
	Accumulated Depreciation—San Diego Agency		14,500
	Wages Payable		1,900

office and branch both must record transactions with one another in their respective accounting systems.

Even though the home office and each branch maintain separate books, all accounts are combined for external reporting in such a way that the external financial statements represent the company as a single economic enterprise. As with the preparation of consolidated financial statements, simply adding together the balances of the accounts contained in each accounting system does not result in the portrayal of a single economic entity. Certain eliminations are needed as well. Overall, the preparation of external accounting reports for a company with a home office and one or more branches is quite similar to the preparation of consolidated financial statements.

Intracompany Accounts

Transactions with external parties are recorded in the normal manner. Transactions between the home office and a branch also are treated in the normal manner except that they are recorded in *intracompany accounts*. These accounts are *reciprocal accounts* between the home office and the branch. When the books of both the home office and the branch are completely up to date, the balance in an intracompany account on the home office books will be equal but opposite that of the related intracompany account on the branch books. For example, if an intracompany account on the home office books has a $10,000 debit balance, the related intracompany account on the branch books should have a credit balance of the same amount.

The intracompany account on the books of the home office often is called Investment in Branch, while the reciprocal account on the branch books may be labeled Home Office. When a company has more than one branch, a separate investment account for each branch is maintained on the home office books.

The balance of the Investment in Branch account indicates the extent of the home office's investment in a particular branch through contributions of cash and the transfer of assets to the branch. The procedures employed by the home office in accounting for its investment in a branch are similar to a parent's application of the equity method in accounting for its investment in a subsidiary. The reciprocal Home Office account on the books of the branch represents the home office's equity in the branch, and the balance is shown in place of owners' equity in the separate financial statements of the branch prepared for internal reporting purposes.

The balances of the two reciprocal accounts are adjusted for the same transactions. The account balances are increased for asset transfers from the home office to the branch and reduced for asset transfers from the branch to the home office. Adjustments to the accounts also are made for profits and losses of the branch, with branch profits leading to an increase in the account balances and branch losses leading to a decrease. Note that increases in the home office's Investment in Branch account are accomplished with debit entries and decreases with credit entries. The opposite is true with respect to the branch's Home Office account.

The reciprocal nature of the Investment in Branch and the Home Office accounts, and the way in which they are affected by various transactions, can be shown as follows:

Investment in Branch (Home Office Books)			Home Office (Branch Books)	
XXXX		Asset transfers to branch		XXXX
	XXXX	Asset transfers from branch	XXXX	
XXXX		Branch income		XXXX
	XXXX	Branch loss	XXXX	

Establishment of Branch

When a company establishes a branch, the transfer of assets to the branch is recorded by the home office in the Investment in Branch account. Similarly, the branch records the transfer with an entry to the Home Office account. To illustrate, assume that Jensen Corporation of St. Paul, Minnesota, establishes a branch in Mayfield, Texas. The home office transfers to the branch $20,000 in cash, new office equipment that cost $5,000, and new store equipment with a cost of $30,000. The home office records the transfer with the following entry:

H(1)	Investment in Mayfield Branch	55,000	
	Cash		20,000
	Office Equipment		5,000
	Store Equipment		30,000
	Transfer of assets to Mayfield branch.		

(*Note:* As in previous chapters, journal entries are numbered consecutively throughout the chapter so that each entry is uniquely identified. Those entries made on home office books are designated in this chapter by *H*, while those on branch books are identified with *B*.)

Jensen's Mayfield branch records the transfer of assets from the home office with the following entry:

B(2)	Cash	20,000	
	Office Equipment	5,000	
	Store Equipment	30,000	
	Home Office		55,000
	Transfer of assets from home office.		

Note that after both the home office and the branch have recorded the transfer, the Investment in Mayfield Branch account on the home office books and the Home Office account on the branch books have reciprocal balances of $55,000. A separate balance sheet prepared for the Mayfield branch immediately after the transfer appears as follows:

Mayfield Branch of Jensen Corporation
Balance Sheet

Assets:		Liabilities:	
Cash	$20,000		
Office Equipment	5,000		
Store Equipment	30,000	Home Office:	$55,000
Total	$55,000	Total	$55,000

While branch financial statements may be prepared for internal reporting purposes, external accounting reports reflect the activities and position of the company as a whole. The accounts of the home office and its branches are combined in preparing external accounting reports to reflect the single enterprise consisting of the home office and its branches. Classification of the Investment in Mayfield Branch account and the Home Office account is not an issue because both accounts are eliminated in preparing financial statements for external use.

Recognition of Branch Income

Income for each branch is computed periodically in the normal manner. Branches seldom compute income taxes on individual branch income or record income tax expense on their books. Because the home office and its branches are not separate legal entities, income taxes are computed for the company as a whole. Tax expense could be allocated to the branches by the home office, but this usually is not done because it would add little to operational control.

All of a branch's revenue and expense accounts are closed to its income summary in the normal manner. The balance of the income summary represents the branch's income for the period and is closed to the Home Office account. The Home Office account serves in place of retained earnings and other owners' equity accounts on the books of the branch. When the branch's income is reported to the home office, an entry is made on the home office books to recognize the income of the branch and to increase the recorded amount of the home office's investment in the branch.

For example, assume there is a credit balance of $63,000 in the Mayfield branch's Income Summary account at the end of the period. The Income Summary account is closed with the following entry on the books of the Mayfield branch:

B(3)	Income Summary	63,000	
	Home Office		63,000
	Close income summary.		

Upon receiving a report of Mayfield's income for the period, the home office records the following entry:

H(4)	Investment in Mayfield Branch	63,000	
	Mayfield Branch Income		63,000
	Record Mayfield branch income.		

These entries maintain the reciprocal relationship of the Investment in Mayfield Branch account and the Home Office account. When financial statements are prepared for the company as a whole, the Investment in Mayfield Branch account, the Home Office account, and the Mayfield Branch Income account all must be eliminated.

Merchandise Shipments to a Branch

A branch that buys and sells merchandise may be required to obtain all its merchandise from the home office, or it may be permitted to acquire some merchandise from external parties. Purchases of merchandise from external parties are recorded by the branch in the normal manner. If Jensen's Mayfield branch purchases $5,000 of merchandise from an independent wholesaler, and the branch uses a perpetual inventory system, the transaction is recorded by the branch as follows:

B(5)	Inventory	5,000	
	Cash (or Accounts Payable)		5,000
	Record purchase of inventory from external party.		

No entry with respect to this transaction is made on the books of the home office.

When inventory is transferred from the home office to a branch, both the home office and the branch must record the transfer. The dollar amount assigned to the inventory that is transferred is referred to as a *transfer price*. Merchandise is transferred from the home office to a branch either at the original cost to the home office or at some amount in excess of that cost.

Merchandise Billed at Cost   Merchandise transferred from the home office and billed to the branch is recorded by the branch in the same way as inventory purchased from external parties, except the credit is to the Home Office account. The transfer of inventory is treated by both the home office and the branch in the same way as the transfer of any other asset, assuming a perpetual inventory system is used. Thus, the journal entries to record a transfer of inventory at cost are similar to entries H(1) and B(2).

To see this, assume that Jensen's home office transfers inventory with a cost of $8,000 to its Mayfield branch. The transfer is recorded on the home office books with the following entry:

H(6)	Investment in Mayfield Branch	8,000	
	Inventory		8,000
	Transfer of inventory to Mayfield branch.		

The branch records the merchandise as an asset in the same inventory account used to record purchases from external parties and also recognizes the home office's increased equity in its net assets with the following entry:

B(7)	Inventory	8,000	
	Home Office		8,000
	Transfer of inventory from home office.		

No profit is recognized by the home office on the transfer. The full amount of the profit is recognized by the branch when it sells the inventory to external parties.

Freight Charges on Merchandise Shipments Freight costs incurred in shipping merchandise from the home office to a branch become part of the cost of the branch inventory. For example, assume that Jensen Corporation's home office pays $100 to transport $8,000 of merchandise to the Mayfield branch. The transfer is recorded by the home office with the following entry:

H(8)	Investment in Mayfield Branch	8,100	
	Inventory		8,000
	Cash		100
	Transfer of inventory to Mayfield branch and payment of shipping charges.		

The Mayfield branch records the transfer as follows:

B(9)	Inventory	8,100	
	Home Office		8,100
	Transfer of inventory from home office.		

Merchandise Billed in Excess of Cost Companies sometimes transfer inventory from the home office to a branch and bill the branch for an amount greater than the home office's cost. This may occur, for example, when the home office and each branch are treated as profit centers for internal reporting and evaluation purposes.

When the home office incurs costs and provides a service, such as by acquiring inventory at lower prices through volume purchases or by manufacturing the inventory, the company may choose to allocate the profit on the sale of the inventory between the home office and the selling branch. This can be done by billing the branch for inventory transfers at an amount greater than the home office's cost. The home office is credited with profit equal to the difference between its cost and the transfer price to the branch; this difference is referred to as the *intracompany profit*. The branch's profit is the difference between the transfer price (the branch's cost) and the selling price to external parties.

While companies may employ various types of internal-responsibility accounting systems, external accounting reports must reflect inventory at its original cost to the company (unless market is lower) and may not include profits until the inventory is sold to external parties. Unrealized profits must be eliminated in the preparation of financial statements for external use. This is accomplished by using a workpaper similar to that used in preparing consolidated financial statements.

Usually the home office records its profit on inventory shipments to its branches in a separate account, allowing it to defer recognition of profits on intracompany sales until the inventory is sold to external parties by the branches. Each branch normally records inventory acquired from the home office in an account separate from inventory purchased from external parties so that the intracompany profit can be more easily identified.

To examine the treatment of intracompany profit included in shipments to a branch, assume that Jensen's home office acquires merchandise for $12,000 and ships it to the Mayfield branch, billing the branch for $15,000. The home office records the shipment with the following entry:

H(10)	Investment in Mayfield Branch	15,000	
	Inventory		12,000
	Unrealized Intracompany Profit		3,000
	Transfer of inventory to Mayfield branch,		
	billed in excess of cost.		

The $3,000 intracompany profit is unrealized because the inventory has not been sold to an external party. Recognition of the profit is deferred until the branch sells the merchandise externally.

The branch records receipt of the shipment with the following entry:

B(11)	Inventory—From Home Office	15,000	
	Home Office		15,000
	Transfer of inventory from home office.		

This entry records the inventory at the cost to the branch without separately recognizing the intracompany profit included in the transfer price. A separate inventory account is established in this case to facilitate eliminating the unrealized intracompany profit when external accounting reports are prepared for the company as a whole. When such reports are prepared while the inventory is still on hand, workpaper entries are needed to eliminate the Unrealized Intracompany Profit balance against the Inventory—From Home Office account. Thus the $3,000 unrealized intracompany profit is eliminated, and the inventory is reported at its $12,000 original cost to the company.

When the branch sells the inventory acquired from the home office, it recognizes a profit for the difference between the external selling price and the transfer price from the home office. Once the inventory has been sold externally, the home office recognizes the intracompany profit that it previously had deferred. For example, if the Mayfield branch sold 80 percent of the inventory transferred from the home office, the intracompany profit would be recognized by the home office with the following entry:

H(12)	Unrealized Intracompany Profit	2,400	
	Mayfield Branch Income		2,400
	Recognize intracompany profit:		
	$3,000 × .80		

This entry is appropriate if, for internal reporting purposes, the intracompany profit is to be attributed to the Mayfield branch.

Alternatively, the company may feel that the intracompany profit should be allocated to the home office for services that it has provided. In that case, the intracompany profit is recognized with the following entry on the books of the home office in place of entry H(12):

H(12a)	Unrealized Intracompany Profit	2,400	
	Realized Profit on Branch Shipments		2,400
	Recognize intracompany profit:		
	$3,000 × .80		

Accounting for Branch Fixed Assets

Normal procedures are followed in accounting for branch fixed assets recorded on the books of the branch. No special procedures are required in accounting for the purchase of fixed assets by the branch or the subsequent depreciation of those assets. On the other hand, if the fixed assets are purchased by the home office for the branch and the branch records the fixed assets on its books, an entry is required on the books of both the home office and the branch.

As an illustration of this, assume that Jensen's home office purchases $30,000 of store equipment for the Mayfield branch. The home office records the purchase with the following entry:

H(13)	Investment in Mayfield Branch	30,000	
	Cash		30,000
	Purchase of equipment for Mayfield		
	branch.		

The purchase is recorded by the branch with the following entry:

B(14)	Store Equipment	30,000	
	Home Office		30,000
	Record purchase of equipment by		
	home office.		

Some companies account for branch fixed assets on the books of the home office rather than on the books of the branch. This may provide the home office with better control over branch fixed assets and may facilitate the computation of depreciation for the company as a whole. For example, a company might establish depreciation policies to be applied to all fixed assets within the company. Some companies use group or composite depreciation methods, which may be applied most easily on a companywide basis.

When branch fixed assets are recorded only on the home office books, no entry is needed on the books of the branch if the home office makes the purchase. For example, if Jensen's home office purchases $30,000 of store equipment for the Mayfield branch, and the equipment is recorded on the books of the home office rather than the branch, the home office records the purchase as follows:

H(15)	Store Equipment—Mayfield Branch	30,000	
	Cash		30,000
	Purchase of equipment for Mayfield branch.		

No entry is recorded on the books of the branch.

If the branch purchases fixed assets that are recorded on the books of the home office, entries are needed by both the home office and the branch. As an example, assume that Jensen's Mayfield branch purchases $30,000 of store equipment to be used by the branch but carried on the home office books. The branch records the purchase with the following entry:

B(16)	Home Office	30,000	
	Cash		30,000
	Purchase of equipment.		

The purchase is recorded by the home office as follows:

H(17)	Store Equipment—Mayfield Branch	30,000	
	Investment in Mayfield Branch		30,000
	Record purchase of branch equipment by Mayfield branch.		

Because the branch purchases an asset that is carried on the home office books, the balances of both the Home Office account and the Investment in Mayfield Branch account are reduced. The transaction is treated as if the branch had purchased equipment for the home office.

Apportionment of Expenses

Branch expenses incurred and paid by the branch are recorded directly on the books of the branch. In some cases, however, the home office assigns expenses to a branch. These assigned expenses might be of several types:

a. Expenses incurred by the branch but paid by the home office; for example, inventory purchased from external parties by the branch and billed to the home office.

b. Expenses incurred by the home office on behalf of the branch; for example, depreciation on branch equipment carried on the home office books, or the cost of an advertising campaign for the branch commissioned by the home office.

c. Allocations of costs incurred by the home office; for example, a portion of the cost of a general advertising campaign, or a portion of the general home office overhead.

In some cases, these costs might be apportioned against branch income and recorded only on the books of the home office. Often, however, the branch to which the costs are apportioned is notified of the apportioned amounts and records the expenses on its own books. In this way, the income computed by the branch on its books includes all expenses deemed related to the branch.

As an illustration of the treatment of apportioned home office costs, assume that Jensen's home office incurs the following costs assigned to its Mayfield branch:

Utilities expenses (costs incurred by Mayfield branch and billed to home office master account)	$14,000
Depreciation expense (on Mayfield branch assets carried on home office books)	3,000
General overhead (allocated to branches based on gross sales)	18,000
Total	$35,000

Jensen's home office already has recorded these expenses in the normal manner, as if they related to the home office. Periodically, the home office notifies the branch of the apportioned expenses. The home office records the following entry upon notifying the Mayfield branch of the $35,000 of apportioned expenses:

H(18)	Investment in Mayfield Branch	35,000	
	Utilities Expense		14,000
	Depreciation Expense		3,000
	General Overhead Expense		18,000
	Apportion expenses to Mayfield branch.		

Upon notification of the expenses by the home office, the branch records the expenses as follows:

B(19)	Utilities Expense	14,000	
	Depreciation Expense	3,000	
	General Overhead Expense	18,000	
	Home Office		35,000
	Record expenses apportioned from home office.		

Without these entries, the home office income would be understated and the branch income overstated. While omission of these entries has no effect on the income of the company as a whole, the separate income amounts of the home office and branch may be important for internal reporting purposes.

Financial Statements for the Company as a Whole

While a home office and its branches may maintain separate books for internal record-keeping and evaluation purposes, the external accounting reports represent the home office and its branches as a single entity; the reporting entity is the company as a whole. Therefore, in the preparation of the company's financial statements, the accounts of the home office and its branches are combined. Intracompany or reciprocal account balances must be eliminated because they relate to activities within the company rather than activities between the company and external parties.

In the preparation of financial statements for the company as a whole, a workpaper normally is used to facilitate combining the accounts of the home office and its branches and eliminating the intracompany accounts. If a complete set of statements is prepared, a three-part workpaper similar to that illustrated in the consolidations chapters might be used to combine the accounts of the home office and branch. The workpaper is comparable to the consolidation workpaper except that the branch's Home Office account replaces the subsidiary's stockholders' equity in the workpaper. As in the preparation of consolidated financial statements, all eliminations are made in the workpaper and not on the separate books of the units being combined.

As an illustration of the basic workpaper entries needed to prepare external financial statements for a company with branch operations, assume the following with respect to Jensen Corporation's fiscal year ending December 31, 19X1:

1. Jensen Corporation's Mayfield branch reports a profit of $63,000 for 19X1.

2. The balance in Jensen's Investment in Mayfield Branch account is $133,000 on December 31, 19X1. The balance in the Mayfield branch's Home Office account is computed as follows:

Preclosing balance, December 31, 19X1	$ 70,000
Mayfield branch 19X1 income	63,000
Postclosing balance, December 31, 19X1	$133,000

3. A total of $3,000 is credited to Jensen's Unrealized Intracompany Profit account on shipments to the Mayfield branch during 19X1:

Intracompany profit realized by year-end	$2,400
Intracompany profit unrealized at year-end	600
Total 19X1 intracompany profit	$3,000

The intracompany profit realized by year-end is apportioned to the home office and recorded on the home office books in an account titled Realized Profit on Branch Shipments. The Unrealized Intracompany Profit account is reduced accordingly, leaving it with a year-end balance of $600.

4. On December 31, 19X1, the Mayfield branch has $8,000 of inventory on hand acquired from the home office; the inventory is carried in a separate account from inventory purchased externally.

In the December 31, 19X1, workpaper used to prepare Jensen Corporation's financial statements, the following entries are needed:

E(20)	Mayfield Branch Income	63,000	
	Home Office, preclosing balance	70,000	
	Investment in Mayfield Branch		133,000
	Eliminate intracompany accounts.		
E(21)	Realized Profit on Branch Shipments	2,400	
	Cost of Goods Sold		2,400
	Eliminate home office profit from cost of goods sold.		
E(22)	Unrealized Intracompany Profit	600	
	Inventory—From Home Office		600
	Eliminate unrealized intracompany profit from inventory.		
E(23)	Inventory	7,400	
	Inventory—From Home Office		7,400
	Reclassify inventory from home office: $8,000 − $600		

(As in the consolidations chapters, *E* is used to designate workpaper eliminating entries. These entries do not appear on the books of either the home office or the branch.)

Entry E(20) eliminates the reciprocal intracompany accounts so the financial statements appear as those of the single reporting enterprise. Because a full set of financial statements is being prepared, the individual income and expense accounts of the branch are combined with the like items of the home office. In total, the revenue and expense items of the branch net to an amount equal to the branch income recorded on the home office books. To avoid counting the branch income twice, the branch income included on the home office books is eliminated. Because the individual revenue and expense accounts of the branch are to be carried to the company financial statements, they are not eliminated.

In effect, entry E(20) can be viewed in two parts. The first part eliminates the branch income recorded on the home office books as well as the portion of the investment account increase stemming from the home office's recognition of branch income:

E(20a)	Mayfield Branch Income	63,000	
	Investment in Mayfield Branch		63,000

The second part of entry E(20) eliminates the remaining balance of the investment account against the reciprocal preclosing balance of the branch's Home Office account:

E(20b) Home Office, preclosing balance	70,000	
Investment in Mayfield Branch		70,000

This part of the entry eliminates the balances that would have been in the two reciprocal accounts if there had been no branch income. The debit to the preclosing balance of the Home Office account is analogous to the elimination of beginning retained earnings in the investment elimination entry for the preparation of consolidated financial statements.

Entry E(21) eliminates the account used by the home office to recognize intracompany profits on shipments to the branch that have been resold to external parties. This entry also reduces the cost of goods sold recorded by the branch. Cost of goods sold is reduced by the amount of the home office's profit included in the branch's cost of the inventory sold. While this entry has no effect on the company's income, it is needed to state correctly the individual income statement items from the perspective of the company as a whole.

Entry E(22) eliminates the unrealized intracompany profit from the branch's ending inventory, bringing the inventory back to its original cost. Entry E(23) classifies all the inventory together rather than segregating that shipped to the branch from the home office.

A workpaper for combining the accounts of a home office and a branch is illustrated in the next section.

Accounting for Branch Operations Illustrated

As a summary illustration of accounting for branch operations, assume that Ulmer, Inc., of Rockford, Illinois, a distributor of office equipment, establishes a branch sales office in Palm Beach, Florida. The home office sells both to retailers and to its Florida branch, with the profit on intercompany sales allocated to the home office. Also assume the following:

a. Ulmer establishes its Florida branch in 19X1 by transferring $30,000 in cash. In addition, the home office transfers $100,000 of new store equipment and fixtures to the Florida branch.

b. During 19X1, the home office purchases $260,000 of merchandise and the Florida branch purchases $50,000 of merchandise from external parties.

c. During the year, the home office transfers merchandise to the Florida branch with a total transfer price of $110,000. The merchandise cost the home office $70,000.

d. The home office sells merchandise costing $254,000 to external parties for $500,000 during the year and collects $480,000 on account. The Florida branch sells merchandise costing it $128,000 to external parties for $200,000 and collects $158,000 on account. Of the merchandise sold by the Florida branch, $38,000 had been purchased from external parties.

e. The Florida branch remits $70,000 in cash to the home office.

f. The home office incurs various operating expenses of $133,000 during the year. The Florida branch incurs various operating expenses of $34,000.

g. The home office pays $390,000 on account during 19X1, and the Florida branch pays $77,000 on account.

h. Ulmer declares and pays dividends of $50,000.

i. At the end of 19X1, the home office records depreciation of $30,000, and the Florida branch records depreciation of $6,000.

j. At the end of 19X1, the branch inventory on hand that had been purchased from external parties had cost $12,000. The branch inventory on hand that had been transferred from the home office had cost the home office $15,000 and been billed to the branch at $20,000.

The journal entries to record the 19X1 activities on the books of Ulmer's home office and the Florida branch are shown in Figure 11-2.

The workpaper to prepare financial statements for Ulmer, Inc., for 19X1 appears in Figure 11-3. The first two columns of the workpaper are the account balances from the books of the home office and the Florida branch. The next two columns are for the workpaper entries needed to eliminate or adjust account balances so they reflect the position and activities of the home office and the branch as a single entity. The final column shows the totals for each account item, where each total consists of the balance from the home office books plus the balance from the branch books, with the sum increased or decreased by any amounts in the elimination columns. The amounts in the last column are those that appear in the financial statements for the company as a whole.

The following eliminating entries are needed in the workpaper presented in Figure 11-3 for the preparation of Ulmer's 19X1 financial statements:

E(24)	Florida Branch Income	32,000	
	Home Office, preclosing balance	170,000	
	Investment in Florida Branch		202,000
	Eliminate intracompany accounts.		
E(25)	Realized Profit on Branch Shipments	35,000	
	Cost of Goods Sold		35,000
	Eliminate home office profit from cost of goods sold.		
E(26)	Unrealized Intracompany Profit	5,000	
	Inventory—From Home Office		5,000
	Eliminate unrealized intracompany profit from inventory.		
E(27)	Inventory	15,000	
	Inventory—From Home Office		15,000
	Reclassify inventory from home office.		

There are several important points to note regarding the workpaper illustrated in Figure 11-3:

1. The workpaper is divided into three sections, one each for the income statement, the retained earnings statement, and the balance sheet. The entire last line of the income statement section of the workpaper carries down to the retained earnings section; the entire last line of the retained earnings section carries down to the balance sheet section.

2. Because the home office records the income of the Florida branch on its books, the total income of the home office in the first column is equal to the total income of the company in the last column.

3. The home office's Florida Branch Income and its Investment in Florida Branch are eliminated in entry E(24) along with the Florida branch's preclosing balance of the Home Office account. The remainder of the Home Office account (the change resulting from the branch's current-period income) is eliminated by the carrydown totals from the income statement portion of the workpaper.

4. The branch's Home Office account replaces retained earnings in the branch's trial balance for the retained earnings and balance sheet sections of the workpaper.

5. The $5,000 of Unrealized Intracompany Profit from the home office's trial balance is eliminated by entry E(26), and the carrying amount of the branch's inventory is reduced to the original cost to the company (home office).

6. The $35,000 of Realized Profit on Branch Shipments included in the home office's trial balance equals total intracompany profit for the period ($110,000 − $70,000) minus the $5,000 of intracompany profit unrealized at the end of the year. This amount is eliminated with entry E(25), and Cost of Goods Sold is reduced to the original cost to the company (home office) of the merchandise sold.

7. As with the consolidation workpapers in previous chapters, the totals of the balance sheet debits and credits must be equal, the debits and credits of each elimination entry must be equal, and the totals of the debit and credit elimination columns at the bottom of the workpaper must be equal.

The financial statements for Ulmer, Inc., prepared from the workpaper in Figure 11-3 are shown in Figure 11-4.

ADDITIONAL CONSIDERATIONS

Transactions between Branches

Branches sometimes transfer assets or services from one to another. While there are several ways of accounting for such transfers, a commonly used approach is to treat the transfers as if they went through the home office. The branches involved in an interbranch transfer generally account for the transfer as if they are dealing with the home office rather than with another branch. For example, if Jensen Corporation's Mayfield branch transfers $5,000 of cash and inventory costing $10,000 to the Fairmont branch, the Mayfield branch records the following entry:

B(28)	Home Office	15,000	
	Cash		5,000
	Inventory		10,000
	Transfer of cash and inventory to Fairmont branch.		

FIGURE 11-2 Ulmer, Inc., home office and branch entries, 19X1.

Home Office Books

Entry	Account	Debit	Credit
(a)	Investment in Florida Branch	130,000	
	Cash		30,000
	Equipment		100,000
	Transfer of cash and equipment to Florida branch.		
(b)	Inventory	260,000	
	Accounts Payable		260,000
	Purchase of inventory.		
(c)	Investment in Florida Branch	110,000	
	Inventory		70,000
	Unrealized Intracompany Profit		40,000
	Transfer of inventory to Florida branch, billed in excess of cost.		
(d)	Accounts Receivable	500,000	
	Sales		500,000
	Record sales of inventory.		
	Cost of Goods Sold	254,000	
	Inventory		254,000
	Record cost of inventory sold.		
	Cash	480,000	
	Accounts Receivable		480,000
	Record collections on account.		
(e)	Cash	70,000	
	Investment in Florida Branch		70,000
	Cash remittance from Florida branch.		
(f)	Operating Expenses	133,000	
	Accounts Payable		133,000
	Record 19X1 operating expenses.		

Florida Branch Books

Entry	Account	Debit	Credit
(a)	Cash	30,000	
	Equipment	100,000	
	Home Office		130,000
	Transfer of cash and equipment from home office.		
(b)	Inventory	50,000	
	Accounts Payable		50,000
	Purchase of inventory.		
(c)	Inventory—From Home Office	110,000	
	Home Office		110,000
	Transfer of inventory from home office.		
(d)	Accounts Receivable	200,000	
	Sales		200,000
	Record sales of inventory.		
	Cost of Goods Sold	128,000	
	Inventory		38,000
	Inventory—From Home Office		90,000
	Record cost of inventory sold.		
	Cash	158,000	
	Accounts Receivable		158,000
	Record collections on account.		
(e)	Home Office	70,000	
	Cash		70,000
	Cash remittance to home office.		
(f)	Operating Expenses	34,000	
	Accounts Payable		34,000
	Record 19X1 operating expenses.		

Home office books:

	Debit	Credit
(g) Accounts Payable	390,000	
Cash		390,000
Record payments on account.		
(h) Dividends Declared	50,000	
Cash		50,000
Record 19X1 dividends paid.		
(i) Depreciation Expense	30,000	
Accumulated Depreciation		30,000
Record 19X1 depreciation.		
(j) Unrealized Intracompany Profit	35,000	
Realized Profit on Branch Shipments		35,000
Recognize portion of intracompany profit realized: $40,000 − $5,000		

Closing entries:

	Debit	Credit
Investment in Florida Branch	32,000	
Florida Branch Income		32,000
Record income from Florida branch.		
Sales	500,000	
Florida Branch Income	32,000	
Realized Profit on Branch Shipments	35,000	
Cost of Goods Sold		254,000
Operating Expenses		133,000
Depreciation Expense		30,000
Income Summary		150,000
Close revenue and expense accounts.		
Income Summary	150,000	
Retained Earnings		150,000
Close income summary.		
Retained Earnings	50,000	
Dividends Declared		50,000
Close dividends declared.		

Branch books:

	Debit	Credit
Accounts Payable	77,000	
Cash		77,000
Record payments on account.		
Depreciation Expense	6,000	
Accumulated Depreciation		6,000
Record 19X1 depreciation.		
Sales	200,000	
Cost of Goods Sold		128,000
Operating Expenses		34,000
Depreciation Expense		6,000
Income Summary		32,000
Close revenue and expense accounts.		
Income Summary	32,000	
Home Office		32,000
Close income summary.		

FIGURE 11-3 December 31, 19X1, workpaper for Ulmer, Inc., combined home office and branch financial statements.

Item	Home Office	Florida Branch	Eliminations Debit		Eliminations Credit		Combined
Sales	500,000	200,000					700,000
Florida Branch Income	32,000		(24)	32,000			
Realized Profit on Branch Shipments	35,000		(25)	35,000			
Credits	567,000	200,000					700,000
Cost of Goods Sold	254,000	128,000			(25)	35,000	347,000
Depreciation	30,000	6,000					36,000
Other Expenses	133,000	34,000					167,000
Debits	(417,000)	(168,000)					(550,000)
Net Income, carry forward	150,000	32,000		67,000		35,000	150,000
Retained Earnings, January 1	285,000						285,000
Home Office, preclosing balance		170,000	(24)	170,000			
Net Income, from above	150,000	32,000		67,000		35,000	150,000
	435,000	202,000					435,000
Dividends Declared	(50,000)						(50,000)
Retained Earnings, December 31, carry forward	385,000	202,000		237,000		35,000	385,000
Cash	47,000	41,000					88,000
Accounts Receivable	75,000	42,000					117,000
Inventory	52,000	12,000	(27)	15,000			79,000
Inventory—From Home Office		20,000			(26)	5,000	
					(27)	15,000	
Land	105,000						105,000
Buildings and Equipment	545,000	100,000					645,000
Investment in Florida Branch	202,000				(24)	202,000	
Debits	1,026,000	215,000					1,034,000
Accumulated Depreciation	105,000	6,000					111,000
Accounts Payable	31,000	7,000					38,000
Common Stock	500,000						500,000
Retained Earnings (and Home Office), from above	385,000	202,000		237,000		35,000	385,000
Unrealized Intracompany Profit	5,000		(26)	5,000			
Credits	1,026,000	215,000		257,000		257,000	1,034,000

Elimination entries:
(24) Eliminate intracompany accounts.
(25) Eliminate home office profit from cost of goods sold.
(26) Eliminate unrealized intracompany profit from inventory.
(27) Reclassify inventory from home office.

FIGURE 11-4 Ulmer, Inc., 19X1 financial statements.

Ulmer, Inc.
Income Statement
For the Year 19X1

Sales		$700,000
Cost of Goods Sold		(347,000)
Gross Margin		$353,000
Expenses:		
Depreciation	$ 36,000	
Other Expenses	167,000	(203,000)
Net Income		$150,000

Ulmer, Inc.
Retained Earnings Statement
For the Year 19X1

Retained Earnings, January 1, 19X1	$285,000
Net Income, 19X1	150,000
Less: Dividends	(50,000)
Retained Earnings, December 31, 19X1	$385,000

Ulmer, Inc.
Balance Sheet
December 31, 19X1

Assets:			Liabilities:		
Cash		$ 88,000	Accounts Payable		$ 38,000
Accounts Receivable		117,000			
Inventory		79,000			
Land		105,000	Stockholders' Equity:		
Buildings and Equipment	$645,000		Common Stock	$500,000	
Less: Accumulated					
Depreciation	(111,000)	534,000	Retained Earnings	385,000	885,000
Total Assets		$923,000	Total Liabilities and Equity		$923,000

The Fairmont branch records the transfer with the following entry:

B(29)	Cash	5,000	
	Inventory	10,000	
	Home Office		15,000
	Transfer of cash and inventory from		
	Mayfield branch.		

The transfer is recorded by the home office as follows:

```
H(30)  Investment in Fairmont Branch              15,000
           Investment in Mayfield Branch                      15,000
       Transfer of cash and inventory from
       Mayfield branch to Fairmont branch.
```

Unrealized Profits in Beginning Branch Inventory

Intracompany profits included in a branch's beginning inventory are recognized on the home office books as being realized whenever the merchandise is sold by the branch. The treatment is the same as if the intracompany transfer had occurred in the current period. In the period in which the branch sells the inventory to external parties, the home office reduces its Unrealized Intracompany Profit account and increases its Realized Profit on Branch Shipments account (assuming the intracompany profit is to be attributed to the home office). When financial statements are prepared for the company as a whole, the balance of the Realized Profit on Branch Shipments account is eliminated against cost of goods sold and any remaining unrealized intracompany profits are eliminated against the carrying amount of the inventory.

Use of a Periodic Inventory System

The illustrations presented throughout the chapter were based on use of a perpetual inventory system. If a company uses a periodic inventory system, the home office and branch entries are somewhat different from those used under a perpetual inventory system. As an illustration of this difference, assume that in the Jensen Corporation example used earlier in the chapter, Jensen's home office ships inventory to its Mayfield branch and bills the branch for the inventory's original cost of $8,000. Under a periodic inventory system, the home office records the shipment of inventory as follows:

```
H(31)  Investment in Mayfield Branch             8,000
           Shipments to Branch                              8,000
       Transfer of inventory to Mayfield branch.
```

The balance of the Shipments to Branch account is subtracted from the total of beginning inventory and purchases in the computation of the home office's cost of goods sold for the period. This reduces the total goods available for sale and avoids an overstatement of cost of goods sold.

The branch records the transfer of inventory with the following entry:

```
B(32)  Shipments from Home Office               8,000
           Home Office                                      8,000
       Transfer of inventory from home office.
```

The Shipments from Home Office account on the branch books is included in the computation of the branch's cost of goods sold in the same way as purchases; it increases the branch's total goods available for sale.

The home office's Shipments to Branch account and the branch's Shipments from Home Office account are reciprocal accounts and are eliminated against one another in the workpaper when financial statements are prepared for the company as a whole.

Divisional Reporting

Companies typically establish internal management control systems to help assure that individuals within the organization work toward its overall goals. There are many different aspects of a management control system, and each company's system is unique in certain respects. However, a crucial feature of all management control systems is the internal reporting system.

Companies may be organized in many different ways for internal reporting purposes. Usually a company defines certain responsibility centers, and the internal reporting system is structured along responsibility center lines, with each responsibility center expected to achieve certain objectives. For example, a profit center is responsible for achieving set profit goals, a cost center for not exceeding budgeted costs, and a production center for filling output quotas.

One organizational approach to responsibility accounting is the home office and branch structure discussed in this chapter. However, other reporting structures commonly are found in practice as well. A multicorporate enterprise may report along subsidiary lines, as discussed in earlier chapters. A single company with multiple operations might establish different divisions and report along divisional lines. Divisions might be organized by geographic location, product line, or any of a number of other factors relevant to the company.

Often, divisions established as profit centers are treated as autonomous units for accounting purposes. Each division may have its own accounting system and prepare separate financial statements for internal reporting purposes. For external reporting, however, the accounts of all of a company's divisions must be combined; the individual divisions are not separate legal or reporting entities (in most organizational structures). For example, most of General Motors' domestic automotive operations are conducted through a single corporation with different divisions (for example, Chevrolet, Buick), although its new Saturn operations have been separately incorporated as a subsidiary.

While many different approaches to divisional reporting are found in practice, most are quite similar to the home office and branch procedures discussed earlier in this chapter, or represent a combination of those procedures and the parent-subsidiary procedures presented in earlier chapters. Regardless of the internal accounting procedures used, the accounts of the divisions are combined and intracompany accounts eliminated for external reporting. If divisions sell inventory or other assets or services to one another, as is often the case, any intracompany profit that is unrealized from the company's viewpoint must be eliminated when financial statements are prepared for external reporting.

SUMMARY OF KEY CONCEPTS AND TERMS

Companies often conduct their activities in more than one location. Locations away from a company's home office are referred to by various names, but two main types of outlying operations are sales agencies and branches. Sales agencies usually take orders that are filled by the home office. They usually have little autonomy, do not stock merchandise, and do not have separate accounting systems.

Branches vary in the degree of autonomy. Most branches have greater autonomy than sales agencies. They usually do stock merchandise and frequently have their own accounting systems.

A branch office's books consist of a self-balancing set of accounts, similar to the books of a separate company. However, a Home Office account replaces the owners' equity accounts found on the books of separate companies. The Home Office account indicates the home office's equity in the branch.

The Home Office account on the books of the branch is reciprocal to the Investment in Branch account on the home office books. Both accounts are increased by asset transfers from the home office to the branch and by branch profits. Both accounts are decreased by asset transfers from the branch to the home office and by branch losses.

While companies often prepare separate accounting reports for the home office and each branch for internal use, the external accounting reports must reflect the activities and position of the company as a whole. The accounts of the home office and the branches are combined to prepare financial statements for external reporting. A workpaper normally is used to facilitate the process of combining home office and branch accounts. In addition, certain account balances must be eliminated or changed so that the results reflect a single company. The reciprocal Home Office and Investment in Branch accounts are eliminated, and the amounts reported as cost of goods sold and ending inventory are adjusted for any intracompany profit recorded by the home office on shipments of merchandise to its branches.

Branch office	Reciprocal accounts
Home office	Sales agency
Intracompany accounts	Transfer price
Intracompany profit	

QUESTIONS

Q11-1 Distinguish between a sales agency and a branch.

Q11-2 How does a sales agency's accounting system usually differ from that employed by a branch?

Q11-3 Distinguish between a home office and a branch.

Q11-4 Why do companies establish sales agencies and branches?

Q11-5 For a company with a home office and numerous branches, why are separate accounting records often maintained for each of the branches when financial statements for external reporting purposes are prepared only for the company as a whole?

Q11-6 In what way are the accounting systems employed by agencies and branches related to the degree of their autonomy?

Q11-7 What are intracompany accounts? Give two examples.

Q11-8 What is meant by a reciprocal relationship? Of what significance are reciprocal relationships for branch accounting?

Q11-9 What items are recorded in the home office's Investment in Branch account? What causes the balance in this account to change?

Q11-10 What items are recorded in a branch's Home Office account? What causes the balance in this account to change?

Q11-11 When is branch income recognized on the books of the home office? How is the home office's Investment in Branch account affected by the income recognition?

Q11-12 What is the accounting treatment for freight charges incurred in shipping inventory from the home office to a branch? Why?

Q11-13 What is a transfer price? Of what significance are transfer prices in accounting for branch operations?

Q11-14 What is intracompany profit? How is unrealized intracompany profit treated for external reporting purposes?

Q11-15 Why might a home office transfer inventory to a branch office and bill the branch for an amount higher than cost?

Q11-16 Why are certain account balances eliminated or adjusted in combining home office and branch accounts for external reporting purposes?

CASES

C11-1 Contrasting Sales Agency and Branch Accounting Systems

Bailey Products, Inc., maintains a total of 11 sales agencies throughout California. Each agency carries a limited number of inventory samples and relies primarily on lavishly illustrated catalogs in presenting the merchandise available for sale. Orders are taken at each of the agency offices and transmitted daily to one of the two main sales distribution offices located in Van Nuys and Oakland. All inventory is shipped from one of the two distribution offices. While individual agency offices do accept cash payments, all cash received is deposited daily in local branches of the Western United Bank. The amounts are credited to the company's account at the Oakland branch of Western United Bank, and only Bailey's home office has access to the funds. Most merchandise is sold on credit, and all billings emanate from and remittances are mailed to Bailey's home office.

Chesapeake Distributors, Inc., with its home office in Towson, Maryland, serves the mid-Atlantic region through four branch offices. Each branch carries a full line of inventory, makes deliveries, and collects accounts. Most inventory is purchased by the home office and transferred to the branches at cost plus 25 percent. For internal reporting purposes, each branch is treated as a profit center.

Required

Describe the main elements of the accounting system that you would expect to be used by Bailey Products. Compare that accounting system with the one that you would expect to be used by Chesapeake Distributors. Indicate why you would expect each of the differences to exist.

C11-2 Comparison of Branch and Subsidiary Accounting

Nieminsky Corporation owns all the stock of four subsidiaries through which most of the company's activities are conducted. Although the subsidiaries are involved in similar activities, they operate autonomously and are treated as profit centers.

Banks Manufacturing, Inc., is a single corporation with no subsidiaries. The company is organized around its home office and three manufacturing plants. The manufacturing plants are established as profit centers and are responsible for producing and selling their assigned products. All raw materials and equipment are purchased by the home office and transferred to the plants at amounts in excess of cost. Periodically, the plants remit to the home office cash collected from sales.

Required

a. What similarities would you expect to find in the accounting systems of Nieminsky and Banks? What differences would you expect?

b. Compare the process of preparing consolidated financial statements for Nieminsky with the process of preparing Banks's external accounting reports.

EXERCISES

E11-1 Establishing a Branch

Diversified Industries operated primarily in the western United States. Wishing to expand its sales and operations into the eastern part of the country, Diversified established a separate branch in New Jersey in 19X2. The New Jersey branch maintained its own accounting records. The following transactions occurred during 19X2:

1. Cash of $80,000 and inventory costing $150,000 were transferred to the newly established branch.

2. Equipment was purchased for $120,000 by Diversified Industries and given to the branch. The equipment was recorded in the records of the branch.

3. The branch purchased additional inventory for $35,000 on account.

4. It cost $300 to ship the inventory and $1,000 to ship the equipment to the branch. Freight charges were paid by the home office.

5. The branch used $50,000 of its cash to purchase a small warehouse to store the inventory acquired from the home office.

Required

Prepare the journal entries recorded by the home office of Diversified Industries and by the New Jersey branch for each of the transactions.

E11-2 Recording Branch Activities

In 19X6, Sunshine Products elected to establish a branch in a nearby state in order to take advantage of favorable tax laws for companies owning property there. Sunshine's home office and branch were involved in the following transactions during 19X8:

1. The branch purchased inventory of $80,000 from Bosco Manufacturing and immediately made payment.

2. Sunshine's home office shipped inventory costing $120,000 to the branch and billed the branch for $180,000.

3. By the end of the period, the branch had sold $150,000 of its purchases from the home office for $240,000 and all the inventory purchased from Bosco Manufacturing for $86,000. No cash was collected at the time of sale.

4. Sunshine Products elected to apportion home office costs of $20,000 in advertising charges, $35,000 of depreciation charges, and $12,000 of utility costs to the branch.

5. The branch collected $235,000 on its receivables and paid the home office the full amount owed on its inventory purchase.

Required

Prepare the journal entries recorded by Sunshine Products' home office and branch on each of the transactions.

E11-3 Investment in Operating Division

Major Manufacturing Corporation established a new divisional operation on the west coast in order to manufacture and sell new products in that market more cheaply. The new division was started with $1,000,000 in cash. In addition, the following transfers took place:

1. Inventory, which had cost Major Manufacturing Corporation $300,000 to produce, was sold to the new division for $450,000 on account.

2. The division resold $240,000 of the items purchased from the head office for $530,000.

3. Total income reported by the division in its first year of operations was $55,000.

4. The division paid $290,000 that it owed on account to the head office.

5. The division was granted authority to borrow $400,000 from its local bank and purchase a future plant site. The money was borrowed and the site purchased before the end of the year.

Required

Compute the balance in the Investment in Western Division account on the books of Major Manufacturing's head office at the end of the first year of the division's operations.

E11-4 Determining Income Statement Totals

Bean Corporation has a branch in a nearby town and regularly ships inventory to the branch. During 19X2, Bean Corporation purchased items costing $30,000 and transferred

$20,000 of the units to the branch at a billing price of $45,000. Bean Corporation sold 60 percent of the remaining units to Separate Company for $11,000. The branch sold 70 percent of the units purchased from the home office during 19X2 for $58,000.

Required

a. Give the journal entries recorded by Bean's home office and branch during 19X2 related to inventory transactions.
b. Determine:
   (1) Cost of goods sold recorded by the branch for 19X2
   (2) Sales recorded by the branch for 19X2
   (3) Cost of goods sold for Bean Corporation as a whole for 19X2
   (4) Sales for Bean Corporation as a whole for 19X2

E11-5 Inventory Transfers

Short Products Corporation, a manufacturer of electronics gear, established a separate branch in another city in 19X6. During 19X6, Short produced inventory for $200,000 and sold it to the branch for $280,000. The branch sold 25 percent of the inventory in 19X6 for $105,000 and 75 percent in 19X7 for $350,000. Both Short and its branch used perpetual inventory systems.

Required

a. Give all journal entries related to the inventory transfers during 19X6 recorded on the books of Short Products Corporation's (1) home office; (2) branch.

b. Give the eliminating entries needed on December 31, 19X6, to remove the effects of the inventory transfer in preparing financial statements for Short Products Corporation.

E11-6 Inventory Transfers in Consecutive Years

Flash Electronics routinely transfers inventory to its branch operation located in another state. In 19X6, Flash's home office sold inventory costing $240,000 to its branch for $300,000. The branch sold 45 percent of the inventory in 19X6 for $180,000 and the remaining 55 percent in 19X7 for $295,000. In 19X7, Flash Electronics transferred $150,000 of inventory to its branch for $225,000. The branch sold one-third of the inventory in 19X7 for $140,000 and two-thirds in 19X8 for $280,000.

Required

a. Prepare the journal entries to be recorded during 19X7 by Flash Electronics' (1) home office and (2) branch with regard to the inventory transactions.

b. Give the eliminating entries needed on December 31, 19X7, to remove the effects of the inventory transfers in preparing financial statements for Flash Electronics.

E11-7 Sale of Land Transferred to Branch

On January 1, 19X3, Amalgamated Wholesalers, Inc., created a separate branch in New York City by transferring to the branch cash of $40,000, inventory with a book value of $120,000, and land with a book value of $150,000. At the time, the inventory had a fair value of $180,000, and the land was worth $190,000. The transfers were recorded at fair value by both the home office and the branch.

The branch purchases all its inventory from the home office. During 19X3, Amalgamated Wholesalers purchased additional inventory for $200,000 and sold it to the branch for $280,000. Both the home office and the branch use a fifo cost flow assumption for inventory.

In 19X3, the branch decided not to build on the land transferred from the home office and sold it for $165,000. An income statement prepared by the branch for 19X3 contained the following items:

Sales		$450,000
Cost of Goods Sold	$320,000	
Rent Expense	40,000	
Loss on Sale of Land	25,000	(385,000)
Contribution to Profits		$ 65,000

Required

a. Give the entries to be recorded on the books of the home office of Amalgamated Wholesalers during 19X3 related to its investment in the branch.

b. Give the workpaper eliminating entries needed for December 31, 19X3, to prepare financial statements for Amalgamated Wholesalers.

E11-8* Transfers between Branches

Bright Corporation already has a branch in Brandenburg and wishes to establish a new branch in Dullesville. On March 15, 19X5, Bright Corporation provides the branch in Dullesville with cash of $40,000 and land of $50,000. In addition, equipment with a book value of $120,000 and inventory of $70,000 is transferred from the branch in Brandenburg to Dullesville. The new branch immediately uses $22,000 in cash to purchase additional inventory.

Required

Record the journal entries for the home office and each branch for 19X5.

E11-9* Periodic Inventory Valuation

Mining Products Corporation established a branch near several of its major customers and transferred a substantial amount of inventory to the branch in hopes of improving product delivery time to its customers. During 19X6, the home office purchased goods for $40,000 and immediately shipped the items to the branch, billing the branch for $60,000. The items were resold for $85,000 by the branch before year-end. Both the home office and the branch use periodic inventory systems.

Required

a. Prepare the journal entries recorded by the home office and branch during 19X6 in connection with the inventory transfer and sale. Omit closing entries.

b. Give the eliminating entry or entries needed to remove the effects of the intracompany inventory sale in preparing Mining Products Corporation financial statements at the end of 19X6.

E11-10* Inventory Profits under Periodic Inventory System

Both Dizzy World and its branch operation use periodic inventory systems. On January 1, 19X5, the branch held $14,000 of inventory purchased from Dizzy World's home office. The inventory had cost the home office $9,000, and transportation charges of $1,500 were paid by the home office to deliver the units to the branch. During 19X5, Dizzy World purchased $200,000 of inventory and sold $80,000 of it to the branch for $100,000; freight charges paid by the home office for delivery to the branch were $4,800. On December 31, 19X5, the branch continued to hold $30,000 of the units purchased from Dizzy's home office during 19X5. The branch recorded total sales of $118,000 for the year.

Required

a. Present the entries recorded on the books of the home office and the branch for 19X5.

b. Give the workpaper entries needed to eliminate the effects of the intracompany inventory transfers in preparing the financial statements of Dizzy World for 19X5.

PROBLEMS

P11-11 Creation of a Branch Operation

Slick Auto Sales decided to create a branch in Mason City at the start of 19X3. The branch operation had the following transactions during 19X3:

1. Automobiles costing $350,000 and cash of $200,000 were transferred from the home office.

2. The branch purchased on account additional automobile inventory of $400,000 from other distributors.

3. Sales of $650,000 were made by the branch during the period. The cost of these sales was $425,000. Cash of $600,000 was collected from sales during the year.

4. Advertising costs of $40,000, sales commissions of $65,000, and other operating costs of $45,000 were incurred and paid by the branch.

5. The branch paid $370,000 on account to other distributors and returned $120,000 to the home office.

Required

   a. Record each of the transactions on the books of the branch.

   b. Prepare an income statement for the branch for 19X3.

   c. Prepare a balance sheet as of December 31, 19X3, for the branch.

P11-12 Inventory Sold to Branch

Plastic Products Corporation created a branch to market its plastic window signs for automobiles. The balance sheets of the home office and branch contained the following amounts on December 31, 19X6:

Item	Home Office	Branch
Cash	$ 70,000	$ 20,000
Accounts Receivable	110,000	60,000
Inventory	200,000	68,000
Inventory—From Home Office		32,000
Land	50,000	70,000
Buildings and Equipment	500,000	300,000
Less: Accumulated Depreciation	(240,000)	(120,000)
Investment in Branch	305,000	
	$995,000	$430,000
Accounts Payable	$ 53,000	$ 25,000
Bonds Payable	300,000	
Notes Payable		100,000
Common Stock	200,000	
Retained Earnings	430,000	
Home Office		305,000
Unrealized Intracompany Profit	12,000	
	$995,000	$430,000

During the year, Plastic Products Corporation shipped $50,000 of inventory to the branch and billed it $80,000. The branch resold 60 percent of the inventory before the end of the period.

Required

   a. Give the eliminating entries needed to prepare a balance sheet for Plastic Products Corporation as of December 31, 19X6.

   b. Prepare a December 31, 19X6, balance sheet for Plastic Products Corporation.

P11-13   Asset Transfers to Multiple Branches

Gold Products Company has branches in Silverton and Durango. Balance sheet amounts for the company's home office and branches on December 31, 19X4, are as follows:

Item	Home Office	Silverton Branch	Durango Branch
Cash	$ 81,000	$ 20,000	$ 15,000
Accounts Receivable	100,000	40,000	25,000
Inventory	260,000	50,000	44,000
Inventory—From Home Office		70,000	56,000
Land	70,000	30,000	20,000
Buildings and Equipment	700,000	350,000	200,000
Less: Accumulated Depreciation	(280,000)	(120,000)	(80,000)
Investment in Silverton Branch	395,000		
Investment in Durango Branch	260,000		
	$1,586,000	$440,000	$280,000
Accounts Payable	$ 110,000	$ 45,000	$ 20,000
Bonds Payable	400,000		
Common Stock	300,000		
Retained Earnings	700,000		
Home Office		395,000	260,000
Unrealized Intracompany Profits:			
Silverton Branch	60,000		
Durango Branch	16,000		
	$1,586,000	$440,000	$280,000

The home office sells inventory to the branches at a constant markup. During 19X4, Gold Products Company transferred $200,000 of inventory to the Silverton branch and billed the branch for $280,000. Gold Products also transferred inventory costing $60,000 to the Durango branch and billed the branch for $84,000. In addition, Gold Products purchased equipment on December 31, 19X4, for $35,000 and immediately sold it to the branch in Silverton for $75,000.

Required

a. Give the eliminating entries needed to prepare a December 31, 19X4, balance sheet for Gold Products Company.

b. Prepare a balance sheet workpaper and a balance sheet for Gold Products Company as a whole as of December 31, 19X4.

P11-14 Sale of Depreciable Asset to Branch

Expando Corporation established a branch in Edgarville on January 1, 19X7, by transferring cash of $100,000 and buildings and equipment billed to the branch at $200,000. The depreciable assets transferred had been purchased on January 1, 19X2, by Expando for $240,000 and had an expected economic life of 15 years from the date of original purchase and 10 years from the time of transfer to the branch. Straight-line depreciation is used by both the home office and the branch. During 19X9, Expando transferred inventory costing $45,000 to the branch for $70,000. The branch resold 40 percent of the inventory before December 31, 19X9.

The following balance sheets are provided by Expando for its home office and its Edgarville branch as of December 31, 19X9:

Item	Home Office	Edgarville Branch
Cash	$ 50,000	$ 40,000
Accounts Receivable	90,000	80,000
Inventory	150,000	78,000
Inventory—From Home Office		42,000
Land	30,000	40,000
Buildings and Equipment	400,000	200,000
Less: Accumulated Depreciation	(240,000)	(60,000)
Investment in Edgarville Branch	350,000	
	$830,000	$420,000
Accounts Payable	$ 47,000	$ 5,000
Bonds Payable	300,000	
Notes Payable		65,000
Common Stock	100,000	
Retained Earnings	340,000	
Home Office		350,000
Unrealized Intracompany Profit	43,000	
	$830,000	$420,000

Required

a. Give the workpaper eliminating entries needed to prepare a balance sheet for Expando Corporation as of December 31, 19X9.

b. Prepare a December 31, 19X9, balance sheet for Expando Corporation.

P11-15 Trial Balance with Intracompany Land Transfer

Trial balances for Alpine Company's home office and Resort branch on December 31, 19X4, are as follows:

Item	Home Office Debit	Home Office Credit	Resort Branch Debit	Resort Branch Credit
Cash	$ 50,000		$ 60,000	
Accounts Receivable	80,000		40,000	
Inventory	110,000		70,000	
Land	60,000		80,000	
Buildings and Equipment	370,000		240,000	
Investment in Resort Branch	340,000			
Cost of Goods Sold	170,000		105,000	
Depreciation Expense	25,000		15,000	
Other Expenses	60,000		10,000	
Dividends Declared	30,000			
Accumulated Depreciation		$ 130,000		$ 60,000
Accounts Payable		91,000		90,000
Bonds Payable		200,000		
Common Stock		150,000		
Retained Earnings		380,000		
Home Office				320,000
Unrealized Intracompany Profit		24,000		
Sales		300,000		150,000
Resort Branch Income		20,000		
	$1,295,000	$1,295,000	$620,000	$620,000

The Resort branch conducts all its operations separately from those of Alpine's home office. In 19X2, the Resort branch paid $44,000 to the home office for land that Alpine had purchased for $20,000 several years earlier.

Required

Complete a December 31, 19X4, workpaper for the preparation of financial statements for Alpine Company.

P11-16 Journal Entries for Branch Operations

Shoreline Corporation established a branch operation in the city of Oceanport on January 1, 19X2. The balance sheet for Shoreline Corporation on December 31, 19X1, was as follows:

Shoreline Corporation
Balance Sheet
December 31, 19X1

Cash	$160,000	Accounts Payable	$ 30,000
Accounts Receivable	120,000	Bonds Payable	400,000
Inventory	210,000	Common Stock	200,000
Land	80,000	Additional Capital	70,000
Buildings and Equipment	400,000	Retained Earnings	110,000
Less: Accumulated			
Depreciation	(160,000)		
	$810,000		$810,000

The following transactions occurred during 19X2:

1. Shoreline Corporation transferred $100,000 of cash and $80,000 of inventory to the new branch. The inventory cost Shoreline Corporation $56,000 to produce.

2. The branch purchased $50,000 of inventory from other companies and recorded sales of $200,000 for the period. Cost of goods sold for the period consisted of $40,000 of purchases from outsiders and $60,000 of inventory transferred from the home office. A total of $170,000 was collected on account before year-end.

3. The home office purchased $300,000 of inventory and sold $320,000 of goods to external parties for $460,000. A total of $375,000 was collected on account during 19X2.

4. The branch remitted $65,000 to the home office as partial payment for inventory. Shoreline declared and paid a dividend of $15,000.

5. The home office recorded depreciation of $35,000 for 19X2 and had other operating expenses of $55,000. The branch recorded rent expense of $36,000 for leased facilities and had other operating expenses of $40,000.

Required

a. Present the journal entries that would appear on the books of Shoreline's home office for 19X2. Include closing entries.

b. Present the journal entries that would appear on the books of Shoreline's Oceanport branch office for 19X2. Include closing entries.

c. Compute the balance of Shoreline's retained earnings as of December 31, 19X2.

P11-17 Trial Balance with Inventory Profits

Dependable Appliance Corporation is considering establishing a number of sales branches to assist in selling its product line. As an experiment, it established a branch in New York City in 19X2 and has operated it for 3 years. During 19X5, Dependable shipped $60,000 of inventory to the branch and billed it for $90,000. On December 31, 19X5, the branch held $18,000 of inventory purchased by the home office for $12,000. The following amounts were reported in the trial balances of the home office and the branch on December 31, 19X5:

Item	Home Office Debit	Home Office Credit	New York Branch Debit	New York Branch Credit
Cash	$ 60,000		$ 55,000	
Accounts Receivable	70,000		40,000	
Inventory	110,000		80,000	
Land	80,000		40,000	
Buildings and Equipment	700,000		400,000	
Investment in New York Branch	430,000			
Dividends Declared	20,000			
Cost of Goods Sold	240,000		120,000	
Depreciation Expense	30,000		15,000	
Other Expenses	20,000		35,000	
Accumulated Depreciation		$ 350,000		$165,000
Accounts Payable		90,000		20,000
Bonds Payable		300,000		
Common Stock		200,000		
Home Office				400,000
Retained Earnings		460,000		
Unrealized Intracompany Profit		6,000		
Sales		300,000		200,000
New York Branch Income		30,000		
Realized Intracompany Profit		24,000		
	$1,760,000	$1,760,000	$785,000	$785,000

Required

a. Prepare and complete a workpaper as of December 31, 19X5, to develop financial statements for Dependable Appliance Corporation.

b. Prepare a 19X5 income statement and balance sheet for Dependable Appliance Corporation.

P11-18 Workpaper for Home Office and Multiple Branches

Ortegren Sales Company is located in Arlington, Texas. Its balance sheet accounts at the beginning of the year are as follows:

Cash	$ 20,000	
Accounts Receivable	25,000	
Inventory	41,000	
Land	52,000	
Buildings and Equipment	90,000	
Accumulated Depreciation		$ 21,000
Accounts Payable		18,000
Notes Payable		30,000
Common Stock		100,000
Retained Earnings		59,000
	$228,000	$228,000

At the beginning of the year, the company establishes branches in Denton and Houston. The company uses a perpetual inventory system. The following transactions occur during the year:

1. The home office purchases equipment on account for $40,000 and immediately transfers half to each of the two branches at cost.

2. The home office transfers cash of $3,000 to the Denton branch and $5,000 to the Houston branch.

3. The company sells inventory to unrelated parties at a 40 percent gross profit and transfers inventory to its branches at a 20 percent gross profit. During the year, the home office has sales of $175,000 to unrelated parties and transfers inventory to the Denton branch at a $140,000 price and to the Houston branch at a $150,000 price.

4. The branches sell their inventory, all acquired from the home office, at a 25 percent gross profit. During the year, the Denton branch has sales of $136,000, and the Houston branch has sales of $152,000.

5. Operating expenses during the year, excluding cost of goods sold and depreciation, total $85,000 for the home office, $13,000 for the Denton branch, and $11,000 for the Houston branch.

6. Selected balance sheet accounts at the end of the year are as follows:

	Home Office	Denton Branch	Houston Branch
Accounts Receivable	$28,000	$11,000	$14,000
Inventory	45,000	38,000	36,000
Accounts Payable	20,000	1,000	2,000
Notes Payable	30,000	35,000	40,000
Accumulated Depreciation	28,000	4,000	4,000

7. During the year, the Denton branch transfers $135,000 of cash to the home office, and the Houston branch transfers $151,000.

Required

a. Record the transactions for the year on the books of (1) the Denton branch; (2) the Houston branch; (3) the home office (include recognition of branch income).

b. Present a workpaper with the appropriate eliminations for the preparation of annual financial statements for Ortegren Sales Company.

P11-19* **Trial Balance with Beginning Inventory Profit**

Reliable Products Corporation operated a branch in a nearby community to facilitate sales and to enhance customer service. Trial balances for the company's home office and branch on December 31, 19X2, are as follows:

Item	Home Office Debit	Home Office Credit	Branch Debit	Branch Credit
Cash	$ 70,000		$ 60,000	
Accounts Receivable	80,000		90,000	
Inventory	150,000		55,000	
Inventory—From Home Office			45,000	
Land	85,000		50,000	
Buildings and Equipment	600,000		400,000	
Investment in Branch	310,000			
Cost of Goods Sold	410,000		170,000	
Depreciation Expense	30,000		20,000	
Other Expenses	50,000		30,000	
Dividends Declared	25,000			
Accumulated Depreciation		$ 370,000		$170,000
Accounts Payable		60,000		20,000
Bonds Payable		300,000		
Notes Payable				200,000
Common Stock		100,000		
Retained Earnings		390,000		
Home Office Balance				280,000
Unrealized Intracompany Profit		15,000		
Sales		500,000		250,000
Branch Income		30,000		
Realized Profit on Branch Shipments		45,000		
	$1,810,000	$1,810,000	$920,000	$920,000

During 19X1, Reliable Products shipped inventory costing $90,000 to its branch and billed the branch $150,000. At the end of the period, inventory that included intracompany profit of $20,000 remained unsold. During 19X2, Reliable Products shipped $80,000 of inventory to its branch and billed the branch for $120,000. The branch sold all the inventory held over from 19X1 in 19X2. At the end of 19X2, the branch still held some of the inventory transferred from the home office during the year.

Required

Develop and complete a workpaper for the preparation of 19X2 financial statements for Reliable Products Corporation.

P11-20* Company with Multiple Branches

Stewart Corporation operates two branches, one in Meakinburg and the other in Riverdale. On December 31, 19X5, the trial balances for the company's home office and its branches are as follows:

Item	Home Office	Meakinburg Branch	Riverdale Branch
Cash	$ 54,000	$ 60,000	$ 20,000
Accounts Receivable	100,000	90,000	40,000
Inventory	150,000	100,000	80,000
Land	60,000	50,000	20,000
Buildings and Equipment	600,000	400,000	300,000
Investment in Meakinburg Branch	310,000		
Investment in Riverdale Branch	225,000		
Cost of Goods Sold	310,000	170,000	130,000
Depreciation Expense	30,000	20,000	15,000
Other Expenses	50,000	30,000	20,000
Dividends Declared	16,000		
	$1,905,000	$920,000	$625,000
Accumulated Depreciation	$ 370,000	$170,000	$125,000
Accounts Payable	28,000	20,000	10,000
Bonds Payable	500,000		
Notes Payable		200,000	100,000
Common Stock	100,000		
Home Office		280,000	210,000
Retained Earnings	437,000		
Unrealized Intracompany Profit	20,000		
Sales	400,000	250,000	180,000
Meakinburg Branch Income	30,000		
Riverdale Branch Income	15,000		
Realized Intracompany Profit	5,000		
	$1,905,000	$920,000	$625,000

During 19X5, the Meakinburg branch purchased inventory for $13,000 and sold it to the Riverdale branch for $18,000. The Riverdale branch resold all this inventory before December 31, 19X5. On December 31, 19X5, Stewart Corporation purchased equipment for $100,000 and immediately transferred it to the Meakinburg branch for a payment of $120,000. There were no other transactions between the home office and the branches in 19X5.

Required

a. Develop and complete a workpaper for the preparation of Stewart Corporation's 19X5 financial statements.

b. Present Stewart Corporation's 19X5 income statement and balance sheet.

P11-21* Company with Periodic Inventory System

Drydock Industries decided to establish a small boatyard near Virginia Beach and to treat it as a branch for accounting purposes. On January 1, 19X7, the branch held inventory containing intracompany profits of $20,000. During 19X7, Drydock transferred $70,000 of inventory to the branch and billed it for $120,000. On December 31, 19X7, the branch held inventory on which Drydock had recorded profits of $32,000. Total inventories held by Drydock Industries' home office and its branch on December 31, 19X7, were $150,000 and $100,000, respectively. Drydock uses a periodic inventory system; the branch does not use separate accounts for inventory acquired from the home office. Trial balances for the company's home office and branch on December 31, 19X7, were as follows:

	Home Office		Branch	
Item	Debit	Credit	Debit	Credit
Cash	$ 70,000		$ 60,000	
Accounts Receivable	80,000		90,000	
Inventory	120,000		80,000	
Land	85,000		50,000	
Buildings and Equipment	600,000		400,000	
Investment in Branch	310,000			
Purchases	440,000		70,000	
Shipments from Home Office			120,000	
Depreciation Expense	30,000		20,000	
Other Expenses	50,000		30,000	
Dividends Declared	25,000			
Accumulated Depreciation		$ 370,000		$170,000
Accounts Payable		50,000		20,000
Bonds Payable		300,000		
Notes Payable				200,000
Common Stock		100,000		
Retained Earnings		390,000		
Home Office				280,000
Unrealized Intracompany Profit		32,000		
Sales		430,000		250,000
Shipments to Branch		70,000		
Branch Income		30,000		
Realized Intracompany Profit		38,000		
	$1,810,000	$1,810,000	$920,000	$920,000

Required

a. Develop a workpaper for the preparation of 19X7 financial statements for Drydock Industries.

b. Prepare a 19X7 income statement and balance sheet for Drydock Industries.

CHAPTER 12

MULTINATIONAL ACCOUNTING: FOREIGN CURRENCY TRANSACTIONS

Many companies, large and small, depend on international markets for supplies of goods and for sales of their products. Every day the business press carries stories about the effects of export and import activity on the U.S. economy and the large flows of capital among the world's major countries. Also reported are changes in the exchange rates of the major currencies of the world, such as "The dollar weakened today against the yen." This chapter and Chapter 13 discuss the accounting issues associated with companies that operate internationally.

A company operating in international markets is subject to normal business risks such as lack of demand for its products in the foreign marketplace, labor strikes, and transportation delays in getting its products to the foreign customer. In addition, the U.S. entity may incur foreign currency risks whenever it conducts transactions in other currencies. For example, if a U.S. company acquires a machine on credit from a German manufacturer, the German company may require payment in German marks (*DM* for "deutsche mark"). This means the U.S. company must eventually use a foreign currency broker or a bank to exchange U.S. dollars for German marks in order to pay for the machine. In the process, the U.S. company may experience foreign currency gains or losses from fluctuations in the value of the U.S. dollar relative to the German mark.

Multinational enterprises (MNEs) often transact in a variety of currencies as a result of their export and import activities. There are now approximately 150 different currencies around the world, but most international trade is settled in seven major currencies that have shown stability and general acceptance over time: the U.S. dollar, the British pound, the Canadian dollar, the French franc, the German mark, the Japanese yen, and the Swiss franc. The International Monetary Fund (IMF) is an organization that provides financial assistance to many countries and promotes international monetary cooperation, currency stability, and trade. Among the 150 members of the IMF are the leaders of the seven major industrial democracies—the United States, Britain, Canada, France, Germany, Italy, and Japan. These seven countries are sometimes referred to as The Group of Seven because of their dominance of the IMF.

Currency names and symbols often reflect a country's nationalistic pride and history. For example, the U.S. dollar receives its name from a variation of the German word *Taler*, the name of a silver piece that was first minted in 1518 and became the chief coin of Europe and the new world. Some historians argue that the dollar symbol ($) is derived from a capital letter *U* superimposed over a capital letter *S*. The greenback as we know it today was first printed in 1862, in the midst of the Civil War, and now is issued by the 12 Federal Reserve banks scattered across the United States. The U.S. dollar can be identified in virtually every corner of the world, as it has become one of the most widely traded currencies.

THE ACCOUNTING ISSUES

Accountants must be able to record and report transactions involving exchanges of U.S. dollars and foreign currencies. *Foreign currency transactions* of a U.S. company include sales, purchases, and other transactions giving rise to a transfer of foreign currency or recording receivables or payables which are *denominated*— that is, numerically specified to be settled—in a foreign currency. Because financial statements of virtually all U.S. companies are prepared using the U.S. dollar as the reporting currency, transactions denominated in other currencies must be restated to their U.S. dollar equivalents before they can be recorded in the U.S. company's books and included in its financial statements. This process of restating foreign currency transactions to their U.S. dollar equivalent values is termed *translation*.

In addition, many large U.S. corporations have multinational operations, such as foreign-based subsidiaries or branches. For example, a U.S. auto manufacturer may have manufacturing subsidiaries in Canada, Mexico, Spain, and Great Britain. The foreign subsidiaries prepare their financial statements in the currency of their countries; for example, the Mexican subsidiary reports its operations in pesos. The foreign currency amounts in the financial statements of these subsidiaries have to be translated, that is, restated, into their U.S. dollar equivalents, before they can be consolidated with the financial statements of the U.S. parent company that uses the U.S. dollar as its reporting currency unit.

This chapter presents the accounting procedures for recording and reporting foreign transactions. Chapter 13 presents the procedures for combining or consolidating a foreign entity with a U.S. parent company. **FASB Statement No. 52**, "Foreign Currency Translation" (FASB 52), issued in 1981, serves as the primary guide for accounting for transactions that require payment or receipt of foreign currency and for the methods used to translate foreign currency financial statements to statements prepared in dollars.

FOREIGN CURRENCY EXCHANGE RATES

Before 1972, most major currencies were valued on the basis of a gold standard whereby their international values were fixed per ounce of gold. However, in 1972, most countries signed an agreement to permit the values of their currencies to "float" based on the supply and demand for their currencies. The resulting *foreign currency exchange rates* between currencies are established daily by foreign exchange brokers who serve as agents for individuals or countries wishing to deal in foreign currencies. Some countries, such as Chile, maintain an official fixed rate of currency exchange and have established fixed exchange rates for dividends remitted outside the country. These official rates may be changed at any time, and companies doing business abroad should contact the government of the foreign country to ensure that the companies are in compliance with any currency exchange restrictions.

The Determination of Exchange Rates

A country's currency is much like any other commodity, and exchange rates change because of a number of economic factors affecting the supply of and demand for a nation's currency. For example, if a nation is experiencing high levels of inflation, the purchasing power of its currency will decrease. This reduction in the value of a currency is reflected by a decrease in the positioning of that country's currency relative to other nations' currencies. Other factors causing exchange rate fluctuations are a nation's balance of payments, changes in a country's interest rate and investment levels, and the stability and process of governance. For example, if the United States had a higher average interest rate than Great Britain, the international investment community would seek to invest in the United States, thus increasing the demand for U.S. dollars relative to British pounds. The dollar would increase in value relative to the pound because of the increased demand. Exchange rates are determined daily and published in several sources, including *The Wall Street Journal*. Figure 12-1 presents an example of a typical daily business press report for selected foreign exchange rates. The rates illustrated in the table are representative averages of the relationships between the U.S. dollar and the other currencies over the last 5 years. They are not meant to illustrate current exchange rates. Current exchange rates may be obtained from most business publications and from many metropolitan newspapers.

The business press sometimes mentions the European Currency Unit (ECU) which is not a single currency, but rather is a "basket" of several European currencies that serves as the currency for the European Monetary System. The ECU will increase in use as the European economic community continues to form and integrate financial operations.

Direct versus Indirect Exchange Rates

As indicated in Figure 12-1, the relative value of one currency to another may be expressed in two different ways: either *directly* or *indirectly*.

FIGURE 12-1 Foreign exchange rates for selected major currencies.

Country	(U.S. Dollar Equivalent) Direct Exchange Rate	(Currency per U.S. Dollar) Indirect Exchange Rate
Australia (dollar)	.7700	1.2987
Belgium (franc):		
Commercial rate	.0306	32.68
Brazil (new cruzado)	.0045	222.22
Britain (pound)	1.8500	.5405
30-day forward	1.8450	.5420
90-day forward	1.8400	.5435
180-day forward	1.8200	.5495
Canada (dollar)	.8700	1.1495
30-day forward	.8650	1.1561
90-day forward	.8550	1.1696
180-day forward	.8500	1.1765
Chile (peso official rate)	.0030	333.33
China (yuan)	.1915	5.2220
France (franc)	.1850	5.4054
30-day forward	.1851	5.4025
90-day forward	.1855	5.3908
180-day forward	.1852	5.4000
Germany (mark)	.6000	1.6667
30-day forward	.5900	1.6950
90-day forward	.5800	1.7241
180-day forward	.5500	1.8182
Greece (drachma)	.0058	172.41
Hong Kong (dollar)	.1280	7.8125
India (rupee)	.0520	19.2307
Ireland (pound)	1.6800	.5952
Israel (shekel)	.4960	2.0161
Italy (lira)	.0008	1250.00
Japan (yen)	.0070	142.86
30-day forward	.0071	140.85
90-day forward	.0073	136.99
180-day forward	.0075	133.33
Mexico (peso)	.0003	3333.33
Spain (peseta)	.0102	98.0392
Sweden (krona)	.1725	5.7965
Switzerland (franc)	.7300	1.3698
30-day forward	.7310	1.3680
90-day forward	.7350	1.3605
180-day forward	.7400	1.3514
Taiwan (dollar)	.0370	27.03

Direct Exchange Rate The direct exchange rate is the number of *local currency units (LCU)* needed to acquire one *foreign currency unit (FCU)*. From the viewpoint of a U.S. entity, the ratio is expressed as follows, with the LCU, the U.S. dollar, in the numerator:

$$\frac{\text{U.S. dollar equivalent value}}{1 \text{ FCU}}$$

The direct exchange rate is used most often in accounting for foreign operations and transactions because the financial statements of the U.S. entity are measured in dollars and the foreign currency–denominated accounts must be restated to their U.S. dollar equivalent values. For example, if $.60 can be exchanged for DM 1 (1 German mark), the direct exchange rate of the dollar versus the German mark is $.60 = DM 1, as follows:

$$\frac{\$.60}{\text{DM } 1} = \$.60$$

Indirect Exchange Rate   The indirect exchange rate is the reciprocal of the direct exchange rate:

$$\frac{1 \text{ FCU}}{\text{U.S. dollar equivalent value}}$$

For the German mark example, the indirect exchange rate is:

$$\frac{\text{DM } 1}{\$.60} = \text{DM } 1.6667$$

This is also expressed as DM 1.6667 = $1 to show the number of foreign currency units that may be obtained for 1 U.S. dollar. Note that the direct and indirect rate are inversely related and that both state the same relationship between two currencies. Some slight differences between the two rates may be found in the exchange markets because of brokers' commissions.

Changes in Exchange Rates

A change in an exchange rate is referred to as a *strengthening* or *weakening* of one currency against another. For example, the exchange rate of the U.S. dollar versus the German mark changed as follows:

	January 1	July 1	December 31
Direct exchange rate (U.S. dollar equivalent of 1 FCU)	$.6000	$.5500	$.5800
Indirect exchange rate (FCU per 1 U.S. dollar)	DM 1.6667	DM 1.8182	DM 1.7241

Between January 1 and July 1, the direct exchange rate has decreased, indicating that it takes less U.S. currency to acquire 1 German mark. Note that the cost of 1 mark was $.60 on January 1, but decreased to $.55 on July 1. This means that the value of the U.S. currency has risen relative to the mark. This is termed a *strengthening* of the dollar versus the mark. Alternatively, looking at the indirect exchange rate, 1 U.S. dollar can acquire 1.6667 marks on January 1, but it can acquire more marks, 1.8182, on July 1. Thus the relative value of the dollar versus the mark is greater on July 1 than on January 1.

Imports from Germany would be less expensive for U.S. consumers on July 1 than on January 1 because of the strengthening of the dollar. For example, assume that a German manufacturer is selling a German-made automobile for DM 50,000. To determine the U.S. dollar equivalent value of the DM 50,000 on January 1, the following equation is used:

U.S. dollar equivalent value		Foreign currency units		Direct exchange rate
$30,000	=	DM 50,000	×	$.60

Between January 1 and July 1, the direct exchange rate decreased as the dollar strengthened relative to the mark. On July 1, the U.S. dollar equivalent value of the DM 50,000 is:

U.S. dollar equivalent value		Foreign currency units		Direct exchange rate
$27,500	=	DM 50,000	×	$.55

While a strengthening of the dollar is favorable for U.S. companies purchasing goods from another country, it adversely affects U.S. companies selling products in that country. Following a strengthening of the dollar, U.S. exports to Germany would be more expensive for German customers. For example, assume a U.S. manufacturer is selling a U.S.–made machine for $10,000. To determine the foreign currency (mark) equivalent value of the $10,000 on January 1, the following equation is used:

Foreign currency equivalent value		U.S. dollar units		Indirect exchange rate
DM 16,667	=	$10,000	×	DM 1.6667

On July 1, after a strengthening of the dollar, the machine would cost the German customer DM 18,182, as follows:

Foreign currency equivalent value		U.S. dollar units		Indirect exchange rate
DM 18,182	=	$10,000	×	DM 1.8182

This substantial increase in cost could result in the German customer's deciding not to acquire the machine from the U.S. company. Thus, a U.S. company's international sales can be seriously affected by changes in foreign currency exchange rates.

Between July 1 and December 31, the direct exchange rate has increased, indicating that it now takes more dollars to acquire marks. On July 1, a mark costs $.55, but on December 31, the relative cost for 1 mark has increased to $.58. This means that the value of the U.S. currency has dropped relative to the mark. This is termed a *weakening* of the dollar against the mark. Another way to view this change is to note that the indirect exchange rate has decreased, indicating that 1 dollar now acquires fewer marks than on July 1. On July 1, 1 U.S. dollar can acquire 1.8182 marks, but on December 31, 1 U.S. dollar can acquire fewer marks, 1.7241, indicating that the relative value of the dollar has dropped between July 1 and December 31.

The relationships between currencies, imports, and exports is summarized in Figure 12-2.

During the latter part of the 1970s, the dollar consistently weakened against other major currencies because of several factors, including the high inflation the United States experienced. This weakening did help the United States' balance of trade, because it reduced the quantity of then–more expensive imports, while making U.S.-made goods less expensive in other countries. In the first half of the 1980s, the dollar consistently strengthened relative to other currencies. Not only was the U.S. economy strong and producing goods more efficiently, but high interest rates attracted large foreign investment in the U.S. capital markets. A stronger dollar added to the foreign trade deficit by making imports less expensive and U.S.-made goods more expensive on the world market. Beginning in 1986 and continuing through the early 1990s, the dollar again weakened relative to the major international currencies.

These changes in the international value of the dollar affect any consumer acquiring imported goods. A weakening dollar means that imports become more expensive while a strengthening dollar means that imports become less expensive.

FIGURE 12-2 Relationships between currencies and exchange rates.

	January 1	July 1	December 31
Direct exchange rate: 1 DM =	$.6000	$.5500	$.5800

U.S. dollar relative
  to foreign currency
		Dollar
		  strengthens
			Dollar
			  weakens

Direct exchange rate		Decreases	Increases
Price of 1 FCU (mark)		Decreases	Increases
Imports into U.S.		Less expensive	More expensive
Exports from U.S.		More expensive	Less expensive
Indirect exchange rate: $1 =	DM 1.6667	DM 1.8182	DM 1.7241
FCU relative to U.S. dollar		FCU weakens	FCU strengthens

Spot Rates versus Current Rates

FASB 52 refers to the use of both spot rates and current rates for measuring foreign operations. The spot rate is the exchange rate for immediate delivery of currencies. The current rate is defined simply as the spot rate on the entity's balance sheet date.

Forward Exchange Rates

A third exchange rate is the rate on future, or forward, exchanges of currencies. Figure 12-1 shows these exchange rates for the major international currencies for 30, 90, and 180 days forward. Active markets in *forward exchange contracts* are maintained for companies wishing to receive, or deliver, major international currencies. The advantage of a forward exchange market is that the U.S. dollar equivalent value of a future receipt or disbursement of foreign currency units may be fixed at the time a contract is made. For example, a U.S. company may have a liability in British pounds due in 30 days. Rather than wait 30 days to buy the pounds and risk having the dollar weaken in value relative to the pound, the company can buy a 30-day forward exchange contract at the forward exchange rate in effect on the contract date. The contract enables the buyer to receive British pounds from an exchange broker 30 days from the contract date at a price fixed now by the contract.

The next section of the chapter presents the accounting for import and export transactions, and for forward exchange contracts.

FOREIGN CURRENCY TRANSACTIONS

As defined earlier, foreign currency transactions are economic activities denominated in a currency other than the entity's recording currency. These transactions may be:

1. Purchases or sales of goods or services (imports or exports) whose prices are stated in a foreign currency
2. Loans payable or receivable in a foreign currency
3. The purchase or sale of forward exchange contracts
4. Purchase or sale of foreign currency units

One of the parties in a foreign exchange transaction must exchange its own currency for another country's currency. The normal business practice is to require settlement of the transaction in the domestic currency of the selling or lending company, but the agreement between the parties may state otherwise.

For financial statement purposes, transactions denominated in a foreign currency must be translated into the currency used by the reporting company. Additionally, at each balance sheet date—interim as well as annual—account balances denominated in a currency other than the entity's reporting currency must be adjusted to reflect changes in exchange rates during the period since the last balance sheet date or since the foreign currency transaction date if it occurred during the period. This adjustment restates the foreign currency–denominated accounts to their U.S. dollar equivalent values as of the balance sheet date. The adjustment in equivalent U.S. dollar values is a *foreign currency transaction gain or loss* for the entity when exchange rates have changed. For example, assume that a U.S. company acquires DM 10,000 from its bank on January 1, 19X1, for use in future purchases from German companies. The direct exchange rate is $.6000 = DM 1; thus the company pays the bank $6,000 for the DM 10,000. The following entry records this exchange of currencies:

```
January 1, 19X1
    (1)   Foreign Currency Units (DM)                         6,000
                Cash                                                     6,000
```

The foreign currency units account is typically reported as a separate item in the current assets section of the balance sheet, immediately below cash rather than being included with cash, because the foreign currency units cannot be used in the United States with the same freedom of exchange as U.S. dollars. The parenthetical DM notation (DM) is used after the debit account to indicate that the asset is German marks, but for accounting purposes it is recorded and reported in its U.S. dollar equivalent value. This translation to the U.S. equivalent value is required in order to add the value of the foreign currency units to all the company's other accounts that are reported in dollars.

On July 1, 19X1, the exchange rate is $.5800 = DM 1 as represented in the following time line:

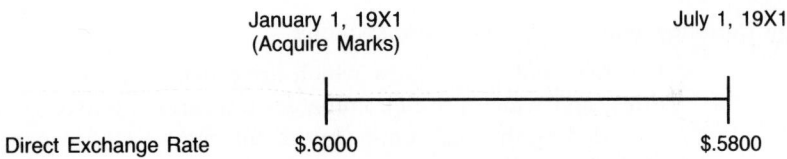

	January 1, 19X1 (Acquire Marks)	July 1, 19X1
Direct Exchange Rate	$.6000	$.5800

By holding the foreign currency units during a time when the dollar strengthens relative to the mark, the company experiences a foreign currency transaction loss, as follows:

```
Equivalent dollar value of DM 10,000 on January 1:
    DM 10,000 × $.6000                                    $6,000
Equivalent dollar value of DM 10,000 on July 1:
    DM 10,000 × $.5800                                     5,800
Foreign currency transaction loss                        $  200
```

If the U.S. company prepares financial statements on July 1, the following adjusting entry is required:

```
July 1, 19X1
    (2)   Foreign Currency Transaction Loss                   200
                Foreign Currency Units (DM)                             200
```

The foreign currency transaction loss is the result of a foreign currency transaction and is included in this period's income statement, usually as a separate item under "Other Income or Loss." Some accountants use the account title Exchange Loss instead of the longer title Foreign Currency Transaction Loss. In this book, the longer, more descriptive account title is used in order to communicate fully the source of the loss. The Foreign Currency Units account is reported on the balance sheet at a value of $5,800, its equivalent U.S. dollar value on that date.

In the previous examples, the U.S. company used the U.S. dollar as its primary currency for performing its major financial and operating functions, that is, as its *functional currency*. Also, the U.S. company prepared its financial statements in U.S. dollars, its *reporting currency*. Any transactions denominated in currencies other than the U.S. dollar require translation to their equivalent U.S. dollar values. Generally, the majority of cash transactions of a business take place in the *local currency* of the country in which the entity operates. The U.S. dollar is the functional currency for virtually all companies based in the United States. A company operating in Germany usually uses the German mark as its functional currency. In this chapter, the local currency is assumed to be the entity's functional and reporting currency. The few exceptions to this general case are discussed in Chapter 13.

Illustrations of various types of foreign currency transactions are given in the sections that follow. Note that different exchange rates are used to value selected foreign currency transactions, depending on a number of factors such as management's reason for entering the foreign currency transaction, the nature of the transaction, and the timing of the transaction.

Foreign Currency Import and Export Transactions

Payables and receivables which arise from transactions with foreign-based entities, and which are denominated in a foreign currency, must be measured and recorded by the U.S. entity in the currency used for its accounting records—the U.S. dollar. The relevant exchange rate for settlement of a transaction denominated in a foreign currency is the spot exchange rate on the date of settlement. At the time the transaction is settled, payables or receivables denominated in foreign currency units must be adjusted to their current U.S. dollar equivalent value. If financial statements are prepared before the foreign currency payables or receivables are settled, their account balances must be adjusted to their U.S. dollar equivalent values as of the balance sheet date, using the current rate on the balance sheet date.

An overview of the required accounting for an import or export foreign currency transaction on credit is as follows:

1. *Transaction Date.* Record the purchase or sale transaction at the U.S. dollar equivalent value using the spot rate of exchange on this date.

2. *Balance Sheet Date.* Adjust the payable or receivable to its U.S. dollar equivalent, end-of-period value using the current exchange rate. Recognize any exchange gain or loss for the change in rates between the transaction and balance sheet dates.

3. *Settlement Date.* First adjust the foreign currency payable or receivable for any changes in the exchange rate between the balance sheet date (or transaction date if transaction occurs after the balance sheet date) and the settlement date, recording any exchange gain or loss as required. Then record the settlement of the foreign currency payable or receivable.

 This adjustment process is required because the FASB adopted what is called the *two-transaction approach*, which views the purchase or sale of an item as a separate transaction from the foreign currency commitment. By adopting the two-transaction approach to foreign currency transactions, the FASB established the general rule that foreign currency exchange gains or losses resulting from the revaluation of assets or liabilities denominated in a foreign currency must be recognized currently in the income statement of the period in which the exchange rate changes. A few exceptions to this general rule are allowed and are discussed later in this chapter.

Illustration of Foreign Purchase Transaction   Figure 12-3 illustrates the journal entries used to measure and record a purchase of goods from a foreign supplier denominated either in the entity's local currency or in a foreign currency. On the left side of Figure 12-3, the transaction is denominated in U.S. dollars, the recording and reporting currency of the U.S. company; on the right side, the transaction is denominated in Japanese yen (¥). The U.S. company is subject to a foreign currency transaction gain or loss only if the transaction is denominated in the foreign currency. If the foreign transaction is denominated in U.S. dollars, no special accounting problems exist and no currency rate adjustments are necessary.

The following information describes the case:

1. On October 1, 19X1, Peerless Products, a U.S. company, acquired goods on account from Tokyo Industries, a Japanese company, for $14,000, or 2,000,000 yen.

2. Peerless Products prepared financial statements at its year-end of December 31, 19X1.

3. Settlement of the payable was made on April 1, 19X2.

The direct spot exchange rates of the U.S. dollar equivalent value of 1 yen were as follows:

Date	Direct Exchange Rate
October 1, 19X1 (transaction date)	$.0070
December 31, 19X1 (balance sheet date)	.0080
April 1, 19X2 (settlement date)	.0076

A timeline may help to clarify the relationships between the dates and the economic events, as follows:

FIGURE 12-3 Comparative U.S. company journal entries for foreign purchase transaction denominated in dollars versus foreign currency units.

	If Denominated in U.S. Dollars	If Denominated in Japanese Yen	

October 1, 19X1 (date of purchase)

Inventory	14,000	
Accounts Payable	14,000	

Inventory   14,000
  Accounts Payable (¥)   14,000
    $14,000 = ¥2,000,000 × $.0070 spot rate

December 31, 19X1 (balance sheet date)

No entry

Foreign Currency Transaction Loss   2,000
  Accounts Payable (¥)   2,000
  Adjust payable denominated in foreign currency to
  current U.S. dollar equivalent and recognize
  exchange loss:

$ 16,000	= ¥2,000,000 × $.0080	Dec. 31 spot rate
−14,000	= ¥2,000,000 × $.0070	Oct. 1 spot rate
$ 2,000	= ¥2,000,000 × ($.0080 − $.0070)	

(handwritten: Dec 31 > Oct, Loss)

April 1, 19X2 (settlement date)

Accounts Payable (¥)   800
  Foreign Currency Transaction Gain   800
  Adjust payable denominated in foreign currency
  to current U.S. dollar equivalent and recognize
  exchange gain:

$ 15,200	= ¥2,000,000 × $.0076	Apr. 1 spot rate
−16,000	= ¥2,000,000 × $.0080	Dec. 31 spot rate
$ 800	= ¥2,000,000 × ($.0076 − $.0080)	

(handwritten: Ap < Dec 31)

Foreign Currency Units (¥)   15,200
  Cash   15,200
  Acquire FCU to settle debt:
  $15,200 = ¥2,000,000 × $.0076 April 1 spot rate

Accounts Payable (¥)   15,200
  Foreign Currency Units (¥)   15,200

Accounts Payable	14,000	
Cash	14,000	

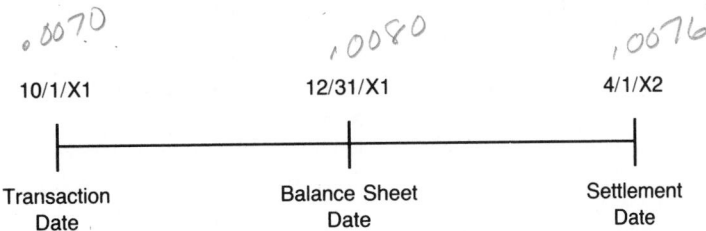

Accounts relating to transactions denominated in yen are noted by the parenthetical symbol for the yen (¥) after the account title. As you proceed through the example, you should especially note the assets and liabilities denominated in the foreign currency and the adjustment needed to reflect their current values by use of the U.S. dollar equivalent rate of exchange.

Key Observations from Illustration If the purchase contract is denominated in dollars, the foreign entity (Tokyo Industries) bears the foreign currency exchange risk. If the transaction is denominated in yen, then the U.S. company (Peerless Products Corporation) is exposed to exchange rate gains and losses. The accounts relating to liabilities denominated in foreign currency units must be valued at the spot rate, with any foreign currency transaction gain or loss recognized in the period's income. The purchase contract includes specification of the denominated currency as agreed upon by the two parties.

On October 1, 19X1, the purchase is recorded on the books of Peerless Products. The U.S. dollar equivalent value of 2,000,000 yen on this date is $14,000 (¥2,000,000 × $.0070).

On December 31, 19X1, the balance sheet date, the payable denominated in foreign currency units must be adjusted to its current U.S. dollar equivalent value. The direct exchange rate has increased since the date of purchase, indicating that the U.S. dollar has weakened relative to the yen. Therefore, on December 31, 19X1, $16,000 is required to acquire 2,000,000 yen (¥2,000,000 × $.0080), whereas, on October 1, 19X1, only $14,000 was required to obtain 2,000,000 yen (¥2,000,000 × $.0070). This increase in the exchange rate requires the recognition of a $2,000 foreign currency transaction loss if the transaction is denominated in yen, the foreign currency unit. No entry is made if the transaction is denominated in U.S. dollars, because Peerless has a liability for $14,000 regardless of the changes in exchange rates.

The payable is settled on April 1, 19X2. If the payable is denominated in U.S. dollars, no adjustment is necessary and the liability is extinguished by payment of $14,000. However, assets and liabilities denominated in foreign currency units must again be adjusted to their present U.S. dollar equivalent values. The dollar has strengthened between December 31, 19X1, and April 1, 19X2, as shown by the decrease in the direct exchange rate. In other words, fewer dollars are needed to acquire 2,000,000 yen on April 1, 19X2, than on December 31, 19X1. Accounts Payable is adjusted to its current dollar value, and an $800 foreign currency transaction gain [¥2,000,000 × ($.0076 − $.0080)] is recognized for the change in rates since the balance sheet date. Peerless acquires 2,000,000 yen, paying an exchange broker the spot exchange rate of $15,200 (¥2,000,000 × $.0076).

Finally, Peerless extinguishes its liability denominated in yen by paying Tokyo Industries the 2,000,000 yen.

Understanding the revaluations may be easier by viewing the process within the perspective of a T-account. The following T-account posts the entries in Figure 12-3:

Accounts Payable (¥)

	19X1
	Oct. 1 14,000 (¥2,000,000 × $.0070)
	Dec. 31 2,000 [¥2,000,000 × ($.0080 − $.0070)]
	Dec. 31 16,000 Balance (¥2,000,000 × $.0080)
19X2	
Apr. 1 800	
[¥2,000,000 × ($.0076 − $.0080)]	
Apr. 1 settlement	
(¥2,000,000 × $.0076) 15,200	
	Apr. 2 -0- Balance

Some accountants combine the revaluation and settlement entries into one entry. Under this alternative approach, the following entries would be made on April 1, 19X2, the settlement date, instead of the entries presented for that date in Figure 12-3:

April 2, 19X2
(3) Foreign Currency Units (¥)   15,200
       Cash   15,200
    Acquire foreign currency.

(4) Accounts Payable (¥)   16,000
       Foreign Currency Transaction Gain   800
       Foreign Currency Units (¥)   15,200
    Settle foreign currency payable and recognize
    gain from change in exchange rates since
    December 31, 19X1.

There are no differences in the final balances between the one-entry approach shown above and the two-entry approach used in Figure 12-3.

In summary, if the transaction is denominated in U.S. dollars, Peerless Products has no foreign currency exchange exposure; Tokyo Industries bears the risk of foreign currency exposure. If the transaction is denominated in yen, however, Peerless has a foreign currency exchange risk. The assets and liabilities denominated in foreign currency units must be valued at their U.S. dollar equivalent values and a foreign currency transaction gain or loss must be recognized on that period's income statement.

Forward Exchange Contracts

Companies operating internationally often enter into forward exchange contracts with foreign currency brokers for the exchange of different currencies at specified future dates at specified rates. The FASB recognized three major purposes of forward exchange contracts:

1. To hedge an exposed foreign currency net asset or liability position
2. To hedge an identifiable foreign currency commitment
3. To speculate in foreign currency markets

Because the economic substance of the forward contract depends on its use, the FASB established different accounting treatments for each of the three purposes.

Forward exchange contracts are acquired from foreign currency brokers. Typically, these contracts are written for one of the seven major international currencies. They are available for virtually any time period up to 12 months forward, but most are for relatively short time periods, usually between 30 and 180 days. The forward exchange rate differs from the spot rate because of the different economic factors involved in the determination of a future versus spot rate of exchange. For hedging transactions, if the forward rate is greater than the spot rate, the difference between the forward and spot rate is termed a *premium on the forward exchange contract*; that is, the foreign currency is selling at a premium in the forward market. If the forward rate is less than the spot rate, the difference is a *discount on the forward exchange contract*; that is, the foreign currency is selling at a discount in the forward market. The premium or discount is generally amortized by the straight-line method over the term of the forward contract and the amortized amount is reported as a financial expense or revenue.

The following three cases illustrate the accounting for the three uses of forward exchange contracts.

Case 1: Hedging an Exposed Foreign Currency Net Asset or Liability Position A company that has trade receivables or other assets denominated in a foreign currency greater than liabilities denominated in that currency incurs a foreign currency risk from its *exposed net asset position*. Alternatively, the company has an *exposed net liability position* if liabilities denominated in a foreign currency exceed receivables denominated in that currency.

The most common use of forward exchange contracts is for *hedging an exposed foreign currency position—either a net asset or a net liability position*. A hedge is a transaction that balances a foreign exchange payable with a receivable in the same foreign currency, thus balancing the risk of foreign exchange fluctuations. For example, a U.S. company acquiring goods from a Swiss company may be required to make payment in Swiss francs. If the transaction is denominated in Swiss francs, the U.S. company is exposed to the effects of changes in exchange rates between the dollar and Swiss franc. To protect itself from fluctuations in the value of the Swiss franc, the U.S. company can enter into a forward exchange contract to receive francs at the future settlement date. The U.S. company will then use these francs to settle its foreign currency commitment arising from the foreign purchase transaction.

Alternatively, a U.S. company could have a receivable denominated in a foreign currency that it could also hedge with a forward exchange contract. In this case, the U.S. company contracts to *deliver* foreign currency units to the forward exchange broker at a future date in exchange for U.S. dollars.

The relevant exchange rate for valuing a forward exchange contract that hedges an exposed foreign currency position is the same rate as used to value the foreign currency receivable or payable. Therefore, this type of forward exchange contract is valued at its equivalent U.S. dollar value using the spot exchange rate. These contracts must also be adjusted for changes in the exchange rates just as is done for the foreign currency payable or receivable.[1]

Illustration of Hedging an Exposed Net Liability Position The following example shows the accounting for a hedge of an exposed foreign currency position with a forward exchange contract. For purposes of this example, assume the following:

1. On October 1, 19X1, Peerless Products purchases goods on account from Tokyo Industries in the amount of 2,000,000 yen.

2. This transaction is denominated in yen, and Peerless Products hedges its exposed foreign currency liability with a forward exchange contract for the receipt of 2,000,000 yen from a foreign exchange broker.

3. The term of the forward exchange contract is equal to the 6-month credit period extended by Tokyo Industries.

4. December 31 is the year-end of Peerless Products, and the payable is settled on April 1, 19X2.

The relevant direct exchange rates are as follows:

	U.S. Dollar Equivalent Value of 1 Yen	
Date	Spot Rate	Forward Exchange Rate
October 1, 19X1 (transaction date)	$.0070	$.0075 (180-day)
December 31, 19X1 (balance sheet date)	$.0080	
April 1, 19X2 (settlement date)	$.0076	

[1] In practice, some accountants argue that a forward contract is executory in nature and should not be recorded until the contract is settled with the exchange broker. Although the company can break its agreement with the exchange broker, virtually all forward contracts are completed. If no entry is made on the date the forward contract is negotiated, no gain or loss is recognized on the hedged foreign currency receivable or payable before its settlement and the revaluations are not recorded. We believe the forward exchange contract should be recorded and reported in the financial statements. Therefore, this chapter records the forward exchange contract on the date it is negotiated and also accounts for the revaluations for both the forward contract and the hedged foreign currency receivable or payable. This not only provides the necessary process for analyzing the subsequent revaluations, but also reports the economic substance of the forward exchange contract.

A time line for these transactions is as follows:

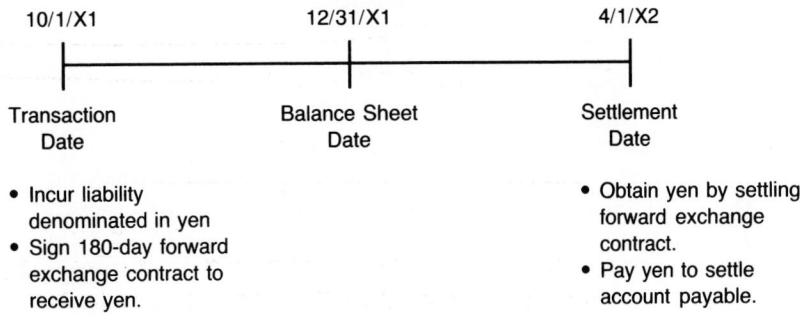

10/1/X1	12/31/X1	4/1/X2
Transaction Date	Balance Sheet Date	Settlement Date

- Incur liability denominated in yen
- Sign 180-day forward exchange contract to receive yen.

- Obtain yen by settling forward exchange contract.
- Pay yen to settle account payable.

The following entries record the events for this illustration.

October 1, 19X1

(5)	Inventory	14,000	
	Accounts Payable (¥)		14,000
	Purchase inventory on account:		
	$14,000 = ¥2,000,000 × $.0070		

(6)	Foreign Currency Receivable from Exchange Broker (¥)	14,000	
	Premium on Forward Contract	1,000	
	Dollars Payable to Exchange Broker ($)		15,000
	Purchase forward contract to receive 2,000,000 yen:		
	$14,000 = ¥2,000,000 × $.0070 Oct. 1 spot rate		
	15,000 = ¥2,000,000 × $.0075 forward rate		

These entries record the purchase of inventory on credit, which is denominated in yen, and the signing of a 6-month forward exchange contract to receive 2,000,000 yen in exchange for $15,000. The premium on the forward contract is the result of the difference between the spot rate ($.0070) and the future rate ($.0075) and is reported as a contra account to the related liability to the exchange broker. The amount payable to the exchange broker is denominated in U.S. dollars, whereas the receivable from the broker is denominated in yen. The necessary entries for the transaction and its settlement are posted to T-accounts in Figure 12-4.

The required adjusting entries on December 31, 19X1, Peerless's fiscal year-end, are:

(7)	Foreign Currency Receivable from Exchange Broker (¥)	2,000	
	Foreign Currency Transaction Gain		2,000
	Adjust receivable denominated in yen to current U.S. dollar equivalent value:		
	$ 16,000 = ¥2,000,000 × $.0080 Dec. 31 spot rate		
	−14,000 = ¥2,000,000 × $.0070 Oct. 1 spot rate		
	$ 2,000 = ¥2,000,000 × ($.0080 − $.0070)		

FIGURE 12-4 T-accounts for the illustration of a hedge of an exposed net liability.

Foreign Currency Receivable from Broker (¥)				Accounts Payable (¥)		
(6)	14,000				(5)	14,000
(7)	2,000				(8)	2,000
Bal. 12/31	16,000				Bal. 12/31	16,000
		(10)	800	(11)	800	
		(14)	15,200	(15)	15,200	
Bal. 4/1	-0-				Bal. 4/1	-0-

Premium on Forward Contract				Dollars Payable to Exchange Broker ($)		
(6)	1,000				(6)	15,000
		(9)	500			
Bal. 12/31	500				Bal. 12/31	15,000
		(12)	500	(13)	15,000	
Bal. 4/1	-0-				Bal. 4/1	-0-

Foreign Currency Units (¥)			
(14)	15,200	(15)	15,200
Bal. 4/1	-0-		

(8) Foreign Currency Transaction Loss	2,000	
Accounts Payable (¥)		2,000
Adjust payable denominated in yen to		
current U.S. dollar equivalent value:		
¥2,000,000 × ($.0080 − $.0070)		
(9) Financial Expense	500	
Premium on Forward Contract		500
Amortize premium over term of		
contract; half of term expired:		
$1,000 × 90 days/180 days		

The direct exchange spot rate has increased between October 1, 19X1, the date of the foreign currency transaction, and December 31, 19X1, the balance sheet date. As previously illustrated, this means that the U.S. dollar has weakened relative to the yen because it takes more U.S. currency to acquire 1 yen at year-end (1 yen = $.0080) than at the initial date of the purchase transaction (1 yen = $.0070), and a U.S. company with a liability in yen experiences an exchange loss. The U.S. dollar equivalent values of the foreign currency–denominated accounts at October 1, 19X1, and December 31, 19X2, are:

	U.S. Dollar Equivalent Values of Foreign Currency-Denominated Accounts		Foreign Currency Transaction Gain (Loss)
Accounts	**October 1, 19X1 (Transaction Date)**	**December 31, 19X1 (Balance Sheet Date)**	
Foreign Currency Receivable from Exchange Broker (¥)	$14,000 (a)	$16,000 (b)	$2,000
Accounts Payable (¥)	14,000 (a)	16,000 (b)	(2,000)

(a) 2,000,000 yen × $.0070 October 1 spot rate
(b) 2,000,000 yen × $.0080 December 31 spot rate

On October 1, the U.S. dollar equivalent value of the foreign currency receivable from the broker is $14,000. Because of the increase in the value of the yen relative to the dollar (i.e., the weakening of the dollar versus the yen), the U.S. dollar equivalent value of the receivable on December 31, 19X1, increases to $16,000, resulting in a foreign currency transaction gain of $2,000. For the U.S. company, the U.S. dollar equivalent value of the liability has increased to $16,000, resulting in a foreign currency transaction loss of $2,000. The hedge of the foreign currency payable with an offsetting forward exchange receivable contract balances the exchange loss of $2,000 from the accounts payable denominated in yen with the $2,000 exchange gain from the forward contract. The company does not show any net exchange gain or loss in its income statement for the period. The only income statement effect is a financial expense of $500 from the amortization of the premium on the forward contract for half the term of the 6-month contract [$1,000 × (3 months/6 months)].

The required entries on April 1, 19X2, the settlement date, are:

(10)	Foreign Currency Transaction Loss	800	
	Foreign Currency Receivable from Exchange Broker (¥)		800

    Adjust receivable to spot rate on settlement date:

$ 15,200 = ¥2,000,000 × $.0076 Apr. 1, 19X2, spot rate
− 16,000 = ¥2,000,000 × $.0080 Dec. 31, 19X1 spot rate
$ 800 = 2,000,000 yen × ($.0076 − $.0080)

(11)	Accounts Payable (¥)	800	
	Foreign Currency Transaction Gain		800

    Adjust payable denominated in yen to spot rate on settlement date:
    ¥2,000,000 × ($.0076 − $.0080)

(12)	Financial Expense	500	
	Premium on Forward Contract		500

    Amortize remainder of premium on forward exchange contract:
    $1,000 × 90 days/180 days

(13)	Dollars Payable to Exchange Broker ($)	15,000	
	Cash		15,000
	Deliver U.S. dollars to currency broker		
	as specified in forward contract.		
(14)	Foreign Currency Units (¥)	15,200	
	Foreign Currency Receivable from		
	Exchange Broker (¥)		15,200
	Receive 2,000,000 yen from exchange broker;		
	valued at Apr. 1, 19X2, spot rate:		
	¥2,000,000 × $.0076		
(15)	Accounts Payable (¥)	15,200	
	Foreign Currency Units (¥)		15,200
	Pay 2,000,000 yen to Tokyo Industries, Inc.,		
	in settlement of liability denominated in yen.		

The direct exchange spot rate has decreased from the $.0080 rate on the balance sheet date to $.0076 on April 1, 19X2, the settlement date, indicating that the U.S. dollar has strengthened relative to the yen. Fewer dollars are needed to acquire the same number of yen on the settlement date than were needed on the balance sheet date. During this period, an exchange loss is realized on an asset denominated in yen, and an exchange gain is recognized on a liability in yen. The U.S. dollar equivalent values of the foreign currency–denominated accounts on December 31, 19X1, and April 1, 19X2, were:

	U.S. Dollar Equivalent Values of Foreign Currency–Denominated Accounts		Foreign Currency Transaction Gain (Loss)
Accounts	**December 31, 19X1 (Balance Sheet Date)**	**April 1, 19X2 (Settlement Date)**	
Foreign Currency Receivable from Exchange Broker (¥)	$16,000 (a)	$15,200 (b)	$(800)
Accounts Payable (¥)	16,000 (a)	15,000 (b)	800

(a) ¥2,000,000 × $.0080 December 31, 19X1 spot rate
(b) ¥2,000,000 × $.0076 April 1, 19X2 spot rate

On December 31, 19X1, the U.S. dollar equivalent value of the foreign currency receivable from the broker is $16,000. Because the yen weakened relative to the dollar, the foreign currency receivable on April 1, 19X2, is lower in U.S. dollar equivalent value, and an exchange loss of $800 is recognized. The U.S. dollar equivalent value of the foreign currency payable is $16,000 on December 31, 19X1, but because the yen weakened (i.e., the dollar strengthened) during the period from December 31, 19X1, to April 1, 19X2, the U.S. dollar equivalent value of the payable decreases to $15,200 on April 1, 19X2. This results in an $800 foreign currency transaction gain during this period.

The forward exchange contract hedges the foreign currency liability position. In 19X2, the net effect is to offset the $800 exchange gain from the liability denominated in yen with the $800 exchange loss from the forward contract receivable denominated in yen. The only income statement effect is the amortization of the remaining 3 months of the premium on the forward contract ($500 = $1,000 × ⅜). Finally, Peerless pays the forward contract price of $15,000 to the exchange broker and receives the 2,000,000 yen, which it then uses to extinguish its account payable to Tokyo Industries. Note that after settlement, all account balances in Figure 12-4 are reduced to zero.

If Peerless Products had a foreign currency receivable, it could also hedge its exposed net asset position by acquiring a forward exchange contract to deliver foreign currency to the exchange broker. In this case, the forward exchange contract would specify the receivable in U.S. dollars with a foreign currency payable to the exchange broker denominated in the foreign currency. The forward exchange contract would be settled when Peerless gives the foreign currency units it has received to the broker in exchange for U.S. dollars. The assets and liabilities denominated in foreign currency units must be revalued to their U.S. dollar equivalent values in the same manner as for the import illustration.

The following illustrations present an overview of the accounting for a forward exchange contract on the day the forward contract is signed. For purposes of the illustrations, both a premium and a discount are presented for the forward exchange contract by assuming two different values for the spot rate ($.0070 and $.0078) on the day the forward contract is signed.

Illustration A: Hedging an Exposed Net Liability Position of 2,000,000 Yen   Sign forward exchange contract to purchase 2,000,000 yen at a forward exchange rate of $.0075:

	(1) Spot Rate = $.0070		(2) Spot Rate = $.0078	
Foreign Currency Receivable from Exchange Broker (¥)	14,000		15,600	
Premium on Forward Contract	1,000		–0–	
Discount on Forward Contract		–0–		600
Dollars Payable to Exchange Broker ($)		15,000		15,000

$14,000 = ¥2,000,000 × $.0070 spot rate
1,000 = premium because forward rate of $.0075 > spot rate of $.0070
15,000 = ¥2,000,000 × $.0075 forward rate

$15,600 = ¥2,000,000 × $.0078 spot rate
600 = discount because forward rate of $.0075 < spot rate of $.0078
15,000 = ¥2,000,000 × $.0075 forward rate

Illustration B: Hedging an Exposed Net Asset Position of 2,000,000 Yen   Sign forward exchange contract to sell 2,000,000 yen at a forward exchange rate of $.0075:

	(1) **Spot Rate = $.0070**	(2) **Spot Rate = $.0078**
Dollars Receivable from Exchange Broker ($)	15,000	15,000
Discount on Forward Contract	–0–	600
Premium on Forward Contract	1,000	–0–
Foreign Currency Payable to		
Exchange Broker (¥)	14,000	15,600

$15,000 = ¥2,000,000 × $.0075 forward rate
  1,000 = premium because forward rate of
          $.0075 > spot rate of $.0070
 14,000 = ¥2,000,000 × $.0070 spot rate

$15,000 = ¥2,000,000 × $.0075 forward rate
   600 = discount because forward rate of
          $.0075 < spot rate of $.0078
 15,600 = ¥2,000,000 × $.0078 spot rate

In any case, the premium or discount on the forward contract is amortized over the life of the forward exchange contract. In Illustrations A(1) and B(2), the amortization increases financial expense. In Illustrations A(2) and B(1), the amortization decreases financial expense, or is amortized to financial income.

Case 2: Hedging an Identifiable Foreign Currency Commitment A company may expose itself to foreign currency risk *before* a purchase or sale transaction occurs. For example, a company may sign a noncancelable order to purchase goods from a foreign entity in the future, to be paid for in the foreign currency. By agreeing to a purchase price in the present for a future purchase, the company has accepted an *identifiable foreign currency commitment* although the purchase has not yet occurred; that is, the purchase contract is still executory. The company will not pay until after delivery of the goods; therefore, it is exposed to changes in currency exchange rates before the transaction date (the date of delivery of the goods).

In **FASB 52**, the FASB recognized the many variations used by management in *hedging identifiable foreign currency commitments* and allowed broad latitude in defining a hedge position. The only requirements established for this type of hedge are:[2]

1. The foreign currency transaction is designated as, and is effective as, a hedge of a foreign currency commitment.
2. The foreign currency commitment is firm.

A hedge transaction does not necessarily have to be coincidental with the exchange risk it is offsetting. For example, a company may offset a currency commitment in a foreign currency with an investment in a second foreign currency as long as the exchange markets in the two foreign currencies move in tandem, or are linked with each other, and are proximate in changes in values in response to

---

[2] *Financial Accounting Standards Board Statement No. 52*, "Foreign Currency Translation," December 1981, par. 17.

new international events. Thus, a U.S. company could possibly offset a foreign currency commitment in British pounds with an investment in French francs and still account for the transaction as a hedge.

Specific accounting criteria are applicable to transactions that hedge a foreign currency commitment. When a foreign currency transaction is a hedge of an identifiable foreign currency commitment, any gain or loss on the hedge is deferred until the related foreign currency transaction is recorded. At that time, the deferred gain or loss on the hedge is an adjustment of the purchase transaction price. Deferring the gain or loss prevents its premature recognition. The forward exchange contract is entered into to offset the exposure to foreign currency exchange risk from a transaction that has not yet occurred. The FASB said it would be appropriate to wait until the completion of the transaction and then determine the net transaction price. One exception is made to this general rule: Losses on hedges of identifiable foreign currency commitments should not be deferred in those cases in which it is estimated that deferral would lead to recognizing losses in later periods.

Whenever balance sheets are prepared, forward exchange contracts written to hedge an identifiable foreign currency commitment must be translated into the entity's reporting currency using the spot rate at the balance sheet date. The entries for a hedge of an identifiable foreign currency commitment are presented in the following illustration.

Illustration of Hedging an Identifiable Foreign Currency Commitment   For purposes of illustration, the import transaction between Peerless Products and Tokyo Industries used throughout this chapter is extended with the following information:

1. On August 1, 19X1, Peerless Products Corporation contracts to purchase special-order goods from Tokyo Industries. The manufacture and delivery of the goods will take place in 60 days (on October 1, 19X1). The contract price is 2,000,000 yen, to be paid by April 1, 19X2, which is 180 days after delivery.

2. On August 1, Peerless Products hedges its foreign currency payable commitment with a forward exchange contract to receive 2,000,000 yen in 240 days (the 60 days until delivery plus 180 days of credit period). The future rate for a 240-day forward contract is $.0073 to 1 yen. The purpose of this 240-day forward exchange contract is twofold. First, for the 60 days from August 1, 19X1, until October 1, 19X1, the forward exchange contract is a hedge of an identifiable foreign currency commitment. For the 180-day period from October 1, 19X1, until April 1, 19X2, the forward exchange contract is a hedge of a foreign currency exposed net liability position.

The relevant exchange rates for this example are as follows:

Date	Spot Rate	Forward Exchange Rate
	U.S. Dollar Equivalent Value of 1 Yen	
August 1, 19X1	$.0065	$.0073 (240-day)
October 1, 19X1	$.0070	$.0075 (180-day)

A time line for the transactions is shown below.

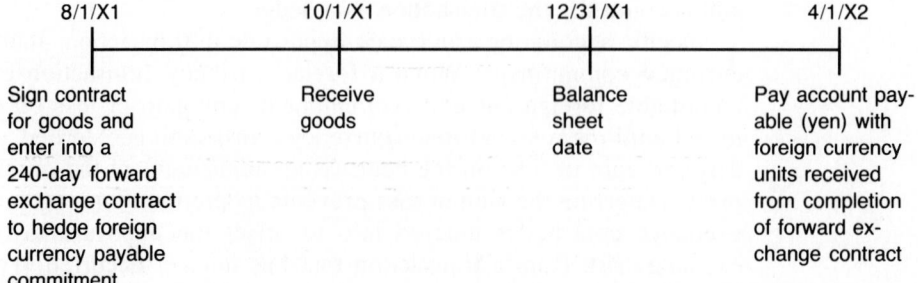

8/1/X1	10/1/X1	12/31/X1	4/1/X2
Sign contract for goods and enter into a 240-day forward exchange contract to hedge foreign currency payable commitment	Receive goods	Balance sheet date	Pay account payable (yen) with foreign currency units received from completion of forward exchange contract

The August 1, 19X1, and October 1, 19X1, entries to account for the forward contract transactions to hedge an identifiable foreign currency commitment are:

August 1, 19X1
(16) Foreign Currency Receivable from Exchange Broker (¥) 13,000
    Premium on Forward Contract 1,600
        Dollars Payable to Exchange Broker ($) 14,600
    Sign forward exchange contract for
    delivery of 2,000,000 yen in 240 days:
    $13,000 = ¥2,000,000 × $.0065 Aug. 1 spot rate
    $14,600 = ¥2,000,000 × $.0073 Aug. 1 forward rate

October 1, 19X1
(17) Foreign Currency Receivable from Exchange Broker (¥) 1,000
        Deferred Exchange Gain 1,000
    Adjust receivable denominated in foreign
    currency to current U.S. dollar equivalent:
    $ 14,000 = ¥2,000,000 × $.0070 Oct. 1 spot rate
    −13,000 = ¥2,000,000 × $.0065 Aug. 1 spot rate
    $ 1,000 = ¥2,000,000 × ($.0070 − $.0065)

(18) Deferred Exchange Loss 400
        Premium on Forward Contract 400
    Amortize contract premium to deferred loss
    for period between date of foreign currency
    commitment and date of receipt of goods:
    $1,600 = 60 days/240 days

(19) Inventory 13,400
    Deferred Exchange Gain 1,000
        Accounts Payable (¥) 14,000
        Deferred Exchange Loss 400
    Record accounts payable at spot rate
    and recognize deferred gain and loss as
    adjustments of purchase price:
    $14,000 = ¥2,000,000 × $.0070 Oct. 1 spot rate

Key Observations from Illustration The August 1, 19X1, entry records the signing of the forward exchange contract that is used to hedge the identifiable foreign currency commitment arising from the noncancelable purchase agreement. In entry (18), the premium on forward contract is amortized over the 240-day term of the forward contract using the straight-line method of amortization. The $400 amortization between August 1 and October 1 is deferred and recognized as an adjustment of the purchase price in this illustration. Alternatively, companies may account for the amortization of the premium as a financial expense and adjust the purchase price for only the change in the spot rates. The remaining $1,200 of unamortized premium on the forward contract ($1,200 = $1,600 − $400 amortized) is amortized as a financial expense over the period from October 1, 19X1, to April 1, 19X2.

The October 1, 19X1, entry (17) adjusts the foreign currency receivable to its equivalent dollar value on that date by recording an increase in the receivable and recognizing a deferred exchange gain for the increase in the direct exchange rate since August 1. The purchase price is then adjusted by the deferred exchange gain and the deferred loss, and the payable denominated in yen is recognized. At this point, the company has an exposed net liability position, which is hedged, and the subsequent accounting follows the accounting for an exposed foreign currency liability position as presented in Case 1 earlier in the chapter.

Case 3: Speculation in Foreign Currency Markets An entity may also decide to speculate in foreign currency as with any other commodity. For example, a U.S. company expects that the dollar will strengthen against the Swiss franc, that is, that the direct exchange rate will decrease. In this case, the U.S. company might *speculate with a forward exchange contract* to sell francs for future delivery, expecting to be able to purchase them at a lower price at the time of delivery.

The economic substance of this foreign currency speculation is to expose the investor to foreign exchange risk for which the investor expects to earn a profit. The exchange rate for valuing accounts related to speculative foreign exchange contracts is the forward rate for the remaining term of the forward contract. The gain or loss on a speculative forward contract is computed by determining the difference between the forward exchange rate on the date of contract (or on the date of a previous valuation) and the forward exchange rate available for the remaining term of the contract. In addition, because the speculative forward exchange contract is often sold before settlement, no separate accounting is given to the premium or discount on the forward contract.

Illustration of Speculation with Forward Contract The following example illustrates the accounting for a U.S. company entering into a speculative forward exchange contract in Swiss francs (SFr), a currency in which it has no receivables, payables, or commitments.

1. On October 1, 19X1, Peerless Products entered into a 180-day forward exchange contract to deliver SFr 4,000 at a forward rate of $.74 = SFr 1, when the spot rate was $.73 = SFr 1. Thus, the forward contract was to deliver SFr 4,000 and receive $2,960 (SFr 4,000 × $.74).

2. On December 31, 19X1, the balance sheet date, the forward rate for a 90-day forward contract was $.78 = SFr 1, and the spot rate for francs was $.75 = SFr 1.

3. On April 1, 19X2, the company acquired SFr 4,000 in the open market and delivered the francs to the broker, receiving the agreed forward contract price of $2,960. At this date, the spot rate was $.77 = SFr 1.

A summary of the direct exchange rates for this illustration is presented below.

Date	Spot Rate	Forward Rate
	U.S. Dollar Equivalent of 1 Franc	
October 1, 19X1	$.73	$.74 (180-day)
December 31, 19X1	.75	.78 (90-day)
April 1, 19X2	.77	

A time line of the economic events is as follows:

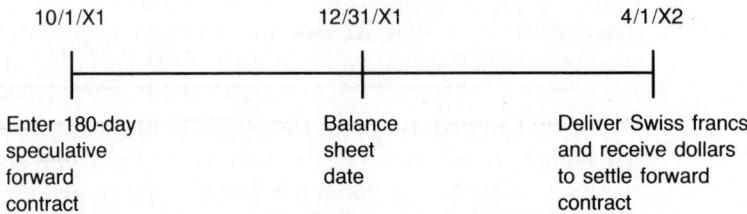

10/1/X1	12/31/X1	4/1/X2
Enter 180-day speculative forward contract	Balance sheet date	Deliver Swiss francs and receive dollars to settle forward contract

The entries for these transactions are presented below.

October 1, 19X1
(20) Dollars Receivable from Exchange Broker ($) ... 2,960
    Foreign Currency Payable to Exchange Broker (SFr) ... 2,960
    Enter into speculative forward exchange contract:
    SFr 4,000 × $.74, the 180-day forward rate

December 31, 19X1
(21) Foreign Currency Transaction Loss ... 160
    Foreign Currency Payable to Exchange Broker (SFr) ... 160
    Recognize speculation loss on forward contract for
    difference between initial 180-day forward
    rate and forward rate for remaining term
    to maturity of contract of 90 days:
    SFr 4,000 × ($.78 − $.74)

April 1, 19X2
(22) Foreign Currency Units (SFr) ... 3,080
    Cash ... 3,080
    Acquire foreign currency units (SFr)
    when spot rate is $.77 = SFr 1:
    SFr 4,000 × $.77 spot rate

(23) Foreign Currency Payable to Exchange Broker (SFr) ... 40
    Foreign Currency Transaction Gain ... 40
    Revalue foreign currency payable to spot rate:
    SFr 4,000 × ($.78 − $.77)

(24)	Foreign Currency Payable to Exchange Broker (SFr)	3,080	
	Foreign Currency Units (SFr)		3,080
	Deliver foreign currency units to exchange		
	broker in settlement of forward contract:		
	SFr 4,000 × $.77 spot rate		
(25)	Cash	2,960	
	Dollars Receivable from Exchange Broker ($)		2,960
	Receive U.S. dollars from exchange broker		
	as contracted.		

Key Observations from Illustration The October 1 entry records the payable of 4,000 Swiss francs to the exchange broker. The payable is denominated in a foreign currency, but must be translated into U.S. dollars used as the reporting currency of Peerless Products. For speculative contracts, the forward exchange contract accounts are translated using the forward exchange rate for the remaining term of the contract, and no separate accounting is made for the premium on the forward exchange contract.

The December 31 entry adjusts the payable denominated in foreign currency to its appropriate balance at the balance sheet date. The payable, Foreign Currency Payable to Exchange Broker, is adjusted for the increase in the forward exchange rate from October 1, 19X1. The foreign currency transaction loss is reported on the income statement, usually under "Other Income (Loss)."

Entry (22), the first April 1 entry, shows the acquisition of the 4,000 francs in the open market, at the spot rate of $.77 = SFr 1. These francs will be used to settle the foreign currency payable to the exchange broker. The next entry, entry (23), revalues the foreign currency payable to its current U.S. dollar equivalent value using the spot rate of exchange, and recognizes the speculation gain. The next two entries on this date, entries (24) and (25), recognize the settlement of the forward contract with the delivery of the 4,000 francs to the exchange broker and the receipt of the $2,960 agreed to when the contract was signed on October 1, 19X1. The $40 foreign currency transaction gain is the difference between the value of the foreign currency contract on December 31 using the forward rate and the value of the foreign currency units on April 1 using the spot rate.

Note that the company has speculated and lost, because the dollar actually weakened against the Swiss franc. The net loss on the speculative forward contract was $120, which is the difference between the $160 loss recognized in 19X1 and the $40 gain recognized in 19X2.

Although this example shows a delivery of foreign currency units with a forward exchange contract, a company may also arrange a future contract for the receipt of foreign currency units. In this case, the October 1 entry would be as follows:

October 1, 19X1

(26)	Foreign Currency Receivable from Exchange Broker (SFr)	2,960	
	Dollars Payable to Exchange Broker ($)		2,960
	Sign forward exchange contract for		
	future receipt of foreign currency units:		
	SFr 4,000 × $.74		

FIGURE 12-5 Overview of accounting for forward exchange contracts.

Type of Forward Exchange Contract	Exchange Rate Used to Value Foreign Currency Balance Sheet Accounts	Accounting for Exchange Gain or Loss	Accounting for Forward Contract Premium or Discount
1. Hedge of an exposed position	Current spot rate	Generally no net exchange gain or loss	Amortized against operating income over term of contract
2. Hedge of an identifiable foreign currency commitment	Current spot rate	Deferred to transaction date; then adjustment of dollar basis of transaction	May be deferred to transaction date as with exchange gain or loss
3. Speculation	Current forward rate for remaining term of contract	Included currently in income statement	No separate accounting recognition

The remainder of the accounting is similar to that of a delivery contract, except that the company records an exchange gain on December 31 because it has a receivable denominated in a foreign currency that has now strengthened relative to the dollar.

Figure 12-5 presents a summary of the accounting methods employed for the three uses of forward exchange contracts. The major differences between the treatments are the different exchange rates used to value the items denominated in the foreign currency, the treatments of the exchange gain or loss on hedges of an identifiable foreign currency commitment, and the alternative treatments for the premium or discount on the forward exchange contract.

Foreign Exchange Matrix

The relationships between changes in exchange rates and the resulting exchange gains and losses are summarized in Figure 12-6. For example, if a company has an account receivable denominated in a foreign currency, the exposed net monetary asset position will result in the recognition of an exchange gain if the direct exchange rate increases, but an exchange loss if the exchange rate decreases. If a company offsets an asset denominated in a foreign currency with a liability also denominated in that currency, the company has protected itself from any changes in the exchange rate because any gain is offset by an equal exchange loss.

ADDITIONAL CONSIDERATIONS

Interperiod Tax Allocation for Foreign Currency Gains (Losses)

Temporary differences in the recognition of foreign currency gains or losses between tax accounting and GAAP accounting require interperiod tax allocation. Generally, the accrual method of recognizing the effects of changes in exchange

FIGURE 12-6 Foreign exchange matrix.

Transactions or Accounts Denominated in Foreign Currency Units	Direct Exchange Rate Changes	
	Exchange Rate Increases (dollar has weakened)	Exchange Rate Decreases (dollar has strengthened)
Net monetary asset position, for example: (1) Foreign Currency Units (2) Accounts Receivable (3) Foreign Currency Receivable from Exchange Broker	EXCHANGE GAIN	EXCHANGE LOSS
Net monetary liability position, for example: (1) Accounts Payable (2) Bonds Payable (3) Foreign Currency Payable to Exchange Broker	EXCHANGE LOSS	EXCHANGE GAIN

rates in the period of change differs from the general election for recognizing exchange gains for tax purposes in the period of actual conversion of the foreign currency–denominated item. The temporary difference is recognized in accordance with **FASB Statement No. 109**, "Accounting for Income Taxes" (FASB 109).

Hedges of a Net Investment in a Foreign Entity

In the earlier discussions of the use of forward exchange contracts as a hedging instrument, the exchange risks from transactions denominated in a foreign currency could be offset. This same concept is applied by U.S. companies that view a net investment in a foreign entity as a long-term commitment that exposes them to foreign currency risk. A number of balance sheet management tools are available for a U.S. company to hedge its net investment in a foreign affiliate. Management may use forward exchange contracts, other foreign currency commitments, or certain intercompany financing arrangements, including intercompany transactions. For example, a U.S. parent company could borrow 10,000 British pounds to hedge against an equivalent net asset position of its British subsidiary. Any effects of exchange rate fluctuations between the pound and the dollar would be offset by the investment in the British subsidiary and the loan payable.

The general rule is that exchange gains and losses related to hedging transactions are not included in determining income. Chapter 13 introduces a special stockholders' equity account, cumulative translation adjustment, which is used to accumulate the exchange rate adjustments on transactions that are intended to hedge a net investment in a foreign entity.

SUMMARY OF KEY CONCEPTS AND TERMS

Virtually all companies have foreign transactions. The general rule is that accounts resulting from transactions denominated in foreign currency units must be valued and reported at their equivalent U.S. dollar values. These accounts must be adjusted to recognize the effects of changes in the exchange rates, and a foreign currency transaction gain or loss is recognized for the period.

Forward exchange contracts can be written (1) to hedge an exposed foreign asset or liability position, (2) to hedge an identifiable foreign currency commitment, or (3) to speculate in foreign currency markets. Generally, no net exchange gain or loss is shown for a hedged activity because of the offset of exchange gains and losses. On the other hand, speculation may result in a gain or loss for the period because of changes in the forward exchange rate.

Foreign currency exchange rate
Foreign currency transaction
 gain or loss
Foreign currency transactions
Foreign currency units (FCU)
Forward exchange contract
Functional currency
Hedging an exposed foreign currency
 position—either a net asset or a net
 liability position

Hedging identifiable foreign
 currency commitments
Local currency
Local currency units (LCU)
Reporting currency
Speculation with a forward
 exchange contract

QUESTIONS

Q12-1 Explain the difference between indirect and direct exchange rates.

Q12-2 What is the direct exchange rate if a U.S. company receives $1.15 in Canadian currency in exchange for $1.00 in U.S. currency?

Q12-3 The U.S. dollar strengthened against the German mark. Will imports from Germany into the United States be more expensive in U.S. dollars or less expensive? Explain why.

Q12-4 Differentiate between a foreign transaction and a foreign currency transaction. Give an example of each.

Q12-5 What types of economic factors affect currency exchange rates? Give an example of a change in an economic factor that results in a weakening of the local currency unit versus a foreign currency unit.

Q12-6 How are assets and liabilities that are denominated in a foreign currency measured on the transaction date? On the balance sheet date?

Q12-7 When are foreign currency transaction gains or losses recognized in the financial statements? Where are these gains or losses reported in the financial statements?

Q12-8 Sun Company, a U.S. corporation, has an account payable of $200,000 denominated in Canadian dollars. If the direct exchange rate increases, will Sun Company experience a foreign currency transaction gain or loss on this payable?

Q12-9 What are some ways a U.S. company can hedge against the risk of changes in the exchange rates for foreign currencies?

Q12-10 Distinguish between an exposed net asset position and an exposed net liability position.

Q12-11 Explain why a difference usually exists between a currency's spot rate and forward rate. Give two reasons why this difference is usually positive when a company enters into a contract to receive foreign currency at a future date.

Q12-12 A forward exchange contract may be used (1) to hedge an exposed foreign currency position, (2) to hedge an identifiable foreign currency commitment, or (3) to speculate in foreign currency markets. What are the main differences in accounting for these three uses?

Q12-13 How should the following accounts be reported on the financial statements, if shown at all?
  a. Foreign Currency Receivable from Broker
  b. Foreign Currency Transaction Loss
  c. Foreign Currency Transaction Gain
  d. Dollars Payable to Exchange Broker
  e. Premium on Forward Contract
  f. Foreign Currency Units
  g. Accounts Payable (denominated in a foreign currency)

Q12-14 For hedges of an exposed foreign currency position, how are premiums or discounts on forward exchange contracts determined? How are the premiums or discounts accounted for over the life of the forward exchange contract?

CASES

C12-1 Effects of Changing Exchange Rates

Since the early 1970s, the U.S. dollar has both increased and decreased in value against other currencies such as the Japanese yen, the Swiss franc, and the German mark. The value of the U.S. dollar, as well as the value of currencies of other countries, is determined by the balance between the demand for and the supply of the currency on the foreign exchange markets. A drop in the value of the U.S. dollar has a widespread impact not only on consumers and businesses that deal with their counterparts overseas, but also on consumers and businesses that operate solely within the United States.

Required

a. Identify the factors that influence the demand for and supply of the U.S. dollar on the foreign exchange markets.

b. Explain the effects a drop in value of the U.S. dollar in relation to other currencies on the foreign exchange markets has on:
  (1) The sales of a U.S. business firm that exports part of its output to foreign countries.
  (2) The costs of a U.S. business firm that imports from foreign countries part of the inputs used in the manufacture of its products.

c. Explain why and how consumers and business firms that operate solely within the United States are affected by the drop in value of the U.S. dollar in relation to other currencies on the foreign exchange markets.

EXERCISES

E12-1 Exchange Rates

The direct foreign exchange rates in U.S. dollars are:

1 British pound   = $1.90
1 Canadian dollar = $ .85

Required

a. What are the indirect exchange rates for the British pound and the Canadian dollar?
b. How many pounds must a British company pay to purchase goods costing $9,500 from a U.S. company?
c. How many U.S. dollars must be paid for a purchase costing 4,000 Canadian dollars?

E12-2 Changes in Exchange Rates

Upon arrival at the international airport in the country of Canteberry, Charles Alt exchanged $200 into florins, the local currency unit. Charles received 1,000 florins in exchange for the $200 of U.S. currency. After completing his business, and upon departure from Canteberry's international airport, he exchanged his remaining 100 florins into $15 of U.S. currency.

Required

a. Determine the currency exchange rates for each of the cells in the following matrix for Charles Alt's business trip to Canteberry:

	Arrival Date	Departure Date
Direct Exchange Rate		
Indirect Exchange Rate		

b. Discuss and illustrate whether the U.S. dollar strengthened or weakened relative to the florin during Mr. Alt's stay in Canteberry.
c. Did Mr. Alt experience a foreign currency transaction gain or a loss on the 100 florins he held during his visit to Canteberry and converted to U.S. dollars at the departure date? Explain your answer.

E12-3 Basic Understanding of Foreign Exposure

The Hi-Stakes Company has a number of importing and exporting transactions. Importing activities result in payables, and exporting activities result in receivables. (LCU represents the local currency unit of the foreign entity.)

Required

a. If the direct exchange rate increases, does the dollar weaken or strengthen relative to the other currency? If the indirect exchange rate increases, does the dollar weaken or strengthen relative to the other currency?

b. Indicate in the following table whether Hi-Stakes will have a foreign currency transaction gain (G), loss (L), or not be affected (NA) by changes in the direct or indirect exchange rates for each of the four situations presented.

Transaction	Settlement Currency	Direct Exchange Rate		Indirect Exchange Rate	
		Increases	Decreases	Increases	Decreases
Importing	Dollar				
Importing	LCU				
Exporting	Dollar				
Exporting	LCU				

E12-4 Account Balances

Noble Company had the following foreign currency transactions:

1. On November 1, 19X1, Noble sold goods to a company located in Munich, Germany. The receivable was to be settled in German marks on February 1, 19X2, with the receipt of DM 100,000 by Noble Company.

2. On November 1, 19X1, Noble purchased machine parts from a company located in Berlin, Germany. Noble is to pay DM 25,000 on February 1, 19X2.

The direct exchange rates for the following dates were:

> November 1, 19X1   DM 1 = $.60
> December 31, 19X1   DM 1 = $.50
> February 1, 19X2   DM 1 = $.55

Required

a. Prepare T-accounts for the following five accounts related to the transactions above: Foreign Currency Units (DM), Accounts Receivable (DM), Accounts Payable (DM), Foreign Currency Transaction Loss, and Foreign Currency Transaction Gain.

b. Within the T-accounts you have prepared, appropriately record the following items:
1. The November 1, 19X1, export transaction (sale).
2. The November 1, 19X1, import transaction (purchase).
3. The December 31, 19X1, year-end adjustment required of the foreign currency–denominated receivable of DM 100,000.
4. The December 31, 19X1, year-end adjustment required of the foreign currency–denominated payable of DM 25,000.
5. The February 1, 19X2, adjusting entry to determine the U.S. dollar equivalent value of the foreign currency receivable on that date.
6. The February 1, 19X2, adjusting entry to determine the U.S. dollar equivalent value of the foreign currency payable on that date.
7. The February 1, 19X2, settlement of the foreign currency receivable.
8. The February 1, 19X2, settlement of the foreign currency payable.

E12-5 Determining Year-End Account Balances for Import and Export Transactions

Delaney, Inc. has several transactions with foreign entities. Each transaction is denominated in the local currency unit of the country in which the foreign entity is located. For each of the following independent cases, determine the December 31, 19X2, year-end balance in the appropriate accounts for the case. Write "NA" for "not applicable" in the space provided below if that account is not relevant to the specific case.

Case 1 On November 12, 19X2, Delaney Company purchased goods from a foreign company at a price of LCU 40,000 when the direct exchange rate was 1 LCU = $.45. The account has not been settled as of December 31, 19X2, when the exchange rate has decreased to 1 LCU = $.40.

Case 2 On November 28, 19X2, Delaney Company sold goods to a foreign entity at a price of LCU 20,000 when the direct exchange rate was 1 LCU = $1.80. The account has not been settled as of December 31, 19X2, when the exchange rate has increased to 1 LCU = $1.90.

Case 3 On December 2, 19X2, Delaney Company purchased goods from a foreign company at a price of LCU 30,000 when the direct exchange rate was 1 LCU = $.80. The account has not been settled as of December 31, 19X2, when the exchange rate has increased to 1 LCU = $.90.

Case 4 On December 12, 19X2, Delaney Company sold goods to a foreign entity at a price of LCU 2,500,000 when the direct exchange rate was 1 LCU = $.003. The account has not been settled as of December 31, 19X2, when the exchange rate has decreased to 1 LCU = $.0025.

Required

Provide the December 31, 19X2, year-end balances on the records of Delaney, Inc., for each of the following applicable items:

	Accounts Receivable	Accounts Payable	Foreign Currency Transaction Exchange Loss	Foreign Currency Transaction Exchange Gain
Case 1	_____	_____	_____	_____
Case 2	_____	_____	_____	_____
Case 3	_____	_____	_____	_____
Case 4	_____	_____	_____	_____

E12-6 Transactions with Foreign Companies

Harris, Inc. had the following transactions:

1. On May 1, Harris, Inc. purchased parts from a Japanese company for a U.S. dollar equivalent value of $8,400, to be paid on June 20. The exchange rates were:

5/1

R. Inv.   8400
   A/p   8400

e/20 A/p   8400
   Cash   8400

May 1	1 yen =	$.0070
June 20	1 yen =	.0075

2. On July 1, Harris, Inc. sold products to a French customer for a U.S. dollar equivalent of $10,000, to be received on August 10. The exchange rates were:

7[c A/R   10,000
   SALES   10,000

8/10 Cash   10,000
   A/R   10,000

July 1	1 franc =	$.20
August 10	1 franc =	.22

Required

a. Assume the two transactions are denominated in U.S. dollars. Prepare the entries required for the dates of the transactions and their settlement in U.S. dollars.

b. Assume the two transactions are denominated in the applicable local currency units of the foreign entities. Prepare the entries required for the dates of the transactions and their settlement in the local currency units of the Japanese company (yen) and the French customer (franc).

E12-7 Foreign Purchase Transaction

On December 1, 19X1, Rone Imports, a U.S. company, purchased clocks from Switzerland for 15,000 francs (SFr), to be paid on January 15, 19X2. Rone's fiscal year ends on December 31, and Rone's reporting currency is the U.S. dollar. The exchange rates are:

December 1, 19X1	1 SFr = $.70
December 31, 19X1	1 SFr = .66
January 15, 19X2	1 SFr = .68

Required

a. In which currency is the transaction denominated?

b. Prepare journal entries for Rone Imports to record the purchase, the adjustment on December 31, and the settlement.

E12-8 Adjusting Entries for Foreign Currency Balances

Jane Deer Farm Implements deals with foreign entities. Some transactions are denominated in U.S. dollars and others in foreign currencies. A summary of accounts receivable and accounts payable on December 31, 19X1, before adjustments for the effects of changes in exchange rates during 19X1, follows.

Accounts receivable:	
In U.S. dollars	$172,300
In 500,000 French francs (FF)	92,500
Accounts payable:	
In U.S. dollars	41,400
In 17,600,000 yen (¥)	123,200

The spot rates on December 31, 19X1, were:

FF 1 = $.194
¥1 = $.0068

The average exchange rates during the collection and payment period in 19X2 are:

FF 1 = $.19
¥1 = $.0070

Required

a. Prepare the adjusting entries on December 31, 19X1.
b. Record the collection of the accounts receivable in 19X2.
c. Record the payment of the accounts payable in 19X2.

E12-9 Purchase with Forward Exchange Contract

Merit & Family purchased engines from Germany for 30,000 marks on March 10, with payment due on June 8. Also, on March 10, Merit acquired a 90-day forward contract to purchase 30,000 marks at a forward rate of DM 1 = $.58. The forward contract was acquired to hedge Merit & Family's exposed net liability position in marks. The spot rates were:

March 10	DM 1 = $.57
June 8	DM 1 = .60

Required

Prepare journal entries for Merit & Family to record the purchase of the engines, entries associated with the forward contract, and entries for the payment of the foreign currency payable.

E12-10 Purchase with Forward Exchange Contract and Intervening Fiscal Year-End

Easy Company purchased equipment from Switzerland for 100,000 francs on December 16, 19X3, with payment due on February 14, 19X4. On December 16, 19X3, Easy also acquired a 60-day forward contract to purchase francs at a forward rate of SFr 1 = $.74. The spot rates were:

December 16, 19X3	1 SFr = $.73
December 31, 19X3	1 SFr = .72
February 14, 19X4	1 SFr = .70

Required

Prepare journal entries for Easy Company to record the purchase of equipment, all entries associated with the forward contract, the adjusting entries on December 31, 19X3, and entries to record the payment on February 14, 19X4.

E12-11 **Foreign Currency Transactions** [AICPA Adapted]

Select the correct answer for each of the following questions.

1. Dale, Inc., a U.S. company, bought machine parts from a German company on March 1, 19X1, for 30,000 marks, when the spot rate for marks was $.4895. Dale's year-end was March 31, when the spot rate was $.4845. On April 20, 19X1, Dale paid the liability with 30,000 marks acquired at a rate of $.4945. Dale's income statements should report a foreign exchange gain or loss for the years ended March 31, 19X1 and 19X2 of:

	19X1	19X2
a.	$0	$0
b.	$0	$150 loss
c.	$150 loss	$0
d.	$150 gain	$300 loss

2. Marvin Company's receivable from a foreign customer is denominated in the customer's local currency. This receivable of 900,000 local currency units (LCU) has been translated into $315,000 on Marvin's December 31, 19X5, balance sheet. On January 15, 19X6, the receivable was collected in full when the exchange rate was 3 LCU to $1. The journal entry Marvin should make to record the collection of this receivable is:

		Debit	Credit
a.	Foreign Currency Units	300,000	
	Accounts Receivable		300,000
b.	Foreign Currency Units	300,000	
	Exchange Loss	15,000	
	Accounts Receivable		315,000
c.	Foreign Currency Units	300,000	
	Deferred Exchange Loss	15,000	
	Accounts Receivable		315,000
d.	Foreign Currency Units	315,000	
	Accounts Receivable		315,000

$\frac{1}{3} \times 900,000$

3. On July 1, 19X1, Black Company lent $120,000 to a foreign supplier, evidenced by an interest-bearing note due on July 1, 19X2. The note is denominated in the currency of the borrower and was equivalent to 840,000 local currency units (LCU) on the loan date. The note principal was appropriately included at $140,000 in the receivables section of Black's December 31, 19X1, balance sheet. The note principal was repaid to Black on the July 1, 19X2, due date when the exchange rate was 8 LCU to $1. In its income statement for the year ended December 31, 19X2, what amount should Black include as a foreign currency transaction gain or loss on the note principal?
   a. $0.
   b. $15,000 loss.
   c. $15,000 gain.
   d. $35,000 loss.

4. If 1 Canadian dollar can be exchanged for 90 cents of United States money, what fraction should be used to compute the indirect quotation of the exchange rate expressed in Canadian dollars?
   a. 1.10/1.
   b. 1/1.10.

c. 1/.90.
d. .90/1.

5. On July 1, 19X4, Bay Company borrowed 1,680,000 local currency units (LCU) from a foreign lender, evidenced by an interest-bearing note due on July 1, 19X5, which is denominated in the currency of the lender. The U.S. dollar equivalent of the note principal was as follows:

Date	Amount
7/1/X4 (date borrowed)	$210,000
12/31/X4 (Bay's year-end)	240,000
7/1/X5 (date repaid)	280,000

In its income statement for 19X5, what amount should Bay include as a foreign exchange gain or loss on the note principal?
a. $70,000 gain.
b. $70,000 loss.
c. $40,000 gain.
d. $40,000 loss.

6. A sale of goods was denominated in a currency other than the entity's functional currency. The sale resulted in a receivable that was fixed in terms of the amount of foreign currency that would be received. The exchange rate between the functional currency and the currency in which the transaction was denominated changed. The effect of the change should be included as a:

a. Separate component of stockholders' equity whether the change results in a gain or a loss.
b. Separate component of stockholders' equity if the change results in a gain, and as a component of income if the change results in a loss.
c. Component of income if the change results in a gain, and as a separate component of stockholders' equity if the change results in a loss.
d. Component of income whether the change results in a gain or a loss.

7. A December 15, 19X6, purchase of goods was denominated in a currency other than the entity's functional currency. The transaction resulted in a payable that was fixed in terms of the amount of foreign currency, and was paid on the settlement date, January 20, 19X7. The exchange rates between the functional currency and the currency in which the transaction was denominated changed at December 31, 19X6, resulting in a loss that should:

a. Not be reported until January 20, 19X7, the settlement date.
b. Be included as a separate component of stockholders' equity at December 31, 19X6.
c. Be included as a deferred charge at December 31, 19X6.
d. Be included as a component of income from continuing operations for 19X6.

E12-12   Sale in Foreign Currency

Hydro Company sold water-pumping equipment to Spain for 3,000,000 pesetas (P) on October 1, with payment due in 6 months. The exchange rates were:

October 1, 19X1	1 peseta = $.014
December 31, 19X1	1 peseta = .017
April 1, 19X2	1 peseta = .016

Required

a. Did the dollar strengthen or weaken relative to the peseta during the period from October 1 to December 31? Did it strengthen or weaken between January 1 and April 1 of the next year?

b. Prepare all required journal entries for Hydro Company as a result of the sale and settlement of the foreign transaction, assuming its fiscal year ends on December 31.

c. Did Hydro Company have an overall net gain or net loss from its foreign currency exposure?

E12-13 Sale with Forward Exchange Contract

Alman Company sold pharmaceuticals to a Swedish company for 200,000 kronor (SKr) on April 20, with settlement to be in 60 days. On the same date, Alman entered into a 60-day forward contract to sell 200,000 kronor at a forward rate of 1 krona = $.167 in order to hedge its exposed foreign currency receivable. The spot rates were:

| April 20 | SKr 1 = $.170 |
| June 19 | SKr 1 = .165 |

Required

a. Record all necessary entries related to the foreign transaction and the forward contract.

b. Compare the effects on net income of Alman's hedging use of the forward exchange contract versus the effects if Alman had not hedged its foreign currency receivable.

E12-14 Foreign Currency Transactions [AICPA Adapted]

Choose the correct answer for each of the following questions.

1. On November 15, 19X3, Chow, Inc., a U.S. company, ordered merchandise FOB shipping point from a German company for 200,000 marks. The merchandise was shipped and invoiced on December 10, 19X3. Chow paid the invoice on January 10, 19X4. The spot rates for marks on the respective dates were:

November 15, 19X3	$.4955
December 10, 19X3	.4875
December 31, 19X3	.4675
January 10, 19X4	.4475

In Chow's December 31, 19X3 income statement, the foreign exchange gain is:
a. $9,600.
b. $8,000.
c. $4,000.
d. $1,600.

2. Stees Corporation had the following foreign currency transactions during 19X2:
   (1) Merchandise was purchased from a foreign supplier on January 20, 19X2, for the U.S. dollar equivalent of $90,000. The invoice was paid on March 20, 19X2, at the U.S. dollar equivalent of $96,000.
   (2) On July 1, 19X2, Stees borrowed the U.S. dollar equivalent of $500,000 evidenced by a note that was payable in the lender's local currency on July 1, 19X4. On December 31, 19X2, the U.S. dollar equivalents of the principal amount and accrued interest were $520,000 and $26,000, respectively. Interest on the note is 10 percent per annum.

   In Stees' 19X2 income statement, what amount should be included as a foreign exchange loss?
   a. $0.
   b. $6,000.
   c. $21,000.
   d. $27,000.

3. On September 1, 19X1, Cott Corporation received an order for equipment from a foreign customer for 300,000 local currency units (LCU) when the U.S. dollar equivalent was $96,000. Cott shipped the equipment on October 15, 19X1, and billed the customer for 300,000 LCU when the U.S. dollar equivalent was $100,000. Cott received the customer's remittance in full on November 16, 19X1, and sold the 300,000 LCU for $105,000. In its income statement for the year ended December 31, 19X1, Cott should report a foreign exchange gain of:
   a. $0.
   b. $4,000.
   c. $5,000.
   d. $9,000.

4. On April 8, 19X3, Trul Corporation purchased merchandise from an unaffiliated foreign company for 10,000 units of the foreign company's local currency. Trul paid the bill in full on March 1, 19X4, when the spot rate was $.45. The spot rate was $.60 on April 8, 19X3, and was $.55 on December 31, 19X3. For the year ended December 31, 19X4, Trul should report a transaction gain of:
   a. $1,500.
   b. $1,000.
   c. $500.
   d. $0.

E12-15 Sale with Forward Contract and Fiscal Year-End

Software House, Inc., sold computer software to a Netherlands company for 80,000 guilders (G) on May 21, with collection due in 60 days. On the same day, Software House entered into a 60-day forward contract to sell 80,000 guilders at a forward rate of G 1 = $.204. Software House's fiscal year ends on June 30. The spot rates were:

May 21	G 1 = $.210
June 30	G 1 = .200
July 20	G 1 = .197

Required

Prepare journal entries for Software House, Inc., to record: **(a)** the sale of software, **(b)** the forward contract, **(c)** the adjusting entries on June 30, **(d)** the July 20 collection of the receivable, and **(e)** the July settlement of the forward contract.

E12-16 Hedge of a Purchase Commitment

On November 1, 19X2, Arden, Inc. contracted to purchase subassemblies from England for 20,000 pounds (£). The parts were to be delivered on January 30, 19X3, and payment would be due on March 1, 19X3. On November 1, 19X2, Arden entered into a 120-day forward contract to receive 20,000 pounds at a forward rate of £1 = $1.82. The forward contract was acquired to hedge the foreign currency commitment. The spot rates were:

November 1, 19X2	£1 = $1.85
December 31, 19X2	£1 = 1.88
January 30, 19X3	£1 = 1.83
March 1, 19X3	£1 = 1.86

Required

a. What is Arden's net exposure to changes in the exchange rate of pounds for dollars between November 1, 19X2, and March 1, 19X3?

b. Prepare all journal entries from November 1, 19X2, through March 1, 19X3 for the purchase of the subassemblies, the forward exchange contract, and the foreign currency transaction. Assume Arden's fiscal year ends on December 31, 19X2.

E12-17 Gain or Loss on Speculative Forward Exchange Contract

On December 1, 19X1, Sycamore Company acquired a 90-day speculative forward contract to sell 120,000 German marks (DM) at a forward rate of DM 1 = $.58. The rates are as follows:

Date	Spot Rate	Forward Rate for March 1
December 1, 19X1	DM 1 = $.60	DM 1 = $.58
December 31, 19X1	DM 1 = .59	DM 1 = .56
March 1, 19X2	DM 1 = .57	

Required

a. Prepare a schedule showing the effects of this speculation on 19X1 income before income taxes.

b. Prepare a schedule showing the effects of this speculation on 19X2 income before income taxes.

E12-18 Speculation in a Foreign Currency

Nick Andros of Streamline suggested that the company speculate in foreign currency as a partial hedge against its operations in the cattle market, which fluctuates like a commodity market. On October 1, 19X1, Streamline bought a 180-day forward contract to purchase 50,000,000 yen (¥) at a forward rate of ¥1 = $.0075 when the spot rate was $.0070. Other exchange rates were as follows:

FC REX × B
$ PAY × B
G or L
dureclly hit $
NO peem
or
DSC

Date	Spot Rate	Forward Rate for March 31, 19X2
December 31, 19X1	$.0073	$.0076
March 31, 19X2	.0072	

Required

a. Prepare all journal entries related to Streamline Company's foreign currency speculation from October 1, 19X1, through March 31, 19X2, assuming the fiscal year ends on December 31, 19X1.

b. Did Streamline Company gain or lose on its purchase of the forward contract? Explain.

PROBLEMS

P12-19 Multiple-Choice Questions on Foreign Currency Transactions

Special Importers purchased carved jadeite, the rarer variety of jade, from China for 100,000 yuan on November 1, 19X3. Payment is due on January 30, 19X4. On November 1, 19X3, the company also entered into a 90-day forward contract to purchase 100,000 yuan. The rates were as follows:

Date	Spot Rate	Forward Rate
November 1, 19X3	$.190	$.196 (90-day)
December 31, 19X3	.188	.193 (30-day)
January 30, 19X4	.185	

Required

Select the correct answer for each of the following questions.

1. The entry on November 1, 19X3, to record the forward contract includes a:
   a. Debit to Foreign Currency Receivable from Exchange Broker, 100,000 yuan.
   b. Debit to Foreign Currency Receivable from Exchange Broker, $19,600.
   c. Credit to Premium on Forward Contract, $600.
   d. Credit to Dollars Payable to Exchange Broker, $19,600.

2. The entries on December 31, 19X3, include a:
   a. Debit to Financial Expense, $300.
   b. Credit to Foreign Currency Payable to Exchange Broker, $200.
   c. Credit to Foreign Currency Receivable from Exchange Broker, $200.
   d. Credit to Foreign Currency Receivable from Exchange Broker, $19,600.

3. The entries on January 30, 19X4, include a:
   a. Debit to Dollars Payable to Exchange Broker, $19,000.
   b. Credit to Cash, $19,600.
   c. Credit to Premium on Forward Contract, $600.
   d. Credit to Foreign Currency Receivable from Exchange Broker, $19,600.

4. The entries on January 30, 19X4, include a:
   a. Debit to Financial Expense, $400.
   b. Debit to Dollars Payable to Exchange Broker, $19,600.
   c. Credit to Foreign Currency Units (yuan), $19,000.
   d. Credit to Foreign Currency Payable to Exchange Broker, $18,500.

5. The entries on January 30, 19X4 include a:
   a. Debit to Foreign Currency Units (yuan), $18,500.
   b. Debit to Dollars Payable to Exchange Broker, $18,500.
   c. Credit to Foreign Currency Transaction Gain, $600.
   d. Credit to Foreign Currency Receivable from Exchange Broker, $19,600.

P12-20 Foreign Purchases

Ladin Manufacturing buys materials and parts from foreign companies. The following are selected transactions.

1. On January 10, Ladin Manufacturing purchased metal parts from a German supplier for 60,000 marks. The exchange rate was DM 1 = $.600 on January 10 and DM 1 = $.580 on February 15 when payment was made.

2. Ladin purchased fabrics from a Swiss company for 50,000 Swiss francs (SFr) on March 5, with payment due on April 4. On March 5, Ladin acquired a 30-day forward contract to purchase francs at a forward rate of 1 franc = $.7310. The spot rates were:

March 5	SFr 1 = $.7300
April 4	SFr 1 = .7280

3. Additional parts were purchased from a plant in Mexico on April 10 for $16,000, when the exchange rate was 1 peso = $.0003. Payment was made in dollars on April 30, when the exchange rate was 1 peso = $.0002.

Required

Prepare journal entries to record Ladin Manufacturing's foreign transactions, including the purchases, the use of forward contracts, and the settlements of the liabilities.

P12-21 Foreign Sales

Tone Manufacturing sells many of its products overseas. The following are some selected transactions.

1. Tone sold electronic subassemblies to a firm in France for 120,000 French francs (FF) on June 6, when the exchange rate was FF 1 = $.1850. Collection was made on July 3, when the rate was FF 1 = $.1853.

2. On July 22, Tone sold personal computers to a company in London for 30,000 pounds (£), with payment due on September 20. Also on July 22, Tone entered into a 60-day forward contract to sell 30,000 pounds at a forward rate of £1 = $1.840. The spot rates were:

July 22	£1 = $1.820
September 20	£1 = 1.850

3. Tone sold storage devices to a Canadian firm for C$36,000 (Canadian dollars) on October 11, with payment due on November 10. On October 11, Tone entered into a 30-day forward contract to sell Canadian dollars at a forward rate of C$1 = $.8650. The spot rates were as follows:

October 11	C$1 = $.8500
November 10	C$1 = .8450

Required

Prepare journal entries to record Tone Manufacturing's foreign sales of its products, use of forward contracts, and settlements of the receivables.

P12-22 Foreign Currency Transactions

Globe Shipping is an importer and exporter. The following are some transactions with foreign companies.

1. Globe Shipping sold blue jeans to a French importer on January 15 for $7,400, when the exchange rate was FF 1 = $.185. Collection, in dollars, was made on March 15, when the exchange rate was $.180.

2. On March 8, Globe Shipping purchased woolen goods from Ireland for 7,000 pounds (IR£). The exchange rate was IR£1 = $1.68 on March 8, but the rate was $1.66 when payment was made on May 1.

3. On May 12, Globe Shipping signed a contract to purchase toys made in Taiwan for 80,000 Taiwan dollars (NT$). The toys were to be delivered 80 days later on August 1, and payment was due on September 9, which was 40 days after delivery. Also, on May 12 Globe Shipping entered into a 120-day forward contract to buy Taiwan dollars at a forward rate of NT$1 = $.0376. The spot rates were as follows:

May 12	NT$1 = $.0370
August 1	NT$1 = .0375
September 9	NT$1 = .0372

4. Globe Shipping sold microcomputers to a German enterprise on June 6 for 150,000 marks. Payment was due in 90 days, on September 4. On July 6, Globe Shipping entered into a 60-day forward contract to sell marks at a forward rate of DM 1 = $.580. The spot rates were as follows:

June 6	DM 1 = $.600
July 6	DM 1 = .590
September 4	DM 1 = .585

Required

Prepare all necessary journal entries for Globe Shipping to account for the foreign transactions, including the sales and purchases of inventory, forward contracts, and settlements.

P12-23 Three Uses of Forward Exchange Contracts

On December 1, 19X1, Micro World, Inc. entered into a 120-day forward contract to purchase 100,000 marks (DM). Micro World's fiscal year ends on December 31. The direct exchange rates were as follows:

Date	Spot Rate	Forward Rate for March 31
December 1, 19X1	$.600	$.609
December 31, 19X1	.610	.612
January 30, 19X2	.608	.605
March 31, 19X2	.602	

Required

Prepare all journal entries for Micro World, Inc., for the following *independent* situations:

a. The forward contract was to hedge the purchase of furniture for 100,000 marks on December 1, 19X1, with payment due on March 31, 19X2.

b. The forward contract was to hedge the agreement made on December 1, 19X1, to purchase furniture on January 30, with payment due on March 31, 19X2.

c. The forward contract was for speculative purposes only.

CHAPTER 13

MULTINATIONAL ACCOUNTING: TRANSLATION OF FOREIGN ENTITY STATEMENTS

When a U.S. multinational company prepares its financial statements for reporting to its stockholders, it must include its foreign-based operations measured in U.S. dollars and reported using U.S. GAAP. These foreign operations may be subsidiaries, branches, or investments of the U.S. company. This chapter presents the translation of the financial statements of a foreign business entity into U.S. dollars, a conversion that is necessary before the statements can be combined or consolidated with the U.S. company's statements, which are already reported in dollars.

Accountants preparing financial statements must consider both the differences in accounting principles and the differences in currencies used to measure the foreign entity's operations. For example, a British subsidiary of a U.S. company provides the parent with statements measured in British pounds sterling, using the British system of accounting, which is different from U.S. accounting methods and measures. The U.S. parent company must typically perform the following steps in the translation and consolidation of the British subsidiary:

1. Receive British subsidiary's financial statements, which are reported in pounds sterling.

2. Restate the statements to conform to U.S. generally accepted accounting principles.

3. Translate the statements measured in pounds sterling into their equivalent U.S. dollar amounts. Each foreign entity account balance must be individually translated into its U.S. dollar equivalent, as follows:

$$\begin{array}{c} \text{Account measured} \\ \text{in foreign currency} \\ \text{units} \end{array} \times \begin{array}{c} \text{appropriate} \\ \text{exchange rate} \end{array} = \begin{array}{c} \text{account measured in} \\ \text{U.S. dollar} \\ \text{equivalent value} \end{array}$$

4. Consolidate the translated subsidiary's accounts, which are now measured in dollars, with the parent company's accounts.

DIFFERENCES IN ACCOUNTING PRINCIPLES

Methods used to measure economic activity differ around the world. These differences have developed from the many different needs of the users in various countries. Most international accountants agree that there are four major models of accounting:

1. The U.S. model, which focuses on the information needs of the common stockholder through the application of generally accepted accounting principles.

2. The British model, which focuses on the information needs of bondholders, creditors, and preferred stockholders.

3. The French-Italian-Spanish model, which is based on the information needs of the taxing authorities.

4. The German and Scandinavian countries model, which is extremely conservative and uses large numbers of reserves to reduce income to its lowest level possible.

Countries following the basic U.S. accounting model are Japan, the Philippines, and Taiwan. Countries following the British model are India, Hong Kong, Malaysia, and Pakistan. Canada, Israel, and Mexico have adopted accounting methods reflecting both the British model and the U.S. model.

A number of countries allow companies to recognize appreciation write-ups in their assets. Most countries do not allow the use of the lifo inventory method. In addition, many countries require that the financial records be maintained according to the tax policies of the country, and because these countries use the tax system to affect public policy as well as to raise revenue, many unique accounting requirements are found.

Several international groups have worked to "harmonize" the world's many different accounting methods by attempting to develop a uniform set of international accounting standards. The International Accounting Standards Committee (IASC) has issued a number of pronouncements on the disclosure of selected financial statement items such as depreciation, accounting policies used, inventories, and research and development activities.[1] The general thrust of this organization has been to promote greater disclosure of the methods used to prepare the

---

[1] The International Accounting Standards Committee (IASC) is a private voluntary organization. The IASC does not have any authority to require adherence to its pronouncements but relies on the pledges of its member groups, such as the AICPA in the United States, to support its efforts.

financial statements, but the IASC has also published several pronouncements on accounting in economic environments of rapidly changing prices (inflation).

Until a set of international accounting standards is available, a U.S. company must ensure that its foreign economic activities are measured using U.S. GAAP before the translation process begins. Some companies do this by issuing a set of accounting standards to all their foreign subsidiaries and branches. Others make all the transformations in their home office.

DETERMINING THE FUNCTIONAL CURRENCY

FASB 52 provides specific guidelines for translating foreign currency financial statements. The translation process begins with a determination of whether each foreign affiliate's *functional currency* is also its reporting currency. A U.S. company may have foreign affiliates in many different countries. Each affiliate must be analyzed to determine its individual functional currency.

FASB 52 defines an entity's functional currency as:

> . . . the currency of the primary economic environment in which the entity operates; normally, that is the currency of the environment in which an entity primarily generates and expends cash.[2]

Figure 13-1 presents the six indicators that must be assessed in order to determine an entity's functional currency: cash flows, sales prices, sales markets, expenses, financing, and intercompany transactions. Most foreign affiliates use their local currency as the functional currency because the majority of cash transactions of a business generally take place in the currency of the country in which the entity operates. Also, the foreign affiliate usually has active sales markets in its own country and obtains financing from local sources.

Some foreign-based entities, however, use a functional currency different from the local currency: for example, a subsidiary in France may conduct virtually all of its business in Spain, or a branch or a subsidiary of a U.S. company operating in Britain may well use the U.S. dollar as its major currency although it maintains its accounting records in British pounds sterling. The following factors would indicate that the U.S. dollar is the functional currency for the British subsidiary: most of its cash transactions are in U.S. dollars; its major sales markets are in the United States; production components are generally obtained from the United States; and the U.S. parent is primarily responsible for financing the British subsidiary.

The functional currency approach was adopted by the FASB after considering the following objectives of the translation process:[3]

a. Provide information that is generally compatible with the expected economic effects of a rate change on an enterprise's cash flows and equity.

---

[2] *Financial Accounting Standards Board Statement No. 52*, "Foreign Currency Translation," 1981, par. 5.
[3] *FASB 52*, par. 4.

FIGURE 13-1 Functional currency indicators.

Indicator	Factors Indicating Foreign Currency (Local Currency) Is the Functional Currency	Factors Indicating U.S. Dollar (Parent's Currency) Is the Functional Currency
Cash flows	Primarily in foreign currency and do not affect parent's cash flows	Directly impact the parent's current cash flows and are readily available to the parent company
Sales prices	Primarily determined by local competition or local government regulation; not generally responsive to changes in exchange rates	Responsive to short-term changes in exchange rates and worldwide competition
Sales markets	Active local sales markets for company's products; might be significant amounts of exports	Sales markets mostly in parent's country, or sales contracts are denominated in parent's currency
Expenses	Labor, materials, and other costs are primarily local costs	Production components generally obtained from the parent company's country
Financing	Primarily obtained from, and denominated in, local currency units; entity's operations generate funds sufficient to service financing needs	Primarily from the parent, or other dollar-denominated financing
Intercompany transactions and arrangements	Few intercompany transactions with parent	Frequent intercompany transactions with parent, or foreign entity is an investment or financing arm for the parent

b. Reflect in consolidated statements the financial results and relationships of the individual consolidated entities as measured in their functional currencies in conformity with U.S. generally accepted accounting principles.

The functional currency approach requires the translation of all the foreign entity's transactions into the functional currency of the foreign entity. If an entity has transactions denominated in other than its functional currency, the foreign transactions must be adjusted to their equivalent functional currency value before the company may prepare financial statements.

Functional Currency Designation in Highly Inflationary Economies

An exception to the criteria for selecting a functional currency is specified when the foreign entity is located in countries such as Argentina, Brazil, and Peru, which have experienced severe inflation. Severe inflation is defined as inflation exceeding 100 percent over a 3-year period.[4] The FASB concluded that the

---

[4] *FASB 52*, par. 11.

volatility of hyperinflationary currencies distorts the financial statements if the local currency is used as the foreign entity's functional currency. Therefore, in cases of operations located in highly inflationary economies, the reporting currency of the U.S. parent—the U.S. dollar—should be used as the foreign entity's functional currency. This exception prevents unrealistic asset values and income statement charges if the hyperinflation is ignored and normal translation procedures are used. For example, assume a foreign subsidiary constructed a building that cost 1,000,000 pesos when the exchange rate was $.05 = 1 peso. Further assume that because of hyperinflation in the foreign subsidiary's country, the exchange rate becomes $.00005 = 1 peso. The translated values of the building at the time it was constructed and after the hyperinflation are:

	Date of Construction		After Hyperinflation	
Amount (pesos)	Rate	Translated Amount	Rate	Translated Amount
1,000,000	$.05	$50,000	$.00005	$50

The translated values after the hyperinflation do not reflect the building's market value or historical cost. Thus, the FASB required the use of the U.S. dollar as the functional currency in cases of hyperinflation in order to give some stability to the financial statements.

Once a foreign affiliate's functional currency is chosen, it should be used consistently. However, if changes in economic circumstances necessitate a change in the designation of the foreign affiliate's functional currency, the accounting change should be treated as a change in estimate: current and prospective treatment only, no restatement of prior periods.

TRANSLATION VERSUS REMEASUREMENT OF FOREIGN FINANCIAL STATEMENTS

Two different methods are used to restate foreign entity statements to U.S. dollars: (1) the *translation* of the foreign entity's functional currency statements into U.S. dollars, and (2) the *remeasurement* of the foreign entity's statements into the functional currency of the entity. The statements must then be translated if the functional currency is *not* the U.S. dollar. No additional work is needed if the functional currency is the U.S. dollar.

Translation is used when the local currency is the foreign entity's functional currency. This is the normal case in which, for example, a U.S. company's French subsidiary uses the French franc as its recording and functional currency. The subsidiary's statements must be translated from the French franc into the U.S. dollar.

Remeasurement is the restatement of the foreign entity's financial statements from the local currency measures used by the entity into the foreign entity's functional currency. Remeasurement is required only when the functional currency is different from the currency used to maintain the books and records of the foreign entity. For example, a relatively self-contained British sales branch of a U.S. company may use the U.S. dollar as its functional currency, but may select the British pound as its recording and reporting currency. Of course, if the British branch uses the dollar for both its functional and its reporting currency, no translation or remeasurement is necessary: its statements are already measured in dollars and are ready to be combined with the U.S. home office statements.

The most frequent application of remeasurement is for affiliates located in countries experiencing hyperinflation. For example, an Argentinian subsidiary of a U.S. parent records and reports its financial statements in the local currency, the Argentine peso. However, because the Argentine economy experiences inflation exceeding 100 percent over a 3-year period, the U.S. dollar is the functional currency for reporting purposes and the subsidiary's statements must then be remeasured from Argentine pesos into U.S. dollars.

The following presents an overview of the methods a U.S. company would use to restate a foreign affiliate's financial statements in U.S. dollars.

Currency in Which the Foreign Affiliate's Books and Records Are Maintained	Functional Currency	Restatement Method
Local currency (i.e., currency of the country in which the foreign entity is located)	Local currency	Translation to U.S. dollars
Local currency	U.S. dollar	Remeasurement to U.S. dollars
U.S. dollar	U.S. dollar	No restatement necessary; already in U.S. dollars

The conceptual reasons for the two different methods come from a consideration of the primary objective of the translation process: to provide information that shows the expected impact of exchange rate changes on the U.S. company's cash flows and equity. Foreign affiliates fall into two groups. Those in the first group are relatively self-contained entities that generate and spend local currency units. The local currency is the functional currency for this group of entities. These foreign affiliates may reinvest the currency they generate or may distribute funds to their home office or parent company in the form of dividends. Exchange rate changes do not directly affect the U.S. parent company's cash flows. Rather, the rate changes affect the foreign affiliate's net assets (assets minus liabilities), and therefore the U.S. parent company's net investment in the entity.

The second group of foreign affiliates is made up of entities that are an extension of the U.S. company. These affiliates operate in a foreign country but are directly affected by changes in exchange rates because they are dependent on the U.S. economy for sales markets, production components, or financing. For this group, the U.S. dollar is the functional currency. There is a presumption that the effect of exchange rate changes on the foreign affiliate's net assets will directly affect the U.S. parent company's cash flows, so the exchange rate adjustments are reported in the U.S. parent's income.

Translation and remeasurement include different adjustment procedures and may result in significantly different consolidated financial statements. Both methods are illustrated in this chapter.

TRANSLATION OF FUNCTIONAL CURRENCY STATEMENTS INTO THE REPORTING CURRENCY OF THE U.S. COMPANY

Typically, a business entity transacts and records most of its business activity in the local currency. Therefore, the local currency of the foreign entity is its functional currency. The translation of the foreign entity's statement into U.S. dollars is a relatively straightforward process.

The FASB felt that the underlying economic relationships presented in the financial statements of the foreign entity should not be distorted or changed during the translation process from the functional currency of the foreign entity into the currency of the U.S. parent. For example, if the foreign entity's functional currency statements report a current ratio of 2:1 and a gross margin of 60 percent of sales, these relationships should pass through the translation process into the reporting currency of the U.S. parent. It is important to be able to evaluate the performance of the foreign entity's management with the same economic measures used to operate the foreign entity. In order to maintain the economic relationships in the functional currency statements, the account balances must be translated by a comparable exchange rate.

The translation is made by using the current exchange rate for *all* assets and liabilities. This rate is the spot rate on the balance sheet date. The income statement items—revenue, expenses, gains, and losses—should be translated at the exchange rate on the dates on which the underlying transactions occurred, although for practical purposes a weighted-average exchange rate for the period may be used for these items with the assumption that revenues and expenses are recognized evenly over the period. However, if a material gain or loss results from a specific event, the exchange rate on the date of the event, rather than the average exchange rate, should be used to translate the results of the transaction.

The stockholders' equity accounts, other than retained earnings, are translated at historical exchange rates, that is, those existing on the date the parent company acquired the investment in the foreign entity. This is necessary to complete the elimination of the parent company's investment account against the foreign subsidiary's capital accounts in the consolidation process. The subsidiary's translated retained earnings are carried forward from the previous period with additions for this period's income and deductions for dividends declared during the period. Dividends are translated at the exchange rate on the date of declaration. It is interesting to observe that if the foreign entity has not paid its declared dividend by the end of its fiscal period, it has a dividends payable account that is translated at the current rate. Nevertheless, the dividend deduction from retained earnings is translated using the exchange rate on the date of dividend declaration.

In summary, the translation of the foreign entity's financial statements from its functional currency into the reporting currency of the U.S. company is made as follows:

Income statement accounts:
   Revenue and expenses   Generally, weighted-average exchange rate for period covered by statement

Balance sheet accounts:
   Assets and liabilities   Current exchange rate on balance sheet date
   Stockholders' equity   Historical exchange rates

Because a variety of rates are used to translate the foreign entity's individual accounts, the trial balance debits and credits after translation generally are not equal. The balancing item to make the translated trial balance debits equal the credits is called the *cumulative translation adjustment.*

Balance Sheet Presentation of Cumulative Translation Adjustment

The cumulative translation adjustment resulting from the translation process is not included in the income statement. **FASB 52** mandates the balance sheet statement presentation of the translation adjustment as follows:

> Translation adjustments are an inherent result of the process of translating a foreign entity's financial statements from the functional currency to U.S. dollars. Translation adjustments are *not* included in determining net income for the period but are disclosed and accumulated in a separate component of consolidated equity until sale or until complete or substantially complete liquidation of the net investment in the foreign entity takes place.[5]

The reason for accumulating the translation adjustment balancing item in the balance sheet is that the adjustments relate to the net asset investment (assets minus liabilities) of the foreign entity, not to current operations. The translation adjustment may have a debit or credit balance. Regardless of the balance, the translation adjustment account is a component of stockholders' equity and typically is presented on the balance sheet between additional paid-in capital and retained earnings. It may, however, also be shown after retained earnings. The account is usually titled Cumulative Translation Adjustment or a similarly descriptive name.

Illustration of Translation and Consolidation of a Foreign Subsidiary

In Chapter 12, the examples illustrated the effects of a dollar that was strengthening against the mark during 19X1. In the examples for the remainder of this

---

[5] *FASB 52*, Introductory Summary, p. ii.

chapter, the dollar weakens against the mark during 19X1. Thus, in Chapters 12 and 13, changes in exchange rates in both directions will have been illustrated.

To examine the consolidation of a foreign subsidiary, assume the following facts:

1. On January 1, 19X1, Peerless Products, a U.S. company, purchased 80 percent of the outstanding capital stock of German Company, a firm located in Berlin, Germany, for $54,000, which is $6,000 above book value. (The proof of the differential is shown at the end of the next section of the chapter.) The excess of cost over book value is attributable to goodwill amortizable over 10 years. Balance sheet accounts in a trial balance format for both companies immediately *before* the acquisition are presented in Figure 13-2.

2. The local currency for German Company is the mark (DM), which is also its functional currency.

3. On October 1, 19X1, the subsidiary declared and paid dividends of DM 12,500.

4. The subsidiary received $4,200 in a sales transaction with a U.S. company when the exchange rate was $.60 = DM 1. The subsidiary still has this foreign currency on December 31, 19X1.

5. Relevant direct spot exchange rates ($/DM1) are:

Date	Rate
January 1, 19X1	$.60
October 1, 19X1	.68
December 31, 19X1	.70
19X1 average	.65

FIGURE 13-2 Balance sheet accounts for the two companies on December 31, 19X0, immediately before acquisition of 80 percent of German Company's stock by Peerless Products, a U.S. company.

	Peerless Products	German Company
Cash	$ 350,000	DM 5,000
Receivables	75,000	20,000
Inventory	100,000	15,000
Land	175,000	-0-
Plant and Equipment	800,000	100,000
Total Debits	$1,500,000	DM 140,000
Accumulated Depreciation	$ 400,000	DM 10,000
Accounts Payable	100,000	5,000
Bonds Payable	200,000	25,000
Common Stock	500,000	80,000
Retained Earnings, 12/31/X0	300,000	20,000
Total Credits	$1,500,000	DM 140,000

Date-of-Acquisition Translation Workpaper   Figure 13-3 presents the translation of German Company's trial balance on January 1, 19X1. This illustration assumes that the subsidiary's books and records are maintained in German marks, the subsidiary's functional currency.

The translation of the subsidiary's trial balance from the functional currency (DM) into dollars, the reporting currency of the U.S. parent, is made using the *current rate method.* The appropriate historical rate used to translate the stockholders' equity accounts depends on the accounting method used to account for the business combination, as follows:

1. *Purchase Accounting* The subsidiary's stockholders' equity accounts are translated using the current rate on the date of the parent company's purchase of the subsidiary's stock.

2. *Pooling Accounting* The subsidiary's stockholders' equity accounts are translated using the exchange rate in effect on the date the subsidiary originally issued its stock. This is consistent with the retroactive restatement required under the pooling of interests method.

The entry made by Peerless Products to record the purchase of 80 percent of German Company's stock is:

```
January 1, 19X1
    (1)  Investment in German Company Stock            54,000
             Cash                                                54,000
         Purchase of German Company stock.
```

FIGURE 13-3 Workpaper to translate foreign subsidiary on January 1, 19X1, the date of acquisition. The functional currency is the German mark.

Item	Trial Balance, DM	Exchange Rate, $/DM	Trial Balance, $
Cash	5,000	.60	3,000
Receivables	20,000	.60	12,000
Inventory	15,000	.60	9,000
Plant and Equipment	100,000	.60	60,000
Total Debits	140,000		84,000
Accumulated Depreciation	10,000	.60	6,000
Accounts Payable	5,000	.60	3,000
Bonds Payable	25,000	.60	15,000
Common Stock	80,000	.60	48,000
Retained Earnings	20,000	.60	12,000
Total Credits	140,000		84,000

Note: $.60 is direct exchange rate on January 1, 19X1.

The differential on January 1, 19X1, the date of acquisition, is computed as follows:

1/1/X1	P	Investment cost		$54,000
80%		Book value of investment:		
		Common stock	$48,000	
		Retained earnings	12,000	
		Total	$60,000	
	G	Percent of German Company's stock acquired by Peerless Company	× .80	
		Book value acquired by Peerless Company		(48,000)
		Differential (excess of cost over book value) attributable to goodwill		$ 6,000

A graphic representation of the acquisition is as follows:

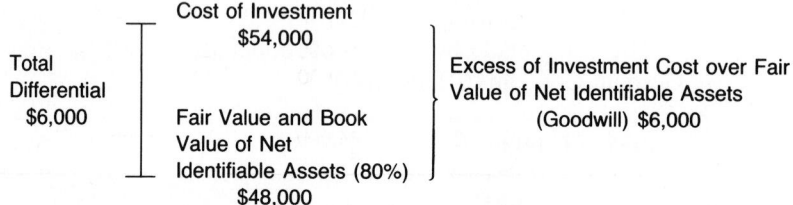

Date-of-Acquisition Consolidated Balance Sheet The consolidated balance sheet workpaper for Peerless Products and its German subsidiary on January 1, 19X1, is presented in Figure 13-4. The consolidation process is identical to the date-of-acquisition consolidations presented in Chapter 4. The eliminating entries are as follows:

E(2)	Common Stock—German Company	48,000	
	Retained Earnings	12,000	
	Differential	6,000	
	Investment in German Company Stock		54,000
	Noncontrolling Interest		12,000
	Eliminate investment balance:		
	$12,000 = ($48,000 + $12,000) × .20		
E(3)	Goodwill	6,000	
	Differential		6,000
	Assign differential.		

Subsequent to Date of Acquisition The accounting subsequent to the date of acquisition is very similar to the accounting used for domestic subsidiaries. The

FIGURE 13-4 January 1, 19X1, workpaper for consolidated balance sheet, date of acquisition; 80 percent purchase at more than book value.

	Peerless Products	German Company	Eliminations Debit	Eliminations Credit	Consolidated
Cash	296,000	3,000			299,000
Receivables	75,000	12,000			87,000
Inventory	100,000	9,000			109,000
Land	175,000				175,000
Plant and Equipment	800,000	60,000			860,000
Investment in German Co.					
Stock	54,000			(2) 54,000	
Differential			(2) 6,000	(3) 6,000	
Goodwill			(3) 6,000		6,000
Total Debits	1,500,000	84,000			1,536,000
Accumulated Depreciation	400,000	6,000			406,000
Accounts Payable	100,000	3,000			103,000
Bonds Payable	200,000	15,000			215,000
Common Stock	500,000	48,000	(2) 48,000		500,000
Retained Earnings	300,000	12,000	(2) 12,000		300,000
Noncontrolling Interest				(2) 12,000	12,000
Total Credits	1,500,000	84,000	72,000	72,000	1,536,000

Elimination entries:
(2) Eliminate investment balance.
(3) Assign differential.

major differences are due to the effects of changes in the exchange rates of the foreign currency.

Translation of Foreign Subsidiary's Postacquisition Trial Balance Figure 13-5 illustrates the translation of German Company's December 31, 19X1, trial balance.

Note the account Foreign Currency Units in the trial balance of the German subsidiary. This account represents the $4,200 of U.S. dollars held by the subsidiary. Because this account is denominated in a currency other than the subsidiary's reporting currency, German Company made an adjusting journal entry to revalue the account from the amount originally recorded using the exchange rate on the date the company received the currency to that amount's equivalent exchange value at the end of the year.

The subsidiary made the following entry on its books when it received the U.S. dollars:

(4)	Foreign Currency Units ($)	DM 7,000	
	Sales		DM 7,000
	Record sales and receipt of 4,200 U.S. dollars at spot exchange rate on date of receipt: DM 7,000 = $4,200/$.60 exchange rate		

FIGURE 13-5 December 31, 19X1, translation of foreign subsidiary's trial balance. The German mark is the functional currency.

Item	Balance, DM	Exchange Rate	Balance, $
Cash	21,500	.70	15,050
Foreign Currency Units	6,000	.70	4,200
Receivables	21,000	.70	14,700
Inventory	10,000	.70	7,000
Plant and Equipment	100,000	.70	70,000
Cost of Goods Sold	45,000	.65	29,250
Operating Expenses	29,000	.65	18,850
Foreign Currency Transaction Loss	1,000	.65	650
Dividends Paid	12,500	.68	8,500
Total Debits	246,000		168,200
Accumulated Depreciation	15,000	.70	10,500
Accounts Payable	6,000	.70	4,200
Bonds Payable	25,000	.70	17,500
Common Stock	80,000	.60	48,000
Retained Earnings (1/1)	20,000	(a)	12,000
Sales	100,000	.65	65,000
Total	246,000		157,200
Translation Adjustment			11,000
Total Credits			168,200

(a) Carry forward from January 1, 19X1, workpaper.

At the end of the period, the subsidiary adjusted the foreign currency units (the U.S. dollars) to the current exchange rate ($.70 = DM 1) by making the following entry:

(5) Foreign Currency Transaction Loss		DM 1,000	
Foreign Currency Units ($)			DM 1,000

Adjust account denominated in foreign currency units to current exchange rate:

$4,200/$.70	DM 6,000
Less: Preadjusted balance	DM (7,000)
Foreign currency transaction loss	DM (1,000)

The foreign currency transaction loss is a component of the subsidiary's net income, and the Foreign Currency Units account is classified as a current asset on the subsidiary's balance sheet. The subsidiary's net income consists of the following elements:

Sales	DM 100,000
Cost of Goods Sold	(45,000)
Operating Expenses	(29,000)
Foreign Currency Transaction Loss	(1,000)
Net Income	DM 25,000

Because the German mark is the foreign entity's functional currency, the subsidiary's statements must be translated into U.S. dollars using the *current rate method*. The assets and liabilities are translated using the current exchange rate at the balance sheet date ($.70), the income statement accounts are translated using the average rate for the period ($.65), and the stockholders' equity accounts are translated using the appropriate historical exchange rates ($.60 and $68). The dividends are translated at the October 1 rate ($.68), which was the exchange rate at the time the dividends were declared. The example assumes the dividends were paid on October 1, the same day they were declared. If the dividends had not been paid by the end of the year, the liability dividends payable would be translated at the current exchange rate of $.70 = DM 1.

One of the analytical features provided by the current method is that many of the ratios management uses to manage the foreign subsidiary are the same in U.S. dollars as they are in the foreign currency unit. This relationship is true for the assets and liabilities of the balance sheet and the revenue and expenses of the income statement, because the translation for these accounts uses the same exchange rate—the current rate for the assets and liabilities, the average exchange rate for the income statement accounts. Thus, the scale of these accounts has changed, but not their relative amounts within their respective statements. This relationship is not true when the ratio includes numbers from both the income statement and the balance sheet, or when a stockholders' equity account is included with an asset or liability. The following table illustrates the relative relationships within the financial statements, using the data in Figure 13-5:

	Measured in DM	Measured in U.S. Dollars
Current ratio:		
Current assets	DM 58,500	$40,950
Current liabilities	DM 6,000	$ 4,200
Current ratio	9.75	9.75
Cost of goods sold as a percentage of sales:		
Cost of goods sold	DM 45,000	$29,250
Sales	DM 100,000	$65,000
Percent	45%	45%

The Translation Adjustment account in Figure 13-5 arises because the investee's assets and liabilities are translated at the current rate, whereas other rates are used for the stockholders' equity and income statement account balances. Although the translation adjustment may be thought of as a balancing item to make the trial balance debits equal the credits, the effects of changes in the exchange rates during the period should be calculated to prove the accuracy of the translation process. This proof for 19X1, the year of acquisition, is provided in Figure 13-6.

The proof begins with determination of the effect of changes in the exchange rate on the beginning investment and on the elements that alter the beginning investment. Note that only events affecting the stockholders' equity accounts will change the net assets investment. In this example, the changes to the investment account occurred from income of DM 25,000 and dividends of DM 12,500. There were no changes in the stock outstanding during the year. The beginning net investment is translated using the exchange rate at the beginning of the year. The income and dividends are translated using the exchange rate at the date the transactions occurred. The income was earned evenly over the year; thus the average exchange rate for the period is used to translate income. The ending net assets position is translated using the exchange rate at the end of the year. The cumulative translation adjustment at the beginning of the year is zero in this example because the subsidiary was acquired on January 1, 19X1.

The Translation Adjustment account has a credit balance because the spot exchange rate at the end of the first period of ownership is higher than the exchange rate at the beginning of the period or the average for the period. If the exchange rate had decreased during the period, Translation Adjustment would have a debit balance.

FIGURE 13-6 Proof of translation adjustment as of December 31, 19X1. The German mark is the functional currency.

Peerless Products and Subsidiary Proof of Translation Adjustment Year Ended December 31, 19X1			
	DM	Translation Rate	$
Net assets at beginning of year	100,000	.60	60,000
Adjustment for changes in net assets position during year:			
Net income for year	25,000	.65	16,250
Dividends paid	(12,500)	.68	(8,500)
Net assets translated at:			
Rates during year			67,750
Rates at end of year	112,500	.70	78,750
Change in cumulative translation adjustment during year—net increase			11,000
Cumulative translation adjustment—1/1			-0-
Cumulative translation adjustment—12/31			11,000

Entries on Parent Company's Books Entries on the parent company's books are made to recognize the dollar equivalent values of the parent's share of the subsidiary's income, amortization of the excess of cost over book value, a cumulative translation adjustment for the parent's differential, and the dividends received from the foreign subsidiary. In addition, the parent company must recognize its share of the translation adjustment arising from the translation of the subsidiary's financial statements. The parent company's translation adjustment from the foreign investment is reported as a separate component of the parent company's stockholders' equity.

The entries Peerless Products makes to account for its investment in German Company are presented below. The dividend was received by Peerless Products on October 1, 19X1, and immediately converted to U.S. dollars, as follows:

October 1, 19X1
(6)	Cash	6,800	
	Investment in German Company Stock		6,800
	Dividend received from foreign subsidiary:		
	DM 12,500 × .80 ownership × $.68 exchange rate		

December 31, 19X1
(7)	Investment in German Company Stock	13,000	
	Income from Subsidiary		13,000
	Equity in net income of foreign subsidiary:		
	DM 25,000 × .80 × $.65 average exchange rate		
(8)	Investment in German Company Stock	8,800	
	Translation Adjustment		8,800
	Parent's share of change in translation adjustment		
	from translation of subsidiary's accounts:		
	$11,000 × .80		

If some time passed between the declaration and payment of dividends, the parent company would record dividends receivable from foreign subsidiary on the declaration date. This account would be denominated in a foreign currency and would be adjusted to its current exchange rate on the balance sheet date and on the payment date, just like any other account denominated in a foreign currency. Any foreign transaction gain or loss resulting from the adjustment procedure would be included in the parent's income for the period.

The Differential The allocation and amortization of the excess of cost over book value require special attention in the translation of a foreign entity's financial statements. The differential does not exist on the books of the foreign subsidiary; it is part of the parent's investment account. However, the translated book value of the foreign subsidiary is a major component of the investment account on the parent's books and is directly related to a foreign-based asset. **FASB 52** requires that the allocation and amortization of the difference between the investment cost and its book value be made in terms of the functional currency of the foreign subsidiary and that these amounts then be translated at the appropriate exchange rates on the workpaper balance sheet date. The periodic amortization affects the income statement and is therefore measured at the average exchange rate used to translate other income statement accounts. On the other hand, the remaining unamortized balance of the differential is reported in the balance sheet and is translated at the current exchange rate used for balance sheet accounts. The effect of this difference in rates is shown in the parent company's translation adjustment account as a revision of part of the parent's original investment in the subsidiary.

Peerless Products amortizes the goodwill over a period of 10 years. The goodwill amortization is presented below.

	German Marks	Translation Rate	U.S. Dollars
Income statement:			
Differential at beginning of year	DM 10,000	.60	$6,000
Amortization this period			
(DM 10,000/10 years)	(1,000)	.65	(650)
Remaining balances	DM 9,000		$5,350
Balance Sheet:			
Remaining balance on			
12/31/X1 translated at			
year-end exchange rate	DM 9,000	.70	$6,300
Difference to			
translation adjustment			$ 950

Entry (9) below recognizes the amortization of the differential for the period. Entry (10) records the portion of the translation adjustment on the increase in the differential for the investment in the foreign subsidiary.

(9)	Income from Subsidiary	650	
	Investment in German Company Stock		650
	Amortization of goodwill:		
	$650 = DM 1,000 × $.65 average exchange rate		
(10)	Investment in German Company Stock	950	
	Translation Adjustment		950
	Recognize translation adjustment on increase in		
	differential.		

It is important to note that the $950 translation adjustment from the differential is attributed solely to the parent company. Noncontrolling Interest is not assigned any portion of this translation adjustment. This $950 translation adjustment is attributable to the excess of cost paid over the book value of the assets, and therefore is added to the differential, which is a component of the investment in the foreign subsidiary, thereby resulting in a debit to the investment account on the parent company's books.

The December 31, 19X1, balance in the Investment in German Company Stock account is $69,300, as shown in the following T-account. The numbers in parentheses are the corresponding journal entry numbers from the text.

Investment in German Company Stock

(1)	Purchase price	54,000			
			(6)	Dividends	6,800
(7)	Equity income	13,000			
(8)	Share of subsidiary's translation adjustment	8,800			
			(9)	Amortization of differential	650
(10)	Translation adjustment on differential	950			
	Balance, 12/31/X1	69,300			

Subsequent Consolidation Workpaper The consolidation workpaper is prepared after the translation process is completed. The process of consolidation is the same as for a domestic subsidiary, except for two major differences: (1) The translation adjustment arising from the translation of the foreign subsidiary's accounts is divided between the parent's stockholders' equity and noncontrolling interest, and (2) as shown previously, the goodwill amortization for the period is translated at the income statement rate (average for the period), whereas the ending goodwill balance is translated at the balance sheet rate (current exchange rate). As shown in entry (10), a translation adjustment must be computed on the differential and assigned as part of the parent company's investment in the foreign subsidiary.

The workpaper is presented in Figure 13-7. The trial balance for German Company is obtained from the translated amounts computed earlier in Figure 13-5. The workpaper entries are presented below in journal entry form. These entries are *not* made on either company's books; they are only in the workpaper elimination columns.

E(11)	Income from Subsidiary	12,350	
	Dividends Declared		6,800
	Investment in German Company Stock		5,550
	Eliminate income from subsidiary:		
	$12,350 = $13,000 equity share − $650 amortization		
E(12)	Income to Noncontrolling Interest	3,250	
	Dividends Declared		1,700
	Noncontrolling Interest		1,550
	Assign income to noncontrolling interest:		
	$3,250 = $16,250 subsidiary income × .20		
	$1,700 = $8,500 dividends × .20		

FIGURE 13-7 December 31, 19X1, consolidated workpaper prepared after translation of foreign statements.

Item	Peerless Products	German Company	Eliminations Debit		Eliminations Credit		Consolidated
Sales	400,000	65,000					465,000
Income from Subsidiary	12,350		(11)	12,350			
Credits	412,350	65,000					465,000
Cost of Goods Sold	170,000	29,250					199,250
Operating Expenses	90,000	18,850	(17)	650			109,500
Foreign Currency Transaction Loss		650					650
Debits	(260,000)	(48,750)					(309,400)
							155,600
Income to Noncontrolling Interest			(12)	3,250			(3,250)
Net Income, carry forward	152,350	16,250		16,250			152,350
Retained Earnings, 1/1	300,000	12,000	(13)	12,000			300,000
Net Income, from above	152,350	16,250		16,250			152,350
	452,350	28,250					452,350
Dividends Declared	(60,000)	(8,500)			(11)	6,800	(60,000)
					(12)	1,700	
Retained Earnings, 12/31	392,350	19,750		28,250		8,500	392,350
Cash	432,800	15,050					447,850
Dollars Held by Sub		4,200					4,200
Receivables	75,000	14,700					89,700
Inventory	100,000	7,000					107,000
Land	175,000						175,000
Plant and Equipment	800,000	70,000					870,000
Investment in German Co. Stock	69,300				(11)	5,550	
					(13)	54,000	
					(14)	8,800	
					(15)	950	
Differential			(13)	6,000	(16)	6,950	
			(15)	950			
Goodwill			(16)	6,950	(17)	650	6,300
Debits	1,652,100	110,950					1,700,050
Accumulated Depreciation	450,000	10,500					460,500
Accounts Payable	100,000	4,200					104,200
Bonds Payable	200,000	17,500					217,500
Capital Stock	500,000	48,000	(13)	48,000			500,000
Retained Earnings, from above	392,350	19,750		28,250		8,500	392,350
Translation Adjustment	9,750	11,000	(14)	11,000			9,750
Noncontrolling Interest					(12)	1,550	
					(13)	12,000	
					(14)	2,200	15,750
Credits	1,652,100	110,950		101,150		101,150	1,700,050

Key to eliminations:
(11) Eliminate income from subsidiary.
(12) Assign income to noncontrolling interest.
(13) Eliminate beginning investment account balance.
(14) Eliminate translation adjustment.
(15) Eliminate adjustment to differential.
(16) Assign differential to goodwill.
(17) Amortize differential.

E(13)	Common Stock—German Co.	48,000	
	Retained Earnings, January 1, 19X1	12,000	
	Differential	6,000	
	Investment in German Co. Stock		54,000
	Noncontrolling Interest		12,000
	Eliminate beginning-of-period investment balance and establish noncontrolling interest's share of beginning equity of subsidiary: $12,000 = ($48,000 + $12,000) × .20		
E(14)	Translation Adjustment—German Co.	11,000	
	Investment in German Co. Stock		8,800
	Noncontrolling Interest		2,200
	Eliminate translation adjustment resulting from translation of subsidiary's end-of-period trial balance.		
E(15)	Differential	950	
	Investment in German Co. Stock		950
	Eliminate end-of-period differential adjustment that was recorded in investment account.		
E(16)	Goodwill	6,950	
	Differential		6,950
	Assign differential, including periodic adjustment of $950, to goodwill: $6,950 = $6,000 + $950 differential adjustment		
E(17)	Operating Expenses—Amortization of Goodwill	650	
	Goodwill		650
	Amortize differential: $650 = DM 1,000 × $.65		

When the equity method is used by the parent company and there are no intercompany revenue transactions, the parent's income and retained earnings are equal to the consolidated income and consolidated retained earnings. This makes it possible to verify the amounts reported on the consolidated financial statements.

Noncontrolling interest shares in the $11,000 translation adjustment which was assigned to the subsidiary because the source of this adjustment is the translation of the financial statements of the foreign subsidiary. Total noncontrolling interest in the subsidiary's net assets at year-end can be proved as follows:

Common stock ($48,000 × .20)		$ 9,600
Retained earnings:		
Beginning retained earnings ($12,000 × .20)	$2,400	
Add: Net income ($16,250 × .20)	3,250	
Less: Dividends ($8,500 × .20)	(1,700)	
Total retained earnings		3,950
Translation adjustment ($11,000 × .20)		2,200
Total noncontrolling interest		$15,750

The $11,000 translation adjustment assigned to the subsidiary as shown in Figure 13-7 is eliminated in entry E(14). As a result, the final balance of the translation adjustment reported in the consolidated balance sheet is $9,750, which is carried forward from the parent company's trial balance.

REMEASUREMENT OF THE BOOKS OF RECORD INTO THE FUNCTIONAL CURRENCY

A second method of restating foreign affiliates' financial statements in U.S. dollars is remeasurement. Although remeasurement is not as commonly used as translation, some situations exist in which the functional currency of the foreign affiliate is not its local currency. Remeasurement is similar to translation in that its goal is to obtain equivalent U.S. dollar values for the foreign affiliate's accounts so they may be combined or consolidated with the U.S. company's statements. The exchange rates used for remeasurement, however, are different from those used for translation, resulting in different dollar values for the foreign affiliate's accounts.

The FASB provided examples of several situations requiring remeasurement:[6]

1. A foreign sales branch or subsidiary of a U.S. manufacturer which primarily takes orders from foreign customers for U.S.–manufactured goods, which bills and collects from foreign customers, and which might have a warehouse to provide for timely delivery of the product to those foreign customers. In substance, this foreign operation may be the same as the export sales department of a U.S. manufacturer.

2. A foreign division, branch, or subsidiary which primarily manufactures a subassembly that is shipped to a U.S. plant for inclusion in a product that is sold to customers located in the U.S. or in different parts of the world.

3. A foreign shipping subsidiary which primarily transports ore from a U.S. company's foreign mines to the United States for processing in a U.S. company's smelting plants.

4. A foreign subsidiary which is primarily a conduit for Eurodollar borrowings to finance operations in the United States.

In most cases, the foreign affiliate may be thought of as a direct production or sales arm of the U.S. company, but it uses the local currency to record and report its operations. In addition, foreign entities located in highly inflationary economies, defined as economies having a cumulative 3-year inflation rate exceeding 100 percent, must use the dollar as their functional currency, and their statements are remeasured into U.S. dollars. Many South American countries have experienced hyperinflation, with some countries having annual inflation rates in excess of 100 percent. If the foreign affiliate uses the U.S. dollar as both its functional and

---

[6] The examples were provided in the exposure draft of **FASB 52** but were not included in the final draft of the standard. The FASB did not want the examples to limit remeasurement to those cases in which the U.S. dollar is the functional currency.

its reporting currency, no remeasurement is necessary, because its operations are already reported in U.S. dollars.

The remeasurement process should produce the same end result as if the foreign entity's transactions had been initially recorded in dollars. For this reason, certain transactions and account balances are converted to their U.S. dollar equivalents using a historical exchange rate, the spot exchange rate at the time the transaction originally occurred. The remeasurement process divides the balance sheet into monetary and nonmonetary accounts. Monetary assets and liabilities, such as cash, short-term or long-term receivables, and short-term or long-term payables, have their amounts fixed in terms of the units of currency. These accounts are subject to gains or losses from changes in exchange rates. Nonmonetary assets are accounts such as inventories, and plant and equipment, which are not fixed in relation to exchange rates.

The monetary accounts are remeasured using the current exchange rate. The appropriate historical exchange rate is used to remeasure nonmonetary balance sheet account balances and related revenue, expense, gain, and loss account balances. A list of the accounts to be remeasured with the appropriate historical exchange rate is provided in Figure 13-8.[7]

Because of the variety of rates used to remeasure the foreign currency trial balance, the debits and credits of the U.S. dollar equivalent trial balance will probably not be equal. In this case, the balancing item is a *remeasurement gain or loss*, which is included in the period's income statement.

FIGURE 13-8 Accounts to be remeasured using historical exchange rates.

Marketable securities carried at cost:
  Equity securities
  Debt securities not intended to be held until maturity
Inventories carried at cost
Prepaid expenses such as insurance, advertising, and rent
Property, plant, and equipment
Accumulated depreciation on property, plant, and equipment
Patents, trademarks, licenses, and formulas
Goodwill
Other intangible assets
Deferred charges and credits, except deferred income taxes and policy acquisition costs for life
  insurance companies
Deferred income
Common stock
Preferred stock carried at issuance price
Revenue and expenses related to nonmonetary items, for example:
  Cost of goods sold
  Depreciation of property, plant, and equipment
  Amortization of intangible items such as goodwill, patents, licenses, etc.
  Amortization of deferred charges or credits except deferred income taxes and policy acquisition
    costs for life insurance companies

Source: FASB No. 52, par. 48.

[7] *FASB 52, par. 48.*

Statement Presentation of Remeasurement Gain or Loss

Any exchange gain or loss arising from the remeasurement process is included in the current period's income statement, usually under "Other Income." Various account titles are used, such as Foreign Exchange Gain (Loss), Currency Gain (Loss), Exchange Gain (Loss), or Remeasurement Gain (Loss). The title Remeasurement Gain (Loss) is used here because it is most descriptive of the source of the item. The remeasurement gain or loss is included in the period's income because if the transactions had originally been recorded in U.S. dollars, the exchange gains and losses would have been recognized this period as part of the adjustments required for valuation of foreign transactions denominated in a foreign currency. Upon completion of the remeasurement process, the financial statements of the foreign entity are presented as they would have been if the U.S. dollar had been used to record the transactions in the local currency as they occurred.

Illustration of Remeasurement of a Foreign Subsidiary

German Company again is used, this time to present remeasurement of financial statements. The only difference between the previous example of translation and the current example is that the functional currency of the foreign subsidiary is now assumed to be the U.S. dollar rather than the German mark. German Company maintains its books and records in marks in order to provide required reports to the German government. Since the dollar is the functional currency, the financial statements of the German Company will be remeasured into dollars. Once the foreign affiliate's statements are remeasured, the consolidation process is the same as for a domestic subsidiary.

Remeasurement of Foreign Subsidiary's Postacquisition Trial Balance The subsidiary's trial balance must be remeasured from the German mark into the U.S. dollar as shown in Figure 13-9. The current exchange rate is used to remeasure the monetary accounts, and the appropriate historical exchange rates are used for each of the nonmonetary accounts.

Three items need special attention. First, the plant and equipment is remeasured using the historical rate of the date the parent company acquired the foreign subsidiary. If the subsidiary purchases any additional plant or equipment after the parent has acquired the stock of the subsidiary, the additional plant or equipment will be remeasured using the exchange rate on the date of the purchase of the additional plant. The same cautionary note is applicable for the other nonmonetary items. It is important to maintain a record of the subsidiary's acquisition or disposition of nonmonetary assets and equities after the foreign subsidiary's stock is acquired to ensure that the proper exchange rates are used to remeasure these items. Recall that the business combination was accounted for as a purchase; therefore, the appropriate historical rate is the spot rate on the date the parent purchased the foreign subsidiary's stock. If the combination was

FIGURE 13-9 December 31, 19X1, remeasurement of the foreign subsidiary's trial balance. The U.S. dollar is the functional currency.

Item	Balance, DM	Exchange Rate	Balance, $
Cash	21,500	.70	15,050
Foreign Currency Units	6,000	.70	4,200
Receivables	21,000	.70	14,700
Inventory	10,000	.69	6,900
Plant and Equipment	100,000	.60	60,000
Cost of Goods Sold	45,000	(a)	28,100
Operating Expenses	29,000	(b)	18,600
Foreign Currency Transaction Loss	1,000	.65	650
Dividends Paid	12,500	.68	8,500
Total Debits	246,000		156,700
Accumulated Depreciation	15,000	.60	9,000
Accounts Payable	6,000	.70	4,200
Bonds Payable	25,000	.70	17,500
Common Stock	80,000	.60	48,000
Retained Earnings	20,000	(c)	12,000
Sales	100,000	.65	65,000
Total	246,000		155,700
Remeasurement Gain			1,000
Total Credits			156,700

	In Marks	Exchange Rate	In Dollars
(a) Cost of Goods Sold:			
Beginning Inventory	15,000	.60	9,000
Purchases	40,000	.65	26,000
Goods Available	55,000		35,000
Less: Ending Inventory	(10,000)	.69	(6,900)
Cost of Goods Sold	45,000		28,100
(b) Operating Expenses:			
Cash Expenses	24,000	.65	15,600
Depreciation Expense	5,000	.60	3,000
	29,000		18,600

(c) Carry forward from January 1, 19X1, workpaper.

accounted for as a pooling, then the appropriate historical spot rates would be the rates on the dates the subsidiary originally issued the stock and acquired the nonmonetary assets, not the later date on which the parent company acquired the subsidiary's stock.

Second, the cost of goods sold consists of transactions that occurred at various exchange rates. The beginning inventory was acquired when the rate was $.60 = DM 1. Purchases of inventory were made at different times during the year and the average rate of $.65 was used for the remeasurement exchange rate. For purposes of illustration, the example assumes that ending inventory was acquired when the direct exchange rate was $.69 = DM 1 and the fifo inventory method is used.

Third, the operating expenses are also incurred at different exchange rates. The depreciation expense is remeasured at $.60 = DM 1 because it is associated with a nonmonetary account, Plant and Equipment, which is remeasured at the historical exchange rate of $.60 = DM 1. The average exchange rate is used to remeasure the remaining operating expenses because they are assumed to be incurred evenly throughout the period.

The remeasurement gain is recognized in this period's income statement. The remeasurement exchange gain is a balancing item to make total debits and total credits equal, but it can be proved by analyzing changes in the monetary items during the period. The complete proof is shown at the end of this chapter.

Subsequent Consolidation Workpaper The consolidation workpaper for the remeasurement case is presented in Figure 13-10. The accounts for German Company are obtained from the remeasured accounts computed in Figure 13-9. The remeasurement gain is included in the trial balance of the German subsidiary because the source of this account is the remeasurement of the subsidiary's accounts. The noncontrolling interest is allocated a portion of the remeasurement gain through its equity in the subsidiary's net income ($3,730 = $18,650 × .20).

The Income from Subsidiary account can be proved as follows:

Income from Subsidiary

		Parent's share of subsidiary income: ($18,650 × .80)	14,920
Amortization of goodwill ($6,000/10 years)	600		
		Balance, 12/31/X1	14,320

In the consolidated income statement, the remeasurement gain account is usually offset against the foreign currency transaction loss account, generating, in this example, a net gain of $350 ($1,000 − $650). This gain is reported in the other income section of the income statement.

The remainder of the consolidation process is identical with the process for a domestic subsidiary. Note that the goodwill of $5,400 shown on the consolidated balance sheet is the unamortized portion of the initial $6,000 amount ($5,400 = $6,000 − $600). No special adjustments are required for goodwill when using the remeasurement process.

FIGURE 13-10 December 31, 19X1, consolidation workpaper prepared after remeasurement of foreign statements.

	Peerless Products	German Company	Eliminations Dr	Eliminations Cr	Consolidated
Sales	400,000	65,000			465,000
Remeasurement Gain		1,000			1,000
Income from Subsidiary	14,320		(18) 14,320		
Credits	414,320	66,000			466,000
Cost of Goods Sold	170,000	28,100			198,100
Operating Expenses	90,000	18,600	(22) 600		109,200
Foreign Currency Transaction Loss		650			650
Debits	(260,000)	(47,350)			(307,950)
					158,050
Income to Noncontrolling Interest			(19) 3,730		(3,730)
Net Income, carry forward	154,320	18,650	18,650		154,320
Retained Earnings, 1/1	300,000	12,000	(20) 12,000		300,000
Net Income, from above	154,320	18,650	18,650		154,320
	454,320	30,650			454,320
Dividends Declared	(60,000)	(8,500)		(18) 6,800	(60,000)
				(19) 1,700	
Retained Earnings, 12/31	394,320	22,150	30,650	8,500	394,320
Cash	432,800	15,050			447,850
Dollars Held by Sub		4,200			4,200
Receivables	75,000	14,700			89,700
Inventory	100,000	6,900			106,900
Land	175,000				175,000
Plant and Equipment	800,000	60,000			860,000
Investment in German Co. Stock	61,520			(18) 7,520	
				(20) 54,000	
Differential			(20) 6,000	(21) 6,000	
Goodwill			(21) 6,000	(22) 600	5,400
Debits	1,644,320	100,850			1,689,050
Accumulated Depreciation	450,000	9,000			459,000
Accounts Payable	100,000	4,200			104,200
Bonds Payable	200,000	17,500			217,500
Common Stock	500,000	48,000	(20) 48,000		500,000
Retained Earnings, from above	394,320	22,150	30,650	8,500	394,320
Noncontrolling Interest				(19) 2,030	
				(20) 12,000	14,030
Credits	1,644,320	100,850	90,650	90,650	1,689,050

Elimination entries:
   (18) Eliminate income and dividends from subsidiary.
   (19) Assign income and dividends to noncontrolling interest.
   (20) Eliminate beginning investment account balance.
   (21) Assign beginning differential to goodwill.
   (22) Amortize goodwill.

The eliminating entries are as follows:

E(18)	Income from Subsidiary		14,320	
	Dividends Declared			6,800
	Investment in German Co. Stock			7,520
	Eliminate income from subsidiary:			
	$6,800 = $8,500 dividends × .80			
E(19)	Income to Noncontrolling Interest		3,730	
	Dividends Declared			1,700
	Noncontrolling Interest			2,030
	Assign income to noncontrolling interest:			
	$3,730 = $18,650 subsidiary income × .20			
	$1,700 = $8,500 dividends × .20			
E(20)	Common Stock—German Co.		48,000	
	Retained Earnings, January 1, 19X1		12,000	
	Differential		6,000	
	Investment in German Co. Stock			54,000
	Noncontrolling Interest			12,000
	Eliminate beginning-of-period investment balance and			
	establish noncontrolling interest's share of beginning			
	equity of subsidiary:			
	$12,000 = ($48,000 + $12,000) × .20			
E(21)	Goodwill		6,000	
	Differential			6,000
	Assign differential to goodwill.			
E(22)	Operating Expenses—Amortization of Goodwill		600	
	Goodwill			600
	Amortize goodwill.			

Summary of Translation versus Remeasurement

A comparison of Figures 13-7 and 13-10 shows that the reported income of the foreign subsidiary differs between translation and remeasurement. The primary reason that subsidiary income is approximately 15 percent higher when the dollar is the functional currency ($18,650 versus $16,250 under translation) is that the U.S. dollar weakened against the German mark during the year. This results in a remeasurement gain for the subsidiary because it was transacting in the stronger currency (the mark) during the period. Furthermore, the cost of goods sold and operating expenses of the subsidiary are remeasured at a lower exchange rate, resulting in a higher income.

When the functional currency is the dollar, the nonmonetary items on the balance sheet are remeasured using historical exchange rates. In this example, the direct exchange rate has increased during the period; therefore, the nonmonetary accounts are lower when remeasured than when translated. A summary of the differences between the translation and remeasurement methods is presented in Figure 13-11.

FIGURE 13-11 Summary of the translation and remeasurement processes.

Item	Translation Process	Remeasurement Process
Foreign entity's functional currency	Local currency unit	U.S. dollar
Method used	Current rate method	Monetary-nonmonetary method
Income statement accounts:		
Revenue	Weighted-average exchange rate	Weighted-average exchange rate, except revenue related to nonmonetary items (historical exchange rate)
Expenses	Weighted-average exchange rate	Weighted-average exchange rate, except costs related to nonmonetary items (historical exchange rate)
Balance sheet accounts:		
Monetary accounts	Current exchange rate	Current exchange rate
Nonmonetary accounts	Current exchange rate	Historical exchange rates
Stockholders' equity capital accounts	Historical exchange rates	Historical exchange rates
Retained earnings	Prior period's balance plus income less dividends	Prior period's balance plus income less dividends
Exchange rate adjustments arising in process	Translation adjustment accumulated in stockholders' equity	Remeasurement gain or loss included in period's income statement

FOREIGN INVESTMENTS AND UNCONSOLIDATED SUBSIDIARIES

Most companies consolidate their foreign subsidiaries in conformity with **FASB Statement No. 94,** "Consolidation of All Majority-Owned Subsidiaries" (FASB 94). In some cases these operations are not consolidated, owing to criteria that apply to foreign subsidiaries. Generally, a parent company consolidates a foreign subsidiary, except when one of the following conditions becomes so severe that the U.S. company owning a foreign company may not be able to exercise the necessary level of economic control over the foreign subsidiary's resources and financial operations to warrant consolidation:

1. Restrictions on foreign exchange in the foreign country
2. Restrictions on transfers of property in the foreign country
3. Other governmentally imposed uncertainties

An unconsolidated foreign subsidiary is reported as an investment on the U.S. parent company's balance sheet. The U.S. investor company must use the equity method if it has the ability to exercise "significant influence" over the investee's financial and operating policies. If the equity method cannot be applied, the cost method is used to account for the foreign investment, recognizing income only as dividends are received.

When the equity method is used for an unconsolidated foreign subsidiary, the financial statements of the investee are either remeasured or translated, depending on the determination of the functional currency. If remeasurement is used, the foreign entity's statements are remeasured to dollars and the investor records its percentage of the investee's income and makes necessary amortizations of any differential. A shortcut approach is available for translation: multiply the foreign affiliate's net income measured in foreign currency units by the average exchange rate during the period and then recognize the parent company's percentage share of the translated net income. In addition, the investor must recognize its share of the translation adjustment arising from the translation of the foreign entity's financial statements. The investor's share of the translation adjustment from its foreign investees is reported on the investor's balance sheet as a separate component of stockholders' equity and also as an adjustment of the carrying value of the investment account. The entries on the investor's books are the same under the equity method whether the subsidiary is consolidated or reported as an unconsolidated investment.

Liquidation of a Foreign Investment

The translation adjustment account is directly related to a company's investment in a foreign entity. If the investor sells a substantial portion of its stock investment, **FASB Interpretation No. 37**, ''Accounting for Translation Adjustments upon Sale of Part of an Investment in a Foreign Entity'' (FIN 37), requires that the pro rata portion of the accumulated translation adjustment account attributable to that investment be included in computing the gain or loss on the disposition of the investment. For example, if the parent company sold off 30 percent of its investment in a foreign subsidiary, 30 percent of the related cumulative translation adjustment would be removed from the translation adjustment account and included in determining the gain or loss on the disposition of the foreign investment.

DISCLOSURE REQUIREMENTS

Disclosures required by **FASB 52** focus on the two major items that arise from foreign transactions and operations:

1. The aggregate foreign transaction gain or loss included in determing net income
2. The cumulative translation adjustment, which is a component of the stockholders' equity section

The aggregate foreign transaction gain or loss included in income must be separately disclosed in the income statement or in an accompanying note. This includes gains or losses recognized from foreign currency transactions, forward exchange contracts, and any remeasurement gain or loss. If not disclosed as a one-line item on the income statement, this disclosure is usually a one-sentence footnote summarizing the company's foreign operations.

Under the translation method, the analysis of the changes that occurred during the period in the stockholders' equity cumulative translation adjustment can be provided in a separate schedule, in the notes to the financial statements, or as part of a statement of changes in stockholders' equity. **FASB 52** requires the following minimum disclosures for this analysis:[8]

1. The beginning and ending amount of cumulative translation adjustment balances.

2. The aggregate adjustment for the period resulting from translation of foreign currency statements and gains and losses from hedges of a net investment in a foreign entity and intercompany long-term investment transactions.

3. The amount of income taxes for the period allocated to the cumulative translation adjustment account.

4. The amounts transferred from the cumulative translation account and included in determining net income for the period as a result of the sale of some portion or all of an investment in a foreign entity.

Item 2 refers to hedges of a net investment in a foreign entity. These are transactions that management designates as hedges of a net investment, and are effective as hedges. For example, a U.S. parent company may borrow 50,000 German marks from a bank to hedge an equivalent net assets position of its German subsidiary. Currency exchange rate changes will affect the subsidiary's net assets and the parent company's loan payable balance to the bank equally, thus offsetting the parent's foreign exposure. The foreign currency transaction exchange gain or loss on the parent's hedge of its net foreign investment is recorded in the cumulative translation adjustment account, thus not affecting the income for the period. The intercompany long-term investment transactions referred to in item 2, and income taxes, referred to in item 3, are discussed in the "Additional Considerations" section later in this chapter.

The disclosures may be presented as part of the consolidated statement of stockholders' equity or as a separate footnote. In addition to these disclosures, **FASB 52** also requires the disclosure of exchange rate changes that occur after the balance sheet date and their effect on unsettled foreign currency transactions, if significant. Figure 13-12 presents the footnote form that may be used to fulfill the disclosure requirements for an analysis of the cumulative translation adjustment account. The numbers used in this illustration are a composite of several published annual reports and are presented to provide a frame of reference for the necessary disclosures.

The example of Peerless Products and German Company would have just a one-line disclosure because the beginning-of-the-year balance was zero and Peerless did not enter into any hedges of its net investment in the foreign subsidiary, nor did it sell any part of its investment in German Company during the year. Therefore, Peerless Products would report just the ending balance of $9,750, as presented in Figure 13-7.

[8] *FASB 52*, pars. 30–32.

FIGURE 13-12 Footnote disclosure of cumulative translation adjustment.

	Year Ended December 31		
	19X3	**19X2**	**19X1**
Cumulative currency translation adjustment at beginning of year	$16,800	$11,600	$18,700
Changes during the year:			
Translation adjustments and gains and losses from specified hedges and intercompany balances	(3,200)	5,800	(8,000)
Income taxes allocated to translation adjustments and hedges	200	(600)	900
Amounts related to dispositions of investments	(800)		
Cumulative currency translation adjustment at end of year	$13,000	$16,800	$11,600

ADDITIONAL CONSIDERATIONS IN ACCOUNTING FOR FOREIGN OPERATIONS AND ENTITIES

Special topics in accounting for multinational enterprises are covered in this section. Although many of these additional considerations are very technical, study of this section will complement your understanding of the many issues of accounting for foreign entities.

Proof of Remeasurement Exchange Gain

The chapter presentation of the remeasurement process for the German subsidiary shown in Figure 13-9 showed the $1,000 remeasurement gain as a balancing item needed to achieve trial balance equality. This balancing item can be proved, and the proof is shown in Figure 13-13. The analysis primarily involves the monetary items, because they are remeasured from the exchange rate at the beginning of the period, or on the date of the generating transaction, to the current exchange rate at the end of the period. The increase or decrease in net monetary assets resulting from remeasurement is recognized as an exchange gain or loss in the current period.

Schedule 1 presents the net monetary positions at the beginning and end of the year. The DM 22,500 change in the net monetary position is the change from a net liability opening balance of DM 5,000 to a net monetary asset position ending balance of DM 17,500. Schedule 2 presents the detailed effects of exchange rate changes on the foreign entity's net monetary position during this period. The beginning net monetary position is included using the exchange rate at the beginning of the year. Then, all increases and decreases in the net monetary accounts are added or deducted using the exchange rates at the time the transactions occurred. Other sources of increases or decreases in the monetary accounts would include financing and investing transactions such as purchases of plant or equipment, issuance of long-term debt, or selling stock. The computed net mone-

FIGURE 13-13 Proof of the remeasurement exchange gain for the year ended December 31, 19X1. The functional currency is the U.S. dollar.

Proof of Remeasurement Gain
Remeasurement of German Company
For Year Ended December 31, 19X1

Schedule 1
Statement of Net Monetary Positions

	End of Year	Beginning of Year
Monetary assets:		
Cash	DM 21,500	DM 5,000
Foreign currency units	6,000	-0-
Receivables	21,000	20,000
Total	DM 48,500	DM 25,000
Less: Monetary equities:		
Accounts payable	DM 6,000	DM 5,000
Bonds payable	25,000	25,000
Total	DM 31,000	DM 30,000
Net monetary liabilities		DM (5,000)
Net monetary assets	DM 17,500	
Increase in net monetary assets during year	DM 22,500	

Schedule 2
Analysis of Changes in Monetary Accounts

	DM	Exchange Rate	U.S. $
Exposed net monetary liability position, 1/1	(5,000)	.60	(3,000)
Adjustments for changes in net monetary position during year:			
Increases:			
From operations:			
Sales	100,000	.65	65,000
From other sources	-0-		-0-
Decreases:			
From operations:			
Purchases	(40,000)	.65	(26,000)
Cash expenses	(24,000)	.65	(15,600)
Foreign currency transaction loss	(1,000)	.65	(650)
From dividends	(12,500)	.68	(8,500)
From other uses	-0-		-0-
Net monetary position prior to remeasurement at year-end rates			11,250
Exposed net monetary asset position, 12/31	17,500	.70	12,250
Remeasurement gain			1,000

tary position at the end of the year using the transaction-date exchange rates ($11,250) is then compared with the year-end net monetary position using the year-end exchange rate ($12,250). Because of the increasing exchange rate, the net assets position at the end of the year was higher when remeasured using the December 31, 19X1, exchange rate of $.70. This means that the U.S. dollar equivalent value of the net monetary assets at the end of the year increased from $11,250 to $12,250 and that a remeasurement gain of $1,000 should be recognized. If the U.S. dollar equivalent value of the December 31, 19X1, exposed net monetary assets position, as remeasured with the December 31 exchange rate, would have been lower than the computed value of $11,250, then a remeasurement loss would have been recognized for the reduction in the U.S. dollar equivalent value of the net assets.

Statement of Cash Flows

The statement of cash flows is a link between two balance sheets. Individual companies have some latitude and flexibility in preparing the statement of cash flows. A general rule is that accounts reported in the statement of cash flows should be restated in U.S. dollars using the same rates as used for balance sheet and income statement purposes. Because the average exchange rate is used in the income statement and the ending spot exchange rate (current rate) is used in the balance sheet, a balancing item for the differences in exchange rates appears in the statement of cash flows. This balancing item can be analyzed and traced to the specific accounts that generate the difference, but it does not affect the net change in the cash flow for the period.

Lower-of-Cost-or-Market Inventory Valuation under Remeasurement

The application of the lower-of-cost-or-market rule to inventories requires special treatment when the recording currency is not the entity's functional currency and, therefore, the foreign entity's financial statements must be remeasured into the functional currency. The historical cost of inventories must first be remeasured using historical exchange rates to determine the functional currency historical cost value. Then these remeasured costs are compared with the market value of the inventories translated using the current rate. The final step is to compare the cost and market, now both in the functional currency, and to recognize any appropriate write-downs to market. The comparison is made in functional currency values, not local or recording currency values; therefore, it is possible to have a write-down appear in the functional currency statements and not on the subsidiary's books, or on the subsidiary's books and not in the consolidated statements.

To illustrate the application of the lower-of-cost-or-market method, assume that a German subsidiary acquired DM 10,000 of inventory when the direct exchange rate was $.69. At the end of the year, the direct exchange rate had decreased to $.60. The estimated net realizable value of the inventory (ceiling) is

DM 11,000; its replacement cost is DM 10,000; and the net realizable value less a normal profit margin (floor) is DM 8,000. The valuation of the inventory is first specified in the local currency unit (mark), and then evaluated after remeasurement into its functional currency, the U.S. dollar, using the end-of-period exchange rate, as follows:

	DM	Exchange Rate	U.S. $
Historical cost	DM 10,000	$.69	$6,900
Net realizable value (ceiling)	DM 11,000	$.60	$6,600
Replacement cost	10,000	.60	6,000
Net realizable value less normal profit (floor)	8,000	.60	4,800

The market value of the inventory is DM 10,000, or $6,000 in U.S. dollars. Note that no write-down was recorded by the subsidiary because the historical cost of the inventory was the same as market. However, the comparison in functional currency (U.S. dollar) values shows that a write-down of $900 is required to write the inventory down from its functional currency historical cost of $6,900 to its functional currency market value of $6,000.

Intercompany Transactions

A U.S. parent or home office may have many intercompany sales or purchases transactions with its foreign affiliate which create intercompany receivables or payables. The process of translating receivables or payables denominated in a foreign currency was discussed in Chapter 12. For example, assume that a U.S. company has a foreign currency–denominated receivable from its foreign subsidiary. The U.S. company would first revalue the foreign currency–denominated receivable to its U.S. dollar equivalent value as of the date of the financial statements. After the foreign affiliate's statements have been translated or remeasured, depending upon the foreign affiliate's functional currency, the intercompany payable and receivable should be at the same U.S. dollar value and can be eliminated.

FASB 52 does provide for an exception when the intercompany foreign currency transactions will not be settled within the forseeable future. These intercompany transactions may be considered part of the net investment in the foreign entity. The translation adjustments on these long-term receivables or payables are deferred and accumulated as part of the cumulative translation account. For example, a U.S. parent company may loan its German subsidiary $10,000 for which the parent does not expect repayment for the foreseeable future. Under the translation method, the dollar-denominated loan payable account of the subsidiary would first be adjusted for the effects of any changes in exchange rates during the period. Any exchange gain or loss adjustment relating to this intercompany note should be classified as part of the cumulative translation adjustment account in stockholder's equity, not in the subsidiary's income for the period. The same result would occur whether the long-term intercompany financing was denominated in U.S. dollars or the local currency—in our example, the mark. Thus, where financing is regarded as part of the long-term investment in the foreign entity, any exchange gain or loss adjustments on that financing are accumulated in the cumulative translation adjustment account in stockholders' equity.

A particularly interesting problem arises when unrealized intercompany profits occur from transactions between the parent and foreign subsidiary. The problem is how to eliminate the profit across currencies that are changing in value relative to each other. For example, assume that the parent, Peerless Products Company, made a downstream sale of inventory to its German subsidiary. The goods cost the parent $10,000, but were sold to the subsidiary for DM 20,000 when the exchange rate was $.65 = DM 1, resulting in an intercompany profit of $3,000 ($13,000 − $10,000). The goods are still in the inventory of the subsidiary at the end of the year when the current exchange rate is $.70 = DM 1. The relevant facts are summarized as follows:

	Measured in U.S. Dollars	Measured in German Marks
Initial inventory transfer date ($.65 = DM 1):		
Selling price (DM 20,000 × $.65)	$13,000	DM 20,000
Cost to parent	(10,000)	
Intercompany profit	$ 3,000	
Balance sheet date ($.70 = DM 1):		
Inventory translation ($14,000 = DM 20,000 × $.70)	$14,000	DM 20,000

There are two issues here:

1. At what amount should the ending inventory be shown on the consolidated balance sheet—the original intercompany transfer price of $13,000 (DM 20,000 × $.65), or the present equivalent exchange value of $14,000 (DM 20,000 × $.70 current exchange rate)?

2. What amount should be eliminated for the unrealized intercompany gain—the original intercompany profit of $3,000, or the balance sheet date exchange equivalent of the intercompany profit of $4,000 ($14,000 present exchange value less $10,000 original cost to parent)?

FASB 52 provides the following guidance to answer these questions.[9]

> The elimination of intercompany profits that are attributable to sales or other transfers between entities that are consolidated, combined, or accounted for by the equity method in the enterprise's financial statements shall be based on the exchange rates at the dates of the sales or transfers. The use of reasonable approximations or averages is permitted.

[9] *FASB 52*, par. 25

Therefore, for the example, the eliminating entry for the intercompany profit is:

E(23)	Cost of Goods Sold	3,000	
	Ending Inventory		3,000
	Elimination of unrealized intercompany profit based on exchange rates at date of transfer.		

The inventory is shown on the consolidated balance sheet at $11,000, which is an increase of $1,000 over the initial cost to the parent company. This increase will result in a corresponding increase in a credit to the translation adjustment component of stockholders' equity. The FASB stated that changes in exchange rates occurring *after* the date of the intercompany transaction are independent of the initial inventory transfer.

Income Taxes

Interperiod tax allocation is required whenever temporary differences exist in the recognition of revenue and expenses for income statement purposes and for tax purposes. Exchange gains and losses from foreign currency transactions require the recognition of a deferred tax if they are included in income but not recognized for tax purposes in the same period.

Generally, no deferral is required for translation adjustments, because these are a component of stockholders' equity. However, an exception to this general rule exists for the portion of the translation adjustment related to the subsidiary's undistributed earnings that are included in the parent's income. **APB Opinion No. 23**, "Accounting for Income Taxes—Special Areas" (APB 23), presumes that a temporary difference exists for the undistributed earnings of a subsidiary unless the earnings are indefinitely reinvested in the subsidiary. Deferred taxes need not be recognized if the undistributed earnings will be indefinitely reinvested in the subsidiary. However, if the parent expects to eventually receive the presently undistributed earnings of a foreign subsidiary, deferred tax recognition is required and the tax entry recorded by the parent should include a debit to the translation adjustment rather than to additional income tax, as follows:

(24)	Translation Adjustment	x,xxx	
	Deferred Taxes Payable		x,xxx

Translation when a Third Currency Is the Functional Currency

There may be a few cases in which the foreign subsidiary maintains its books and records in the local currency unit, but has a third currency as its functional currency. For example, assume that our subsidiary, German Co., maintains its records in its local currency, the mark. If the subsidiary conducts many of its business activities in the Swiss franc, management may conclude that the Swiss franc is the subsidiary's functional currency. In the case in which the entity's books and records are not expressed in its functional currency, the following two-step process must be used:

1. Remeasure the subsidiary's financial statements into the functional currency. In our example, the financial statements expressed in German marks would be remeasured into Swiss francs. The remeasurement process would be the same as illustrated earlier in the chapter. The statements would now be expressed in the entity's functional currency, the Swiss franc.

2. The statements expressed in Swiss francs are then translated into U.S. dollars using the translation process illustrated in the chapter.

As indicated above, this occurrence would not be common in practice, but is a consideration for foreign subsidiaries that have very significant business activities in a currency other than the currency of the country in which the subsidiary is physically located. This discussion does indicate that it is important to first determine the foreign entity's functional currency before beginning the translation process.

SUMMARY OF KEY CONCEPTS AND TERMS

The restatement of a foreign affiliate's financial statements in U.S. dollars may be made using the translation or remeasurement method, depending on the foreign entity's functional currency. Most foreign affiliates' statements are translated using the current rate method because the local currency unit is typically the functional currency. If the U.S. dollar is the functional currency, remeasurement is used to convert the foreign entity's statements from the local currency into dollars. The choice of functional currency affects the valuations of the foreign entity's accounts reported on the consolidated financial statements.

Because translation or remeasurement is performed with different exchange rates applied to balance sheet and income statement accounts, a balancing item called a "translation adjustment" or "remeasurement gain or loss" is created in the process. The translation adjustment is proportionally divided between the parent company and the noncontrolling interest. The parent company's share is reported in the equity section of the consolidated balance sheet. The noncontrolling interest's share is a direct adjustment to noncontrolling interest reported in the consolidated balance sheet. The remeasurement gain or loss is reported in the consolidated income statement.

Cumulative translation adjustment	Remeasurement
Current rate method	Remeasurement gain or loss
Functional currency	Translation

QUESTIONS

Q13-1   Define the following terms: (a) local currency unit, (b) recording currency, and (c) reporting currency.

Q13-2   What factors are used to determine a reporting entity's functional currency? Provide at least one example for which a company's local currency may not be its functional currency.

Q13-3   Some accountants are seeking to harmonize international accounting standards. What is meant by the term "harmonize"? How might harmonization result in better financial reporting for a U.S. parent company with many foreign investments?

Q13-4   A Canadian-based subsidiary of a U.S. parent uses the Canadian dollar as its functional currency. Describe the methodology for translating the subsidiary's financial statements into the parent's reporting currency.

Q13-5   A U.S. company has a foreign sales branch located in Spain. The Spanish branch has selected the U.S. dollar for its functional currency. Describe the methodology for remeasuring the branch's financial statements into the U.S. company's reporting currency.

Q13-6   Discuss the accounting treatment and disclosure of translation adjustments. When does the translation adjustment have a debit balance? When does it have a credit balance?

Q13-7   Where is the remeasurement gain or loss shown in the consolidated financial statements?

Q13-8   When the functional currency is the foreign affiliate's local currency, why are the stockholders' equity accounts translated at historical exchange rates? How is retained earnings computed?

Q13-9   Comment on the following statement: "The use of the current exchange rate method of translating a foreign affiliate's financial statements allows for an assessment of foreign management by the same ratio criteria used to manage the foreign affiliate."

Q13-10   A U.S. company paid more than book value in acquiring a foreign affiliate. How is this excess reported in the consolidated balance sheet and income statement in subsequent periods when the functional currency is the local currency unit of the foreign affiliate?

Q13-11   What is the logic behind the parent company's recognizing its share, on its books, of the translation adjustment arising from the translation of its foreign subsidiary?

Q13-12   Are all foreign subsidiaries consolidated? Why or why not?

Q13-13   Describe the accounting for a foreign investment that is not consolidated with the U.S. company.

Q13-14   What are the minimum disclosure requirements for reporting the cumulative translation adjustment in the consolidated financial statements?

Q13-15*   Describe the basic problem of eliminating intercompany transactions with a foreign affiliate.

CASES

C13-1   Determining a Functional Currency

Following are descriptions of several independent situations.

[handwritten margin notes: a. Peso's; D. # because of inflation; C. Remeasurement]

1. Rockford Company has a subsidiary in Argentina. The subsidiary does not have much debt, because of the high interest costs resulting from the average annual inflation rate exceeding 100 percent. Most of its sales and expense transactions are denominated in Argentinian pesos, and the subsidiary attempts to minimize its receivables and payables. Although the subsidiary owns a warehouse, the primary asset is inventory that it receives from the Rockford Company. The Argentinian government requires all companies located in Argentina to provide the central government with a financial report using the Argentinian system of accounts and government-mandated forms for financial statements.

[handwritten margin notes: a Pesos; b. # pg 716; c.]

2. JRB International is located in Dallas, Texas, and is the world's largest manufacturer of electronic stirrups. The company acquires the raw materials for its products from around the world and begins the assembly process in Dallas. It then sends the partially completed units to its subsidiary in Mexico for completion of the assembly. Mexico has been able to hold its inflation rate under 100 percent over the last 3 years. The subsidiary is required to pay its employees and local vendors in Mexican pesos. The parent company provides all financing for the Mexican subsidiary, and the subsidiary sends all its production back to the warehouse in Dallas, from which it is shipped as orders are received. The subsidiary provides the Mexican government with financial statements.

[handwritten margin notes: a Pound; B Pound; C. Translation]

3. Huskie, Inc. maintains a branch office in Great Britain. The branch office is fairly autonomous because it must find its own financing, sets its own local marketing policies, and is responsible for controlling its own costs. The branch receives weekly shipments from Huskie, Inc., which it then conveys to its customers. The pound sterling is used to pay the subsidiary's employees and to pay for the weekly shipments.

[handwritten margin notes: a lira; B Franc; C. R- Franc/lira; Translate from lira to #]

4. The Hola Company has a foreign subsidiary located in a rural area of Italy, right next to the French-Italian border. The subsidiary hires virtually all its employees from France and makes most of its sales to companies in France. The majority of its cash transactions are maintained in the French franc. However, it is required to pay local property taxes and sales taxes in Italian lira and to provide annual financial statements to the Italian government.

Required

For each of these independent cases, determine:

    a. The foreign entity's reporting currency in which its books and records are maintained
    b. The foreign entity's functional currency
    c. The process to be used to restate the foreign entity's financial statements into the reporting currency of the United States–based parent company

C13-2 Principles of Consolidating and Translating Foreign Accounts
[AICPA Adapted]

Petie Products Company was incorporated in Wisconsin in 19X0 as a manufacturer of dairy supplies and equipment. Since incorporating, Petie has doubled in size about every 3 years and is now considered one of the leading dairy supply companies in the country.

During January 19X4, Petie established a subsidiary, Cream, Ltd., in the emerging nation of Kolay. Petie owns 90 percent of the outstanding capital stock of Cream; the remaining 10 percent of Cream's outstanding capital stock is held by Kolay citizens, as required by Kolay law. The investment in Cream, accounted for by Petie by the equity method, represents about 18 percent of the total assets of Petie at December 31, 19X7, the close of the accounting period for both companies.

Required

a. What criteria should Petie Products Company use in determining whether it would be appropriate to prepare consolidated financial statements with Cream, Ltd., for the year ended December 31, 19X7? Explain.

b. Independent of your answer to part (*a*), assume it has been appropriate for Petie and Cream to prepare consolidated financial statements for each year, 19X4 through 19X7. Before consolidated financial statements can be prepared, the individual account balances in Cream's December 31, 19X7, adjusted trial balance must be translated into dollars. The Kola (K) is the functional currency for the subsidiary. For each of the 10 accounts listed below, taken from Cream's adjusted trial balance, specify what exchange rate (for example, average exchange rate for 19X7, current exchange rate on December 31, 19X7) should be used to translate the account balance into dollars and explain why that rate is appropriate. Number your answers to correspond with the accounts listed below.

  (1) Cash in Kolay National Bank
  (2) Trade Accounts Receivable (all from 19X7 revenue)
  (3) Supplies Inventory (all purchased during the last quarter of 19X7)
  (4) Land purchased in 19X4
  (5) Short-Term Note Payable to Kolay National Bank
  (6) Capital Stock (no par or stated value and all issued in January 19X4)
  (7) Retained Earnings, January 1, 19X7
  (8) Sales Revenue
  (9) Depreciation Expense (on buildings)
 (10) Salaries Expense

EXERCISES

E13-1 Multiple-Choice Questions on Translation and Remeasurement
[AICPA Adapted]

For each of the seven cases presented below, work the case twice and select the best answer. First assume that the foreign currency is the functional currency; then assume that the U.S. dollar is the functional currency.

1. Certain balance sheet accounts in a foreign subsidiary of Shaw Company on December 31, 19X1, have been restated in United States dollars as follows:

	Restated at	
	Current Rates	Historical Rates
Accounts Receivable, Current	$100,000	$110,000
Accounts Receivable, Long-Term	50,000	55,000
Prepaid Insurance	25,000	30,000
Patents	40,000	45,000
Total	$215,000	$240,000

non-mon.

What total should be included in Shaw's balance sheet for December 31, 19X1, for the above items?

a. $215,000.
b. $225,000.
c. $230,000.
d. $240,000.

2. A wholly-owned foreign subsidiary of Nick, Inc. has certain expense accounts for the year ended December 31, 19X4, stated in local currency units (LCU) as follows:

	LCU
Depreciation of Equipment (related assets were purchased January 1, 19X2)	120,000
Provision for Uncollectible Accounts	80,000
Rent	200,000

The exchange rates at various dates were as follows:

	Dollar Equivalent of 1 LCU
January 1, 19X2	$.50
Average for the year ended December 31, 19X4	.44
December 31, 19X4	.40

What total dollar amount should be included in Nick's income statement to reflect the above expenses for the year ended December 31, 19X4?

a. $160,000.
b. $168,000.
c. $176,000.
d. $183,200.

3. Linser Corp. owns a foreign subsidiary with 2,600,000 local currency units (LCU) of property, plant, and equipment before accumulated depreciation on December 31, 19X4. Of this amount, 1,700,000 LCU were acquired in 19X2 when the rate of exchange was 1.5 LCU = $1, and 900,000 LCU were acquired in 19X3 when the rate of exchange was 1.6 LCU = $1. The rate of exchange in effect on December 31, 19X4, was 1.9 LCU = $1. The weighted average of exchange rates that were in effect during 19X4 was 1.8 LCU = $1. Assuming that the property, plant, and equipment are depreciated using the straight-line method over a 10-year period with no salvage value, how much depreciation expense relating to the foreign subsidiary's property, plant, and equipment should be charged in Linser's income statement for 19X4?

a. $144,444.
b. $162,000.
c. $169,583.
d. $173,333.

4. On January 1, 19X1, Pat Company formed a foreign subsidiary. On February 15, 19X1, Pat's subsidiary purchased 100,000 local currency units (LCU) of inventory. 25,000 LCU of the original inventory purchased on February 15, 19X1, made up the entire

inventory on December 31, 19X1. The exchange rates were 2.2 LCU = $1 from January 1, 19X1, to June 30, 19X1, and 2 LCU = $1 from July 1, 19X1, to December 31, 19X1. The December 31, 19X1, inventory balance for Pat's foreign subsidiary should be restated in United States dollars in the amount of:

a. $10,500.
b. $11,364.
c. $11,905.
d. $12,500.

5. At what rates should the following balance sheet accounts in the foreign currency financial statements be restated into United States dollars?

	Equipment	Accumulated Depreciation of Equipment
a.	Current	Current
b.	Current	Average for year
c.	Historical	Current
d.	Historical	Historical

6. A credit balancing item resulting from the process of restating a foreign entity's financial statement from the local currency unit to U.S. dollars should be included as a (an):
a. Separate component of stockholders' equity.
b. Deferred credit.
c. Component of income from continuing operations.
d. Extraordinary item.

7. A foreign subsidiary of the Bart Corporation has certain balance sheet accounts on December 31, 19X2. Information relating to these accounts in U.S. dollars is as follows:

	Restated at	
	Current Rates	**Historical Rates**
Marketable Securities carried at cost	$ 75,000	$ 85,000
Inventories carried at average cost	600,000	700,000
Refundable Deposits	25,000	30,000
Goodwill	55,000	70,000
	$755,000	$885,000

What total should be included in Bart's balance sheet on December 31, 19X2, as a result of the above information?

a. $755,000.
b. $780,000.
c. $870,000.
d. $880,000.

Transaction changes hit
both
Restatement only hits
Remeasurement

E13-2 Multiple-Choice Translation and Foreign Currency Transactions
[AICPA Adapted]

For each of the three cases presented below, select the best answers under each of two alternative assumptions: **(a)** the LCU is the functional currency and the translation method is appropriate; and **(b)** the U.S. dollar is the functional currency and the remeasurement method is appropriate.

1. Gate, Inc. had a credit adjustment of $30,000 for the year ended December 31, 19X2, from restating its foreign subsidiary's accounts from their local currency units into U.S. dollars. Additionally, Gate had a receivable from a foreign customer payable in the customer's local currency. On December 31, 19X1, this receivable for 200,000 local currency units (LCU) was correctly included in Gate's balance sheet at $110,000. When the receivable was collected on February 15, 19X2, the U.S. dollar equivalent was $120,000. In Gate's 19X2 consolidated income statement, how much should be reported as foreign exchange gain?
   a. $0.
   b. $10,000.
   c. $30,000.
   d. $40,000.

2. Bar Corporation had a realized foreign exchange loss of $13,000 for the year ended December 31, 19X2, and must also determine whether the following items will require year-end adjustment:
   (1) Bar had a $7,000 credit resulting from the restatement in dollars of the accounts of its wholly owned foreign subsidiary for the year ended December 31, 19X2.
   (2) Bar had an account payable to an unrelated foreign supplier payable in the supplier's local currency. The U.S dollar equivalent of the payable was $60,000 on the October 31, 19X2, invoice date, and it was $64,000 on December 31, 19X2. The invoice is payable on January 30, 19X3.

   What is the amount of the net foreign exchange loss that should be reported in Bar's 19X2 consolidated income statement?
   a. $6,000.
   b. $10,000.
   c. $13,000.
   d. $17,000.

3. The balance in Simpson Corp.'s foreign exchange loss account was $15,000 on December 31, 19X2, before any necessary year-end adjustment relating to the following:
   (1) Simpson had a $20,000 debit resulting from the restatement in dollars of the accounts of its wholly owned foreign subsidiary for the year ended December 31, 19X2.
   (2) Simpson had an account payable to an unrelated foreign supplier, payable in the supplier's local currency on January 27, 19X3. The U.S. dollar equivalent of the payable was $100,000 on the November 28, 19X2, invoice date, and it was $106,000 on December 31, 19X2.

   In Simpson's 19X2 consolidated income statement, what amount should be included as foreign exchange loss?
   a. $41,000.
   b. $35,000.

c. $21,000.

d. $15,000.

E13-3   Translation

On January 1, 19X1, Popular Creek Corporation organized RoadTime Company as a subsidiary in Switzerland with an initial investment cost of SFr 60,000. RoadTime's December 31, 19X1, trial balance in Swiss francs (SFr) is as follows:

	Debit	Credit
Cash	SFr 7,000	
Accounts Receivable (net)	20,000	
Receivable from Popular Creek	5,000	
Inventory	25,000	
Plant and Equipment	100,000	
Accumulated Depreciation		SFr 10,000
Accounts Payable		12,000
Bonds Payable		50,000
Common Stock		60,000
Sales		150,000
Cost of Goods Sold	70,000	
Depreciation Expense	10,000	
Operating Expense	30,000	
Dividends Paid	15,000	
Total	SFr 282,000	SFr 282,000

Additional information:

1. The receivable from Popular Creek is denominated in Swiss francs. Popular Creek's books show a payable to RoadTime at $4,000.

2. Purchases of inventory goods are made evenly during the year. Items in the ending inventory were purchased November 1.

3. Equipment is depreciated by the straight-line method with a 10-year life and no residual value. A full year's depreciation is taken in the year of acquisition. The equipment was acquired on March 1.

4. The dividends were declared and paid on November 1.

5. Exchange rates were as follows:

January 1	SFr 1 = $.73
March 1	SFr 1 = .74
November 1	SFr 1 = .77
December 31	SFr 1 = .80
19X1 Average	SFr 1 = .75

6. The Swiss franc is the functional currency.

Required

Prepare a schedule translating the December 31, 19X1, trial balance from Swiss francs to dollars.

E13-4   Proof of Translation Adjustment

Refer to the data in Exercise 13-3.

Required

a. Prepare a proof of the translation adjustment computed in Exercise 13-3.
b. Where is the translation adjustment reported on the consolidated financial statements of Popular Creek Corporation and its foreign subsidiary?

E13-5   Remeasurement

Refer to the data in Exercise 13-3, but assume that the dollar is the functional currency for the foreign subsidiary.

Required

Prepare a schedule remeasuring the December 31, 19X1, trial balance from Swiss francs to dollars.

E13-6*   Proof of Remeasurement Gain (Loss)

Refer to the data in Exercises 13-3 and 13-5.

Required

a. Prepare a proof of the remeasurement gain or loss computed in Exercise 13-5.
b. How should this remeasurement gain or loss be reported on the consolidated financial statements of Popular Creek Corporation and its foreign subsidiary?

E13-7   Remeasurement and Translation of Cost of Goods Sold

Kinder Company is a subsidiary of Bell Corporation and is located in London, England, where the currency is the British pound (£). Data on Kinder's inventory and purchases are as follows:

Inventory, January 1, 19X1	£18,000
Purchases during 19X1	82,000
Inventory, December 31, 19X1	22,500

The beginning inventory was acquired during the fourth quarter of 19X0, and the ending inventory was acquired during the fourth quarter of 19X1. Purchases were made evenly over the year. Exchange rates were as follows:

Fourth quarter of 19X0	£1 = $1.79
January 1, 19X1	£1 = 1.82
Average during 19X1	£1 = 1.83
Fourth quarter of 19X1	£1 = 1.84
December 31, 19X1	£1 = 1.85

Required

a. Show the remeasurement of cost of goods sold for 19X1, assuming the U.S. dollar is the functional currency.

b. Show the translation of cost of goods sold for 19X1, assuming the British pound is the functional currency.

E13-8 Equity-Method Entries for a Foreign Subsidiary

Arc Company is located in Ireland. The local currency is the Irish pound (IR£). On January 1, 19X1, Stone Company purchased a 70 percent interest in Arc Company for $350,000, which resulted in an excess of cost-over-market value of $34,400. The goodwill has a 10-year life. Stone uses the equity method to account for its investment.

Arc's December 31, 19X1, trial balance has been translated into dollars, requiring a translation adjustment debit of $5,200. Arc's net income translated into dollars is $80,000. Arc declared and paid a IR£ 12,000 dividend on November 3.

Relevant exchange rates are as follows:

January 1, 19X1	IR£1 = $1.72
Average for 19X1	IR£1 = $1.65
November 3, 19X1	IR£1 = $1.64
December 31, 19X1	IR£1 = $1.60

Required

a. Record the dividend received by Stone Company from Arc Company.

b. Prepare the entries to record Stone Company's equity in the net income of Arc Company and the parent's share of the translation adjustment.

c. Show a calculation of the goodwill reported on the consolidated balance sheet of December 31, 19X1, and the translation adjustment from goodwill.

d. Record the amortization of goodwill on Stone's books.

E13-9 Purchase versus Pooling of a Foreign Company

Westwind, Inc., is located in Los Angeles; Chali, Ltd., is located in Bangkok, Thailand. Chali's capital stock was issued on January 2, 19X1, and its plant and equipment were acquired at the same time. The plant and equipment are depreciated by the straight-line method over a 10-year life with no residual value.

Westwind acquired all the ownership interest of Chali on January 1, 19X3. Selected information from Chali's balance sheet for December 31, 19X4, measured in Thailand bahts (B), is as follows:

Inventory	B 1,640,000
Plant and Equipment	3,400,000
Accumulated Depreciation	1,360,000
Liabilities	300,000
Common Stock	1,600,000

Exchange rates were as follows:

January 2, 19X1	B 1 = $.045
January 1, 19X3	B 1 = .042
December 31, 19X4	B 1 = .040
Average rate for 19X4	B 1 = .041

The average cost method of inventory valuation is used by the subsidiary. Management has determined that the U.S. dollar is the functional currency of the foreign subsidiary.

Required

   a. Show the remeasurement of the five selected accounts on December 31, 19X4, assuming that the acquisition was accounted for as a pooling of interests.
   b. Show the remeasurement of the five selected accounts on December 31, 19X4, assuming the acquisition was accounted for as a purchase.

E13-10*   Lower-of-Cost-or-Market

The ending inventory of a foreign subsidiary of a U.S. company has a cost of 5,000 local currency units. This inventory was acquired when the exchange rate was 1 LCU = $.40. The dollar is the functional currency of the foreign subsidiary and the inventories are valued at lower-of-cost-or-market.

Required

For each of the following four independent cases, **(a)** determine the inventory amount reported on the balance sheet of the foreign subsidiary, and **(b)** prepare a schedule showing how the inventory is remeasured and the inventory amount that would be reported in the consolidated balance sheet.

	Case 1	Case 2	Case 3	Case 4
Replacement cost	LCU 6,000	LCU 6,000	LCU 4,000	LCU 5,000
Net realizable value	7,000	6,000	7,000	4,000
Net realizable value less a normal profit margin	5,000	4,000	4,500	3,000
Direct exchange rate at year-end	$.35	$.30	$.45	$.40

E13-11*   Intercompany Transactions

Hawk Company sold inventory to United Ltd., an English subsidiary. The goods cost Hawk $8,000 and were sold to United for $12,000 on November 27, payable in British pounds. The goods are still on hand at the end of the year on December 31. The British pound (£) is the functional currency of the English subsidiary. The exchange rates were:

November 27   £1 = $1.60
December 31   £1 = 1.70

Required

a. At what dollar amount is the ending inventory shown in the trial balance of the consolidation workpaper?

b. What amount is eliminated for the unrealized intercompany gross profit, and at what amount is the inventory shown on the consolidated balance sheet?

PROBLEMS

P13-12   Parent Company Journal Entries and Translation

On January 1, 19X1, Par Company purchased all the outstanding stock of North Bay Company, located in Canada, for $120,000. On January 1, 19X1, the direct exchange rate for the Canadian dollar (C$) was C$1 = $.80. The book value of North Bay Company on January 1, 19X1, was C$90,000. The fair value of North Bay's plant and equipment was C$10,000 greater than book value, and the plant and equipment is being depreciated over 10 years, with no salvage value. The remainder of the differential is attributable to goodwill which is amortized over 10 years.

During 19X1, North Bay Company earned C$20,000 in income and declared and paid C$8,000 in dividends. The dividends were declared and paid in Canadian dollars when the exchange rate was C$1 = $.75. On December 31, 19X1, Par Company continues to hold the Canadian currency received from the dividend. On December 31, 19X1, the direct exchange rate is C$1 = $.70. The average exchange rate during 19X1 was C$1 = $.75. Management has determined that the Canadian dollar is the appropriate functional currency for North Bay Company.

Required

a. Prepare a schedule showing the differential allocation and amortization for 19X1. The schedule should present both Canadian dollars and U.S. dollars.

b. Par Company uses the basic equity method to account for its investment. Provide the entries that Par Company would record in 19X1 for its investment in North Bay Company for the following items:

(1) Purchase of investment in North Bay Company
(2) Equity accrual for Par's share of North Bay's income
(3) Recognition of dividend declared and paid by North Bay Company
(4) Amortization of differential
(5) Recognition of translation adjustment on differential

c. Prepare a schedule showing the proof of the translation adjustment for North Bay Company as a result of the translation of the subsidiary's accounts from Canadian dollars to U.S. dollars. Then provide the entry that Par Company would record for its share of the translation adjustment resulting from the translation of the subsidiary's accounts.

d. Provide the entry required by Par Company to restate the C$8,000 in the Foreign Currency Units account into its year-end U.S. dollar equivalent value.

P13-13 Translation and Calculation of Translation Adjustment

On January 1, 19X4, Alum Corporation acquired Franco Company, a French subsidiary, by purchasing all the common stock at book value. Franco's trial balances on January 1, 19X4, and December 31, 19X4, expressed in French francs (FF), are as follows:

	January 1, 19X4 Debit	January 1, 19X4 Credit	December 31, 19X4 Debit	December 31, 19X4 Credit
Cash	FF 62,000		FF 57,700	
Accounts Receivable (net)	83,900		82,000	
Inventories	95,000		95,000	
Prepaid Insurance	5,600		2,400	
Plant and Equipment	250,000		350,000	
Accumulated Depreciation		FF 67,500		FF 100,000
Intangible Assets	42,000		30,000	
Accounts Payable		20,000		24,000
Income Taxes Payable		30,000		27,000
Interest Payable		1,000		1,100
Notes Payable		20,000		20,000
Bonds Payable		120,000		120,000
Common Stock		80,000		80,000
Additional Paid-In Capital		150,000		150,000
Retained Earnings		50,000		50,000
Sales				500,000
Cost of Goods Sold			230,000	
Insurance Expense			3,200	
Depreciation Expense			32,500	
Amortization Expense			12,000	
Operating Expense			152,300	
Dividends Paid			25,000	
Total	FF 538,500	FF 538,500	FF 1,072,100	FF 1,072,100

Additional information:

1. Franco uses fifo inventory valuation. Purchases were made uniformly during 19X4. Ending inventory for 19X4 is comprised of units purchased when the exchange rate was $.25.

2. The insurance premium for a 2-year policy was paid on October 1, 19X3.

3. Plant and equipment were acquired as follows:

Date	Cost
January 1, 19X1	FF 200,000
July 10, 19X2	50,000
April 7, 19X4	100,000

4. Plant and equipment are depreciated using the straight-line method and a 10-year life with no residual value. A full month's depreciation is taken in the month of acquisition.

5. The intangible assets are patents acquired on July 10, 19X2, at a cost of FF 60,000. The estimated life is 5 years.

6. The common stock was issued on January 1, 19X1.

7. Dividends of FF 10,000 were declared and paid on April 7. On October 9, FF 15,000 of dividends were declared and paid.

8. Exchange rates were as follows:

January 1, 19X1	FF 1 = $.45
July 10, 19X2	FF 1 = .40
October 1, 19X3	FF 1 = .34
January 1, 19X4	FF 1 = .30
April 7, 19X4	FF 1 = .28
October 9, 19X4	FF 1 = .23
December 31, 19X4	FF 1 = .20
19X4 average	FF 1 = .25

Required

a. Prepare a schedule translating the December 31, 19X4, trial balance of Franco Company from francs to dollars.

b. Prepare a schedule calculating the cumulative translation adjustment as of the end of 19X4. The net assets on January 1, 19X4, were FF 280,000.

P13-14* Remeasurement and Proof of Remeasurement Gain or Loss

Refer to the information in Problem 13-13. Assume that the dollar is the functional currency.

Required

a. Prepare a schedule remeasuring the December 31, 19X4, trial balance of Franco Company from francs to dollars.

b. Prepare a schedule providing a proof of the remeasurement gain or loss.

P13-15 Translation

Alamo, Inc. purchased 80 percent of the outstanding stock of Western Ranching Company, a company located in Australia, on January 1, 19X3. The purchase price was A$200,000, and A$40,000 of the differential was allocated to plant and equipment which is amortized over a 10-year period. The remainder of the differential was attributable to goodwill. Alamo, Inc. amortizes goodwill over 10 years. Western Ranching Company's trial balance on December 31, 19X3, in Australian dollars (A$) is as follows:

TRANSLATION
R

	Debit	Credit
Cash	A$ 44,100	
Accounts Receivable (net)	72,000	
Inventory	86,000	
Plant and Equipment	240,000	
Accumulated Depreciation		A$ 60,000
Accounts Payable		53,800
Payable to Alamo, Inc.		10,800
Interest Payable		3,000
12% Bonds Payable		100,000
Premium on Bonds		5,700
Common Stock		90,000
Retained Earnings		40,000
Sales		579,000
Cost of Goods Sold	330,000	
Depreciation Expense	24,000	
Operating Expenses	131,500	
Interest Expense	5,700	
Dividends Paid	9,000	
Total	A$942,300	A$942,300

Handwritten annotations (rates): .60, .60, .60, .65 (Acq. at avg when sub purch), .70 (when sub purch), .60 .70, .60 .60, .60 .60, .60 .60, .60 .60, .60 .60, .70 .70, .70 .70 (same), .65 .65, .65, .65 .70, .65 .65, .65 .65, .67 .67

Net Assets A130,000 .70 / 91,000 / 87800 .65 / (9000) .67 / 208,800 .60

Rates end of yr

Additional information:

1. Western Ranching Company uses average cost for cost of goods sold. Inventory increased by A$20,000 during the year. Purchases were made uniformly during 19X3. The ending inventory was acquired at the average exchange rate for the year.

2. Plant and equipment were acquired as follows:

Date	Cost
January, 19X1	A$180,000
January 1, 19X3	60,000

3. Plant and equipment are depreciated using the straight-line method, a 10-year life, and no residual value.

4. The payable to Alamo, Inc., is in Australian dollars. Alamo's books show a receivable from Western Ranching Company of $6,480.

5. The 10-year bonds were issued on July 1, 19X3, for A$106,000. The premium is amortized on a straight-line basis. The interest is paid on April 1 and October 1.

6. The dividends were declared and paid on April 1.

7. Exchange rates were as follows:

January, 19X1	A$1 = $.93
August, 19X1	A$1 = $.88
January 1, 19X3	A$1 = $.70
April 1, 19X3	A$1 = $.67
July 1, 19X3	A$1 = $.64
December 31, 19X3	A$1 = $.60
19X3 average	A$1 = $.65

Handwritten (Remeasurement):
Rem
Beg Inv 66,000 × .70
Purch 350,000 × .65
Goods Avail 416,000
Ending Inv (86,000) × .65
CGS 330,000

Required

a. Prepare a schedule translating the December 31, 19X3, trial balance of Western Ranching Company from Australian dollars to U.S. dollars.

b. Prepare a schedule providing a proof of the translation adjustment.

P13-16   Parent Company Journal Entries and Translation

Refer to the information given in Problem 13-15 for Alamo and its subsidiary, Western Ranching. Assume that the Australian dollar (A$) is the functional currency and that Alamo uses the basic equity method for accounting for its investment in Western Ranching Company.

Required

Prepare the entries that would be recorded by Alamo, Inc. in 19X3 for its investment in Western Ranching. Your entries should include the following:

1. Record the initial investment on January 1, 19X3.

2. Record the dividend received by the parent company.

3. Recognize the parent company's share of the equity income of the subsidiary.

4. Record the amortizations of the differential.

5. Recognize the translation adjustment required by the parent from the adjustment of the differential.

6. Recognize the parent company's share of the translation adjustment resulting from the translation of the subsidiary's accounts.

Provide the necessary documentation and support for the amounts recorded in the journal entries, including a schedule of the translation adjustment related to the differential.

P13-17   Consolidation Workpaper after Translation

Refer to the information given in Problems 13-15 and 13-16 for Alamo and its subsidiary, Western Ranching. Assume that the Australian dollar (A$) is the functional currency and that Alamo uses the basic equity method for accounting for its investment in Western Ranching Company. A December 31, 19X3, trial balance for Alamo, Inc. is presented below. Use this trial balance for completing this problem.

Item	Debit	Credit
Cash	$ 38,000	660
Accounts Receivable (net)	140,000	
Receivable from Western Ranching	6,480	
Inventory	128,000	
Plant and Equipment	500,000	
Investment in Western Ranching	152,064	
Cost of Goods Sold	600,000	
Depreciation Expense	28,000	
Operating Expenses	204,000	
Interest Expense	2,000	
Dividends Declared	50,000	
Translation Adjustment	22,528	
Accumulated Depreciation		$ 90,000
Accounts Payable		60,000
Interest Payable		2,000
Common Stock		500,000
Retained Earnings, January 1, 19X3		179,656
Sales		1,000,000
Income from Subsidiary		39,416
Total	$1,871,072	$1,871,072

Required

a. Prepare a set of eliminating entries, in general journal form, for the entries required to prepare a three-part consolidation workpaper as of December 31, 19X3.

b. Prepare a three-part consolidation workpaper as of December 31, 19X3.

P13-18* Remeasurement

Refer to the information in Problem 13-15. Assume the U.S. dollar is the functional currency.

Required

a. Prepare a schedule remeasuring the December 31, 19X3, trial balance of Western Ranching Company from Australian dollars to U.S. dollars.

b. Prepare a schedule providing a proof of the remeasurement gain or loss. The subsidiary's net monetary liability position on January 1, 19X3, was A$80,000.

P13-19 Parent Company Journal Entries and Remeasurement

Refer to the information given in Problems 13-15 and 13-18 for Alamo and its subsidiary, Western Ranching. Assume that the U.S. dollar is the functional currency and that Alamo uses the basic equity method for accounting for its investment in Western Ranching Company.

Required

Prepare the entries that would be recorded by Alamo, Inc. in 19X3 for its investment in Western Ranching. Your entries should include the following:

1. Record the initial investment on January 1, 19X3.
2. Record the dividend received by the parent company.
3. Recognize the parent company's share of the equity income from the subsidiary.
4. Record the amortizations of the differential.

Provide the necessary documentation and support for the amounts recorded in the journal entries.

P13-20 Consolidation Workpaper after Remeasurement

Refer to the information given in Problems 13-15 and 13-19 for Alamo and its subsidiary, Western Ranching. Assume that the U. S. dollar is the functional currency and that Alamo uses the basic equity method for accounting for its investment in Western Ranching Company. A December 31, 19X3, trial balance for Alamo, Inc. is presented below. Use this trial balance for completing this problem.

Item	Debit	Credit
Cash	$ 38,000	
Accounts Receivable (net)	140,000	
Receivable from Western Ranching	6,480	
Inventory	128,000	
Plant and Equipment	500,000	
Investment in Western Ranching	178,544	
Cost of Goods Sold	600,000	
Depreciation Expense	28,000	
Operating Expenses	204,000	
Interest Expense	2,000	
Dividends Declared	50,000	
Accumulated Depreciation		$ 90,000
Accounts Payable		60,000
Interest Payable		2,000
Common Stock		500,000
Retained Earnings, January 1, 19X3		179,656
Sales		1,000,000
Income from Subsidiary		43,368
Total	$1,875,024	$1,875,024

Required

  a. Prepare a set of eliminating entries, in general journal form, for the entries required to prepare a three-part consolidation workpaper as of December 31, 19X3.
  b. Prepare a three-part consolidation workpaper as of December 31, 19X3.

P13-21 Foreign Currency Remeasurement [AICPA Adapted]

On January 1, 19X1, the Kiner Company formed a foreign subsidiary that issued all its currently outstanding common stock on that date. Selected accounts from the balance sheets, all of which are shown in local currency units, are as follows:

	December 31	
	19X2	**19X1**
Accounts Receivable (net of allowance for uncollectible accounts of 2,200 LCU on December 31, 19X2, and 2,000 LCU on December 31, 19X1)	40,000	35,000
Inventories, at cost	80,000	75,000
Property, Plant, and Equipment (net of allowance for accumulated depreciation of 31,000 LCU on December 31, 19X2, and 14,000 LCU on December 31, 19X1)	163,000	150,000
Long-Term Debt	100,000	120,000
Common Stock, authorized 10,000 shares, par value 10 LCU per share; issued and outstanding, 5,000 shares on December 31, 19X2, and December 31, 19X1	50,000	50,000

Additional information:

1. Exchange rates are as follows:

January 1, 19X1–July 31, 19X1	2 LCU = $1
August 1, 19X1–October 31, 19X1	1.8 LCU = $1
November 1, 19X1–June 30, 19X2	1.7 LCU = $1
July 1, 19X2–December 31, 19X2	1.5 LCU = $1
Average monthly rate for 19X1	1.9 LCU = $1
Average monthly rate for 19X2	1.6 LCU = $1

2. An analysis of the accounts receivable balance is as follows:

	19X2	19X1
Accounts Receivable:		
Balance at beginning of year	37,000	
Sales (36,000 LCU per month in 19X2 and 31,000 LCU per month in 19X1)	432,000	372,000
Collections	(423,600)	(334,000)
Write-offs (May 19X2 and December 19X1)	(3,200)	(1,000)
Balance at end of year	42,200	37,000

	19X2	19X1
Allowance for Uncollectible Accounts:		
Balance at beginning of year	2,000	
Provision for uncollectible accounts	3,400	3,000
Write-offs (May 19X2 and December 19X1)	(3,200)	(1,000)
Balance at end of year	2,200	2,000

3. An analysis of inventories, for which the first-in, first-out inventory method is used, is as follows:

	19X2	19X1
Inventory at beginning of year	75,000	
Purchases (June 19X2 and June 19X1)	335,000	375,000
Goods available for sale	410,000	375,000
Inventory at end of year	(80,000)	(75,000)
Cost of goods sold	330,000	300,000

4. On January 1, 19X1, Kiner's foreign subsidiary purchased land for 24,000 LCU and plant and equipment for 140,000 LCU. On July 4, 19X2, additional equipment was purchased for 30,000 LCU. Plant and equipment is being depreciated on a straight-line basis over a 10-year period with no residual value. A full year's depreciation is taken in the year of purchase.

5. On January 15, 19X1, 7 percent bonds with a face value of 120,000 LCU were issued. These bonds mature on January 15, 19X7, and the interest is paid semiannually on July 15 and January 15. The first interest payment was made on July 15, 19X1.

Required

Prepare a schedule remeasuring the selected accounts into U.S. dollars for December 31, 19X1, and December 31, 19X2, respectively, assuming the U.S. dollar is the functional currency for the foreign subsidiary. The schedule should be prepared using the following form:

Item	Balance, in LCU	Appropriate Exchange Rate	Remeasured into U.S. Dollars
December 31, 19X1:			
Accounts Receivable (net)			
Inventories			
Property, Plant, and Equipment (net)			
Long-Term Debt			
Common Stock			
December 31, 19X2:			
Accounts Receivable (net)			
Inventories			
Property, Plant, and Equipment (net)			
Long-Term Debt			
Common Stock			

P13-22 Foreign Currency Translation

Refer to the information in Problem 13-21 for Kiner Company and its foreign subsidiary.

Required

Prepare a schedule translating the selected accounts into U.S. dollars as of December 31, 19X1, and December 31, 19X2, respectively, assuming that the local currency unit is the functional currency for the foreign subsidiary.

CHAPTER 14

SEGMENT AND INTERIM REPORTING

REPORTING FOR SEGMENTS

Diversification into new products and multinational markets during the 1960s and early 1970s created a need for disaggregated information about the individual segments or components of an enterprise. This information need was addressed by the Accounting Principles Board, the Financial Executives Institute, the National Association of Accountants, the Securities Exchange Commission, and, finally, the Financial Accounting Standards Board.

Large, diversified companies can be viewed as a portfolio of assets operated as divisions or subsidiaries, often multinational in scope. The various components of a large company may have different profit rates, different degrees and types of risk, and different opportunities for growth. The central issue for accountants is how to develop and disclose the information necessary to reflect these essential differences. The following discussion presents the accounting standards for reporting an entity's industry components, foreign operations, and major customers.

SEGMENT REPORTING ACCOUNTING ISSUES

In 1967, the APB issued **Statement No. 2**, "Disclosure of Supplemental Financial Information by Diversified Companies," which recommended voluntary disclosure of segment information. In 1969, the SEC required line-of-business reporting in registration statements of new stock issues and in 1970 extended this requirement to Form 10-K, the report filed annually by all publicly held companies. Using extensive research reports prepared by the National Association of

Accountants[1] and the Financial Executives Institute,[2] the FASB issued **FASB Statement No. 14**, "Financial Reporting for Segments of a Business Enterprise" (FASB 14), in December 1976. This pronouncement requires the supplemental disclosure of revenue, profits, assets, and other information for selected industry segments of an entity as well as disclosures about its foreign operations. **FASB 14** has undergone several minor amendments, but its major provisions still serve as the basic standards for disclosure of industry segments and foreign operations.

The FASB faced three critical issues in the preparation of **FASB 14**. First, it had to establish guidelines for defining reportable segments. The second issue was to determine the types of disclosure required for each segment defined in the first step. The third issue was to address the myriad technical aspects of disaggregating an enterprise into its constituent pieces, such as the mechanism for reporting intersegment transactions and the impact of cost allocations on segment incomes.

The task of defining segment income was particularly interesting. Accountants make many subjective estimates and allocations in income determinations and asset valuations. The question is whether the income reported for each segment should include directly traceable expenses only, or whether it should also include an allocation of common costs, such as for companywide advertising or a central purchasing department. One accounting researcher has stated that all allocations are arbitrary, that is, not completely verifiable with empirical evidence, and therefore net income after deducting any allocated costs is arbitrary.[3] The FASB decided that common costs can and should be allocated on a reasonable basis and that the resulting measures of segment income are useful measures of a segment's contribution to the company. For example, the cost of a shared purchasing department might be allocated on an average order size basis, and the cost of a shared quality control department might be allocated on a units-of-production basis. Common costs also may be aggregated into "logical and homogeneous expense pools" and then allocated on the basis of an activity or output measure that has a beneficial or causal relationship with the cost.[4] For example, all advertising costs may be aggregated into a single expense pool and then allocated to the specific industry segments on the basis of the ratio of each segment's revenues to total combined revenues.

INFORMATION ABOUT OPERATIONS IN DIFFERENT INDUSTRIES

Many entities are diversified across several industries. Each industry may be subject to unique competitive factors and may react differently to changes in the economic environment. For example, a large company such as Johnson & John-

[1] M. Backer and R. McFarland, *External Reporting for Segments of a Business,* National Association of Accountants (New York), 1968.
[2] R. Mautz, *Financial Reporting by Diversified Companies,* Financial Executives Research Foundation (New York), 1968.
[3] A. Thomas, *The Allocation Problem: Part Two,* American Accounting Association (Sarasota, Fla.), 1974.
[4] *Cost Accounting Standards Board, Standard No. 403,* "Allocation of Home Office Expenses to Segments," 1972.

son operates in three major industrial segments: consumer, pharmaceutical, and professional. Its products include disposable contact lenses, baby products, surgical products, antibody therapies, and cold and flu medications. A conglomerate may operate in several consumer markets, each with different characteristics. In addition, a company is exposed to different risks in each of the markets in which it acquires its factors of production. Consolidated statements present all these heterogeneous factors in a single-entity context. The purpose of segment reporting is to allow financial statement users to look behind the consolidated totals to the individual components that constitute the entity.

Several different approaches can be used to cut up the consolidated entity "pie" into meaningful pieces. A company may be broken down by types of production processes (for example, labor-intensive versus capital-intensive), by markets served (for example, consumer versus industrial), or by type of product (for example, machine tools, clothing, entertainment). Defining reportable segments sets the stage for determining the scope and significance of the supplemental information.

Defining Reportable Segments

The process of determining *reportable industry segments*, that is, industry segments for which supplemental disclosures must be provided, begins with identification of a company's industry components and then the application of significance tests to determine which are reportable. **FASB 14** defines an industry segment as:

> A component of an enterprise engaged in providing a product or service or a group of related products and services primarily to unaffiliated customers (i.e., customers outside the enterprise) for a profit.[5]

This definition is broad and often difficult to apply. The disaggregation process begins with identifying the company's present profit centers. A profit center is the smallest separate operating unit for which revenue and expense information is accumulated. It could be a department, a division, or a subsidiary. Generally, a company's profit centers each operate within only one industry. However, large profit centers that include several different industry components must be analyzed and divided into separate industry groups of related products on the basis of related risks and profitability of the products, similarity of production processes, or similarity of markets and marketing methods.

Ten Percent Significance Rules Once the entity is divided into its industry segments, significance tests (*10 percent significance rules*) must be applied to determine which of the segments are reportable. **FASB 14** requires that supplemental information be disclosed in the annual report for any industry segment satisfying at least one of the following tests:[6]

---

[5] *Financial Accounting Standards Board Statement No. 14*, "Financial Reporting for Segments of a Business Enterprise," December 1976, par. 10.

[6] *FASB 14*, par. 15.

1. Its revenue (including both sales to unaffiliated customers and intersegment sales or transfers) is 10 percent or more of the combined revenue (sales to unaffiliated customers and intersegment sales or transfers) of all of the enterprise's industry segments.
2. The amount of its operating profit or loss is 10 percent or more of the greater, in absolute amount, of
   a. The combined operating profit of all industry segments that earned an operating profit, or
   b. The combined operating loss of all industry segments that suffered an operating loss.
3. Its identifiable assets are 10 percent or more of the combined identifiable assets of all industry segments.

Note that the revenue test includes intersegment sales or transfers. The FASB felt that the full impact of a particular segment on the entire enterprise should be measured. However, any segment that is primarily engaged in providing services or products to other segments is not separately disclosed. These vertically integrated operations, such as the extractive, refining, and retailing operations of an integrated oil company, are not separately reported so long as most of the output from the extractive and refining operations is not sold to unaffiliated customers (that is, third-party customers outside the integrated oil company).

Operating profit or loss is defined as revenue minus operating expenses. Operating expenses arising from shared facilities are allocated to segments on a reasonable basis. However, **FASB 14** specifically excludes the following items from the determination of segment operating profit or loss:[7]

1. Revenue earned at the corporate level and not derived from the operations of any industry segment
2. General corporate expenses
3. Interest expense (except for financial services segments)
4. Domestic and foreign income taxes
5. Equity in income or loss from unconsolidated subsidiaries and other unconsolidated investees
6. Gain or loss from discontinued operations
7. Extraordinary items
8. Noncontrolling interest
9. Cumulative effect of a change in accounting principle

Identifiable assets are those operating assets that can be directly identified with the operations of an industry segment. Identifiable assets include the tangible and intangible assets that are used by a segment. Allowance for uncollectible accounts and accumulated depreciation are included in computing identifiable assets. Identifiable assets also include an allocated portion of assets used jointly by two or more industry segments; however, those assets directly traceable to the general corporate office should be separated from the assets of other segments and

[7] *FASB 14*, par. 10.

reported separately. Identifiable assets of nonfinancing industry segments do not include any intersegment investments or financing receivables from other industry segments—the focus is on operating assets. An exception to the exclusion of financing assets is made for determining the identifiable assets of a finance segment as discussed below.

Special Rules for Financing Segments Financing segments are sometimes created by entities to manage the external financing needs of the consolidated entity, to provide financing for customers wishing to acquire the company's products, or to manage the leasing and other financing functions of the entity. For example, the major auto manufacturers maintain separate financing operations to finance consumers' purchases of their vehicles. General Motors Acceptance Corporation (GMAC) is one of the largest financing operations of this kind.

The FASB established special rules for determining the revenue, operating profits or loss, and identifiable assets of financing segments. Recall that the general rule is that financing and investing items are not included in any of the three 10 percent significance tests. However, because of the financial nature of the financing segments, both financing and investing items are included for determining the revenue, operating profit, and identifiable assets for financing segments. The following rules apply to financing segments:

1. Revenue for a financing segment includes interest or other financial revenue from external sources *and* from intersegment loans, advances, or other financing transactions.

2. Operating profit or loss for a financing segment includes directly traceable costs, allocated common costs, *and* interest or other financing charges incurred with external parties, or resulting from intersegment financing transactions.

3. Identifiable assets for a financing segment include the tangible and intangible operating assets used by the segment *and* any intersegment loans, advances, or other financing assets generated by the financing segment.

After determining the revenues, operating profit or loss, and identifiable assets for the financing segments, these are then included with the revenues, operating profit or loss, and identifiable assets of the nonfinancing industry segments to compute the three 10 percent significance tests. The key point is that the revenue, operating profit or loss, and identifiable assets of financing segments include both external and intersegment financing and investing items.

Figure 14-1 presents an overview of the three 10 percent significance tests and the other disclosure tests required by **FASB 14**. This figure is presented here for reference during the following discussion and illustration of these disclosure tests.

Illustration of 10 Percent Tests Figure 14-2 represents the consolidated financial statements for Peerless Products Corporation and Special Foods, Inc. Information for the example is as follows:

1. Peerless owns 80 percent of Special Foods' common stock. Special Foods reports a profit of $50,000 for 19X1 and pays dividends of $30,000. The December

FIGURE 14-1 Significance tests for **FASB Statement No. 14** disclosures.

	Revenue Tests		Operating Profit Tests		Identifiable Assets Tests
Industry segments:					
Separately reportable industry segments	A segment's combined revenue from unaffiliated and intersegment customers is ≥ 10 percent of the total combined revenue of all industry segments.	(or)	A segment's operating profit or loss is ≥ 10 percent of the greater of (a) combined operating profit of all industry segments earning a profit, or (b) combined operating loss of all industry segments incurring operating losses.	(or)	A segment's identifiable assets are ≥ 10 percent of the combined identifiable assets of all industry segments.
Dominant industry comprehensive disclosure test	A segment's revenue from unaffiliated customers is > 90 percent of the combined revenue from both unaffiliated and intersegment customers.	(and)	A segment's operating profit or loss is > 90 percent of the greater of (a) combined operating profit of all industry segments earning a profit, or (b) combined operating loss of all industry segments incurring operating losses.	(and)	A segment's identifiable assets are > 90 percent of the combined identifiable assets of all industry segments.
75 percent comprehensive disclosure test	The sum of revenue from sales to unaffiliated customers by all separately reportable segments is ≥ 75 percent of the total revenue from unaffiliated customers by all segments.				
Foreign operations:					
Reportable geographic area operations	Revenue of foreign operations from sales to unaffiliated customers is ≥ 10 percent of consolidated revenue.			(or)	Identifiable assets of foreign operations are ≥ 10 percent of consolidated total assets.
Export Sales	Export sales made by domestic operations to unaffiliated foreign customers is ≥ 10 percent of consolidated revenue.				
Major customers	Revenue from a single customer or the federal, state, or local government is ≥ 10 percent of the entity's total revenue.				

FIGURE 14-2 Consolidated financial statements for Peerless Products Company and Subsidiary.

Peerless Products Company and Subsidiary
Consolidated Statement of Income and Retained Earnings
Year Ended December 31, 19X1

Revenues:	
Sales	$572,000
Income from Investment in Barclay	32,000
Expenses and Deductions:	
Cost of Goods Sold	(267,000)
Depreciation and Amortization	(70,000)
Other Expenses	(15,000)
Interest Expense	(30,000)
Income to Noncontrolling Interest	(10,000)
Income Taxes	(62,000)
Net Income	$150,000
Retained Earnings, January 1	300,000
Less: Dividends	(60,000)
Retained Earnings, December 31	$390,000

Peerless Products Corporation and Subsidiary
Consolidated Balance Sheet
December 31, 19X1

Cash		$ 131,000
Accounts Receivable		125,000
Inventory		165,000
Investment in Barclay Stock		184,000
Land		215,000
Building and Equipment	$1,400,000	
Less: Accumulated Depreciation	(770,000)	630,000
Total Assets		$1,450,000
Accounts Payable		$ 200,000
Bonds Payable		300,000
Noncontrolling Interest		60,000
Common Stock		500,000
Retained Earnings		390,000
Total Liabilities and Stockholders' Equity		$1,450,000

31, 19X1, balances in Special Foods' stockholders' equity accounts total $300,000, of which the noncontrolling interest is 20 percent.

2. Peerless acquires 40 percent of Barclay Company stock on January 1, 19X1, for a cost of $160,000, which is equal to the book value of the stock on that date. The equity method is used to account for this investment. Barclay Company earns $80,000 in profit during 19X1 and pays $20,000 in dividends.

Segment disclosure provides a breakdown of the consolidated totals into their constituent parts. The items that appear in the consolidated statements and must be disaggregated are sales of $572,000 and total assets of $1,450,000. In the segment analysis, operating profit is also used; however, this figure is not presented directly on the consolidated income statement and must be computed separately.

Figure 14-3 is a workpaper used to perform the disaggregation from the consolidated totals into the various segments. Figure 14-3 also includes additional data necessary for the preparation of the annual report footnote disclosure presented later in this chapter.

Additional information for this illustration is as follows:

1. The consolidated entity of Peerless Products and Special Foods comprises five different industry segments as well as a central corporate administration. The industry segments are defined by management as Food I roducts, Plastic and Packaging, Consumer and Commercial, Health and Scientific, and Chemicals. Each of the two legal entities—Peerless Products and Special Foods—operates in more than one industry segment.

2. On January 1, 19X1, the Food Products segment of Special Foods issues a $100,000, 12 percent note payable to the Plastic and Packaging segment of Peerless Products. The intercompany interest is $12,000 for the year and is properly eliminated from the consolidated statements.

3. Each industry segment makes sales to unaffiliated customers. In addition, $28,000 of intersegment sales are made during the year by the Food Products, the Plastic and Packaging, and the Consumer and Commercial segments. The cost of these intersegment sales is $18,000. These goods are still in the ending inventories of the purchasing industry segments. Specific revenue information is presented in Figure 14-3.

4. Figure 14-3 also presents the operating profit and loss information for each segment. Note that a total of $315,000 of costs is directly traceable to the specific industry segments.

5. A computer costing $30,000 is acquired during the year. The computer is used for production scheduling and control and is being depreciated by the straight-line method over a period of 3 years ($30,000 ÷ 3 years = $10,000 per year). The annual expense of this computer is allocated on the basis of use, which is monitored by the computer itself. These allocated costs are shown in Figure 14-3 immediately below the costs directly traceable to each industry segment.

6. The intersegment interest expense from the intercompany note is attributable to the Food Products segment, and the intercompany interest income is earned by the Plastic and Packaging segment.

7. Items excludable from segment operating profit and loss are general corporate expenses, income from the investment in Barclay, and interest (both between segments and to unaffiliated lenders). These items are noted in the other items section of Figure 14-3. This information is collected to reconcile the consolidated totals and because it is part of the segment disclosure footnote.

FIGURE 14-3 Workpaper to analyze Peerless Products Corporation and Subsidiary's industry segments.

Peerless Products Corporation and Special Foods, Inc.
Segmental Disclosure Workpaper

Item	Industry Segments					Corporate Administration	Combined	Intersegment Eliminations	Consolidated
	Food Products	Plastic and Packaging	Consumer and Commercial	Health and Scientific	Chemicals				
Revenue:									
Sales to unaffiliated customers	317,000	95,000	41,000	86,000	33,000		572,000		572,000
Intersegment sales	6,000	18,000	4,000				28,000	(28,000)	
Total revenue	323,000	113,000	45,000	86,000	33,000		600,000	(28,000)	572,000
Operating costs:									
Directly traceable operating expenses	(110,000)	(35,000)	(68,000)	(61,000)	(41,000)		(315,000)	18,000	(297,000)
Allocated costs	(3,000)	(1,000)	(2,000)	(3,000)	(1,000)		(10,000)		(10,000)
Operating profit	210,000	77,000	(25,000)	22,000	(9,000)		275,000	(10,000)	265,000
Other items:									
General corporate expenses						(45,000)	(45,000)		(45,000)
Income from investment		32,000					32,000		32,000
Interest expense— unaffiliated		(30,000)					(30,000)		(30,000)
Interest expense— intersegment	(12,000)						(12,000)	12,000	
Interest income— intersegment		12,000					12,000	(12,000)	
Income from continuing operations before taxes	198,000	91,000	(25,000)	22,000	(9,000)	(45,000)	232,000	(10,000)	222,000
Assets:									
Identifiable with segment	411,000	275,000	100,000	310,000	80,000		1,176,000	(10,000)	1,166,000
General corporate assets						100,000	100,000		100,000
Investments		184,000					184,000		184,000
Intersegment notes		100,000					100,000	(100,000)	
Total assets	411,000	559,000	100,000	310,000	80,000	100,000	1,560,000	(110,000)	1,450,000

8. The assets section of Figure 14-3 presents the assets identifiable with each segment. Included in the identifiable assets is the $20,000 book value ($30,000 less $10,000 of accumulated depreciation) of the production computer.

The specific significance tests that Peerless Products and subsidiary must use to determine reportable industry segments are as follows:

a. Ten Percent Revenue Test The first 10 percent test is applied to each industry segment's total revenue as a percentage of the combined revenue of all industry segments before elimination of intersegment transfers and sales. If an industry segment's total revenue is 10 percent or more of the combined revenue of all segments, then the segment is separately reportable and supplementary disclosures must be provided for it in the annual report.

The 10 percent revenue tests are applied as follows:

Segment	Segment Revenue	Percent of Combined Revenue of $600,000	Reportable Segment
Food Products	$323,000	53.8%	Yes
Plastic and Packaging	113,000	18.8	Yes
Consumer and Commercial	45,000	7.5	No
Health and Scientific	86,000	14.3	Yes
Chemicals	33,000	5.5	No
Total	$600,000	100.0%*	

*Unrounded percents for segments total to 100 percent.

The revenue test shows that the following industry segments are separately reportable: Food Products, Plastic and Packaging, and Health and Scientific. A common shortcut is to compute 10 percent of the denominator of the test (for Peerless and its subsidiary, $600,000 $\times$ .10) and then compare each of the segments' total revenue with that fraction. In this case, reportable segments are those with $60,000 or more in total revenue.

b. Ten Percent Operating Profit (Loss) Test The operating profit or loss test is the second test to determine which industry segments are separately reportable. The test is to determine if a segment's operating profit or loss is equal to or greater than 10 percent of the absolute value of either the combined operating profits or the combined operating losses of the industry segments, whichever is greater.

Because two segments had operating losses for the year, separate tabulations are made, as follows:

Segment	Operating Profits	Operating Losses
Food Products	$210,000	
Plastic and Packaging	77,000	
Consumer and Commercial		$(25,000)
Health and Scientific	22,000	
Chemicals		(9,000)
Totals	$309,000	$(34,000)

The greater absolute total is the $309,000 of operating profits. This amount becomes the denominator for the 10 percent operating profit or loss test. Because this test is based on absolute amounts, all numbers are treated as positive numbers. The test is shown below.

Segment	Operating Profit (Loss)	Percent of Test Amount of $309,000	Separately Reportable
Food Products	$210,000	68.0%	Yes
Plastic and Packaging	77,000	24.9	Yes
Consumer and Commercial	(25,000)	8.1	No
Health and Scientific	22,000	7.1	No
Chemicals	(9,000)	2.9	No

The Food Products and Plastic and Packaging segments are separately reportable using the operating profit or loss test.

c. Identifiable Assets Test   The last of the three tests to determine if a segment is separately reportable is the 10 percent identifiable assets test. The combined identifiable assets of Peerless and Special Foods are used for this test. The difference of $10,000 between combined identifiable assets of $1,176,000 and consolidated identifiable assets of $1,166,000 is the unrealized intercompany inventory profit from intersegment inventory transactions that has not been realized in sales to third parties. This $10,000 difference is eliminated in the consolidation process.

The 10 percent significance rule is applied to identifiable assets as follows:

Segment	Segment Identifiable Assets	Percent of Test Amount of $1,176,000	Separately Reportable
Food Products	$ 411,000	34.9%	Yes
Plastic and Packaging	275,000	23.4	Yes
Consumer and Commercial	100,000	8.5	No
Health and Scientific	310,000	26.4	Yes
Chemicals	80,000	6.8	No
Total	$1,176,000	100.0%	

The Food Products, Plastic and Packaging, and Health and Scientific segments are separately reportable using the 10 percent identifiable assets test; that is, their identifiable assets are equal to or greater than 10 percent of the combined identifiable assets ($117,600 = $1,176,000 × .10).

Figure 14-4 summarizes the results of the three tests. Recall that a segment is separately reportable if it meets any one of the three 10 percent tests. The following segments are separately reportable under the three tests: Food Products, Plastic and Packaging, and Health and Scientific. The remaining segments, Consumer and Commercial, and Chemicals, are not separately reportable under any of the three tests. Supplemental industry information must therefore be reported in the annual report for the three separately reportable segments, and information for the remaining two nonreportable segments may be combined under the heading "Other Segments."

FIGURE 14-4 Summary of reportable industry segments: 10 percent tests.

	Food Products	Plastic and Packaging	Consumer and Commercial	Health and Scientific	Chemicals
Revenue test	Yes	Yes	No	Yes	No
Operating profit (loss) test	Yes	Yes	No	No	No
Identifiable assets test	Yes	Yes	No	Yes	No

Comprehensive Disclosure Tests

After determining which of the segments are reportable under any of the three 10 percent tests, the company must apply three comprehensive tests. The purpose of these tests is to place practical limits (both minimum and maximum) on the number of reportable segments for which the supplemental disclosures must be made. The three comprehensive tests are (1) the *dominant industry segment test*, (2) the *75 percent revenue test*, and (3) the *maximum number of reportable segments test*.

Dominant Industry Segment Test If a company has one industry segment that constitutes more than 90 percent of the combined revenue, operating profits (losses), and identifiable assets of all industry segments, then the consolidated financial statements are sufficient to provide information on the risks and profitability of the dominant industry component of the company. Such a company is required to provide only a brief footnote describing its dominant segment; no further industry breakdowns are required. For Peerless Products and Special Foods, there is more than one reportable segment; no dominant segment exists.

Seventy-five Percent Revenue Test The total revenue from sales to unaffiliated customers by all separately reportable segments must equal at least 75 percent of the total revenue from sales to unaffiliated customers by all segments. The reporting company must identify additional industry segments as reportable until this test is met. Peerless Products and Special Foods, with three reportable segments, compute the 75 percent test as follows:

Sales to unaffiliated customers by reportable segments:		
Food Products	$317,000	
Plastic and Packaging	95,000	
Health and Scientific	86,000	
Total of reportable segments		$498,000
Revenue from unaffiliated customers for all industry segments		572,000
Reportable segments' percentage of revenue ($498,000 ÷ $572,000)		87.1%

Because this percentage is equal to or greater than 75 percent, no further segments must be separately reported. Had the percentage been less than 75 percent, additional individual industry segments would have been required to be treated as reportable until the 75 percent test was met.

Maximum Number of Reportable Segments Test   The last overall test places an upper limit on the number of reportable segments. A practical limit of about 10 segments is used because above that number, the supplemental information may become overly detailed. A company having more than about 10 reportable segments should consider combining the most closely related segments. Peerless Products and Special Foods have just three reportable segments.

In addition to these overall tests, companies must exercise judgment to determine the individual segments to be reported. For example, a segment may meet or fail a specific test because of some unusual situation, such as an abnormally high profit or loss on a one-time contract. The concept of interperiod comparability should be followed in deciding whether or not the segment should be disclosed in the current period. Companies should separately report segments that have been reported in prior years but fail the current period's significance tests because of abnormal occurrences. Similarly, companies need not separately report a segment that has met a 10 percent test on a one-time basis only because of abnormal circumstances. A company is required, however, to indicate why a reportable segment is not disclosed.

Finally, if a segment becomes reportable in the current period but has not been reported separately in earlier periods, the prior year's comparative segment disclosures, which are included in the current year's annual report, should be restated to obtain comparability of financial data.

Reporting Segment Information

The specific disclosures required for each reportable segment are defined in **FASB 14**. In segment reporting, the following must be disclosed for *each* segment determined to be separately reportable:[8]

1. *Revenue.* The segment's revenue, including both sales to unaffiliated customers and intersegment sales, and the basis of accounting for intersegment sales and transfers.
2. *Operating Profit or Loss.* The segment's operating profit or loss. In addition, the nature and amount of any unusual or infrequently occurring items that are included in operating profit or loss should be disclosed.
3. *Identifiable Assets.* The aggregate carrying amount of the segment's identifiable assets.

---

[8] *FASB 14*, pars. 22–27.

4. *Other Related Information for Each Segment:*
   a. Aggregate provisions for depreciation, depletion, and amortization.
   b. Capital expenditures.
   c. Equity in net income and the investment in equity method investees whose operations are vertically integrated with a reportable segment.
   d. The effect of any change in accounting principles.

Companies are allowed to present these disclosures in separate schedules, as part of the main financial statements, or in the footnotes. Most companies present footnote disclosures with accompanying schedules. An example of a commonly used disclosure format is presented in Figure 14-5 for Peerless Products and Special Foods. The figure presents the information on the industry segments used in the example and only the current year's data. In practice, however, companies usually provide comparative data for at least one prior fiscal period together with the current period's information.

The segment disclosures are reconciled to the amounts reported on the company's consolidated statements. Specific disclosures are made for each segment, and the amounts are then reconciled to the consolidated amounts by eliminating any intersegment transactions. For Peerless and its subsidiary, intersegment sales of $28,000, including $10,000 unrealized profit, must be eliminated. The consolidated income statement reports $572,000 in sales. The consolidated balance sheet reports $1,450,000 of total assets. This reconciliation is required by **FASB 14**.

Segment disclosures are not required in interim reports. Also, segment disclosures need not be made by companies whose securities are not traded on a stock exchange or in the over-the-counter market.

INFORMATION ABOUT FOREIGN OPERATIONS AND EXPORT SALES

Multinational entities have operations in several different countries. **FASB 14** includes disclosure guidelines for presentation of the revenue, operating profits, and identifiable assets for these operations. In essence, the entity is required to make another disaggregation of its consolidated "pie," this time into pieces differentiated by geographic area rather than by industry segments. Companies must separately disclose domestic and significant foreign operations.

Foreign operations include all operations located outside the United States (or other home country of the entity), but do not include unconsolidated foreign subsidiaries or foreign investees. Foreign operations are broken down by country or groups of related countries. The additional disclosures provide investors, creditors, and other external users with information that can be used to assess the potential risks incurred by the company's involvement in foreign markets. Indeed, an investment in a Latin American country may carry different risks from the same dollar amount of investment in Great Britain or Italy. A typical identification of foreign markets is presented in the Coca-Cola Company's annual report. Coca-Cola reports five geographic areas: United States, Latin America, European Community, Northeast Europe and Africa, and Canada and Pacific.

FIGURE 14-5 Required footnote disclosure for Peerless Products Corporation and Subsidiary's industry segments.

FOOTNOTE X:
INFORMATION ABOUT THE COMPANY'S OPERATIONS IN DIFFERENT INDUSTRY SEGMENTS

Item	Food Products	Plastic and Packaging	Health and Scientific	Others	Intersegment Eliminations	Consolidated
			Industry Segments			
Sales to unaffiliated customers	$317,000	$ 95,000	$ 86,000	$ 74,000		$ 572,000
Intersegment sales	6,000	18,000		4,000	$(28,000)	
Total revenue	$323,000	$113,000	$ 86,000	$ 78,000	$(28,000)	$ 572,000
Operating profit	$210,000	$ 77,000	$ 22,000	$ (34,000)	$(10,000)	$ 265,000
Other items:						
General corporate expenses						(45,000)
Income from investments						32,000
Interest expense— unaffiliated						(30,000)
Income from continuing operations before taxes						$ 222,000
Identifiable assets	$411,000	$275,000	$310,000	$180,000	$(10,000)	$1,166,000
General corporate assets						$ 100,000
Investments						184,000
Total assets						$1,450,000
Depreciation expense	$ 24,000	$ 16,000	$ 11,000	$ 4,000		
Capital expenditures	$ 60,000	$ 21,000	$ 16,000	$ 14,000		

Many of the specific procedures for determining reportable geographic segments are similar to those used for determining reportable industry segments. Minor differences are noted throughout the following discussion.

Defining Reportable Foreign Operations

The first step in defining reportable foreign operations is to classify the consolidated entity's operations into domestic and aggregate foreign. Tests are then applied to determine if the aggregate foreign operations are significant. Two tests are used instead of the three used for industry segments. Aggregate foreign operations are significant if either of the following two tests is met:[9]

1. Revenue generated by the enterprise's foreign operations from sales to unaffiliated customers is 10 percent or more of consolidated revenue as reported in the enterprise's income statement.

2. Identifiable assets of the enterprise's foreign operations are 10 percent or more of consolidated total assets as reported in the enterprise's balance sheet.

The operating profit or loss test is not used for foreign operations because of the many differences in tax structures and accounting practices in different geographic areas.

If the aggregate foreign operations are significant, they are then divided into individual geographic areas and the two 10 percent tests are applied to each individual foreign area to determine if it is separately reportable. Operations in two or more foreign countries may be grouped into a single geographic area on the basis of:

> . . . proximity, economic affinity, similarities of business environments, and the nature, scale, and degree of interrelationship of the operations in various countries.[10]

Illustration of 10 Percent Significance Tests for Foreign Operations   Figure 14-6 presents information about the domestic and foreign operations of Peerless Products and its subsidiary, Special Foods. The geographic areas are determined by management based on an assessment of proximity and similarity of profitability and risks. The information consists of a disaggregation of the consolidated totals into domestic and individual foreign geographic areas. The entity's corporate administration center is located in the United States, which the company has defined as its domestic area. Aggregate foreign revenues and aggregate foreign identifiable assets are determined to be significant by the 10 percent tests, as follows:

$$\frac{\text{Aggregate foreign operations' sales to unaffiliated customers}}{\text{Consolidated revenue}} = \frac{\$192{,}000}{\$572{,}000} = 33.6\%$$

$$\frac{\text{Aggregate foreign operations' identifiable assets}}{\text{Consolidated assets}} = \frac{\$\ 596{,}000}{\$1{,}450{,}000} = 41.1\%$$

If aggregate foreign operations were not significant, no separate geographical area disclosure would be required and no further tests on specific geographical areas would be made. However, once aggregate foreign operations are found to be significant, the next step is to separately analyze each individual foreign area to determine which specific areas are significant, and therefore separately report-

---

[9] *FASB 14*, par. 32.
[10] *FASB 14*, par. 34.

FIGURE 14-6 Workpaper to analyze Peerless Products Corporation and Subsidiary's foreign operations.

Peerless Products Corporation and Special Foods
Foreign Operations Disclosure Workpaper

Item	Geographic Area				Combined	Interarea Eliminations	Consolidated
	Domestic	Europe	South America	Australia			
Revenues:							
Sales to unaffiliated customers	380,000	116,000	28,000	48,000	572,000		572,000
Intracompany sales between geographic areas	6,000				6,000	(6,000)	
Total revenue	386,000	116,000	28,000	48,000	578,000	(6,000)	572,000
Operating profit	184,000	51,000	16,000	15,000	266,000	(1,000)	265,000
Other items:							
General corporate expenses	(45,000)				(45,000)		(45,000)
Interest expense— unaffiliated	(30,000)				(30,000)		(30,000)
Income from investment	32,000				32,000		32,000
Income from continuing operations before taxes	141,000	51,000	16,000	15,000	223,000	(1,000)	222,000
Assets:							
Identifiable to geographic area	571,000	420,000	108,000	68,000	1,167,000	(1,000)	1,166,000
General corporate assets	100,000				100,000		100,000
Investments	184,000				184,000		184,000
Total assets	855,000	420,000	108,000	68,000	1,451,000	(1,000)	1,450,000

able. The remainder of the illustration is directed at testing the individual foreign areas.

Revenue is separated between sales to unaffiliated customers and intracompany sales between geographic areas. For example, the domestic operation made intracompany sales of $6,000 to other geographic areas. Of course, these intracompany sales are excluded from the revenue reported in the consolidated income statement. Note that the intracompany sales between geographic areas total $6,000, which is different from the $28,000 in intersegment sales shown in Figure 14-3. The reason for this difference is that some of the intersegment sales were made to affiliates within the same geographic area. The company's assets are also disaggregated into domestic operations and specific foreign areas.

a. Ten Percent Revenue Test for Individual Foreign Operations The 10 percent revenue test to determine reportable foreign operations measures the proportion of consolidated sales to unaffiliated customers in each geographic area. The test is as follows:

Geographic Area	Sales to Unaffiliated Customers	Percent of Consolidated Revenues of $572,000	Separately Reportable
Domestic	$380,000	66.4%	Yes
Europe	116,000	20.3	Yes
South America	28,000	4.9	No
Australia	48,000	8.4	No
Total	$572,000	100.0%	

Recall that the revenue test for industry segments is based on segment revenue as a percentage of total combined revenue before any eliminations for intersegment transactions. Both the numerator and the denominator are different for the foreign operations revenue test. The numerator for the foreign operations revenue test does not include intracompany sales, and the denominator is consolidated sales. The 10 percent revenue test determines that the domestic area and the European geographic area are each separately reportable.

b. Identifiable Assets Test for Individual Foreign Operations The 10 percent identifiable assets test measures the proportion of identifiable assets for each geographic area. Again, this test differs from the assets test used for industry segments. The test for reportable geographic segments uses consolidated total assets, while the industry segment test uses combined identifiable assets.

The 10 percent identifiable assets test for foreign operations is applied as follows:

Geographic Area	Identifiable Assets	Percent of Total Consolidated Assets of $1,450,000	Separately Reportable
Domestic	$571,000	39.4%	Yes
Europe	420,000	29.0	Yes
South America	108,000	7.4	No
Australia	68,000	4.7	No

The identifiable assets test shows that the domestic area operation and Europe are both separately reportable. The company is not required to report the South American and Australian areas separately because the percentages are less than 10 percent. Although the company could voluntarily disclose information about the South American and Australian areas, most companies are reluctant to disclose more than is required by GAAP for fear that the additional disclosures could be used by competitors to determine the company's level of investment and profitability of operations in individual geographic areas.

Both tests indicate that the domestic area and Europe are each separately reportable. Supplemental revenue, profitability, and asset information must be presented for these two areas. The South American and Australian geographic areas are combined under the heading "Other Foreign Operations" without further elaboration.

Required Foreign Operations Disclosures

FASB 14 requires the disclosure of the following information for each reportable foreign operation:[11]

1. *Revenue*. Revenue for each geographic area broken down by sales to unaffiliated companies and intracompany sales or transfers.

2. *Profitability Information*. Operating profit or loss, net income, or some other measure of profitability between operating profit and net income.

3. *Identifiable Assets*. The carrying value of identifiable assets for each geographic area.

The typical format for footnote disclosure of foreign operations is presented for the consolidated entity in Figure 14-7. As with the industry segment disclosure, the foreign operations information must be reconciled to the amounts reported in the consolidated financial statements.

Reporting Export Sales

FASB 14 also requires the separate disclosure of significant export sales made by a company's *domestic operations* to unaffiliated foreign customers. The measure of significance is again 10 percent. The test measures the proportion of domestic operations' sales to unaffiliated foreign customers. If these export sales are 10 percent or more of consolidated revenue, they must be disclosed in total and by geographic area to which the sale was made. This disclosure is required whether or not the company reports information about industry segments or geographic areas. The export sales information is usually presented in a footnote in the annual report.

INFORMATION ABOUT MAJOR CUSTOMERS

The final supplemental disclosure required by **FASB 14** is information about major customers. If the company sells a large percentage of its products to a few customers, then its profits and risks are directly related to the performance of those few customers.

An important issue is how to define an individual customer. **FASB Statement No. 30**, "Disclosure of Information about Major Customers" (FASB 30), amended **FASB 14** on this matter. For purposes of applying the disclosure test, each of the following is considered to be an individual customer: any single

---

[11] *FASB 14*, par. 35.

FIGURE 14-7 Required footnote disclosure schedule for Peerless Products Corporation and Subsidiary's foreign operations.

FOOTNOTE Y:
INFORMATION ABOUT THE COMPANY'S OPERATIONS IN DIFFERENT GEOGRAPHIC AREAS

Item	Geographic Area			Interarea Eliminations	Consolidated
	Domestic	Europe	Others		
Sales to unaffiliated customers	$380,000	$116,000	$ 76,000		$ 572,000
Intracompany sales between geographic areas	6,000			$(6,000)	
Total revenue	$386,000	$116,000	$ 76,000	$(6,000)	$ 572,000
Operating profit	$184,000	$ 51,000	$ 31,000	$(1,000)	$ 265,000
Other items:					
General corporate expenses					$ (45,000)
Investment income					32,000
Interest expense					(30,000)
Income from continuing operations before taxes					$ 222,000
Identifiable assets	$571,000	$420,000	$176,000	$(1,000)	$1,166,000
General corporate assets					$ 100,000
Investments					184,000
Total assets					$1,450,000

customer (including a group of persons or companies under common control), the federal government, a state government, a local government, or a foreign government. Significant customers are determined using a 10 percent of total revenue test; that is, disclosures are required when 10 percent or more of the entity's total revenue is generated from a single customer. The disclosures include the amount of sales to each significant customer and the industry segments making the sales. The names of the individual customers need not be disclosed. The disclosures are usually made by a footnote in the annual report.

This concludes the discussion of segment reporting. The remainder of the chapter presents another major area of financial disclosure: interim financial reporting.

INTERIM FINANCIAL REPORTING

Interim reports, which cover a time period of less than 1 year, are as important to investors and other statement users as annual financial reports. The interim report is, in many ways, a smaller version of the annual report. It includes an abbreviated income statement, balance sheet, statement of cash flows, and selected footnotes and other disclosures for the interim period being reported, as well as comparative data for prior interim periods. The purpose of interim reporting is to provide investors and other interested parties with contemporary reports on the operating progress of the entity.

Interim reports are used to assess the entity's performance and to estimate any turning points in the income trend of the business. Rapid stock market reactions to the release of interim information indicate that investors and other financial statement users look closely at these reports.

In addition, the SEC requires the inclusion of selected quarterly financial data in a footnote in the annual financial report. This disclosure requirement means that the independent auditors must review the company's interim reports made during the fiscal year and note any errors or restatements. Because of the wide use of interim reports and their importance in economic decision making, accountants must be aware of the methods and procedures used in preparing them.

THE FORMAT OF THE INTERIM FINANCIAL REPORT

The SEC requires quarterly financial reports within 45 days after the end of each quarter, except that the annual report may be used in place of the last interim report of the fiscal year. Interim reports generally contain the following items:

1. An income statement for the most recent quarter of the current fiscal period and a comparative income statement for the same quarter for the prior fiscal year.

2. Income statements for the cumulative year-to-date time period and for the corresponding period of the prior fiscal year.

3. A condensed balance sheet at the end of the current quarter and a condensed balance sheet at the end of the prior fiscal year. However, companies should include the balance sheet as of the end of the corresponding interim period of the previous year if it is necessary for an understanding of the impact of seasonal fluctuations on the company's financial condition.

4. A statement of cash flows as of the end of the current cumulative year-to-date period, and for the same time span for the prior year.

5. Footnotes that update those in the last annual report. These interim footnotes summarize any changes in measurement or major economic events that have occurred since the end of the most recent fiscal year.

6. A report by management analyzing and discussing the results for the latest interim period.

ACCOUNTING ISSUES

Interim reporting presents accountants with several technical and conceptual measurement issues. Most of these center on the accounting concept of periodicity and division of the annual period.

The use of interim reports to provide timely information is a fairly recent development. Many firms began publishing interim reports voluntarily in the late 1940s. These early reports raised substantive accounting issues because no standards existed to guide their presentation. Some firms' first three quarterly reports suggested a significant profit for the year, and then arbitrary and questionable fourth-quarter adjustments reconciled to an actual loss for the year. The lack of established guidelines led to experimentation with a variety of cost allocations among periods, resulting in unrealistic patterns of quarterly income. It was not until 1973, when the Accounting Principles Board issued **APB Opinion No. 28**, "Interim Financial Reporting" (APB 28), that guidelines were finally standardized.

Discrete versus Integral View of Interim Reporting

Two divergent views of interim reporting were held before the release of **APB 28**. The *discrete theory of interim reporting* views each interim period as a basic accounting period to be evaluated as if it were an annual accounting period. Any end-of-period adjustments and deferrals would be determined using the same accounting principles used for the annual report.

The *integral theory of interim reporting* views an interim period as an installment of an annual period. Under this view, recognition and adjustment of certain income or expense items may be affected by judgments about the expected results of the entire year's operations. For example, expenses that normally would be charged to operations in one period for annual accounting purposes could be deferred and expensed in several interim periods based on an allocation using sales volume, production levels, or some other basis.

To examine the differences between these two theories, assume that Peerless Products Corporation incurred a $20,000 cost at the beginning of the second quarter of its fiscal year for an advertising campaign intended to generate sales revenue for the remainder of the year. Under the discrete view, the entire $20,000 must be charged against income in the second quarter. Under the integral view, however, the advertising cost could initially be recorded as a deferred cost and expensed over the second, third, and fourth interim periods. The allocation to the individual periods could be made on the basis of the sales volume generated or some other appropriate basis. Under the integral view, one interim period would not bear the entire expense that benefits more than one interim period.

Both views were applied in practice, and it was up to the Accounting Principles Board to settle the conflict. The integral view was selected as the primary theory for interim reporting, although some modifications of this theory were made so that reports would conform closely to the results of operations for the year.

Accounting Pronouncements on Interim Reporting

APB 28 standardized the preparation and reporting of interim income statements. The opinion defines the income elements and the measurement of costs on an interim basis. Also the opinion provides guidance for the annual report footnote summarizing the published interim disclosures and explaining any adjustments required to make the interim figures total the annual figures. This conformance to the annual report increases the reliability of the published interim statements and also brought interim reporting under the view of the external auditors who review the footnotes in the annual report as part of the audit.

FASB Statement No. 3, "Reporting Accounting Changes in Interim Financial Statements" (FASB 3), amended **APB 28**. **FASB 3** details the interim statement presentation of accounting changes requiring a cumulative effect treatment discussed in **APB Opinion No. 20**, "Accounting Changes" (APB 20). Generally, the approach required by **FASB 3** for interim reports is consistent with the logic and objectives of **APB 20**.

FASB Interpretation No. 18, "Accounting for Income Taxes in Interim Periods" (FIN 18), also amended **APB 28**. This interpretation tackles the difficult problems of measuring the tax provision for interim reports when the actual tax expense is based on annual income. The interpretation allows estimates and judgments in order to obtain a reasonable relationship between the reported interim operating income and the related income tax provision. Examples of accounting for taxes in interim statements are presented later in this chapter.

REPORTING STANDARDS FOR INTERIM INCOME STATEMENTS

The form of the interim income statement is the same as the form of the annual income statement. Some differences exist in the measurement of specific components of income because of the shorter time period. In general, the accounting standards used for interim statements are the same as those used for the annual statements, although **APB 28** provides an abundance of technical assistance to measure and report on an interim basis. Figure 14-8 presents an overview of the major accounting principles used for the interim income statement. The technical requirements relevant to interim reporting are discussed in the following sections.

Revenue

One of the most significant elements of the interim income statement is revenue from sales. Investors wish to assess the revenue-generating capability of the entity, so they compare revenue of the current interim period with revenue of the corresponding interim periods of prior years. **APB 28** states that:

> Revenue from products sold or services rendered should be recognized as earned during an interim period on the same basis as followed for the full year.[12]

Thus, revenue must be recognized and reported in the period in which earned and cannot be deferred to other periods in order to present a more stable revenue stream. Revenue from seasonal businesses, such as in agriculture, food products, wholesale or retail outlets, and amusements, cannot be manipulated to eliminate seasonal trends.

---

[12] *APB Opinion No. 28*, "Interim Financial Reporting," American Institute of Certified Public Accountants (New York), 1973, par. 11.

FIGURE 14-8 Overview of interim income statement accounting principles.

Revenue	Recognize as earned during an interim period on same basis as used for annual reporting.
Cost of goods sold	Product costs for interim period recognized on same basis as used for annual reporting, except for interims: • Estimated gross profit rates may be used to determine interim cost of goods sold. • Temporary liquidations of lifo-base inventories are charged to cost of goods sold using expected replacement cost of the items. • Lower-of-cost-or-market valuation method allows for loss recoveries for increases in market prices in later interim periods of the same fiscal year. • Standard costs systems should use same procedures as for annual reporting except that price variances or volume or capacity variances expected to be absorbed by end of the year should be deferred.
All other costs and expenses	Expense as incurred or allocate among interim periods based on benefit received or other systematic and rational basis.
Income taxes	Based on estimated annual effective tax rate, with recognition of tax benefits of an operating loss if benefits are assured beyond a reasonable doubt; second and subsequent quarters are based on changes in cumulative amount of tax computed, including changes in estimates.
Disposal of a segment, or extraordinary, unusual, infrequently occurring, and contingent items	Recognize in interim period in which they occur.
Accounting changes: 1. Cumulative effect–type	Make effective and determine cumulative effect on retained earnings as of beginning of first interim period of fiscal year.
2. Retroactive type	Restate prior interims of current fiscal period and interims of prior years.
3. Adoption of lifo	Make effective as of beginning of first interim period of fiscal year.

The APB considered the issue of seasonality to be very important. Businesses that experience material seasonal variations in their revenue are encouraged to supplement their interim reports with information for 12-month periods ending at the interim date for the current and preceding years. Such disclosures reduce the possibility that users of the reports might make unwarranted inferences about the annual results from an interim report with material seasonal variation.

Cost of Goods Sold and Inventory

Cost of goods sold is generally the largest single expense on the interim income statement. The interim cost of goods sold should be computed as follows:

Those costs and expenses that are associated directly with or allocated to the products sold or to the services rendered for annual reporting purposes . . . should be similarly treated for interim reporting purposes.[13]

[13] Ibid., par. 13.

Although this provision requires use of the same methods for interim and annual reports, **APB 28** permits the following practical modifications to this general rule:[14]

1. Estimated gross profit rates *may be used* to determine an interim period's cost of goods sold, thus eliminating the need for a physical inventory count in each interim period.

2. Companies that use lifo inventory valuation may experience a *temporary liquidation of lifo-base* inventories. Such temporary reductions of inventories expected to be replaced by the end of the fiscal year should *not* be expensed through cost of goods sold at historical cost. Instead, the expected replacement cost of the liquidated portion of the lifo base should be used for the interim period's cost of goods sold.

3. Inventory losses due to a decline in market prices *are recognized* in the period of decline using the lower-of-cost-or-market valuation method. Recoveries of market prices in later interim periods of the same fiscal year *should be recognized as gains (recoveries of prior losses) in the later interim period*. Temporary market declines that are expected to reverse by the end of the fiscal year need not be recognized on the interim date, because no loss is expected for the fiscal year.

4. Companies using a standard cost system for inventories should use the *same procedures* for computing and reporting variances in an interim period as used for the fiscal year. However, purchase price variances or volume or capacity variances that are expected to be absorbed by the end of the fiscal year should be deferred at the interim period and should not be included in the interim income.

Illustration of Temporary LIFO Liquidation   The reason that the interim treatment of lifo inventory liquidations differs from the annual treatment of lifo liquidations is that the inventory is expected to be replaced by the end of the fiscal year. Interim income for the period of the temporary liquidation would be overstated if cost of goods sold were charged with the lower lifo inventory costs in a time of rising prices. The following example illustrates this point.

1. During the third quarter of its fiscal year, Special Foods, Inc., experienced a temporary liquidation of 2,000 units in its lifo base owing to seasonal fluctuations. The lifo unit cost is $25. The liquidation is normal, and the company plans to replace the liquidated inventory during the early part of the next (fourth) interim period.

2. The estimated replacement cost of the inventory is $35 per unit.

The entry in the third interim period to account for the temporary inventory liquidation is:

---

[14] Ibid., par. 14.

(1) Cost of Goods Sold	70,000	
Inventory		50,000
Excess of Replacement Cost over Lifo		
Cost of Inventory Liquidated		20,000

Record temporary lifo inventory liquidation:
$70,000 = 2,000 units × $35
$50,000 = 2,000 units × $25 lifo cost

The interim income statement presents cost of goods sold at the expected replacement cost. The Excess of Replacement Cost over Lifo Cost of Inventory Liquidated should be shown as a current liability on the interim balance sheet, although some accountants net this against the inventory reported on the interim balance sheet.

When the inventory is replaced at $36 per unit during the fourth quarter, the following entry is made:

(2) Cost of Goods Sold	2,000	
Inventory	50,000	
Excess of Replacement Cost over Lifo Cost		
of Inventory Liquidated	20,000	
Accounts Payable		72,000

Record replacement of lifo inventory liquidation:
$50,000 = 2,000 × $25 lifo cost
$72,000 = 2,000 × $36

The actual replacement price of $36 is different from the estimated replacement price of $35. The difference is an adjustment to cost of goods sold in the replacement period. The third quarter's interim report is not retroactively restated. If the liquidated inventory is not replaced by the end of the fiscal year, the liability account is written off to Cost of Goods Sold, decreasing the reported annual cost of goods sold to its correct amount.

Illustration of Market Write-Down and Recovery The following example illustrates the use of the lower-of-cost-or-market (LCM) method for interim reports:

1. At the beginning of its fiscal year, Peerless Products Corporation has 10,000 units of inventory on hand with a fifo cost of $10 each.
2. No additional purchases are made during the year.
3. The sales and market costs at the end of each quarter during the fiscal year are as follows:

Quarter	Units Sold in Quarter	Unit Market Values at End of Quarter
1	2,000	$ 7
2	2,000	6
3	2,000	7
4	2,000	11

Peerless is not certain of the cause of the reductions in market value and is considering them to be permanent; therefore, the reductions are recognized in the quarter in which they occur. No recognition is required if the reductions are anticipated to be temporary, with recovery by year-end.

Figure 14-9 presents the calculations needed to adjust the Inventory account of Peerless Products to the lower of cost or market. At the end of the first quarter, the inventory is written down by $24,000, and a loss is recognized on the interim income statement. Many companies report this write-down as part of their cost of goods sold because it is associated with inventory. By the end of the second quarter an additional write-down of $6,000 is required. The third-quarter interim report shows a loss recovery of $4,000 due to an increase in inventory replacement costs. Note that this is a recovery of valuation losses recognized in prior quarters. In quarter 4, the market price of $11 is $1 higher than the initial cost of the inventory. A $6,000 loss recovery on the ending inventory of the 2,000 units is recognized to bring the inventory valuation from $7 per unit to its original cost of

FIGURE 14-9 Interim lower-of-cost-or-market analysis of the Inventory account of Peerless Products Corp.

		Inventory		
Quarter	Item	Units	Unit Price	Dollars
	Balance, beginning of year	10,000	$10	$100,000
1	Inventory sold, first quarter	(2,000)	$10	(20,000)
	Adjustment to market:			
	[8,000 units × ($10 − $7)]	8,000	(3)	(24,000)
	Balance, end of first quarter	8,000	$ 7	$ 56,000
2	Inventory sold, second quarter	(2,000)	$ 7	(14,000)
	Adjustment to market:			
	[6,000 units × ($7 − $6)]	6,000	(1)	(6,000)
	Balance, end of second quarter	6,000	$ 6	$ 36,000
3	Inventory sold, third quarter	(2,000)	$ 6	(12,000)
	Market price recovery:			
	[4,000 units × ($6 − $7)]	4,000	1	4,000
	Balance, end of third quarter	4,000	$ 7	$ 28,000
4	Inventory sold, fourth quarter	(2,000)	$ 7	(14,000)
	Market price recovery:			
	[2,000 units × ($7 − $10)]	2,000	3	6,000
	Balance, end of fourth quarter	2,000	$10(a)	$ 20,000

(a) Note that although market value is $11, inventory valuation cannot exceed cost.

$10 per unit. Note that the inventory may not be valued at an amount in excess of cost.

A graphical representation of the market prices during the year is presented in Figure 14-10. Note that after decreasing during the first two quarters, the market price increases during the third and fourth quarters. At year-end, the price is $11 per unit, which is above the initial cost for the inventory.

Another way to view the effects of the write-downs is to compute the amount that would be reported in each quarter's cost of goods sold. This amount would include the costs assigned to the goods sold during the quarter plus the effects of any inventory write-downs and less the effects of any recoveries of losses recognized in prior interim periods. These market adjustments are normally treated as adjustments of cost of goods sold in order to represent all the product costs in one location on the income statement. The following table shows the computation of cost of goods sold for each quarter:

Quarter	Costs Assigned to Goods Sold	Ending Inventory Write-Down to Market or (Loss Recovery)	Total
1	2,000 units × $10	8,000 units × $3	$44,000
2	2,000 units × $7	6,000 units × $1	20,000
3	2,000 units × $6	(4,000 units × $1)	8,000
4	2,000 units × $7	(2,000 units × $3)	8,000

If the reductions in market value in quarters 1 and 2 were considered temporary, no write-downs need to be recognized and therefore no loss recoveries would be recognized in quarters 3 and 4. The total of the cost of goods sold reported for the interims must reconcile to the amount reported on the annual financial statements. Note that the year-end market price ($11) is greater than the market price at the beginning of the year ($10). On the annual statement:

$$8,000 \text{ units} \times \$10 \text{ unit price} = \$80,000$$

FIGURE 14-10 Graph of market prices of inventory.

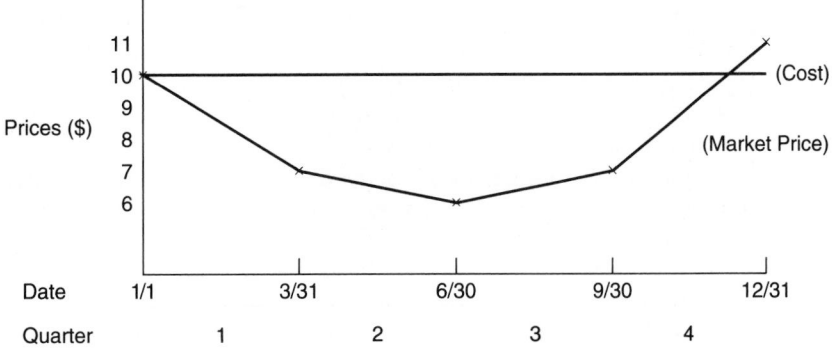

On the interim statements:

Quarter 1	$44,000
Quarter 2	20,000
Quarter 3	8,000
Quarter 4	8,000
Total	$80,000

In order to focus on the main points of the example, it was assumed that no additional inventory was acquired during the year. Of course, in actual practice, most companies do make continuous inventory acquisitions. These purchases would be added to inventory at whatever cost flow method was used by the company. The lower-of-cost-or-market valuation method would be applied at the end of each quarter in the same manner as in the example, and the losses or loss recoveries would be recognized.

All Other Costs and Expenses

The integral view adopted by the APB is most evident when dealing with period costs. A number of allocations and estimates are required for dealing with these costs, as follows:

> Costs and expenses other than product costs should be charged to income in interim periods as incurred, or be allocated among interim periods based on an estimate of time expired, benefit received or activity associated with the periods.[15]

The choice between immediate recognition of the expenditure on the interim period's income statement and deferral and allocation to several periods' interim income statements is based on a subjective evaluation of the periods that benefit by the expenditure. Although most expenditures are charged to the interim period in which they are incurred, the following examples illustrate when an expenditure may be deferred and allocated to several periods:[16]

1. Some costs such as major machinery repairs are expensed for annual reporting purposes but clearly benefit more than one interim period. Such costs should be deferred and allocated to the interim periods that benefit from the expenditure.

2. Quantity discounts offered to customers based on annual sales should be estimated and charged to sales during each of the interim periods rather than being recognized only in the fourth interim period.

3. Property taxes should be deferred or accrued to ensure an appropriate allocation to each interim period.

4. Major advertising costs may be deferred in the period incurred and allocated to the other interim periods that benefit. The allocation may be made on the basis

---

[15] *APB 28*, par. 15.
[16] Ibid., par. 16.

of the expected sales volume in each interim period that benefits from the advertising.

Illustration of Deferral and Allocation of Advertising Costs   On April 1, the beginning of the second quarter of Peerless Products and Subsidiary's consolidated fiscal year, a cost of $20,000 was incurred for an advertising campaign expected to benefit the last three quarters of the current year. Consolidated sales for the second, third, and fourth quarters are expected to total $400,000. Consolidated interim statements are prepared as of March 31, June 30, September 30, and December 31. No advertising expense was shown in the first interim period ending March 31, and the only advertising cost during the year is the $20,000 incurred on April 1.

The $20,000 cost is recorded as a prepaid asset when incurred and then charged to Advertising Expense in each of the interim periods benefited, as shown in Figure 14-11. The allocation base selected is the quarterly sales in the periods benefited as a percentage of the estimated total sales for the period of benefit.

At the beginning of the third quarter (July 1), $15,000 of advertising cost remains in Prepaid Advertising. If actual quarterly sales differ from the estimated amounts, then the allocation procedure is revised for the change in estimate. For example, if on September 30, management determines the consolidated sales for the third quarter, ending on September 30, to be $120,000 and estimates that fourth-quarter sales will be $180,000, then the remaining balance of $15,000 in Prepaid Advertising is allocated to the third quarter as follows:

$$\$6,000 = \frac{\$120,000}{\$300,000} \times \$15,000$$

The fourth quarter is charged for any remaining balance in the Prepaid Advertising account.

FIGURE 14-11 Accounting for advertising costs that benefit more than one interim period.

Date	Quarterly Sales	Debit Advertising Expense	Credit Prepaid Advertising	Balance in Prepaid Advertising
April 1				$20,000
June 30	$100,000	$ 5,000(a)	$ 5,000	15,000(b)
September 30	100,000	5,000	5,000	10,000
December 31	200,000	10,000	10,000	-0-
Totals	$400,000	$20,000	$20,000	

(a) $5,000 = ($100,000/$400,000) × $20,000.
(b) $15,000 = $20,000 − $5,000.

Accounting for Income Taxes in Interim Periods

The *interim income tax* computation poses a particularly troublesome problem for accountants because the actual tax burden is computed on income for the entire fiscal year. In addition, temporary differences between tax accounting and GAAP accounting require the recognition of deferred taxes. Nevertheless, the interim tax provision is a significant item and requires estimates and a number of subjective evaluations based on the anticipated annual tax. The first step is to determine the effective annual tax rate for use in computing the interim income tax provision.

Estimating the Annual Effective Tax Rate   Estimates are a normal part of the accounting cycle, and the interim income tax provision is based on an estimate of the annual tax rate, as follows:

> At the end of each interim period the company should make its best estimate of the effective tax rate expected to be applicable for the full fiscal year. The rate so determined should be used in providing for income taxes on a current year-to-date basis. The effective tax rate should reflect anticipated . . . tax credits, foreign tax rates, percentage depletion, capital gains rates, and other available tax planning alternatives. However, in arriving at this effective tax rate no effect should be included for the tax related to significant unusual or extraordinary items that will be separately reported or reported net of their related tax effect in reports for the interim period or for the fiscal year.[17]

The estimate of the annual rate is updated each interim period. The effective rate includes all available tax credits and rate adjustments. Items such as unusual or infrequent events, discontinued operations, cumulative effects of accounting changes, and extraordinary items should be treated separately along with their related tax effects. The reporting process is illustrated below.

Illustration of Estimating Annual Effective Tax Rate   Figure 14-12 illustrates the computation of the tax rate. While proceeding through the example note the adjustments, such as the differences between tax accounting and GAAP accounting, necessary to determine the annual rate. Following are data for the illustration:

1. Peerless Products and its subsidiary expect to earn consolidated income from continuing operations of $225,000 for the 19X1 fiscal year.

2. Permanent differences between accounting income and tax income are expected to be $2,000 for goodwill amortization and an exclusion of $27,000 for dividends received from investments in stocks of other companies.

3. The combined federal and state income tax rate is estimated to be 38 percent (30 percent federal and 8 percent state), and the company expects to be eligible for a $22,000 business tax credit related to new job development expenditures and employee retraining costs.

---

[17] *APB 28*, par. 19.

FIGURE 14-12 Estimation of annual effective tax rate.

	Estimated Annual Amounts
Income from continuing operations	$225,000
Adjust for permanent differences:	
Add goodwill amortization	2,000
Deduct dividends received exclusion	(27,000)
Estimated annual taxable income	$200,000
Combined federal and state income taxes	× 38%
Estimated annual taxes before tax credits	$ 76,000
Deduct business tax credit	(22,000)
Estimated income taxes for year	$ 54,000
Divide by estimated annual income from continuing operations	$225,000
Estimated effective annual tax rate on continuing operations ($54,000 ÷ $225,000)	24%

The estimated effective tax rate of 24 percent computed in Figure 14-12 is used to determine the income tax provision for the first quarter. Assuming the first-quarter earnings were $20,000, the following entry records the tax provision:

```
(3)  Income Tax Expense                    4,800
         Income Taxes Payable                       4,800
     Record first-quarter tax provision:
     $4,800 = $20,000 × .24 effective tax rate
```

Updating the Annual Estimated Rate in Subsequent Interim Periods Assume that second-quarter actual earnings are $25,000, for a cumulative total for the year to date of $45,000 ($20,000 + $25,000). The consolidated entity must first recompute its estimate of its effective annual tax rate based on the updated information it has at the end of the second quarter, such as additional differences between taxable and accounting income or a better estimate of projected annual earnings. Assuming the new estimated effective annual tax rate is 34 percent because of changes in the estimated amount of the available business tax credit and other changes in estimates, this rate replaces the 24 percent rate used at the end of the first quarter.

The new estimated tax rate is used to compute the estimated year-to-date income tax provision at the end of the second interim period, as follows:

Actual cumulative income for first two quarters ($20,000 + $25,000)	$45,000
Updated estimated effective annual tax rate	× .34
Cumulative income tax provision (expense)	$15,300
Less: Income tax provision made in first quarter	(4,800)
Income tax provision required in second quarter	$10,500

Peerless Products and its subsidiary report an income tax expense of $10,500 on the second-quarter consolidated income statement. The tax provision is cumulative, and the first quarter's provision is *not* retroactively restated for the change in the estimate of the annual tax rate.

The example does not include any temporary differences between accounting income and taxable income that result in deferred taxes. Temporary differences do *not* affect the estimate of the tax provision. Instead, the recognition of any temporary difference is made in the entry to record the tax provision and associated tax liability. For example, if $2,000 of the second-quarter income of $25,000 is due to a temporary difference in which accounting income is greater than tax income, the following entry would be made to recognize the provision and deferral:

```
(4)  Income Tax Expense                          10,500
         Deferred Tax Liability                              680
         Income Taxes Payable                             9,820
     Record second-quarter tax provision:
     $680 = $2,000 × .34 updated effective tax rate
```

Losses and Operating Loss Carrybacks and Carryforwards   An interesting problem is presented to accountants when a company has a year-to-date loss as of the end of an interim period. Normally, an operating loss creates a tax benefit (that is, reduces tax payable) because the loss can be carried back against the operating income shown in previous years and the company may file a claim for a refund of taxes paid in prior years. After the carryback portion of an operating loss is depleted, any remaining operating loss is carried forward against future operating income. These carryback and carryforward provisions, however, apply only to annual results, not to interim results.

These and other special tax problems are discussed in **FIN 18**. The first part of the interpretation deals with the numerous alternative income trends possible, such as an operating loss for year to date but income anticipated for the year, or operating income for year to date but loss expected for the year. The possible combinations of interim and annual results are too numerous to show here, but one special case is covered. This special case is the determination of the tax benefit for a company with a year-to-date operating loss but with the expectation of an annual income. The issue is how to determine and report the income tax for the interim periods.

FASB Statement No. 106, "Accounting for Income Taxes" (FASB 106), also addresses the issue of accounting for income taxes in an interim period. **FASB 106** affirms the general rule that the realization of a tax benefit must be assured beyond a reasonable doubt before the benefit may be recognized in the financial statements.[18] The assurance needed to recognize a tax benefit on interim statements is described as follows:[19]

[18] *Financial Accounting Standards Board Statement No. 106*, "Accounting for Income Taxes," 1992, pars. 190–195.

[19] *Financial Accounting Standards Board Interpretation No. 18*, "Accounting for Income Taxes in Interim Periods," 1977, par. 18.

1. Prior periods of income are present against which the current loss can be applied as a loss carryback.

2. Tax credits are available (for example, a business tax credit) at a sufficient level to offset the tax effect of the operating loss.

3. The company has established seasonal patterns of income in subsequent interim periods.

In any of these three cases, the company can recognize a tax benefit of a to-date operating loss. If the realization of the tax benefit of an operating loss is not assured, then the company cannot show any tax benefit on the interim statements.

Illustration of Interim Operating Loss Figure 14-13 presents the computation of the tax or benefit that should be shown on the interim statements if a company experiences a year-to-date loss but anticipates an annual income. For example, assume that the consolidated entity of Peerless Products Corporation and Special Foods, Inc., has an actual first-quarter loss of $40,000 but expects an annual income of $222,000. The estimated annual tax rate is 24 percent. The consolidated entity has a normal seasonal variation of losses in the first quarter followed by profits in subsequent quarters. Therefore, the tax benefit of the operating loss of $9,600 ($40,000 × .24) is assured beyond a reasonable doubt, and the tax benefit is shown in the loss quarter.

A partial income statement for the first quarter is presented below. Note how the tax benefit reduces the reported net loss.

Peerless Products and Special Foods
Partial Interim Consolidated Income Statement
First Quarter Ended March 31, 19X1

Operating Loss before Income Tax Effect	$(40,000)
Less: Tax Benefit of Operating Loss	9,600
Net Loss	$(30,400)

FIGURE 14-13 Interim analysis when tax benefit of operating loss is assured.

Reporting Period	Continuing Income (Loss) before Taxes — Reporting Period	Year-to-Date	Estimated Annual Effective Tax Rate, %	Tax or (Benefit) — Year-to-Date[a]	Less Previously Provided	Reported in Period
First quarter	$ (40,000)	$ (40,000)	24	$(9,600)		$ (9,600)
Second quarter	20,000	(20,000)	34	(6,800)	$(9,600)	2,800
Third quarter	80,000	60,000	34	20,400	(6,800)	27,200
Fourth quarter	162,000	222,000	27.9[b]	62,000	20,400	41,600
Fiscal year	$222,000					$62,000

[a] Year-to-date: continuing income (loss) × estimated annual effective tax rate.
[b] Rounded off.

FIGURE 14-14 Interim analysis when operating loss benefit is not assured.

Reporting Period	Continuing Income (Loss) before Taxes		Estimated Annual Effective Tax Rate, %	Tax or (Benefit)		
	Reporting Period	Year-to-Date		Year-to-Date	Less Previously Provided	Reported in Period
First quarter	$ (40,000)	$ (40,000)		$ -0-		$ -0-
Second quarter	20,000	(20,000)		-0-	$ -0-	-0-
Third quarter	80,000	60,000	34	20,400	-0-	20,400
Fourth quarter	162,000	222,000	27.9	62,000	20,400	41,600
Fiscal year	$222,000					$62,000

As shown earlier in Figure 14-2, Peerless Products and Subsidiary's actual annual income tax provision for 19X1 was $62,000. The year-to-date tax provision in the fourth quarter should equal the total actual annual provision, and the amount of tax reported in the fourth quarter is the balance necessary to reach the amount of the annual provision. Therefore, the actual annual income tax rate on continuing income for 19X1 was 27.9% ($62,000 annual tax provision ÷ $222,000 annual income from continuing operations before the deduction for income to non-controlling interest).

If the realizability of the tax benefit from the operating loss is not assured beyond a reasonable doubt, then no tax benefit should be shown. This case is presented in Figure 14-14. Note that the actual annual provisions are identical; the differences are in the interim presentations.

Disposal of a Segment or Extraordinary, Unusual, Infrequently Occurring, and Contingent Items

APB 28 requires the measurement and reporting of major nonoperating items on the same basis as used to prepare the annual report. In addition, unusual and infrequently occurring items must be separately noted to highlight their nonordinary nature. The interim accounting for these items is presented in the following provision:

Extraordinary items should be disclosed separately and included in the determination of net income for the interim period in which they occur. In determining materiality, extraordinary items should be related to the estimated income for the full fiscal year. Effects of disposals of a segment of a business and unusual and infrequently occurring transactions and events that are material with respect to the operating results of the interim period . . . should be reported separately. . . . Extraordinary items, gains or losses from disposal of a segment of a business, and unusual or infrequently occurring items should not be prorated over the balance of the fiscal year.[20]

[20] *APB 28*, par. 21.

Contingencies or other major uncertainties that could affect the company must also be disclosed on the same basis as that used in the annual report. This disclosure is required to provide information on items that might affect the fairness of the interim report. The procedures for measuring and reporting contingencies in both interim and annual reports are presented in **FASB Statement No. 5**, "Accounting for Contingencies" (FASB 5).

ACCOUNTING CHANGES IN INTERIM PERIODS

Accounting for changes in accounting principles or estimates should be presented in interim reports in the same manner as in annual reports. **APB 20** provides the guidelines for treatments of changes in annual reports. Changes in estimates are handled currently and prospectively, that is, from the change date forward in time, because estimates are a normal part of the accounting process.

Changes in accounting principles present additional problems because of the different methods used to present various types of changes. The alternatives are (1) cumulative effect changes, such as a change in depreciation method, (2) retroactive adjustment changes, such as a change *from* the lifo method of inventory pricing, and (3) special exceptions, such as a change *to* the lifo inventory method. **FASB Statement No. 3**, "Reporting Accounting Changes in Interim Financial Statements" (FASB 3), embraces the general recommendation that accounting changes, if made, should be made during the first interim period of a fiscal year.

Cumulative Effect Accounting Changes

Consistent with the view that all accounting changes should be made effective as of the beginning of the fiscal period, the cumulative effect of the accounting change on retained earnings is computed at the beginning of the fiscal year and reported in the first interim period's income statement. If a cumulative effect type of change is made during an interim period subsequent to the first one, the prior interim reports must be restated as if the change had been made effective as of the first day of the fiscal year. The effect of this provision is to make all changes effective as of the beginning of the fiscal period and to use the new accounting method to present all the interim reports for the fiscal year. Pro forma earnings per share figures are required to allow comparison with prior years' interim income statements.

Retroactive-Type Accounting Changes

If a change in accounting principle requires the restatement of prior years' financial statements, it also requires the restatement of previously issued interim financial statements in the same manner as for the annual statements. For example if a company acquires a subsidiary in the third quarter and consolidates it on a pooling of interests basis, the first two quarters' interim reports, as well as the previous years' interims, should be restated to reflect the pooling.

Adoption of LIFO

In the case of the adoption of lifo, neither the cumulative effect nor the necessary pro forma information is usually available on an annual basis. However, for interim reporting purposes, the change to lifo should be made effective as of the first interim period of the fiscal year of the change. If the change is actually made in a later interim period, such as the third quarter of the year, the previously issued interim reports must be restated as if the lifo inventory method had been adopted as of the beginning of the fiscal year.

SUMMARY OF KEY CONCEPTS AND TERMS

Segment disclosures about the specific industries of an entity and foreign areas in which an entity operates provide information about the different risks and profitability of each of the individual components that the entity comprises. These additional disclosures are useful in assessing past performance and prospects of future performance. A critical issue is the definition of a segment. The FASB allows management the flexibility it needs to disaggregate its operations but imposes several significance tests to determine which segments are separately reportable.

Interim reports must be issued by publicly held corporations so users of the information can assess corporate performance and make predictions about results for the annual fiscal period. The major issues are the measurement and disclosure problems of breaking down the annual reporting period into smaller parts. The FASB selected the integral theory of interim reporting, which views an interim period as an integral part of an annual period. Many of the technical problems revolve around cost of goods sold and income taxes. Estimates based on expected annual results are allowed when determining both of these costs. Even with the estimation and measurement problems, interim reports are primary disclosure vehicles that are quickly and carefully evaluated by investors and other users of financial statements.

Discrete theory of interim reporting
Dominant industry segment test
Identifiable assets
Integral theory of interim reporting
Interim income tax
Interim reports

Maximum number of reportable
 segments test
Reportable industry segments
75 percent revenue test
10 percent significance rules

QUESTIONS

Q14-1 How might information on a company's operations in different industries be helpful to investors?

Q14-2 What is the relationship between the FASB's definition of an industry segment and a company's profit centers?

Q14-3 What are the three 10 percent significance tests used to determine reportable segments under **FASB 14**? Give the numerator and denominator for each of the tests.

Q14-4 Specifically, what information is excluded from the determination of a segment's operating profit or loss? Why do you think the FASB excluded these items?

Q14-5 A company has 10 industry segments, of which the largest 5 account for 80 percent of the combined revenues of the company. What considerations are important in determining the number of segments that are separately reportable? How are the remaining segments reported?

Q14-6 What are the special rules for determining the revenue, operating profit or loss, and identifiable assets of financing segments?

Q14-7 Only two significance tests are used to determine separately reportable foreign operations. What are these two tests? Why isn't the third test used to assess foreign operations?

Q14-8 What information must be disclosed about a company's export sales? Where is this information disclosed in the annual report?

Q14-9 What information must be disclosed about a company's major customers? Are the names of customers disclosed?

Q14-10 How can interim reports be used by investors to identify a company's seasonal trends?

Q14-11 Distinguish between the discrete and integral views of interim reporting. Which view is used in **APB Opinion No. 28**?

Q14-12 How is revenue recognized on an interim basis?

Q14-13 Describe the basic rules for computing cost of goods sold and inventory on an interim basis. In what circumstances are estimates permitted to determine costs?

Q14-14 How does the application of the lower-of-cost-or-market valuation method for inventories differ between interim statements and annual statements?

Q14-15 How might the accounting for an advertising campaign expenditure of $200,000 in the first quarter of a company's fiscal year differ between the integral theory and the discrete theory of interim reporting?

Q14-16 Describe the process of updating the estimate of the effective tax rate in the second quarter of a company's fiscal year.

Q14-17 How is the tax benefit of an interim period's operating loss treated if the future realizability of the tax benefit is *not* assured beyond a reasonable doubt?

Q14-18 How are extraordinary items reported on an interim basis?

Q14-19 The Allied Company made a change in depreciation accounting during the third quarter of its fiscal year. This change is a cumulative effect type of accounting change. Describe the effect of this accounting change on prior interim reports and on the third quarter's interim report.

CASES

C14-1 Segment Disclosures [CMA Adapted]

Chemax, Inc., manufactures a wide variety of pharmaceuticals, medical instruments, and other related medical supplies. Eighteen months ago the company developed and began to market a new product line of antihistamine drugs under various trade names. Sales and profitability of this product line during the current fiscal year greatly exceeded management's expectations. The new product line will account for 10 percent of the company's total sales and 12 percent of the company's operating income for the fiscal year ending June 30, 19X0. Management believes sales and profits will be significant for several years.

Chemax is concerned that its market share and competitive position may suffer if it discloses the volume and profitability of its new product line in its annual financial statements. Management is not sure how **FASB 14**, ''Financial Reporting for Segments of a Business Enterprise,'' applies in this case.

Required

a. What is the purpose of requiring segment information in financial statements?

b. Identify and explain the factors that should be considered when attempting to decide how products should be grouped to determine a single business segment.

c. What options, if any, does Chemax, Inc., have with the disclosure of its new antihistamine product line? Explain your answer.

C14-2 Matching Revenue and Expenses for Interim Periods

Periodic reporting adds complexity to accounting by requiring estimates, accruals, deferrals, and allocations. Interim reporting creates even greater difficulties in matching revenue and expenses.

Required

a. Explain how revenue, product costs, gains, and losses should be recognized for interim periods.

b. Explain how determination of cost of goods sold and inventory differs for interim period reports versus annual reports.

c. Explain the treatment of period costs at interim dates.

d. Explain the treatment of the following items for interim financial statements:
   (1) Long-term contracts
   (2) Advertising
   (3) Seasonal revenue
   (4) Flood loss
   (5) Annual major repairs and maintenance to plant and equipment during the last 2 weeks in December

EXERCISES

E14-1 Reportable Segments

Amalgamated Products has seven industry segments. Data on the segments are as follows:

Segments	Revenues	Operating Profit (Loss)	Identifiable Assets
Electronics	$ 42,000	$ (8,600)	$ 73,000
Bicycles	105,000	30,400	207,000
Sporting Goods	53,000	(4,900)	68,000
Home Appliances	147,000	23,000	232,000
Gas & Oil Equipment	186,000	11,700	315,000
Glassware	64,000	(19,100)	96,000
Hardware	178,000	38,600	194,000
	$775,000	$71,100	$1,185,000

Included in the $105,000 revenue of the Bicycles segment are sales of $25,000 made to the Sporting Goods segment.

Required

   a. Indicate which segments are reportable.
   b. Do the reportable segments include a sufficient portion of total revenue? Explain.

E14-2 Multiple-Choice Questions on Segment Reporting [AICPA Adapted]

Select the correct answer for each of the following questions.

   1. Barbee Corporation discloses supplementary industry segment information for its two reportable segments. Data for 19X2 are available as follows:

	Segment E	Segment W
Sales	$750,000	$250,000
Traceable operating expenses	325,000	130,000

Additional 19X2 expenses are as follows:

Indirect operating expenses	$120,000
General corporate expenses	100,000

Appropriately selected common expenses are allocated to segments based on the ratio of each segment's sales to total sales. The 19X2 operating profit for Segment E was:
   a. $260,000.
   b. $335,000.
   c. $395,000.
   d. $425,000.

   2. The profitability information that should be reported for each reportable segment of a business enterprise consists of:
   a. An operating profit or loss figure consisting of segment revenue less traceable costs and allocated common costs.
   b. An operating profit or loss figure consisting of segment revenue less traceable costs but not allocated common costs.
   c. An operating profit or loss figure consisting of segment revenue less allocated common costs but not traceable costs.
   d. Segment revenue only.

   3. Dutko Co. has three lines of business, each of which is a significant industry segment. Company sales aggregated $1,800,000 in 19X2, of which Segment 3 contributed 60 percent. Traceable costs were $600,000 for Segment 3 from a total of $1,200,000 for the company as a whole. In addition, $350,000 of common costs are allocated in the ratio of a segment's income before common costs to the total income before common costs. For Segment 3 Dutko should report a 19X2 operating profit of:
   a. $200,000.
   b. $270,000.
   c. $280,000.

d. $480,000.

e. None of the above.

4. The Stein Company is a diversified company that discloses supplemental financial information on its industry segments. The following information is available for 19X2:

	Sales	Traceable Costs	Allocable Costs
Segment A	$400,000	$225,000	
Segment B	300,000	240,000	
Segment C	200,000	135,000	
Totals	$900,000	$600,000	$150,000

Allocable costs are assigned based on the ratio of a segment's income before allocable costs to total income before allocable costs. This is an appropriate method of allocation. The operating profit for Segment B for 19X2 is:

a. $0.

b. $10,000.

c. $30,000.

d. $50,000.

e. None of the above.

5. Selected data for a segment of a business enterprise are to be reported separately in accordance with **FASB 14** when the revenue of the segment exceeds 10 percent of the:

a. Combined net income of all segments' reporting profits.

b. Total revenue obtained in transactions with outsiders.

c. Total revenue of all the enterprise's industry segments.

d. Total combined revenue of all segments reporting profits.

6. Kimber Company operates in four different industries, each of which is appropriately regarded as a reportable segment. Total sales for 19X2 for all segments combined were $1,000,000. Sales for Segment 2 were $400,000, and the traceable costs were $150,000. Total common costs for all the segments combined were $500,000. Kimber allocates common costs based on the ratio of a segment's sales to total sales, an appropriate method of allocation. The operating profit to be reported for Segment 2 for 19X2 is:

a. $50,000.

b. $125,000.

c. $200,000.

d. $250,000.

e. None of the above.

7. The following information pertains to Reding Corporation for the year ended December 31, 19X3:

Sales to unaffiliated customers	$2,000,000
Intersegment sales of products similar to those sold to unaffiliated customers	600,000
Interest earned on loans to other industry segments	40,000

All of Reding's segments are engaged solely in manufacturing operations. Reding has a reportable segment if that segment's revenue exceeds:
a. $264,000.
b. $260,000.
c. $204,000.
d. $200,000.

8. In financial reporting for segments of a business enterprise, the operating profit or loss of a segment should include:
a. Federal income taxes.
b. Interest expense even though a segment's operations are not principally of a financial nature.
c. Revenue earned at the corporate level.
d. Common costs allocated on a reasonable basis.

9. In financial reporting for segments of a business enterprise, which of the following assets should be included as an identifiable asset of Segment A?
a. An intangible asset used by Segment A.
b. An advance from a nonfinancial segment to another segment.
c. An allocation of a tangible asset used for general corporate purposes and *not* used in the operations of any particular segment.
d. An allocation of a tangible asset used by another segment that transfers products to industry Segment A.

10. Snow Corporation's revenue for the year ended December 31, 19X2, was as follows:

Consolidated revenue per income statement	$1,200,000
Intersegment sales	180,000
Intersegment transfers	60,000
Combined revenue of all industry segments	$1,440,000

Snow has a reportable industry segment if that segment's revenue exceeds:
a. $6,000.
b. $24,000.
c. $120,000.
d. $144,000.

11. Porter Corporation is engaged solely in manufacturing operations. The following data (consistent with prior years' data) pertain to the industries in which operations were conducted for the year ended December 31, 19X1:

Industry Segment	Total Revenue	Operating Profit	Identifiable Assets at 12/31/X1
A	$10,000,000	$1,750,000	$20,000,000
B	8,000,000	1,400,000	17,500,000
C	6,000,000	1,200,000	12,500,000
D	3,000,000	550,000	7,500,000
E	4,250,000	675,000	7,000,000
F	1,500,000	225,000	3,000,000
	$32,750,000	$5,800,000	$67,500,000

In its segment information for 19X1, how many reportable segments does Porter have?
a. Three.
b. Four.
c. Five.
d. Six.

12. Boecker is a multidivisional corporation which has both intersegment sales and sales to unaffiliated customers. Boecker should report segment financial information for each segment meeting which of the following criteria?
a. Segment operating profit or loss is 10 percent or more of consolidated profit or loss.
b. Segment operating profit or loss is 10 percent or more of combined operating profit or loss of all company segments.
c. Segment revenue is 10 percent or more of combined revenue of all company segments.
d. Segment revenue is 10 percent or more of consolidated revenue.

E14-3 Multiple-Choice Questions on Interim Reporting [AICPA Adapted]

Select the correct answer for each of the following questions.

1. In considering interim financial reporting, how did the Accounting Principles Board conclude that such reporting should be viewed?
a. As a "special" type of reporting that need not follow generally accepted accounting principles.
b. As useful only if activity is evenly spread throughout the year so that estimates are unnecessary.
c. As reporting for a basic accounting period.
d. As reporting for an integral part of an annual period.

2. Which of the following is an inherent difficulty in determining the results of operations on an interim basis?
a. Cost of sales reflects only the amount of product expense allocable to revenue recognized as of the interim date.
b. Depreciation on an interim basis is a partial estimate of the actual annual amount.
c. Costs expensed in one interim period may benefit other periods.
d. Revenue from long-term construction contracts accounted for by the percentage-of-completion method is based on annual completion, and interim estimates may be incorrect.

3. Which of the following reporting practices is permissible for interim financial reporting?
a. Use of the gross profit method for interim inventory pricing.
b. Use of the direct costing method for determining manufacturing inventories.
c. Deferral of unplanned variances under a standard cost system until year-end.
d. Deferral of non-temporary inventory market declines until year-end.

4. On January 1, 19X2, Harris, Inc., paid property taxes on its plant, for the calendar year 19X2, amounting to $40,000. In March 19X2, Harris made annual major repairs to its machinery amounting to $120,000. These repairs will benefit the entire calendar year's operations. How should these expenses be reflected in Harris's quarterly income statements?

	Three Months Ended:			
	March 31, 19X2	June 30, 19X2	September 30, 19X2	December 31, 19X2
a.	$ 22,000	$46,000	$46,000	$46,000
b.	40,000	40,000	40,000	40,000
c.	70,000	30,000	30,000	30,000
d.	160,000	-0-	-0-	-0-

5. An inventory loss from market decline of $420,000 occurred for the Wenger Company in April 19X2. The company recorded this loss in April 19X2 after its March 31, 19X2, quarterly report was issued. None of this loss was recovered by the end of the year. How should this loss be reflected in Wenger's quarterly income statements?

	Three Months Ended:			
	March 31, 19X2	June 30, 19X2	September 30, 19X2	December 31, 19X2
a.	$ -0-	$ -0-	$ -0-	$420,000
b.	-0-	140,000	140,000	140,000
c.	-0-	420,000	-0-	-0-
d.	105,000	105,000	105,000	105,000

6. A company that uses the last-in, first-out (lifo) method of inventory costing finds, at an interim reporting date, that there has been a partial liquidation of the base-period inventory level. The decline is considered temporary, and the base inventory will be replaced before year-end. The amount shown as inventory on the interim reporting date should:
   a. Not give effect to the lifo liquidation, and cost of sales for the interim reporting period should include the expected cost of replacement of the liquidated lifo base.
   b. Be shown at the actual level, and cost of sales for the interim reporting period should reflect the decrease in lifo base-period inventory level.
   c. Not give effect to the lifo liquidations, and cost of sales for the interim reporting period should reflect the decrease in the lifo base-period inventory level.
   d. Be shown at the actual level, and the decrease in inventory level should not be reflected in the cost of sales for the interim reporting period.

7. During the second quarter of 19X1, Camerton Company sold a piece of equipment at a $12,000 gain. What portion of the gain should Camerton report in its income statement for the second quarter of 19X1?
   a. $12,000.
   b. $6,000.
   c. $4,000.
   d. $0.

8. On March 15, 19X1, Burge Company paid propety taxes of $180,000 on its factory building for calendar year 19X1. On April 1, 19X1, Burge made $300,000 in unanticipated repairs to its plant equipment. The repairs will benefit operations for the remainder of the calendar year. What total amount of these expenses should be included in Burge's quarterly income statement for the 3 months ended June 30, 19X1?

a. $75,000.
b. $145,000.
c. $195,000.
d. $345,000.

9. The SRB Company had an inventory loss from a market price decline which occurred in the first quarter. The loss was not expected to be restored in the fiscal year. However, in the third quarter the inventory had a market price recovery that exceeded the first-quarter decline. For interim financial reporting, the dollar amount of net inventory should:
    a. Decrease in the first quarter by the amount of the market price decline and increase in the third quarter by the amount of the market price recovery.
    b. Decrease in the first quarter by the amount of the market price decline and increase in the third quarter by the amount of the decrease in the first quarter.
    c. Not be affected in the first quarter and increase in the third quarter by the amount of the market price recovery that exceeded the amount of the market price decline.
    d. Not be affected in either the first quarter or the third quarter.

10. For external reporting purposes, it is appropriate to use estimated gross profit rates to determine the cost of goods sold for:

	Interim Financial Reporting	Year-End Financial Reporting
a.	Yes	Yes
b.	Yes	No
c.	No	Yes
d.	No	No

E14-4 Temporary Lifo Liquidation

During June, Kissick Hardware, which uses a perpetual inventory system, sold 920 units from its lifo-base inventory, which had originally cost $12 per unit. The replacement cost is expected to be $21 per unit. Kissick is reducing inventory levels, and expects to replace only 640 of these units by December 31, the end of the fiscal year.

Required

a. Prepare the entry in June to record the sale of the 920 units.
b. Prepare the entry for the replacement of the 640 units in August at an actual cost of $19.80 per unit.

E14-5 Inventory Write-Down and Recovery

Comeback Co., a calendar-year entity, had 9,000 medical instruments in its beginning inventory for 19X2. On December 31, 19X1, the instruments had been adjusted down to $10.20 per unit, which was the lower of average cost or market, from an actual average cost of $10.55 per unit. No additional units were purchased during 19X2. The following additional information is provided for 19X2:

Quarter	Date	Inventory, (units)	Replacement Cost
1	March 31, 19X2	8,000	$10.10
2	June 30, 19X2	7,500	10.35
3	September 30, 19X2	6,000	9.90
4	December 31, 19X2	4,000	10.00

Required

Determine the cost of goods sold for each quarter, and verify the total cost of goods sold by computing annual cost of goods sold on a lower-of-cost-or-market basis.

E14-6 Multiple-Choice Questions on Income Taxes at Interim Dates
[AICPA Adapted]

Select the correct answer for each of the following questions.

1. According to **APB Opinion No. 28**, "Interim Financial Reporting," income tax expense in an income statement for the first interim period of an enterprise's fiscal year should be computed by:
   a. Applying the estimated income tax rate for the full fiscal year to the pretax accounting income for the interim period.
   b. Applying the estimated income tax rate for the full fiscal year to the taxable income for the interim period.
   c. Applying the statutory income tax rate to the pretax accounting income for the interim period.
   d. Applying the statutory income tax rate to the taxable income for the interim period.

2. Neil Company, which has a fiscal year ending January 31, had the following pretax accounting income and estimated effective annual income tax rates for the first three quarters of the year ended January 31, 19X2:

Quarter	Pretax Accounting Income	Estimated Effective Annual Income Tax Rate at End of Quarter, %
First	$60,000	40
Second	70,000	40
Third	40,000	45

Neil's income tax expenses in its interim income statement for the third quarter are:
   a. $18,000.
   b. $24,500.
   c. $25,500.
   d. $76,500.
   e. None of the above.

3. Beckett Corporation expects to sustain an operating loss of $100,000 for the full year ending December 31, 19X3. Beckett operates entirely in one jurisdiction, where the tax rate is 40 percent. Anticipated tax credits for 19X3 total $10,000. No permanent differences are expected. Realization of the full tax benefit of the expected operating

loss and realization of anticipated tax credits are assured beyond any reasonable doubt because they will be carried back. For the first quarter ended March 31, 19X3, Beckett reported an operating loss of $20,000. How much of a tax benefit should Beckett report for the interim period ended March 31, 19X3?

a. $0.

b. $8,000.

c. $10,000.

d. $12,500.

e. None of the above.

4. The computation of a company's third-quarter provision for income taxes should be based on earnings:

a. For the quarter at an expected annual effective income tax rate.

b. For the quarter at the statutory rate.

c. To date at an expected annual effective income tax rate less prior quarters' provisions.

d. To date at the statutory rate less prior quarters' provisions.

E14-7 Significant Foreign Operations

Information about the domestic and foreign operations of Conrad, Inc., is as follows:

	Geographic Area					
	United States	**Europe**	**South America**	**Israel**	**South Pacific**	**Total**
Sales to unaffiliated customers	$364,000	$252,000	$72,000	$58,000	$47,000	$ 793,000
Interarea sales between affiliates	38,000	19,000	6,000			63,000
Total revenue	$402,000	$271,000	$78,000	$58,000	$47,000	$ 856,000
Operating profit	$ 34,500	$ 22,500	$11,300	$ 3,200	$ 4,500	$ 76,000
Identifiable assets	$509,000	$439,000	$93,000	$66,000	$75,000	$1,182,000
Interarea loans	30,000	10,000				40,000
Total assets	$539,000	$449,000	$93,000	$66,000	$75,000	$1,222,000

Required

Prepare schedules showing appropriate tests to determine which geographic areas are significant.

E14-8 Major Customers

Sales by Knight, Inc., to major customers are as follows:

Customer	Sales
State of Illinois	$2,700,000
Cook County, Illinois	3,500,000
U.S. Treasury Department	3,900,000
U.S. Department of Defense	2,200,000
Bank of England	4,650,000
Philips NV	2,850,000
Honda	5,400,000

Required

If worldwide sales total $43,000,000 for the year, which of Knight's customers should be disclosed as major customers?

E14-9 Estimated Annual Tax Rates

Sword Orbit, Inc., estimates total federal and state tax rates to be 40 percent. Sword's first-quarter earnings are $200,000, and expected annual earnings are $1,200,000. For the year, goodwill amortization will be $50,000, premiums for life insurance on officers will be $10,000, and dividend exclusions are expected to be $70,000. A business tax credit of $40,000 should be available.

Required

    a. Estimate Sword Orbit's effective combined federal and state tax rate for the year.
    b. Prepare the entry to record the tax provision for the first quarter.

E14-10 Operating Loss Tax Benefits

Igloo Technology has a first-quarter operating loss of $150,000 and expects the following income for the other three quarters:

Second quarter	$100,000
Third quarter	300,000
Fourth quarter	450,000

Igloo estimated the effective annual tax rate at 45 percent at the end of the first quarter and changed it to 50 percent at the end of the third quarter. The company has a normal seasonal pattern of losses in the first quarter and income in the other quarters.

Required

Prepare a schedule computing the tax or tax benefits that should be shown on the interim statements.

E14-11 Disclosure Tests Including a Finance Segment

Badger Corporation has prepared the following data, in thousands of dollars, for its industry segments for the year ended December 31, 19X4:

	Textiles	Paper Goods	Finance	General Corporate
Revenues:				
Sales:				
Unaffiliated	$ 800	$ 400		
Intersegment	50	10		
Interest revenue:				
From external			$ 60	
From intersegment	10		40	
Income from equity				
investments				$ 30
Total revenue	$ 860	$ 410	$ 100	$ 30
Expenses:				
Cost of sales	$ 400	$ 180		
Depreciation	30	10	$ 10	$ 10
Other directly traceable costs	100	80	40	40
Allocated common costs	40	30	10	20
Interest expense:				
To external	5		30	10
To intersegment	20	30		
Income tax (benefit)	100	40	5	(20)
Net income	$ 165	$ 40	$ 5	$(30)
Asset data:				
Identifiable operating assets	$3,000	$2,000	$ 100	$ 50
Investments				120
Loans to external parties			500	
Intersegment loans	100		400	
Total assets	$3,100	$2,000	$1,000	$170

Required

a. Apply the three 10 percent significance tests to determine which of the segments are separately reportable.

b. Use the comprehensive disclosure tests to determine if the separately reportable segments comprise sufficient disclosure of Badger Corporation's industry segments.

E14-12 Industry Segment and Geographic Area Revenue Tests

The Symbiotic Chemical Company has four major industry segments and operates both in the U.S. domestic market and in several foreign markets. Information about its revenue from the specific industry segments and its foreign activities for the year 19X2 is as follows:

Sales to Unaffiliated Customers (in thousands)

Industry Segment	Domestic	Foreign	Total
Ethical Drugs	$300		$300
Nonprescription Drugs	325	$100	425
Generic Drugs	125	245	370
Industrial Chemicals	70		70

Sales to Affiliated Customers (in thousands)

Industry Segment	Domestic	Foreign	Total
Ethical Drugs	$20		$ 20
Nonprescription Drugs	50	$ 40	90
Generic Drugs	40	60	100
Industrial Chemicals	10		10

All the foreign revenues of the Nonprescription Drugs segment, both to unaffiliated and intersegment customers, were attributable to a Taiwanese division of the company. This division operates exclusively in the Asian geographic area, except for a sale of $10,000 from the division to a U.S. subsidiary of the company. All other foreign operations of the company take place exclusively within the Latin American countries.

Required

    a. Determine which of the company's industry segments are separately reportable under the revenue test for segment reporting.

    b. Determine which of the geographic areas (Domestic, Asian, and Latin American) are separately reportable under the revenue test for segment reporting.

    c. Prepare a schedule for disclosing the company's revenue by industry segment for 19X2.

    d. Prepare a schedule for disclosing the company's revenue by geographic area for 19X2.

E14-13 Different Reporting Methods for Interim Reports [CMA Adapted]

Listed below are six independent cases on how accounting facts might be reported on an individual company's interim financial reports.

    a. Bean Company was reasonably certain it would have an employee strike in the third quarter. As a result, the company shipped heavily during the second quarter but plans to defer the recognition of the sales in excess of the normal sales volume. The deferred sales will be recognized as sales in the third quarter when the strike is in progress. Bean Company management thinks this is more nearly representative of normal second- and third-quarter operations.

    b. Green, Inc., takes a physical inventory at year-end for annual financial statement purposes. Inventory and cost of sales reported in the interim quarterly statements are based on estimated gross profit rates because a physical inventory would result in a cessation of operations.

    c. ER Company is planning to report one-fourth of its annual pension expense each quarter.

d. Fair Corporation wrote down inventory to reflect the lower of cost or market in the first quarter of 19X1. At year-end, the market price exceeds the original acquisition cost of this inventory. Consequently, management plans to write the inventory back up to its original cost as a year-end adjustment.

e. Carson Company realized a large gain on the sale of investments at the beginning of the second quarter. The company wants to report one-third of the gain in each of the remaining quarters.

f. Ring Corporation has estimated its annual audit fee. Management plans to prorate this expense equally over all four quarters.

Required

For the six cases, state whether the method proposed for interim reporting is acceptable under generally accepted accounting principles applicable to interim financial data. Support each answer with a brief explanation.

PROBLEMS

P14-14 Segment Reporting Workpaper and Schedules

West Corporation reported the following consolidated data for 19X2:

Sales	$ 810,000
Consolidated income before taxes	128,000
Total assets	1,200,000

Data reported for West's four divisions are as follows:

	Division A	Division B	Division C	Division D
Sales to outsiders	$280,000	$130,000	$340,000	$60,000
Intersegment sales	60,000		18,000	12,000
Traceable costs	245,000	90,000	290,000	82,000
Identifiable assets	400,000	105,000	500,000	75,000

Intersegment sales are priced at cost and all goods have been subsequently sold to non-affiliates. Some joint production costs are allocated to the divisions based on total sales. These joint costs were $45,000 in 19X2. The company's corporate center had $20,000 of general corporate expenses and $120,000 of identifiable assets.

Required

Each question below is unrelated to the others.

a. The divisions are industry segments.
  (1) Prepare a segmental disclosure worksheet for the company.
  (2) Prepare schedules showing which segments are reportable.
b. Assume that each division operates in an individual geographic area and Division A is in

the domestic area and the other divisions operate in separate foreign areas. Prepare schedules showing which geographic areas are reportable.

c. Determine the amount of sales to an outside customer that would cause that outside customer to be classified as a major customer under the criteria of **FASB 14**.

P14-15 Segment Reporting Workpaper and Schedules

Calvin, Inc., has operating segments in five different industries: apparel, building, chemical, furniture, and machinery. Data for the five segments for 19X1 are as follows:

	Apparel	Building	Chemical	Furniture	Machinery
Sales to nonaffiliates	$870,000	$750,000	$55,000	$95,000	$180,000
Intersegment sales			5,000	15,000	140,000
Cost of goods sold	480,000	450,000	42,000	78,000	150,000
Selling expenses	160,000	40,000	10,000	20,000	30,000
Other traceable expenses	40,000	30,000	6,000	12,000	18,000
Allocated general corporate expenses	80,000	75,000	7,000	13,000	25,000
Identifiable assets	610,000	560,000	80,000	90,000	140,000
Depreciation expense	60,000	50,000	10,000	11,000	25,000
Capital expenditures	20,000	30,000			15,000

Additional information:

1. The corporate headquarters had general corporate expenses totaling $235,000. For internal reporting purposes $200,000 were allocated to the divisions based on their cost of goods sold.

2. Headquarters had assets of $125,000.

Required

a. Prepare a segmental disclosure workpaper for Calvin, Inc.

b. Prepare schedules to show which segments are separately reportable.

c. Prepare the information about the company's operations in different industry segments as required by **FASB 14**.

P14-16 Interim Income Statement

Chris, Inc., has accumulated information for its second-quarter income statement for 19X2:

Sales	$850,000
Cost of goods sold	420,000
Operating expenses	230,000

Additional information:

1. First-quarter income before taxes was $100,000, and the estimated effective annual tax rate was 40 percent. At the end of the second quarter, expected annual income is

$600,000, and a dividend exclusion of $30,000 and a business tax credit of $15,000 are anticipated. The combined state and federal tax rate is 50 percent.

2. The cost of goods sold of $420,000 is determined by the lifo method and includes 7,500 units from the base layer, at a cost of $12 per unit. However, you have determined that these units are expected to be replaced at a cost of $26 per unit.

3. The operating expenses of $230,000 include a $60,000 factory rearrangement cost incurred in April. You have determined that the second quarter will receive about 25 percent of the benefits from this project, with the remainder benefiting the third and fourth quarters.

Required

a. Calculate the expected annual effective tax rate at the end of the second quarter for Chris, Inc.

b. Prepare the income statement for the second quarter of 19X2. Your solution should include a computation of income tax (or benefit) with the following headings:

	Operating Income (Loss) before Taxes		Estimated	Tax (Benefit)		
Interim Period	Current Period	Year-to-Date	Annual Effective Tax Rate	Year-to-Date	Less Previously Provided	Reported in This Period

P14-17 Interim Income Statement

At the end of the second quarter of 19X1, Malta Corporation assembled the following information:

1. The first quarter resulted in a $90,000 loss before taxes. During the second quarter, sales were $1,200,000; purchases were $650,000; and operating expenses were $320,000.

2. Cost of goods sold is determined by the fifo method. The inventory at the end of the first quarter was reduced by $4,000 to a lower-of-cost-or-market figure of $78,000. During the second quarter, replacement costs recovered, and by the end of the period, market value exceeded the ending inventory cost by $1,250.

3. The ending inventory is estimated by the gross profit method. The estimated gross profit rate is 46 percent.

4. At the end of the first quarter, the effective annual tax rate was estimated at 45 percent. At the end of the second quarter, expected annual income is $600,000. An investment tax credit of $15,000 and goodwill amortization of $75,000 are expected for the year. The combined state and federal tax rate is 40 percent.

5. The tax benefits from operating losses are assured beyond a reasonable doubt. Prior years' income totaling $50,000 is available for operating loss carrybacks.

Required

a. Calculate the expected annual effective tax rate at the end of the second quarter for Malta Corporation.

b. Prepare the income statement for the second quarter of 19X1. Your solution should include a computation of income tax (or benefit) for the first and second quarters.

P14-18 Grouping Foreign Operations

For many years, the Clark Company operated exclusively in the United States, but recently it expanded its operations to the Pacific Rim countries of New Zealand, Singapore, and Australia. After a modest beginning in these countries, recent successes have resulted in an increased level of operations in each of these countries. The company is currently considering the method by which it should group its foreign operations. Alternatives considered include presenting all foreign activity as a single geographic area, grouping various geographic areas, and presenting each of the separately reportable segments and then disclosing the nonseparately reportable segment(s) as one group. Operating information (in thousands of U.S. dollars) for the company's domestic and foreign operations is presented below.

	U.S.	New Zealand	Singapore	Australia
Sales to unaffiliated	$2,500	$320	$ 60	$120
Interarea sales	100		10	
Operating expenses	1,820	290	70	30
Identifiable assets	2,200	280	140	80

In addition, common costs of $120,000 are to be allocated to operations on the basis of the ratio of an area's sales to nonaffiliates to total company sales to nonaffiliates.

Required

a. Determine the operating profit or loss for each geographic segment.
b. Determine if the company must separately report any of its foreign operations.
c. Determine which, if any, of the three individual foreign geographic segments is separately reportable.
d. Discuss the possible advantages or disadvantages of grouping the foreign segments into the following groups for purposes of determining the separately reportable geographic areas:
  (1) New Zealand, Singapore, and Australia as one group
  (2) New Zealand and Australia as one group
  (3) New Zealand and Singapore as one group
  (4) Singapore and Australia as one group

P14-19 Interim Accounting Changes

During the third quarter of its 19X2 fiscal year, the Square Q Company is considering the methods of accounting for accounting changes on its interim statements. Preliminary data are available for the third quarter of 19X2, ending on September 30, 19X2, prior to any adjustments required for any accounting changes. The company's tax rate is 40 percent of income. Selected interim data, in thousands of dollars, for the company are presented below:

Quarter Ended	Net Sales	Gross Profit	Earnings from Continuing Operations	Net Earnings
19X2				
March 31	$388	$133	$27	$26
June 30	406	135	30	35
September 30 (preliminary)	428	151	32	32
19X1:				
March 31	394	139	27	28
June 30	416	151	32	31
September 30	403	148	31	31
December 31	385	134	11	12

Required

For each of the following *independent* cases, present the comparative interim financial data for the company for the three quarters of 19X2, and the comparative data for 19X1, assuming that in a meeting on the last day of the third quarter of 19X2, the company decides to make an accounting change, as specified below.

a. The company decides to change to the lifo method of inventory. If the lifo method had been used as of January 1, 19X2, beginning inventories would have been $20,000 lower than reported. As of September 30, 19X2, the inventories would have been $32,000 lower under lifo. The $12,000 difference between January 1, 19X2, and September 30, 19X2, occurred evenly over the first three quarters of 19X2.

b. The company decides to switch from the straight-line method of depreciation to the accelerated method of depreciation. The accounting department has prepared the following schedule of data, in thousands of dollars, comparing straight-line and accelerated depreciation for each of the interim periods:

Quarter Ended	Straight-Line	Accelerated
19X2:		
March 31	$45	$45
June 30	45	44
September 30	45	42
19X1:		
March 31	40	50
June 30	40	48
September 30	40	47
December 31	40	45

The accounting department determined that there would be no difference in accumulated depreciation prior to January 1, 19X1.

c. The company decides to change its method of accounting for recognizing sales revenue on its long-term contracts. The company had been using the completed contract method, but changed to the percentage-of-completion method. The accounting department prepared an analysis of the sales and gross profit recognition under each of the two methods, in thousands of dollars, as follows:

	Completed Contract		Percentage-of-Completion	
Quarter Ended	**Sales**	**Gross Profit**	**Sales**	**Gross Profit**
19X2				
March 31	$ 80	$ 20	$60	$30
June 30	-0-	-0-	55	30
September 30	100	50	70	40
19X1				
March 31			60	40
June 30	150	100	40	20
September 30	-0-	-0-	50	30
December 31	60	40	50	30

P14-20 Interim Reporting and Accounting Changes [CMA Adapted]

The Locke Company is a publicly held manufacturing company whose fiscal year ends March 31. On December 1, 19X3, after several months of discussion and analysis, the management of Locke decided for financial reporting purposes to change from accelerated depreciation to straight-line depreciation and to increase the warranty expense accrual. These revisions are to be effective immediately, but they will not affect tax accounting procedures.

The table below presents the accelerated depreciation for the past two quarters and the estimated amount for the third quarter of the current fiscal year as reported for financial statement purposes. The table also presents the recalculated figures for the same periods under the straight-line method. The accumulated depreciation as of April 1, 19X3, amounted to $980,000 under the accelerated depreciation method but would have been only $700,000 if straight-line depreciation had been used.

Fiscal Quarter	**Accelerated Depreciation (actual amount used for financial reporting purposes)**	**Straight-Line Depreciation (recalculated amounts)**
Fiscal year 3/31/X4:		
First (4/1/X3–6/31/X3)	$62,000	$50,000
Second (7/1/X3–9/30/X3)	58,000	50,000
Third (10/1/X3–12/31/X3, estimated)	55,000	50,000

Locke Company has a 1-year warranty on its products. Management has been accruing warranty expense at the rate of 1.00 percent of net sales. The balance of the accrued warranty account as of April 1, 19X3, was $47,000. The data presented in the following table show the actual warranty accruals and expenditures for the past six quarters and the estimates for the current third quarter. Actual warranty expenditures have exceeded the accrual for future quarters if a 1.00 percent accrual rate continues to be used. Consequently, management has decided to increase the accrual rate to 1.25 percent of net sales effective with the third quarter of the current year:

Fiscal Quarter	Accrued Warranty Expenses at 1%	Actual Warranty Expenditures
Fiscal year 3/31/X3:		
First (4/1/X2–6/30/X2)	$40,000	$32,000
Second (7/1/X2–9/30/X2)	42,000	35,000
Third (10/1/X2–12/31/X2)	45,000	42,000
Fourth (1/1/X3–3/31/X3)	35,000	44,000
Fiscal year 3/31/X4:		
First (4/1/X3–6/30/X3)	43,000	47,000
Second (7/1/X3–9/30/X3)	46,000	55,000
Third (10/1/X3–12/31/X3, est.)	50,000	58,000

The estimated financial results and related earnings per share for the third quarter and for the 9 months ending December 31 for the current fiscal year are shown below. The third-quarter and 9-month data presented for the current fiscal year were compiled before the two accounting revisions were implemented. The company has issued only common stock and has no dilutive securities. One million shares of common stock have been outstanding for the past 2 years. Locke Company is subject to a 40 percent income tax rate.

	Fiscal Year Ending 3/31/X4	
	Third Quarter (10/1/X3–12/31/X3)	Nine Months (4/1/X3–12/31/X3)
Income before extraordinary items	$600,000	$1,500,000
Extraordinary loss, net of related income tax effect	400,000	1,000,000
Net income	$200,000	$ 500,000
Earnings per share:		
Earnings before extraordinary loss	$.60	$1.50
Extraordinary loss	.40	1.00
Net earnings	$.20	$ .50

Required

a. Discuss the disclosure requirements for current- and prior-year data which Locke Company would need to make in its interim financial statements as a consequence of the change in depreciation method and the increase in warranty expense accrual.

b. Locke Company will prepare and distribute to its stockholders interim financial statements at the end of the third quarter of the current fiscal year. These statements will present third-quarter and year-to-date data following generally accepted accounting procedures. Present the financial results and related earnings per share data as they would appear in the interim financial statments issued at the end of the third quarter, reflecting the change in depreciation method and the increase in warranty expense accrual. Explain your presentation completely, showing supporting calculations.

CHAPTER 15

SEC REPORTING

Since its creation in 1934, the Securities and Exchange Commission (SEC) has had a significant impact on the capital formation process by which companies obtain capital from investors. The SEC is an independent federal agency responsible for regulating securities markets, in which stocks and bonds of the major companies trade, and for the "full and fair disclosure" of financial information so investors may make informed investment decisions. The ability of companies to raise capital in the stock markets and the millions of shares that are traded daily are both indications of the SEC's success in maintaining an effective marketplace for companies issuing securities and for investors seeking capital investments.

HISTORY OF SECURITIES REGULATION

The need for regulation has gone hand in hand with the offering of securities to the general public. In the thirteenth century, King Edward I of England established a Court of Aldermen to regulate security trades in London. In the latter part of the eighteenth century, England's Parliament passed several acts, termed the Bubble Acts, to control questionable security schemes that had become popular. In 1790, the New York Stock Exchange was created to serve as a clearinghouse for securities trades between members of the exchange. The need for additional sources of capital paralleled the advent of the industrial revolution and the growth of commerce in the United States. Some individuals took advantage of this situation and offered securities of fictitious companies for sale to the general public or used financial reports that were not factual about the offering company's financial picture. In 1911, because of the lack of any federal security regulatory laws, several states began passing what were called "blue sky laws" to regulate the offering of securities by companies made up only of "blue sky," that is, which did not have a sound financial base.

The era of the 1920s was one of heavy stock speculation by many individuals. Business executives, cabdrivers, and assembly-line workers all wanted to participate in the many stock opportunities that existed at that time. Unfortunately, a number of abuses were occurring in the marketplace. For example, certain speculators sought to manipulate selected stock prices by issuing untrue press releases about companies' operations or managements. Companies were not required to be audited, and some of them issued false and misleading financial statements. Investors were using excessive amounts of margin; that is, they were borrowing heavily to invest in stocks. And some employees of companies were using inside information—information that had not been released to the public—to purchase or sell their company's stock for personal advantage.

The month of October, 1929, is often viewed as the beginning of the great depression. Stock prices plunged to record lows within just a few weeks as panic took over the market. It became obvious that some form of federal regulation was necessary in order to restore confidence in the stock market. The Federal Securities Acts of 1933 and 1934 were part of President Franklin D. Roosevelt's New Deal legislation. The Securities Act of 1933 regulated the initial distribution of security issues by requiring companies to make "full and fair" disclosure of their financial affairs before their securities could be offered to the public. The Securities Exchange Act of 1934 required the periodic updating of financial information for all companies whose stocks were traded on a stock exchange. In addition, the 1934 act created the Securities and Exchange Commission and assigned it the responsibility of administering both the 1933 and 1934 acts.

The SEC has the legal responsibility to regulate trades of securities and to determine the types of financial disclosures that a publicly held company must make. Although the SEC has the ultimate legal authority to establish the disclosure requirements, it has worked closely with the accounting profession to prescribe the accounting principles and standards used to measure and report companies' financial conditions and results of operations. The SEC's role is to assure full and fair disclosure; it does not guarantee the investment merits of any security. Stock markets still operate on a *caveat emptor* basis, "let the buyer beware." The SEC has consistently taken the position that investors must have the necessary information to make their own assessments of the risk and return attributes of a security.

The present role of the SEC is particularly complex. In 1935, its first year of full activity, only 284 new securities were registered for sale to the general public. Now the number of new securities being registered for sale has grown to over 5,000 per year. The SEC also regulates over 10,000 securities brokers and dealers and must monitor stock exchange volumes often surpassing 100 million shares a day. The SEC continues to work to facilitate the registration and filing process and is extending its development of an electronic filing system known as EDGAR (Electronic Data Gathering Analysis and Retrieval). Under this system, firms may file electronically directly by use of computers which should not only facilitate the data transfer, but also make public data more quickly available. A number of firms use EDGAR and it is expected that this means of filing will increase over time.

SECURITIES AND EXCHANGE COMMISSION

Organizational Structure of the Commission

The Commission consists of five members appointed by the President of the U.S., with the advice and consent of the Senate. Figure 15-1 is an organizational chart of the Commission showing the separate divisions and offices that must report directly to the Commission. The major divisions, and their primary responsibilities, are as follows:

1. *Division of Corporation Regulation.* Assists in the regulation of public utilities and advises federal courts in bankruptcies of publicly held companies.

2. *Division of Corporation Finance.* Develops and administers the disclosure requirements for the securities acts and reviews all registration statements and other issuer-oriented disclosures. This is the division with which accountants are most familiar because all registration forms are submitted to it.

3. *Division of Enforcement.* Directs enforcement activities of the Commission by investigating individuals who may be in violation of the securities acts and by preparing injunctive actions or other sanctions to prohibit further violations.

4. *Division of Investment Management Regulation.* Regulates investment advisers and investment companies.

5. *Division of Market Regulation.* Regulates national securities exchanges, brokers, and dealers of securities.

These divisions are supported by several offices, of which one of the most important is the Office of the Chief Accountant. This office assists the Commis-

FIGURE 15-1 Organizational structure of the Securities and Exchange Commission.

The Commission

| Division of Corporation Regulation | Division of Corporation Finance | Division of Enforcement | Division of Investment Management Regulation | Division of Market Regulation |

| Office of the Chief Accountant | Office of Economic Research | Office of the General Counsel | Office of Policy Planning |

Regional Offices and Branches

sion by studying current accounting issues and preparing position papers for the Commission to consider. The other offices offer the Commission advice on a variety of economic and regulatory matters.

Laws Administered by the SEC

In addition to the Securities Acts of 1933 and 1934, the Commission is responsible for administering other laws established to regulate companies or individuals involved with the securities markets. The laws are as follows:

1. *Public Utility Holding Company Act of 1935.* This act prohibits artificial pyramids of capital in public utilities and allows the Commission to restructure those "holding companies" whose only purpose is to concentrate the stock voting power in a few individuals.

2. *Trust Indenture Act of 1939.* This act requires a trustee to be appointed for sales of bonds, debentures, and other debt securities of public corporations, thus bringing in a bonded expert to administer the debt.

3. *Investment Company Act of 1940.* This act controls companies such as mutual funds that invest funds for the public. These companies must be audited annually, with the auditor reporting directly to the SEC.

4. *Investment Advisors Act of 1940.* This act requires complete disclosure of information about investment advisers including their backgrounds, business affiliations, and bases for compensation.

5. *Securities Investor Protection Act of 1970.* This act created the Securities Investor Protection Corporation (SIPC), an entity responsible for insuring investors from possible losses if an investment house enters bankruptcy. A small fee is added to the cost of each stock trade to cover the costs of the SIPC.

6. *Foreign Corrupt Practice Act of 1977.* This act amended the 1934 Securities Exchange Act. It requires accurate and fair recording of financial activities and requires management to maintain an adequate system of internal control.

7. *Federal Bankruptcy Acts.* The SEC provides assistance to the courts when a publicly held company declares bankruptcy. The primary concern of the SEC in these cases is the protection of security holders.

The Regulatory Structure

Many people beginning a study of the regulatory structure of the SEC are overwhelmed by the myriad of regulations, acts, guides, and releases the SEC uses to perform its tasks. It is easier to understand how the SEC operates after obtaining a basic understanding of these public documents and the nature of the SEC's pronouncements. Figure 15-2, which will be referenced throughout the chapter, presents an overview of this regulatory structure.

The Securities Act of 1933 and the Securities Exchange Act of 1934 are broken down into rules, regulations, forms, guides, and releases. The rules generally provide specific definitions for complying with the acts. The regulations establish

FIGURE 15-2 The regulatory structure.

Item	Contents
Securities Act of 1933	Statute regulating initial registration and sale of securities.
Securities Act rules	Basic definitions of Securities Act terms such as *offers, distribution, participation,* and *accredited investor.*
Securities Act regulations	Detailed requirements of registration. At the present time there are six regulations (Regulations A, B, C, D, E, F), of which two (A and D) specify exemptions from registration requirements for small or private stock offerings.
Securities Act forms	Content of registration forms. The most frequently used forms are Form 1-A for small offerings of securities and Forms S-1, S-2, and S-3, which are general registration forms.
Securities Act industry guides	Specifications of additional disclosures required in registration statements of companies in special industries such as oil and gas, banking, and real estate.
Securities Act releases (SRs)	Announcements amending or adopting new rules, guides, forms, or policies under the 1933 act. Approximately 6,000 releases have been published. These are noted with a prefix; for example, for release number 6,000, Release 33-6000.
Securities Exchange Act of 1934	Regulation of security trading and requirements for periodic reports by publicly held companies.
Exchange Act rules	Specific reporting requirements of over-the-counter securities, special reports required by stockholders who own 5 percent or more of a company's outstanding stock, and prohibition of manipulative and deceptive devices or contrivances.
Exchange Act forms	Specification of the content of periodic reports. The most commonly used forms are Form 10-K (annual report), Form 10-Q (quarterly report), and Form 8-K (current events report).
Exchange Act industry guides	Additional periodic reporting requirements of companies in specialized industries such as electric and gas utilities, oil and gas, and banking.
Securities Exchange Act releases (SRs)	Announcements of amendments or adoptions of new rules, guides, forms, or policy statements pertaining to the 1934 act. Over 15,000 have been issued, identified with a prefix; for example, for number 15,000, Release 34-15000.
Regulation S-X (Reg. S-X)	Articles specifying the form and content of financial disclosures: financial statements, schedules, footnotes, reports of accountants, and pro forma disclosures.
Regulation S-K (Reg. S-K)	Articles specifying disclosure rules of nonfinancial items to be included in registration statements, annual reports, and proxy statements. Major items are description of business, management's discussion and analysis, disagreements with accountants, and required information about new stock issues.
Financial Reporting Releases (FRRs)	Amendments to Securities Act, additional disclosure requirements, and other current issues regarding accounting and auditing principles and standards. *Financial Reporting Release No. 1* is a codification of the accounting and auditing materials in the 307 Accounting Series Releases published between 1933 and 1982.
Accounting and Auditing Enforcement Releases (AAERs)	Announcements of enforcement actions involving accountants practicing before the SEC. Includes discussion of the findings and opinions (including sanctions against the accountants involved) of enforcement hearings held by the Commission. *AAER No. 1* is a codification of all enforcement topics previously included in the Accounting Series Releases.
Staff Accounting Bulletins (SABs)	New or revised administrative practices and interpretations used by the Commission's staff in reviewing financial statements.

compliance requirements; for example, the regulations of the 1933 act detail specific reporting requirements for special cases such as small companies. The forms specify the format of the reports to be made under each of the acts. The guides provide specified additional disclosure requirements for selected industries such as oil and gas, and banks. The releases are used for amendments or adoptions of new requirements under the acts.

Two major regulations, *Regulation S-X* and *Regulation S-K*, govern the preparation of financial statements and associated disclosures made in reports to the SEC. Specifically, Regulation S-X presents the rules for preparing financial statements, footnotes, and the auditor's report. Regulation S-K covers all the nonfinancial items, such as management's discussion and analysis of the company's operations and present financial position.

The SEC needed some reporting vehicle to inform accountants about changes made in disclosure requirements, regulatory changes in the auditor-client relationship, and the results of enforcement actions taken against participants in the financial disclosure or securities trading process. Before 1982, the Commission used Accounting Series Releases (ASRs) for this purpose and had issued 307 ASRs covering a wide range of topics. In 1982, these ASRs were classified as covering either financial accounting topics or enforcement actions and codified into a more organized reporting format.

The *Financial Reporting Releases* (FRRs) disclose amendments or adoptions of new rules that affect preparers of financial statements and other disclosures. The *Accounting and Auditing Enforcement Releases* (AAERs) present the results of enforcement actions taken against accountants or other participants in the filing process. Most of these actions result from the filing of a false or misleading statement. The *Staff Accounting Bulletins* (SABs) allow the Commission's staff to make announcements on technical issues with which it is concerned as a result of reviews of SEC filings. The SABs are not formal actions of the Commission; nevertheless, most preparers do follow these bulletins because they represent the views of the staff that will be reviewing their companies' filings.

The *SEC Docket* is a weekly publication of the SEC that presents current information about changes to regulations, significant actions taken by the Commission, and enforcement actions filed each week. The *SEC Docket* is an important resource for persons who must remain current on SEC matters.

INTEGRATED DISCLOSURE SYSTEM

In 1980, the SEC undertook a project to reduce the duplicative disclosures companies were required to make for the annual report and in each additional filing with the SEC; that is, the Commission sought to integrate all the disclosures. For this *integrated disclosure system* the Commission adopted a standard financial reporting package for the annual report and then provided that "incorporation by reference" could be made from the annual report to other SEC reports by citing the appropriate annual report page number on which the required information appears. In addition, the Commission adopted a *basic information package (BIP)*, which includes the most important information investors and others need in order to assess a company's financial risk.

The five classes of information constituting the BIP are presented in Figure 15-3 and are as follows.

1. *Market Price of and Dividends on Common Equity and Related Security Matters.* This part of the package provides investors with dividend information, including any restrictions on the company's ability to pay future dividends.

2. *Selected Financial Data.* Companies are required to provide 5-year trend data on summary statistics representing the company's ability to earn income and service its debt. Many companies provide more than the minimum required, often disclosing 7 to 10 years of summary data.

3. *Management's Discussion and Analysis of Financial Condition and Results of Operations.* **Management discussion and analysis** (MDA) provides analysis of the

FIGURE 15-3 Basic information package (BIP).

1. Market price of and dividends on common equity and related security matters:
   a. Markets in which stock is traded
   b. Quarterly common stock price for the last 2 years
   c. Approximate number of common stockholders
   d. Frequency and amount of dividends during the last 2 years
   e. Any restrictions on the issuer's present or future ability to pay dividends
2. Selected financial data:
   a. Net sales or operating revenue
   b. Income (loss) from continuing operations
   c. Income (loss) from continuing operations per share
   d. Total assets
   e. Long-term obligations, including capital leases and redeemable preferred stock
3. Management's discussion and analysis of financial condition and results of operations (MDA):
   a. Discussion of liquidity, capital resources, and results of operations
   b. Discussion of any known matters that materially affect or are expected to affect the company's financial condition and results of operations
   c. Discussion of causes for material changes in line items of financial statements for all years presented
   d. Discussion of the impact of inflation and changing prices on the company's sales and income from continuing operations
4. Audited financial statements and supplementary data not covered by the auditors' report:
   a. Income statements and statements of cash flows for the last 3 years
   b. Balance sheets for the last 2 years
   c. Required footnotes, including condensed interim data and inflation disclosures
5. Other information:
   a. Brief description of business
   b. Major operating developments such as bankruptcies or major dispositions or acquisitions of assets
   c. Industry and foreign segment information
   d. Description of major properties currently owned
   e. Description of major active legal proceedings
   f. Information about management: backgrounds, remuneration, and major transactions between members of management and the company
   g. Selected industry-specific disclosures for insurance, banking, and other regulated industries

company's financial condition and changes in financial condition. The focus is on discussion of the company's present and future prospects for liquidity, capital resources, and changes in operations. Management must disclose unused lines of credit and capital budgeting plans and must perform a line-by-line analysis of the causes of changes in the financial statements presented. Financial analysts are extremely interested in management's assessment of the company's present and expected financial position. This disclosure is one of the most important in the annual report.

4. *Audited Financial Statements and Supplementary Data.* The company must provide audited statements, including 3 years of income statements and statements of cash flows so investors may determine trends, and the last 2 years' balance sheets. In addition, all required footnotes must accompany the financial statements.

5. *Other Information.* This category includes a brief description of the business, details relating to operations and management, and disclosures required of special industries such as insurance and banking.

ISSUING SECURITIES: THE REGISTRATION PROCESS

Companies wishing to sell securities to the general public are required by the Securities Act of 1933 to register those securities with the SEC. The registration process requires extensive disclosure about the company, its management, and the intended use of the proceeds from the issue. The registrant must also provide audited financial statements. Several types of enterprises are exempt from this offering requirement because they are governed by separate regulatory bodies. The exempted entities include not-for-profit organizations such as schools, government units such as cities or park districts, and common carriers.

Certain private and small offerings may be issued with less than the full disclosure required in the general registration statement. Regulation A deals specifically with small issues. This regulation exempts from full disclosure requirements issues of less than $1.5 million of stock sales during any 12-month period. These small issues must still be registered, but the registration is in the form of an "offering statement," which contains limited information about the company. Regulation D covers limited offerings to "accredited investors," defined as individuals earning more than $100,000 income per year and having a net worth exceeding $750,000. Companies may offer up to $5 million in securities within a 12-month period to these individuals with only a limited amount of financial disclosure.

The offering process usually begins with the selection of an investment banker, also called an "underwriter," who assists the company in the registration process by providing marketing information and ultimately directing the distribution of the securities. The underwriting agreement is a contract between the company and the underwriter and specifies such items as the underwriter's responsibilities and the final disposition of any unsold securities remaining at the end of the public offering. In some cases the underwriter agrees to purchase any remaining securities; in others, the company is required to withdraw any unsold securities. An offering team comprises the company, the underwriter, the company's independent accountant, the company's legal counsel, and experts such as appraisers or engineers who may be required. Typically, the underwriter requires a "comfort letter" from the accountant to indicate that the company has fulfilled all the accounting requirements in the registration process.

The Registration Statement

The process of issuing begins with the preparation of the registration statement. The company must select 1 from among approximately 20 different forms the SEC currently has for registering securities. The most common are *Form S-1*, *Form S-2*, and *Form S-3*. Others are required when registering stock option plans, foreign issues, limited issuances under Regulation D, and special types of offerings. Form S-1 is the most comprehensive registration statement; Form S-2 is an abbreviated form for present registrants who have other publicly traded stock; Form S-3 is a brief form available for large, established registrants whose stock has been trading for several years.

Form S-1 has two different levels of disclosure. Part I, often referred to as the "prospectus," is intended primarily for investors and includes the basic information package as well as information about the intended use of the proceeds, a description of the securities being offered, and the plan of distribution, including the name of the principal underwriter. Filings for bond issues must include summary information about the ratio of earnings to fixed charges so investors are informed about some of the financial risk the new bond issue adds to the company. Part II of Form S-1 includes more detailed information, such as a listing of the expenses of issuing and distributing the new security, additional information about directors and officers, and additional financial statement schedules. The registration statement must be signed by the principal executive, financial, and accounting officers, as well as a majority of the company's board of directors. The company then submits its registration statement to an SEC review by the Division of Corporation Finance.

SEC Review and Public Offering

Most first-time registrants receive a "customary review," which is a thorough examination by the SEC and may result in acceptance or, alternatively, a *comment letter* specifying the deficiencies that must be corrected before the securities may be offered for sale. Established companies that already have stock widely traded generally are subject to a summary review or a cursory review. Once the registration statement becomes effective, the company may begin selling securities to the public. This review period is 20 days unless the company receives a comment letter from the SEC.

Between the time the registration statement is presented to the SEC and its effective date, the company may issue a *preliminary prospectus,* referred to as a *red herring prospectus*, which provides tentative information to investors about an upcoming issue. The name "red herring" comes from the red ink used on the cover of this preliminary prospectus, indicating that it is not an offering statement and that the securities being discussed are not yet available for sale. In addition, the company generally prepares a "tombstone ad" in the business press to inform investors of the upcoming offering. These ads are bordered in black ink, whence the title.

The time period between the initial decision to offer securities and the actual sale may exceed 120 days. In the interim, many factors may affect the stock market and may decrease the company's ability to obtain capital. In 1982, the SEC devised the *shelf registration* rule for large, established companies with other issues of stock already actively traded. These companies file a registration statement with the SEC for a stock issue that may be "brought off the shelf" and, with the aid of an underwriter, updated within a very short time, usually 2 to 3 days. A shelf registration is limited to 10 percent of the company's currently outstanding stock, but allows large companies to select the optimal time to sell their stock.

Accountants' Legal Liability in the Registration Process

Accountants play a key role in the preparation of the registration statement. The company's own accountants prepare the initial financial disclosures, which are then audited by the company's independent accountants. The 1933 act created a very broad legal liability for all participants in the registration process, and this legal exposure is particularly high for accountants because financial disclosures make up the majority of the registration statement. Accountants are liable for any materially false or misleading information *to the effective date* of the registration statement. The underwriters handling the sale of the securities will often require a "comfort letter" from the registrant's public accountants for the period between the filing date and the effective date. This comfort letter provides additional evidence that the public accountant has not found any adverse financial changes since the filing date. Plaintiffs suing the accountant are not required to show they relied on the registration statement, only that the statement was wrong at the effective date! Accountants have a "due diligence" defense, the result of interpretations by the courts as to what is generally required in a reasonable investigation of the company's financial position; however, the broad legal exposure causes many anxieties for accountants involved with the offering of securities.

PERIODIC REPORTING REQUIREMENTS

The Securities Exchange Act of 1934 regulates the trading of securities and imposes reporting requirements on companies whose securities trade on one of the stock exchanges. The 1933 act requires registration for the issuance of each additional security a company wishes to sell to the public. The 1934 act also requires that each class of security a company has outstanding must be registered. For example, if a company wishes to sell 1 million new shares of its common stock to the public, it must have the common stock class registered under the 1934 act and then must register the additional issue under the 1933 act. In addition, recall that smaller companies with net assets less than $3 million and fewer than 500 shareholders are exempted from the registration requirements of the 1933 act. Once a company exceeds these minimum criteria, it must register its outstanding securities for the first time using Form 10 defined by the 1934 act. The information required by Form 10 is similar to the prospectus information required in Form S-1 under the 1933 act.

The 1934 act also requires publicly held companies to file periodic financial disclosures as updates on their economic activities. The three basic forms used for this updating are Form 10-K, Form 10-Q, and Form 8-K.

Form 10-K must be filed within 90 days after the end of the company's fiscal year. Although the report is broken into four parts, the general format is similar to the company's annual report to shareholders. Parts I, II, and III contain the basic information package, including the financial statements, often incorporated by reference to the annual report. Part IV contains additional schedules and exhibits. However, Form 10-K differs from the annual report by providing specific information relevant to the security holders, such as description of any matters submitted to a vote of security holders; discussion of any disagreements with external auditors; management compensation and major ownership blocks; and schedules detailing selected asset and liability accounts, including accounts receivable, property, plant, and equipment, the company's investments in other enterprises, and indebtedness of the company and its affiliates.

Form 10-Q is the interim report of the SEC. It is due within 45 days after the end of each quarter except the fourth quarter, when the 10-K is issued. Part I of Form 10-Q includes comparative financial statements prepared in accordance with **APB 28**; these interim statements need not be audited. Essentially, the company provides financial statements for the most recent quarter, cumulative statements from the beginning of the fiscal period, and comparative statements for the equivalent quarters in the preceding fiscal year.

Part II of Form 10-Q is an update on significant matters occurring since the last quarter. These include new legal proceedings, changes in the rights of securities, defaults on senior securities, increases or decreases in the number of securities outstanding, and other materially important events affecting security holders.

Form 8-K is used to disclose unscheduled material events. This form is due within 15 days after the occurrence of a "current event," defined as follows:

1. A change in the control of the registrant
2. Acquisition or disposal of major assets
3. Bankruptcy or receivership of the registrant
4. Changes in the registrant's certifying accountants
5. Resignations of one or more of the registrant's directors
6. Any other events deemed to be of material importance to security holders

The purpose of Form 8-K is to provide public disclosure of these significant events on a relatively contemporaneous basis.

For changes in the registrant's certifying accountants, Form 8-K must include the following: the date the former auditor resigned or was dismissed, a statement describing and fully discussing any material disagreements with the former auditors over accounting or auditing standards over the past 24 months, a statement stating if the former auditor's opinion was qualified in any way for the past 2 years and describing the nature of any qualification, and a letter from the former auditor as an exhibit to Form 8-K which states if the former auditor agrees or disagrees with the facts as stated in the Form 8-K, as presented by the registrant.

Accountants' Legal Liability in Periodic Reporting

The 1934 Securities Exchange Act provides for a limited level of legal exposure from involvement in the preparation and filing of periodic reports. Civil liability is imposed for filing materially false or misleading statements. The accountant's liability for registration statements under the 1933 act extends to the date the registration becomes effective. Plaintiffs suing accountants under the 1934 act must show that a periodic report contains a misleading material fact and that they suffered a loss because they relied on that report. Accountants are provided with good faith defenses to combat any lawsuits brought under the 1934 act.

FOREIGN CORRUPT PRACTICES ACT OF 1977

In the mid-1970s, Congress held a number of public hearings which brought to light that millions of dollars in bribes had been paid to high government officials of other countries by United States–based companies seeking to win defense or consumer product contracts. Alarmed by the size and scope of these activities, Congress passed the *Foreign Corrupt Practices Act of 1977* (FCPA) as a major amendment to the Securities Exchange Act of 1934. The FCPA has two major sections: Part I prohibits foreign bribes, and Part II requires publicly held companies to maintain an adequate system of internal control and accurate records.

Under Part I, individuals associated with U.S. companies are prohibited from bribing foreign governmental or political officials for the purpose of securing a contract or otherwise increasing the company's business. Small compensating or agents' fees to lower-level civil servants are allowed if the purpose of these fees is to facilitate a transaction that is already in process, such as to obtain shipping permits or to acquire local licenses in a foreign country. Both civil and criminal sanctions can be imposed on individuals making foreign bribes.

Part II of the FCPA has had a significant impact on both corporate accountants and independent auditors. This part requires all public companies, whether operating internationally or not, to keep detailed records that accurately and fairly reflect their financial transactions and to develop and maintain an adequate internal control system. An internal control system should ensure that all major transactions are fully authorized, that transactions are properly recorded and reported, that the company's assets are safeguarded, and that management's policies are properly carried out.

Although the FCPA was not specific about the types of internal controls necessary, it defined the following as important aspects of a good internal control system: (1) strong budgetary controls, (2) an objective internal audit function that helps develop, document, and then monitor the control system, (3) an active audit committee from the company's board of directors, and (4) a review of the internal control system by the independent auditors. The FCPA allows for the development of "tailored" control procedures that best serve the company. In addition, the FCPA indicated that the cost of an internal control procedure should not outweigh its benefit to the firm.

The FCPA also had a significant effect on independent auditors by requiring them to evaluate a company's internal controls and to communicate any material weaknesses in those controls to the company's top management and board of directors. Initially, the SEC considered having the external auditor offer an opinion in the annual report on the adequacy of the company's internal control system, to be published next to the auditor's audit opinion. However, the SEC reconsidered and dropped this idea, although many companies ask their external auditors for a separate assessment and opinion on their internal control systems beyond that required for the periodic audit of their financial statements. The total impact of the FCPA is still unclear. Subsequent proposals offered by the SEC itself have somewhat softened the foreign bribery section of the act; however, Part II of the FCPA, dealing with internal control, has certainly increased the interest of companies in maintaining strong internal control systems.

CORPORATE GOVERNANCE ACTIVITIES

The SEC has established regulations guiding certain management actions and increasing management's accountability to the security holders of the enterprise. Three areas are of particular note: proxy statements, insider trading rules, and audit committees.

Proxy statements are solicitations submitted to stockholders for actions such as election of directors, changes in the corporate charter, appointment of an independent auditor, issuance of new securities or modification of outstanding securities, or plans for a major business combination. In many cases, voting on these matters takes place at the annual meeting. The proxy is the solicitation of the stockholder's voting right and is often in the form of a checkoff ballot which management encourages the stockholder to return to be voted at the annual meeting.

Proxy statements may also be used by individual stockholders, or a group of stockholders, for proposals that are in opposition to management. For example, a stockholder group may oppose a recent action by management and solicit other stockholders for support of their opposing position. At times, the business press carries news of proxy battles between management and nonmanagement groups which each are soliciting stockholders' support. The SEC sets requirements in the following areas for shareholder proposals that are in opposition to management:

1. *Eligibility.* The proponent must own a security with voting privileges.

2. *Attendance.* The proponent or a designate must be in attendance at the annual meeting to present the proposal.

3. *Timeliness*. The proposal must be received at least 90 days prior to the mailing date of the proxy statement.

4. *Rejected Proposals*. The proposal cannot relate to a similar proposal that has been rejected within the last 5 years.

The proxy statement includes a variety of information about the committees of the board of directors, executive compensation and share ownership, and a copy of the most recent annual report of the company.

Insider trading rules have been established to prohibit company officers, directors, major investors, or anyone else who has gained access to nonpublic information about a company from profiting from that information through purchase or sale of the company's stock. Accountants, including independent auditors, are most certainly subject to insider trading rules. The SEC analyzes unusual share-trading data for evidence of insider abuses. In addition, officers, directors, and stockholders owning more than 10 percent of the shares of each class of securities are required to report their holdings and any transactions in those securities. The SEC's enforcement structure aggressively seeks out evidence of insider trading and actively prosecutes abuses as discovered.

The *audit committee* is a subcommittee of a company's board of directors. This committee is typically comprised of nonmanagement directors and is assigned the responsibility to work with both the external auditor aand internal auditors to ensure that management fulfills its fiduciary responsibilities to maintain an adequate system of financial reporting and internal control. The audit committee meets regularly with the external auditor during the audit process to review the scope and progress of the audit, and to receive reports on any investigative matters related to financial reporting and internal control. The audit committee also often monitors the activities of the internal audit department and receives the results of reviews conducted by the internal audit staff. Although the SEC does not require audit committees, the New York Stock Exchange does, and the SEC has supported the use of audit committees to assist in enhancing the independence of the external auditors. Some companies now include a letter from the chairman of the audit committee within the annual report to shareholders to show the activities of the audit committee during the fiscal period and to indicate the importance that the company's board of directors places on the need for independent, nonmanagement interaction with both the external and internal auditing functions.

THE SEC'S POLICY-SETTING RESPONSIBILITIES

The 1933 and 1934 securities acts provided the SEC with broad regulatory powers to determine the accounting and reporting standards for publicly traded companies. The SEC has generally relied on the accounting profession to establish accounting standards. The profession's rule makers are closer to the daily business environment and can identify emerging issues, as well as obtain the general acceptance of practicing accountants for any changes in accounting policies.

Nevertheless, the SEC has ultimate legal authority to establish accounting and reporting standards for publicly owned companies. This authority was dramatically evidenced in a 1938 financial accounting series release, the fourth in its series, in which the Commission stated:

> In cases where financial statements filed with the Commission pursuant to its rules and regulations under the Securities Act or the Exchange Act are prepared in accordance with accounting principles for which there is no substantial support, such financial statements will be presumed to be misleading or inaccurate despite disclosures contained in the certificate of the accountant or in footnotes to the statements provided the matters involved are material.[1]

The Commission went on to state that any principles it prescribed would have "substantial authoritative support." A cooperative working relationship was formed between the Commission and the accounting profession's standard-setting body and was reaffirmed in 1973 when the Commission issued its **Accounting Series Release No. 150**, "Statement of Policy on the Establishment and Improvement of Accounting Principles and Standards" (ASR 150), explicitly stating that the principles, standards, and practices established by the FASB have substantial authoritative support. However, the Commission can and does issue policy statements that supersede or amend accounting principles issued by the FASB. Several such instances are discussed later in the chapter.

In 1976, this cooperative working relationship between the SEC and FASB was threatened by a congressional subcommittee report signed by Senator Lee Metcalf and titled "The Accounting Establishment." This extremely long report sharply criticized the public accounting profession for not being sufficiently independent from the clients it serves. The report concluded with the recommendation that the SEC take a much stronger role in prescribing accounting principles. However, the SEC has continued to support the primary establishment of principles in the private sector by the FASB.

The Commission continues to provide leadership in selected areas of financial disclosure. One of these is the definition of *materiality*, which has eluded the FASB. The definition of materiality is important because immaterial items do not need separate disclosure. The SEC uses a prudent-investor rule: Would a prudent investor be affected by the separate disclosure of an item? A general rule is that material items are those amounting to more than 10 percent of a general balance sheet category, or more than 5 percent of total assets. Some small items, however, may be considered material to a prudent investor, and separate disclosure must be made of such small items as amounts due to or from officers and directors of the company, accrued tax liability, and selected important valuation accounts such as allowance for inventory write-downs.

The cooperation between the SEC and FASB has worked with varying levels of success. The FASB is sensitive to the changes in the business world and attempts

---

[1] *Financial Reporting Release No. 1*, "Codification of Financial Reporting Policies," Securities and Exchange Commission (Washington, D.C.), 1982, par. 101.

to react quickly to these changes by promulgating new accounting standards when needed. The SEC, however, continues to fulfill its responsibility by issuing releases on subjects that it feels must be addressed. Most practicing accountants believe that the FASB should continue to have primary responsibility for establishing accounting standards.

MAJOR DISCLOSURE REQUIREMENTS

Virtually every SEC accounting release reminds registrants of the commitment to full and fair disclosure of financial information needed by investors. The SEC has taken the lead in requiring inflation disclosures and disclosures about a company's liquidity position. These and other areas are discussed here.

Management Discussion and Analysis

The management discussion and analysis (MDA) of a company's financial condition and results of operations is part of the basic information package (BIP) required in all major filings with the SEC. The SEC has taken the leadership role in requiring management to analyze and discuss the financial statements for investors, and this discussion often extends to three or more pages of the annual report. The financial statements are, after all, management's expressions of the economic consequences of their decisions made during the period. Management has the clearest picture of the company's financial environment. A key element in the MDA is a view that is both historical and forward-looking of the company's liquidity and solvency. The SEC recognizes that investors are particularly concerned with a company's ability to generate adequate amounts of cash to meet short-term and long-term cash needs.

Although management is given a flexible format in which to make its narrative and analytical explanation, the discussion must include the following five items:

1. *Specific Information about the Company's Liquidity, Capital Resources, and Results of Operations.* With regard to liquidity, management must discuss its cash flows and its sources of liquidity, including any unused lines of credit. Capital commitments, such as the company's capital budget plans, must be included in a discussion of capital resources. The results of operations must include a discussion of any unusual items affecting the company, any new products, or other changes that may significantly affect the future progress of the company.

2. *The Impact of Inflation and Changing Prices on Net Sales and Revenues and on Income from Continuing Operations.* Companies already making these disclosures elsewhere in the financial report are not required to duplicate them in the MDA.

3. *Material Changes in Line Items of the Consolidated Financial Statements from Prior-Period Amount.* This line-by-line analytical review must include the reasons for significant changes between the fiscal periods presented in the financial statements.

4. *Known Material Events and Uncertainties That May Make Historical Financial Information Not Indicative of Future Operations or Future Conditions.*

5. *Any Other Information the Company Believes Necessary for an Understanding of Its Financial Condition, Changes in Financial Condition, and Results of Operations.*

The MDA is continually being monitored and will undoubtedly be amended to include new analyses the SEC feels are important for investors.

At one time, the SEC considered requiring a companion report to the auditor's statement to be signed by the management of the company. This "report of management" was prompted by the internal controls requirement of the Foreign Corrupt Practices Act of 1977. The report typically contains four paragraphs: (1) a statement that management is responsible for the statements, (2) a discussion of the company's internal control environment, (3) a discussion of the board of directors audit committee, and (4) any other information, such as the adoption of a set of ethical standards. The frequency of this report has increased each year since its advent in 1977, and is likely to be included in most annual reports in the future. Consequently, because of its wide acceptance, the SEC withdrew its position making this report mandatory.

Annual Report Disclosures

The SEC gained regulatory control over the annual report to shareholders by requiring a copy of the annual report to be mailed with proxy solicitations made by management. In this way, the Commission has continued to decrease the differences in information disclosures between Form 10-K and the annual report by controlling both. This section covers several disclosure areas in which the SEC has adopted positions that have forged the path toward greater disclosures in the annual report.

Cash Flow Data and Compensating Balances The SEC has consistently held that the presentation of cash flow data on a per-share basis confounds the reader and is not a substitute for income measured under an accrual accounting system. However, the Commission has encouraged the presentation of cash flow data in tabular form in the footnotes when accompanied by a full discussion of how they were measured. In 1987, the FASB issued **FASB Statement No. 95**, "Statement of Cash Flows" (FASB 95), requiring full disclosure of a company's cash flows in a primary financial statement.

Compensating balances are demand deposits that a company must maintain because of existing borrowing arrangements. For example, a company may be required to maintain a balance of $1 million on deposit in a non-interest-bearing account in order to have assurance of a $10 million line of credit against which future cash may be borrowed. The effect of compensating balances is to reduce management's flexibility over the funds held on deposit and to increase the effective rate of interest on the line of credit. For these reasons, compensating balances and short-term borrowing arrangements must be disclosed in the footnotes of the annual report.

Selected footnote disclosures are also required on accounts receivables. For example, total retainages on long-term contracts, the portion of the contract price retained until completion of the contract, must be disclosed together with any unbilled receivables that are expected to be collected after 1 year. Both these disclosures provide information on the future liquidity of the company.

LIFO Inventory The SEC supports the use of lifo because it approximates a current cost for cost of goods sold. However, in **ASR No. 293**, the Commission pointed out several observed abuses of the lifo method, such as shifting items between inventories and using minor product changes to manipulate reported income. The continued use of lifo will be carefully monitored to ensure that firms are not violating the basic concept of lifo.

In 1981, the Internal Revenue Service modified its position and allowed companies using lifo to make fifo comparisons in the annual report. The SEC felt that the disclosures of lifo income versus fifo income may diminish the information value of the lifo-based income because shareholders might look only at the fifo disclosures. Therefore, any fifo-based disclosures must be limited to the footnotes or the MDA and are not to be included in the president's letter, press releases, or the primary financial statements.

Intercorporate Investments The SEC has continued to lead the way in requiring detailed disclosures of intercorporate investments. An intercorporate structure may be of a parent company, one or more consolidated subsidiaries, one or more unconsolidated subsidiaries, or a number of less-than-majority-owned investees. The basic premise of a consolidated entity is that the parent company controls the affairs of its constituent companies and that there is a relatively free flow of funds among the various companies making up the consolidated entity. The key issue is that consolidated financial statements may not adequately present the fact that the parent company cannot exercise full control over the transfer of funds among its affiliates because of restrictions imposed by regulatory bodies, borrowing arrangements, or foreign governments. In these cases, footnotes to the annual report must fully disclose any restrictions on retained earnings or dividends of any company that is part of the consolidated entity.

To determine if this additional footnote disclosure is necessary, the consolidated entity must first determine the total portion of consolidated net assets for which transfer is restricted. To this is added any consolidated net assets in the form of equity in undistributed earnings of companies in which the entity has 50 percent or less ownership. If the total of the restricted assets and equity in earnings is greater than 25 percent of total consolidated net assets, then the additional footnote disclosure must be made. Also, the footnotes must disclose the amount of consolidated retained earnings representing undistributed earnings of entities accounted for by the equity method and in which ownership is 50 percent or less.

In some circumstances, the SEC requires separate financial statements for the parent company only, for significant unconsolidated subsidiaries, and for other companies in which ownership is 50 percent or less. These separate financial statements are not required in the annual report to shareholders; however, registration statements and other filings with the Commission may require these separate footnote disclosures in addition to the primary consolidated financial statements, as follows:

1. Statements by the parent company alone must be provided whenever any subsidiary's assets restricted from transfer to the parent because of loan agreements or other restrictions exceed 25 percent of the total consolidated assets.

2. Separate audited financial statements for unconsolidated subsidiaries and for companies in which ownership is 50 percent or less must be provided in the consolidated annual report whenever such investees' assets or income exceeds 20 percent of consolidated total assets or net income. However, whenever the total assets or income of unconsolidated subsidiaries and companies in which ownership is 50 percent or less exceeds 10 percent of the consolidated total assets or net income, then the consolidated report must include summarized information about the unconsolidated and other investee companies. This summarized information must include the combined totals for all unconsolidated subsidiaries and other investees in which ownership is 50 percent or less for each of the following items: assets, liabilities, revenues, and expenses.

Other Disclosures   The Commission has also established several other reporting requirements for additional disclosures in the footnotes of the annual report to shareholders. In **Accounting Series Release No. 149**, "Notice of Adoption of Amendment to Regulation S-X to Provide for Improved Disclosure of Income Tax Expense" (ASR 149), the Commission adopted rules that require reconciliation between the effective income tax indicated by the income statement and the statutory income tax rate as well as the reasons for and tax effects of temporary differences resulting in deferred income taxes. **Accounting Series Release No. 280**, "General Revision of Regulation S-X" (ASR 280), added the requirement to disclose separately both domestic and foreign pretax income in the income tax footnote.

Footnote disclosure is also required of the following items:

1. Legal proceedings on environmental actions and any government proceedings if possible sanction is greater than $100,000.

2. Any restrictions on the company's ability to pay dividends.

3. Supplemental schedules detailing property, plant, and equipment (PPE) if PPE less accumulated depreciation is more than 25 percent of total assets at both the beginning and the end of the year.

4. Material related-party transactions if amounts involved are more than 10 percent of a general category on a balance sheet or more than 5 percent of total assets. These include transactions between management and the company and between parent and subsidiary companies.

5. Disclosures of any unusual risks and uncertainties such as declines in the value of marketable securities, significant dependence on a small number of projects, or declines in the loan loss reserves of financial institutions.

Specialized Industry Disclosures

Banks, insurance companies, and oil and gas companies all operate in highly regulated environments. The key issue is the type of financial disclosure these companies must make to shareholders. For example, insurance regulatory bodies require the computation of several loss reserves that have no specific parallel in accrual accounting. These statutory reserves reduce income below that reported under GAAP. In virtually all cases, the Commission has stated that disclosures intended for shareholders must be prepared using accrual accounting and that specific information about the unique aspects of these industries should be disclosed in the footnotes as supplementary schedules, tables, or narrative discussions.

Because banks have extensive lending and investing activities, they are required to provide additional footnote disclosures in their reports to shareholders for the following items: (1) loans to officers, directors, and stockholders and (2) certificates of deposit (CDs) and time deposits (TDs) in denominations of $100,000 or more, broken down between foreign and domestic investments. The balance sheet must disclose the market value of investment securities, and the income statement must present investment securities' gains and losses as a separate subcategory of other income, not as a distinct second item of revenue generation.

Insurance companies are highly regulated by various state insurance commissions. Their financial reports to shareholders must be prepared using GAAP with one consolidated financial report encompassing all lines of insurance for multiline companies offering a variety of different types of insurance. GAAP accounting for insurance companies is defined in **FASB Statement No. 60**, "Accounting and Reporting by Insurance Companies" (FASB 60). Multiline insurance companies must disclose in footnotes a breakdown of their various types of insurance, such as life, property and liability, and title insurance. In addition, the footnotes must disclose the amounts of statutory income (that is, income determined using insurance accounting) and any significant statutory restrictions on dividends. Finally, the companies must break down their investments in bonds and notes, preferred stock, and common stock into two categories—fixed maturities and equity securities—both on the balance sheet and in an investment summary schedule.

The Commission has had a significant impact on disclosures made by oil and gas companies. In 1975, the Commission was directed by the Energy Policy and Conservation Act to provide accounting principles that would enable the Department of Energy to develop a reliable energy data base. In 1977, the FASB issued **FASB Statement No. 19**, "Financial Accounting and Reporting by Oil and Gas Producing Companies" (FASB 19), which supported the successful-efforts method of determining income. In 1978, the SEC issued **ASR No. 253** defining "Reserve Recognition Accounting" (ASR 253), which recognized oil and gas reserves as assets in the balance sheet. Also, this ASR allowed companies to use either the successful-efforts or the full cost method of computing income. Reserve recognition accounting required footnote disclosure of (1) known oil and gas reserve quantities, (2) estimated future net revenue computed at current prices, and (3) the present value of future net revenue. Obviously, companies have major problems of measuring and valuing proven reserves that are still underground. The FASB later allowed both the full cost and the successful-efforts methods and has issued a number of pronouncements defining the required footnote disclosures for oil and gas producing companies. Generally, these footnotes present information on the net quantities of proven oil and gas reserves and a summary of the costs related to oil and gas activities. In 1981, the SEC withdrew its requirement for reserve recognition accounting in an acknowledgment that the disclosures required by the FASB were adequate.

Information outside Financial Statements

The Commission has taken the lead in requiring many additional footnote disclosures not directly related to the financial statements. Three of the more important areas of disclosure addressed by the SEC are as follows.

Inflation Disclosures The issue of reporting the effects of inflation has been with us since the early days of the accounting profession. In the 1960s, the APB released a report promoting the general price level adjustment of financial statements. The SEC took an alternative view and in 1976 issued **ASR No. 190**, "Disclosure of Certain Replacement Cost Data" (ASR 190), which required disclosures based on a modified form of current value accounting. **ASR 190** required footnote disclosure of the replacement costs of inventories and gross plant for companies in which these two items exceeded $100 million and were more than 10 percent of total assets. The disclosures did not have to be audited by the company's auditors, but the independent accountants were expected to review them. This requirement placed the SEC and the FASB at different ends of the spectrum of disclosing inflation's effects on the company. A compromise was reached when the FASB issued **Statement No. 33**, "Financial Reporting and Changing Prices" (FASB 33), requiring disclosure of both constant dollar and current cost information, and the SEC withdrew **ASR 190. FASB Statement No. 89**, "Financial Reporting and Changing Prices" (FASB 89), superseded **FASB 33**, and now firms are encouraged, but not required, to disclose supplementary information on changing prices. Nevertheless, the fact that the FASB compromised in **FASB 33** by requiring both disclosures clearly shows the tremendous impact the SEC can and does have on the determination of accounting principles.

Pro Forma Disclosures *Pro forma disclosures* are essentially "what if" financial presentations often taking the form of summarized financial statements. Pro forma statements are used to show the effects of major transactions that occur after the end of the fiscal period, or that have occurred during the year and are not fully reflected in the company's historical cost financial statements. The SEC requires these to be presented whenever the company has made a significant business combination or disposition, a corporate reorganization, an unusual asset exchange, or a restructuring of existing indebtedness. A pro forma condensed income statement presented in the footnotes shows the impact of the transaction on the company's income from continuing operations, thereby helping investors to focus on the specific effects of the major transaction. The pro forma balance sheet includes all the adjustments reflecting the full impact of the transaction. Investors therefore have (1) the historical cost primary financial statements, which report these items as discontinued operations or as a cumulative effect accounting change, and (2) the pro forma statements, which restate the company's financial condition to include these items.

Financial Forecasts The Commission has consistently encouraged the use of financial forecasts in financial disclosures because they present the investor with information about future expectations of the company's risk and return. The concern is with the methods used to arrive at these figures, and the Commission has provided specific guidelines for the preparation and disclosure of forecasts. In addition to the forecasts themselves, the company must disclose the major assumptions underlying them. In order to encourage the use of forecasts, the SEC established "safe harbor" rules for companies preparing forecasts in a reasonable manner and in good faith. These safe harbor rules limit a company's liability for errors of judgment in these disclosures.

ADDITIONAL CONSIDERATIONS

The following section contains special topics that can enhance your understanding of the impact the SEC has had on auditing practices and on accounting firms.

Influence on the Practice of Auditing

The SEC has consistently taken the lead in requiring the independence of the auditor from the client company and in defining the parameters of the audit function. The SEC insists on strict independence of the auditor as the best protection of the public investors' need for full and fair disclosure of a company's financial position and performance. Many of the present auditing standards are results of actions taken by the Commission. In addition to its registration review process, the SEC's Division of Enforcement has actively investigated instances of possible false or misleading statements that may have been caused by the failure of generally accepted auditing standards (GAAS). For example, although fraud detection is not one of the primary goals of an audit, the Commission has consistently examined major litigation involving management frauds, including notorious cases such as McKesson-Robbins, Equity Funding, Penn Central, and

Stirling Homex, and has repeatedly questioned if the auditing standards applied in each of these cases were adequate and why the fraud was not uncovered earlier. Although auditors cannot be the "police officers" of business, it is apparent that the SEC will continue to insist that auditors use every possible device to explore situations in which management fraud is suspected.

AICPA's Division of Firms

In 1977, the American Institute of Certified Public Accountants (AICPA) divided its member CPA firms into two groups: the SEC Practice Section and the Private Companies Section. In the *AICPA's division of firms*, only those auditing firms belonging to the SEC Practice Section are permitted to practice before the Commission by auditing publicly traded companies and providing SEC-related services. Each CPA firm elects the section to which it wishes to belong. Firms in the SEC Practice Section have a number of quality review standards to which its members must subscribe. These firms are subject to peer reviews, in which one auditing firm is selected to review another auditing firm's client workpapers and audit procedures. In addition, each firm in the SEC Practice Section must maintain continuing education programs for its professional staff and partners, and the primary partner on an SEC client company must be rotated periodically to ensure "fresh looks" at the client over evenly spaced intervals. The SEC Practice Section is aided by a public oversight board that establishes policies for the section.

The Private Companies Section is made up of auditing firms that do not provide SEC-related services. A different set of quality standards that includes a requirement for continuing education is imposed on these firms.

The division of auditing firms has received both positive and negative responses from accountants. On one hand, many accountants support independence and continued review to assure top-quality services for publicly traded companies. On the other hand, some accountants disagree with the intrusion on the auditor-client relationship, especially the requirement to rotate partners on SEC clients. Dividing auditing firms into two groups has had some favorable outcomes by requiring comprehensive continuing education programs and by providing a mechanism for an auditing firm offering SEC services to undergo an extensive self-evaluation. The benefits seem to outweigh the costs.

SUMMARY OF KEY CONCEPTS AND TERMS

Since its creation in 1934, the SEC has played a significant role in the development of financial disclosures necessary for investor confidence in the capital formation process. The Commission has consistently worked for full and fair disclosure of information it considers necessary so investors can assess the risk and returns of companies wishing to offer their securities to the public. The SEC has taken the leadership in a myriad of reporting issues, predominantly in reporting liquidity and solvency measures, inflation reporting, and a management narrative of the company's performance.

Although the SEC has the statutory responsibility to develop and maintain accounting principles used for financial reporting, it has permitted the rule-making bodies of the accounting profession to take the initiative in establishing accounting principles and reporting standards. The cooperation has worked with varying success over the years. The SEC has shown its willingness and capacity to assume the lead in those areas in which it feels the private sector is not moving rapidly enough. It is expected that this arrangement will continue in the future.

AICPA's division of firms	Management discussion and analysis
Accounting and Auditing Enforcement Releases	Periodic reporting forms: Form 10-K, Form 10-Q, Form 8-K
Audit committees	Preliminary prospectus
Basic information package (BIP)	Pro forma disclosures
Comment letter	Proxy statement
Compensating balances	Registration statements: Form S-1,
Financial Reporting Releases	Form S-2, Form S-3
Foreign Corrupt Practices Act of 1977	Regulation S-K
	Regulation S-X
Insider trading rules	Shelf registration
Integrated disclosure system	Staff Accounting Bulletins

QUESTIONS

Q15-1 What is the basis of the SEC's legal authority to regulate accounting principles?

Q15-2 Which securities act—the 1933 or 1934 act—regulates the initial registration of securities? Which regulates the periodic reporting of publicly traded companies?

Q15-3 Which division of the SEC receives the registration statements of companies wishing to make public offerings of securities? Which division investigates individuals or firms who may be in violation of a security act?

Q15-4 Which law requires that companies maintain accurate accounting records and an adequate system of internal control? What is meant by an "adequate system of internal control"?

Q15-5 What does Regulation S-X cover? What is included in Regulation S-K?

Q15-6 What are the objectives of the integrated disclosure system?

Q15-7 Present the five major items included in the basic information package.

Q15-8 What types of public offerings of securities are exempted from the comprehensive registration requirements of the SEC?

Q15-9 When can a company use a Form S-1 registration form? In what circumstances must the company use a Form S-3 registration form?

Q15-10 Define the following terms, which are part of the SEC terminology: (a) customary review, (b) comment letter, (c) red herring prospectus, (d) shelf registration.

Q15-11 What is included in Form 10-K? When must a 10-K be filed with the SEC?

Q15-12 Must interim reports submitted to the SEC be audited? What is the role of the public accountant in the preparation of Form 10-Q?

Q15-13 What types of items are reported on Form 8-K?

Q15-14 What is a proxy? What must be included in the proxy material submitted to security holders?

Q15-15 Describe Parts I and II of the Foreign Corrupt Practices Act. What is the impact of this act on companies and public accountants?

Q15-16 What types of information must be disclosed in the management discussion and analysis? Must the MDA be included in interim reports filed with the SEC?

Q15-17 In what areas has the SEC assumed a leadership role in promoting increased disclosures in the annual report?

Q15-18 What is the SEC's position on reporting the effects of inflation in the annual report to stockholders?

Q15-19* What role has the SEC played in defining the relationship between public accountants (external, independent auditor) and publicly traded companies?

CASES

C15-1   Objectives of Securities Acts [CMA Adapted]

During the late 1920s, approximately 55 percent of all personal savings in the United States were used to purchase securities. Public confidence in the business community was extremely high as stock values doubled and tripled in short periods of time. The road to wealth was believed to be through the stock market, and everyone who was able participated. Thus, the public was severely affected when the Dow Jones Industrial Average fell 89 percent between 1929 and 1933. The public outcry arising from this decline in stock prices motivated the passage of major federal laws regulating the securities industry.

Required

a. Describe the investment practices of the 1920s that contributed to the erosion of the stock market.

b. Explain the basic objectives of each of the following:
   (1) Securities Act of 1933.
   (2) Securities Exchange Act of 1934.

c. More recent legislation has resulted from abuses in the securities industry. Explain the provisions of the Foreign Corrupt Practices Act of 1977.

C15-2   Roles of SEC and FASB [CMA Adapted]

The development of accounting theory and practice has been influenced directly and indirectly by many organizations and institutions. Two of the most important institutions have been the Financial Accounting Standards Board (FASB) and the Securities and Exchange Commission (SEC).

The FASB is an independent body that was established in 1972. The FASB is composed of seven persons who represent public accounting and fields other than public accounting.

The SEC is a governmental regulatory agency that was created in 1934 to administer the Securities Act of 1933 and the Securities Exchange Act of 1934. These acts and the creation of the SEC resulted from the widespread collapse of business and the securities markets in the early 1930s.

Required

a. What official role does the SEC have in the development of financial accounting theory and practice?

b. What is the interrelationship between the FASB and the SEC with respect to the development and establishment of financial accounting theory and practice?

C15-3 SEC Organization and Responsibilities [CMA Adapted]

The U.S. Securities and Exchange Commission (SEC) was created in 1934 and consists of five commissioners and a staff of approximately 1,900. The SEC professional staff is organized into five divisions and several principal offices. The primary objectives of the SEC are to support fair securities markets and to foster enlightened shareholder participation in major corporate decisions. The SEC has a significant presence in financial markets and corporation-shareholder relations and has the authority to exert significant influence on entities whose actions lie within the scope of its authority. The SEC chair has identified enforcement cases and full disclosure filings as major activities of the SEC.

Required

a. The SEC must have some "license" to exercise power. Explain where the SEC receives its authority.
b. Discuss in general terms the major ways in which the SEC:
   (1) Supports fair securities markets
   (2) Fosters enlightened shareholder participation in major corporate decisions
c. Describe the means by which the SEC attempts to assure the material accuracy and completeness of registrants' financial disclosure filings.

C15-4 Proxy Solicitations [CMA Adapted]

The Securities and Exchange Commission has the authority to regulate proxy solicitations. This authority is derived from the Securities and Exchange Act of 1934 and is closely tied to the disclosure objective of this act. Regulations established by the SEC require corporations to mail a proxy statement to each shareholder shortly before the annual shareholder meeting.

Required

a. Explain the purpose of proxy statements.
b. Identify four types of events or actions for which proxy statements normally are solicited.
c. Identify the conditions that must be met in order to have a dissident shareholder proposal included in a proxy statement.

C15-5 Registration Process [CMA Adapted]

Bandex Inc. has been in business for 15 years. The company has compiled a record of steady but not spectacular growth. Bandex's engineers have recently perfected a product that has an application in the small computer market. Initial orders have exceeded the company's capacity and the decision has been made to expand.

Bandex has financed past growth from internally generated funds, and since the initial stock offering 15 years ago, no further shares have been sold. Bandex's finance committee has been discussing methods of financing the proposed expansion. Both short-term and long-term notes were ruled out because of high interest rates. Mel Greene, the chief financial officer, said, "It boils down to either bonds, preferred stock, or additional common stock." Alice Dexter, a consultant employed to help in the financing decision, stated, "Regardless of your choice, you will have to file a registration statement with the SEC."

Bob Schultz, Bandex's chief accountant for the past 5 years, stated, "I've coordinated the filing of all the periodic reports required by the SEC—10-Ks, 10-Qs, and 8-Ks. I see no reason why I can't prepare a registration statement also."

Required

a. Identify the circumstances under which a firm must file a registration statement with the Securities and Exchange Commission (SEC).

b. Explain the objectives of the registration process required by the Securities Act of 1933.

c. Identify and explain the SEC publications Bob Schultz would use to guide him in preparing the registration statement.

C15-6   Form 10-K [CMA Adapted]

The Jerford Company is a well-known manufacturing company with several wholly owned subsidiaries. The company's stock is traded on the New York Stock Exchange, and the company files all appropriate reports with the Securities and Exchange Commission. Jerford Company's financial statements are audited by a public accounting firm.

Part A   Jerford Company's annual report to stockholders for the year ended December 31, 19X4, contained the following phrase in boldface type: **"The Company's 10-K is available upon written request."**

Required

a. What is form 10-K, who requires that the form be completed, and why is the phrase "The Company's 10-K is available upon written request" shown in the annual report?

b. What information not normally included in the company's annual report could be ascertained from the 10-K?

c. Indicate three items of financial information that are often included in annual reports that are not required for the 10-K.

Part B   Jerford Company changed independent auditors during 19X4. Consequently, the financial statements were certified by a different public accounting firm in 19X4 than in 19X3.

Required

What information is Jerford Company responsible for filing with the SEC with respect to this change in auditors? Explain your answer completely.

C15-7 Form 8-K [CMA Adapted]

The purpose of the Securities Act of 1933 is to regulate the initial offering of a firm's securities by ensuring that investors are given full and fair disclosure of all pertinent information about the firm. The Securities Exchange Act of 1934 was passed to regulate the trading of securities on secondary markets and to eliminate abuses in the trading of securities after their initial distribution. To accomplish these objectives, the 1934 act created the Securities and Exchange Commission. Under the auspices of the SEC, public companies must not only register their securities but must also periodically prepare and file Forms 8-K, 10-K, and 10-Q.

Required

a. With regard to Form 8-K, discuss:
  (1) The purpose of the report
  (2) The timing of the report
  (3) The format of the report
  (4) The role of financial statements in the filing of the report
b. Identify five circumstances under which the Securities and Exchange Commission requires the filing of Form 8-K.
c. Discuss how the filing of Form 8-K fosters the purpose of the SEC.
d. Does the SEC pass judgment on securities based on information contained in periodic reports? Explain your answer.

C15-8 Audit Committees [CMA Adapted]

An early event leading to the establishment of audit committees as a regular subcommittee of boards of directors occurred in 1940 as part of the consent decree relative to the McKesson-Robbins scandal. An audit committee composed of outside directors was required as part of the consent decree. (A consent decree is the formal statement issued in an enforcement action when a person agrees to terms of a disciplinary nature without admitting to the allegations in the complaint.)

Since June 1978, the New York Stock Exchange (NYSE) has required all domestic listed members to establish and maintain an audit committee composed solely of directors independent of management. The SEC has advised audit committees, boards of directors, and managements about factors which should be considered in determining whether to engage their independent accountants to perform nonaudit services.

Despite the increasing interest in audit committees and the official actions taken as described above, no specific role, duties, or liabilities have been established for them by the SEC, the NYSE, or any of the accounting organizations. Nevertheless, a commonly accepted set of duties and expectations has developed for the conduct and performance of audit committees.

Required

a. Explain the role the audit committee generally assumes with respect to the annual audit conducted by the company's external auditors.
b. Identify duties other than those associated with the annual audit which might be assigned to the audit committee by the board of directors.

c. Discuss the relationship which should exist between the audit committee and a company's internal audit staff.

d. Explain why board members appointed to serve on the audit committee should be outside (independent of management) board members.

EXERCISES

E15-1 **Organization Structure and Regulatory Authority of the SEC** [CMA Adapted]

Select the correct answer for each of the following questions.

1. Two interesting and important topics concerning the SEC are the role the Commission plays in the development of accounting principles and the impact it has had and will continue to have on the accounting profession and business in general. Which of the following statements about the SEC's authority on accounting practice is false?
   a. The SEC has the statutory authority to regulate and to prescribe the form and content of financial statements and other reports it receives.
   b. Regulation S-X of the SEC is the principal source of the form and content of financial statements to be included in registration statements and financial reports filed with the Commission.
   c. The SEC has little if any authority over disclosures in corporate annual reports mailed to shareholders with proxy solicitations. The type of information disclosed and the format to be used are left to the discretion of management.
   d. If the Commission disagrees with some presentation in the registrant's financial statements but the principles used by the registrant have substantial authoritative support, the SEC often will accept footnotes to the statements in lieu of correcting the statements to the SEC view, provided the SEC has not previously expressed its opinion on the matter in published material.

2. The Securities and Exchange Commission was established in 1934 to help regulate the U.S. securities market. Which of the following statements is true about the SEC?
   a. The SEC prohibits the sale of speculative securities.
   b. The SEC regulates only securities offered for public sale.
   c. Registration with the SEC guarantees the accuracy of the registrant's prospectus.
   d. The SEC's initial influences and authority have diminished in recent years as the stock exchanges have become more organized and better able to police themselves.
   e. The SEC's powers are broad with respect to enforcement of its reporting requirements as established in the 1933 and 1934 acts but narrow with respect to new reporting requirements because these require confirmation by Congress.

3. The Securities and Exchange Commission is organized into several divisions and principal offices. The organization unit that reviews registration statements, annual reports, and proxy statements that are filed with the Commission is:
   a. The Office of the Chief Accountant.
   b. The Division of Corporation Finance.
   c. The Division of Enforcement.
   d. The Division of Market Regulation.
   e. The Office of the Comptroller.

4. Regulation S-X:
   a. Specifies the information that can be incorporated by reference from the annual report into the registration statement filed with the SEC.
   b. Specifies the regulation and reporting requirements of proxy solicitations.
   c. Provides the basis for generally accepted accounting principles.
   d. Specifies the general form and content requirements of financial statements filed with the SEC.
   e. Provides explanations and clarifications of changes in accounting or auditing procedures used in reports filed with the SEC.

5. The Securities Exchange Act of 1934 specifies the types of companies that must report periodically to the SEC. Which one of the following types of companies is not required to report to the SEC under this act?
   a. Banks subject to the Federal Reserve Board.
   b. Companies whose securities are listed on the National Securities Exchange.
   c. Companies whose securities are traded over the counter, if those companies have total assets in excess of $1 million and 500 or more stockholders.
   d. Companies whose securities are traded over the counter that voluntarily elect to comply with the reporting requirements even though they have total assets less than $1 million and less than 500 stockholders.
   e. Companies with over 300 stockholders of a class of securities that is registered under the Securities Act of 1933.

6. Which of the following is not a purpose of the Securities Exchange Act of 1934?
   a. To establish federal regulation over securities exchanges and markets.
   b. To prevent unfair practices on securities exchanges and markets.
   c. To discourage and prevent the use of credit in financing excessive speculation in securities.
   d. To approve the securities of corporations which are to be traded publicly.
   e. To control unfair use of information by corporate insiders.

7. Regulation S-K disclosure requirements of the Securities and Exchange Commission deal with the company's business, properties, and legal proceedings; selected 5-year summary financial data; management's discussion and analysis of financial condition and results of operations; and:
   a. The form and content of the required financial statements.
   b. The requirements for filing interim financial statements.
   c. Unofficial interpretations and practices regarding securities laws disclosure requirements.
   d. Supplementary financial information such as quarterly financial data and information on the effects of changing prices.
   e. The determination of the proper registration statement form to be used in any specific public offering of securities.

E15-2 Role of SEC in Establishing Disclosure Standards [CMA Adapted]

Select the correct answer for each of the following questions.

1. The role of the Securities and Exchange Commission regarding financial accounting for public companies is that the SEC:

    a. Promulgates generally accepted accounting principles.

    b. Adopts pronouncements of the Financial Accounting Standards Board in every case.

    c. Regularly adopts requirements that conflict with the pronouncements of the Financial Accounting Standards Board.

    d. Makes regulations and rules pertaining to filings with the SEC but not to annual or quarterly reports to shareholders.

    e. Makes regulations and rules pertaining more to disclosure outside the financial statements than to the setting of accounting measurement principles.

2. The primary intent of the integrated disclosure rules issued by the Securities and Exchange Commission is:

    a. To reduce the influence of SEC rgulations in public financial reporting.

    b. To replace generally accepted accounting principles with Regulation S-X.

    c. To replace Regulation S-X with generally accepted accounting principles.

    d. To minimize the differences between published financial reports and financial reports filed on Form 10-K.

    e. To integrate the materiality criteria of Regulation S-X with generally accepted accounting principles.

3. The SEC's system of integrated disclosure of financial information sets forth criteria for management discussion and analysis of financial conditions and results of operations. One of these criteria is that:

    a. Forward-looking information is encouraged but not required to be disclosed.

    b. A discussion of financial conditions for the most recent 7 fiscal years be included.

    c. Information about the effects of inflation be provided only when the registrant is already subject to the reporting requirement of **FASB 89**, ''Financial Reporting and Changing Prices.''

    d. An analysis of income from foreign operations be included even if such operations are not material to the results of the firm.

    e. Identification of all equity security investments in defense contracts and oil and gas subsidiaries be included whether or not such investments are material to the overall financial statements and operations.

4. The underlying concept of the SEC's integrated disclosure program, which took effect for fiscal years ending after December 15, 1980, recognizes:

    a. The need for more detailed regulatory requirements to maintain separate generally accepted accounting principles and SEC disclosures.

    b. That no basic information can be described as common to the annual report and the 10-K.

    c. The efficient capital markets concept, i.e., widely followed companies produce information for the public in various forms, resulting in less need for a specific disclosure format.

    d. Recent actions to provide oversight of the SEC by the senior technical committees of professional organizations.

    e. The elimination of the need for an unqualified auditor's opinion on financial statements filed with the SEC.

5. SEC regulations provide for a procedure known as ''incorporation by reference.'' Which of the following best illustrates the concept of incorporation by reference?

a. Incorporation of a partnership by reference to the U.S. tax code.
b. Incorporation of proprietorship or partnership.
c. Inclusion of information on officers' remuneration in Form 10-K by reference to the same information in the proxy statement to shareholders.
d. Footnote reference to market data per share since incorporation.
e. Footnote disclosure that financial statements are incorporated into the annual report by reference from Form 10-K.

6. Which one of the following is a required disclosure in the annual reports of companies registered with the Securities and Exchange Commission?
   a. Audited balance sheets for the last 4 years.
   b. Audited summary of earnings for the last 10 years.
   c. Identification of registrar and transfer agent.
   d. Identification of significant research projects.
   e. Range of market prices of the common stock of the registrant for each quarter of the last 2 years.

7. The management discussion and analysis section of Form 10-K has been revised by the SEC's integrated disclosure system. The revised management discussion section does not require a description of:
   a. Factors affecting financial condition as well as the results of operations.
   b. Factors affecting international markets and currency exchange.
   c. Factors that are likely to increase or decrease liquidity materially.
   d. Material commitments for capital expenditures, including the purpose of and source of financing for such commitments.
   e. The impact of inflation and changing prices on net sales and revenue and on income from continuing operations.

8. Non–financial statement disclosures are specified in:
   a. Regulation S-K.
   b. Financial Reporting Releases.
   c. Staff Accounting Bulletins.
   d. Accounting and Auditing Enforcement Releases.
   e. Regulation S-X.

9. Staff Accounting Bulletins (SABs) issued by the SEC:
   a. Specify the information that can be incorporated by reference from the annual report into the registration statement filed with the SEC.
   b. Specify the regulations and reporting requirements of proxy solicitations.
   c. Provide explanations, interpretations, and procedures used by the SEC in administering the federal securities laws.
   d. Specify the general form and content requirements of financial statements filed with the SEC.
   e. Provide explanations and clarifications of changes in accounting or auditing procedures used in reports filed with the SEC.

10. Financial Reporting Releases (FRRs), called Accounting Series Releases (ASRs) before 1982, issued by the SEC:
    a. Provide the basis for generally accepted accounting principles.
    b. Specify the regulations and reporting requirements of proxy solicitations.
    c. Provide explanations, interpretations, and procedures.

    d. Specify the general form and content requirements of financial statements filed with the SEC.

    e. Provide explanations and clarifications of changes in accounting or auditing procedures used in reports filed with the SEC.

E15-3 Registration of New Securities [CMA Adapted]

Select the correct answer for each of the following questions.

1. In the registration and sales of new securities issues, the SEC:

    a. Endorses the investment merit of a security by allowing its registration to "go effective."

    b. Provides a rating of the investment quality of the security.

    c. May not allow the registration to "go effective" if it judges the security's investment risk to be too great.

    d. Allows all registrations to "go effective" if the issuing company's external accountant is satisfied that disclosures and representations are not misleading.

    e. Does not makes any guarantees regarding the material accuracy of the registration statement.

2. The 1933 Securities Act provides for a 20-day waiting period between the filing and the effective date of the registration. During this waiting period the registrant is prohibited from:

    a. Preparing any amendments to the registration statement.

    b. Announcing the prospective issue of the securities being registered.

    c. Accepting offers to purchase the securities being registered from potential investors.

    d. Placing an advertisement indicating by whom orders for the securities being registered will be accepted.

    e. Issuing a prospectus in preliminary form.

3. Before turning over the proceeds of a securities offering to a registrant, the underwriters frequently require a "comfort letter" from the public accountant. The purpose of the comfort letter is:

    a. To remove the public distrust of a red herring by converting the letter into a prospectus.

    b. To find out if the public accountant found any adverse financial change between the date of audit and the effective date of the securities offering.

    c. To gain comfort from the public accountant's audit of the stub period financial statements contained in the registration statement.

    d. To meet SEC regulations requiring the public accountant to give an opinion as an expert on the financial statements of the registrant.

    e. To conform to New York Stock Exchange (NYSE) member requirements that a comfort letter from a public accountant be obtained before public sale of securities.

E15-4 Reporting Requirements of the SEC [CMA Adapted]

Select the correct answer for each of the following questions.

1. Form 10-K is filed with the SEC to update the information a company supplied when filing a registration statement under the Securities and Exchange Act of 1934. Form 10-K is a report that is filed:

a. Annually within 90 days of the end of a company's fiscal year.

b. Semiannually within 30 days of the end of a company's second and fourth fiscal quarters.

c. Quarterly within 45 days of the end of each quarter.

d. Monthly within 2 weeks of the end of each month.

e. Within 15 days of the occurrence of significant events.

2. Regulation S-X disclosure requirements of the Securities and Exchange Commission (SEC) deal with:

a. Changes in and disagreements with accountants on accounting and financial disclosure.

b. Management's discussion and analysis of the financial condition and the results of operations.

c. The requirements for filing interim financial statements and pro forma financial information.

d. Summary information, risk factors, and the ratio of earnings to fixed charges.

e. Information concerning recent sales of unregistered securities.

3. Form 10-Q is filed with the SEC to keep both investors and experts apprised of a company's operations and financial position. Form 10-Q is a report that is filed within:

a. 90 days after the end of the fiscal year covered by the report.

b. 45 days after the end of each of the first three quarters of each fiscal year.

c. 90 days after the end of an employee stock purchase plan fiscal year.

d. 15 days after the occurrence of a significant event.

e. 60 days after the end of the fiscal year covered by the report.

4. The SEC has substantially increased the disclosure requirements on Form 10-Q quarterly reports to the point where all but one of the following items must be disclosed. Select the item that need not be filed with the quarterly 10-Q.

a. Signature of either the chief financial officer or chief accounting officer.

b. Management analysis of reasons for material changes in the amount of revenue and expense items from one quarter to the next.

c. In case of a change in accounting principle, a letter indicating that the public accountant believes the new principle is preferable for measuring business operations.

d. Income statements for the most recent quarter, the equivalent quarter from the preceding year, and year-to-date data for both years.

e. A statement by the public accountant that he or she has reviewed the financial data in Form 10-Q and that all necessary adjustments are reflected in the statements.

5. A significant event affecting a company registered under the Securities and Exchange Act of 1934 should be reported on:

a. Form 10-K.

b. Form 10-Q.

c. Form S-1.

d. Form 8-K.

e. Form 11-K.

6. Within 15 days after the occurrence of any event that is of material importance to the stockholders, a company must file a Form 8-K information report with the SEC to disclose the event. An example of the type of event required to be disclosed is:
   a. A salary increase to the officers.
   b. A contract to continue to employ the same certified public accounting firm as in the prior year.
   c. A change in projected earnings per share from $12.00 to $12.11 per share.
   d. The purchase of bank certificates of deposit.
   e. The acquisition of a large subsidiary other than in the ordinary course of business.

7. Form 8-K must generally be submitted to the SEC within 15 days after the occurrence of a significant event. Which one of the following is not an event that would be reported by Form 8-K?
   a. The replacement of the registrant company's external auditor.
   b. A material change in accounting principle.
   c. The resignation of one of the directors of the registrant company.
   d. A significant acquisition or disposition of assets.
   e. A change in control of the registrant company.

8. Which one of the following items is not required to be included in a company's periodic 8-K report filed with the SEC when significant events occur?
   a. Acquisition or disposition of a significant amount of assets.
   b. Instigation or termination of material legal proceedings other than routine litigation incidental to the business.
   c. Change in certifying public accountant.
   d. Election of new vice president of finance to replace the retiring incumbent.
   e. Default in the payment of principal, interest, or sinking fund installment.

E15-5 Corporate Governance [CMA Adapted]

Select the correct answer for each of the following questions.

1. A major impact of the Foreign Corrupt Practices Act of 1977 is that registrants subject to the Securities Exchange Act of 1934 are required to:
   a. Keep records that reflect the transactions and dispositions of assets and to maintain a system of internal accounting controls.
   b. Provide access to records by authorized agencies of the federal government.
   c. Record all correspondence with foreign nations.
   d. Prepare financial statements in accordance with international accounting standards.
   e. Produce full, fair, and accurate periodic reports on foreign commerce, foreign political party affiliations, or both.

2. The requirements of the Foreign Corrupt Practices Act of 1977 to devise and maintain an adequate system of internal accounting control is assigned in the act to the:
   a. Chief financial officer.
   b. Board of directors.
   c. Director of internal auditing.
   d. Company's external auditor.
   e. Company as a whole with no designation of specific persons or positions.

3. As far as the SEC is concerned, the existence of a public company's reasonably effective system of internal accounting control:
   a. Is a matter that requires no specific disclosure or comment by management in annual reports or filings with the SEC.
   b. Is not required if financial statements can be presented in accordance with generally accepted accounting principles.
   c. Must be specifically attested to in the audit report of the registrant's external accounting firm.
   d. Is required only to the extent necessary to deter company personnel from bribing foreign governmental or political officials.
   e. Is a matter about which the SEC has no authority under federal law.

4. Shareholders may ask or allow others to enter their vote at a shareholders' meeting that they are unable to attend. The document furnished to shareholders to provide background information for their vote is a:
   a. Registration statement.
   b. Proxy statement.
   c. 10-K report.
   d. Prospectus.
   e. Proxy.

5. Formation and meaningful utilization of an audit committee of the board of directors is required of publicly traded companies that are subject to the rules of the:
   a. Securities and Exchange Commission.
   b. Financial Accounting Standards Board.
   c. New York Stock Exchange.
   d. National Association of Securities Dealers.
   e. SEC Practice Section of the American Institute of Certified Public Accountants' Division of Firms.

6. An audit committee of the board of directors consisting of outside directors should be objective in arbitrating disputes between a company's top management and the external auditor because audit committee members:
   a. Have only limited contacts with the external auditor.
   b. Have no direct responsibility for the results of a company's operations.
   c. Usually have no influence on the hiring of the external auditor.
   d. Rely on opinions of senior management in resolving disputes with the external auditor.
   e. Are required by the Securities Exchange Act of 1934 to oversee the progress of the annual external audit.

7. An external auditor's involvement with Form 10-Q that is being prepared for filing with the SEC would most likely consist of:
   a. An audit of the financial statements included in Form 10-Q.
   b. A compilation report on the financial statements included in Form 10-Q.
   c. Issuing a comfort letter that covers stub-period financial data.
   d. Issuing an opinion on the internal controls under which the Form 10-Q data were developed.
   e. A review of the interim financial statements included in Form 10-Q.

CHAPTER 16

PARTNERSHIPS: FORMATION, OPERATION, AND CHANGES IN MEMBERSHIP

The number of partnerships in the United States has been estimated to be between 1.5 and 2.0 million, second only to sole proprietorships, which number in excess of 15 million businesses. In contrast, there are about 1 million corporations in the United States. Accountants are often called on to aid in the formation and operation of partnerships to ensure proper measurement and valuation of the partnership's transactions. This chapter focuses on the formation and operation of partnerships, including accounting for the addition of new partners and the retirement of a present partner. Chapter 17 presents the accounting for the termination and liquidation of partnerships.

Partnerships are a popular form of business because they are easy to form and because they allow several individuals to combine their talents and skills in a particular business venture. In addition, partnerships provide a means of obtaining more equity capital than a single individual can obtain and allow the sharing of risks for rapidly growing businesses. Partnerships are particularly common in the service professions, especially law, medicine, and accounting. These professions have generally not adopted the corporate form of business because of their long-standing tradition of close professional association with clients and the total commitment of the professional's business and personal assets to the propriety of the advice and service given to clients.

Accounting for partnerships requires recognition of several important factors. First, from an accounting viewpoint, the partnership is a separate business entity. From a legal viewpoint, however, a partnership, like a sole proprietorship, is not separate from the owners. The Internal Revenue Code views the partnership form as a conduit only, not separable from the business interests of the individual partners. Therefore several differences exist between tax and financial accounting for specific events, such as the value assigned to assets contributed in the formation of the partnership. This chapter presents the generally accepted accounting principles of partnership accounting. A brief discussion of the tax aspects of a partnership is presented in Appendix A to this chapter.

Second, although many partnerships account for their operations using accrual accounting, some partnerships use the cash basis or modified cash basis of accounting. These alternatives are allowed because the partnership records are maintained for the partners and must reflect their information needs. The partnership's financial statements are usually prepared only for the partners, but occasionally for the partnership's creditors. Unlike publicly traded corporations, most partnerships are not required to have annual audits of their financial statements. Although many partnerships adhere to generally accepted accounting principles (GAAP), deviations from GAAP are found in practice. The specific needs of the partners should be the primary criteria for determining the accounting policies to be used for a specific partnership.

NATURE OF PARTNERSHIP ENTITY

The partnership form of business has several unique elements because of its legal and accounting status. The following section describes the major characteristics which distinguish the partnership form of organization.

Definition of a Partnership

The *Uniform Partnership Act* (UPA) has been the general governing authority for partnerships since its adoption by virtually all the states. Accountants advising partnerships must be familiar with this act because it describes many of the rights of each partner and of creditors during creation, operation, and liquidation of the partnership. Section 6 of the UPA defines a partnership as an "association of two or more persons to carry on as co-owners a business for profit." This definition encompasses three distinct factors:

1. *Association of Two or More Persons.* The "persons" are usually individuals; however, they could be corporations or other partnerships.

2. *To Carry On as Co-Owners.* A partnership is an aggregation of partners' individual rights. This means that all partners are co-owners of partnership property and are co-owners of the profits or losses of the partnership.

3. *Business for Profit.* A partnership may be formed to perform any legal business, trade, profession, or other service. However, the partnership must attempt to make a profit; therefore, not-for-profit organizations, such as fraternal groups, may not be partnerships.

Formation of a Partnership

A primary advantage of the partnership form of entity is ease of formation. The agreement to form a partnership may be as informal as a handshake or as formal as a many-paged agreement typically termed the *articles of copartnership*. Each partner must agree to the formation agreement, and partners are strongly advised to have a formal written agreement in order to avoid potential problems that may arise during the operation of the business. It is usually true that if the potential partners cannot agree on the various operating aspects before a partnership is formed, then many future disputes may arise that could cause severe management problems and that might seriously imperil the operations of the partnership.

The articles of copartnership should include the following items:

1. The name of the partnership and the names of the partners.

2. The type of business to be conducted by the partnership and the duration of the partnership agreement.

3. The initial capital contribution of each partner and the method by which future capital contributions are to be accounted for.

4. A complete specification of the profit or loss distribution, including salaries, interest on capital balances, bonuses, limits on withdrawals in anticipation of profits, and the percentages used to distribute any residual profit or loss.

5. Procedures used for changes in the partnership, such as admission of new partners and the retirement of a partner.

6. Other aspects of operations the partners decide on, such as the management rights of each partner, election procedures, and accounting methods.

Each partner should sign the partnership agreement to indicate acceptance of the terms. A carefully prepared partnership agreement can eliminate many of the more common types of problems and disputes that may arise in the future operations of the partnership.

Other Major Characteristics of Partnerships

Several other characteristics are germane to a partnership.

Limited Life   A partnership legally terminates as a business entity each time there is a change in membership. This legal termination is called a "dissolution of the partnership." Most partnerships include provisions in their articles of copartnership for changes in membership so that the business is not interrupted. These provisions provide procedures for electing new partners and for valuing a partner's capital balance at the time of death or retirement, thus ensuring continued business operations during the period of change.

Agency Relationship   Each partner is a co-owner of the partnership assets and liabilities. Creditors view each partner as an agent of the partnership capable of transacting business in the name of the partnership. Consequently, any partner can bind the partnership when acting within the scope of the partnership activities. For example, partner A signs a lease in the partnership name, even though the articles of copartnership specify that only partner B may sign leases. The partnership is still bound by the lease because the other party to the lease can assume mutual agency of each partner. Any legal remedy is strictly between partners A and B.

Unlimited Liability Because partnerships are not incorporated, all partners in a *general partnership* have unlimited liability. In the event the partnership fails and its assets are not sufficient to pay its liabilities, partnership creditors may take recourse by obtaining liens or attachments against the personal assets of any or all of the partners. Generally, creditors will take action against the partner with the most liquid assets. This means that any individual partner may be required to pay the partnership's creditors from personal assets in an amount exceeding his or her capital balance in the partnership. This unlimited liability of partners differs from the corporate form of business, in which an investor's ultimate loss is limited to the amount invested in the corporation's stock.

Many persons view unlimited liability as the major disadvantage of the partnership form of business. For this reason, sometimes people become *limited partners* in a *limited partnership.* The liability of limited partners is limited to the amount of their investment, but they are restricted as to the types of management acts they may perform. They cannot actively participate in the management of the partnership, but their personal assets are not placed in jeopardy as a result of their membership in the partnership. Limited partners must be identified as such to creditors and others doing business with the partnership. All partnerships must have at least one general partner whose liability is not limited.

ACCOUNTING FOR THE FORMATION OF A PARTNERSHIP

At the formation of a partnership, it is necessary to assign a proper value to the noncash assets and liabilities contributed by the partners. An item contributed by a partner becomes partnership property co-owned by all partners. The partnership must clearly distinguish between capital contributions and loans made to the partnership by individual partners. Loan arrangements should be evidenced by promissory notes or other legal documents necessary to show that a loan arrangement exists between the partnership and an individual partner.

The contributed assets should be valued at their fair values, which may require appraisals or other valuation techniques. Liabilities assumed by the partnership should be valued at the present value of the remaining cash flows.

The individual partners must agree to the percentage of equity that each will have in the net assets of the partnership. Generally, the capital balance is determined by the proportionate share of each partner's capital contribution. For example, if A contributes 70 percent of the net assets in a partnership with B, then A will have a 70 percent capital share and B will have a 30 percent capital share. In recognition of intangible factors, such as a partner's special expertise or necessary business connections, however, partners may agree to any proportional division of capital. Therefore, before recording the initial capital contribution, all partners must agree on the valuation of the net assets and on each partner's capital share.

Illustration of Accounting for Partnership Formation

The following illustration is used as the basis for the remaining discussion in this chapter. Alt, a sole proprietor, has been developing software for several types of microcomputers. The business has the following account balances as of December 31, 19X0:

Cash	3,000	
Inventory	7,000	
Equipment	20,000	
Accumulated Depreciation—Equipment		5,000
Liabilities		10,000
Alt, Capital		15,000

Alt needs additional technical assistance to meet the increasing sales and offers Blue an interest in the business. Alt and Blue agree to form a partnership. Alt's business is audited, and its net assets are appraised. The audit and appraisal disclose that $1,000 of liabilities has not been recorded, inventory has a market value of $9,000, and the equipment has a fair value of $19,000.

Alt and Blue prepare and sign articles of copartnership that include all significant operating policies. Blue will contribute $10,000 cash for a one-third capital interest. The AB Partnership is to acquire all of Alt's business and assume its debts.

The entry to record the initial capital contribution on the partnership's books is:

January 1, 19X1			
(1)	Cash	13,000	
	Inventory	9,000	
	Equipment	19,000	
	Liabilities		11,000
	Alt, Capital		20,000
	Blue, Capital		10,000
	Formation of AB Partnership by capital contributions of Alt and Blue.		

Key Observations from Illustration   Note that the partnership is an accounting entity separate from each of the partners, and that the assets and liabilities are recorded at their market values at the time of contribution. No accumulated depreciation is carried forward from the sole proprietorship to the partnership. All liabilities are recognized and recorded.

The capital of the partnership is $30,000. This is the sum of the individual partners' capital accounts and is also the value of the partnership's assets less liabilities. The fundamental accounting equation—assets less liabilities equals capital—is used often in partnership accounting. Blue is to receive a one-third capital interest in the partnership with a contribution of $10,000. In this case, his capital interest is equal to his capital contribution.

Each partner's capital interest recorded does not necessarily have to equal his or her capital contribution. The partners could decide to divide the total capital equally regardless of the source of the contribution. For example, although Alt contributed $20,000 of the $30,000 partnership capital, he could agree to $15,000 as his initial capital balance and permit Blue the remaining $15,000 as a capital credit. On the surface this may not seem to be a reasonable action by Alt, but it is possible that Blue has some particularly important business experience needed by the partnership and Alt agrees to the additional credit to Blue in recognition of his experience and skills. The key point is that the partners may allocate the capital contributions in any manner they desire. The accountant must be sure that all partners agree to the allocation and must then record it accordingly.

ACCOUNTING FOR OPERATIONS OF A PARTNERSHIP

A partnership provides services or sells products in pursuit of profit. These transactions are recorded in the appropriate journals and ledger accounts. Many partnerships use accrual accounting and generally accepted accounting principles to maintain their books because GAAP results in better measures of income than alternative accounting methods such as the cash basis or modified cash basis. Partnership financial statements are prepared for the partners and occasionally for partnership creditors. Some partnerships may deviate from GAAP accounting for simplicity of record keeping or to reflect current asset values for an ongoing partnership. Although most partnerships are not audited, in the event an audit is made of a partnership that does not follow GAAP, the partnership's financial statements will not receive a "clean" or unqualified opinion because of its departures from GAAP. Accountants often encourage the use of GAAP for financial statement purposes because the partners may then compare the partnership's financial statements with those of other business entities; and if a creditor requires audited financial statements as a condition for a loan to the partnership, the partnership's statements are not restricted from receiving an unqualified audit opinion.

Partners' Accounts

The partnership may maintain several accounts for each partner in its accounting records. These *partners' accounts* are as follows:

Capital Accounts   The initial investment of a partner, any subsequent capital contributions, profit or loss distributions, and any withdrawals of capital by the partner are ultimately recorded in the partner's capital account. Each partner has one capital account, which usually has a credit balance. On occasion, a partner's capital account may have a debit balance, called a *deficiency* or sometimes termed a *deficit*, which occurs because the partner's share of losses and withdrawals exceeds his or her capital contribution and share of profits. A deficiency is usually eliminated by additional capital contributions. The balance in the capital account represents the partner's share of the net assets of the partnership.

Drawing Accounts   Partners generally make withdrawals of assets from the partnership during the year in anticipation of profits. A separate drawing account often is used to record the periodic withdrawals and is then closed to the partner's capital account at the end of the period. For example, the following entry is made in the AB Partnership's books for a $3,000 cash withdrawal by Blue on May 1, 19X1:

```
May 1, 19X1
    (2)  Blue, Drawing                          3,000
             Cash                                           3,000
         Withdrawal of $3,000 by Blue.
```

Noncash drawings should be valued at their market values at the date of the withdrawal. A few partnerships make an exception to the rule of market value for withdrawals of inventory by the partners. They record withdrawals of inventory at cost, thereby not recording a gain or loss on these drawings.

Loan Accounts The partnership may look to its present partners for additional financing. Any loans between a partner and the partnership should always be accompanied by proper loan documentation such as a promissory note. A loan from a partner is shown as a payable on the partnership's books, the same as any other loan. Unless all partners agree otherwise, the partnership is obligated to pay interest on the loan to the individual partner. Note that interest is *not* required to be paid on capital investments unless the partnership agreement states that capital interest is to be paid. Interest on loans is recorded as an operating expense by the partnership. Alternatively, the partnership may lend money to a partner, in which case it records a loan receivable from the partner. Again, unless it is otherwise agreed by all partners, these loans should bear interest and the interest income is recognized on the partnership's income statement. The following entry is made to record a $4,000, 10 percent, 1-year loan from Alt to the partnership on July 1, 19X1:

```
July 1, 19X1
    (3)  Cash                                    4,000
             Loan Payable to Alt                            4,000
         Sign loan agreement with partner Alt.
```

The loan payable to Alt is reported in the partnership's balance sheet. A loan from a partner is a related-party transaction for which separate footnote disclosure is required, and it must be reported as a separate balance sheet item, not included with other liabilities.

ALLOCATING PROFIT OR LOSS TO PARTNERS

Profit or loss is allocated to the partners at the end of each period in accordance with the partnership agreement. If no partnership agreement exists, section 18 of the UPA declares that profits and losses are to be shared equally by all partners. Virtually all partnerships have a profit or loss allocation agreement. The agreement must be followed precisely, and if it is unclear, then the accountant should make sure that all partners agree to the profit or loss distribution. Many problems and later arguments can be avoided by carefully specifying the profit or loss distribution in the articles of copartnership.

A wide range of *profit distribution plans* is found in the business world. Some partnerships have straightforward distribution plans, while others have extremely complex ones. It is the accountant's responsibility to distribute the profit or loss according to the partnership agreement regardless of how simple or complex that agreement is. Profit distributions are similar to dividends for a corporation: these distributions should not be included on the income statement, regardless of how the profit is distributed. Profit distributions are recorded directly into the partner's capital accounts, not as expense items.

Most partnerships use one or more of the following distribution methods:

1. Preselected ratio
2. Interest on capital balances
3. Salaries to partners
4. Bonuses to partners

Preselected ratios are usually the result of negotiations between the partners. Ratios for profit distributions may be based on the percentage of total partnership capital, time and effort invested in the partnership, or a variety of other factors. Often, smaller partnerships split profits evenly among the partners. In addition, some partnerships have different ratios if the firm suffers a loss versus earns a profit. The partnership form of business allows a wide selection of profit distribution ratios to meet the individual desires of the partners.

Distributing partnership income based on interest on capital balances recognizes the contribution of the partners' capital investments to the profit-generating capacity of the partnership. This interest on capital is not an expense of the partnership; it is a distribution of profits. If one or more of the partners' services are important to the partnership, the profit distribution agreement may provide for salaries or bonuses. Again, these salaries paid to partners are a form of profit distribution and are not an expense of the partnership. Occasionally, the distribution process may depend on the size of the profit or may differ if the partnership has a loss for the period. For example, salaries to partners might be paid only if revenue exceeds expenses by a certain amount. The accountant must carefully read the articles of copartnership to determine the precise profit distribution plan for the specific circumstances at the time.

The profit or loss distribution is recorded with a closing entry at the end of each period. The revenue and expenses are closed into an income summary account or directly into the partners' capital accounts. In the examples which follow, an income summary account is used, the balance of which is net income or net loss after the revenue and expense accounts are closed and before the income or loss is distributed to the partners' capital accounts.

Illustrations of Profit Allocation

During 19X1, the AB Partnership earns $45,000 of revenue and incurs $35,000 in expenses, leaving a profit of $10,000 for the year. Alt maintains a capital balance of $20,000 during the year, but Blue's capital investment varies during the year as follows:

Date	Debit	Credit	Balance
January 1			$10,000
May 1	$3,000		7,000
September 1		$500	7,500
November 1	1,000		6,500
December 31			6,500

The debits of $3,000 and $1,000 are recorded in Blue's drawing account, while the additional investment is credited to his capital account.

Arbitrary Profit Sharing Ratio   Alt and Blue could agree to share profits in a ratio unrelated to their capital balances or to any other operating feature of the partnership. For example, the partners might agree to share profits or losses in the ratio of 60 percent to Alt and 40 percent to Blue. Some partnership agreements specify this ratio as 3:2. The following schedule illustrates how the net income is distributed using a 3:2 profit sharing ratio:

	Alt	Blue	Total
Profit sharing percentage	60%	40%	100%
Net income			$10,000
Allocate 60:40	$6,000	$4,000	(10,000)
Total	$6,000	$4,000	$ -0-

This schedule shows how net income is distributed to the partners' capital accounts. The actual distribution is accomplished by closing the Income Summary account. In addition, the drawing accounts are closed to the capital accounts at the end of the period.

December 31, 19X1

(4)	Blue, Capital		4,000	
	Blue, Drawing			4,000
	Close Blue's drawing account.			
(5)	Revenue		45,000	
	Expenses			35,000
	Income Summary			10,000
	Close revenue and expenses.			
(6)	Income Summary		10,000	
	Alt, Capital			6,000
	Blue, Capital			4,000
	Distribute profit in accordance with partnership agreement.			

Interest on Capital Balances   The articles of copartnership may provide for interest to be credited on the partners' capital balances as part of the distribution of profits. The rate of interest is often a stated percentage, but some partnerships use an interest rate that is determined by reference to current U.S. Treasury rates or current money market rates.

As stated earlier, interest calculated on partners' capital is not an expense of operating the business. The calculation is made after net income is determined in order to decide how the income is to be distributed.

Particular caution must be exercised whenever interest on capital balances is included in the profit distribution plan. For example, the amount of the distribution can be significantly different depending on whether the interest is computed on beginning capital balances, ending capital balances, or average capital balances for the period. Most provisions for interest on capital specify that a weighted-average capital should be used. This method explicitly recognizes the time span each capital level is maintained during the period. For example, Blue's weighted-average capital balance for 19X1 is computed as follows:

Date	Debit	Credit	Balance	Months Maintained	Months Times Dollar Balance
January 1			$10,000	4	$40,000
May 1	$3,000		7,000	4	28,000
September 1		$500	7,500	2	15,000
November 1	1,000		6,500	2	13,000
Total				12	$96,000
Average capital ($96,000 ÷ 12 months)					$ 8,000

If Alt and Blue agreed to allow interest of 15 percent on the weighted-average capital balances with any remaining profit to be distributed in the 60:40 ratio, the distribution of the $10,000 profit would be calculated as follows:

	Alt	Blue	Total
Profit percentage	60%	40%	100%
Average capital	$20,000	$8,000	
Net income			$10,000
Interest on average capital (15%)	$ 3,000	$1,200	(4,200)
Residual income			$ 5,800
Allocate 60:40	3,480	2,320	(5,800)
Total	$ 6,480	$3,520	$ -0-

Salaries   Salaries to partners are often included as part of the profit distribution plan to recognize and compensate for differing amounts of personal services partners provide to the business. It is a general precept of partnership accounting that salaries to partners are not operating expenses but rather are part of the profit distribution plan. This precept is closely related to the proprietary concept of owner's equity. According to the proprietary theory, the proprietor invests capital and personal services in pursuit of income. The earnings are a result of those two investments. The same logic applies to the partnership form of organization. Some partners invest capital, while others may invest personal time. Those who invest capital are typically rewarded with interest on their capital balances; those who invest personal time are rewarded with salaries. However, both interest and salaries are a result of the respective investments and are used not in the determination of income but rather in the determination of the proportion of income to be credited to each partner's capital account. An interesting question arises if the partnership experiences losses. Can salaries to the partners during the year be treated as a distribution of profits? While any amounts actually paid to partners during the year are really drawings made in anticipation of profits, the agreed salary amounts usually are added to the loss and that total is then distributed to the partners' capital accounts. Caution should be exercised if the partnership experiences a loss during the year. Some partnership agreements specify different distributions for profit than for losses. The accountant must be especially careful to follow precisely the partnership agreement when distributing the period's profit or loss to the partners.

To examine partnership salaries, assume that the partnership agreement provides for salaries of $2,000 to Alt and $5,000 to Blue. Any remainder is to be distributed in the profit and loss sharing ratio of 60:40 percent. The profit distribution is calculated as follows:

	Alt	Blue	Total
Profit percentage	60%	40%	100%
Net income			$10,000
Salary	$2,000	$5,000	(7,000)
Residual income			$ 3,000
Allocate 60:40	1,800	1,200	(3,000)
Total	$3,800	$6,200	$ -0-

Bonuses Bonuses are sometimes used as a means of providing additional compensation to partners who have provided services to the partnership. Bonuses are typically stated as a percentage of income either before or after the bonus. Sometimes the partnership agreement requires a minimum income to be earned before a bonus is calculated. The bonus is easily calculated by deriving and solving an equation. For example, a bonus of 10 percent of income in excess of $5,000 is to be credited to Blue's capital account before distributing the remaining profit. In Case 1 the bonus is computed as a percentage of income *before* subtracting the bonus. In Case 2 the bonus is computed as a percentage of income *after* subtracting the bonus.

Case 1:

$$\text{Bonus} = X\%(\text{NI} - \text{MIN})$$

where $X\%$ = the bonus percentage
NI = net income before bonus
MIN = minimum amount of income before bonus

$$Bonus = .10(\$10,000 - \$5,000) = \$500$$

Case 2:

$$
\begin{aligned}
Bonus &= X\%(NI - MIN - Bonus) \\
&= .10(\$10,000 - \$5,000 - Bonus) \\
&= .10(\$5,000 - Bonus) \\
&= \$500 - .10\ Bonus \\
1.10\ Bonus &= \$500 \\
Bonus &= \$454.55
\end{aligned}
$$

The distribution of net income based on Case 2 is calculated as follows:

	Alt	Blue	Total
Profit percentage	60%	40%	100%
Net income			$10,000
Bonus to partner		$ 455	(455)
Residual income			$ 9,545
Allocate 60:40	$5,727	3,818	(9,545)
Total	$5,727	$4,273	$ -0-

Multiple Bases of Profit Allocation

A partnership agreement may describe a combination of several allocation procedures to be used to distribute profit. For example, the profit and loss agreement of the AB Partnership specifies the following allocation method:

1. Interest of 15 percent on weighted-average capital balances
2. Salaries of $2,000 for Alt and $5,000 for Blue
3. A bonus of 10 percent to be paid to Blue on partnership income exceeding $5,000 before subtracting the bonus, partners' salaries, and interest on capital balances
4. Any residual to be allocated in the ratio of 60 percent to Alt and 40 percent to Blue

The partnership agreement should also contain a provision to specify the allocation process in the event that partnership income is not sufficient to satisfy all the allocation procedures. Some partnerships specify a profit distribution to be followed to whatever extent is possible. Most agreements specify that the entire process is to be completed and any remainder is to be allocated in the profit and loss ratio as illustrated in the following schedule:

	Alt	Blue	Total
Profit percentage	60%	40%	100%
Average capital	$20,000	$8,000	
Net income:			$10,000
Step 1:			
Interest on average capital (15 percent)	$ 3,000	$1,200	(4,200)
Remaining after step 1			$ 5,800
Step 2:			
Salary	2,000	5,000	(7,000)
Deficiency after step 2			$(1,200)
Step 3:			
Bonus		500	(500)
Deficiency after step 3			$(1,700)
Step 4:			
Allocate 60:40	(1,020)	(680)	1,700
Total	$ 3,980	$6,020	$ -0-

In this case, the first two distribution steps created a deficiency. The AB Partnership agreement provided that the entire profit distribution process must be completed and any deficiency distributed in the profit and loss ratio. A partnership agreement could specify that the profit distribution process stop at any point in the event of an operating loss or the creation of a deficiency. Again, it is important for the accountant to have a thorough knowledge of the partnership agreement before beginning the profit distribution process.

Special Profit Allocation Methods

Some partnerships distribute net income on the basis of other criteria. For example, most public accounting partnerships distribute profit on the basis of partnership "units." A new partner acquires a certain number of units and additional units are assigned by a firmwide compensation committee for obtaining new clients, for providing the firm with specific areas of industrial expertise, for serving as a local office's managing partner, or for accepting a variety of other responsibilities.

Other partnerships may devise profit distribution plans that reflect the earnings of the partnership. For example, some medical or dental partnerships allocate profit on the basis of billed services. Other criteria may be number or size of clients, years of service with the firm, or the partner's position within the firm. An obvious advantage of the partnership form of organization is the flexibility it allows partners for the distribution of profits.

PARTNERSHIP FINANCIAL STATEMENTS

A partnership is a separate reporting entity for accounting purposes, and the three financial statements—income statement, balance sheet, and statement of cash flows—typically are prepared for the partnership at the end of each reporting period. Interim statements may also be prepared to meet the information needs of the partners. In addition to the three basic financial statements, a *statement of partners' capital* is usually prepared to present the changes in the partners' capital accounts for the period. The statement of partners' capital for the AB Partnership for 19X1 under the multiple-base profit distribution plan illustrated in the prior section is presented below.

AB Partnership
Statement of Partners' Capital
For the Year Ended December 31, 19X1

	Alt	Blue	Total
Balance, January 1, 19X1	$20,000	$10,000	$30,000
Add: Additional investment		500	500
Net income distribution	3,980	6,020	10,000
	$23,980	$16,520	$40,500
Less: Withdrawal		(4,000)	(4,000)
Balance, December 31, 19X1	$23,980	$12,520	$36,500

CHANGES IN MEMBERSHIP

Changes in the membership of a partnership occur with the addition of new partners or the retirement of present partners. New partners are often a primary source of additional capital or needed business expertise. The legal structure of a partnership requires that the *admission of a new partner* be subject to the unanimous approval of the present partners. Furthermore, public announcements are typically made about new partner additions so that third parties transacting business with the partnership are aware of the change in the partnership. Section 17 of the Uniform Partnership Act specifies that a new partner is liable for all obligations of the partnership incurred before the new partner's admission date, but the extent of liability for preexisting debts is limited to the new partner's capital investment.

The retirement or *withdrawal of a partner from a partnership* results in the legal dissolution of the partnership. A dissolution does not require termination of the business. A dissolution means that the partnership's books are brought up to date through any necessary adjusting entries and the withdrawing partner's capital account is determined as of the date of the withdrawal. Appropriate recognition then is given to the withdrawal of the partner.

The admission of a new partner or retirement of a present partner results in a new partnership, although daily operations of the business generally are not affected. Because a new partnership is formed, many partnerships use the transactions surrounding the change as evidence for revaluing the existing assets of the partnership or for recording previously unrecognized goodwill. This practice of *asset revaluation* and *goodwill recognition* constitutes a marked difference from corporation practice. The justification given to revaluing assets at the time of the change in the membership of the partnership is to state fully the true economic condition of the partnership at the time of the change in membership and to assign the changes in asset values and goodwill to the partners who have been managing the business during the time the changes in values occurred. Indeed, many accountants feel this revaluation is necessary to value properly each partner's present equity in the partnership.

A new partner may be admitted by (1) acquiring part of an existing partner's interest directly in a private transaction with the selling partner or (2) by investing additional capital in the partnership.

New Partner Purchases an Interest

An individual may acquire a partnership interest directly from one or more of the present partners. In this type of transaction, cash or other assets are exchanged outside the partnership, and the only entry necessary on the partnership's books is a reclassification of the total capital of the partnership.

A concept used with some frequency is book value. The *book value of a partnership* is simply the total amount of the capital, which is also the difference between total assets and total liabilities. Book value is important because it serves as a basis for asset revaluations or goodwill recognition.

For purposes of this discussion, assume that after operations and partners' withdrawals during 19X1 and 19X2, AB Partnership has a book value of $30,000 and profit percentages on January 1, 19X3, as shown below:

	Capital Balance	Profit Percentage
Alt	$20,000	60
Blue	10,000	40
Total	$30,000	100

The following information describes the case:

1. On January 1, 19X3, Alt and Blue invite Cha to become a partner in their business. The resulting partnership will be called the ABC Partnership.

2. Cha purchases a one-fourth interest in the partnership capital directly from Alt and Blue for a total cost of $9,000, paying $5,900 to Alt and $3,100 to Blue. Cha will have a capital credit of $7,500 ($30,000 × .25) in a proportionate reclassification from Alt and Blue's capital accounts.

3. Cha will be entitled to a 25 percent interest in the profits or losses of the partnership. The remaining 75 percent interest will be divided between Alt and Blue in their old profit ratio of 60:40 percent. The resulting profit and loss percentages after the admission of Cha are:

Partner	Profit Percentage
Alt	45 (75% of .60)
Blue	30 (75% of .40)
Cha	25
Total	100

In this example, Cha's 25 percent share of partnership profits or losses is the same as her one-fourth capital interest. These two percentage shares do not have to be the same. As was described earlier in the chapter, a partner's capital interest may change over time because of profit distributions, withdrawals, or additional investments in capital. Furthermore, Cha could have acquired her entire capital interest directly from either partner. It is not necessary that a new partner directly purchasing an interest do so in a proportionate reclassification from each of the prior partners.

The transaction is between Cha and the individual partners and is not reflected on the partnership's books. The only entry in this case is to reclassify the partnership capital. Alt and Blue each provide one-fourth of their capital to Cha, as follows:

```
January 1, 19X3
  (7)  Alt, Capital                                    5,000
       Blue, Capital                                   2,500
            Cha, Capital                                          7,500
       Reclassify capital to new partner.
       From Alt: $5,000 = $20,000 × .25
       From Blue: $2,500 = $10,000 × .25
```

In this case the capital credit to Cha is only $7,500, although $9,000 is paid for the one-fourth interest. The payment of $9,000 implies that the fair value of the partnership is $36,000, calculated as follows:

$$\$9,000 = \text{fair value} \times .25$$
$$\$36,000 = \text{fair value}$$

The book value of the partnership is $30,000 before Cha's investment. The payment of $9,000 is made directly to the individual partners, and it does not become part of the partnership's assets. The $6,000 difference between the partnership's fair value and its new book value could be due to understated assets or possibly to unrecognized goodwill.

Alt and Blue could use the evidence from Cha's acquisition to revalue the partnership's assets and fully reflect the changes in values that have taken place before the admission of Cha. Failure to do so could result in Cha's sharing proportionately in the increases in value when the increases are realized. For example, if the partnership has land that is undervalued by $6,000 and if the land is sold after Cha is admitted to the partnership, Cha will share in the gain on the sale of the land according to the profit ratio. To avoid this possible problem, some partnerships revalue the assets at the time a new partner is admitted, even if the new partner purchases the partnership interest directly from the present partners. In this case, Alt and Blue could recognize the increase in the value of the land immediately before the admission of Cha and properly allocate the increase to their capital accounts in their 60:40 profit ratio, as follows:

(8)	Land	6,000	
	Alt, Capital		3,600
	Blue, Capital		2,400
	Revaluation of land before admission of new partner.		

Note that the total resulting capital of the partnership is now $36,000 ($30,000 prior plus the $6,000 revaluation). The transfer of a one-fourth capital credit to Cha is recorded as follows:

(9)	Alt, Capital	5,900	
	Blue, Capital	3,100	
	Cha, Capital		9,000
	Reclassify capital to new partner:		
	$5,900 = $23,600 × .25		
	$3,100 = $12,400 × .25		
	$9,000 = $36,000 × .25		

A partnership has wide latitude in recognizing goodwill or revaluing assets. The partnership's accountant should ensure that sufficient evidence exists for any revaluation in order to prevent valuation abuses. Corroborating evidence such as appraisals or an extended period of excess earnings help support asset valuations.

New Partner Invests in Partnership

A new partner may acquire a share of the partnership by investing in the business. In this case, the partnership receives the cash or other assets. Three cases can exist when a new partner invests in a partnership:

Case 1. The new partner's investment is equal to the new partner's proportion of the partnership's book value.

Case 2. The investment is for *more* than the new partner's proportion of the partnership's book value. This indicates that the partnership's prior net assets are undervalued on the books or that unrecorded goodwill exists.

Case 3. The investment is for *less* than the new partner's proportion of the partnership's book value. This suggests that the partnership's prior net assets are overvalued on the books of the partnership or that the new partner may be contributing goodwill in addition to other assets.

The first step in determining how to account for the admission of a new partner is to compute the ***new partner's proportion of the partnership's book value*** as follows:

$$
\begin{array}{c}
\text{New partner's} \\
\text{proportion of} \\
\text{the partnership's} \\
\text{book value}
\end{array}
=
\left(
\begin{array}{c}
\text{prior} \\
\text{capital of} \\
\text{present} \\
\text{partners}
\end{array}
+
\begin{array}{c}
\text{investment} \\
\text{of new} \\
\text{partner}
\end{array}
\right)
\times
\begin{array}{c}
\text{percentage} \\
\text{of capital} \\
\text{to new} \\
\text{partner}
\end{array}
$$

The new partner's proportion of the partnership's book value is compared with the amount of the investment made by the new partner to determine the procedures to be followed in accounting for his or her admission. Figure 16-1 presents an overview of the three cases presented above. Step 1 is to compare the new partner's investment with his or her proportion of the partnership's book value. Note that this is done before any revaluations or recognition of goodwill. Step 2 is to determine the specific admission method. Three different methods are available to the partnership to account for the admission of a new partner when there is a difference between the new partner's investment and his or her proportion of the partnership's book value. The three methods are: (1) revalue net assets, (2) recognize goodwill, or (3) use the ***bonus method***. Under the revaluation of net assets and goodwill recognition methods, the historical cost bases of the partnership's net assets are adjusted during the admission of the new partner. Some partners object to this departure from historical cost and prefer to use the bonus method which uses capital interest transfers among the partners to align the total resulting capital of the partnership. Under the bonus method, net assets remain at their historical cost bases to the partnership. The choice of method of accounting for the admission of a new partner is up to the partners.

There are several parallels between accounting for the admission of a new partner and accounting for an investment in the stock of another company. If a new partner pays more than book value, the excess of cost over book value, that is, the positive differential, may be due to unrecognized goodwill or to undervalued assets—the same cases as in accounting for the differential for stock investments. If book value equals the investment cost, then no differential exists, indicating that the book values of the net assets are equal to their fair values. If the new partner's investment is less than the proportionate book value, that is, an excess of book value over cost exists, then the assets of the partnership may be overvalued. Therefore, the only concept unique to partnership accounting is the use of the bonus method. Figure 16-1 serves as a guide through the following discussion.

The AB Partnership example presented earlier is again used to illustrate the three cases. A review of the major facts for this example follows:

1. The January 1, 19X3, capital of the AB Partnership is $30,000. Alt's balance is $20,000, and Blue's balance is $10,000. Alt and Blue share profits in the ratio of 60:40.

2. Cha is invited into the partnership. Cha will have a one-fourth capital interest and a 25 percent share of profits. Alt and Blue will share the remaining 75 percent of profits in the ratio of 60:40, resulting in Alt having a 45 percent share of any profits and Blue having a 30 percent share.

FIGURE 16-1 Overview of accounting for admission of a new partner.

Step 1: Compare Proportionate Book Value and Investment of New Partner	Step 2: Alternative Methods to Account for Admission	Key Observations
Investment cost > book value (Case 2)	1. Revalue net assets up to market value and allocate to prior partners. 2. Record unrecognized goodwill and allocate to prior partners. 3. Assign bonus to prior partners.	• Prior partners receive asset valuation increase, goodwill, or bonus indicated by the excess of new partner's investment over book value of the capital share initially assignable to new partner. • Recording asset valuation increase or prior partners' goodwill increases total resulting partnership capital.
Investment cost = book value (Case 1)	1. No revaluations, bonus, or goodwill.	• No additional allocations necessary because new partner will receive a capital share equal to the amount invested. • Total resulting partnership capital equals prior partners' capital plus investment of new partner.
Investment cost < book value (Case 3)	1. Revalue net assets down to market value and allocate to prior partners. 2. Recognize goodwill brought in by new partner. 3. Assign bonus to new partner.	• Prior partners are assigned the reduction of asset values occurring before admission of the new partner. Alternatively, new partner is assigned goodwill or bonus as part of admission incentive. • Recording asset valuation decrease reduces total resulting capital, while recording new partner's goodwill increases total resulting capital.

Case 1: Investment Equals Proportion of the Partnership's Book Value The total book value of the partnership before the admission of the new partner is $30,000, and the new partner, Cha, is buying a one-fourth capital interest for $10,000.

The amount of a new partner's investment is often the result of negotiations between the prior partners and the prospective partner. As with any acquisition or investment, the investor must determine the market value of the investment. In the case of a partnership, the prospective partner attempts to ascertain the market value and earning power of the partnership's net assets. The investment by the new partner is then a function of the percentage of partnership capital being acquired. In this case, Cha must feel that the $10,000 investment required is a fair price for a one-fourth interest in the resulting partnership; otherwise, she would not make the investment.

After the amount of investment is agreed upon, it is possible to calculate the new partner's proportionate book value. For a $10,000 investment, Cha will have a one-fourth interest in the partnership, as follows:

Investment in partnership	$10,000
New partner's proportionate book value:	
($30,000 + $10,000) × .25	(10,000)
Difference (investment = book value)	$ -0-

Because the amount of the investment ($10,000) is equal to the new partner's 25 percent proportionate book value ($10,000 = 40,000 × .25), there is an implication that the net assets are fairly valued. Total resulting capital is equal to the prior partners' capital ($30,000) plus the tangible investment of the new partner ($10,000). Note that the capital credit assigned to the new partner is her share of the total resulting capital of the partnership, after her admission as partner. The entry on the partnership's books is:

```
January 1, 19X3
   (10)  Cash                                      10,000
            Cha, Capital                                     10,000
         Admission of Cha for one-fourth interest
         upon investment of $10,000.
```

The following schedule presents the key concepts in Case 1:

	Prior Capital	New Partner's Tangible Investment	New Partner's Proportion of Partnership's Book Value (25%)	Total Resulting Capital	New Partner's Share of Total Resulting Capital (25%)
Case 1:					
New partner's investment equals proportionate book value	$30,000	$10,000	$10,000		
No revaluations, bonus, or goodwill				$40,000	$10,000

Case 2: New Partner's Investment Greater than Proportion of the Partnership's Book Value   In some cases a new partner may invest more in an existing partnership than his or her proportionate share of the partnership's book value. This means that the partner perceives some value in the partnership that is not reflected on the books of account.

For example, Cha invests $11,000 for a one-fourth capital interest in the ABC Partnership. The first step is to compare the new partner's investment with the new partner's proportionate book value, as follows:

Investment in partnership	$11,000
New partner's proportionate book value:	
($30,000 + $11,000) × .25	(10,250)
Difference (investment > book value)	$ 750

Cha has invested $11,000 for an interest with a book value of $10,250, thus paying an excess of $750 over the present book value.

Generally, an excess of investment over the respective book value of the partnership interest indicates that the partnership's prior net assets are undervalued or that the partnership has some unrecorded goodwill. Three alternative accounting treatments exist in this case:

1. *Revalue Assets Upward.* Under this alternative:
    a. Asset book values are increased to their market values.
    b. The prior partners' capital accounts are increased for their respective shares of the increase in the book values of the assets.
    c. Total resulting capital of the partnership is the prior capital balances plus the amount of asset revaluation plus the new partner's investment.
2. *Record Unrecognized Goodwill.* With this method:
    a. Unrecognized goodwill is recorded.
    b. The prior partners' capital accounts are increased for their respective shares of the goodwill.
    c. Total resulting capital of the partnership is the prior capital balances plus the goodwill recognized plus the new partner's investment.
3. *Use Bonus Method.* Essentially, the bonus method is a transfer of capital balances among the partners. This method is used when the partners do not wish to record adjustments in asset accounts and do not want to recognize goodwill. Under this method:
    a. The prior partners' capital accounts are increased for their respective shares of the bonus paid by the new partner.
    b. Total resulting capital of the partnership is the prior capital balances plus the new partner's investment.

Any one of the three alternatives may be used by the partnership. The decision is usually a result of negotiations between the prior partners and the prospective partner. The revaluation of assets or recognition of goodwill is criticized by some accountants because it results in a marked departure from the historical cost principle and differs from the accepted accounting principles in **APB Opinion No. 17**, "Intangible Assets" (APB 17), which prohibits corporations from recognizing goodwill that has not been acquired by purchase. Accountants who support the recognition of goodwill point out that whenever a new partner is admitted to the partnership, the old partnership is legally dissolved and a new partnership entity is formed. Therefore the basis of valuation for new entities is the fair value of the assets acquired by the newly formed entity. Consequently, assets should be recorded at their fair values and should include previously unrecognized goodwill. Finally, accountants who use the goodwill or asset revaluation methods argue that the goal of partnership accounting is to state fairly the relative capital equities of the partners, and this may require different accounting procedures from those used in corporate entities.

The accountant's function is to ensure that any estimates used in the valuation process are based on the best evidence available. Subjective valuations that could impair the fairness of the presentations made in the partnership's financial statements should be avoided or minimized.

Illustration of Revaluation of Assets Approach   Assume that Cha paid a $750 excess ($11,000 − $10,250) over her proportionate book value because the partnership owns land with a book value of $4,000 but a recent appraisal indicates the land has a market value of $7,000. The prior partners decide to use the admission of the new partner to recognize the increase in value of the land and to assign this increase to the capital accounts of the prior partners. The increase in land value is allocated to the partners' capital accounts in the profit and loss ratio that existed during the time of the increase. Alt's capital is increased by $1,800 (60 percent of the $3,000 increase), and Blue's capital is increased by $1,200 (40 percent of the $3,000). The partnership makes the following entry for the revaluation of the land:

(11) Land	3,000	
Alt, Capital		1,800
Blue, Capital		1,200
Revalue partnership land to market value.		

The $11,000 investment by Cha brings the partnership's total resulting capital to $44,000, as follows:

Prior capital of AB Partnership	$30,000
Revaluation of land to market value	3,000
Cha's investment	11,000
Total resulting capital of ABC Partnership	$44,000

Cha is acquiring a one-fourth interest in the total resulting capital of the ABC Partnership. Cha's capital credit, *after revaluing the land*, is calculated as follows:

$$\frac{\text{New partner's share of}}{\text{total resulting capital}} = (\$30,000 + \$3,000 + 11,000) \times .25 = \$11,000$$

The entry to record the admission of Cha into the partnership is:

(12) Cash	11,000	
Cha, Capital		11,000
Admission of Cha for one-fourth capital		
interest in ABC Partnership.		

When the land is eventually sold, Cha will participate in the gain or loss calculated on the basis of the new $7,000 book value, which is the land's market value at the time of her admission into the partnership. The entire increase in the value of the land before the admission of Cha belongs to the prior partners.

Illustration of Goodwill Recognition   An entering partner may be paying an excess because of unrecognized goodwill, indicated by high profitability of the partnership. Some partnerships use the change in membership as an opportunity to record unrecognized goodwill that has been created by the prior partners. Recording unrecognized goodwill is allowed for partnership accounting because of the need to establish appropriate capital equity among the partners. As noted earlier, this is an exception to the general rule established in **APB 17**, but the information needs of the partners and specific purposes of the partnership's financial statements justify the exception.

Generally, the amount of goodwill is determined by negotiations between the prior and prospective partners and is based on estimates of future earnings. For example, the prior and new partners may agree that, due to the efforts of the prior partners, the partnership has superior earnings potential and that $3,000 of goodwill should be recorded to recognize this fact. The new partner's negotiated investment cost will be based partly on the earnings potential of the partnership. Alternatively, goodwill may be estimated from the amount of the new partner's investment. For example, in this case, Cha is investing $11,000 for a one-fourth interest; therefore, she must feel the total resulting partnership capital is $44,000 ($11,000 × 4). The estimated goodwill is $3,000 as follows:

Step 1:		
25% of estimated total resulting capital	$11,000	
Estimated total resulting capital		
(11,000 ÷ .25)	$44,000	
Step 2:		
Estimated total resulting capital	$44,000	
Total net assets not		
including goodwill ($30,000 prior		
plus $11,000 invested by Cha)	(41,000)	
Estimated goodwill	$ 3,000	

The unrecorded goodwill is recorded, and the prior partners' capital accounts are credited for the increase in assets. The adjustments to the capital accounts are in the profit and loss ratio that existed during the periods the goodwill was developed. Alt's capital is increased by 60 percent of the goodwill, and Blue's by 40 percent. The entries to record goodwill and the admission of Cha are as follows:

(13)	Goodwill	3,000	
	Alt, Capital		1,800
	Blue, Capital		1,200
	Recognize unrecorded goodwill.		
(14)	Cash	11,000	
	Cha, Capital		11,000
	Admission of Cha to partnership for a		
	one-fourth capital interest:		
	$44,000 × .25		

Another reason for recording goodwill is that the new partner may want her capital balance to equal the amount of investment made. The investment is based on the market value of the partnership, and for this equality to occur, the partnership must restate its prior net assets to their fair values.

It is important to note that the $11,000 credit to Cha's capital account is one-fourth of the total resulting capital of ABC Partnership of $44,000 as follows:

$$\text{New partner's share of total resulting capital} = (\$30,000 + \$3,000 + \$11,000) \times .25 = \$11,000$$

In future periods, the goodwill will be amortized against partnership earnings before net income is distributed to the partners. Consequently, Cha's future profit distribution will be affected by the goodwill recognized at the time of her admission into the partnership.

Illustration of Bonus Method   Some partnerships are averse to recognizing asset revaluations or unrecorded goodwill when a new partner is admitted. Instead, they record a portion of the new partner's investment as a bonus to the existing partners in order to align the capital balances properly at the time of the admission of the new partner. In this case, the $750 excess paid by Cha is a bonus allocated to the prior partners in their profit and loss ratio of 60 percent to Alt and 40 percent to Blue. The total resulting capital of the ABC Partnership consists of $30,000 prior capital of Alt and Blue plus the $11,000 investment of Cha. No additional capital is recognized by revaluing assets. The value of the capital credit acquired by the new partner is calculated as:

$$\text{New partner's share of total resulting capital} = (\$30,000 + \$11,000) \times .25 = \$10,250$$

The entry to record the admission of Cha under the bonus method is as follows:

(15) Cash	11,000	
Alt, Capital		450
Blue, Capital		300
Cha, Capital		10,250
Admission of Cha with bonus to		
Alt and Blue.		

Cha may dislike the bonus method because her capital balance is $750 less than her investment in the partnership. This is one of the disadvantages of the bonus method.

A comparison of the goodwill and bonus methods shows that the differences between the two methods is reconciled in future periods by the amortization of goodwill. If no future changes are made in the membership of the partnership, and the profit and loss percentages remain the same, the goodwill of $3,000 recognized in the second alternative is amortized and the partners' capital balances will be the same as with the bonus method. Apart from any other future changes in the partners' capital accounts, the comparison is as follows:

	Partner			
	Alt	Blue	Cha	Total
Profit percentage	45%	30%	25%	100%
Capital balance under goodwill method at time of Cha's admission	$21,800	$11,200	$11,000	$44,000
Goodwill of $3,000 amortized	(1,350)	(900)	(750)	(3,000)
Capital balance after amortization	$20,450	$10,300	$10,250	$41,000
Capital balance under bonus method	$20,450	$10,300	$10,250	$41,000

Again, the capital balances after the goodwill is amortized are equal to the capital balances under the bonus method only if the profit and loss ratio remains constant during the period of goodwill amortization. However, if the ratio changes because of changes in partnership members or changes in the profit agreement, then the goodwill and bonus methods will result in different capital balances for each of the partners. In effect, the goodwill method adjusts the capital balances by amortization of the goodwill over time, whereas the bonus method makes the capital adjustments at the time the new partner is admitted.

The following schedule presents the key concepts for Case 2:

	Prior Capital	New Partner's Tangible Investment	New Partner's Proportion of Partnership's Book Value (25%)	Total Resulting Capital	New Partner's Share of Total Resulting Capital (25%)
Case 2: New partner's investment greater than proportionate book value	$30,000	$11,000	$10,250		
1. Revalue assets by increasing land $3,000				$44,000	$11,000
2. Recognize $3,000 goodwill for prior partners				$44,000	$11,000
3. Bonus of $750 to prior partners				$41,000	$10,250

Case 3: New Partner's Investment Less than Proportion of the Partnership's Book Value It is possible that a new partner may pay less than his or her proportionate share of the partnership's book value. For example, Cha invests $8,000 for a one-fourth capital interest in the ABC Partnership. The first step is to

compare the new partner's investment with the new partner's proportionate book value, as follows:

Investment in partnership	$ 8,000
New partner's proportionate book value:	
($30,000 + $8,000) × .25	(9,500)
Difference (investment < book value)	$(1,500)

The fact that Cha's investment is less than the book value of a one-fourth interest in the partnership indicates that the partnership has overvalued assets or the prior partners recognize that Cha is contributing additional value in the form of expertise or skills she possesses which are needed by the partnership. In this case, Cha is investing $8,000 in cash and an additional amount that may be viewed as goodwill.

As with Case 2, in which the investment is greater than the book value acquired, there are three alternative approaches when the investment is less than the book value acquired. The three approaches are as follows:

1. *Revalue Assets Downward.* Under this alternative:
   a. Asset book values are decreased to recognize the reduction in their values.
   b. The prior partners' capital accounts are decreased for their respective shares of the decrease in the values of the assets.
   c. Total resulting capital of the partnership is the prior capital balances less the amount of the asset valuation write-down plus the new partner's investment.
2. *Recognize Goodwill Brought in by the New Partner.* In this approach:
   a. Goodwill or other intangible benefits brought in by the new partner is recorded and also included in the new partner's capital account.
   b. The prior partners' capital accounts remain unchanged.
   c. Total resulting capital of the partnership is the prior capital balances plus the new goodwill brought in plus the new partner's tangible investment.
3. *Use Bonus Method.* Under the bonus method:
   a. The new partner is assigned a bonus from the prior partners' capital accounts, which are decreased for their respective shares of the bonus paid to the new partner.
   b. Total resulting capital of the partnership is the prior capital balances plus the new partner's investment.

Illustration of Revaluation of Assets Approach   Assume that the reason Cha paid only $8,000 for a one-fourth interest in the partnership is that inventory currently recorded at a book value of $14,000 has a fair market value of only $8,000 because of the obsolescence of several items. The partners agree to write down the inventory to its fair value before admission of the new partner. The write-down is allocated to the prior partners in the profit and loss ratio that existed during the period of the inventory decline: 60 percent to Alt and 40 percent to Blue. The write-down is recorded as follows:

(16)	Alt, Capital	3,600	
	Blue, Capital	2,400	
	Inventory		6,000
	Revalue inventory to market.		

Note that the total capital of the partnership has now been reduced from $30,000 to $24,000 as a result of the $6,000 write-down. The value of Cha's share of total resulting capital of the ABC Partnership, *after the write-down*, is calculated as follows:

$$\text{New partner's share of total resulting capital} = (\$24,000 + \$8,000) \times .25 = \$8,000$$

The entry to record the admission of Cha as a partner in the ABC Partnership is:

(17)	Cash	8,000	
	Cha, Capital		8,000
	Admission of Cha to partnership.		

Cha's recorded capital credit is equal to her investment because the total partnership capital of $32,000 ($24,000 + $8,000) now represents the fair value of the partnership.

Illustration of Recording Goodwill for New Partner   The prior partners may offer Cha a one-fourth capital interest in the ABC Partnership for an investment of $8,000 because Cha has essential business experience, skills, customer contacts, reputation, or other ingredients of goodwill that she will bring into the partnership. The amount of goodwill brought in by the new partner is usually determined through negotiations between the prior partners and the prospective partner. For example, Alt, Blue, and Cha may agree that Cha's abilities will generate excess earnings for the resulting ABC Partnership. They agree that Cha should be given $2,000 of goodwill recognition at the time she joins the partnership in recognition of her anticipated excess contribution to the future earnings of the partnership. The negotiated goodwill is recognized and is added to her tangible investment to determine the amount of capital credit.

Alternatively, the amount of goodwill brought in by the new partner may be estimated from the amount of the total capital being retained by the prior partners. In this case, the prior partners are retaining a 75 percent interest in the partnership and allowing the new partner a 25 percent capital interest. The dollar amount of the prior partners' 75 percent interest is $30,000. Cha's investment of $8,000 plus goodwill makes up the remaining 25 percent. The amount of goodwill brought into the partnership by Cha is determined as follows:

Step 1:	
75% of estimated total resulting capital	$30,000
Estimated total resulting capital	
($30,000 ÷ .75)	$40,000

Step 2:

Estimated total resulting capital	$40,000
Total net assets not including goodwill	
($30,000 + $8,000)	(38,000)
Estimated goodwill	$ 2,000

Note that the estimate of goodwill for the new partner is made using the information from the prior partners' interests. Earlier, in Case 2, the estimate of goodwill to the prior partners was made using the information from the new partner's investment. A useful mnemonic to remember how to estimate goodwill is to use the opposite partners' information for the estimate:

Use new partner to estimate goodwill to prior partners; use prior partners to estimate goodwill to new partner.

The entry to record the admission of Cha into the ABC Partnership is:

(18)	Cash	8,000	
	Goodwill	2,000	
	Cha, Capital		10,000
	Admission of Cha to partnership.		

Note that the total resulting capital of the ABC Partnership is now $40,000, with Alt and Blue together having a 75 percent interest and Cha having a 25 percent interest.

Illustration of Bonus Method   The admission of Cha as a new partner with a one-fourth interest in the ABC Partnership for an investment of only $8,000 may be accounted for by recognizing a bonus given to Cha from the prior partners. The bonus of $1,500 is the difference between the new partner's $9,500 book value and her $8,000 investment. The prior partners' capital accounts are reduced by $1,500 in their profit and loss ratio of 60 percent for Alt and 40 percent for Blue, and Cha's capital account is credited for $9,500, as follows:

(19)	Cash	8,000	
	Alt, Capital	900	
	Blue, Capital	600	
	Cha, Capital		9,500
	Admission of Cha to partnership.		

Note that the amount of the capital credit assigned to the new partner is her share of the total resulting capital, as follows:

$$\text{New partner's share of total resulting capital} = (\$30,000 + \$8,000) \times .25 = \$9,500$$

The following schedule presents the key concepts for Case 3:

	Prior Capital	New Partner's Tangible Investment	New Partner's Proportion of Partnership's Book Value (25%)	Total Resulting Capital	New Partner's Share of Total Resulting Capital (25%)
Case 3: New partner's investment less than proportionate book value	$30,000	$8,000	$9,500		
1. Revalue assets by decreasing inventory by $6,000.				$32,000	$ 8,000
2. Recognize goodwill of $2,000 for new partner.				$40,000	$10,000
3. Bonus of $1,500 to new partner.				$38,000	$ 9,500

Summary and Comparison of Accounting for Investment of New Partner Figure 16-2 presents the entries made in each of the three cases discussed above. In addition, the capital balances of each of the three partners immediately after the admission of Cha are presented to the right of the journal entries.

Summarizing the alternative methods of accounting for the investment of a new partner:

Case 1. New partner's investment *equals* his or her proportion of the partnership's book value.

1. The new partner's capital credit is equal to his or her investment.

2. No goodwill or bonus is recognized in this case.

Case 2. New partner's investment is *greater than* his or her proportion of the partnership's book value.

1. The revaluation of an asset or recognition of goodwill increases the total resulting capital of the partnership. The increase is allocated to the prior partners in their profit and loss ratio.

2. After recognition of the asset revaluation or unrecorded goodwill, the new partner's capital credit is equal to his or her investment and to his or her percentage of the total resulting capital.

3. Under the bonus method, the total resulting capital of the partnership is the sum of the prior partnership's capital plus the investment by the new partner. The capital credit recorded for the new partner is less than the investment but is equal to his or her percentage of the resulting partnership capital.

Case 3. New partner's investment is *less than* his or her proportion of the partnership's book value.

1. Under the revaluation of assets approach, the write-down of the assets reduces the prior partners' capital in their profit and loss ratio. The new partner's capital is then credited for the amount of the investment.

FIGURE 16-2 Summary of accounting for investment of new partner: journal entries and capital balances after admission of new partner.

Case 1: New partner's investment equals proportionate book value. Cha invests $10,000 cash for one-fourth capital interest.

Cash	10,000		Alt	$20,000
Cha, Capital		10,000	Blue	10,000
			Cha	10,000
			Total	$40,000

Case 2: New partner's investment greater than proportionate book value. Cha invests $11,000 cash for one-fourth capital interest.

(a) Revalue assets:

Land	3,000		Alt	$21,800
Alt, Capital		1,800	Blue	11,200
Blue, Capital		1,200	Cha	11,000
Cash	11,000		Total	$44,000
Cha, Capital		11,000		

(b) Recognize goodwill for prior partners:

Goodwill	3,000		Alt	$21,800
Alt, Capital		1,800	Blue	11,200
Blue, Capital		1,200	Cha	11,000
Cash	11,000		Total	$44,000
Cha, Capital		11,000		

(c) Bonus to prior partners:

Cash	11,000		Alt	$20,450
Alt, Capital		450	Blue	10,300
Blue, Capital		300	Cha	10,250
Cha, Capital		10,250	Total	$41,000

Case 3: New partner's investment less than proportionate book value. Cha invests $8,000 cash for a one-fourth capital interest.

(a) Revalue assets:

Alt, Capital	3,600		Alt	$16,400
Blue, Capital	2,400		Blue	7,600
Inventory		6,000	Cha	8,000
Cash	8,000		Total	$32,000
Cha, Capital		8,000		

(b) Recognize goodwill for new partner:

Cash	8,000		Alt	$20,000
Goodwill	2,000		Blue	10,000
Cha, Capital		10,000	Cha	10,000
			Total	$40,000

(c) Bonus to new partner:

Cash	8,000		Alt	$19,100
Alt, Capital	900		Blue	9,400
Blue, Capital	600		Cha	9,500
Cha, Capital		9,500	Total	$38,000

2. Under the goodwill method, goodwill is assigned to the new partner, and the total resulting capital of the partnership is increased. The new partner's capital is credited for his or her percentage interest in the total resulting capital of the partnership.

3. The bonus method results in a transfer of capital from the prior partners to the new partner. The total resulting capital of the new partnership is equal to the prior capital plus the investment of the new partner. The new partner's capital credit is greater than the investment made but is equal to his or her percentage of the total resulting capital.

Determining a New Partner's Investment Cost

In the previous sections, the amount of the new partner's contribution has been provided. In some instances, accountants are asked to determine the amount of cash investment the new partner should be asked to contribute. The basic principles of partnership accounting provide the means to solve this question. For example, let us continue the basic example from the chapter, for which partners Alt and Blue wish to admit Cha as a new partner. The prior partnership capital was $30,000 and the partners wish to invite Cha into the partnership for a one-fourth interest.

Assume that the prior partners, Alt and Blue, agree that the assets of the partnership should be revalued up by $3,000 to recognize the increase in value of the land held by the partnership. The question is how much Cha, the new partner, should be asked to invest for her one-fourth interest.

When determining the new partner's investment cost, it is important to note the total resulting capital of the partnership and the percentage of ownership interest retained by the prior partners. In this example, the prior partners retain a three-fourths' interest in the resulting partnership, for which their 75 percent capital interest is $33,000, the $30,000 of prior capital plus the $3,000 from the revaluation of the land, as follows:

75% of total resulting capital	$33,000
Total resulting capital	$44,000
Less prior partners' capital	(33,000)
Cash contribution required of new partner	$11,000

Note that this is simply another way of evaluating the admission process as was discussed in the asset revaluation illustration under Case 2.

In some cases, the amount of bonus may be determined prior to the determination of the cash contribution required from the new partner. For example, assume that Alt and Blue agree to give Cha a bonus of $1,500 for joining the partnership. The following schedule determines the amount of cash investment required of Cha, the new partner:

Prior capital of Alt and Blue	$30,000
Less bonus given to Cha upon admission	(1,500)
Capital retained by Alt and Blue	$28,500
75% of the total resulting capital	$28,500
Total resulting capital	
($28,500 ÷ .75)	$38,000
Less prior partners' capital	(28,500)
Capital credit required of new partner	$ 9,500
Less bonus to new partner from prior partners	(1,500)
Cash contribution required of new partner	$ 8,000

This second example is another way of viewing the bonus to new partner method under Case 3 as presented earlier. The key is to determine the amount of capital that will be retained by the prior partners for their percentage share in the total resulting capital of the partnership after admitting the new partner. The new partner's cash contribution can be computed simply by determining the amount of the capital credit that will be assigned to him or her and then recognizing any bonuses that will be used to align the capital balances.

Retirement of a Partner from the Partnership

When a partner retires or withdraws from a partnership, the partnership is dissolved but the remaining partners may wish to continue operating the business. The articles of copartnership should specify the procedures to be followed by the partnership to ensure that the agreement of the partners is carried out. The primary accounting issue is the proper measurement of the retiring partner's capital account. This sometimes requires a determination of the fair value of the partnership at the time the partner retires, including the computation of partnership income since the end of the last fiscal period.

Most partnerships have covenants in their partnership agreements to guide the process of accounting for retirement of a partner. For example, in some large public accounting firms, retiring partners receive only the book value of their capital accounts, not the fair value. Other partnerships may require that the partnership's net assets be appraised and that the retiring partner receive the proportionate share of the fair value of the business.

The retiring partner is still personally liable for any partnership debts accumulated before the withdrawal date, but is not responsible for any partnership debts incurred after the retirement date. Therefore, it is especially important to determine all liabilities that exist on the retirement date.

Some partnerships have an audit performed whenever a change in partners is made. This audit establishes the accuracy of the book values of the assets and liabilities. On occasion, accounting errors are found during an audit. Errors should be corrected and the partners' capital accounts adjusted based on the profit and loss ratio that existed in the period in which the errors were made. For example, if an audit disclosed that 3 years ago depreciation expense was charged for $4,000 less than it should have been, the error is corrected with a prior period adjustment, and the partners' capital accounts are charged with their respective shares of the adjustment based on their profit and loss ratio of 3 years ago.

Generally, the existing partners buy out the retiring partner either by making a direct acquisition or by having the partnership acquire the retiring partner's interest. If the present partners directly acquire the retiring partner's interest, then the only entry on the partnership's books is to record the reclassification of capital among the partners. If the partnership acquires the retiring partner's interest, then the partnership must record the reduction of total partnership capital and the corresponding reduction of assets paid to the retiring partner. For example, assume that Alt retires from the ABC Partnership when his capital account has a balance of $55,000, after recording all increases in the net assets of the partnership including income earned up to the date of the retirement. The entry made by the ABC Partnership is:

(20)	Alt, Capital	55,000	
	Cash		55,000
	Retirement of Alt.		

If the partnership is unable to pay the total of $55,000 to Alt at the time of retirement, it must recognize a liability for the remaining portion.

Often, a partnership pays a "retirement premium" for a retiring partner. The premium is usually treated as a bonus from the other partners, allocated in the remaining profit and loss ratio. For example, if the ABC Partnership agrees to pay Alt $65,000 at the time of retirement, the bonus of $10,000 ($65,000 paid less $55,000 capital balance) reduces the capital accounts of Blue and Cha in their profit ratio. Blue has a 30 percent interest, and Cha has a 25 percent interest in the net income of the ABC Partnership. The sum of their respective shares is 55 percent (30 percent + 25 percent), and their relative profit percentages, rounded to the nearest percentage, are 55 percent for Blue and 45 percent for Cha, computed as follows:

	Prior Profit Percentage	Remaining Profit Percentage
Alt	45	0
Blue	30	55 (30/55)
Cha	25	45 (25/55)
Total	100	100

The entry to record the retirement of Alt is:

(21)	Alt, Capital	55,000	
	Blue, Capital	5,500	
	Cha, Capital	4,500	
	Cash		65,000
	Retirement of Alt.		

The $10,000 bonus paid to Alt is allocated to Blue and Cha in their respective profit ratios. Blue is charged for 55 percent, and Cha is charged for the remaining 45 percent.

Sometimes partners wish to leave a partnership badly enough to accept less than their current capital balances upon retirement. In that case, a bonus may be assigned to the remaining partners. For example, Alt agrees to accept $50,000 cash upon retirement even though his capital balance is $55,000. The $5,000 remaining balance is distributed as a bonus to Blue and Cha in their respective profit and loss ratio.

Occasionally, a partnership uses the retirement of a partner and dissolution of the old partnership to record unrecognized goodwill. In this case, the partnership may record the retiring partner's share only, or it may impute the entire amount of goodwill based on the retiring partner's profit percentage. If total goodwill is imputed, the remaining partners also receive their respective shares of the total goodwill recognized. Many accountants criticize recording goodwill on the retirement of a partner on the same theoretical grounds as they criticize recording unrecognized goodwill on the admission of a new partner. Nevertheless, partnership accounting allows the recognition of goodwill at dissolution.

For example, if a $10,000 premium is paid to Alt and only Alt's share of unrecognized goodwill is to be recorded, the partnership makes the following entries at the time of Alt's retirement:

(22)	Goodwill	10,000	
	Alt, Capital		10,000
	Recognize Alt's share of goodwill.		
(23)	Alt, Capital	65,000	
	Cash		65,000
	Retirement of Alt.		

SUMMARY OF KEY CONCEPTS AND TERMS

Accounting for partnerships recognizes the unique aspects of this form of business organization. Profits must be distributed to partners in accordance with the partnership agreement or, in the absence of agreement, in accordance with the Uniform Partnership Act. The partnership is a separate accounting entity but not a separate legal or tax entity. For financial accounting purposes, noncash capital investments are recorded at their fair values at the time of the contribution to the partnership.

A partnership is legally dissolved when a new partner is admitted to the partnership or when a present partner retires. From a legal viewpoint, a new partnership is formed after each change in membership. From a practical point of view, however, the business often continues to operate. Some partnerships use the dissolution as an opportunity to revalue assets or to recognize unrecorded goodwill, thus adjusting their capital accounts for changes in the values of the net assets of the partnership. Others adhere more closely to the historical cost method of accounting and use the bonus method of realigning capital accounts for changes in the relative equity positions of the partners when membership changes. A variety of alternative methods are allowed for partnership accounting. The key is to find accounting policies that meet the needs of the partners and partnership. Flexibility is provided in partnership accounting to meet those needs.

Admission of a new partner:
  Asset revaluation
  Bonus method
  Goodwill recognition
Articles of copartnership
Book value of a partnership
General partnership
Limited partnership

New partner's proportion of the
  partnership's book value
Partners' accounts
Profit distribution plans
Statement of partners' capital
Uniform Partnership Act
Withdrawal of a partner from a
partnership

APPENDIX A: Tax Aspects of a Partnership

The Internal Revenue Service views the partnership form of organization as a temporary aggregation of some of the individual partners' rights. The partnership is not a separate taxable entity. Therefore, the individual partners must report their share of the partnership income or loss on their personal tax returns, whether withdrawn or not. This sometimes creates cash flow problems for partners who leave their share of income in the partnership and permit the partnership to use the income for growth. In such cases, the partners must pay income tax on income that was not distributed to them. However, this tax conduit feature also offers special tax features to the individual partners. For example, charitable contributions made by the partnership are reported on the partners' individual tax returns. Also, any tax-exempt income earned by the partnership is passed through to the individual partners.

This pass-through benefits individual partners when the business has an operating loss. The individual partners can recognize their shares of the partnership loss on their own tax returns, thereby offsetting other taxable income. If the business is incorporated, the loss does not pass through to the stockholders.

TAX BASIS OF ASSET INVESTMENTS

The accounting basis for capital investments versus the tax basis is computed differently. For tax purposes, a partnership must value the assets invested in the partnership at the tax basis of the individual partner who invests the assets. For example, assume partner A contributes a building to the AB Partnership. The building originally cost $6,000 and has been depreciated $2,000, leaving a book value of $4,000. The building has a market value of $10,000. For tax purposes, the partnership records the building at $4,000, the adjusted basis of partner A.

This tax valuation differs from the amount that is recognized under generally accepted accounting principles. A basic concept in GAAP is to value asset transfers between separate reporting entities at their respective fair market values. In this case, the partnership records the building at its fair value of $10,000 for accounting purposes. Most partnerships maintain their accounting records and financial statements using GAAP, and they use a separate adjusting schedule at the end of each period to report the results for tax purposes on Form 1065, the partnership tax information form.

In addition to asset transfers, a partnership may also assume the liabilities associated with an asset. For example, if the building was subject to a mortgage of $2,000 which was assumed by the AB Partnership together with the building, partner A benefits because the other partners have assumed a portion of the mortgage that originally was owed entirely by A.

A partner's tax basis in a partnership is the sum of the following:

The partner's tax basis of any assets contributed to the partnership
Plus the partner's share of other partners' liabilities assumed by the partnership
Less the amount of the partner's liabilities assumed by the other partners

To illustrate, A contributes the building discussed above. The building has an adjusted tax basis of $4,000 ($6,000 cost less $2,000 depreciation) and is subject to a mortgage of $2,000. The market value of the building is $10,000. B contributes machinery that has a book value of $15,000 and a market value of $20,000 and is subject to a note payable of $5,000. The partners agree to share equally in the liabilities assumed by the AB Partnership. The tax basis of each partner in the partnership is calculated as follows:

	Partner A	Partner B
Tax basis of assets contributed	$4,000	$15,000
Partner's share of other partner's liabilities assumed by partnership:		
Partner A: ($\frac{1}{2}$ of $5,000)	2,500	
Partner B: ($\frac{1}{2}$ of $2,000)		1,000
Partner's liabilities assumed by other partners:		
Partner A: ($\frac{1}{2}$ of $2,000)	(1,000)	
Partner B: ($\frac{1}{2}$ of $5,000)		(2,500)
Tax basis of partner's interest	$5,500	$13,500

The tax basis of each partner is used for tax recognition of gains or losses on subsequent disposals of the partner's investment in the partnership.

For GAAP purposes, each partner's investment is based on the fair value of the assets less liabilities assumed. Thus, in the above case, partner A's accounting basis is $8,000 ($10,000 market value of the building less $2,000 mortgage), and partner B's accounting basis is $15,000 ($20,000 market value of the equipment less $5,000 note payable). Any asset disposal gain or loss in the accounting financial statements is based on the valuations made using GAAP. A separate schedule of tax bases for each of the partners is typically maintained in case the information is required for a partner's individual tax return.

SUBCHAPTER S CORPORATIONS

Certain corporations meeting strict guidelines may elect to be taxed as if they were partnerships. Corporations having only one class of stock with less than 35 shareholders and meeting some special income classification tests may elect the Subchapter S alternative. The Subchapter S corporation does not pay taxes on its income. Instead the shareholders must include their share of corporate income or loss in their personal returns, whether or not the income has been distributed as dividends. This alternative eliminates the double taxation of corporate income: first, as taxable income to the corporation, and second, as taxable dividend income to the shareholder.

APPENDIX B: Joint Ventures

A joint venture is a business entity owned, operated, and jointly controlled by a small group of investors as a separate and specific business project organized for the mutual benefit of the ownership group. Many joint ventures are short-term associations of two or more parties to fulfill a specific project such as the development of real estate, joint oil or gas drilling efforts, the financing of a joint production center, or the financing of a motion picture effort. Many international efforts to expand production or markets involve joint ventures either with foreign-based companies or with foreign governments. A recent phenomenon is the formation of research joint ventures in which two or more corporations agree to share the costs and eventual research accomplishments of a separate research laboratory. Each venturer typically participates in the overall management of the venture. The venturers might not have equal ownership interests, and a venturer's share could be as low as 5 or 10 percent, and as high as 90 or 95 percent. Many joint ventures of only two venturers have the ownership share divided equally, and these are called 50 percent–owned ventures.

A joint venture may be organized as a corporation, partnership, or undivided interest. A corporate joint venture is usually formed for long-term projects such as the development and sharing of technical knowledge among a small group of companies. The incorporation of the joint venture formalizes the legal relationships between the venturers and limits each investor's liability to the amount of the investment in the venture. The venture's stock is not traded publicly, and the venturers usually have other business transactions between them. Accounting for a corporate joint venture is guided by **APB 18**, which states:

> The Board concludes that the equity method best enables investors in corporate joint ventures to reflect the underlying nature of their investment in those ventures. Therefore, investors should account for investments in common stock of corporate joint ventures by the equity method. . . .[1]

If the venturer has control of the joint venture through majority stock ownership, the controlling venturer should consolidate the subsidiary and recognize a noncontrolling interest for the other venturers' interests.

A partnership joint venture is accounted for as any other partnership. Typically, the joint venture has its own accounting records, and all facets of partnership accounting presented in the chapter apply to these partnerships. Some joint ventures are accounted for on the books of one of the venturers; however, this combined accounting does not fully reflect the fact that the joint venture is a separate reporting entity. The partners, the venturers, each maintain an investment account on their books for their share of the partnership venture capital. The investment in the partnership account is debited for the initial investment and for the investor's share of subsequent profits. Withdrawals and shares of losses are credited to the investment account. The balance in the investment

---

[1] *APB Opinion No. 18*, "The Equity Method of Accounting for Investments in Common Stock," American Institute of Certified Public Accountants (New York), 1971, par. 16.

account should correspond to the balance in the partner's capital account shown on the joint venture partnership's statements.

In 1971, the AICPA issued **Accounting Interpretation No. 2**, "Investments in Partnerships and Ventures" (AIN 2 of APB 18), which specified that many of the provisions of **APB 18** are appropriate for accounting for investments in partnerships and unincorporated joint ventures. In particular, intercompany profits should be eliminated and the investor-partners should record their shares of the venture's income or loss in the same manner as with the equity method. For financial reporting purposes, if the joint venture is in fact controlled by one of the investor-venturers, that venturer should consolidate the joint venture into its financial statements. If joint control is maintained by all investor-venturers, then the one-line equity method should be used to report the investment in the joint venture.

Accounting for unincorporated joint ventures that are undivided interests usually follows the method of accounting used by partnerships. An undivided interest exists when each investor-venturer owns a proportionate share of each asset and is proportionately liable for its share of each liability. Some established industry practices, especially in oil and gas venture accounting, provide for a pro rata recognition of assets, liabilities, revenue, and expenses of the venture. For example, assume that A Company and B Company are each 50 percent investors in a joint venture, called JTV, for the purposes of oil exploration. The JTV venture has plant assets of $500,000 and long-term liabilities of $200,000. Therefore, A Company and B Company each have an investment of $150,000 ($300,000 × .50). Under the equity method, the investment would be reported in A and B companies' balance sheets as an investment in joint venture of $150,000. However, under pro rata recognition, often termed "proportionate consolidation," the balance sheet of each of the companies would report its share of the assets and liabilities of JTV. In this case, assets of $250,000 ($500,000 × .50) and liabilities of $100,000 ($200,000 × .50) would be added to the present assets and liabilities of each of the investor-venturers. The proportionate share of the assets and liabilities should be added to similar items in the investor's financial statements. The same pro rata method is also used for the joint venture's revenue and expenses. A comparison of the equity method and the proportionate consolidation for venturer A Company is presented in Figure 16-3.

FIGURE 16-3 Comparative balance sheets for reporting a joint venture.

	Balance Sheets of A Company		
	Before Joint Venture	Equity Method	Proportionate Consolidation
Current Assets	$250	$100	$100
Property, Plant, and Equipment	400	400	650
Investment in Joint Venture	-0-	150	-0-
Total	$650	$650	$750
Current Liabilities	$100	$100	$100
Long-Term Debt	300	300	400
Stockholders' Equity	250	250	250
Total	$650	$650	$750

Real estate development is often carried out through joint ventures. Accounting for noncontrolling interests in real estate joint ventures is guided by the AICPA's **Statement of Position 78-9**, "Accounting for Investments in Real Estate Ventures" (SOP 78-9). **SOP 78-9** recommends that the equity method be used to account for noncontrolling investments in corporate or noncorporate real estate ventures.

Additional footnote disclosures are also made for joint ventures to present additional detail about the formation and operation of the joint venture, the methods of accounting used, and a summary of the joint venture's financial position and earnings.

Another form of business association is the syndicate. Syndicates are usually short-term and have a defined single purpose such as developing a financing proposal for a corporation. Syndicates are typically very informal; nevertheless, the legal relationships between the parties should be clearly specified before beginning the project.

QUESTIONS

Q16-1   Why is the partnership form of business organization sometimes preferred over the corporate or sole proprietorship forms?

Q16-2   What is the Uniform Partnership Act, and what is its relevance to partnership accounting?

Q16-3   What types of items are typically included in the articles of copartnership?

Q16-4   Define the following features of a partnership: (a) limited life, (b) agency relationship, and (c) unlimited liability.

Q16-5   Under what circumstances would a partner's capital account have a debit, or deficiency, balance? How is the deficiency usually eliminated?

Q16-6   A partnership agreement specifies that profits will be shared in the ratio of 4:6:5. What percentage of profits will each partner receive? Allocate a profit of $60,000 to each of the three partners.

Q16-7   The Good-Nite partnership agreement includes a profit distribution provision for interest on capital balances. Unfortunately, the provision does not state the specific capital balance to be used in computing the profit share. What choices of capital balances are available to the partners? What is the preferred capital balance to be used in an interest allocation? Why?

Q16-8   Are salaries to partners an expense of the partnership? Why or why not?

Q16-9   Define dissolution of a partnership. What types of events cause a dissolution to occur? Must a partnership terminate business upon dissolution?

Q16-10   What is the book value of a partnership? Does book value also represent the market value of the partnership?

Q16-11   Present the arguments for and against the bonus method of recognizing the admission of a new partner.

Q16-12   In which cases of admission of a new partner is the new partner's capital credit equal to the investment made? In which cases of admission of a new partner is the new partner's capital credit less than or greater than the amount of the investment?

Q16-13   Aabel, a partner in the ABC Partnership, receives a bonus of 15 percent of income. If income for the period is $20,000, what is Aabel's bonus, assuming the bonus is computed as a percentage of income before the bonus? What is the bonus if it is computed as a percentage of income *after* deducting the bonus?

Q16-14   Caine, a new partner in the ABC Partnership, has invested $12,000 for a one-third interest in a partnership with a prior capital of $21,000. What is the implied true value of the ABC partnership? If the partners agree to recognize goodwill for the difference between the book value and true value, present the entries the ABC partnership should make upon admission of Caine.

Q16-15A S. Horton contributes assets with a book value of $5,000 to a partnership. The assets have a market value of $10,000 and a remaining liability of $2,000 that is assumed by the partnership. If the liability is shared equally with the other three partners, what is the basis of Horton's contribution for tax purposes? For GAAP purposes?

Q16-16B What is a joint venture? How are corporate joint ventures accounted for on the books of the investor companies?

CASES

C16-1 Partnership Agreement

J. Nitty and G. Gritty are considering the formation of a partnership to operate a crafts and hobbies store. They have come to you to obtain information about the basic elements of a partnership agreement. Partnership agreements usually specify an income-and-loss-sharing ratio. The agreements may also provide for such additional income and loss sharing features as salaries, bonuses, and interest allowances on invested capital.

Required

   a. Discuss why there may be a need for partnership agreement features in addition to the income and loss sharing ratio.
   b. Discuss the arguments in favor of recording salary and bonus allowances to partners as expenses included in computing net income.
   c. What are the arguments against recording salary and bonus allowances to partners as expenses of the partnership?
   d. Some partnership agreements contain a provision for interest on invested capital in distributing income to the individual partners. List the additional provisions that should be included in the partnership agreement so the interest amounts can be computed.

C16-2 Comparisons of Bonus, Goodwill, and Asset Revaluation Methods

Bill, George, and Anne are partners in the BGA Partnership. A difference of opinion exists among the partners as to how to account for the admission of Newt, a new partner. The three present partners have the following positions:

Bill wants to use the bonus method.
George feels the goodwill method is best.
Anne wants to revalue the existing tangible assets.

You have been called in to advise the three partners.

Required

Prepare a memo discussing the three different methods of accounting for the admission of a new partner, including consideration of the effects on partnership capital in the year Newt is admitted, and the effects on the capital balances in future years.

EXERCISES

E16-1 Multiple Choice on Initial Investment [AICPA Adapted]

Select the correct answer for each of the following questions.

1. On May 1, 19X9, Cathy and Mort formed a partnership and agreed to share profits and losses in the ratio of 3:7, respectively. Cathy contributed a parcel of land that cost her $10,000. Mort contributed $40,000 cash. The land was sold for $18,000 on May 1, 19X9, immediately after formation of the partnership. What amount should be recorded in Cathy's capital account on formation of the partnership?
   a. $18,000.
   b. $17,400.
   c. $15,000.
   d. $10,000.

2. On July 1, 19X8, a partnership was formed by James and Short. James contributed cash. Short, previously a sole proprietor, contributed property other than cash, including realty subject to a mortgage, which was assumed by the partnership. Short's capital account at July 1, 19X8 should be recorded at:
   a. Short's book value of the property at July 1, 19X8.
   b. Short's book value of the property less the mortgage payable at July 1, 19X8.
   c. The fair value of the property less the mortgage payable at July 1, 19X8.
   d. The fair value of the property at July 1, 19X8.

3. A partnership is formed by two individuals who were previously sole proprietors. Property other than cash which is part of the initial investment in the partnership would be recorded for financial accounting purposes at the:
   a. Proprietors' book values or the fair value of the property at the date of the investment, whichever is higher.
   b. Proprietors' book values or the fair value of the property at the date of the investment, whichever is lower.
   c. Proprietors' book values of the property at the date of the investment.
   d. Fair value of the property at the date of the investment.

4. Mutt and Jeff formed a partnership on April 1 and contributed the following assets:

	Mutt	**Jeff**
Cash	$150,000	$ 50,000
Land		310,000

   The land was subject to a mortgage of $30,000, which was assumed by the partnership. Under the partnership agreement, Mutt and Jeff will share profit and loss in the ratio of one-third and two-thirds respectively. Jeff's capital account at April 1 should be:
   a. $300,000.
   b. $330,000.
   c. $340,000.
   d. $360,000.

5. On July 1, Mabel and Pierre formed a partnership, agreeing to share profits and losses in the ratio of 4:6 respectively. Mabel contributed a parcel of land that cost her $25,000. Pierre contributed $50,000 cash. The land was sold for $50,000 on July 1, 4 hours after

formation of the partnership. How much should be recorded in Mabel's capital account on formation of the partnership?

a. $10,000.
b. $20,000.
c. $25,000.
d. $50,000.

E16-2 Division of Income—Multiple Bases

The partnership of Jordan and Pippen has the following provisions in the partnership agreement:

1. The partners are to earn 10 percent interest on the average capital.
2. Jordan and Pippen are to earn salaries of $25,000 and $15,000, respectively.
3. Any remaining income or loss is to be divided between Jordan and Pippen in a 70:30 ratio.

Jordan's average capital is $50,000 and Pippen's is $30,000.

Required

Prepare an income distribution schedule assuming the income of the partnership is **(a)** $80,000; **(b)** $20,000.

E16-3 Division of Income—Interest on Capital Balances

Case and Hand are partners. Their capital accounts during 19X1 were as follows:

Case, Capital				Hand, Capital			
8/28	6,000	1/1	40,000	3/5	9,000	1/1	60,000
		4/3	8,000			7/6	7,000
		10/31	3,000			10/7	5,000

Net income of the partnership is $40,000 for the year. The partnership agreement provides for the division of income as follows:

1. Each partner is to be credited 9 percent interest on his average capital.
2. Any remaining income or loss is to be divided equally.

Required

Prepare an income distribution schedule.

E16-4 Allocation of Partnership Income [AICPA Adapted]

The partnership of Doug, Pat, and Neil was formed on January 1, 19X1. The original investments were as follows:

Doug	$ 80,000
Pat	$120,000
Neil	$180,000

According to the partnership agreement, net income or loss will be divided among the respective partners as follows:

1. Salaries of $12,000 for Doug, $10,000 for Pat, and $8,000 for Neil.
2. Interest of 8 percent on the average capital balances not including regular drawings against shares of net income by Doug, Pat, and Neil during the year.
3. Remainder divided equally.

Additional information:

1. Net income of the partnership for the year ended December 31, 19X1, was $70,000.
2. Doug invested an additional $20,000 in the partnership on July 1, 19X1.
3. Neil withdrew $30,000 from the partnership on October 1, 19X1.
4. Doug, Pat, and Neil each made regular drawings against their shares of net income during 19X1 of $10,000.

Required

a. Prepare a schedule showing the division of net income among the three partners. Show supporting computations in good form.

b. Prepare a statement of partners' capital at December 31, 19X1. Show supporting computations in good form.

E16-5 Multiple-Choice Questions on Admission of a Partner

Arne and Jackson are partners with capital of $40,000 and $20,000. They share income in a 3:1 ratio. Little is to become a partner with a one-fifth interest in capital and income.

Required

Select the correct answer for each of the following questions.

1. If no goodwill or bonus is recorded, Little must invest:
   a. $12,000.
   b. $14,000.
   c. $15,000.
   d. $16,000.

2. If goodwill is to be recorded and Little invests $18,000, the amount of goodwill is:
   a. $2,400.
   b. $3,000.
   c. $12,000.
   d. $30,000.

3. If goodwill is to be recorded and Little invests $13,000, the amount of goodwill is:
   a. $1,600.
   b. $2,000.

    c. $8,000.

    d. $15,000.

4. If Little invests $17,000 and goodwill is not recorded, Little's capital account will be credited:

    a. $12,000.

    b. $15,000.

    c. $15,400.

    d. $17,000.

E16-6   Admission of a Partner

In the LTM partnership, the capital balances of Linda, Tom, and Matt, who share income in the ratio of 7:2:1, are:

Linda	$260,000
Tom	140,000
Matt	50,000

Required

    a. If no goodwill or bonus is recorded, how much must Anne invest for a one-fourth interest?

    b. Prepare journal entries for the admission of Anne if she invests $100,000 for a one-fifth interest and goodwill is recorded.

    c. Prepare journal entries for the admission of Anne if she invests $225,000 for a 20 percent interest and total capital will be $675,000.

E16-7   Admission of a Partner

Jeff and Kristie, partners in the J & K partnership, have capital balances of $100,000 and $40,000 and share income in a ratio of 4:1, respectively. Brad is to be admitted into the partnership with a 20 percent interest in the business.

Required

Record the admission of Brad for each of the following independent situations:

    a. Brad invests $60,000, and goodwill is to be recorded.

    b. Brad invests $60,000. Total capital is to be $200,000.

    c. Brad purchases the 20 percent interest by paying Jeff $22,000 and Kristie $11,000. Brad is assigned 20 percent of each of Jeff's and Kristie's capital accounts.

    d. Brad invests $32,000. Total capital is to be $172,000.

    e. Brad invests $32,000, and goodwill is to be recorded.

E16-8   Multiple-Choice Questions on the Admission of a Partner

Select the correct answer for each of the following questions.

The following balance sheet is for the partnership of Alex, Betty, and Claire, and relates to questions 1 and 2:

Cash	$ 20,000
Other Assets	180,000
	$200,000
Liabilities	$ 50,000
Alex, Capital (40%)	37,000
Betty, Capital (40%)	65,000
Claire, Capital (20%)	48,000
Total Liabilities and Capital	$200,000

(*Note:* Figures shown parenthetically reflect agreed profit and loss sharing percentages.)

1. If the assets are fairly valued on the above balance sheet and the partnership wishes to admit Denise as a new one-sixth-interest partner without recording goodwill or bonus, Denise should contribute cash or other assets of:
   a. $40,000.
   b. $36,000.
   c. $33,333.
   d. $30,000.

2. If assets on the initial balance sheet are fairly valued, Alex and Betty consent and Denise pays Claire $51,000 for her interest; the revised capital balances of the partners would be:
   a. Alex, $38,000; Betty, $66,500; Denise, $51,000.
   b. Alex, $38,500; Betty, $66,500; Denise, $48,000.
   c. Alex, $37,000; Betty, $65,000; Denise, $51,000.
   d. Alex, $37,000; Betty, $65,000; Denise, $48,000.

3. On December 31, 19X4, Alan and Dave are partners with capital balances of $80,000 and $40,000, and they share profit and losses in the ratio of 2:1, respectively. On this date Scott invests $36,000 cash for a one-fifth interest in the capital and profit of the new partnership. The partners agree that the implied partnership goodwill is to be recorded simultaneously with the admission of Scott. The total implied goodwill of the firm is:
   a. $4,800.
   b. $6,000.
   c. $24,000.
   d. $30,000.

4. Boris and Richard are partners who share profits and losses in the ratio of 6:4, respectively. On May 1, 19X9, their respective capital accounts were as follows:

Boris	$60,000
Richard	50,000

On that date, Lisa was admitted as a partner with a one-third interest in capital and profits for an investment of $40,000. The new partnership began with a total capital of $150,000. Immediately after Lisa's admission, Boris's capital should be:

    a. $50,000.
    b. $54,000.
    c. $56,667.
    d. $60,000.

5. At December 31, Rod and Sheri are partners with capital balances of $40,000 and $20,000, and they share profits and losses in the ratio of 2:1, respectively. On this date Pete invests $17,000 in cash for a one-fifth interest in the capital and profit of the new partnership. Assuming that goodwill is not recorded, how much should be credited to Pete's capital account on December 31?
    a. $12,000.
    b. $15,000.
    c. $15,400.
    d. $17,000.

6. The capital accounts of the partnership of Ella, Nick, and Brandon are presented below with their respective profit and loss ratios:

Ella	$139,000	(½)
Nick	209,000	(⅓)
Brandon	96,000	(⅙)

Tony was admitted to the partnership when he purchased directly, for $132,000, a proportionate interest from Ella and Nick in the net assets and profits of the partnership. As a result, Tony acquired a one-fifth interest in the net assets and profits of the firm. Assuming implied goodwill is not to be recorded, what is the combined gain realized by Ella and Nick upon the sale of a portion of their interests in the partnership to Tony?
    a. $0.
    b. $43,200.
    c. $62,400.
    d. $82,000.

7. Fred and Ralph are partners who share profits and losses in the ratio of 7:3, respectively. Their respective capital accounts are as follows:

Fred	$35,000
Ralph	30,000

They agreed to admit Lute as a partner with a one-third interest in the capital and profits and losses, upon an investment of $25,000. The new partnership will begin with a total capital of $90,000. Immediately after Lute's admission, what are the capital balances of Fred, Ralph, and Lute, respectively?
    a. $30,000, $30,000, $30,000.
    b. $31,500, $28,500, $30,000.
    c. $31,667, $28,333, $30,000.
    d. $35,000, $30,000, $25,000.

8. If A is the total capital of a partnership before the admission of a new partner, B is the total capital of the partnership after the investment of a new partner, C is the amount of the new partner's investment, and D is the amount of capital credit to the new partner, then there is:

a. A bonus to the new partner if $B = A + C$ and $D < C$.
b. Goodwill to the old partners if $B > (A + C)$ and $D = C$.
c. Neither bonus nor goodwill if $B = A - C$ and $D > C$.
d. Goodwill to the new partner if $B > (A + C)$ and $D < C$.

E16-9   Withdrawal of a Partner

In the ABC partnership, Anderson's capital is $50,000, Beaman's is $30,000, and Chapman's is $40,000. They share income in a 3:1:1 ratio. Chapman is retiring from the partnership.

Required

Prepare journal entries to record Chapman's withdrawal according to each of the following independent assumptions:

a. Chapman is paid $48,000, and no goodwill is recorded.
b. Chapman is paid $50,000, and only his share of the goodwill is recorded.
c. Chapman is paid $45,000, and all implied goodwill is recorded.

E16-10   Retirement of a Partner

On January 1, 19X1, Eddy decides to retire from the partnership of Cobb, Davis, and Eddy, who share profits and losses in the ratio of 3:2:1 respectively. The following condensed balance sheets present the account balances immediately before and, for six independent cases, after Eddy's retirement.

Accounts	Balances prior to Eddy's Retirement	Balances after Eddy's Retirement					
		Case 1	Case 2	Case 3	Case 4	Case 5	Case 6
Assets:							
Cash	$ 90,000	$ 10,000	$ 16,000	$ 25,000	$ 16,000	$ 50,000	$ 90,000
Other Assets	200,000	200,000	200,000	200,000	200,000	220,000	200,000
Goodwill	10,000	10,000	14,000	10,000	34,000	10,000	10,000
Total Assets	$300,000	$220,000	$230,000	$235,000	$250,000	$280,000	$300,000
Liabilities and Capital:							
Liabilities	$ 60,000	$ 60,000	$ 60,000	$ 60,000	$ 60,000	$ 60,000	$ 60,000
Cobb, Capital	80,000	74,000	80,000	83,000	92,000	110,000	80,000
Davis, Capital	90,000	86,000	90,000	92,000	98,000	110,000	160,000
Eddy, Capital	70,000	–0–	–0–	–0–	–0–	–0–	–0–
Total Liabilities and Capital	$300,000	$220,000	$230,000	$235,000	$250,000	$280,000	$300,000

Required

Prepare the necessary journal entries to record Eddy's retirement from the partnership for each of the six independent cases.

PROBLEMS

P16-11 Admission of a Partner

Sandi and Bernie sell electronic equipment and supplies through their partnership. They wish to expand their computer lines and decide to admit Chester to the partnership. Sandi's capital is $100,000, Bernie's capital is $80,000, and they share income in a ratio of 3:2.

Required

Record the admission of Chester for each of the following independent situations:

a. Chester directly purchases half of Bernie's investment in the partnership for $46,500.

b. Chester invests the amount needed to give him a one-third interest in the capital of the partnership if no goodwill or bonus is recorded.

c. Chester invests $56,000 for a one-fourth interest. Goodwill is to be recorded.

d. Sandi and Bernie agree that some of the inventory is obsolete. The inventory account is decreased before Chester is admitted. Chester invests $52,000 for a one-fourth interest.

e. Chester directly purchases a one-fourth interest by paying Sandi $32,000 and Bernie $36,000. The land account is increased before Chester is admitted.

f. Chester invests $40,000 for a one-fifth interest in the total capital of $220,000.

g. Chester invests $60,000 for a one-fifth interest. Goodwill is to be recorded.

P16-12 Division of Income

C. Eastwood, A. North, and M. West are manufacturers' representatives in the architecture business. Their capital accounts in the ENW partnership for 19X1 were as follows:

C. Eastwood, Capital				A. North, Capital				M. West, Capital			
9/1	8,000	1/1	30,000	3/1	9,000	1/1	40,000	8/1	12,000	1/1	50,000
		5/1	6,000			7/1	5,000			4/1	7,000
						9/1	4,000			6/1	3,000

Required

For each of the following independent income-sharing agreements, prepare an income distribution schedule.

a. Salaries are $15,000 to Eastwood, $20,000 to North, and $18,000 to West. Eastwood receives a bonus of 5 percent of net income after deducting his bonus. Interest is 10 percent of ending capital balances. Any remainder is divided by Eastwood, North, and West in a 3:3:4 ratio. Net income was $78,960.

b. Interest is 10 percent of weighted-average capital balances. Salaries are $24,000 to Eastwood, $21,000 to North, and $25,000 to West. North receives a bonus of 10 percent of net income after deducting the bonus and her salary. Any remainder is divided equally. Net income was $68,080.

c. West receives a bonus of 20 percent of net income after deducting the bonus and the salaries. Salaries are $21,000 to Eastwood, $18,000 to North, and $15,000 to West. Interest is 10 percent of beginning capital balances. Any remainder is divided by Eastwood, North, and West in an 8:7:5 ratio. Net income was $92,940.

P16-13   Determining a New Partner's Investment Cost

The following condensed balance sheet is presented for the partnership of Der, Egan, and Oprins, who share profits and losses in the ratio of 4:3:3, respectively.

Cash	$ 40,000	Accounts Payable	$150,000
Other Assets	710,000	Der, Capital	260,000
		Egan, Capital	180,000
		Oprins, Capital	160,000
Total Assets	$750,000	Total Liabilities and Capital	$750,000

Assume that the partnership decides to admit Snider as a new partner with a one-fourth interest.

Required

For each of the following independent cases, determine the amount that Snider must contribute in cash or other assets.

a. No goodwill or bonus is to be recorded.

b. Goodwill of $30,000 is to be recorded and allocated to the prior partners.

c. A bonus of $24,000 is to be paid by Snider and allocated to the prior partners.

d. The prior partners, Der, Egan, and Oprins, agree to give Snider $10,000 of goodwill upon admission into the partnership.

e. Other assets are revalued for an increase of $20,000, and goodwill of $40,000 is recognized and allocated to the prior partners at the time of the admission of Snider.

f. The partners agree that total resulting capital should be $820,000 and no goodwill should be recognized.

g. Other assets are revalued down by $30,000 and a bonus of $30,000 is paid to Snider at the time of admission.

P16-14   Division of Income

The Melchiorri Dough Company is a partnership that sells pizza and pasta. The partnership agreement provides for 10 percent interest on invested capital, salaries of $14,000 to Tony and $18,000 to Vince, and a bonus for Tony. The 19X1 capital accounts were as follows:

Tony, Capital				Vince, Capital			
8/1	15,000	1/1	40,000	7/1	10,000	1/1	60,000
		4/1	5,000			9/1	22,500

Required

For each of the following independent situations, prepare an income distribution schedule.

a. Interest is based on weighted-average capital balances. The bonus is 5 percent and is calculated on net income after deducting the bonus. In 19X1, net income was $42,630. Any remainder is divided between Tony and Vince in a 2:3 ratio, respectively.

b. Interest is based on ending capital balances after deducting salaries, which the partners normally withdraw during the year. The bonus is 12.5 percent and is calculated on net income after deducting the bonus and salaries. Net income was $126,950. Any remainder is divided equally.

c. Interest is based on beginning capital balances. The bonus is 8 percent and is calculated on net income after deducting the bonus. Net income was $52,650. Any remainder is divided between Tony and Vince in a 5:2 ratio, respectively.

P16-15 Withdrawal of a Partner

Johnson, Miller, and Wilson have operated a tax service as a partnership. Miller has decided to retire from the partnership. Before Miller's withdrawal, the books are closed, and the following balance sheet is prepared:

Assets		Liabilities and Capital	
Cash	$ 60,000	Accounts Payable	$ 15,000
Accounts Receivable	14,000	Johnson, Capital	35,000
Library (net)	30,000	Miller, Capital	50,000
Furniture (net)	56,000	Wilson, Capital	60,000
Total	$160,000	Total	$160,000

Johnson, Miller, and Wilson share income in a 2:3:5 ratio.

Required

Prepare journal entries for Miller's withdrawal in each of the following independent situations:

a. Miller is to receive $47,000 because the partners agree that the furniture is overvalued. The carrying value of the furniture is reduced.

b. The partners agree that the library is undervalued by $8,000. After recording the increase, Miller is paid the amount in his capital account.

c. Johnson and Wilson allow Baxter to purchase Miller's interest in the partnership for $57,000. No goodwill is recognized.

d. Miller receives $56,300. The bonus method is used.

e. Miller receives $56,300, and his share of the goodwill is recorded.

f. Miller receives $56,300, and the total implied goodwill is recorded.

P16-16 Multiple Choice—Initial Investments, Division of Income, Admission and Retirement of a Partner.

Select the correct answer for each of the following questions.

1. Kiddo and Bucko contribute assets to form a partnership. Initial investments are as follows:

	Book Value	Market Value
Kiddo:		
Land	$ 5,000	$ 4,000
Office equipment	15,000	12,000
Notes payable	12,000	11,000
Bucko:		
Inventory	10,000	10,000
Building	32,000	40,000
Mortgage payable	33,000	36,000

After they record the initial investments, the credit balances in the capital accounts are:
a. Kiddo, $4,000; Bucko, $17,000.
b. Kiddo, $8,000; Bucko, $9,000.
c. Kiddo, $5,000; Bucko, $14,000.
d. Kiddo, $9,000; Bucko, $6,000.

Questions 2 and 3 are based on the following information:

Melissa and Michael have the following income sharing agreement for their partnership:

1. Melissa and Michael are to receive salaries of $24,000 and $30,000.
2. Melissa will get a bonus of 10 percent of income after deducting the bonus.
3. Any remainder is divided in a ratio of Melissa 5:Michael 1.

2. If income before the bonus is $66,000, Melissa's share of the income is:
a. $30,000.
b. $35,000.
c. $39,000.
d. $41,000.

3. If income before the bonus is $33,000, Melissa's share of the income is:
a. $7,000.
b. $12,000.
c. $15,000.
d. $27,000.

Questions 4, 5, and 6 are based on the following information:

Ken and Steve are partners who share income in a 2:3 ratio. Their capital balances are $50,000 and $40,000. Gary is to become a partner with a one-fourth interest in capital and income.

4. If Gary invests $25,000, the amount of goodwill recorded will be:
a. $3,750.
b. $5,000.

   c. $10,000.

   d. $15,000.

5. If Gary invests $20,000 and total capital will be $110,000, Ken's capital balance after Gary's admission will be:

   a. $47,000.

   b. $47,750.

   c. $50,000.

   d. $53,000.

6. If Gary directly purchases his interest by paying Ken $15,000 and Steve $12,000, Steve's capital balance after Gary's admission will be:

   a. $28,000.

   b. $30,000.

   c. $39,000.

   d. $43,600.

Questions 7 and 8 are based on the following information:

The capital balances and income percentages of partners Doug, June, and Barb are as follows:

Doug	$50,000	48%
June	60,000	22
Barb	40,000	30

7. Barb retires and is paid $46,000. Assuming the total implicit goodwill is recorded, Doug's capital balance after Barb's retirement is:

   a. $51,800.

   b. $54,800.

   c. $57,200.

   d. $59,600.

8. Barb retires and is paid $45,000. Assuming the bonus method is used, Doug's capital balance after Barb's retirement will be:

   a. $46,571.

   b. $46,875.

   c. $50,000.

   d. $53,429.

P16-17   Division of Income

Candy, Davis, and Evans, who are accountants, agreed to combine their individual practices into a partnership as of January 1, 19X3. The partnership includes the following features.

1. Each partner's capital contribution was the net amount of assets and liabilities taken over by the partnership, which were as follows:

	Candy	Davis	Evans
Cash	$ 5,000	$ 5,000	$ 5,000
Accounts receivable	14,000	6,000	16,000
Furniture and library	4,300	2,500	6,200
Total debits	$23,300	$13,500	$27,200
Allowance for depreciation	$ 2,400	$ 1,500	$ 4,700
Accounts payable	300	1,400	700
Total credits	$ (2,700)	$ (2,900)	$ (5,400)
Capital contributions	$20,600	$10,600	$21,800

Each partner guaranteed the collectibility of receivables.

2. Evans leased office space and was bound by the lease until June 30, 19X3. The monthly rental was $600. The partners agreed to occupy Evans's office space until the expiration of the lease and to pay the rent. The partners concurred that the rent was too high for the space and that a fair rental value is $450 per month. The excess rent is to be charged to Evans at year-end. On July 1, the partners moved to new quarters with a monthly rental of $500.

3. No salaries are to be paid to the partners. The individual partners are to receive 20 percent of the gross fees billed to their respective clients during the first year of the partnership. After deducting operating expenses (excluding the excess rent), the residual profit should be credited to the partners' capital accounts in the following ratios: Candy, 40 percent; Davis, 35 percent; Evans, 25 percent.

4. On April 1, 19X3, Flint was admitted to the partnership. Flint is to receive 20 percent of the fees from new business obtained after April 1, after deducting expenses applicable to that new business. Expenses (excluding the excess rent) are to be apportioned to the new business in the same ratio that total expenses for the entire year, other than bad debt losses, bore to total gross fees.

5. The following information pertains to the partnership's activities in 19X3.

   a. Fees were billed as follows:

Candy's clients	$ 44,000
Davis's clients	24,000
Evans's clients	22,000
New business:	
Before April 1	6,000
After April 1	24,000
Total	$120,000

   b. Total expenses, excluding depreciation and uncollectible accounts expenses, were $29,350, including the total amount paid for rent. Depreciation is to be computed at the rate of 10 percent of the original cost of the furniture and library for each partner. Depreciable assets purchased during 19X3, on which half a year's depreciation is to be taken, totaled $5,000.

   c. Cash withdrawals charged to the partners' accounts during the year were:

Candy	$ 5,200
Davis	4,400
Evans	5,800
Flint	2,500
Total cash withdrawals	$17,900

d. Of Candy's and Davis's receivables, $1,200 and $450, respectively, proved to be uncollectible and were charged against their capital accounts. A new client billed in March for $1,600 had been adjudged bankrupt, and a settlement of 50 cents on the dollar was made.

Required

a. Determine the profit for 19X3.
b. Prepare a schedule showing how the profit for 19X3 is to be divided.
c. Prepare a statement of partners' capital for the year ended December 31, 19X3.

P16-18 Partnership Accounting—Comprehensive [AICPA Adapted]

You have been engaged to prepare financial statements for the partnership of Highland, Kelly, and Walt as of June 30, 19X2. You have obtained the following information from the partnership agreement as amended and from the accounting records.

1. The partnership was formed originally by Highland and Bayles on July 1, 19X1. At that date:

Bayles contributed $400,000 cash.

Highland contributed land, building, and equipment with fair market values of $110,000, $520,000, and $185,000, respectively. The land and building were subject to a mortgage securing an 8 percent per annum note (interest rate of similar notes at July 1, 19X1). The note is due in quarterly payments of $5,000 plus interest on January 1, April 1, July 1, and October 1 of each year. Highland made the July 1, 19X1, principal and interest payment personally. The partnership then assumed the obligation for the remaining $300,000 balance.

The agreement further provided that Highland had contributed a certain intangible benefit to the partnership due to her many years of business activity in the area to be served by the new partnership. The assigned value of this intangible asset plus the net tangible assets she contributed gave Highland a 60 percent initial capital interest in the partnership.

Highland was designated the only active partner with an annual salary of $24,000 plus an annual bonus of 4 percent of net income after deducting her salary but before deducting interest on partners' capital investments (see below). Both the salary and the bonus are operating expenses of the partnership.

Each partner is to receive a 6 percent return on his or her average capital investment, such interest to be an expense of the partnership.

All remaining profits or losses are to be shared equally.

2. On October 1, 19X1, Bayles sold his partnership interest and rights as of July 1, 19X1, to Walt for $370,000. Highland agreed to accept Walt as a partner if he would contribute sufficient cash to meet the October 1, 19X1, principal and interest payment on the mortgage note. Walt made the payment from personal funds.

3. On January 1, 19X2, Highland and Walt admitted a new partner, Kelly. Kelly invested $150,000 cash for a 10 percent capital interest based on the initial investments at July 1, 19X1, of Highland and Bayles. At January 1, 19X2, the book value of the partnership's assets and liabilities approximated their fair market values. Kelly contributed no intangible benefit to the partnership.

Similar to the other partners, Kelly is to receive a 6 percent return on his average capital investment. His investment also entitled him to 20 percent of the partnership's profits or losses as defined above. However, for the year ended June 30, 19X2, Kelly would receive one-half of his pro rata share of the profits or losses.

4. The accounting records show that on February 1, 19X2, Other Miscellaneous Expenses had been charged $3,600 in payment of hospital expenses incurred by Highland's 8-year-old daughter.

5. All salary payments to Highland have been charged to her drawing account. On June 1, 19X2, Walt made a $33,000 withdrawal. These are the only transactions recorded in the partners' drawing accounts.

6. Presented below is a trial balance which summarizes the partnership's general ledger balances at June 30, 19X2. The general ledger has not been closed.

	Debit	Credit
Current Assets	$ 307,100	
Fixed Assets, net	1,285,800	
Current Liabilities		$157,000
8 Percent Mortgage Note Payable		290,000
Highland, Capital		515,000
Kelly, Capital		150,000
Walt, Capital		400,000
Highland, Drawing	24,000	
Kelly, Drawing	–0–	
Walt, Drawing	33,000	
Sales		872,600
Cost of Sales	695,000	
Administrative Expenses	16,900	
Other Miscellaneous Expenses	11,100	
Interest Expense	11,700	

Required

Prepare a workpaper to adjust the net (income) loss and partners' capital accounts for the year ended June 30, 19X2, and to close the net income loss to the partners' capital accounts at June 30, 19X2. Supporting schedules should be in good form. Amortization of goodwill, if any, is to be over a 10-year period. Ignore all tax considerations. Use the following column headings and begin with balances per books as shown.

Highland, Kelly, and Walt
Adjustments to Net Income and Partners' Capital
June 30, 19X2

	Net (Income) Loss	Partners' Capital			Other Accounts	
		Highland	Kelly	Walt	Amount	Name
Book balances at 6/30/X2*	$(137,900)	$(515,000)	$(150,000)	$(400,000)		

* Parentheses indicate credit amount.

P16-19 Partnership Accounting—Cash to Accrual Comprehensive [AICPA Adapted]

The partnership of Abbott, Robinson, and Stevens engaged you to adjust its accounting records and convert them uniformly to the accrual basis in anticipation of admitting Kingston as a new partner. Some accounts are on the accrual basis and others are on the cash basis. The partnership's books were closed at December 31, 19X6, by the bookkeeper, who prepared the general ledger trial balance that appears below.

Abbott, Robinson, and Stevens
General Ledger Trial Balance
December 31, 19X6

	Debit	Credit
Cash	$ 10,000	
Accounts Receivable	40,000	
Inventory	26,000	
Land	9,000	
Buildings	50,000	
Allowance for Depreciation of Buildings		$ 2,000
Equipment	56,000	
Allowance for Depreciation of Equipment		6,000
Goodwill	5,000	
Accounts Payable		55,000
Allowance for Future Inventory Losses		3,000
Abbott, Capital		40,000
Robinson, Capital		60,000
Stevens, Capital		30,000
Totals	$196,000	$196,000

Your inquiries disclosed the following:

1. The partnership was organized on January 1, 19X5, with no provision in the partnership agreement for the distribution of partnership profits and losses. During 19X5, profits were distributed equally among the partners. The partnership agreement was amended effective January 1, 19X6, to provide for the following profit and loss sharing ratio: Abbott, 50 percent; Robinson, 30 percent; and Stevens, 20 percent. The amended partnership agreement also stated that the accounting records were to be maintained on the accrual basis and that any adjustments necessary for 19X5 should be allocated according to the 19X5 distribution of profits.

2. The following amounts were not recorded as prepayments or accruals:

	December 31	
	19X6	**19X5**
Prepaid insurance	$700	$ 650
Advances from customers	200	1,100
Accrued interest expense	-0-	450

The advances from customers were recorded as sales in the year the cash was received.

3. In 19X6, the partnership recorded a provision of $3,000 for anticipated declines in inventory prices. You convinced the partners that the provision was unnecessary and the provision and related allowance should be removed from the books.

4. The partnership charged equipment purchased for $4,400 on January 3, 19X6, to expense. The equipment has an estimated life of 10 years and an estimated salvage value of $400. The partnership depreciates its capitalized equipment on the double-declining-balance method.

5. The partners agreed to establish an allowance for uncollectible accounts at 2 percent of current accounts receivable and 5 percent of past-due accounts. At December 31, 19X5, the partnership had $54,000 of accounts receivable, of which only $4,000 was past due. At December 31, 19X6, 15 percent of accounts receivable was past due, of which $4,000 represented sales made in 19X5 and was generally considered collectible. The partnership had written off uncollectible accounts in the year the accounts became worthless as follows:

	Account Written Off	
	19X6	**19X5**
19X6 accounts	$ 800	-0-
19X5 accounts	1,000	$250

6. Goodwill was recorded on the books in 19X6 and credited to the partners' capital accounts in the profit and loss sharing ratio in recognition of an increase in the value of the business resulting from improved sales volume. No amortization of goodwill was recorded. The partners agreed to write off the goodwill before admitting the new partner.

Required

a. Prepare the journal entries to convert the accounting records to the accrual basis and to correct the books before admitting the new partner.

b. Without prejudice to your solution to part (**a**) above, assume that the assets were properly valued and that the adjusted total of the partners' capital account balances at December 31, 19X6, was $140,000. On that date, Kingston invested $55,000 in the partnership. Record the admission of Kingston using the goodwill method. Kingston is to be granted a one-fourth interest in the partnership. The other partners will retain their 50:30:20 income-sharing ratio for the remaining three-fourths' interest.

P16-20A   Initial Investments and Tax Bases [AICPA Adapted]

The DELS partnership was formed by combining individual accounting practices on May 10, 19X1. The initial investments were as follows:

	Current Value	Tax Basis
Delaney:		
Cash	8,000	8,000
Building	60,000	32,000
Mortgage payable, assumed by DELS	36,000	36,000
Engstrom:		
Cash	9,000	9,000
Office furniture	23,000	17,000
Note payable, assumed by DELS	10,000	10,000
Lahey:		
Cash	$12,000	$12,000
Computers and printers	18,000	21,000
Note payable, assumed by DELS	15,000	15,000
Simon:		
Cash	21,000	21,000
Library (Books and periodicals)	7,000	5,000

Required

a. Prepare the journal entry to record the initial investments, using GAAP accounting.

b. Calculate the tax basis of each partner's capital if Delaney, Engstrom, Lahey, and Simon agree to assume equal amounts for the payables.

CHAPTER 17

PARTNERSHIPS: LIQUIDATION

Because of the normal risks of doing business, the majority of partnerships begun in any one year fail within 3 years and require termination and liquidation. The termination of a partnership's business is often an emotional event for the partners. The partners may have had high expectations for the business when it began and invested a large amount of personal resources and time in the business. The end of the partnership often is the end of these business dreams. Accountants usually assist in the liquidation process and must recognize the legitimate rights of the many parties involved in the partnership: individual partners, creditors of the partnership and the individual partners, customers, and others doing business with the partnership.

The Uniform Partnership Act has 45 sections, of which 16 deal specifically with the termination and dissolution of a partnership. Most of these sections discuss the specific rights of third-party creditors who have extended credit to the partnership. These outside creditors have first claim to the partnership's assets and, because of the unlimited liability of each partner, may have claims against individual partners' personal assets. This chapter presents the concepts that accountants must know if they offer professional services to partnerships undergoing liquidation.

OVERVIEW OF PARTNERSHIP LIQUIDATIONS

The Uniform Partnership Act (UPA) governs partnership terminations and liquidations. The basic liquidation provisions contained in the UPA are discussed briefly in the following section.

Dissolution, Termination, and Liquidation of a Partnership

Dissolution is a legal concept indicating a change in the legal relationship between partners. *Termination* is the end of the normal business function of the partnership. The partnership is no longer a going concern at the point of termination. *Liquidation* is the sale of the partnership assets, payment of the partnership's liabilities, and distribution of any remaining assets to the individual partners.

Dissolution is defined in Section 29 of the UPA as "the change in the relation of the partners," usually as a result of a new partner's entering the partnership or a partner's leaving the partnership because of death, retirement, or voluntary withdrawal. The major causes of a dissolution are:

1. A new partner is admitted or a partner withdraws.
2. The specified term or task of the partnership has been completed.
3. All partners agree to dissolve the partnership.
4. The partnership or an individual partner is bankrupt.
5. By court decree:
   a. A partner is declared insane.
   b. A partner seriously breaches the partnership agreement.
   c. The court determines that a partnership may be operated only at a loss.

The dissolution of a partnership does not necessarily mean the partnership must stop doing business, close its doors, and liquidate. As discussed in Chapter 16, many partnerships go through legal dissolution without any effect on their day-to-day operations. For example, the admission of a new partner requires the legal dissolution of the old partnership and the creation of a new partnership. Accounting for this dissolution requires the determination of each partner's capital balance on the date of dissolution. The new partnership may then continue doing business as it did immediately before the admission of the new partner.

In most instances of dissolution, a partnership may easily avoid termination and liquidation by including provisions in the partnership agreement for the continuation of business after the dissolution. Certain dissolutions, however, require the termination of business regardless of provisions in the partnership agreement. A partnership must immediately terminate its activities if:

1. A court so decrees.
2. The partnership is bankrupt.
3. The partnership's business becomes illegal.

The partnership agreement should include the necessary continuation provisions if the partners wish to avoid termination in other than the above three required instances. The partnership agreement should also specify if a special liquidation profit and loss sharing ratio is to be used in lieu of the normal profit and loss sharing ratio. If the partnership agreement does not provide for a special liquidation sharing ratio, then the same ratio used to distribute the operating profit or loss is used during liquidation.

The liquidation of a partnership may take place over a period of several months after the date of termination. The partners may seek the best possible prices for the partnership's assets and may not wish to accept a forced sale price—for example, the price at a public auction. This phase-out period requires accounting for the liquidation activities of the partnership. In addition, the legal rights of the partners and creditors must be fully protected.

Priority of Claims

At the point of partnership liquidation, the assets and liabilities of the partnership are directly intertwined with those of the individual partners' personal assets and liabilities because of the unlimited liability of each partner. The Uniform Partnership Act establishes the priorities for creditors' claims against the assets available to pay the partnerships' liabilities. Two concepts are important here: the marshaling of assets and the right of offset.

Marshaling of Assets   Section 40 of the UPA presents the order of creditors' rights against the partnership's assets and the personal assets of the individual partners, the *marshaling of assets*. The order in which claims against the partnership's assets will be marshaled, or satisfied, is as follows:

1. Partnership creditors other than partners
2. Partners' claims other than capital and profits, such as loans payable and accrued interest payable
3. Partners' claims to capital or profits, to the extent of credit balances in capital accounts

The order of claims against the personal assets of individual partners is as follows:

1. Personal creditors of individual partners
2. Partnership creditors for unpaid partnership liabilities, regardless of a partner's capital balance in the partnership

These priorities are illustrated with the liquidation of the ABC Partnership, whose partners, Alt, Blue, and Cha, decide to terminate the business on May 1, 19X5. The AB Partnership was formed on January 1, 19X1. Cha was admitted into the partnership on January 1, 19X3, and the name of the business was changed to the ABC Partnership. For purposes of this illustration, assume that Alt remained in the partnership and, in 19X4, the partners agreed to a realignment of their profit and loss sharing percentages to more closely conform with the efforts of each partner. The profit and loss sharing percentages after realignment in 19X4 and the balances of each of the three partners' capital and loan accounts on May 1, 19X5, are as follows:

	Partners		
	Alt	**Blue**	**Cha**
Profit and loss percentage	40%	40%	20%
Partnership capital account	$34,000	$10,000	$12,000
Partnership loan payable to Cha			4,000

The three partners also prepare personal net worth statements (discussed in the appendix to this chapter), including the expected net capital and loan values of each partner's investment in the ABC Partnership, which show the following:

	Alt	Blue	Cha
Personal assets	$150,000	$12,000	$42,000
Personal liabilities	(86,000)	(16,000)	(14,000)
Net worth (deficit)	$ 64,000	$ (4,000)	$28,000

Partners Alt and Cha are personally solvent; that is, their personal assets are greater than their personal liabilities. Blue, on the other hand, is personally insolvent, which means that his personal liabilities of $16,000 exceed his personal assets of $12,000.

If the partnership is insolvent, that is, partnership liabilities exceed partnership assets, the deficit must be made up by additional contributions from individual partners. The UPA provides that additional contributions should be made in the profit and loss ratio of the solvent partners. The partnership creditors, however, are not required to wait for individual partners to make additional contributions of capital. Because of the unlimited liability of each partner for partnership obligations, the partnership's creditors can make claims against any partner's individual assets for the unpaid partnership liabilities. In our example, the unpaid partnership creditors might make a claim against the net assets of partner Alt, because Alt has the greatest net worth and may have the most liquid assets. Alt's personal creditors will have first claims to Alt's personal assets. Alt's remaining assets then become available to pay any unsettled partnership liabilities. Should Alt have to pay partnership debts, he would have legal recourse against Cha for Cha's proportionate share of the unpaid partnership liabilities. Blue is unable to contribute to the partnership because his personal creditors have claims to all his personal assets.

Blue's personal creditors have claims only against Blue's assets. One of these assets is his investment in the ABC Partnership. Blue's creditors may claim partnership assets to the extent of the credit balance in Blue's capital account, but not for more than that credit balance.

Right of Offset In the example above, the partnership has a $4,000, 12 percent, interest-bearing loan payable to partner Cha. The loan was originally recorded by the partnership with the following journal entry:

(1)	Cash	4,000	
	Loan Payable to Partner Cha		4,000
	Record loan payable to partner.		

All financing arrangements should be supported with proper documentation such as promissory notes to indicate clearly that the cash received by the partnership was not an additional capital contribution.

Loans payable to a partner have a higher priority in liquidation than partners' capital balances, but a lower priority than liabilities to outside creditors. However, the legal *right of offset* allows a deficit in a partner's capital account to be offset by a loan payable to that partner. For example, if Cha had a $2,000 deficit in her capital account at the end of the liquidation process, $2,000 of the loan payable to her would be offset against the deficit as follows:

(2)	Loan Payable to Partner Cha	2,000	
	Cha, Capital		2,000
	Offset deficit in Cha's capital account		
	with loan payable.		

The remaining $2,000 loan payable to partner Cha is then paid to Cha.

For purposes of simplifying the illustration, and to focus on the major issues of partnership liquidation, assume that a provision of the initial note between Cha and the partnership is that the 12 percent interest ceases accruing at the point the partnership terminates as a going concern. Please note that this provision is not required as part of a partnership termination. No part of the UPA requires a partner to give up any property rights to interest for loans between the partnership and a partner. Unless otherwise specifically agreed upon, a loan between the partnership and a partner continues to bear interest until extinguished or until the loan is utilized as an offset to remedy an actual deficit in that partner's capital account. In fact, section 18(c) of the UPA states that a partner who, in the aid of the partnership, provides payments or advances that are not capital shall be paid interest from the date of the payment or advance.

Cautions about Offsetting Partners' Loans and Capital Because the right of offset of capital defects arising during liquidation has been recognized by the courts, some accountants combine, at the beginning of the liquidation process, the net amount of loans payable to a partner, or loans receivable from a partner, with the partner's capital account. The offset of a loan payable to a partner increases that partner's capital account, while the offset of a loan receivable from a partner reduces the amount of that partner's capital account. The practical effect of this procedure is to utilize fully the potential right of offset at the beginning of the liquidation process in anticipation of any deficit capital balances. However, please note that the legal right of offset allows for the offset of a loan payable only with the amount of an actual deficit in a partner's capital account. It is important to maintain specific identification of a loan payable (or receivable) between the partnership and a partner because of the following considerations:

1. *If the loan payable (or receivable) continues to be interest-bearing during the liquidation process,* the interest continues to accrue and must be recorded proportionately as a charge (or credit) against each partner's capital account for the amount of interest expense (revenue), and as interest payable (receivable) of the partnership. Note that according to the marshaling of assets priority, interest on a loan payable to a partner has a lower priority in liquidation than claims from external creditors of the partnership.

2. *If the loan is secured by a property interest,* it has specific legal rights above other unsecured interests. Separately retaining the loan payable (or receivable) in the records during the liquidation process ensures that the specific legal rights will be maintained.

3. *Actual offsetting of receivables from partners against partners' capitals may be considered a cancellation of the receivable* and should be performed with caution. The elimination of receivables from partners' accounts should be done only with the agreement of all partners. Although offsetting loans receivable against capital accounts is typical practice, all partners should carefully consider and evaluate all legal rights of the partnership before the receivable offset is approved.

The specific utilization of the right of offset is discussed and illustrated in this chapter in order to separately preserve the identification of the loans with partners.

Statement of Partnership Realization and Liquidation   To guide and summarize the partnership liquidation process, a *statement of partnership realization and liquidation* may be prepared. The statement, often called a "statement of liquidation," is the basis of the journal entries made to record the liquidation. It presents, in workpaper form, the effects of the liquidation on the balance sheet accounts of the partnership. The statement shows the conversion of assets into cash, the allocation of any gains or losses to the partners, and the distribution of cash to creditors and partners. This statement is a basic feature of accounting for a partnership liquidation and is presented and illustrated in the remainder of the chapter.

LUMP-SUM LIQUIDATIONS

A *lump-sum liquidation* of a partnership is one in which all the assets are converted into cash within a very short time, outside creditors are paid, and a single, lump-sum payment is made to the partners for their capital interests. Although most partnership liquidations take place over an extended period, as illustrated later, the lump-sum liquidation is an excellent focal point for presenting the major concepts of partnership liquidation.

Realization of Assets

Typically, a partnership experiences losses on the disposal of its assets. A partnership may have a "Going out of Business" sale in which its inventory is marked down well below normal selling price to encourage immediate sale. Often, the remaining inventory may be sold to companies that specialize in acquiring assets of liquidating businesses. The partnership's furniture, fixtures, and equipment may also be offered at a reduced price or sold to liquidators.

The accounts receivable are usually collected by the partnership. Sometimes the partnership offers a large cash discount for the prompt payment of any remaining receivables whose collection may otherwise delay terminating the partnership. Alternatively, the receivables may be sold to a factor. A factor is a business that specializes in acquiring accounts receivables and immediately paying cash to the seller of the receivables. The partnership records the sale of the receivables as it would any other asset. Typically, the factor acquires only the best of a business's receivables at a price below face value, but some factors are willing to buy all receivables and pay a significantly lower price than face value.

Before any distributions of assets may be made to the partners, either liabilities to outside creditors must be paid in full or the necessary funds may be placed in an escrow account. The escrow agent, usually a bank, uses the funds only for payment of the partnership's liabilities.

Expenses of Liquidation

The liquidation process usually begins with scheduling the partnership's known assets and liabilities. The names and addresses of creditors and the amounts owed to each are specified. As diligent as the effort usually is, additional, unscheduled creditors may become known during the liquidation process. The liquidation process also involves some expenses, such as additional legal and accounting costs. The partnership may also incur costs of disposing of the business, such as special advertising and costs of locating specialized equipment dealers. These expenses are allocated to partners' capital accounts in the profit and loss distribution ratio.

Illustration of Lump-Sum Liquidation

The following illustration is used to present the lump-sum liquidation of the ABC Partnership in which Alt, Blue, and Cha are partners. A condensed trial balance of the company on May 1, 19X5, the day the partners decide to liquidate the business, is presented below.

ABC Partnership
Trial Balance
May 1, 19X5

Cash	$ 10,000	
Noncash Assets	90,000	
Liabilities		$ 40,000
Loan Payable to Partner Cha		4,000
Alt, Capital (40%)		34,000
Blue, Capital (40%)		10,000
Cha, Capital (20%)		12,000
Total	$100,000	$100,000

The basic accounting equation, assets − liabilities = owners' equity, applies to partnership accounting. In this case, owners' equity is the sum of the partners' capital accounts, as follows:

$$\text{Assets } - \text{ Liabilities } = \text{ Owners' Equity}$$
$$\$100,000 - \$44,000 = \$56,000$$

The following three cases illustrate the partnership liquidation concepts that are used commonly. Each case begins with the May 1, 19X5, trial balance of the ABC Partnership. The terms of the note between Cha and the partnership state that the interest on the note stops accruing at the point the partnership ceases operating as a going concern, May 1, 19X5, in this example. The amount of cash realized from the disposal of the noncash assets is different for each of the three cases, and the effects of the different realizations are shown in the statement of partnership realization and liquidation presented for each case.

Case 1: Partnership Solvent and No Deficits in Partners' Capital Accounts   The noncash assets are sold for $80,000 on May 15, 19X5, at a $10,000 loss. The outside creditors are paid their $40,000 on May 20, and the remaining $50,000 cash is distributed to the partners on May 30, 19X5.

The statement of realization and liquidation for Case 1 is presented in Figure 17-1. Note that parentheses are used to indicate credit amounts in the workpapers used throughout this chapter. The statement includes only balance sheet accounts across the columns with all noncash assets presented together as a single total. Once a business has entered liquidation, the balance sheet accounts are the only relevant ones; the income statement is for a going concern. The process of

FIGURE 17-1 Case 1: Partnership solvent; no deficits in partners' capital accounts.

ABC Partnership
Statement of Partnership Realization and Liquidation
Lump-Sum Liquidation

	Cash	Noncash Assets	Liabilities	Cha Loan	Capital Balance Alt, 40%	Blue, 40%	Cha, 20%
Preliquidation balances	10,000	90,000	(40,000)	(4,000)	(34,000)	(10,000)	(12,000)
Sale of assets and distribution of $10,000 loss	80,000	(90,000)			4,000	4,000	2,000
	90,000	-0-	(40,000)	(4,000)	(30,000)	(6,000)	(10,000)
Payment to outside creditors	(40,000)		40,000				
	50,000	-0-	-0-	(4,000)	(30,000)	(6,000)	(10,000)
Lump-sum payments to partners:							
Partner's loan	(4,000)			4,000			
Partners' capital	(46,000)				30,000	6,000	10,000
Postliquidation balances	-0-	-0-	-0-	-0-	-0-	-0-	-0-

Note: Parentheses indicate credit amount.

liquidation is presented in the order of occurrence in the rows of the workpaper. Thus, the workpaper includes the entire realization and liquidation process and is the basis for the journal entries to record the liquidation.

Other important observations are as follows:

1. The preliquidation balances are obtained from the May 1, 19X5, trial balance.

2. The $10,000 loss is distributed directly to the partners' capital accounts.

3. Outside creditors are paid before any assets are distributed to partners.

4. Technically, the partnership's loan payable to partner Cha is paid before any payments to partners for capital balances.

5. The postliquidation balances are all zero, indicating the accounts are all closed and the partnership is fully liquidated and terminated.

The statement of partnership realization and liquidation is the basis for the following journal entries to record the liquidation process:

May 15, 19X5			
(3)	Cash	80,000	
	Alt, Capital	4,000	
	Blue, Capital	4,000	
	Cha, Capital	2,000	
	Noncash Assets		90,000
	Realization of all noncash assets of the ABC Partnership and distribution of $10,000 loss using profit and loss ratio.		
May 20, 19X5			
(4)	Liabilities	40,000	
	Cash		40,000
	Pay outside creditors.		
May 30, 19X5			
(5)	Cha, Loan	4,000	
	Alt, Capital	30,000	
	Blue, Capital	6,000	
	Cha, Capital	10,000	
	Cash		50,000
	Lump-sum payments to partners.		

Case 2: Partnership Solvent and Deficit Created in Partner's Capital Account A deficit in a partner's capital account can occur if the credit balance of a partner's capital account is too low to absorb his or her share of losses. A capital deficit may be created at any time in the liquidation process. Such deficits may be remedied by either of the following two means:

1. The partner invests cash or other assets to eliminate the capital deficit.

2. The partner's capital deficit is distributed to the other partners in their resulting profit and loss sharing ratio.

The approach used depends on the solvency of the partner with the capital deficit. A partner who is personally solvent and has sufficient net worth to eliminate the capital deficit must make an additional investment in the partnership to cover the deficit. On the other hand, if the partner is personally insolvent—that is, personal liabilities exceed personal assets—then section 40 of the UPA requires the remaining partners to absorb the insolvent partner's deficit by allocating it to their capital accounts in their resulting profit and loss sharing ratio.

The following lump-sum distribution illustrates these points:

1. The three partners' personal financial statements are as follows:

	Alt	Blue	Cha
Personal assets	$150,000	$12,000	$42,000
Personal liabilities	(86,000)	(16,000)	(14,000)
Net worth (deficit)	$ 64,000	$(4,000)	$28,000

Blue is personally insolvent; Alt and Cha are personally solvent.

2. The noncash assets of the partnership are sold for $35,000 on May 15, 19X5, and the $55,000 loss is allocated to the partners' capital accounts.

3. The outside creditors are paid $40,000 on May 20, 19X5.

4. The remaining $5,000 cash is distributed to the partners as a lump-sum payment on May 30, 19X5.

The statement of partnership realization and liquidation for Case 2 is presented in Figure 17-2.

The following observations emerge from this illustration:

1. The loss of $55,000 on the realization of noncash assets is allocated in the partners' profit and loss sharing ratio of 40 percent for Alt, 40 percent for Blue, and 20 percent for Cha. Blue's $22,000 share of the loss on disposal creates a $12,000 deficit in his capital account. Blue is personally insolvent and is unable to make an additional investment to remove the capital deficit.

2. The outside creditors are paid before any distributions are made to the partners.

3. Blue's $12,000 deficit is distributed to Alt and Cha in their resulting profit and loss ratio. Alt absorbs two-thirds (40/60) of Blue's deficit, and Cha absorbs one-third (20/60).

4. The distribution of Blue's deficit creates a deficit in Cha's capital account. The right of offset is used to eliminate the deficit with the loan payable to partner Cha. Note that the right of offset is only for the amount of the capital deficit, not for the entire amount of the loan.

5. Lump-sum payments are made to Cha for the remaining $1,000 of the loan payable and to Alt for his $4,000 capital credit.

6. All postliquidation balances are zero, indicating the completion of the liquidation process.

Case 3: Partnership Is Insolvent and Deficit Created in Partner's Capital Account A partnership is insolvent when existing cash and cash generated from the

FIGURE 17-2 Case 2: Partnership solvent; deficit created in personally insolvent partner's capital account.

ABC Partnership
Statement of Partnership Realization and Liquidation
Lump-Sum Liquidation

	Cash	Noncash Assets	Liabilities	Cha Loan	Capital Balance Alt, 40%	Capital Balance Blue, 40%	Capital Balance Cha, 20%
Preliquidation balances	10,000	90,000	(40,000)	(4,000)	(34,000)	(10,000)	(12,000)
Sale of assets and							
distribution of $55,000 loss	35,000	(90,000)			22,000	22,000	11,000
	45,000	-0-	(40,000)	(4,000)	(12,000)	12,000	(1,000)
Payment to outside creditors	(40,000)		40,000				
	5,000	-0-	-0-	(4,000)	(12,000)	12,000	(1,000)
Distribution of deficit of							
insolvent partner:						(12,000)	
40/60 X $12,000					8,000		
20/60 X $12,000							4,000
	5,000	-0-	-0-	(4,000)	(4,000)	-0-	3,000
Offset Cha's deficit with loan				3,000			(3,000)
	5,000	-0-	-0-	(1,000)	(4,000)	-0-	-0-
Lump-sum payments to							
partners:							
Partner's loan	(1,000)			1,000			
Partner's capital	(4,000)				4,000		
Postliquidation balances	-0-	-0-	-0-	-0-	-0-	-0-	-0-

Note: Parentheses indicate credit amount.

sale of the assets is not sufficient to pay the partnership's liabilities. In this case, the individual partners are liable for the remaining unpaid partnership liabilities. The following illustration presents an insolvent partnership and a deficit in one of the partner's capital accounts.

1. Alt and Cha are personally solvent, and Blue is personally insolvent as in Case 2.
2. The noncash assets are sold for $20,000 on May 15, 19X5.
3. The outside creditors are paid $40,000 on May 20, 19X5.

The statement of partnership realization and liquidation for Case 3 is presented in Figure 17-3.

The following observations are made from this illustration:

1. The loss of $70,000 is allocated to the partners in their profit and loss sharing ratio. This allocation creates deficits of $18,000 in Blue's capital account and $2,000 in Cha's capital account.

FIGURE 17-3 Case 3: Partnership insolvent; deficit created in personally insolvent partner's capital account.

ABC Partnership
Statement of Partnership Realization and Liquidation
Lump-Sum Liquidation

	Cash	Noncash Assets	Liabilities	Cha Loan	Alt, 40%	Blue, 40%	Cha, 20%
					Capital Balance		
Preliquidation balances	10,000	90,000	(40,000)	(4,000)	(34,000)	(10,000)	(12,000)
Sale of assets and distribution of $70,000 loss	20,000	(90,000)			28,000	28,000	14,000
	30,000	-0-	(40,000)	(4,000)	(6,000)	18,000	2,000
Distribution of deficit of insolvent partner:						(18,000)	
40/60 X $18,000					12,000		
20/60 X $18,000							6,000
	30,000	-0-	(40,000)	(4,000)	6,000	-0-	8,000
Offset deficit with loan				4,000			(4,000)
	30,000	-0-	(40,000)	-0-	6,000	-0-	4,000
Contribution by Alt and Cha	10,000				(6,000)		(4,000)
	40,000	-0-	(40,000)	-0-	-0-	-0-	-0-
Payment to outside creditors	(40,000)		40,000				
Postliquidation balances	-0-	-0-	-0-	-0-	-0-	-0-	-0-

Note: Parentheses indicate credit amount.

2. Because Blue is personally insolvent, his $18,000 deficit is distributed to Alt and Cha in their profit and loss sharing ratio of 40:60 for Alt and 20:60 for Cha. The distribution of Blue's deficit results in a $6,000 deficit for Alt and an $8,000 deficit for Cha.

3. The loan payable to partner Cha is used to offset $4,000 of Cha's $8,000 capital deficit.

4. Alt and Cha make additional capital contributions to remedy their respective capital deficits of $6,000 and $4,000.

5. The $40,000 of partnership cash now available is used to pay outside creditors.

6. The postliquidation balances are zero, indicating completion of the partnership liquidation.

In Case 3, Alt and Cha made additional capital contributions to eliminate their capital deficits. In the event either partner fails to eliminate a debit balance in his or her capital account, the partnership's creditors could attach any solvent partner's personal assets in excess of personal liabilities as a means of collecting unpaid partnership liabilities. In this example, Alt's deficit of $6,000 and Cha's deficit of $4,000 constitute the partnership insolvency of $10,000. The partnership's creditors could attach Alt's personal assets for the entire $10,000 unpaid liability, regardless of Alt's capital balance. The concept of unlimited liability means that the partnership creditors' claims against a specific partner's assets are not limited by the partner's capital balance. Of course, Alt would, in this case, have a legal remedy against Cha for Cha's portion of the partnership insolvency.

INSTALLMENT LIQUIDATIONS

An *installment liquidation* is one that typically requires several months to complete and includes periodic, or installment, payments to the partners during the liquidation period. Most partnership liquidations take place over an extended period in order to obtain the largest possible amount from the realization of the assets. The partners typically receive periodic payments during the liquidation because they require funds for personal purposes.

Installment liquidations involve the distribution of cash to partners before complete liquidation of the assets occurs. The accountant must be especially cautious when distributing available cash, because future events may change the amounts to be paid to each partner. For this reason, the following practical guides are used to assist the accountant in determining the safe installment payments to the partners.

1. Distribute no cash to the partners until all liabilities and actual and potential liquidation expenses are paid or provided for by reserving the necessary cash.
2. Anticipate the worst, or most restrictive, possible case before determining the amount of cash installment each partner receives:
   a. Assume that all remaining noncash assets will be written off as a loss; that is, assume that nothing will be realized on asset disposals.
   b. Assume that deficits created in the capital accounts of partners will be distributed to the remaining partners; that is, assume that deficits will not be eliminated by additional partner capital contributions.
3. After the accountant has assumed the worst possible cases, the remaining credit balances in loan and capital accounts represent safe distributions of assets and cash that may be distributed to partners in those amounts.

Illustration of Installment Liquidation

The same illustration used in the lump-sum liquidation of the ABC Partnership is now used to illustrate liquidation in installments. Alt, Blue, and Cha decide to liquidate their business over a period of time and to receive installment distributions of available cash during the liquidation process.

The condensed trial balance of the ABC Partnership on May 1, 19X5, the day the partners decide to liquidate the business, is presented below. Each partner's profit and loss sharing percentage is also shown.

ABC Partnership
Trial Balance
May 1, 19X5

Cash	$ 10,000	
Noncash Assets	90,000	
Liabilities		$ 40,000
Loan Payable to Partner Cha		4,000
Alt, Capital (40%)		34,000
Blue, Capital (40%)		10,000
Cha, Capital (20%)		12,000
Total	$100,000	$100,000

The following describes this case.

1. The partners' net worth statements on May 1, 19X5, are as follows:

	Alt	Blue	Cha
Personal assets	$150,000	$12,000	$42,000
Personal liabilities	(86,000)	(16,000)	(14,000)
Net worth (deficit)	$ 64,000	$ (4,000)	$28,000

Blue is personally insolvent; Alt and Cha are personally solvent.

2. The terms of the note between Cha and the partnership state that the interest on the loan payable to Cha stops accruing at the point the partnership ceases operating as a going concern. This date is determined to be May 1, 19X5.

3. The noncash assets are sold as follows:

Date	Book Value	Proceeds	Loss
5/15/X5	$55,000	$45,000	$10,000
6/15/X5	30,000	15,000	15,000
7/15/X5	5,000	5,000	

4. The outside creditors are paid $40,000 on May 20.

5. The partners agree to maintain a $10,000 cash reserve during the liquidation process to pay for any liquidation expenses.

6. The partners agree to distribute the available cash at the end of each month; that is, installment liquidations will be made on May 31 and June 30. The final cash distributions to partners will be made on July 31, 19X5, the end of the liquidation process.

Figure 17-4 presents the statement of partnership realization and liquidation for the installment liquidation of the ABC Partnership.

FIGURE 17-4 Installment liquidation workpaper.

ABC Partnership
Statement of Partnership Realization and Liquidation
Installment Liquidation

					Capital Balance		
	Cash	Noncash Assets	Liabilities	Cha Loan	Alt, 40%	Blue, 40%	Cha, 20%
Preliquidation balances, May 1	10,000	90,000	(40,000)	(4,000)	(34,000)	(10,000)	(12,000)
May 19X5:							
Sale of assets and distribution of $10,000 loss	45,000	(55,000)			4,000	4,000	2,000
	55,000	35,000	(40,000)	(4,000)	(30,000)	(6,000)	(10,000)
Payment to outside creditors	(40,000)		40,000				
	15,000	35,000	-0-	(4,000)	(30,000)	(6,000)	(10,000)
Payment to partners (Schedule 1, Figure 17-5)	(5,000)			1,000	4,000		
	10,000	35,000	-0-	(3,000)	(26,000)	(6,000)	(10,000)
June 19X5:							
Sale of assets and distribution of $15,000 loss	15,000	(30,000)			6,000	6,000	3,000
	25,000	5,000	-0-	(3,000)	(20,000)	-0-	(7,000)
Payment to partners (Schedule 2, Figure 17-5)	(15,000)			3,000	10,000		2,000
	10,000	5,000	-0-	-0-	(10,000)	-0-	(5,000)
July 19X5:							
Sale of assets at book value	5,000	(5,000)					
	15,000	-0-	-0-	-0-	(10,000)	-0-	(5,000)
Payment of $7,500 in liquidation costs	(7,500)				3,000	3,000	1,500
	7,500	-0-	-0-	-0-	(7,000)	3,000	(3,500)
Distribution of deficit of insolvent partner:						(3,000)	
40/60 X $3,000					2,000		
20/60 X $3,000							1,000
	7,500	-0-	-0-	-0-	(5,000)	-0-	(2,500)
Payment to partners	(7,500)				5,000		2,500
Postliquidation balances, July 31	-0-	-0-	-0-	-0-	-0-	-0-	-0-

Note: Parentheses indicate credit amount.

Transactions during May 19X5   The events during May 19X5 result in a distribution of $5,000 to the partners. The procedure to arrive at this amount is as follows:

1. The sale of $55,000 of assets results in a loss of $10,000, which is distributed to the three partners in their profit and loss sharing ratio.
2. Payments of $40,000 are made to outside creditors for the known liabilities.
3. Available cash is distributed to the partners on May 31, 19X5.

In order to determine the safe payment of cash to be distributed to partners, the accountant must make some assumptions about the future liquidation of the remaining assets. Assuming the worst possible situation, the remaining $35,000 of assets will result in a total loss. Before making a cash distribution to the partners, the accountant prepares a *schedule of safe payments to partners* using the worst-case assumptions. Figure 17-5 presents the schedule of safe payments to partners as of May 31, 19X5.

The schedule begins with the partners' capital and loan balances as of May 31. The potential right of offset is applied fully in this worst-case plan to fully reflect the loss-bearing capability of Cha. This is not an actual offset, but rather is for worst-case planning only. If the loan had continued to be interest-bearing during liquidation, interest would continue to accrue and would be recorded on the statement of realization and liquidation until the loan was extinguished or utilized for offset against an actual deficit. Therefore, under this worst-case set of assumptions as of May 31, 19X5, Cha's May 31 loan balance of $4,000 is combined with her $10,000 capital balance because the loan payable could be used, if necessary, to eliminate a deficit in her capital account resulting from losses during the liquidation process. The partners agreed to withhold $10,000 for possible liquidation expenses. In addition, the noncash assets have a remaining balance of $35,000 on May 31. A worst-case assumption is a complete loss on the noncash assets and $10,000 of liquidation expenses, totaling $45,000 of charges to be distributed to the partners' capital accounts. The capital accounts of Alt, Blue, and Cha would be charged for $18,000, $18,000, and $9,000, respectively, for their shares of the $45,000. These assumptions result in a pro forma deficit in Blue's capital account. This is not an actual deficit that must be remedied! It is merely the result of applying the worst-case assumptions.

Continuing such worst-case planning, the accountant assumes that Blue is insolvent (which happens to be true in this example) and distributes the pro forma deficit in Blue's capital account to Alt and Cha in their profit and loss sharing ratio of 40:60 to Alt and 20:60 to Cha. The resulting credit balances indicate the amount of cash that may be safely distributed to the partners. The May 31 cash distribution is shown in Figure 17-4. The available cash of $5,000 is distributed to Alt and Cha, with the $1,000 paid to Cha reducing the loan payable because loan arrangements have a higher priority in liquidation than capital amounts. The ending balances should satisfy the equality of assets and equities of the accounting equation. If the equality has been destroyed, an error has occurred that must be

FIGURE 17-5 Schedule of safe payment to partners for an installment liquidation.

ABC Partnership
Schedule of Safe Payment to Partners

	Partner		
	Alt, 40%	**Blue, 40%**	**Cha, 20%**
Schedule 1, May 31, 19X5			
Computation of distribution of cash available on May 31, 19X5:			
Capital and loan balances, May 31, before cash distribution	(30,000)	(6,000)	(14,000)
Assume full loss of $35,000 on remaining noncash assets and $10,000 in possible future liquidation expenses	18,000	18,000	9,000
	(12,000)	12,000	(5,000)
Assume Blue's potential deficit must be absorbed by Alt and Cha:		(12,000)	
40/60 × $12,000	8,000		
20/60 × $12,000			4,000
Safe payment to partners, May 31	(4,000)	-0-	(1,000)
Schedule 2, June 30, 19X5			
Computation of distribution of cash available on June 30, 19X5:			
Capital and loan balances, June 30	(20,000)	-0-	(10,000)
Assume full loss of $5,000 on remaining noncash assets and $10,000 in possible future liquidation expenses	6,000	6,000	3,000
	(14,000)	6,000	(7,000)
Assume Blue's potential deficit must be absorbed by Alt and Cha:		(6,000)	
40/60 × $6,000	4,000		
20/60 × $6,000			2,000
Safe payment to partners, June 30	(10,000)	-0-	(5,000)

Note: Parentheses indicate credit amount.

corrected before proceeding further. As of May 31, after the installment distribution, the accounting equation is:

Assets − Liabilities = Owners' Equity
$45,000 − $3,000 = $42,000

Transactions during June 19X5 Figure 17-4 continues with transactions for June 19X5, as follows:

1. Noncash assets of $30,000 are sold on June 15 for a loss of $15,000. The loss is distributed to the partners in their profit and loss sharing ratio, resulting in a zero capital balance for Blue.

2. On June 30, 19X5, available cash is distributed as an installment payment to the partners.

The schedule of safe payments to partners as of June 30, 19X5, in Figure 17-5 shows how the amounts of distribution are calculated. A worst-case plan assumes that the remaining noncash assets of $5,000 must be written off as a loss and that the $10,000 cash in reserve will be completely used for liquidation expenses. This pro forma loss of $15,000 is allocated to the partners in their profit and loss sharing ratio, which creates a $6,000 deficit in Blue's capital account. Continuing the worst-case scenario, it is assumed Blue will not eliminate this debit balance. Therefore, the $6,000 potential deficit is allocated to Alt and Cha in their resulting profit and loss sharing ratio of 40:60 to Alt and 20:60 to Cha. The resulting credit balances in the partners' capital accounts show the amount of cash that can be distributed safely. Only $15,000 of the available cash is distributed to Alt and Cha on June 30, as shown in Figure 17-4. Of the $5,000 paid to Cha, $3,000 repays the loan payable. The remaining $2,000 reduces Cha's capital account.

Transactions during July 19X5   The last part of Figure 17-4 shows the completion of the liquidation transactions during July 19X5.

1. The remaining assets are sold at their book values.

2. Actual liquidation costs of $7,500 are paid and allocated to the partners in their profit and loss sharing ratio, creating a deficit of $3,000 in Blue's capital account. The remaining $2,500 of the $10,000 reserved for the expenses is released for distribution to the partners.

3. Because Blue is personally insolvent and cannot contribute to the partnership, the $3,000 deficit is distributed to Alt and Cha in their profit and loss sharing ratio. Note that this is an actual deficit, not a pro forma deficit.

4. The $7,500 of remaining cash is paid to Alt and Cha to the extent of their capital balances. After this last distribution, all account balances are zero, indicating the completion of the liquidation process.

Cash Distribution Plan

At the beginning of the liquidation process, it is common for accountants to prepare a *cash distribution plan,* which gives the partners an idea of the installment cash payments each will receive as cash becomes available to the partnership. The actual installment distributions are determined using the statement of realization and liquidation, supplemented with the schedule of safe payments to partners as presented in the last section of the chapter. The cash distribution plan is a pro forma projection of the application of cash as it becomes available.

Loss Absorption Power   A basic concept of the cash distribution plan at the beginning of the liquidation process is *loss absorption power* (LAP). An individual partner's LAP is defined as the maximum loss that can be realized by the partnership before that partner's capital and loan account balances are extinguished. For planning purposes, the potential rule of offset is applied fully and loan accounts become available for capital deficits. Thus loan accounts are fully offset against the capital accounts before a partner's LAP is computed. This offset is just for planning purposes; any actual offsets will be performed as necessary during the liquidation process. The loss absorption power is a function of two elements, as follows:

$$\text{LAP} = \frac{\text{partner's capital and loan account balances}}{\text{partner's profit and loss share}}$$

For example, Alt has a capital account credit balance of $34,000 and a 40 percent share in the profits and losses of ABC Partnership. Alt's LAP is:

$$\text{LAP} = \frac{\$34,000}{.40} = \$85,000$$

This means that $85,000 in losses on disposing of noncash assets or from additional liquidation expenses would eliminate the credit balance in Alt's capital account, as follows:

$$\$85,000 \times .40 = \$34,000$$

Illustration of Cash Distribution Plan   The following illustration is based on the ABC Partnership example. A trial balance of the balance sheet accounts of the ABC Partnership on May 1, 19X5, the day the partners decide to liquidate the business, is presented below.

ABC Partnership
Trial Balance
May 1, 19X5

Cash	$ 10,000	
Noncash Assets	90,000	
Liabilities		$ 40,000
Loan Payable to Partner Cha		4,000
Alt, Capital (40%)		34,000
Blue, Capital (40%)		10,000
Cha, Capital (20%)		12,000
	$100,000	$100,000

The partners ask for a cash distribution plan as of May 1, 19X5, to determine the distributions of cash as it becomes available during the liquidation process. Such a plan always provides for payment to the outside creditors before any distributions may be made to the partners. Figure 17-6 presents the cash distribution plan as of May 1, the beginning date of the liquidation process.

FIGURE 17-6 Cash distribution plan for liquidating partnership.

ABC Partnership
Cash Distribution Plan
May 1, 19X5

	Loss Absorption Power			Capital and Loan Accounts		
	Alt	Blue	Cha	Alt	Blue	Cha
Profit and loss sharing percentages				40%	40%	20%
Preliquidation capital and loan account balances, May 1, 19X5				(34,000)	(10,000)	(16,000)
Loss absorption power (LAP) (Capital and loan accounts ÷ profit and loss ratio)	(85,000)	(25,000)	(80,000)			
Decrease highest LAP to next-highest LAP: Decrease Alt by $5,000 (cash distribution: $5,000 × .40 = $2,000)	5,000			2,000		
	(80,000)	(25,000)	(80,000)	(32,000)	(10,000)	(16,000)
Decrease LAPs to next-highest level: Decrease Alt by $55,000 (cash distribution: $55,000 × .40 = $22,000)	55,000			22,000		
Decrease Cha by $55,000 (cash distribution: $55,000 × .20 = $11,000)			55,000			11,000
	(25,000)	(25,000)	(25,000)	(10,000)	(10,000)	(5,000)
Decrease LAPs by distributing cash in profit and loss sharing percentages	40%	40%	20%			

Summary of Cash Distribution Plan

Step 1: First $40,000 to outside creditors			
Step 2: Next $10,000 to liquidation expenses			
Step 3: Next $2,000 to Alt	2,000		
Step 4: Next $33,000 to Alt and Cha in their respective profit and loss ratios	22,000		11,000
Step 5: Any additional distributions in the partners' profit and loss ratio	40%	40%	20%

Note: Parentheses indicate credit amount.

The important observations from this illustration are as follows:

1. The cash distribution plan does not distinguish between partners' capital and loan accounts. Because of the potential right of offset, the balances of such accounts are combined for purposes of the cash distribution plan. Cha's beginning amount of $16,000 in Figure 17-6 is the sum of the $4,000 loan and the May 1 capital balance of $12,000.

2. The loss absorption power of each partner is computed as the partner's preliquidation capital and loan balances divided by that partner's profit and loss sharing percentage. Alt has the highest LAP ($85,000), Cha has the next highest ($80,000), and Blue has the lowest ($25,000). Each partner's LAP is the amount of loss that would completely eliminate his or her net capital credit balance. Alt is the least vulnerable to a loss, and Blue is the most vulnerable.

3. The least vulnerable partner will be the first to receive any cash distributions after payment of creditors. Alt will be the only partner to receive cash until his LAP is decreased to the level of the next highest partner, Cha. To decrease Alt's LAP by $5,000 requires the payment of $2,000 ($5,000 × .40) to Alt. After payment of $2,000 to Alt, his new loss absorption power will be the same as Cha's, calculated as Alt's remaining capital balance of $32,000 divided by his profit and loss sharing percentage of 40 percent ($32,000 ÷ .40 = $80,000).

4. Alt's and Cha's LAPs are now equal, and they will receive cash distributions until their LAPs are each decreased to the next highest level, the $25,000 of Blue. Multiplying the $55,000 by the two partners' profit and loss sharing ratios shows how much of the next available cash can be safely paid to each partner. Alt and Cha will receive cash distributions in their profit and loss sharing ratio. As the next $33,000 of cash becomes available, it will be distributed to Alt and Cha in the ratio of 40:60 to Alt and 20:60 to Cha.

5. Finally, when all three partners have the same LAPs, any remaining cash is distributed in their profit and loss sharing ratio.

The summary of the cash distribution plan on the bottom of Figure 17-6 is provided to the partners. From this summary, partners are able to determine the relative amounts each will receive as cash becomes available to the partnership.

Figure 17-7 presents the combined capital and loan account balances for each of the partners in the ABC Partnership during the installment liquidation period from May 1, 19X5, through July 31, 19X5. The installment payments to partners are computed on the statement of partnership realization and liquidation (Figure 17-4) using a schedule of safe distributions to partners (Figure 17-5). Figure 17-7 shows that the actual distributions of available cash conform to the cash distribution plan prepared at the beginning of the liquidation process.

ADDITIONAL CONSIDERATIONS

Incorporation of a Partnership

As a partnership continues to grow, the partners may decide to incorporate the business in order to have access to additional equity financing, to limit their personal liability, to obtain selected tax advantages, or to achieve other sound business purposes. At the time of incorporation, the partnership is terminated, and the assets and liabilities are revalued to their market values. The gain or loss on revaluation is allocated to the partners' capital accounts in the profit and loss sharing ratio.

FIGURE 17-7 Confirmation of cash distribution plan.

ABC Partnership
Combined Capital and Loan Account Balances
May 1, 19X5, through July 31, 19X5

	Partner		
	Alt, 40%	Blue, 40%	Cha, 20%
Preliquidation balances, May 1	(34,000)	(10,000)	(16,000)
May loss of $10,000 on disposal of assets	4,000	4,000	2,000
	(30,000)	(6,000)	(14,000)
May 31 distribution of $5,000 available cash to partners:			
First $2,000	2,000		
Next $3,000:			
40/60 to Alt	2,000		
20/60 to Cha			1,000
	(26,000)	(6,000)	(13,000)
June loss of $15,000 on disposal of assets	6,000	6,000	3,000
	(20,000)	-0-	(10,000)
June 30 distribution of $15,000 available cash to partners:			
40/60 to Alt	10,000		
20/60 to Cha			5,000
	(10,000)	-0-	(5,000)
Liquidation costs of $7,500	3,000	3,000	1,500
	(7,000)	3,000	(3,500)
Distribution of Blue's deficit	2,000	(3,000)	1,000
	(5,000)	-0-	(2,500)
Final payment of $7,500 to partners on July 31, 19X5:			
40/60 to Alt	5,000		
20/60 to Cha			2,500
Postliquidation balances, July 31	-0-	-0-	-0-

Note: Parentheses indicate credit amount.

Capital stock in the new corporation is then distributed in proportion to the capital accounts of the partners. The corporation may continue to use the partnership's accounting journals and ledgers to record its entries. In this case, the partners' capital accounts are closed, and the newly issued stock is recorded at the appropriate par value and any additional paid-in capital. If the corporation decides to open a new set of accounting records, the partnership's books are closed with the receipt of the new corporation's stock for the partnership's assets and liabilities and the subsequent distribution of the stock to the partners in proportion to their capital credits.

The ABC Partnership's trial balance on May 1, 19X5, as shown previously, is used to illustrate incorporation of a partnership. Instead of liquidating the partnership as shown throughout the chapter, assume the partners agree to incorporate the partnership.

The new corporation is to be called the Peerless Products Corporation. The new corporation will keep the partnership's books. At the time of conversion from a partnership to a corporation, all assets and liabilities should be appraised and valued at their market values. Any gain or loss must be distributed to the partners in their profit and loss sharing ratios. Assume the noncash assets have a market value of $80,000. The $10,000 loss to market value is allocated to the partners' capital accounts before the incorporation, as follows:

(6)	Alt, Capital	4,000	
	Blue, Capital	4,000	
	Cha, Capital	2,000	
	Noncash Assets		10,000
	Recognize loss on reduction of assets to		
	market values.		

Of course, in practice, specific asset accounts would be used instead of the general classification of noncash assets. Gains on asset revaluations also may occur when a successful partnership elects to incorporate.

Now that all assets and liabilities are at their respective fair values, the corporation issues 4,600 shares of $1 par common stock in exchange for the partners' capital interests in the partnership. The entry to record the stock distribution is:

(7)	Alt, Capital	30,000	
	Blue, Capital	6,000	
	Cha, Capital	10,000	
	Comon stock		4,600
	Paid-In Capital in Excess of Par		41,400
	Stock distributed to prior partners.		

If Peerless Products Corporation decides to open a new set of books, entries are made by the corporation to acquire the partnership assets and liabilities and by the partnership to receive the stock and distribute it to the partners. The entry on the corporation's books is:

(8)	Cash	10,000	
	Noncash Assets	80,000	
	Liabilities		40,000
	Loan Payable to Cha		4,000
	Common Stock		4,600
	Paid-In Capital in Excess of Par		41,400
	Issuance of stock for partnership's assets		
	and liabilities.		

The partners make the following entry on the partnership's books:

(9)	Investment in Peerless Products Stock	46,000	
	Liabilities	40,000	
	Loan Payable to Partner Cha	4,000	
	Cash		10,000
	Noncash Assets		80,000
	Receipt of stock in Peerless Products for partnership's net assets.		

Recall that the noncash assets were reduced to their fair values in entry (6) above. To distribute the stock to the partners and close the partnership's books, the final entry is:

(10)	Alt, Capital	30,000	
	Blue, Capital	6,000	
	Cha, Capital	10,000	
	Investment in Peerless Products Stock		46,000
	Distribution of Peerless Products stock to partners.		

SUMMARY OF KEY CONCEPTS AND TERMS

The termination and liquidation of a partnership are often traumatic times for partners. The Uniform Partnership Act provides guides to the liquidation process and specifies the legal rights of the partners and of partnership creditors.

Dissolution is a change in the relationship between the partners. Not all dissolutions require termination, which is the cessation of normal business functions, or liquidation, which is the disposal of assets, payment of liabilities, and distribution of remaining cash to partners. Termination and liquidation can be avoided by carefully preparing the articles of copartnership to allow continuation of the business when a new partner is admitted or a partner retires. Liquidation may be voluntary or involuntary. The most common reasons for involuntary liquidation are court decrees or bankrupt partnerships.

During the liquidation process, accountants must be aware of the priority of claims against partnership assets and against the partners' personal assets. The Uniform Partnership Act provides for the marshaling of assets and the right of offset. Marshaling of assets establishes priorities of the claims against assets; the right of offset means the loans payable to partners or receivable from partners may be offset against their capital accounts.

Liquidation can involve a single lump-sum payment to partners. Most liquidations, however, take several months and involve installment payments to partners during the liquidation process. Liquidations are facilitated by the preparation of the statement of partnership realization and liquidation, a workpaper summarizing the liquidation process and serving as a basis for the journal entries to record the events. Installment payments to partners are determined on a worst-case basis using a schedule of safe payments to partners, which assumes that all noncash assets will be written off and that partners with debit balances in their capital accounts will not be able to remedy the deficiencies.

A cash distribution plan provides partners with information about the installment payments they will receive as cash becomes available to the partnership. The plan is prepared at the beginning of the liquidation process. Actual cash distributions during the liquidation process are determined with the statement of partnership realization and liquidation. The concept of loss absorption power (LAP) is central to the development of the cash distribution plan. Loss absorption power is the amount of partnership loss required to eliminate a given partner's capital credit balance. The loss absorption power is determined by dividing a partner's net capital credit balance by his or her profit and loss sharing percentage.

The incorporation of a partnership requires the revaluation of partnership assets and liabilities to their market values. The corporation may take over the partnership's accounting records, or the partnership books may be closed, when the corporation's stock is distributed to the partners.

Cash distribution plan	Marshaling of assets
Dissolution (of a partnership)	Right of offset
Installment liquidation	Schedule of safe payments to partners
Liquidation (of a partnership)	Statement of partnership realization and liquida-
Loss absorption power	tion
Lump-sum liquidation	Termination (of a partnership)

APPENDIX: Partners' Personal Financial Statements

At the beginning of the liquidation process, partners are usually asked for personal financial statements in order to determine each partner's personal solvency. Guidelines for preparing personal financial statements are found in **Statement of Position 82-1**, "Personal Financial Statements" (SOP 82-1).[1]

Personal financial statements consist of the following:

1. Statement of financial condition, or personal balance sheet, which presents the person's assets and liabilities at a point in time
2. Statement of changes in net worth, or personal income statement, which presents the primary sources of changes in the person's net worth

The statement of financial condition shows the person's assets and liabilities, with net worth as the difference between the two. In general, the accrual basis of accounting should be used to determine the person's assets and liabilities, and comparative statements are usually provided. However, unlike a balance sheet of a business that is based on historical cost, the assets in the personal statement of financial condition are stated at their estimated

---

[1] *Accounting Standards Division of AICPA (Statement of Position 82-1),* "Accounting and Financial Reporting for Personal Financial Statements," 1982.

current values. The liabilities are stated at the lower of the discounted value of future cash payments or the current cash settlement amount. Also included among liabilities are the estimated taxes that would be paid if all the assets were converted to cash and all the liabilities were paid.

Assets and liabilities are presented in their order of liquidity and maturity, not as current and noncurrent. **SOP 82-1** provides guidelines for determining the current value of a person's assets and liabilities. The primary valuation methods are discounted value of future cash flows, current market prices of marketable securities or other investments, and appraisals of properties. The liabilities are stated at their discounted cash flow value or current liquidation value. The accountant uses applicable tax laws, carryover provisions, and other regulations to compute the estimated tax liability from the conversion of assets.

The statement of changes in net worth presents the major sources of income. Both realized and unrealized income are recognized. A commercial business's income statement does not recognize holding gains on marketable securities, but such gains are recognized on an individual's statement of changes in net worth.

ILLUSTRATION OF PERSONAL FINANCIAL STATEMENTS

The following illustration presents Alt's personal financial condition as of May 1, 19X5, the day the partners decide to liquidate the ABC Partnership. Alt's net worth on this date is as follows:

Personal assets	$150,000
Personal liabilities	(86,000)
Net worth	$ 64,000

Statement of Financial Condition

Alt's statement of financial condition on May 1, 19X5, is presented in Figure 17-8 along with the prior year's statement. The 19X5 statement illustrates the following:

1. Receivables due to Alt from other people have a present value of $3,500.

2. Alt has two investments, one of which is his interest in the ABC Partnership, valued at estimated current market value, which in this case is also equal to its book value of $34,000. The marketable security investments are shown at market value.

3. The cash surrender value of life insurance is presented net of any loans payable on the policies.

4. Alt's residence and personal effects are presented at their appraised values.

5. Liabilities are presented at their estimated current liquidation value or the discounted value of the future cash flows.

6. The estimated income taxes on the difference between the estimated current values of assets and liabilities and their tax bases is the amount of income tax Alt would be liable for if all assets were converted to cash and all liabilities were paid.

7. Net worth is the difference between the estimated current value of Alt's assets and liabilities including estimated tax.

FIGURE 17-8 Personal statement of financial condition.

C. Alt
Statement of Financial Condition
May 1, 19X5 and 19X4

	Year	
	19X5	19X4
Assets		
Cash	$ 4,000	$ 2,500
Receivables	3,500	4,000
Investments:		
Marketable securities	5,000	4,000
ABC Partnership	34,000	26,000
Cash surrender value of life insurance	4,000	3,000
Residence	84,000	76,000
Personal effects	15,500	12,500
Total assets	$150,000	$128,000
Liabilities and Net Worth		
Charge accounts	$ 2,000	$ 3,000
Income taxes—current-year balance	1,200	800
10 percent note payable	6,000	10,000
Mortgage payable	60,000	62,000
Estimated income taxes on the difference between the estimated current values of assets and liabilities and their tax bases	16,800	12,200
Net worth	64,000	40,000
Total liabilities and net worth	$150,000	$128,000

Statement of Changes in Net Worth

Alt's statement of changes in net worth, shown in Figure 17-9, illustrates the following:

1. The statement separates the realized and unrealized changes in net worth. Realized changes are cash flows to or from Alt that have already taken place. Unrealized changes are equivalent to holding gains or losses. They have not yet been converted to cash. For example, Alt received $3,000 from the ABC Partnership during the year ended May 1, 19X5. In addition, Alt's partnership interest increased by $8,000 during the year.

2. Alt realized a total of $42,200 in cash flows during the year ended May 1, 19X5. The primary source was a salary of $37,000 from full-time employment outside the ABC Partnership.

3. The major realized decrease in net worth during the year ended May 1, 19X5, was for personal expenditures of $19,200.

FIGURE 17-9 Personal statement of changes in net worth.

C. Alt
Statement of Changes in Net Worth
For the Years Ended May 1, 19X5, and 19X4

	Year Ended May 1	
	19X5	19X4
Realized increases in net worth:		
Salary	$ 37,000	$ 35,000
Dividends and interest income	800	400
Distribution from ABC Partnership	3,000	1,000
Gains on sales of marketable securities	1,400	1,200
	$ 42,200	$ 37,600
Realized decreases in net worth:		
Income taxes	$ 8,200	$ 7,800
Interest expense	1,400	700
Real estate taxes	2,400	2,200
Personal expenditures	19,200	18,900
	$(31,200)	$(29,600)
Net realized increase in net worth	$ 11,000	$ 8,000
Unrealized increases in net worth:		
Marketable securities	$ 1,600	$ 400
ABC Partnership	8,000	5,000
Residence	8,000	4,000
	$ 17,600	$ 9,400
Unrealized decreases in net worth:		
Increase in estimated income taxes on the difference between the estimated current values of assets and liabilities and their tax bases	(4,600)	(4,400)
Net unrealized increase in net worth	$ 13,000	$ 5,000
Net increase in net worth:		
Realized and unrealized	$ 24,000	$ 13,000
Net worth at beginning of period	40,000	27,000
Net worth at end of period	$ 64,000	$ 40,000

4. Unrealized increases of $17,600 during the year were primarily from an increase in the value of Alt's personal residence ($8,000) and an increase in the investment value of Alt's partnership interest in the ABC Partnership ($8,000). Unrealized holding gains of $1,600 are available in Alt's investments in marketable securities.

5. The change in the estimated tax liability is an unrealized decrease because this amount is due only if Alt converts these assets to cash.

6. The net unrealized changes in net worth are added to the net realized changes in net worth to obtain the total change in Alt's net worth for each year. Alt's net worth increased by $13,000 during the year ended May 1, 19X4, and by $24,000 during the year ended May 1, 19X5.

Footnote Disclosures

Sufficient footnote disclosures should accompany the two personal financial statements. The footnotes should describe the following:

1. The methods used to value the major assets.

2. The names and nature of businesses in which the person has major investments.

3. The methods and assumptions used to compute the estimated tax bases and a statement that the tax provision in an actual liquidation will probably differ from the estimate because the actual tax burden will then be based on actual realizations determined by market values at the point of liquidation.

4. Maturities, interest rates, and other details of any receivables and debt.

5. Any other information needed to present fully the person's net worth.

QUESTIONS

Q17-1 What are the major causes of a dissolution? What are the accounting implications of a dissolution?

Q17-2 Explain the marshaling of assets procedure in a partnership liquidation.

Q17-3 X, Y, and Z are partners. The partnership is liquidating, and partner Z is personally insolvent. What implications may this have for partners X and Y?

Q17-4 Define the right of offset in a partnership liquidation. When will the right of offset be used in a liquidation?

Q17-5 Contrast a lump-sum liquidation with an installment liquidation.

Q17-6 How is a deficit in a partner's capital account eliminated if he or she is personally insolvent?

Q17-7 The DEF Partnership has total assets of $55,000. Partner D has a capital credit of $6,000, partner E has a capital deficit of $20,000, and partner F has a capital credit of $8,000. Is the DEF Partnership solvent or insolvent?

Q17-8 If a partnership is insolvent, and some partners have positive capital balances but others have deficits, against which partners may partnership creditors proceed to satisfy their claims?

Q17-9 How are a partner's personal payments to partnership creditors accounted for on the partnership's books?

Q17-10 What is the schedule of safe payments to partners used for?

Q17-11 In what ratio are losses during liquidation assigned to the partners' capital accounts? Is this ratio used in all instances?

Q17-12 The installment liquidation process uses a worst-case assumption in computing the payments to partners. What does this worst-case assumption mean?

Q17-13 Define loss absorption power and explain its importance in the determination of cash distributions to partners.

Q17-14 Partner A has a capital credit of $25,000. Partner B's capital credit is also $25,000. Partners A and B share profits and losses in a 60:40 ratio, respectively. Which partner will receive the first payment of cash in an installment liquidation?

Q17-15* Explain the process of incorporating a partnership.

CASES

C17-1   Cash Distributions to Partners

The partnership of A. Bull and T. Bear is in the process of termination. The partners have disagreed on virtually every decision and have decided to liquidate the present business, with each partner taking his own clients from the partnership. Bull wants cash distributed as it becomes available, while Bear feels no cash should be distributed until all the assets are sold and all liabilities are settled. You are called in to aid in the termination and liquidation process.

Required

How would you respond to each of the partners' requests?

C17-2   Cash Distributions to Partners

Alexander and Bell agreed to liquidate their partnership. You have been asked to assist them in this process, and you prepare the following balance sheet for the date of the beginning of the liquidation. The profit sharing percentages are in parentheses next to the capital account balances.

Cash	$ 40,000
Loan Receivable from Alexander	10,000
Other Assets	200,000
Total	$250,000
Accounts Payable	$ 30,000
Loan Payable to Bell	100,000
Alexander, Capital (50%)	80,000
Bell, Capital (50%)	40,000
Total	$250,000

Bell is demanding that the loan to her be paid before any cash is distributed to Alexander. Alexander feels the available cash should be paid to him until his capital account is reduced to $40,000, the same as Bell's. Alexander will then pay the loan receivable to the partnership with the cash received. You have been asked to reconcile the argument.

Required

How would you advise in this case?

EXERCISES

E17-1   Multiple-Choice Questions on Partnership Liquidations

Select the correct answer for each of the following questions.

Questions 1, 2, and 3 are based on the following information:

The balance sheet for the partnership of Joan, Charles, and Thomas, whose shares of profits and losses are 40, 50, and 10 percent, is as follows:

Cash	$ 50,000	Accounts Payable	$150,000
Inventory	360,000	Joan, Capital	160,000
		Charles, Capital	45,000
		Thomas Capital	55,000
Total Assets	$410,000	Total Liabilities and Equities	$410,000

1. If the inventory is sold for $300,000, how much should Joan receive upon liquidation of the partnership?
   a. $48,000.
   b. $100,000.
   c. $136,000.
   d. $160,000.

2. If the inventory is sold for $180,000, how much should Thomas receive upon liquidation of the partnership?
   a. $28,000.
   b. $32,500.
   c. $37,000.
   d. $55,000.

3. The partnership will be liquidated in installments. As cash becomes available, it will be distributed to the partners. If inventory costing $200,000 is sold for $140,000, how much cash should be distributed to each partner at this time?

	Joan	Charles	Thomas
a.	$56,000	$70,000	$14,000
b.	$16,000	$20,000	$ 4,000
c.	$32,000	$ 0	$ 8,000
d.	$20,000	$ 0	$20,000

4. In accounting for the liquidation of a partnership, cash payments to partners after all nonpartner creditors' claims have been satisfied, but before the final cash distribution, should be according to:
   a. The partners' relative profit and loss sharing ratios.
   b. The final balances in partner capital accounts.
   c. The partners' relative share of the gain or loss on liquidations.
   d. Safe payments computations.

5. After all noncash assets have been converted into cash in the liquidation of the Adam and Kay partnership, the ledger contains the following account balances:

	Debit	Credit
Cash	$47,000	
Accounts Payable		$32,000
Loan Payable to Adam		15,000
Adam, Capital	7,000	
Kay, Capital		7,000

Available cash should be distributed with $32,000 going to accounts payable and:

a. $15,000 to the loan payable to Adam.

b. $7,500 each to Adam and Kay.

c. $8,000 to Adam and $7,000 to Kay.

d. $7,000 to Adam and $8,000 to Kay.

Questions 6 and 7 are based on the following information.

F, A, S, and B are partners sharing profits and losses equally. The partnership is insolvent and is to be liquidated. The status of the partnership and each partner is as follows:

	Partnership Capital Balance	Personal Assets (exclusive of partnership interest)	Personal Liabilities (exclusive of partnership interest)
F	$(15,000)	$100,000	$40,000
A	(10,000)	30,000	60,000
S	20,000*	80,000	5,000
B	30,000*	1,000	28,000
Total	$ 25,000*		

* Deficit

6. The partnership creditors:

  a. Must first seek recovery against S because she is personally solvent and has a negative capital balance.

  b. Will *not* be paid in full regardless of how they proceed legally because the partnership assets are less than the partnership liabilities.

  c. Will have to share A's interest in the partnership on a pro rata basis with A's personal creditors.

  d. Have first claim to the partnership assets before any partner's personal creditors have rights to the partnership assets.

7. The partnership creditors may obtain recovery of their claims:

  a. In the amount of $6,250 from each partner.

  b. From the personal assets of either F or A.

  c. From the personal assets of either S or B.

  d. From the personal assets of either F or S for all or some of their claims.

E17-2 Multiple-Choice on Partnership Liquidation [AICPA Adapted]

Select the correct answer for each of the following questions.

1. On January 1, 19X7, the partners of Casey, Dithers, and Edwards, who share profits and losses in the ratio of 5:3:2, respectively, decided to liquidate their partnership. On this date the partnership condensed balance sheet was as follows:

Assets		Liabilities and Capital	
Cash	$ 50,000	Liabilities	$ 60,000
Other Assets	250,000	Casey, Capital	80,000
		Dithers, Capital	90,000
		Edwards, Capital	70,000
Total	$300,000	Total	$300,000

On January 15, 19X7, the first cash sale of other assets with a carrying amount of $150,000 realized $120,000. Safe installment payments to the partners were made the same date. How much cash should be distributed to each partner?

	Casey	Dithers	Edwards
a.	$15,000	$51,000	$44,000
b.	$40,000	$45,000	$35,000
c.	$55,000	$33,000	$22,000
d.	$60,000	$36,000	$24,000

2. In a partnership liquidation, the final cash distribution to the partners should be made in accordance with the:
   a. Partners' profit and loss sharing ratio.
   b. Balances of the partners' loan and capital accounts.
   c. Ratio of the capital contributions by the partners.
   d. Ratio of capital contributions less withdrawals by the partners.

The following balance sheet is for the partnership of Art, Blythe, and Cooper and relates to questions 3 through 5:

Assets		Liabilities and Capital	
Cash	$ 20,000	Liabilities	$ 50,000
Other Assets	180,000	Art, Capital (40%)	37,000
		Blythe, Capital (40%)	65,000
		Cooper, Capital (20%)	48,000
Total	$200,000	Total	$200,000

Figures shown parenthetically reflect agreed profit and loss sharing percentages.

3. If the firm, as shown on the original balance sheet, is dissolved and liquidated by selling assets in installments, and if the first sale of noncash assets having a book value of $90,000 realizes $50,000 and all cash available after settlement with creditors is distributed, the respective partners would receive (to the nearest dollar):

	Art	Blythe	Cooper
a.	$8,000	$ 8,000	$ 4,000
b.	$6,667	$ 6,667	$ 6,666
c.	$ 0	$13,333	$ 6,667
d.	$ 0	$ 3,000	$17,000

4. If the facts are as in question 3 except that $3,000 cash is to be withheld, the respective partners would then receive (to the nearest dollar):

	Art	Blythe	Cooper
a.	$6,800	$ 6,800	$ 3,400
b.	$5,667	$ 5,667	$ 5,666
c.	$ 0	$11,333	$ 5,667
d.	$ 0	$ 1,000	$16,000

5. If each partner properly received some cash in the distribution after the second sale, if the cash to be distributed amounts to $12,000 from the third sale, and if unsold assets with an $8,000 book value remain, ignoring questions 3 and 4, the respective partners would receive:

	Art	Blythe	Cooper
a.	$ 4,800	$ 4,800	$ 2,400
b.	$ 4,000	$ 4,000	$ 4,000
c.	37/150	65/150	48/150
	of	of	of
	$12,000	$12,000	$12,000
d.	$ 0	$ 8,000	$ 4,000

6. The following condensed balance sheet is presented for the partnership of Arnie, Bart, and Kurt, who share profits and losses in the ratio of 4:3:3, respectively:

Assets		Liabilities and Capital	
Cash	$100,000	Liabilities	$150,000
Other Assets	300,000	Arnie, Capital	40,000
		Bart, Capital	180,000
		Kurt, Capital	30,000
Total	$400,000	Total	$400,000

The partners agreed to dissolve the partnership after selling the other assets for $200,000. Upon dissolution of the partnership, Arnie should have received:

a. $0.

b. $40,000.

c. $60,000.

d. $70,000.

E17-3 Marshaling of Assets

The Good Times Company, a partnership, has assets of $32,000 and liabilities of $40,000. The partners' personal finances are as follows:

	Heather	Drew
Capital balance in partnership	$(9,000)	$17,000*
Personal assets (exclusive of partnership interest)	35,000	40,000
Personal liabilities (exclusive of partnership interest)	28,000	34,000

* Deficit

Required

Prepare a schedule showing the distribution of assets according to the marshaling of assets.

E17-4 Lump-Sum Liquidation

Amp, Volt, and Watt are partners in the Electric Company and share profits in a 5:3:2 ratio. The balance sheet on June 30, 19X1, when they decide to liquidate the business, is as follows:

Assets		Liabilities and Equities	
Cash	$ 20,000	Liabilities	$ 30,000
Amp, Loan	15,000	Volt, Loan	10,000
Noncash Assets	135,000	Amp, Capital	80,000
		Volt, Capital	36,000
		Watt, Capital	14,000
Total Assets	$170,000	Total Liabilities and Equities	$170,000

The noncash assets are sold for $95,000. Rather than require payments, all partners agree to offset the receivable from Amp against his capital credit.

Required

    a. Prepare a statement of partnership realization and liquidation.
    b. Prepare the required journal entries to account for the liquidation of the Electric Company.

E17-5 Schedule of Safe Payments to Partners

Will and Rogers are partners who share profits and losses in a 2:3 ratio. The partnership will be liquidated in installments. Some noncash assets have been sold, but other assets with a book value of $63,000 remain. Liabilities are now $8,000, and liquidation expenses are expected to be $3,600. The capital balances are $46,000 for Will and $34,000 for Rogers.

Required

Prepare a schedule of safe payments to partners to show how the $25,000 in cash should be divided.

E17-6 Schedule of Safe Payments to Partners

Partners Miller and Bell have decided to liquidate their business. The ledger shows the following account balances:

Cash	$ 25,000	Accounts Payable	$15,000
Inventory	120,000	Bell, Loan (12%)	60,000
		Miller, Capital	65,000
		Bell, Capital	5,000

Miller and Bell share profits and losses in a 8:2 ratio. The 12 percent note payable to Bell contains a provision that interest ceases accruing at the date the business terminates as a going concern. During the first month of liquidation, half the inventory is sold for $40,000, and $10,000 of the accounts payable is paid. During the second month, the rest of the inventory is sold for $30,000, and the remaining accounts payable are paid. Cash is distributed at the end of each month, and the liquidation is completed at the end of the second month.

Required

Prepare a statement of partnership realization and liquidation with a schedule of safe payments for the 2-month liquidation period.

E17-7 Partnership Liquidation with an Interest-Bearing Note

Refer to the data in Exercise 17-6 for the Miller and Bell partnership. Use the same facts, but now assume that the 12 percent note payable to Bell continues to accrue interest during the liquidation process. At the end of the first month, it is estimated that additional interest of $120 is possible on the note payable to Bell until the note is extinguished.

Required

Prepare a statement of partnership realization and liquidation with a schedule of safe payments to partners for the 2-month liquidation period.

E17-8 Cash Distribution Plan

Aken, Prince, and Bird share profits and losses for their APB Partnership in a ratio of 2:3:5. When they decide to liquidate, the balance sheet is as follows:

Assets		Liabilities and Equities	
Cash	$ 40,000	Liabilities	$ 50,000
Aken, Loan	10,000	Bird, Loan	20,000
Other Assets	200,000	Aken, Capital	55,000
		Prince, Capital	75,000
		Bird, Capital	50,000
Total Assets	$250,000	Total Liabilities and Equities	$250,000

Liquidation expenses are expected to be negligible. No interest accrues on loans with partners after termination of the business.

Required

Prepare a cash distribution plan for the APB Partnership.

E17-9 Confirmation of Cash Distribution Plan

Refer to the data in Exercise 17-8. During the liquidation process for the APB Partnership, the following events occurred:

1. During the first month of liquidation, noncash assets with a book value of $85,000 were sold for $65,000, and $21,000 of the liabilities were paid.

2. During the second month, the remaining noncash assets were sold for $79,000, and the rest of the outside creditors were paid, and the partners agreed to offset Aken's loan against his capital balance.

3. Cash is distributed to partners at the end of each month.

Required

Prepare a statement of partnership realization and liquidation with a schedule of safe payments to partners for the liquidation period.

E17-10 Cash Distribution Plan

Foster, Allen, Smith, and Bradley decide to liquidate their partnership. They share profits in a ratio of 3:2:4:1. Their capital accounts and loans payable of the partnership are as follows:

	Loan	Capital
Foster	$14,000	$40,000
Allen		45,000
Smith	18,000	50,000
Bradley		25,000

Noncash assets total $195,000, and other liabilities are $28,000. Liquidation expenses will not be material. No interest accrues on loans with partners during liquidation of the business.

Required

Prepare a cash distribution plan for the FASB Partnership.

E17-11* Incorporation of a Partnership

When Alice and Betty decided to incorporate their partnership, the trial balance was as follows:

	Debit	Credit
Cash	$ 8,000	
Accounts Receivable (net)	22,400	
Inventory	36,000	
Equipment (net)	47,200	
Accounts Payable		$ 17,200
Alice, Capital (60%)		62,400
Betty, Capital (40%)		34,000
Total	$113,600	$113,600

The partnership's books will be closed, and new books will be used for A & B Corporation. The following additional information is available:

1. The estimated fair values of the assets are:

Accounts Receivable	$21,600
Inventory	32,800
Equipment	40,000

2. All assets and liabilities are transferred to the corporation.
3. The common stock is $10 par. Alice and Betty receive a total of 7,100 shares.
4. The partners' profit and loss sharing ratio is shown in the trial balance.

Required

    a. Prepare the entries on the partnership's books to record **(1)** the revaluation of assets, **(2)** the transfer of the assets to the A & B Corporation and the receipt of the common stock, and **(3)** the closing of the books.
    b. Prepare the entries on A & B Corporation's books to record the assets and the issuance of the common stock.

E17-12A   Multiple-Choice on Personal Financial Statements [AICPA Adapted]

Select the correct answer for each of the following questions.

    1. On December 31, 19X7, Judy is a fully vested participant in a company-sponsored pension plan. According to the plan's administrator, Judy has at that date the nonforfeitable right to receive a lump sum of $100,000 on December 28, 19X8. The discounted amount of $100,000 is $90,000 at December 31, 19X7. The right is not contingent on Judy's life expectancy and requires no future performance on Judy's part. In Judy's December 31, 19X7, personal statement of financial condition, the vested interest in the pension plan should be reported at:
    a. $0.
    b. $90,000.
    c. $95,000.
    d. $100,000.

    2. On December 31, 19X7, Mr. and Mrs. McManus owned a parcel of land held as an investment. The land was purchased for $95,000 in 19X0, and was encumbered by a mortgage with a principal balance of $60,000 at December 31, 19X7. On this date the fair value of the land was $150,000. In the McManuses' December 31, 19X7, personal statement of financial condition, at what amount should the land investment and mortgage payable be reported?

	Land Investment	Mortgage Payable
a.	$150,000	$60,000
b.	$ 95,000	$60,000
c.	$ 90,000	$ 0
d.	$ 35,000	$ 0

    3. Rich Drennen's personal statement of financial condition at December 31, 19X6, shows net worth of $400,000 before consideration of employee stock options owned on that date. Information relating to the stock options is as follows:

1. Options are to purchase 10,000 shares of Oglesby Corporation stock.
2. Option exercise price is $10 a share.
3. Options expire on June 30, 19X7.
4. Market price of the stock is $25 a share on December 31, 19X6.
5. Assume that exercise of the options in 19X7 would result in ordinary income taxable at 35 percent.

After giving effect to the stock options, Drennen's net worth at December 31, 19X6 would be:

a. $497,500.
b. $550,000.
c. $562,500.
d. $650,000.

4. Nancy Emerson owns 50 percent of the common stock of Marks Corporation. Emerson paid $25,000 for this stock in 19X3. At December 31, 19X8, it was ascertained that Emerson's 50 percent stock ownership in Marks had a current value of $185,000. Marks's cumulative net income and cash dividends declared for the 5 years ended December 31, 19X8, were $300,000 and $30,000 respectively. In Emerson's personal statement of financial condition at December 31, 19X8, what amount should be reported as her net investment in Marks?

a. $25,000.
b. $160,000.
c. $175,000.
d. $185,000.

5. In a personal statement of financial condition, which of the following should be reported at estimated current values?

	Investments in Closely Held Businesses	Investments in Leaseholds
a.	Yes	Yes
b.	Yes	No
c.	No	No
d.	No	Yes

6. Personal financial statements should include which of the following statements?

	Financial Condition	Changes in Net Worth	Cash Flows
a.	No	Yes	Yes
b.	Yes	No	No
c.	Yes	Yes	No
d.	Yes	Yes	Yes

7. A business interest that constitutes a large part of an individual's total assets should be presented in a personal statement of financial condition as:

a. A single amount equal to the proprietorship equity.
b. A single amount equal to the estimated current value of the business interest.
c. A separate listing of the individual assets and liabilities, at cost.
d. Separate line items of both total assets and total liabilities, at cost.

8. Personal financial statements should report assets and liabilities at:
   a. Historical cost.
   b. Historical cost and, as additional information, at estimated current values at the date of the financial statements.
   c. Estimated current values at the date of the financial statements.
   d. Estimated current values at the date of the financial statements and, as additional information, at historical cost.

9. The following information pertains to marketable equity securities owned by Kent:

	Fair Value at December 31		Cost in
Stock	19X3	19X2	19X0
City Manufacturing, Inc.	$95,500	$93,000	$89,900
Tri Corporation	3,400	5,600	3,600
Zee, Inc.		10,300	15,000

The Zee stock was sold in January 19X3 for $10,200. In Kent's personal statement of financial condition at December 31, 19X3, what amount should be reported for marketable equity securities?
   a. $93,300.
   b. $93,500.
   c. $94,100.
   d. $98,900.

10. Personal financial statements should report an investment in life insurance at the:
   a. Face amount of the policy less the amount of premiums paid.
   b. Cash value of the policy less the amount of any loans against it.
   c. Cash value of the policy less the amount of premiums paid.
   d. Face amount of the policy less the amount of any loans against it.

11. Mrs. Taft owns a $150,000 insurance policy on her husband's life. The cash value of the policy is $125,000, and there is a $50,000 loan against the policy. In the Tafts' personal statement of financial condition at December 31, 19X3, what amount should be shown as an investment in life insurance?
   a. $150,000.
   b. $125,000.
   c. $100,000.
   d. $75,000.

E17-13A Personal Financial Statements

Leonard and Michelle have asked you to prepare their statement of changes in net worth for the year ended August 31, 19X3. They have properly prepared the following comparative statement of financial condition based upon estimated current values as required by **SOP 82-1.**

Leonard and Michelle
Statement of Financial Condition
August 31, 19X3 and 19X2

Assets		19X3	19X2
Cash		$ 3,600	$ 6,700
Marketable securities		4,900	16,300
Residence		94,800	87,500
Personal effects		10,000	10,000
Cash surrender value of life insurance		3,200	5,600
Investment in farm business:			
Farm land	$ 42,000		$32,100
Farm equipment	22,400		9,000
Note payable on farm equipment	(10,000)		-0-
Net investment in farm		54,400	41,100
Total assets		$170,900	$167,200

Liabilities and Net Worth	19X3	19X2
Credit card	$ 2,400	$ 1,500
Income taxes payable	11,400	12,400
Mortgage payable on residence	71,000	76,000
Estimated income taxes on the difference between the estimated current values of assets and liabilities and their tax bases	19,700	16,500
Net worth	66,400	60,800
Total liabilities and net worth	$170,900	$167,200

Additional information:

1. Leonard and Michelle's total salaries during the fiscal year ended August 31, 19X3, were $44,300; farm income was $6,700; personal expenditures were $43,500, interest and dividends received were $1,400.

2. Marketable securities that were purchased in 19X1 at a cost of $11,000 and having a current market value of $11,000 on August 31, 19X2, were sold on March 1, 19X3, for $10,700. No additional marketable securities were purchased or sold during the fiscal year.

3. The values of the residence and farm land are based upon year-end appraisals.

4. On August 31, 19X3, Leonard purchased a used combine at a cost of $14,000. A down payment of $4,000 was made, and a 5-year, 10 percent note payable was signed for the $10,000 balance owed. No other farm equipment was purchased or sold during the fiscal year.

5. The cash surrender value of the life insurance policy increased during the fiscal year by $1,600. However, Leonard borrowed $4,000 against the policy on September 1, 19X2. Interest at 15 percent for the first year of this loan was paid when due on August 31, 19X3.

6. Federal income taxes of $12,400 were paid during the 19X3 fiscal year.

7. Total mortgage payments made during the year were $9,000, which included payments of principal and interest.

Required

Using the comparative statement of financial condition and additional information provided, prepare the statement of changes in net worth for the year ended August 31, 19X3.

(Hint: It will be helpful to use T-accounts to determine several realized and unrealized amounts. An analysis of the cash, personal effects, and credit card accounts should not be required to properly complete the statement.)

PROBLEMS

P17-14 Lump-Sum Liquidation

Taylor, Olsen, and Moyer are partners sharing profits in the ratio of 4:3:2, respectively. The partnership and two of the partners are currently unable to make full payment of their obligations to creditors. The balance sheet of the partnership and an enumeration of the assets and liabilities of the separate partners are as follows:

TOM Partnership
Balance Sheet
April 1, 19X1

Assets		Liabilities and Equities		
Cash	$ 500	Accounts Payable		$37,000
Other Assets	60,500	Capital:		
		Taylor	$10,000	
		Olsen	6,000	
		Moyer	8,000	
				24,000
Total Assets	$61,000	Total Liabilities and Equities		$61,000

Assets and Liabilities of Partners T, O, and M
Excluding Partnership Interests

Partner	Cash and Cash Value of Personal Assets	Liabilities
Taylor	$31,000	$20,000
Olsen	9,450	11,900
Moyer	4,000	5,000

Required

a. Assuming that "other assets" are converted into $33,500 in cash, prepare a partnership realization and liquidation statement.

b. Prepare a schedule indicating the distribution of partners' personal assets according to the provisions of the Uniform Partnership Act.

P17-15 Installment Liquidation

The trial balance of the NOT Partnership on April 30, 19X1, is presented below. The profit and loss percentages are shown in the trial balance.

	Debit	Credit
Cash	$ 15,000	
Accounts Receivable (net)	85,000	
Inventory	82,000	
Plant Assets (net)	120,000	
Accounts Payable		$ 90,000
Otter, Loan		15,000
Nate, Capital (60%)		80,000
Otter, Capital (20%)		57,000
Trin, Capital (20%)		60,000
Total	$302,000	$302,000

The partnership is being liquidated. Liquidation activities are as follows:

	May	June	July
Accounts receivable collected	$40,000	$28,000	$ 13,000
Noncash assets sold:			
Book value	44,000	35,000	123,000
Selling price	50,000	30,000	80,000
Accounts payable paid	65,000	25,000	
Liquidation expenses:			
Paid during month	3,500	3,000	2,500
Anticipated for remainder			
of liquidation process	6,000	4,000	

Cash is distributed at the end of each month, and the liquidation is completed by July 31, 19X1. No interest accrues on Otter's loan during the liquidation.

Required

Prepare a statement of partnership realization and liquidation for the NOT Partnership with schedules of safe payments to partners.

P17-16 Installment Liquidation [AICPA Adapted]

On January 1, 19X1, the partners of Able, Black, and Ciou, who share profits and losses in the ratio of 5:3:2, respectively, decide to liquidate their partnership. The partnership trial balance at this date is as follows:

	Debit	Credit
Cash	$ 18,000	
Accounts Receivable	66,000	
Inventory	52,000	
Machinery and Equipment, net	189,000	
Able, Loan	30,000	
Accounts Payable		$ 53,000
Black, Loan		20,000
Able, Capital		118,000
Black, Capital		90,000
Ciou, Capital		74,000
Total	$355,000	$355,000

The partners plan a program of piecemeal conversion of assets in order to minimize liquidation losses. All available cash, less an amount retained to provide for future expenses, is to be distributed to the partners at the end of each month. No interest accrues on partners' loans during liquidation. A summary of the liquidation transactions is as follows:

January, 19X1:

1. $51,000 was collected on accounts receivable; the balance is uncollectible.

2. $38,000 was received for the entire inventory.

3. $2,000 liquidation expenses were paid.

4. $50,000 was paid to outside creditors, after offset of a $3,000 credit memorandum received on January 11, 19X1.

5. $10,000 cash was retained in the business at the end of the month for potential unrecorded liabilities and anticipated expenses.

February, 19X1:

6. $4,000 liquidation expenses were paid.

7. $6,000 cash was retained in the business at the end of the month for potential unrecorded liabilities and anticipated expenses.

March, 19X1:

8. $146,000 was received on sale of all items of machinery and equipment.

9. $5,000 liquidation expenses were paid.

10. The $30,000 loan from Able is approved by the partners for offset against his capital account.

11. No cash was retained in the business.

Required

Prepare a statement of partnership liquidation for the partnership with schedules of safe payments to partners.

P17-17 Cash Distribution Plan

The partnership of Fox, Gold, and Hare has asked you to assist it in winding up the affairs of the business. You compile the following information.

1. The trial balance of the partnership on June 30, 19X1, is:

	Debit	Credit
Cash	$ 6,000	
Accounts Receivable (net)	22,000	
Inventory	14,000	
Plant and Equipment (net)	99,000	
Loan to Fox	12,000	
Loan to Hare	7,500	
Accounts Payable		$ 17,000
Fox, Capital		67,000
Gold, Capital		45,000
Hare, Capital		31,500
Total	$160,500	$160,500

2. The partners share profits and losses as follows: Fox, 50 percent; Gold, 30 percent; and Hare, 20 percent.

3. The partners are considering an offer of $100,000 for the accounts receivable, inventory, and plant and equipment as of June 30. The $100,000 will be paid to creditors and the partners in installments, the number and amounts of which are to be negotiated.

Required

Prepare a cash distribution plan as of June 30, 19X1, showing how much cash each partner will receive if the offer to sell the assets is accepted.

P17-18 Installment Liquidation

Refer to the facts in Problem 17-17. The partners have decided to liquidate their partnership by installments instead of accepting the offer of $100,000. Cash is distributed to the partners at the end of each month. No interest on partners' loans accrues during liquidation. A summary of the liquidation transactions follows:

July:
   $16,500 collected on accounts receivable; balance is uncollectible.
   $10,000 received for the entire inventory.
   $1,000 liquidation expense paid.
   $17,000 paid to outside creditors.
   $8,000 cash retained in the business at the end of the month.

August:
   $1,500 in liquidation expenses paid.
   As part payment of his capital, Hare accepted an item of special equipment that he developed which had a book value of $4,000. The partners agreed that a value of $10,000 should be placed on this item for liquidation purposes.
   $2,500 in cash retained in the business at the end of the month.

September:
   $75,000 received on sale of remaining plant and equipment.
   The partners agree to allow the offset of the loans to Fox and Hare against their capital accounts.
   $1,000 liquidation expenses paid. No cash retained in the business.

Required

Prepare a statement of partnership realization and liquidation with supporting schedules of safe payments to partners.

P17-19 Cash Distribution Plan

Ring, Long, Martin, and Newman are considering dissolving their partnership. They plan to sell the assets gradually so that losses will be minimized. The partners share profits and losses as follows: Ring, 40 percent; Long, 30 percent; Martin, 20 percent; and Newman, 10 percent. No interest accrues on partners' loans during liquidation. The partnership's trial balance as of May 1, 19X2, the date on which liquidation begins, is:

	Debit	Credit
Cash	$ 500	
Receivables	18,800	
Inventory, May 1, 19X2	45,500	
Equipment (net)	32,200	
Accounts Payable		$ 3,500
Ring, Loan		4,000
Long, Loan		9,000
Ring, Capital		25,000
Long, Capital		21,000
Martin, Capital		23,500
Newman, Capital		11,000
Total	$97,000	$97,000

Required

a. Prepare a statement as of May 1, 19X2, showing how cash will be distributed among partners as it becomes available.

b. On May 31, 19X2, if cash of $19,400 becomes available, and liquidation costs of $12,000 have been incurred, how will the cash be distributed to creditors, liquidation cost items, and partners?

CHAPTER 18

GOVERNMENTAL ENTITIES: INTRODUCTION AND GENERAL FUND ACCOUNTING

In the early 1990s, the combined annual spending of federal, state, and local governments exceeded $2.0 trillion. This is the equivalent of $8,100 for each person in the United States, or approximately $21,000 per family. Government purchases of goods and services constitute approximately 20 percent of the total gross national product of the United States.[1]

The first part of this chapter presents an introduction to the accounting and reporting requirements for state and local government units. The major concepts of governmental accounting are discussed and illustrated in this part. The last part of this chapter presents a comprehensive illustration of accounting for the general fund of a city. The comprehensive illustration reviews and integrates the concepts presented in the first part of the chapter. Chapter 19 continues the comprehensive illustration for the remainder of the discussion on state and local governmental accounting and reporting.

Each of the 50 states follows relatively uniform accounting standards; however, some states have unique statutory provisions for selected items. Local governments are political subdivisions of state government. The 80,000 local government units in the United States are classified as (1) general-purpose local governments, such as counties, cities, towns, villages, and townships, (2) special-purpose local governments, such as soil conservation districts, and (3) authorities and agencies, such as the New York Port Authority and local housing authorities. Authorities and agencies differ from other government units because they typ-

---

[1] Annual reports of the national income and product accounts, including aggregate revenues and expenditures of government entities, are presented in the *Survey of Current Business*, published periodically by the U.S. Department of Commerce.

ically do not have taxing power and may sell only revenue bonds, not general obligation bonds.

Governmental entities have operating objectives different from those of commercial entities; therefore, governmental accounting is different from accounting for commercial enterprises. The major differences between governmental and for-profit entities are as follows:

1. Governmental accounting must recognize that government units collect resources and make expenditures to fulfill societal needs. Society expects government units to develop and maintain an infrastructure of highways, streets, and sewer and sanitation systems, as well as to provide public protection, recreation, and cultural services.

2. Except for some proprietary activities such as utilities, government entities do not have a general profit motive. Police and fire departments do not have a profit motive; instead, these units must be evaluated on their ability to provide for society's needs.

3. Government operations have legal authorization for their existence, revenue raising through the power of taxation, and mandated expenditures they must make to provide their services. The governmental accounting system must make it possible to determine and demonstrate compliance with finance-related legal and contractual provisions. Government units are subject to extensive regulatory oversight through laws, grant restrictions, bond indentures, and a variety of other legal constraints.

4. Governmental entities use comprehensive budgetary accounting which serves as a significant control mechanism and provides the basis for comparing actual operations against budgeted amounts. The budget is a legally established statutory control vehicle.

5. The primary emphasis in governmental accounting is to measure and report on management's stewardship of the financial resources committed to the objectives of the government unit. Accountability for the flow of economic resources is a chief objective of government accounting. The managers of the government unit must be able to show they are in compliance with the many legal regulations governing its operations.

6. Governmental entities typically are required to establish separate funds to carry out their various missions. Each fund is an independent accounting and fiscal entity and is responsible for using its own resources to accomplish its specific responsibilities.

7. Many fund entities do not record fixed assets or long-term debt. These fund entities record the purchase of assets such as equipment and buildings as expenditures of the period. A separate accounting of the fixed assets and long-term debt is maintained in a set of auxiliary accounts within the government unit.

EXPENDABILITY OF RESOURCES VERSUS CAPITAL MAINTENANCE OBJECTIVES

The major differences between commercial and governmental accounting are due to the objectives of the entities. In commercial enterprises, the emphasis is on the measurement of the flow of all economic resources of the firm. The accrual method of accounting is used to match the revenues and expenses during a period with the objective of measuring profitability. The company's balance sheet contains both current and noncurrent assets and liabilities, and the change in retained earnings reflects the company's ability to maintain its capital investment.

In contrast, the major focus for many of the operations within a governmental entity is the flow of current resources available to provide services to the public. The emphasis is on the expendability of the resources to accomplish the objectives and purposes of the governmental entity. Operating authorization is initiated by a budget that is passed by the legislative governing body. Managers of governmental units must be very careful to ensure that resources are expended in full and complete compliance with the legal and financial restrictions placed upon the governmental entity. The focus on expendability affects many of the accounting and financial reporting standards of governmental entities.

FINANCIAL REPORTING OF GOVERNMENTAL ENTITIES

Governmental entities provide financial reports for use by their governing bodies, such as a city council; their resource providers, such as the public; and other interested parties, such as persons issuing credit to the entity, its employees, suppliers, and primary constituents. Governmental reporting entities actually produce two different types of financial reports. The first is the general-purpose financial statements (GPFS), which are comparable to the annual report of a commercial enterprise. This report is used by parties external to the governmental reporting entity, such as credit grantors, to assess its performance. The second report is the comprehensive annual financial report (CAFR), which incorporates the information from the general-purpose financial statements and also includes additional information on specific aspects of the governmental reporting entity. This report is directed to the government entity's governing body or other persons desiring detailed information on the entity.

The financial statements report on the primary government unit and its component units for which the primary government unit has financial accountability. A governmental unit may have a variety of boards, commissions, authorities, or other component units under its control. **GASB Statement No. 14**, "The Financial Reporting Entity" (GASB 14) states that financial accountability exists if the primary government appoints a majority of an organization's governing body and

(a) is able to impose its will on the organization, or
(b) possesses a financial benefit or assumes a financial burden for the organization.[2]

GASB 14 is effective for financial statements for periods beginning after December 15, 1992.

Persons not familiar with governmental reporting are sometimes surprised to see a combined balance sheet for a governmental entity that may have as many as

[2] GASB Statement 14, "The Financial Reporting Entity," Governmental Accounting Standards Board (Norwalk, Conn.), 1991, para. 21.

10 separate columns, each column corresponding to a separate accounting entity within the government unit. A statement of revenues and expenditures for a government unit includes a comparison between actual and budgeted amounts for the fiscal year. A variety of other accounting and financial reporting differences exist between governmental entities and commercial entities because of different information needs and different types of operations between the two types of entities.

HISTORY OF GOVERNMENTAL ACCOUNTING

Before 1984, the development of accounting principles for local government units was directed by the Municipal Finance Officers Association (MFOA). In 1934, the National Committee on Municipal Accounting, a committee of the MFOA, published the first statement on local governmental accounting. The report was entitled *A Tentative Outline—Principles of Municipal Accounting*. In 1968, the National Committee on Governmental Accounting, the successor committee, published *Governmental Accounting, Auditing, and Financial Reporting* (GAAFR). Some governmental accountants call it the "blue book," after the color of its cover. The GAAFR is periodically updated to include the most recent governmental financial reporting standards; major revisions were made in 1980 and 1988.

In 1974, the American Institute of Certified Public Accountants published an industry audit guide, *Audits of State and Local Governmental Units,* in which it stated that "except as modified in this guide, they [GAAFR] constitute generally accepted accounting principles."[3] In March 1979, the National Council on Governmental Accounting (NCGA) issued its **Statement No. 1**, "Governmental Accounting and Financial Reporting Principles" (NCGA 1), which established a set of accounting principles for governmental reporting.

In 1984, the Financial Accounting Foundation created a companion group to the Financial Accounting Standards Board. The Governmental Accounting Standards Board (GASB) is now responsible for maintaining and developing accounting and reporting standards for state and local governmental entities. In **GASB Statement No. 1**, "Authoritative Status of NCGA Pronouncements and AICPA Industry Audit Guide" (GASB 1), released in July 1984, the GASB stated that all NCGA statements and interpretations issued and in effect on that date were accepted as generally accepted accounting principles for governmental accounting. In 1985, the GASB published a codification of the existing GAAP for state and local governments entitled *Codification of Governmental Accounting and Financial Reporting Standards*. The first section of the codification is virtually identical with **NCGA 1** as amended by subsequent NCGA statements. Section 2 presents the financial reporting issues for government entities. Sections 3 and 4 present specific balance sheet and operating statement topics. The GASB continues to

---

[3] *Committee on Governmental Accounting and Auditing,* "Audits of State and Local Governmental Units," American Institute of Certified Public Accountants (New York), 1974, pp. 8–9.

publish updated codifications periodically. The codification is an authoritative source for accounting and financial reporting principles for government units.

Accounting for government units is given the general description of fund accounting to distinguish it from accounting for commercial entities. This chapter presents an overview of fund accounting and illustrates accounting in the general fund, typically the largest single part of most government units. Chapter 19 presents the accounting for the remaining funds of a government entity.

DEFINITIONS AND TYPES OF FUNDS

Fund accounting must recognize the unique aspects of government operations. Government units must provide a large range of services, such as fire and police protection, water and sewerage, legal courts, and construction of public buildings and other facilities. In addition, government units receive their resources from many different sources and must make expenditures in accordance with legal restrictions.

The operations of a government unit must also be broken down into periodic reporting intervals of fiscal years because the management of these public operations may change as a result of elections or new appointments. Thus, governmental accounting must recognize the many different purposes, the different sources of revenue, the mandated expenditures, and the fiscal periodicity of the government unit. To accomplish the objectives of the government unit, the unit establishes a variety of *funds* as fiscal and accounting entities of the government unit. The second principle of governmental accounting presented in the 1990 GASB codification states:

> Governmental accounting systems should be organized and operated on a fund basis. A fund is defined as a fiscal and accounting entity with a self-balancing set of accounts recording cash and other financial resources, together with all related liabilities and residual equities or balances, and changes therein, which are segregated for the purpose of carrying on specific activities or attaining certain objectives in accordance with special regulations, restrictions, or limitations.[4]

Different funds are established for the specific functions that a government must provide. Most funds obtain resources from taxes on property, income, or commercial sales; they may also obtain resources as grants from other government agencies, from fines or licenses, and from charges for services. Each fund must make its expenditures in accordance with its specified purposes. For example, a fund established for fire protection cannot be used to provide school buses for the local school. The fire department may make expenditures only directly related to its function—providing fire protection.

Each fund has its own asset and liability accounts, and its own revenue and expenditures accounts. The term *expenditures* refers to the outflow of resources in funds providing government services. Separate financial statements must be

---

[4] Governmental Accounting Standards Board, *Codification of Governmental Accounting and Financial Reporting Standards*, 3d ed., 1990, Section 1100.102, p. 33.

prepared for each fiscal period for each fund. In this manner, governing bodies or other interested parties may assess the financial performance of each fund in the fulfillment of the specific purpose for which it was established.

Types of Funds and Account Groups

Governmental accounting systems are established on a fund basis in three major categories: governmental, proprietary, and fiduciary. Figure 18-1 presents an overview of each of the funds and provides a brief description of the types of activities accounted for in each fund.

Governmental Funds   Four *governmental funds* are used to provide basic government services to the public. The governmental fund category is subdivided into the following four fund types: (1) *general fund*, (2) *special revenue funds*, (3) *capital projects funds*, and (4) *debt service funds*. The number of governmental funds maintained by the governmental entity is based on the legal and operating requirements of the governmental entity. The 1990 GASB codification states that governmental entities should attempt to maintain only the minimum number of funds necessary, consistent with legal and operating requirements. Unnecessary funds result in inflexibility, undue complexity, and inefficient financial administration. Only one general fund may be created by each governmental entity, but more than one of each of the other types of governmental funds may be created, based on the specific needs of the entity. For example, some governmental entities establish a separate capital projects fund for each major capital project.

Before 1987, many government units used a fifth governmental fund, the *special assessments fund*, to record the construction and financing of public improvements deemed to benefit a limited group of people. These public improvements, such as sewerage additions, streetlights in a specific neighborhood, or new sidewalks or streets in a specific area, are paid for over time by a special tax assessment on the properties that benefited from the improvement. However, in January 1987 the GASB issued **Statement No. 6,** "Accounting and Financial Reporting for Special Assessments," (GASB 6) which requires that these activities be recorded in other government funds if the government unit is obligated in any manner on the debt issued to finance the construction. In most cases, the government unit will provide some type of general governmental commitment on the debt issue. Thus, the capital projects fund is typically used to account for the construction phase of these capital improvements, and the long-term debt financing is reported along with the other long-term debt of the government unit. In those very few cases in which the government unit has absolutely no commitment on the debt issue, the debt is not shown as part of the government unit. Other uses of special assessment bonds are discussed in Chapter 19.

Financial Reporting for Governmental Funds   Financial reporting must consider not only the form and nature of the financial statements but also the reporting period selected. Government units must provide both annual and interim reports, just as do commercial entities. However, many alternative reporting dates are

FIGURE 18-1 Governmental funds and account groups.

Fund or Account Group	Description
	Governmental Funds
1. General fund	Accounts for all financial resources except those required to be accounted for in another fund. Includes transactions for general government services provided by the executive, legislative, and judicial operations of the governmental entity.
2. Special revenue funds	Accounts for the proceeds of revenue sources that are legally restricted for specified purposes. Includes resources and expenditures for operations such as public libraries when a separate tax is levied for their support.
3. Capital projects funds	Accounts for financial resources for the acquisition or construction of major capital projects that benefit many citizens, such as parks and municipal buildings. This fund is in existence only during the acquisition or construction of the facilities and is closed once the project is completed.
4. Debt service funds	Accounts for the accumulation of resources for, and the payment of, long-term debt principal and interest. This fund is used for servicing the long-term debt of the government.
	Proprietary Funds
5. Internal service funds	Accounts for the financing of goods or services provided by one department or agency to other departments or agencies of the government unit. The services are usually provided on a cost-reimbursement basis and are offered only to other government agencies, not the general public. Examples are municipal motor vehicle pools, city print shops, and central purchasing operations.
6. Enterprise funds	Accounts for operations of government units that charge for services provided to the general public. Includes those activities financed in a manner similar to private business enterprises where the intent of the governing body is to recover the costs of providing goods or services to the general public on a continuing basis through user charges. Also includes those operations that the governing body intends to operate at a profit. Examples include sports arenas, municipal electric utilities, and municipal bus companies.
	Fiduciary Funds
7. Trust funds	Accounts for assets held by a government unit in a trustee capacity. An example of a trust fund is a trust created from a citizen's gift for use in the development of a city's park system.
8. Agency funds	Accounts for assets held by a government unit in an agency capacity for employees, or for other government units. An example is the city employees' payroll withholding for health insurance premiums.
	Account Groups
9. General fixed assets account group	This account group maintains a record of fixed assets acquired by the governmental-type funds. Proprietary funds maintain their own fixed assets in their accounts.
10. General long-term debt account group	This account group maintains a record of the unmatured, general long-term liabilities of the governmental-type funds.

used by government units. Some states allow their local governments to select their own reporting dates; however, many states prescribe a specific reporting date for each type of government unit. Several states use the old federal fiscal year ending on June 30. Other states require a different date, such as April 30 or December 31. Some states have accepted the new federal fiscal year ending on September 30 as their reporting period. The nature of the reports is the same regardless of the reporting date selected.

The balance sheet for each of the governmental funds includes the following classifications:

Condensed Balance Sheet for a Governmental Fund

Current Assets	$XXXX	Current Liabilities		$ XX
		Fund Balance:		
		Reserved	$X	
		Unreserved	X	
				XX
		Total Liabilities		
Total Assets	$XXXX	and Fund Balance		$XXXX

The focus of the balance sheet is on the dollars available to be expended to fulfill the fund's objectives. Long-term productive assets (buildings, equipment, etc.) or long-term liabilities are *not* reported within the individual governmental funds. Separate, nonfund accounting reports are used for the government unit's long-term productive assets and long-term debt. Short-term debt, however, such as from vouchers payable or tax anticipation notes payable, are included in the governmental funds. Tax anticipation notes are a common short-term financing instrument of many government units and represent loans obtained using future taxes as collateral for the notes. Most states restrict these borrowings to those taxes that have been levied but not yet collected. These notes payable are paid from the first tax collections of the tax levy to which the notes are related. The account Fund Balance replaces the stockholders' equity section found on commercial operations' balance sheets, because no common stock exists and the general public is the theoretical owner of the fund. Fund Balance reports the difference between the assets and liabilities of the fund and is divided between Unreserved, which is the amount that may still be expended, and Reserved, which is the amount that is restricted from being expended. The various types of restricted reserves are presented later in the chapter.

Each of the governmental funds must also prepare a statement of revenues, expenditures, and changes in fund balance. This is the major operating statement of the fund and replaces the combined income statement and statement of retained earnings of a commercial enterprise.

The statement of revenues, expenditures, and changes in fund balance has three major sections:

1. *Operating Section.* The top section includes the revenues less expenditures for the period, with the difference shown as the excess of revenues over expenditures (or excess of expenditures over revenues).

2. *Other Financing Sources or Uses.* The middle section includes nonrevenue items such as bond proceeds and some interfund transfers.

3. *Reconciliation of Unreserved Fund Balance.* The bottom section reconciles the ending balance in Unreserved Fund Balance for **(a)** the results of operations, **(b)** other financing sources or uses, **(c)** changes in the portion of the fund balance classified as reserved and **(d)** any equity transfers with other funds.

This major operating statement is referenced often during the chapter. An understanding of its basic format, which follows, is important.

Statement of Revenues, Expenditures, and Changes in Fund Balance

Revenues	$X,XXX
Expenditures	XXX
Excess of Revenues over Expenditures	$ XX
Other Financing Sources or Uses	X
Excess of Revenues and Other Items over Expenditures and Other Items	$ XX
Fund Balance, Beginning of Fiscal Period	X
Changes in Reserves of Fund Balance	X
Fund Balance, End of Fiscal Period	$ XX

Actually, two formats of this operating statement are used in governmental financial reporting. The first statement is a presentation of only actual amounts for the fiscal period, as presented above. However, funds that have a legally adopted operating budget for the period must also present another statement that is an expanded format of the operating statement above. This second statement is similar to the first, except it has three columns: the first column is for the budgeted amounts for each line item reported, the second column is for the actual amounts of each item for the period, and the third column is for a comparison of the budgeted versus actual amounts for the period. This expanded version is called the statement of revenues, expenditures, and changes in fund balance—budget and actual. The budget versus actual comparison allows users of the financial statements to determine if the governmental entity remained within budgeted constraints for the period.

Proprietary Funds   Some activities of a government unit, such as operation of a public swimming pool or operation of a municipal water system, are similar to those of commercial enterprises. The objective of the government unit is to recover its costs in these operations through a system of user charges. The two types of *proprietary funds* are (5) *internal service funds* and (6) *enterprise funds* (See Figure 18-1).

Accounting and reporting for a proprietary fund is identical to accounting for a commercial operation. The balance sheet of each proprietary fund reports all assets, including long-term assets, and reports all liabilities, including long-term liabilities. Instead of common stock, however, the balance sheet shows contributed capital and a retained earnings balance. The capital is usually contributed by the general fund. An income statement and a statement of cash flows are also prepared for each proprietary fund. A complete discussion of proprietary funds is presented in Chapter 19.

Fiduciary Funds   The last classification consists of the *fiduciary funds*, which account for assets held by the government unit for others. The major types of fiduciary funds are (7) *trust funds* and (8) *agency funds*.

Some governmental units have pension trust funds that they classify as fiduciary funds. A complete discussion of fiduciary funds, including pension funds, is presented in Chapter 19.

Account Groups   In addition to the eight funds, governmental accounting also requires the establishment of two accounting entities, termed *account groups*, to record the general long-term assets and general long-term debt of the governmental unit that have been generated by the governmental-type funds. For example, when the general fund records an expenditure for a fixed asset, that asset is not recorded on the books of the general fund; instead, an accounting record of the acquisition of the fixed asset is maintained in the general long-term asset account group. Proprietary funds account for their own fixed assets or long-term debt within those funds. The two self-balancing account groups are not funds, inasmuch as they do not receive resources or make expenditures. They are simply accounting records used to maintain an inventory and control of the governmental entity's general fixed assets and long-term debt. The two account groups are (9) *general fixed assets account group (GFAAG)* and (10) *general long-term debt account group (GLTDAG)*.

The financial reporting for these two account groups is in the form of schedules listing the general long-term assets and general long-term debt. Specific examples of the two account groups are presented in Chapter 19.

MEASUREMENT FOCUS AND BASIS OF ACCOUNTING

The *basis of accounting* refers to the timing of recognizing a transaction for financial reporting purposes. For example, the cash basis recognizes transactions when cash is received or paid. The accrual basis recognizes transactions when the transaction or event takes place. The *modified accrual method* is a hybrid system that includes some aspects of accrual accounting and some aspects of cash-basis accounting. The modified accrual method is used when the measurement focus of the governmental entity is the flow of current financial resources and the proper expendability of the resources for the designated purposes, and determination of the available resources remaining to be expended. The accrual method is used when the measurement focus of the governmental entity is the flow of all economic resources available within a particular time period, thereby allowing for a comparison of revenues and expenses and a focus on maintenance of capital.

In May 1990, the GASB took the rather unusual position of issuing a statement that does not become effective until June 15, 1994. The statement was the result of extensive task force and standards board work on the Measurement Focus and Basis of Accounting project that was commonly identified by its acronym, MFBA. In **GASB Statement No. 11**, "Measurement Focus and Basis of Accounting—Governmental Fund Operating Statements" (GASB 11), the GASB stated that *interperiod equity* is essential to accountability in governmental financial accounting and established it as an objective of financial reporting. The principle of interperiod equity shows whether revenues were raised during a period in an amount sufficient to pay for the services provided within that period. With the required disclosures, governmental entities should be able to determine if current-year citizens are paying for current-year services, and not shifting the cost of current services to future-year taxpayers.

The postponement of the effective date of **GASB 11** to fiscal periods beginning after June 15, 1994, was to provide time for additional work on other projects under consideration by the GASB that might affect the reporting standards for governmental entities. Implementation of **GASB 11** may be delayed or specific issues may be modified, as is common for such pronouncements. The major provisions of **GASB 11** are as follows:

> The measurement focus for governmental fund operating statements should be the flow of financial resources measurement focus. The operating results expressed using this measurement focus show the extent to which financial resources obtained during a period are sufficient to cover claims incurred during that period against financial resources. This measurement focus considers financial resources only and uses an accrual basis of accounting.
>
> Revenues, operating expenditures, and interfund operating and residual equity transfers are the result of transactions or events that affect financial resources. Also, the acquisition, disposition, and long-term financing of capital assets and the long-term financing of certain nonrecurring projects or activities that have long-term economic benefit are transactions that affect financial resources. The flow of financial resources measurement focus does not, however, report an operating statement effect for the issuance and repayment of operating debt.[5]

If the full provisions of **GASB 11** are implemented, relatively minor modifications will be made to some specific aspects of the basic governmental accounting model. The discussion and illustrations in Chapters 18 and 19 of the text present the major dimensions of the governmental accounting model, and any changes that are made in the future can be assimilated into your understanding of governmental accounting.

---

[5] *Governmental Accounting Standards Board Statement No. 11*, "Measurement Focus and Basis of Accounting," 1990, Summary.

Basis of Accounting—Governmental Funds

Under accounting standards that remain effective until June 15, 1994, the modified accrual method is used to account for the four governmental funds. The modified accrual method is applied as follows:

1. *Revenue* is recorded in the accounting period in which it is both measurable and available to finance expenditures made during the current fiscal period.

2. *Expenditures* are recognized in the period in which the liabilities are both measurable and incurred.

"Measurable" means that the amount of the revenue or expenditure may be objectively determined. "Available" means due or past due and receivable within the current period, and collected within the current period or expected to be collected soon enough thereafter to be used to pay liabilities of the current period. The definition of "soon enough thereafter" has been stated as a period of not more than 60 days after the end of the current fiscal period.

Recognition of Revenue   Under the modified accrual method, some revenues are recognized on the accrual basis, and some revenues are recognized on the cash basis. Note that the revenue must be both measurable and available before recognition can occur. Revenues normally recognized under the accrual basis include property taxes, firm intergovernmental grants and revenues, interest on investments and delinquent taxes, and regularly billed charges for services. Revenues normally recognized under the cash basis method include income taxes, fees for licenses and permits, fines and forfeits, parking meter receipts, and intergovernmental grants or revenues that have some reasonable probability of being withdrawn. Detailed discussion of several revenue items is presented in the remainder of this section.

1. *Property Taxes.* The accrual basis of accounting is used to record property tax revenue when the taxes are levied. The receivable is recorded and revenue is accrued for those taxes applicable to and collectible within the current fiscal period, or within a short time after the end of the fiscal period. Generally, taxes are billed in the period of the levy. A *levy* gives the governmental entity the legal right to collect property taxes and to attach a legally enforceable lien against any property on which taxes are not paid. For example, a city council approves a budget which then becomes the legal basis for imposing a property tax levy. The city clerk then files the budget with the appropriate property tax collecting agent such as the county treasurer's office, which determines the necessary tax rate and sends out the tax bills. The levy is for a specific year and for the dollar amount determined by multiplying the assessed valuation of the property by the tax rate. The property owner pays the tax, which is then forwarded by the county treasurer to the city for expenditure.

NCGA Interpretation No. 3, "Revenue Recognition—Property Taxes" (NCGA 3), specifies that property taxes must be collectible within a maximum of 60 days after the end of the current fiscal period to be recognized as revenue in the current period. Taxes collectible 60 days after the current period ends are deferred and accounted for as next period's revenue.

Some governmental entities bill property owners in advance of the fiscal year to which the revenue is to be applied. If property taxes receivable are not available for current expenditures, or if they are collected in advance of the year for which they are levied, they are recorded as a credit in a deferred revenue account such as Deferred Revenue—Property Tax. The deferred amounts are reclassified as revenue in the period the taxes become available for current expenditure.

Revenue from another government unit or tax-exempt entity in lieu of taxes, such as a payment by a university to a city for police and fire protection, should be accrued and recorded as revenue when it becomes billable.

Revenue from property taxes should be recorded net of any uncollectibles or abatements. The Property Taxes Receivable account is debited for the full amount of the taxes levied, with estimated uncollectibles recorded separately in an allowance account reported as a contra account to the receivable.

2. *Interest on Investments and Delinquent Taxes.* Interest on investments or delinquent property taxes is accrued in the period in which the interest is earned. The governmental funds may temporarily invest available cash in interest-generating financial instruments such as certificates of deposit and federal or state securities. Governmental entities should carefully determine the credit risks and market risks of possible investments in order to minimize their potential loss. Governmental funds report their own current and long-term financial investments, and any accrued interest receivable, as assets of the funds.

3. *Income Taxes and Sales Taxes.* Self-assessed taxes such as income taxes and sales taxes are recorded when taxpayer liability, measurability, and collectibility clearly have been established. Typically, this occurs only when the tax returns have been filed and the tax paid. Sales taxes collected by another government unit (for example, the state government) may be accrued prior to receipt by the government unit to which they will be distributed (for example, a city) if the taxes are both measurable and available for expenditure. Measurability in this case is based on an estimate of the sales taxes to be received, and availability is based on the ability of the governing entity to obtain current resources through credit by using future sales tax collections as collateral for the loan.

4. *Miscellaneous Revenue.* Miscellaneous revenues such as license fees, fines, parking meter revenue, and charges for services are recorded when the cash is received because these cannot be predicted accurately.

5. *Grants, Entitlements, and Shared Revenue.* These are resources received from other government units. *Grants* are contributions from another government unit to be used for a specified purpose, activity, or facility. *Entitlements* are payments local governments are entitled to receive as determined by the federal government. *Shared revenue* is from revenue such as taxes on the retail sale of gasoline collected by the state. This revenue is levied by one government unit but shared with others on some predetermined basis. Grants are recognized as revenue in the period in which the local government receives an irrevocable right to the grant. This may be at the point the grant is authorized, but, in practice, most government units wait until the cash is received because the grant may be withdrawn by the grantor. Some grants are made to reimburse a government unit for expenditures made in accordance with legal requirements. The revenue from such grants should be recognized only when the expenditure is made.

NCGA Statement No. 2, "Grant, Entitlement, and Shared Revenue Accounting and Reporting by State and Local Governments" (NCGA 2), indicates that the legal and contractual requirements of the grant or entitlement should be reviewed carefully to determine the proper accounting.

Proceeds from the sale of bonds are not revenue. These proceeds are reported as other financing sources on the statement of revenues, expenditures, and changes in fund balance. Although bond sales do increase the resources available for expenditure, bonds must be repaid, while revenue of the government unit does not need to be repaid.

Recognition of Expenditures   Expenditures are recorded in the period in which the related liability is both measurable and incurred. Specific examples are as follows:

1. Costs for personal services, such as wages and salaries, are generally recorded in the period paid because they are normal, recurring expenditures of a government unit.

2. Goods and services obtained from outside the government entity are recorded as expenditures in the period in which they are received.

3. Capital outlays for equipment, buildings, and other long-term facilities are recorded as expenditures in the period of acquisition.

4. Interest on long-term debt is recorded in the period in which it is legally payable.

Basis of Accounting—Proprietary Funds

The two major proprietary funds are the internal service fund and the enterprise fund. Proprietary funds are established for government operations that have a management focus of income determination and capital maintenance; therefore, the accrual method is used to account for these funds in the same manner as for profit-seeking corporate entities. Proprietary funds record their own long-term assets, and depreciation is recognized on these assets. Long-term debt is recorded and interest is accrued as for commercial operations.

Basis of Accounting—Fiduciary Funds

Fiduciary fund revenues and expenditures (or expenses) should be accounted for based on the objective of the fund. Agency funds have a focus on the flow of current resources that are held in agency by the governing unit. The governing unit is the temporary custodian of these resources. The modified accrual method of accounting should be used for agency funds. An example of an agency fund is a county's billing and collecting taxes on behalf of other governmental entities, such as a city and a school district. After collection is completed on the "tax roll," the county properly distributes the taxes in accordance with each governmental entity's approved levy.

Trust funds can be either expendable or nonexpendable. For example, assume a long-term resident of a city bequeathed $100,000 to the city to be used to acquire and develop a tract of land for a city park. In this case, the trust fund principal, and any investment income, is expendable to satisfy the terms of the bequest. The modified accrual method is appropriately used to account for this expendable trust. In contrast, if the trust agreement specified that the $100,000 principal of the trust could not be expended, but only the interest from the investment of the principal is available for use by the city, the trust principal is nonexpendable. For nonexpendable trusts, capital maintenance is the primary focus and the accrual method of accounting is used. Therefore, the terms of the trust agreement must be closely examined to determine the basis of accounting to be used.

BUDGETARY ASPECTS OF GOVERNMENT OPERATIONS

Budgets are used in governmental accounting to assist in management control and to provide the legal authority to levy taxes, collect revenue, and make expenditures in accordance with the budget. Budgets establish the objectives and priorities of governing units.

For state governments, budgets are proposed by governors and debated by the legislative bodies. After passage, the budget usually becomes part of the fiscal period's state law. For local governments, the mayor or the major administrator may propose the budget. Public hearings and discussions of the budget are then held by governing boards such as the city council, county board, or township board prior to the adoption of the final budget.

A government unit may have several types of budgets, including the following:

1. *Operating Budgets.* Operating budgets specify expected revenue from the various sources provided by law. The operating budget includes expected expenditures for various line items, such as payrolls of employees, supplies, and goods and services to be obtained from outside the governing unit. Operating budgets are used in the general fund, special revenue funds, and sometimes the debt service funds.

2. *Capital Budgets.* A capital budget is prepared to provide information about proposed construction projects such as new buildings or street projects. Capital budgets are used in the capital projects funds.

Although proprietary funds may prepare budgets, these do not serve as a primary control vehicle. Budgets in the proprietary funds are advisory in much the same way budgets are used in commercial entities.

Recording the Operating Budget

Budgets are such an important control vehicle that those governmental funds with legally adopted annual operating budgets should enter their budgets into the formal accounting records. Capital budgets are not normally entered into the formal accounting records. Recording the operating budgets permits better management control and facilitates a year-end comparison of budgeted and actual amounts. This comparison is required as part of the financial reporting for the funds that must have operating budgets. A budget-actual comparison provides an assessment of management's stewardship of the governmental entity and allows citizens and others to determine if the governmental entity remained within its operating budgetary limits.

To help understand the process of accounting for operating budgets, this text uses the technique illustrated in the 1988 edition of *Governmental Accounting, Auditing and Financial Reporting* (GAAFR),[6] in which the budgetary accounts are identified with all capital letters. Capitalization of the budgetary accounts clearly separates the budgetary nominal accounts from the operating accounts of the governmental unit. Although budgetary accounts are not capitalized in actual practice, this convention is helpful in learning the following material.

The recording of the operating budget for the general fund is shown with the following example. Assume that the January 1, 19X1, the first day of the new fiscal period, the city council of Barb City approves the operating budget for the general fund, providing for $900,000 in revenue and $850,000 in expenditures. Approval of the budget provides the legal authority to levy the local property taxes and to appropriate resources for the expenditures. The term *appropriation* is the legal description of the authority to expend resources. The entry made in the general fund's accounting records on this date is:

January 1, 19X1		
(1) ESTIMATED REVENUES CONTROL	900,000	
APPROPRIATIONS CONTROL		850,000
BUDGETARY FUND BALANCE UNRESERVED		50,000
Record general fund budget for year.		

Note the word CONTROL used as part of the account titles. In governmental accounting, control accounts often are used in the major journals, with subsidiary accounts recording the detail behind each control account. This method is similar to a commercial entity's using a control account for its accounts receivable and then using subsidiary ledgers for the specific customer transactions. Throughout this chapter, the control account level is illustrated in order to focus on the major issues. In practice, detailed accounting is maintained for each separate classification of revenue and appropriation, either in the major journal or in a subsidiary ledger. The AICPA uses both control-level accounts and budgetary accounts on

---

[6] *Governmental Accounting, Auditing and Financial Reporting*, Government Finance Officers Association (Chicago), 1988.

the Uniform CPA Examination, although it does not capitalize the letters of the budgetary accounts used in the exam.

The ESTIMATED REVENUES CONTROL account is an *anticipatory asset*; that is, the government unit anticipates receiving resources from the revenue sources listed in the budget. The APPROPRIATIONS CONTROL account is an *anticipatory liability*; that is, the government unit anticipates incurring expenditures and liabilities for the budgeted amount. The excess of estimated revenues over anticipated expenditures is the budget surplus and is recorded to BUDGETARY FUND BALANCE UNRESERVED, which is a fund equity account. Some approved budgets have budget deficits in which expected expenditures exceed anticipated revenue. These budgets are recorded with a debit to BUDGETARY FUND BALANCE UNRESERVED.

Recording the budget in the governmental entity's books makes the budget a formal accounting control mechanism for the fiscal period. At the end of the year, after the appropriate financial statements have been prepared, all the budgetary accounts are closed.

ACCOUNTING FOR EXPENDITURES

The governmental funds and expendable trust funds use a variety of controls over expenditures to ensure that each expenditure is made in accordance with any legal restrictions on the fund.

The Expenditure Process

The expenditure process in governmental accounting comprises the following sequential steps: appropriation, encumbrance, expenditure, and disbursement.

Step 1: Appropriation   The budget provides the appropriating authority to make future expenditures. The general, special revenue, and often the debt service funds, prepare operating budgets. The capital projects fund prepares capital budgets.

The appropriation was recorded in the budget entry made previously in entry (1) for the general fund of Barb City. Recall that a total of $850,000 in anticipated expenditures was approved in the budget.

Step 2: Encumbrance   An *encumbrance* is a reservation of part of the budgetary appropriation and is recognized at the time an order is placed for goods or services. Encumbrances are a unique element of governmental accounting. Their purpose is to ensure that the expenditures within a period do not exceed the budgeted appropriations. The appropriation level was established by the approved budget and sets the legal maximum that may be expended for each budgeted item. The managers of the governmental unit must be sure that they do not exceed this budgetary authority. Thus, encumbrances provide a control system and safeguard for governmental unit administrators.

When an order is placed for goods or services to be received from outside the governmental unit, the budgeted appropriation is encumbered for the estimated cost of the order. Encumbrances are of greatest use when an order is placed and a period of time expires before delivery. Payroll costs, immaterial costs, and costs for goods acquired from within the government entity typically are not encumbered because these are normal and recurring and the managers of the government unit are able to predict these costs based on past experiences and other administrative controls, such as employment agreements.

A sensible approach should be used with an encumbrance system. For example, it is not necessary to establish an individual encumbrance when an employee orders a pad of paper. Rather, a blanket purchase order with a maximum dollar amount, for example, a total of $500, should be prepared and encumbered and then it can serve as the control for small, routine supply purchases. Encumbrances provide the unit administrators with an important accounting control to fulfill their responsibilities to manage within an approved budget.

To illustrate encumbrance accounting, assume that on August 1, 19X1, Barb City completed a purchase order (PO) for goods from an outside vendor that are estimated to cost $15,000. The entry to record this application of part of the budgeted appropriation authority for the period is:

August 1, 19X1
(2)	ENCUMBRANCES	15,000	
	BUDGETARY FUND BALANCE RESERVED FOR ENCUMBRANCES		15,000
	Record order for goods estimated to cost $15,000.		

Note that the ENCUMBRANCES account is a budgetary account which is reserving part of the appropriation authority of the budget. For detailed accounting, governmental entities often maintain a subsidiary ledger including accounts for specific types of encumbrances to correspond to each specific type of appropriation. For purposes of this illustration, the single title ENCUMBRANCES is used to indicate a control-level account to focus attention on the major aspects of governmental accounting. It is important to note that the BUDGETARY FUND BALANCE RESERVED FOR ENCUMBRANCES is a *reservation* (or restriction) *of the budgetary fund balance* and not an actual liability.

Step 3: Expenditure An *expenditure* and a corresponding liability are recorded when the governmental entity receives the goods or services ordered in step 2 above. When the goods are received, the encumbrance entry is reversed for the amount encumbered and the expenditure is recorded for the actual cost to the governmental entity. Although the actual cost is typically very close to the encumbered amount, some differences may exist because of partially completed orders, less expensive replacements, or unforeseen costs. Assume that the goods are received on September 20, 19X1, at an actual cost of $14,000. The entries to reverse the encumbrance for the goods and to record the actual expenditure are:

September 20, 19X1

(3)	BUDGETARY FUND BALANCE RESERVED		
	FOR ENCUMBRANCES	15,000	
	ENCUMBRANCES		15,000
	Reverse encumbrance for goods.		
(4)	Expenditures	14,000	
	Vouchers Payable		14,000
	Receive goods at cost of $14,000.		

At any time, the remaining appropriating authority available to the fund managers can be determined by the following equation:

$$\begin{matrix} \text{Appropriating} \\ \text{authority} \\ \text{remaining} \\ \text{available} \end{matrix} = \text{APPROPRIATIONS} - (\text{ENCUMBRANCES} + \text{Expenditures})$$

Step 4: Disbursement   A disbursement is the payment of cash for expenditures. Disbursements usually must be approved by the governing board or council as an additional level of control over expenditures.

Virtually all governmental entities use a comprehensive voucher system to control cash outflows. The governing board receives a schedule of vouchers to be approved for payment by vote of the board. This is usually one of the early agenda items in any board or council meeting as a vote is taken to "pay all bills." Checks are then written and delivered to the supplier of the goods. If the Barb City council approved the voucher at its October 8 meeting and a check was prepared in the amount of $14,000 and mailed on October 15, 19X1, the following entry would record the disbursement:

October 15, 19X1

(5)	Vouchers Payable	14,000	
	Cash		14,000
	Payment of voucher for goods received.		

Classification of Expenditure Transactions and Accounts

Governmental accounting places many controls over expenditures, and much of the financial reporting focuses on the various aspects of an expenditure. Expenditures should be classified by fund, function (or program), organizational unit, activity, character, and principal classes of objects. Figure 18-2 describes the major expenditure classifications.

Many governmental units have a comprehensive chart of accounts, with specific coding digits, that provide the basis for classifying each expenditure. For example, an expenditure journal entry might specify the expenditure account to be charged as number 421.23-110. The chart of accounts shows that the 421.23

FIGURE 18-2 Major expenditure classifications for governmental funds.

Classification	Description
Fund	The fund is identified to show the specific source of the expenditure. For example, the general fund would be noted for expenditures from that fund.
Function (or program)	Functions are group-related activities directed at accomplishing a major service or regulatory responsibility. Standard classifications of function include general government; public safety; highway and streets; sanitation; health and welfare; culture and recreation; and education.
Organizational unit	Classifying by organizational unit maintains accountability by each unit director. The organizational unit is determined by the governmental unit's organization chart. For example, public safety could be broken down into police, fire, corrections, protective inspection (such as plumbing and electrical code inspections), and other protection (such as flood control, traffic engineering, and examination of licensed occupations).
Activity	Activities within a function are recorded to maintain a record of the efficiency of each activity. For example, the police function could be broken down into the following activities: police administration, crime control and investigation, traffic control, police training, support service (such as communication services and ambulance services), special detail services, and police station and building maintenance. Each of these activities could be broken down further, if desired.
Character	Character classifications are based primarily on the period the expenditures are anticipated to benefit. Four major character classifications are current, capital outlay, debt service, and intergovernmental.
Object class	Object class is a grouping of types of items purchased or services obtained. For example, operating expenditures include personal services, purchased and contractual services, and commodities. Each of these objects could be further broken down, depending on the information needs of the governing entity. For example, purchased services could include utility services, cleaning services (such as custodial, lawn care, and snow plowing), repair and maintenance services, rentals, construction services, and other purchased services, such as insurance or printing.

account is for public safety: police—crime control and investigation—patrol, as follows:

> 420.   Public safety
>   421.   Police
>   421.2 Crime control and investigation
>   421.23   Patrol

The -110 suffix shows that this expenditure is for personal services in the form of salaries and wages for regular employees. It is not unusual for some accounting systems to have 11- to 14-digit accounts classifying each individual transaction. The level of specificity in the chart of accounts depends upon the information needs of the particular governing entity. Classifying information with such specificity allows the governing entity to maintain complete data base control over the expenditure information which it can use at any time in aggregate or relational analysis. For the examples in this chapter, only the expenditure control level is presented; in practice, a complete specification of the expenditure is made.

Outstanding Encumbrances at End of Fiscal Period

In the Barb City example earlier, the goods were received within the same fiscal period in which they were ordered. But what happens if the goods are ordered in one fiscal year and received in the next year? In this case the encumbrance is not reversed before the end of the fiscal period.

Accounting for these outstanding encumbrances depends on the policy of the government unit. The government may allow outstanding encumbrances to lapse; that is, the government unit is not required to honor these encumbrances carried over to the new year, and the new year's budget must rebudget them. In virtually all cases, the encumbrances will be rebudgeted and honored; however, this policy specifically recognizes the legal authority of the new governing board to determine its own expenditures. A second method is to carry over the encumbrances as nonlapsing spending authority. This method recognizes the practical aspects of encumbrances outstanding at the end of a fiscal period. Either method may be used in governmental accounting.

To illustrate the differences between the lapsing and nonlapsing methods of accounting for encumbrances, assume the following:

1. On August 1, 19X1, $15,000 of goods are ordered and an appropriate entry is made to record the encumbrance.

2. The goods have not yet been received on December 31, 19X1, the end of the fiscal period.

3. The goods are received on February 1, 19X2, at an actual cost of $14,000.

Figure 18-3 presents a comparison of the journal entries that would be required under each of the two methods of accounting for unfilled encumbrances at year-end.

Outstanding Encumbrances Lapse at Year-End   The closing entries on December 31, 19X1, close the remaining budgetary encumbrances and establish a reserve of the actual fund balance on the December 31, 19X1 balance sheet. Although the 1988 GAAFR recommends that a reserve for lapsing encumbrances be reported on the balance sheet, the GASB codification allows the alternative of just footnote disclosure of lapsing open orders at year-end that are expected to be honored in the next fiscal period. If just footnote disclosure is used, the governmental unit would not have the second closing entry which establishes the reserve of the actual fund balance on the balance sheet.

At the beginning of 19X2, the new governing board must decide if it will honor the outstanding encumbrances by including them in the 19X2 budgeted appropria-

FIGURE 18-3 Comparison of accounting for lapsing and nonlapsing encumbrances at year-end.

Item	Outstanding Encumbrances Lapse at Year-End		Outstanding Encumbrances Do Not Lapse at Year-End	
December 31, 19X1:				

Close remaining budgetary encumbrances.	BUDGETARY FUND BALANCE
	  RESERVED FOR ENCUMBRANCES
	  ENCUMBRANCES
		15,000
		15,000
			BUDGETARY FUND BALANCE
			  RESERVED FOR ENCUMBRANCES
			  ENCUMBRANCES
				15,000
				15,000

Reserve actual fund balance for outstanding encumbrances at end of 19X1 expected to be honored in 19X2.	Unreserved Fund Balance
	  Fund Balance Reserved
	    for Encumbrances
		15,000
		
		15,000
			Unreserved Fund Balance
			  Fund Balance Reserved
			    for Encumbrances
				15,000
				
				15,000

January 1, 19X2:				

Reverse prior-year encumbrance reserve.	Fund Balance Reserved
	  for Encumbrances
	    Unreserved Fund Balance
		15,000
		15,000
			—	

Establish budgetary control over encumbrances renewed from prior period.	ENCUMBRANCES
	  BUDGETARY FUND BALANCE
	    RESERVED FOR ENCUMBRANCES
		15,000
		
		15,000
			—	

Reclassify reserve from prior year.	—		Fund Balance Reserved
			  for Encumbrances
			  Fund Balance Reserved
			    for Encumbrances—19X1
				15,000
				
				15,000

February 1, 19X2:				

Receive goods and remove budgetary reserve for encumbrances.	BUDGETARY FUND BALANCE
	  RESERVED FOR ENCUMBRANCES
	  ENCUMBRANCES
		15,000
		15,000
			—	

Record actual expenditure for goods received.	Expenditures
	  Vouchers Payable
		14,000
		14,000
			Expenditures—19X1
			  Vouchers Payable
				14,000
				14,000

December 31, 19X2:				

Close expenditures account.	Unreserved Fund Balance
	  Expenditures
		14,000
		14,000
			Fund Balance Reserved
			  for Encumbrances—19X1
			  Expenditures—19X1
			  Unreserved Fund Balance
				15,000
				
				14,000
				1,000

tions. If the governing board decides to honor the outstanding purchase orders, an entry is made on January 1, 19X2, to establish budgetary control over the expenditure. A "fresh start" new spending authority is established and the sequence of entries continues as if this is a new order and purchase completed during 19X2.

If the new governing board decides not to honor outstanding encumbrances, then the following entry is made on January 1, 19X2, to record the cancellation of the open encumbrance:

January 1, 19X2

(6) Fund Balance Reserved for Encumbrances	15,000	
Unreserved Fund Balance		15,000
Eliminate reserve for outstanding		
encumbrances not being renewed.		

If the governmental unit used only footnote disclosure for open encumbrances at the end of 19X1, then no entry would be required. The governmental unit would simply cancel the order with the external vendor.

Outstanding Encumbrances at Year-End Are Nonlapsing   Some governing units carry over the appropriations authority from prior periods as nonlapsing encumbrances. In this case, the budget for the second fiscal period does *not* show these carryovers. Some governmental accountants feel this method is realistic for many situations in which orders placed with outside vendors cannot easily be canceled.

The 19X1 year-end closing entries presented in Figure 18-3 show the required reservation of the actual fund balance. Note that these are the same two entries as under the lapsing method with balance sheet recognition of the reserve of the fund balance. The differences between the two methods become apparent during the second fiscal period. Under the nonlapsing method, it is important to identify separately expenditures made from spending authority carried over from prior periods. Typically this is done in a reclassification entry on the first day of the second fiscal period, which dates the Fund Balance Reserved for Encumbrances. No budgetary entry is made in the second year because the appropriation authority comes from the first year's budget. When the goods are received, the expenditures account is also dated to indicate that the expenditure authority emanated from 19X1.

At the end of 19X2, the Expenditures—19X1 account is closed directly to the Fund Balance Reserved for Encumbrances—19X1. Note that the $1,000 difference between the actual cost of $14,000 and the reserved amount of $15,000 is closed to Unreserved Fund Balance because the actual cost is less than the amount encumbered from the prior year's appropriation authority. If the actual cost is greater than the reserve, then the difference must be approved as part of the appropriation authority for 19X2.

Key Observations from the Illustration   GASB standards require only actual expenditures made during the period to be reported on the statement of revenues, expenditures and changes in fund balance. For the budget-actual operating statement comparison, the ninth (of 12) basic principles of governmental accounting, as stated in the 1990 GASB codification, is that "budgetary comparisons should be included in the appropriate financial statements and schedules for governmental funds for which an annual budget has been adopted."[7] The lapsing method is

---

[7] Governmental Accounting Standards Board, *Codification of Governmental Accounting and Financial Reporting Standards*, 3d ed., 1990, Section 1100.109, p. 36.

preferred under generally accepted accounting principles because it includes all anticipated expenditures for a year in that year's budget. Furthermore, the lapsing method explicitly recognizes the legal responsibility of the governing board for operations within each period. A comparison between actual expenditures and the budget for those expenditures can then be made in the statement of revenues, expenditures, and changes in fund balance—budget and actual, for the years 19X1 and 19X2 as follows:

Lapsing Method

---

1. Statement of revenues, expenditures, and changes in fund balance (GAAP basis)

	Actual
19X1:	
Expenditures	$ 0
19X2:	
Expenditures	$14,000

2. Statement of revenues, expenditures, and changes in fund balance—budget and actual (budgetary basis)

	Budget	Actual	Over (Under) Budget
19X1:			
Expenditures	$15,000	$ 0	$(15,000)
19X2:			
Expenditures	$15,000	$14,000	$ (1,000)

The 19X1 budget-actual comparison shows the variance of $15,000 resulting from the unfilled encumbrance at the fiscal year-end. The 19X2 comparison shows that the $15,000 was rebudgeted and reappropriated for 19X2, and that the actual expenditure was $1,000 less than the budgeted amount for the period.

Under the nonlapsing method, expenditures made during the current year from the prior year's appropriation are separately reported in the expenditures sections of the statement of revenues, expenditures, and changes in fund balance. Note that this statement presents all actual expenditures made during the year, including those from the appropriating authority of the prior year. The most significant difference in financial statement presentation between the lapsing and nonlapsing methods occurs in the budget versus actual comparison in the statement of revenues, expenditures, and changes in fund balance—budget and actual. Under the nonlapsing method, the budget and actual columns include both actual expenditures and encumbrances in recognition of the budgetary basis used. The budget-actual comparison under the nonlapsing method for the two years, 19X1 and 19X2, is as follows:

Nonlapsing Method

---

1. Statement of revenues, expenditures, and changes in fund balance (GAAP basis)

	Actual
19X1:	
Expenditures	$ 0
19X2:	
Expenditures—prior year's appropriation	$14,000

2. Statement of revenues, expenditures, and changes in fund balance—budget and actual (budgetary basis)

	Budget	**Actual**	**Over (Under) Budget**
19X1:			
Expenditures and encumbrances:			
Under current year's appropriation	$15,000	$15,000	$ -0-
19X2:			
Expenditures and encumbrances:			
Under current year's appropriation	$ -0-	$ -0-	$ -0-

Note that the nonlapsing method reports different actual expenditures in the budget versus actual statement from those reported in the GAAP operating statement.

The method of accounting for open encumbrances at year-end is based on the governmental unit's budgetary policy, and both methods are found in practice. The comprehensive example presented later in this chapter uses the lapsing method because of its widespread use and because of its preference under generally accepted accounting principles.

Expenditures for Inventory

Most governmental units maintain small amounts of inventory in office supplies. A first issue is to determine which of two methods should be followed to account for the expenditure of inventories. The first method recognizes the entire expenditure for inventory in the period the supplies are acquired. This is called the *purchase* method. The second method is the *consumption* method and recognizes expenditures for only the amount of inventory used in the period. The specific method to follow depends on the policy of the governing unit and how inventory expenditures are included in the budget.

A second issue is whether or not inventory should be shown as an asset on the balance sheet of the governmental funds. Inventory is not an expendable asset; that is, it may not be spent as the governing entity wishes. NCGA 1 states that inventory should be shown on the balance sheets for governmental funds if the amount of inventory is material. Immaterial inventories need not be shown on the balance sheet. If the inventory is material, it is presented as an asset on the balance sheet; an amount equal to the inventory also should be shown as a reservation of the fund balance, indicating that that amount is no longer expendable.

Figure 18-4 presents the entries to account for inventories under both the purchase method and the consumption method. The illustration assumes that Barb City acquires $2,000 of inventory on November 1, 19X1, having held no inventory previously. On December 31, 19X1, the end of Barb City's fiscal year, a physical count shows $1,400 still in stock. During 19X2, $900 of this inventory is used, resulting in a $500 remaining balance of supplies on December 31, 19X2.

Purchase Method of Accounting for Inventories Under the purchase method, the entire amount of inventory acquired is charged to Expenditures in the period acquired. On December 31, 19X1, the end of the fiscal year, an adjusting entry is made to recognize the $1,400 remaining inventory as an asset and to restrict the fund balance for the nonexpendable portion applicable to inventories.

The expenditure of $2,000 is closed into Unreserved Fund Balance for 19X1 in a closing entry made at the end of the fiscal year. The December 31, 19X1, balance sheet includes the inventory of supplies as an asset in the amount of $1,400, and Fund Balance Reserved for Inventories is shown as a fund balance reserve for $1,400. The 19X1 operating statement shows a $2,000 expenditure for supplies.

At the end of 19X2, an adjusting entry is made to recognize the use of the $900 of supplies of the $1,400 remaining from the 19X1 purchase. This entry reduces the reservation of the fund balance and decreases inventory. At the end of 19X2,

FIGURE 18-4 Comparison of accounting for inventories—purchase versus consumption method.

Item	Purchase Method of Accounting		Consumption Method of Accounting	
November 1, 19X1:				
Record acquisition of	Expenditures	2,000	Expenditures	2,000
$2,000 of inventory.	Vouchers Payable	2,000	Vouchers Payable	2,000
December 31, 19X1:				
Recognize ending	Inventory of Supplies	1,400	Inventory of Supplies	1,400
inventory of $1,400.	Fund Balance Reserved		Expenditures	1,400
	for Inventories	1,400		
			Unreserved Fund Balance	1,400
			Fund Balance Reserved	
			for Inventories	1,400
December 31, 19X2:				
Record remaining	Fund Balance Reserved		Expenditures	900
inventory of $500, with	for Inventories	900	Inventory of Supplies	900
$900 of supplies having	Inventory of Supplies	900		
been consumed during			Fund Balance Reserved	
19X2.			for Inventories	900
			Unreserved Fund Balance	900

Inventory of Supplies is $500, and Fund Balance Reserved for Inventories is $500, for the remaining unused supplies.

In summary, the expenditure of $2,000 is recognized in the period in which the supplies are purchased. No expenditures are recognized in subsequent periods, although some of the supplies are used in those periods.

Consumption Method of Accounting for Inventories   Under the consumption method, expenditures for a period are reported just for the amount consumed. In this case, the budget for the period should be based on the expected amount of use so the budgeted and actual amounts compared at the end of the year are on the same basis.

A net expenditure of $600 ($2,000 − $1,400) for supplies used is reported in 19X1, the year the supplies were acquired. With $500 of inventory remaining at the end of 19X2, an expenditure of $900 is reported in the 19X2 operating statement, to show the amount of supplies consumed during 19X2. The consumption method relates the expenditures with the use of the inventory.

A comparison of selected account balances under the purchase method and consumption method shows the different amounts that are reported under these two methods:

	Purchase Method	Consumption Method
19X1:		
Expenditures	$2,000	$ 600
Inventory of Supplies	1,400	1,400
19X2:		
Expenditures	0	900
Inventory of Supplies	500	500

Note that the choice of methods has no effect on the balance sheet amounts; the only effect is on the period in which the expenditures for inventory are reported.

Both inventory methods are used in practice. The method to be used by a specific government unit depends on its budgeting policy. If the government unit includes all inventory acquisitions in its appropriations for the period, the purchase method should be used. If the government unit includes just the expected amount of inventory to be used during a period in that period's appropriations, the consumption method should be used.

Accounting for Prepayments and Fixed Assets

Governmental entities may acquire insurance or equipment that has an economic life of more than 1 year. Accounting for these acquisitions depends on which fund expends the resources for the acquisition. The governmental funds are concerned with the expendability and control over available resources, and account for the acquisitions of equipment, or other prepayments, as expenditures. In the governmental funds, the entire amount of the cost of the acquisition of equipment and other capital assets is recognized as an expenditure in the year the asset is acquired. No capital assets are recorded in the general fund; they are treated as expenditures of the period.

The proprietary funds are concerned with capital maintenance and account for acquisitions of capital assets in the same manner as used in commercial entities. Thus, the accounting for the purchase of a capital asset is different in the four governmental funds from that used in the proprietary funds.

The fifth principle (part a) of the 1990 GASB governmental accounting codification covers the accounting for fixed assets:

> Fixed assets related to specific proprietary funds or trust funds should be accounted for through those funds. All other fixed assets of a governmental unit should be accounted for through the General Fixed Assets Account Group.[8]

The sixth principle of the GASB codification presents the valuation standards for fixed assets, as follows:

> Fixed assets should be accounted for at cost or, if the cost is not practicably determinable, at estimated cost. Donated fixed assets should be recorded at their estimated fair value at the time received.[9]

For example, assume that Barb City acquires a truck. The acquisition is made from the resources of, and accounted for in, the general fund. The encumbrance is $12,000, but the actual cost is $12,500 because of minor modifications required by the city. The general fund makes the following entries to account for the acquisition of the truck:

(7)	ENCUMBRANCES	12,000	
	BUDGETARY FUND BALANCE RESERVED		
	FOR ENCUMBRANCES		12,000
	Order truck at estimated cost of $12,000.		
(8)	BUDGETARY FUND BALANCE RESERVED		
	FOR ENCUMBRANCES	12,000	
	ENCUMBRANCES		12,000
	Cancel reserve for truck received.		
(9)	Expenditures	12,500	
	Vouchers Payable		12,500
	Receive truck at actual cost of $12,500.		

The truck is not recorded as an asset in the general fund; it is an expenditure in this fund. A record of the acquisition of capital assets acquired by the governmental funds is maintained in the general fixed assets account group, but that record is only for control purposes. The general fixed assets account group is illustrated in Chapter 19.

---

[8] Governmental Accounting Standards Board, *Codification of Governmental Accounting and Financial Reporting Standards*, 3d ed., 1990, Section 1100.105, p. 35.

[9] Ibid., Section 1100.106, p. 35.

Depreciation of Fixed Assets   The seventh governmental accounting principle in the 1990 GASB codification covers depreciation of fixed assets, as follows:

a. Depreciation of general fixed assets should not be recorded in the accounts of governmental funds. Depreciation of general fixed assets may be recorded in cost accounting systems or calculated for cost finding analyses, and accumulated depreciation may be recorded in the general fixed assets account group.

b. Depreciation of fixed assets accounted for in a proprietary fund should be recorded in the accounts of that fund. Depreciation is also recognized in those trust funds where expenses, net income, and/or capital maintenance are measured.[10]

In commercial, for-profit accounting, depreciation matches the cost of providing goods or services with revenues earned. However, the governmental funds' focus is on the financial resources available to provide the services to society; therefore, depreciation is not required in the governmental funds. Some accountants feel that the governmental funds should reflect depreciation of fixed assets in order to determine the full cost of providing services, even though the matching principle is not applicable to these funds. Nevertheless, under present governmental accounting standards, the governmental funds do not recognize depreciation.

The proprietary funds recognize depreciation as a part of providing goods or services to their customers. For example, a municipal electrical utility, operating as a proprietary fund, records its own fixed assets, and records depreciation on them as part of the expenses associated with earning revenue. Depreciation expense is shown on the proprietary fund's income statement as with commercial, for-profit organizations.

Long-Term Debt and Capital Leases

Commercial, profit-seeking businesses recognize long-term debt and capital leases as noncurrent liabilities. The debt or capital lease is entered into to use to earn income, and the liability is recognized under the flow of all economic resources measurement model. However, accounting for long-term liabilities in governmental funds is directly affected by the flow of current financial resources measurement focus model. Principle 5 (part b) of the 1990 GASB codification states:

Long-term liabilities of proprietary funds and trust funds should be accounted for through those funds. All other unmatured general long-term liabilities of the governmental unit, including special assessment debt for which the government is obligated in some manner, should be accounted for through the General Long-Term Debt Account Group.[11]

Thus, the governmental funds, which include the general fund, record the proceeds from a bond issue as a debit to Cash and a credit to Bond Issue Proceeds, another financing source. Bond issue proceeds are not revenue because the bonds

[10] Ibid., Section 1100.107, p. 35.
[11] Ibid., Section 1100.105, p. 35.

must be repaid. Other financing sources are shown in the middle section of the statement of revenues, expenditures, and other changes in fund balances. Bonds or capital leases are not reported on the governmental funds' balance sheets.

INTERFUND TRANSFERS AND TRANSACTIONS

A basic concept in governmental accounting is that each fund is a separate entity and has separate sources of resources, sometimes including the power to levy and collect taxes. The revenues of each fund must then be expended in accordance with the budget and restrictions established by law. Because a single government entity has a number of separate funds, it sometimes becomes necessary to transfer resources from one fund to another. *Interfund transfers and transactions* are resource flows between fund entities. In a consolidated financial statement for a commercial entity, intercompany transactions are eliminated in order to report only the effect of transactions with external entities. Governmental accounting, on the other hand, requires the separate maintenance and reporting of interfund items. The governing body must approve any interfund transfers and transactions in order to provide a public record and to prevent distortion of fund uses. Many governmental entities include interfund transfers and transactions anticipated during a fiscal year in the operating budgets for the year. Budgetary entries for interfund transfers and transactions are illustrated in the comprehensive example of Sol City presented later in this chapter. Interfund transfers must be accounted for carefully to ensure that the legal and budgetary restrictions are followed and that resources intended for one fund are not used in another.

Five types of interfund items are found in governmental accounting. Three are *interfund transactions*: (1) quasi-external transactions, (2) reimbursements, and (3) financing transactions. The other two are *interfund transfers*: (4) operating transfers and (5) residual equity transfers. Interfund transfers are reported separately in each fund's financial statements. The five interfund items are discussed below and illustrated in Figure 18-5.

Quasi-External Transactions

Quasi-external interfund transactions are transactions that would be treated as revenue, expenditures, or expenses if they involved parties external to the government unit. However, because they involve only other funds of the government unit, they are termed quasi-external transactions. Quasi-external transactions are still reported as revenue, expenditures, or expenses, but these transactions are different because they are entirely within the government unit. These interfund transactions are normal and recurring items, usually involving at least one proprietary fund. Two examples are as follows:

1. The general fund purchases goods or services from an internal service or enterprise fund.
2. Payments are made to the general fund from the enterprise fund in lieu of taxes, such as payments for fire and police protection.

FIGURE 18-5 Interfund transactions and transfers.

Item	Entry in General Fund		Entry in Other Fund	
1. Quasi-external transaction			**INTERNAL SERVICE FUND:**	
	Expenditures	100	Due from General Fund	100
	Due to Internal Service Fund	100	Revenue from Billings	100
	Due to Internal Service Fund	100	Cash	100
	Cash	100	Due from General Fund	100
2. Reimbursement for expenditures			**CAPITAL PROJECTS FUND:**	
	Cash	3,000	Expenditures	3,000
	Expenditures	3,000	Cash	3,000
3. Financing transaction and repayment			**INTERNAL SERVICE FUND:**	
	Due from Internal Service Fund	4,000	Cash	4,000
	Cash	4,000	Due to General Fund	4,000
	Cash	4,000	Due to General Fund	4,000
	Due from Internal Service Fund	4,000	Cash	4,000
4. Operating transfer			**CAPITAL PROJECTS FUND:**	
	Operating Transfer Out to		Cash	10,000
	Capital Projects Fund	10,000	Operating Transfer In	
	Cash	10,000	from General Fund	10,000
5. Residual equity transfer			**CAPITAL PROJECTS FUND:**	
	Cash	15,000	Residual Equity Transfer Out	
	Residual Equity Transfer In		to General Fund	15,000
	from Capital Projects Fund	15,000	Cash	15,000

Usually these transfers involve the recognition of a receivable or payable because of the time lag between the purchase of the services and the disbursement of funds. A "Due to (or from)" account is used for short-term interfund receivables and payables rather than a formal Vouchers Payable account.

The illustration of a quasi-external transaction in Figure 18-5 assumes that the general fund of Barb City uses an auto from the city motor pool. The motor pool operates as an internal service fund. The general fund is billed $100 based on mileage and pays the bill 30 days later.

Reimbursements

A reimbursement transaction is for the reimbursement of a fund's expenditure or expense which was initially made from the fund, but which is properly chargeable to another fund. These initial payments are sometimes made either because of improper classification to the wrong fund, or for expediency within the governmental entity. The reimbursement from one fund to another is recorded as a reduction of the expenditure in the fund initially recording the expenditure and a recording of the expenditure in the proper fund for the appropriate amount. Two examples are as follows:

1. An expenditure properly chargeable to the special revenue fund is initially recorded and paid by the general fund, and the general fund subsequently is reimbursed by the special revenue fund.

2. The general fund records and pays for an expenditure to provide preliminary architectural work on the planning for a new sports arena. The general fund is later reimbursed from the sports arena enterprise fund.

The illustration of a reimbursement in Figure 18-5 assumes that the general fund of Barb City recorded a $3,000 expenditure for a bill from outside consultants that is later discovered to be properly chargeable to the capital projects fund. Upon notification, the capital projects fund reimbursed the general fund and properly recorded the expenditure in its fund.

Financing Transactions: Loans and Advances

State law may allow lending or borrowing activities between funds. The loans must be repaid, usually within 1 year or before the end of the fiscal period. Loans and advances are not shown on a fund's statement of revenues, expenditures, and changes in fund balance; however, all outstanding loans or advances must be shown on the balance sheet as payables or receivables. Interest usually is not charged on interfund financing arrangements. If interest is charged, it is accounted for in the funds in the same manner as other interest income or expense.

Some governments distinguish between short-term and long-term financing arrangements by using the term "Advances to (or from)" to denote a long-term agreement and "Due to (or from)" for a short-term agreement.

The illustration of an interfund financing transaction in Figure 18-5 assumes Barb City's general fund loans the internal service fund $4,000 for 2 months. The general fund reports a receivable for the amount of the loan until the loan is repaid.

Operating Transfers

Operating transfers include all interfund transfers that are not classified as one of the other four interfund items. The general fund often transfers resources into another fund to be used by the receiving fund for its own operations; occasionally, the general fund receives resources from other funds. Such transfers are not fund revenues or expenditures but are instead called "operating transfers." These transfers are classified under "Other Financing Sources or Uses" in the operating financial statements of the funds. The reason that the receiving fund does not recognize these transfers as revenue is that the issuing fund has already properly recognized these resources as revenue. Thus, the recording of these transfers as other financing sources eliminates the possibility of double-counting the same resources as revenue in two different funds of the combined governmental entity. Examples include:

1. A transfer of resources, such as cash or other assets, is made from the general fund to an enterprise fund or internal service fund that has an operating deficit that must be eliminated.

2. A transfer of resources from the general fund to a capital projects fund is made to help finance new construction.

3. A transfer of resources from the general fund to the debt service fund is made to pay principal and interest.

The illustration of an operating transfer in Figure 18-5 assumes that the general fund of Barb City agrees to provide $10,000 to the capital projects fund toward the construction of a new library. The Operating Transfer Out account in the general fund is closed to its Unreserved Fund Balance at the end of the fiscal period. The capital projects fund also closes its Operating Transfer In account at the end of the fiscal period to its Unreserved Fund Balance.

Residual Equity Transfers

Residual equity interfund transfers are nonrecurring or nonroutine transfers of equity between funds. They are accounted for as changes in the fund balance in both the paying and receiving funds. The following are examples of residual equity transfers:

1. A contribution from the general fund is made to establish an internal service fund or an enterprise fund.

2. The capital project fund transfers its remaining resources to the general fund or debt service fund when the capital project is completed and the capital projects fund is closed.

Residual equity transfers must be distinguished from operating transfers. Operating transfers are routine transfers from one ongoing fund to another, such as a subsidy for an operating deficit. Residual equity transfers are for the creation or termination of a fund.

Some governments account for residual equity transfers directly in the fund balance. Most, however, use an intermediate account entitled Residual Equity Transfer Out to (or In from) the other fund involved. The intermediate account approach is used here to provide a complete presentation of the interfund transfer.

The illustration of a residual equity transfer in Figure 18-5 assumes that the general fund of Barb City receives $15,000 from the capital projects fund upon completion of the library building. In accordance with the city charter, the Capital Projects Fund transfers its remaining balance in the library project fund and closes out the fund upon completion of the library project.

At the end of the year, the general fund closes the Residual Equity Transfer from Capital Projects Fund account to Unreserved Fund Balance, as follows:

(10)	Residual Equity Transfer In from		
	Capital Projects Fund	15,000	
	Unreserved Fund Balance		15,000
	Close residual equity transfer account.		

On the books of the capital projects fund, the Residual Equity Transfer Out to General Fund account is closed to Unreserved Fund Balance, as follows:

(11)	Unreserved Fund Balance	15,000	
	Residual Equity Transfer Out to		
	General Fund		15,000
	Close equity transfer out to general fund.		
	Capital Projects Fund balance is now zero.		

Residual equity transfers are reported in the bottom part of the statement of revenues, expenditures, and changes in fund balance as an adjustment of the Unreserved Fund Balance Account. A good way to remember the definition of

FIGURE 18-6 Overview of general fund.

Item	Description
Measurement focus	Flow of current financial resources—expendability
Accounting basis	Modified accrual
Budgetary basis	Operating budget
Financial statements	1. Balance sheet
	2. Statement of revenues, expenditures, and changes in fund balance
	3. Statement of revenues, expenditures, and changes in fund balance—budget and actual
Balance sheet:	
Current assets	Includes current financial resources such as cash, certificates of deposit, and property taxes receivable accrued and allowance for uncollectible taxes estimated.
	Material inventories reported.
Long-term productive assets (buildings, etc.)	Fixed assets not reported in general fund.
Current liabilities	Vouchers payable is primary current liability. Interfund financing also included as liabilities (or assets).
Long-term debt	Governmental unit long-term debt not reported in general fund.
Fund balance	Unreserved fund balance and reservations of fund balance, e.g., encumbrances and inventories.
Statement of revenues, expenditures, and changes in fund balance:	
Revenue	Recorded when measurable and available. Some revenues accrued and others recognized under cash basis accounting. Quasi-external transactions also included in revenues (or expenditures).
Expenditures	Recognized in period measurable and incurred.
Other financing sources and uses	Includes bond issue proceeds and operating transfers.
Changes in fund balance	Reconciles changes in unreserved fund balance during period, including changes in reservations of fund balance and residual equity transfers.

residual equity transfers is that these are transfers of equity to initiate or terminate a fund.

OVERVIEW OF ACCOUNTING AND FINANCIAL REPORTING FOR GENERAL FUND

Figure 18-6 presents an overview of the accounting for the general fund, including accounting for the interfund transactions and transfers on the general fund's operating statement, the statement of revenues, expenditures, and changes in fund balance. Note that the interfund financing transactions are reported only on the fund's balance sheet.

COMPREHENSIVE ILLUSTRATION OF ACCOUNTING FOR THE GENERAL FUND

The following example illustrates the accounting for the general fund of Sol City for the January 1, 19X2, to December 31, 19X2, fiscal year. The entries are presented by topic, not necessarily in chronological order. The balance sheet for the general fund as of December 31, 19X1, presented in Figure 18-7, represents the opening balances for fiscal 19X2.

Adoption of the Budget

The city council adopts the budget for fiscal 19X2 as presented in Figure 18-8. The budget summarizes the four major functions of the city: general government, streets and highways, public safety (fire and police), and sanitation. In the complete budget used by the city council, the expenditures in each of the four

FIGURE 18-7 General fund balance sheet at the beginning of 19X2.

<table>
<tr><td colspan="3" align="center">Sol City
General Fund
Balance Sheet
December 31, 19X1</td></tr>
<tr><td>Assets:</td><td></td><td></td></tr>
<tr><td>Cash</td><td></td><td>$ 50,000</td></tr>
<tr><td>Property Taxes Receivable—Delinquent</td><td>$100,000</td><td></td></tr>
<tr><td>Less: Allowance for Uncollectibles—Delinquent</td><td>(5,000)</td><td>95,000</td></tr>
<tr><td>Inventory of Supplies</td><td></td><td>14,000</td></tr>
<tr><td>Total Assets</td><td></td><td>$159,000</td></tr>
<tr><td>Liabilities and Fund Balance:</td><td></td><td></td></tr>
<tr><td>Vouchers Payable</td><td></td><td>$ 30,000</td></tr>
<tr><td>Fund Balance:</td><td></td><td></td></tr>
<tr><td>Reserved for Encumbrances</td><td>$ 11,000</td><td></td></tr>
<tr><td>Reserved for Inventories</td><td>14,000</td><td></td></tr>
<tr><td>Unreserved</td><td>104,000</td><td>129,000</td></tr>
<tr><td>Total Liabilities and Fund Balance</td><td></td><td>$159,000</td></tr>
</table>

FIGURE 18-8 General fund operating budget for fiscal 19X2.

Sol City
General Fund
Operating Budget
For Period of January 1, 19X2, to December 31, 19X2

Estimated Revenue:		
Property Taxes	$775,000	
Grants	55,000	
Sales Taxes	25,000	
Miscellaneous	20,000	
Total Estimated Revenue		$ 875,000
Appropriations:		
General Government	$200,000	
Streets and Highways	75,000	
Public Safety	400,000	
Sanitation	150,000	
Total Appropriations		(825,000)
Excess of Estimated Revenue over Appropriations		$ 50,000
Interfund Transfers:		
Operating Transfers out to Capital Projects Fund	$ (20,000)	
Residual Equity Transfer to Initiate Internal Service Fund	(10,000)	
Total Interfund Transfers		(30,000)
Excess of Estimated Revenue and Interfund Transfers over Appropriations and Interfund Transfers		$ 20,000

functions are broken down into the following categories: personal services, supplies, other services and charges, and capital outlay. The public safety budget includes a budgeted capital outlay of $50,000 for a new fire truck.

Among the city's accounting policies are the following:

1. *Consumption Method for Inventories.* The city budgets supplies inventory on the consumption method, including only the costs of expected inventory use during the year.

2. *Lapsing Method of Accounting for Encumbrances.* The city uses the lapsing method for accounting for any encumbrances outstanding at the end of fiscal periods. The APPROPRIATIONS CONTROL for fiscal 19X2 includes a reappropriation of the $11,000 of outstanding encumbrances as of December 31, 19X1.

3. *Use of Control Accounts.* The city uses a comprehensive system of control accounts for its major journals. The following accounts have extensive subsidiary ledgers that correspond to the entries made in the journal: ESTIMATED REVENUES CONTROL, APPROPRIATIONS CONTROL, ENCUMBRANCES, and Expenditures. The specific detail supporting each of these control accounts is maintained in the subsidiary records. For purposes of focusing on the major aspects of governmental accounting, the Sol City illustration includes just the control-level entries.

4. *Budgeted Interfund Transactions and Transfers.* The city includes in the budget all anticipated interfund transactions and transfers during the fiscal year. The general fund is expected to have the following interfund transfers:

OPERATING TRANSFER:
Out to capital projects fund $20,000
RESIDUAL EQUITY TRANSFER:
Out to internal service fund   10,000

The operating transfer out to the capital projects fund is to pay for the city's share of a municipal courthouse addition project, and the residual equity transfer out is to initiate the internal service fund.

The following entries are made to record the budget and to renew the lapsing encumbrances from the prior period:

January 1, 19X2

(12)	ESTIMATED REVENUES CONTROL	875,000	
	APPROPRIATIONS CONTROL		825,000
	ESTIMATED OPERATING TRANSFER OUT		20,000
	ESTIMATED RESIDUAL EQUITY TRANSFER OUT		10,000
	BUDGETARY FUND BALANCE UNRESERVED		20,000
	Record budget for fiscal 19X2.		
(13)	Fund Balance Reserved for Encumbrances	11,000	
	Unreserved Fund Balance		11,000
	Reverse prior-year encumbrances reserve.		
(14)	ENCUMBRANCES	11,000	
	BUDGETARY FUND BALANCE RESERVED FOR ENCUMBRANCES		11,000
	Renew encumbrances from prior period as included in budgeted appropriations in 19X2.		

(*Note*: The technique of capitalizing the account titles of all budgetary accounts is continued through the comprehensive illustration. This technique is used in the text to assist differentiation of the budgetary from the operating accounts. In practice, the budget accounts are not capitalized.)

Property Tax Levy and Collection

Most municipalities obtain the majority of their revenue from property taxes. Property taxes should be recorded on the date they are levied. Revenue is recorded if the property taxes are measurable and available for current expenditures. A deferred revenue account is credited if the property taxes are not available for current expenditures. For Sol City, the property taxes are due within the fiscal period and therefore are recorded as revenue as of the levy date. Note that a provision for uncollectibles must be recorded and this provision is a reduction of property tax revenue, not a bad debts expense as in commercial accounting. Governmental funds have no such account as bad debts expense. The receivables are classified as current, collectible within this period; or delinquent, for past-due accounts.

The entries in Sol City's general fund for the transactions relating to property taxes are as follows:

(15)	Property Taxes Receivable—Current	785,000	
	Allowance for Uncollectible Taxes—Current		10,000
	Revenue—Property Tax		775,000
	Property taxes levied for this fiscal year.		
(16)	Cash	791,000	
	Property Taxes Receivable—Current		695,000
	Property Taxes Receivable—Delinquent		96,000
	Collect portion of property taxes including $96,000 of past due accounts.		
(17)	Allowance for Uncollectible Taxes—Delinquent	4,000	
	Property Taxes Receivable—Delinquent		4,000
	Write off remaining $4,000 of delinquent property taxes.		
(18)	Allowance for Uncollectible Taxes—Delinquent	1,000	
	Allowance for Uncollectible Taxes—Current	5,000	
	Revenues—Property Tax		6,000
	Revise estimate of uncollectibles from $10,000 to $5,000 and close remaining $1,000 balance of allowance account for delinquent accounts.		
(19)	Property Taxes Receivable—Delinquent	90,000	
	Allowance for Uncollectible Taxes—Current	5,000	
	Property Taxes Receivable—Current		90,000
	Allowance for Uncollectible Taxes—Delinquent		5,000
	Reclassify remaining receivables and allowance account from current to delinquent.		

Other Revenue

Other sources of income are grants from other government units, a portion of the sales tax collected on retail sales made within the city, and miscellaneous revenue from parking meters, fines, and licenses. Grants from other government units should be recognized as revenue when the grants become available and measurable. The city's policy is to recognize these grants as they are received because they may be withdrawn by the grantor at any time up to the actual transmittal of the monies. In our example, the city receives only 60 percent of the expected grant that had been budgeted at $55,000. Sales tax revenue may be accrued if the city can make a good estimate of the amount to be received and if the sales tax revenue is available for current expenditures. It is the policy of the city to recognize the sales taxes when received. Miscellaneous revenue is recognized as received.

The entries to record the other sources of income are:

(20) Cash	33,000	
Revenue—Grant		33,000
Receive only 60 percent of expected grant.		
(21) Cash	32,000	
Revenue—Sales Tax		32,000
Receive sales tax revenue from state.		
(22) Cash	18,000	
Revenue—Miscellaneous		18,000
Receive miscellaneous revenue from fines, license fees, minor disposals of equipment, and other sources.		

Expenditures

The appropriations were recorded in the budget entry (entry 12), together with a renewal of the encumbrances carried over from the prior period under the lapsing method of accounting for encumbrances (entries 13 and 14). Orders for goods and services from outside vendors are encumbered, and a voucher system is used. Recall that internal payroll typically is not encumbered by a governmental entity.

The entries for the encumbrances, expenditures, and disbursements made in Sol City's general fund during the year are as follows:

(23) ENCUMBRANCES	210,000	
BUDGETARY FUND BALANCE RESERVED FOR ENCUMBRANCES		210,000
Encumber for purchase orders for goods and services ordered from outside vendors.		
(24) BUDGETARY FUND BALANCE RESERVED FOR ENCUMBRANCES	5,000	
ENCUMBRANCES		5,000
Reverse encumbrance for portion of order that is not deliverable because item has been discontinued.		
(25) BUDGETARY FUND BALANCE RESERVED FOR ENCUMBRANCES	190,000	
ENCUMBRANCES		190,000
Reverse reserve for partial order of goods received.		
(26) Expenditures	196,000	
Vouchers Payable		196,000
Receive goods at actual cost of $196,000 that had been encumbered for $190,000. Difference due to increase in cost of items. Includes supplies for inventory.		
(27) BUDGETARY FUND BALANCE RESERVED FOR ENCUMBRANCES	11,000	
ENCUMBRANCES		11,000
Reverse reserve for goods received that were ordered in prior year.		

(28)	Expenditures	9,000	
	Vouchers Payable		9,000
	Receive goods ordered in prior year. Actual cost is $9,000 on encumbered amount of $11,000. Difference due to price reduction as part of special sale.		
(29)	Expenditures	550,000	
	Vouchers Payable		550,000
	Payroll costs to employees for period.		
(30)	Vouchers Payable	730,000	
	Cash		730,000
	Vouchers approved by city council and paid during period.		

Acquisition of Capital Asset

The budget for the fire department includes $50,000 for a new fire truck. This capital outlay is accounted for as any other expenditure of available resources. The resources for the fire truck are encumbered at the time the order is placed with the truck manufacturer. A record of the acquisition is made in the general fixed assets group of accounts for inventory purposes. The entries in the general fund for the acquisition of the fire truck are:

(31)	ENCUMBRANCES	50,000	
	BUDGETARY FUND BALANCE RESERVED FOR ENCUMBRANCES		50,000
	Order fire truck at estimated cost of $50,000.		
(32)	BUDGETARY FUND BALANCE RESERVED FOR ENCUMBRANCES	50,000	
	ENCUMBRANCES		50,000
	Reverse reserve for fire truck received.		
(33)	Expenditures	58,000	
	Vouchers Payable		58,000
	Receive fire truck at actual cost of $58,000 due to approved additional items required to meet new fire code.		
(34)	Vouchers Payable	58,000	
	Cash		58,000
	Voucher approved and disbursement made for fire truck.		

Interfund Transfers and Transactions

The anticipated interfund items are included in the budget for the fiscal period. They include the estimated residual equity transfer of $10,000 to initiate the internal service fund and the estimated operating transfer of $20,000 for capital improvements to a capital projects fund. In addition to these transfers, the general fund also has a quasi-external transaction with the internal service fund for services received in the amount of $1,000, and it lends the enterprise fund $3,000.

The following entries in the general fund record the general fund's side of the interfund transfers and transactions during the year. Chapter 19 continues the comprehensive example of Sol City, and presents the entries for these interfund transactions and transfers in each of the related funds so that both sides of accounting for interfund items are illustrated for the Sol City example.

(35)	Residual Equity Transfer Out to Internal Service Fund	10,000	
	Due to Internal Service Fund		10,000
	Recognize the residual equity transfer out and associated payable to the internal service fund as included in the budget.		
(36)	Operating Transfer Out to Capital Projects Fund	20,000	
	Due to Capital Projects Fund		20,000
	Recognize the operating transfer out and associated liability to the capital projects fund as included in the budget.		
(37)	Due to Internal Service Fund	10,000	
	Cash		10,000
	Pay cash to internal service fund for payable from residual equity transfer out previously recognized.		
(38)	Due to Capital Projects Fund	20,000	
	Cash		20,000
	Pay cash to capital projects fund for payable from operating transfer out previously recognized.		
(39)	Expenditures	1,000	
	Due to Internal Service Fund		1,000
	Recognize payable for quasi-external transaction with internal service fund for goods received.		
(40)	Due to Internal Service Fund	1,000	
	Cash		1,000
	Pay cash to eliminate payable.		
(41)	Due from Enterprise Fund	3,000	
	Cash		3,000
	City Council approves loan to enterprise fund to be repaid in 90 days.		

Adjusting Entries

Certain adjusting entries are required to state correctly the balance sheet items for the year. Assume that a physical count of the inventory shows an ending balance of $17,000 on December 31, 19X2. This is a net increase of $3,000 from the beginning balance of $14,000.

The policy of the general fund is to recognize inventory as an asset and to report a reserve against fund balance for the ending balance. Recall that the city is using the consumption method of accounting for inventories. The entries required to adjust the ending balance of the supplies inventory are:

(42) Inventory of Supplies   3,000
       Expenditures   3,000
       Adjust ending inventory to $17,000 and
       reduce expenditures to net amount
       consumed during the period.

(43) Unreserved Fund Balance   3,000
       Fund Balance Reserved for Inventories   3,000
       Adjust the reserve for inventories from
       beginning balance of $14,000 to its ending
       balance of $17,000.

Closing Entries

The final set of entries closes the nominal accounts. The format presented first reverses the budget entry and then closes the operating revenues and expenditures. Some governmental entities close the accounts in a slightly different order by closing budgeted revenue against actual revenue, and budgeted appropriations against actual expenditures. The specific order of closing the accounts has no impact on the final effect; all budgetary accounts and nominal operating accounts must be closed at year-end.

A preclosing trial balance is presented in Figure 18-9. Recall that the city is using the lapsing method of accounting for encumbrances open at the end of the fiscal year. The closing entries for the general fund of Sol City for fiscal 19X2 are as follows:

December 31, 19X2
(44) APPROPRIATIONS CONTROL   825,000
       ESTIMATED OPERATING TRANSFER OUT   20,000
       ESTIMATED RESIDUAL EQUITY TRANSFER OUT   10,000
       BUDGETARY FUND BALANCE UNRESERVED   20,000
          ESTIMATED REVENUES CONTROL   875,000
       Close budgetary accounts.

(45) BUDGETARY FUND BALANCE RESERVED
       FOR ENCUMBRANCES   15,000
          ENCUMBRANCES   15,000
       Close remaining encumbrances by reversing
       remaining budgetary balance.

(46) Unreserved Fund Balance   15,000
       Fund Balance Reserved for Encumbrances   15,000
       Reservation of fund balance for encumbrances that
       lapse but are expected to be honored in 19X3.

FIGURE 18-9 Preclosing trial balance for general fund.

Sol City
General Fund
Preclosing Trial Balance
December 31, 19X2

	Debit	Credit
Cash	$ 102,000	
Property Taxes Receivable—Delinquent	90,000	
Allowance for Uncollectible Taxes—Delinquent		$ 5,000
Due from Enterprise Fund	3,000	
Inventory of Supplies	17,000	
Vouchers Payable		55,000
Fund Balance Reserved for Inventories		17,000
Unreserved Fund Balance		112,000
Revenue—Property Tax		781,000
Revenue—Grant		33,000
Revenue—Sales Tax		32,000
Revenue—Miscellaneous		18,000
Expenditures	811,000	
Operating Transfer Out to Capital Projects Fund	20,000	
Residual Equity Transfer Out to Internal Service Fund	10,000	
ESTIMATED REVENUES CONTROL	875,000	
APPROPRIATIONS CONTROL		825,000
ESTIMATED OPERATING TRANSFER OUT		20,000
ESTIMATED RESIDUAL EQUITY TRANSFER OUT		10,000
ENCUMBRANCES	15,000	
BUDGETARY FUND BALANCE RESERVED FOR ENCUMBRANCES		15,000
BUDGETARY FUND BALANCE UNRESERVED		20,000
Total	$1,943,000	$1,943,000

(47)	Revenue—Property Tax	781,000	
	Revenue—Grant	33,000	
	Revenue—Sales Tax	32,000	
	Revenue—Miscellaneous	18,000	
	Expenditures		811,000
	Operating Transfer Out to Capital Projects Fund		20,000
	Unreserved Fund Balance		33,000
	Close operating statement accounts.		
(48)	Unreserved Fund Balance	10,000	
	Residual Equity Transfer Out to Internal Service Fund		10,000
	Close residual equity transfer.		

A reconciliation of the Unreserved Fund Balance account is used to determine its ending balance of $120,000, as follows:

Unreserved Fund Balance

		Bal. 1/1/X2	104,000
(43)	3,000	(13)	11,000
		Bal. Preclosing	112,000
(46)	15,000	(47)	33,000
(48)	10,000		
		Bal. 12/31/X2	120,000

Financial Statements for the General Fund

Three major statements are required for Sol City's general fund:

1. Balance sheet as of December 31, 19X2, with comparative amounts for the prior year-end.

2. Statement of revenues, expenditures, and changes in fund balance—budgeted versus actual, for the 19X2 fixcal year, with comparative amounts for the prior year.

3. Statement of revenues, expenditures, and changes in fund balance, for the 19X2 fiscal year, with comparative amounts for the prior year.

The only difference between the second and third statements is the budget-actual comparison presented in the second statement; just the actual amounts are presented in the third statement. Although this may seem like duplication of information, governmental funds having legally adopted annual operating budgets must provide both forms of the operating statement to fulfill the reporting objective of a budget-actual comparison. Governmental funds not having an operating budget provide only statements 1 and 3 above.

For purposes of the illustration, the December 31, 19X2, balance sheet and just 19X2's statement of revenues, expenditures, and changes in fund balance—budget versus actual, are presented for the general fund. Additional reports also must be presented that include the general fund, and these additional reports are discussed in the comprehensive financial reporting section in Chapter 19. The balance sheet as of December 31, 19X2, is presented in Figure 18-10.

The balance sheet includes the supplies inventory for $17,000 and the associated reservation of fund balance, reflecting that this portion of the fund balance is not expendable. The $3,000 receivable from the financing interfund transaction with the enterprise fund is shown as a current asset. The outstanding encumbrances of $15,000 are a reservation of fund balance indicating that a portion of the year's appropriation has been used but that the ordered goods or services have not yet been received.

The statement of revenues, expenditures, and changes in fund balance, with a comparison between budgeted and actual operating results for the period, is presented in Figure 18-11.

FIGURE 18-10 General fund balance sheet at the end of the fiscal period.

Sol City
General Fund
Balance Sheet
December 31, 19X2

Assets:		
Cash		$102,000
Property Taxes Receivable—Delinquent	$ 90,000	
Less: Allowance for Uncollectibles—Delinquent	(5,000)	85,000
Due from Enterprise Fund		3,000
Inventory of Supplies		17,000
Total Assets		$207,000
Liabilities and Fund Balance:		
Vouchers Payable		$ 55,000
Fund Balance:		
Reserved for Encumbrances	$ 15,000	
Reserved for Inventories	17,000	
Unreserved	120,000	
		152,000
Total Liabilities and Fund Balance		$207,000

The statement of revenues, expenditures, and changes in fund balance is made up of three major sections:

1. *Operating Section.* Revenues less expenditures, resulting in an excess of revenues over expenditures for the period. Expenditures include the quasi-external interfund transactions.

2. *Other Financing Sources (Uses).* This section includes operating transfers and nonrevenue proceeds such as bond issues.

3. *Reconciliation of Unreserved Fund Balance.* The ending balance in Unreserved Fund Balance is reconciled for (a) the results of operations, (b) other financing sources or uses, (c) changes in the balances of fund balance reserves since the beginning of the fiscal period, and (d) residual equity transfers.

Revenues should be classified by major sources, and expenditures by major functions. Although the entries presented in the illustrations for Sol City did not break down the expenditures by function (general government, streets and highways, public safety, and sanitation), this breakdown is done in the actual governmental accounting process, so each expenditure can be classified by both function and object (personal services, supplies, and other services and charges. The amounts presented in the actual expenditures section in Figure 18-11 are the assumed amounts from a comprehensive accounting system. Total expenditures do reconcile to the expenditures recorded in the Sol City illustration.

The statement of revenues, expenditures, and changes in fund balance reconciles to the ending amount in the unreserved fund balance. An alternative accept-

FIGURE 18-11 General fund statement of revenues, expenditures, and changes in fund balance—budget and actual, for fiscal 19X2.

**Sol City
General Fund
Statement of Revenues, Expenditures, and Changes
in Fund Balance—Budget and Actual
For Fiscal Year Ended December 31, 19X2**

	Budget	Actual	Over (Under) Budget
Revenues:			
Property Taxes	$775,000	$781,000	$ 6,000
Grants	55,000	33,000	(22,000)
Sales Taxes	25,000	32,000	7,000
Miscellaneous	20,000	18,000	(2,000)
Total Revenues	$875,000	$864,000	$(11,000)
Expenditures:			
Current:			
General Government	$200,000	$206,000	$ 6,000
Streets and Highways	75,000	71,000	(4,000)
Public Safety	350,000	335,000	(15,000)
Sanitation	150,000	141,000	(9,000)
Capital Outlay:			
Public Safety	50,000	58,000	8,000
Total Expenditures	$825,000	$811,000	$(14,000)
Excess of Revenues over Expenditures	$ 50,000	$ 53,000	$ 3,000
Other Financing Sources (Uses):			
Operating Transfer Out to Capital Projects Fund	(20,000)	(20,000)	-0-
Excess of Revenues and Other Sources over Expenditures and Other Uses	$ 30,000	$ 33,000	$ 3,000
Deduct: Increase in Reserve for Encumbrances	-0-	(4,000)	(4,000)
Increase in Reserve for Inventories	-0-	(3,000)	(3,000)
Increase in Unreserved Fund Balance	$ 30,000	$ 26,000	$ (4,000)
Unreserved Fund Balance, January 1	104,000	104,000	-0-
Residual Equity Transfer Out to Internal Service Fund	(10,000)	(10,000)	-0-
Unreserved Fund Balance, December 31	$124,000	$120,000	$ (4,000)

able format, used by some governmental entities, is to reconcile to total fund balance of $152,000. Most government units reconcile to unreserved fund balance because this provides better disclosure of the changes in the reserves of the fund balance and focuses on the remaining resources that may be expended.

SUMMARY OF KEY CONCEPTS AND TERMS

Accounting for state and local government units requires the use of fund accounting to recognize properly the variety of services and objectives of the government unit. Funds are separate fiscal and accounting entities established to segregate, control, and account for resource flows. Three types of funds are used by government units: governmental funds, of which the general fund is usually the largest; proprietary funds; and fiduciary funds. The basis of accounting for each fund depends on the fund's objective. Governmental funds are concerned with the amount of resources that may be expended to fulfill the objective of the fund; therefore, the modified accrual method is used to measure the revenue and expenditures for them. Proprietary funds are concerned with capital maintenance and income determination, and the full accrual method is used for them. Accounting for the fiduciary funds is based on the objectives of the fund, and the modified accrual or full accrual method is used, as appropriate.

Under the modified accrual method, revenue is recognized when it is both measurable and available for financing expenditures of the period. A major source of revenue is property tax levies, but other sources may include sales taxes, grants from other government units, and fines, licenses, or permits. Expenditures are recognized in the period in which the related liability is both measurable and incurred. The expenditure process usually begins with a budget, which establishes the spending authority for the fund. Encumbrances are used for purchases outside the government entity to recognize the use of a portion of the spending authority for the period and to avoid overspending the expenditure authority. Encumbrances outstanding at the end of a fiscal period are reported as a reserve of the fund balance and may be accounted for as lapsing or nonlapsing. Another type of fund balance reserve is a reserve for inventories, which is used if the amount of inventory is material.

The general fund is responsible for offering many of the usual services of government units. Fire and police protection, the local government's administrative and legislative functions, and many other basic services are administered through the general fund. The modified accrual method of accounting is used to account for revenue and expenditure transactions. No long-term assets or long-term debt is recorded in the general fund; separate account groups are used to maintain records of these items.

Interfund transfers and transactions must be evaluated carefully to ensure that the legal and budgetary controls of the local government unit are not violated. Five types of interfund transactions and transfers exist: (1) quasi-external transactions, (2) reimbursements, (3) financing transactions, (4) operating transfers, and (5) residual equity transfers. All interfund transactions are shown on the financial statements of the government unit. The disclosure made depends on the type of transaction or transfer. Types 1, 2, 4, and 5 are shown on the operating statement, the statement of revenues, expenditures, and changes in fund balance. Type 3, financing transactions, is shown as a receivable or payable on the balance sheet.

Account groups	Governmental funds
Appropriations	Interfund transfers and transactions
Basis of accounting	Interperiod equity
Budgets	Measurement focus of funds
Encumbrance	Modified accrual method
Expenditure	Proprietary funds
Fiduciary funds	Reservation of the budgetary fund balance
Funds	Revenue

QUESTIONS

Q18-1 What is a fund? How does a fund receive resources?

Q18-2 What are the eight funds generally used by local and state governments? Briefly state the purpose of each fund.

Q18-3 Are the general fixed assets and general long-term debt account groups accounted for as funds? Why or why not?

Q18-4 Compare the modified accrual method with the accrual accounting method.

Q18-5 Which of the two, the modified accrual method or the accrual method, is used for funds for which expendability is the concern? Why?

Q18-6 When are property taxes recognized as revenue in the general fund?

Q18-7 How are taxpayer-assessed income and sales taxes recognized in the general fund? Why?

Q18-8 What is meant by "budgetary accounting"? Explain the accounting for expected revenue and anticipated expenditures.

Q18-9 Are all expenditures encumbered?

Q18-10 Why do some government units not report small amounts of inventories of supplies in their balance sheets?

Q18-11 What are the main differences between the lapsing and nonlapsing methods of accounting for encumbrances outstanding at the end of the fiscal year? What are the differences in accounting between the lapsing and nonlapsing methods when accounting for the actual expenditure in the subsequent year?

Q18-12 When is the expenditure for inventories recognized under the purchase method? Under the consumption method?

Q18-13 Explain the difference between an operating interfund transfer and a residual equity interfund transfer. Give examples of each.

Q18-14 Where is an operating interfund transfer reported on the general fund's financial statements?

Q18-15 Explain the accounting for quasi-external interfund transactions. Where are they reported on the general fund's financial statements?

Q18-16 The general fund agrees to lend the enterprise fund $2,000 for 3 months. How is this interfund loan reported on the financial statements of the general fund?

Q18-17 Explain how an expenditure may be classified by **(1)** function, **(2)** activity, and **(3)** object within the financial statements of a government unit.

CASES

C18-1 Budget Theory

Governmental accounting gives substantial recognition to budgets, with budgets being recorded in the accounts of the governmental unit.

Required

a. What is the purpose of a governmental accounting system, and why is the budget recorded in the accounts of a governmental unit? Include in your discussion the purpose and significance of appropriations.

b. Describe when and how (1) a governmental unit records its budget and (2) closes out the budgetary accounts.

C18-2 Municipal versus Financial Accounting

William Bates is executive vice president of Mavis Industries, Inc., a publicly held industrial corporation. Bates has just been elected to the city council of Gotham City. Before assuming office as a city councilman, he asks you to explain the major differences that exist in accounting and financial reporting for a large city when compared with a large industrial corporation.

Required

a. Describe the major differences that exist in the purpose of accounting and financial reporting and in the type of financial reports of a large city when compared with a large industrial corporation.

b. Why are inventories often ignored in accounting for local governmental units? Explain.

c. Under what circumstances should depreciation be recognized in accounting for local governmental units? Explain.

EXERCISES

E18-1 Multiple-Choice Questions on the General Fund [AICPA Adapted]

Select the correct answer for each of the following questions.

1. One of the differences between accounting for a governmental (not-for-profit) unit and a commercial (for-profit) enterprise is that a governmental unit should:
   a. *Not* record depreciation expense in any of its funds.
   b. Always establish and maintain complete self-balancing accounts for each fund.
   c. Use only the cash basis of accounting.
   d. Use only the modified accrual basis of accounting.

2. Belle Valley incurred $100,000 of salaries and wages for the month ended March 31, 19X2. How should this be recorded on that date?

	Debit	Credit
a. Expenditures—Salaries and Wages	100,000	
Vouchers Payable		100,000
b. Salaries and Wages Expense	100,000	
Vouchers Payable		100,000
c. Encumbrances—Salaries and Wages	100,000	
Vouchers Payable		100,000
d. Fund Balance	100,000	
Vouchers Payable		100,000

3. Which of the following should be accrued as revenue by the general fund of a local government?
   a. Sales taxes held by the state that will be remitted to the local government.
   b. Parking meter revenue.
   c. Sales taxes collected by merchants.
   d. Income taxes currently due.

4. Which of the following expenditures is normally recorded on the accrual basis in the general fund?
   a. Interest.
   b. Personal services.
   c. Inventory items.
   d. Prepaid expenses.

5. Which of the following accounts of a governmental unit is credited when taxpayers are billed for property taxes?
   a. Estimated Revenue.
   b. Revenue.
   c. Appropriations.
   d. Fund Balance Reserved for Encumbrances.

6. When fixed assets purchased from general fund revenue were received, the appropriate journal entry was made in the general fixed assets account group. What account, if any, should have been debited in the general fund?
   a. No journal entry should have been made in the general fund.
   b. Fixed Assets.
   c. Expenditures.
   d. Due from General Fixed Assets Account Group.

7. The initial transfer of cash from the general fund in order to establish an internal service fund would require the general fund to credit Cash and debit:
   a. Accounts Receivable—Internal Service Fund.
   b. Unreserved Fund Balance.
   c. Fund Balance Reserved for Encumbrances.
   d. Operating Transfers Out.

E18-2 Multiple-Choice Questions on the Accounting Basis of Funds
[AICPA Adapted]

Select the correct answer for each of the following questions.

1. Which of the following funds of a governmental unit uses the modified accrual basis of accounting?
   a. Debt service.
   b. Internal service.
   c. Enterprise.
   d. Nonexpendable trust.

2. Revenue of a municipality should be recognized in the accounting period in which it becomes available and measurable for a:

	Governmental Fund	Proprietary Fund
a.	Yes	No
b.	Yes	Yes
c.	No	Yes
d.	No	No

3. A state governmental unit should use which basis of accounting for each of the following types of funds?

	Governmental	Proprietary
a.	Cash	Modified accrual
b.	Modified accrual	Modified accrual
c.	Modified accrual	Accrual
d.	Accrual	Accrual

4. Which of the following funds of a governmental unit recognizes revenue and expenditures under the same basis of accounting as the general fund?
   a. Debt service.
   b. Enterprise.
   c. Internal service (intragovernmental service).
   d. Nonexpendable pension trust.

5. Under the modified accrual basis of accounting, which of the following taxes is usually recorded before it is received in cash?
   a. Property.
   b. Income.
   c. Gross receipts.
   d. Gift.

E18-3 Multiple-Choice Questions on Budgets, Expenditures, and Revenue
[AICPA Adapted]

Select the correct answer for each of the following questions.

1. Which of the following steps in the acquisition of goods and services occurs first?
   a. Appropriation.
   b. Encumbrance.
   c. Budget.
   d. Expenditure.

2. What account is used to earmark the fund balance to recognize the contingent obligations of goods ordered but not yet received?
   a. Appropriations.
   b. Encumbrances.
   c. Obligations.
   d. Fund Balance Reserved for Encumbrances.

3. When the Estimated Revenues Control account of a governmental unit is closed out at the end of the fiscal year, the excess of revenue over estimated revenue is:
   a. Debited to Unreserved Fund Balance.

b. Debited to Fund Balance Reserved for Encumbrances.
c. Credited to Unreserved Fund Balance.
d. Credited to Fund Balance Reserved for Encumbrances.

4. The Carson City general fund issued purchase orders of $630,000 to vendors and suppliers. Which of the following entries should be made to record this transaction?

	Debit	Credit
a. Encumbrances	630,000	
Budgetary Fund Balance		
Reserved for Encumbrances		630,000
b. Expenditures	630,000	
Vouchers Payable		630,000
c. Expenses	630,000	
Accounts Payable		630,000
d. Budgetary Fund Balance		
Reserved for Encumbrances	630,000	
Encumbrances		630,000

5. The following balances are included in the subsidiary records of Dogwood's Parks and Recreation Department on March 31, 19X2:

Appropriations—Supplies	$7,500
Expenditures—Supplies	4,500
Encumbrances—Supply Orders	750

How much does the department have available for additional purchases of supplies?

7500 - (4500+750)

a. $0.
b. $2,250.
c. $3,000.
d. $6,750.

6. The board of commissioners of the City of Elgin adopted its budget for the year ending July 31, 19X2, which indicated revenue of $1,000,000 and appropriations of $900,000. If the budget is formally integrated into the accounting records, what is the required journal entry?

	Debit	Credit
a. Memorandum entry only		
b. Appropriations Control	900,000	
Budgetary Fund Balance Unreserved	100,000	
Estimated Revenues Control		1,000,000
c. Estimated Revenues Control	1,000,000	
Appropriations Control		900,000
Budgetary Fund Balance Unreserved		100,000
d. Revenue Receivable	1,000,000	
Expenditures Payable		900,000
Budgetary Fund Balance Unreserved		100,000

7. Which of the following accounts of a governmental unit is credited when the budget is recorded?

a. Encumbrances.

    b. Budgetary Fund Balance Reserved for Encumbrances.

    c. Estimated Revenue Control.

    d. Appropriations Control.

8. Which of the following accounts of a governmental unit is debited when supplies previously ordered are received?

    a. Encumbrances.

    b. Budgetary Fund Balance Reserved for Encumbrances.

    c. Vouchers Payable.

    d. Appropriations Control.

9. Which of the following situations will increase the fund balance of a governmental unit at the end of the fiscal year?

    a. Appropriations are less than expenditures and budgetary fund balance reserved for encumbrances.

    b. Appropriations are less than expenditures and encumbrances.

    c. Appropriations are more than expenditures and encumbrances.

    d. Appropriations are more than estimated revenue.

10. Which of the following accounts of a governmental unit is credited to close it out at the end of the fiscal year?

    a. Appropriations Control.

    b. Revenue—Property Tax.

    c. Budgetary Fund Balance Reserved for Encumbrances.

    d. Encumbrances.

E18-4 Multiple-Choice Questions on the General Fund [AICPA Adapted]

Select the correct answer for each of the following questions.

1. On December 31, 19X3, Fox City paid a contractor $4,500,000 for the total cost of a new city hall built in 19X3 on city-owned land. Financing for the capital project was provided by a $3,000,000 general obligation bond issue sold at face amount on December 31, 19X3, with the remaining $1,500,000 transferred from the general fund. What account and amount should be reported in Fox's 19X3 financial statements for the general fund?

    a. Other Financing Sources Control $4,500,000.

    b. Expenditures Control $4,500,000.

    c. Other Financing Sources Control $3,000,000.

    d. Other Financing Uses Control $1,500,000.

2. The following information pertains to Lion City's general fund for 19X3:

Appropriations	$6,500,000
Expenditures	5,000,000
Other financing sources	1,500,000
Other financing uses	2,000,000
Revenues	8,000,000

After Lion's general fund accounts were closed at the end of 19X3, the fund balance increased by:

    a. $3,000,000.

b. $2,500,000.

c. $1,500,000.

d. $1,000,000.

3. The following information pertains to Tine City:

19X3 governmental fund revenues that became measurable and available in time to be used for payment of 19X3 liabilities	$16,000,000
Revenues earned in 19X1 and 19X2 and included in the $16,000,000 indicated above	2,000,000
Sales taxes collected by merchants in 19X3 but not required to be remitted to Tine until January 19X4	3,000,000

For the year ended December 31, 19X3, Tine should recognize revenues of:

a. $14,000,000.

b. $16,000,000.

c. $17,000,000.

d. $19,000,000.

Questions 4 through 6 are based on the following information:

Fleck Township's fiscal year ends on July 31. During the year ended July 31, 19X3, Fleck received a state grant of $150,000 to finance the purchase of a senior citizens' recreation bus, and an additional $15,000 grant to be used for bus operations during the year ended July 31, 19X3. Only $125,000 of the capital grant was used during the year ended July 31, 19X3 for the bus purchase, but the entire operating grant of $15,000 was disbursed during the year.

Fleck's governing body adopted its general fund budget for the year ending July 31, 19X4, comprising estimated revenues of $50,000,000 and appropriations of $40,000,000. Fleck formally integrates its budget into the accounting records.

4. The senior citizens' recreation bus program is accounted for as part of Fleck's general fund. What amount should Fleck report as grant revenues for the year ended July 31, 19X3, in connection with the state grants?

a. $165,000.

b. $150,000.

c. $140,000.

d. $125,000.

5. When Fleck records budgeted revenues, Estimated Revenues Control should be:

a. Debited for $10,000,000.

b. Credited for $10,000,000.

c. Debited for $50,000,000.

d. Credited for $50,000,000.

6. The $10,000,000 budgeted excess of revenues over appropriations should be:

a. Debited to Budgetary Fund Balance Unreserved.

b. Credited to Budgetary Fund Balance Unreserved.

c. Debited to Estimated Excess Revenues Control.

d. Credited to Estimated Excess Revenues Control.

7. When Micro records its annual budget, which of the following control accounts indicates the amount of the authorized spending limitation for the year ending December 31, 19X3?
   a. Reserved for Appropriations.
   b. Appropriations.
   c. Budgetary Fund Balance Reserved for Encumbrances.
   d. Encumbrances.

8. In Micro's general fund balance sheet presentation at December 31, 19X3, which of the following expenditures should be classified as fixed assets?

	Structural Alterations to Firehouse	Mayor's Office Furniture
a.	No	No
b.	No	Yes
c.	Yes	No
d.	Yes	Yes

9. For state and local governmental units, generally accepted accounting principles require that encumbrances outstanding at year-end be reported as:
   a. Expenditures.
   b. Reservations of fund balance.
   c. Deferred liabilities.
   d. Current liabilities.

E18-5 Encumbrances at Year-End

Fargo ordered new office equipment for $12,500 on April 20, 19X1. The office equipment had not been received by June 30, 19X1, the end of Fargo's fiscal year.

Required

a. Assume that outstanding encumbrances lapse at year-end.
   (1) Prepare the entries required on June 30, 19X1.
   (2) Assuming that the city council accepts outstanding encumbrances in its budget for the next fiscal period (19X2), prepare entries on July 1, 19X1.
   (3) Prepare entries on July 24, 19X1, when the equipment was received with an invoice for $12,750.
b. Assume that outstanding encumbrances are nonlapsing.
   (1) Prepare the entries required on June 30, 19X1.
   (2) Prepare the entry required on July 1, 19X1, to identify the expenditure with 19X1.
   (3) Prepare the entry on July 24, 19X1, when the equipment was received with an invoice for $12,750.
   (4) Prepare the closing entry on June 30, 19X2, assuming the expenditure is netted against 19X2 expenditures.

E18-6 Accounting for Inventories of Office Supplies

Georgetown purchased supplies on August 8, 19X2, for $3,600. At the end of the fiscal year on September 30, the inventory of supplies was $2,800.

Required

a. Assume that Georgetown uses the consumption method of accounting for inventories.
   (1) Prepare the entry for the purchase on August 8, 19X2.
   (2) Prepare the entries required on September 30, 19X2, including the closing of the Expenditures account.
   (3) Assuming the supplies were used during 19X3, prepare the entries on September 30, 19X3.

b. Assume that Georgetown uses the purchase method of accounting for inventories.
   (1) Prepare the entry for the purchase on August 8, 19X2.
   (2) Prepare the entries required on September 30, 19X2, including the closing of the Expenditures account.
   (3) Assuming the supplies were used during 19X3, prepare the entry on September 30, 19X3.

E18-7 Accounting for Prepayments and Capital Assets

Required

Prepare journal entries for the Iron City general fund for the following, including any adjusting and closing entries on December 31, 19X1:

   1. Acquired a 3-year fire insurance policy for $5,400 on September 1, 19X1.
   2. Ordered new furniture for the city council meeting room on September 17, 19X1, at an estimated cost of $15,600. The furniture was delivered on October 1. The actual cost was $15,200. The estimated life of the furniture is 10 years, with no residual value.
   3. Acquired supplies on November 4, 19X1, for $1,800. Iron City uses the consumption method of accounting. Supplies on hand on December 31 were $1,120.

E18-8 Interfund Transfers and Transactions

During 19X1, the following transfers and transactions between funds took place in the city of Jackson:

   1. A transfer of $12,000 was made on March 1 from the general fund to establish a building maintenance service fund. Jackson uses intermediate residual equity transfer accounts to account for this type of transfer.
   2. On April 1, the general fund made an $8,000, 6-month loan to the building maintenance service fund.
   3. On April 15, $2,400 was transferred to the debt service fund to pay interest.
   4. The Jackson transportation service fund billed the general fund $825 for April on May 5. The general fund paid the bill on May 25.

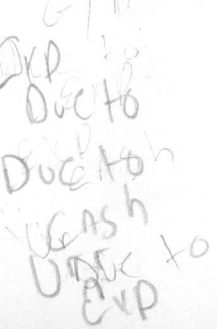

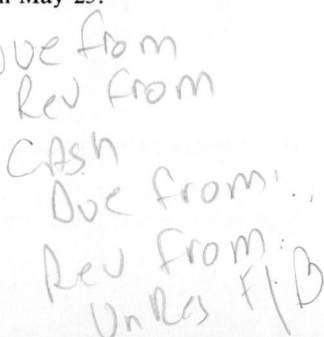

Required

a. Prepare journal entries for the general fund and the other fund involved that should be recorded at the time of each transfer or transaction.

b. For each transfer or transaction, prepare the appropriate closing entries for the general fund and the other fund for the year ended June 30, 19X1.

E18-9 Closing Entries

The preclosing trial balance for the general fund of Kokomo is given below.

	Debit	Credit
Cash	$ 75,000	
Due from Motor Pool	17,600	
Inventory of Supplies	12,000	
Vouchers Payable		$ 42,000
Fund Balance Reserved for Inventories		12,000
Unreserved Fund Balance		36,000
Property Tax Revenue		953,000
Miscellaneous Revenue		24,600
Expenditures	928,000	
Operating Transfer Out to Library	35,000	
Estimated Revenues Control	965,000	
Appropriations Control		950,000
Encumbrances	21,000	
Budgetary Fund Balance Reserved for Encumbrances		21,000
Budgetary Fund Balance Unreserved		15,000
	$2,053,600	$2,053,600

Kokomo uses the consumption method of accounting for inventories, and the lapsing method of accounting for encumbrances.

Required

Prepare the closing entries for the general fund.

E18-10 Closing Entries and Balance Sheet

The preclosing trial balance at December 31, 19X1 for the general fund of Lone Wolf is given below.

	Debit	Credit
Cash	$ 90,000	
Property Taxes Receivable—Delinquent	100,000	
Allowance for Uncollectibles—Delinquent		$ 7,200
Due from Other Funds	14,600	
Vouchers Payable		65,000
Due to Other Funds		8,400
Unreserved Fund Balance		119,000
Property Tax Revenue		1,130,000
Miscellaneous Revenue		40,000
Expenditures	1,100,000	
Operating Transfer Out	40,000	
Residual Equity Transfers Out	25,000	
Estimated Revenues Control	1,200,000	
Appropriations Control		1,145,000
Estimated Residual Equity Transfer Out		25,000
Encumbrances	32,000	
Budgetary Fund Balance Reserved for Encumbrances		32,000
Budgetary Fund Balance Unreserved		30,000
	$2,601,600	$2,601,600

Lone Wolf uses the purchase method of accounting for inventories and the lapsing method of accounting for encumbrances.

Required

a. Prepare the closing entries for the general fund.
b. Prepare a general fund balance sheet at December 31, 19X1.

E18-11 Statement of Revenues, Expenditures, and Changes in Fund Balance

Refer to the preclosing trial balance in Exercise 18-10. Assume the balances on December 31, 19X0, were as follows:

Fund Balance Reserved for Encumbrances	$28,000
Unreserved Fund Balance	91,000

Required

Prepare a general fund statement of revenues, expenditures, and changes in fund balance for fiscal 19X1, showing actual figures only.

E18-12 Calculation of Property Tax Levy for Municipality [AICPA Adapted]

The comptroller of the city of Big River recently resigned. In the comptroller's absence, the deputy comptroller attempted to calculate the amount of money required to be raised from property taxes for the general fund for the fiscal year ending June 30, 19X1. The calculation is to be made as of January 1, 19X0, to serve as a basis for the following fiscal year. The mayor has requested you to review the deputy comptroller's calculations and to obtain other necessary information to prepare a formal statement for the general fund which will disclose the amount of money required to be raised from property taxes for the fiscal year ending June 30, 19X1. Following are the calculations prepared by the deputy comptroller:

City resources other than proposed tax levy:		
Estimated general fund working balance, January 1, 19X0		$ 352,000
Estimated receipts from property taxes		
(January 1, 19X0—June 30, 19X0)		2,222,000
Estimated revenues from investments		
(January 1, 19X0—June 30, 19X1)		442,000
Estimated proceeds from sale of general obligation		
bonds in August, 19X0		3,000,000
		$6,016,000
General fund requirements:		
Estimated expenditures (January 1, 19X0—June 30, 19X0)		$1,900,000
Proposed appropriations (July 1, 19X0—June 30, 19X1)		4,300,000
		$6,200,000

Additional information:

1. The general fund working balance required by the city council for July 1, 19X1, is $175,000.

2. Property tax collections are due in March and September of each year. Your review indicates that during the month of February, 19X0, estimated expenditures will exceed available funds by $200,000. Pending collection of property taxes in March 19X0, this deficiency will have to be met by the issuance of 30-day tax-anticipation notes of $200,000 at an estimated interest rate of 9 percent per year.

3. The proposed general obligation bonds will be issued by the city water fund, which is a separate enterprise fund, and will be used for the construction of a new water pumping station.

Required

Prepare a statement as of January 1, 19X0, calculating the property tax levy required for the City of Big River General Fund for the fiscal year ending June 30, 19X1.

PROBLEMS

P18-13 General Fund Entries [AICPA Adapted]

The following information was abstracted from the accounts of the general fund of the City of Noble after the books had been closed for the fiscal year ended June 30, 19X2:

	Postclosing Trial Balance, June 30, 19X1	Transactions July 1, 19X1–June 30, 19X2		Postclosing Trial Balance, June 30, 19X2
		Debit	Credit	
Cash	$700,000	$1,820,000	$1,852,000	$668,000
Taxes Receivable	40,000	1,870,000	1,828,000	82,000
	$740,000			$750,000
Allowance for Uncollectible				
Taxes	$ 8,000	8,000	10,000	$ 10,000
Vouchers Payable	132,000	1,852,000	1,840,000	120,000
Fund Balance:				
Reserve for				
Encumbrances			70,000	70,000
Unreserved	600,000	70,000	20,000	550,000
	$740,000			$750,000

Additional information:

The budget for the fiscal year ended June 30, 19X2, provided for estimated revenue of $2,000,000 and appropriations of $1,940,000. Encumbrances of $1,070,000 were made during the year.

Required

Prepare proper journal entries to record the budgeted and actual transactions for the fiscal year ended June 30, 19X2. Include closing entries.

P18-14   General Fund Entries

The following are some events and transactions related to the general fund of Mount Pleasant that took place during fiscal 19X2:

1. The budget included estimated revenue from property taxes, $925,000; sales taxes, $45,000; appropriations, $910,000; and estimated residual equity transfer out, $40,000.

2. Mount Pleasant uses the lapsing method of accounting for encumbrances. The appropriations included encumbrances of $14,000 from 19X1.

3. The property tax levy was $940,000, and estimated uncollectibles were $15,000.

4. Property taxes of $860,000 were collected; $4,500 was written off. Remaining receivables and allowance were reclassified from current to delinquent.

5. Received $48,000 sales tax revenue from the state.

6. Ordered a personal computer, $3,600.

7. The personal computer was received; actual cost was $3,750.

8. Made the residual equity transfer of $40,000 to establish a city motor pool.

9. Transferred $12,000 to the debt service fund to pay interest.

10. Received supplies (no encumbrances), $750. Supplies are charged to expenditures as acquired.

11. Loaned the motor pool fund $10,000 for 6 months.

12. Received a statement from the motor pool for $320 and paid the bill 2 weeks later.

Required

Prepare journal entries for the general fund to record these events and transactions.

P18-15   General Fund Entries [AICPA Adapted]

The trial balances shown below were taken from the accounts of the Omega City general fund before the books had been closed for the fiscal year ended June 30, 19X2.

	Trial Balance, July 1, 19X1	Trial Balance, June 30, 19X2
Cash	$400,000	$ 700,000
Taxes Receivable	150,000	170,000
Allowance for Uncollectible Taxes	(40,000)	(70,000)
Estimated Revenues Control	—	3,000,000
Expenditures	—	2,900,000
Encumbrances	—	91,000
	$510,000	$6,791,000
Vouchers Payable	$ 80,000	$ 408,000
Due to Other Funds	210,000	142,000
Fund Balance Reserved for Encumbrances	60,000	—
Unreserved Fund Balance	160,000	220,000
Revenue from Taxes	—	2,800,000
Miscellaneous Revenues	—	130,000
Appropriations Control	—	2,980,000
Budgetary Fund Balance Reserved for Encumbrances	—	91,000
Budgetary Fund Balance Unreserved	—	20,000
	$510,000	$6,791,000

Additional information:

1. The estimated taxes receivable for the year ended June 30, 19X2, were $2,870,000, and the taxes collected during the year totaled $2,810,000. Miscellaneous revenue of $130,000 was also collected during the year.

2. Encumbrances in the amount of $2,700,000 were recorded. In addition, the $60,000 of lapsed encumbrances from the 19X1 fiscal year was renewed.

3. During the year, the general fund was billed $142,000 for services performed on its behalf by other city funds (debit Expenditures).

4. An analysis of the transactions in the Vouchers Payable account for the year ended June 30, 19X2, is as follows:

	Debit (Credit)
Current expenditures (liquidating all encumbrances to date except for renewed 19X1 commitment)	$(2,700,000)
Expenditures applicable to previous year	(58,000)
Vouchers for payments to other funds	(210,000)
Cash payments during year	2,640,000
Net change	$ (328,000)

5. On May 10, 19X2, encumbrances were recorded for the purchase of next year's supplies at an estimated cost of $91,000.

Required

On the basis of the data presented, reconstruct the original detailed journal entries that were required to record all transactions for the fiscal year ended June 30, 19X2, including the recording of the current year's budget. Do not prepare closing entries for June 30, 19X2.

P18-16 General Fund Closing Entries and Statements

The unadjusted trial balance for the general fund of Quincy on June 30, 19X2, is given below.

	Debit	Credit
Cash	$ 100,000	
Property Taxes Receivable—Delinquent	108,000	
Allowance for Uncollectibles—Delinquent		$ 8,400
Due from Data Processing Fund	10,000	
Estimated Revenues Control	1,450,000	
Operating Transfers Out	25,000	
Residual Equity Transfers Out	50,000	
Encumbrances	23,000	
Expenditures	1,360,000	
Vouchers Payable		44,000
Due to Printing Service Fund		2,600
Property Tax Revenue		1,390,000
Grant Revenue		40,000
Miscellaneous Revenue		32,000
Appropriations Control		1,400,000
Estimated Residual Equity Transfers Out		50,000
Budgetary Fund Balance Reserved for Encumbrances		23,000
Unreserved Fund Balance		136,000
	$3,126,000	$3,126,000

Additional information:

1. Quincy uses the lapsing method for outstanding encumbrances. Fund Balance Reserved for Encumbrances on June 30, 19X1, was $28,300. The encumbrances were renewed.

2. Unreserved Fund Balance, June 30, 19X1, was $107,700.

3. Quincy uses the consumption method of accounting for inventories. There were no supplies on hand on June 30, 19X1. Supplies on hand on June 30, 19X2, cost $8,000.

Required

a. Prepare adjusting and closing entries for the general fund.
b. Prepare a balance sheet for the general fund as of June 30, 19X2.
c. Prepare a statement of revenues, expenditures, and changes in fund balance for fiscal 19X2, showing actual figures only.

P18-17   General Fund Entries and Statements

The balance sheet of the general fund of Ruby Valley on June 30, 19X1, is given below.

Ruby Valley
Balance Sheet—General Fund
June 30, 19X1

Assets

Cash		$103,000
Property Taxes Receivable—Delinquent	$ 80,000	
Less: Allowance for Uncollectibles—Delinquent	(8,000)	72,000
Inventory of Supplies		11,000
Total Assets		$186,000

Liabilities and Fund Balance

Vouchers Payable		$ 42,000
Fund Balance:		
Reserve for Encumbrances	$ 18,000	
Reserve for Inventories	11,000	
Unreserved	115,000	144,000
Total Liabilities and Fund Balance		$186,000

Budget and transaction information for fiscal 19X2 is as follows:

1. Estimated revenue:

Property taxes	$1,280,500
Grants	100,000
Miscellaneous	40,000

The property tax levy was $1,300,000, of which uncollectible taxes were estimated at $1\frac{1}{2}$ percent.

2. Appropriations were $1,320,000; estimated residual equity transfers out, $25,000; and estimated operating transfers out, $36,000. Ruby Valley uses the nonlapsing method to account for encumbrances. The appropriations included $50,000 for a new elevator.

3. Cash receipts were as follows:

Property taxes—delinquent	$ 69,000
Property taxes—current	1,245,000
Grants from the state	90,000
Miscellaneous revenue	46,000
Residual equity transfer from	
capital projects fund	30,000

The remaining property taxes from fiscal 19X1 were written off, and those remaining from 19X2 were reclassified. The allowance for uncollectibles for 19X2 was reduced to $7,500.

4. The general fund issued purchase orders totaling $1,296,000, of which $120,000 were outstanding at year-end. Actual expenditures were $1,200,000, including $20,000 for 19X1 encumbrances, $27,000 for supplies, and $45,000 for a new elevator. Vouchers paid totaled $1,187,000. The supplies on hand on June 30, 19X2, were $6,700. Ruby Valley uses the consumption method to account for inventories.

5. Other cash payments and transfers were as follows:

Operating transfer out	$40,000
Residual equity transfer out	25,000
Loan to the computer center	20,000

Required

a. Prepare entries to summarize the general fund budget and transactions for fiscal 19X2.

b. Prepare an unadjusted trial balance.

c. Prepare adjusting and closing entries for the general fund.

d. Prepare a balance sheet for the general fund as of June 30, 19X2.

e. Prepare a statement of revenues, expenditures, and changes in fund balance for fiscal 19X2, showing budget, actual, and variance amounts.

P18-18   General Fund Entries and Statements

The postclosing trial balance of the general fund of the town of Pine Ridge on December 31, 19X1, is as follows:

	Debit	Credit
Cash	$111,000	
Property Taxes Receivable—Delinquent	90,000	
Allowance for Uncollectibles—Delinquent		$ 9,000
Vouchers Payable		31,000
Fund Balance Reserved for Encumbrances		21,000
Unreserved Fund Balance		140,000
	$201,000	$201,000

Additional information related to 19X2:

1. Estimated revenue: property taxes, $1,584,000 from a tax levy of $1,600,000 of which 1 percent was estimated uncollectible; sales taxes, $250,000; and miscellaneous, $43,000. Appropriations totaled $1,800,000; estimated operating transfers out, $40,000; and estimated residual equity transfers out, $37,000. Appropriations included outstanding purchase orders from 19X1 of $21,000, and $40,000 for office furniture. Pine Ridge uses the lapsing method for outstanding encumbrances.

2. Cash receipts: property taxes, $1,590,000, including $83,000 from 19X1; sales taxes, $284,000; licenses and fees, $39,000; and a loan from the motor pool, $10,000. The remaining property taxes from 19X1 were written off, and those remaining from 19X2 were reclassified.

3. Orders were issued for $1,760,000 in addition to the acceptance of the $21,000 outstanding purchase orders from 19X1. A total of $48,000 of purchase orders still was

outstanding at the end of 19X2. Actual expenditures were $1,748,000, including $42,000 for office furniture. Vouchers paid totaled $1,753,000.

4. Other cash payments and transfers were as follows:

Loan to central stores	$13,000
Operating transfers out	40,000
Residual equity transfer out	37,000

Required

    a. Prepare entries to summarize the general fund budget and transactions for 19X2.
    b. Prepare a preclosing trial balance.
    c. Prepare closing entries for the general fund.
    d. Prepare a balance sheet for the general fund as of December 31, 19X2.
    e. Prepare a statement of revenues, expenditures, and changes in fund balance for 19X2, showing budget, actual, and variance amounts.

P18-19 General Fund Entries

The following financial activities affecting Johnson City's general fund took place during the year ended June 30, 19X1. The following budget was adopted:

Estimated revenue:	
Property taxes	$4,500,000
Licenses and permits	300,000
Fines	200,000
	$5,000,000
Appropriations:	
General government	$1,500,000
Police services	1,200,000
Fire department services	900,000
Public works services	800,000
Acquisition of fire engines	400,000
	$4,800,000

Additional information related to 19X1:

    1. Property tax bills totaling $4,650,000 were mailed. It was estimated that $300,000 of this amount would be delinquent and $150,000 would be uncollectible.
    2. Property taxes totaling $3,900,000 were collected. The $150,000 previously estimated to be uncollectible remained unchanged, but $750,000 was reclassified as delinquent. It is estimated that the delinquent taxes will be collected soon enough after June 30, 19X1, to make them available to finance obligations incurred during the year ended June 30, 19X1. There was no balance of uncollected taxes on July 1, 19X0.
    3. Tax anticipation notes in the face amount of $300,000 were issued.
    4. Other cash collections were as follows:

Licenses and permits	$270,000
Fines	200,000
Sale of public works equipment	
(original cost, $75,000)	15,000
	$485,000

5. The following purchase orders were executed:

	Total	Outstanding on June 30, 19X1
General government	$1,050,000	$ 60,000
Police services	300,000	30,000
Fire department services	150,000	15,000
Public works services	250,000	10,000
Fire engines	400,000	-0-
	$2,150,000	$115,000

No encumbrances were outstanding on June 30, 19X0.

6. The following vouchers were approved:

General government	$1,440,000
Police services	1,155,000
Fire department services	870,000
Public works services	700,000
Fire engines	400,000
	$4,565,000

7. Vouchers totaling $4,600,000 were paid.

Required

Prepare journal entries to record the foregoing financial activities in the general fund, assuming separate appropriation and expenditure accounts are maintained for each function of the city. Omit explanations. Ignore interest accruals.

P18-20   General Fund Entries [AICPA Adapted]

The general fund trial balance of the city of Prescott for December 31, 19X2, was as follows:

	Debits	**Credits**
Cash	$ 62,000	
Taxes Receivable—Delinquent	46,000	
Estimated Uncollectible Taxes—Delinquent		$ 8,000
Stores Inventory—Program Operations	18,000	
Vouchers Payable		28,000
Fund Balance Reserved for Stores Inventory		18,000
Fund Balance Reserved for Encumbrances		12,000
Unreserved Fund Balance		60,000
	$126,000	$126,000

Collectible delinquent taxes are expected to be collected within 60 days after the end of the year. Prescott uses the purchases method to account for stores inventory and the nonlapsing method to account for encumbrances outstanding from a prior year. The following data pertain to 19X3 general fund operations:

1. Budget adopted:

Revenue and other financing sources:	
Taxes	$220,000
Fines, forfeits, and penalties	80,000
Miscellaneous revenue	100,000
Share of bond issue proceeds	200,000
	$600,000

Expenditures and other financing uses:	
Program operations	$300,000
General administration	120,000
Stores—program operations	60,000
Capital outlay	80,000
Periodic transfer to capital projects fund	20,000
	$580,000

2. Taxes were assessed at an amount that would result in revenue of $220,800, after deduction of 4 percent of the tax levy as uncollectible.
3. Orders placed but not received:

Program operations	$176,000
General administration	80,000
Capital outlay	60,000
	$316,000

4. The city council designated $20,000 of the unreserved fund balance for possible future appropriation for capital outlay.

5. Cash collections and transfer:

Delinquent taxes	$ 38,000
Current taxes	226,000
Refund of overpayment of invoice for purchase of equipment	4,000
Fines, forfeits, and penalties	88,000
Miscellaneous revenue	90,000
Share of bond issue proceeds	200,000
Transfer of remaining fund balance of a discontinued fund	18,000
	$664,000

6. Eliminated encumbrances for items received:

	Estimated	Actual
Prior year—program operations	$ 12,000	$ 12,000
Program operations	144,000	154,000
General administration	84,000	80,000
Capital outlay	62,000	62,000
	$302,000	$308,000

7. Additional vouchers:

Program operations	$188,000
General administration	38,000
Capital outlay	18,000
Operating transfer to capital projects fund	20,000
	$264,000

8. Mr. Harris, a taxpayer, overpaid his 19X3 taxes by $2,000. He applied for a $2,000 credit against his 19X4 taxes. The city council granted his request.

9. Vouchers paid totaled $580,000.

10. Stores inventory on December 31, 19X3, amounted to $12,000.

Required

Prepare journal entries to record the effects of the presented data, assuming Prescott maintains separate appropriation and expenditure accounts for each function of the city. Omit explanations.

CHAPTER 19

GOVERNMENTAL ENTITIES: SPECIAL FUNDS AND ACCOUNT GROUPS

In addition to the general fund, discussed in Chapter 18, governments have a number of other funds and account groups. This chapter presents the accounting and financial reporting requirements for (1) the three remaining governmental funds, (2) the two proprietary funds, (3) the fiduciary funds, and (4) the two account groups. A local government uses as many of these special funds and account groups as necessary for its operations or as required by law. The typical fund organization for a local government is presented in Figure 19-1. In practice, the funds and account groups are often identified with the acronyms from the first letters of their titles, as follows:

Governmental funds:

GF	General fund
SRF	Special revenue funds
DSF	Debt service funds
CPF	Capital projects funds

Proprietary funds:

EF	Enterprise funds
ISF	Internal service funds

Fiduciary funds:

ETF	Expendable trust funds
NTF	Nonexpendable trust funds
PTF	Pension trust funds
AF	Agency funds

Account groups:

GFAAG	General fixed assets account group
GLTDAG	General long-term debt account group

FIGURE 19-1 Funds and account groups for a governmental entity.

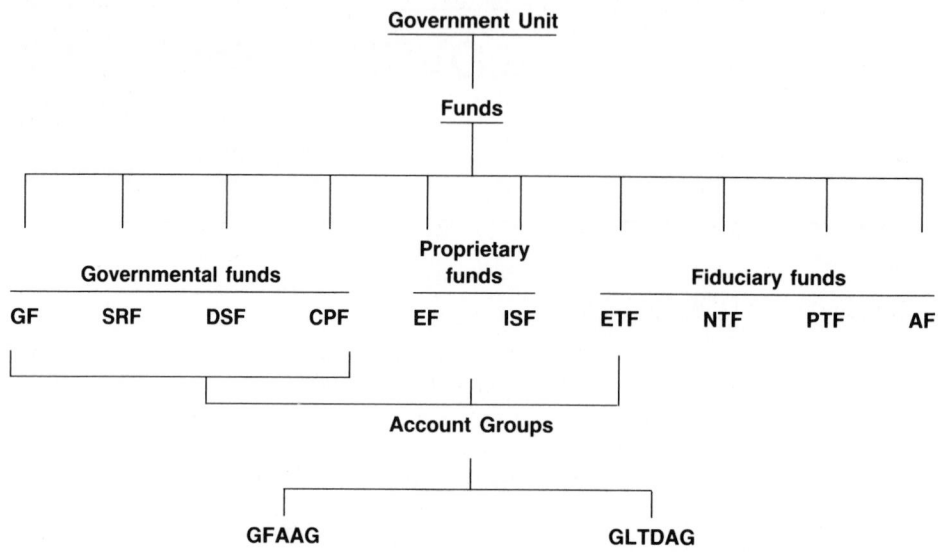

The "number of funds principle" is stated in the 1990 GASB codification as follows:

> Governmental units should establish and maintain those funds required by law and sound financial administration. Only the minimum number of funds consistent with legal and operating requirements should be established, however, because unnecessary funds result in inflexibility, undue complexity, and inefficient financial administration.[1]

A general rule followed in many governmental entities is that all activities should be accounted for in the general fund unless specifically required by law or GAAP to be accounted for in another fund. This rule does not prohibit the creation of additional funds, but places a reasonable restraint on the proliferation of additional funds. The structure of funds discussed in this chapter is the typical one used in most state and local government systems.

One event may require entries in several funds and account groups. For example, the construction of a new municipal building through the issuance of general obligation bonds requires entries in a capital projects fund, a debt service fund, the general fixed assets account group, and the general long-term debt account group. In addition, interfund transactions require entries in two or more funds.

This chapter continues the example of Sol City started in Chapter 18, where the entries and financial reports for the general fund were presented for 19X2. Sol

---

[1] Governmental Accounting Standards Board, *Codification of Governmental Accounting and Financial Reporting Standards*, 3d ed., 1990, Section 1100.104, p. 34.

City uses the lapsing method of accounting for encumbrances, the consumption method for inventories, and records all expected budgetary accounts, including anticipated interfund transactions. The techniques of capitalizing all budgetary accounts, and recording journal entries at the control level, are continued from Chapter 18. The final section of this chapter presents comprehensive financial reports for Sol City.

Figure 19-2 presents an overview of the major accounting and financial standards for the individual funds and account groups. This figure can be used as a continual reference point during study of Chapter 19.

SPECIAL REVENUE FUNDS

Some government resources may be restricted for specific purposes, such as construction of the state highway system, maintenance of public parks, or operation of the public school system, city libraries, and museums. The necessary revenue often comes from special tax levies or federal or state government grants. Some minor revenue may be earned through user charges, but these charges are usually not sufficient to fully fund the service. *Special revenue funds* are used to account for such restricted resources. The governmental entity has a separate special revenue fund for each different activity of this type. Thus, a city may have several special revenue funds.

Accounting for special revenue funds is the same as for the general fund. The modified accrual basis of accounting is used, no fixed assets or depreciation are recorded in a special revenue fund, the operating budget is typically recorded in the accounts, and no long-term debt is recorded in a special revenue fund. The financial reports are the same as for the general fund: the balance sheet; and the statement of revenues, expenditures, and changes in fund balance, both actual only and a budget versus actual comparison.

Special revenue fund accounting and financial reporting are not illustrated in the chapter because the principles were covered in Chapter 18 in the discussion of the general fund. The focus of this chapter is on the unique or interesting aspects of governmental accounting and financial reporting.

CAPITAL PROJECTS FUNDS

Capital projects funds account for the acquisition or construction of major capital facilities or improvements that benefit the public. Examples are the construction of libraries, civic centers, fire stations, courthouses, bridges, major streets, and city municipal buildings. A separate capital projects fund is created at the time the project is approved and ceases at the completion of the project. Each project or group of related projects is accounted for in a separate capital projects fund.

Accounting for capital projects funds is similar to accounting for the general fund. The modified accrual basis of accounting is used, no fixed assets or depreciation are recorded in the capital projects funds, and no long-term debt is recorded in these funds. Capital projects funds, however, typically do not have

FIGURE 19-2 Overview of accounting and financial reporting for individual funds and account groups.

	Governmental Type Funds				Proprietary Funds		Fiduciary Funds	
	General Fund	Special Revenue Funds	Capital Projects Funds	Debt Service Funds	Enterprise Funds	Internal Service Funds	Non-expendable Trust Funds	Expendable Trust and Agency Funds
Measurement focus	Expendability	Expendability	Expendability	Expendability	Capital maintenance	Capital maintenance	Capital maintenance	Expendability
Basis of accounting	Modified accrual	Modified accrual	Modified accrual	Modified accrual	Accrual	Accrual	Accrual	Modified accrual
Budgetary basis recorded(a)	Operating budget recorded	Operating budget recorded	Capital budget usually not recorded	Perhaps	None recorded	None recorded	None recorded	Perhaps
Long-term productive assets (buildings, equipment, etc.) recorded	No	No	No	No	Yes	Yes	Yes	No
Long-term debt recorded	No	No	No	No	Yes	Yes	Yes	No
Encumbrances	Yes	Yes	Yes	No	No	No	No	Possibly
Financial statements:								
Balance sheet	X	X	X	X	X	X	X	X
Revenues, expenditures, and changes in fund balance	X	X	X	X				
Revenues, expenditures, and changes in fund balance—budget and actual(b)	X	X	X	Perhaps				
Revenues, expenses, and changes in retained earnings					X	X		
Revenues, expenses, and changes in fund balance							X	X (trust)
Statement of cash flows					X	X	X	
Changes in assets and liabilities								X (agency)

Nonfund Account Groups

General Fixed Assets Account Group	General Long-Term Debt Account Group
Schedule of assets	Schedule of amount available for repayment
Schedule of resources used to acquire assets	Schedule of amount to be provided for repayment
	Schedule of the maturity value of general-obligation long-term debt

(a)Budgetary accounts are used when a legally adopted annual operating budget is passed. Debt service funds typically do not use operating budgets. Expendable trusts may have an operating budget. Agency funds typically do not record budgets.

(b)The statement of revenues, expenditures, and changes in fund balances, budget and actual, is required for funds with a legally adopted annual operating budget.

annual operating budgets. A capital budget is prepared as a basis for selling bonds to finance a project, and the capital budget is the control mechanism for the length of the project. The capital budget for the project may, or may not, be formally recorded in the accounts. Theoretically, encumbrances are part of the budgetary system and encumbrances should flow from the appropriating authority of the budget. However, encumbrances may be recorded even if the capital project budget is not recorded. Encumbrances maintain an ongoing accounting record of the expenditure commitments that have been made on a project. The reserve for encumbrances reported on the periodic balance sheet for the capital projects fund can be determined from the information in the recorded budgetary encumbrance accounts.

The capital projects fund records capital outlays as expenditures. Thus, no fixed assets are recorded in this fund. A record of the construction in progress, however, may be maintained in the general fixed assets account group.

The financial statements for capital projects funds are the balance sheet and the statement of revenues, expenditures, and changes in fund balance. Note that no budget and actual comparison operating statement is required because capital projects funds typically prepare capital budgets on a project basis rather than an annual basis. If the capital projects fund does prepare and have a legally adopted annual operating budget, then a budget-actual operating statement would have to be prepared.

Illustration of Transactions

On January 1, 19X2, Sol City establishes a capital projects fund to account for a capital addition to the municipal courthouse. The expected cost of the addition is $120,000. A $100,000, 10 percent general obligation bond issue is sold at 102, for total proceeds of $102,000. The bond is a 5-year serial bond with equal amounts of $20,000 to be paid each year, until the debt is extinguished. The bond proceeds are not revenue to the capital projects fund; they are reported in the other financing sources section of the statement of revenues, expenditures, and changes in fund balance. Sol City chose not to formally enter the project budget into the accounts, but does use an encumbrance system for control over project expenditures.

The capital projects fund is not entitled to the $2,000 premium on the sale of bonds. This premium is transferred as an operating transfer out to the debt service fund immediately upon receipt. The debt service fund records the receipt of the transfer as an operating transfer in (see entry 15 later in this chapter). The premium is viewed as an adjustment of the interest rate, not as a part of the funds expendable by the capital projects fund. If bonds are sold at a discount, either the amount expended for the improvement must be decreased or the general fund must make up the difference to par.

In addition, a federal grant for $10,000 is received as financial support for part of the capital addition, and the capital projects fund receives an operating transfer of $20,000 from the city's general fund. Recall that an operating transfer is an interfund transaction in which resources are moved from one fund, usually from the general fund, to another fund to be used for the operations of the receiving fund. The general fund records this transfer of $20,000 as an operating transfer out (see entry 36 in Chapter 18). The following entries are recorded for the 19X2 fiscal year.

Capital Projects Revenue and Bond Proceeds   The sale of the bonds and receipt of the federal grant and operating transfer in are recorded as follows:

(1)	Cash	102,000	
	Other Financing Sources—Bond Issue Proceeds		102,000
	Issue $100,000 of bonds at 102.		
(2)	Operating Transfer Out to Debt Service Fund	2,000	
	Cash		2,000
	Forward bond premium to debt service fund.		
(3)	Cash	10,000	
	Revenue—Federal Grant		10,000
	Received federal grant to be applied to courthouse addition.		
(4)	Due from General Fund	20,000	
	Operating Transfer In from General Fund		20,000
	Establish receivable for transfer in from general fund.		
(5)	Cash	20,000	
	Due from General Fund		20,000
	Receive transferred resources from general fund.		

Entry (3) recognizes the $10,000 grant from the federal government as revenue at the time the grant is received. Some grants from the federal government are termed "expenditure-driven" grants, for which revenue can be recognized only as expenditures are incurred in conformity with the grant agreement. For these expenditure-driven grants, the local government unit credits a deferred revenue, instead of revenue, at the time of receipt of the grant, and then recognizes the revenue from the grant as approved expenditures are made.

Capital Projects Fund Expenditures   The following encumbrances, expenditures, and disbursements are recorded in 19X2:

(6)	ENCUMBRANCES	110,000	
	BUDGETARY FUND BALANCE RESERVED FOR ENCUMBRANCES		110,000
	Issue construction contract for $100,000.		
(7)	BUDGETARY FUND BALANCE RESERVED FOR ENCUMBRANCES	110,000	
	ENCUMBRANCES		110,000
	Project is completed and reverse reserve for encumbrances.		

(8)	Expenditures	118,000	
	Contract Payable		108,000
	Contract Payable—Retained Percentage		10,000
	Actual construction cost of courthouse		
	addition is $118,000. Additional cost		
	is approved. Contract terms include retained		
	percentage of $10,000 until full and final		
	acceptance of project.		
(9)	Expenditures	6,000	
	Vouchers Payable		6,000
	Additional items for courthouse addition.		
(10)	Vouchers Payable	6,000	
	Contract Payable	108,000	
	Cash		114,000
	Pay current portion of construction		
	contract and vouchers.		

In entry (8), Contract Payable is credited for $108,000 for the current portion due, and Contract Payable—Retained Percentage is credited for $10,000. In entry (10), the $108,000 current portion of the contract liability is paid in full. A normal practice of government units is to have a retained percentage of the total amount due under a construction contract held back to ensure that the contractor fully completes the project to the satisfaction of the governmental unit. For example, a city may stipulate that 10 percent of the total contract price is retained until the project is fully completed and accepted. This retainage payable is released and paid upon final acceptance of the project by the government unit.

Closing Entries in the Capital Projects Fund   The nominal accounts are closed with the following entries:

(11)	Revenue—Federal Grant	10,000	
	Unreserved Fund Balance	114,000	
	Expenditures		124,000
	Close operating accounts of revenue and		
	expenditures.		
(12)	Other Financing Sources—Bond Issue Proceeds	102,000	
	Unreserved Fund Balance		102,000
	Close other financing sources.		
(13)	Operating Transfer In from General Fund	20,000	
	Operating Transfer Out to Debt Service Fund		2,000
	Unreserved Fund Balance		18,000
	Close interfund transfers.		

No encumbrances are outstanding as of the end of the fiscal year. At this point, the Unreserved Fund Balance account has a credit balance of $6,000. Upon completion and final approval of a capital project, the remaining fund balance is transferred either to the general fund or to the debt service fund, depending on the policy of the government unit. The transfer is a residual equity transfer out for the capital projects fund and a residual equity transfer in for the receiving fund because it involves the one-time transfer of the remaining equity in the capital projects fund. In the example above, Sol City decided that the fund should remain open through the first part of the next fiscal year in case any minor modifications of the new courthouse addition are required. If no further modifications are required, and the courthouse addition project is officially accepted, the $10,000 in the Contract Payable—Retained Percentage account is paid to the contractor. Any remaining resources in the capital projects fund are transferred and the capital projects fund is closed.

Financial Statements for Capital Projects Funds

The financial statements for capital projects funds are a balance sheet and the statement of revenues, expenditures, and changes in fund balance. Note that no budget versus actual operating statement is required because the capital projects fund typically uses a capital budget rather than an operating budget. The balance sheet and statement of revenues, expenditures, and changes in fund balance for 19X2, the first year of the capital project's existence, are presented in Figures 19-3 and 19-4, respectively.

The Sol City capital projects fund was created on January 1, 19X2, the date the capital addition was approved and the serial bonds were sold. The only asset remaining after construction is completed is $6,000 of cash. The $102,000 of proceeds from the bond issue is reported among other financing sources in Figure 19-4, with a reduction for the transfer of the $2,000 premium to the debt service fund, and the transfer in of $20,000, netting out the large excess of expenditures over revenue in the amount of $114,000. The statement of revenues, expenditures, and changes in fund balance reconciles to the $6,000 unreserved fund balance at the end of the fiscal period.

DEBT SERVICE FUNDS

Debt service funds account for the accumulation and use of resources for the payment of general long-term debt principal and interest. A government may have several types of general long-term debt obligations, as follows:

1. *Serial Bonds.* The most common form of debt issued by governments is in the form of serial bonds. The bonds are repaid in installments over the life of the debt. A serial bond is called "regular" if the installments are equal, "irregular" if they are not equal.

2. *Term Bonds.* This form of debt is less frequent now than in the past. The entire principal of the debt is due at the maturity date.

3. *Special Assessment Bonds.* Special assessment bonds are secured by tax liens on the property located within the government unit. Typically the government unit also becomes obligated in some manner to assume the payment of the debt in the event of default by the property owners. Special assessment bonds

FIGURE 19-3 Capital projects fund balance sheet as of the end of the fiscal period.

Sol City
Capital Projects Fund
Balance Sheet
December 31, 19X2

Assets:		
Cash		$16,000
Total Assets		$16,000
Liabilities and Fund Balance:		
Contracts Payable—Retained Percentage		$10,000
Fund Balance:		
Unreserved	$6,000	$ 6,000
Total Liabilities and Fund Balance		$16,000

FIGURE 19-4 Capital projects fund statement of revenues, expenditures, and changes in fund balance for fiscal 19X2.

Sol City
Capital Projects Fund
Statement of Revenues, Expenditures, and
Changes in Fund Balance
For Fiscal Year Ended December 31, 19X2

Revenue:	
Grants	$ 10,000
Total Revenue	$ 10,000
Expenditures:	
Capital Outlay:	
Buildings	$ 124,000
Total Expenditures	$ 124,000
Excess of Expenditures over Revenues	$(114,000)
Other Financing Sources (Uses):	
Proceeds of General Obligation Bonds	102,000
Operating Transfer Out to Debt Service Fund	(2,000)
Operating Transfer In from General Fund	20,000
Excess of Revenue and Other Sources over Expenditures and Other Uses	$ 6,000
Increase in Unreserved Fund Balance	$ 6,000
Unreserved Fund Balance, January 1	-0-
Unreserved Fund Balance, December 31	$ 6,000

may be used to finance capital projects, or to acquire other assets, such as ambulances or fire engines, necessary to operate the government unit. Special assessment bonds sold to acquire enterprise fund assets, however, should be accounted for within the enterprise fund. The special assessment feature simply states the source of financing and means of repayment.

4. *Notes and Warrants.* These consist of debt typically issued for 1 or 2 years. These debts are usually secured by specific tax revenue, which may be used only to repay the debt. Property tax anticipation warrants are an example.

5. *Capital Leases.* Government units must record capital leases in accordance with generally accepted accounting principles. These leases then become long-term liabilities of the government unit.

Some government units service long-term debt directly from the general fund, thereby eliminating the need for a debt service fund as a separate fiscal, accounting, and reporting entity. However, if a government entity has several long-term general obligations outstanding, it may be required by bond indentures or other regulations to establish a separate debt service fund for each obligation to account for the proper servicing of that debt.

The accounting and financial reporting for debt service funds are the same as for the general fund. The modified accrual basis of accounting is used, and only that portion of the long-term debt that has matured and is currently payable is recorded in the debt service funds. At the time of issue, the long-term debt is recorded in the general long-term debt account group (GLTDAG). Often, entries in the debt service fund must be coordinated with entries in the GLTDAG. As debt is paid off, the expenditure is recorded in the debt service fund and a related entry is made in the GLTDAG to record the reduction in the government entity's outstanding debt. The separation of the servicing of the debt from the record keeping of the total debt outstanding provides an additional locus of administrative control and management over a critical area for governmental entities.

Interest payable on long-term debt is not accrued; interest is recognized as a liability only when it comes due and payable. The "when due" recognition of interest matches the debt service expenditures with the resources accumulated to repay the debt. This approach prevents an understatement of the debt service fund balance. For example, if interest is accrued before it is actually due, the fund balance may show a deficit because of the excess of liabilities over assets. The function of the debt service fund is to accumulate resources to pay debt principal and interest as they become due. Thus, the when-due recognition of interest is consistent with the fund's objectives.

Illustration of Transactions

Sol City establishes a debt service fund to service the $100,000, 5-year, 10 percent serial bond issued on January 1, 19X2, to finance the capital project courthouse addition. The bond initially sold at a premium of $2,000. The resources to pay the bond principal and interest as they become due will be obtained from a property tax levy specifically for debt service.

Adoption of Debt Service Fund Budget   Debt service funds are not required to adopt annual operating budgets because the fund's expenditures are generally mandated by bond agreements and an operating budget may be viewed as unnecessarily redundant. Nevertheless, there is no restriction against having an operating budget for the debt service fund as part of a comprehensive budgeting system for a government entity, as illustrated below.

The annual operating budget for the debt service fund is adopted at the time the fund is created to service the serial bonds sold for the courthouse addition. Appropriations of $30,000 are budgeted to pay $20,000 of maturing principal and $10,000 of interest for the year. Sol City budgets all expected interfund transactions, and the anticipated operating transfer in of the $2,000 premium on the serial bonds sold is part of the entry to record the budget.

(14)	ESTIMATED REVENUES CONTROL	30,000	
	ESTIMATED OPERATING TRANSFER IN	2,000	
	APPROPRIATIONS CONTROL		30,000
	BUDGETARY FUND BALANCE UNRESERVED		2,000
	Adopt budget for 19X2.		

The budgetary accounts ESTIMATED REVENUES CONTROL and APPROPRIATIONS CONTROL are used to account for servicing serial bonds.

Debt Service Fund Revenue and Other Financing Sources   The debt service fund obtains revenue from a specified property tax levy in this example. The bond premium received from the capital projects fund is recognized as an operating transfer in. Note that the capital projects fund records this transfer as an operating transfer out (see entry 2 earlier in this chapter). The entries to record the receipt of the bond premium and the levy and collection of taxes are as follows:

(15)	Cash	2,000	
	Operating Transfer In from Capital Projects Fund		2,000
	Receive bond premium from capital projects fund.		
(16)	Property Taxes Receivable	35,000	
	Allowance for Uncollectible Taxes		5,000
	Revenue—Property Tax		30,000
	Levy property taxes and provide for		
	allowance for uncollectible taxes.		
(17)	Cash	30,000	
	Property Taxes Receivable		30,000
	Receive portion of property taxes.		
(18)	Property Taxes Receivable—Delinquent	5,000	
	Allowance for Uncollectible Taxes	5,000	
	Property Taxes Receivable		5,000
	Revenue—Property Tax		3,000
	Allowance for Uncollectible Taxes—Delinquent		2,000
	Reclassify remaining property taxes as delinquent		
	and reduce allowance for uncollectible taxes		
	from $5,000 to $2,000.		

Debt Service Fund Expenditures   The primary expenditures of the debt service fund are for the first annual payment of principal and for interest on the serial bonds payable. An encumbrance system is typically not used for matured principal and interest because the debt agreement serves as the expenditure control mechanism.

(19)	Expenditures	20,000	
	Matured Bonds Payable		20,000
	Recognize matured portion of serial bond: $100,000 ÷ 5 years		
(20)	Expenditures	10,000	
	Matured Interest Payable		10,000
	Recognize interest due this period: $100,000 × .10 × 1 year		
(21)	Matured Bonds Payable	20,000	
	Matured Interest Payable	10,000	
	Cash		30,000
	Pay first year's installment plus interest on bond.		
(22)	Expenditures	2,000	
	Vouchers Payable		2,000
	Incur other expenditures for supplies and miscellaneous items.		
(23)	Vouchers Payable	1,000	
	Cash		1,000
	Pay approved vouchers; remaining vouchers not yet approved.		

Closing Entries in the Debt Service Fund   The nominal accounts are closed as follows:

(24)	APPROPRIATIONS CONTROL	30,000	
	BUDGETARY FUND BALANCE UNRESERVED	2,000	
	ESTIMATED REVENUES CONTROL		30,000
	ESTIMATED OPERATING TRANSFER IN		2,000
	Close budgetary accounts.		
(25)	Revenue—Property Tax	33,000	
	Expenditures		32,000
	Unreserved Fund Balance		1,000
	Close operating revenue and expenditures.		
(26)	Operating Transfer In from Capital Projects Fund	2,000	
	Unreserved Fund Balance		2,000
	Close interfund transfer.		

If the debt service fund services term bonds, a different budgetary account system is used. The following budgetary entry would be made for term bonds for the periods prior to the maturity date:

REQUIRED CONTRIBUTIONS		XXX
REQUIRED EARNINGS		X
BUDGETARY FUND BALANCE UNRESERVED		XXX

The budgetary amounts are determined based on a computation of the contributions needed each period to be invested, earning a given return to accumulate to the amount required for the payment of the bonds. The debt service fund would then receive resources from the general fund or from a tax levy, which it would invest until the term bonds became due. In the period the term bonds reach maturity, the debt service fund pays the matured principal and interest from its available resources. The debt service fund reports its investments as an asset of the fund because this fund is expected to invest any excess cash in temporary investments in order to maximize the return from its resources. Most temporary investments are made in low-risk U.S. Treasury securities or in certificates of deposit from large banks. Interest income is accrued as earned.

Financial Statements for Debt Service Funds

The financial statements of the debt service fund are the same as required for the general fund. The balance sheet and statement of revenues, expenditures, and changes in fund balance are presented in Figures 19-5 and 19-6. The fund was created on January 1, 19X2, the date the serial bonds were sold. The Over (Under) Budget variance column in the statement of revenues, expenditures, and changes in fund balance shows an excess of revenue over expenditures of $1,000. This may be computed as the $3,000 in revenue over budget less the $2,000 in expenditures over budget. The actual column shows the reconciliation to the $3,000 ending balance in the unreserved fund account.

FIGURE 19-5 Debt service fund balance sheet as of the end of the fiscal period.

Sol City
Debt Service Fund
Balance Sheet
December 31, 19X2

Assets:		
Cash		$1,000
Property Taxes Receivable—Delinquent	$5,000	
Less: Allowance for Uncollectibles—Delinquent	(2,000)	3,000
Total Assets		$4,000
Liabilities and Fund Balance:		
Vouchers Payable		$1,000
Fund Balance:		
Unreserved	$3,000	3,000
Total Liabilities and Fund Balance		$4,000

FIGURE 19-6 Debt service fund statement of revenues, expenditures, and changes in fund balance—budget and actual, for fiscal 19X2.

Sol City
Debt Service Fund
Statement of Revenues, Expenditures, and Changes
in Fund Balance—Budget and Actual
For Fiscal Year Ended December 31, 19X2

	Budget	Actual	Over (Under) Budget
Revenue:			
Property Taxes	$30,000	$33,000	$3,000
Total Revenue	$30,000	$33,000	$3,000
Expenditures:			
Miscellaneous	$ -0-	$ 2,000	$2,000
Debt Service:			
Principal Retirement	20,000	20,000	-0-
Interest Charges	10,000	10,000	-0-
Total Expenditures	$30,000	$32,000	$2,000
Excess of Revenue over Expenditures	$ -0-	$ 1,000	$1,000
Other Financing Sources (Uses):			
Operating Transfer In from Capital Projects Fund	2,000	2,000	-0-
Increase in Unreserved Fund Balance	$ 2,000	$ 3,000	$1,000
Unreserved Fund Balance, January 1	-0-	-0-	-0-
Unreserved Fund Balance, December 31	$ 2,000	$ 3,000	$1,000

GENERAL FIXED ASSETS ACCOUNT GROUP (GFAAG)

The *general fixed assets account group* is not a fund; it does not receive or expend resources. It is simply a self-balancing accounting record of fixed assets belonging to the government unit that were acquired by the expendable funds: the general fund, special revenue funds, capital projects funds, debt service funds, and expendable trust funds. Recall that these funds record the acquisition of fixed assets by recording a current expenditure. The capital maintenance funds—enterprise funds, internal service funds, and nonexpendable trust funds—record fixed assets in their own funds.

Only fixed assets, such as buildings and equipment, are recorded in the GFAAG. Records of financial assets, such as investments in bonds or other securities, are maintained in the individual funds. The general fixed assets account group includes the following records:

1. A listing of the major types of fixed assets, such as land, buildings, improvements, machinery, and construction in progress.

2. A record of the source of the funds used to acquire each asset, including the name of the fund from which the resources were expended.

According to the sixth principle of governmental accounting presented in the 1990 GASB codification, the basis of fixed assets is cost. Donated assets are recorded at their market values on the date of receipt.

Government units may obtain assets through purchases, construction, gift, or by one of the methods unique to governmental entities: foreclosure for nonpayment of taxes, eminent domain for public access needs, and escheat for assets unclaimed after a sufficient time interval by their owners. Property records are maintained for each item of property owned by the government. Evidence of this record is usually by inventory tag attached to each item. Subsidiary property ledgers are maintained by (1) type or class of property, (2) organization unit in which the property is located, and (3) function and activity served by the property. Automated inventory systems can be organized to record all increases in property by a multidigit inventory number that registers all necessary information at the time the asset is brought into the government unit. Annual property inventories are taken to discern the current state of the property items.

Governmental accounting principles make it optional for local governments to record infrastructure assets such as roads, bridges, curbs and gutters, streets and sidewalks, drainage systems, and lighting systems. This exception is provided to reduce the amount of bookkeeping required in the general fixed assets account group for assets that have little risk of being lost or stolen.

Illustration of Accounting in General Fixed Assets Account Group

Sol City records in the general fixed assets account group all fixed assets acquired by expendable funds except infrastructure assets such as sidewalks and streets. As of January 1, 19X2, the city owns the following assets:

Asset	Original Cost
Buildings	$400,000
Improvements other than buildings	25,000
Machinery and equipment	185,000
Total	$610,000

All these assets were acquired from general fund revenue.

Depreciation is generally not recorded in the general fixed assets account group, because government units are concerned with the expendability of funds, not measuring income. However, the seventh governmental accounting principle provides that a record of accumulated depreciation may be kept in the general fixed assets group if the governing body finds depreciation records helpful for decision making. If accumulated depreciation is recorded in the general fixed assets group, the debit is to Investment in General Fixed Assets and the credit is to Accumulated Depreciation. Sol City, like most government units, does not report accumulated depreciation.

The general fixed assets group is typically just a record of the acquisition value of the assets acquired by the government. The cost of each asset is retained in the record until the asset is retired, at which time the acquisition entry is reversed.

During 19X2, Sol City had the following long-term asset transactions:

1. Acquisition of a new fire truck by the general fund. The general fund records an expenditure of $58,000 for the purchase of a new fire truck that is financed from general revenues (see entry 33 in Chapter 18).

2. Construction of a courthouse addition in the capital projects fund. The capital projects fund records expenditures of $124,000 for the construction of the courthouse addition (see entries 8 and 9 earlier in this chapter). The capital projects fund receives its resources from the following sources: (*a*) $100,000 from the issuance of bonds; (*b*) $20,000 as an operating transfer in from the general fund, of which $14,000 is expended and $6,000 still remains in the capital projects fund; and (*c*) $10,000 as a federal government grant.

3. Sale for $2,000 of old office equipment that had an original cost of $10,000. The general fund records the $2,000 as miscellaneous revenue (see entry 22 in Chapter 18).

Assets Acquired   Entries to record the increase in property items during the year are as follows:

(27)	Machinery and Equipment	58,000	
	Investment in General Fixed Assets—From		
	General Fund Revenue		58,000
	Record acquisition of fire truck.		
(28)	Buildings	124,000	
	Investment in General Fixed Assets—		
	From Capital Projects Fund Bond Receipts		100,000
	Investment in General Fixed Assets—From		
	General Fund Revenue		14,000
	Investment in General Fixed Assets—From		
	Federal Government Grant		10,000
	Record courthouse addition.		

Any assets received as gifts would be recorded at their fair market values by a debit to the specific asset and a credit to Investment in General Fixed Assets—Gifts. Sol City did not receive any donated assets during the year.

It is possible to record assets still under construction at the end of a fiscal period. These are reported as Construction in Progress with the fund source also identified, as follows:

Construction in Progress	XXX	
Investment in General Fixed Assets—(source of resources)		XXX

This assures a contemporary record in the general fixed assets account group of all properties of the government entity, even partially completed ones. Upon completion of construction, the following entry is made:

Buildings (or other asset type)	XXX	
Construction in Progress		XXX

Sol City did not have any assets under construction at the end of the year.

Assets Retired During 19X2, Sol City sells old office equipment. The general fund had acquired the assets a number of years ago at an initial cost of $10,000. The equipment is sold at public auction at a price of $2,000. The general fund receives and records the $2,000 as miscellaneous revenue.

In cases of material receipts from the sales of retired assets, the general fund should record the proceeds as a credit to Other Financing Sources—Sales of Retired Assets. However, when the proceeds are very small, and not expected to be recurring, the general fund can record these receipts as miscellaneous revenue.

The entry in the general fixed assets account group to record the disposal is:

(29) Investment in General Fixed Assets—From		
General Fund Revenue	10,000	
Machinery and Equipment		10,000
Record retirement of office equipment.		

Note that this is simply the reversal of the entry that was recorded when the asset was acquired. The selling price is not relevant for the entry in the general fixed assets account group.

Financial Statement for General Fixed Assets Account Group

The general fixed assets account group reports a schedule of the fixed assets at the end of the fiscal year. This schedule lists the types of assets, followed by a listing of the sources of assets. The schedule for Sol City's general fixed assets account group is presented in Figure 19-7.

FIGURE 19-7 Schedule of general fixed assets as of the end of the fiscal year.

Sol City
Schedule of General Fixed Assets
December 31, 19X2

General Fixed Assets:	
Buildings	$524,000
Improvements Other Than Buildings	25,000
Machinery and Equipment	233,000
Total General Fixed Assets	$782,000
Investments in General Fixed Assets from:	
General Fund Revenue	$672,000
Capital Projects Fund Bond Receipts	100,000
Federal Government Grants	10,000
Total Investments in General Fixed Assets	$782,000

GENERAL LONG-TERM DEBT ACCOUNT GROUP (GLTDAG)

The *general long-term debt account group* is an accounting record of all general long-term obligations of the government unit, except for the long-term obligations accounted for in the capital maintenance funds: the enterprise funds, the internal service funds, and the nonexpendable trust funds. Recall that expendable funds record the proceeds of a bond issuance under "Other Financing Sources—Bond Issue Proceeds." Thus, the GLTDAG is necessary because the expendable funds do not record long-term debt. In addition, the GLTDAG is necessary to ensure that the government unit does not exceed its legal debt limit, which is usually stated as a percentage of the assessed value of taxable properties, and that a full and complete record of the maturing principal on the government entity's long-term debt is maintained.

The general long-term debt account group is not a fund; it does not receive or expend resources. It is only an accounting record of the following items:

1. The amount of financial resources available in the debt service fund for the retirement of the principal of long-term debt.

2. The amount remaining to be provided for the retirement of long-term debt principal.

3. The unmatured principal of general long-term bonds, notes, warrants, capitalized leases, and other long-term debt of the government unit. Note that just the unmatured principal is recorded in the GLTDAG; the matured portion of the principal and the matured interest on the debt is recorded in the debt service fund. Current liabilities are recorded in the appropriate funds.

The par or maturity value is the amount recorded in the GLTDAG even if bonds are issued at a discount or premium. However, the use of deep-discount bonds by some government units has created an exception to the general rule of not recording discounts. *Deep-discount bonds* are issued at stated interest rates that are significantly lower than effective interest rates, resulting in a significant discount from the face value of the bonds. Governmental accounting standards specify that when the stated interest rate is less than 75 percent of the effective interest rate, the bonds should be classified in the deep-discount category. Deep-discount bonds are presented in the GLTDAG at face value less the discount. The discount is then amortized over the life of the bond using either the effective-interest method or the straight-line method of amortization.

The general long-term debt account group is a companion record to the debt service fund, which is responsible for servicing debt principal and interest. This relationship is most evident in the requirement for the general long-term debt account group to record separately the amount of financial resources available in the debt service funds to extinguish the principal of the long-term debt.

Illustration of Accounting in General Long-Term Debt Account Group

Sol City has a general long-term debt account group to record its general obligations. At the beginning of 19X2, the city had no outstanding long-term debt. During 19X2, Sol City had the following transactions affecting long-term debt:

1. On January 1, 19X2, $100,000 par value of 5-year serial bonds are issued to finance the courthouse addition. The bond is sold at $102,000 and the $2,000 premium is immediately transferred from the capital projects fund to the debt service fund. The capital projects fund records the proceeds from the bond under "Other Financing Sources—Bond Issue Proceeds" (see entries 1 and 2 earlier in this chapter).

2. During 19X2, the debt service fund receives $35,000 in resources, of which $23,000 is available to service the principal on the serial bonds.

3. The first installment of $20,000 of principal becomes due on the serial bonds and is paid by the debt service fund. The debt service fund records an expenditure for the $20,000 due and payable on the principal of the bond (see entry 19 earlier in this chapter).

General Obligation Debt Issued   The issuance of the $100,000 par value serial bonds to finance the capital project courthouse addition is recorded in the GLTDAG as:

(30)	Amount to Be Provided for Payment of		
	Serial Debt Principal	100,000	
	Serial Bonds Principal Payable		100,000
	Issue 5-year serial bonds.		

Amount Available in Debt Service Fund   The relationship between the general long-term debt account group and the debt service fund is shown by the following required entry in the GLTDAG as resources become available in the debt service fund to retire the principal of the debt:

(31)	Amount Available in Debt Service Fund	23,000	
	Amount to Be Provided for Payment of		
	Serial Debt Principal		23,000
	Record resources available in debt service		
	fund for debt principal.		

The $23,000 amount of current financial resources available in the debt service fund to pay principal consists of $33,000 from property tax revenue plus $2,000 from the receipt of the bond premium, less $2,000 in operating expenditures and $10,000 required for interest on the debt.

Payment of Bond Principal by Debt Service Fund   When the debt service fund records the liability for the matured portion of the bond principal in preparation for the bond retirement, the following entry is made in the general long-term debt account group:

(32)	Serial Bonds Principal Payable	20,000	
	Amount Available in Debt Service Fund		20,000
	Record first annual serial bond installment		
	recognized by debt service fund.		

The first installment of bond principal is then paid by the debt service fund (see entry 21 earlier in this chapter).

Financial Statement for General Long-Term Debt Account Group

The general long-term debt account group reports a schedule of the amount available for payment of debt principal, the amount to be provided for future payment of principal, and the total long-term debt outstanding. This schedule is presented in Figure 19-8. The $3,000 balance of the account Amount Available in Debt Service Fund is also the ending balance in the unreserved fund balance of the debt service fund. Again, the relationship between the general long-term debt account group and the debt service fund is evident.

ENTERPRISE FUNDS

Governments sometimes offer goods or services for sale to the public. The amounts charged to customers are intended to recover all or most of the cost of these goods or services. For example, a city may operate electric, gas, and water utilities; transportation systems such as buses, trains, and subways; airports; sports arenas; parking lots and garages; and public housing. Such operations are accounted for in *enterprise funds*. Enterprise funds differ from special revenue funds in that the costs of enterprise fund activities are recovered by user charges. Therefore, the primary difference between establishing a special revenue fund and an enterprise fund is the source of revenue.

Enterprise funds are proprietary funds, and the basis of accounting is the same as for commercial entities. The accrual method is used to measure revenue and expenses. Proprietary funds report fixed assets, which are depreciated, and long-term debt, if issued, and they focus on income determination and capital maintenance. The financial statements for a proprietary fund are the same as for com-

FIGURE 19-8 Schedule of general long-term debt as of the end of the fiscal year.

Sol City
Schedule of General Long-term Debt
December 31, 19X2

Amount Available and to Be Provided:	
Amount Available in Debt Service Fund	$ 3,000
Amount to Be Provided	77,000
Total Amount Available and to Be Provided	$80,000
General Long-Term Debt Payable:	
Serial Bonds Payable	$80,000
Total General Long-Term Debt Payable	$80,000

mercial entities: the balance sheet; the income statement, which in governmental accounting is called the statement of revenues, expenses, and changes in retained earnings; and the statement of cash flows.

Budgeting in the proprietary funds also has the same role as in commercial entities. A budget may be prepared for management planning purposes; however, the budget is not entered into the accounts.

Illustration of Transactions

Sol City has a municipal water utility that it operates as an enterprise fund. The trial balance of the water utility as of January 1, 19X2, the first day of the 19X2 fiscal year, is presented below.

Sol City
Trial Balance for Water Utility Enterprise Fund
January 1, 19X2

Cash	$ 9,000	
Machinery and Equipment	94,000	
Buildings	40,000	
Accumulated Depreciation—Machinery and Equipment		$ 15,000
Accumulated Depreciation—Buildings		2,000
Bonds Payable, 5%		100,000
Contributed Capital		20,000
Retained Earnings		6,000
Totals	$143,000	$143,000

One difference between balance sheet accounts for commercial entities and for proprietary funds is the lack of a stockholders' equity section in governmental accounting. The general public is the theoretical owner of all governmental assets. Furthermore, no stock certificates are issued; therefore a Contributed Capital account is used instead of Common Stock and Additional Paid-In Capital. Other interesting differences are the large relative amounts of fixed assets and long-term debt. This is because enterprise funds typically require large investments in productive assets in order to provide the necessary level of service to the public, and these investments are usually financed by long-term revenue bonds.

The water utility sells its product to the residents of Sol City based on a user charge. In addition to water revenue, the water utility receives a $3,000 short-term interfund loan from the general fund and obtains its office supplies from the city's centralized purchasing operation, which is accounted for as an internal service fund. During the year, the water utility acquires a new pump costing $6,000.

Enterprise Fund Revenues   The water utility provides service during the period and bills its customers for the amount of water used. These transactions are recorded as follows:

(33)	Accounts Receivable	40,000	
	Revenue		40,000
	Bill customers for water used as indicated by meter readings.		

(34)	Cash	32,000	
	Accounts Receivable		32,000
	Collect portion of accounts receivable.		

Capital Asset Acquisition   The water utility acquires a new pump during the year.

(35)	Equipment	6,000	
	Vouchers Payable		6,000
	Receive new pump for wellhouse.		

(36)	Vouchers Payable	6,000	
	Cash		6,000
	Pay voucher for new pump.		

Interfund Transactions   Several interfund transactions occur during the year. First, in an interfund financing transaction, the water utility receives $3,000 from the general fund as a short-term loan to be repaid within 1 year. The general fund records this as a short-term receivable, Due From Enterprise Fund (see entry 41 in Chapter 18). Second, the utility acquires its office supplies from the internal service fund in a quasi-external interfund transaction. The internal service fund reports this as a quasi-external revenue transaction (see entry 50 later in this chapter).

(37)	Cash	3,000	
	Due to General Fund		3,000
	Recognize payable for loan from general fund.		

(38)	General Operating Expenses	3,000	
	Due to Internal Service Fund		3,000
	Receive office supplies from centralized purchasing department at a cost of $3,000.		

(39)	Due to Internal Service Fund	2,000	
	Cash		2,000
	Approve payment of $2,000 to centralized purchasing department for supplies received.		

Enterprise Fund Expenses   The water utility fund incurs $9,000 of operating expenses during the period. In addition, several adjusting journal entries are required at the end of the fiscal year to recognize additional expenses. Note that these adjusting entries are similar to those of a commercial entity.

(40)	General Operating Expenses	9,000	
	Vouchers Payable		9,000
	Incur operating expenses during year.		

(41)	Vouchers Payable	6,000	
	Cash		6,000
	Pay approved vouchers for operating expenses.		

(42)	Bad Debt Expense	3,000	
	Allowance for Uncollectibles		3,000
	Provide for expected uncollectible accounts.		

(43)	Depreciation Expense	18,000	
	Accumulated Depreciation—Buildings		3,000
	Accumulated Depreciation—Machinery and		
	Equipment		15,000
	Recognize depreciation expense for year.		

(44)	Interest Expense	5,000	
	Accrued Interest Payable		5,000
	Accrue interest on bond payable:		
	$100,000 × .05 × 1 year		

Closing Entries in the Enterprise Fund   The nominal accounts are closed, and the period's profit or loss is determined as follows:

(45)	Revenue	40,000	
	General Operating Expenses		12,000
	Bad Debt Expense		3,000
	Depreciation Expense		18,000
	Interest Expense		5,000
	Profit and Loss Summary		2,000
	Close nominal accounts into profit and loss summary.		

(46)	Profit and Loss Summary	2,000	
	Retained Earnings		2,000
	Close profit and loss summary into retained earnings.		

Financial Statements for Enterprise Funds

Three financial statements are required for enterprise funds, similar to those required for commercial entities. The three are: the balance sheet (Figure 19-9); the statement of revenues, expenses, and changes in retained earnings (Figure 19-10); and the statement of cash flows (Figure 19-11). In practice, comparative figures are also presented for the prior fiscal period.

The balance sheet is similar to that required for commercial entities. Enterprise funds report their own fixed assets, investments, and long-term liabilities. The statement of revenues, expenses, and changes in retained earnings is similar to the income statement for commercial enterprises. A separation of operating and nonoperating revenues and expenses is made to provide greater information value on the operations of the enterprise funds.

The statement of cash flows for enterprise funds is specified by **GASB Statement No. 9,** "Reporting Cash Flows of Proprietary and Nonexpendable Trust Funds and Governmental Entities That Use Proprietary Fund Accounting" (GASB 9). This standard, effective for fiscal years beginning after December 15, 1989, provides a format that differs somewhat from the three-section format of the

FIGURE 19-9 Enterprise fund balance sheet as of the end of the fiscal period.

Sol City
Enterprise Fund
Balance Sheet
December 31, 19X2

Assets:		
Cash		$ 30,000
Accounts Receivable	$ 8,000	
Less: Allowance for Uncollectibles	(3,000)	5,000
Machinery and Equipment	$100,000	
Less: Accumulated Depreciation	(30,000)	70,000
Buildings	$ 40,000	
Less: Accumulated Depreciation	(5,000)	35,000
Total Assets		$140,000
Liabilities and Fund Equity:		
Vouchers Payable		$ 3,000
Accrued Interest Payable		5,000
Due to Other Funds		4,000
Bonds Payable, 5%		100,000
Fund Equity:		
Contributed Capital	$ 20,000	
Retained Earnings	8,000	28,000
Total Liabilities and Fund Equity		$140,000

FIGURE 19-10 Enterprise fund statement of revenues, expenses, and changes in retained earnings for fiscal 19X2.

Sol City
Enterprise Fund
Statement of Revenues, Expenses, and
Changes in Retained Earnings
For Fiscal Year Ended December 31, 19X2

Operating Revenues:	
Revenues	$40,000
Total Revenues	$40,000
Operating Expenses:	
General Operating	$12,000
Bad Debts	3,000
Depreciation	18,000
Total Operating Expenses	$33,000
Operating Income	$ 7,000
Nonoperating Expenses:	
Interest Expense	5,000
Net Income for the Year	$ 2,000
Retained Earnings, January 1	6,000
Retained Earnings, December 31	$ 8,000

FIGURE 19-11 Enterprise fund statement of cash flows for fiscal 19X2.

Sol City
Enterprise Fund
Statement of Cash Flows
For the Year Ended December 31, 19X2

Cash Flows from Operating Activities:		
Cash Received from Customers	$32,000	
Cash Payments for Goods and Services	(6,000)	
Cash Paid to Internal Service Fund for Supplies	(2,000)	
Net Cash Provided by Operating Activities		$24,000
Cash Flows from Noncapital Financing Activities:		
Cash Received from General Fund for Noncapital Loan	$ 3,000	
Net Cash Provided by Noncapital Financing Activities		3,000
Cash Flows from Capital and Related Financing Activities:		
Acquisition of Capital Asset	$(6,000)	
Net Cash Used for Capital and Related Financing Activities		(6,000)
Cash Flows from Investing Activities		-0-
Net Increase in Cash		$21,000
Cash at Beginning of Year		9,000
Cash at End of Year		$30,000
Reconciliation of Operating Income to Net Cash Provided by		
Operating Activities:		
Operating Income		$ 7,000
Adjustments to Reconcile Operating Income to Net Cash Provided		
by Operating Activities:		
Depreciation	$18,000	
Provision for Uncollectible Accounts	3,000	
Change in Assets and Liabilities:		
Increase in Accounts Receivable	(8,000)	
Increase in Vouchers Payable	3,000	
Increase in Due to Internal Service Fund for Operating Supplies	1,000	
Total Adjustments		17,000
Net Cash Provided by Operating Activities		$24,000

statement of cash flows for commercial entities. Because of the large number of capital asset acquisition and financing transactions in proprietary funds, the GASB specified four sections of the statement of cash flows, as follows:

1. *Cash Flows from Operating Activities.* This first section includes all transactions from providing services and delivering goods. It includes cash flows from quasi-external transactions and reimbursements from other funds.

2. *Cash Flows from Noncapital Financing Activities.* This second section includes activities such as borrowing or repaying money for purposes other than to acquire, construct, or improve capital assets. It includes cash received from, or paid to, other funds except that which is specifically specified for capital asset use.

3. *Cash Flows from Capital and Related Financing Activities.* This third section includes all activities clearly related to, or attributable to, the acquisition, disposition, construction, or improvement of capital assets. This section also includes the interest paid on borrowings for capital assets.

4. *Cash Flows from Investing Activities.* This fourth section includes all investing activities, and acquisition and disposition of debt or equity instruments.

In addition to the statement of cash flows, proprietary funds are also required to provide a supplementary schedule that reconciles the cash flow from operating activities with the operating income or loss reported on the statement of revenues, expenses, and changes in retained earnings.

INTERNAL SERVICE FUNDS

Internal service funds account for the financing of goods or services provided by one department or agency to other departments or agencies, on a cost reimbursement basis. These services are not available to the general public, making the internal service fund different from the enterprise fund. Examples are motor vehicle pools, central computer facilities, printing shops, and centralized purchasing and storage facilities. Separate internal service funds are established for each of these functions maintained by the local government unit.

Accounting and financial reporting for internal service funds are the same as for enterprise funds or for commercial entities. The accrual basis is used to measure revenue and expenses, and the balance sheet may include fixed assets, which are depreciated, and long-term debt, if issued. The statement of revenue, expenses, and changes in retained earnings reports the fund's income for the period. The statement of cash flows is also required.

Illustration of Transactions

Sol City decides to establish a centralized purchasing and storage function as an internal service fund. This centralized purchasing department provides office supplies to all other funds of the local government on a user-charge basis. After acquiring the necessary supplies, the centralized purchasing department makes the following sales:

Buying Fund	Selling Price	Cost to Internal Service Fund
General fund	$1,000	$ 500
Enterprise fund	3,000	1,500

The following entries are made during the year to record the activities of the centralized purchasing and storage department.

Establishment of Internal Service Fund and Acquisition of Inventories The fund is started with a residual equity transfer from the general fund in the amount of $10,000, which the internal service fund then uses to acquire inventory and equipment. The general fund records this transfer as a residual equity transfer out (see entries 35 and 37 in Chapter 18).

(47) Cash	10,000	
Contributed Capital		10,000
Receive residual equity transfer from		
general fund to initiate centralized		
purchasing and storage function.		
(48) Inventory	8,000	
Vouchers Payable		8,000
Acquire inventory of supplies.		
(49) Machinery and Equipment	3,000	
Vouchers Payable		3,000
Acquire equipment.		

Internal Service Fund Revenue The revenue of the internal service fund is earned by selling supplies to other funds and billing them for the value of the supplies. The billing rate is typically established at more than the operating costs of the internal service fund so that the fund may acquire replacement assets or new assets.

(50) Due from General Fund	1,000	
Due from Enterprise Fund	3,000	
Billings to Departments		4,000
Recognize revenue from providing supplies		
to general fund and enterprise fund.		
(51) Cash	3,000	
Due from General Fund		1,000
Due from Enterprise Fund		2,000
Collect portion of receivables.		

The general fund records the $1,000 for supplies as a quasi-external expenditure transaction (see entry 39 in Chapter 18). The enterprise fund records the $3,000 as a quasi-external expenditure transaction (see entry 38 earlier in this chapter).

Internal Service Fund Expenses The internal service fund incurs $4,000 of operating expenses, including payroll, during the period. In addition, cost of goods sold of $2,000 and $1,000 of depreciation expense are recognized in adjusting entries. The $9,000 of vouchers paid include a voucher in the amount of $3,000 for the equipment acquired in entry (49) above.

(52) General Operating Expenses	4,000	
Vouchers Payable		4,000
Incur operating expenses.		
(53) Vouchers Payable	9,000	
Cash		9,000
Pay approved vouchers.		

(54)	Cost of Goods Sold	2,000	
	Inventory		2,000
	Recognize cost of supplies sold.		

(55)	Depreciation Expense	1,000	
	Accumulated Depreciation		1,000
	Depreciation of equipment.		

Closing Entries in the Internal Service Fund The closing entries for the internal service fund are presented below. "Profit and Loss Summary" is used here in the closing process; however, some government units use an account called Excess of Net Billings over Costs to perform the same function.

(56)	Billings to Departments	4,000	
	Profit and Loss Summary	3,000	
	Cost of Goods Sold		2,000
	General Operating Expenses		4,000
	Depreciation Expense		1,000
	Close revenue and expenses.		

(57)	Retained Earnings	3,000	
	Profit and Loss Summary		3,000
	Close Profit and Loss Summary		
	to Retained Earnings.		

Financial Statements for Internal Service Funds

The financial statements required for internal service funds are the same as those required for enterprise funds. The balance sheet and statement of revenues, expenses, and changes in retained earnings are presented in Figures 19-12 and 19-13. A statement of cash flows is also required as presented in Figure 19-14.

TRUST FUNDS

Trust funds account for resources held by a government unit in a trustee capacity. The government acts as a fiduciary for monies or properties held on behalf of individuals, employees, or other government entities. Trust funds may be *expendable* or *nonexpendable*, depending on the terms of the trust arrangement. Because these two types of trusts have different objectives, the accounting and financial reporting requirements for them differ. Examples of trust funds are public employee pension and retirement funds, endowments to governmental units for parks or equipment, and certain federal grant programs. A nonexpendable trust fund is illustrated first, and then an expendable trust is presented. Public employee pension funds are discussed in the "Additional Considerations" section at the end of the chapter.

Illustration of Nonexpendable Trust Fund

Nonexpendable trust funds must preserve the fund principal; therefore, the accrual basis of accounting is used to measure income and capital maintenance. The

FIGURE 19-12 Internal service fund balance sheet as of the end of the fiscal period.

Sol City
Internal Service Fund
Balance Sheet
December 31, 19X2

Assets:		
Cash		$ 4,000
Due from Other Funds		1,000
Inventory of Supplies		6,000
Machinery and Equipment	$ 3,000	
Less: Accumulated Depreciation	(1,000)	2,000
Total Assets		$13,000
Liabilities and Fund Equity:		
Vouchers Payable		$ 6,000
Fund Equity:		
Contributed Capital	$10,000	
Retained Earnings (deficit)	(3,000)	7,000
Total Liabilities and Fund Equity		$13,000

FIGURE 19-13 Internal service fund statement of revenues, expenses, and changes in retained earnings for fiscal 19X2.

Sol City
Internal Service Fund
Statement of Revenues, Expenses, and
Changes in Retained Earnings
For Fiscal Year Ended December 31, 19X2

Operating Revenue:	
Billings to Departments	$ 4,000
Total Revenue	$ 4,000
Operating Expenses:	
Cost of Goods Sold	$ 2,000
General Operating	4,000
Depreciation	1,000
Total Operating Expenses	$ 7,000
Net Operating Loss for Period	$(3,000)
Retained Earnings, January 1	-0-
Retained Earnings, December 31	$(3,000)

FIGURE 19-14 Internal service fund statement of cash flows for fiscal 19X2.

Sol City
Internal Service Fund
Statement of Cash Flows
For the Year Ended December 31, 19X2

Cash Flows from Operating Activities:		
Cash Received from Customers	$ 3,000	
Cash Payments for Goods and Services	(6,000)	
Net Cash Used by Operating Activities		$(3,000)
Cash Flows from Noncapital Financing Activities:		
Cash Received from General Fund for Noncapital Activities	$ 7,000	
Net Cash Provided by Noncapital Financing Activities		7,000
Cash Flows from Capital and Related Financing Activities:		
Cash Received from General Fund for Capital Activity	$ 3,000	
Acquisition of Capital Asset	$(3,000)	
Net Cash Used for Capital and Related Financing Activities		-0-
Cash Flows from Investing Activities		-0-
Net Increase in Cash		$ 4,000
Cash at Beginning of Year		-0-
Cash at End of Year		$ 4,000
Reconciliation of Operating Income to Net Cash Used by		
Operating Activities:		
Operating Loss		$(3,000)
Adjustments to Reconcile Operating Income to Net Cash Used		
by Operating Activities:		
Depreciation	$ 1,000	
Change in Assets and Liabilities:		
Increase in Due from Other Funds from Billings	(1,000)	
Increase in Inventory of Supplies	(6,000)	
Increase in Vouchers Payable	6,000	
Total Adjustments		-0-
Net Cash Used by Operating Activities		$(3,000)

financial reports for a nonexpendable trust fund are the same as for a commercial entity: balance sheet; statement of revenues, expenses, and changes in retained earnings; and statement of cash flows.

On January 1, 19X2, Sol City receives a $100,000 bequest from a long-term resident of the city. The will stipulates that the $100,000 is to be invested and the income is to be used to provide a transportation service for the city's disabled and senior citizens. The entries in this nonexpendable trust fund during 19X2 are as follows:

Nonexpendable Trust Fund Established   The fund is established on January 1, 19X2:

(58)	Cash	100,000	
	Fund Balance—Endowment Principal		100,000
	Accept nonexpendable trust.		

Investment and Interest   The trustee of the fund acquires $100,000 face value, high-grade, 8 percent government securities at 90 to yield an effective interest rate of 10 percent.

(59)	Investment in Bonds	90,000	
	Cash		90,000
	Acquire $100,000 par value government securities at 90.		

(60)	Accrued Interest Receivable	8,000	
	Investment in Bonds	1,000	
	Interest Revenue		9,000
	Accrue interest and amortize discount:		
	$8,000 = $100,000 × .08, nominal rate		
	$9,000 = $90,000 × .10, effective rate		

(61)	Cash	8,000	
	Accrued Interest Receivable		8,000
	Collect accrued interest on securities.		

Any capital gain or loss on the sale of investments is an adjustment of Fund Balance—Endowment Principal. Capital gains or losses are not part of the expendable income.

Interfund Transactions   The income from the bonds is transferred to an expendable trust fund to be used to provide transportation in accordance with the endowment restrictions. This operating transfer out will be made periodically for the time specified in the endowment in order to transfer revenue earned in one fund to another fund that will make the required expenditure. Note that the operating transfer is recognized when income is recorded, but cash is transferred only as it becomes available.

(62)	Operating Transfer Out to Expendable Trust Fund	9,000	
	Due to Expendable Trust Fund		9,000
	Recognize liability to expendable trust fund for income from investments.		

(63)	Due to Expendable Trust Fund	8,000	
	Cash		8,000
	Forward available cash to expendable trust fund.		

Closing Entries in the Nonexpendable Trust Fund   The nominal accounts are closed, as follows:

(64)	Interest Revenue	9,000	
	Operating Transfer Out to Expendable Trust Fund		9,000
	Close revenue and operating transfer out.		

Illustration of Expendable Trust Fund

Expendable trust funds account for resources that may be expended. Therefore, the modified accrual basis of accounting is used for these funds, and the accounting and financial reporting are the same as for the general fund.

Sol City establishes an expendable trust fund to account for the resources made available from the investment of the nonexpendable endowment.

Transfer In of Resources The expendable trust fund receives its resources from the nonexpendable trust fund (see entries 62 and 63):

(65)	Due from Nonexpendable Trust Fund	9,000	
	Operating Transfer In from Nonexpendable Trust Fund		9,000
	Recognize receivable for operating transfer.		
(66)	Cash	8,000	
	Due from Nonexpendable Trust Fund		8,000
	Receive cash from nonexpendable trust fund.		

Expenditures in the Expendable Trust Fund The expendable trust fund incurs transportation costs of $5,000:

(67)	Expenditures	5,000	
	Vouchers Payable		5,000
	Record transportation service costs.		
(68)	Vouchers Payable	4,000	
	Cash		4,000
	Pay portion of vouchers.		

If the expendable trust fund acquires any long-term productive assets, the acquisition is recorded as an expenditure in the expendable trust fund and a record of the increase in fixed assets is maintained in the general fixed assets account group.

Closing Entries in the Expendable Trust Fund The nominal accounts are closed:

(69)	Operating Transfer In from Nonexpendable Trust Fund	9,000	
	Expenditures		5,000
	Unreserved Fund Balance		4,000
	Close operating transfer in and expenditures.		

Financial Statements for the Trust Funds

The financial statements required for the nonexpendable trust fund are the same as required for commercial entities because the fund measures income and capital maintenance. The balance sheet for the nonexpendable trust fund is presented in Figure 19-15, and the statement of revenues, expenses, and changes in retained earnings is presented in Figure 19-16. The ending fund balance for the nonexpend-

FIGURE 19-15 Trust funds balance sheets as of the end of the fiscal period.

Sol City
Trust Funds
Balance Sheets
December 31, 19X2

	Nonexpendable Trust (Principal)	Expendable Trust (Income)
Assets:		
Cash	$ 10,000	$4,000
Due from Nonexpendable Trust Fund		1,000
Investments	91,000	
Total Assets	$101,000	$5,000
Liabilities and Fund Balance:		
Vouchers Payable		$1,000
Due to Expendable Trust Fund	$ 1,000	
Fund Balance:		
Endowment Principal	100,000	
Unreserved		4,000
Total Liabilities and Fund Balance	$101,000	$5,000

FIGURE 19-16 Nonexpendable trust fund statement of revenues, expenses, and changes in fund balance for fiscal 19X2.

Sol City
Nonexpendable Trust Fund
Statement of Revenues, Expenses, and
Changes in Fund Balance
For Fiscal Year Ended December 31, 19X2

Operating Revenue:	
Interest Revenue	$ 9,000
Total Operating Revenue	$ 9,000
Operating Expenses	$ -0-
Operating Income	$ 9,000
Nonoperating Item:	
Operating Transfer Out	9,000
Net Income	$ -0-
Fund Balance—Endowment Principal:	
January 1	-0-
Endowment Contribution	100,000
Fund Balance—Endowment Principal:	
December 31	$100,000

FIGURE 19-17 Statement of cash flows for nonexpendable trust fund for fiscal 19X2.

Sol City
Nonexpendable Trust Fund
Statement of Cash Flows
For the Year Ended December 31, 19X2

Cash Flows from Operating Activities:		
Interest Received	$ 8,000	
Net Cash Provided by Operating Activities		$ 8,000
Cash Flows from Noncapital Financing Activities:		
Cash Received from Bequest	$100,000	
Cash Paid to Expendable Trust Fund	(8,000)	
Net Cash Provided by Noncapital Financing Activities		92,000
Cash Flows from Capital and Related Financing Activities		–0–
Cash Flows from Investing Activities:		
Purchase of Investments	$ 90,000	
Net Cash Used for Investing Activities		(90,000)
Net Increase in Cash		$10,000
Cash at Beginning of Year		–0–
Cash at End of Year		$10,000
Reconciliation of Operating Income to Net Cash Provided by Operating Activities:		
Operating Income		$ 9,000
Adjustments to Reconcile Operating Income to Net Cash Provided by Operating Activities:		
Change in Assets and Liabilities:		
Increase in Investment in Bonds (amortization)	$ (1,000)	
Total Adjustments		(1,000)
Net Cash Provided by Operating Activities		$ 8,000

able trust fund is $100,000, the initial amount of the principal endowment. The investment in governmental securities is reported at $91,000, the original acquisition price of $90,000 plus the $1,000 discount amortized during the period. The statement of cash flows for the nonexpendable trust fund is presented in Figure 19-17.

The balance sheet for the expendable trust fund is presented in Figure 19-15. The statement of revenues, expenditures, and changes in fund balance for the expendable trust fund is presented in Figure 19-18. The statement of revenues, expenditures, and changes in fund balance reconciles to the ending balance in the unreserved fund balance of the expendable trust fund.

AGENCY FUNDS

Agency funds account for resources held by a government unit as an agent for individuals, private organizations, other funds, or other government units. Examples are tax collection funds that collect property taxes and then distribute them to local government units, and employee benefit funds for such items as dental

FIGURE 19-18 Expendable trust fund statement of revenues, expenditures, and changes in fund balance for fiscal 19X2.

Sol City
Expendable Trust Fund
Statement of Revenues, Expenditures, and
Changes in Fund Balance
For Fiscal Year Ended December 31, 19X2

Revenue:	$ -0-
Expenditures:	
Transportation Service	$ 5,000
Total Expenditures	$ 5,000
Excess of Expenditures over Revenue	$(5,000)
Other Financing Sources (Uses):	
Operating Transfer in from Nonexpendable Trust Fund	9,000
Excess of Revenue and Other Sources Over Expenditures and Other Uses	$ 4,000
Increase in Fund Balance	$ 4,000
Fund Balance—Endowments, January 1	-0-
Fund Balance—Endowments, December 31	$ 4,000

insurance or charitable contributions that employees authorize as withholdings from their paychecks.

The modified accrual basis of accounting is used to account for agency funds. Because agency funds are custodial in nature, assets always equal liabilities and there is no fund equity. The required financial statements include a balance sheet and a statement of changes in assets and liabilities.

Illustration of Transactions in an Agency Fund

Sol City has established an agency fund to account for the employees' share of health insurance, which is deducted from the employees' paychecks and then forwarded to the insurance company.

Agency Fund Receipts and Disbursements   The receipts and disbursements in the agency fund during 19X2 are as follows:

(70)	Cash	9,000	
	Due to Insurance Company		9,000
	Employees' contributory share of health insurance deducted from payroll checks.		
(71)	Due to Insurance Company	9,000	
	Cash		9,000
	Pay liability to insurance company for employees' share of insurance cost.		

The statement of changes in assets and liabilities is presented in Figure 19-19.

FIGURE 19-19 Statement of changes in assets and liabilities for an agency fund.

Sol City
Health Insurance Agency Fund
Statement of Changes in Assets and Liabilities
For Fiscal Year Ended December 31, 19X2

	Balance, January 1	Additions	Deductions	Balance, December 31
Assets:				
Cash	$-0-	$9,000	$9,000	$-0-
Liabilities:				
Due to Insurance				
Company	-0-	9,000	9,000	-0-

FINANCIAL REPORTING FOR A GOVERNMENT UNIT

The discussion on financial reporting has focused on the statements required for each individual fund. It is important now to examine the format of the report for the governmental financial reporting entity as a whole.

A governmental entity issues two different types of financial reports. The *general-purpose financial statements (GPFS)* are used for external financial reporting to credit grantors and others interested in comparing the operations of the governmental entity with other types of entities. The *comprehensive annual financial report (CAFR)* includes the information from the general-purpose financial statements but also contains much more information and detail on the operations of the governmental entity. The CAFR is intended for readers interested in the details of operating and financial information available for governmental entities.

The Government Finance Officers' Association (GFOA) provides local governments with the opportunity to have their external financial reports evaluated for conformance to a high level of reporting standards. Those local governments deemed to meet the high standards of financial reporting of the GFOA receive a *certificate of achievement*, which the local government may include in its external financial reports. This certificate assures users of the statements that high reporting standards have been satisfied.

The Financial Reporting Pyramid

Three different levels of aggregation are required for reporting the financial operations and condition of a governmental financial reporting entity.

1. Individual Fund Financial Statements These are the statements prepared for each fund and illustrated in this chapter. In addition, major component units included within the governmental reporting entity may also have condensed individual financial statements.

2. Combining Financial Statements   Combining financial statements are used to bring together the financial statements for similar types of funds and certain other component units. For example, if the local government has four different capital projects funds, each capital projects fund is presented in a separate column. The columns are then aggregated and a single set of combining financial statements for all the capital projects funds is prepared.

The combining statements are prepared from the individual fund statements. In this manner, users of the financial statements may, in one set of financials, see the aggregates for each of the governmental entity's fund types—all the debt service funds as one, all the internal service funds as one, and so on. In addition, separate combining statements are required for the discretely presented component units of a governmental entity. For example, if a primary government unit has component units of a parks and recreation commission, a transit authority, an airport authority, and a convention center authority, each of these component units would be included in a combining statement of component units. Because the Sol City example has just one of each type of fund, and no component units, no combining statements are required for the city.

3. Combined Financial Statements   These are the aggregation of all funds and component units into one financial statement. For example, the combined balance sheet includes the combining balance sheet from each of the individual fund types and the account groups, including all governmental proprietary and fiduciary funds and the two account groups. Separate columns are used for each fund type and account group, and for the discretely presented component units of the primary government unit. A combined balance sheet is presented in Figure 19-20, and a combined statement of revenues, expenditures, and changes in fund balance is presented in Figure 19-21.

These three levels are sometimes referred to as a *reporting pyramid*, with the individual fund statements at the bottom of the pyramid, the combining statements at the middle level, and the combined statements at the top.

The Reporting Entity

An important decision is to determine which units should be included within the governmental entity's financial reports—for example, which boards, commissions, authorities, agencies, or other component units are under the control of the reporting entity and should be included within its financials. **GASB 14** defines the financial reporting entity based on financial accountability, as follows:

> a. The primary government is financially accountable if it appoints a voting majority of the organization's governing body and (1) it is able to impose its will on that organization or (2) there is a potential for the organization to provide specific financial benefits to, or impose specific financial burdens on, the primary government.

FIGURE 19-20 Combined balance sheet—all fund types and account groups.

Sol City
Combined Balance Sheet—All Fund Types and Account Groups
December 31, 19X2

	Governmental Funds				Proprietary Funds		Fiduciary Funds		Account Groups		Total— (Memorandum Only) Reporting Entity December 31, 19X2
	General Fund	Special Revenue Fund	Debt Service Fund	Capital Projects Fund	Enterprise Fund	Internal Service Fund	Nonexpendable Trust Funds	Expendable Trust and Agency Funds	General Fixed Assets	General Long-Term Debt	
Cash	$102,000	$15,000	$1,000	$16,000	$30,000	$4,000	$10,000	$4,000			$182,000
Receivables:											
Taxes	90,000	3,000	5,000								98,000
Accounts					8,000						8,000
Allowance for Uncollectibles	(5,000)	(2,000)	(2,000)		(3,000)						(12,000)
Due from Other Funds	3,000					1,000		1,000			5,000
Inventory of Supplies	17,000					6,000					23,000
Investments							91,000				91,000
Improvements Other than Buildings									$ 25,000		25,000
Machinery and Equipment					100,000	3,000			233,000		336,000
Less: Accumulated Depreciation					(30,000)	(1,000)					(31,000)
Buildings					40,000				524,000		564,000
Less: Accumulated Depreciation					(5,000)						(5,000)
Amount Available										$ 3,000	3,000
Amount to Be Provided										77,000	77,000
Total Assets	$207,000	$16,000	$4,000	$16,000	$140,000	$13,000	$101,000	$5,000	$782,000	$80,000	$1,364,000
Vouchers Payable	$ 55,000	$ 3,000	$1,000		$ 3,000	$ 6,000		$1,000			$ 69,000
Contract Payable—Retained Percentage				$10,000							10,000
Accrued Liabilities					5,000						5,000
Due to Other Funds					4,000		$ 1,000				5,000
Revenue Bonds Payable					100,000						100,000
General Obligation Serial Bonds Payable										$80,000	80,000
Total Liabilities	$ 55,000	$ 3,000	$1,000	$10,000	$112,000	$ 6,000	$ 1,000	$1,000	$ -0-	$80,000	$ 269,000
Fund Equity:											
Contributed Capital					$ 20,000	$10,000					$ 30,000
Investment in General Fixed Assets									$782,000		782,000
Retained Earnings					8,000	(3,000)					5,000
Fund Balance:											
Reserved for Encumbrances	$ 15,000	$ 6,000									21,000
Reserved for Inventories	17,000										17,000
Reserved for Endowments							$100,000				100,000
Unreserved	120,000	7,000	3,000	6,000				4,000			140,000
Total Fund Equity	$152,000	$13,000	$3,000	$ 6,000	$ 28,000	$ 7,000	$100,000	$4,000	$782,000	$ -0-	$1,095,000
Total Liabilities and Fund Equity	$207,000	$16,000	$4,000	$16,000	$140,000	$13,000	$101,000	$5,000	$782,000	$80,000	$1,364,000

FIGURE 19-21 Combined statement of revenues, expenditures, and changes in fund balance.

Sol City
Combined Statement of Revenues, Expenditures, and Changes in Fund Balance—
All Governmental Fund Types and Expendable Trust Funds
December 31, 19X2

	Governmental Funds				Fiduciary Fund	Total—(Memorandum Only) Reporting Entity December 31, 19X2
	General Fund	Special Revenue Fund	Debt Service Fund	Capital Projects Fund	Expendable Trust	
Revenues:						
Property Taxes	$781,000	$62,000	$33,000			$ 876,000
Sales Taxes	32,000					32,000
Intergovernmental Grants	33,000			$ 10,000		43,000
Miscellaneous	18,000					18,000
Total Revenues	$864,000	$62,000	$33,000	$ 10,000	$ -0-	$ 969,000
Expenditures:						
Current:						
General Government	$206,000					$ 206,000
Streets and Highways	71,000					71,000
Public Safety	335,000					335,000
Sanitation	141,000					141,000
Culture and Recreation		$49,000				49,000
Miscellaneous			$ 2,000		$ 5,000	7,000
Capital Outlay	58,000			$ 124,000		182,000
Debt Service:						
Principal Retirement			20,000			20,000
Interest Charges			10,000			10,000
Total Expenditures	$811,000	$49,000	$32,000	$ 124,000	$ 5,000	$1,021,000
Excess of Revenues over (under) Expenditures	$ 53,000	$13,000	$ 1,000	$(114,000)	$(5,000)	$ (52,000)
Other Financing Sources (Uses):						
Proceeds of Bond Issue				102,000		102,000
Operating Transfers In			2,000	20,000	9,000	31,000
Operating Transfers Out	(20,000)			(2,000)		(22,000)
Excess of Revenues and Other Sources over Expenditures and Other Uses	$ 33,000	$13,000	$ 3,000	$ 6,000	$ 4,000	$ 59,000
Changes in Reserves:						
Increase in Reserves	(7,000)	(6,000)				(13,000)
Increase (Decrease) in Fund Balance	$ 26,000	$ 7,000	$ 3,000	$ 6,000	$ 4,000	$ 46,000
Unreserved Fund Balance, 1/1	104,000	-0-	-0-	-0-	-0-	104,000
Residual Equity Transfers	(10,000)					(10,000)
Unreserved Fund Balance, 12/31	$120,000	$ 7,000	$ 3,000	$ 6,000	$ 4,000	$ 140,000

b. The primary government may be financially accountable if an organization is fiscally dependent on the primary government regardless of whether the organization has (1) a separately elected governing board, and (2) a governing board appointed by a higher level of government, or (3) a jointly appointed board.[2]

The criteria indicate that a primary government unit may be financially accountable for organizations with boards not appointed by the primary government unit. For example, some organizations are fiscally dependent on a primary government entity for issuance of debt, approval of budgets, or tax levies. Whenever the primary government is still financially accountable for these organizations, they should be included in its financial statements as component units. Through the legislative body and the chief executive, the primary government entity may act as the oversight unit over many such component units. Separately issued financial reports of component units are called *component unit financial reports (CUFRs).*

The financial statements of the reporting entity should allow users to distinguish between the primary government and its major component units. Two financial reporting approaches are used: *discrete presentation of component units* and *blending of component units.* A discrete presentation, by a separate column in the financials, is used for most component units. The presentation of component units should be separated from the primary government unit's columnar presentation. For example, if a primary government unit has several component units, the combined balance sheet would have the following organization:

Accounts	Primary Government's Fund Types and Account Groups	Totals— (Memorandum Only) Primary Government	Component Units	Totals— (Memorandum Only) Reporting Entity

The primary government unit's fund types and account groups are presented in several columns, as shown in Figure 19-21. The discretely presented component units are typically presented together in one column to correspond to the aggregate combining statement for these component units. The GASB favored just one column for reporting these component units in the combined financial statements, but did allow for multicolumnar reporting if the primary government unit judges that fuller disclosure can be beneficial. The Sol City example did not have any discretely presented component units, so the Sol City reporting entity is comprised of just the primary government unit. Note that the totals columns are labeled "Memorandum Only." This denotes that these totals are not logically comparable to a consolidation.

Blending of component units is used for component units that are legally separate from the primary government unit but are so intertwined that they are, in substance, the same as the primary government unit. For example, a city could have a legally separate unit that manages a public housing authority exclusively

---

[2] *GASB Statement No. 14*, "The Financial Reporting Entity," Governmental Accounting Standards Board (Norwalk, Conn.), 1991, par. 21.

for the city. The board of the housing authority is comprised of the city mayor and two city council members. In this case, the public housing authority is substantively the same as the city government, and the housing authority's financial statements should be blended into the city's by including the housing authority's balances and transactions in the appropriate combining statements of the city, the primary governing unit. The only exception in blending is that the blended component unit's general fund should be reported as a special revenue fund for the city. This maintains the separate and distinct nature of the primary governing unit's general fund.

General-Purpose Financial Statements (GPFS)

The general-purpose financial statements must include the following six items:

1. Combined balance sheet—all fund types and account groups for the primary government unit and blended component units, and for its discretely presented component units.
2. Combined statement of revenues, expenditures, and changes in fund balance—all governmental fund types and expendable trust funds for the primary government unit and blended component units, and for its discretely presented component units.
3. Combined statement of revenues, expenditures, and changes in fund balance—budgeted and actual—all governmental fund types and expendable trust funds for the primary government unit and blended component units with a legally adopted annual operating budget. Budget-actual comparisons are not required for discretely reported component units.
4. Combined statement of revenues, expenses, and changes in retained earnings—all proprietary fund types, nonexpendable trusts, and pension trust funds for the primary government unit and blended component units, and for its discretely presented component units.
5. Combined statement of cash flows—all proprietary fund types and nonexpendable trusts for the primary government unit and blended component units, and for its discretely presented component units.
6. Notes to financial statements, including:
   a. Summary of significant accounting policies.
   b. Schedules of long-term debt and fixed asset information.
   c. Commitments, legal violations, litigations, and contingent liabilities.
   d. Individual disclosure of significant component units, and other disclosures essential for fair presentation to distinguish between information pertaining to the primary government (including its blended component units) and information pertaining to its discretely presented component units. Financial information about the major component units may be presented either by including the combining statements for the component units or by providing condensed individual component unit financial reports.

The general-purpose financial statements also include the auditor's opinion and other miscellaneous disclosures about the government unit.

Comprehensive Annual Financial Report (CAFR)

As its name implies, the comprehensive annual financial report (CAFR) is more comprehensive than the government unit's general-purpose financial statements. The CAFR is intended to provide detailed information for governing bodies, for resource providers, for oversight bodies, and for the various constituents of the government unit. The CAFR, which includes the GPFS, has three major sections, each with several subsections, as follows:

1. Introductory section
   a. Title page and table of contents
   b. Transmittal letter from chief financial officer of government unit
   c. Certificate of achievement from GFOA, if received
2. Financial section
   a. Auditor's report
   b. General-purpose financial statements (GPFS)
   c. Combining financial statements
   d. Individual fund and component unit financial reports
   e. Schedule disclosure required by state law or debt covenants
3. Statistical section, including:
   a. Expenditures in each fund by function and activity
   b. Revenue in each fund by source
   c. Property tax levies and collections
   d. Special assessment collections
   e. Property values, demographic statistics, and other miscellaneous statistics

In addition to the GPFS and CAFR, the government unit may also publish condensed summary data in the so-called popular report format. These are summaries of information from the CAFR that are intended to be easily understood digests of the financial information. They are often presented to the public as graphic displays or other summarized formats.

Interim Reporting

Government units generally are not required to publish interim reports, although many prepare monthly or quarterly reports to determine the current progress of compliance with legal and budgetary limitations and to plan for changes in events or developments that were not foreseen when the annual budget was prepared. Interim reports are a valuable internal management control instrument; they typically are not made available to the general public.

Auditing Government Entities

Most government units are audited annually because of state or federal requirements or because long-term creditors demand audited statements as part of the debt agreements. The audit of a government unit is different from the audit of a commercial entity. The auditor not only must express an opinion on the fairness of the audited entity's financial statements in conformity with applicable accounting principles, but must also assess the audited entity's compliance with legal or contractual provisions of state law, debt covenants, terms of grants from other government entities, and other restrictions on the government unit.

The Single Audit Act of 1984 is a federal law specifying the audit requirements for all state and local governments receiving federal financial assistance. The audit act requires auditors to determine (1) if the financial statements fairly present the government's financial condition, (2) if the government unit has an internal control system to provide reasonable assurance that it is managing federal financial assistance programs in compliance with applicable laws and regulations, and (3) if the government unit has complied with laws and regulations that may have a material effect on each federal program. The auditors not only issue the standard audit report, but also must issue special reports on items (2) and (3) above. The Single Audit Act does not apply to all government units receiving federal financial assistance. Government units receiving more than $100,000 in any one year must fully comply; units receiving between $25,000 and $100,000 in any one year may elect the single audit covering all three items or may have an audit examination on just items (2) and (3). Government units receiving less than $25,000 in any one year are exempt from the provisions of the act.

ADDITIONAL CONSIDERATIONS

Accounting for Pension Trust Funds

Many states, and some local governments, now have public employee retirement systems (PERS), which either supplement or replace federal social security. Some PERS are created for employees of specific governments, such as all municipal employees, while some are for employees within certain functional fields, such as teachers, firefighters, or police officers. Employees included in a PERS contribute a percentage of their salaries, and the employer also makes a contribution. The advantage of a PERS to a local government unit is that the required employer contribution is typically less than that required by the FICA, thereby saving the government and the taxpayers additional costs. Several states now fund their PERS on a terminal funding or pay-as-you-go basis, and the state's share of the contribution to the PERS is usually reduced or eliminated during a period of economic hardship for the state. As a consequence, many states have substantial unfunded liabilities to their PERS.

A PERS is a pension trust fund responsible for receiving resources from employees or government units, investing the fund resources, and calculating and paying pensions or other benefits to beneficiaries. Pension trust funds are classified as fiduciary fund types, similar to nonexpendable trust funds. The accrual method is used to measure revenue and expenses. The primary revenue is from employee and employer contributions and investment income. The primary expenses are the annuity payments made to retired employees or death benefits paid to relatives of deceased employees.

The required financial statements of a pension trust fund are the same as for a proprietary fund, except that a statement of cash flows is not required of pension trust funds. The two statements required of pension trust funds are a balance sheet and a statement of revenues, expenses, and changes in fund balance. In addition, the fund must report on its actuarial soundness. This additional information includes how contribution rates are determined and how they fulfill the financial objectives of the plan, the actuarial assumptions and method, and a schedule of information about the pension values of active members and payments made to retired members of the plan.

SUMMARY OF KEY CONCEPTS AND TERMS

This chapter completes the disussion of accounting and financial reporting principles used by local and state governments. Governments generally use four governmental funds, two proprietary funds, three trust funds, and two account groups. The basis of accounting used in each of these fund types depends on whether management's focus is expendability or capital maintenance. The account groups are not funds; they are self-balancing records of the government unit's general long-term debt and general fixed assets. In commercial accounting, one event is recorded in one journal; in fund accounting, an event may affect two or three different funds and account groups.

Governmental reporting entities present two financial reporting formats. The first is the general-purpose financial statements (GPFS), which include the combined financial statements for the governmental reporting entities' funds. The second reporting format is the comprehensive annual financial report (CAFR). The CAFR includes the GPFS but also reports additional operating and financial details about governmental reporting entities.

Agency funds
Blending of component units
Capital projects funds
Certificate of achievement
Combined financial statements
Component unit financial reports
  (CUFR)
Comprehensive annual financial report
  (CAFR)
Debt service funds
Discrete presentation of component
  units
Enterprise funds

Expendable trust funds
General fixed assets account group
  (GFAAG)
General long-term debt account group
  (GLTDAG)
General-purpose financial statements
  (GPFS)
Individual fund financial statements
Internal service funds
Nonexpendable trust funds
Reporting entity
Reporting pyramid
Special revenue funds

APPENDIX: Other Governmental Entities—
Public School Systems and the Federal Government

In addition to local and state governmental entities, two other governmental entities—public schools and the federal government—have pervasive influences on the lives of citizens. This appendix presents a brief overview of the basic accounting and financial reporting requirements for these two government entities.

PUBLIC SCHOOL SYSTEMS

In the United States today, over 50 million students attend approximately 14,000 public elementary and secondary school systems employing about 2.5 million teachers and expending over $100 billion dollars annually. Many others attend one of the myriad of private schools formed by religious or other groups.

Accounting and Financial Reporting for Public School Systems

Accounting for public schools is similar to accounting for local or state governments. The modified accrual basis of accounting is used for most funds, and the financial statements for a school district are similar to those of a local government. Over half of school district revenue is obtained from local property taxes; the remaining sources are fees for services, state education aid, and federal grants to education. Most school districts have an elected school board that serves as a public policy-making body for the school system.

The fund structure for a school district is similar to the fund structure for a local or state government. School district funds include the general fund, special revenue funds, capital projects funds, debt service funds, enterprise funds, internal service funds, and trust and agency funds. In addition, school districts should have general fixed assets and general long-term debt account groups.

The school district's general fund resources are expended for costs directly associated with the education process: teachers' salaries, books and supplies, etc. Special revenue funds may include specific funds for operations, building, and maintenance (OBM) of the physical facilities of the school district, as well as the transportation special revenue fund, which is responsible for acquiring and maintaining the buses for transporting children to and from the schools.

Public school systems have a public hearing on the annual budget, which is then approved by the school board or other governing body. The budget, which is entered into the accounts, specifies the revenue from the three basic sources: local property taxes and fees, state school aid, and federal sources. The expenditures are broken down into the following three dimensions: *program*, such as gifted, vocational, elementary, secondary, and adult/continuing education; *function*, such as guidance counselors, instructional staff, school administration, and student transportation; and *object*, such as salaries, employee benefits, purchased services, and supplies and materials.

The department of education of each state receives the annual reports from each school district. Typically these financial statements must be audited by independent auditors. The formal statements include a combined balance sheet for all funds and a combined statement of revenues, expenditures, and changes in fund balance. Other statements required are the same as for other government units. In addition, the comprehensive annual financial report for a school district includes a variety of other disclosures relevant to the school district, such as the cost per student, the debt capacity of the district, and the assessed valuation of all property included in the school district.

FEDERAL GOVERNMENT ACCOUNTING

An accounting structure for the federal government has been part of the U.S. statutes since 1789. The following individuals or entities have significant roles in the federal budgeting and expending process:

	Executive Branch	**Legislative Branch**
	President	Congress
	Office of Management and Budget (OMB)	General Accounting Office (GAO)
	Secretary of the Treasury	Congressional Budget Office (CBO)
	Federal agencies	

The President of the United States directs that the annual budget be prepared by the director of the Office of Management and Budget, who is a member of the President's staff. The director of the OMB then consults with the various federal agencies and the Secretary of the Treasury and prepares the budget that the President presents to Congress. The Congressional Budget Office then evaluates the executive budget and may propose that Congress present one of its own. After the legislative process runs its course and the budget is approved, Congress provides the authority for the executive branch to obtain revenue through taxation or other charges. The primary agency responsible for obtaining revenue is the Internal Revenue Service, which is an agency of the Department of the Treasury.

The fund arrangement of the federal government is as follows:

	Federal Funds	**Trust or Custodian Funds**
	General fund	Trust funds
	Special funds	Deposit funds
	Revolving funds	
	Management funds	

The federal government has only one general fund, which is responsible for collecting and expending resources that are not dedicated to specific purposes. Special funds are similar to special revenue funds of a local government. These funds are earmarked by law for specific purposes. Although the federal government has many special funds, the dollar amounts involved in these funds are typically small. Revolving funds are similar to internal service funds of a local government. These funds carry out a cycle of intragovernmental business-type operations. Management funds account for the resources merged from two or more individual appropriations in order to carry out a common purpose or project, such as a drug enforcement program involving several government agencies.

The trust or custodian funds are similar to the trust and agency funds of a local government. The largest trust fund is the Federal Old Age and Survivors Trust Fund, more commonly known as the social security fund. Deposit fund accounts are created to account for deductions from federal employees' pay for such items as federal or state withholding taxes and health insurance premiums.

The appropriation-expenditure process is a little different for the federal government than for local government units. The federal budget provides the appropriation authority for the federal government. This appropriation authority is then allocated to the various agencies through a process of apportionments made by the Office of Management and Budget. The apportionment is then divided among the agency's programs and activities by a process of allotments. The agency then makes obligations by incurring costs for services provided. These obligations are then liquidated through the preparation of vouchers, which are submitted to the Department of the Treasury for payment.

Federal Agency Accounting

Most federal activities are carried out through agencies that are subdivisions of the federal government. A major difference between accounting for local and state governments and the agencies of the federal government is that federal agencies must use the accrual basis of accounting to measure their activities. In addition, the accounting system must provide information on each agency's obligations (encumbrances), expended obligations (expenditures), applied costs (expenses), and cash disbursements. The accrual system provides more disclosures on the actual costs of providing services for a period than the modified accrual basis does.

The fiscal period for the federal government is from October 1 to September 30 of the next calendar year. Each agency of the federal government must provide a statement of financial position (balance sheet), a statement of operations, a statement of sources and application of funds, and a statement of changes in the investment of the United States. An illustrative statement of financial position is presented in Figure 19-22. The following are observations on Figure 19-22:

1. The account Fund Balances with the U.S. Treasury is used instead of cash.

2. The equipment is depreciated, resulting in an Accumulated Depreciation account.

3. The investment of the U.S. Government is the difference between the assets and liabilities. The investment is divided between the invested capital and the unexpended appropriations. The Invested Capital account includes the amounts invested in inventory, fixed assets, leasehold improvements, and other assets necessary to provide the agency's services.

4. The account Unexpended Appropriations is the amount of appropriations that is still available for obligation.

FIGURE 19-22 Statement of financial position for a federal agency.

Federal Agency
Statement of Financial Position
As of September 30, 19X2

Assets

Current Assets:		
Fund Balances with U.S. Treasury	$ 300,000	
Inventories	26,000	$ 326,000
Fixed Assets:		
Equipment	$2,400,000	
Less: Accumulated Depreciation	(500,000)	1,900,000
Total Assets		$2,226,000

Liabilities and Investment of the U.S. Government

Current Liabilities:		
Accounts Payable		$ 85,000
Investment of the U.S. Government:		
Invested Capital	$2,131,000	
Unexpended Appropriations	10,000	2,141,000
Total Liabilities and Investment of the U.S. Government		$2,226,000

Audits of Federal Agencies

The comptroller general of the United States is the head of the General Accounting Office (GAO). The GAO is an agency of the legislative branch of the federal government and works with the Department of the Treasury, an executive department, to develop and maintain the federal government's accounting system. The GAO reviews the accounting systems of each executive agency each year from both a financial and a compliance perspective. The compliance part of the audit ensures that the agency fulfilled all legal and budgetary restrictions. Exceptions are reported to Congress, which then communicates them to the executive branch, thus completing the cycle that began when the executive branch first proposed the annual budget to Congress.

QUESTIONS

Q19-1 In what circumstances would a government unit use a special revenue fund rather than a general fund?

Q19-2 Which governmental funds use operating budgets? Which use capital budgets?

Q19-3 How is interest on long-term debt accounted for in the debt service fund?

Q19-4 What are the major differences between a special revenue fund and an enterprise fund?

Q19-5 What is the basis of accounting in the proprietary funds? Why?

Q19-6 What financial statements must be prepared for the governmental funds? For the enterprise funds?

Q19-7 Is the accounting basis for nonexpendable trust funds the same as for expendable trust funds? Why or why not?

Q19-8 Are all a government unit's fixed assets accounted for in the general fixed assets account group? Why or why not?

Q19-9 Does the general long-term debt account group account for all the long-term debt of the government unit? Why or why not?

Q19-10 Is interest payable accounted for in the general long-term debt account group?

Q19-11 What is the relationship between the debt service fund and the general long-term debt account group?

Q19-12 Explain the difference between combining financial statements and combined financial statements.

Q19-13 What information is presented in the comprehensive annual financial report that is not presented in the general-purpose financial statements?

Q19-14 What is the certificate of achievement? How is it received?

Q19-15 Explain the difference in financial reporting between reporting a component unit as a blended organization or as a discretely presented organization.

CASES

C19-1 Basis of Accounting and Reporting Issues

The accounting system of Barb City is organized and operated on a fund basis. Among the types of funds used are a general fund, a special revenue fund, and an enterprise fund.

Required

a. Explain the basic differences in revenue recognition between the accrual basis of accounting and the modified accrual basis of accounting in relation to governmental accounting.

b. What basis of accounting should be used for each of the following funds: **(1)** general fund, **(2)** special revenue fund, **(3)** enterprise fund?

c. Discuss the accounting procedures for fixed assets and long-term liabilities related to the general fund and to the enterprise fund.

d. How should the balance sheets of the general fund, the special revenue fund, and the enterprise fund be handled when preparing the comprehensive annual financial report? Why?

C19-2 Capital Projects, Debt Service, and Internal Service Funds

The funds of Lake City include a debt service fund, a capital projects fund, and an internal service fund.

Required

a. Explain the use of capital projects funds. Include what they account for, the basis of accounting used, unusual entries and accounts, and financial statements.

b. Explain the use of debt service funds. Include what they account for, the basis of accounting used, unusual entries and accounts, and financial statements.

c. Explain the use of internal service funds. Include what they account for, the basis of accounting used, unusual entries and accounts, and financial statements.

EXERCISES

E19-1 Multiple-Choice Questions on Budgets [AICPA Adapted]

Select the correct answer for each of the following questions.

1. Which of the following funds of a governmental unit integrates budgetary accounts into the accounting system?
   a. Enterprise.
   b. Special revenue.
   c. Internal service.
   d. Nonexpendable trust.

Items 2 through 4 are based on the following data:

The board of commissioners of Sugar Creek adopted its budget for the year ending July 31, 19X1, consisting of estimated revenue of $30,000,000 and appropriations of $29,000,000. Sugar Creek formally integrates its budget into the accounting records.

2. What entry should be made for budgeted revenue?
   a. Memorandum entry only.
   b. Debit Estimated Revenue Receivable, $30,000,000.
   c. Debit Estimated Revenues Control, $30,000,000.
   d. Credit Estimated Revenues Control, $30,000,000.

3. What entry should be made for budgeted appropriations?
   a. Memorandum entry only.
   b. Credit Estimated Expenditures Payable, $29,000,000.
   c. Credit Appropriations Control, $29,000,000.
   d. Debit Estimated Expenditures, $29,000,000.

4. What entry should be made for the budgeted excess of revenue over appropriations?
   a. Memorandum entry only.
   b. Credit Budgetary Fund Balance Unreserved, $1,000,000.
   c. Debit Estimated Excess Revenue, $1,000,000.
   d. Debit Excess Revenue Receivable, $1,000,000.

5. When the budget of a governmental unit is adopted and the estimated revenues exceed the appropriations, the excess is:
   a. Credited to Budgetary Fund Balance Unreserved.
   b. Debited to Budgetary Fund Balance Unreserved.
   c. Credited to Fund Balance Reserved for Encumbrances.
   d. Debited to Fund Balance Reserved for Encumbrances.

6. The Estimated Revenue account of a governmental unit is credited when:
   a. The budget is closed out at the end of the year.
   b. The budget is recorded.
   c. Property taxes are recorded.
   d. Property taxes are collected.

E19-2 Multiple-Choice Questions on Governmental Funds [AICPA Adapted]

Select the correct answer for each of the following questions.

1. On December 31, 19X1, Tiffin Township paid a contractor $2,000,000 for the total cost of a new firehouse built in 19X1 on township-owned land. Financing was by means of a $1,500,000 general obligation bond issue sold at face amount on December 31, 19X1, with the remaining $500,000 transferred from the general fund. What should be reported on Tiffin's financial statements for the capital projects fund?
   a. Revenue, $1,500,000; Expenditures, $1,500,000.
   b. Revenue, $1,500,000; Other Financing Sources, $500,000; Expenditures, $2,000,000.
   c. Revenue, $2,000,000; Expenditures, $2,000,000.
   d. Other Financing Sources, $2,000,000; Expenditures, $2,000,000.

2. Fixed assets should be accounted for in the general fixed assets account group for:

	Governmental Funds	Proprietary Funds
a.	No	Yes
b.	No	No
c.	Yes	No
d.	Yes	Yes

3. Which of the following funds of a governmental unit uses the same basis of accounting as the special revenue fund?
   a. Internal service.

    b. Expendable trust.

    c. Nonexpendable trust.

    d. Enterprise.

4. A debt service fund of a municipality is an example of which of the following types of funds?

    a. Fiduciary.

    b. Governmental.

    c. Proprietary.

    d. Internal service.

5. Revenue of a special revenue fund of a governmental unit should be recognized in the period in which the:

    a. Revenue becomes available and measurable.

    b. Revenue becomes available for appropriation.

    c. Revenue is billable.

    d. Cash is received.

6. Which of the following funds of a governmental unit would use the general long-term debt account group to account for unmatured general long-term liabilities?

    a. Capital projects.

    b. Nonexpendable trust.

    c. Internal service.

    d. Enterprise.

7. Which of the following funds of a governmental unit would use the general fixed assets account group to account for fixed assets?

    a. Internal service.

    b. Enterprise.

    c. Nonexpendable trust.

    d. Expendable trust.

8. Taxes collected and held by a municipality for a school district would be accounted for in a(n):

    a. Enterprise fund.

    b. Intragovernmental (internal) service fund.

    c. Agency fund.

    d. Special revenue fund.

9. Interest expense on bonds payable should be recorded in a debt service fund:

    a. At the end of the fiscal period if the interest due date does not coincide with the end of the fiscal period.

    b. When bonds are issued.

    c. When legally payable.

    d. When paid.

10. Which of the following funds frequently does not have a fund balance?

    a. General fund.

    b. Agency fund.

    c. Special revenue fund.

    d. Capital projects fund.

E19-3   Multiple-Choice Questions on Proprietary Funds [AICPA Adapted]

Select the correct answer for each of the following questions.

1. Which of the following accounts could be included in the balance sheet of an enterprise fund?

	Reserve for Encumbrances	Revenue Bonds Payable	Retained Earnings
a.	No	No	Yes
b.	No	Yes	Yes
c.	Yes	Yes	No
d.	No	No	No

2. Customers' meter deposits that cannot be spent for normal operating purposes would most likely be classified as restricted cash in the balance sheet of which fund?
   a. Internal service.
   b. Expendable trust.
   c. Agency.
   d. Enterprise.

3. Which fund is not an expendable fund?
   a. Capital projects.
   b. General.
   c. Special revenue.
   d. Internal service.

4. If a governmental unit established a data processing center to service all agencies within the unit, the data processing center should be accounted for as a(n):
   a. Capital projects fund.
   b. Internal service fund.
   c. Agency fund.
   d. Trust fund.

5. Recreational facilities run by a governmental unit and financed on a user-charge basis would be accounted for in which fund?
   a. General.
   b. Trust.
   c. Enterprise.
   d. Capital projects.

6. The Underwood Electric Utility Fund, which is an enterprise fund, had the following:

Prepaid insurance paid in December 19X1	$ 43,000
Depreciation for 19X1	129,000
Provision for doubtful accounts for 19X1	14,000

What amount should be reflected in the statement of revenue and expenses of the Underwood Electric Utility Fund for the above items?
   a. $(43,000).
   b. $0.
   c. $129,000.
   d. $143,000.

7. Which of the following funds of a governmental unit uses the same basis of accounting as an enterprise fund?
   a. Special revenue.
   b. Internal service.
   c. Expendable trust.
   d. Capital projects.

8. Fixed assets utilized in a city-owned utility are accounted for in which of the following?

	Enterprise Fund	General Fixed Assets Group of Accounts
a.	No	No
b.	No	Yes
c.	Yes	No
d.	Yes	Yes

9. Which of the following funds of a governmental unit would include retained earnings in its balance sheet?
   a. Expendable pension trust.
   b. Internal service.
   c. Special revenue.
   d. Capital projects.

10. Which of the following funds of a governmental unit would account for general long-term debt in the accounts of the fund?
   a. Special revenue.
   b. Capital projects.
   c. Internal service.
   d. General.

E19-4 Multiple-Choice Questions on Fiduciary Funds and Account Groups
[AICPA Adapted]

Select the correct answer for each of the following questions.

1. John Adams donated a building to Valley View in 19X3. Adams's original cost of the property was $100,000. Accumulated depreciation on the date of the gift amounted to $60,000. Fair market value on the date of the gift was $300,000. In the general fixed assets account group, at what amount should Valley View record this donated fixed asset?
   a. $300,000.
   b. $100,000.
   c. $40,000.
   d. $0.

2. Which type of fund can be either expendable or nonexpendable?
   a. Debt service.
   b. Enterprise.
   c. Trust.
   d. Special revenue.

3. The amount to be provided for retirement of general long-term debt is in an account of a governmental unit that would be included in the:

a. Assets section of the general long-term debt account group.

b. Assets section of the debt service fund.

c. Liabilities section of the general long-term debt account group.

d. Liabilities section of the debt service fund.

4. The following items were among Wyatt Township's expenditures from the general fund during the year ended July 31, 19X1:

Minicomputer for tax collector's office	$22,000
Furniture for Township Hall	40,000

How much should be classified as fixed assets in Wyatt's general fund balance sheet for July 31, 19X1?

a. $0.

b. $22,000.

c. $40,000.

d. $62,000.

5. Xenia issued the following bonds during the year ended June 30, 19X1:

Revenue bonds to be repaid from admission fees collected by the Xenia Zoo enterprise fund	$200,000
General obligation bonds issued for the Xenia water and sewer enterprise fund, which will service the debt	300,000

How much of these bonds should be accounted for in Xenia's general long-term debt account group?

a. $0.

b. $200,000.

c. $300,000.

d. $500,000.

6. Which of the following would be included in the combined statement of revenues, expenditures, and changes in fund balance—budget and actual, in the comprehensive annual financial report of a governmental unit?

	Enterprise Fund	General Fixed Asset Account Group
a.	Yes	Yes
b.	Yes	No
c.	No	Yes
d.	No	No

E19-5 Multiple-Choice Questions on Special Funds and Account Groups

Select the correct answer to the following questions.

1. The following information for the year ended June 30, 19X3, pertains to a proprietary fund established by Oakbrook in connection with Oakbrook's public parking facilities:

Receipts from users of parking facilities	$400,000
Expenditures:	
Parking meters	210,000
Salaries and other cash expenses	90,000
Depreciation of parking meters	70,000

For the year ended June 30, 19X3, this proprietary fund should report net income of:
a. $0.
b. $30,000.
c. $100,000.
d. $240,000.

2. The following proceeds received by Maple City in 19X3 are legally restricted to expenditure for specified purposes:

Donation by a benefactor mandated to an expendable trust fund to provide meals for the needy	$300,000
Sales taxes to finance the maintenance of tourist facilities in the shopping district	900,000

What amount should be accounted for in Maple's special revenue funds?
a. $0.
b. $300,000.
c. $900,000.
d. $1,200,000.

3. The following fund types used by Hodge City had total assets at December 31, 19X3, as follows:

Special revenue funds	$100,000
Agency funds	150,000
Trust funds	200,000

Total fiduciary fund assets amounted to:
a. $200,000.
b. $300,000.
c. $350,000.
d. $450,000.

4. During 19X3, Hill City recorded the following receipts from self-sustaining activities paid for by users of the services rendered:

Municipal bus system	$1,000,000
Operation of water supply and sewage plant	1,800,000

What amount should be accounted for in Hill's enterprise funds?
a. $2,800,000.
b. $1,800,000.

    c. $1,000,000.

    d. $0.

5. Vista County collects property taxes levied within its boundaries and receives a 1 percent fee for administering these collections on behalf of the municipalities located in the
county. In 19X3, Vista collected $1,000,000 for its municipalities and remitted $990,000
to them after deducting fees of $10,000. In the initial recording of the 1 percent fee,
Vista's agency fund should credit:

    a. Fund Balance—Agency Fund, $10,000.

    b. Fees Earned—Agency Fund, $10,000.

    c. Due to Vista County General Fund, $10,000.

    d. Revenues Control, $10,000.

6. In 19X3, Mint Village received $5,000,000 of bond proceeds to be used for capital
projects. Of this amount, $1,000,000 was expended in 19X3. Expenditures for the
$4,000,000 balance were expected to be incurred in 19X4. These bond proceeds should
be recorded in capital projects funds for:

    a. $5,000,000 in 19X3.

    b. $5,000,000 in 19X4.

    c. $1,000,000 in 19X3 and $4,000,000 in 19X4.

    d. $1,000,000 in 19X3 and in the general fund for $4,000,000 in 19X3.

7. Fort City operates a centralized data processing center through an internal service fund,
to provide data processing services to Fort's other governmental units. In 19X3, this
internal service fund billed Fort's water and sewer fund $100,000 for data processing
services. How should the internal service fund record this billing?

	Debit	Credit
a. Memoranda entry only	—	—
b. Due from Water and Sewer Fund	$100,000	
Data Processing Department		
Expenses		$100,000
c. Intergovernmental Transfers	$100,000	
Interfund Exchanges		$100,000
d. Due from Water and Sewer Fund	$100,000	
Operating Revenues Control		$100,000

8. Pond City received a gift of a new fire engine from a local resident. The fair market value
of this fire engine was $200,000. The entry to be made in the general fixed assets account
group for this gift is:

	Debit	Credit
a. Machinery and Equipment	$200,000	
Investment in General Fixed		
Assets from Private Gifts		$200,000
b. Investments in General Fixed Assets	$200,000	
Gift Revenue		$200,000
c. General Fund Assets	$200,000	
Private Gifts		$200,000
d. Memorandum entry only	—	—

E19-6 Capital Projects Fund Entries

York established a capital projects fund for the construction of a walkway over Kish Avenue from the courthouse to the parking garage. The estimated cost is $300,000. The county commission agreed to provide a $100,000 grant. A 9 percent, $200,000 bond issue was sold at 102.5. The York City Council awarded a construction contract for $275,000 on March 1, 19X1. The walkway was completed on November 10, 19X1, and the actual cost was $282,000. The city council approved payment of the extra cost. The walkway was carpeted at a cost of $7,400. On December 15, 19X1, the city council gave the final approval of payment for the walkway. The fund balance was transferred to the debt service fund.

Required

Prepare entries for the capital projects fund to record the following:

  a. Receipt of the county grant, sale of the bonds, and transfer of the bond premium.
  b. Issue of the construction contract, actual cost, carpeting, and payment.
  c. Closing of the nominal accounts.
  d. Transfer of the balance to the debt service fund.

E19-7 Debt Service Fund Entries and Statement

York established a debt service fund to account for the bonds issued to finance the walkway (see Exercise 19-6). The 9 percent, $200,000 bond issue was sold at 102.5 on January 1, 19X1. It is a 10-year serial bond issue. The funds to pay the interest and annual principal will be from a property tax levy.

Additional information:

  1. The operating budget for 19X1 included estimated revenue of $38,000 and appropriations of $20,000 for principal and $18,000 for interest and an estimated operating transfer of $5,000 from the capital projects fund.
  2. The property tax levy was for $40,000, and an allowance for uncollectibles of $4,000 was established. Collections totaled $36,000. The remaining taxes were reclassified as delinquent, and the allowance was reduced to $1,000. The bond premium was received from the capital projects funds.
  3. The current portion of the serial bonds and the interest due this year were recorded and paid. Other expenses charged to the debt service fund totaled $1,800, and $1,500 was paid.
  4. The nominal accounts were closed.

Required

  a. Prepare entries for the debt service fund for 19X1.
  b. Prepare a statement of revenues, expenditures, and changes in fund balance for 19X1.

E19-8 Enterprise Fund Entries and Statements

Augusta has a municipal water and gas utility district (MUD). The trial balance on January 1, 19X1, was as follows:

	Debit	Credit
Cash	$ 92,000	
Accounts Receivable	25,000	
Inventory of Supplies	8,000	
Land	120,000	
Plant and Equipment	480,000	
Accumulated Depreciation		$ 80,000
Vouchers Payable		15,000
Bonds Payable, 6%		500,000
Contributed Capital		100,000
Retained Earnings		30,000
	$725,000	$725,000

Additional information for 19X1:

1. Charges to customers for water and gas were $420,000; collections were $432,000.

2. A loan of $30,000 for 2 years was received from the general fund.

3. The water and gas lines were extended to a new development at a cost of $75,000. The contractor was paid.

4. Supplies were acquired from central stores (internal service fund) for $12,400. Operating expenses were $328,000, and interest expense was $30,000. Payment was made for the interest and the payable to central stores, and $325,000 of the vouchers were paid.

5. Adjusting entries were as follows: Bad Debts Expense, $6,300; Depreciation Expense, $32,000; Supplies on Hand, $5,200.

Required

a. Prepare entries for the MUD enterprise fund for 19X1, and prepare closing entries.

b. Prepare a balance sheet for the fund for December 31, 19X1.

c. Prepare a statement of revenues, expenses, and changes in retained earnings for 19X1.

d. Prepare a statement of cash flows for 19X1.

E19-9 Internal Service Fund Entries [AICPA Adapted]

Eagle Rock operates a central garage through an internal service fund to provide garage space and repairs for all city-owned and operated vehicles. The central garage fund was established by a contribution of $300,000 from the general fund on July 1, 19X1, at which time the building was acquired. The afterclosing trial balance on June 30, 19X3, was as follows:

	Debit	Credit
Cash	$ 50,000	
Due from General Fund	20,000	
Inventory of Supplies	80,000	
Land	60,000	
Building	300,000	
Accumulated Depreciation—Building		$ 20,000
Machinery and Equipment	75,000	
Accumulated Depreciation—Machinery and Equipment		12,000
Vouchers Payable		38,000
Contribution from General Fund		300,000
Retained Earnings		215,000
	$585,000	$585,000

The following information applies to the fiscal year ended June 30, 19X4:

1. Supplies were purchased on account for $74,000.

2. The inventory of supplies on June 30, 19X4, was $58,000, which agreed with the physical count taken.

3. Salaries and wages paid to employees totaled $230,000, including related costs.

4. A billing was received from the enterprise fund for utility charges totaling $30,000 and was paid.

5. Depreciation of the building was recorded in the amount of $10,000. Depreciation of the machinery and equipment amounted to $8,000.

6. Billings to other departments for services rendered to them were as follows:

General fund	$262,000
Water and sewer fund	84,000
Special revenue fund	32,000

7. Uncollected interfund receivable balances on June 30, 19X4, were as follows:

General fund	$ 6,000
Special revenue fund	16,000

8. Vouchers payable on June 30, 19X4, were $14,000. All other vouchers were paid.

Required

a. For fiscal 19X4, prepare journal entries to record all the transactions in the central garage fund accounts.

b. Prepare closing entries for the central garage fund on June 30, 19X4.

E19-10   Internal Service Fund Entries and Statements

The Bellevue City printing shop had the following trial balance on January 1, 19X2:

	Debit	Credit
Cash	$ 24,600	
Due from Other Funds	15,600	
Inventory of Supplies	9,800	
Furniture and Equipment	260,000	
Accumulated Depreciation		$ 50,000
Vouchers Payable		12,000
Contributed Capital		200,000
Retained Earnings		48,000
	$310,000	$310,000

Additional information:

1. During 19X2, the printing shop acquired supplies for $96,000, furniture for $1,500, and a copier for $3,200.

2. Printing jobs billed to other funds amounted to $292,000; cash received from other funds, $287,300; costs of printing jobs, $204,000, including $84,000 of supplies; operating expenses, $38,000, including $8,400 of supplies; depreciation expense, $23,000; vouchers paid, $243,000.

Required

a. Prepare entries for the printing shop for 19X2, including closing entries.

b. Prepare a balance sheet for the fund on December 31, 19X2.

c. Prepare a statement of revenues, expenses, and changes in retained earnings for 19X2.

d. Prepare a statement of cash flows for 19X2.

E19-11   Trust Funds Entries and Statements

The city of Sycamore received an endowment of $500,000 from a former resident who is a professional golfer. The $500,000 is to be invested, and the income is to be used to develop a junior golf program at the public golf courses.

Additional information:

1. A nonexpendable trust fund was established on July 5, 19X1. The trust acquired $400,000 of 10 percent government bonds at 105. The remainder was invested in certificates of deposit.

2. On January 1, 19X2, the trustee received $20,000 in interest from the bonds and recorded $1,000 amortization.

3. By March 31, interest income from the certificates of deposit totaled $6,000. The $25,000 (interest less amortization) was transferred to an expendable trust fund, where it will be used to develop a junior golf program.

4. On June 30, 19X2, the trustee recorded $20,000 interest receivable and $1,000 amortization, and recognized a liability to the expendable trust fund for $19,000. Also, she recorded $1,800 other interest which was then transferred to the expendable fund.

5. The expendable trust fund incurred salary, promotion, and supplies expenses of $21,500. Vouchers totaling $18,200 were paid. On June 30, 19X2, supplies on hand were $780. The fund uses the purchase method of accounting for inventories.

Required

a. Prepare entries for the nonexpendable and expendable trust funds for fiscal 19X2, including adjusting and closing entries.

b. Prepare a balance sheet with a column for each trust fund as of June 30, 19X2.

c. Prepare a statement of revenues, expenses, and changes in retained earnings for the nonexpendable trust fund for fiscal 19X2.

d. Prepare a statement of revenues, expenses, and changes in fund balance for the expendable trust fund for fiscal 19X2.

PROBLEMS

P19-12 Capital Projects Fund Entries and Balance Sheet [AICPA Adapted]

During the fiscal year ended June 30, 19X1, Prescott authorized the construction of a new library and sale of general obligation bonds to finance the construction. The authorization imposed the following restrictions:

Construction cost was not to exceed $5,000,000.
Annual interest rate was not to exceed 9 percent.

The following transactions related to financing and construction of the library occurred during fiscal 19X2:

1. On July 1, 19X1, the city issued $5,000,000 of 30-year, 8 percent general obligation bonds for $5,100,000. The semiannual interest dates are December 31 and June 30. The premium of $100,000 was transferred to the library debt service fund.

2. On July 3, 19X1, the library capital projects fund invested $4,900,000 in short-term commercial paper. These purchases were at face value with no accrued interest. Interest on cash invested by the library capital projects fund must be transferred to the library debt service fund. The fiscal 19X2 estimated interest to be earned was $140,000.

3. On July 5, 19X1, the city signed a contract with Ace Construction Company to build the library for $4,980,000.

4. On January 15, 19X2, the library capital projects fund received $3,040,000 from the maturity of short-term notes purchased on July 3. The cost of these notes was $3,000,000. The interest of $40,000 was transferred to the library debt service fund.

5. On January 20, 19X2, Ace Construction Company properly billed the city $3,000,000 for work performed on the new library. The contract calls for 10 percent retention until final inspection and acceptance of the building. The library capital projects fund paid Ace $2,700,000.

6. On June 30, 19X2, the library capital projects fund made the proper adjusting entries (including accrued interest receivable of $103,000) and closing entries.

Required

a. Prepare in good form journal entries to record the six preceding sets of facts in the library capital projects fund. List the transaction numbers (1 through 6), and give the necessary entry or entries. Do not record journal entries in any other fund or group of accounts.

b. Prepare in good form a balance sheet for the Prescott library capital projects fund as of June 30, 19X2.

P19-13 Adjusting Entries for General Fund and Account Groups [AICPA Adapted]

On June 30, 19X2, the end of the fiscal year, the Wadsworth Park District prepared the following trial balance for the general fund:

	Debit	Credit
Cash	$ 47,250	
Taxes Receivable—Current	31,800	
Allowance for Uncollectibles—Current		$ 1,800
Temporary Investments	11,300	
Inventory of Supplies	11,450	
Buildings	1,300,000	
Estimated Revenues Control	1,007,000	
Appropriations Control		1,000,000
Revenue—State Grants		300,000
Bonds Payable		1,000,000
Vouchers Payable		10,200
Expenditures	848,200	
Debt Service from Current Funds	130,000	
Capital Outlays (Equipment)	22,000	
Revenue—Taxes		1,008,200
Unreserved Fund Balance		81,800
Budgetary Fund Balance Unreserved		7,000
	$3,409,000	$3,409,000

An examination of the records disclosed the following information:

1. The recorded estimate of losses for the current year taxes receivable was considered to be adequate.

2. The local government unit gave the park district 20 acres of land to be used for a new community park. The unrecorded estimated value of the land was $50,000. In addition, a state grant of $300,000 was received, and the full amount was used in payment of contracts pertaining to the construction of the park. Purchases of playground equipment costing $22,000 were paid from general funds.

3. Five years ago, a 4 percent, 10-year sinking fund bond issue in the amount of $1,000,000 for constructing park buildings was sold; it is still outstanding. Interest on the issue is payable at maturity. Budgetary requirements of a contribution of $130,000 to the debt service fund were met. Of this amount, $100,000 represents the fifth equal contribution for principal repayment.

4. Outstanding purchase orders not recorded in the accounts at year-end totaled $2,800.

5. A physical inventory of supplies at year-end revealed $6,500 of the supplies on hand. Wadsworth uses the consumption method of accounting for inventories.

6. Except where indicated to the contrary, all recordings were made in the general fund.

Required

a. Prepare the adjusting entries to correct the general fund records.

b. Prepare the adjusting entries for the general fixed assets account group and the general long-term debt account group.

P19-14   Adjusting Entries for General Fund and Account Groups [AICPA Adapted]

You have been engaged to examine the financial statements of Fairfield for the year ended June 30, 19X2. You discover that all transactions were recorded in the general fund. The general fund trial balance as of June 30, 19X2, was:

	Debit	Credit
Cash	$ 16,800	
Short-Term Investments	40,000	
Accounts Receivable	11,500	
Taxes Receivable—Current Year	30,000	
Tax Anticipation Notes Payable		$ 50,000
Appropriations Control		400,000
Expenditures	382,000	
Estimated Revenues Control	320,000	
Revenue		360,000
General Property	85,400	
Bonds Payable	52,000	
Unreserved Fund Balance		207,700
Budgetary Fund Balance Unreserved	80,000	
	$1,017,700	$1,017,700

Your audit disclosed the following additional information:

1. The accounts receivable and revenue include $1,500 due to the city's water utility for the sale of its scrap.

2. The balance in Taxes Receivable—Current Year is now considered delinquent, and the town estimates that $24,000 will be uncollectible.

3. On June 30, 19X2, the town retired, at face value, 6 percent general obligation serial bonds totaling $40,000. The bonds were issued 5 years ago, at face value of $200,000. Interest paid during the year ended June 30, 19X2, was charged to Bonds Payable.

4. During the year, supplies totaling $128,000 were purchased and charged to Expenditures. The town conducted a physical inventory of supplies on hand for June 30, 19X2, and this physical count disclosed that supplies totaling $84,000 were used. Fairfield uses the consumption method of accounting for inventories.

5. Expenditures for the year ended June 30, 19X2, included $11,200 applicable to purchase orders issued in the prior year. Outstanding purchase orders as of June 30, 19X2, not recorded in the accounts amounted to $17,500. Fairfield used the nonlapsing method.

6. On June 28, 19X2, the State Revenue Department informed the town that its share of a state-collected, locally shared tax would be $34,000.

7. During the year, equipment with a book value of $7,900 was removed from service and sold for $4,600. In addition, new equipment costing $90,000 was purchased. The transactions were recorded in General Property.

8. During the year, 100 acres of land was donated to the town for use as an industrial park. The land had a value of $125,000. No recording of this donation has been made.

Required

a. Prepare formal reclassification and adjusting journal entries for the general fund as of June 30, 19X2. Account titles should be respected if acceptable, though different.

b. Prepare adjusting journal entries for the general long-term debt account group and the general fixed assets account group as of June 30, 19X2.

c. Prepare closing entries for the general fund as of June 30, 19X2.

P19-15   Entries for Funds and Account Groups [AICPA Adapted]

The following transactions represent practical situations frequently encountered in accounting for municipal governments. Each transaction is independent of the others.

1. The city council of Green Acres adopted a general operating budget in which revenue is estimated at $695,000 and anticipated expenditures are $650,000.

2. Taxes of $160,000 are levied for the special revenue fund of Hiawatha. One percent is estimated to be uncollectible.

3. On July 25, 19X2, office supplies estimated to cost $2,390 are ordered by Ivyton, which operates on the calendar-year basis and does not use a perpetual inventory system. The supplies are received on August 9, 19X2, accompanied by an invoice for $2,500.

4. On October 10, 19X2, the general fund of Junction City repaid to the utility fund a loan of $1,000 plus $40 interest. The loan had been made earlier in the fiscal year.

5. A prominent citizen died and left 10 acres of undeveloped land to Kezar Falls for a future school site. The donor's cost of the land was $55,000. The fair market value of the land at the date of death was $90,000.

6. On March 1, 19X2, Lakeland issued 6 percent special assessment bonds, payable March 1, 19X7, at face value of $90,000. The city is obligated in the event the property owners default. Interest is payable annually. Lakeland, which operates on the calendar-year basis, will use the proceeds to finance a curbing project. On October 29, 19X2, the cost of the completed project was $84,000. The contract had not been encumbered or paid.

7. A citizen of Montague donated common stock valued at $32,000 to the city. Under the terms of an agreement, the principal amount is not to be expended. Income from the stock must be used for college scholarships. On December 14, 19X2, dividends of $1,100 are received and transferred to the endowment income fund.

8. On February 1, 19X3, the city of Northstar, which operates on a calendar-year basis, issued 6 percent general obligation bonds with a face value of $300,000. Interest is payable annually on February 1. Total proceeds were $308,000; the premium was transferred to the debt service fund for ultimate payment of principal. The bond issue was floated to finance the construction of an addition to the city hall, estimated to cost $300,000. On December 30, 19X3, the addition was completed at a cost of $297,000, all of which was paid.

Required

For each of the transactions described, prepare the necessary journal entries for all the funds and groups of accounts involved. Indicate the fund or group in which each entry would be made by using the following format:

Fund or Group	**Journal Entry**

P19-16 Entries for Funds and Account Groups [AICPA Adapted]

Olivia Village was recently incorporated and began financial operations on July 1, 19X2, the beginning of its fiscal year. The following transactions occurred during this first fiscal year, July 1, 19X2, to June 30, 19X3:

1. The village council adopted a budget for general operations for the fiscal year ending June 30, 19X3. Revenue was estimated at $400,000. Legal authorizations for budgeted expenditures were $394,000.

2. Property taxes were levied in the amount of $390,000; it was estimated that 2 percent of this amount would prove uncollectible. These taxes are available as of the date of levy to finance current expenditures.

3. During the year, a resident of the village donated marketable securities valued at $50,000 to the village under the terms of a trust agreement. The terms of the trust agreement stipulated that the principal amount is to be kept intact. The use of revenue generated by the securities is restricted to financing college scholarships for needy students. Revenue earned and received on these marketable securities amounted to $5,500 through June 30, 19X3, and was transferred to the endowment income fund.

4. A general fund transfer of $5,000 was made in order to establish an internal service fund to provide for a permanent investment in inventory.

5. The village decided to install lighting in the village park, and a special assessment project was authorized to install the lighting at a cost of $75,000. The city is obligated if the property owners default on their special assessments. Special assessment bonds were issued in the amount of $72,000, and the first year's special assessment of $24,000 was levied against the village's property owners. The remaining $3,000 for the project will be contributed from the village's general fund.

6. The special assessments for the lighting project are due over a 3-year period, and the first year's assessments of $24,000 were collected. The $3,000 transfer from the village's general fund was received by the lighting capital projects fund.

7. A contract for $75,000 was let for the installation of the lighting. The capital projects fund was encumbered for the contract. On June 30, 19X3, the contract was completed and the contractor was paid.

8. During the year, the internal service fund purchased various supplies at a cost of $1,900.

9. Cash collections recorded by the general fund during the year were as follows:

Current property taxes	$386,000
Licenses and permit fees	7,000

The allowance for estimated uncollectible taxes is adjusted to $4,000.

10. The village council decided to build a village hall at an estimated cost of $500,000 to replace space occupied in rented facilities. The village does not record project authorizations. It was decided that general obligation bonds bearing interest at 6 percent would be issued. On June 30, 19X3, the bonds were issued at face value of $500,000, payable in 20 years. No contracts have been signed for this project, and no expenditures have been made, nor has an annual operating budget been prepared.

11. A fire truck was purchased for $15,000 and the voucher was approved and paid by the general fund. This expenditure was previously encumbered for $15,000.

Required

Prepare journal entries to record properly each of these transactions in the appropriate fund, funds, or account groups of Olivia Village for the fiscal year ended June 30, 19X3. Use the following funds and account groups: general fund, capital projects fund, internal service fund, endowment principal fund, endowment income fund, general long-term debt account group, and general fixed assets account group. Each journal entry should be numbered to correspond to the transactions. Do not prepare closing entries for any fund. Your answer sheet should be organized as follows:

Fund or Group	Journal Entry

P19-17   Entries to Adjust Account Balances [AICPA Adapted]

You have been assigned by the town of Papillion to examine its June 30, 19X1, balance sheet. You are the first CPA to be engaged by the town, and you find that acceptable methods of municipal accounting have not been employed. The town clerk stated that the books had not been closed and presented the following preclosing trial balance of the general fund as of June 30, 19X1:

	Debit	Credit
Cash	$150,000	
Taxes Receivable—Current Year	59,200	
Allowance for Uncollectibles—Current		$ 18,000
Taxes Receivable—Delinquent	8,000	
Allowance for Uncollectibles—Delinquent		10,200
Estimated Revenues Control	310,000	
Appropriations Control		348,000
Donated Land	27,000	
Expenditures—Building Addition Constructed	50,000	
Expenditures—Serial Bonds Paid	16,000	
Other Expenditures	280,000	
Special Assessment Bonds Payable		100,000
Revenue		354,000
Accounts Payable		26,000
Unreserved Fund Balance		82,000
Budgetary Fund Balance Unreserved	38,000	
	$938,200	$938,200

Additional information:

1. The estimated losses of $18,000 for current-year taxes receivable were determined to be a reasonable estimate. The delinquent taxes allowance account should be adjusted to $8,000, the remaining delinquent taxes.

2. Included in the Revenue account is a credit of $27,000, representing the value of land donated by the state as a grant-in-aid for construction of a municipal park.

3. Operating supplies ordered in the prior fiscal year and chargeable to that year were received, recorded, and consumed in July 19X0. The outstanding purchase orders for these supplies, which were not recorded in the accounts on June 30, 19X0, amounted to $8,800. The vendors' invoices for these supplies totaled $9,400. Appropriations lapse 1 year after the end of the fiscal year for which they are made.

4. Outstanding purchase orders on June 30, 19X1, for operating supplies totaled $2,100. These purchase orders were not recorded on the books.

5. The special assessment bonds were sold in June 19X1 to finance a street-paving project. No contracts have been signed for this project, and no expenditures have been made from the capital projects fund. The city is obligated for the bonds if the property owners default.

6. The balance in the Revenue account includes credits for $20,000 for a note issued to a bank to obtain cash in anticipation of tax collections and for $1,000 for the sale of scrap iron from the town's water plant. The note was still outstanding on June 30, 19X1. The operations of the water plant are accounted for in the water fund.

7. The Expenditures—Building Addition Constructed account balance is the cost of an addition to the town hall building. This addition was constructed and completed in June 19X1. The general fund recorded the payment as authorized.

8. The Expenditures—Serial Bonds Paid account reflects the annual retirement of general obligation bonds issued to finance the construction of the town hall. Interest payments of $7,000 for the bond issue are included in other expenditures.

Required

a. Prepare the formal adjusting and closing journal entries for the general fund for the fiscal year ended June 30, 19X1.

b. The foregoing information disclosed by your examination was recorded only in the general fund even though other funds or groups of accounts were involved. Prepare the formal adjusting journal entries for any other funds or groups of accounts involved.

P19-18 Capital Projects Fund Entries and Statements

During the fiscal year ended June 30, 19X3, West City Council authorized construction of a new city hall building, and the sale of serial bonds to finance the construction. The following transactions, related to financing and constructing the city hall, occur during fiscal 19X3:

1. On August 1, 19X2, West issues $5,000,000 of serial bonds for $5,080,000. Interest is payable annually and the first retirement of $500,000 is due on July 31, 19X7. The premium is transferred to the debt service fund.

2. The old city hall, which had a recorded cost of $650,000, is torn down. The cost of razing the old building is $45,000, net of salvage value. This cost was included in the capital budget, but was not encumbered. The cost is vouchered and paid.

3. West signs a contract with Roth Construction Co. to build the city hall for $4,500,000. The contract cost is to be encumbered. Construction is to be completed during fiscal 19X4.

4. Roth Construction Co. bills West $2,000,000 for construction completed during fiscal 19X3. Ten percent of the billings will be retained until final acceptance of the new city hall.

Required

   a. For each of the transactions above, prepare the necessary journal entries for all the funds or account groups involved. Indicate the fund or account group in which the entry is made by giving its initials in the left margin: CPF, DSF, GFAAG, or GLTDAG. Give the closing entries for the capital projects fund.

   b. Prepare a balance sheet for the capital projects fund at June 30, 19X3.

   c. Prepare a statement of revenues, expenditures, and changes in fund balance for the capital projects fund for the fiscal year ended June 30, 19X3.

P19-19 Workpaper for Allocation of Joint Tax Collections [AICPA Adapted]

In compliance with a newly enacted state law, DeKalb County assumed the responsibility of collecting all property taxes levied within its boundaries as of July 1, 19X1. A composite property tax rate per $100 of net assessed valuation was developed for the fiscal year ending June 30, 19X2, and is presented below.

DeKalb County General Fund	$ 6.00
Sycamore City General Fund	3.00
Cortland Township General Fund	1.00
	$10.00

All property taxes are due in quarterly installments, and when collected, are then distributed to the governmental units represented in the composite rate. In order to administer collection and distribution of such taxes, the county has established a tax agency fund.

Additional information:

   1. In order to reimburse the county for estimated administration expenses of operating the tax agency fund, the tax agency fund is to deduct 2 percent from the tax collections each quarter for Sycamore City and Cortland Township. The total amount deducted is to be remitted to the DeKalb County general fund.

   2. Current-year tax levies to be collected by the tax agency fund are as follows:

	Gross Levy	Estimated Amount to Be Collected
DeKalb County	$3,600,000	$3,500,000
Sycamore City	1,800,000	1,740,000
Cortland Township	600,000	560,000
	$6,000,000	$5,800,000

   3. Cortland Township was charged back $10,000 because of an error in the original computation of its current gross tax levy and the estimated amount to be collected.

4. As of September 30, 19X1, the tax agency fund has received $1,440,000 in first-quarter payments. On October 1, 19X1, this fund made a distribution to the three governmental entities.

Required

For the period July 1, 19X1, through October 1, 19X1, prepare journal entries, using a workpaper format, to record the effects of the transactions described above. The workpaper should have the following headings:

Account	DeKalb County Tax Agency Fund		DeKalb County General Fund		Sycamore City General Fund		Cortland Township General Fund	
	Debit	Credit	Debit	Credit	Debit	Credit	Debit	Credit

P19-20 Workpaper to Correct Municipal Trial Balance [AICPA Adapted]

White City was incorporated and began operations on January 1, 19X3. The budget approved by the city council was recorded, but the cash basis was used in White's books for all 19X3 transactions. White has decided to use encumbrance accounting. White's cash-basis general fund trial balance at December 31, 19X3, is presented below.

Debits	
Cash	$477,800
Expenditures	145,000
Estimated Revenues	228,200
Total	$851,000

Credits	
Appropriations Control	$204,000
Revenues	216,800
Bonds Payable	400,000
Premium on Bonds Payable	6,000
Fund Balance Unreserved	24,200
Total	$851,000

Additional information:

	Budgeted	Actual
Revenues		
Property Taxes	$205,200	$192,000
Licenses	14,800	15,800
Fines	8,200	9,000
Totals	$228,200	$216,800
Appropriations		
Services	$ 90,000	$ 77,000
Supplies	38,000	22,000
Equipment	76,000	46,000
Totals	$204,000	$145,000

It was estimated that 5 percent of the property taxes would not be collected. Accordingly, property taxes were levied to yield the budgeted amount of $205,200. Taxes of $192,000 had been collected by December 31, 19X3, and it was expected that all remaining collectible taxes would be received by February 28, 19X4.

Supplies of $8,000 and equipment of $20,000 were received, but the vouchers were unpaid at December 31, 19X3. Purchase orders were still outstanding for supplies and equipment not yet received, in the amounts of $2,400 and $7,600.

It was decided to record $3,400 physical inventory of supplies on hand on December 31, 19X3. In conformity with a city ordinance, expenditures are based on purchases rather than usage.

On November 1, 19X3, White issued 4 percent general obligation, 20-year bonds of $400,000 at $101\frac{1}{2}$. Interest is payable each May 1 and November 1. Cash from the bond premium is to be set aside in the debt service fund and restricted for eventual retirement of bond principal. The bonds were issued to finance the construction of a firehouse, but no contracts had been executed by December 31, 19X3.

Required

Prepare a workpaper with the following format. Using the workpaper you have prepared, show all adjustments and distributions to the proper funds or account groups, before closing entries, in conformity with generally accepted accounting principles applicable to governmental entities.

| | | Adjustments | | | Debt | Capital | Account Groups | |
Account	Trial Balance	Debit	Credit	General Fund	Service Fund	Projects Fund	General Fixed Assets	General Long-Term Debt
Debits:								
Cash	$477,800							
Expenditures	145,000							
Estimated revenues	228,200							
Totals	$851,000							
Credits:								
Appropriations	$204,000							
Revenues and other financing sources	216,800							
Bonds payable	400,000							
Premium on bonds payable	6,000							
Fund balance	24,200							
Totals	$851,000							

CHAPTER 20

NOT-FOR-PROFIT ENTITIES: COLLEGES AND UNIVERSITIES

This chapter provides a bridge between fund accounting for local governmental entities and accounting for other not-for-profit entities. Accounting for colleges and universities is based on the principles of fund accounting presented in Chapters 18 and 19, but includes several unique aspects because of the operating objectives and sources of revenue of these institutions. This chapter presents the financial reporting principles for colleges and universities.

OVERVIEW OF ACCOUNTING FOR COLLEGES AND UNIVERSITIES

There are over 2,400 colleges and universities in the United States. Some offer 2-year programs, some offer 4-year programs, and others offer a wide selection of both undergraduate and graduate programs. Public and private institutions provide a large variety of liberal arts, science, and professional programs for our society. Public colleges and universities receive a significant portion of their operating resources from state governments. Private colleges and universities receive most of their resources from tuition and fees, but they use most of the same accounting and financial reporting principles as public institutions.

In 1973, the AICPA published *Audits of Colleges and Universities* as a guide to auditors. In 1974, *College and University Business Administration* (CUBA) was published by the National Association of College and University Business Officers (NACUBO). The differences between these two documents were relatively minor, and in 1974 the Accounting Standards Division of the AICPA issued **Statement of Position-74**, "Financial Accounting and Reporting by Colleges and Universities" (SOP-74), which amended the audit guide to conform to the 1974 CUBA. The comprehensive college and university illustration presented in this chapter is adapted from CUBA. CUBA is actually a loose-leaf service and is updated periodically. The 1974 edition has undergone slight revisions since its issuance.

GASB Statement No. 15, "Governmental College and University Accounting and Financial Reporting Models" (GASB 15), provides that public colleges and universities may follow the AICPA (NACUBO) accounting and financial reporting model. The alternative model is the governmental model of accounting and reporting as presented in Chapters 18 and 19. Because virtually all public colleges and universities follow the AICPA model, this chapter presents the accounting and financial reporting requirements established by that model. The chapter presents the major financial statements required for colleges and universities and then illustrates the transactions and entries that are reported in them. A financial statement orientation seems the most direct approach to learning the accounting and disclosure requirements for colleges and universities.

Fund Structure for Colleges and Universities

Colleges and universities use six major funds to account for their resources. Endowments and gifts from alumni are a major source of resources for many institutions, and several funds are established to account for these resources. Colleges and universities also use a subfund structure, often termed "funds within a fund." This chapter illustrates the accounting and financial reporting for each of the funds and *subfunds*. The fund structure for colleges and universities recommended by CUBA is as follows:

Fund Group	Major Subfunds
1. Current funds	Current funds—unrestricted
	Current funds—restricted
2. Loan funds	
3. Endowment and similar funds	Endowment funds
	Term endowment funds
	Quasi-endowment funds
4. Annuity and life income funds	Annuity funds
	Life income funds
5. Plant funds	Unexpended funds
	Funds for renewals and replacements
	Funds for retirement of indebtedness
	Investment in plant
6. Agency funds	

Accounting for the funds of colleges and universities is in many ways similar to fund accounting for government units. Both account for the revenue and expenditures in the expendable funds. Both use budgets to plan and monitor operations. Both use a system of encumbrances to account for purchase orders issued. Both have interfund transactions and transfers. Finally, both present combined balance sheets and operating statements for the period.

Several differences exist, however, relating to funds received. Colleges and universities must distinguish between *restricted funds* and *unrestricted funds*. Restrictions may be externally imposed by the grantors of gifts or endowments. In addition, the governing board of the university, sometimes called a "board of regents" or a "board of trustees," may *designate* monies for specific purposes. However, the government board may not *restrict* a fund. Therefore, whenever the term *restricted* is used in college and university accounting, it refers to an externally imposed constraint on the use of funds, not an internally imposed designation. **Financial Accounting Concepts Statement No. 6**, "Elements of Financial Statements" (FAC 6), specifies three mutually exclusive groups of assets: permanently restricted net assets, temporarily restricted net assets, and unrestricted net assets.

Figure 20-1 presents an overview of the accounting and financial reporting for colleges and universities as a basic reference for use throughout this chapter. Accounting and financial reporting for each of the fund groups and subfunds is now discussed and illustrated.

UNRESTRICTED CURRENT FUND

The **unrestricted current fund** accounts for the resources that may be expended to carry out the primary purposes of the institution—instruction, research, and public service—and that are not restricted to specific purposes. The unrestricted current fund is similar in purpose to the general fund of a state or local government entity.

FIGURE 20-1 Overview of college and university accounting and reporting.

	Fund Groups						
	Current Funds						
	Unrestricted	Restricted	Loan	Endowment and Similar	Annuity and Life Income	Plant	Agency
Accounting basis	Accrual	Revenue recognized to extent of resources expended.	Contributions and transfers are credited directly to fund balances. Expendable resources are transferred to current funds except for capital outlay and debt retirement, which are accounted for in the plant funds.				No revenue recognized.
Financial statements	Statement of current funds revenue, expenditures, and other changes						
	Statement of changes in fund balance						
	Balance sheet (combined)						

Accounting Basis and Financial Statements   The accounting basis of the unrestricted current fund is the accrual method, as used for commercial entities. Instead of net income, however, the difference between revenue and expenditures is accounted for as a net change to fund balance.

The three financial statements required for the unrestricted current fund are a balance sheet; a statement of revenue, expenditures, and other changes; and a statement of changes in fund balances. Comparative amounts for the preceding fiscal period are also required as part of each of the statements. The general format of these statements is quite similar to that used by local and state governments.

Revenue   The typical revenue and expenditure accounts used in the unrestricted current fund are presented in Figure 20-2. The primary sources of revenue include tuition and fees from students; grants from government sources, both state and federal; gifts from individuals; income from investments; and revenue from sales of services. A significant source of revenue in the unrestricted current fund is from auxiliary enterprises. These are the many operations of a college or university not directly related to the educational mission. Auxiliary enterprises include the student union, cafeterias, bookstores, residence halls, and intercollegiate athletics.

Expenditures   Major expenditures are related to the primary missions of the college or university. In addition to instruction, research, and public service, the

FIGURE 20-2 Classification of current funds revenue, expenditures, and transfers.

Revenue	Expenditures and Transfers
Tuition and fees	Educational and general:
Appropriations:	Instruction
Federal, state, and local	Research
Grants and contracts:	Public service
Federal, state, and local	Academic support, e.g., libraries, computing
Private gifts, grants, and contracts	services
Endowment income	Student services, e.g., dean of students, financial aid administration, career guidance and placement, intramural athletics
Sales and services of educational activities, e.g., testing services, film rentals	Institutional support, e.g., alumni office, legal counsel, purchasing, central accounting
Sales and services of auxiliary enterprises, e.g., residence halls, food services, university union, hospitals, athletic programs	Operation and maintenance of plant
Other sources	Scholarships and fellowships
Independent operations	Mandatory transfers
	Nonmandatory transfers
	Auxiliary enterprises and others:
	Expenditures
	Mandatory transfers

institution must also provide libraries, computing facilities, student services offices, and other support facilities. Each of these functions is individually represented in the accounts.

Budgets Colleges and universities normally prepare detailed budgets by function, object, department, and expenditure class. These budgets are typically entered into the accounts as with governmental accounting, but with a minor difference: instead of using BUDGETARY FUND BALANCE for the difference between budgeted revenue and expenditures, colleges and universities use an account called UNALLOCATED BUDGET BALANCE. The format for the budget entry is:

UNREALIZED REVENUE	XXX,XXX	
ESTIMATED EXPENDITURES		XXX,XXX
UNALLOCATED BUDGET BALANCE		XX

The budgetary accounts are closed at the end of the fiscal period.

Special Conventions of Revenue and Expenditure Recognition

Colleges and universities have several special conventions of recognizing revenue and expenditures in the unrestricted current fund. These are as follows:

1. Tuition and Fee Remissions/Waivers and Uncollectible Accounts Tuition and fees are primary revenue sources for the unrestricted current fund. In college and university accounting, the full amount of the standard rate for tuition and fees is recognized as revenue. University-provided scholarships, fellowships, tuition and fee remissions or waivers, and uncollectible accounts are accounted for as expenditures. Although many scholarships typically are available within a university or college, the unrestricted current fund accounts for only those sponsored directly by the university. Other scholarships from alumni or corporate funds that are administered by the university are accounted for in other funds. An example of university-sponsored scholarships are those given by the athletic department for its student athletes. The university first recognizes revenue at the standard rate of tuition and fees and then records the scholarship as a debit to expenditure for the athletic department. Another example is the tuition remission (reduction) that is often given to graduate students who accept teaching assistantships. The university records revenue for the graduate student's tuition at the standard rate and then records the tuition remission as an expenditure of the year in which the graduate student is a teaching assistant.

Uncollectible accounts are recorded as expenditures, similar to bad debts expense for commercial entities. An estimate of uncollectible accounts receivable is usually made and recorded as an expenditure. The allowance for uncollectibles is credited and reported as a contra account to the accounts receivable. As specific accounts receivable are determined to be uncollectible, the allowance is debited and the specific receivable is credited.

2. Tuition and Fee Reimbursements for Withdrawals from Coursework Students withdrawing from classes after the beginning of the class term may be able to collect a reimbursement or return of some of the tuition and fees paid at the beginning of the term. College and university accounting requires reimbursements of tuition and fees to be recorded as a reduction of revenue. When the check to the student is approved, the university debits revenues from tuition and fee reimbursements and credits cash or accounts receivable.

3. Academic Terms That Span Two Fiscal Periods Some academic terms may begin in one fiscal year of the university and be completed in another. This is often true for summer school sessions. College and university accounting requires that the tuition and fees collected for a term of instruction be recognized as revenue in the fiscal year in which the term is predominantly conducted, along with all expenditures incurred to finance that term. For example, if tuition and fees are collected at the beginning of summer school which takes place predominantly in the next fiscal period, the university records the collection as a debit to cash and a credit to deferred revenue. The deferred revenue, and any deferred expenditures, are then recognized as revenue and expenditures of the next fiscal period.

Transfers and Board-Designated Funds

As with governmental accounting, colleges and universities may have a variety of interfund transfers. The terms *mandatory transfer* and *nonmandatory transfer,* however, are unique to college and university accounting and reporting. The 1974 edition of CUBA provides a definition and explanation of these transfers, as summarized in the following:

Mandatory transfers are transfers out of the current funds group to other funds resulting from binding legal agreements on financing or renewals and replacements of educational plant, and from grant agreements with agencies of the federal government, donors, or other organizations requiring matching gifts and grants from the governing board to the loan fund or other funds.

Nonmandatory transfers are discretionary transfers specified by the governing board for a variety of purposes such as new additions to plant, increases in loan funds, payments on debt principal, and repairs and replacements of plant. Nonmandatory transfers may also be made from the loan, endowment, or annuity funds to the current funds.

Mandatory and nonmandatory transfers are reported separately in the financial statements of the current funds similarly to transfers in or out for governmental funds. Of course, a transfer out of one fund of the college or university must be accounted for as a transfer in to another fund.

The governing board may designate unrestricted current fund resources for specific purposes in future periods. These *board-designated funds* are internal designations similar to appropriations of retained earnings for a commercial entity. The governing board may impose or remove a designation at its own volition. For example, it might designate $50,000 of future expenditures in the unrestricted current fund for development of a foreign student counseling office. Such designations are usually reported in the footnotes to the financial statements, but they may be shown as allocations of part of the fund balance in the unrestricted current fund balance sheet.

Investments

Colleges and universities are allowed to value investments at cost, at the lower of cost or market, or at market. The method selected, however, must be used for all funds. If the market method is used, market values above the cost of the investment are reported as realized gains. Some colleges and universities combine their investments into a common pool administered by an investment expert. At the end of each reporting period, the gains and losses of the investment pool are allocated to the individual funds, based on the relative value of each fund's investment. For example, if the unrestricted current fund provided half the resources for the common investment pool, half the period's investment gain or loss is allocated to the unrestricted current fund, which then makes the appropriate entries to recognize the gain or loss and revalue its investment based on the report received from the investment pool.

Donations of stock or other investments are recorded by the university at the current market value on the date of receipt. The amount recorded is the basis for subsequent recognition of gains or losses.

Contributions

Both public and private colleges and universities seek contributions from alumni, business firms, and other supporting persons, in order to enhance their educational programs and other activities. These contributions are essential for the vitality of higher education. Some institutions have relatively freestanding foundations that solicit contributions and provide financial support for the many programs of the institution. For example, a foundation may initiate a fund drive for undergraduate scholarships through a telethon of alumni. The foundation collects the alumni's contributions and prepares the scholarship checks to the persons selected by various departments or by the institution. Foundations that are legally independent of the college or university are not included in its financial statements. Foundations that are an integral part of the college or university have their current funds and other funds blended into the institution's financial statements.

Contributions of Property   The general rule is that *contributions of property* are recognized as revenue for the fair value of the contribution. Fair value may, in some cases, be determined by appraisal or other market valuation techniques. It is particularly important to separate restricted contributions from unrestricted contributions. If the donor specifies that the contribution is restricted only to a specific purpose, the university must determine if the restriction can be met. For example, some restrictions may be illegal, and the university must refuse to accept, or must return, any donations that have an illegal restriction. The restricted resources that are accepted are recorded in restricted current funds and expended in accordance with the restriction. For example, many alumni provide funds for scholarship support for students in a particular department or academic area. The college or university must ensure that those funds are expended only for scholarships, and only for students in the specific department stated by the donor. Unrestricted contributions are recorded in unrestricted current funds and expended in accordance with the institution's needs as determined by its administrators or governing board. Some contributions are in the form of endowments for which the principal must be maintained for some stated period. These contributions are recorded in a separate endowment fund.

Contributions of Services *Contributions of services*, such as volunteer service by students for a new student orientation program, are usually not recorded as revenue. Although volunteer services are important for the university, the FASB has specified that contributions of services are to be recognized as an expenditure with an equivalent amount recorded as revenue only in those cases where the services received (1) create or enhance other assets, (2) are provided by entities that normally provide those services for compensation, or (3) are substantially the same as services normally purchased by the recipient. Because of these constraints, few public universities record revenue for any contributed services. Some religious-based colleges record revenue, with an offsetting amount to an expenditure, for the fair value of contributed lay teaching services. This recognition is made to report the full cost of the teaching mission of these private colleges.

Depreciation

Before 1987, most universities did not report depreciation on their academic buildings and equipment because depreciation is not an expenditure of resources. CUBA and the AICPA did, however, allow an accumulated depreciation allowance to be reported under the investment in plant on the balance sheet in order to permit institutions to use depreciation in evaluating performance and to reflect the cost of providing university services. The CUBA and AICPA standards stated that depreciation should *not* be recognized in the current funds.

In 1987, **FASB Statement No. 93,** "Recognition of Depreciation by Not-for-Profit Organizations" (FASB 93), specified that all not-for-profit organizations, including colleges and universities, should report depreciation in general-purpose external financial statements. The depreciation should be reported as an expenditure in the fund using the assets during the period. The institution may select the method of depreciation and the estimated useful lives of the fixed assets. Those few institutions that did recognize depreciation prior to **FASB 93** tended to use the straight-line method and long lives for the assets.

In January 1988, the GASB responded with **GASB Statement No. 8**, "Applicability of FASB Statement No. 93, Recognition of Depreciation by Not-for-Profit Organizations, to Certain State and Local Governmental Entities" (GASB 8). **GASB 8** specified that public colleges and universities may continue to depreciate their tangible assets in accordance with the AICPA guidelines. **GASB 8** is not applicable to private colleges and universities. Under the jurisdictional guidelines of the GASB, its governmental accounting standards are applicable only to governmental entities. The FASB standards are applicable to all other entities. As a result, a lack of comparability exists between public and private institutions.[1]

Private colleges and universities must show depreciation expense in accordance with **FASB 93** standards. Depreciation must be recognized on long-lived tangible assets, other than works of art or historical treasures that have cultural, aesthetic, or historical value that is worth preserving perpetually, and whose holders have the ability to preserve that value and are doing so. The depreciation is reported as an expenditure of the fund that uses the tangible long-lived assets during the period. This means that the unrestricted current fund of a private college or university is required to report a depreciation expenditure for the cost of using tangible assets. Thus, private colleges and universities must report depreciation expenditures for the libraries, the student unions, the athletic buildings, the dormitories, and all other physical assets they own and use. The amount of depreciation expenditure in the unrestricted current fund can be quite high due to reporting depreciation on all the buildings and equipment used in the primary missions of the institution.

FASB 93 requires disclosure of the following items: (1) the depreciation for the period, (2) the balances of the major classes of depreciable assets, (3) the accumulated depreciation at the balance sheet date, and (4) the method used to compute depreciation for the major classes of depreciable assets.

Illustration of Transactions

Sol City University, a small public liberal arts university, maintains a complete fund accounting structure including budgets and encumbrances. The budgetary and encumbrance accounts are not presented in this illustration, in order to focus on those aspects of college and university accounting that differ from governmental accounting. Sol City University uses the cost method of accounting for investments. The university's operations for the 19X2 fiscal year, ending June 30, 19X2, are presented below. The balance sheet for the current funds, both unrestricted and restricted, is presented in Figure 20-3. The statement of revenue, expenditures, and other changes is presented in Figure 20-4 along with comparative data for 19X1.

Key Observations about Formats of Statements Figure 20-3 presents the balance sheet for both types of current funds: the unrestricted current fund and the restricted current funds. Although the current funds are presented within one balance sheet, a separation must be maintained between the two subfunds. Note

[1] In response to the difference with depreciation, in September 1988, the FASB issued *FASB Statement No. 99*, "Deferral of the Effective Date of Recognition of Depreciation by Not-for-Profit Organizations" (FASB 99). **FASB 99** deferred the effective date of **FASB 93** until after January 1, 1990, in an effort to provide additional time to resolve the issues raised by the differences.

FIGURE 20-3 Balance sheet for current funds.

Sol City University
Balance Sheet—Current Funds
June 30, 19X2
(with comparative figures for June 30, 19X1)

	19X2	19X1
Assets		
Current Funds:		
Unrestricted:		
Cash	$105,000	$ 55,000
Investments, at cost	235,000	180,000
Accounts Receivable, less allowance		
of $10,000 in 19X1, $9,000 in 19X2	114,000	88,000
Inventories, at lower of cost or market	45,000	40,000
Prepaid Expenses and Deferred		
Charges	14,000	10,000
Total Unrestricted	$513,000	$373,000
Restricted:		
Cash	$179,000	$ 56,000
Investments, at cost	124,000	83,000
Accounts Receivable, less allowance		
of $4,000 each year	34,000	80,000
Total Restricted	$337,000	$219,000
Total Current Funds	$850,000	$592,000
Liabilities and Fund Balances		
Current Funds:		
Unrestricted:		
Accounts Payable	$ 63,000	$ 50,000
Accrued Liabilities	10,000	8,000
Students' Deposits	15,000	18,000
Due to Other Funds	79,000	60,000
Deferred Credits	15,000	10,000
Fund Balance:		
Unallocated	281,000	227,000
Board-Designated	50,000	-0-
Total Unrestricted	$513,000	$373,000
Restricted:		
Accounts Payable	$ 7,000	$ 3,000
Fund Balance	330,000	216,000
Total Restricted	$337,000	$219,000
Total Current Funds	$850,000	$592,000

FIGURE 20-4 Statement of current funds revenue, expenditures, and other changes.

Sol City University
Statement of Current Funds Revenue, Expenditures, and Other Changes
For Year Ended June 30, 19X2

	Current Year			Prior-Year Total
	Unrestricted	Restricted	Total	
Revenue:				
Tuition and fees	$ 1,300,000		$ 1,300,000	$ 1,150,000
Government appropriations	650,000		650,000	250,000
Government grants and contracts	20,000	$ 212,000	232,000	500,000
Private gifts, grants, and contracts	425,000	190,000	615,000	425,000
Endowment income	255,000	105,000	360,000	185,000
Auxiliary enterprises	1,100,000		1,100,000	1,050,000
Expired term endowment	20,000		20,000	
Total current revenue	$ 3,770,000	$ 507,000	$ 4,277,000	$ 3,560,000
Expenditures and mandatory transfers:				
Educational and general:				
Instruction	$ 1,480,000	$ 245,000	$ 1,725,000	$ 1,650,000
Research	50,000	200,000	250,000	325,000
Public service	65,000	12,000	77,000	88,000
Academic support	125,000		125,000	112,000
Student services	100,000		100,000	95,000
Institutional support	275,000		275,000	220,000
Operation and maintenance of plant	110,000		110,000	100,000
Scholarships and fellowships	45,000	50,000	95,000	90,000
Educational and general expenditures	$ 2,250,000	$ 507,000	$ 2,757,000	$ 2,680,000
Mandatory transfers for:				
Principal and interest	45,000		45,000	25,000
Renewals and replacements	50,000		50,000	40,000
Loan fund matching grant	1,000		1,000	
Total educational and general	$ 2,346,000	$ 507,000	$ 2,853,000	$ 2,745,000
Auxiliary enterprises:				
Expenditures	$ 915,000		$ 915,000	$ 865,000
Mandatory transfers for:				
Principal and interest	75,000		75,000	125,000
Renewals and replacements	35,000		35,000	35,000
Total auxiliary enterprises	$ 1,025,000	$ -0-	$ 1,025,000	$ 1,025,000
Total expenditures and mandatory transfers	$(3,371,000)	$(507,000)	$(3,878,000)	$(3,770,000)
Net increase (decrease) in fund balance before other transfers and additions (deductions)	$ 399,000	$ -0-	$ 399,000	$ (210,000)
Other transfers and additions (deductions):				
Excess of restricted receipts over transfers to revenue		128,000	128,000	120,000
Refunded to grantors		(14,000)	(14,000)	
Nonmandatory transfer: Unrestricted gifts to other funds	(325,000)		(325,000)	(260,000)
Portion of quasi-endowment gains appropriated	30,000		30,000	
Net increase in fund balances	$ 104,000	$ 114,000	$ 218,000	$ (350,000)

that no long-term assets are reported in the current funds. The long-term assets are reported in the separate plant funds.

Figure 20-4 presents the operating statement for the current funds. Again, both the unrestricted and restricted subfunds are presented, this time in columnar format. The statement of current funds revenue, expenditures, and other changes has three major sections, as follows:

1. *Revenue*, which reports the revenue of the institution by major source;

2. *Expenditures and mandatory transfers*, which reports the educational expenditures by major function, reports the mandatory transfers between the current funds and other funds of the institution, and separately reports the expenditures made by the auxiliary enterprises;

3. *Other transfers and additions (deductions)*, which reports nonmandatory transfers between current funds and other funds, and reports other revenue or expenditure items.

The following illustration and journal entries are tied to the financial statements. This chapter takes a financial statement approach to the study of college and university accounting. The journal entries will be primarily in the sequence of the items as reported on the operating statement and the balance sheet for each fund in order to relate the accounting with the financial reporting required for colleges and universities. To focus on the major aspects of accounting for colleges and universities, the budgetary entries are not included in the illustration. Although most universities do record annual budgets in the accounting records, the illustration focuses on the operating accounts and the balance sheet accounts. Colleges and universities also typically use an extensive encumbrance system, similar to that used in state and local government entities. Again, in order to focus on the primary issues, the illustrations in this chapter do not include encumbrance accounting. The unrestricted current fund, which is the major subfund of the current funds, is considered first.

Revenue   Figure 20-4 presents the revenue sources for the unrestricted current fund of Sol City University. Net tuition and fees revenue is $1,300,000. Initially, $1,320,000 was charged at standard rates, and a total of $1,275,000 of tuition and fees was collected in cash, of which $20,000 was later reimbursed to withdrawing students. A receivable of $45,000 is recorded for tuition reductions/waivers for university-supported scholarships and fellowships. These tuition reductions are included in revenue for the period at the standard tuition rate in order to measure fully the revenue obtainable before reductions are allowed. The tuition reductions are shown later as an expenditure (see entry 9 later in this chapter).

(1)	Cash	1,275,000	
	Accounts Receivable	45,000	
	Revenue—Tuition and Fees		1,320,000
	Tuition and fees revenues are recorded.		
	Accounts receivable of $45,000 recognized		
	for tuition reductions expected.		

(2)	Revenue—Tuition and Fees	20,000	
	Cash		20,000

Reimbursement of tuition and fees to
students withdrawing from classes.

The next source of revenue presented in Figure 20-4 is from government appropriations and grants. The university receives $650,000 of appropriations from the federal and state governments. An additional $20,000 of government grants is received from the restricted current fund for reimbursement of indirect overhead costs for lab equipment that are incurred by the unrestricted current fund in connection with a government grant.

(3)	Cash	670,000	
	Revenue—Government Appropriations		650,000
	Revenue—Government Grants and		
	Contracts		20,000

Governmental appropriations and grants,
including $20,000 for cost recovery.

The next source of revenue on Figure 20-4 is from private gifts, grants, and contracts. The university receives $425,000 of gifts from alumni and grants from foundations. In addition, the university receives $255,000 from an endowed trust owned by the university that distributes its income to the university but maintains its principal intact. The endowment principal is reported in the university's endowment fund. The entries in the unrestricted current fund are:

(4)	Cash	425,000	
	Revenue—Private Gifts, Grants, and		
	Contracts		425,000
	Private gifts and grants.		
(5)	Cash	255,000	
	Revenue—Endowment Income		255,000
	Income from endowment.		

The university's auxiliary enterprise earns $1,100,000 in revenue, including $20,000 from the sale of used equipment, and provides an allowance of $9,000 on its accounts receivable. Unlike governmental accounting, in which the provision for uncollectibles is a reduction of revenue, colleges and universities record the provision for uncollectible receivables as an expenditure.

(6)	Cash	977,000	
	Accounts Receivable	123,000	
	Expenditures—Auxiliary Enterprises	9,000	
	Allowance for Uncollectibles		9,000
	Revenue—Auxiliary Enterprises		1,100,000
	Auxiliary enterprises' revenue.		

According to a trust endowed by an alumna some years ago, $20,000 of endowment principal is to be distributed to the university in 19X2. The amount is paid to the unrestricted current fund from the endowment fund.

(7) Cash	20,000	
Revenue—Expired Term Endowments		20,000
Receive expired term endowment.		

Expenditures   Figure 20-4 presents the expenditures for the unrestricted current fund, classified by function. The expenditures in the unrestricted current fund for the 19X2 fiscal year are listed below. Entry (8) accounts for the major educational and general expenditures, of which $2,003,000 is paid in cash, after approval of the appropriate vouchers; $40,000 is from use of inventories of supplies; a total of $73,000 of expenditures is made on credit; and $79,000 is expended by other funds, which must be reimbursed. The institutional support expenditures include $20,000 of indirect overhead costs in support of a government grant for cancer research.

(8) Expenditures—Instruction	1,480,000	
Expenditures—Research	50,000	
Expenditures—Public Service	65,000	
Expenditures—Academic Support	125,000	
Expenditures—Student Services	100,000	
Expenditures—Institutional Support	275,000	
Expenditures—Operation and Maintenance of		
Plant	110,000	
Cash		2,003,000
Inventories		40,000
Prepaid Expenses and Deferred Charges		10,000
Accounts Payable		63,000
Accrued Liabilities		10,000
Due to Other Funds		79,000
Educational and general expenditures.		

Included in the instruction expenditures above is $50,000 that the unrestricted current fund incurred for long-term tangible assets such as lab and office equipment. Similar to the general fund in governmental accounting, the current funds may acquire assets. Colleges and universities, however, do not have a general long-term assets account group. Instead, a separate investment in plant fund is used to record acquisitions of plant assets by either the current funds or other plant funds. Large acquisitions of plant assets should not be made from the current funds, but rather should be under the control of the capital budget and included in the plant funds, as shown later in the chapter.

The university's financial aid committee approves $45,000 in tuition aid and reductions, which are included in revenue in entry (1) and which are now shown separately as an expenditure.

(9)	Expenditures—Scholarships and Fellowships	45,000	
	Accounts Receivable		45,000
	Tuition reductions.		

Expenditures for auxiliary enterprises, including the student union bookstore, cafeteria, and residence halls, are recorded. Note that entry (6) includes a provision for uncollectibles for $9,000 which is an expenditure.

(10)	Expenditures—Auxiliary Enterprises	906,000	
	Vouchers Payable (Cash)		906,000
	Auxiliary enterprises expenditures.		

Transfers   Figure 20-4 shows that the unrestricted current fund makes several mandatory transfers out to other funds. A total of $120,000 in mandatory transfers to the plant funds is required by a loan agreement for the purpose of retirement of debt. The $120,000 is allocated $45,000 to educational and $75,000 to auxiliary enterprises. A transfer of $85,000 to the plant funds is mandated for renewals and replacements. This transfer is allocated $50,000 to educational and $35,000 to auxiliary enterprises. A $1,000 mandatory transfer to the loan fund is required by the terms of a donor's contribution. The transfers are summarized below.

Mandatory Transfer Out to	Amount	Purpose
Plant funds	$120,000	Retirement of indebtedness
Plant funds	85,000	Renewals and replacements
Loan funds	1,000	Matching contribution

In addition to authorizing the mandatory transfers, the board of trustees also stipulates a total of $325,000 of nonmandatory transfers from unrestricted gifts accepted during the period, as follows:

Nonmandatory Transfer Out to	Amount	Purpose
Loan funds	$ 15,000	Increase amounts available
Endowment and similar funds	275,000	Establish endowment
Plant funds	35,000	Increase unexpended amounts

The governing board specified a $30,000 nonmandatory transfer in to the unrestricted current fund of a portion of investment gains realized in the endowment fund, as follows:

Nonmandatory Transfer In from	Amount	Purpose
Endowment and similar funds	$30,000	Distribution of investment gains

The entries for these transactions are as follows:

(11)	Mandatory Transfer Out to Plant Funds	120,000	
	Mandatory Transfer Out to Plant Funds	85,000	
	Mandatory Transfer Out to Loan Funds	1,000	
	Cash		206,000
	Required transfers out.		
(12)	Nonmandatory Transfer Out to Loan Funds	15,000	
	Nonmandatory Transfer Out to Endowment and		
	Similar Funds	275,000	
	Nonmandatory Transfer Out to Plant Funds	35,000	
	Nonmandatory Transfer In from Endowment		
	and Similar Funds		30,000
	Cash		295,000
	Voluntary transfers.		

At the end of the accounting period, the transfers out and in are closed to Fund Balance with all other nominal accounts, including budgetary accounts and revenue and expenditures. The closing process is the same as for local and state governmental funds and is not presented. As shown in Figure 20-4, the revenue and expenditures are reflected in the statement of current funds revenue, expenditures, and other changes.

Other Transactions Figure 20-3 presents the balance sheet for the unrestricted current fund. The following journal entries record the transactions during the period affecting just balance sheet accounts.

(13)	Investments	55,000	
	Cash		55,000
	Acquire additional investments.		
(14)	Cash	88,000	
	Allowance for Uncollectibles	10,000	
	Accounts Receivable		98,000
	Collect $88,000 of accounts receivable and write		
	off $10,000 of accounts.		
(15)	Inventories	45,000	
	Cash		45,000
	Acquire additional inventories of supplies.		
(16)	Prepaid expenses	14,000	
	Cash		14,000
	Incur costs for prepaid expenses.		
(17)	Accounts Payable	50,000	
	Accrued Liabilities	8,000	
	Due to Other Funds	60,000	
	Cash		118,000
	Pay liabilities outstanding at beginning of fiscal		
	period.		

(18)	Cash	5,000	
	Deferred Credits		5,000
	Receive monies applicable to next year's operations.		

(19)	Students' Deposits	3,000	
	Cash		3,000
	Return $3,000 of students' deposits.		

The Deferred Credits account in entry (18) is for unearned revenue of the university. For example, toward the end of the fiscal year, the university may begin collecting fees for its summer school session, which is predominantly offered in the next fiscal year. These receipts are applicable to the next fiscal year and are reported as unearned until earned through the offering of the summer school session in the next fiscal period.

The governing board designates a $50,000 reserve of the fund balance for future research grants. The entry to record this designation is:

(20)	Fund Balance	50,000	
	Board-Designated Reserve for Research Grants		50,000
	Governing board's designation of fund balance.		

The account Board-Designated Reserve for Research Grants is reported as part of the fund balance in the balance sheet.

RESTRICTED CURRENT FUND

Restricted current fund resources are available for current operating purposes subject to restrictions imposed by donors, grantors, or other external agencies. The restricted current fund for a university or college is similar in purpose to the special revenue funds for a state or local government entity. These resources are separated from unrestricted current funds because of the externally imposed restrictions on their use. Restricted gifts or grants are recorded as increases in cash and the fund balance, but they are not recognized as revenue until the terms of the acceptance agreement are fulfilled and the resources are expended in the manner specified by the grantor. For example, assume an alumnus contributes $75,000 for use in acquiring new microcomputer equipment for the business school of XYZ College. The restricted current fund of XYZ College would record the contribution as follows:

| (21) | Cash | 75,000 | |
| | Fund Balance | | 75,000 |

If the college acquires $50,000 of computers as its first phase under the terms of the grantor's gift, it will make the following entry:

(22) Expenditures—Educational	50,000	
Fund Balance	50,000	
Cash		50,000
Revenue—Gifts		50,000

In theory and in practice, the revenue is not earned until the expenditure takes place. In this manner, the restricted current fund always reports revenue equal to expenditures in the statement of current funds revenue, expenditures, and other changes. The fund balance of this fund may change, however, because of gifts and contributions that have been received but not used or because of other transfers affecting the fund balance.

Illustration of Transactions

Sol City University has a restricted current fund to account for resources received subject to restrictions imposed by the granting person or agency. The balance sheets in Figure 20-3 and the statement of current funds revenue, expenditures, and other changes in Figure 20-4 report the effects of the following transactions in the restricted current fund.

Revenue and Other Additions to Fund Balance The university accepts two large restricted grants during the year. The first is $300,000 from the federal government, to be used for cancer research. This grant includes $20,000 to cover the indirect overhead costs of the university in administering the grant. The second grant is for $250,000 from a private foundation for use in developing a Center for New Technologies, which is to present seminars on changing technologies.

Entries to record the receipt of the grants are:

(23) Cash	300,000	
Fund Balance		300,000
Receive federal cancer research grant. Includes $20,000 for reimbursement of indirect overhead costs incurred in administration of grant.		
(24) Cash	250,000	
Fund Balance		250,000
Receive grant to establish Center for New Technologies.		

Revenue may be recognized only to the extent that expenditures are incurred in accordance with the terms of the grant (the expenditures are reported in entry 28 later in this chapter). As shown in Figure 20-4, the university expends a total of $212,000 of the government grant. In addition, the Center for New Technologies is established and staffed at a cost of $190,000 for the year. Additional costs for the center are expected in the future. The entries to record revenue for the restricted current fund are:

(25)	Fund Balance	212,000	
	Revenue—Government Grants		212,000
	Revenue for cancer research project		
	recognized to equal expenditures on project.		

(26)	Fund Balance	190,000	
	Revenue—Private Grants		190,000
	Center established at cost of $190,000.		

The restricted current fund also receives $105,000 of income from an endowment established by C. Alt, an alumnus. The university must maintain the endowment principal, but the income from the endowment is available to be expended specifically for use in the undergraduate business program. The endowment is included in the university's endowment fund. The $105,000 of endowment income is immediately expended in accordance with the donor's restriction. The entry to record the endowment income in the restricted current fund is:

(27)	Cash	105,000	
	Revenue—Endowment Income		105,000
	Receive income from C. Alt endowment for		
	undergraduate business program.		

Expenditures and Other Deductions   As shown in Figure 20-4, the restricted current fund had a total of $507,000 of expenditures during the period. The expenditures include the $212,000 for the cancer research project, the $190,000 for the Center for New Technologies, and the $105,000 as specified in the C. Alt endowment. They are now classified by the nature of the expenditure, not the source of the revenue. Accounts payable increase by $7,000; remaining expenditures are all paid in cash after the appropriate vouchers are approved.

(28)	Expenditures—Instruction	245,000	
	Expenditures—Research	200,000	
	Expenditures—Public Service	12,000	
	Expenditures—Scholarships	50,000	
	Cash		500,000
	Accounts Payable		7,000
	Expenditures for various programs made in		
	accordance with external restrictions.		

The government research grant provides for reimbursement of $20,000 of indirect overhead costs incurred in administering the grant. These overhead costs are incurred in the unrestricted current fund, and $20,000 is reimbursed to that fund. Recall that the unrestricted current fund recognized both the revenue and expenditure for the $20,000 (see entries 3 and 8 earlier in this chapter).

(29)	Fund Balance	20,000	
	Cash		20,000
	Reimburse indirect overhead expenditures in		
	unrestricted current fund. Cash forwarded.		

After studying several small gifts from outside donors, the university decides that specific restrictions could not be satisfied. The university therefore returns the gifts to the individual donors.

(30) Fund Balance   14,000
      Cash   14,000
      Return restricted gifts to donors.

Other Transactions Figure 20-3 shows the effects of other transactions in the restricted current fund during the period affecting just balance sheet accounts, as follows:

(31) Investments   41,000
      Cash   41,000
      Acquire additional investments.

(32) Cash   46,000
      Accounts Receivable   46,000
      Collect accounts receivable of $46,000.

(33) Accounts Payable   3,000
      Cash   3,000
      Pay accounts payable outstanding at beginning of
      19X2 fiscal period.

Closing entries are required to close the nominal accounts for the period.

Financial Statements for the Restricted Current Fund

The balance sheet and statement of current funds revenue, expenditures, and other changes are presented in Figures 20-3 and 20-4. In the statement of revenue, expenditures, and other changes (Figure 20-4), revenue of $507,000 equals the expenditures of $507,000. This is because revenue is recognized only after the expenditures are made and the terms of the restrictions are met. The other transfers section includes $128,000 as the excess of restricted fund receipts over revenue recognized. The $232,000 expended of the government grant includes the $20,000 transferred to the unrestricted fund in entry (29).

Gift or Grant	Amount Received	Amount Expended	Remainder
Government grant for cancer research	$300,000	$232,000	$ 68,000
Foundation grant for technologies	250,000	190,000	60,000
Total	$550,000	$422,000	$128,000

Figure 20-5 presents a combined statement of changes in fund balances for both of the current funds—unrestricted and restricted—as well as for all the other funds of Sol City University. This statement is one of the three required statements for colleges and universities. The three are a combined balance sheet for all funds; a statement of current funds revenue, expenditures, and other changes; and a statement of changes in fund balances. The combined balance sheet for all funds simply combines the individual funds' balance sheets. That process is illustrated later in the chapter.

The statement of changes in fund balances in Figure 20-5 for all funds shows how some of the information from Figure 20-4 is used. Figure 20-5 presents the total amount of restricted grants ($300,000 and $250,000) as increases to fund balance, whereas Figure 20-4 reports the amount expended as revenue, with the remaining excess shown among other additions. Both statements report the same net changes in each of the fund balances for the period.

LOAN FUNDS

Loan funds account for resources that may be loaned to students, faculty, or staff. The resources are provided by private individuals, foundations and businesses, and governments. A loan fund is intended to be *revolving;* that is, as the outstanding loans are repaid, the proceeds are then made available to other borrowers. Furthermore, the interest on the loans is expected to offset the administrative costs of the loan fund and the losses from uncollectibles.

Donors may restrict the type of loan recipient; therefore, the fund capital must be separated between restricted loan fund balance and unrestricted loan fund balance. No revenue or expense accounts are used in the loan fund; all transactions affecting the fund balance are recorded directly to the fund balance account. Interest on loans outstanding is credited to the fund balance on the accrual basis. Investment income is also accrued. Estimated provisions for losses on loans may be necessary to value properly the amount of loans outstanding. An allowance for uncollectible loans should be used if the amount of uncollectibles can be estimated. Writing off losses in the period the loans become uncollectible is permitted if the allowance method is not used. Actual or estimated losses from loans or investment transactions are debited directly to the fund balance.

Two financial statements are required for loan funds: the balance sheet, as presented in Figure 20-6, and the statement of changes in fund balance, as incorporated into Figure 20-5. No operating statement is required because loan funds do not have revenues or expenditures.

Illustration of Transactions

Sol City University has a loan fund to provide financial aid support for students and short-term emergency loans to faculty. The initial loan fund is subject to certain operating restrictions, but any additional amounts contributed by the university are available as unrestricted resources. A balance sheet for the loan fund is presented in Figure 20-6. The loan fund uses the direct write-off method of accounting for uncollectible loans because uncollectibles are expected to be minor. The following entries record the transactions in the loan fund during the 19X2 fiscal year.

FIGURE 20-5 Statement of changes in fund balances.

Sol City University
Statement of Changes in Fund Balances
For Year Ended June 30, 19X2

	Current Funds		Loan Funds	Endowment and Similar Funds	Annuity and Life Income Funds	Plant Funds			
	Unrestricted	Restricted				Unexpended	Renewals, Replacements	Retirement of Indebtedness	Investment in Plant
Revenue and other additions:									
Unrestricted current fund revenue	$3,770,000								
Expired term endowment						$ 25,000			
Government appropriations—restricted						40,000			
Government grants and contracts—restricted		$300,000							
Private gifts, grants, contracts—restricted		250,000	$ 50,000	$750,000	$400,000	55,000		$ 33,000	$ 20,000
Endowment and investment income—restricted		105,000	6,000	15,000	8,000	10,000	$ 3,000	4,000	
Realized gains on investments—unrestricted			4,000	55,000		5,000	2,000	3,000	
Realized gains on investments—restricted			3,000	25,000					
Interest on loans receivable			10,000						
U.S. government advances									
Expended for plant facilities (including $50,000 charged to current funds)									800,000
Retirement of indebtedness									100,000
Matured annuity and life income—restricted				5,000					
Total revenue and other additions	$3,770,000	$655,000	$ 73,000	$850,000	$408,000	$135,000	$ 5,000	$ 40,000	$920,000
Expenditures and other deductions:									
Educational and general	$2,250,000	$507,000							
Auxiliary enterprises	915,000								
Indirect costs recovered		20,000							
Refunded to grantors		14,000							
Loan cancellations and write-offs			$ 5,000						
Administrative and collection costs			1,000					$ 1,000	
Adjustment of actuarial liability for annuities payable					$ 51,000				
Expended for plant facilities						$600,000	$150,000		
Retirement of bond indebtedness								100,000	
Interest on indebtedness								106,000	
Disposal of plant facilities									$ 60,000
Expired term endowments			3,000	$ 45,000					
Matured annuity and life income—restricted					5,000				
Accumulated depreciation									500,000
Total expenditures and other deductions	$(3,165,000)	$(541,000)	$ (9,000)	$ (45,000)	$ (56,000)	$(600,000)	$(150,000)	$(207,000)	$(560,000)
Transfers among funds—additions (deductions):									
Mandatory:									
Principal and interest	$ (120,000)							$120,000	
Renewals and replacements	(85,000)						$ 85,000		
Loan fund matching grant	(1,000)		$ 1,000						
Nonmandatory:									
Unrestricted gifts allocated	(325,000)		15,000	$275,000		$ 35,000			
Portion of quasi-endowment funds investment gains appropriated	30,000			(30,000)					
Total transfers	$ (501,000)	$ -0-	$ 16,000	$245,000	$ -0-	$ 35,000	$ 85,000	$120,000	$ -0-
Net increase (decrease) for the year	$ 104,000	$114,000	$ 80,000	$1,050,000	$352,000	$ (430,000)	$ (60,000)	$ (47,000)	$ 360,000
Fund balance at beginning of year	227,000	216,000	250,000	5,950,000	1,251,000	1,060,000	190,000	147,000	18,670,000
Fund balance at end of year	$ 331,000	$330,000	$330,000	$7,000,000	$1,603,000	$630,000	$130,000	$100,000	$19,030,000

FIGURE 20-6 Balance sheet for loan funds.

**Sol City University
Balance Sheet—Loan Funds
June 30, 19X2**
(with comparative figures for June 30, 19X1)

	19X2	19X1
Assets		
Cash	$ 3,000	$ 10,000
Investments (at cost)	50,000	50,000
Loans to Students, Faculty, and Staff	275,000	190,000
Due from Unrestricted Current Funds	2,000	
Total Loan Funds	$330,000	$250,000
Liabilities and Fund Balances		
Fund Balances:		
U.S. Government Grants	$ 25,000	$ 17,000
University Funds:		
Restricted	240,000	183,000
Unrestricted	65,000	50,000
Total Loan Funds	$330,000	$250,000

Additions to Fund Balance As shown in Figure 20-5, the loan fund had the following transactions that increased the loan fund balance during the 19X2 fiscal year:

(34) Cash 50,000
    Fund Balance—Restricted 50,000
    Fund-raising effort increases amount of loan money available. Donors specifiy restrictions on funds.

(35) Cash 6,000
    Fund Balance—Restricted 6,000
    Receive investment income.

(36) Cash 19,000
    Fund Balance—Restricted 4,000
    Investments 15,000
    Sell investment for realized gain of $4,000.

(37) Cash 3,000
    Fund Balance—Restricted 3,000
    Receive interest on loans outstanding.

(38) Cash 10,000
    Fund Balance—U.S. Government Grants 10,000
    Receive U.S. government advance on loan fund monies.

Deductions from Fund Balance   Figure 20-5 reports the following transactions decreasing the loan fund balance during the 19X2 fiscal year:

(39)	Fund Balance—Restricted	5,000	
	Cash		5,000
	Return $5,000 to grantors because restrictions can no longer be met.		
(40)	Fund Balance—Restricted	1,000	
	Loans Receivable		1,000
	Loan written off as uncollectible.		
(41)	Fund Balance—Restricted	3,000	
	Cash		3,000
	Administrative and collection costs.		

Transfers   The loan fund receives two transfers from the unrestricted current fund. The first is a mandatory transfer in of $1,000 to match a contribution by a private donor. The second is a nonmandatory transfer in of $15,000 as the loan fund's allocated portion of unrestricted gifts. The entries are made directly to fund balance rather than to a transfer account; however, the nature of the transfer must be noted because transfers are reported separately in the statement of changes in fund balance, as shown in Figure 20-5. Recall that the unrestricted current fund accounts for these as transfers out (see entries 11 and 12 earlier in this chapter).

(42)	Cash	16,000	
	Fund Balance—Restricted		1,000
	Fund Balance—Unrestricted		15,000
	Transfers in from unrestricted current funds.		

Other Transactions   Figure 20-6 shows the effects of several other transactions in the loan fund during the year that affect only balance sheet accounts, as follows:

(43)	Investments	15,000	
	Cash		15,000
	Acquire additional investments.		
(44)	Loans Receivable	86,000	
	Cash		86,000
	Issue new loans.		
(45)	Due from Unrestricted Current Fund	2,000	
	Cash		2,000
	Recognize receivable from unrestricted current fund for reimbursable costs.		
(46)	Fund Balance—U.S. Government Grants	2,000	
	Fund Balance—Restricted		2,000
	U.S. grant reallocated to restricted fund balance in accordance with terms of grant.		

ENDOWMENT AND SIMILAR FUNDS

Endowment funds account for resources that may not be expended currently. The endowment fund obtains resources from gifts, appreciation of principal, and transfers in from other funds.

Universities and colleges typically maintain three different types of endowments as described below.

1. *Endowments* are gifts from external parties given in perpetuity. The fund principal is never expended.

2. *Term endowments* are gifts for which the donor has specified a date or event after which the funds may be expended.

3. *Quasi-endowments* are established by the governing board, usually from unrestricted gifts received in the unrestricted current fund.

Decreases in fund balance occur from the termination of term endowments and also from the transmission of endowed resources to other funds in accordance with the endowment agreements.

Accounting for endowments is the same as for loan funds. Interest revenue is accrued at the end of the fiscal year. Some universities recognize the appreciation in the market value of the endowment investments as income in the period of the appreciation. Most, however, follow the more traditional and conservative method of maintaining their investments at cost or at lower of cost or market. In the latter case, the full amount realized on a sale of an investment normally is reinvested as a part of the principal balance.

Income from endowment investments may be recognized by a university in one of two ways. The endowment fund may first record all investment income on endowments and then transfer the income to another fund where it may be expended in accordance with the terms of the endowment acceptance agreement. Alternatively, the university may record income from endowment investments directly in the receiving fund, with no income entry in the endowment fund. Either method results in the same net effect on the university's financial statements. Sol City University uses the prevalent method of recording income from investments directly in the receiving fund in which it can be expended.

When the college or university receives the cash from the endowment investment, it must distribute the cash to the proper fund. For investment income available for unrestricted purposes, the cash is distributed to the unrestricted current fund which also recognizes the revenue. For example, in Figure 20-4 the unrestricted current fund of Sol City University reports $255,000 revenue from an endowment which specified that the income from the endowment could be used for any purpose deemed proper by the governing board (see entry 5 earlier in this chapter). If the investment income is to be used for specified restricted purposes, it is recorded in the specific fund, such as the restricted current fund, loan fund, plant fund, or as specified in the gift agreement. For example, the restricted fund reports $105,000 as cash received and revenue from an endowment restricting the income for use by the undergraduate business school (see entry 27 earlier in this chapter). Investment income must be recognized in the endowment fund if the terms of the gift agreement specify that the income is to be added to the endowment principal. This is sometimes the case for term endowments or endowments for which a certain minimum amount of principal must be retained in the endowment fund.

Individuals may establish private endowment trusts administered by entities outside the university, such as a bank, which pay the income to the university. These private endowments are not included in the university's endowment fund because the university does not own or possess the funds. Such private endowments are typically described in footnotes in the university's annual report.

Illustration of Transactions

Sol City University establishes a fund to account for endowments received from external parties and also for its internally developed endowment-type funds. Transactions in this fund during the 19X2 fiscal year are presented below. The balance sheet for the fund is presented in Figure 20-7, and the results of the transactions are presented in the statement of changes in fund balances in Figure 20-5. No operating statement is required because the endowment and similar funds do not recognize revenue or expenditures; all changes are recorded directly against fund balance.

Additions to Fund Balance As reported in Figure 20-5, the endowment and similar funds receive two large grants totaling $750,000 from external parties. The first is an endowment of $495,000, the income from which is to be used to establish a program in small business management. The second grant is a 3-year term endowment of $255,000. Income earned is to be used in the nursing program. At

FIGURE 20-7 Balance sheet for endowment fund.

Sol City University
Balance Sheet—Endowment and Similar Funds
June 30, 19X2
(with comparative figures for June 30, 19X1)

	19X2	19X1
Assets		
Cash	$ 50,000	$ 50,000
Investments (at cost)	6,950,000	5,900,000
Total Endowment and Similar Funds	$7,000,000	$5,950,000
Liabilities and Fund Balances		
Fund Balances:		
Endowments	$3,900,000	$3,360,000
Term Endowment	1,920,000	1,710,000
Quasi-Endowment	1,180,000	880,000
Total Endowment and Similar Funds	$7,000,000	$5,950,000

the end of the 3 years, the endowment principal is to be expended to buy new equipment for the medical school. The fund also receives investment income of $15,000 and realizes gains of $80,000, which are to be added to the initial endowment principal in the allocation of $55,000 for unrestricted and $25,000 for restricted fund balances. In addition, the fund receives $5,000 from the annuity and life income fund in accordance with the agreement made with the private donor.

(47)	Cash	750,000	
	Fund Balance—Endowment		495,000
	Fund Balance—Term Endowment		255,000
	Receive two endowments from external parties.		
(48)	Cash	15,000	
	Fund Balance—Endowment		15,000
	Receive investment income that is added to the endowment principal.		
(49)	Cash	180,000	
	Investments		100,000
	Fund Balance—Quasi-Endowment		55,000
	Fund Balance—Endowment		25,000
	Realize gains on investment transactions. A total of $55,000 is attributable to quasi-endowment investments and the remaining gain of $25,000 is attributable to endowment investments.		
(50)	Cash	5,000	
	Fund Balance—Endowment		5,000
	Receive $5,000 from annuity and life income funds in accordance with terms of donor agreement.		

Deductions from Fund Balance   As reported in Figure 20-5, a term endowment of $45,000 expires during the year. Of the $45,000 principal, $20,000 is transmitted to the unrestricted current funds and $25,000 to the unexpended plant fund. The unrestricted current fund recorded the $20,000 as revenue (see entry 7 earlier in this chapter). The unexpended plant fund records revenue of $25,000 (see entry 63 later in this chapter).

(51)	Fund Balance—Term Endowment	45,000	
	Cash		45,000
	Term endowment expires, and distribute remaining principal.		

Transfers   The endowment fund receives $275,000 from the unrestricted current fund as its portion of unrestricted gifts. The amount is recognized as a quasi-endowment fund balance in compliance with the governing board's directions.

(52)	Cash	275,000	
	Fund Balance—Quasi-Endowment		275,000
	Nonmandatory transfers in from unrestricted current fund.		

Recall that the unrestricted current fund recorded the transfer as a nonmandatory transfer out (see entry 12 presented earlier in this chapter).

The endowment fund makes a nonmandatory transfer out to the unrestricted current fund for its portion of the investment gains realized on quasi-endowment investments.

(53)	Fund Balance—Quasi-Endowment	30,000	
	Cash		30,000
	Nonmandatory transfer out to unrestricted current fund.		

The unrestricted current fund recorded the transfer as a nonmandatory transfer in (see entry 12 presented earlier in this chapter).

Other Transactions   Figure 20-7 presents the effects of the other transactions during the period that affect only balance sheet accounts. Additional investments are acquired during the year.

(54)	Investments	1,150,000	
	Cash		1,150,000
	Additional investments acquired.		

ANNUITY AND LIFE INCOME FUNDS

Annuity and life income funds account for resources that are given to a university provided that the university agrees to make periodic payments to a designated recipient. In the case of *annuity funds,* the agreement stipulates that periodic payments are made to the recipient for a specified amount for a specified period of time, such as 20 years. If the recipient dies prior to the end of the 20 years, the continued application of the annuity funds is determined by the agreement. The agreement may specify that the recipient's beneficiaries will receive the remaining annuity payments, or the agreement may specify that the death of the recipient releases the annuity fund resources to the university. *Life income funds* distribute income earned to the individuals as long as they live. When the person dies, the remaining life income fund resources become the property of the university and are used as specified in the gift agreement. The major difference between annuity and life funds is that annuity funds pay a specified amount periodically, whereas life income fund payments vary with the amount of income earned.

Accounting for annuity and life income funds is similar to accounting for endowment funds, with one major difference. At the time the university accepts an annuity income gift, it must recognize an annuity payable for the present value of the expected future amounts that will be paid under the terms of the agreement. This requires actuarial assumptions as to expected earnings rates, the length of time the payments will be made, and so on. For life income funds, no payable is recorded at the time of the gift, because the university does not obligate itself to any payments beyond the income from the fund's investments.

FIGURE 20-8 Balance sheet for annuity and life income funds.

Sol City University
Balance Sheet—Annuity and Life Income Funds
June 30, 19X2
(with comparative figures for June 30, 19X1)

	19X2	19X1
Assets		
Annuity Funds:		
Cash	$ 28,000	$ 23,000
Investments (at cost)	1,630,000	1,505,000
Total Annuity Funds	$1,658,000	$1,528,000
Life Income Funds:		
Cash	$ 8,000	$ 8,000
Investment (at cost)	1,017,000	870,000
Total Life Income Funds	$1,025,000	$ 878,000
Total Annuity and Life Income Funds	$2,683,000	$2,406,000
Liabilities and Fund Balances		
Annuity Funds:		
Annuities Payable	$1,075,000	$1,150,000
Fund Balance	583,000	378,000
Total Annuity Funds	$1,658,000	$1,528,000
Life Income Funds:		
Income Payable	$ 5,000	$ 5,000
Fund Balances	1,020,000	873,000
Total Life Income Funds	$1,025,000	$ 878,000
Total Annuity and Life Income Funds	$2,683,000	$2,406,000

Two financial statements are required for the annuity and life income funds. The first is the balance sheet, as presented in Figure 20-8, and the second is the statement of changes in fund balance, as presented in Figure 20-5.

Illustration of Transactions

Sol City University has established separate annuity and life income subfunds, for which the balance sheets are presented in Figure 20-8. The transactions in these funds are also reported on the statement of changes in fund balances in Figure 20-5. Entries for the transactions in these two subfunds during the 19X2 fiscal year are presented below.

Annuity Fund Additions to Fund Balances   The annuity fund accepts an annuity-based gift from an alumna who specifies that she receive a monthly payment of $1,000 for 10 years. The gift consists of cash of $210,000 and securities having a market value of $125,000 at the time of the gift. The university's actuaries compute the present value of the annuity as $82,000 based on various actuarial assumptions. The initial present value of the liability recorded upon receipt of the gift is for the principal portion only; the remaining portion of the annuity payments is expected to be earned from investment income. The entry to record the acceptance of the gift is:

(55)	Cash	210,000	
	Investments	125,000	
	Annuities Payable		82,000
	Fund Balance—Annuity		253,000
	Accept annuity-based gift.		

The $253,000 is included as part of the $400,000 increase in the fund balance of the annuity and life income funds as reported in Figure 20-5. The remainder of the $400,000 increase is from a $147,000 addition to life income funds which is discussed later in this section.

Annuity Fund Deductions from Fund Balance   The university's actuaries reassess the existing annuities and modify some of their present value estimates based on changes in the actuarial assumptions, primarily a lower rate of return on investment than originally expected. This revision results in an increase in the present values of some of the annuities payable, as follows:

(56)	Fund Balance—Annuity	51,000	
	Annuities Payable		51,000
	Actuarial reassessment of present values of		
	annuities.		

A matured annuity is transferred to the endowment fund upon completion of the terms of the annuity agreement, as follows:

(57)	Fund Balance—Annuity	5,000	
	Cash		5,000
	Transmit matured annuity to endowment fund.		

Recall that the endowment fund recorded this transfer as an increase to its fund balance (see entry 50 presented earlier in this chapter).

Other Annuity Fund Transactions   Figure 20-8 presents the effects of other transactions in the annuity fund, which include the receipt of investment income and the payment of annuities. A portion of the investment income is allocated to Annuities Payable for the amount of the increase in the present value of the annuities payable after the revision in entry (56), and the remainder of the investment income is recorded as an addition to fund balance. Recall that the initial present value recorded upon receipt of the gift was for the principal portion only. The present value of the annuity increases as payments become due.

(58)	Cash	50,000	
	Annuities Payable		42,000
	Fund Balance—Annuity		8,000
	Investment income.		

(59)	Annuities Payable	250,000	
	Cash		250,000
	Pay current annuities due.		

Life Income Fund Additions to Fund Balance   The university accepts a gift of stock from an alumnus and agrees that the alumnus will receive the income from the stock for the remainder of his life. The stock has a market value of $147,000 at the time of acceptance. The entry to record the receipt of the gift is:

(60)	Investments	147,000	
	Fund Balance—Life Income		147,000
	Accept life income gift.		

No payable is recorded, because there is no obligation to make any payments until income is earned. The $147,000 is included in the $400,000 increase in fund balance for the combined annuity and life income funds reported in Figure 20-5.

Other Life Income Fund Transactions   The investments in the life income fund earn $60,000 during the year. This income is payable to the donors of the gifts and is a liability in the fund. The liablity is extinguished by payments to the individual life income recipients. Figure 20-8 presents the effects of the following entries:

(61)	Cash	60,000	
	Income Payable		60,000
	Income from investments.		

(62)	Income Payable	60,000	
	Cash		60,000
	Pay income to individual recipients.		

PLANT FUNDS

Colleges and universities maintain four different *plant subfunds*. Each subfund has its own purpose, as follows:

1. *Unexpended Plant Fund.* This subfund accounts for the expendable resources to be used to acquire or construct fixed assets. Building projects are recorded in this subfund during the period of construction.

2. *Fund for Renewals and Replacements.* This subfund accounts for resources to be used for remodeling, renovation, or replacement of existing fixed assets.

3. *Fund for Retirement of Indebtedness.* This subfund accounts for resources to be used to service the debt incurred to acquire or construct fixed assets. This subfund is similar to debt service funds of local governments.

4. *Investment in Plant.* This subfund accounts for the institution's fixed assets, debt related to plant, and net investment in plant.

The flows within and among the four subfunds are presented in Figure 20-9. Additions to the investment in plant subfund occur when plant assets are contributed to the university, when other funds acquire plant assets, and when building projects or renewals and improvements are completed. In addition, retirement of principal in the retirement of indebtedness subfund increases the university's net investment in plant.

A college or university may issue bonds, incur a mortgage, or use other borrowings for construction of plant assets. The liability is shown in the unexpended plant fund until the construction project is completed, at which time the liability is transferred to the investment in plant fund. Interest on debt during the construction phase is treated in several different ways. Some universities pay the interest costs during construction directly out of the unexpended plant fund. In this case, the interest cost is typically capitalized as part of the construction cost of the asset and is included in the amount transferred to investment in plant. Other universities account for interest during construction as a financing expenditure, not part of the capitalized cost of the asset. In this case, the retirement of

FIGURE 20-9 Additions to and deductions from plant fund subfunds.

Additions	Deductions
Unexpended Plant Fund	
Government or private gifts of grants restricted to plant funds Income and gains from investments Sale of bonds, mortgages, or other borrowings Transfers in from other fund groups	Disbursements for completed plant acquisition or construction[a] Investment losses
Fund for Renewals and Replacements	
Income and gains from investments Transfers in from other fund groups for renewals and replacements	Disbursements for renewals and replacements[a] Investment losses
Fund for Retirement of Indebtedness	
Income and gains from investments Government or private gifts or grants restricted to debt retirement Transfers in from other fund groups for retirement of indebtedness	Payments for retirement of principal[b] Payments for interest Administration costs Investment losses
Investment in Plant	
Government or private gifts or plant Plant acquisitions or construction financed from resources in other plant funds or current funds Retirements of principal portion of debt	Disposal of plant assets Accumulated depreciation Transfers in of bonds, mortgages, or other borrowings

[a] See second addition to investment in plant.
[b] See third addition to investment in plant.

indebtedness subfund normally pays interest during construction. Interest costs after the completion of the building are treated as a periodic expenditure from the retirement of indebtedness subfund.

Depreciation

The recognition of depreciation of a university's plant and equipment is different for public institutions as opposed to private institutions. **GASB 8** established the depreciation guidelines for public colleges and universities, which permits the recognition of an accumulated depreciation allowance to be reported in the investment in plant balance sheet. If a public university elects to recognize depreciation in the investment in plant subfund, the amount reported as depreciation reduces the fund balance in that plant subfund and must be reported in the statement of changes in fund balances. Public institutions should not recognize depreciation in either the statement of current funds revenue, expenditures, and other changes or the statement of changes in unrestricted current funds balance. For private colleges and universities, **FASB 93** requires the recognition of depreciation expense in the fund using the plant or equipment during the period. Therefore, for a private college using fund accounting, the individual funds must report depreciation in their general-purpose external financial statements. For the current funds, depreciation is reported in the operating statement that includes the period's revenue, expenditures, and other changes. The following example of Sol City University follows the guidelines in **GASB 8** because the illustration states that the university is a public university.

Sol City University has established all four subfunds of the plant fund. The balance sheet for the four subfunds is presented in Figure 20-10. The results of transactions in the four subfunds are presented in the statement of changes in fund balances in Figure 20-5.

Illustration of Transactions in Unexpended Plant Fund

The unexpended plant fund accounts for the resources available for acquisition of fixed assets. Projects under construction are accounted for in this subfund until they are completed and transferred to the investment in plant subfund. This subfund also reports any debt outstanding on projects during construction. Records are maintained on a project-by-project basis.

Additions to Unexpended Plant Fund Balance As reported in Figure 20-5, the unexpended plant fund receives resources from the endowment fund, from state government appropriations, from private gifts, and from investment activity, as follows:

(63)	Cash	25,000	
	Fund Balance—Restricted		25,000
	Receive distribution from endowment fund.		

FIGURE 20-10 Balance sheet for plant funds.

Sol City University
Balance Sheet—Plant Funds
June 30, 19X2
(with comparative figures for June 30, 19X1)

Assets

	19X2	19X1
Plant Funds:		
Unexpended:		
Cash	$ 163,000	$ 205,000
Investments (at cost)	642,000	795,000
Due from Unrestricted Current Funds	75,000	60,000
Total Unexpended	$ 880,000	$ 1,060,000
Renewals and Replacements:		
Cash	$ 3,000	$ 2,000
Investments (at cost)	75,000	143,000
Deposits with Trustees	50,000	45,000
Due from Other Funds	2,000	-0-
Total Renewals and Replacements	$ 130,000	$ 190,000
Retirement of Indebtedness:		
Cash	$ 25,000	$ 70,000
Deposits with Trustees	75,000	77,000
Total Retirement of Indebtedness	$ 100,000	$ 147,000
Investment in Plant:		
Land	$ 250,000	$ 250,000
Land Improvements	600,000	550,000
Buildings	13,830,000	13,030,000
Equipment	7,100,000	7,100,000
Library Books	50,000	40,000
Accumulated Depreciation	(1,500,000)	(1,000,000)
Total Investment in Plant	$20,330,000	$19,970,000
Total Plant Funds	$21,440,000	$21,367,000

Liabilities and Fund Balances

	19X2	19X1
Plant Funds:		
Unexpended:		
Notes Payable	$ 50,000	$ -0-
Bonds Payable	200,000	-0-
Fund Balances:		
Restricted	520,000	930,000
Unrestricted	110,000	130,000
Total Unexpended	$ 880,000	$ 1,060,000
Renewals and Replacements:		
Fund Balances:		
Restricted	$ 28,000	$ 90,000
Unrestricted	102,000	100,000
Total Renewals and Replacements	$ 130,000	$ 190,000
Retirement of Indebtedness:		
Fund Balances:		
Restricted	$ 93,000	$ 63,000
Unrestricted	7,000	84,000
Total Retirement of Indebtedness	$ 100,000	$ 147,000
Investment in Plant:		
Bonds Payable	$ 1,100,000	$ 1,200,000
Mortgages Payable	200,000	100,000
Net Investment in Plant	19,030,000	18,670,000
Total Investment in Plant	$20,330,000	$19,970,000
Total Plant Funds	$21,440,000	$21,367,000

(64)	Cash	40,000	
	Fund Balance—Restricted		40,000
	Receive government appropriation for new construction.		

(65)	Cash	55,000	
	Fund Balance—Restricted		55,000
	Receive private gifts for acquiring fixed assets.		

(66)	Cash	10,000	
	Fund Balance—Restricted		10,000
	Investment income.		

(67)	Cash	158,000	
	Investments		153,000
	Fund Balance—Restricted		5,000
	Sell investments at gain.		

Entry (63) reports the distribution received from the endowment fund. Recall that the endowment fund recorded the distribution as a reduction of its fund balance (see entry 51 presented earlier in this chapter).

Deductions from Unexpended Plant Fund Balance The primary construction project during the period is a $700,000 addition to the business school building. A mortgage payable is obtained in the amount of $100,000. The remaining resources needed for the construction project are currently available in the fund and are taken from the fund balance restricted for the business building addition of $545,000 and the unrestricted fund balance of $55,000. Figure 20-5 reports the $600,000 of net resources expended from the unexpended plant fund ($700,000 − $100,000 of mortgage payable).

(68)	Cash	100,000	
	Mortgage Payable		100,000
	University signs mortgage for business building addition.		

(69)	Construction in Progress	700,000	
	Cash		700,000
	Construction costs of business building project.		

(70)	Mortgage Payable	100,000	
	Fund Balance—Restricted	545,000	
	Fund Balance—Unrestricted	55,000	
	Construction in Progress		700,000
	Complete business building addition and transfer to investment in plant subfund.		

Entry (70) transfers the completed building addition and the $100,000 mortgage payable to the investment in plant fund. This transfer will be examined further in the discussion under that subfund.

Transfers In to Unexpended Plant Fund   The unexpended plant fund subfund receives a nonmandatory transfer in from the unrestricted current fund for its portion of unrestricted gifts.

(71)	Cash	35,000	
	Fund Balance—Unrestricted		35,000
	Nonmandatory transfer in from unrestricted		
	current fund.		

The unrestricted current fund recorded this transfer as a nonmandatory transfer out (see entry 12 presented earlier in this chapter).

Other Transactions in Unexpended Plant Fund   Figure 20-10 presents the effects of other transactions affecting only balance sheet accounts. The unexpended plant fund also begins preparing for an addition to the science building. Notes payable and bonds payable are issued to obtain monies for financing the project, which will begin in the early part of the next fiscal period.

(72)	Cash	250,000	
	Notes Payable		50,000
	Bonds Payable		200,000
	Issue debt for science building addition.		

An increase of $15,000 is recognized in the receivable from the unrestricted current fund for reimbursable items (see entry 8 earlier in this chapter).

(73)	Due from Other Funds	15,000	
	Cash		15,000
	Increase in receivable.		

Illustration of Transactions in Renewals and Replacements

The fund for renewals and replacements subfund (R&R fund) receives most of its resources from other funds, primarily the unrestricted current fund. The R&R fund is used for minor repair or replacement projects on the university's fixed assets. Major construction projects are accounted for in the unexpended plant fund.

The transactions in Sol City University's R&R fund are presented below.

Additions to R&R Fund Balance   Figure 20-5 presents the results of the increases in the renewal and replacement fund balance from investment transactions and income, as follows:

(74)	Cash	3,000	
	Fund Balance—Restricted		3,000
	Investment income.		

(75)	Cash	70,000	
	Investments		68,000
	Fund Balance—Restricted		2,000
	Sell investments at gain.		

Deductions from R&R Fund Balance A total of $150,000 of resources is used for a variety of renewal and replacement projects on campus. The restricted fund balance for specific R&R projects is charged for $67,000 of the costs for the period. The remaining R&R costs of $83,000 are charged to the unrestricted fund balance.

(76)	Fund Balance—Restricted	67,000	
	Fund Balance—Unrestricted	83,000	
	Cash		150,000
	R&R projects during year.		

The university's net investment in plant assets is increased by these R&R projects (see entry 90 later in this chapter).

Transfers In to R&R Fund The primary source of resources is a mandatory transfer in from the unrestricted current fund for renewals and replacements.

(77)	Cash	85,000	
	Fund Balance—Unrestricted		85,000
	Mandatory transfer in from unrestricted current fund.		

The unrestricted current fund recorded this transfer as a mandatory transfer out (see entry 11 presented earlier in this chapter).

Other Transactions in R&R Plant Fund Figure 20-10 presents the effects of other transactions affecting the balance sheet accounts. The receivable from the unrestricted current fund is increased by $2,000 for reimbursable items (see entry 8 earlier in the chapter), and an additional $5,000 is deposited with external trustees as required by debt agreements.

(78)	Due from Other Funds	2,000	
	Cash		2,000
	Receivable from unrestricted current fund.		
(79)	Deposits with Trustees	5,000	
	Cash		5,000
	Increase deposits with trustees.		

Illustration of Transactions in Retirement of Indebtedness

The retirement of indebtedness subfund is responsible for servicing the debt incurred in acquiring the university's fixed assets. Transactions in Sol City University's retirement of indebtedness plant fund are presented below.

Additions to Retirement of Indebtedness Fund Balance The retirement of indebtedness subfund receives $33,000 in private gifts and earns investment income and records a gain on the sale of investments. Figure 20-5 reports the effects of the following entries on the fund balance.

(80)	Cash	33,000	
	Fund Balance—Restricted		33,000
	Receive private gift for retirement of debt.		
(81)	Investments	50,000	
	Cash		50,000
	Acquire investments.		
(82)	Cash	4,000	
	Fund Balance—Restricted		4,000
	Receive investment income.		
(83)	Cash	53,000	
	Investments		50,000
	Fund Balance—Restricted		3,000
	Sell investments at a gain.		

Deductions from Retirement of Indebtedness Fund Balance The major deductions from the retirement of indebtedness subfund are for the payment of interest of $106,000 and for principal retirement of $100,000. The total of $206,000 in debt reduction is allocated between restricted and unrestricted fund balances. In addition, administrative expenses of $1,000 are paid during the year. Figure 20-5 presents the effects on fund balance from the following transactions.

(84)	Fund Balance—Restricted	10,000	
	Fund Balance—Unrestricted	196,000	
	Cash		206,000
	Pay interest of $106,000 and principal of $100,000.		
(85)	Fund Balance—Unrestricted	1,000	
	Cash		1,000
	Pay administrative expenses.		

The $100,000 of principal retirement increases the university's net investment in plant assets (see entry 92 later in this chapter).

Transfers In to Retirement of Indebtedness Fund The retirement of indebtedness subfund receives a mandatory transfer in from the unrestricted current fund.

(86)	Cash	120,000	
	Fund Balance—Unrestricted		120,000
	Receive mandatory transfer in.		

The unrestricted current fund recorded this transfer as a mandatory transfer out (see entry 11 presented earlier in this chapter).

Other Transactions in Retirement of Indebtedness Fund The trustees for the external debt return $2,000 on deposit with them. The return is due to the fulfillment of specified debt agreements. Figure 20-10 shows the effect on the balance sheet from this transaction.

(87)	Cash	2,000	
	Deposits with Trustees		2,000
	Receive portion of deposit with trustee.		

Illustration of Transactions in Investment in Plant

The fourth subfund of the plant fund records the university's net investment in plant. The investment in plant is increased for the costs of fixed assets acquired by the other funds and for the retirement of debt by the retirement of indebtedness subfund. The investment in plant is decreased by disposals of fixed assets. The investment in plant section of the balance sheet reports the costs of fixed plant assets; outstanding long-term debt incurred for the acquisition or construction of those assets is reported in the balance sheet as liabilities. The account Net Investment in Plant rather than Fund Balance is used to report the difference between assets and liabilities.

Sol City University has the following transactions in its investment in plant subfund during the 19X2 fiscal year.

Additions to Net Investment in Plant Figure 20-5, the statement of changes in fund balances, reports several increases in the fund balance of this subfund during 19X2. The investment in plant subfund is increased by the following private gifts:

(88)	Library Books	10,000	
	Equipment	10,000	
	Net Investment in Plant		20,000
	Receive donated books and equipment with a		
	market value of $20,000.		

The investment in plant assets was increased by a total of $800,000 from the university's resources during the year. Several funds have provided the resources for the additional investment, as follows:

1. The total cost of the business building addition is $700,000, of which $600,000 is paid from existing resources. The remaining $100,000 is obtained from a mortgage payable that is still outstanding. Note that the unexpended plant fund recorded the use of the $600,000 from its available resources and recorded the transfer of the mortgage payable to the investment in plant fund (see entry 70 presented earlier in this chapter).

2. A total of $150,000 is expended for building renewals and replacements. The renewals and replacements plant fund recorded the $150,000 reduction of its resources for this work (see entry 76 presented earlier in this chapter).

3. The unrestricted current fund expended $50,000 for plant assets which it recorded as an expenditure of the period (see entry 8 presented earlier in this chapter).

The effects of these transactions on the Net Investment in Plant fund balance are reported in Figure 20-5, the statement of changes in fund balances. Note that the $100,000 of resources provided by the mortgage payable for the business building addition do not change the fund balance and are not reported in Figure 20-5. The net investment in fund balance will be changed when the mortgage payable is paid off. Until paid off, the mortgage payable is reported as a liability of the investment in plant fund on the balance sheet, as presented in Figure 20-10. The entries to record the additions to net investment in plant assets are:

(89)	Buildings	650,000	
	Land Improvements	50,000	
	Net Investment in Plant		600,000
	Mortgage Payable		100,000
	Business building addition completed.		
(90)	Buildings	150,000	
	Net Investment in Plant		150,000
	Renewals and replacements in R&R subfund.		
(91)	Equipment	50,000	
	Net Investment in Plant		50,000
	Equipment acquired by unrestricted current fund.		

Bond debt principal of $100,000 is paid during the year (see entry 84 earlier in this chapter). The bonds were sold many years ago to finance the acquisition of a continuing education center.

(92)	Bonds Payable	100,000	
	Net Investment in Plant		100,000
	Debt principal paid by retirement of		
	indebtedness subfund.		

Deductions from Investment in Plant Figure 20-5, the statement of changes in fund balances, reports several deductions from the university's investment in plant during the period. Used auxiliary enterprises' equipment with an original cost of $60,000 is sold for $20,000. The $20,000 is recorded as revenue in the unrestricted current fund (see entry 6 earlier in the chapter).

(93)	Net Investment in Plant	60,000	
	Equipment		60,000
	Dispose of used equipment.		

Sol City University recognizes depreciation on its buildings and equipment in order to obtain more complete information on the costs of providing services. Depreciation of $500,000 is recognized, using the straight-line method.

(94)	Net Investment in Plant	500,000	
	Accumulated Depreciation		500,000
	Recognize depreciation.		

Note that the governmental accounting standards presented in **GASB 8** do not require a public university to recognize depreciation. This is an option that some universities use to obtain a more complete report on the costs of maintaining an extensive physical plant. Public universities that do recognize depreciation should do so only as part of the investment in plant fund. Depreciation is not an expenditure under governmental accounting standards. If depreciation is recognized by public universities, it must be reported on the statement of changes in fund balance for the investment in plant fund, as in Figure 20-5. The depreciation is also accumulated and reported as such on the balance sheet for the investment in plant funds, as in Figure 20-10.

Private universities must record depreciation and allocate it to the specific fund that uses the assets. In most cases, this means that the unrestricted current fund of a private university will show an expenditure for depreciation.

AGENCY FUNDS

Similar to the agency fund used by local government units, the *agency fund* of a college accounts for the collection and disbursement of assets held in a custodial relationship. Examples are employees' payroll deductions for health insurance premiums or other items, and funds collected by the university on behalf of other organizations. For example, the university may collect student government fees as part of its tuition collection process. The university then holds these fees until they are requested by the student government organization.

The agency fund does not report a fund balance, because total assets always equal total liabilities. Any income on investments is added to the appropriate liability accounts. Because of this equality, the agency fund is not included in the statement of changes in fund balance; however, the agency fund prepares a balance sheet of its assets and liabilities, as presented in Figure 20-11.

Illustration of Transactions

Sol City University established an agency fund to account for the collection and disbursement of the student government's fees collected during student registration. The following cash transactions occur in the agency fund during the 19X2 fiscal year:

(95)	Cash		60,000	
		Deposits Held in Custody for Others		60,000
		Collect student government fees.		
(96)	Investments		20,000	
		Cash		20,000
		Additional investments.		
(97)	Deposits Held in Custody for Others		50,000	
		Cash		50,000
		Disburse fees as requested by student government.		

FIGURE 20-11 Balance sheet of agency fund.

Sol City University
Balance Sheet—Agency Fund
June 30, 19X2
(with comparative figures for June 30, 19X1)

	19X2	19X1
Assets		
Cash	$25,000	$35,000
Investments (at cost)	30,000	10,000
Total Agency Funds	$55,000	$45,000
Liabilities and Fund Balances		
Deposits Held in Custody for Others	$55,000	$45,000
Total Agency Funds	$55,000	$45,000

FINANCIAL REPORTING FOR A UNIVERSITY ENTITY

The annual report for a university includes three basic financial statements: the combined balance sheet; the statement of current funds revenue, expenditures, and other changes (Figure 20-4); and the statement of changes in fund balances (Figure 20-5). The combined balance sheet is displayed in either the "pancake" format or the columnar format. The *"pancake" display format* is also often termed the "layered" format and is simply a combination of the individual funds' balance sheets presented earlier in the chapter, as follows:

Sol City University
Combined Balance Sheet—All Funds
June 30, 19X2

	Assets	Liabilities and Fund Balances
Unrestricted current fund balance sheet		
Restricted current fund balance sheet		
Loan funds balance sheet		
Endowment and similar funds balance sheet		
Annuity and life income funds balance sheet		
Plant funds balance sheet		
Agency funds balance sheet		

The *columnar display format* for the combined balance sheet is gaining in use. The columnar display has a column for each fund, often presented with comparative figures for the preceding fiscal period. An example of the columnar display format for the combined balance sheet is presented in Figure 20-12. Note that each fund has its own discrete column, that a Total of All Funds column is

FIGURE 20-12 Columnar display format for combined balance sheet of a college or university.

Sol City University
Combined Balance Sheet
June 30, 19X2
(with comparative figures for June 30, 19X1)

	Current Unrestricted 19X2	Current Unrestricted 19X1	Current Restricted 19X2	Current Restricted 19X1	Loan 19X2	Loan 19X1	Endowment and Similar 19X2	Endowment and Similar 19X1
Assets								
Cash	$105,000	$ 55,000	$179,000	$ 56,000	$ 3,000	$ 10,000	$ 50,000	$ 50,000
Investments, at cost	235,000	180,000	124,000	83,000	50,000	50,000	6,950,000	5,900,000
Deposits with Trustees								
Accounts Receivable	123,000	98,000	38,000	84,000				
Less: Allowance for								
Uncollectibles	(9,000)	(10,000)	(4,000)	(4,000)				
Loans to Students,								
Faculty, & Staff					275,000	190,000		
Due from Other Funds					2,000			
Inventories	45,000	40,000						
Prepaid Expenses and								
Deferred Charges	14,000	10,000						
Investment in Plant, net								
Total Assets	$513,000	$373,000	$337,000	$219,000	$330,000	$250,000	$7,000,000	$5,950,000
Liabilities and Fund Balances								
Accounts Payable	$ 63,000	$ 50,000	$ 7,000	$ 3,000				
Accrued Liabilities	10,000	8,000						
Students' Deposits	15,000	18,000						
Due to Other Funds	79,000	60,000						
Deferred Credits	15,000	10,000						
Annuities and Income								
Payable								
Notes Payable								
Bonds Payable								
Mortgages Payable								
Deposits Held in								
Custody								
Fund Balance:								
Unrestricted:								
Allocated	50,000				$ 65,000	$ 50,000		
Unallocated	281,000	227,000						
Restricted:								
Temporarily			330,000	216,000	240,000	183,000	$3,100,000	$2,590,000
Permanently							3,900,000	3,360,000
U.S. Government								
Grants					25,000	17,000		
Net Investment in								
Plant								
	$513,000	$373,000	$337,000	$219,000	$330,000	$250,000	$7,000,000	$5,950,000

	Annuity and Life Income		Plant		Agency		Total, All Funds	
	19X2	19X1	19X2	19X1	19X2	19X1	19X2	19X1
	$ 36,000	$ 31,000	$ 191,000	$ 277,000	$25,000	$35,000	$ 589,000	$ 514,000
	2,647,000	2,375,000	717,000	938,000	30,000	10,000	10,753,000	9,536,000
			125,000	122,000			125,000	122,000
							161,000	182,000
							(13,000)	(14,000)
							275,000	190,000
			77,000	60,000			79,000	60,000
							45,000	40,000
							14,000	10,000
			20,330,000	19,970,000			20,330,000	19,970,000
	$2,683,000	$2,406,000	$21,440,000	$21,367,000	$55,000	$45,000	$32,358,000	$30,610,000
							$ 70,000	$ 53,000
							10,000	8,000
							15,000	18,000
							79,000	60,000
							15,000	10,000
	$1,080,000	$1,155,000					1,080,000	1,155,000
			$ 50,000				50,000	
			1,300,000	$ 1,200,000			1,300,000	1,200,000
			200,000	100,000			200,000	100,000
					$55,000	$45,000	55,000	45,000
							115,000	50,000
			219,000	314,000			500,000	541,000
	1,603,000	1,251,000	641,000	1,083,000			5,914,000	5,323,000
							3,900,000	3,360,000
							25,000	17,000
			19,030,000	18,670,000			19,030,000	18,670,000
	$2,683,000	$2,406,000	$21,440,000	$21,367,000	$55,000	$45,000	$32,358,000	$30,610,000

presented, and that full disclosure is made of the restricted versus unrestricted resources of the university.

SUMMARY OF KEY CONCEPTS AND TERMS

Colleges and universities use a fund accounting system to account for their activities. A separation must be preserved within the funds for restrictions imposed by external donors on the types of expenditures that may be made from their contributions to the university. These restrictions may appear in any of the fund types, except agency funds. The accrual basis of accounting is used in the unrestricted current fund. In the restricted current fund, revenue is recognized to the extent of the resources expended in accordance with the restrictions. Therefore, in the restricted current funds, revenue equals expenditures. The plant funds expend resources for capital outlays for fixed assets, and also service the debt associated with the fixed assets of the college or university. The unexpended plant subfund accounts for fixed assets during construction. At completion, the costs are transferred to the investment in plant fund, which is a subfund of the plant fund.

A unique aspect of college and university accounting is the need for mandatory and nonmandatory transfers between funds. For example, the unrestricted current fund may be required to transfer monies to the retirement of indebtedness plant subfund in order to provide for the retirement of debt used to finance fixed assets. These transfers must be reported separately in the statement of current funds revenue, expenditures, and other changes, and in the statement of changes in fund balances. In addition, the college or university provides a combined balance sheet of all funds, typically presented in either the "pancake" or the columnar format.

Agency funds
Annuity and life income funds
Board-designated funds
Columnar display format for combined balance sheet
Contributions of property
Contributions of services
Endowment funds
Loan funds
Mandatory transfer
Nonmandatory transfer

Plant subfunds (Unexpended plant fund, Fund for renewals and replacements, Fund for retirement of indebtedness, and Investment in plant fund)
"Pancake" or layered display format for combined balance sheet
Restricted current fund
Subfunds
Unrestricted current fund

QUESTIONS

Q20-1 What is NACUBO, and what is its involvement in the development of accounting standards for colleges and universities?

Q20-2 What does the term *restricted* mean in college and university accounting?

Q20-3 What is the basis of accounting used in the two current funds?

Q20-4 Which of the seven funds used by colleges and universities expends resources within its own fund? Which funds transfer expendable resources?

Q20-5 Differentiate between mandatory and nonmandatory transfers. Where are these shown in the financial statements of a college or university?

Q20-6 Are board-designated resources restricted? Why or why not?

Q20-7 How are tuition scholarships reported by a college or university?

Q20-8 What are auxiliary enterprises?

Q20-9 A donor contributes $10,000 to a university, restricted for use in acquiring micro-computers for the college of business. Which fund records this contribution? In which fund is the expenditure for the microcomputers recorded?

Q20-10 For the restricted current fund, do expenditures always equal revenue? Why?

Q20-11 Do colleges and universities record depreciation? Why or why not?

Q20-12 What is a quasi-endowment? How does this differ from other forms of endowments?

Q20-13 What is the difference between an annuity fund and a life income fund? Which fund records a payable to the donor at the time of the contribution to the college or university?

Q20-14 What are the four subfunds of the plant fund? Which subfund accounts for projects under construction?

Q20-15 Which fund services the long-term debt associated with the fixed assets of the college or university?

Q20-16 What is the "pancake," or layered, format of a balance sheet?

CASE

C20-1   Basis of Accounting and Reporting Issues

Central University uses the following types of funds: unrestricted current fund, restricted current fund, and plant fund.

Required

a. Explain the revenue recognition process used in the restricted current fund. Will total revenue always be equal to total expenditures in this fund? Why?

b. Define the differences between mandatory and nonmandatory transfers. Where are the two types of transfers reported in the university's financial statements?

c. Do universities record depreciation? Why or why not?

EXERCISES

E20-1   Multiple-Choice Questions on Identification of Funds and Accounting for Colleges and Universities [AICPA Adapted]

Select the correct answer for each of the following questions.

1. Which of the following should be used in accounting for public colleges and universities?
   a. Fund accounting and accrual accounting.
   b. Fund accounting but *not* accrual accounting.
   c. Accrual accounting but *not* fund accounting.
   d. Neither accrual accounting nor fund accounting.

2. Which of the following should be included in a university's current funds revenue?

	Unrestricted Gifts	Expended Restricted Current Funds	Unexpended Restricted Current Funds
a.	Yes	Yes	Yes
b.	Yes	Yes	No
c.	Yes	No	No
d.	No	No	Yes

3. Which of the following is utilized for current expenditures by a university?

	Unrestricted Current Funds	Restricted Current Funds
a.	No	No
b.	No	Yes
c.	Yes	No
d.	Yes	Yes

4. The plant funds group of a university includes which of the following subgroups?

	Investment in Plant Funds	Unexpended Plant Funds
a.	No	Yes
b.	No	No
c.	Yes	No
d.	Yes	Yes

5. The current funds group of a university includes which of the following subgroups?

	Term Endowment Funds	Life Income Funds
a.	No	No
b.	No	Yes
c.	Yes	Yes
d.	Yes	No

6. Which of the following should be included in the current funds revenues of a university?

	Tuition Waivers	Unrestricted Bequests
a.	Yes	No
b.	Yes	Yes
c.	No	Yes
d.	No	No

7. Which of the following receipts is properly recorded as restricted current funds on the books of a university?
   a. Tuition.
   b. Student laboratory fees.
   c. Housing fees.
   d. Research grants.

8. Funds established at a college by donors who have stipulated that the principal is nonexpendable but that the income generated may be expended by current operating funds would be accounted for in the:
   a. Quasi-endowment fund.
   b. Endowment fund.

c. Term endowment fund.

d. Agency fund.

9. Funds which the governing board of an institution, rather than a donor or other outside agency, has determined are to be retained and invested for other than loan or plant purposes would be accounted for in the:

a. Quasi-endowment fund.

b. Endowment fund.

c. Agency fund.

d. Restricted current fund.

E20-2 **Multiple-Choice Questions on Current Funds Transactions** [AICPA Adapted]

Select the correct answer for each of the following questions.

1. Abbey University's unrestricted current funds comprised the following:

Assets	$5,000,000
Liabilities (including deferred revenues of $100,000)	3,000,000

The fund balance of Abbey's unrestricted current funds was:

a. $1,900,000.

b. $2,000,000.

c. $2,100,000.

d. $5,000,000.

2. For the summer session of 19X2, Pacific University assessed its students $1,700,000 (net of refunds), covering tuition and fees for educational and general purposes. However, only $1,500,000 was expected to be realized, because scholarships totaling $150,000 were granted to students, and tuition remissions of $50,000 were allowed to faculty members' children attending Pacific. What amount should Pacific include in the unrestricted current funds as revenues from student tuition and fees?

a. $1,500,000.

b. $1,550,000.

c. $1,650,000.

d. $1,700,000.

3. Tuition waivers for which there is *no* intention of collection from the student should be classified by a university as:

	Revenue	Expenditures
a.	No	No
b.	No	Yes
c.	Yes	Yes
d.	Yes	No

4. For the fall semester of 19X1, Dover University assessed its students $2,300,000 for tuition and fees. The net amount realized was only $2,100,000 because of the following revenue reductions:

Refunds occasioned by class cancellations and student withdrawals	$ 50,000
Tuition remissions granted to faculty members' families	10,000
Scholarships and fellowships	140,000

How much should Dover report for the period for unrestricted current fund revenue from tuition and fees?

a. $2,100,000.
b. $2,150,000.
c. $2,250,000.
d. $2,300,000.

5. During the years ended June 30, 19X2 and 19X3, Belmont College conducted a cancer research project financed by a $2,000,000 gift from an alumnus. This entire amount was pledged by the donor on July 10, 19X1, although he paid only $500,000 on that date. The gift was restricted to the financing of this particular research project. During the 2-year research period, Belmont's related gift receipts and research expenditures were as follows:

	Year Ended June 30	
	19X2	**19X3**
Gift receipts	$1,200,000	$ 800,000
Cancer research expenditures	900,000	1,100,000

How much gift revenue should Belmont report in the restricted column of its statement of current funds revenue, expenditures, and other changes for the year ended June 30, 19X3?

a. $0.
b. $800,000.
c. $1,100,000.
d. $2,000,000.

6. An increase in Oak College's restricted current funds balance could be reported as an excess of:

a. Transfers to revenues over restricted receipts.
b. Restricted receipts over transfers to revenues.
c. Revenues over expenditures and mandatory transfers.
d. Revenues and mandatory transfers over expenditures.

7. The following information was available from Forest College's accounting records for its current funds for the year ended March 31, 19X0:

Restricted gifts received:	
Expended	$100,000
Not expended	300,000
Unrestricted gifts received:	
Expended	600,000
Not expended	75,000

What amount should be included in current funds revenues for the year ended March 31, 19X0?

a. $600,000.
b. $700,000.
c. $775,000.
d. $1,000,000.

Items 8 through 10 are based on the following information pertaining to Global University as of June 30, 19X1, and for the year then ended:

Unrestricted current funds comprised $7,500,000 of assets and $4,500,000 of liabilities (including deferred revenues of $150,000). Among the receipts recorded during the year were unrestricted gifts of $550,000 and restricted grants totaling $330,000, of which $220,000 was expended during the year for current operations and $110,000 remained unexpended at the close of the year.

Volunteers from the surrounding communities regularly contribute their services to Global and are paid nominal amounts to cover their travel costs. During the year, the total amount paid to these volunteers aggregated $18,000. The gross value of services performed by them, determined by reference to equivalent wages available in that area for similar services, amounted to $200,000. Global University normally purchases the types of contributed services and the university feels the contributed services enhance its assets.

8. At June 30, 19X1, the fund balance of Global's unrestricted current fund was:
   a. $7,500,000.
   b. $3,150,000.
   c. $3,000,000.
   d. $2,850,000.

9. For the year ended June 30, 19X1, what amount should be included in Global's current funds revenue for the unrestricted gifts and restricted grants?
   a. $550,000.
   b. $660,000.
   c. $770,000.
   d. $880,000.

10. For the year ended June 30, 19X1, what amount should Global record as expenditures for the volunteers' services?
    a. $218,000.
    b. $200,000.
    c. $18,000.
    d. $0.

E20-3 Multiple-Choice Questions on Noncurrent Funds [AICPA Adapted]

Select the correct answer for each of the following questions.

1. The following funds were among those on Trent University's books at April 30, 19X1:

Funds to be used for acquisition of additional
properties for university purposes (unexpended
at 4/30/X1) $3,000,000

> Funds set aside for debt service charges and
> for retirement of indebtedness on university's
> properties   5,000,000

How much of the above-mentioned funds should be included in plant funds?
a. $0.
b. $3,000,000.
c. $5,000,000.
d. $8,000,000.

2. On January 2, 19X2, Jane Nicholas established a $500,000 trust, the income from which is to be paid to Main University for general operating purposes. The Sycamore National Bank was appointed by Nicholas as trustee of the fund. What journal entry is required on Main's books at the time the trust is established?

	Debit	Credit
a. Memorandum entry only	—	—
b. Cash	$500,000	
Endowment Fund Balance		$500,000
c. Nonexpendable Endowment Fund	$500,000	
Endowment Fund Balance		$500,000
d. Expendable Funds	$500,000	
Endowment Fund Balance		$500,000

3. In the loan fund of a college or university, each of the following types of loans would be found except:
a. Student.
b. Staff.
c. Building.
d. Faculty.

4. On July 31, 19X2, Bentum College showed the following amounts to be used for:

Renewal and replacement of college properties	$200,000
Retirement of indebtedness on college properties	300,000
Purchase of physical properties for college purposes, but unexpended at 7/31/X2	400,000

What total amount should be included in Bentum's plant funds at July 31, 19X2?
a. $900,000.
b. $600,000.
c. $400,000.
d. $200,000.

5. The following information pertains to interest received by Beech University from endowment fund investments for the year ended June 30, 19X0:

	Received	Expended for Current Operations
Unrestricted	$300,000	$100,000
Restricted	500,000	75,000

What amount should be credited to endowment income for the university for the year ended June 30, 19X0?

a. $800,000.
b. $375,000.
c. $175,000.
d. $100,000.

E20-4 Journal Entries for Unrestricted Current Fund

The following are selected transactions of the unrestricted current fund of Eden University:

1. Eden received a total of $720,000 appropriations from the federal and state governments.

2. Tuition and fees collected were $2,160,000. In addition, tuition waivers of $180,000 are expected on $270,000 of tuition yet to be collected.

3. Nonmandatory transfers of $124,000 to endowment funds and $37,000 to loan funds and a mandatory transfer of $60,000 to plant funds for retirement of debt were made.

4. The dairy store is an auxiliary enterprise. Sales were $120,000 and collections $106,000; $900 was established for uncollectibles. Expenses were as follows: dairy products, $40,000; salaries, $45,000; other expenses, $30,000. Vouchers payable totaled $7,300.

5. University expenditures included $2,050,000 for instruction, $42,000 for research, $260,000 for student services, and $180,000 for plant operations. Of this total, $75,000 was for supplies used and $38,000 of payables remain at year-end.

6. Student financial aid approved $172,000 of tuition reductions.

7. Received $11,500 in deposits from resident students.

Required

Prepare journal entries for the transactions in the unrestricted current fund.

E20-5 Journal Entries for Restricted Current Fund

The following are selected transactions of the restricted current fund of Eden University:

1. The alumni association transferred in $36,000 for support of faculty.

2. During the year, $32,500 of the funds transferred from the alumni association was spent for travel and research by the faculty.

3. A grant of $100,000 was received from the state for a study of water resources.

4. Expenditures for the water resources project were as follows: salaries, $45,000; equipment, $9,600; other expenses, $14,000.

5. Cash was transferred to the unrestricted current fund to cover indirect overhead costs of $16,000.

Required

Prepare journal entries for the transactions in the restricted current fund.

E20-6 Journal Entries for Plant Fund

The following are selected transactions of the plant funds of Eden University:

1. Received $60,000 from unrestricted current funds for retirement of debt.
2. Received $800,000 from state appropriations for an addition to the library.
3. Paid interest of $24,000 and principal of $100,000; $40,000 of the total was from restricted fund balances.
4. The new science building was completed. The $5,800,000 total included costs of $450,000 for sidewalks, parking lots, and landscaping. Bonds payable for $1,200,000 are outstanding for this project.
5. Equipment purchased for the science building totaled $1,600,000, of which $220,000 was from notes payable that remain outstanding.
6. Old library equipment with a book value of $16,000 was junked in preparation for the addition to the library.
7. Received $125,000 from the endowment fund for equipment for the science building.

Required

Prepare journal entries in the plant fund subfunds for the transactions. Indicate the subfund in which each entry would be made by using the following format:

Subfund **Journal Entry**

E20-7 Journal Entries for Loan Fund

The following are selected transactions of the loan fund of Eden University:

1. Received $37,000 from unrestricted current fund and $24,000, with restrictions, from the alumni association.
2. Invested $8,000 in government securities.
3. Made loans to students of $42,000 and to faculty of $15,000.
4. Received interest income: $2,700, restricted.
5. Administration costs paid were $3,200.
6. Sold investments for $21,000, which was a loss of $700, restricted.
7. Received repayments from students of $18,200 plus $680 interest.
8. Wrote off student loans totaling $1,100.

Required

Prepare journal entries for the transactions in the loan fund.

E20-8 Journal Entries for Endowment Fund

The following are selected transactions of the endowment fund of Eden University:

1. The endowment fund received $124,000 from the unrestricted current fund according to the board of regents' instructions.

2. Received a 5-year term endowment of $200,000, with the income to be used for business reference materials and with the principal to be used for copying equipment.

3. A term endowment of $125,000 expired and was transferred to unexpended plant funds to buy equipment for the new science building.

4. Purchased investments totaling $280,000.

5. Received $6,000 interest and dividends on endowment investments.

6. Sold quasi-endowment investments for $210,000, realizing a gain of $17,000.

7. Received $62,000 from annuity fund for endowment.

Required

Prepare journal entries in the endowment fund for the transactions.

E20-9 Journal Entries for Annuity and Life Income Fund

The following are selected transactions of the annuity and life income fund of Eden University:

1. Eden received investments from Joan Fisher, an alumna, with the stipulation that she receive the income from the investments for the remainder of her life. The market value was $245,000.

2. Income from life income fund investments totaled $78,000.

3. Income from annuity fund investments totaled $62,000, of which $12,000 was allocated to annuities payable.

4. Annuity payments were $340,000.

5. Eden received stocks and bonds valued at $325,000 from Don Garnet, Class of 1955, with the agreement that he receive $2,500 a month for 15 years. The present value of the annuity was estimated at $228,000.

6. An expired annuity worth $62,000 was transferred to the endowment fund.

Required

Prepare journal entries in the annuity and life income funds for the transactions.

PROBLEMS

P20-10 Balances in Annuity, Plant, and Current Funds [AICPA Adapted]

The bookkeeper for Hillside College resigned on March 1, 19X2, after preparing the following general ledger trial balance data and analysis of cash as of February 28, 19X2:

	Debit	Credit
Cash for General Unrestricted Current Operations	$258,000	
Cash for Restricted Current Uses	30,900	
Stock Donated by Jane Irwin	11,000	
Bonds Donated by Dick Miller	150,000	
Land	22,000	
Building	33,000	
General Current Operating Expenses	38,000	
Faculty Recruitment Expenses	4,100	
Mortgage Payable on Plant Assets		$ 30,000
Income from Gifts for General Operations		210,000
Income from Gifts for Restricted Uses		196,000
Student Fees		31,000
Fund Balance		80,000
Total	$547,000	$547,000

Hillside College
Analysis of Cash
For the 6 Months Ended February 28, 19X2

Cash for unrestricted current operations:			
Balance, September 1, 19X1		$ 80,000	
Add: Student fees	$ 31,000		
Gift from Diane Nugent	210,000	241,000	
		$321,000	
Deduct: General current operating expenses	$ 38,000		
Payment on land and building mortgage	25,000	(63,000)	$258,000
Cash for restricted uses:			
Gift from Diane Nugent for faculty recruitment		$ 35,000	
Less: Faculty recruitment expenses		(4,100)	30,900
Checking account balance, February 28, 19X2			$288,900

An accountant has been engaged to determine the proper balances for the school as of August 31, 19X2, the close of the school's fiscal year. An examination disclosed the following information:

1. Jane Irwin donated 100 shares of Go Company stock in September 19X1 with a market value of $110 per share on the date of donation. The terms of the restricted gift provide that the stock and any income therefrom are to be retained intact. At any date designated by the board of trustees, the assets are to be liquidated and the proceeds used as a down payment to assist the college's president in acquiring a personal residence. If proceeds are not sufficient to equal the down payment, the board authorized the difference to be covered from unrestricted cash, but not to exceed $1,000. The college will not retain any financial interest in the residence.

2. Dick Miller donated 6 percent bonds in September 19X1 with par and market values of $150,000 on the date of donation. Annual payments of $3,500 are to be made to the donor during his lifetime. Interest in excess of these payments is to be used for current operations in the following fiscal year. Upon the donor's death, the fund is to be used to construct a school cafeteria. The actuarially determined present value of the annuity is $50,000. Interest of $9,000 was received in April 19X2, of which $400 was allocated to annuities payable.

3. No transactions have been recorded on the school's books since February 28, 19X2. An employee of the school prepared the following analysis of the checking account for the period from March 1 through August 31, 19X2:

Balance, March 1, 19X2			$288,900
Deduct: General current operating expenses	$ 14,000		
Purchase of equipment	47,000	$(61,000)	
Less: Student fees		8,000	
Net expenses		$(53,000)	
Down payment for president's residence	$(11,200)		
Less: Sale of 100 shares of Go stock	10,600	(600)	
Net outflows			(53,600)
			$235,300
Add: Interest on 6% bonds		$ 9,000	
Less: Payments to Dick Miller		(3,500)	5,500
Balance, August 31, 19X2			$240,800

The accountant feels that previous records were very poorly kept and recommends that they be closed and that new records be established for each appropriate fund. Furthermore, the payments on the mortgage and purchase of equipment should be transferred to an investment in plant fund. The board of trustees accepts the recommendations, and the old set is closed.

Required

Prepare a journal entry to establish correct preclosing balances as of August 31, 19X2, for each of the following:

a. Annuity fund.
b. Investment in plant fund.
c. Restricted current fund (including expenditure and revenue accounts for the year).
d. Unrestricted current fund (including expenditure and revenue accounts for the year).

Use an operating expenditures account, since detail on operational expenditures is not provided, and record the transfers to the plant fund for the payments of the mortgage and purchase of equipment.

P20-11 Entries and Statement of Changes in Fund Balance for Current Funds
[AICPA Adapted]

A partial balance sheet of Midland University as of the end of its fiscal year ended July 31, 19X2, follows.

Midland University
Current Funds Balance Sheet
July 31, 19X2

Assets

Unrestricted:

Cash	$200,000
Accounts Receivable (tuition and fees, less allowance for doubtful accounts of $15,000)	360,000
Prepaid Expenses	40,000
Total Unrestricted	$600,000

Restricted:

Cash	$ 10,000
Investments	210,000
Total Restricted	$220,000
Total Current Funds	$820,000

Liabilities and Fund Balance

Unrestricted:

Accounts Payable	$100,000
Due to Other Funds	40,000
Deferred Revenue—Tuition and Fees	25,000
Fund Balance	435,000
Total Unrestricted	$600,000

Restricted:

Accounts Payable	$ 5,000
Fund Balance	215,000
Total Restricted	$220,000
Total Current Funds	$820,000

The following information pertains to the year ended July 31, 19X3:

1. Cash collected from students' tuition totaled $3,000,000. Of this $3,000,000, $362,000 represented accounts receivable outstanding on July 31, 19X2, $2,500,000 was for current-year tuition, and $138,000 was for tuition applicable to the semester beginning in August 19X3.

2. Deferred revenue on July 31, 19X2, was earned during the year ended July 31, 19X3.

3. Accounts receivable on July 31, 19X2, which were not collected during the year ended July 31, 19X3, were determined to be uncollectible and were written off against the allowance account. On July 31, 19X3, the allowance account was estimated at $10,000.

4. During the year, an unrestricted appropriation of $60,000 was made by the state. This state appropriation was to be paid to Midland sometime in August 19X3.

5. During the year, unrestricted cash gifts of $80,000 were received from alumni. Midland's board of trustees transferred $30,000 of these gifts to the student loan fund.

6. During the year, restricted fund investments costing $25,000 were sold for $31,000. Restricted fund investments were purchased at a cost of $40,000. Investment income of $18,000 was earned and collected during the year.

7. Unrestricted general expenses of $2,500,000 were recorded in the voucher system. On July 31, 19X3, the unrestricted accounts payable balance was $75,000.

8. The restricted accounts payable balance on July 31, 19X2, was paid.

9. The $40,000 due to other funds on July 31, 19X2, was paid to the plant fund as required.

10. One-quarter of the prepaid expenses on July 31, 19X2, expired during the current year and pertained to general education expense. There was no addition to prepaid expenses during the year.

Required

a. Prepare journal entries in summary form to record the foregoing transactions for the year ended July 31, 19X3. Number each entry to correspond with the number indicated in the description of its respective transaction. Your answer sheet should be organized as follows:

| | | Current Funds | | | |
| | | Unrestricted | | Restricted | |
Entry No.	Accounts	Debit	Credit	Debit	Credit

b. Prepare a statement of changes in fund balances for the year ended July 31, 19X3.

P20-12 Entries and Statement of Changes for Current and Endowment Funds
[AICPA Adapted]

The current funds balance sheet of Worthmore University as of the end of its fiscal year ended June 30, 19X2, follows.

Worthmore University
Current Funds Balance Sheet
June 30, 19X2

Assets

Unrestricted:		
Cash	$210,000	
Accounts Receivable (student tuition and fees, less allowance for doubtful accounts of $9,000)	341,000	
State Appropriations Receivable	75,000	$626,000
Restricted:		
Cash	$ 7,000	
Investments	60,000	67,000
Total Current Funds		$693,000

Liabilities and Fund Balances

Unrestricted:		
Accounts Payable	$ 45,000	
Deferred Revenue	66,000	
Fund Balance	515,000	$626,000
Restricted:		
Fund Balance		67,000
Total Current Funds		$693,000

The following transactions occurred during the fiscal year ended June 30, 19X3:

1. On July 7, 19X2, a gift of $100,000 was received from an alumnus. The alumnus requested that half the gift be restricted to the purchase of books for the university library and the remainder be used for the establishment of an endowed scholarship fund. The alumnus further requested that the income generated by the scholarship fund be used annually to award a scholarship to a qualified disadvantaged student. On July 20, 19X2, the board of trustees resolved that the funds of the newly established scholarship endowment fund would be invested in savings certificates. On July 21, 19X2, the savings certificates were purchased.

2. Revenue from student tuition and fees applicable to the year ended June 30, 19X3, amounted to $1,900,000. Of this amount, $66,000 was collected in the prior year, and $1,686,000 was collected during the year ended June 30, 19X3. In addition, on June 30, 19X3, the university had received cash of $158,000 representing deferred revenue fees for the session beginning July 1, 19X3.

3. During the year ended June 30, 19X3, the university had collected $349,000 of the outstanding accounts receivable at the beginning of the year. The balance was determined to be uncollectible and was written off against the allowance account. On June 30, 19X3, the allowance account was increased by $3,000.

4. During the year, interest charges of $6,000 were earned and collected on late student fee payments.

5. During the year the state appropriation was received. An additional unrestricted appropriation of $50,000 was made by the state but had not been paid to the university as of June 30, 19X3.

6. An unrestricted gift of $25,000 cash was received from alumni of the university.

7. During the year, restricted investments of $21,000 were sold for $26,000. Investment income amounting to $1,900 was received.

8. During the year unrestricted operating expenses of $1,777,000 were recorded. On June 30, 19X3, $59,000 of these expenses remained unpaid.

9. Restricted current funds of $13,000 were spent for authorized purposes during the year.

10. The accounts payable on June 30, 19X2, were paid during the year.

11. During the year, $7,000 interest was earned and received on the savings certificates purchased in accordance with the board of trustees' resolutions, as discussed in transaction 1.

Required

a. Prepare journal entries for the unrestricted and restricted current funds and the endowment fund. Number the transactions as given, and use the following format:

Event   **Fund**   **Journal Entry**

b. Prepare a statement of changes in fund balances for the year ended June 30, 19X3.

P20-13   Entries for University Funds [AICPA Adapted]

City College has the following funds:

Unrestricted current fund	Restricted current fund
Student loan fund	Endowment fund
Unexpended plant fund	Investment in plant
Annuity fund	

The following transactions and events occurred during 19X1:

January 1

City College, which previously held no endowment funds, received five gifts as a result of an appeal for funds. The campaign closed December 31, and all gifts received are to be recorded as of January 1. The gifts are as follows:

1. From S. Baker, $20,000, the principal to be held intact and the income to be used to endow scholarships for worthy students.

2. From J. Drew, $40,000, the principal to be held intact and the income to be used to endow scholarships for worthy students.

3. From M. Feldman, $60,000, the principal to be held intact and only the interest to be loaned to students. All income is to be available for loans; all losses from student loans are to be charged against income.

4. From C. Hanson, $200,000. During her lifetime, semiannual payments of $7,500 are to be made to the donor. After her death, the fund is to be used to construct or purchase a residence hall for students. Since Hanson is seriously ill, no present value of the annuity is established.

5. From T. Jordan, 1,000 shares of Pine Company stock, which had a market value on this date of $150 per share. Such shares are to be held for not more than 5 years and all income received therefrom held intact. The donation is to be recorded in the unexpended plant fund. At any date designated by the board of trustees during this period, all assets are to be liquidated and the proceeds used to build a student health center.

6. The board of trustees consolidated the assets of the Baker and Drew funds into a pooled investments account (in the proportion of their principal accounts) and purchased $60,000 of Northwestern bonds at par. Interest rate: 8 percent; interest dates: January 1 and July 1.

7. The cash of the Feldman fund is used to purchase $60,000, 10 percent bonds of Dandy, Inc., at par value plus $1,500 accrued interest. Interest dates: April 1 and October 1.

8. The $200,000 cash of the Hanson fund is used to purchase $200,000, 6 percent U.S. Treasury notes at par. Interest dates: January 1 and July 1.

April 1–July 1

9. All interest receivable on July 1 has been received as stipulated on bonds and notes owned and has been transferred to the proper fund when necessary. Dividends of $4,000 are received on Pine Company stock.

10. Payment is made to C. Hanson in accordance with the terms of the gift. A loan of cash is authorized from the endowment fund to cover the overdraft created.

11. Northwestern bonds with a par of $40,000 are sold at 102. No commission is involved; the gain is an addition to principal.

12. A loan of $500 is made to D. Lind from the Feldman student loan fund.

October 1

13. Notice is received of the death of C. Hanson. Since there is no liability to the estate, no entry need be made at this point.

14. An award of $400 is made from the Drew scholarship fund.

15. U.S. Treasury notes with a par of $200,000 held by the Hanson fund are sold at 101 and accrued interest. The endowment fund loan is repaid and the remaining proceeds are transferred to the unexpended plant fund.

16. Interest of $3,000 due on bonds of the Feldman fund is received.

17. D. Lind paid $100 principal and $15 interest on his student loan.

18. The board of trustees purchased a building suitable for a residence hall for $500,000, using the available funds from the C. Hanson gift as partial payment and issuing a 20-year mortgage for the balance of $296,500.

Required

Prepare journal entries to record the transactions and events. Number the transactions as given, and use the following format:

Event	Fund	Journal Entry

P20-14   Entries and Statements for University Current Funds

The trial balances of the current funds of Modern University on June 30, 19X1, were as follows:

	Debit	Credit
Unrestricted Current Fund:		
Cash	$ 420,000	
Investments	425,000	
Accounts Receivable	155,000	
Allowance for Uncollectibles		$ 14,000
Inventories	115,000	
Vouchers Payable		140,000
Deposits		30,000
Deferred Revenue		116,000
Fund Balance		815,000
	$1,115,000	$1,115,000
Restricted Current Fund:		
Cash	$ 80,000	
Investments	300,000	
Vouchers Payable		$ 17,000
Fund Balance		363,000
	$ 380,000	$ 380,000

The following transactions occurred during the 19X2 fiscal year:

		Unrestricted	Restricted
1.	Collections:		
	Tuition and fees	$4,200,000	
	State appropriations	1,150,000	
	Federal grants	200,000	$1,250,000
	Private gifts and grants	1,050,000	650,000
	Endowment income	850,000	500,000
	Auxiliary enterprises	2,300,000	
	Accounts receivable	140,000	

Included in the $4,200,000 of tuition and fees is $90,000 applicable to fiscal year 19X3.

2. The accounts receivable belong to auxiliary enterprises. Accounts written off totaled $10,000. The allowance was adjusted to $12,000 on June 30, 19X2. Accounts receivable on June 30, 19X2, totaled $125,000.

		Unrestricted	Restricted
3.	Salaries and wages paid:		
	Instruction	$2,340,000	$360,000
	Research	430,000	110,000
	Academic support	560,000	
	Student services	580,000	150,000
	Institutional support	440,000	
	Plant operations	670,000	
	Auxiliary enterprises	820,000	410,000

4. Vouchers payable in the unrestricted fund on June 30, 19X2, were for:

Plant operations	$ 30,000
Auxiliary enterprises	55,000

All vouchers payable (from both funds) on June 30, 19X1, were paid.

5. Inventories purchased by the unrestricted fund during the year were $1,820,000. Inventories were used for:

Instruction	$ 780,000
Research	135,000
Academic support	140,000
Student services	150,000
Institutional support	145,000
Plant operations	230,000
Auxiliary enterprises	260,000

6. Other expenditures paid from restricted cash were for:

Instruction	$ 400,000
Research	210,000
Student services	360,000
Auxiliary enterprises	375,000

7. The restricted fund balances on June 30, 19X1, were:

Federal grants	$ 183,000
Private gifts and grants	100,000
Endowment income	80,000

Restricted cash is expended from the following sources:

Federal grants	$1,200,000
Private gifts and grants	700,000
Endowment income	475,000

8. Mandatory transfers out of unrestricted cash:

Educational and general:	
Principal and interest	$ 220,000
Renewals and replacements	195,000
Auxiliary enterprises:	
Principal and interest	200,000
Renewals and replacements	175,000

9. Nonmandatory transfers of unrestricted cash to other funds totaled $355,000.

10. Deposits from students increased $3,000. Deposits are recorded in the unrestricted current fund.

11. Deferred revenue is related to tuition and fees. Deferred revenue on June 30, 19X1, was related to fiscal year 19X2.

12. Other expenditures paid from unrestricted cash were for:

Instruction	$ 420,000
Research	80,000
Academic support	75,000
Student services	110,000
Institutional support	90,000
Plant operations	125,000
Auxiliary enterprises	145,000

13. Government bonds were purchased from unrestricted cash in the amount of $150,000 and from restricted cash in the amount of $40,000.

Required

a. Prepare journal entries in the current funds for the transactions.

b. Prepare a comparative combined balance sheet for the unrestricted current funds on June 30, 19X1, and June 30, 19X2.

c. Prepare a statement of current funds revenue, expenditures, and other changes, with one column for unrestricted and a second column for restricted, for the year ended June 30, 19X2.

P20-15 Budgeting for a College [AICPA Adapted]

Forest College is developing schedules for its overall budget projection for the 19X1–X2 academic year. Relevant data from the prior year, 19X0–X1, include:

	Undergraduate	Graduate
Enrollment	4,200	1,300
Average number of credit hours carried each year per student	30	24
Average number of students per class	25	14
Average faculty teaching load in credit hours per year (number of classes taught multiplied by 3 credit hours per class)	(8 × 3) 24	(6 × 3) 18
Average faculty salary and benefits	$50,000	$60,000
Tuition per credit hour (no other fees required)	$200	$300

Changes projected for 19X1–X2 and additional information:

1. Enrollments are expected to increase by 5 percent for both undergraduate and graduate programs.

2. Average faculty salary and benefits are expected to increase by 3 percent.

3. Forest has not previously used graduate students for teaching undergraduates, but will do so for 19X1–X2. All of the projected increased undergraduate enrollment will be taught by graduate students. Forest will recruit these graduate teaching assistants (TAs) in addition to the 5 percent student increase indicated. Each TA will carry half an average graduate student course load and half an average undergraduate faculty teaching load. TAs will receive a full remission of tuition fees and $10,000 in salary and benefits. For budgeting purposes, the tuition remission is considered both a tuition revenue and a tuition scholarship.

4. Nonfaculty costs (excluding scholarships) for 19X1–X2 are to be budgeted by fixed and variable elements derived from estimates of cost at the following two levels of registration:

Total student credit hours (both undergraduate and graduate)	140,000	180,000
Total estimated nonfaculty costs	$21,960,000	$22,320,000

Required

  a. Prepare the following 19X1–X2 budget schedules for each program—undergraduate and graduate:
    (1) Projected enrollment
    (2) Projected student credit hours
    (3) Projected number of full-time faculty and TAs
    (4) Projected salaries and benefits for full-time faculty and TAs
    (5) Projected tuition revenue
  b. (1) Calculate the fixed and variable elements in the nonfaculty costs.
    (2) Calculate the budgeted nonfaculty costs, including scholarships for the TAs, for the 19X1–X2 academic year.

CHAPTER 21

NOT-FOR-PROFIT ENTITIES: HEALTH CARE PROVIDERS, VOLUNTARY HEALTH AND WELFARE ORGANIZATIONS, AND OTHER ENTITIES

This chapter presents the accounting and financial reporting principles used by health care providers such as hospitals and nursing homes, voluntary health and welfare organizations such as the Red Cross and United Way, and other not-for-profit organizations such as professional or fraternal associations. Common accounting features of these not-for-profit entities are the use of the accrual basis of accounting and the use of funds to account for their activities.

HEALTH CARE PROVIDERS

The health care environment is currently undergoing a revolution. Rapidly growing costs of providing medical care are forcing hospitals to merge at an increasing rate in order to consolidate the types of services offered. The cost of new technology is also requiring health care providers to reevaluate their missions to the communities they serve.

Although the major focus of the first section of this chapter is on hospitals, the accounting and financial reporting guidelines for hospitals are the same as those used by all health care providers included within the scope of the AICPA's 1990 audit and accounting guide, *Audits of Providers of Health Care Services.*[1] The 1990 audit and accounting guide applies to the following health care entities:

1. Clinics, medical group practices, individual practice associations, individual practitioners, and other ambulatory care organizations
2. Continuing-care retirement communities

---

[1] *Audits of Providers of Health Care Services,* American Institute of Certified Public Accountants (New York), 1990.

3. Health maintenance organizations and similar prepaid health care plans

4. Home health agencies

5. Hospitals

6. State and local government-owned health care entities that use enterprise fund accounting and reporting

7. Nursing homes that provide skilled, intermediate, and less intensive levels of health care

8. Organizations whose primary activities are the planning, organization, and oversight of entities providing health care services, such as parent or holding companies of health care providers[2]

Audit guides provide an authoritative source for selecting accounting and financial reporting procedures. **FASB Statement No. 32**, "Specialized Accounting and Reporting Principles and Practices in AICPA Statements of Position and Guides on Accounting and Auditing Matters" (FASB 32), states that the audit and accounting guides are preferable accounting principles for purposes of justifying a change in accounting principles under **APB Opinion No. 20**, "Accounting Changes" (APB 20). The audit and accounting guides provide extensive guidance for the entities discussed in this chapter. These guides are published regularly by the AICPA and address the specific issues in selected industries. Because audit and accounting guides represent authoritative support, and because they are so widely used in practice, extensive reference is made to several of them in the chapter discussion and illustrations.

Hospitals may be classified as profit-seeking or as not-for-profit entities. Some hospitals now operate as investor-owned, profit-oriented chains. These investor-owned hospitals seek additional financial resources through sales of stocks and issuance of large amounts of debt. Profit-seeking hospitals provide the same types of financial reports as commercial entities, whereas not-for-profit hospitals use a format somewhat closer to other nonprofit organizations in presenting their financial results. Not-for-profit hospitals are often affiliated with a university, a religious group, or a civic association. Not-for-profit hospitals are discussed in this chapter because of the large number of these hospitals and because of their unique accounting and financial reporting issues.

Hospital Accounting

Guidance for hospital accounting is provided by several sources. The first is the audit and accounting guide for health care providers published by the AICPA. This audit guide is continually updated, and new editions are published periodically, with the most recent revision in 1990. The audit guide presents both audit guidelines and financial accounting and reporting guidelines for health care providers.

---

[2] Ibid., p. ix.

Two professional associations, the American Hospital Association (AHA) and the Hospital Financial Management Association (HFMA), are also active in developing and improving hospital management, accounting, and financial reporting. The comprehensive hospital illustration presented later in this chapter is an adaptation of the financial statements for a hospital presented in the 1990 *Audits of Providers of Health Care Services*.

In this chapter, it is assumed that the hospital is a separate reporting entity, and is not a component unit of any other governmental or private organization. In the few cases in which a hospital is operated by a governmental entity, such as a city, the 1990 GASB codification states that the hospital's accounts should be reported as a discrete enterprise fund, as a component unit of the city, using the accounting guidelines in the AICPA's hospital audit and accounting guide.[3]

Hospital Fund Structure Hospitals have two major fund classes: general and restricted. The general fund is the primary operating fund for hospitals, and most economic transactions are recorded in this fund.

Restricted funds account for assets received from donors or other third parties who have imposed certain restrictions on their use. The restricted funds are often termed "holding" funds because they must hold the restricted assets and transfer expendable resources to the general funds for expenditure. Figure 21-1 presents an overview of the fund structure and financial reporting for hospitals.

General Fund The *general fund* accounts for the resources received and expended in the primary health care mission of the hospital. The basis of accounting is the accrual method in order to measure fully all expenses of providing services during the period. Depreciation is included in the operating expenses. Fixed assets are included in the fund, on the theory that the governing board may use these assets in any manner desired.

The governing board may establish *board-designated resources* within the general fund. For example, the board may designate resources for the expansion of the hospital, for retirement of debt, or for some other purpose. The American Hospital Association has recommended that a separate fund within the general fund group be established for board-designated resources; however, the AICPA's hospital audit guide presents these designated resources as part of a single general fund.

Restricted Funds All *restricted funds* account for resources whose use is restricted by the donor. The major types of restricted funds are (1) the specific-purpose fund, (2) the plant replacement and expansion fund, and (3) the endowment fund. A hospital may also have restricted loan funds and annuity and life income funds; however, few hospitals use these funds and they are not discussed in this chapter. Hospitals account for restricted loan funds and annuity and life income funds in the same way as colleges and universities, as presented in Chapter 20.

---

[3] *Codification of Governmental Accounting and Financial Reporting Standards,* 3d ed., Governmental Accounting Standards Board, 1990, Section *H.5.102,* p. 441.

FIGURE 21-1 Overview of hospital accounting and reporting.

		Fund Groups		
			Restricted	
	General	Specific Purpose	Plant Replacement and Expansion	Endowment
Accounting basis	Accrual	Contributions, transfers, and other changes are credited directly to fund balances. Resources are held until transferred to general fund for expenditures.		
Distinguishing features		Resources restricted for specific operating purposes.	Resources restricted for additions to plant assets.	Principal must be preserved.
Financial statements	Statement of revenue and expenses			
	Statement of cash flows			
	Balance sheet (combined)			
	Statement of changes in fund balances			

Specific-purpose funds are restricted for *specific operating purposes.* For example, a donor may specify that a donation of $25,000 may be used only for maternity care. The donation is held in the specific-purpose fund until the maternity expenditure is approved in the general fund, at which time the specific-purpose fund transfers the resources to the general fund.

Plant replacement and expansion restricted funds account for contributions to be used only for additions to fixed assets. When the general fund approves or makes the appropriate expenditures for the fixed assets, the plant replacement and expansion fund transfers the resources to the general fund.

Endowment funds account for resources when the principal must be preserved. The income from these resources is usually available for either a restricted or a general purpose. Endowments may be either permanent or term. Term endowments are for limited time periods, for example, 5 or 10 years, or until a specific event occurs, such as the death of the donor. After the term expires, the principal of the fund is used by the governing board in accordance with the gift agreement.

Financial Statements for a Hospital

Accounting for a hospital is, in many respects, a hybrid of commercial accounting and fund accounting. The financial statements of the hospital reflect this dual nature. A hospital must provide four statements: (1) a balance sheet, (2) a statement of revenue and expenses for the general fund, (3) a statement of changes in fund balances, and (4) a statement of cash flows for the general fund. The statements are quite comparable to those of a commercial entity and are presented later in the chapter as part of a comprehensive illustration.

Revenue and Expense Classifications Revenue and expenses are measured only in the general fund. Restricted funds record transfers and contributions directly to their fund balances. *Operating revenue and expenses* arise from on-going major or central operations. Gains or losses from transactions that are peripheral or incidental to the provision of health care services are classified as *nonoperating* items. The specific elements of operating revenue and nonoperating gains are as follows:

1. *Operating revenue*
   a. *Patient service revenue* represents the gross revenue of the hospital, measured at normally established rates, earned from various inpatient and outpatient centers.
   b. *Contractual adjustments* are reported as a direct deduction from patient service revenue. Contractual adjustments are reductions from standard rates that are specified in contracts with third-party payors such as insurance companies or medicare.
   c. *Other operating revenue* is from nonpatient sources such as television rentals, cafeteria sales, sales in gift shops operated by the hospital, and tuition on educational programs provided by the hospital. Transfers from the restricted funds for reimbursement or payment of approved operating expenditures are also included here.
2. *Nonoperating gains* are derived from sources other than patient care, patient services, and related activities. Nonoperating gains include unrestricted gifts, investment income, unrestricted income transferred in from endowment funds, donated services, and sales of hospital properties.

The patient service revenue is the gross amount of billings at the normal billing rate. This reports the full earning capacity of the hospital. Some hospitals are required to perform a certain amount of charity care for which no revenue is recognized. The charity cases are imposed by the terms of certain federal medical-care grant programs for construction of hospital facilities. Charity care helps ensure that indigent persons living in the region served by the hospital may obtain adequate medical services. When charity care is provided, no revenue is recognized, but disclosure of the estimated amount of charity care is presented in the footnotes to the financial statements.

Contractual Adjustments A major deduction from patient service revenue results from the involvement of third-party payors in the medical reimbursement process. Insurance companies or government units (especially the federal government) reimburse less than the full standard rate for medical services provided to patients covered by insurance or government-provided services such as medicare. These third-party payors may stipulate limits on the amount of costs they will pay. A hospital may have a standard rate for a specific service but may contract with the third-party payor to accept a lower amount for that service. For example, medicare establishes specific reimbursement rates for various services, termed a "diagnosis-related group" (DRG). The hospital makes a contractual adjustment from its normal service charge, and this adjustment is shown as a deduction from gross patient service revenue.

Interfund Transfers for Property, Plant, and Equipment   Note that interfund transfers of resources from the restricted plant funds for property, plant, or equipment replacements or additions are *not* recognized as either a revenue or a gain. Interfund transfers into the general fund for property, plant, or equipment are recorded directly as a change to the general fund's fund balance because these resources increase the permanent capital of the hospital.

General Fund Expenses   The major expenses in the general fund are for nursing services, other professional services, depreciation, bad debts, and the general and administrative costs of the hospital. These costs are recognized on the accrual basis of accounting, similar to commercial entities. Hospitals that self-insure for malpractice costs should recognize an expense and a liability for malpractice costs in the period during which the incidents that give rise to the claims occur, if it is probable that liabilities have been incurred and the amounts of the losses can be reasonably estimated. Any expenses related to fund-raising should be classified separately. Patients pay physicians directly for their medical services.

Donations   Hospitals often receive a wide variety of services from volunteers. For example, retired physicians or pharmacists may voluntarily work part-time in their professional roles. In addition, the hospital may receive donations of supplies or equipment. The rules on accounting for donations and contributions to hospitals are as follows:

1. *Donated Services.* Because it is often difficult to place a value on donated services, their values are usually not recorded. However, if all the following conditions exist, the estimated value of the donated services is reported as an expense and a corresponding amount is reported as contributions.[4] The 1990 hospital audit and accounting guide specifies that a recorded contribution from donated services should be classified as a nonoperating gain.
   a. The services performed are significant and form an integral part of the efforts of the entity; the services would be performed by salaried personnel if donated services were not available for the entity to accomplish its purpose; and the entity would continue this program or activity.
   b. The entity controls the employment and duties of the service donors and is able to influence their activities in a way comparable to the control it would exercise over employees with similar responsibilities.
   c. The entity has a clearly measurable basis for the amount to be recorded.
2. *Donated Assets.* Donated assets are reported at fair market value at the date of the contribution.[5]

[4] AICPA, *Audits of Providers of Health Care Services*, p. 15.
[5] Ibid., pp. 14–15.

a. Donated assets, other than property, plant, and equipment, are reported in the statement of revenue and expenses of the general fund if unrestricted, or as additions to the appropriate fund balance if restricted. Unrestricted donated assets, other than property, plant, and equipment, are reported as either other operating revenue or a nonoperating gain, depending on whether the donated asset is to be used in the normal, ongoing operations of the health care entity, or is used in a peripheral activity. For example, the donation of disposable medical supplies is recorded by a debit to inventory and a credit to other operating revenue. For restricted gifts, when restrictions no longer apply, the restricted resources are transferred to the general fund as a nonoperating gain.

b. Donations of property and equipment, or of assets to be used to acquire property or equipment, are reported in a restricted fund. These contributions are added directly to the restricted fund balance. When the property or equipment is placed in service, the transfer is made from the restricted fund to the general fund. This transfer is not shown on the statement of revenue and expenses; rather, it is a transfer directly to the general fund's fund balance and is shown on the statement of changes in fund balances. The rationale for not recognizing revenue (or gain) for transfers of plant and equipment to the general fund is that the donation of plant or equipment is a contribution to the long-term capital of the hospital, not just to current operations.

Appropriate expense accounts are charged as the donated assets are consumed. For example, donated supplies such as medicines, linen, and disposable medical items are charged to an expense as used from inventory. For donated physical plant or equipment having an estimated economic life of more than 1 year, depreciation is charged to each period in which the plant or equipment is used.

Balance Sheet Items   The general fund records receivables, investments, property, plant, and equipment, assets whose use is limited, and long-term debt.

Receivables   Receivables may include amounts due from patients, third-party payors, other insurers of health care, pledges or grants, and interfund transactions. Receivables should be accrued at the anticipated realizable amount. Thus, the realizable amounts may include reductions due to contractual agreements with third-party payors, or provider practices, such as allowing courtesy discounts to medical staff members and employees. An allowance for uncollectibles is recognized for estimated bad debts. It is important not to include receivables for charity care services. Charity care cases should not be recognized as revenue, nor should receivables be recognized for charity care services. Receivables from pledges of future contributions are reported in the period the pledge is made, net of an allowance for uncollectible amounts.

Investments   Investments are initially recorded at cost if purchased, or at fair value at the date of receipt if received as a gift. Investments in debt securities should be reported at amortized cost if the intent is to hold the securities to maturity. Debt investments are reported at the lower of cost or market if the hospital does not intend to hold them to maturity. Marketable equity securities are reported at the lower of aggregate cost or market in accordance with **FASB 12**, "Accounting for Certain Marketable Equity Securities." Investments in stock accounted for under the equity method are reported in accordance with **APB 18**, "The Equity Method of Accounting for Investments in Common Stock." Some hospitals receive income from trusts that donors have established with fiduciaries, such as banks. If the hospital does not own the trust or its investments, then the independent trusts are not an asset of the hospital and are not reported on the hospital's balance sheet. Footnote disclosure may be made of major independent endowment or trust agreements that benefit the hospital.

Plant Assets   Property, plant, and equipment is reported, together with any accumulated depreciation, in the general fund. Depreciation is recorded in the general fund because the use of assets is part of the cost of providing medical services. The assets are reported in the general fund because they are available for use in any manner deemed necessary by the governing board.

Assets Whose Use Is Limited   *Assets whose use is limited* under terms of debt indentures, trust arrangements, third-party reimbursements, or other similar arrangements should be reported in a separate section within the general fund's balance sheet. For example, a hospital sells bonds from which the proceeds are limited to use for capital improvements. The cash received at the bond issuance date is classified as an asset whose use is limited. Another example is assets received from medicare reimbursements that are specified to pay for the depreciation of assets used to provide services to medicare patients. These depreciation reimbursement resources may be used only to acquire or replace capital assets. A third example of the type of assets reported in the assets whose use is limited section of the general fund's balance sheet is assets set aside for identified purposes by the hospital's governing board and over which the board retains control.

Long-Term Debt   The general fund also accounts for the hospital's long-term debt and pays the principal and interest as it becomes due. The debt is shown in the general fund's balance sheet. This differs from most other not-for-profit entities for which a separate fund is established to service debt or the debt is serviced by the plant funds.

Comprehensive Illustration of Hospital Accounting and Financial Reporting

Sol City Community Hospital provides medical care for the region surrounding Sol City. The hospital has established the following four funds: (1) general, (2) specific purpose, (3) plant replacement and expansion, and (4) endowment.

Entries to record transactions in each of the four funds during the 19X2 fiscal year, ending December 31, 19X2, are presented in the next section of the chapter. First the financial statements for the period are presented, and then the transactions from which these statements resulted are discussed. The balance sheet for both the general and the restricted funds is presented in Figure 21-2. Note that the

FIGURE 21-2 Balance sheet for a hospital.

Sol City Community Hospital
Balance Sheet
December 31, 19X2 and 19X1

	19X2	19X1
General Funds		
Assets		
Current:		
Cash	$ 25,000	$ 10,000
Receivables	460,000	400,000
Less: Estimated Uncollectibles	(40,000)	(30,000)
Due from Specific-Purpose Fund	80,000	
Inventories	50,000	60,000
Prepaid Expenses	15,000	20,000
Total Current Assets	$ 590,000	$ 460,000
Other:		
Investments	$ 250,000	$ 300,000
Property, Plant, and Equipment	3,550,000	3,200,000
Less: Accumulated Depreciation	(1,150,000)	(1,000,000)
Total Other Assets	$2,650,000	$2,500,000
Assets Whose Use Is Limited:		
Board-Designated Reserves:		
Cash	$ 10,000	$ -0-
Investments	200,000	200,000
Total Assets Whose Use Is Limited	$ 210,000	$ 200,000
Total Assets	$3,450,000	$3,160,000
Liabilities and Fund Balance		
Current:		
Notes Payable to Bank	$ 65,000	$ 70,000
Current Portion of Long-Term Debt	50,000	60,000
Accounts Payable	50,000	90,000
Accrued Expenses	30,000	25,000
Estimated Malpractice Costs Payable	30,000	-0-
Advances from Third Parties	160,000	125,000
Deferred Revenue	5,000	5,000
Total Current Liabilities	$ 390,000	$ 375,000
Long-Term Debt:		
Mortgage Payable	1,050,000	1,100,000
Total Liabilities	$1,440,000	$1,475,000
Fund Balance	2,010,000	1,685,000
Total Liabilities and Fund Balance	$3,450,000	$3,160,000

(Continued)

FIGURE 21-2 (*continued*)

	19X2	19X1
Restricted Funds		
Assets		
Specific-Purpose Fund:		
Cash	$ 13,000	$ 2,000
Investments	90,000	20,000
Total Assets—Specific-Purpose Fund	$ 103,000	$ 22,000
Plant Replacement and Expansion Fund:		
Cash	$ 50,000	$ 200,000
Pledges Receivable—Net of Allowance for Uncollectibles	15,000	120,000
Investments	140,000	18,000
Total Assets—Plant Replacement and Expansion Fund	$ 205,000	$ 338,000
Endowment Fund:		
Cash	$ 15,000	$ 10,000
Investments	1,400,000	1,000,000
Total Assets—Endowment Fund	$1,415,000	$1,010,000
Liabilities and Fund Balances		
Specific-Purpose Fund:		
Due to General Fund	$ 80,000	$ -0-
Fund Balances:		
Education	$ 7,000	$ 8,000
Research	16,000	14,000
	$ 23,000	$ 22,000
Total Liabilities and Fund Balance—Specific-Purpose Fund	$ 103,000	$ 22,000
Plant Replacement and Expansion Fund:		
Fund Balance	$ 205,000	$ 338,000
Total Liabilities and Fund Balance—Plant Replacement and Expansion Fund	$ 205,000	$ 338,000
Endowment Fund:		
Fund Balances:		
Permanent Endowment	$1,215,000	$ 800,000
Term Endowment	200,000	210,000
Total Liabilities and Fund Balances—Endowment Fund	$1,415,000	$1,010,000

balance sheet is presented in what is generally termed the "pancake" style. All funds are presented in one balance sheet, with the general fund above the restricted funds. The alternative columnar display format is also acceptable. The columnar format has a separate column for each fund. The choice of display format is made by the hospital's governing board, based on its preferences. The GASB continues to explore alternative display formats, but does allow for choices among widely accepted current alternatives. The statement of revenue and expenses is presented in Figure 21-3. These two statements, as well as the statement of changes in fund balances and the statement of cash flows, are discussed after the journal entries for the general fund are illustrated.

FIGURE 21-3 Statement of revenue and expenses for the general fund for a hospital.

Sol City Community Hospital
Statement of Revenue and Expenses for the General Fund
For the Year Ended December 31, 19X2

Operating revenue:		
Patient services	$2,600,000	
Contractual adjustments	(240,000)	
Net patient services revenue		$2,360,000
Other operating revenue:		
Miscellaneous revenue sources	$ 60,000	
From specific-purpose fund reimbursement	120,000	180,000
Total operating revenue		$2,540,000
Operating expenses:		
Nursing services	$ 800,000	
Other professional services	630,000	
General services	700,000	
Fiscal services	100,000	
Administrative services	80,000	
Medical malpractice costs	30,000	
Bad debts	60,000	
Depreciation	200,000	
Total operating expenses		2,600,000
Operating loss		$ (60,000)
Nonoperating gains:		
Expired term endowment	$ 10,000	
Unrestricted gifts and bequests	65,000	
Unrestricted income from endowment funds	60,000	
Income and gains from board-designated funds	10,000	
Disposal of hospital assets	5,000	
Donated services	10,000	
Total nonoperating gains		160,000
Excess of revenue and gains over expenses		$ 100,000

General Fund The transactions in the general fund for 19X2 are presented in the order in which they appear in the financial statements. The first series of entries for the operating revenue, the operating expenses, and nonoperating items illustrate the transactions affecting the statement of revenue and expenses in Figure 21-3. Other transactions shown affect only the balance sheet in Figure 21-2.

Operating Revenue The hospital provides patient services of $2,600,000, measured at standard rates. From this amount, $240,000 is deducted for contractual adjustments with third-party payors, as follows:

(1)	Accounts Receivable	2,600,000	
	Patient Services Revenue		2,600,000
	Gross charges at standard rates.		
(2)	Contractual Adjustments	240,000	
	Accounts Receivable		240,000
	Deduction from gross revenue for contractual adjustments.		

Other operating revenue totaling $180,000 is earned during the year, including $30,000 from normal nonpatient care services offered by the hospital on an ongoing basis, $30,000 from donated medicines and medical supplies that were added to current inventories, and a $120,000 transfer in from a specific-purpose restricted fund for reimbursement of certain operating expenditures related to education and research. The restricted fund pays only $40,000 of these expenditures; the remaining $80,000 is recorded as a receivable by the general fund.

(3)	Cash	30,000	
	Inventories	30,000	
	Other Operating Revenue—Cafeteria Sales		20,000
	Other Operating Revenue—TV Rentals		4,000
	Other Operating Revenue—Vending Machine Commissions		6,000
	Other Operating Revenue—Donated Supplies		30,000
	Miscellaneous revenue sources.		
(4)	Cash	40,000	
	Due from Specific-Purpose Fund	80,000	
	Other Operating Revenue—Specific-Purpose Grant		120,000
	Record payment and receivable for reimbursement of operating expenditures made in accordance with restricted gift.		

Entry (4) presents the entry in the general fund to record the interfund transfer from the specific-purpose fund. The rationale for classifying the transfer as other operating revenue is that the resources from the specific-purpose fund are being transferred to pay for operating costs incurred in the general fund. Therefore, the operating costs associated with the specific-purpose agreement are matched with the "other operating revenue" resulting from the transfer. The specific-purpose fund also records this interfund transfer (see entry 23 later in this chapter).

Operating Expenses The hospital incurs $2,600,000 in operating expenses for nursing and other professional care, for general and administrative expenses, for bad debts expense, and for depreciation. Fiscal services expense includes interest expense on the hospital's debt. The hospital recognized $30,000 in estimated malpractice costs that are probable and reasonably estimated. Cash payments are made for $2,125,000 of the total operating expenses, and the remainder is consumption of prepaid assets, allowance for uncollectibles, depreciation, and increases in liabilities. The hospital receives donated services valued at $10,000, which are recognized as other professional expenses with a corresponding amount recognized as nonoperating gain.

(5)	Nursing Services Expense	800,000	
	Other Professional Services Expense	620,000	
	General Services Expense	700,000	
	Fiscal Services Expense	100,000	
	Administrative Services Expense	80,000	
	Medical Malpractice Costs	30,000	
	Bad Debts Expense	60,000	
	Depreciation Expense	200,000	
	Cash		2,125,000
	Allowance for Uncollectibles		60,000
	Inventories		90,000
	Prepaid Expenses		5,000
	Accumulated Depreciation		200,000
	Accounts Payable		50,000
	Accrued Expenses		30,000
	Estimated Medical Malpractice Costs Payable		30,000
	Record operating expenses.		
(6)	Other Professional Services Expense	10,000	
	Nonoperating Gain—Donated Services		10,000
	Receive donated services.		

Entry (6) records the fair value of donated services both as a debit for the operating expense and as a credit for the nonoperating gain. Therefore, donated services do not affect the bottom line of the hospital's statement of revenue and expenses, but they do affect the amounts shown for the expenses and nonoperating gains sections of the statement.

Nonoperating Gains The hospital has $150,000 of additional nonoperating gains, as follows:

(7)	Cash	10,000	
	Nonoperating Gain—Transfer from Expired Term Endowment		10,000
	Receive expired term endowment now available for expenditure in the general fund.		
(8)	Cash	65,000	
	Nonoperating Gain—Unrestricted Gifts and Bequests		65,000
	Receive unrestricted gifts.		

(9)	Cash	60,000	
	Nonoperating Gain—Unrestricted Income from Endowment Income		60,000
	Unrestricted interest earnings on endowment fund investments deposited in the general fund.		

(10)	Cash—Limited Use	10,000	
	Nonoperating Gain—Income and Gains from Board-Designated Funds		10,000
	Earnings on general fund's resources reserved by hospital's governing board.		

(11)	Cash	55,000	
	Accumulated Depreciation	50,000	
	Property, Plant, and Equipment		100,000
	Nonoperating Gain—Gain on Disposal of Equipment		5,000
	Sell hospital asset.		

Entries (7) and (9) record the interfund transfers in from the endowment fund. The endowment fund also records these interfund transfers (see entries 34 and 35 later in the chapter). Note that these are unrestricted resources to be used by the general fund. These transfers are recorded as nonoperating gains in order to reflect the fact that they are not derived from providing patient care.

A net increase in resources from the sale of unrestricted assets is recorded as a nonoperating gain in the general fund. Entry (11) records the disposal of used hospital assets. Note that $10,000 of nonoperating gain was recognized in entry (6) as part of the donation of other professional services also recognized in the operating expenses section.

Other Transactions in the General Fund   The remaining transactions during the 19X2 fiscal year affect only the balance sheet accounts. Transactions affecting only the asset accounts include collecting receivables, acquiring inventory, selling an investment, and purchasing additional physical plant assets, as follows:

(12)	Cash	2,250,000	
	Allowance for Uncollectibles	50,000	
	Accounts Receivable		2,300,000
	Collect some receivables and write off $50,000 as uncollectible.		

(13)	Inventories	50,000	
	Cash		50,000
	Acquire inventories.		

(14)	Cash	50,000	
	Investments		50,000
	Sell investment at cost.		

(15)	Property, Plant, and Equipment	425,000	
	Cash		225,000
	Cash—Limited Use		200,000
	Purchase new plant, using both limited cash and unlimited cash.		

Transactions affecting the current liability accounts include paying current liabilities and recording the receipt of cash in advance of billings from third parties. The hospital reclassified the portion of the long-term mortgage that is currently due. The entries for these events are:

(16)	Notes Payable to Bank	5,000	
	Current Portion of Long-Term Debt	60,000	
	Accounts Payable	90,000	
	Accrued Expenses	25,000	
	Cash		180,000
	Pay liabilities outstanding at beginning of period.		
(17)	Cash	35,000	
	Advances from Third Parties		35,000
	Increase in cash received from third parties for deposits in advance of service billings.		
(18)	Mortgage Payable	50,000	
	Current Portion of Long-Term Debt		50,000
	Reclassify current portion of long-term debt.		

Two interfund transfers are made between the general fund and the restricted plant funds. Transfers into the general fund involving property, plant, and equipment are recorded directly to fund balance. These transfers are not a revenue or gain because contributions for long-term physical assets are considered increases in the long-term capital of the hospital. The first transfer is for $25,000 of donated equipment that is placed into service. The donation of the equipment initially is recognized in the restricted plant fund until the hospital began using the asset. Upon installation into service, the value of the donated equipment is transferred from the restricted plant fund to the general fund. The second transfer from the restricted plant fund is for $200,000, which is to be used for the acquisition of plant assets. The entries for these two transfers are:

(19)	Property, Plant, and Equipment	25,000	
	Fund Balance		25,000
	Transfer from restricted plant fund for donated equipment placed into service.		
(20)	Cash—Limited Use	200,000	
	Fund Balance		200,000
	Receive transfer in from restricted plant replacement and expansion fund for use in acquiring plant assets.		

The restricted plant fund also records these interfund transfers (see entries 28 and 29 later in the chapter).

FIGURE 21-4 Statement of changes in fund balances for a hospital.

Sol City Community Hospital
Statement of Changes in Fund Balances
For the Year Ended December 31, 19X2

General Fund

Balance, January 1, 19X2	$1,685,000
Transfers from plant replacement and expansion fund	225,000
Excess of revenue over expenses	100,000
Balance, December 31, 19X2	$2,010,000

Restricted Funds

Specific-purpose fund:

Balance, January 1, 19X2	$ 22,000
Restricted gifts	115,000
Investment interest	6,000
Transfers to general fund for:	
Education	(61,000)
Research	(59,000)
Balance, December 31, 19X2	$ 23,000

Plant replacement and expansion fund:

Balance, January 1, 19X2	$ 338,000
Restricted gifts	85,000
Investment interest	7,000
Transfers to general fund	(225,000)
Balance, December 31, 19X2	$ 205,000

Endowment fund:

Balance, January 1, 19X2	$1,010,000
Investment interest and dividends	60,000
Restricted gifts	415,000
Transfers to general fund	(70,000)
Balance, December 31, 19X2	$1,415,000

Closing entries, required for all nominal accounts, are not presented because the focus here is on other aspects of hospital accounting and because the closing process for a hospital is the same as for any other accounting entity.

Financial Statements for the General Fund Hospitals must provide four financial statements, similar to those of a commercial entity. The statements are:

1. Balance sheet (Figure 21-2)
2. Statement of revenue and expenses for the general fund (Figure 21-3)
3. Statement of changes in fund balance (Figure 21-4)
4. Statement of cash flows for the general fund (Figure 21-5)

The combined balance sheet presents both the general fund and the restricted funds. Accounting for the restricted funds is illustrated in the next section of the

FIGURE 21-5 Statement of cash flows of the general fund for a hospital.

Sol City Community Hospital
Statement of Cash Flows for General Fund
For the Year Ended December 31, 19X2

Cash Flows from Operating Activities and Gains and Losses:	
Excess of Revenue and Gains over Expenses	$ 100,000
Adjustments to Reconcile Revenue and Gains in Excess of Expenses and Losses	
to Net Cash Provided by Operating Activities and Gains and Losses:	
Depreciation	200,000
Gain on Sale of Hospital Assets	(5,000)
Increase in Net Patient Accounts Receivable	(50,000)
Increase in Due from Specific-Purpose Fund	(80,000)
Decrease in Inventories	10,000
Decrease in Prepaid Expenses	5,000
Decrease in Short-Term Note Payable to Bank	(5,000)
Decrease in Accounts Payable and Accrued Expenses	(35,000)
Increase in Estimated Malpractice Costs Payable	30,000
Increase in Advances from Third Parties	35,000
Net Cash Provided by Operating Activities and Gains and Losses	$ 205,000
Cash Flows from Investing Activities:	
Purchase of Property, Plant, and Equipment	$(425,000)
Transfer In from Restricted Plant Fund	200,000
Sale of Used Hospital Assets	55,000
Sale of Investments	50,000
Increase in Cash for Limited Use	(10,000)
Net Cash Used by Investing Activities	$(130,000)
Cash Flows from Financing Activities:	
Payment of Current Portion of Long-Term Debt	$ (60,000)
Net Cash Used by Financing Activities	$ (60,000)
Net Increase in Cash	$ 15,000
Cash at Beginning of Year	10,000
Cash at End of Year	$ 25,000

chapter. The statement of revenue and expenses reports only transactions in the general fund because restricted funds do not recognize revenue or expenses but make all entries directly to fund balance.

The statement of changes in fund balances reports the additions to and deductions from each of the fund balances during the period. The general fund section includes transfers from the plant replacement and expansion fund, which are reported as a decrease in the plant fund. In addition, the general fund reports additions to its fund balance from the excess of revenue over expenses.

The hospital's financial statements presented in this chapter are patterned after those presented in the AICPA's 1990 *Audits of Providers of Health Care*. Transfers from the restricted funds for acquiring fixed assets are shown only in the statement of changes in fund balances.

The statement of cash flows for the general fund (Figure 21-5) is a required statement. Either the direct or the indirect method may be used to display net cash flows from operations. Under the direct method, the specific inflows and outflows from operations are presented. Under the indirect method, the statement begins with revenue and gains in excess of expenses and losses as presented on the statement of revenue and expenses for the general fund. It then presents the adjustments necessary to reconcile the net amount shown on the statement of revenue and expenses with the cash flow that is provided by operating activities. Figure 21-5 presents the indirect method because of its popularity and wide use by hospitals. The statement of cash flows is similar to that required of commercial, profit-seeking entities. The three categories of operating activities, investing activities, and financing activities are the same as for commercial entities.

In addition to the primary financial statements for the present fiscal period, with comparatives for the prior period, hospitals are required to present extensive footnotes similar to those of a commercial entity. A specific footnote disclosure is required to report the estimated value of charity care services provided by the hospital during the period.

Specific-Purpose Fund Sol City Community Hospital has a specific-purpose restricted fund to accept restricted gifts for use by the hospital for other than acquiring plant assets. Gifts and other transfers are recorded directly in the restricted fund balance. The specific-purpose fund does not make expenditures; it holds the restricted resources until the general fund satisfies the terms of the restriction, usually by making the appropriate operating expenditure or by having the restricted expenditure approved by the governing board, whereupon the resources are transferred from the specific-purpose fund to the general fund to pay for the operating expenditure.

The specific-purpose restricted fund typically invests its cash and receives interest or dividends from its investments. A variety of investment transactions can affect the fund balance. Nevertheless, the specific fund is only a holding fund for restricted resources until they are released for use by the hospital.

The following entries record the transactions in Sol City Community Hospital's specific-purpose fund during the 19X2 fiscal year and are reflected in the balance sheet in Figure 21-2 and the statement of changes in fund balances in Figure 21-4.

Additions to Specific-Purpose Fund Balance The specific-purpose fund receives $6,000 of interest income from its investment of funds from a restricted gift to support the hospital's research activity. Restricted gifts of $115,000 are received in response to a community fund-raising effort. The restricted gifts are allocated to the two fund balances based on donors' specifications.

```
(21)  Cash                                       6,000
          Fund Balance—Research                          6,000
          Interest on investment of research
          gift resources.
```

```
(22)  Cash                                            115,000
           Fund Balance—Education                                60,000
           Fund Balance—Research                                 55,000
           Receive restricted gifts.
```

Deductions from Specific-Purpose Fund Balance   The specific-purpose fund is notified that the general fund fulfilled the terms of agreements for specific restricted grants totaling $120,000. The specific-purpose fund acknowledged its liability to the general fund and made an interfund transfer of $40,000 in cash, with the remaining balance to be forwarded soon. The $80,000 liability is still outstanding at the end of the fiscal period.

```
(23)  Fund Balance—Education                          61,000
       Fund Balance—Research                           59,000
           Cash                                                  40,000
           Due to General Fund                                   80,000
           Receive notice from general fund
           of fulfillment of restrictions.
```

This interfund transaction was also recorded in the general fund (see entry 4 earlier in the chapter).

Other Transactions in Specific-Purpose Fund   A transaction in the specific-purpose fund affecting only balance sheet accounts is presented below:

```
(24)  Investments                                      70,000
           Cash                                                  70,000
           Acquire additional investments.
```

Financial Statements for the Specific-Purpose Fund   The specific-purpose fund prepares the balance sheet shown in Figure 21-2 and the statement of changes in fund balance shown in Figure 21-4.

Plant Replacement and Expansion Fund   The plant replacement and expansion fund, sometimes called the "plant fund," is used to account for restricted resources given to the hospital to be used only for additions or major modifications to the physical plant. This fund is used as a holding fund until the expenditures for plant assets are approved in the general fund by the governing board. The resources are then transferred to the general fund.

A primary source of resources for the plant replacement and expansion fund is from fund-raising efforts in the communities served by the hospital. Hospitals often ask potential donors to sign pledges specifying a giving level for a period of time, for example, $100 per month for the next 12 months. The pledges become receivables of the fund, and typically require a substantial allowance for uncollectibles. The fund records the net contribution directly to fund balance at the time the pledge is received.

The entries recorded in Sol City Community Hospital's plant replacement and expansion fund during 19X2 are presented below and are reflected in the balance sheet in Figure 21-2 and the statement of changes in fund balances in Figure 21-4.

Additions to Plant Fund Balance   Increases in the plant replacement and expansion fund during the period are a donation of equipment with a fair value of $25,000 that is recorded in the restricted plant fund until the equipment is placed into service; a donation of $60,000 for use to acquire additional medical equipment; and the receipt of $7,000 of interest on the plant fund's investments. Entries to record these events are presented below.

(25)	Property, Plant, and Equipment	25,000	
	Fund Balance		25,000
	Receive donated equipment with fair value of $25,000.		
(26)	Cash	60,000	
	Fund Balance		60,000
	Receive restricted gifts for use to acquire equipment.		
(27)	Cash	7,000	
	Fund Balance		7,000
	Receive interest on fund's investments.		

Deductions from Plant Fund Balance   Deductions from the plant fund during the year are two interfund transfers to the general fund. The first is the transfer of $25,000 of donated equipment that is placed into service, and the second is the transfer of $200,000 to the general fund for expenditures for fixed assets. These two interfund transfers are also recorded in the general fund (see entries 19 and 20 earlier in the chapter).

(28)	Fund Balance	25,000	
	Property, Plant, and Equipment		25,000
	Transfer donated equipment to general fund at time of placement into service.		
(29)	Fund Balance	200,000	
	Cash		200,000
	Transfer cash to general fund for use in acquiring plant assets.		

Other Transactions in Plant Funds   Other transactions affecting only the asset or liability accounts of the plant funds are a collection of pledges made by individual donors during the last capital fund-raising drive, and the acquisition of additional investments in the fund. Entries for these transactions are presented below.

(30)	Cash	105,000	
	Pledges Receivable (net)		105,000
	Collect net pledges receivable.		

(31)	Investments	122,000	
	Cash		122,000
	Increase investments.		

Financial Statements for the Plant Replacement and Expansion Fund   This fund provides a balance sheet as shown in Figure 21-2 and a statement of changes in fund balances as shown in Figure 21-4.

Endowment Fund   The hospital has an endowment fund to account for resources for which the principal must be maintained, either in perpetuity or for a specified term. The income from the investments in the endowment fund is transferred to the funds to which it applies. If the income from the investments is available for unrestricted uses, the general fund recognizes this income as a nonoperating revenue. If the investment income is restricted, it is transferred to the appropriate restricted fund.

The balance sheet in Figure 21-2 and the statement of changes in fund balance in Figure 21-4 include the entries in Sol City Community Hospital's endowment fund for 19X2.

Additions to Endowment Fund Balance   The endowment fund earns $60,000 in interest and dividends from its permanent endowment investments. The terms of the endowment gift agreement specify that the income from investments should be transferred to the general fund for use by the hospital board in any manner deemed proper. In addition, a total of $415,000 in new permanent endowments is received.

(32)	Cash	60,000	
	Fund Balance—Permanent Endowment		60,000
	Interest and dividends from investments.		
(33)	Cash	415,000	
	Fund Balance—Permanent Endowment		415,000
	Receive additional endowments.		

Deductions from Endowment Fund Balance   The endowment fund makes two transfers to the general fund. The first is for the $60,000 of investment income; the second is the transfer of an expired term endowment that became available for any purpose deemed suitable by the hospital board.

(34)	Fund Balance—Permanent Endowment	60,000	
	Cash		60,000
	Transfer investment income to general fund.		
(35)	Fund Balance—Term Endowment	10,000	
	Cash		10,000
	Transfer expired term endowment to general fund.		

These interfund transactions are also recorded in the general fund (see entries 7 and 9 earlier in the chapter).

Other Transactions in Endowment Fund The endowment fund acquires additional investments during 19X2, as follows:

(36) Investments	400,000	
Cash		400,000
Acquire additional investments.		

Financial Statements for the Endowment Fund The transactions illustrated above are reflected in the endowment fund's balance sheet in Figure 21-2 and in the statement of changes in fund balances in Figure 21-4.

Summary of Hospital Accounting and Financial Reporting

The major operating activities of a hospital take place in the general fund. The restricted funds are holding funds that transfer resources to the general fund for expenditures upon satisfaction of their respective restrictions. The accrual basis of accounting is used in the general fund in order to measure fully the revenue and costs of providing health care. Patient services revenue is reported at gross amounts measured at standard billing rates. A deduction for contractual adjustments is then made to arrive at net patient services revenue. Other operating revenue is recognized for ongoing nonpatient services, such as cafeteria sales and television rentals, and donated supplies and medicines. Charity care services are presented only in the footnotes; no revenue is recognized for them. Operating expenses in the general fund include depreciation, bad debts, and the value of recognized donated services that are in support of the basic services of the hospital. Not all donated services are recognized. Nonoperating gains and losses include unrestricted gifts, the contribution value of recognized donated services, and sales of hospital properties. Donated property and equipment is first recorded in a restricted fund, such as plant fund, until placed into service, at which time it is transferred to the general fund. Donated assets are recorded at their fair market values at the date of gift.

The financial statements of a hospital are (1) the balance sheet, (2) the statement of revenue and expenses for the general fund, (3) the statement of changes in fund balances, and (4) the statement of cash flows for the general fund.

VOLUNTARY HEALTH AND WELFARE ORGANIZATIONS

Voluntary health and welfare organizations (VHWO) provide a variety of social services. Examples of such organizations are the United Way, the American Heart Association, the March of Dimes, the American Cancer Society, the Red Cross, and the Salvation Army. These organizations solicit funds from the community at large and typically provide their services for no fee, or they may charge a nominal fee to those with the ability to pay.

The accounting and financial reporting principles for VHWOs are provided in the AICPA's *Audits of Voluntary Health and Welfare Organizations*, first issued in 1974, and revised in 1988.[6] This audit guide requires the use of generally accepted accounting principles for VHWOs. VHWOs are typically audited, and the audited reports are made available to contributors and to others interested in the financial condition of the organization. The federal government normally provides tax-exempt status to these organizations. Another source for accounting and reporting guidelines for VHWOs is the *Standards of Accounting and Financial Reporting for Voluntary Health and Welfare Organizations*, published by the combined group of the National Health Council, the National Assembly of National Voluntary Health and Social Welfare Organizations, and the United Way of America.[7] The standards book represents an effort to incorporate the most recent accounting and financial reporting standards, and the most recent actual experiences of the largest VHWOs in the United States. The most recent edition, the third, was revised and published in 1988. The standards book is informally referred to as "the black book" after the color of its cover. Because the standards book is used by the largest VHWOs, "the black book" does represent a source that should be familiar to accountants working with VHWOs. There are few differences in guidelines between the audit guide and the standards book. The following discussion of VHWOs follows the AICPA's audit guide because the audit guide presents the most authoritative pronouncement on VHWO accounting, but with differences between the audit guide and the standards book noted, where appropriate.

Accounting for a VHWO

The accrual basis of accounting is required for VHWOs in order to measure fully the resources available to the organization. Depreciation is reported as an operating expense each period because the omission of depreciation would result in an understatement of the costs of providing the organization's services. Therefore, accounting for VHWOs is similar to other not-for-profit organizations, except for special financial statements that report on the important aspects of VHWOs. An overview of the accounting and financial reporting principles for a VHWO is presented in Figure 21-6.

VHWO Fund Structure   The audit guide does not require a specific type of fund structure, but most VHWOs use the following structure of four funds:

1. *Current Unrestricted Fund*. The ***current unrestricted fund*** accounts for the unrestricted expendable resources of the VHWO and is comparable to the general fund of a hospital.

---

[6] *Audits of Voluntary Health and Welfare Organizations*, 2d ed., American Institute of Certified Public Accountants (New York), 1988.
[7] *Standards of Accounting and Financial Reporting for Voluntary Health and Welfare Organizations*, 3d ed., National Health Council, Inc. (Washington D.C.), 1988.

FIGURE 21-6 Overview of voluntary health and welfare organization accounting and reporting.

	Fund Groups			
	Current Funds			
	Unrestricted	**Restricted**	**Land, Buildings, and Equipment**	**Endowment**
Accounting basis	Accrual	Accrual	Accrual	Contributions and transfers are credited directly to fund balances. Expendable resources are transferred to other funds.
Distinguishing features		Restricted for only operating purposes.	Includes additions to plant and debt service.	
Financial statements	Balance sheet (combined)			
	Statement of support, revenue, and expenses and changes in fund balances			
	Statement of functional expenses			

2. *Current Restricted Funds.* The ***current restricted funds*** account for resources available for specific operating purposes, subject to restrictions imposed by donors or grantors.

3. *Land, Buildings, and Equipment Fund.* The land, buildings, and equipment fund is sometimes termed the "plant fund." This fund accounts for the resources restricted to, or board-designated for, the land, buildings, and equipment of the VHWO. This fund also includes any long-term debt incurred to acquire plant assets and is responsible for servicing that debt through payments of debt principal and interest.

4. *Endowment Funds.* The endowment funds account for resources received for which the principal must be maintained. Income from the endowment is typically available for operating purposes and is transferred to one of the other funds.

A major feature of VHWOs is that public support and revenue and expenses are recorded in the current unrestricted fund, the current restricted fund, and in the land, buildings, and equipment fund. This record of public support, revenue, and expenses is necessary to provide detailed information on the financial statements for the public support and revenues received by each fund.

Depreciation expense is recorded in the land, buildings, and equipment fund, not in the current unrestricted fund. The endowment fund typically records transfers and contributions directly to fund balance. The endowment fund transfers expendable resources to one of the other funds, usually the current unrestricted fund, as investment income is earned on the investments in the endowment fund.

A few VHWOs have two other types of funds: custodian accounts and loan and annuity funds. Custodian accounts include resources received from donors that may be expended only on instructions from the donor. Loan and annuity funds account for assets held to make loans or to pay annuities to recipients. The VHWO usually obtains title to the resources remaining in the annuity funds at the end of the annuity. These funds are accounted for in the same manner as endowment funds.

Financial Statements for a VHWO

A VHWO must provide the following financial statements: (1) a balance sheet; (2) a statement of support, revenue, and expenses and changes in fund balances; and (3) a statement of functional expenses.

The financial statements are designed primarily for those who are interested in the organizations as "outsiders," not members of management. These include contributors, beneficiaries of services, creditors and potential creditors, and related organizations. A clear distinction should be maintained between restricted resources and those resources available for expenditure for the organization's major missions. For example, **FASB Concepts Statement No. 6**, "Elements of Financial Statements" (FAC 6) divides assets of not-for-profit organizations into three mutually exclusive classes: permanently restricted net assets, temporarily restricted net assets, and unrestricted net assets. Restricted resources are subject to externally imposed constraints, not internal or board-designated decisions that may be changed by the governing board of the VHWO. In addition, readers of the general-purpose financial statements should be able to clearly evaluate management's performance in accomplishing the objectives of the VHWO.

Balance Sheet for a VHWO   Figure 21-7 presents a balance sheet for a VHWO. Two alternative formats may be used to display the balance sheet information, as follows:

a. *Columnar Format.* The columnar format has a separate column for each fund, and a total for all funds. Recent practice has moved more to the columnar format, and this is the format suggested in the 1988 National Health Council's standards book. Figure 21-7 presents the columnar format for a VHWO.

b. *"Pancake" Format.* The "pancake," or layered, format presents separate balance sheet information for each fund in a layered display, with the current unrestricted fund on the top, and proceeding down through each of the funds. No total is presented for all funds. The "pancake" format was used to present the hospital's balance sheet information in Figure 21-2, earlier in this chapter.

Either format may be used to present the VHWO's combined balance sheet for all funds. The assets and liabilities should be segregated into current and noncurrent classifications. Major balance sheet accounts are as follows.

Pledges from Donors   The current unrestricted fund includes net *pledges receivable* of $78,400 in 19X2. The accrual basis of accounting recognizes the receivable

FIGURE 21-7 Balance sheet for a voluntary health and welfare organization.

Voluntary Health and Welfare Service
Balance Sheet
For the Year Ended December 31, 19X2
(with comparative totals for 19X1)

	Current Funds		Land, Buildings, and Equipment Fund	Endowment Fund	19X2 Total	19X1 Total
	Unrestricted	Restricted				
Assets						
Current Assets:						
Cash	$ 64,100	$ 800	$ 4,100	$ 3,000	$ 72,000	$ 71,200
Short-Term Investments	24,000	6,000			30,000	38,000
Receivables:						
Program Service Fees, net of allowance for uncollectibles	1,200				1,200	1,000
Pledges Receivable, net of allowance for uncollectibles	78,400				78,400	61,600
Interfund Receivable (Payable)	1,800	(1,800)				
Inventory	6,400				6,400	8,300
Prepaid Expenses	8,000				8,000	7,200
Total Current Assets	$183,900	$5,000	$ 4,100	$ 3,000	$196,000	$187,300
Noncurrent Investments	248,000			136,500	384,500	346,900
Land, Buildings, and Equipment Less: Accumulated Depreciation			125,500		125,500	114,800
Total Assets	$431,900	$5,000	$129,600	$139,500	$706,000	$649,000
Liabilities and Fund Balances						
Current Liabilities:						
Accounts Payable	$ 16,100				$ 16,100	$ 12,400
Accrued Expenses	4,800				4,800	4,300
Support and Revenue Designated for Subsequent Periods	12,000				12,000	13,100
Total Current Liabilities	$ 32,900				$ 32,900	$ 29,800
Mortgage Payable			$ 21,000		21,000	23,000
Amounts Payable under Capital Lease			8,000		8,000	7,000
Total Liabilities	$ 32,900		$ 29,000		$ 61,900	$ 59,800
Fund Balances:						
Current Unrestricted:						
Designated by the Governing Board for:						
Long-Term Investment	$238,000				$238,000	$218,000
Purchase of New Equipment	64,000				64,000	60,000
Research	21,000				21,000	12,000
Undesignated—available	76,000				76,000	58,000
Current Restricted for:						
Professional Education		$1,000			1,000	2,000
Research		4,000			4,000	6,000
Land, Buildings, and Equipment Fund:						
Unexpended, Restricted			$ 4,100		4,100	3,000
Equity in Fixed Assets			96,500		96,500	91,600
Endowment Fund				$139,500	139,500	138,600
Total Fund Balances	$399,000	$5,000	$100,600	$139,500	$644,100	$589,200
Total Liabilities and Fund Balances	$431,900	$5,000	$129,600	$139,500	$706,000	$649,000

and associated revenue at the time the pledge is received and becomes legally enforceable. Of course, an adequate allowance for uncollectibles must be recognized. Pledges or other contributions applicable to future periods should be reported as a deferred revenue, for example, "Support and Revenue Designated for Subsequent Periods." The following illustrates the accounting for pledges of $100,000, of which $15,000 is attributable to future periods. Experience shows that 20 percent of pledges are uncollectible for this organization. An allowance for uncollectibles is recognized in the amount of $20,000 ($17,000 for current pledges receivable and $3,000 for pledges receivable in the future). Note that both current support and deferred revenue for a future period are recorded net of estimated uncollectibles.

(37)	Pledges Receivable	100,000	
	Allowance for Uncollectible Pledges		20,000
	Support—Contributions		68,000
	Support and Revenue Designated		
	for Subsequent Periods		12,000
	Receive pledges.		

Of the $85,000 ($100,000 − $15,000) of pledges for the current fiscal year, $71,000 is collected, requiring an adjustment of Support—Contributions for the $3,000 in pledges collected above the initial estimate of $68,000 ($85,000 × .80 estimated collectible). The remaining $14,000 of pledges receivable in the current year are written off against the allowance as uncollectible.

(38)	Cash	71,000	
	Allowance for Uncollectible Pledges	3,000	
	Pledges Receivable		71,000
	Support—Contributions		3,000
	Collect pledges including $3,000		
	above initial estimate of collectibility.		
(39)	Allowance for Uncollectible Pledges	14,000	
	Pledges Receivable		14,000
	Write off uncollectible pledges.		

In subsequent years, the deferred support (Support and Revenue Designated for Subsequent Periods) is reclassified as a current support (Support—Contributions), and the pledge collections are recorded.

Investments Investments may be purchased or donated to the organization. Purchased investments should be recorded at cost. Securities donated to the organization should be recorded at their fair market values at the dates of the gifts. If the market value of the investment falls below the recorded book value, and it can be reasonably anticipated that the organization will suffer a loss on disposal of the investment, then a provision for the reduction of value to market should be made in the period of decline in the value. The carrying of investments at full market value is also an acceptable method; however, the same basis of accounting (cost, lower-of-cost-or-market, or full market value) should be used by all funds. If the market value method is used, appreciation gains (or reductions in value) are separately identified as unrealized gains (losses) in the organization's operating statement. Transfers of investments from one fund to another should be made at market value, with any gains or losses in valuation recorded by the fund making the transfer.

Investment income from investments in the unrestricted fund is reported as unrestricted income. Income from investments in the restricted funds, other than endowment funds, should be included in the revenue of the restricted funds, unless legally available for unrestricted purposes. If the investment income is available for unrestricted purposes, the income should be recognized in the current unrestricted fund. Transaction gains and losses on investments of the restricted funds are typically reported in the restricted funds.

Special conventions have been developed for endowment fund investments. Unless restricted to a specific purpose, endowment fund investment income should be recognized in the current unrestricted fund. Restricted endowment investment income should be reported in the appropriate restricted fund. Transaction gains and losses on investments of endowment funds are typically considered principal transactions in the endowment fund, and the same restrictions that apply to the endowment principal apply to any net realized gains from investments of that principal.

Land, Buildings, and Equipment The land, buildings, and equipment fund accounts for the fixed assets, the depreciation expense, and the accumulated depreciation on the fixed assets. The basis of fixed assets is cost, and donated assets are recorded at their fair market values at the dates of the gifts. Donations of fixed assets that will be sold by the organization in the near future are equivalent to other contributions, and should be separately reported in the unrestricted fund until sold. For example, assume the VHWO receives land as a donation. The VHWO plans to sell the land and use the proceeds from the sale in supporting the entity's program services. The land should be recorded at fair value in the unrestricted fund and reported as land held for resale, until sold.

A VHWO may use any one of the methods of depreciation available to commercial entities. Not-for-profit entities are not required to depreciate assets such as works of art or other historically valuable assets in instances in which the not-for-profit entity has made a commitment to preserve the value of the art or historically valuable asset, and has shown the capacity to do so.

Liabilities Each fund recognizes its own liabilities. Note that the land, buildings, and equipment fund accounts for the long-term mortgage payable. The land, buildings, and equipment fund is responsible for servicing the debt associated with fixed assets. However, it is not unusual for the current unrestricted fund to pay the mortgage and record a fund balance transfer to the land, buildings, and equipment fund. For example, assume the current unrestricted fund pays a mortgage payment of $2,000 from its resources. The current unrestricted fund records the following entry:

(40) Fund Balance—Undesignated, Available	2,000	
Cash		2,000
Pay mortgage from current unrestricted fund resources.		

The land, buildings, and equipment fund, which is responsible for servicing the debt associated with fixed assets, concurrently makes the following entry:

(41)	Mortgage Payable	2,000	
	Fund Balance—Equity in Fixed Assets		2,000
	Mortgage payment made by current		
	unrestricted fund.		

Fund Balances The governing board of the VHWO may designate specific purposes for the resources in the unrestricted fund. For example, the current unrestricted fund balance in Figure 21-7 includes board-designated funds for long-term investments, for purchases of new equipment, and for research purposes. The balance sheet reflects the current designations of these resources, but the governing board may change these at any time.

The land, buildings, and equipment fund balance is separated between expended (equity in fixed assets) and unexpended amounts. The unexpended fund balance represents the amount of resources that may still be expended for fixed assets.

Statement of Support, Revenue, and Expenses and Changes in Fund Balances Figure 21-8 presents the major operating statement of VHWOs, entitled the statement of support, revenue, and expenses and changes in fund balances, which has the following format:

Public support and revenue:	
Public support	$XXX
Revenue	X
Total support and revenue	$XXX
Expenses:	
Program services	$ XX
Supporting services	X
Total expenses	$ XX
Excess (deficiency) of public support	
and revenue over expenses	$ X
Fund balances, beginning of year	XX
Other changes in fund balances	X
Fund balances, end of year	$XXX

The National Health Council's "black book" of standards for VHWOs has a slightly different designation for the operating statement. Its operating statement is entitled "statement of revenue, expenses, and changes in fund balances." A difference between the AICPA's VHWO audit guide and the standards book is that the audit guide separately notes the word "support" in the title of the statement, while the standards book treats public support as a normal revenue source. This minor difference is not significant to the format of the statement.

Public Support *Public support* contributions includes pledges from donors. Contributions are reported net of estimated uncollectible pledges. Costs of special

FIGURE 21-8 Statement of support, revenue, and expenses and changes in fund balances for a voluntary health and welfare organization.

Voluntary Health and Welfare Service
Statement of Support, Revenue, and Expenses and Changes in Fund Balance
For the Year Ended December 31, 19X2
(with comparative totals for 19X1)

	Current Funds		Land, Buildings and Equipment Fund	Endowment Fund	19X2 Total	19X1 Total
	Unrestricted	Restricted				
Public support and revenue:						
Public support:						
Received directly:						
Contributions, net of estimated uncollectible pledges	$627,000	$27,000	$ 12,000	$ 2,000	$668,000	$662,000
Legacies and bequests	15,000			6,000	21,000	21,500
Donated services	3,000				3,000	2,000
Received indirectly:						
Collected through affiliated units	2,800				2,800	1,900
Allocation from federated fund-raising effort (net of fund-raising expenses)	45,300				45,300	44,600
Total public support	$693,100	$27,000	$ 12,000	$ 8,000	$740,100	$732,000
Revenue:						
Membership dues	$ 6,100				$ 6,100	$ 5,800
Program service fees	700				700	600
Sales of materials (net of costs)	200				200	300
Endowment and investment income	36,400	$ 500			36,900	39,400
Gains (losses) on investments	12,000			$ 1,000	13,000	(2,000)
Total revenue	$ 55,400	$ 500		$ 1,000	$ 56,900	$ 44,100
Total support and revenue	$748,500	$27,500	$ 12,000	$ 9,000	$797,000	$776,100

Expenses:						
Program services:						
Research	$245,000	$25,000	$ 4,300		$274,300	$261,000
Public health education	91,000		1,000		92,000	87,000
Professional training	104,000		2,000		106,000	103,000
Community services	97,400		1,200		98,600	75,000
Total program services	$537,400	$25,000	$ 8,500	$ -0-	$570,900	$526,000
Supporting services:						
Management and general	$ 91,200		$ 500		$ 91,700	$104,000
Fund-raising	64,000		500		64,500	54,600
Total supporting services	$155,200	$ -0-	$ 1,000	$ -0-	$156,200	$158,600
Payments to national organization	$ 15,000		$ 9,500	$ -0-	$ 15,000	$ 12,000
Total expenses	$707,600	$25,000			$742,100	$696,600
Excess (deficiency) of public support and revenue over expenses	$ 40,900	$ 2,500	$ 2,500	$ 9,000	$ 54,900	$ 79,500
Fund balances, beginning of year	364,100	2,500	82,100	140,500	589,200	509,700
Expired endowment principal transferred to unrestricted fund	10,000			(10,000)		
Acquisition of fixed assets by unrestricted fund	(14,000)		14,000			
Mortgage payment by unrestricted fund	(2,000)		2,000			
Fund balances, end of year	$399,000	$ 5,000	$100,600	$139,500	$644,100	$589,200

fund-raising efforts are deducted directly from the support obtained. The contributions received as a result of a federated fund-raising effort with other not-for-profit organizations is also reported net of the special fund-raising costs. Normal fund-raising costs from the VHWO's own ongoing fund-raising efforts are deducted as a supporting services expense within the expenses section of the statement.

A VHWO records restricted contributions differently from hospitals and colleges and universities. Restricted contributions are recognized as public support and are reported with other revenue in the period in which the restricted contribution is received, unless the contribution is specified for future periods, in which case it is deferred. The VHWO need not wait until the conditions of the restriction are met to report the contribution in its operating statement. However, the restricted contribution must be spent in accordance with the donor's wishes.

Donated Materials and Services A VHWO often relies heavily on *donated materials and services.* Donated materials should be recorded at fair value when received. If the donated materials are used in one of the VHWO's program services, then the recorded value of the materials should be reported as an expense in the period used. If the donated materials simply pass through the VHWO to its charitable beneficiaries, then the VHWO is acting as an agent, and the materials would not then be recorded as a contribution or an expense.

Donated services are an essential part of a VHWO. Because of the difficulty of valuing these services, they often are not recorded as contributions. However, if donated services are significant, they should be recognized by the VHWO if the following three conditions are satisfied:

1. The services performed are a normal part of the program or supporting services and would otherwise be performed by salaried personnel.

2. The organization exercises control over the employment and duties of the donors of the services.

3. The organization has a clearly measurable basis for the amount.

If these three conditions are satisfied, the value of donated services should be reported as part of the public support and also as an expense in the period in which the services are provided. As an example of donated services, assume that a CPA donates audit services with an estimated value of $3,000. The VHWO makes the following entry in the current unrestricted fund to recognize the donated services:

(42) Expenses—Supporting Services	3,000	
Support—Donated Services		3,000
CPA donates audit.		

Revenue Although the majority of a VHWO's resources are obtained from public support, most VHWOs earn some revenue from membership dues or from investment activities. This revenue is recognized using the accrual method.

Expenses Expenses are separated into program services and supporting services, in order to provide contributors and others with information on the full cost of providing the essential programs. Program services include the cost of printing brochures, training those who provide special programs, research expenses, and the salaries of those who conduct programs. Supporting services include electricity and heating costs for the headquarters, salaries of the general manager and office personnel, and operating costs of a central record-keeping system. Routine fund-raising costs are reported as a supporting service expense for the VHWO.

The entry to record depreciation expense of $9,500 for 19X2 is recorded in the land, buildings, and equipment fund. An allocation is made to each of the program services and supporting services, based on square footage used or some other reasonable basis. For example, an allocation of the $9,500 of depreciation, based on square footage occupied, to each of the program and supporting services is recorded with the following entry in the land, buildings, and equipment fund:

(43)	Research—Depreciation	4,300	
	Public Health—Depreciation	1,000	
	Professional Training—Depreciation	2,000	
	Community Services—Depreciation	1,200	
	Management and General—Depreciation	500	
	Fund-Raising—Depreciation	500	
	Accumulated Depreciation		9,500
	Record depreciation for 19X2.		

Joint Costs of Informational Materials That Include a Fund-Raising Appeal   Not-for-profit entities often prepare informational materials that include a direct or indirect message soliciting funds. The issue is how to record the cost of these materials. Should these costs be a program expense or a fund-raising expense? Many VHWOs prefer to classify such costs as program rather than fund-raising to highlight the fulfillment of the basic service mission of the VHWO. Users of the general-purpose financial statements are concerned with the amounts that VHWO organizations spend to solicit contributions, as opposed to the amounts spent for program services. **Statement of Position No. 87-2**, "Accounting for Joint Costs of Informational Materials and Activities of Not-for-Profit Organizations That Include a Fund-Raising Appeal" (SOP 87-2), provides the accounting guidelines for the allocation of these types of costs. **SOP 87-2** states that if a not-for-profit entity cannot show that a program or management function has been conducted in conjunction with the appeal for funds, then the entire cost of the informational materials or activities should be reported as a fund-raising expense. However, if it can be demonstrated that a bona fide program or management function has been conducted in conjunction with the appeal for funds, then the *joint costs of informational materials* are allocated between programs and fund-raising. Evidence of a bona fide program intent in a brochure would be an appeal designed to motivate its audience to action other than providing financial support to the organization. An informational content of a brochure might include a description of the symptoms of a disease and the actions an individual should take if one or more of the symptoms occur. Thus, the content of the message, and the intended audience, are significant factors. **SOP 87-2** leaves it to management to determine the basis of any allocations required of these joint costs.

Other Changes in Fund Balances The other changes in fund balances section includes transfers between funds. These transfers may be recorded directly in fund balances, or they may be recorded in nominal accounts such as Transfer In from Endowment Fund, which is then closed to Fund Balance at the end of the period. Of course, a transfer in from one fund must be matched with a transfer out reported in another fund.

In the land, buildings, and equipment fund, a reclassification from unexpended to expended fund balance is made when a fixed asset is purchased. For example, assume the land, buildings, and equipment fund acquires a fixed asset at a cost of $14,000. The entries to record this acquisition in the land, buildings, and equipment fund are:

(44)	Land, Buildings, and Equipment	14,000	
	Cash		14,000
	Acquire equipment at a cost of $14,000.		
(45)	Fund Balance—Unexpended	14,000	
	Fund Balance—Equity in Fixed Assets		14,000
	Reclassify fund balance from unexpended to expended for fixed assets acquired.		

However, it is not uncommon for the current unrestricted fund to acquire fixed assets. In this case, a fund balance transfer is made from the current unrestricted fund to the land, buildings, and equipment fund. Thus, regardless of which fund acquires the fixed asset, accounting for fixed assets is recorded in the land, buildings, and equipment fund. For example, assume the current unrestricted fund acquires the equipment with $14,000 of its resources. The entry in the current unrestricted fund is:

(46)	Fund Balance—Undesignated, Available	14,000	
	Cash		14,000
	Acquire equipment with current unrestricted fund resources.		

The land, buildings, and equipment fund concurrently records the following entry:

(47)	Land, Buildings, and Equipment	14,000	
	Fund Balance—Equity in Fixed Assets		14,000
	Equipment acquisition by current unrestricted fund resources transferred into land, buildings, and equipment fund.		

Although it is not unusual for the unrestricted fund to directly acquire fixed assets, this practice should be discouraged because it reduces the control over the asset acquisition process of the organization. It is preferable for the unrestricted fund to first transfer the necessary resources to the land, buildings, and equipment fund, and then the land, buildings, and investment fund may acquire the fixed assets through its management and control processes.

When restrictions on endowment fund principal lapse, the resources released should be transferred to the current unrestricted fund, or to a restricted fund in accordance with the terms of the original gift or bequest. This transfer is recorded as a change to fund balance, not as an expense of the endowment fund, nor as a revenue of the receiving fund. If no terms are provided in the original gift, then expired endowments are transferred to the current unrestricted fund.

Statement of Functional Expenses   The third and last statement for VHWOs is the *statement of functional expenses*. This statement details the items reported in the expenses section of the statement of support, revenue, and expenses and changes in fund balances in Figure 21-8. Figure 21-9 is a standard format for the statement of functional expenses. The expense categories are presented across the columns. The rows are the specific nature of the items comprising these expense categories from the various funds.

The statement of functional expenses includes depreciation of $9,500 for the year, allocated among the various programs and supporting services. The AICPA VHWO audit guide states that total expenses before depreciation must be presented, and depreciation is then reported as a separate item. This provides an indication of the outflow of resources that are a part of each expense class. The National Health Council's standards' book uses the same title and format for this third statement, but does not separate depreciation; rather, depreciation is included with the other functional expenses. Total expenses of $742,100 in Figure 21-8 are analyzed and reconciled on the statement of functional expenses in Figure 21-9.

Summary of Accounting and Financial Reporting for VHWOs

The accounting and financial reporting requirements for VHWOs are specified in the AICPA's audit guide for these organizations. A VHWO uses several funds to account for its operations. The accrual basis of accounting is used in the current unrestricted and current restricted funds and in the land, buildings, and equipment fund. Depreciation expense and debt service costs are accounted for in the land, buildings, and equipment fund. Resources restricted for specific operating purposes are accounted for in the current restricted fund. Resources restricted for other than operating purposes are recorded in other restricted funds.

A VHWO provides three financial statements: (1) a balance sheet, (2) a statement of support, revenue, and expenses and changes in fund balance, and (3) a statement of functional expenses. Public support for the current period is reported along with revenues for the period. Support applicable to future periods is deferred. The statement of functional expenses is an analysis of all expenses for the organization, including depreciation, broken down into types of expenses, such as salaries, supplies, and conferences. The expenses are summarized by individual program services and by individual supporting services.

FIGURE 21-9 Statement of functional expenses for a voluntary health and welfare organization.

Voluntary Health and Welfare Service
Statement of Functional Expenses
Year Ended December 31, 19X2
(with comparative totals for 19X1)

	Program Services					Supporting Services			Total Program and Supporting Services Expenses	
	Research	Public Health Education	Professional Training	Community Services	Total	Management and General	Fund Raising	Total	19X2	19X1
Salaries	49,000	58,200	51,100	53,800	212,100	66,100	34,100	100,200	312,300	347,000
Employee benefits	2,800	2,900	2,900	2,900	11,500	4,100	1,000	5,100	16,600	16,800
Payroll taxes, etc.	2,400	3,100	2,600	2,900	11,000	3,600	1,800	5,400	16,400	15,500
Total salaries and related expenses	54,200	64,200	56,600	59,600	234,600	73,800	36,900	100,700	345,300	379,300
Professional fees	200	1,000	5,200	1,600	8,000	3,000	1,500	4,500	12,500	12,000
Supplies	400	600	1,000	1,000	3,000	2,100	3,000	5,100	8,100	7,900
Telephone	400	1,400	1,200	4,300	7,300	2,500	7,200	9,700	17,000	16,800
Postage and shipping	400	3,200	900	2,800	7,300	2,600	6,000	8,600	15,900	14,300
Occupancy	1,000	3,400	6,000	9,000	19,400	3,000	1,000	4,000	23,400	20,500
Rental of equipment	200	800	3,400	400	4,800	600	100	700	5,500	4,800
Printing and publications	600	11,200	6,500	1,400	19,700	900	7,400	8,300	28,000	23,000
Travel	1,600	2,000	10,800	4,200	18,600	1,100	200	1,300	19,900	21,500
Conferences and meetings	800	1,800	10,500	1,600	14,700	1,400	600	2,000	16,700	16,300
Awards and grants	209,300	1,200	600	10,300	221,400				221,400	157,500
Other expenses	900	200	1,300	1,200	3,600	200	100	300	3,900	4,200
Total expenses before depreciation	270,000	91,000	104,000	97,400	562,400	91,200	64,000	155,200	717,600	678,100
Depreciation of buildings and equipment	4,300	1,000	2,000	1,200	8,500	500	500	1,000	9,500	6,500
Total functional expenses	274,300	92,000	106,000	98,600	570,900	91,700	64,500	156,200	727,100	684,600
Payments to national office									15,000	12,000
Total expenses									742,100	696,600

OTHER NOT-FOR-PROFIT ENTITIES

A variety of other not-for-profit organizations (ONPOs) exist for which accounting records must be maintained and financial reports must be prepared. The AICPA provides audit and accounting guidelines in *Audits of Certain Nonprofit Organizations*.[8] This audit and accounting guide includes **AICPA Statement of Position No. 78-10**, "Accounting Principles and Reporting Practices for Certain Nonprofit Organizations" (SOP 78-10), which is an authoritative source for accounting for ONPOs. Examples of other not-for-profit organizations include:

Cemetery organizations	Private and community foundations
Civic organizations	Private elementary and secondary schools
Fraternal organizations	Professional associations
Labor unions	Public broadcasting stations
Libraries	Religious organizations
Museums	Research and scientific organizations
Other cultural institutions	Social and country clubs
Performing arts organizations	Trade associations
Political parties	Zoological and botanical societies

Accounting for ONPOs

Fund Structure for an ONPO Fund accounting is used to account for ONPOs in a manner similar to accounting for VHWOs. Although no specific fund structure is recommended in the audit and accounting guide, most ONPOs use the following funds:

1. *Unrestricted Operating Fund.* The **unrestricted operating fund** accounts for all unrestricted resources received and the expenses incurred for the primary purposes of the organization.

2. *Restricted Operating Fund.* The **restricted operating fund** accounts for resources received from donors or grantors with restrictions imposed on their use.

3. *Land, Buildings, and Equipment Fund.* This fund accounts for the organization's resources restricted to, or expended for, the acquisition of the organization's fixed assets. The land, buildings, and equipment fund records fixed assets and the long-term debt on those assets. This fund also records depreciation on fixed assets.

4. *Endowment Fund.* The endowment fund accounts for the principal of gifts and bequests accepted with donor-specified restrictions relating to maintenance of principal or distribution of income.

Accounting within these four funds is comparable to accounting for VHWOs. The accrual basis of accounting is used to recognize revenue and expenses in the

[8] *Audits of Certain Nonprofit Organizations*, 2d ed., American Institute of Certified Public Accountants (New York), 1987.

first three funds above. Transactions in the endowment fund are recorded directly to fund balance rather than to revenue and expenses, and the endowment fund transfers its resources to another fund for expenditure. Figure 21-10 presents an overview of the accounting and financial reporting for ONPOs. The primary operating statement for an ONPO is the statement of support and revenue, expenses, capital additions, and changes in fund balance, generally called the *statement of activity*.

In addition to the four funds already cited, a few ONPOs may include an annuity and life income fund and a deposit and loan fund. Accounting for these two funds is similar to accounting for an endowment fund.

The audit and accounting guide recognizes that smaller, less complex ONPOs need flexibility in accounting, and allows funds of smaller organizations to be combined. An ONPO may simplify its accounting and financial reporting by using only two fund types to account for its operations: unrestricted and restricted. Some smaller ONPOs use the cash basis of accounting to record their transactions. As an ONPO increases in size and becomes more complex, however, a more complete fund structure should be implemented and the accrual method should be used. The remaining discussion in this chapter assumes a complete fund structure and the accrual method.

Support and Capital Additions The audit and accounting guide covering ONPOs specifies the accounting for *support* and *capital additions* for ONPOs. Separate designation is important because the ONPO's statement of activity has a separate section to report support and another section in which capital additions are reported.

FIGURE 21-10 Overview of accounting and reporting for other not-for-profit organizations.

	Fund Groups			
	Operating Funds		**Land, Buildings, and Equipment**	**Endowment**
	Unrestricted	**Restricted**		
Accounting basis	Accrual	Accrual	Accrual	Contributions and transfers are credited directly to fund balances. Expendable resources are transferred to other funds.
Financial statements	Balance sheets			
	Statement of activity			
	Statement of cash flows			

1. *Support.* Support is expendable gifts, grants, and bequests for the program or service activities of the ONPO. These donations may be unrestricted, or may have donor-imposed restrictions limiting the manner or time period in which the donated resources may be used for a program or service. An example of support is a restricted donation that may be used only for providing a specific program activity of the ONPO.

2. *Capital Additions.* Capital additions are gifts, grants, or bequests restricted by the donor or grantor for endowment, plant, or loan purposes, either permanently or for a specified period of time. Capital additions do not include donor-restricted gifts for program or supporting services. An example of a capital addition is a donation that must be used for acquisitions of plant and equipment.

An ONPO accounts for restricted support as deferred public support until an expenditure of restricted or unrestricted funds is made. For example, assume a donor makes a contribution of $10,000 for a specific program. The ONPO makes the following entry for this restricted gift in its restricted operating fund:

(48)	Cash	10,000	
	Deferred Support—Contributions		10,000
	Record restricted gift for specific program.		

The account Deferred Support—Contributions is a liability account.

At the time the organization incurs expenses for the specified program, the contribution is recognized as current public support and reported as revenue of the period in the organization's statement of activity. For example, assume that the organization spends $8,000 for the specified program during the current fiscal period. Current support revenue of $8,000 is reclassified from the deferred support liability. The remaining $2,000 of the initial $10,000 gift is maintained as a liability in the restricted operating fund. The restricted operating fund makes the following entries:

(49)	Expenses (specified program)	8,000	
	Cash		8,000
	Incur expenses for program specified in restricted gift.		
(50)	Deferred Support—Contributions	8,000	
	Support—Contributions		8,000
	Reclassify portion of restricted gift for expenses incurred for specified program.		

It does not matter if the governing board decides to use unrestricted resources when the actual services are performed and expenses incurred. The conditions of the restriction are met as soon as any costs are incurred for the program to which the restricted contribution is directed. The unrestricted operating fund is reimbursed by the restricted operating fund for any expenditures it makes for restricted programs or services.

Donated Services   ONPOs typically receive *donated services*. **SOP 78-10** specifies four criteria that must be met in order to recognize donated services as public support and, concurrently, as an expense of the period.[9]

1. The services performed are significant and form an integral part of the efforts of the organization; the services would be performed by salaried personnel if they were not donated by volunteers; and the organization would continue this program or activity.

2. The ONPO controls the employment and duties of the persons donating the service.

3. The ONPO has a clearly measurable basis for the amount to be recorded.

4. The program services of the ONPO are not principally intended for the benefit of the organization's members.

The fourth criterion prevents the recognition of most donated services for ONPOs because many of these organizations are established principally for the benefit of their members. Accordingly, donated and contributed services are not normally recorded by organizations such as religious communities, professional and trade associations, labor unions, political parties, fraternal organizations, and social and country clubs.

Donated Materials   Donated materials, if significant, should be recorded at fair market value, provided the ONPO has a clearly measurable and objective basis for determining the market value. If the donation of materials is recorded, it is typically recognized as support, and an entry is then made to record the expense in the period the materials are used. If the donated materials pass directly through the ONPO to its charitable beneficiaries, and the ONPO acts only as an agent to facilitate the distribution of the donated materials, then the organization is not required to record either the contribution or the distribution.

Accounting for Investments   Health care providers report their investments at cost, or at lower of cost or market. VHWOs may report their investments at either cost or market. An ONPO uses the following rules to value its investments:

1. When there is both the ability and the intent to hold marketable debt securities to maturity, they should be reported at amortized cost, market value, or the lower of amortized cost or market value.

2. Marketable equity securities and marketable debt securities that are not expected to be held to maturity should be reported at either market value or the lower-of-cost-or-market value. If the market value method is used, unrealized gains and losses from changes in the market value should be recognized in the same manner as realized gains and losses and reported on the ONPO's statement of activity for the period.

---

[9] *Statement of Position No. 78-10,* "Accounting Principles and Reporting Practices for Certain Nonprofit Organizations," American Institute of Certified Public Accountants (New York), 1978, par. 67.

Not-for-profit organizations may pool their investments from several funds in order to centralize the investment activity under the direction of an investment expert. The *market value unit method* may be used to account for pooled investments. Under the market value unit method, a fund is assigned a number of units based on the fund's contribution to the pool and the total fair market value of all investments in the pool at the time of the contribution. For example, an investment pool has assigned a total of 10,000 units to investments with a fair market value of $300,000. Therefore, the value of each unit is $30. If the endowment fund of an ONPO contributes $60,000 to the investment pool at this time, it would receive 2,000 units with a value of $30 each. Income distributions, including gains and losses from investment activity, are then allocated to the various funds by dividing the total income by the number of units in the pool. If the investment fund realizes income of $36,000 during the period, the value of each unit increases by $3 ($36,000/12,000 units). The endowment fund then records income of $6,000 ($3 × 2,000 units).

Depreciation Expense and Accumulated Depreciation   The land, buildings, and equipment fund records depreciation expense and accumulated depreciation on fixed assets. In addition, this fund accounts for acquisitions of assets and for servicing debt on the fixed assets. The land, buildings, and equipment fund may receive resources from other funds, especially from the unrestricted operating fund, for acquisitions or debt service. These interfund transfers are accounted for as changes directly to fund balances, not as revenue or expense items. Temporary fund balance accounts for these transfers may be used, such as "transfers out" from the transmitting fund and "transfers in" to the land, buildings, and equipment fund.

Financial Statements for an ONPO

The principal purpose of the financial statements of an ONPO is to explain how the resources have been used to carry out the organization's objectives. Therefore, the statements should disclose the nature and source of the resources, any restrictions on the resources, the principal programs and their costs, and the organization's ability to continue to carry out its objectives. An ONPO must provide the following three financial statements: (1) a balance sheet, (2) a statement of activity, and (3) a statement of cash flows. The following illustrations of the balance sheet and statement of activity are modeled after those presented in **SOP 78-10**. The required statement of cash flows is similar to that required for commercial entities.

Balance Sheet for an ONPO   Figure 21-11 presents a balance sheet for a nonprofit organization that renovates and preserves historical buildings in Sol City. The name of the organization is the Ellwood Historical Society. The society has its own governing board and is not associated with a government. The illustrated balance sheet separately reports each of the two operating funds;

FIGURE 21-11 Balance sheet for an other not-for-profit organization (ONPO).

Ellwood Historical Society
Balance Sheet
June 30, 19X1

	Operating Funds		Land, Buildings, and Equipment Fund	Endowment Funds	Total, All Funds
	Unrestricted	Restricted			
Assets					
Cash	$ 32,000	$ 4,000	$ 16,000	$ 2,000	$ 54,000
Accounts Receivable, less allowance for uncollectibles	17,500				17,500
Pledges Receivable, less allowance for uncollectibles			28,000		28,000
Inventories	3,000				3,000
Investments	84,000	26,000		100,000	210,000
Land, Buildings, and Equipment, net of accumulated depreciation			242,000		242,000
Other Assets	6,500				6,500
Total Assets	$143,000	$30,000	$286,000	$102,000	$561,000
Liabilities and Fund Balances					
Accounts Payable and Accrued Expenses	$ 28,000				$ 28,000
Deferred Support		$30,000			30,000
Long-Term Debt			$178,000		178,000
Total Liabilities	$ 28,000	$30,000	$178,000	$ -0-	$236,000
Fund Balances:					
Unrestricted:					
Designated by Governing Board:					
For Long-Term Investment	$ 84,000				$ 84,000
Undesignated	31,000				31,000
Restricted—Nonexpendable				$102,000	102,000
Net Investment in Plant			$108,000		108,000
Total Fund Balances	$115,000	$ -0-	$108,000	$102,000	$325,000
Total Liabilities and Fund Balances	$143,000	$30,000	$286,000	$102,000	$561,000

however, it is also acceptable to report the operating funds together in one column. Either the columnar format or the "pancake" format is allowed for presenting the balance sheet of an ONPO. Figure 21-11 uses the columnar format because of its increasing use in practice.

The operating funds include deferred amounts for contributions received that are applicable to future periods. In addition, the fund balances of the operating funds are separated into board-designated amounts and undesignated amounts. Board-designated resources are similar to an appropriation of retained earnings of a commercial entity.

The land, buildings, and equipment fund reports both the fixed assets and the long-term debt on the fixed assets. The fund balance is reported as "Net Investment in Plant."

Statement of Activity A statement of activity for the historical society, presented in Figure 21-12, reports the support, revenue, expenses, capital additions, transfers, and changes in fund balance during the fiscal period.

The format for the statement of activity is as follows:

Support and revenue	$XXX
Expenses:	
Program services	XX
Support services	XX
Excess (deficiency) of support and revenue over expenses before capital additions	$ X
Capital additions	XX
Excess (deficiency) of support and revenue over expenses after capital additions	$ XX
Fund balances at the beginning of the year	XXX
Interfund transfers	X
Fund balances at the end of the year	$XXX

Note that capital additions are reported in a separate section below support and expenses.

The title of the statement may vary, depending on the actual circumstances of the ONPO. The illustration uses the title "Statement of Support and Revenue, Expenses, Capital Additions, and Changes in Fund Balance." Other organizations may use just the title "Statement of Activity." The statement of activity is comparable to the statement of support, revenue, and expenses and changes in fund balances for a VHWO. The only difference is that the statement of activity for an ONPO reports capital additions in a separate section. Capital additions are gifts, grants, and bequests to endowment or plant funds, which are restricted by donors either permanently or for an extended period of time. Capital additions do not include restricted gifts for programs or supporting services. Restricted gifts for programs or services are reported as deferred support until the conditions of the restrictions are satisfied or expenses are incurred for the program, at which time the support is recognized for the period. Therefore, the restricted operating fund reports revenue equal to expenses for each period.

FIGURE 21-12 Statement of activity for an other not-for-profit organization (ONPO).

Ellwood Historical Society
Statement of Support, Revenue, Expenses,
Capital Additions, and Changes in Fund Balances
For the Year Ended June 30, 19X1

	Operating Funds		Land, Buildings, and Equipment Fund	Endowment Funds	Total, All Funds
	Unrestricted	Restricted			
Support and revenue:					
Support:					
Contributions	$130,000	$60,000			$190,000
Donated services	3,000				3,000
Total support	$133,000	$60,000	$ -0-	$ -0-	$193,000
Revenue:					
Membership dues	$ 16,000				$ 16,000
Admission fees	12,000				12,000
Investment income	12,200	$ 2,600			14,800
Gain on sale of equipment			$ 5,000		5,000
Total revenue	$ 40,200	$ 2,600	$ 5,000	$ -0-	$ 47,800
Total support and revenue	$173,200	$62,600	$ 5,000	$ -0-	$240,800
Expenses:					
Program services:					
Community education	$ 84,000	$43,400	$ 12,000		$139,400
Research	6,000	16,200	2,000		24,200
Auxiliary activities	18,000		1,000		19,000
Total program services	$108,000	$59,600	$ 15,000	$ -0-	$182,600
Supporting services:					
General administrative	$ 16,000	$ 2,000	$ 2,000		$ 20,000
Fund-raising	12,000	1,000			13,000
Total supporting services	$ 28,000	$ 3,000	$ 2,000	$ -0-	$ 33,000
Total expenses	$136,000	$62,600	$ 17,000	$ -0-	$215,600
Excess (deficiency) of support and revenue over expenses before capital additions	$ 37,200	$ -0-	$(12,000)	$ -0-	$ 25,200
Capital additions:					
Contributions and bequests			$ 16,000	$100,000	$116,000
Net gain on investment transactions				12,000	12,000
Total capital additions	$ -0-	$ -0-	$ 16,000	$112,000	$128,000
Excess (deficiency) of support and revenue over expenses after capital additions	$ 37,200		$ 4,000	$112,000	$153,200
Fund balances at beginning of year	71,800		100,000	-0-	171,800
Transfers:					
Equipment acquisitions by unrestricted fund	(4,000)		4,000		
Transfer of expired term endowment	10,000			(10,000)	
Fund balances at end of year	$115,000	$ -0-	$108,000	$102,000	$325,000

The $17,000 of expense shown in Figure 21-12 in the land, buildings, and equipment fund represents depreciation which is allocated to the individual program services and support services expense accounts. The land, buildings, and equipment fund also is responsible for servicing the long-term debt on the ONPO's fixed assets.

Statement of Cash Flows   Figure 21-13 presents the statement of cash flows for the illustrated historical society. The statement presents cash flows from all funds. The cash flows from operations section begins with the excess (deficiency) of support and revenue over expenses before capital additions, and capital additions are reported separately.

Summary of Accounting and Financial Reporting for ONPOs

Accounting for ONPOs is similar to accounting for VHWOs. The accrual basis of accounting is used in the two operating funds and in the land, buildings, and equipment fund. Transactions in the endowment fund are recorded directly to fund balance.

The audit and accounting guide, and **SOP 78-10**, are the authoritative sources of accounting and financial reporting principles for ONPOs. The balance sheet, statement of activity, and statement of cash flows are reported by ONPOs. The statement of activity reports public support and revenue for the period. Capital additions are reported separately on the statement of activity. Capital additions result from gifts to the land, buildings, and equipment fund, or the endowment funds, which have been restricted by the donors either permanently or for an extended period of time.

The land, buildings, and equipment fund records fixed assets, long-term debt on the fixed assets, and depreciation.

SUMMARY OF KEY CONCEPTS AND TERMS

Health care providers, voluntary health and welfare organizations, and other not-for-profit entities use the accrual basis of accounting to measure revenue and expenses. Health care providers have one primary operating fund—the general fund—in which most transactions occur. The restricted funds for a health care provider are funds used to hold resources until the conditions of the restrictions are met and the resources are transferred to the general fund. Hospitals record gross patient revenue and then provide an appropriate deduction for contractual adjustments. Donated medical supplies and medicines are other operating revenue. Donated services are a nonoperating gain; donated equipment is credited directly to fund balance.

VHWOs and ONPOs recognize revenue and expenses in the operating funds and in the land, buildings, and equipment fund. Public support is reported in the major operating statement in the period in which the contribution is received unless it is intended for future periods, in which case a deferred revenue is

FIGURE 21-13 Statement of cash flows for an other not-for-profit organization (ONPO).

Ellwood Historical Society
Statement of Cash Flows
For the Year Ended June 30, 19X1

	Operating Funds		Land, Buildings, and Equipment Fund	Endowment Funds	Total, All Funds
	Unrestricted	Restricted			
Net Cash Flows from Operating Activities:					
Excess (Deficiency) of Support and Revenue over Expenses before Capital Additions	$37,200		$(12,000)		$ 25,200
Capital Additions			16,000	$ 112,000	128,000
Adjustments to reconcile excess of support and revenue over expenses after capital additions with net cash flow from operating activities:					
Depreciation			17,000		17,000
Net Increase in Deferred Support		$2,000			2,000
Net Increase in Receivables, Inventory, and Payables	(18,000)				(18,000)
Gain on Sale of Assets			(5,000)		(5,000)
Net Cash Flows from Operating Activities	$19,200	$2,000	$ 16,000	$ 112,000	$149,200
Cash Flows from Investing Activities:					
Sale of Investments	$ 3,000				$ 3,000
Sale of Equipment			$ 8,000		8,000
Acquisition of Equipment	(4,000)				(4,000)
Purchase of Investments				$(100,000)	(100,000)
Net Cash Flows from Investing Activities	$ (1,000)	$ -0-	$ 8,000	$(100,000)	$ (93,000)
Cash Flows from Financing Activities:					
Transfer of Expired Term Endowment	$10,000			$ (10,000)	
Reduction of Long-Term Debt			$ (9,000)		$ (9,000)
Net Cash Flows from Financing Activities	$10,000	$ -0-	$ (9,000)	$ (10,000)	$ (9,000)
Net Increase in Cash	$28,200	$2,000	$ 15,000	$ 2,000	$ 47,200
Cash Balance at Beginning of Year	3,800	2,000	1,000	-0-	6,800
Cash Balance at End of Year	$32,000	$4,000	$ 16,000	$ 2,000	$ 54,000

recognized. Donated services may be included as both a public support item and an expense item, although donated services are typically not recorded.

The financial statements of a VHWO include a statement of functional expenses. The financial statements of an ONPO include a statement of activity. Although several similarities exist in the major financial statements of these two not-for-profit entities, the statements have several differences in format because of the different operating and financial aspects of the entities. Capital additions are reported separately in the statement of activity for an ONPO. VHWOs are not required to present a statement of cash flows, while ONPOs provide a statement of cash flows for all funds.

Health care providers:
  Assets whose use is limited
  Board-designated resources
  General fund
  Nonoperating gains
  Operating revenue
  Restricted funds
Voluntary health and welfare organizations:
  Current funds (unrestricted and restricted)
  Donated materials and services
  Joint costs of informational materials

Pledges receivable
Public support
Statement of functional expenses
Other not-for-profit organizations:
  Capital additions
  Donated services
  Market value unit method
  Operating funds (unrestricted and restricted)
  Statement of activity
  Support

QUESTIONS

Q21-1 What is the basis of accounting in a hospital's general fund? Its restricted funds?

Q21-2 How are donated services accounted for by a hospital? How does it account for donated equipment and donated medical supplies?

Q21-3 A donor contributes $15,000 to be used for operating costs in the intensive care unit. How does the hospital account for this contribution? How does it account for the expenditure of the $15,000?

Q21-4 What are the components of operating revenue of a hospital?

Q21-5 In which fund is a gain on the sale of hospital properties recorded by a hospital? How is the gain reported in the hospital's financial statements?

Q21-6 Is depreciation accounted for by a hospital? Why or why not?

Q21-7 What is the basis of accounting for the unrestricted current fund of a VHWO? What is the basis for the restricted funds?

Q21-8 Where are fixed assets recorded for a VHWO? Is depreciation recorded for a VHWO?

Q21-9 An individual contributes $10,000 to a VHWO for restricted use in a public health education service. How does the VHWO account for this contribution? How does it account for the expenditure of the $10,000?

Q21-10 Explain the accounting for pledges from donors to a VHWO.

Q21-11 Do VHWOs report all public support received in the period in their major operating financial statement? Identify that which is not included.

Q21-12 How do VHWOs account for donated services?

Q21-13 Describe the statement of functional expenses.

Q21-14 An alumna of a sorority donates $12,000 to the sorority for restricted use in a community service activity of the sorority. How is the contribution accounted for by this ONPO? How is the expenditure of the $12,000 accounted for?

Q21-15 Are donated services received by an ONPO accounted for in the same manner as donated services received by hospitals? Why or why not?

Q21-16 What is the market value unit method of accounting for investments?

Q21-17 Should a rotary club, an ONPO, report depreciation expense? Why or why not?

Q21-18 Describe the statement of activity for an ONPO. Compare it with the statement of support, revenue, and expenses and changes in fund balances for a VHWO.

Q21-19 Give an example of a capital addition for an ONPO. How are capital additions reported in the financial statements?

CASES

C21-1 Accounting for Donations

Hospitals, voluntary health and welfare organizations, and other not-for-profit organizations often rely heavily on donations of volunteers' time and donations of equipment, supplies or other assets.

Required

a. Specify the criteria to be used to determine the accounting for donated services to (1) hospitals, (2) voluntary health and welfare organizations, and (3) other not-for-profit organizations. Discuss the reasons for any differences in the accounting criteria used.

b. How are donations of capital assets, such as equipment, accounted for by hospitals? Is depreciation recorded on these donations? Why or why not?

c. How are cash contributions accounted for by (1) hospitals, (2) voluntary health and welfare organizations, and (3) other not-for-profit organizations?

C21-2 Public Support to an Other Not-for-Profit Organization

L. Dawnes has just been elected treasurer of the local professional association of registered nurses. The association provides public health messages for the community as well as services for members. She is now preparing financial statements for the year and comes to you for advice on accounting for the proceeds from a major fund drive that occurred during the year. The nursing association received $25,000 in unrestricted donations and $15,000 in restricted donations that are restricted to public health advertisements. A total of $6,000 has been incurred for public health advertising since the restricted donations were received.

The former treasurer accounted for the $40,000 of donations as revenue in the unrestricted fund. L. Dawnes feels this may not be correct because it does not disclose the restricted nature of the donations for the public health messages.

Required

a. Discuss the accounting and financial statement disclosure to be used to account for the $25,000 of unrestricted donations to the professional association.

b. How should the $15,000 of restricted contributions have been accounted for at the time of the donation? How should they have been reported on this year's financial statements?

EXERCISES

E21-1 Multiple-Choice Questions on Hospital Accounting [AICPA Adapted]

Select the correct answer for each of the following questions.

Questions 1 through 3 are based on the following data:

Under Dodge Hospital's established rate structure, the hospital would have earned patient service revenue of $5,000,000 for the year ended December 31, 19X3. However, Dodge did not expect to collect this amount, because of contractual adjustments of $500,000 to third-party payors. In May 19X3, Dodge purchased bandages from Hunt Supply Co. at a cost of $1,000. However, Hunt notified Dodge that the invoice was being canceled and that the bandages were being donated to Dodge. On December 31, 19X3, Dodge had board-designated assets consisting of $40,000 in cash and investments of $700,000.

1. For the year ended December 31, 19X3, how much should Dodge record as patient service revenue?
   a. $4,500,000.
   b. $5,000,000.
   c. $5,500,000.
   d. $5,740,000.

2. For the year ended December 31, 19X3, Dodge should record the donation of bandages as:
   a. A $1,000 reduction in operating expenses.
   b. Nonoperating gain of $1,000.
   c. Other operating revenue of $1,000.
   d. A memorandum entry only.

3. How much of Dodge's board-designated assets should be included in the general fund grouping?
   a. $0.
   b. $40,000.
   c. $700,000.
   d. $740,000.

4. Donated medicines that normally would be purchased by a hospital should be recorded at fair value and should be credited directly to:
   a. Other operating revenue.
   b. Other nonoperating gain.
   c. Fund balance.
   d. Deferred revenue.

5. Which of the following would normally be included in other operating revenue of a not-for-profit hospital?
   a. Unrestricted interest income from an endowment fund.
   b. An unrestricted gift.
   c. Donated services.
   d. Tuition received from an educational program.

6. An unrestricted gift pledge from an annual contributor to a not-for-profit hospital made in December 19X1 and paid in March 19X2 would generally be credited to:
   a. Nonoperating gain in 19X1.
   b. Nonoperating gain in 19X2.
   c. Operating revenue in 19X1.
   d. Operating revenue in 19X2.

7. An organization of high school seniors assists patients at Lake Hospital. These students are volunteers and perform services that the hospital would not otherwise provide, such as wheeling patients in the park and reading to patients. Lake has no employer-employee relationship with these volunteers, who donated 5,000 hours of service to Lake in 19X2. At the minimum wage, these services would amount to $18,750, while it is estimated that the fair value of these services was $25,000. In Lake's 19X2 statement of revenues and expenses, what amount should be reported as nonoperating gain?
   a. $25,000.
   b. $18,750.
   c. $6,250.
   d. $0.

8. Which of the following would be included in the general funds of a not-for-profit hospital?
   a. Permanent endowments.
   b. Term endowments.
   c. Board-designated funds originating from previously accumulated income.
   d. Plant expansion and replacement funds.

9. During the year ended December 31, 19X1, Greenacre Hospital received the following donations stated at their respective fair values:

Employee services from members of a religious group	$100,000
Medical supplies from an association of physicians. These supplies were restricted for indigent care and were used for such purpose in 19X1.	30,000

   How much operating revenue and nonoperating gain from donations should Greenacre report in its 19X1 statement of revenue and expenses?
   a. $0.
   b. $30,000.
   c. $100,000.
   d. $130,000.

10. Johnson Hospital's property, plant, and equipment (net of depreciation) consists of the following:

Land	$ 500,000
Buildings	10,000,000
Movable equipment	2,000,000

What amount should be included in the restricted fund grouping?
a. $0.
b. $2,000,000.
c. $10,500,000.
d. $12,500,000.

11. Depreciation should be recognized in the financial statements of:
a. Proprietary (for-profit) hospitals only.
b. Both proprietary and not-for-profit hospitals.
c. Both proprietary and not-for-profit hospitals, only when they are affiliated with a college or university.
d. All hospitals, as a memorandum entry not affecting the statement of revenue and expenses.

12. On March 1, 19X1, J. Rowe established a $100,000 endowment fund, the income from which is to be paid to Central Hospital for general operating purposes. Central does not control the fund's principal. Rowe appointed Sycamore National Bank as trustee of this fund. What journal entry is required by Central to record the establishment of the endowment?

	Debit	Credit
a. Cash	$100,000	
Nonexpendable endowment fund		$100,000
b. Cash	100,000	
Endowment fund balance		100,000
c. Nonexpendable endowment fund	100,000	
Endowment fund balance		100,000
d. Memorandum entry only	—	—

E21-2 Entries for a Hospital General Fund

The following are transactions of the general fund of Eden Hospital for the 19X1 fiscal year ending December 31, 19X1.

1. The value of patient services provided is $4,800,000.
2. Operating expenses total $4,740,000, as follows:

Nursing services	$1,500,000
Other professional services	1,000,000
Fiscal services	200,000
General services	1,300,000
Bad debts	100,000
Administration	240,000
Depreciation	400,000

Accounts credited for operating expenses other than depreciation:

Cash	$3,860,000
Allowance for Uncollectibles	100,000
Accounts Payable	150,000
Inventories	180,000
Donated Services	50,000

3. Contractual adjustments of $180,000 are allowed as deductions from gross patient revenues.

4. A transfer of $160,000 is received from specific-purpose funds. This transfer is for payment of approved operating costs in accordance with the terms of the restricted grant.

5. Eden receives $125,000 of unrestricted gifts.

6. Accounts receivable are collected except for $65,000 written off.

Required

a. Prepare journal entries in the general fund for each of the transactions.

b. Prepare the statement of revenue and expenses for the general fund of Eden Hospital.

E21-3   Entries for Other Hospital Funds

The following are selected transactions of the specific-purpose fund, the plant fund, and the endowment fund of Eden Hospital:

1. The endowment fund received new permanent endowments totaling $240,000 and new term endowments totaling $80,000.

2. The plant replacement and expansion fund received pledges of $1,800,000 for the new wing. Uncollectibles were estimated at 15 percent.

3. The specific-purpose fund received gifts of $65,000 for research and $25,000 for education.

4. Interest and dividends received on investments were:

Endowment fund (permanent)	$120,000
Plant fund	50,000
Specific-purpose fund (research)	24,000

5. The specific-purpose fund was notified that the general fund fulfilled the agreements related to restricted gifts as follows:

Research	75,000
Education	25,000

Cash of $60,000 was transferred to the general fund, with the balance to be sent later.

6. Investments made:

Endowment fund	$300,000
Plant fund	200,000
Specific-purpose fund	80,000

Required

Prepare journal entries for the transactions in the specific-purpose fund, plant fund, and endowment fund, as appropriate.

E21-4   Multiple-Choice Questions on Voluntary Health and Welfare Organization Accounting [AICPA Adapted]

Select the correct answer for each of the following questions.

1. Which basis of accounting should a voluntary health and welfare organization use?
   a. Cash basis for all funds.
   b. Modified accrual basis for all funds.
   c. Accrual basis for all funds.
   d. Accrual basis for some funds and modified accrual basis for other funds.

Questions 2 and 3 are based on the following data:

Morgan Service Center is a voluntary welfare organization funded by contributions from the general public. During 19X3, unrestricted pledges of $900,000 were received, half of which were payable in 19X3, with the other half payable in 19X4 for use in 19X4. It was estimated that 10 percent of these pledges would be uncollectible. In addition, Helen Ladd, a social worker on Morgan's permanent staff, earning $20,000 annually for a normal workload of 2,000 hours, contributed an additional 800 hours of her time to Morgan at no charge.

2. How much should Morgan report as net contribution support for 19X3 with respect to the pledges?
   a. $0.
   b. $405,000.
   c. $810,000.
   d. $900,000.

3. How much should Morgan record in 19X3 for contributed service expenses?
   a. $0.
   b. $800.
   c. $4,000.
   d. $8,000.

4. A voluntary health and welfare organization received a pledge in 19X1 from a donor specifying that the amount pledged be used in 19X3. The donor paid the pledge in cash in 19X2. The pledge should be accounted for as:
   a. A deferred credit in the balance sheet at the end of 19X1 and as support in 19X2.
   b. A deferred credit in the balance sheet at the end of 19X1 and as support in 19X3.
   c. Support in 19X1.
   d. Support in 19X2 and *no* deferred credit in the balance sheet at the end of 19X1.

5. Beacon Fund, a voluntary welfare organization funded by contributions from the general public, received unrestricted pledges of $200,000 during 19X2. It was estimated that 10 percent of these pledges would be uncollectible. By the end of 19X2, $130,000 of the pledges had been collected. It was expected that $50,000 more would be collected in

19X3 and that the balance of $20,000 would be written off as uncollectible. What amount should Beacon include under public support in 19X2 for net contributions?

    a. $200,000.

    b. $180,000.

    c. $150,000.

    d. $130,000.

Items 6 through 8 are based on the following:

In 19X0, Community Helpers, a voluntary health and welfare organization, received a bequest of a $100,000 certificate of deposit maturing in 19X5. The testator's only stipulations were that this certificate be held until maturity and that the interest revenue be used to finance salaries for a preschool program. Interest revenue for 19X5 was $8,000. When the certificate was redeemed, the board of trustees adopted a formal resolution designating $20,000 of the proceeds for the future purchase of equipment for the preschool program.

6. In regard to the certificate of deposit, what should be reported in the Endowment Fund column of the 19X5 statement of support, revenue, and expenses and changes in fund balances?

    a. Legacies and bequests, $100,000.

    b. Direct reduction of fund balance for transfer to current unrestricted fund, $100,000.

    c. Transfer to land, building, and equipment fund, $20,000.

    d. Revenues control, $100,000.

7. What should be reported in the Current Unrestricted Funds column of the 19X5 statement of support, revenue, and expenses and changes in fund balances?

    a. Investment income, $8,000.

    b. Direct reduction of fund balance for transfer to land, building, and equipment fund, $20,000.

    c. Direct addition to fund balance for transfer from endowment fund, $100,000.

    d. Public support, $108,000.

8. What should be reported in the 19X5 year-end current unrestricted funds balance sheet?

    a. Fund balance designated for preschool program, $28,000; undesignated fund balance, $80,000.

    b. Fund balance designated for purchase of equipment, $20,000; undesignated fund balance, $80,000.

    c. Fund balance designated for preschool program salaries, $8,000; undesignated fund balance, $80,000.

    d. Undesignated fund balance, $72,000.

9. In a statement of support, revenue, and expenses and changes in fund balances of a voluntary health and welfare organization, depreciation expense should:

    a. Be included as an element of expense.

    b. Be included as an element of other changes in fund balances.

    c. Be included as an element of support.

    d. Not be included.

E21-5 Entries for Voluntary Health and Welfare Organizations

The following are the 19X2 transactions of the Midwest Heart Association, which has the following funds and fund balances on January 1, 19X2:

Current unrestricted fund	$281,000
Current restricted fund	87,000
Land, buildings, and equipment fund	163,000
Endowment fund	219,000

1. Unrestricted pledges total $700,000, of which $150,000 are for future years. Uncollectible pledges are estimated at 8 percent.

2. Restricted grants total $150,000, of which $50,000 are for future years.

3. A total of $520,000 of current pledges are collected, and $30,000 of remaining uncollected current pledges are written off.

4. The land, buildings, and equipment fund spends $9,300 for office equipment.

5. The current unrestricted fund pays $3,000 for the mortgage payment due on the buildings. The land, buildings, and equipment fund is responsible for servicing the debt associated with fixed assets.

6. Interest and dividends received are $27,200 on unrestricted investments and $5,400 on restricted investments. An endowment investment with a recorded value of $5,000 is sold for $6,000, resulting in a realized transaction gain of $1,000.

7. Depreciation is recorded and allocated as follows:

Community services	$ 12,000
Public health education	7,000
Research	10,000
Fund-raising	15,000
General and administrative	9,000

8. Other operating costs of the unrestricted current fund are:

Community services	$250,600
Public health education	100,000
Research	81,000
Fund-raising	39,000
General and administrative	61,000

9. Clerical services donated during the fund drive total $2,400. These are not part of the expenses reported in item 8. It has been determined that these donated services should be recorded.

Required

a. Prepare journal entries for the transactions in the two current funds, the land, buildings, and equipment fund, and the endowment fund.

b. Prepare a statement of support, revenue, and expenses and changes in fund balances for 19X2.

E21-6 Multiple-Choice Questions on Other Nonprofit Organizations [AICPA Adapted]

Select the correct answer for each of the following questions.

1. On January 2, 19X2, a nonprofit botanical society received a gift of an exhaustible fixed asset with an estimated useful life of 10 years and no salvage value. The donor's cost of this asset was $20,000, and its fair market value at the date of the gift was $30,000. What amount of depreciation of this asset should the society recognize in its 19X2 financial statements?

a. $3,000.
b. $2,500.
c. $2,000.
d. $0.

2. In 19X1, a nonprofit trade association enrolled five new member companies, each of which was obligated to pay nonrefundable initiation fees of $1,000. These fees were receivable by the association in 19X1. Three of the new members paid the initiation fees in 19X1, and the other two new members paid their initiation fees in 19X2. Annual dues (excluding initiation fees) received by the association from all of its members have always covered the organization's costs of services provided to its members. It can be reasonably expected that future dues will cover all costs of the organization's future services to members. Average membership duration is 10 years because of mergers, attrition, and economic factors. What amount of initiation fees from these five new members should the association recognize as revenue in 19X1?

a. $5,000.
b. $3,000.
c. $500.
d. $0.

3. Roberts Foundation received a nonexpendable endowment of $500,000 in 19X3 from Multi Enterprises. The endowment assets were invested in publicly traded securities. Multi did not specify how gains and losses from dispositions of endowment assets were to be treated. No restrictions were placed on the use of dividends received and interest earned on fund resources. In 19X4, Roberts realized gains of $50,000 on sales of fund investments, and received total interest and dividends of $40,000 on fund securities. The amount of these capital gains, interest, and dividends available for expenditure by Roberts's unrestricted current fund is:

a. $0.
b. $40,000.
c. $50,000.
d. $90,000.

4. In July 19X2, Ross donated $200,000 cash to a church with the stipulation that the revenue generated from this gift be paid to him during his lifetime. The conditions of this donation are that after Ross dies, the principal may be used by the church for any purpose voted on by the church elders. The church received interest of $16,000 on the $200,000 for the year ended June 30, 19X3, and the interest was remitted to Ross. In the church's June 30, 19X3 annual financial statements:

a. $200,000 should be reported as deferred support in the balance sheet.
b. $184,000 should be reported under support and revenue in the activity statement.
c. $16,000 should be reported under support and revenue in the activity statement.
d. The gift and its terms should be disclosed only in notes to the financial statements.

5. The following expenditures were among those incurred by a nonprofit botanical society during 19X4:

Printing of annual report	$10,000
Unsolicited merchandise sent to encourage contributions	20,000

What amount should be classified as fund-raising costs in the society's activity statement?

a. $0.
b. $10,000.
c. $20,000.
d. $30,000.

6. Birdlovers, a community foundation, incurred $5,000 in management and general expenses during 19X1. In Birdlovers' statement of revenue, expenses, and changes in fund balance for the year ended December 31, 19X1, the $5,000 should be reported as:
   a. A contra account offsetting revenue and support.
   b. Part of program services.
   c. Part of supporting services.
   d. A direct reduction of fund balance.

7. In 19X3, the board of trustees of Burr Foundation designated $100,000 from its current funds for college scholarships. Also in 19X3, the foundation received a bequest of $200,000 from an estate of a benefactor who specified that the bequest was to be used for hiring teachers to tutor handicapped students. What amount should be accounted for as current restricted funds?
   a. $0.
   b. $100,000.
   c. $200,000.
   d. $300,000.

Items 8 through 10 are based on the following information:

United Together, a labor union, had the following receipts and expenses for the year ended December 31, 19X2:

Receipts:	
Per capita dues	$680,000
Initiation fees	90,000
Sales of organizational supplies	60,000
Nonexpendable gift restricted by donor for loan purposes for 10 years	30,000
Nonexpendable gift restricted by donor for loan purposes in perpetuity	25,000
Expenses:	
Labor negotiations	500,000
Fund-raising	100,000
Membership development	50,000
Administrative and general	200,000

Additional information:

The union's constitution provides that 10 percent of the per capita dues are designated for the strike insurance fund to be distributed for strike relief at the discretion of the union's executive board.

8. In United Together's statement of activity for the year ended December 31, 19X2, what amount should be reported under the classification of revenue for both undesignated and designated funds?
   a. $740,000.
   b. $762,000.
   c. $770,000.
   d. $830,000.

9. In United Together's statement of activity for the year ended December 31, 19X2, what amount should be reported under the classification of program services?
   a. $850,000.
   b. $600,000.
   c. $550,000.
   d. $500,000.

10. In United Together's statement of activity for the year ended December 31, 19X2, what amount should be reported under the classification of capital additions?
   a. $55,000.
   b. $30,000.
   c. $25,000.
   d. $0.

E21-7   Statement of Activity for an Other Nonprofit Organization

The following is a list of selected account balances in the unrestricted operating fund for the Pleasant School:

	Debit	Credit
Fund Balance, July 1, 19X1		$ 420,000
Tuition and Fees		1,200,000
Contributions		165,000
Auxiliary Activities Revenue		40,000
Investment Income		32,000
Other Revenue		38,000
Instruction	$1,050,000	
Auxiliary Activities Expenses	37,000	
Administration	250,000	
Fund-Raising	28,000	
Transfer to Plant Funds	130,000	
Transfer from Endowment Funds		12,000

Required

Prepare a statement of activity for the unrestricted operating fund of the Pleasant School for the year ended June 30, 19X2.

PROBLEMS

P21-8 Hospital Worksheet [AICPA Adapted]

Riverwood Hospital's postclosing trial balance at December 31, 19X8, is as follows:

	Debits	Credits
Cash	$ 60,000	
Investment in U.S. Treasury Bills	400,000	
Investment in Corporate Bonds	500,000	
Interest Receivable	10,000	
Accounts Receivable	50,000	
Inventory	30,000	
Land	100,000	
Building	800,000	
Equipment	170,000	
Allowance for Depreciation		$ 410,000
Accounts Payable		20,000
Notes Payable		70,000
Endowment Fund Balance		520,000
Other Fund Balances		1,100,000
	$2,120,000	$2,120,000

Riverwood, which is a nonprofit hospital, did not maintain its books in conformity with the principles of hospital fund accounting. Effective January 1, 19X9, Riverwood's board of trustees voted to adjust the December 31, 19X8, general ledger balances, and to establish separate funds for the general fund, the endowment funds, and the plant replacement and expansion fund.

Additional account information:

1. "Investment in Corporate Bonds" pertains to the amount required to be accumulated under a board policy to invest cash equal to accumulated depreciation until the funds are needed for asset replacement. The $500,000 balance at December 31, 19X8, is less than the full amount required because of errors in computation of building depreciation for past years. Included in the allowance for depreciation is a correctly computed amount of $90,000 applicable to the equipment.

2. Endowment Fund Balance has been credited with the following:

Donor's bequest of cash	$300,000
Gains on sales of securities	100,000
Interest and dividends earned in 19X6, 19X7, and 19X8	120,000
Total	$520,000

The terms of the bequest specify that the principal, plus all gains on sales of investments, is to remain fully invested in U.S. government or corporate securities. At December 31, 19X8, $400,000 was invested in U.S. Treasury bills. The bequest further specifies that interest and dividends earned on investments are to be used for payment of current operating expenses.

3. Land comprises the following:

Donation of land in 19X0, at appraised value	$ 40,000
Appreciation in fair value of land, determined by independent appraiser in 19X4	60,000
Total	$100,000

4. Building comprises the following:

Hospital building completed 40 years ago, when operations were started (estimated useful life of 50 years), at cost	$720,000
Installation of elevator 20 years ago (estimated useful life of 20 years), at cost	80,000
Total	$800,000

Required

Prepare a workpaper with the format presented below. Enter the adjustments necessary to restate the general ledger account balance properly. Distribute the adjusted balances to separate fund accounts, and complete the workpaper. Formal journal entries are not required, but supporting computations should be referenced to the workpaper adjustments.

Riverwood Hospital
Workpaper to Adjust General Ledger Balances
and to Establish Funds
January 1, 19X9

Account	Trial Balance Dec. 31, 19X8	Adjustments Debits	Adjustments Credits	General Fund	Endowment Fund	Plant Replacement and Expansion Fund
Cash	60,000					
Investment in U.S. Treasury Bills	400,000					
Investment in Corporate Bonds	500,000					
Interest Receivable	10,000					
Accounts Receivable	50,000					
Inventory	30,000					
Land	100,000					
Building	800,000					
Equipment	170,000					
Debits	2,120,000					
Allowance for Depreciation	410,000					
Accounts Payable	20,000					
Notes Payable	70,000					
Endowment Fund Balance	520,000					
Other Fund Balances	1,100,000					
Credits	2,120,000					

P21-9 Entries and Statement of Activity for an Other Nonprofit Organization
[AICPA Adapted]

In 1950 a group of civic-minded merchants in Eldora organized the "Committee of 100" for the purpose of establishing the Community Sports Club, a nonprofit sports organization for local youth. Each of the committee's 100 members contributed $1,000 toward the club's capital and in turn received a participation certificate. In addition, each participant agreed to pay dues of $200 a year for the club's operations. All dues have been collected in full by the end of each fiscal year ending March 31. Members who have discontinued their participation have been replaced by an equal number of new members through transfer of the participation certificates from the former members to the new ones. Following is the club's trial balance for April 1, 19X2:

	Debit	Credit
Cash	$ 9,000	
Investments (at market, equal to cost)	58,000	
Inventories	5,000	
Land	10,000	
Building	164,000	
Accumulated Depreciation—Building		$130,000
Furniture and Equipment	54,000	
Accumulated Depreciation— Furniture and Equipment		46,000
Accounts Payable		12,000
Participation Certificates (100 at $1,000 each)		100,000
Cumulative Excess of Revenue over Expenses		12,000
	$300,000	$300,000

Transactions for the year ended March 31, 19X3, were as follows:

Collections from participants for dues	$20,000
Snack bar and soda fountain sales	28,000
Interest and dividends received	6,000
Additions to voucher register:	
House expenses	17,000
Snack bar and soda fountain	26,000
General and administrative	11,000
Vouchers paid	55,000
Assessments for capital improvements not yet incurred (assessed on March 20, 19X3; none collected by March 31, 19X3; deemed 100% collectible during year ending March 31, 19X4)	10,000
Unrestricted bequest received	5,000

Adjustment data:

1. Investments are valued at market, which amounted to $65,000 on March 31, 19X3. There were no investment transactions during the year.
2. Depreciation for year:

Building	$4,000
Furniture and equipment	8,000

3. Allocation of depreciation:

House expenses	$9,000
Snack bar and soda fountain	2,000
General and administrative	1,000

4. Actual physical inventory on March 31, 19X3, was $1,000 and pertains to the snack bar and soda fountain.

Required

a. Record the transactions and adjustments in journal entry form for the year ended March 31, 19X3. Omit explanations.
b. Prepare the appropriate all-inclusive activity statement for the year ended March 31, 19X3.

P21-10   Balance Sheet and Entries for a Hospital [AICPA Adapted]

You have been hired to provide accounting assistance to Grace Hospital. The December 31, 19X1, balance sheet was prepared by a bookkeeper who thought hospitals reported funds as follows:

Grace Hospital
Balance Sheet
As of December 31, 19X1

Assets			Liabilities and Fund Balances		

General Fund

Cash		$ 20,000	Accounts Payable		$ 16,000
Accounts Receivable	$ 37,000		Accrued Expenses		6,000
Less: Allowance for Uncollectible			Total Liabilities		$ 22,000
Accounts	(7,000)	30,000			
Inventory of Supplies		14,000	Fund Balance		42,000
Total		$ 64,000	Total		$ 64,000

Plant Fund

			Mortgage Bonds		
Cash		$ 53,800	Payable		$ 150,000
Investments		71,200	Fund Balance:		
Land		400,000	Investment in Plant		$2,021,000
Buildings	$1,750,000		Reserved for Plant Improvement		
Less: Accumulated Depreciation	(430,000)	1,320,000	and Replacement		220,000
Equipment	$ 680,000				$2,241,000
Less: Accumulated Depreciation	(134,000)	546,000			
Total		$2,391,000	Total		$2,391,000

Endowment Fund

Cash		$ 6,000	Fund Balance		$ 266,000
Investments		260,000			
Total		$ 266,000	Total		$ 266,000

During 19X2, the following transactions occurred:

1. Gross charges for patient services, all charged to Accounts Receivable, were as follows:

Room and board charges	$780,000
Charges for other professional services	321,000

2. Deductions from gross earnings were as follows:

Contractual adjustments	$15,000

3. The general fund paid $18,000 to retire mortgage bonds payable with an equivalent fair value.

4. During the year, the general fund received general contributions of $50,000 and income from endowment fund investments of $6,500. The general fund has been designated to receive income earned on endowment fund investments.

5. New equipment costing $26,000 was acquired from general fund resources. The plant replacement and expansion fund reimbursed the general fund for the $26,000. An X-ray machine which originally cost $24,000 and which had an undepreciated cost of $2,400 was sold for $500.

6. Vouchers totaling $1,191,000 were issued for the following items:

Administrative service expense	$120,000
Fiscal service expense	95,000
General service expense	225,000
Nursing service expense	520,000
Other professional service expense	165,000
Supplies	60,000
Expenses accrued as of December 31, 19X1	6,000

7. The provision for uncollectible accounts is increased by $30,000. Collections on accounts receivable totaled $985,000. Accounts written off as uncollectible amounted to $11,000.

8. Cash payments on vouchers payable during the year were $825,000.

9. Supplies of $37,000 were issued to nursing services.

10. On December 31, 19X2, accrued interest income on plant fund investments was $800.

11. Depreciation of buildings and equipment was as follows:

Buildings	$44,000
Equipment	73,000

12. On December 31, 19X2, an accrual of $6,100 was made for fiscal service expense on mortgage bonds.

Required

a. Restate the balance sheet of Grace Hospital as of December 31, 19X1, to reflect the fact that hospitals do not have an investment in plant funds. (*Hint*: The $53,800 cash and $71,200 investments belong to a restricted plant replacement and expansion fund, and the other assets reported in the plant fund are properly included in the general fund.)

b. Prepare journal entries to record the transactions for 19X2 in the general fund, the plant replacement and expansion fund, and the endowment fund. Assume that the plant fund balances have been transferred to the appropriate funds as indicated in part **a** of this problem. Omit explanations.

P21-11 Entries and Statements for General Fund of a Hospital

The postclosing trial balance of the general fund of Serene Hospital on December 31, 19X1, was:

	Debit	Credit
Cash	$ 125,000	
Accounts Receivable	400,000	
Allowance for Uncollectibles		$ 50,000
Due from Specific-Purpose Fund	40,000	
Inventories	95,000	
Prepaid Expenses	20,000	
Investments	900,000	
Property, Plant, and Equipment	6,100,000	
Accumulated Depreciation		1,500,000
Accounts Payable		150,000
Accrued Expenses		55,000
Deferred Revenue—Reimbursement		75,000
Bonds Payable		3,000,000
Fund Balance		2,850,000
	$7,680,000	$7,680,000

During 19X2 the following transactions occurred:

1. The value of patient services provided was $6,160,000.
2. Contractual adjustments of $330,000 from patients' bills were approved.
3. Operating expenses totaled $5,600,000, as follows:

Nursing services	$1,800,000
Other professional services	1,200,000
Fiscal services	250,000
General services	1,550,000
Bad debts	120,000
Administration	280,000
Depreciation	400,000

Accounts credited for operating expenses other than depreciation:

Cash	$4,580,000
Allowance for Uncollectibles	120,000
Accounts Payable	170,000
Accrued Expenses	35,000
Inventories	195,000
Prepaid Expenses	30,000
Donated Services	70,000

4. Received $75,000 cash from specific-purpose fund for partial reimbursement of $100,000 for operating expenditures made in accordance with a restricted gift. The receivable increased by the remaining $25,000 to an ending balance of $65,000.
5. Payments for inventories were $176,000 and for prepaid expenses were $24,000.
6. Received $85,000 income from endowment fund investments.
7. Sold an X-ray machine that had cost $30,000 and had accumulated depreciation of $20,000 for $17,000.
8. Collected $5,800,000 receivables and wrote off $132,000.
9. Acquired investments amounting to $60,000.
10. Income from board-designated investments was $72,000.
11. Paid the beginning balance in Accounts Payable and Accrued Expenses.
12. Deferred Revenue—Reimbursement increased $20,000.

13. Received $140,000 from the plant replacement and expansion fund for use in acquiring fixed assets.

14. Net receipts from the cafeteria and gift shop were $63,000.

Required

a. Prepare journal entries to record the transactions for the general fund. Omit explanations.

b. Prepare a comparative balance sheet for the general fund for 19X2 and 19X1.

c. Prepare a statement of revenue and expenses of the general fund for 19X2. Include changes in the fund balance at the bottom of the statement.

d. Prepare a statement of cash flows for the general fund for 19X2.

P21-12   Statements for Current Funds of a Voluntary Health and Welfare Organization [AICPA Adapted]

Following are the adjusted current funds trial balances of Community Association for Handicapped Children, a voluntary health and welfare organization, on June 30, 19X4:

Community Association for Handicapped Children
Adjusted Current Funds Trial Balances
June 30, 19X4

	Unrestricted		Restricted	
	Debit	**Credit**	**Debit**	**Credit**
Cash	$ 40,000		$ 9,000	
Bequest Receivable			5,000	
Pledges Receivable	12,000			
Accrued Interest Receivable	1,000			
Investments (at cost, which approximates market)	100,000			
Accounts Payable and Accrued Expenses		$ 50,000		$ 1,000
Deferred Revenue		2,000		
Allowance for Uncollectible Pledges		3,000		
Fund Balances, July 1, 19X3:				
Designated		12,000		
Undesignated		26,000		
Restricted				3,000
Transfers of Expired Endowment Fund Principal		20,000		
Contributions		300,000		15,000
Membership Dues		25,000		
Program Service Fees		30,000		
Investment Income		10,000		
Deaf Children's Program Expenses	120,000			
Blind Children's Program Expenses	150,000			
Management and General Services	45,000		4,000	
Fund-Raising Services	8,000		1,000	
Provision for Uncollectible Pledges	2,000			
	$478,000	$478,000	$19,000	$19,000

Required

    a. Prepare a statement of support, revenue, expenses, and changes in fund balances, separately presenting each current fund, for the year ended June 30, 19X4.

    b. Prepare a balance sheet separately presenting each current fund as of June 30, 19X4. Use the "pancake," or layered, format for the balance sheet.

P21-13 Workpaper for Transactions of a Voluntary Health and Welfare Organization [AICPA Adapted]

    Children's Agency, a voluntary health and welfare organization, conducts two programs: a medical services program and a community information services program. It had the following transactions during the year ended June 30, 19X2:

    1. Received the following contributions:

Unrestricted pledges	$800,000
Restricted cash	95,000
Building fund pledges	50,000
Endowment fund cash	1,000

    2. Collected the following pledges:

Unrestricted	450,000
Building fund	20,000

    3. Received the following unrestricted cash revenues:

From theater party (net of direct costs)	12,000
Bequests	10,000
Membership dues	8,000
Interest and dividends	5,000

    4. Program expenses incurred (processed through vouchers payable):

Medical services	60,000
Community information services	15,000

    5. Services expenses incurred (processed through vouchers payable):

General administration	150,000
Fund-raising	200,000

    6. Fixed assets purchased with unrestricted cash   18,000

    7. Depreciation of all buildings and equipment in the land, buildings, and equipment fund was allocated as follows:

Medical services program	4,000
Community information services program	3,000
General administration	6,000
Fund raising	2,000

8. Paid vouchers payable 330,000

Required

Prepare a workpaper with the column headings presented below. Record the journal entries (without explanations) for the preceding transactions. With credit amounts placed in parentheses, insert the amounts in the proper columns for each of the following funds:

Current fund—unrestricted
Current fund—restricted
Land, buildings, and equipment fund
Endowment fund

Number the journal entries to coincide with the transaction numbers indicated.

Children's Agency
Journal Entries
For the Year Ended June 30, 19X2

Account Title	Current Fund Unrestricted Dr.	Cr.	Restricted Dr.	Cr.	Land, Buildings, and Equipment Fund Dr.	Cr.	Endowment Fund Dr.	Cr.

P21-14 Comparative Journal Entries for a Government Entity and a Voluntary Health and Welfare Organization [AICPA Adapted]

Listed below are four independent transactions or events that relate to a local government and to a voluntary health and welfare organization:

1. A disbursement of $25,000 was made from the general fund (or its equivalent) for the cash purchase of new equipment.
2. An unrestricted cash gift of $100,000 was received from a donor.
3. Listed common stocks with a total carrying value of $50,000, exclusive of any allowance, were sold by an endowment fund for $55,000, before any dividends were earned on these stocks. There are no restrictions on the gain.
4. General obligation bonds payable with a face amount of $1,000,000 were sold at par, with the proceeds required to be used solely for construction of a new building. This building was completed at a total cost of $1,000,000, and the total amount of bond issue proceeds was disbursed toward this cost. Disregard interest capitalization.

Required

a. For each of the above-listed transactions or events, prepare journal entries, without explanations, specifying the affected funds and account groups and showing how these transactions or events should be recorded by a local government whose debt is serviced by general tax revenue.

b. For each of the above-listed transactions or events, prepare journal entries, without explanations, specifying the affected funds and showing how these transactions or events should be recorded by a voluntary health and welfare organization that maintains a separate land, building, and equipment fund. The voluntary health and welfare organization uses temporary "transfer in" and "transfer out" accounts for interfund transactions affecting fund balances.

CHAPTER 22

CORPORATIONS IN FINANCIAL DIFFICULTY

A life cycle exists for businesses as for individuals. The business press carries stories daily of companies in financial difficulty and management's actions necessary in these companies, including, in some cases, the final action of corporate bankruptcy. In 1990, one of the low points of the economic recession that began in 1989, over 60,000 industrial and commercial businesses failed. This was a 20 percent increase over the average annual number of business failures during 1987–89. Untold thousands of other companies used alternate courses of action, such as debt restructuring and agreements with creditors, in order to work themselves out of financial difficulty.

Companies get into financial difficulty for a large variety of reasons. A company may suffer from continued losses from operations, overextended credit to customers, poor management of working capital, failure to react to changes in economic conditions, inadequate financing, and a host of other reasons for not sustaining a viable economic position. A company's liquidity problems often become cumulative. Failing to make a sufficient level of sales, a company cannot obtain adequate financing, then begins to miss debt payments, and the vicious cycle of financial difficulty is under way. At this point, outside creditors may decide to exercise their claims and demand payment of their debts. The debtor company has a number of alternative courses open to it. It may try to reach an agreement with its creditors to postpone required payments, it may turn its assets over to its creditors to liquidate, or it may take the legal remedy of bankruptcy.

A company may petition the courts for bankruptcy for other reasons, such as to protect itself from an onslaught of legal suits. Several companies have also attempted to void union contracts by petitioning for bankruptcy. The courts are still defining the exact limits of bankruptcy, and each case must be decided individually.

Insolvency is defined as a condition in which a company is unable to meet debts as the debts mature. The insolvent company is unable to meet its liabilities. Before 1978, creditors had to show that the debtor was insolvent before they could petition for relief in a bankruptcy court. Because of changes in the bankruptcy law in 1978, insolvency is no longer a necessary pre-condition for bankruptcy.

A company in financial difficulty has a large number of alternatives, of which bankruptcy is only a final course. This chapter presents the range of major actions typically used by a company experiencing financial problems.

COURSES OF ACTION

Bankruptcy is the final step for a financially distressed business. Prior to that, however, management usually tries to work closely with the company's creditors to provide for the creditors' claims while also attempting to ensure the continuing existence of the firm. A variety of nonjudicial arrangements with creditors are available. If these fail, the company usually ends up in a judicial action under the direction of a bankruptcy court.

Nonjudicial Actions

Formal agreements between the company and its creditors are legally binding but are not administered by a court. The major nonjudicial actions include debt restructuring and voluntary asset assignments.

Debt Restructuring Arrangements   Arrangements between a debtor company and one or more of its creditors are common for companies in temporary financial difficulty. The debtor may solicit an extension of due dates of its debt, ask for a decrease of the interest rate on the debt, or ask for a modification of other terms of the debt contract. Creditors are usually willing to extend concessions to a debtor rather than risk the legal expense and ill will from legal action against a previously valuable debtor. Many banks, for example, prefer to continue to work with a customer who is in temporary financial difficulty rather than force that customer into bankruptcy. Experience has shown that banks eventually realize a larger portion of their receivable, and continue to have a future customer, if they assist the debtor with financial problems by restructuring the debt. Accounting for these *troubled debt restructurings* is presented in **FASB Statement No. 15**, "Accounting by Debtors and Creditors for Troubled Debt Restructurings" (FASB 15), issued in 1977. Examples of troubled debt restructurings are presented later in this chapter.

Another form of debt restructuring arrangement is the *composition agreement*. In this case, creditors agree to accept less than the face amount of their claims. The advantage to the creditors is that they receive an immediate cash payment and usually negotiate the timing of the remaining cash payments. Although creditors receive less than the full amount, they are assured of receiving most of their receivables. Composition agreements typically involve all the creditors, although some creditors may not be willing to agree to the composition. In some cases, the consenting group of creditors agree to allow the dissenting creditors to be paid in full if it means the debtor can return to profitable operations. Accounting for composition agreements is also covered by **FASB 15.**

Creditors' Committee Management Under *creditors' committee management*, the creditors may agree to assist the debtor in managing the most efficient payment of creditors' claims. Most creditors' committees are advisory and counsel closely with the debtor because the creditors do not want to assume additional liabilities and problems of actual operation of the debtor. Forming a creditors' committee is a nonjudicial action usually initiated with a *plan of settlement* proposed by the debtor. The plan of settlement is a detailed document that includes a schedule of payments listing the specific debts and the anticipated payments. The creditors then work closely with the debtor to enact the plan.

In some extreme cases, creditors may decide to assume operating control of the debtor company. The creditors appoint a trustee who assumes management responsibility for the debtor company. The trustee reports to the creditors with recommendations for the eventual settlement of claims. The trustee may attempt to work out a payment schedule or may recommend bankruptcy as the best alternative. The advantage of the creditors' committee management in these extreme cases is that creditors have operating control of the debtor and receive a full report of the debtor's financial condition. The disadvantage to the creditors of assuming operating control is that they incur a greater risk if the debtor enters bankruptcy because, as managers before the bankruptcy, they may be held responsible. The advantage to the debtor is that the creditors are attempting to assist the debtor out of its financial difficulty and may return operating control once the financial problems are solved, without resorting to legal action.

Voluntary Asset Assignment A voluntary asset agreement is the placement of the debtor's assets under the control of a trustee appointed by the creditors. The trustee then sells the assets and liquidates the debts. The advantage of a voluntary asset assignment is that the debtor avoids the legal costs and reporting requirements of a judicial bankruptcy. However, a voluntary asset assignment does result in the liquidation of a company's assets.

Judicial Actions

Bankruptcy is a judicial action administered by bankruptcy courts and bankruptcy judges under the Bankruptcy Reform Act of 1978. The Bankruptcy Act is composed of eight chapters, numbered as follows:

Chapter 1 General Provisions
Chapter 3 Case Administration
Chapter 5 Creditors, the Debtor, and the Estate
Chapter 7 Liquidation
Chapter 9 Adjustment of Debts of a Municipality

Chapter 11 Reorganization
Chapter 13 Adjustment of Debts of an Individual with Regular Income
Chapter 15 United States Trustees

Chapters 1, 3, and 5 present the definitions and operating provisions of the act. Chapters 7 and 11 deal with corporations. Chapter 9 deals with municipal governments and Chapter 13 with individual bankruptcies. Chapter 15 provides for the appointment of trustees to assist bankruptcy judges with the administration of the act.

Either the debtor or its creditors may decide that a judicial action is best in the individual circumstances. The debtor may file a *voluntary petition* seeking judicial protection in the form of an **order of relief** against the initiation or continuation of legal claims by the creditors against the debtor. Alternatively, creditors may file an *involuntary petition* against the debtor. Certain conditions must exist before creditors may file a petition. First, with regard to the debtor, the debtor is generally not paying debts as they become due, or within the last 120 days a custodian has been appointed by other creditors, by the debtor, or by some other agency to take possession of the debtor's assets. Second, with regard to creditors, if more than 12 creditors exist, then 3 or more must combine to file the petition, and these must have aggregate unsecured claims of at least $5,000.

Once a petition is filed, the bankruptcy court evaluates the company and determines if present management should continue to manage the company or if a trustee should be appointed by the court. Appointments of trustees are common whenever creditors make allegations of management fraud or gross management incompetence.

The Bankruptcy Reform Act provides for two major alternatives under the protection of the bankruptcy court. These two alternatives are often known by the chapters of the Bankruptcy Act. The first is **reorganization under Chapter 11**, in which the debtor is provided judicial protection for a rehabilitation period during which it can eliminate unprofitable operations, obtain new credit, develop a new company structure with sustainable operations, and work out agreements with its creditors. The second alternative is a **liquidation under Chapter 7** of the Bankruptcy Act. A Chapter 7 liquidation is often administered by a trustee appointed by the court. The debtor's assets are sold and its liabilities extinguished as the business is liquidated. The major difference between a reorganization and a liquidation is that the debtor continues as a business after a reorganization, whereas the business does not survive a liquidation. Both of these alternatives are illustrated later in the chapter. First, the accounting for troubled debt restructurings, a common initial procedure for companies in financial difficulty, is presented.

TROUBLED DEBT RESTRUCTURING

FASB 15 prescribes the accounting for troubled debt restructurings. Not all renegotiations of debt covenants are covered by this standard; the restructuring must be a concession granted by a creditor to a debtor in financial difficulties.

Renegotiations between a debtor and a creditor because of changes in the competitive general economic environment are not troubled debt restructurings and are not included in this standard.

The most common form of troubled debt restructuring is a modification of the debt terms to alleviate the short-term cash needs of the debtor. For example, the creditor may reduce the current interest rate, forgive some of the accrued interest or principal, or modify some other term of the debt agreement. Another common form of troubled debt restructuring is the creditor's acceptance of assets or equity with a fair value less than the amount of the debt, because the creditor feels it is the best alternative to maximize recoverability of the receivable from the debtor in financial difficulty. For example, the creditor may accept land with a fair value of $50,000 in exchange for extinguishing a debt of $65,000, because the creditor feels the $50,000 is the maximum amount it will be able to collect. The key issue is how to account for and report the troubled debt restructuring on the books of the creditor and the debtor companies.

FASB 15 specifies that the carrying value of the debt must be compared with the total future cash flows related to the debt, or with the fair value of the consideration exchanged in extinguishment of that debt. This comparison is made to determine if a gain or loss should be recognized on the transaction as follows:

$$\text{Restructuring difference} = \text{CV} - \text{TFCF} \quad or \quad \text{CV} - \text{FV}$$

$$
\begin{aligned}
\text{where} \quad \text{CV} &= \text{carrying value of the debt} \\
\text{TFCF} &= \text{total future cash flows} \\
\text{FV} &= \text{fair value of noncash items}
\end{aligned}
$$

The carrying value of the debt is the book value of the debt on the books of the creditor or debtor plus accrued interest as of the date of the restructuring. If the debtor and creditor agree to extinguish the current debt through an immediate payment of cash, transfer of noncash assets, or transfer of an equity interest, a *restructuring difference* is computed as the difference between the carrying value of the debt and the fair value of the consideration exchanged. The debtor recognizes a gain and the creditor a loss for the amount of the restructuring difference. The debtor's gain, if material, should be reported as an extraordinary gain in its income statement. The debtor's legal fees and other direct costs incurred are accounted for in the following manner: if an equity interest is transferred, the fees and direct costs incurred reduce the amount recorded for the equity interest; in other restructurings, the fees and direct costs are deducted in measuring the gain on the restructuring.

A creditor typically provides for uncollectibles with an allowance for uncollectibles and the creditor's restructuring loss is charged against the allowance. If the creditor has not anticipated adequately for uncollectibles, the restructuring difference is reported by the creditor as a loss for the period. The creditor's legal expenses and other costs associated with preparing the agreement should be recognized as an operating expense of the period.

In a debt restructuring involving a modification of terms, the total future cash flows are the aggregate of all cash payments after the restructuring takes place as specified in the restructuring agreement. Any immediate cash payments or transfers of assets or equity reduces the book value of the debt prior to computing a gain or loss. The following decision rules are then used:

1. *CV ≤ TFCF: No gain or loss; future interest.* If the carrying value of the debt is less than, or equal to, the total future cash flows, no gain or loss is shown and the debtor's future effective interest expense on this debt, and the creditor's effective interest income is the restructuring difference between the carrying value and the future cash flows.

2. *CV > TFCF: Debtor gain and creditor loss, no future interest.* If the carrying value of the debt is greater than the total future cash flows, then the debtor recognizes a restructuring gain and the creditor recognizes a restructuring loss for the amount of the restructuring difference. In this case the current book value of the debt is greater than the total amount of cash that will be received—obviously, the book value must be reduced. The debtor's gain, if material, is reported as an extraordinary item. The creditor's loss is typically written off against the allowance for uncollectibles. Once a gain or loss has been recognized, no future interest income on this debt contract is reported by the creditor and no future interest expense on this debt is reported by the debtor.

Some accounting theorists are concerned that a comparison of a present amount (carrying value of the debt) and a future amount (total future cash flows) is inherently inconsistent in logic. Although the FASB also noted this in its deliberations before the release of **FASB 15**, the Board felt that any alternative to **FASB 15**'s requirements of accounting for restructuring agreements would have resulted in major default actions by creditors against debtors. **FASB 15** results in fewer losses by creditors in restructurings involving modification of terms than the accounting standards that existed before the issuance of **FASB 15**. Thus, **FASB 15** encourages creditors to work with the debtor during a period of financial difficulty rather than initiate legal action on the default.

The decision rules presented in **FASB 15** are illustrated in the next section of the chapter.

Illustration of Troubled Debt Restructurings

The following illustration demonstrates the accounting for various forms of a troubled debt restructuring. Peerless Products Corporation is financially distressed and is evaluating a variety of restructuring alternatives. Following are observations about Peerless Products Corporation:

1. On December 31, 19X6, the company has an unsecured current liability of $30,000 to the Creditor Company, on which $3,000 interest has been accrued and is unpaid.

2. Peerless Products Corporation has been negotiating with Creditor Company to restructure the current debt of $33,000 ($30,000 + $3,000). The three alternatives are presented below.

Alternative 1: Transfer of Cash in Full Settlement of Debt The first alternative is the transfer of $27,000 in full settlement of the carrying value of the debt. The restructuring difference between the carrying value of the debt and total future cash flow of the restructuring agreement is computed as follows:

Carrying value of the debt:		
Principal	$30,000	
Accrued interest (10% for 1 year)	3,000	$33,000
Total future cash flows		(27,000)
Restructuring difference		$ 6,000

The total future cash flows of $27,000 are less than the $33,000 carrying value of the debt. If the creditor agrees to the restructuring, the debtor recognizes a restructuring gain of $6,000 and the creditor recognizes a restructuring loss in the same amount.

The entry required for Peerless Products Corporation, the debtor company, is:

December 31, 19X6		
(1) Notes Payable	30,000	
Accrued Interest Payable	3,000	
Cash		27,000
Gain on Restructuring of Debt		6,000
Restructure and settle debt.		

The gain on restructuring of debt, if material, is reported as an extraordinary item on the income statement.

The entry required for Creditor Company is:

December 31, 19X6		
(2) Cash	27,000	
Allowance for Uncollectibles	6,000	
Notes Receivable		30,000
Accrued Interest Receivable		3,000
Restructure and settle receivable.		

If Creditor Company had not provided adequately for uncollectible receivables, a loss account is debited instead of the allowance for uncollectibles. A loss is normally reported as an operating loss on the creditor's income statement.

Alternative 2: Transfer of Noncash Assets in Settlement of Debt In the second alternative, Peerless Products Corporation agrees to transfer inventory with a book value of $45,000 and a fair value of $26,000 to Creditor Company in full settlement of the $33,000 debt. When noncash assets are transferred in a restructuring agreement, the assets must be revalued to their fair values *before* determining the restructuring difference. The gain or loss is shown on the debtor's income statement as an operating item resulting from the disposal of assets. Therefore, Peerless Products Corporation recognizes a loss on disposal of its inventory for the $19,000 decline in its inventory from its book value of $45,000 to its fair value of $26,000. The revaluation is typically made in the journal entry summarizing the troubled debt restructuring.

The restructuring difference is computed as follows:

Carrying value of the debt:		
Principal	$30,000	
Accrued Interest	3,000	$33,000
Fair value of assets transferred		(26,000)
Restructuring difference		$ 7,000

The carrying value of the debt is greater than the fair value of the assets transferred; therefore, the debtor recognizes a restructuring gain of $7,000, and the creditor recognizes a $7,000 loss.

The entry made on Peerless Products' books is:

December 31, 19X6

(3)	Notes Payable	30,000	
	Accrued Interest Payable	3,000	
	Loss on Disposal of Inventory	19,000	
	Inventory		45,000
	Gain on Restructuring of Debt		7,000
	Restructure and settle debt.		

The $19,000 loss on the disposal of inventory reduces the inventory from its $45,000 book value to its $26,000 fair value before the restructuring difference is computed. The $33,000 carrying value of the debt is extinguished by the $26,000 fair value of the inventory. Therefore, a restructuring gain of $7,000 is recognized by the debtor company.

The entry on the creditor's books is:

December 31, 19X6

(4)	Inventory	26,000	
	Allowance for Uncollectibles	7,000	
	Notes Receivable		30,000
	Accrued Interest Receivable		3,000
	Restructure and settle receivable.		

The noncash asset is recorded at its fair value. The allowance for uncollectibles is charged for the difference between the $26,000 value received and the $33,000 book value of the debt.

The creditor may also accept the debtor's common stock or other equity as settlement of the debt. The stock is recorded at its fair value, and the restructuring difference is computed as in the case of the transfer of a noncash asset. It may seem unusual that a creditor would accept stock of a company that is experiencing financial difficulty, but the creditor may feel that the company is viable and that the stock is a reasonable long-term investment.

Alternative 3: Modification of Terms   A common technique of debt restructuring is to modify some of the terms of the original debt contract. Modification of terms may include:

1. Reduction of the stated interest rate for the remainder of the original debt
2. Extension of the maturity date of the original debt at a lower rate of interest
3. Reduction of part of the face amount of the original debt
4. Reduction in the accrued interest

Accounting for a modification of debt terms is included in **FASB 15**. The restructuring difference is computed as the difference between the carrying value of the debt and the total future estimated cash flows under the new terms. If the carrying value of the debt is greater than the total future estimated cash flows, the debtor recognizes a gain for the restructuring difference and the creditor recognizes a loss for the same amount. If the carrying value of the debt is less than the total future cash flows, no gain or loss is recognized and the new effective interest rate is determined based on the amount of the restructuring difference. The following cases illustrate these points.

Case A: Carrying Value of Debt Greater than Modified Total Future Cash Flows—Debtor Gain and Creditor Loss Recognized   Peerless Products Corporation, the debtor, owes $30,000 principal plus $3,000 accrued interest to Creditor Company. On December 31, 19X6, the two entities agree to the following modification of terms on the debt contract:

1. Forgive accrued interest of $3,000.
2. Reduce the interest rate from 10 percent to 5 percent.
3. Extend the maturity for 1 additional year to December 31, 19X7.

The restructuring difference as of the date of the modification of terms is:

Carrying value of the debt:		
Principal	$30,000	
Accrued interest	3,000	$33,000
Total future estimated cash flows:		
Total future principal	$30,000	
Total future contractual interest		
($30,000 × .05 × 1 year)	1,500	(31,500)
Restructuring difference		$ 1,500

The $33,000 carrying value of the debt is greater than the $31,500 total future estimated cash flows. The debtor recognizes a $1,500 restructuring gain, and the creditor recognizes a $1,500 restructuring loss. Because a gain and loss is recognized, **FASB 15** states that no interest expense or interest income is recognized on this debt in future periods. Therefore, although the restructuring calls for contractual interest of 5 percent for a 1-year period, this amount is included in the remaining book value of the debt as of the restructuring date and is not recognized as accounting interest income (creditor's financial statements) or interest expense (debtor's financial statements).

The entry required for Peerless Products Corporation, the debtor, on December 31, 19X6, the date of the modification of terms agreement, is:

```
December 31, 19X6
  (5)  Accrued Interest Payable                    3,000
       Notes Payable (10%)                        30,000
            Notes Payable (5%)                              31,500
            Gain on Restructuring of Debt                    1,500
       Modify terms of debt.
```

The total future cash flows of $31,500 are recorded as restructured debt, and the original debt and accrued interest are written off. The gain, if material, is shown as an extraordinary item on Peerless Products Corporation's income statement.

When Peerless Products Corporation repays the debt on December 31, 19X7, it makes the following entry:

```
December 31, 19X7
  (6)  Notes Payable (5%)                         31,500
            Cash                                            31,500
       Pay restructured debt.
```

Although the terms of the restructuring agreement specify a contractual interest rate of 5 percent, no interest expense is recorded.

In this situation, Creditor Company records a loss of $1,500 and a receivable of $31,500 when the debt is restructured. At the time the receivable is collected, no interest income is recorded. The entries are as follows:

```
December 31, 19X6
  (7)  Notes Receivable (5%)                      31,500
       Allowance for Uncollectibles                1,500
            Notes Receivable (10%)                          30,000
            Accrued Interest Receivable                      3,000
       Modify terms with debtor.

December 31, 19X7
  (8)  Cash                                       31,500
            Notes Receivable (5%)                           31,500
       Collect restructured receivable.
```

Case B: Carrying Value of Debt Less than Modified Total Future Cash Flows: No Gain and Loss Recognized Peerless Products Corporation, the debtor, and

Creditor Company agree to the following modification of terms for the debt of $30,000 and $3,000 of accrued interest:

1. Forgive $500 of accrued interest.
2. Reduce contracted interest from 10 percent to 5 percent.
3. Extend maturity for 1 additional year to December 31, 19X7.

The first step is to determine the restructuring difference on December 31, 19X6, the date of the troubled debt restructuring.

Carrying value of the debt:		
Principal	$30,000	
Accrued interest	3,000	$33,000
Total future estimated cash flows:		
Total future principal	$30,000	
Remaining accrued interest not forgiven	2,500	
Total future contractual interest		
($30,000 × .05 × 1 year)	1,500	(34,000)
Restructuring difference		$ (1,000)

No gain or loss is recognized in this case, because the $33,000 carrying value of the debt is less than the total future estimated cash flows resulting from the restructuring. The entry required on Peerless Products Corporation's books on December 31, 19X6, the restructuring date, is:

December 31, 19X6		
(9) Accrued Interest Payable	3,000	
Notes Payable (10%)	30,000	
Notes Payable (5%)		33,000
Modify terms of debt.		

On December 31, 19X7, Peerless Products Corporation must pay a total of $34,000, which includes $33,000 to extinguish the restructured debt and $1,000 of interest expense. The entry on December 31, 19X7, is:

December 31, 19X7		
(10) Interest Expense	1,000	
Notes Payable (5%)	33,000	
Cash		34,000
Pay restructured debt and interest.		

The actual interest rate for the restructured debt may be found by solving the present value formula for the interest rate, as follows:

$$\text{Present value} = \text{present value factor} \times \text{future amount}$$

where the present value is the present book value of debt; the present value factor (PVF) is the factor from the "present value of $1" table for one period, which is the term of the debt; and the future value is the total future cash flows. Therefore

$$\$33,000 = \text{PVF} \times \$34,000$$

and
$$\text{PVF} = \frac{\$33,000}{\$34,000} = .9705$$

In a present value of $1 table, the factor .9705 is found for 1 year in the 3 percent column. Therefore, the interest rate is approximately 3 percent. For this 1-year example, the interest rate may be approximated by a more direct manner, as follows:

$$\frac{\$1,000}{\$33,000} = .0303, \text{ or } 3.03 \text{ percent interest rate}$$

Although the restructuring agreement shows the contractual interest rate as 5 percent, the interest income and interest expense reported on the creditor's and debtor's income statements are reported at an effective interest rate of 3.03 percent. The difference between the 5 percent and the 3.03 percent becomes part of the restructured debt principal. For notes payable of more than 1 year in length, the computed effective rate of interest would be used to determine the amount of interest expense to be reported for each year.

Other Considerations

Some restructuring agreements contain provisions for contingent payments. For example, the agreement may specify that the debtor must pay an additional amount if its future net income exceeds a certain level. At the time of the restructuring agreement, contingent amounts should be included in the estimated total future cash payments by both the debtor and creditor if the conditions established in **FASB Statement No. 5,** "Accounting for Contingencies" (FASB 5), for a recognition of a loss contingency have been met. This standard requires contingencies to be recognized as payables in the first period in which it is probable that a liability has been incurred and the amount can be reasonably estimated. If these conditions are not met, the debtor should include the contingent payments in its computation of estimated future cash flows only to the extent necessary to avoid recognizing a restructuring gain; the creditor would not include the contingent payments until the conditions of **FASB 5** were met.

At the time of a debt restructuring, the debtor is required to make supplementary footnote disclosures in its financial reports describing the major features of the restructuring plan, the aggregate gain on restructuring the payables and any related income tax effects, the net gain or loss on transfers of assets in accordance with the plan, and the per-share effects of the aggregate gain on restructuring of the payables net of related income tax effects. For periods after the restructuring, the debtor must disclose amounts that are contingently payable and the terms under which these contingencies become payable.

Creditors must disclose, either in the financial statements or in the notes, specific information about troubled debt restructurings. These disclosures include the amount of restructured receivables, the amount of interest income that would have been recorded on those receivables if they had not been restructured, the actual amount of interest income on the restructured receivables, and the amount of any commitments to lend additional funds to debtors owing receivables for which the terms were modified.

The next section of the chapter presents corporate reorganizations administered under the Bankruptcy Act. Troubled debt restructurings are often a part of the reorganization effort as the debtor attempts to rehabilitate itself and return to profitable operations.

CHAPTER 11 REORGANIZATIONS

Chapter 11 of the Bankruptcy Reform Act of 1978 allows for legal protection from creditors' actions during a time needed to reorganize the debtor company and return its operations to a profitable level. Reorganizations are administered by the bankruptcy court, and trustees are often appointed by the court to direct the reorganization. Reorganizations are typically described by the four P's of reorganization. A company in financial distress *petitions* the bankruptcy court for *protection* from its creditors. If granted protection, the company receives an order of relief to suspend making any payments on its pre-petition debt. The company continues to operate while it prepares a ***plan of reorganization***, which serves as an operating guide during the reorganization. The *proceeding* includes the actions that take place from the time the petition is filed until the company completes the reorganization.

The petition must discuss the alternative of liquidating the debtor and distributing the expected receipts to the creditors. The plan of reorganization is the essence of any reorganization. The plan must include a complete description of the expected debtor actions during the reorganization period and how these actions will be in the best interest of the debtor and its creditors. A *disclosure statement* is transmitted to all creditors and other parties eligible to vote on the plan of reorganization. The disclosure statement includes information that would enable a reasonable investor or creditor to make an informed judgment about the worthiness of the plan and how the plan will affect that person's financial interest in the debtor company. The bankruptcy court then evaluates the responses to the plan from creditors and other parties, and either confirms the plan of reorganization or rejects it. Confirmation of the plan implies that the debtor, or an appointed trustee, will fully follow the plan. The reorganization period may be as short as a few months or as long as several years. Most reorganizations require more than 1 year; however, the time span of the proceeding depends on the complexity of the reorganization.

Statement of Position No. 90-7, "Financial Reporting by Entities in Reorganization under the Bankruptcy Code" (SOP 90-7),[1] provides guidance for financial reporting for companies in reorganization. The financial statements issued by a

[1] *Statement of Position No. 90-7*, "Financial Reporting by Entities in Reorganization under the Bankruptcy Code," American Institute of Certified Public Accountants (New York), 1990.

company during Chapter 11 proceedings should distinguish transactions and events directly associated with the reorganization from those associated with ongoing operations. Companies in reorganization are required to present balance sheets, income statements, and statements of cash flows, but **SOP 90-7** requires these three statements to clearly reflect the unique circumstances related to the reorganization.

The balance sheet of a company in reorganization has the following special attributes:

1. Pre-petition liabilities subject to compromise as part of the reorganization proceeding should be reported separately from liabilities not subject to compromise. Liabilities subject to compromise include unsecured debt and other payables that are incurred before the company entered reorganization. Liabilities that are not subject to change by the reorganization plan include fully secured liabilities incurred before reorganization, and all liabilities incurred after the company enters its petition for reorganization relief.

2. The liabilities should be reported at the expected amount to be allowed by the bankruptcy court. If no reasonable estimation is possible, then the claims should be disclosed in the footnotes.

The income statement of a company in reorganization has the following special requirements:

1. Income statement amounts directly related to the reorganization, such as legal fees and losses on disposals of assets, should be reported separately as reorganization items in the period incurred. However, any gains or losses on discontinued operations, or extraordinary items, should be reported separately according to **APB Opinion 30**, "Reporting the Results of Operations."

2. Some of the interest income earned during reorganization is a result of the debtor not being required to pay debt and thus investing the available resources in interest-bearing sources. Such interest income should be reported separately as a reorganization item. The extent to which reported interest expense differs from the contractual interest on the company's debt should be disclosed, either parenthetically on the face of the income statement, or within the footnotes.

3. Earnings per share is disclosed, but any anticipated changes to the number of common shares or common stock equivalents outstanding as a result of the reorganization plan should be disclosed.

The statement of cash flows of a company in reorganization has the following special features:

1. **SOP 90-7** prefers the direct method of presenting cash flows from operations, but if the indirect method is used, then the company must also disclose separately the operating cash flows associated with the reorganization.

2. Cash flows related to the reorganization should be reported separately from those from regular operations. For example, excess net interest received as a result of the company's not paying its debts during reorganization should be reported separately.

Fresh Start Accounting

The basic view of a reorganization is that it is a fresh start for the company. However, it is difficult to determine if a Chapter 11 reorganization results in a new entity for which fresh start accounting should be used, or if the reorganization results in a continuation of the prior entity. **SOP 90-7** stated that fresh start reporting should be used as of the confirmation date of the plan of reorganization if both the following conditions occur:[2]

1. The reorganization value of the assets of the emerging entity immediately before the date of confirmation is less than the total of all post-petition liabilities and allowed claims, and

2. Holders of existing voting shares immediately before confirmation receive less than 50 percent of the voting shares of the emerging entity. This implies that the prior shareholders have lost control of the emerging company.

Fresh start accounting results in a new reporting entity. First, the company is required to compute the *reorganization value* of the assets of the emerging entity. Reorganization value represents the fair value of the entity before considering liabilities, and approximates the amount a willing buyer would pay for the assets of the entity. The reorganization value is then allocated to the assets using the allocation of value method in **APB 16** for purchase accounting. Any reorganization value in excess of amounts assignable to identifiable assets is reported as an intangible asset called "reorganization value in excess of amounts allocable to identifiable assets." This excess is then amortized in conformity with **APB 17**, "Intangible Assets." Liabilities of the emerging company are recorded at the present values of the amounts to be paid. Any retained earnings, or deficit, is eliminated. A set of final operating statements is prepared just prior to emerging from reorganization. In essence, the company is a new reporting entity after reorganization.

Companies not qualifying for fresh start accounting should report liabilities at the present values of amounts to be paid, with forgiveness of debt reported as an extraordinary item as specified by **FASB 15**. The companies continue their accounting for assets, as used prior to entering reorganization; however, write-downs of assets for permanent losses should be recognized.

FASB 15 does not apply to troubled debt restructurings in which debtors restate their liabilities generally under the purview of the bankruptcy court. **FASB 15** applies only to specific debt restructuring transactions. This exception is not an issue in the immediate settlement of debt in which the debtor's gain or loss is the difference between the fair value of the consideration given and the carrying value of the debt. The gain or loss is the same under **FASB 15** as under a general restatement of liabilities in a reorganization. However, in cases of modification of terms in a reorganization involving a general restatement of liabilities, the gain or loss is computed as the difference between the carrying value of the debt and the

---

[2] *Statement of Position No. 90-7*, para. 36.

new principal after restructuring of the debt. The future cash flows from interest payments are not included in the computation of the new principal. Thus, in most cases of debt restructuring of companies in reorganization proceedings, the debtor's gain from the debt restructuring is greater than it would have been under **FASB 15**.

Plan of Reorganization

The plan of reorganization is typically a detailed document with a full discussion of all major actions to be taken during the reorganization period. In addition to these major actions, management also continues to manufacture and sell products, collect receivables, and pursue other day-to-day operations. Most plans include detailed discussions of the following:

1. Disposing of unprofitable operations, through either sale or liquidation
2. Restructuring of debt with specific creditors
3. Revaluation of assets and liabilities
4. Reductions or eliminations of claims of original stockholders and issuances of new shares to creditors or others

The plan of reorganization must be approved by at least half of all creditors, who must hold at least two-thirds of the dollar amount of the debtor's total outstanding debt, although the court may still confirm a plan that the necessary number of creditors do not approve, provided the court finds that the plan is in the best interests of all parties and is equitable and fair to those groups not voting approval.

Illustration of a Reorganization

A balance sheet for the Peerless Products Corporation on December 31, 19X6, is presented in Figure 22-1. On January 2, 19X7, Peerless's management petitions the bankruptcy court for a Chapter 11 reorganization in order to obtain relief from debt payments and time to rehabilitate the company and return to profitable operations.

The following time line presents the dates relevant for this example:

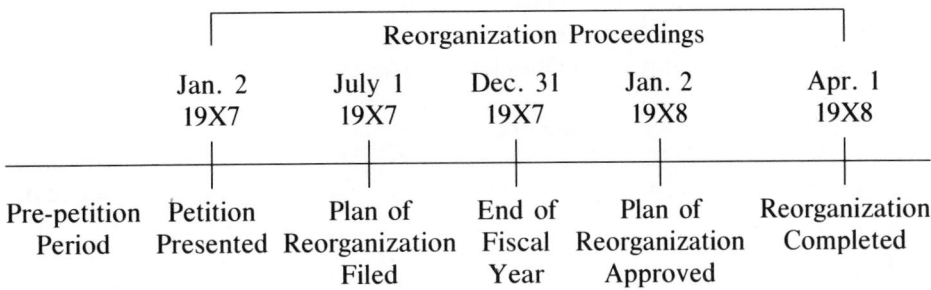

FIGURE 22-1 Balance sheet on the date of corporate insolvency.

Peerless Products Corporation
Balance Sheet
December 31, 19X6

Assets

Cash			$ 2,000
Marketable Securities			8,000
Accounts Receivable		$ 20,000	
Less: Allowance for Uncollectible Accounts		(2,000)	18,000
Inventory			45,000
Prepaid Assets			1,000
Total Current Assets			$ 74,000

Property, Plant, and Equipment:

	Cost	Accumulated Depreciation	Undepreciated Cost	
Land	$ 10,000	$ -0-	$10,000	
Plant	75,000	20,000	55,000	
Equipment	20,000	4,000	16,000	
Total	$105,000	$24,000	$81,000	81,000
Goodwill				20,000
Total Assets				$175,000

Liabilities

Accounts Payable			$ 26,000
Notes Payable:			
Partially Secured		$ 10,000	
Unsecured, 10% interest		80,000	90,000
Accrued Interest			3,000
Accrued Wages			14,000
Total Current Liabilities			$133,000
Mortgages Payable			50,000
Total Liabilities			$183,000

Shareholders' Equity

Preferred Stock		$ 40,000	
Common Stock ($1 par)		10,000	
Retained Earnings (Deficit)		(58,000)	
Total Shareholders' Equity			(8,000)
Total Liabilities and Shareholders' Equity			$175,000

The bankruptcy court accepts the petition and Peerless Products prepares its plan of reorganization. The plan is filed on July 1, 19X7, and the disclosure statement is sent to all creditors and other affected parties. On December 31, 19X7, the company presents its financial statements for the 19X7 fiscal period in which it was in Chapter 11 proceedings. The bankruptcy court approves the reorganization plan on January 2, 19X8, and the reorganization is completed by April 1, 19X8.

Peerless Products Corporation files the plan of reorganization presented in Figure 22-2, together with audited financial statements and other disclosures requested by the bankruptcy court.

Prior to the approval of the plan of reorganization, Peerless Products Corporation continues to operate under the protection of the granted petition of relief. The company makes only court-approved payments on the pre-petition liabilities. The only court-approved payment on pre-petition liabilities is a $2,000 payment on the mortgage payable. On December 31, 19X7, the company issues financial statements for the fiscal year. **SOP 90-7** prescribes the reporting guidelines for companies in reorganization proceedings. A most important reporting concern is that the reorganization amounts be reported separately from other operating amounts. Peerless Products Corporation prepares the following financial statements as of December 31, 19X7: balance sheet (Figure 22-3), income statement (Figure 22-4),

FIGURE 22-2 Plan of reorganization.

Peerless Products Corporation
Plan of Reorganization
Under Chapter 11 of the Bankruptcy Code
(Filed July 1, 19X7)

---

a. The accounts payable of $26,000 will be provided for as follows: (1) $6,000 will be eliminated, (2) $4,000 will be paid in cash, (3) $12,000 of the payables will be exchanged for subordinated debt, and (4) $4,000 of the payables are to be exchanged for 4,000 shares of newly issued common stock.

b. The partially secured notes payable of $10,000 will be provided for as follows: (1) $2,000 will be paid in cash, and (2) the remaining $8,000 will be exchanged for senior debt secured by a lien on equipment.

c. The unsecured notes payable of $80,000 will be provided for as follows: (1) $12,000 are to be eliminated, (2) $14,000 are to be paid in cash, (3) $49,000 are to be exchanged to senior debt secured by a lien against fixed assets, and (4) $5,000 are to be exchanged into 5,000 shares of newly issued common stock.

d. The accrued interest of $3,000 will be provided for as follows: (1) $2,000 will be eliminated, and (2) the remaining $1,000 will be paid in cash.

e. The accrued wages of $14,000 will be provided for as follows: (1) $12,000 will be paid in cash, and (2) the remaining $2,000 will be exchanged into 2,000 shares of newly issued common stock.

f. The preferred shareholders will receive 8,000 shares of newly issued common stock in exchange for their preferred stock.

g. The present common stockholders will receive 1,000 shares of newly issued common stock in exchange for their present common stock.

FIGURE 22-3 Balance sheet for a company in reorganization proceedings.

Peerless Products Corporation
(Debtor-in-Possession)
Balance Sheet
December 31, 19X7

Assets

Cash		$ 40,000
Income Tax Refund Receivable		12,000
Marketable Securities		8,000
Accounts Receivable	$ 6,000	
Less: Allowance for Uncollectibles	(1,000)	5,000
Inventory		37,000
Total Current Assets		$102,000
Property, Plant, and Equipment:	$85,000	
Less: Accumulated Depreciation	(26,000)	59,000
Goodwill		19,000
Total Assets		$180,000

Liabilities

Liabilities Not Subject to Compromise:		
Current Liabilities (post-petition):		
Short-Term Borrowings	$15,000	
Accounts Payable—Trade	10,000	
Noncurrent Liability:		
Mortgage Payable, Fully Secured	48,000	
Total Liabilities Not Subject to Compromise		$ 73,000
Liabilities Subject to Compromise (pre-petition):		
Accounts Payable	$26,000	
Notes Payable, Partially Secured	10,000	
Notes Payable, Unsecured	80,000	
Accrued Interest	3,000	
Accrued Wages	14,000	
Total Liabilities Subject to Compromise		133,000
Total Liabilities		$206,000

Shareholders' Equity

Preferred Stock	$40,000	
Common Stock ($1 par)	10,000	
Retained Earnings (deficit)	(76,000)	
Total Shareholders' Equity		(26,000)
Total Liabilities and Shareholders' Equity		$180,000

FIGURE 22-4 Income statement for a company in reorganization proceedings.

Peerless Products Corporation (Debtor-in-Possession) Income Statement For the Year Ended December 31, 19X7		
Revenue:		
Sales		$120,000
Cost and Expenses:		
Cost of Goods Sold	$110,000	
Selling, Operating, and Administrative	21,000	
Interest (contractual interest $6,000)	3,000	134,000
Earnings before Reorganization Items and Income Tax Benefit		$ (14,000)
Reorganization Items:		
Loss on Disposal of Assets	$ (10,000)	
Professional Fees	(8,000)	
Interest Earned on Accumulated Cash Resulting from Chapter 11 Proceeding	2,000	
Total Reorganization Items		(16,000)
Loss before Income Tax Benefit		$ (30,000)
Income Tax Benefit		12,000
Net Loss		$ (18,000)

and statement of cash flows (Figure 22-5). Note that "Debtor-in-Possession" indicates that Peerless Products continues to manage its own assets, rather than being managed by a court-appointed trustee.

On January 2, 19X8, the bankruptcy court approves the plan of reorganization, as filed. Peerless Products Corporation carries out the plan as shown in Figure 22-6.

An important concept for determining the appropriate accounting for entities in reorganization is the determination of reorganization value. Reorganization value is the fair value of the assets of the entity. Typical methods of determining reorganization value are discounting future cash flows, or appraisals. After extensive analysis, a reorganization value of $195,000 is determined for Peerless Products' assets. Recall that fresh start accounting is appropriate only when both of the following conditions occur: (1) reorganization value is less than total postpetition liabilities and allowed claims, and (2) holders of existing shares of voting stock immediately before the plan of reorganization is approved retain less than 50 percent of the voting shares of the emerging entity. To determine the first

FIGURE 22-5 Statement of cash flows for a company in reorganization proceedings.

Peerless Products Corporation
(Debtor-in-Possession)
Statement of Cash Flows
For the Year Ended December 31, 19X7

Cash Flows Provided by Operating Activities:	
Cash Received from Customers	$133,000
Cash Paid to Suppliers and Employees	(109,000)
Interest Paid	(3,000)
Net Cash Provided by Operating Activities before Reorganization Items	$ 21,000
Operating Cash Flows Used by Reorganization Activities:	
Professional Fees	(8,000)
Interest Received on Cash Accumulated Because of Chapter 11 Proceeding	2,000
Net Cash Used by Reorganization Items	$ (6,000)
Net Cash Provided by Operating Activities and Reorganization Items	$ 15,000
Cash Flows Provided by Investing Activities:	
Proceeds from Sale of Assets Due to Chapter 11 Proceeding	$ 10,000
Net Cash Provided by Investing Activities	$ 10,000
Cash Flows Provided by Financing Activities:	
Net Borrowings under Short-Term Financing Plan	$ 15,000
Principal Payments on Pre-petition Debt Authorized by Court (Mortgage Payable)	(2,000)
Net Cash Provided by Financing Activities	$ 13,000
Net Increase in Cash	$ 38,000
Cash at January 1, 19X7	2,000
Cash at December 31, 19X7	$ 40,000

---

condition for Peerless Products Corporation, a comparison is made on the date the plan of reorganization is approved:

Post-petition liabilities	$ 73,000
Liabilities deferred pursuant to Chapter 11 proceedings	133,000
Total post-petition liabilities and allowed claims	$206,000
Reorganization value	(195,000)
Excess of liabilities over reorganization value	$ 11,000

Note that the first condition for fresh start accounting is present. The second condition for fresh start accounting also occurs, as shown in Figure 22-6. The common shareholders immediately before the plan of reorganization is approved hold only 5 percent of the common stock of the emerging entity. Therefore, fresh

FIGURE 22-6 Recovery analysis for plan of reorganization.

Peerless Corporation
Plan of Reorganization
Recovery Analysis

	Elimination of Debt and Equity	Surviving Debt	Recovery					Total Recovery $	Total Recovery %
			Cash	Senior Debt	Subordinated Debt	Common Stock %	Common Stock Value		
Post-Petition Liabilities	(73,000)	(73,000)						(73,000)	100%
Claims/Interest:									
Accounts Payable	(26,000)	6,000	(4,000)		(12,000)	20%	(4,000)	(20,000)	77
Notes Payable, partially secured	(10,000)		(2,000)	(8,000)				(10,000)	100
Notes Payable, unsecured	(80,000)	12,000	(14,000)	(49,000)		25	(5,000)	(68,000)	85
Accrued interest	(3,000)	2,000	(1,000)					(1,000)	33
Accrued wages	(14,000)		(12,000)			10	(2,000)	(14,000)	100
Total	(133,000)	20,000							
Preferred Shareholders	(40,000)	32,000				40	(8,000)	(8,000)	
Common Shareholders	(10,000)	9,000				5	(1,000)	(1,000)	
Retained Earnings Deficit	76,000	(76,000)							
Total	(180,000)	(15,000)	(33,000)	(57,000)	(12,000)	100%	(20,000)	(195,000)	

Parentheses indicate credit amount.

start accounting is used for Peerless Products Corporation. If both conditions for fresh start accounting are not met, the emerging company is not a new reporting entity and does not revalue its assets.

After intensive study of risk-equivalent companies, the profit potential of the emerging company, and the present value of future cash flows, the capital structure of the emerging company is established as follows:

Post-petition current liabilities	$ 25,000
Post-petition mortgage payable	48,000
Senior debt	57,000
Subordinated debt	12,000
Common stock (new)	20,000
Total post-reorganization capital structure	$162,000

Note that for purposes of the illustration, the newly issued common stock is no-par stock; therefore, no additional paid-in capital is carried forward to the emerging entity. If the assigned value of the newly issued stock is greater than its par value, an additional paid-in capital account would be credited for the excess. The $162,000 of post-reorganization capital is the reorganization value of $195,000 less the $33,000 paid out for the pre-petition liabilities as part of the plan of reorganization.

Peerless Products Corporation prepares entries to record the execution of the plan of reorganization as it transpires between January 1, 19X8, and April 1, 19X8. Figure 22-7 presents a worksheet illustrating the effects of executing the plan of reorganization on the balance sheet accounts of Peerless Products Corporation. The first journal entry records the debt restructuring and the retained earnings adjustment for the gain on the discharge of debt.

January 1, 19X8–April 1, 19X8

(11)	Liabilities Subject to Compromise	133,000	
	Cash		33,000
	Senior Debt		57,000
	Subordinated Debt		12,000
	Common Stock (new)		11,000
	Gain on Debt Discharge		20,000
	Record debt discharge.		

The second journal entry records the exchange of stock for stock. The prior preferred shareholders receive 8,000 shares of newly issued common stock. The prior common shareholders receive 1,000 shares of the newly issued common stock.

January 1, 19X8–April 1, 19X8

(12)	Preferred Stock	40,000	
	Common Stock (old)	10,000	
	Common Stock (new)		9,000
	Additional Paid-In Capital		41,000
	Record exchange of stock for stock.		

FIGURE 22-7 Effect of plan of reorganization on company's balance sheet.

	Pre-confir-mation	Adjustments to Record Confirmation of Plan			Company's Reorganized Balance Sheet
		Debt Discharge	Exchange of Stock	Fresh Start	
Assets					
Cash	40,000	(33,000)			7,000
Income Tax Refund Receivable	12,000				12,000
Marketable Securities	8,000			2,000	10,000
Accounts Receivable (net)	5,000				5,000
Inventory	37,000			(4,000)	33,000
	102,000				67,000
Property, Plant, and Equipment (net)	59,000			26,000	85,000
Goodwill	19,000			(19,000)	
Reorganization Value in Excess of Amounts Allocable to Identifiable Assets				10,000	10,000
Total	180,000	(33,000)		15,000	162,000
Liabilities					
Liabilities Not Subject to Compromise:					
Current Liabilities					
Short-Term Borrowings	(15,000)				(15,000)
Accounts Payable	(10,000)				(10,000)
Noncurrent Liability:					
Mortgage Payable	(48,000)				(48,000)
	(73,000)				(73,000)
Liabilities Subject to Compromise	(133,000)	133,000			
Senior Debt		(57,000)			(57,000)
Subordinated Debt		(12,000)			(12,000)
Total Liabilities	(206,000)	64,000			(142,000)
Shareholders' Equity					
Preferred Stock	(40,000)		40,000		
Common Stock (old)	(10,000)		10,000		
Common Stock (new)		(11,000)	(9,000)		(20,000)
Additional Paid-In Capital			(41,000)	41,000	
Retained Earnings (deficit)	76,000	(20,000)		20,000	
				(76,000)	-0-
Total Shareholders' Equity	26,000	(31,000)	-0-	(15,000)	(20,000)
Total	(180,000)	33,000	-0-	(15,000)	(162,000)

Parentheses indicate credit amount.

The third and last journal entry records the fresh start adjustments of the assigned values of the assets of the emerging entity, and elimination of any retained earnings, or deficit. A comparison between the book values and fair values of the company is presented below. The fair values are determined according to the procedures in **APB 16**, which include requirements for appraisals and reallocations of "negative goodwill." Note that Reorganization Value in Excess of Amounts Allocable to Identifiable Assets is debited for any amount not assignable to other assets. The reorganization value excess is reported as an intangible asset and amortized according to **APB 17**.

	Book Value	Fair Value	Difference
Cash	$ 7,000	$ 7,000	$ –0–
Income Tax Refund Receivable	12,000	12,000	–0–
Marketable securities	8,000	10,000	2,000
Accounts receivable (net)	5,000	5,000	–0–
Inventory	37,000	33,000	(4,000)
Property, plant, and equipment	59,000	85,000	26,000
Goodwill	19,000	–0–	(19,000)
Reorganization value in excess of amounts allocable to identifiable assets	–0–	10,000	10,000
Totals	$147,000	$162,000	$15,000

The entry to record the fresh start revaluation of assets and elimination of the deficit is:

```
April 1, 19X8
  (13)   Marketable Securities                              2,000
         Property, Plant, and Equipment                    26,000
         Reorganization Value in Excess of Amounts
           Allocable to Identifiable Assets                10,000
         Gain on Debt Discharge                            20,000
         Additional Paid-In Capital                        41,000
             Inventory                                                  4,000
             Goodwill                                                  19,000
             Retained Earnings—Deficit                                 76,000
         Record fresh start accounting and eliminate deficit.
```

The last column in Figure 22-7 presents the post-reorganization, new reporting entity's balance sheet.

Some reorganizations are unsuccessful, and the debtor must be liquidated. The major reason for unsuccessful reorganizations is continuing losses from operations and no reasonable likelihood of rehabilitation. Another common reason is the inability to consummate a reorganization plan because of the failure to dispose of an unprofitable subsidiary, a material default of the plan by either the debtor or a creditor, or the inability to effect part of the plan as a result of changes in the economic environment. The debtor company then moves from reorganization into liquidation. Liquidation is the topic of the next section of the chapter.

CHAPTER 7 LIQUIDATIONS

Liquidations are administered by the bankruptcy courts in the interests of creditors and shareholders of the corporation. The intent in liquidation is to maximize the net dollar amount recovered from disposal of the debtor's assets. Bankruptcy courts appoint accountants, attorneys, or experienced business managers as trustees to administer the liquidation. The liquidation process is often completed within 6 to 12 months, during which the trustees must make periodic reports to the bankruptcy court. The entire liquidation process is governed by the Bankruptcy Reform Act of 1978, which describes the specific procedures to be followed and reports to be made. A very important aspect of liquidation is determining the legal rights of each creditor and establishing priorities for those rights.

Classes of Creditors

The Bankruptcy Reform Act specifies three classes of creditors, whose claims have the following priorities: (1) secured creditors, (2) creditors with priority, and (3) unsecured creditors. The priority of claims determines the order and source of payment to each creditor.

Secured Creditors *Secured creditors* have liens, or security interests, on specific assets, often called "collateral." A creditor with such a legal interest in a specific asset has the highest-priority claim on that asset. For example, in Figure 22-1, Peerless Products Corporation's $50,000 mortgage payable is secured by the company's land and plant. On December 31, 19X6, the land and plant have a combined net book value of $65,000 and a fair value of $55,000. The holders of the mortgage have first claim to the proceeds from the sale of the land and plant. Therefore, when the land and plant are sold for $55,000, $50,000 of the proceeds is used to discharge the Mortgage Payable account and the remaining $5,000 is available to the next-lower class of creditor.

Creditors with Priority As defined by the Bankruptcy Reform Act, *creditors with priority* are unsecured creditors, that is, those having no collateral claim against specific assets, who have priority over other unsecured creditors. Creditors with priority are the first to be paid from any proceeds available to unsecured creditors. The Bankruptcy Reform Act presents the following as liabilities with priority:

1. Costs of administering the bankruptcy, including accounting and legal costs for experts appointed by the bankruptcy court.
2. Liabilities arising in the ordinary course of business during the bankruptcy proceedings.

3. Wages, salaries, or commissions, including severance and sick pay earned within 3 months of the date the petition was filed, but limited to $2,000 for each individual.

4. Contributions to employee benefit plans for the last 3 months remaining after elimination of compensation in item 3 above, but constrained by the remainder of the limit of $2,000 per individual.

5. Deposits of customers who made partial payments for the purchase or lease of goods or services that were not delivered. Priority is given to the first $900 per individual; any excess deposit is added to the unsecured claims.

6. Unsecured tax claims of government units, including income taxes, property taxes, excise taxes, and other taxes.

These six groups of creditors are paid from assets available to unsecured creditors. Any remaining monies are then distributed to the general unsecured creditors.

General Unsecured Creditors The lowest priority is given to claims by *general unsecured creditors*. These creditors are paid only after secured creditors and unsecured creditors with priority are satisfied to the extent of any legal limits. Often, the general unsecured creditors receive less than the full amount of their claim. The amounts to be paid to these creditors are usually stated as a percentage of the total claim, such as 55 cents on the dollar, or whatever the specific percentage is. The payment to general unsecured creditors is often termed a "dividend." It is not uncommon for these dividends to be as low as 20 to 25 percent of the total remaining unsecured claims.

"Preference payments," payments made by the debtor to one creditor to the detriment of all other creditors within 90 days before the bankruptcy petition was filed, may usually be recovered from the specific creditor and returned to the cash available for all creditors. Sometimes a member of the debtor's management may assure a creditor that the debtor will pay any claim to that specific creditor. This often occurs during the latter phases of financial difficulty, just before filing a petition for bankruptcy. These management assurances are not binding and do not increase the level of the legal claim against the debtor's assets. The priority of the claims is determined solely in accordance with the Bankruptcy Reform Act.

Statement of Affairs

The *accounting statement of affairs* is the basic accounting report made at the beginning of the liquidation process to present the expected realizable amounts from disposal of the assets, the order of creditors' claims, and the expected amount unsecured creditors will receive as a result of the liquidation. A different report, also entitled the "statement of affairs," is a list of questions the debtor must answer as part of the bankruptcy petition. The following discussion is about the accounting report, not the legal questionnaire.

The statement of affairs is not a going-concern report; it is an important planning report for the anticipated liquidation of a company. The statement of affairs presents the book values of the debtor company's balance sheet accounts, the estimated fair market values of the assets, the order of the claims, and the estimated deficiency to the general unsecured creditors. Common stockholders rarely receive any monies from a liquidating company. The statement of affairs is a planning instrument: the actual liquidation process is recorded on the debtor's books as the transactions occur.

Assume that rather than reorganizing, Peerless made a decision on December 31, 19X6, to enter Chapter 7 bankruptcy on that date. The following illustration begins with the December 31, 19X6, statement of affairs for Peerless Products Corporation shown in Figure 22-8.

1. The report presents the balance sheet accounts in order of priority for liquidation. Current versus noncurrent accounts no longer have importance for Peerless Products Corporation.

2. The report presents estimated current fair values and expected gains or losses on the disposal of the assets. These are only estimates at the point the bankruptcy petition is filed; actual gains or losses will be recorded as realized.

3. In this example, fully secured creditors are expected to have their entire claims of $50,000 satisfied with the proceeds from the disposal of the secured asset. The mortgage payable is expected to be fully satisfied with the proceeds of $55,000 from the sale of the land and plant. The remaining $5,000 will then be available to satisfy unsecured claims.

4. Partially secured creditors will not have their claims completely satisfied from the sale of the collateral asset. Marketable securities having an estimated fair value of $9,000 are used to secure notes payable of $10,000. The first $9,000 of the notes payable will be satisfied; the remaining $1,000 will be added to the general unsecured liabilities.

5. Free assets are available to unsecured creditors. The first unsecured creditors are those with priority as defined by the Bankruptcy Reform Act. Peerless Products Corporation has accrued wages of $14,000 payable to its employees, none of whom has more than $2,000 due. In addition, the company expects to incur $4,000 of expenses to administer the liquidation.

6. All remaining claims are added to the general unsecured liabilities. The total of unsecured claims is $110,000. Only $45,000 is expected to be available to meet these claims. Therefore, the estimated dividend to general unsecured creditors is 41 cents on the dollar ($45,000/$110,000). The estimated deficiency to unsecured creditors is $65,000.

7. The stockholders will not receive anything upon liquidation of the Peerless Products Corporation. Stock is a residual claim to be settled only after all creditors' claims are fully settled. Stockholders typically do not receive anything from a bankruptcy liquidation.

The statement of affairs is a planning instrument prepared only at the beginning of the bankruptcy process. It provides important information to creditors and the

FIGURE 22-8 Accounting statement of affairs.

			Estimated Amount	**Estimated**
		Estimated	**Available**	**Gain or**
Book		**Current**	**to Unsecured**	**(Loss) on**
Values		**Values**	**Claims**	**Realization**

Assets

Book Values		Estimated Current Values	Estimated Amount Available to Unsecured Claims	Estimated Gain or (Loss) on Realization
	(1) Assets pledged with fully secured creditors:			
$ 10,000	Land	$15,000		$ 5,000
55,000	Plant (net)	40,000		(15,000)
		$55,000		
	Less: Mortgage Payable	(50,000)	$ 5,000	
	(2) Assets pledged with partially secured creditors:			
8,000	Marketable Securities	$ 9,000		1,000
	Less: Notes Payable	(10,000)		
	(3) Free Assets:			
2,000	Cash	$ 2,000	2,000	
18,000	Accounts Receivable (net)	18,000	18,000	
45,000	Inventory	26,000	26,000	(19,000)
1,000	Prepaid Assets	-0-	-0-	(1,000)
16,000	Equipment (net)	12,000	12,000	(4,000)
20,000	Goodwill	-0-	-0-	(20,000)
	Estimated amount available		$ 63,000	
	Less: Creditors with priority		(18,000)	
	Net estimated amount available to unsecured creditors (41 cents on the dollar: $45,000/$110,000)		$ 45,000	
	Estimated deficiency to unsecured creditors		65,000	
$175,000				$(53,000)
	Total unsecured debt		$110,000	

(Continued)

bankruptcy court as to the expected monies available to each class of creditors. Once the bankruptcy is under way, the debtor records the transactions on its accounting records as they occur.

ADDITIONAL CONSIDERATIONS

Presented now are the accounting and reporting practices for trustees who act as fiduciaries for the creditors' committee or for the bankruptcy court. Trustees'

FIGURE 22-8 *(Continued)*

Book Values			Estimated Amount Unsecured
		Liabilities and Stockholders' Equity	
	(1)	Fully secured creditors:	
$ 50,000		Mortgage Payable	$50,000
	(2)	Partially secured creditors:	
10,000		Notes Payable—Partially	
		Secured	$10,000
		Less: Marketable Securities	(9,000) $ 1,000
	(3)	Creditors with priority:	
		Estimated liquidation	
-0-		expenses	$ 4,000
14,000		Accrued wages	14,000
			$18,000
	(4)	Remaining unsecured creditors:	
26,000		Accounts Payable	26,000
80,000		Notes Payable—Unsecured	80,000
3,000		Accrued Interest	3,000
	(5)	Stockholders' equity:	
40,000		Preferred Stock	
10,000		Common Stock	
(58,000)		Retained Earnings (Deficit)	
$175,000			$ 110,000

reports are different from the traditional financial statements because the trustees' legal rights and responsibilities differ from those of the debtor company's management.

Also included is a brief presentation on the bankruptcy provisions applicable to individuals. The area of individual bankruptcies is undergoing constant change, and the presentation is only a general guide.

Trustee Accounting and Reporting

Bankruptcy courts appoint trustees to manage a company under Chapter 11 reorganizations in cases of management fraud, dishonesty, incompetence, or gross mismanagement. The trustee then attempts to rehabilitate the business. In Chapter 7 liquidations, the trustee normally has the responsibility to expeditiously liquidate the bankrupt company and pay creditors in conformity with the legal status of their secured or unsecured interests. In some cases under Chapter 7, the court appoints a trustee to operate the company for a short time in an effort to obtain a better price for the company in entirety rather than selling it piecemeal.

Trustees examine the proofs of all creditors' claims against the debtor's bankruptcy estate, that is, the debtor's net assets. Sometimes the trustee receives title to all assets as a *receivership*, becomes responsible for the actual management of the debtor, and must direct a plan of reorganization or liquidation. A trustee who takes title to the debtor's assets in a liquidation must make a periodic financial report to the bankruptcy court, reporting on the progress of the liquidation and on the fiduciary relationship held. When the trustee accepts the assets, the trustee usually establishes a set of accounting records to account for the receivership. The trustee's accounting records include a liability of the trustee which is created to recognize the debtor's interest in the assets accepted by the trustee. This new account is credited for the book value of the assets accepted and is usually named for the debtor company in receivership. The trustee does not transfer the debtor's liabilities, because these remain the legal responsibility of the debtor company. The general form of the trustee's opening entry, accepting the assets of the debtor company, is:

Assets	XXX	
Debtor Company—In Receivership		XXX

The actual entry details the individual asset accounts and includes the debtor's company name.

Statement of Realization and Liquidation   A monthly report, called a *statement of realization and liquidation*, is prepared for the bankruptcy court. It shows the results of the trustee's fiduciary actions beginning at the point the trustee accepts the debtor's assets. The statement has three major sections: assets, supplementary items, and liabilities. The debtor's liabilities are not transferred to the trustee, but the trustee may incur new liabilities that must be reported in the statement of realization and liquidation.

The assets section of the statement is divided into the following four groups:

Assets	
Assets to be realized	Assets realized
Assets acquired	Assets not realized

The assets to be realized are those received from the debtor company. The assets acquired are those subsequently acquired by the trustee. The assets realized are those sold by the trustee; the assets not realized are those remaining under the trustee's responsibility as of the end of the period. Cash is usually not reported in the statement of realization and liquidation because a separate cash flow report is typically made.

The supplementary items section of the report consists of the following two items:

Supplementary Items

Supplementary charges	Supplementary credits

Supplementary charges include the trustee's administration fees and any cash expenses paid by the trustee. Supplementary credits may include any unusual revenue items.

Although the trustee does not record the debtor's liabilities, the trustee settles some of the debtor's payables and may also incur new payables during the receivership. The liabilities section of the statement is divided as follows:

Liabilities

Liabilities liquidated Liabilities not liquidated	Liabilities to be liquidated Liabilities incurred

The liabilities liquidated are creditors' claims settled during the period. The liabilities not liquidated are those outstanding at the end of the reporting period. The liabilities to be liquidated are those debts remaining on the books of the debtor company for whose liquidation the trustee is responsible as of the date of appointment. Finally, the liabilities incurred are new obligations incurred by the trustee.

Illustration of Trustee Accounting and Reporting   On December 31, 19X6, D. Able was appointed trustee in charge of liquidating Peerless Products Corporation. D. Able will be allowed to operate the company for a short period of time to determine if the company can be sold in entirety as opposed to piecemeal. During this time, the trustee must reduce the current short-term debts of Peerless Products Corporation. If a sale in entirety is infeasible, Able is directed to liquidate the company. Able accepts the assets on December 31, 19X6, and makes several transactions during January 19X7. The transactions and the entries made on the books of Peerless Products Corporation and on the books of the trustee are presented in Figure 22-9 and discussed below.

   a. Entry (14) eliminates goodwill by Peerless Products Corporation before transfer of the assets to D. Able, Trustee.

   b. Entry (15) records the transfer of assets from Peerless Products Corporation to D. Able. D. Able recognizes the assets at their book values as reported by Peerless Products Corporation. Accounts receivable are dated as "old" to note that these were part of the transferred assets. The credit for $155,000 to Peerless Products Corporation—In Receivership is a liability of the trustee. On Peerless's books, the reciprocal account, D. Able—Receiver, is a receivable. Note that no liabilities are transferred. These remain on Peerless's books because they are legal responsibilities of Peerless Products Corporation.

FIGURE 22-9 Trustee and debtor company entries during liquidation.

Trustee D. Able's Books			Peerless Products Corporation's Books	

Write off goodwill of $20,000:

Trustee D. Able's Books		Peerless Products Corporation's Books	
(14) (No entry)		Retained Earnings	20,000
		Goodwill	20,000

Transfer of Peerless's assets to trustee:

Trustee D. Able's Books			Peerless Products Corporation's Books		
(15) Cash	2,000		D. Able—Receiver	155,000	
Marketable Securities	8,000		Allowance for Uncollectibles	2,000	
Accounts Receivable (old)	20,000		Accumulated Depreciation	24,000	
Inventory	45,000		Cash		2,000
Prepaid Assets	1,000		Marketable Securities		8,000
Property, Plant, and Equipment	105,000		Accounts Receivable		20,000
Allowance for Uncollectibles (old)		2,000	Inventory		45,000
Accumulated Depreciation		24,000	Prepaid Assets		1,000
Peerless Products Company—In Receivership		155,000	Property, Plant, and Equipment		105,000

Purchases of inventory of $20,000 on account by trustee:

Trustee D. Able's Books			Peerless Products Corporation's Books
(16) Inventory	20,000		(No entry)
Accounts Payable (new)		20,000	

Sales on account by trustee, $85,000. Cost of sales is $50,000, including all the inventory transferred from Peerless Products Corporation.

Trustee D. Able's Books			Peerless Products Corporation's Books
(17) Accounts Receivable (new)	85,000		(No entry)
Sales		85,000	
(18) Cost of Sales	50,000		
Inventory		50,000	

Receivables collected by trustee: Old $12,000   New 44,000

Trustee D. Able's Books			Peerless Products Corporation's Books
(19) Cash	56,000		(No entry)
Accounts Receivable (old)		12,000	
Accounts Receivable (new)		44,000	

Disbursements by trustee:

Old current payables	$30,000
New current payables	4,000
Operating expenses	13,000
Trustee's expenses	5,000

	Receiver's Books		Company's Books	
(20)	Peerless Products Company—in Receivership	30,000	Accounts Payable	20,000
	Accounts Payable (new)	4,000	Notes Payable	10,000
	Operating Expenses	13,000	D. Able—Receiver	30,000
	Trustee's Expenses	5,000		
	Cash	52,000		

Sales of marketable securities for $9,000:

(21)	Cash	9,000	(No entry)	
	Marketable Securities	8,000		
	Gain on Sale of Securities	1,000		

Adjusting entries at end of period:

Provision for bad debts:

Old receivables	$ 1,000
New receivables	2,000
Old receivables written off	2,000
Depreciation expense	10,000
Prepaid expenses expired	1,000

(22)	Uncollectibles Expense	3,000	(No entry)	
	Depreciation Expense	10,000		
	Allowance for Uncollectibles (old)	1,000		
	Allowance for Uncollectibles (new)	2,000		
	Accumulated Depreciation	10,000		
(23)	Allowance for Uncollectibles (old)	2,000		
	Accounts Receivable (old)	2,000		
(24)	Prepaid Costs Expense	1,000		
	Prepaid Assets	1,000		

Closing entries at end of period:

(25)	Sales	85,000	D. Able—Receiver	4,000
	Gain on Sale of Securities	1,000	Retained Earnings	4,000
	Cost of Sales	50,000		
	Operating Expenses	13,000		
	Receiver's Expenses	5,000		
	Prepaid Costs Expense	1,000		
	Bad Debts Expense	3,000		
	Depreciation Expense	10,000		
	Peerless Products Company—In Receivership	4,000		

c. The trustee's transactions are recorded in the normal manner in entries (16) through (19). The only difference is the differentiation between "old" accounts, which were part of the assets transferred, and "new" accounts, which result from the trustee's transactions.

d. The trustee pays $20,000 of Peerless Products Corporation's accounts payable and pays $10,000 for the partially secured note payable. In entry (20), the debit of $30,000 is made to the liability account Peerless Products Company—In Receivership. Peerless Products Corporation makes a corresponding entry to reduce its accounts payable and notes payable, and to reduce the receivable, D. Able—Receiver.

e. The remaining entries (21 through 25), complete the transactions, adjust the books, and close the books at the end of the first period of receivership. Operations resulted in a net income of $4,000 for the period. The closing entry transfers the net income to the receivership account on the trustee's books. A corresponding entry on Peerless Products Corporation's books increases the receiver's account and the retained earnings account.

The entries are the basis of the statement of realization and liquidation for the month of January 19X7. This statement is reported to the bankruptcy court to show the current state of the liquidation process and to report on the fiduciary responsibility of D. Able, the trustee. The statement of realization and liquidation for Peerless Products Corporation, as reported by D. Able, is shown in Figure 22-10.

Following are observations on this statement:

1. The statement begins with an accounting of the assets received from Peerless Products Corporation and those acquired by the trustee. The assets realized section reports the proceeds of the sale of assets. For example, the marketable securities were sold for $9,000, which is $1,000 more than their book value. Sales of inventory are also reported for the amount of the total proceeds. This is the traditional approach used most often in practice, although an alternative sometimes found is to recognize the disposal of the assets at their book values, with the profit or gain element recognized as a supplementary credit. Either method, using gross proceeds or using book value, is allowed in practice. The assets not realized shows the ending book values of remaining assets as of January 31, 19X7. Cash is not included on the statement, because it is already a realized asset. Cash is reported in a separate statement by the trustee.

2. Supplementary items include $13,000 of operating expenses paid, receiver's expenses of $5,000, and the net gain of $4,000 as a balancing item. It is important to note that cost allocations are not included in the supplementary items. For example, the trustee recognized depreciation expense of $10,000, bad debt expense of $3,000, and expiration of prepaid assets of $1,000. These do not appear directly in the statement, but they are shown indirectly. For example, under assets to be realized, depreciable assets are reported as $81,000, while under the assets not realized, the depreciable assets, net, are shown as $71,000. The $10,000 difference is the depreciation expense for the period. Bad debts expense and prepaid expense are treated in a similar way.

FIGURE 22-10 Receiver's statement of realization and liquidation.

Peerless Products Corporation
D. Able, Receiver
Statement of Realization and Liquidation
December 31, 19X6, to January 31, 19X7

Assets

Assets to Be Realized		Assets Realized	
Old receivables (net)	$ 18,000	Old receivables	$ 12,000
Marketable securities	8,000	New receivables	44,000
Old inventory	45,000	Marketable securities	9,000
Prepaid assets	1,000	Sales of inventory	85,000
Depreciable assets (net)	81,000		
Assets Acquired		**Assets Not Realized**	
New receivables	85,000	Old receivables (net)	5,000
New inventory purchased	20,000	New receivables (net)	39,000
		New inventory	15,000
		Depreciable assets (net)	71,000

Supplementary Items

Supplementary Charges		Supplementary Credits	
Operating expenses paid	13,000		
Receiver's expenses	5,000		
Net gain from operations	4,000		

Liabilities

Debts Liquidated		Debts to Be Liquidated	
Old current payables	30,000	Old current payables	133,000
New current payables	4,000	Mortgage payable	50,000
Debts Not Liquidated		**Debts Incurred**	
Old current payables	103,000	New current payables	20,000
New current payables	16,000		
Mortgage payable	50,000		
	$483,000		$483,000

3. The last part of the statement is a report on the liabilities. The trustee is responsible for liquidating the preexisting debts of $183,000 and has incurred additional debt of $20,000 during the month. A total of $34,000 of debts has been liquidated, leaving $169,000 still to be liquidated.

4. The statement balances at a total of $483,000, indicating all items are reported.

The trustee provides a statement of realization and liquidation to the bankruptcy court on a monthly basis. In addition, a short cash flow statement is provided which summarizes the cash receipts and cash disbursements during the period.

The fact that various bankruptcy courts are accepting alternative forms of the statement of realization may create some consternation for accountants providing professional services in several judicial districts. For example, should assets realized be shown at their gross proceeds, or should a net amount be shown with the gain or loss shown in supplementary items? The report format presented in this chapter is the traditional approach accepted by a large majority of courts. Some courts, however, are currently experimenting with other forms of trustee reporting. The experiments now taking place in trustee reporting may eventually lead to a new report that will be a modification of the present statement. Until then, accountants serving as trustees or advising trustees should ascertain from the specific bankruptcy court administering the estate which reporting form to use.

Bankruptcy Provisions for Individuals

In addition to Chapter 7 bankruptcies, individuals have the opportunity to use the provisions of Chapter 13 of the Bankruptcy Reform Act, entitled "Adjustment of Debts of an Individual with Regular Income."

An individual may file for bankruptcy only once every 7 years. In addition, an individual is allowed to retain only the bare minimum of personal properties through a bankruptcy, and certain forms of debts are not dischargeable in bankruptcy.

An individual entering bankruptcy under any of the current provisions is allowed to exempt certain limited property from the bankruptcy estate; that is, the person may retain these properties after bankruptcy. Exempted property guidelines listed in the federal bankruptcy statutes for an individual include the following:

1. Real property or personal property used as a residence, not to exceed $7,500.

2. One motor vehicle, not to exceed $1,200.

3. Household items and wearing apparel for personal use, not to exceed $200 in any particular item.

4. Personal, family, or household jewelry, not to exceed $500.

5. Professional books or tools of trade, not to exceed $750.

6. Accrued dividend, loan value, and so forth of unmatured life insurance contract, not to exceed $4,000.

7. Professionally prescribed health aids.

8. Selected payments such as social security, retirement benefits, disability benefits, alimony, and the like. Some of these are limited to the extent reasonably necessary to provide essential support of the debtor and the debtor's dependents.

Individual judicial jurisdictions may have guidelines that differ from the federal statutes; an attorney should be consulted prior to any personal bankruptcy filing.

In personal bankruptcy, the court uses all the individual debtor's nonexempt assets to liquidate the debtor's liabilities. The debtor is then discharged from all remaining debts except those listed below. In other words, the debtor must repay the following debts even after being declared bankrupt:

1. A tax that was willfully evaded
2. Debts obtained by false pretenses, false representations, or actual fraud
3. Debts that were not scheduled by the debtor in time to permit timely action by the creditors
4. Debts for fraud or defalcation while acting in a fiduciary capacity, for embezzlement, or for larceny
5. Alimony, maintenance, or support obligations
6. Debts due to willful and malicious injury to another entity or its property
7. Most educational loans, unless the loan first became due more than 5 years before the petition date or if an undue hardship would be imposed

Individuals with regular income from wages or a small business and total unsecured debts of less than $100,000 and secured debts of less than $350,000 may file for bankruptcy under Chapter 13. A trustee is appointed by the court to work directly with the debtor to schedule all debts and derive a plan for settling all priority claims. A 3-year limit is imposed on any payment plan unless specially extended by the bankruptcy court to a maximum of 5 years. The advantage of a Chapter 13 bankruptcy is its greater flexibility than afforded by Chapter 11. Chapter 13 allows the debtor to retain control over assets and to work with the trustee under the order of relief given by the bankruptcy court. After completing payments under the plan, the debtor is discharged from all remaining debts except those listed earlier. In addition, the debtor may remain liable for certain long-term secured claims that cannot be exhausted within the duration of the plan, such as the mortgage for a personal residence.

SUMMARY OF KEY CONCEPTS AND TERMS

A variety of actions are available to companies in financial difficulty. A debtor may restructure its existing debt by agreeing to settle its obligation at less than current value or to modify some of the terms of the debt agreement. The debtor's payable may be settled with the transfer of equity or assets, or the terms of the debt may be modified. Not all troubled debt restructurings result in a gain to the debtor or loss to the creditor. A debtor recognizes a gain if its debt is settled for an amount less than the debt's book value or if all future cash flows on the restructured debt are to be less than the book value of the debt at the date of the restructuring. In such circumstances, the creditor recognizes a loss, usually as a charge against its allowance for uncollectibles.

In some cases, creditors may form a committee to manage the debtor's business. In this nonjudicial action, the debtor agrees to comply with the creditors.

The creditors' committee may attempt to rehabilitate the business or may find that liquidation is the best course of action.

Two judicial remedies are available under the Bankruptcy Reform Act of 1978. The first is Chapter 11 reorganization, in which the debtor is given some relief from creditors' claims and can attempt to rehabilitate the business and return it to profitable operations. A trustee is sometimes appointed by the bankruptcy court to advise the debtor. **SOP 90-7** requires that financial statements produced during reorganization proceedings clearly separate the reorganization items from operating items. In addition, **SOP 90-7** prescribes the two conditions that must occur before fresh start accounting may be used by firms emerging from reorganization proceedings. The two conditions are: (1) The post-petition liabilities, plus pre-petition liabilities allowed as claims by the court, must be greater than the reorganization value assigned to the company's assets; and (2) the holders of voting shares immediately prior to confirmation of the plan of reorganization must hold less than 50 percent of the voting shares of the emerging company. Fresh start accounting includes the revaluation of assets and the elimination of any retained earnings, or deficit.

The second judicial remedy is a Chapter 7 liquidation. At the beginning of a judicial action, a statement of affairs is prepared as a planning document to show the expected amounts that will be realized on the liquidation of the business and the order of the creditors' claims against the debtor's assets. During liquidation, the debtor's assets are sold, and the creditors' claims are settled in the order of priority defined by the Bankruptcy Act. Secured claims are satisfied with proceeds of the sale of the corresponding collateral; unsecured claims with priority are then settled. Any remaining cash is distributed to the general unsecured creditors.

Trustees are sometimes appointed by bankruptcy courts to administer the reorganization or liquidation process. A trustee provides a statement of realization and liquidation to the bankruptcy court to report on the progress of the judicial action and on the fiduciary actions of the trustee. The statement presents the assets transferred to the trustee, the additional assets acquired by the trustee, and the ending balance of unrealized assets still to be converted into cash. The statement also reports on the debtor's liabilities discharged by the trustee as well as the additional liabilities incurred by the trustee. Some minor variations of the statement format are found in bankruptcy courts.

Accounting statement of affairs	Receivership
Creditors' committee management	Reorganization under Chapter 11
Creditors with priority	Reorganization value
Fresh start accounting	Restructuring difference
General unsecured creditors	Secured creditors
Liquidation under Chapter 7	Statement of realization and liquidation
Order of relief	Troubled debt restructurings
Plan of reorganization	

QUESTIONS

Q22-1   What are the nonjudicial actions available to a financially distressed company? What judicial actions are available?

Q22-2   What is the difference between a Chapter 7 action and a Chapter 11 bankruptcy action?

Q22-3   Under what circumstances may an involuntary petition for relief be filed? Who files this petition?

Q22-4   What is a troubled debt restructuring? Are all debt restructurings accounted for in the same manner?

Q22-5   Summarize the procedures for determining if a gain or loss from debt restructuring is reported.

Q22-6   Explain the two steps involved with accounting for the transfer of noncash assets in settlement of a restructured debt.

Q22-7   How is a gain from a troubled debt restructuring reported on the debtor's financial statements? How is a loss reported on the creditor's financial statements?

Q22-8   Under what circumstances will a gain be shown by a debtor in a modification of terms of the debt agreement?

Q22-9   How is interest expense computed by the debtor after a modification of terms in which the carrying value of the debt is less than the modified total future cash flows?

Q22-10   What is usually included in the plan of reorganization filed as part of a Chapter 11 reorganization? Does **FASB 15** apply to debt restructurings that are part of a reorganization plan? Explain.

Q22-11   Explain the use of the account Reorganization Value in Excess of Amount Assigned to Identifiable Assets during a Chapter 11 reorganization.

Q22-12   What conditions must occur for a company in reorganization to use fresh start accounting?

Q22-13   What financial statements must be filed by a company during a Chapter 11 reorganization?

Q22-14   What are the rights of creditors with priority in a Chapter 7 liquidation?

Q22-15   Describe the statement of affairs used in planning an anticipated liquidation.

Q22-16* What are the financial reporting responsibilities of a trustee who accepts the debtor company's assets in a Chapter 7 liquidation?

Q22-17* How are the sales of assets reported on the statement of realization and liquidation?

CASES

C22-1 Restructuring of Debt

Elec-Tric, Inc., is experiencing financial difficulties and is seeking ways to settle a $100,000 debt with one of its creditors. The creditor is willing to accept $70,000 in cash or accept land that cost Elec-Tric, Inc., $20,000 but was recently appraised at $90,000. The controller of the company wishes to settle the debt by transferring the land, while the president of the company feels the debt should be settled by transferring the $70,000 in cash.

Required

Discuss the accounting procedures and financial statement disclosures to be used by Elec-Tric, Inc., to account for and report the settlement of the debt with the: (a) transfer of the land; (b) transfer of the $70,000 cash.

C22-2   Creditors' Alternatives

The creditors of the Lost Hope Company have had several meetings with the company's management to discuss the financial difficulties of the company. Lost Hope currently has a significant deficit in retained earnings and has defaulted on several of its debt issues. The options currently open to the creditors are to (1) form a creditors' committee, (2) work with the company in a Chapter 11 reorganization, or (3) go through a Chapter 7 liquidation. The creditors have come to you to seek your advice on the advantages and disadvantages of each of the three options from their viewpoint.

Required

Discuss the advantages and disadvantages to the creditors of each of the three options available. Include a discussion of the probable recovery of each of the creditors' claims and the time period of that recovery.

EXERCISES

E22-1   Multiple-Choice Questions on Debt Restructuring [AICPA Adapted]

Select the correct answer for each of the following questions:

1. On January 1, 19X1, Kalb Company purchased at par 500 of the $1,000 face value, 8 percent bonds of Lane Corporation as a long-term investment. The bonds mature on January 1, 19X9, and pay interest semiannually on July 1 and January 1. Lane incurred heavy losses from operations for several years and defaulted on the July 1, 19X4, and January 1, 19X5, interest payments. Because of the permanent decline in market value of Lane's bonds, Kalb wrote down its investment to $400,000 on December 31, 19X4. Pursuant to Lane's plan of reorganization effected on July 1, 19X5, Kalb received 5,000 shares of $100 par value, 8 percent cumulative preferred stock of Lane in exchange for the $500,000 face value bond investment. The quoted market value of the preferred stock was $70 per share on July 1, 19X5. What amount of loss should be included in the determination of Kalb's net income for 19X5?
   a. $0.
   b. $50,000.
   c. $100,000.
   d. $150,000.

2. On December 31, 19X1, Adam Company entered into a debt restructuring agreement with Laker Company, which was experiencing financial difficulties. Adam restructured a $100,000 note receivable as follows:

   > Reduced the principal obligation to $70,000
   > Forgave $12,000 of accrued interest
   > Extended the maturity date from December 31, 19X1, to December 31, 19X3
   > Reduced the interest rate from 12 percent to 8 percent

Interest was payable annually on December 31, 19X2 and 19X3. In accordance with the agreement, Laker made payments to Adam on December 31, 19X2 and 19X3. How much interest income should Adam report for the year ended December 31, 19X3?

a. $0.
b. $5,600.
c. $8,400.
d. $11,200.

3. Smith Company holds an overdue note receivable of $800,000 plus recorded accrued interest of $64,000. As the result of a court imposed settlement on December 31, 19X0, Smith agreed to the following restructuring agreement:

Reduced the principal obligation to $600,000.
Forgave the $64,000 accrued interest.
Extended the maturity date to December 31, 19X2.
Annual interest of $60,000 is to be paid to Smith on December 31, 19X1 and 19X2.

On December 31, 19X0, Smith must recognize a loss from restructuring of:

a. $144,000.
b. $200,000.
c. $204,000.
d. $264,000.

4. Carling, Inc., is indebted to Dow Finance Company under a $600,000, 10 percent, 5-year note dated January 1, 19X1. Interest, payable annually on December 31, was paid on the December 31, 19X1 and 19X2, due dates. However, during 19X3, Carling experienced severe financial difficulties and is likely to default on the note and interest unless some concessions are made. On December 31, 19X3, Carling and Dow signed an agreement restructuring the debt as follows:

Interest for 19X3 was reduced to $30,000, payable March 31, 19X4.
Interest payments each year were reduced to $40,000 per year for 19X4 and 19X5.
The principal amount was reduced to $400,000.

What is the amount of gain that Carling should report on the debt restructuring in its income statement for the year ended December 31, 19X3?

a. $120,000.
b. $150,000.
c. $200,000.
d. $230,000.

5. For a troubled debt restructuring involving only modification of terms, it is appropriate for a debtor to recognize a gain when the carrying amount of the debt:

a. Exceeds the total future cash payments specified by the new terms.
b. Is less than the total future cash payments specified by the new terms.
c. Exceeds the present value specified by the new terms.
d. Is less than the present value specified by the new terms.

6. Hull Company is indebted to Apex under a $500,000, 12 percent, 3-year note dated December 31, 19X1. Because of Hull's financial difficulties developing in 19X3, Hull owed accrued interest of $60,000 on the note at December 31, 19X3. Under a troubled debt restructuring, on December 31, 19X3, Apex agreed to settle the note and accrued interest for a tract of land having a fair value of $450,000. Hull's acquisition cost of the

land is $360,000. Ignoring income taxes, on its 19X3 income statement Hull should report as a result of the troubled debt restructuring:

	Other Income	Extraordinary Gain
a.	$200,000	$ 0
b.	$140,000	$ 0
c.	$ 90,000	$ 50,000
d.	$ 90,000	$110,000

E22-2   Debt Restructuring

Golden Company experienced cash flow problems during 19X1 and on December 31, 19X1, was unable to pay principal and interest on an $80,000 debt to its principal supplier, Hogan, Inc. In view of Golden's distressed financial condition, Hogan agreed to accept machinery that had cost $120,000 and had accumulated depreciation of $36,000 and a fair value of $75,000, in full satisfaction of the $80,000 debt and $9,600 accrued interest.

Required

Prepare journal entries on the books of Golden Company and Hogan, Inc., to record the troubled debt restructuring on December 31, 19X1.

E22-3   Debt Restructuring

Hook Corporation, a major creditor of financially troubled Inland Company, has agreed to modify the terms of a debt owed to Hook. The debt consists of a $1,500,000, 10 percent note that is due currently, together with accrued interest of $120,000. Hook agreed to extend the due date of the note and accrued interest for 3 years and to reduce the interest rate to 4 percent per annum (on both the maturity value of $1,500,000 and the extended accrued interest of $120,000), with interest to be paid annually.

Required

a. Should a gain on restructuring be recognized by Inland? Explain.
b. Prepare the entry to be made on Inland's books on the date of restructure.

E22-4   Debt Restructuring

Refer to the data described in Exercise 22-3, but assume that the terms of modification of the debt are as follows:

1. Accrued interest of $50,000 is to be canceled.
2. The face value of the note is reduced to $900,000, payable at the end of 3 years. Interest at 10 percent on the new face value and the extended accrued interest is to be paid annually.

Required

a. Should a gain on the restructuring be recognized by Inland? Explain.
b. Prepare the entry on the books of Inland Company to record the restructuring.

c. Prepare the entry on Inland Company's books to record the $97,000 interest payment at the end of the first year after restructuring.

E22-5 Multiple-Choice Questions on Chapter 11 Reorganizations
[AICPA Adapted]

Select the correct answer for each of the following questions.

1. A client has joined other creditors of Jet Company in a composition agreement seeking to avoid the necessity of a bankruptcy proceeding against Jet. Which statement describes the composition agreement?
   a. It provides for the appointment of a receiver to take over and operate the debtor's business.
   b. It must be approved by all creditors.
   c. It provides that the creditors will receive less than the full amount of their claims.
   d. It provides a temporary delay, not to exceed 6 months, in the debtor's obligation to repay the debts included in the composition.

2. Hardluck, Inc., is insolvent. Its liabilities exceed its assets by $13 million. Hardluck is owned by its president, Blank, and members of his family. Blank, whose assets are estimated at less than a million dollars, guaranteed the loans of the corporation. A consortium of banks is the principal creditor of Hardluck, having lent it $8 million, the bulk of which is unsecured. The banks decided to seek reorganization of Hardluck, and Blank has agreed to cooperate. Regarding the proposed reorganization:
   a. Blank's cooperation is necessary since he must sign the petition for a reorganization.
   b. If a petition in bankruptcy is filed against Hardluck, Blank will also have his personal bankruptcy status resolved and relief granted.
   c. Only a duly constituted creditors' committee may file a plan of reorganization of Hardluck.
   d. Hardluck will remain in possession unless a request is made to the court for the appointment of a trustee.

3. Among other provisions, a Chapter 11 plan of reorganization must:
   a. Rank claims according to their liquidation priorities.
   b. Not impair claims of secured creditors.
   c. Provide adequate means for the plan's execution.
   d. Treat all claims alike.

4. A condition that must exist for the filing of an involuntary bankruptcy petition is:
   a. The debtor must have debts of at least $10,000.
   b. If the debtor has 12 or more creditors, a majority of the creditors must sign the petition.
   c. If the debtor has 12 or more creditors, only 1 creditor need sign the petition, but that creditor must be owed at least $5,000.
   d. If the debtor has 12 or more creditors, the required number of creditors signing the petition must be owed at least $5,000 in total.

5. The plan of reorganization must be approved by:
   a. At least one-third of all creditors who hold at least half of the total debt.
   b. At least half of all creditors who hold at least half of the total debt.

c. At least half of all creditors who hold at least two-thirds of the total debt.

d. At least two-thirds of all creditors who hold at least two-thirds of the total debt.

E22-6 Recovery Analysis for a Chapter 11 Reorganization

The plan of reorganizing for Taylor Companies, Inc., was approved by the court, stockholders, and creditors on December 31, 19X1. The plan calls for a general restructuring of all debt of Taylor Companies. The liability and capital accounts of the company on December 31, 19X1, are as follows:

Accounts Payable (post-petition)	$ 30,000
Liabilities Subject to Compromise:	
Accounts Payable	80,000
Notes Payable, 10%, unsecured	150,000
Interest Payable	40,000
Bonds Payable, 12%	200,000
Common Stock, $1 par	100,000
Additional Paid-In Capital	200,000
Retained Earnings (deficit)	(178,000)
Total	$622,000

A total of $30,000 of accounts payable has been incurred since the company filed its petition for relief under Chapter 11. No other liabilities have been incurred since the petition was filed. No payments have been made on the liabilities subject to compromise that existed on the petition date.

Under the terms of the reorganization plan:

1. The accounts payable creditors existing at the date the petition was filed agree to accept $72,000 of net accounts receivable in full settlement of their claims.

2. The holders of the 10 percent notes payable of $150,000 plus $16,000 of interest payable agree to accept land having a fair value of $125,000, and a book value of $85,000.

3. The holders of the 12 percent bonds payable of $200,000 plus $24,000 of interest payable agree to cancel accrued interest of $18,000, accept cash payment of the remaining $6,000 of interest, and accept a secured interest in the equipment of the company in exchange for extending the term of the bonds for an additional year at no interest.

4. The common shareholders agree to reduce the deficit by changing the par value of the stock to $2 per share and eliminating any remaining deficit after recognition of all gains or losses from the debt restructuring transactions specified in the plan of reorganization. The deficit will be eliminated by reducing additional paid-in capital.

Required

a. Prepare a recovery analysis for the plan of reorganization, concluding with the total recovery of each liability and capital component of Taylor Companies.

b. Prepare the journal entries to account for the discharge of the debt and the restructuring of the common equity in fulfillment of the plan of reorganization.

E22-7 Multiple-Choice Questions on Chapter 7 Liquidations

Select the correct answer for each of the following questions.

1. Lear Company ceased doing business and is in bankruptcy. Among the claimants are employees seeking unpaid wages. The following statements describe the possible status of such claims in a bankruptcy proceeding. Which is the *incorrect* statement?
   a. They are entitled to priority.
   b. If a priority is afforded such claims, it cannot exceed $2,000 per wage earner.
   c. Such claims include wages earned within 180 days before the filing of the bankruptcy petition, but not to exceed $2,000 in amount.
   d. The amounts of excess wages not entitled to a priority are mere unsecured claims.

2. The highest priority for payment of unsecured claims in a bankruptcy proceeding is:
   a. Administrative expenses of the bankruptcy.
   b. Unpaid federal income taxes.
   c. Wages up to $2,000 earned within 3 months before the petition.
   d. Wages owed to an insolvent employee.

3. The order of payments for unsecured priority claims in a Chapter 7 bankruptcy case is such that:
   a. Tax claims of government units are paid before claims for administrative expenses incurred by the trustee.
   b. Tax claims of government units are paid before claims of employees for wages.
   c. Claims of employees for wages are paid before administrative expenses incurred by the trustee.
   d. Claims incurred between the filing of an involuntary petition and appointment of a trustee are paid before the claims for contributions to employee benefit plans.

4. Narco is in serious financial difficulty and is unable to meet current unsecured obligations of $30,000 to some 14 creditors who are demanding immediate payment. Narco owes Johnson $5,000, and Johnson has decided to file an involuntary petition against Narco. Which of the following is necessary in order for Johnson to file validly?
   a. Johnson must be joined by at least two other creditors.
   b. Narco must have committed a fraudulent act within 1 year of the filing.
   c. Johnson must allege and subsequently establish that Narco's liabilities exceed Narco's assets upon fair valuation.
   d. Johnson must be a secured creditor.

5. Your client is insolvent under the federal bankruptcy law. Under the circumstances:
   a. So long as the client can meet current debts or claims by its most aggressive creditors, a bankruptcy proceeding is *not* possible.
   b. Such information—that is, insolvency—need *not* be disclosed in the financial statements reported on by your CPA firm so long as you are convinced that the problem is short-lived.
   c. A transfer of assets to a creditor less than 90 days before filing a petition may be a voidable transfer.
   d. Your client *cannot* file a voluntary petition for bankruptcy.

E22-8 Chapter 7 Liquidation

The carrying values and estimated fair values of the assets of Penn, Inc., are:

	Carrying Value	Fair Value
Cash	$ 16,000	$ 16,000
Accounts Receivable	60,000	50,000
Inventory	90,000	65,000
Land	100,000	80,000
Building (net)	220,000	160,000
Equipment (net)	250,000	100,000
Total	$736,000	$471,000

Debts of Penn, Inc., are:

Accounts Payable	$ 95,000
Wages Payable (all have priority)	9,500
Taxes Payable	14,000
Notes Payable (secured by receivables and inventory)	190,000
Interest on Notes Payable	5,000
Bonds Payable (secured by land and building)	220,000
Interest on Bonds Payable	11,000
Total	$544,500

Required

a. Prepare a schedule to calculate the net estimated amount available for general unsecured creditors.

b. Compute the percentage dividend to general unsecured creditors.

c. Prepare a schedule showing the amount to be paid each of the creditor groups upon distribution of the $471,000 estimated to be realizable.

E22-9 Liquidation under Chapter 7

The book values and estimated realizable values of the assets of Royal Company on May 31, 19X1, are as follows:

	Book Value	Realizable Value
Cash	$ 14,700	$ 14,700
Accounts Receivable (net)	65,000	52,000
Inventory	75,000	40,000
Land and Building (net)	190,000	120,000
Equipment (net)	340,000	180,000
Total	$684,700	$406,700

Equities of Royal Company are as follows:

Accounts Payable	$105,000
Wages Payable (all have priority)	24,000
Note Payable (secured by receivables)	40,000
Note Payable (secured by inventory)	80,000
Note Payable (secured by equipment)	150,000
Bonds Payable (secured by land and building)	200,000
Common Stock	160,000
Retained Earnings (deficit)	(74,300)
Total	$684,700

Required

a. Prepare a statement of affairs.

b. Compute the percentage dividend to unsecured creditors.

E22-10* Statement of Realization and Liquidation

A trustee has been appointed for Pace, Inc., which is being liquidated under Chapter 7 of the Bankruptcy Reform Act. The following transactions occurred after the assets were transferred to the trustee:

1. Sales on account by the trustee were $75,000. Cost of goods sold were $60,000, consisting of all the inventory transferred from Pace.
2. The trustee sold all the marketable securities of $12,000 for $10,500.
3. Receivables collected by the trustee:

Old: $21,000 of the $38,000 transferred
New: $47,000

4. Recorded $16,000 depreciation on the plant assets of $96,000 transferred from Pace.
5. Disbursements by the trustee:

Old current payables: $22,000 of the $48,000 transferred
Trustee's expenses: $4,300

Required

Prepare a statement of realization and liquidation according to the traditional approach illustrated in the chapter.

PROBLEMS

P22-11 Debt Restructuring

Quad, Inc., is in serious financial trouble and enters into an agreement with Reed Company, one of its creditors. Quad has a 12 percent note payable due now to Reed Company for $80,000 plus $9,600 accrued interest. Under the terms of the agreement,

Reed will receive machinery that cost $60,000 and has a book value of $32,000 and a fair value of $30,000. Reed agrees to forgive the accrued interest, reduce the note to $50,000, extend the maturity date 2 years, and reduce the interest rate to 6 percent. Interest is due at the end of each year.

Required

a. Record the journal entries on the books of Quad, Inc., for the modification of terms and the future interest payments. Prepare supporting schedules in good form.

b. Assume that instead of Quad's giving the machinery to Reed, it issues to Reed 3,000 shares of its $10 par common stock, which has a market value of $12 per share. All other modifications remain the same.

(1) Record the entry on the date of restructure on the books of Quad, Inc.

(2) Explain how the new interest rate and the interest expense each year will be determined.

P22-12   Chapter 11 Reorganization

During the recent recession, Polydorous, Inc., has accumulated a deficit in retained earnings. Although still operating at a loss, Polydorous posted better results during 19X1. Polydorous is having trouble paying suppliers on time and paying interest when it is due. The company files for protection under Chapter 11 of the Bankruptcy Reform Act of 1978, and has the following liabilities and stockholders' equity accounts at the time the petition is filed:

Accounts Payable	$160,000
Interest Payable	20,000
Notes Payable, 10%, unsecured	340,000
Preferred Stock	100,000
Common Stock, $5 par	150,000
Retained Earnings (deficit)	(80,000)
Total	$690,000

A plan of reorganization is filed with the court, and after review and obtaining creditor and investor votes, the plan is approved by the court. The plan of reorganization includes the following actions:

1. The pre-petition accounts payable will be restructured according to the following: (a) $40,000 will be paid in cash, (b) $20,000 will be eliminated, (c) the remaining $100,000 will be exchanged for a 5-year, secured note payable, paying 12 percent interest.

2. The interest payable will be restructured as follows: $10,000 of the interest will be eliminated, and the remaining $10,000 will be paid in cash.

3. The 10 percent, unsecured notes payable will be restructured as follows: (a) $60,000 of the notes will be eliminated, (b) $10,000 of the notes will be paid in cash, (c) $240,000 of the notes will be exchanged for a 5-year, 12 percent secured note, and (d) the remaining $30,000 will be exchanged for 3,000 shares of newly issued common stock having a par value of $10.

4. The preferred shareholders will exchange their stock for 5,000 shares of newly issued $10 par common stock.

5. The common shareholders will exchange their stock for 2,000 shares of newly issued $10 par common stock.

After extensive analysis, the reorganization value of the company is determined to be $510,000 prior to any payments of cash required by the reorganization plan. An additional $10,000 in current liabilities have been incurred since the petition was filed. After the reorganization is completed, the capital structure of the company will be as follows:

Current liabilities (post-petition)	$ 10,000
Notes payable, 12%, secured	340,000
Common stock ($10 par)	100,000
Post-reorganization capital structure	$450,000

An evaluation of the fair values of the assets was made after the company completed its reorganization, immediately prior to the point the company emerged from the proceedings. The following information is available:

	Book Value	Fair Value
Cash	$ 30,000	$ 30,000
Accounts receivable (net)	140,000	110,000
Inventory	25,000	18,000
Property, plant, and equipment (net)	405,000	262,000
Goodwill	40,000	-0-
	$640,000	$420,000

Required

a. Prepare a plan of reorganization recovery analysis for the liability and stockholders' equity accounts of Polydorous, Inc., on the day the plan of reorganization is approved. (Hint: the liabilities on the plan's approval day are $530,000, which is $520,000 from pre-petition payables plus $10,000 in additional accounts payable incurred post-petition.)

b. Prepare an analysis showing if the company qualifies for fresh start accounting as it emerges from the reorganization.

c. Prepare journal entries for execution of the plan of reorganization with its general restructuring of debt and capital.

d. Prepare the balance sheet for the company on completion of the plan of reorganization.

P22-13 Chapter 11 Reorganization

The balance sheet of Solo, Inc., a company in reorganization proceedings, on March 31, 19X1, is as follows:

Solo, Inc.
Debtor-In-Possession
Balance Sheet
March 31, 19X1

Cash	$ 25,000
Accounts Receivable (net)	95,000
Inventory	160,000
Land	70,000
Plant and Equipment (net)	400,000
Patents	60,000
Goodwill	30,000
Total Assets	$840,000
Liabilities Not Subject to Compromise:	
Accounts Payable—Trade	$ 65,000
Liabilities Subject to Compromise:	
Accounts Payable	190,000
12% Notes Payable, Unsecured	200,000
15% Bonds Payable	400,000
Preferred Stock	50,000
Common Stock ($5 par)	100,000
Additional Paid-In Capital	25,000
Retained Earnings (Deficit)	(190,000)
Total Liabilities and Equity	$840,000

The plan of reorganization was approved on March 31, 19X1, by the court, the stockholders, and the creditors. The plan included the following:

1. The accounts payable creditors subject to compromise agreed to accept the $95,000 of net accounts receivable, and 6,000 shares of newly issued no-par common stock having a value of $36,000 in settlement of their claims of $190,000.

2. The holders of the 12 percent unsecured notes payable for $200,000 agreed to accept the land with a fair value of $100,000, and 6,000 shares of newly issued no-par common stock having a value of $36,000.

3. The holders of the 15 percent bonds payable agreed to reduce the principal of the bonds to $380,000. Interest at 9 percent will be due annually on December 31 of each period from the date the plan of reorganization is approved onward, and the bondholders agreed to extend the maturity date of the bonds for an additional 4 years.

4. The preferred shareholders agreed to accept 1,500 shares of newly issued no-par value common stock having a value of $9,000 in exchange for their preferred stock.

5. The common shareholders agreed to accept 1,500 shares of newly issued no-par-value common stock having a value of $9,000 in exchange for their pre-reorganization shares of common stock.

After extensive analysis, the reorganization value of the company at the date the plan of reorganization is approved is determined to be $730,000 before the payment of any assets as required by the plan of reorganization. The plan of reorganization is then completed and the remaining identifiable assets have fair values as follows:

Cash	$ 25,000
Inventory	150,000
Plant and equipment (net)	255,000
Patents	90,000
	$520,000

After consultation among the creditors, the court, and the management of the company, the post-reorganization capital of the company will be:

Accounts payable	$ 65,000
Bonds payable	380,000
Common stock (no-par)	90,000
	$535,000

Required

a. Prepare a recovery analysis for the plan of reorganization.

b. Prepare an evaluation to determine if the company meets the two conditions necessary for fresh start accounting as it emerges from the Chapter 11 reorganization.

c. Prepare the journal entries to record the execution of the plan of reorganization.

d. Prepare a worksheet presenting the effects of the plan of reorganization on the company's balance sheet.

P22-14   Chapter 7 Liquidation, Statement of Affairs

Name Brand Company is to be liquidated under Chapter 7 of the Bankruptcy Act. The balance sheet on July 31, 19X1, is as follows:

Assets

Cash	$ 5,000
Marketable Securities (at cost)	30,000
Accounts Receivable (net)	105,000
Inventory	160,000
Prepaid Insurance	7,000
Land	80,000
Plant and Equipment (net)	412,000
Franchises	72,000
Total	$871,000

Equities

Accounts Payable	$265,000
Wages Payable	20,000
Taxes Payable	12,000
Interest Payable	37,000
Notes Payable	280,000
Mortgages Payable	220,000
Common Stock ($20 par)	240,000
Retained Earnings (deficit)	(203,000)
Total	$871,000

Additional information:

1. Marketable securities consist of 1,000 shares of Wooly, Inc., common stock. The market value of the stock is $22. The stock was pledged against a $28,000, 10 percent note payable that has accrued interest of $1,400.

2. Accounts receivable of $50,000 are collateral for a $40,000, 12 percent note payable that has accrued interest of $4,000.

3. Inventory with a book value of $79,000 and a current value of $75,000 is pledged against accounts payable of $105,000. The appraised value of the remainder of the inventory is $76,000.

4. Only $1,500 will be recovered from prepaid insurance.

5. Land is appraised at $110,000 and plant and equipment at $340,000.

6. It is estimated that the franchises can be sold for $30,000.

7. All the wages payable qualify for priority.

8. The mortgages are on the land and on a building with a book value of $162,000 and an appraised value of $150,000. The accrued interest on the mortgages is $14,600.

9. Estimated legal and accounting fees for the liquidation are $13,000.

Required

a. Prepare a statement of affairs as of July 31, 19X1.

b. Compute the estimated percentage settlement to unsecured creditors.

P22-15 Chapter 7 Liquidation, Statement of Affairs [AICPA Adapted]

Tower, Inc., advises you that it is facing bankruptcy proceedings. As the company's CPA, you are aware of its condition. The balance sheet of Tower, Inc., on December 31, 19X1, and supplementary data are presented below.

Assets

Cash	$ 2,000
Accounts Receivable (net)	70,000
Inventory, Raw Materials	40,000
Inventory, Finished Goods	60,000
Marketable Securities	20,000
Land	13,000
Buildings (net)	90,000
Machinery (net)	120,000
Goodwill	20,000
Prepaid Expenses	5,000
Total Assets	$440,000

Liabilities and Capital

Accounts Payable	$ 80,000
Notes Payable	135,000
Wages	15,000
Mortgages Payable	130,000
Common Stock	100,000
Retained Earnings (deficit)	(20,000)
Total Liabilities and Capital	$440,000

Additional information:

1. Cash includes a $500 travel advance that has been expended.

2. Accounts receivable of $40,000 have been pledged in support of bank loans of $30,000. Credit balances of $5,000 are netted in the accounts receivable total.

3. Marketable securities consist of government bonds costing $10,000 and 500 shares of Dawson Company stock. The market value of the bonds is $10,000, and the stock is $18 per share. The bonds have $200 of accrued interest due. The securities are collateral for a $20,000 bank loan.

4. Appraised value of raw materials is $30,000 and of finished goods is $50,000. For an additional cost of $10,000, the raw materials could realize $70,000 as finished goods.

5. The appraised value of fixed assets is $25,000 for land, $110,000 for buildings, and $75,000 for machinery.

6. Prepaid expenses will be exhausted during the liquidation period.

7. Accounts payable include $15,000 of withheld payroll taxes and $6,000 owed to creditors who have been reassured by the president of Tower that they would be paid. There are unrecorded employer's payroll taxes in the amount of $500.

8. Wages payable are not subject to any limitations under bankruptcy laws.

9. Mortgages payable consist of $100,000 on land and buildings and $30,000 for a chattel mortgage on machinery. Total unrecorded accrued interest for these mortgages amounts to $2,400.

10. Estimated legal fees and expenses in connection with the liquidation are $10,000.

11. The probable judgment on a pending damage suit is $50,000.

12. You have not rendered an invoice for $5,000 for last year's audit, and you estimate a $1,000 fee for liquidation work.

Required

a. Prepare a statement of affairs. (The book value column should reflect adjustments that properly should have been made as of December 31, 19X1, in the normal course of business.)

b. Compute the estimated settlement per dollar of unsecured liabilities.

P22-16 Financial Statements for a firm in Chapter 11 Proceedings

On January 2, 19X2, the Hobbes Company files a petition for relief under Chapter 11 of the Bankruptcy Act. The company had disastrous operating performance during the recent recession and needs time to reestablish profitable operations. The trial balance on January 2, 19X2, is as follows:

	Debit	Credit
Cash	$ 15,000	
Accounts Receivable (net)	65,000	
Inventory	102,000	
Property, Plant, and Equipment	620,000	
Accumulated Depreciation		$140,000
Accounts Payable		138,000
Notes Payable, 10%		170,000
Bonds Payable, 12%		250,000
Interest Payable		47,000
Preferred Stock		50,000
Common Stock, $1 par		50,000
Additional Paid-In Capital		75,000
Retained Earnings (deficit)	118,000	
	$920,000	$920,000

The following information applies to the 19X2 fiscal year, ending December 31, 19X2. The company is in reorganization proceedings for the entire year, and the plan of reorganization has not been approved as of December 31, 19X2. The debtor remained in possession of the company during the year.

Income data for 19X2:

1. Sales revenue of $246,000 is generated during the year.
2. Cost of goods sold is $170,000 as a result of cost reduction programs installed during the year.
3. Selling, operating, and administrative expenses are $50,000 for the year.
4. Interest expense is $4,000. Contractual interest would have been $51,000 for the year.
5. Reorganization items include $15,000 in fees paid to professionals, and $3,000 of interest earned on cash accumulated as a result of the Chapter 11 proceedings.
6. The income tax of $5,000 on operating income was paid during the year.
7. Discontinued operations included a loss on operations, net of tax, of $16,000, and a gain on the sale of assets, net of tax, of $9,000. The sale of the assets was administered by the court under the Chapter 11 proceedings.

Cash flow data for 19X2:

1. A total of $264,000 is received from customers. This includes $18,000 received on the accounts receivable that were outstanding prior to the filing of the petition.
2. A total of $206,000 is paid to suppliers, employees, and others for operations.
3. The current interest expense of $4,000 is paid during the year. This interest is on post-petition debt.
4. Professional fees of $15,000 are paid, and interest on cash accumulations of $3,000 is received.
5. Net cash used by discontinued operations, excluding the sale of assets, is $3,000.
6. The proceeds from the sale of the discontinued assets is $18,000. This sale was administered by the bankruptcy court.
7. The company borrowed $10,000 in short-term debt as part of a financing plan administered by the court.
8. The court authorized a payment of $10,000 on the bonds payable. The ending cash balance of $72,000 represents an increase of $57,000 during the year.

Other data for 19X2:

1. Through careful working-capital management, the ending inventory is reduced to $88,000. Continued reduction is expected in 19X3.
2. The property, plant, and equipment, net of accumulated depreciation, at the end of 19X2 was $460,000.
3. In addition to the $10,000 short-term borrowings that are part of the court-approved financing plan, the company has post-petition accounts payable of $7,000.

Required

a. Prepare the income statement for the company for the year ending December 31, 19X2.
b. Prepare the statement of cash flows for the company for the year ending December 31, 19X2.
c. Prepare the balance sheet for the company as of December 31, 19X2.

P22-17* Statement of Realization and Liquidation

A trustee, R. Smith, has been appointed for Nelson Company, which is being liquidated under Chapter 7 of the Bankruptcy Reform Act. The trial balance at the beginning of the liquidation on May 1, 19X1, was as follows:

	Debit	Credit
Cash	$ 30,000	
Marketable Securities	12,000	
Accounts Receivable	36,000	
Allowance for Uncollectibles		$ 3,000
Inventory	50,000	
Land	40,000	
Plant and Equipment (net)	110,000	
Goodwill	16,000	
Accounts Payable		95,000
Notes Payable		35,000
Interest Payable		8,000
Mortgages Payable		80,000
Common Stock ($10 par)		150,000
Retained Earnings (deficit)	77,000	
Total	$371,000	$371,000

The following transactions occurred:

1. The goodwill was written off.
2. The assets were transferred to the trustee.
3. The trustee purchased inventory of $24,000 on account.
4. Sales on account by the trustee were $90,000. Cost of goods sold was $60,000, including all the inventory transferred from Nelson.
5. Disbursements by trustee:

Old current payables	$73,000
New current payables	9,000
Operating expenses	15,000
Trustee's expenses	6,000

6. Receivables collected by trustee:

Old	$14,000
New	53,000

7. Marketable securities were sold for $16,000.

8. Adjusting entries on June 30, 19X1:

Provision for uncollectibles:	
Old receivables	$ 2,000
New receivables	4,000
Old receivables written off	3,000
Depreciation expense	12,000

Required

Prepare a statement of realization and liquidation reflecting these transactions according to the traditional approach illustrated in the chapter.

INDEX